W9-ADP-857

Sexual Personae

Sexual Personae

Art and Decadence from

Nefertiti to Emily Dickinson

CAMILLE PAGLIA

Yale University Press *London & New Haven*

Published with assistance from the foundation established in memory of Amasa Stone Mather of the Class of 1907, Yale College.

The author gratefully acknowledges permission to use the following material: "Sex and Violence, or Nature and Art," by Camille Paglia, first appeared (in a somewhat different form) in *Western Humanities Review*, Vol. XLII, No. 1 (Spring 1988). "The Apollonian Androgyne and the *Faerie Queene*," by Camille Paglia (here revised), is reprinted with permission from *English Literary Renaissance* 9.1 (1979), 42–63. "Oscar Wilde and the English Epicene," by Camille Paglia, appeared in a somewhat different form in *Raritan*, Vol. IV, No. 3 (Winter 1985). Poems 656, 1027, and 1711, by Emily Dickinson, are reprinted by permission of the publishers and the Trustees of Amherst College from *The Poems of Emily Dickinson*, edited by Thomas H. Johnson, Cambridge, Mass.: The Belknap Press of Harvard University Press, Copyright 1951, © 1955, 1979, 1983 by The President and Fellows of Harvard College.

Designed by Richard Hendel and set in Linotype Walbaum type by Keystone Typesetting, Inc., Orwigsburg, Pennsylvania Printed in the United States of America by Vail Ballou Press, Binghamton, New York

Library of Congress Cataloging-in-Publication Data
Paglia, Camille, 1947–
   Sexual personae. Art and decadence from Nefertiti to Emily Dickinson / Camille Paglia.
      p. cm.
   Bibliography: p.
   Includes index.
   ISBN 0–300–04396–1 (alk. paper)
   1. Literature, Modern—19th century—History and criticism. 2. Literature, Modern—History and criticism. 3. Romanticism. 4. Paganism in literature. 5. Sex in literature. 6. Decadence (Literary movement) 7. Decadence in literature. 8. Arts. 9. Paganism in art. 10. Sex in art. I. Title.
PN751.P34   1990
809'.03—dc 20   89–31659
                          CIP
                          Rev.

10 9 8 7 6

for my grandmothers

and my aunt

Vincenza Colapietro

Alfonsina Paglia

Lenora Antonelli

Contents

List of Illustrations / ix

Preface / xiii

Acknowledgments / xiv

Chapter 1 Sex and Violence, or Nature and Art / 1

Chapter 2 The Birth of the Western Eye / 40

Chapter 3 Apollo and Dionysus / 72

Chapter 4 Pagan Beauty / 99

Chapter 5 Renaissance Form: Italian Art / 140

Chapter 6 Spenser and Apollo: *The Faerie Queene* / 170

Chapter 7 Shakespeare and Dionysus: *As You Like It* and *Antony and Cleopatra* / 194

Chapter 8 Return of the Great Mother: Rousseau vs. Sade / 230

Chapter 9 Amazons, Mothers, Ghosts: Goethe to Gothic / 248

Chapter 10 Sex Bound and Unbound: Blake / 270

Chapter 11 Marriage to Mother Nature: Wordsworth / 300

Chapter 12 The Daemon as Lesbian Vampire: Coleridge / 317

Chapter 13 Speed and Space: Byron / 347

Chapter 14 Light and Heat: Shelley and Keats / 365

Chapter 15 Cults of Sex and Beauty: Balzac / 389

Chapter 16 Cults of Sex and Beauty: Gautier, Baudelaire, and Huysmans / 408

Chapter 17 Romantic Shadows: Emily Brontë / 439

Chapter 18 Romantic Shadows: Swinburne and Pater / 460

Chapter 19 Apollo Daemonized: Decadent Art / 489

Chapter 20   The Beautiful Boy as Destroyer: Wilde's *The Picture of Dorian Gray* / 512

Chapter 21   The English Epicene: Wilde's *The Importance of Being Earnest* / 531

Chapter 22   American Decadents: Poe, Hawthorne, Melville / 572

Chapter 23   American Decadents: Emerson, Whitman, James / 598

Chapter 24   Amherst's Madame de Sade: Emily Dickinson / 623

Notes / 675

Index / 701

Illustrations

1. *Perseus Cutting Off the Head of Medusa.* Museo Nazionale, Palermo (Alinari/Art Resource). / 48

2. *Venus of Willendorf.* Limestone. Museum of Natural History, Vienna (Alinari/Art Resource). / 55

3. *Chephren.* Green diorite. Egyptian Museum, Cairo (Alinari/Art Resource). / 58

4. *Stele of the Overseer of Magazine of Amon, Nib-Amun, and His Wife, Huy.* Limestone. Metropolitan Museum of Art, New York, Gift of James Douglas, 1890 (90.6.131). / 63

5. *Cat Goddess with One Gold Earring.* Bronze. Metropolitan Museum of Art, New York, Purchase 1958, Fund from Various Donors. / 65

6. *Nefertiti.* Painted limestone with plaster additions. Copy (Marburg/Art Resource). / 67

7. *Nefertiti.* Painted limestone with plaster additions. State Museums, Berlin (Marburg/Art Resource). / 68

8. *Apollo*, from the Temple of Zeus, Olympia. Olympia Museum (Alinari/Art Resource). / 75

9. *Ephesian Artemis.* Marble and bronze. Museo nuovo dei Conservatori, Rome (Alinari/Art Resource). / 76

10. *Athena Parthenos* (Alinari/Art Resource). / 82

11. *Dionysus and Maenads.* Glyptothek, Munich. / 90

12. *Kouros.* Island marble. Metropolitan Museum of Art, New York, Fletcher Fund, 1932 (32.11.1). / 111

13. *The Kritios Boy.* Acropolis Museum, Athens (Alison Frantz). / 112

14. *Byzantine Saints.* Mosaic. Cathedral of Cefalù, Sicily (Alinari/Art Resource). / 113

15. Sandro Botticelli, *St. Sebastian.* State Museums, Berlin (Marburg/Art Resource). / 114

16. *The Benevento Boy.* Louvre, Paris (Marburg/Art Resource). / 119

17. *Antinous.* Museo Nazionale, Naples (Alinari/Art Resource). / 120

18. Benvenuto Cellini, *Perseus with the Head of Medusa.* Loggia dei Lanzi, Florence (Alinari/Art Resource). / 145

19. Donatello, *David.* Bargello, Florence (Alinari/Art Resource). / 147

20. Sandro Botticelli, *The Birth of Venus.* Uffizi, Florence (Alinari/Art Resource). / 151

21. Sandro Botticelli, *Primavera.* Uffizi, Florence (Alinari/Art Resource). / 152

22. Leonardo da Vinci, *Mona Lisa.* Louvre, Paris (Alinari/Art Resource). / 154

23. Leonardo da Vinci, *Virgin and Child with St. Anne.* Louvre, Paris (Alinari/Art Resource). / 155

24. Michelangelo, *Cumaean Sibyl.* Sistine Chapel, Vatican, Rome (Alinari/Art Resource). / 161

25. Michelangelo, *Night.* Medici Chapel, Church of San Lorenzo, Florence (Alinari/Art Resource). / 162

26. Michelangelo, *Giuliano de' Medici.* Medici Chapel, Church of San Lorenzo, Florence (Alinari/Art Resource). / 164

27. Michelangelo, *Dying Slave.* Louvre, Paris (Giraudon/Art Resource). / 166

28. *Homogeneous Tilting Armour.* Metropolitan Museum of Art, New York, The Bashford Dean Memorial Collection, Gift of Helen Farnestock Hubbard, 1929, in Memory of Her Father, Harris C. Farnestock (29.154.1). / 174

29. *Greek Helmet.* Bronze. Metropolitan Museum of Art, New York, Rogers Fund, 1919 (19.192.35). / 175

30. Sandro Botticelli, *Venus and Mars.* National Gallery, London (The Trustees of the National Gallery of Art, London). / 188

31. William Blake, *God Creating Adam.* The Tate Gallery, London. / 275

32. William Blake, *Infant Joy,* from *Songs of Innocence and of Experience.* The British Museum, London (Courtesy of the Trustees of the British Museum). / 277

33. Jean-Auguste-Dominique Ingres, *The Turkish Bath.* Louvre, Paris (Cliché des Musées Nationaux, Paris). / 278

34. Thomas Phillips, *Lord Byron.* Newstead Abbey, Nottingham City Museums. / 360

35. *Elvis Presley* in the film *Speedway.* Museum of Modern Art, New York/Film Stills Archive. / 361

36. Eugène Delacroix, *Death of Sardanapalus.* Louvre, Paris (Cliché des Musées Nationaux, Paris). / 398

37. Dante Gabriel Rossetti, *The Lady Lilith.* Delaware Art Museum, Wilmington, Samuel and Mary R. Bancroft Memorial Collection. / 492

38. Dante Gabriel Rossetti, *Astarte Syriaca.* Manchester City Art Galleries. / 494

39. Dante Gabriel Rossetti, *The Bower Meadow.* Manchester City Art Galleries. / 495

40. Sir Edward Burne-Jones, *The Briar Wood.* Briar Rose Series. Buscot Park, The Faringdon Collection Trust (Photograph: Courtauld Institute of Art, London). / 498

41. Sir Edward Burne-Jones, *The Doom Fulfilled.* Southampton City Art Gallery, U.K. / 499

42. Gustave Moreau, *Helen at the Scaean Gate.* Musée Gustave Moreau, Paris (Cliché des Musées Nationaux, Paris). / 500

43. Gustave Moreau, *Jupiter and Semele.* Musée Gustave Moreau, Paris (Cliché des Musées Nationaux, Paris). / 502

44. Franz von Stuck, *Sin.* Neue Pinakothek, Munich. / 503

45. Aubrey Beardsley, *The Ascension of St. Rose of Lima.* / 509

46. Aubrey Beardsley, *Portrait of Himself,* from *The Yellow Book,* Volume 3. / 510

47. Aubrey Beardsley, *The Climax,* from *Salomé.* / 564

Preface

Sexual Personae seeks to demonstrate the unity and continuity of western culture—something that has inspired little belief since the period before World War I. The book accepts the canonical western tradition and rejects the modernist idea that culture has collapsed into meaningless fragments. I argue that Judeo-Christianity never did defeat paganism, which still flourishes in art, eroticism, astrology, and pop culture.

The first volume of *Sexual Personae* examines antiquity, the Renaissance, and Romanticism from the late eighteenth century to 1900. I demonstrate that Romanticism turns almost immediately into Decadence, which I find throughout major nineteenth-century authors, even Emily Dickinson. The second volume will show how movies, television, sports, and rock music embody all the pagan themes of classical antiquity. My approach throughout the book combines disciplines: literature, art history, psychology, and religion.

What is art? How and why does an artist create? The amorality, aggression, sadism, voyeurism, and pornography in great art have been ignored or glossed over by most academic critics. I fill in the space between artist and art work with metaphors drawn from the Cambridge School of Anthropology. My largest ambition is to fuse Frazer with Freud.

What is sex? What is nature? I see sex and nature as brutal pagan forces. My stress on the truth in sexual stereotypes and on the biologic basis of sex differences is sure to cause controversy. I reaffirm and celebrate woman's ancient mystery and glamour. I see the mother as an overwhelming force who condemns men to lifelong sexual anxiety, from which they escape through rationalism and physical achievement.

I show how much of western life, art, and thought is ruled by personality, which the book traces through recurrent types or personae ("masks"). My title was inspired by Ingmar Bergman's cruel, dreamy masterpiece, *Persona* (1966). My method is a form of sensationalism: I try to flesh out intellect with emotion and to induce a wide range of emotion from the reader. I want to show meaning arising from simple everyday things—cats, grocery stores, bridges, chance encounters—and thereby to liberate criticism and interpretation from their imprisonment in classroom and library.

Acknowledgments

Harold Bloom has been a tremendous source of encouragement and practical help throughout this project. I am very grateful for his warm hospitality to my ideas.

Milton Kessler hugely influenced the way I read and teach literature. I am grateful for the early support of my work by Geoffrey Hartman, Richard Ellmann, Barbara Herrnstein Smith, Richard Tristman, and Alvin Feinman.

My parents, Pasquale and Lydia Paglia, and sister Lenora have provided unflagging spiritual and material support for all my endeavors. Thanks to my extended family: Albert and Angelina Mastrogiacomo, Bruno and Jane Colapietro, Sister Rita Mastrogiacomo, Wanda Hudak, Rico and Jennie DiPietro, and Numa Pompilius.

Friends who heroically gave of their time and effort to advise me on the manuscript are Robert L. Caserio, Bruce Benderson, Heidi Jon Schmidt, James Fessenden, and Kent Christensen. Friends who generously nurtured me over the long haul are Helen Vermeychuk, Elizabeth Davis, Stephen Feld, Ann Jamison, Kristen Lippincott, and Lisa Chedekel.

I would also like to thank Ronald R. Macdonald, John DeWitt, Carmelia Metosh, Kristoffer Jacobson, Gregory Vermeychuk, Rachel Wizner, Margaret W. Ferguson, R. D. Skillings, Jeannette LeBlanc, Jeanne Bloom, Stephen Jarratt, Linda Ferris, Robert A. Goldstein, Carole C. Leher, Cammy Sanes, Frances Fanelli, and Sarah S. Fought.

I am grateful to Ellen Graham, the sponsoring editor, and Judith Calvert, the manuscript editor, for their expert contributions to my book. Financial support was received from the Fels Facilities Fund of Bennington College, the Faculty Research Project Grants of Philadelphia College of the Performing Arts, and the President's Completion Grants of the University of the Arts. Earlier versions of Chapters One, Six, and Twenty-One appeared in *Western Humanities Review, English Literary Renaissance,* and *Raritan.*

Sexual Personae

1

Sex and Violence, or Nature and Art

In the beginning was nature. The background from which and against which our ideas of God were formed, nature remains the supreme moral problem. We cannot hope to understand sex and gender until we clarify our attitude toward nature. Sex is a subset to nature. Sex is the natural in man.

Society is an artificial construction, a defense against nature's power. Without society, we would be storm-tossed on the barbarous sea that is nature. Society is a system of inherited forms reducing our humiliating passivity to nature. We may alter these forms, slowly or suddenly, but no change in society will change nature. Human beings are not nature's favorites. We are merely one of a multitude of species upon which nature indiscriminately exerts its force. Nature has a master agenda we can only dimly know.

Human life began in flight and fear. Religion rose from rituals of propitiation, spells to lull the punishing elements. To this day, communities are few in regions scorched by heat or shackled by ice. Civilized man conceals from himself the extent of his subordination to nature. The grandeur of culture, the consolation of religion absorb his attention and win his faith. But let nature shrug, and all is in ruin. Fire, flood, lightning, tornado, hurricane, volcano, earthquake—anywhere at any time. Disaster falls upon the good and bad. Civilized life requires a state of illusion. The idea of the ultimate benevolence of nature and God is the most potent of man's survival mechanisms. Without it, culture would revert to fear and despair.

Sexuality and eroticism are the intricate intersection of nature and culture. Feminists grossly oversimplify the problem of sex when they reduce it to a matter of social convention: readjust society, eliminate sexual inequality, purify sex roles, and happiness and harmony will reign. Here feminism, like all liberal movements of the past two hundred years, is heir to Rousseau. *The Social Contract* (1762) begins: "Man is born free, and everywhere he is in chains." Pitting benign Romantic nature against corrupt society, Rousseau produced the progressivist strain in nineteenth-century culture, for which social reform was the means to achieve paradise on earth. The bubble of these hopes was burst by the catastrophes of two world wars. But Rousseauism was reborn in the postwar generation of the Sixties, from which contemporary feminism developed.

Rousseau rejects original sin, Christianity's pessimistic view of man born unclean, with a propensity for evil. Rousseau's idea, derived from Locke, of man's innate goodness led to social environmentalism, now the dominant ethic of American human services, penal codes, and behaviorist therapies. It assumes that aggression, violence, and crime come from social deprivation—a poor neighborhood, a bad home. Thus feminism blames rape on pornography and, by a smug circularity of reasoning, interprets outbreaks of sadism as a backlash to itself. But rape and sadism have been evident throughout history and, at some moment, in all cultures.

This book takes the point of view of Sade, the most unread major writer in western literature. Sade's work is a comprehensive satiric critique of Rousseau, written in the decade after the first failed Rousseauist experiment, the French Revolution, which ended not in political paradise but in the hell of the Reign of Terror. Sade follows Hobbes rather than Locke. Aggression comes from nature; it is what Nietzsche is to call the will-to-power. For Sade, getting back to nature (the Romantic imperative that still permeates our culture from sex counseling to cereal commercials) would be to give free rein to violence and lust. I agree. Society is not the criminal but the force which keeps crime in check. When social controls weaken, man's innate cruelty bursts forth. The rapist is created not by bad social influences but by a failure of social conditioning. Feminists, seeking to drive power relations out of sex, have set themselves against nature. Sex *is* power. Identity is power. In western culture, there are no nonexploitative relationships. Everyone has killed in order to live. Nature's universal law of creation from destruction operates in mind as in matter. As Freud, Nietzsche's heir, asserts, identity is conflict. Each generation drives its plow over the bones of the dead.

Modern liberalism suffers unresolved contradictions. It exalts individualism and freedom and, on its radical wing, condemns social orders as oppressive. On the other hand, it expects government to provide materially for all, a feat manageable only by an expansion of authority and a swollen bureaucracy. In other words, liberalism defines government as tyrant father but demands it behave as nurturant mother. Feminism has inherited these contradictions. It sees every hierarchy as repressive, a social fiction; every negative about woman is a male lie designed to keep her in her place. Feminism has exceeded its proper mission of seeking political equality for women and has ended by rejecting contingency, that is, human limitation by nature or fate.

Sexual freedom, sexual liberation. A modern delusion. We are hierarchical animals. Sweep one hierarchy away, and another will take its place, perhaps less palatable than the first. There are hierarchies in nature and alternate hierarchies in society. In nature, brute force is the law, a survival of the fittest. In society, there are protections for the weak. Society is our frail barrier against nature. When the prestige of state and religion is low, men are free, but they find freedom intolerable and seek new ways to enslave themselves, through drugs or depression. My theory is that whenever sexual freedom is sought or achieved, sadomasochism will not be far behind. Romanticism always turns into decadence. Nature is a hard taskmaster. It is the hammer and the anvil, crushing individuality. Perfect freedom would be to die by earth, air, water, and fire.

Sex is a far darker power than feminism has admitted. Behaviorist sex therapies believe guiltless, no-fault sex is possible. But sex has always been girt round with taboo, irrespective of culture. Sex is the point of contact between man and nature, where morality and good intentions fall to primitive urges. I called it an intersection. This intersection is the uncanny crossroads of Hecate, where all things return in the night. Eroticism is a realm stalked by ghosts. It is the place beyond the pale, both cursed and enchanted.

This book shows how much in culture goes against our best wishes. Integration of man's body and mind is a profound problem that is not about to be solved by recreational sex or an expansion of women's civil rights. Incarnation, the limitation of mind by matter, is an outrage to imagination. Equally outrageous is gender, which we have not chosen but which nature has imposed upon us. Our physicality is torment, our body the tree of nature on which Blake sees us crucified.

Sex is daemonic. This term, current in Romantic studies of the past twenty-five years, derives from the Greek *daimon*, meaning a spirit of lower divinity than the Olympian gods (hence my pronunciation "daimonic"). The outcast Oedipus becomes a daemon at Colonus. The word came to mean a man's guardian shadow. Christianity turned the daemonic into the demonic. The Greek daemons were not evil—or rather they were both good and evil, like nature itself, in which they dwelled. Freud's unconscious is a daemonic realm. In the day we are social creatures, but at night we descend to the dream world where nature reigns, where there is no law but sex, cruelty, and metamorphosis. Day itself is invaded by daemonic night. Moment by moment, night flickers in the imagination, in eroticism, subverting our strivings for virtue and order, giving an uncanny aura to objects and persons, revealed to us through the eyes of the artist.

The ghost-ridden character of sex is implicit in Freud's brilliant theory of "family romance." We each have an incestuous constellation of sexual personae that we carry from childhood to the grave and that determines whom and how we love or hate. Every encounter with friend or foe, every clash with or submission to authority bears the perverse traces of family romance. Love is a crowded theater, for as Harold Bloom remarks, "We can never embrace (sexually or otherwise) a single person, but embrace the whole of her or his family romance."[1] We still know next to nothing of the mystery of cathexis, the investment of libido in certain people or things. The element of free will in sex and emotion is slight. As poets know, falling in love is irrational.

Like art, sex is fraught with symbols. Family romance means that adult sex is always representation, ritualistic acting out of vanished realities. A perfectly humane eroticism may be impossible. Somewhere in every family romance is hostility and aggression, the homicidal wishes of the unconscious. Children are monsters of unbridled egotism and will, for they spring directly from nature, hostile intimations of immorality. We carry that daemonic will within us forever. Most people conceal it with acquired ethical precepts and meet it only in their dreams, which they hastily forget upon waking. The will-to-power is innate, but the sexual scripts of family romance are learned. Human beings are the only creatures in whom consciousness is so entangled with animal instinct. In western culture, there can never be a purely physical or anxiety-free sexual encounter. Every attraction, every pattern of touch, every orgasm is shaped by psychic shadows.

The search for freedom through sex is doomed to failure. In sex, compulsion and ancient Necessity rule. The sexual personae of family romance are obliterated by the tidal force of regression, the backwards movement toward primeval dissolution, which Ferenczi identifies with ocean. An orgasm is a domination, a surrender, or a breaking through. Nature is no respecter of human identity. This is why so many men turn away or flee after sex, for they have sensed the annihilation of the

daemonic. Western love is a displacement of cosmic realities. It is a
defense mechanism rationalizing forces ungoverned and ungovern-
able. Like early religion, it is a device enabling us to control our primal
fear.

Sex cannot be understood because nature cannot be understood.
Science is a method of logical analysis of nature's operations. It has
lessened human anxiety about the cosmos by demonstrating the materiality of nature's forces, and their frequent predictability. But science is
always playing catch-up ball. Nature breaks its own rules whenever it
wants. Science cannot avert a single thunderbolt. Western science is a
product of the Apollonian mind: its hope is that by naming and classification, by the cold light of intellect, archaic night can be pushed back
and defeated.

Name and person are part of the west's quest for form. The west
insists on the discrete identity of objects. To name is to know; to know is
to control. I will demonstrate that the west's greatness arises from this
delusional certitude. Far Eastern culture has never striven against nature in this way. Compliance, not confrontation is its rule. Buddhist
meditation seeks the unity and harmony of reality. Twentieth-century
physics, going full circle back to Heracleitus, postulates that all matter
is in motion. In other words, there is no thing, only energy. But this
perception has not been imaginatively absorbed, for it cancels the west's
intellectual and moral assumptions.

The westerner knows by seeing. Perceptual relations are at the heart
of our culture, and they have produced our titanic contributions to art.
Walking in nature, we see, identify, name, *recognize*. This recognition is
our apotropaion, that is, our warding off of fear. Recognition is ritual
cognition, a repetition-compulsion. We say that nature is beautiful. But
this aesthetic judgment, which not all peoples have shared, is another
defense formation, woefully inadequate for encompassing nature's totality. What is pretty in nature is confined to the thin skin of the globe
upon which we huddle. Scratch that skin, and nature's daemonic ugliness will erupt.

Our focus on the pretty is an Apollonian strategy. The leaves and
flowers, the birds, the hills are a patchwork pattern by which we map the
known. What the west represses in its view of nature is the chthonian,
which means "of the earth"—but earth's bowels, not its surface. Jane
Harrison uses the term for pre-Olympian Greek religion, and I adopt it
as a substitute for Dionysian, which has become contaminated with
vulgar pleasantries. The Dionysian is no picnic. It is the chthonian
realities which Apollo evades, the blind grinding of subterranean force,

the long slow suck, the murk and ooze. It is the dehumanizing brutality of biology and geology, the Darwinian waste and bloodshed, the squalor and rot we must block from consciousness to retain our Apollonian integrity as persons. Western science and aesthetics are attempts to revise this horror into imaginatively palatable form.

The daemonism of chthonian nature is the west's dirty secret. Modern humanists made the "tragic sense of life" the touchstone of mature understanding. They defined man's mortality and the transience of time as literature's supreme subjects. In this I again see evasion and even sentimentality. The tragic sense of life is a partial response to experience. It is a reflex of the west's resistance to and misapprehension of nature, compounded by the errors of liberalism, which in its Romantic nature-philosophy has followed the Rousseauist Wordsworth rather than the daemonic Coleridge.

Tragedy is the most western literary genre. It did not appear in Japan until the late nineteenth century. The western will, setting itself up against nature, dramatized its own inevitable fall as a human universal, which it is not. An irony of literary history is the birth of tragedy in the cult of Dionysus. The protagonist's destruction recalls the slaughter of animals and, even earlier, of real human beings in archaic ritual. It is no accident that tragedy as we know it dates from the Apollonian fifth century of Athens' greatness, whose cardinal work is Aeschylus' *Oresteia*, a celebration of the defeat of chthonian power. Drama, a Dionysian mode, turned against Dionysus in making the passage from ritual to mimesis, that is, from action to representation. Aristotle's "pity and fear" is a broken promise, a plea for vision without horror.

Few Greek tragedies fully conform to the humanist commentary on them. Their barbaric residue will not come unglued. Even in the fifth century, as we shall see, a satiric response to Apollonianized theater came in Euripides' decadent plays. Problems in accurate assessment of Greek tragedy include not only the loss of three-quarters of the original body of work but the lack of survival of any complete satyr-play. This was the finale to the classic trilogy, an obscene comic burlesque. In Greek tragedy, comedy always had the last word. Modern criticism has projected a Victorian and, I feel, Protestant high seriousness upon pagan culture that still blankets teaching of the humanities. Paradoxically, assent to savage chthonian realities leads not to gloom but to humor. Hence Sade's strange laughter, his wit amid the most fantastic cruelties. For life is not a tragedy but a comedy. Comedy is born of the clash between Apollo and Dionysus. Nature is always pulling the rug out from under our pompous ideals.

Female tragic protagonists are rare. Tragedy is a male paradigm of rise and fall, a graph in which dramatic and sexual climax are in shadowy analogy. Climax is another western invention. Traditional eastern stories are picaresque, horizontal chains of incident. There is little suspense or sense of an ending. The sharp vertical peaking of western narrative, as later of orchestral music, is exemplified by Sophocles' *Oedipus Rex*, whose moment of maximum intensity Aristotle calls *peripeteia*, reversal. Western dramatic climax was produced by the agon of male will. Through action to identity. Action is the route of escape from nature, but all action circles back to origins, the womb-tomb of nature. Oedipus, trying to escape his mother, runs straight into her arms. Western narrative is a mystery story, a process of detection. But since what is detected is unbearable, every revelation leads to another repression.

The major women of tragedy—Euripides' Medea and Phaedra, Shakespeare's Cleopatra and Lady Macbeth, Racine's Phèdre—skew the genre by their disruptive relation to male action. Tragic woman is less moral than man. Her will-to-power is naked. Her actions are under a chthonian cloud. They are a conduit of the irrational, opening the genre to intrusions of the barbaric force that drama shut out at its birth. Tragedy is a western vehicle for testing and purification of the male will. The difficulty in grafting female protagonists onto it is a result not of male prejudice but of instinctive sexual strategics. Woman introduces untransformed cruelty into tragedy because she is the problem that the genre is trying to correct.

Tragedy plays a male game, a game it invented to snatch victory from the jaws of defeat. It is not flawed choice, flawed action, or even death itself which is the ultimate human dilemma. The gravest challenge to our hopes and dreams is the messy biological business-as-usual that is going on within us and without us at every hour of every day. Consciousness is a pitiful hostage of its flesh-envelope, whose surges, circuits, and secret murmurings it cannot stay or speed. This is the chthonian drama that has no climax but only an endless round, cycle upon cycle. Microcosm mirrors macrocosm. Free will is stillborn in the red cells of our body, for there is no free will in nature. Our choices come to us prepackaged and special delivery, molded by hands not our own.

Tragedy's inhospitality to woman springs from nature's inhospitality to man. The identification of woman with nature was universal in prehistory. In hunting or agrarian societies dependent upon nature, femaleness was honored as an immanent principle of fertility. As culture progressed, crafts and commerce supplied a concentration of resources freeing men from the caprices of weather or the handicap of geography. With nature at one remove, femaleness receded in importance.

Buddhist cultures retained the ancient meanings of femaleness long after the west renounced them. Male and female, the Chinese yang and yin, are balanced and interpenetrating powers in man and nature, to which society is subordinate. This code of passive acceptance has its roots in India, a land of sudden extremes where a monsoon can wipe out 50,000 people overnight. The femaleness of fertility religions is always double-edged. The Indian nature-goddess Kali is creator *and* destroyer, granting boons with one set of arms while cutting throats with the other. She is the lady ringed with skulls. The moral ambivalence of the great mother goddesses has been conveniently forgotten by those American feminists who have resurrected them. We cannot grasp nature's bare blade without shedding our own blood.

Western culture from the start has swerved from femaleness. The last major western society to worship female powers was Minoan Crete. And significantly, that fell and did not rise again. The immediate cause of its collapse—quake, plague, or invasion—is beside the point. The lesson is that cultic femaleness is no guarantee of cultural strength or viability. What did survive, what did vanquish circumstance and stamp its mind-set on Europe was Mycenaean warrior culture, descending to us through Homer. The male will-to-power: Mycenaeans from the south and Dorians from the north would fuse to form Apollonian Athens, from which came the Greco-Roman line of western history.

Both the Apollonian and Judeo-Christian traditions are transcendental. That is, they seek to surmount or transcend nature. Despite Greek culture's contrary Dionysian element, which I will discuss, high classicism was an Apollonian achievement. Judaism, Christianity's parent sect, is the most powerful of protests against nature. The Old Testament asserts that a father god made nature and that differentiation into objects and gender was after the fact of his maleness. Judeo-Christianity, like Greek worship of the Olympian gods, is a sky-cult. It is an advanced stage in the history of religion, which everywhere began as earth-cult, veneration of fruitful nature.

The evolution from earth-cult to sky-cult shifts woman into the nether realm. Her mysterious procreative powers and the resemblance of her rounded breasts, belly, and hips to earth's contours put her at the center of early symbolism. She was the model for the Great Mother figures who crowded the birth of religion worldwide. But the mother cults did not mean social freedom for women. On the contrary, as I will show in a discussion of Hollywood in the sequel to this book, cult-objects are prisoners of their own symbolic inflation. Every totem lives in taboo.

Woman was an idol of belly-magic. She seemed to swell and give birth by her own law. From the beginning of time, woman has seemed an uncanny being. Man honored but feared her. She was the black maw that had spat him forth and would devour him anew. Men, bonding together, invented culture as a defense against female nature. Sky-cult was the most sophisticated step in this process, for its switch of the creative locus from earth to sky is a shift from belly-magic to head-magic. And from this defensive head-magic has come the spectacular glory of male civilization, which has lifted woman with it. The very language and logic modern woman uses to assail patriarchal culture were the invention of men.

Hence the sexes are caught in a comedy of historical indebtedness. Man, repelled by his debt to a physical mother, created an alternate reality, a heterocosm to give him the illusion of freedom. Woman, at first content to accept man's protections but now inflamed with desire for her own illusory freedom, invades man's systems and suppresses her indebtedness to him as she steals them. By head-magic she will deny there ever was a problem of sex and nature. She has inherited the anxiety of influence.

The identification of woman with nature is the most troubled and troubling term in this historical argument. Was it ever true? Can it still be true? Most feminist readers will disagree, but I think this identification not myth but reality. All the genres of philosophy, science, high art, athletics, and politics were invented by men. But by the Promethean law of conflict and capture, woman has a right to seize what she will and to vie with man on his own terms. Yet there is a limit to what she can alter in herself and in man's relation to her. Every human being must wrestle with nature. But nature's burden falls more heavily on one sex. With luck, this will not limit woman's achievement, that is, her action in male-created social space. But it must limit eroticism, that is, our imaginative lives in sexual space, which may overlap social space but is not identical with it.

Nature's cycles are woman's cycles. Biologic femaleness is a sequence of circular returns, beginning and ending at the same point. Woman's centrality gives her a stability of identity. She does not have to become but only to be. Her centrality is a great obstacle to man, whose quest for identity she blocks. He must transform himself into an independent being, that is, a being free of her. If he does not, he will simply fall back into her. Reunion with the mother is a siren call haunting our imagination. Once there was bliss, and now there is struggle. Dim memories of life before the traumatic separation of birth may be the source of Arcadian fantasies of a lost golden age. The western idea of history as a propulsive movement into the future, a progressive or Providential design climaxing in the revelation of a Second Coming, is a male formulation. No woman, I submit, could have coined such an idea, since it is a strategy of evasion of woman's own cyclic nature, in which man dreads being caught. Evolutionary or apocalyptic history is a male wish list with a happy ending, a phallic peak.

Woman does not dream of transcendental or historical escape from natural cycle, since she *is* that cycle. Her sexual maturity means marriage to the moon, waxing and waning in lunar phases. Moon, month, menses: same word, same world. The ancients knew that woman is bound to nature's calendar, an appointment she cannot refuse. The Greek pattern of free will to hybris to tragedy is a male drama, since woman has never been deluded (until recently) by the mirage of free will. She knows there is no free will, since she is not free. She has no choice but acceptance. Whether she desires motherhood or not, nature yokes her into the brute inflexible rhythm of procreative law. Menstrual cycle is an alarming clock that cannot be stopped until nature wills it.

Woman's reproductive apparatus is vastly more complicated than man's, and still ill-understood. All kinds of things can go wrong or cause distress in going right. Western woman is in an agonistic relation to her own body: for her, biologic normalcy is suffering, and health an illness. Dysmenorrhea, it is argued, is a disease of civilization, since women in tribal cultures have few menstrual complaints. But in tribal life, woman has an extended or collective identity; tribal religion honors nature and subordinates itself to it. It is precisely in advanced western society, which attempts to improve or surpass nature and which holds up individualism and self-realization as a model, that the stark facts of woman's condition emerge with painful clarity. The more woman aims for personal identity and autonomy, the more she develops her imagination, the fiercer will be her struggle with nature—that is, with the intractable physical laws of her own body. And the more nature will punish her: do not dare to be free! for your body does not belong to you.

The female body is a chthonian machine, indifferent to the spirit who inhabits it. Organically, it has one mission, pregnancy, which we may spend a lifetime staving off. Nature cares only for species, never individuals: the humiliating dimensions of this biologic fact are most directly experienced by women, who probably have a greater realism and wisdom than men because of it. Woman's body is a sea acted upon by the month's lunar wave-motion. Sluggish and dormant, her fatty tissues are gorged with water, then suddenly cleansed at hormonal high tide. Edema is our mammalian relapse into the vegetable. Pregnancy demonstrates the deterministic character of woman's sexuality. Every pregnant woman has body and self taken over by a chthonian force beyond her control. In the welcome pregnancy, this is a happy sacrifice. But in the unwanted one, initiated by rape or misadventure, it is a horror. Such unfortunate women look directly into nature's heart of darkness. For a fetus is a benign tumor, a vampire who steals in order to live. The so-called miracle of birth is nature getting her own way.

Every month for women is a new defeat of the will. Menstruation was once called "the curse," a reference to the expulsion from the Garden, when woman was condemned to labor pains because of Eve's sin. Most early cultures hemmed in menstruating women by ritual taboos. Orthodox Jewish women still purify themselves from menstrual uncleanness in the *mikveh*, a ritual bath. Women have borne the symbolic burden of man's imperfections, his grounding in nature. Menstrual blood is the stain, the birthmark of original sin, the filth that transcendental religion must wash from man. Is this identification merely phobic, merely misogynistic? Or is it possible there *is* something uncanny about menstrual blood, justifying its attachment to taboo? I will argue that it is not menstrual blood per se which disturbs the imagination—unstanchable as that red flood may be—but rather the albumen in the blood, the uterine shreds, placental jellyfish of the female sea. This is the chthonian matrix from which we rose. We have an evolutionary revulsion from slime, our site of biologic origins. Every month, it is woman's fate to face the abyss of time and being, the abyss which is herself.

The Bible has come under fire for making woman the fall guy in man's cosmic drama. But in casting a male conspirator, the serpent, as God's enemy, Genesis hedges and does not take its misogyny far enough. The Bible defensively swerves from God's true opponent, chthonian nature. The serpent is not outside Eve but in her. She is the garden *and* the serpent. Anthony Storr says of witches, "At a very primitive level, all mothers are phallic."[2] The Devil is a woman. Modern emancipation movements, discarding stereotypes impeding woman's social advance, refuse to acknowledge procreation's daemonism. Nature is serpentine, a bed of tangled vines, creepers and crawlers, probing dumb fingers of fetid organic life which Wordsworth taught us to call pretty. Biologists speak of man's reptilian brain, the oldest part of our upper nervous system, killer survivor of the archaic era. I contend that

the premenstrual woman incited to snappishness or rage is hearing
signals from the reptilian brain. In her, man's latent perversity is manifest. All hell breaks loose, the hell of chthonian nature that modern
humanism denies and represses. In every premenstrual woman struggling to govern her temper, sky-cult wars again with earth-cult.

Mythology's identification of woman with nature is correct. The male
contribution to procreation is momentary and transient. Conception is a
pinpoint of time, another of our phallic peaks of action, from which the
male slides back uselessly. The pregnant woman is daemonically, devil-
ishly complete. As an ontological entity, she needs nothing and no one. I
shall maintain that the pregnant woman, brooding for nine months
upon her own creation, is the pattern of all solipsism, that the historical
attribution of narcissism to women is another true myth. Male bonding
and patriarchy were the recourse to which man was forced by his
terrible sense of woman's power, her imperviousness, her archetypal
confederacy with chthonian nature. Woman's body is a labyrinth in
which man is lost. It is a walled garden, the medieval *hortus conclusus*,
in which nature works its daemonic sorcery. Woman is the primeval fabricator, the real First Mover. She turns a gob of refuse into a spreading
web of sentient being, floating on the snaky umbilical by which she
leashes every man.

Feminism has been simplistic in arguing that female archetypes were
politically motivated falsehoods by men. The historical repugnance to
woman has a rational basis: disgust is reason's proper response to the
grossness of procreative nature. Reason and logic are the anxiety-
inspired domain of Apollo, premiere god of sky-cult. The Apollonian is
harsh and phobic, coldly cutting itself off from nature by its superhuman purity. I shall argue that western personality and western achievement are, for better or worse, largely Apollonian. Apollo's great opponent Dionysus is ruler of the chthonian whose law is procreative
femaleness. As we shall see, the Dionysian is liquid nature, a miasmic
swamp whose prototype is the still pond of the womb.

We must ask whether the equivalence of male and female in Far
Eastern symbolism was as culturally efficacious as the hierarchization
of male over female has been in the west. Which system has ultimately
benefited women more? Western science and industry have freed wom-
en from drudgery and danger. Machines do housework. The pill neutralizes fertility. Giving birth is no longer fatal. And the Apollonian line
of western rationality has produced the modern aggressive woman who
can think like a man and write obnoxious books. The tension and
antagonism in western metaphysics developed human higher cortical

powers to great heights. Most of western culture is a distortion of reality. But reality *should* be distorted; that is, imaginatively amended. The Buddhist acquiescence to nature is neither accurate about nature nor just to human potential. The Apollonian has taken us to the stars.

Daemonic archetypes of woman, filling world mythology, represent the uncontrollable nearness of nature. Their tradition passes nearly unbroken from prehistoric idols through literature and art to modern movies. The primary image is the femme fatale, the woman fatal to man. The more nature is beaten back in the west, the more the femme fatale reappears, as a return of the repressed. She is the spectre of the west's bad conscience about nature. She is the moral ambiguity of nature, a malevolent moon that keeps breaking through our fog of hopeful sentiment.

Feminism dismisses the femme fatale as a cartoon and libel. If she ever existed, she was simply a victim of society, resorting to destructive womanly wiles because of her lack of access to political power. The femme fatale was a career woman *manquée*, her energies neurotically diverted into the boudoir. By such techniques of demystification, feminism has painted itself into a corner. Sexuality is a murky realm of contradiction and ambivalence. It cannot always be understood by social models, which feminism, as an heir of nineteenth-century utilitarianism, insists on imposing on it. Mystification will always remain the disorderly companion of love and art. Eroticism *is* mystique; that is, the aura of emotion and imagination around sex. It cannot be "fixed" by codes of social or moral convenience, whether from the political left or right. For nature's fascism is greater than that of any society. There is a daemonic instability in sexual relations that we may have to accept.

The femme fatale is one of the most mesmerizing of sexual personae. She is not a fiction but an extrapolation of biologic realities in women that remain constant. The North American Indian myth of the toothed vagina (*vagina dentata*) is a gruesomely direct transcription of female power and male fear. Metaphorically, every vagina has secret teeth, for the male exits as less than when he entered. The basic mechanics of conception require action in the male but nothing more than passive receptivity in the female. Sex as a natural rather than social transaction, therefore, really is a kind of drain of male energy by female fullness. Physical and spiritual castration is the danger every man runs in intercourse with a woman. Love is the spell by which he puts his sexual fear to sleep. Woman's latent vampirism is not a social aberration but a development of her maternal function, for which nature has equipped her with tiresome thoroughness. For the male, every act of intercourse is a return to the mother and a capitulation to her. For men, sex is a struggle for identity. In sex, the male is consumed and released again by the toothed power that bore him, the female dragon of nature.

The femme fatale was produced by the mystique of connection between mother and child. A modern assumption is that sex and procreation are medically, scientifically, intellectually "manageable." If we keep tinkering with the social mechanism long enough, every difficulty will disappear. Meanwhile, the divorce rate soars. Conventional marriage, despite its inequities, kept the chaos of libido in check. When the prestige of marriage is low, all the nasty daemonism of sexual instinct pops out. Individualism, the self unconstrained by society, leads to the coarser servitude of constraint by nature. Every road from Rousseau leads to Sade. The mystique of our birth from human mothers is one of the daemonic clouds we cannot dispel by tiny declarations of independence. Apollo can swerve from nature, but he cannot obliterate it. As emotional and sexual beings we go full circle. Old age is a second childhood in which earliest memories revive. Chillingly, comatose patients of any age automatically drift toward the fetal position, from which they have to be pried by nurses. We are tied to our birth by unshakable apparitions of sense-memory.

Rousseauist psychologies like feminism assert the ultimate benevolence of human emotion. In such a system, the femme fatale logically has no place. I follow Freud, Nietzsche, and Sade in my view of the amorality of the instinctual life. At some level, all love is combat, a wrestling with ghosts. We are only *for* something by being *against* something else. People who believe they are having pleasant, casual, uncomplex sexual encounters, whether with friend, spouse, or stranger, are blocking from consciousness the tangle of psychodynamics at work, just as they block the hostile clashings of their dream life. Family romance operates at all times. The femme fatale is one of the refinements of female narcissism, of the ambivalent self-directedness that is completed by the birth of a child or by the conversion of spouse or lover into child.

Mothers can be fatal to their sons. It is against the mother that men have erected their towering edifice of politics and sky-cult. She is Medusa, in whom Freud sees the castrating and castrated female pubes. But Medusa's snaky hair is also the writhing vegetable growth of nature. Her hideous grimace is men's fear of the laughter of women. She that gives life also blocks the way to freedom. Therefore I agree with Sade that we have the right to thwart nature's procreative compulsions, through sodomy or abortion. Male homosexuality may be the most valorous of attempts to evade the femme fatale and to defeat nature. By turning away from the Medusan mother, whether in honor or detestation of her, the male homosexual is one of the great forgers of absolutist western identity. But of course nature has won, as she always does, by making disease the price of promiscuous sex.

The permanence of the femme fatale as a sexual persona is part of the weary weight of eroticism, beneath which both ethics and religion founder. Eroticism is society's soft point, through which it is invaded by chthonian nature. The femme fatale can appear as Medusan mother or as frigid nymph, masquing in the brilliant luminosity of Apollonian high glamour. Her cool unreachability beckons, fascinates, and destroys. She is not a neurotic but, if anything, a psychopath. That is, she has an amoral affectlessness, a serene indifference to the suffering of others, which she invites and dispassionately observes as tests of her power. The mystique of the femme fatale cannot be perfectly translated into male terms. I will speak at length of the beautiful boy, one of the west's most stunning sexual personae. However, the danger of the *homme fatal*, as embodied in today's boyish male hustler, is that he will leave, disappearing to other loves, other lands. He is a rambler, a cowboy and sailor. But the danger of the femme fatale is that *she will stay*, still, placid, and paralyzing. Her remaining is a daemonic burden, the ubiquity of Walter Pater's *Mona Lisa*, who smothers history. She is a thorny symbol of the perversity of sex. She will stick.

We are moving in this chapter toward a theory of beauty. I believe that the aesthetic sense, like everything else thus far, is a swerve from the chthonian. It is a displacement from one area of reality to another, analogous to the shift from earth-cult to sky-cult. Ferenczi speaks of the replacement of animal nose by human eye, because of our upright stance. The eye is peremptory in its judgments. It decides what to see and why. Each of our glances is as much exclusion as inclusion. We select, editorialize, and enhance. Our idea of the pretty is a limited notion that cannot possibly apply to earth's metamorphic underworld, a cataclysmic realm of chthonian violence. We choose not to see this violence on our daily strolls. Every time we say nature is beautiful, we are saying a prayer, fingering our worry beads.

The cool beauty of the femme fatale is another transformation of chthonian ugliness. Female animals are usually less beautiful than males. The mother bird's dull feathers are camouflage, protecting the nest from predators. Male birds are creatures of spectacular display, of both plumage and parade, partly to impress females and conquer rivals and partly to divert enemies from the nest. Among humans, male ritual display is just as extreme, but for the first time the female becomes a lavishly beautiful object. Why? The female is adorned not simply to increase her property value, as Marxism would demystifyingly have it, but to assure her desirability. Consciousness has made cowards of us all. Animals do not feel sexual fear, because they are not rational beings. They operate under a pure biologic imperative. Mind, which has enabled humanity to adapt and flourish as a species, has also infinitely complicated our functioning as physical beings. We see too much, and so have to stringently limit our seeing. Desire is besieged on all sides by anxiety and doubt. Beauty, an ecstasy of the eye, drugs us and allows us to act. Beauty is our Apollonian revision of the chthonian.

Nature is a Darwinian spectacle of the eaters and the eaten. All phases of procreation are ruled by appetite: sexual intercourse, from kissing to penetration, consists of movements of barely controlled cruelty and consumption. The long pregnancy of the human female and the protracted childhood of her infant, who is not self-sustaining for seven years or more, have produced the agon of psychological dependency that burdens the male for a lifetime. Man justifiably fears being devoured by woman, who is nature's proxy.

Repression is an evolutionary adaptation permitting us to function under the burden of our expanded consciousness. For what we are conscious of could drive us mad. Crude male slang speaks of female genitalia as "slash" or "gash." Freud notes that Medusa turns men to stone because, at first sight, a boy thinks female genitals a wound, from which the penis has been cut. They are indeed a wound, but it is the infant who has been cut away, by violence: the umbilical is a hawser sawed through by a social rescue party. Sexual necessity drives man back to that bloody scene, but he cannot approach it without tremors of apprehension. These he conceals by euphemisms of love and beauty. However, the less well-bred he is—that is, the less socialized—the sharper his sense of the animality of sex and the grosser his language. The foulmouthed roughneck is produced not by society's sexism but by society's absence. For nature is the most foulmouthed of us all.

Woman's current advance in society is not a voyage from myth to truth but from myth to new myth. The rise of rational, technological woman may demand the repression of unpleasant archetypal realities. Ferenczi remarks, "The periodic pulsations in feminine sexuality (puberty, the menses, pregnancies and parturitions, the climacterium) require a much more powerful repression on the woman's part than is necessary for the man."[3] In its argument with male society, feminism must suppress the monthly evidence of woman's domination by chthonian nature. Menstruation and childbirth are an affront to beauty and form. In aesthetic terms, they are spectacles of frightful squalor. Modern life, with its hospitals and paper products, has distanced and sanitized these primitive mysteries, just as it has done with death, which used to be a gruelling at-home affair. An awful lot is being swept under the rug: the awe and terror that is our lot.

The woundlike rawness of female genitals is a symbol of the unredeemability of chthonian nature. In aesthetic terms, female genitals are lurid in color, vagrant in contour, and architecturally incoherent. Male genitals, on the other hand, though they risk ludicrousness by their rubbery indecisiveness (a Sylvia Plath heroine memorably thinks of "turkey neck and turkey gizzards"), have a rational mathematical design, a syntax. This is no absolute virtue, however, since it may tend to confirm the male in his abundant misperceptions of reality. Aesthetics stop where sex begins. G. Wilson Knight declares, "All physical love is, in its way, a victory over physical secrecies and physical repulsions."[4] Sex is sloppy and untidy, a return to what Freud calls the infant's polymorphous perversity, a zestful rolling around in every body fluid. St. Augustine says, "We are born between feces and urine." This misogynistic view of the infant's sin-stained emergence from the birth canal is close to the chthonian truth. But excretion, through which nature for once acts upon the sexes equally, can be saved by comedy, as we see in Aristophanes, Rabelais, Pope, and Joyce. Excretion has found a place in high culture. Menstruation and childbirth are too barbaric for comedy. Their ugliness has produced the giant displacement of women's historical status as sex object, whose beauty is endlessly discussed and modified. Woman's beauty is a compromise with her dangerous archetypal allure. It gives the eye the comforting illusion of intellectual control over nature.

My explanation for the male domination of art, science, and politics, an indisputable fact of history, is based on an analogy between sexual physiology and aesthetics. I will argue that all cultural achievement is a projection, a swerve into Apollonian transcendance, and that men are anatomically destined to be projectors. But as with Oedipus, destiny may be a curse.

How we know the world and how it knows us are underlain by shadow patterns of sexual biography and sexual geography. What breaks into consciousness is shaped in advance by the daemonism of the senses. Mind is a captive of the body. Perfect objectivity does not exist. Every thought bears some emotional burden. Had we time or energy to pursue it, each random choice, from the color of a toothbrush to a decision over a menu, could be made to yield its secret meaning in the inner drama of our lives. But in exhaustion, we shut out this psychic supersaturation. The realm of number, the crystalline mathematic of Apollonian purity, was invented early on by western man as a refuge from the soggy emotionalism and bristling disorder of woman and nature. Women who excel in mathematics do so in a system devised by men for the mastery of nature. Number is the most imposing and least creaturely of pacifiers, man's yearning hope for objectivity. It is to number that he—and now she—withdraws to escape from the chthonian mire of love, hate, and family romance.

Even now, it is usually men rather than women who claim logic's superiority to emotion. This they comically tend to do at moments of maximum emotional chaos, which they may have incited and are helpless to stem. Male artists and actors have a cultural function in keeping the line of emotion open from the female to male realms. Every man harbors an inner female territory ruled by his mother, from whom he can never entirely break free. Since Romanticism, art and the study of art have become vehicles for exploring the west's repressed emotional life, though one would never know it from half the deadening scholarship that has sprung up around them. Poetry is the connecting link between body and mind. Every idea in poetry is grounded in emotion. Every word is a palpation of the body. The multiplicity of interpretation surrounding a poem mirrors the stormy uncontrollability of emotion, where nature works her will. Emotion *is* chaos. Every benign emotion has a flip side of negativity. Thus the flight from emotion to number is another crucial strategy of the Apollonian west in its long struggle with Dionysus.

Emotion is passion, a continuum of eroticism and aggression. Love and hate are not opposites: there is only more passion and less passion, a difference of quantity and not of kind. To live in love and peace is one of the outstanding contradictions that Christianity has imposed on its followers, an ideal impossible and unnatural. Since Romanticism, artists and intellectuals have complained about the church's sex rules, but these are just one small part of the Christian war with pagan nature. Only a saint could sustain the Christian code of love. And saints are ruthless in their exclusions: they must shut out an enormous amount of reality, the reality of sexual personae and the reality of nature. Love for all means coldness to something or someone. Even Jesus, let us recall, was unnecessarily rude to his mother at Cana.

The chthonian superflux of emotion is a male problem. A man must do battle with that enormity, which resides in woman and nature. He can attain selfhood only by beating back the daemonic cloud that would swallow him up: mother-love, which we may just as well call mother-hate. Mother-love, mother-hate, for her or from her, one huge conglomerate of natural power. Political equality for women will make very little difference in this emotional turmoil that is going on above and below politics, outside the scheme of social life. Not until all babies are born from glass jars will the combat cease between mother and son. But in a totalitarian future that has removed procreation from woman's hands, there will also be no affect and no art. Men will be machines, without pain but also without pleasure. Imagination has a price, which we are paying every day. There is no escape from the biologic chains that bind us.

What has nature given man to defend himself against woman? Here we come to the source of man's cultural achievements, which follow so directly from his singular anatomy. Our lives as physical beings give rise to basic metaphors of apprehension, which vary greatly between the sexes. Here there can be no equality. Man is sexually compartmentalized. Genitally, he is condemned to a perpetual pattern of linearity, focus, aim, directedness. He must learn to aim. Without aim, urination and ejaculation end in infantile soiling of self or surroundings. Woman's eroticism is diffused throughout her body. Her desire for foreplay remains a notorious area of miscommunication between the sexes. Man's genital concentration is a reduction but also an intensification. He is a victim of unruly ups and downs. Male sexuality is inherently manic-depressive. Estrogen tranquilizes, but androgen agitates. Men are in a constant state of sexual anxiety, living on the pins and needles of their hormones. In sex as in life they are driven *beyond*—beyond the self, beyond the body. Even in the womb this rule applies. Every fetus becomes female unless it is steeped in male hormone, produced by a signal from the testes. Before birth, therefore, a male is already beyond the female. But to be beyond is to be exiled from the center of life. Men know they are sexual exiles. They wander the earth seeking satisfaction, craving and despising, never content. There is nothing in that anguished motion for women to envy.

The male genital metaphor is concentration and projection. Nature gives concentration to man to help him overcome his fear. Man approaches woman in bursts of spasmodic concentration. This gives him the delusion of temporary control of the archetypal mysteries that brought him forth. It gives him the courage to return. Sex is metaphysical for men, as it is not for women. Women have no problem to solve by sex. Physically and psychologically, they are serenely self-contained. They may choose to achieve, but they do not need it. They are not thrust into the beyond by their own fractious bodies. But men are out of balance. They must quest, pursue, court, or seize. Pigeons on the grass, alas: in such parkside rituals we may savor the comic pathos of sex. How often one spots a male pigeon making desperate, self-inflating sallies toward the female, as again and again she turns her back on him and nonchalantly marches away. But by concentration and insistence he may carry the day. Nature has blessed him with obliviousness to his own absurdity. His purposiveness is both a gift and a burden. In human beings, sexual concentration is the male's instrument for gathering together and forcibly fixing the dangerous chthonian superflux of emotion and energy that I identify with woman and nature. In sex, man is driven into the very abyss which he flees. He makes a voyage to nonbeing and back.

Through concentration to projection into the beyond. The male projection of erection and ejaculation is the paradigm for all cultural projection and conceptualization—from art and philosophy to fantasy, hallucination, and obsession. Women have conceptualized less in history not because men have kept them from doing so but because women do not need to conceptualize in order to exist. I leave open the question of brain differences. Conceptualization and sexual mania may issue from the same part of the male brain. Fetishism, for instance, a practice which like most of the sex perversions is confined to men, is clearly a conceptualizing or symbol-making activity. Man's vastly greater commercial patronage of pornography is analogous.

An erection is *a thought* and the orgasm an act of imagination. The male has to will his sexual authority before the woman who is a shadow of his mother and of all women. Failure and humiliation constantly wait in the wings. No woman has to prove herself a woman in the grim way a man has to prove himself a man. He must perform, or the show does not go on. Social convention is irrelevant. A flop is a flop. Ironically, sexual success always ends in sagging fortunes anyhow. Every male projection is transient and must be anxiously, endlessly renewed. Men enter in triumph but withdraw in decrepitude. The sex act cruelly mimics history's decline and fall. Male bonding is a self-preservation society, collegial reaffirmation through larger, fabricated frames of reference. Culture is man's iron reinforcement of his ever-imperiled private projections.

Concentration and projection are remarkably demonstrated by urination, one of male anatomy's most efficient compartmentalizations.

Freud thinks primitive man preened himself on his ability to put out a fire with a stream of urine. A strange thing to be proud of but certainly beyond the scope of woman, who would scorch her hams in the process. Male urination really *is* a kind of accomplishment, an arc of transcendance. A woman merely waters the ground she stands on. Male urination is a form of commentary. It can be friendly when shared but is often aggressive, as in the defacement of public monuments by Sixties rock stars. To piss on is to criticize. John Wayne urinated on the shoes of a grouchy director in full view of cast and crew. This is one genre of self-expression women will never master. A male dog marking every bush on the block is a graffiti artist, leaving his rude signature with each lift of the leg. Women, like female dogs, are earthbound squatters. There is no projection beyond the boundaries of the self. Space is claimed by being sat on, squatter's rights.

The cumbersome, solipsistic character of female physiology is tediously evident at sports events and rock concerts, where fifty women wait in line for admission to the sequestered cells of the toilet. Meanwhile, their male friends zip in and out (in every sense) and stand around looking at their watches and rolling their eyes. Freud's notion of penis envy proves too true when the pubcrawling male cheerily relieves himself in midnight alleyways, to the vexation of his bursting female companions. This compartmentalization or isolation of male genitality has its dark side, however. It can lead to a dissociation of sex and emotion, to temptation, promiscuity, and disease. The modern male homosexual, for example, has sought ecstasy in the squalor of public toilets, for women perhaps the least erotic place on earth.

Man's metaphors of concentration and projection are echoes of both body and mind. Without them, he would be helpless before woman's power. Without them, woman would long ago have absorbed all of creation into herself. There would be no culture, no system, no pyramiding of one hierarchy upon another. Earth-cult must lose to sky-cult, if mind is ever to break free from matter. Ironically, the more modern woman thinks with Apollonian clarity, the more she participates in the historical negation of her sex. Political equality for women, desirable and necessary as it is, is not going to remedy the radical disjunction between the sexes that begins and ends in the body. The sexes will always be jolted by violent shocks of attraction and repulsion.

Androgyny, which some feminists promote as a pacifist blueprint for sexual utopia, belongs to the contemplative rather than active life. It is the ancient prerogative of priests, shamans, and artists. Feminists have politicized it as a weapon against the masculine principle. Redefined, it now means men must be like women and women can be whatever they like. Androgyny is a cancellation of male concentration and projection. Prescriptions for the future by bourgeois academics and writers carry their own bias. The reform of a college English department cuts no ice down at the corner garage. Male concentration and projection are visible everywhere in the aggressive energy of the streets. Fortunately, male homosexuals of every social class have preserved the cult of the masculine, which will therefore never lose its aesthetic legitimacy. Major peaks of western culture have been accompanied by a high incidence of male homosexuality—in classical Athens and Renaissance Florence and London. Male concentration and projection are self-enhancing, leading to supreme achievements of Apollonian conceptualization.

If sexual physiology provides the pattern for our experience of the world, what is woman's basic metaphor? It is mystery, *the hidden*. Karen Horney speaks of a girl's inability to see her genitals and a boy's ability to see his as the source of "the greater subjectivity of women as compared with the greater objectivity of men."[5] To rephrase this with my different emphasis: men's delusional certitude that objectivity is possible is based on the visibility of their genitals. Second, this certitude is a defensive swerve from the anxiety-inducing invisibility of the womb. Women tend to be more realistic and less obsessional because of their toleration for ambiguity, which they learn from their inability to learn about their own bodies. Women accept limited knowledge as their natural condition, a great human truth that a man may take a lifetime to reach.

The female body's unbearable hiddenness applies to all aspects of men's dealings with women. What does it look like in there? Did she have an orgasm? Is it really my child? Who was my real father? Mystery shrouds woman's sexuality. This mystery is the main reason for the imprisonment man has imposed on women. Only by confining his wife in a locked harem guarded by eunuchs could he be certain that her son was also his. Man's genital visibility is a source of his scientific desire for external testing, validation, proof. By this method he hopes to solve the ultimate mystery story, his chthonian birth. Woman is veiled. Violent tearing of this veil may be a motive in gang-rapes and rape-murders, particularly ritualistic disembowellings of the Jack the Ripper kind. The Ripper's public nailing up of his victim's uterus is exactly paralleled in tribal ritual of South African Bushmen. Sex crimes are always male, never female, because such crimes are conceptualizing assaults on the unreachable omnipotence of woman and nature. Every woman's body contains a cell of archaic night, where all knowing must stop. This is the profound meaning behind striptease, a sacred dance of pagan origins which, like prostitution, Christianity has never been able to stamp out. Erotic dancing by males cannot be comparable, for a nude woman carries off the stage a final concealment, that chthonian darkness from which we come.

Woman's body is a secret, sacred space. It is a *temenos* or ritual precinct, a Greek word I adopt for the discussion of art. In the marked-off space of woman's body, nature operates at its darkest and most mechanical. Every woman is a priestess guarding the temenos of dae-monic mysteries. Virginity is categorically different for the sexes. A boy becoming a man quests for experience. The penis is like eye or hand, an extension of self reaching outward. But a girl is a sealed vessel that must be broken into by force. The female body is the prototype of all sacred spaces from cave shrine to temple and church. The womb is the veiled Holy of Holies, a great problem, as we shall see, for sexual polemicists like William Blake who seek to abolish guilt and covertness in sex. The taboo on woman's body is the taboo that always hovers over the place of magic. Woman is literally the occult, which means "the hidden." These uncanny meanings cannot be changed, only suppressed, until they break into cultural consciousness again. Political equality will succeed only in political terms. It is helpless against the archetypal. Kill the imagination, lobotomize the brain, castrate and operate: then the sexes will be the same. Until then, we must live and dream in the daemonic turbulence of nature.

Everything sacred and inviolable provokes profanation and violation. Every crime that *can* be committed *will* be. Rape is a mode of natural aggression that can be controlled only by the social contract. Modern feminism's most naive formulation is its assertion that rape is a crime of violence but not of sex, that it is merely power masquerading as sex. But sex *is* power, and all power is inherently aggressive. Rape is male power fighting female power. It is no more to be excused than is murder or any other assault on another's civil rights. Society is woman's protection against rape, not, as some feminists absurdly maintain, the cause of rape. Rape is the sexual expression of the will-to-power, which nature plants in all of us and which civilization rose to contain. Therefore the rapist is a man with too little socialization rather than too much. World-wide evidence is overwhelming that whenever social controls are weak-ened, as in war or mob rule, even civilized men behave in uncivilized ways, among which is the barbarity of rape.

The latent metaphors of the body guarantee the survival of rape, which is a development in degree of intensity alone of the basic movements of sex. A girl's loss of virginity is always in some sense a violation of sanctity, an invasion of her integrity and identity. Defloration *is* destruction. But nature creates by violence and destruction. The commonest violence in the world is childbirth, with its appalling pain and gore. Nature gives males infusions of hormones for dominance in order to hurl them against the paralyzing mystery of woman, from whom they would otherwise shrink. Her power as mistress of birth is already too extreme. Lust and aggression are fused in male hormones. Anyone who doubts this has probably never spent much time around horses. Stallions are so dangerous they must be caged in barred stalls; once gelded, they are docile enough to serve as children's mounts. The hormonal disparity in humans is not so gross, but it is grosser than Rousseauists like to think. The more testosterone, the more elevated the libido. The more dominant the male, the more frequent his contributions to the genetic pool. Even on the microscopic level, male fertility is a function not only of number of sperm but of their motility, that is, their restless movement, which increases the chance of conception. Sperm are miniature assault troops, and the ovum is a solitary citadel that must be breached. Weak or passive sperm just sit there like dead ducks. Nature rewards energy and aggression.

Profanation and violation are part of the perversity of sex, which never will conform to liberal theories of benevolence. Every model of morally or politically correct sexual behavior *will be subverted*, by nature's daemonic law. Every hour of every day, some horror is being committed somewhere. Feminism, arguing from the milder woman's view, completely misses the blood-lust in rape, the joy of violation and destruction. An aesthetics and erotics of profanation—evil for the sake of evil, the sharpening of the senses by cruelty and torture—have been documented in Sade, Baudelaire, and Huysmans. Women may be less prone to such fantasies because they physically lack the equipment for sexual violence. They do not know the temptation of forcibly invading the sanctuary of another body.

Our knowledge of these fantasies is expanded by pornography, which is why pornography should be tolerated, though its public display may reasonably be restricted. The imagination cannot and must not be policed. Pornography shows us nature's daemonic heart, those eternal forces at work beneath and beyond social convention. Pornography cannot be separated from art; the two interpenetrate each other, far more than humanistic criticism has admitted. Geoffrey Hartman rightly says, "Great art is always flanked by its dark sisters, blasphemy and

pornography."[6] *Hamlet* itself, the cardinal western work, is full of lewdness. Criminals through history, from Nero and Caligula to Gilles de
Rais and the Nazi commandants, have never needed pornography to
stimulate their exquisite, gruesome inventiveness. The diabolic human
mind is quite enough.

Happy are those periods when marriage and religion are
strong. System and order shelter us against sex and nature. Unfortunately, we live in a time when the chaos of sex has broken into the open.
G. Wilson Knight remarks, "Christianity came originally as a tearing
down of taboos in the name of a sacred humanity; but the Church it
gave rise to has never yet succeeded in Christianizing the pagan evil
magic of sex."[7] Historiography's most glaring error has been its assertion that Judeo-Christianity defeated paganism. Paganism has survived
in the thousand forms of sex, art, and now the modern media. Christianity has made adjustment after adjustment, ingeniously absorbing its
opposition (as during the Italian Renaissance) and diluting its dogma to
change with changing times. But a critical point has been reached. With
the rebirth of the gods in the massive idolatries of popular culture, with
the eruption of sex and violence into every corner of the ubiquitous mass
media, Judeo-Christianity is facing its most serious challenge since
Europe's confrontation with Islam in the Middle Ages. The latent paganism of western culture has burst forth again in all its daemonic
vitality.

Paganism never was the unbridled sexual licentiousness portrayed by
missionaries of the young, embattled Christianity. Singling out as typical of paganism the orgies of bored late Roman aristocrats would be as
unfair as singling out as typical of Christianity the sins of renegade
priests or the Vatican revels of Pope Alexander VI. True orgy was a ceremony of the chthonian mother-cults in which there were both sex and
bloodshed. Paganism recognized, honored, and feared nature's daemonism, and it limited sexual expression by ritual formulae. Christianity was a development of Dionysian mystery religion which paradoxically tried to suppress nature in favor of a transcendental other world.
The sole contact with nature that Christianity permitted its followers
was sex sanctified by marriage. Chthonian nature, embodied in great
goddess figures, was Christianity's most formidable opponent. Christianity works best when revered institutions like monasticism or universal marriage channel sexual energy in positive directions. Western civilization has profited enormously from the sublimation Christianity
forced on sex. Christianity works least when sex is constantly stimulated

from other directions, as it is now. No transcendental religion can compete with the spectacular pagan nearness and concreteness of the carnal-red media. Our eyes and ears are drowned in a sensual torrent.

The pagan ritual identity of sex and violence is mass media's chief check to the complacent Rousseauism of modern humanists. The commercial media, responding directly to popular patronage, sidestep the liberal censors who have enjoyed such long control over book culture. In film, popular music, and commercials, we contemplate all the daemonic myths and sexual stereotypes of paganism that reform movements from Christianity to feminism have never been able to eradicate. The sexes are eternally at war. There is an element of attack, of search-and-destroy in male sex, in which there will always be a potential for rape. There is an element of entrapment in female sex, a subliminal manipulation leading to physical and emotional infantilization of the male. Freud notes, apropos of his theory of the primal scene, that a child overhearing his parents having sex thinks male is wounding female and that the woman's cries of pleasure are cries of pain. Most men merely grunt, at best. But woman's strange sexual cries come directly from the chthonian. She is a Maenad about to rend her victim. Sex is an uncanny moment of ritual and incantation, in which we hear woman's barbaric ululation of triumph of the will. One domination dissolves into another. The dominated becomes the dominator.

Every menstruating or childbearing woman is a pagan and primitive cast back to those distant ocean shores from which we have never fully evolved. On the streets of every city, prostitutes, the world's oldest profession, stand as a rebuke to sexual morality. They are the daemonic face of nature, initiates of pagan mysteries. Prostitution is not just a service industry, mopping up the overflow of male demand, which always exceeds female supply. Prostitution testifies to the amoral power struggle of sex, which religion has never been able to stop. Prostitutes, pornographers, and their patrons are marauders in the forest of archaic night.

That nature acts upon the sexes differently is proved by the test case of modern male and female homosexuality, illustrating how the sexes function separately outside social convention. The result, according to statistics of sexual frequency: male satyriasis and female nesting. The male homosexual has sex more often than his heterosexual counterpart; the female homosexual less often than hers, a radical polarization of the sexes along a single continuum of shared sexual nonconformity. Male aggression and lust are the energizing factors in culture. They are men's tools of survival in the pagan vastness of female nature.

The old "double standard" gave men a sexual liberty denied to women. Marxist feminists reduce the historical cult of woman's virginity to her property value, her worth on the male marriage market. I would argue instead that there was and is a biologic basis to the double standard. The first medical reports on the disease killing male homosexuals indicated men most at risk were those with a thousand partners over their lifetime. Incredulity. Who could such people be? Why, it turned out, everyone one knew. Serious, kind, literate men, not bums or thugs. What an abyss divides the sexes! Let us abandon the pretense of sexual sameness and admit the terrible duality of gender.

Male sex is quest romance, exploration and speculation. Promiscuity in men may cheapen love but sharpen thought. Promiscuity in women is illness, a leakage of identity. The promiscuous woman is self-contaminated and incapable of clear ideas. She has ruptured the ritual integrity of her body. It is in nature's best interests to goad dominant males into indiscriminate spreading of their seed. But nature also profits from female purity. Even in the liberated or lesbian woman there is some biologic restraint whispering: keep the birth canal clean. In judiciously withholding herself, woman protects an invisible fetus. Perhaps this is the reason for the archetypal horror (rather than socialized fear) that many otherwise bold women have of spiders and other rapidly crawling insects. Women hold themselves in reserve because the female body is a reservoir, a virgin patch of still, pooled water where the fetus comes to term. Male chase and female flight are not just a social game. The double standard may be one of nature's organic laws.

The quest romance of male sex is a war between identity and annihilation. An erection is a hope for objectivity, for power to act as a free agent. But at the climax of his success, woman is pulling the male back to her bosom, drinking and quelling his energy. Freud says, "Man fears that his strength will be taken from him by woman, dreads becoming infected with her femininity and then proving himself a weakling."[8] Masculinity must fight off effeminacy day by day. Woman and nature stand ever ready to reduce the male to boy and infant.

The operations of sex are convulsive, from intercourse through menstruation and childbirth: tension and distention, spasm, contraction, expulsion, relief. The body is wrenched in serpentine swelling and sloughing. Sex is not the pleasure principle but the Dionysian bondage of pleasure-pain. So much is a matter of *overcoming resistance*, in the body or the beloved, that rape will always be a present danger. Male sex is repetition-compulsion: whatever a man writes in the commentary of his phallic projections must be rewritten again and again. Sexual man is the magician sawing the lady in half, yet the serpent head and tail always live and rejoin. Projection is a male curse: forever to need something or someone to make oneself complete. This is one of the sources of art and the secret of its historical domination by males. The artist is the closest man has come to imitating woman's superb self-containment. But the artist needs his art, his projection. The blocked artist, like Leonardo, suffers tortures of the damned. The most famous painting in the world, the *Mona Lisa,* records woman's self-satisfied apartness, her ambiguous mocking smile at the vanity and despair of her many sons.

Everything great in western culture has come from the quarrel with nature. The west and not the east has seen the frightful brutality of natural process, the insult to mind in the heavy blind rolling and milling of matter. In loss of self we would find not love or God but primeval squalor. This revelation has historically fallen upon the western male, who is pulled by tidal rhythms back to the oceanic mother. It is to his resentment of this daemonic undertow that we owe the grand constructions of our culture. Apollonianism, cold and absolute, is the west's sublime refusal. The Apollonian is a male line drawn against the dehumanizing magnitude of female nature.

Everything is melting in nature. We think we see objects, but our eyes are slow and partial. Nature is blooming and withering in long puffy respirations, rising and falling in oceanic wave-motion. A mind that opened itself fully to nature without sentimental preconception would be glutted by nature's coarse materialism, its relentless superfluity. An apple tree laden with fruit: how peaceful, how picturesque. But remove the rosy filter of humanism from our gaze and look again. See nature spuming and frothing, its mad spermatic bubbles endlessly spilling out and smashing in that inhuman round of waste, rot, and carnage. From the jammed glassy cells of sea roe to the feathery spores poured into the air from bursting green pods, nature is a festering hornet's nest of aggression and overkill. This is the chthonian black magic with which we are infected as sexual beings; this is the daemonic identity that Christianity so inadequately defines as original sin and thinks it can cleanse us of. Procreative woman is the most troublesome obstacle to Christianity's claim to catholicity, testified by its wishful doctrines of Immaculate Conception and Virgin Birth. The procreativeness of chthonian nature is an obstacle to all of western metaphysics and to each man in his quest for identity against his mother. Nature is the seething excess of being.

The most effective weapon against the flux of nature is art. Religion, ritual, and art began as one, and a religious or metaphysical element is still present in all art. Art, no matter how minimalist, is never simply design. It is always a ritualistic reordering of reality. The enterprise of art, in a stable collective era or an unsettled individualistic one, is inspired by anxiety. Every subject localized and honored by art is endangered by its opposite. Art is a *shutting in* in order to *shut out*. Art is a ritualistic binding of the perpetual motion machine that is nature. The first artist was a tribal priest casting a spell, fixing nature's daemonic energy in a moment of perceptual stillness. Fixation is at the heart of art, fixation as stasis and fixation as obsession. The modern artist who merely draws a line across a page is still trying to tame some uncontrollable aspect of reality. Art is spellbinding. Art fixes the audience in its seat, stops the feet before a painting, fixes a book in the hand. Contemplation is a magic act.

Art is order. But order is not necessarily just, kind, or beautiful. Order may be arbitrary, harsh, and cruel. Art has nothing to do with morality. Moral themes may be present, but they are incidental, simply grounding an art work in a particular time and place. Before the Enlightenment, religious art was hieratic and ceremonial. After the Enlightenment, art had to create its own world, in which a new ritual of artistic formalism replaced religious universals. Eighteenth-century Augustan literature demonstrates it is the order in morality rather than the morality in order that attracts the artist. Only utopian liberals could be surprised that the Nazis were art connoisseurs. Particularly in modern times, when high art has been shoved to the periphery of culture, is it evident that art is aggressive and compulsive. The artist makes art not to save humankind but to save himself. Every benevolent remark by an artist is a fog to cover his tracks, the bloody trail of his assault against reality and others.

Art is a temenos, a sacred place. It is ritually clean, a swept floor, the threshing floor that was the first site of theater. Whatever enters this space is transformed. From the bison of cave painting to Hollywood movie stars, represented beings enter a cultic other life from which they may never emerge. They are spellbound. Art is sacrificial, turning its inherent aggression against both artist and representation. Nietzsche says, "Almost everything we call 'higher culture' is based on the spiritualization of *cruelty*."[9] Literature's endless murders and disasters are there for contemplative pleasure, not moral lesson. Their status as fiction, removed into a sacred precinct, intensifies our pleasure by guaranteeing that contemplation cannot turn into action. No lunge by a compassionate spectator can avert the cool inevitability of that hieratic ceremony, ritually replayed through time. The blood that is shed will always be shed. Ritual in church or theater is amoral fixation, dispelling anxiety by formalizing and freezing emotion. The ritual of art is the cruel law of pain made pleasure.

Art makes *things*. There are, I said, no objects in nature, only the gruelling erosion of natural force, flecking, dilapidating, grinding down, reducing all matter to fluid, the thick primal soup from which new forms bob, gasping for life. Dionysus was identified with liquids—blood, sap, milk, wine. The Dionysian is nature's chthonian fluidity. Apollo, on the other hand, gives form and shape, marking off one being from another. All artifacts are Apollonian. Melting and union are Dionysian; separation and individuation, Apollonian. Every boy who leaves his mother to become a man is turning the Apollonian against the Dionysian. Every artist who is compelled toward art, who needs to make words or pictures as others need to breathe, is using the Apollonian to defeat chthonian nature. In sex, men must mediate between Apollo and Dionysus. Sexually, woman can remain oblique, opaque, taking pleasure without tumult or conflict. Woman is a temenos of her own dark mysteries. Genitally, man has a little thing that he must keep dipping in Dionysian dissolution—a risky business! Thing-making, thing-preserving is central to male experience. Man is a fetishist. Without his fetish, woman will just gobble him up again.

Hence the male domination of art and science. Man's focus, directedness, concentration, and projection, which I identified with urination and ejaculation, are his tools of sexual survival, but they have never given him a final victory. The anxiety in sexual experience remains as strong as ever. This man attempts to correct by the cult of female beauty. He is erotically fixated on woman's "shapeliness," those spongy maternal fat deposits of breast, hip, and buttock which are ironically the wateriest and least stable parts of her anatomy. Woman's billowy body reflects the surging sea of chthonian nature. By focusing on the shapely, by making woman a sex-object, man has struggled to fix and stabilize nature's dreadful flux. Objectification is conceptualization, the highest human faculty. Turning people into sex objects is one of the specialties of our species. It will never disappear, since it is intertwined with the art-impulse and may be identical to it. A sex-object is ritual form imposed on nature. It is a totem of our perverse imagination.

Apollonian thing-making is the main line of western civilization, extending from ancient Egypt to the present. Every attempt to repress this aspect of our culture has ultimately been defeated. First Judaism, then Christianity turned against pagan idol-making. But Christianity, with wider impact than Judaism, became the most art-laden, art-dominated religion in the world. Imagination always remedies the defects of religion. The hardest object of Apollonian thing-making is western personality, the glamourous, striving, separatist ego that entered literature in the *Iliad* but, I will show, first appeared in art in Old Kingdom Egypt.

Christianity, wiping out paganism's secular glamours, tried to make spirituality primary. But as an embattled sect, it ended by reinforcing the west's absolutist ego-structure. The hero of the medieval Church militant, the knight in shining armour, is the most perfect Apollonian *thing* in world history. Art books need to be rewritten: there is a direct line from Greek and Roman sculpture through medieval armour to the Renaissance revival of classicism. Arms and armour are not handicrafts but art. They carry the symbolic weight of western personality. Armour is the pagan continuity in medieval Christianity. After the Renaissance released the sensual, idolatrous art-making of classicism, the pagan line has continued in brazen force to today. The idea that the western tradition collapsed after World War One is one of the myopic little sulks of liberalism. I will argue that high culture made itself obsolete through modernism's neurotic nihilism and that popular culture is the great heir of the western past. Cinema is the supreme Apollonian genre, thing-making and thing-made, a machine of the gods.

Man, the sexual conceptualizer and projector, has ruled art because art is his Apollonian response toward and away from woman. A sex object is something to aim at. The eye is Apollo's arrow following the arc of transcendance I saw in male urination and ejaculation. The western eye is a projectile into the *beyond*, that wilderness of the male condition. By no coincidence, Europe first made firearms for gunpowder, which China had invented centuries earlier but found little use for. Phallic aggression and projection are intrinsic to western conceptualization. Arrow, eye, gun, cinema: the blazing lightbeam of the movie projector is our modern path of Apollonian transcendance. Cinema is the culmination of the obsessive, mechanistic male drive in western culture. The movie projector is an Apollonian straightshooter, demonstrating the link between aggression and art. Every pictorial framing is a ritual limitation, a barred precinct. The rectangular movie screen is clearly patterned on the post-Renaissance framed painting. But all conceptualization is a framing.

The history of costume belongs to art history but is too often regarded as a journalistic lady's adjunct to scholarship. There is nothing trivial about fashion. Standards of beauty are conceptualizations projected by each culture. They tell us everything. Women have been the most victimized by fashion's ever-turning wheel, binding their feet or bosom to phantom commands. But fashion is not just one more political oppression to add to the feminist litany. Standards of beauty, created by men but usually consented to by women, ritually limit women's archetypal sexual allure. Fashion is an externalization of woman's daemonic invisibility, her genital mystery. It brings before man's Apollonian eye what that eye can never see. Beauty is an Apollonian freeze-frame: it halts and condenses the flux and indeterminacy of nature. It allows man to act by enhancing the desirability of what he fears.

The power of the eye in western culture has not been fully appreciated or analyzed. The Asian abases the eyes and transfers value into a mystic third eye, marked by the red dot on the Hindu forehead. Personality is inauthentic in the east, which identifies self with group. Eastern meditation rejects historical time. We have a parallel religious tradition: the paradoxical axioms of eastern and western mystics and poets are often indistinguishable. Buddhism and Christianity agree in seeing the material world as *samsara*, the veil of illusion. But the west has another tradition, the pagan, culminating in cinema. The west makes personality and history numinous objects of contemplation. Western personality is a work of art, and history is its stage. The twentieth century is not the Age of Anxiety but the Age of Hollywood. The pagan cult of personality has reawakened and dominates all art, all thought. It is morally empty but ritually profound. We worship it by the power of the western eye. Movie screen and television screen are its sacred precincts.

Western culture has a roving eye. Male sex is hunting and scanning: boys hang yelping from honking cars, acting like jerks over strolling girls; men lunching on girders go through the primitive book of wolf whistles and animal clucks. Everywhere, the beautiful woman is scrutinized and harassed. She is the ultimate symbol of human desire. The feminine is that-which-is-sought; it recedes beyond our grasp. Hence there is always a feminine element in the beautiful young man of male homosexuality. The feminine is the ever-elusive, a silver shimmer on the horizon. We follow this image with longing eyes: maybe this one, maybe this time. The pursuit of sex may conceal a dream of being freed from sex. Sex, knowledge, and power are deeply tangled; we cannot get one without the others. Islam is wise to drape women in black, for the eye is the avenue of eros. Western culture's hard, defined personalities suffer from inflammation of the eye. They are so numerous that they have never been catalogued, except in our magnificent portrait art. Western sexual personae are nodes of power, but they have made a torment of eroticism. From this torment has come our grand tradition of literature and art. Unfortunately, there is no way to separate the whistling ass on his girder from the rapt visionary at his easel. In accepting the gifts of culture, women may have to take the worm with the apple.

Judeo-Christianity has failed to control the pagan western eye. Our thought processes were formed in Greece and inherited by Rome, whose language remains the official voice of the Catholic church. Intellectual inquiry and logic are pagan. Every inquiry is preceded by a roving eye; and once the eye begins to rove, it cannot be morally controlled. Judaism, due to its fear of the eye, put a taboo on visual representation. Judaism is based on word rather than image. Christianity followed suit, until it drifted into pictorialism to appeal to the pagan masses. Protestantism began as an iconoclasm, a breaking of the images of the corrupt Roman church. The pure Protestant style is a bare white church with plain windows. Italian Catholicism, I am happy to say, retains the most florid pictorialism, the bequest of a pagan past that was never lost.

Paganism is eye-intense. It is based on cultic exhibitionism, in which sex and sadomasochism are joined. The ancient chthonian mysteries have never disappeared from the Italian church. Waxed saints' corpses under glass. Tattered armbones in gold reliquaries. Half-nude St. Sebastian pierced by arrows. St. Lucy holding her eyeballs out on a platter. Blood, torture, ecstasy, and tears. Its lurid sensationalism makes Italian Catholicism the emotionally most complete cosmology in religious history. Italy added pagan sex and violence to the ascetic Palestinian creed. And so to Hollywood, the modern Rome: it is pagan sex and violence that have flowered so vividly in our mass media. The camera has unbound daemonic western imagination. Cinema is *sexual showing*, a pagan flaunting. Plot and dialogue are obsolete word-baggage. Cinema, the most eye-intense of genres, has restored pagan antiquity's cultic exhibitionism. Spectacle is a pagan cult of the eye.

There is no such thing as "mere" image. Western culture is built on perceptual relations. From the soaring god-projections of ancient sky-cult to the celebrity-inflating machinery of American commercial promotion, western identity has organized itself around charismatic sexual personae of hierarchic command. Every god is an idol, literally an "image" (Latin *idolum* from Greek *eidolon*). Image is implied visibility. The visual is sorely undervalued in modern scholarship. Art history has attained only a fraction of the conceptual sophistication of literary criticism. And literature and art remain unmeshed. Drunk with self-love, criticism has hugely overestimated the centrality of language to western culture. It has failed to see the electrifying sign language of images.

The war between Judeo-Christianity and paganism is still being waged in the latest ideologies of the university. Freud, as a Jew, may have been biased in favor of the word. In my opinion, Freudian theory overstates the linguistic character of the unconscious and slights the gorgeously cinematic pictorialism of the dream life. Furthermore, arguments by the French about the rationalist limitations of their own culture have been illegitimately transferred to England and America, with poor results. The English language was created by poets, a five-hundred-year enterprise of emotion and metaphor, the richest internal dialogue in world literature. French rhetorical models are too narrow for the English tradition. Most pernicious of French imports is the notion that there is no person behind a text. Is there anything *more* affected, aggressive, and relentlessly concrete than a Parisian intellectual behind his/her turgid text? The Parisian is a provincial when he pretends to speak for the universe. Behind every book is a certain person with a certain history. I can never know too much about that person and that history. Personality is western reality. It is a visible condensation of sex and psyche outside the realm of word. We know it by Apollonian vision, the pagan cinema of western perception. Let us not steal from the eye to give to the ear.

Word-worship has made it difficult for scholarship to deal with the radical cultural change of our era of mass media. Academics are constantly fighting a rearguard action. Traditional genre-criticism is moribund. The humanities must abandon their insular fiefdoms and begin thinking in terms of *imagination,* a power that crosses the genres and unites high with popular art, the noble with the sleazy. There is neither decline nor disaster in the triumph of mass media, only a shift from word to image—in other words, a return to western culture's pre-Gutenberg, pre-Protestant pagan pictorialism.

That popular culture reclaims what high culture shuts out is clear in the case of pornography. Pornography is pure pagan imagism. Just as a poem is ritually limited verbal expression, so is pornography ritually limited visual expression of the daemonism of sex and nature. Every shot, every angle in pornography, no matter how silly, twisted, or pasty, is yet another attempt to *get the whole picture* of the enormity of chthonian nature. Is pornography art? Yes. Art is contemplation and conceptualization, the ritual exhibitionism of primal mysteries. Art makes order of nature's cyclonic brutality. Art, I said, is full of crimes. The ugliness and violence in pornography reflect the ugliness and violence in nature.

Pornography's male-born explicitness renders visible what is invisible, woman's chthonian internality. It tries to shed Apollonian light on woman's anxiety-provoking darkness. The vulgar contortionism of pornography is the serpentine tangle of Medusan nature. Pornography is human imagination in tense theatrical action; its violations are a protest against the violations of our freedom by nature. The banning of pornography, rightly sought by Judeo-Christianity, would be a victory over the west's stubborn paganism. But pornography cannot be banned, only driven underground, where its illicit charge will be enhanced. Pornography's amoral pictorialism will live forever as a rebuke to the humanistic cult of the redemptive word. Words cannot save the cruel flux of pagan nature.

The western eye makes *things*, idols of Apollonian objectification. Pornography makes many well-meaning people uncomfortable because it isolates the voyeuristic element present in all art, and especially cinema. All the personae of art are sex objects. The emotional response of spectator or reader is inseparable from erotic response. As I said, our lives as physical beings are a Dionysian continuum of pleasure-pain. At every moment we are steeped in the sensory, even in sleep. Emotional arousal is sensual arousal; sensual arousal is sexual arousal. The idea that emotion can be separated from sex is a Christian illusion, one of the most ingenious but finally unworkable strategies in Christianity's ancient campaign against pagan nature. Agape, spiritual love, belongs to eros but has run away from home.

We are voyeurs at the perimeters of art, and there is a sadomasochistic sensuality in our responses to it. Art is a scandal, literally a "stumbling block," to all moralism, whether on the Christian right or Rousseauist left. Pornography and art are inseparable, because there is voyeurism and voracity in all our sensations as seeing, feeling beings. The fullest exploration of these ideas is Edmund Spenser's Renaissance epic, *The Faerie Queene*. In this poem, which prefigures cinema by its radiant Apollonian projections, the voyeuristic and sadomasochistic latency in art and sex is copiously documented. Western perception is a daemonic theater of ritual surprise. We may not like what we see when we look into the dark mirror of art.

Sex object, art work, personality: western experience is cellular and divisive. It imposes a graph of marked-off spaces on nature's continuity and flow. We have made Apollonian demarcations that function as ritual preserves against nature; hence our complex criminal codes and elaborate erotics of transgression. The weakness in radical critiques of sex and society is that they fail to recognize that sex needs ritual binding to control its daemonism and secondly that society's repressions *increase* sexual pleasure. There is nothing less erotic than a nudist colony. Desire is intensified by ritual limitations. Hence the mask, harness, and chains of sadomasochism.

The western cells of holiness and criminality are a cognitive advance in human history. Our cardinal myths are Faust, who locks himself in his study to read books and crack the code of nature, and Don Juan, who makes a war of pleasure and counts his conquests by Apollonian number. Both are cellular egos, seducers and criminal knowers, in whom sex, thought, and aggression are fused. This cell separated from nature is our brain and eye. Our hard personalities are imagistic projections from the Apollonian higher cortex. Personae are visible ideas. All facial expressions and theatrical postures, present among animal primates, are fleeting shadows of personae. While Japanese decorum limits facial expressions, western art since the Hellenistic era has recorded every permutation of irony, anxiety, flirtation, and menace. The hardness of our personalities and the tension with which they are set off from nature have produced the west's vulnerability to decadence. Tension leads to fatigue and collapse, "late" phases of history in which sadomasochism flourishes. As I will show, decadence is a *disease of the eye*, a sexual intensification of artistic voyeurism.

The Apollonian *things* of western sex and art reach their economic glorification in capitalism. In the past fifteen years, Marxist approaches to literature have enjoyed increasing vogue. To be conscious of the social context of art seems automatically to entail a leftist orientation. But a theory is possible that is both avant-garde *and* capitalist. Marxism was one of Rousseau's nineteenth-century progeny, energized by faith in the perfectibility of man. Its belief that economic forces are the primary dynamic in history is Romantic naturism in disguise. That is, it sketches a surging wave-motion in the material context of human life but tries to deny the perverse daemonism of that context. Marxism is the bleakest of anxiety-formations against the power of chthonian mothers. Its influence on modern historiography has been excessive. The "great man" theory of history was not as simplistic as claimed; we have barely recovered from a world war in which this theory was proved evilly true. One man *can* change the course of history, for good or ill. Marxism is a flight from the magic of person and the mystique of hierarchy. It distorts the character of western culture, which is based on charismatic power of person. Marxism can work only in pre-industrial societies of homogeneous populations. Raise the standard of living, and the rainbow riot of individualism will break out. Personality and art, which Marxism fears and censors, rebound from every effort to repress them.

Capitalism, gaudy and greedy, has been inherent in western aesthetics from ancient Egypt on. It is the mysticism and glamour of *things*, which take on a personality of their own. As an economic system, it is in the Darwinian line of Sade, not Rousseau. The capitalist survival of the fittest is already present in the *Iliad*. Western sexual personae clash by day and by night. Homer's gleaming bronze-clad warriors are the Apollonian soup cans that crowd the sunny temples of our supermarkets and compete for our attention on television. The west objectifies persons and personalizes objects. The teeming multiplicity of capitalist products is an Apollonian correction of nature. Brand names are territorial cells of western identity. Our shiny chrome automobiles, like our armies of grocery boxes and cans, are extrapolations of hard, impermeable western personality.

Capitalist products are another version of the art works flooding western culture. The portable framed painting appeared at the birth of modern commerce in the early Renaissance. Capitalism and art have challenged and nourished each other ever since. Capitalist and artist are parallel types: the artist is just as amoral and acquisitive as the capitalist, and just as hostile to competitors. That in the age of the merchant-prince art works are hawked and sold like hot dogs supports my argument but is not central to it. Western culture is animated by a visionary materialism. Apollonian formalism has stolen from nature to make a romance of *things*, hard, shiny, crass, and willful.

The capitalist distribution network, a complex chain of factory, transport, warehouse, and retail outlet, is one of the greatest male accomplishments in the history of culture. It is a lightning-quick Apollonian circuit of male bonding. One of feminism's irritating reflexes is its fashionable disdain for "patriarchal society," to which nothing good is ever attributed. But it is patriarchal society that has freed me as a woman. It is capitalism that has given me the leisure to sit at this desk writing this book. Let us stop being small-minded about men and freely acknowledge what treasures their obsessiveness has poured into culture.

We could make an epic catalog of male achievements, from paved roads, indoor plumbing, and washing machines to eyeglasses, antibiotics, and disposable diapers. We enjoy fresh, safe milk and meat, and vegetables and tropical fruits heaped in snowbound cities. When I cross the George Washington Bridge or any of America's great bridges, I think: *men* have done this. Construction is a sublime male poetry. When I see a giant crane passing on a flatbed truck, I pause in awe and reverence, as one would for a church procession. What power of conception, what grandiosity: these cranes tie us to ancient Egypt, where monumental architecture was first imagined and achieved. If civilization had been left in female hands, we would still be living in grass huts. A contemporary woman clapping on a hard hat merely enters a conceptual system invented by men. Capitalism is an art form, an Apollonian fabrication to rival nature. It is hypocritical for feminists and intellectuals to enjoy the pleasures and conveniences of capitalism while sneering at it. Even Thoreau's Walden was just a two-year experiment. Everyone born into capitalism has incurred a debt to it. Give Caesar his due.

The pagan dialectic of Apollonian and Dionysian was sweepingly comprehensive and accurate about mind and nature. Christian love is so lacking its emotional polarity that the Devil had to be invented to focus natural human hatred and hostility. Rousseauism's Christianized psychology has led to the tendency of liberals toward glumness or depression in the face of the political tensions, wars, and atrocities that daily contradict their assumptions. Perhaps the more we are sensitized by reading and education, the more we must repress the facts of chthonian nature. But the insupportable feminist dichotomy between sex and power must go. Just as the hatreds of divorce court expose the dark face beneath the mask of love, so is the truth about nature revealed during crisis. Victims of tornado and hurricane instinctively speak of "the fury of Mother Nature"—how often we hear that phrase as the television camera follows dazed survivors picking through the wreckage of homes and towns. In the unconscious, everyone knows that Jehovah has never gained control of the savage elements. Nature is Pandemonium, an All Devils' Day.

There are no accidents, only nature throwing her weight around. Even the bomb merely releases energy that nature has put there. Nuclear war would be just a spark in the grandeur of space. Nor can radiation "alter" nature: she will absorb it all. After the bomb, nature will pick up the cards we have spilled, shuffle them, and begin her game again. Nature is forever playing solitaire with herself.

Western love has been ambivalent from the start. As early as Sappho (600 B.C.) or even earlier in the epic legend of Helen of Troy, art records the push and pull of attraction and hostility in that perverse fascination we call love. There is a magnetics of eroticism in the west, due to the hardness of western personality: eroticism is an electric forcefield be-

tween masks. The modern pursuit of self-realization has not led to
sexual happiness, because assertions of selfhood merely release the
amoral chaos of libido. Freedom is the most overrated modern idea,
originating in the Romantic rebellion against bourgeois society. But
only *in* society can one *be* an individual. Nature is waiting at society's
gates to dissolve us in her chthonian bosom. Out with stereotypes,
feminism proclaims. But stereotypes are the west's stunning sexual
personae, the vehicles of art's assault against nature. The moment there
is imagination, there is myth. We may have to accept an ethical cleavage
between imagination and reality, tolerating horrors, rapes, and mutilations in art that we would not tolerate in society. For art is our message
from the beyond, telling us what nature is up to. Not sex but cruelty is
the great neglected or suppressed item on the modern humanistic
agenda. We must honor the chthonian but not necessarily yield to it. In
The Rape of the Lock, Pope counsels good humor as the only solution to
sex war. So with our enslavement by chthonian nature. We must accept
our pain, change what we can, and laugh at the rest. But let us see art for
what it is and nature for what it is. From remotest antiquity, western art
has been a parade of sexual personae, emanations of absolutist western
mind. Western art is a cinema of sex and dreaming. Art is form struggling to wake from the nightmare of nature.

2

The Birth of the Western Eye

Mythology begins with cosmogony, the creation of the world. Somehow out of the chaos of matter comes order. The plenum, a soupy fullness, divides itself into objects and beings. Cosmogonies vary among societies. Earth-cult admits the priority and primacy of nature. For Judeo-Christianity, a sky-cult, God creates nature rather than vice versa. His consciousness precedes and engulfs all.

Hebrew cosmogony, in the polemical poetry of Genesis, is lofty in its claims. Creation is rational and systematic. The evolution of forms proceeds majestically, without carnage or cataclysm. God presides with workmanlike detachment. The cosmos is something constructed, a framed dwelling for man. God is a spirit, a presence. He has no name and no body. He is beyond sex and against sex, which belongs to the lower realm. Yet God is distinctly *he*, a father and not a mother. Female-ness is subordinate, an afterthought. Eve is merely a sliver pulled from Adam's belly. Maleness is magic, the potent principle of universal cre-ativity.

The book of Genesis is a male declaration of independence from the ancient mother-cults. Its challenge to nature, so sexist to modern ears, marks one of the crucial moments in western history. Mind can never be free of matter. Yet only by mind *imagining* itself free can culture ad-vance. The mother-cults, by reconciling man to nature, entrapped him in matter. Everything great in western civilization has come from strug-gle against our origins. Genesis is rigid and unjust, but it gave man hope as a man. It remade the world by male dynasty, cancelling the power of mothers.

Jehovah exists somewhere outside his creation, beyond space and time. Most ancient cosmogonies begin with a primeval being who embraces all opposites and contains everything that is or can be. Why should any eternal, self-sufficient god add to what already is? Whether out of loneliness or a craving for drama, primeval deities set off the motion-machine and add to their own troubles. My favorite such god is Egyptian Khepera, who gives birth to the second stage of existence by an act of masturbation: "I had union with my hand, and I embraced my shadow in a love embrace; I poured seed into my own mouth, and sent forth from myself issue in the form of the gods Shu and Tefnut."[1] Logically, primeval hierarchs must dig into themselves to continue the story of creation. Jehovah, as much as Khepera, multiplies by self-compounding.

Virtually all cosmogonies but ours are overtly sexual. The primeval deity may be hermaphroditic, like Egypt's mother goddess Mut, who has both male and female genitals. Or there is wholesale incest, the only sex possible when the in-group is the only group. Developed mythologies ignore the incest or edit it out, as Genesis does in discreetly passing over the question of whom Cain and Abel must marry to get on with history. Similarly, Greek myth stresses Hera as Zeus' wife but makes little of the fact that she is also his sister. In Egypt there never was so stringent a purification of sacred texts, and primitive motifs lingered on to the end. Isis and Osiris are distinctly sister and brother as well as wife and husband. Egyptian gods are tangled in archaic family romance. The mother goddess Hathor, for example, is eerily called "the mother of her father and the daughter of her son." As in Romanticism, identity is regressive and supercondensed. The sexual irregularities of fertility gods are intrinsic to the dark, disorderly mystery of sexual growth.

Judaism, though ascribing artfulness to God, is inhospitable to art in man. Earth-cult's lurid sexual symbolism contains a psychic truth: there is a sexual element in all creation, in nature or art. Khepera eating his own seed is a model of Romantic creativity, where the self is isolated and sexually dual. Khepera bent over himself is a uroboros, the serpent eating its own tail, a magic circle of regeneration and rebirth. The uroboros is the prehistoric track of natural cycle, from which Judaism and Hellenism make a conceptual break. Later in this book, I will argue that Romanticism restores the archaic western past, divining lost or suppressed pagan myths. Incest, erotic solipsism, is everywhere in Romantic poetry. Masturbation, subliminal in Coleridge and Poe, boldly emerges in later Romantics like Walt Whitman, Aubrey Beardsley, and Jean Genet, libidinous solitary dreamers. Khepera is the androgyne as demiurge.

The supreme symbol of fertility religion is the Great Mother, a figure of double-sexed primal power. Many mother goddesses of the Mediterranean world were indiscriminately fused in the syncretism of the Roman empire. They include Egyptian Isis, Cretan and Mycenaean

Gaia and Rhea, Cyprian Aphrodite, Phrygian Cybele, Ephesian Artemis, Syrian Dea, Persian Anaitis, Babylonian Ishtar, Phoenician Astarte, Canaanite Atargatis, Cappadocian Mâ, and Thracian Bendis and Cottyto. The Great Mother embodied the gigantism and unknowability of primeval nature. She descended from the period before agriculture, when nature seemed autocratic and capricious. Woman and nature were in mysterious harmony. Early man saw no necessary connection between coitus and conception, since sexual relations often preceded menstruation. Even today, pregnancy is unpredictable and takes months to show. Woman's fertility, following its own laws, inspired awe and fear.

Though woman was at the center of early symbolism, real women were powerless. A fantasy dogging feminist writing is that there was once a peaceable matriarchy overthrown by warmongering men, founders of patriarchal society. The idea began with Bachofen in the nineteenth century and was adopted by Jane Harrison, that great scholar's one error. Not a shred of evidence supports the existence of matriarchy anywhere in the world at any time. Matriarchy, political rule by women, must not be confused with matrilineage, passive transmission of property or authority through the female side. The matriarchy hypothesis, revived by American feminism, continues to flourish outside the university.

Primitive life, far from peaceable, was submerged in the turbulence of nature. Man's superior strength provided protection to women, particularly in the incapacitating final stages of pregnancy. The polarization of sex roles probably occurred rather early. Men roamed and hunted, while women in their gathering forays ventured no farther from the campsite than they could carry their nursing infants. There was simple logic in this, not injustice. The link between father and child was a late development. Margaret Mead remarks, "Human fatherhood is a social invention."[2] James Joyce says, "Paternity may be a legal fiction."[3] Society had advanced when the male contribution to conception was acknowledged. Both sexes have profited from the consolidation and stability of the family.

The myth of matriarchy may have originated in our universal experience of mother power in infancy. We are all born from a female colossus. Erich Neumann calls the first stage of psychic development "matriarchal."[4] Therefore every person's passage from nursery to society is an overthrow of matriarchy. As history, the idea of matriarchy is spurious, but as metaphor, it is poetically resonant. It is crucial for the interpretation of dreams and art, in which the mother remains dominant. Matriarchy hovers behind art works like the *Venus de Milo, Mona Lisa,* and *Whistler's Mother,* which popular imagination has made culturally archetypal. We will examine the way Romanticism, as part of its archaizing movement, restores the mother to matriarchal power, notably in Goethe, Wordsworth, and Swinburne.

The autonomy of the ancient mother goddesses was sometimes called virginity. A virgin fertility seems contradictory, but it survives in the Christian Virgin Birth. Hera and Aphrodite annually renewed their virginity by bathing in a sacred spring. The same duality appears in Artemis, who was honored both as virgin huntress and patron of childbirth. The Great Mother is a virgin insofar as she is independent of men. She is a sexual dictator, symbolically impenetrable. Males are nonpersons: Neumann elsewhere speaks of "the anonymous power of the fertilizing agent."[5] Thus Joyce's sensual Great Mother, Molly Bloom, sleepily mulls over all the men in her life as "he," implying their casual interchangeability. The Great Mother did not even need a male to fertilize her: the Egyptian goddess Net gives birth to Ra by parthenogenesis or self-fecundation.

The mother goddess gives life but takes it away. Lucretius says, "The universal mother is also the common grave."[6] She is morally ambivalent, violent as well as benevolent. The sanitized pacifist goddess promoted by feminism is wishful thinking. From prehistory to the end of the Roman empire, the Great Mother never lost her barbarism. She is the ever-changing face of chthonian nature, now savage, now smiling. The medieval Madonna, a direct descendant of Isis, is a Great Mother with her chthonian terror removed. She has lost her roots in nature, because it is pagan nature that Christianity rose to oppose.

The masculine side of the Great Mother is often expressed in serpents, wound about her arms or body. Mary trampling the serpent underfoot recalls pagan images in which goddess and serpent are one. The serpent inhabits the womblike underworld of mother earth. It is both male and female, piercing and strangling. Apuleius calls the Syrian goddess "omnipotens et omniparens," all-potent and all-producing.[7] Energy and abundance on so vast a scale can be crushing and cold. The fluid serpent will never be converted to friend.

The goddess' animal fecundity was cruelly dramatized in ritual. Her devotees practiced castration, breast-amputation, self-flagellation or slashing, and dismemberment of beasts. This sacrificial extremity of experience mimics the horrors of chthonian nature. Today such behavior survives only in sexual sadomasochism, universally labeled perverse. I think sadomasochism an archaizing phenomenon, returning the imagination to pagan nature-worship. Lewis Farnell says whipping in vegetation-rites was meant to increase fertility or, more often, "to drive out from the body impure influences or spirits, so that it may become the purer vehicle of divine force."[8] In the Roman Lupercalia, depicted in Shakespeare's *Julius Caesar*, youths ran naked through the streets and struck matrons with leather thongs to stimulate childbearing. Newlyweds are pelted with rice to drive off evil spirits and fertilize the bride. Blows mark a rite of passage into maturity. The kneeling knight is struck with sword on shoulder by his lord. At Catholic Confirmation, the kneeling adolescent is slapped by the bishop. The Orthodox Jewish girl at first menstruation is slapped by her mother. In *Stover at Yale* (1911), the lucky initiate to Skull and Bones is ambushed at night and slammed on the back. Blows are archaic magic, punishing marks of election.

Castration in the mother-cults may have imitated the reaping of crops. Only stone tools could be used for ritual castration; bronze or iron was forbidden, indicating the custom's prehistoric origins. Edith Weigert-Vowinkel endorses the view that the Phrygians borrowed castration from the Semites, who altered it over time to circumcision, and that the celibacy of Catholic priests is a substitute for castration.[9] The halolike tonsure of Catholic monks, like the shaved heads of priests of Isis, is a lesser self-mutilation. By castration, the devotee subordinated himself to the female life force. Contact with the goddess was dangerous. After making love with Aphrodite, Anchises ended up crippled, so that he had to be carried from burning Troy by his son Aeneas. The story that he was punished for boasting of his tryst is likely a late addition. H. J. Rose says of Anchises' handicap, "The business of fertilizing the Great Mother was so exacting as utterly to exhaust the strength of her inferior male partner, who consequently, if he did not die, became a eunuch."[10] Maleness is obliterated by shocks of female power.

Self-castration was a one-way road to ritual impersonation. In the mystery religions, which influenced Christianity, the devotee imitated and sought union with his god. The priest of the Great Mother changed sex in order to become her. Transsexualism was the severe choice, transvestism less so. In ceremonies at Syracuse, men were initiated in Demeter's purple robe. In ancient Mexico, a woman representing the goddess was flayed and her skin put on by a male priest. The Great Mother's eunuch priest was called "she." Thus after Catullus' Attis castrates himself, the pronouns shift from masculine to feminine. Today, etiquette requires one to refer to the urban drag queen as "she," even when he is in male dress.

Spiritual enlightenment produces feminization of the male. Mead says, "The more intricate biological pattern of the female has become a model for the artist, the mystic, and the saint."[11] Intuition or extra-sensory perception is a feminine hearkening to the secret voices in and beyond things. Farnell says, "Many ancient observers noted that women (and effeminate men) were especially prone to orgiastic re-ligious seizure."[12] Hysteria means womb-madness (from the Greek *ustera*, "womb"). Women were sibyls and oracles, subject to prophetic visions. Herodotus speaks of Scythian Enarees, male prophets afflicted by a "female disease," probably sexual impotence.[13] This phenomenon called shamanism migrated northward to Central Asia and has been reported in North and South America and Polynesia. Frazer describes the shaman's stages of sexual transformation, which resemble those of our candidates for sex-reassignment surgery. The religious call may come as a dream in which the man is "possessed by a female spirit." He adopts female speech, hair style, and clothing and finally takes a hus-band.[14] The Siberian shaman, who wears a woman's caftan sewn with large round disks as female breasts, is for Mircea Eliade an example of "ritual androgyny," symbolizing the *coincidentia oppositorum* or recon-ciliation of opposites.[15] Inspired, the shaman goes into a trance and falls unconscious. He may disappear, either to fly over distant lands or to die and be resurrected. The shaman is an archaic prototype of the artist, who also crosses sexes and commands space and time. How many modern transsexuals are unacknowledged shamans? Perhaps it is to poets they should go for counsel, rather than surgeons.

Teiresias, the androgynous Greek shaman, is depicted as an old man with long beard and pendulous female breasts. In Homer, Circe tells Odysseus his quest for home cannot succeed until he descends to the underworld to consult the seer. It is as if Teiresias, in the underworld of racial memory, represents a fullness of emotional knowledge fusing the sexes. The masculine glamour of the *Iliad* is gone. When we first see the hero of the *Odyssey*, he is weeping. The ruling virtues of this poem are female perception and endurance, rather than aggressive action. In Sophocles' *Oedipus Rex*, Teiresias is the hero's double. Teiresias and Oedipus are involuntary initiates into an uncanny range of sexual expe-rience. At the start, Teiresias holds the key to the mystery of plague and perversion. He alone knows the secret of Oedipal family romance, with its inflamed multiplicities of identity: Oedipus is husband *and* son, father *and* brother. At play's end, Oedipus has literally become Teiresias, a blind holy man who pays the price of esoteric knowledge. In *The Waste Land*, T. S. Eliot, following Apollinaire, makes Teiresias the witness and repository of modern sexual miseries.

How did Teiresias become an androgyne? On Mount Cithaeron (where infant Oedipus was exposed), he stumbled upon two snakes mating, for which he was punished by being turned into a woman. Seven years later, he came upon the same sight and was turned back into a man. The tale confirms the terrible consequences of seeing something forbidden to mortals. Thus Actaeon was torn to pieces by his hunting dogs for finding Artemis at her bath. Callimachus claims Teiresias was blinded for accidentally seeing Athena bathing. Hesiod says: "This same Teiresias was chosen by Zeus and Hera to decide the question whether the male or the female has most pleasure in intercourse. And he said: 'Of ten parts a man enjoys one only; but a woman's sense enjoys all ten in full.' For this Hera was angry and blinded him, but Zeus gave him the seer's power."[16] The oldest part of Teiresias' story is the meeting with mating snakes, a chthonian motif. The uncanny or grotesque in myth is evidence of extreme antiquity. The bantering comic tone of Zeus and Hera's domestic dispute marks it as later ornamentation. Charm in myths is a coming in from the chthonian cold.

I adopt the name "Teiresias" for a category of androgyne, the nurturant male or male mother. He can be found in sculptures of classical river gods, in Romantic poetry (Wordsworth and Keats), and in modern popular culture (television talk-show hosts). I take one more model from Greek prophetic transsexualism, the Delphic oracle. Delphi, holiest spot of the ancient Mediterranean, was once dedicated to female deities, as the priestess recalls at the opening of Aeschylus' *Eumenides*. W. F. Jackson Knight asserts that "Delphi means the female generative organ."[17] The delta has been found to symbolize the female pubes in societies as far as the Brazilian jungle. The Delphic oracle was called the Pythia or Pythoness after the giant serpent Pytho, slain by invading Apollo. Legend claims the oracle was maddened by fumes rising from a chasm above the decaying chthonian serpent. But no chasm has been found at Delphi.

The oracle was Apollo's high priestess and spoke for him. Pilgrims, royal and lowly, arrived at Delphi with questions and left with cryptic replies. It was after descending from Delphi that Oedipus collided with his father at the crossroads—a spot in the Greek pastureland still unchanged after three thousand years of ghostly legend. The prophesying oracle was the instrument of the god of poetry, a lyre upon which he played. E. R. Dodds states, "The Pythia became *entheos, plena deo:* the god entered into her and used her vocal organs as if they were his own, exactly as the so-called 'control' does in modern spirit-mediumship; that is why Apollo's Delphic utterances are always couched in the first person, never in the third."[18] This resembles the ventriloquism Frazer ascribes to entranced shamans. Michelangelo uses the Delphic metaphor in a madrigal comparing a Renaissance virago, intellectual and poet Vittoria Colonna, to the oracle: "A man in a woman, indeed a god, speaks through her mouth." The Delphic oracle is a woman invaded by a male spirit. She suffers usurpation of identity, like the mental sextransformations of great dramatists and novelists. I designate as "the Pythoness" another category of androgyne, of which my best example will be the sibylline comedienne Gracie Allen.

The Great Mother is the master image from which split off surrogate subforms of female horrors, like Gorgon and Fury. The vagina dentata literalizes the sexual anxiety of these myths. In the North American Indian version, says Neumann, "A meat-eating fish inhabits the vagina of the Terrible Mother; the hero is the man who overcomes the Terrible Mother, breaks the teeth out of her vagina, and so makes her into a woman."[19] The toothed vagina is no sexist hallucination: every penis is made less in every vagina, just as mankind, male and female, is devoured by mother nature. The vagina dentata is part of the Romantic revival of pagan myth. It is subliminally present in Poe's voracious maelstrom and dank, scythe-swept pit. It overtly appears in the bible of French Decadence, Huysmans' *A Rebours* (1884), where a dreamer is magnetically drawn toward mother nature's open thighs, the "bloody depths" of a carnivorous flower rimmed by "swordblades."[20]

The Greek Gorgon was a kind of vagina dentata. In Archaic art, she is a grinning head with beard, tusks, and outthrust tongue. She has snakes in her hair or around her waist. She runs in swastika form, a symbol of primitive vitality. Her beard, a postmenopausal virilization, turns up on the witches of *Macbeth*. She is like a jack-o'-lantern or death's-head, the spectral night face of mother nature. The gorgoneion or "bodiless head of fright" antedates by many centuries the Gorgon with a woman's body.[21] The Perseus legend obscures an ancient prototype: the hero seizes a trophy that cannot be severed or slain (fig. 1).

Men, never women, are turned to stone by gazing at Medusa. Freud interprets this as the "terror of castration" felt by boys at their first glimpse of female genitals.[22] Richard Tristman feels the staring mechanism involved in male consumption of pornography is a compulsive

1. *Perseus Cutting Off the Head of Medusa*, from the metope of Temple C at Selinus, Sicily, ca. 550–540 B.C.

scrutiny or searching for the missing female penis. That female genitals do resemble a wound is evident in those slang terms "slash" and "gash." Huysmans calls the genital flower a "hideous flesh-wound." Flower, mouth, wound: the Gorgon is a reverse image of the Mystic Rose of Mary. Woman's genital wound is a furrow in female earth. Snaky Medusa is the thorny undergrowth of nature's relentless fertility.

The Gorgon's name comes from the adjective *gorgos*, "terrible, fearful, fierce." *Gorgopos*, "fierce-eyed, terrible," is an epithet of Athena, who wears the Gorgon's head on breast and shield, a gift from Perseus.

It is an apotropaion, a charm to ward off evil spirits, like the giant eye painted on prows of ancient ships. Jackson Knight says of the gorgoneion, "It occurs on shields, on the brow-bands of war-horses, and on the doors of ovens, where it was meant to exclude evil influences from the bread."[23] Jane Harrison compares the Gorgon's head to primitive ritual masks: "They are the natural agents of a religion of fear and 'riddance'. . . . The function of such masks is permanently to 'make an ugly face', *at* you if you are doing wrong, breaking your word, robbing your neighbor, meeting him in battle; *for* you if you are doing right."[24] Apotropaic charms are common in Italy, where belief in the evil eye is still strong. Gold hands and red or gold horns dangle from necks and hang in kitchens next to chains of garlic to drive away vampires. The Mediterranean has never lost its chthonian cultism.

I use the apotropaic gorgoneion in two major ways. Art and religion come from the same part of the mind. Great cult symbols transfer smoothly into artistic experience. Solitary or highly original artists often make apotropaic art. The *Mona Lisa,* for example, seems to have functioned as an apotropaion for Leonardo, who refused to part with it until his death at the court of the French king (hence its presence in the Louvre). Ambiguous Mona Lisa, presiding over her desolate landscape, is a gorgoneion, staring hierarch of pitiless nature.

A second apotropaion: Joyce's dense modernist style. Joyce has only one subject—Ireland. His writing is both a protest against an intolerable spiritual dependency and ironically an immortalization of the power that bound him. Ireland is a Gorgon, in Joyce's words "the Mother Sow who eats her children." Knight compares the mazelike meander design on Greek houses to "tangled thread" charms on British doorsteps: "Tangled drawings are meant to entangle intruders, as the tangled reality of a labyrinthine construction at the approach to a fort actually helps very much to entangle attackers."[25] Language as labyrinth: Joyce's aggressive impenetrability is the hex sign of Harrison's "religion of fear and 'riddance'." We will later examine the creator of the first impenetrable modern style, Henry James. There we return full circle to the Great Mother, for my theory is that James's Decadent late style is the heavy ritual transvestism of a eunuch-priest of the mother goddess.

My third apotropaion: Virginia Woolf's *To the Lighthouse,* a novel as ghost dance, as invocation and exorcism. From Woolf's diary:

> Father's birthday. He would have been 96, 96, yes, today; and could have been 96, like other people one has known: but mer-

cifully was not. His life would have entirely ended mine. What would have happened? No writing, no books—inconceivable.

I used to think of him and mother daily; but writing the *Lighthouse* laid them in my mind. And now he comes back sometimes, but differently. (I believe this to be true—that I was obsessed by them both, unhealthily; and writing of them was a necessary act.)[26]

An apotropaion bars encroachment by the dead. The ghost of Odysseus' mother, let us recall, is thirsty for blood. Unsentimentally, Woolf wishes for no longer years for her father. Contest for life is a Sadean power struggle. *To the Lighthouse* is filled with *imagines*, ancestor masks. The Romans put them in the atrium to keep them out of the bedroom. As family romance, *To the Lighthouse* is the gorgoneion on the oven door, which must be shut to make a room of one's own. The novel has a second ritual pattern: the Eleusinian *heuresis* or "finding again" of Persephone by Demeter. In *To the Lighthouse*, mother and daughter reunite, but only to bid farewell.

Now my other major use of the gorgoneion. The ugly staring Gorgon is *the daemonic eye*. She is the paralyzing animal eye of chthonian nature, the glittering, mesmerizing eye of vampires and seductresses. The tusked Gorgon is *the eye which eats*. In other words, the eye is still bound to biology. It hungers. I will show that the west invented a new eye, contemplative, conceptual, the eye of art. It was born in Egypt. This is the Apollonian solar disk, illuminating and idealizing. The Gorgon is the night eye, Apollo the day. I will argue that the origin of the Greek Apollonian is in Egypt. Greek ideas are creatures of Egyptian formalism. It is untrue the Egyptians had no ideas. There are, I said, ideas in images. Egyptian images made western imagination. Egypt liberated and divinized the human eye. The Apollonian eye is the brain's great victory over the bloody open mouth of mother nature.

Only the Sphinx is as symbolically rich as the Gorgon. There are benign male sphinxes in Egypt, but the famous one is female, born of the incest of half-serpent Echidna with her dog-son Orthus. The Sphinx has a woman's head and bosom, a griffin's wings, and a lion's claws and rump. Her name means "the Throttler" (from the Greek *sphiggo*, "strangle"). The riddle by which she defeats all men but Oedipus is the ungraspable mystery of nature, which will defeat Oedipus anyway. The Gorgon rules the eye, while the Sphinx rules words. She rules them by stopping them, stillborn, in the throat. Poets appeal to the Muse to stave off the Sphinx. In Coleridge's *Christabel*, one of the great horror stories of Romanticism, Muse and Sphinx merge, changing the poet's sex and making him mute. Birth is taking first breath. But the Sphinx of nature throttles us in the womb.

Other subforms of the Great Mother cluster in groups. The Furies or Erinyes are avengers. Without fixed shape in Homer, they first gain one in the *Oresteia*. Hesiod says the Furies sprang from drops of blood falling to earth from Uranus' castration by his son Cronos. They are cruel chthonian emanations of the soil. The motif of seminal splashes recurs in Pegasus' birth from drops of blood from Medusa's severed head—suggesting the Gorgon's half-maleness. In early ritual, throats were cut or blood poured directly on the field to stimulate earth's fertility. The ugly, barbaric Furies are first cousin to Aphrodite. She comes from another seminal splashdown, from the foam cast up by Uranus' castrated organs hitting the sea. It is her arrival on shore, by convenient seashell, that Botticelli depicts in *The Birth of Venus*. Aphrodite is therefore a Fury washed clean of her chthonian origins. Aeschylus gives the Furies a doglike rheum: their eyes drip with pus. They are the daemonic eye as running sore, the impacted, putrefying womb of nature.

The Harpies are servants of the Furies. They are "the Snatchers" (from *harpazo*, "snatch"), airborne pirates, befouling men with their droppings. They represent the aspect of femaleness that clutches and kills in order to feed itself. The archetypal power of Alfred Hitchcock's great saga of malevolent nature, *The Birds* (1963), comes from its reactivation of the Harpy myth, shown as both bird and woman. Keres resemble Harpies as female carriers of disease and pollution. They are smoky intruders from the underworld. Greek art and literature never did crystallize a shape and story for them, so they remain vague. The Sirens, on the other hand, made it into the erotic big time. They are graveyard creatures who appear in Archaic art much like Harpies, as birds with female heads and male beards. Homer's Sirens are twin singers luring sailors to destruction on the rocks: "They sit there in a meadow piled high with the mouldering skeletons of men, whose withered skin still hangs upon their bones."[27] The Sirens are the triumph of matter. Man's spiritual trajectory ends in the rubbish heap of his own mother-born body.

Some female monsters shifted from plural to singular. Lamia, a bisexual Greek and Roman succubus who kidnapped children and drank their blood, was once one of many, like the child-killer Mormo. Joseph Fontenrose calls the Lamiai "*phasmata* that rose from earth in woods and glens," while the Mormones were "wandering *daimones*."[28] Gello, another child-stealer, remains part of Greek superstition today.

The night-stalking vampire Empusa devoured her prey after the sex act. These examples catch myth midcourse. Spooks and goblins, who run in packs in the primeval murk, begin to emerge as personalities. But they must be condensed and refined by the popular imagination or by a great poet.

Circe owes everything to Homer. An Italian sorceress living among pigs has been gorgeously enhanced with cinematic glamour. Lordly in her cold stone house, Circe waves her phallic wand over her subject males, grunting in the slop of infancy. She is the prison of sex, a tomb in a thicket. Circe's Hebrew counterpart is Lilith, Adam's first wife, whose name means "of the night." Harold Bloom says Lilith, originally a Babylonian wind-demoness, sought ascendancy in the sex act: "The vision men call Lilith is formed primarily by their anxiety at what they perceive to be the beauty of a woman's body, a beauty they believe to be, at once, far greater and far less than their own."[29] Like Aphrodite, Circe and Lilith are the ugly made beautiful. Nature's Medusan hag dons her magic mask in the hall of art.

Sexually dominated by him, Circe warns Odysseus of future dangers. Her description of Scylla has relish, for Scylla is her outdoor alter ego, a cliff monster with twelve feet, six heads, and triple rows of teeth who plucks sailors off ships. Like the Harpy, she is a Snatcher, a gnawing female appetite. Scylla's female companion, Charybdis, is her upside-down mirror image. Sucking and spewing three times a day, the killer whirlpool is the womb-vortex of the nature mother. It is probably into Charybdis that Poe's hero sinks in *Descent into the Maelström.* Ovid's Circe stunts Scylla's legs and girds her belly with a pack of wild dogs with "gaping mouths."[30] Scylla becomes a vagina dentata or sexual she-wolf. At the gates of Hell in Milton's *Paradise Lost,* she is Sin, the torso of a beautiful woman ending in a scaly serpent with a scorpion's sting. Her waist is ringed with screeching hellhounds that kennel in her womb. The dogs are insatiable, ulcerating lusts, like the Indian man-eating fish. Sexual disillusion leads to Scylla and Charybdis. King Lear, hanging a white beard on his witchy daughter Goneril, sees woman as animal-loined, a stinking "sulphurous pit" sucking men to hell (IV.vi.97–135). Attraction is repulsion, necessity bondage.

The Great Mother's main disciple is her son and lover, the dying god of Near Eastern mystery religion. Neumann says of Attis, Adonis, Tammuz, and Osiris, "They are loved, slain, buried, and bewailed by her, and are then reborn through her." Maleness is merely a shadow whirled round in nature's eternal cycle. The boy gods are "phallic consorts of the Great Mother, drones serving the queen bee, who are killed off as soon as they have performed their duty of fecundation." Mother-love smothers what it embraces. The dying gods are "delicate blossoms, symbolized by the myths as anemones, narcissi, hyacinths, or violets."

> The youths, who personify the spring, belong to the Great Mother. They are her bondslaves, her property, because they are the sons she has borne. Consequently the chosen ministers and priests of the Mother Goddess are eunuchs. . . . For her, loving, dying, and being emasculated are the same thing.[31]

Masculinity flows from the Great Mother as an aspect of herself and is recalled and cancelled by her at will. Her son is a servant of her cult. There is no going beyond her. Motherhood blankets existence.

The most brilliant perception of *The Golden Bough*, muted by prudence, is Frazer's analogy between Jesus and the dying gods. The Christian ritual of death and redemption is a survival of pagan mystery religion. Frazer says, "The type, created by Greek artists, of the sorrowful goddess with her dying lover in her arms, resembles and may have been the model of the *Pietà* of Christian art."[32] Early Christian and Byzantine Christs were virile, but once the Church settled in Rome, Italy's vestigial paganism took over. Christ relapsed into Adonis. Michelangelo's *Pietà* is one of the most popular works of world art partly because of its pagan evocation of the archetypal mother-relation. Mary, with her unmarked maiden's face, is the mother goddess ever-young and ever-virgin. Jesus is remarkably epicene, with aristocratic hands and feet of morbid delicacy. Michelangelo's androgynous dying god fuses sex and religion in the pagan way. Grieving in her oppressive robes, Mary admires the sensual beauty of the son she has made. His glassy nude limbs slipping down her lap, Adonis sinks back to earth, his strength drained by and returned to his immortal mother.

Freud says, "It is the fate of all of us, perhaps, to direct our first sexual impulse towards our mother."[33] Incest is at the start of all biography and cosmogony. The man who finds his true wife has found his mother. Male mastery in marriage is a social illusion, nurtured by women exhorting their creations to play and walk. At the emotional heart of every marriage is a pietà of mother and son. I will find traces of the archaic incest of mother-cults in Poe and James and in Tennessee Williams' *Suddenly Last Summer*, where a queen mother, ruling a brutal primeval garden, marries her homosexual aesthete son, who is ritually slain and mourned. Female dynamism is the law of nature. Earth husbands herself.

The residual paganism of western culture bursts out full flower in modern show business. An odd phenomenon, over fifty years old, is the cultishness of male homosexuals around female superstars. There is no equivalent taste among lesbians, who as a group in America seem more interested in softball than art and artifice. The female superstar is a goddess, a universal mother-father. Cabaret parodies by female impersonators unerringly find the androgyny in the great stars. Mae West, Marlene Dietrich, Bette Davis, Eartha Kitt, Carol Channing, Barbra Streisand, Diana Ross, Joan Collins, Joan Rivers: all are self-exalting females of cold male will, with subtle sexual ambiguities of manner and look. Judy Garland inspired mob hysteria among male homosexuals. Media reports speak of uncanny shrieking, mass assaults on the stage, blinding showers of bouquets. These were orgiastic eunuch rites at the shrine of the goddess. Photos show posturing men making sensational entrances in Garland's glittery costume, just like transvestite devotees of the ancient Great Mother. Such spectacles became rarer in the Seventies, when American homosexuals went macho. But I sense a return to imaginative sensibility among younger men. Cultishness still thrives among homosexual opera fans, whose supreme diva was tempestuous Maria Callas. I interpret this phenomenon, like pornography and perversion, as more evidence of men's tendency toward sexual conceptualization, for me a biological faculty at the roots of art. One result of the disease claiming so many lives is that homosexuals have been involuntarily rewed to their shamanistic identity, fatal, sacrificial, outcast. To make sexual ideas out of reality, as they did in their fevered cult of the female star, is more profitable to culture than to act out such ideas in bar or bedroom. Art advances by self-mutilation of the artist. The more negative homosexual experience, the more it belongs to art.

Our first exhibit from western art is the so-called Venus of Willendorf, a tiny statuette (height 4⅜") from the Old Stone Age found in Austria (fig. 2). In it we see all the strange laws of primitive earth-cult. Woman is idol and object, goddess and prisoner. She is buried in the bulging mass of her own fecund body.

The Venus of Willendorf is comically named, for she is unbeautiful by every standard. But beauty has not yet emerged as a criterion for art. In the Old Stone Age, art is magic, a ritual recreation of what-is-desired. Cave paintings were not meant to be seen. Their beauty for us is incidental. Bison and reindeer crowd the walls, following rock ridges and grooves. Art was invocation, a summoning: mother nature, let herds return that man might eat. Caves were the bowels of the goddess, and art was a sexual scribbling, an impregnation. It had rhythm and

2. *Venus of Willendorf,*
ca. 30,000 B.C.

vitality but no visual status. The Venus of Willendorf, a cult-image half-molded from a rough stone, is unbeautiful because art has not yet found its relation to the eye. Her fat is a symbol of abundance in an age of famine. She is the too-muchness of nature, which man longs to direct to his salvation.

Venus of Willendorf carries her cave with her. She is blind, masked. Her ropes of corn-row hair look forward to the invention of agriculture. She has a furrowed brow. Her facelessness is the impersonality of primitive sex and religion. There is no psychology or identity yet, because there is no society, no cohesion. Men cower and scatter at the blast of the elements. Venus of Willendorf is eyeless because nature can be seen but not known. She is remote even as she kills and creates. The statuette, so overflowing and protuberant, is ritually invisible. She stifles the eye. She is the cloud of archaic night.

Bulging, bulbous, bubbling. Venus of Willendorf, bent over her own belly, tends the hot pot of nature. She is eternally pregnant. She broods, in all senses. She is hen, nest, egg. The Latin *mater* and *materia*, mother and matter, are etymologically connected. Venus of Willendorf is the nature-mother as primeval muck, oozing into infant forms. She is female but not feminine. She is turgid with primal force, swollen with great expectations. She has no feet. Placed on end, she would topple over. Woman is immobile, weighed down by her inflated mounds of breast, belly, and buttock. Like Venus de Milo, Venus of Willendorf has no arms. They are flat flippers scratched on the stone, unevolved, useless. She has no thumbs and therefore no tools. Unlike man, she can neither roam nor build. She is a mountain that can be climbed but can never move.

Venus is a solipsist, navel-gazing. Femaleness is self-referential and self-replicating. Delphi was called the omphalos or navel of the world, marked by a shapeless holy stone. A black meteorite, a primitive image of Cybele, was brought to Rome from Phrygia to save the city in the last Punic War. The Palladium, a Zeus-sent image of Athena upon which Troy's fate depended, was probably such a meteorite. Today, the Kaaba, the inner sanctuary of the Great Mosque of Mecca, enshrines a meteorite, the Black Stone, as the holiest relic of Islam. The Venus of Willendorf is a kind of meteorite, a quirky found object, lumpish and mystic. The Delphic omphalos-stone was cone, womb, and beehive. The braided cap of Venus of Willendorf is hivelike—prefiguring the provocative beehives of French court wigs and shellacked swinging-Sixties towers. Venus buzzes to herself, queen for all days, woman for all seasons. She sleeps. She is hibernation and harvest, the turning wheel of the year. The egg-shaped Venus thinks in circles. Mind under matter.

Sex, I said, is a descent to the nether realms, a daily sinking from sky-cult to earth-cult. It is abdominal, abominable, daemonic. Venus of Willendorf is going down, disappearing into her own labyrinth. She is a tuber, rooted from a pocket of earth. Kenneth Clark divides female nudes into the Vegetable and the Crystalline Aphrodite. Inert and self-communing, Venus of Willendorf represents the obstacle of sex and vegetable nature. It is at her shrine that we worship in oral sex. In the bowels of the earth mother, we feel but do not think or see. Venus dwindles to a double pubic delta, knees clamped and cramped in the sharp pelvic angle of the wide-hipped childbearing woman, which prevents her from running with ease. Female jiggle is the ducklike waddle of our wallowing Willendorf, who swims in the underground river of liquid nature. Sex is probings, plumbing, secretions, gushings. Venus is drowsing and dowsing, hearkening to the stirring in her sac of waters.

Is the Venus of Willendorf just to female experience? Yes. Woman is trapped in her wavy, watery body. She must listen and learn from something beyond and yet within her. The Venus of Willendorf, blind, tongueless, brainless, armless, knock-kneed, seems a depressing model of gender. Yet woman is depressed, pressed down, by earth's gravitation, calling us back to her bosom. We will see that malign magnetism at work in Michelangelo, one of his great themes and obsessions. In the west, art is a hacking away at nature's excess. The western mind makes definitions. That is, it draws lines. This is the heart of Apollonianism. There are no lines in the Venus of Willendorf, only curves and circles. She is the formlessness of nature. She is mired in the miasmic swamp I identify with Dionysus. Life always begins and ends in squalor. The Venus of Willendorf, slumping, slovenly, sluttish, is in a rut, the womb-tomb of mother nature. Never send to know for whom the belle tolls. She tolls for thee.

How did beauty begin? Earth-cult, suppressing the eye, locks man in the belly of mothers. There is, I insisted, nothing beautiful in nature. Nature is primal power, coarse and turbulent. Beauty is our weapon against nature; by it we make objects, giving them limit, symmetry, proportion. Beauty halts and freezes the melting flux of nature.

Beauty was made by men acting together. Hamlets, forts, cities spread across the Near East after the founding of Jericho (ca. 8000 B.C.), the first known settlement in the world. But it was not until Egypt that art broke its enslavement to nature. High art is nonutilitarian. That is, the art object, though retaining its ritualism, is no longer a tool of something else. Beauty is the art object's license to life. The object exists on its own, godlike. Beauty is the art object's light from within. We know it by the eye. Beauty is our escape from the murky flesh-envelope that imprisons us.

Egypt, making a state, made beauty. The reign of Chephren (fl. 2565 B.C.) gave Egyptian art its supreme style, a tradition to last until the time of Christ (fig. 3). Pharaoh was the state. The concentration of power in one man, a living god, was a great cultural advance. A king's emergence out of feuding tribal chieftains is always a step forward in history, as in the medieval era with its quarrelsome barons. Commerce, technology, and the arts profit when nationalism wins over parochialism. Egypt, the first totalitarian régime, made a mystique out of one-man rule. And in that mystique was the birth of the western eye.

A king, ruling alone, is the head of state, as the people are the body. Pharaoh is a wise eye, never blinking. He unifies the scattered many.

3. *Chephren*, from the pyramid complex at Giza, ca. 2500 B.C.

The unification of upper and lower Egypt, a geographical triumph, was man's first experience of concentration, condensation, conceptualization. Social order and the *idea* of social order emerge. Egypt is history's first romance of hierarchy. Pharaoh, elevated and sublime, contemplated life's panorama. His eye was the sun disk at the apex of the social pyramid. He had *point of view*, an Apollonian sightline. Egypt invented the magic of *image*. The mystique of kingship had to be projected over thousands of miles to keep the nation together. Conceptualization and projection: in Egypt is forged the formalistic Apollonian line that will end in modern cinema, master genre of our century. Egypt invented glamour, beauty as power and power as beauty. Egyptian aristocrats were the first Beautiful People. Hierarchy and eroticism fused in Egypt, making a pagan unity the west has never thrown off. The eros of hierarchical orders, separate but mutually intrusive, is one of the west's most characteristic perversions, later intensified by the Christian taboo upon sex. Egypt makes personality and history numinous. This idea, entering Europe through Greece, remains the principal distinction between western and eastern culture.

A black line on a white page. The Nile, cutting through the desert, was the first straight line in western culture. Egypt discovered linearity, a phallic track of mind piercing the entanglements of nature. The thirty royal dynasties of Egypt were the cascading river of history. Ancient Egypt was a thin band of cultivated land an average of five miles wide but six hundred miles long. An absolutist geography produced an absolutist politics and aesthetics. At its height in the Old Kingdom, pharaonic power created the pyramid, a mammoth design of converging lines. At Giza are remnants of the elevated causeway leading up from the Nile past the Great Sphinx to the pyramid of Chephren. Long causeways, for construction crews and religious processions, were highways into history. Egyptian linearity cut the knot of nature; it was the eye shot forward into the far distance.

The masculine art form of construction begins in Egypt. There were public works before, as in the fabled walls of Jericho, but they did not cater to the eye. In Egypt, construction is male geometry, a glorification of the visible. The first clarity of intelligible form appears in Egypt, the basis of Greek Apollonianism in art and thought. Egypt discovers foursquare architecture, a rigid grid laid against mother nature's melting ovals. Social order becomes a visible aesthetic, countering nature's chthonian invisibilities. Pharaonic construction is the perfection of matter in art. Fascist political power, grandiose and self-divinizing, creates the hierarchical, categorical superstructure of western mind.

Pyramids are man-mountains to rival nature, ladders to the sun of sky-cult. Colossalism, monumentality. The ideal human figure in Egypt is a pillar, an element of architecture and geometry. The gigantism of pro-creative nature has been masculinized and hardened. Egypt had little wood but lots of stone. Stone makes an art of permanence. The body is an obelisk, square, phallic, sky-pointing, an Apollonian line defying time and organic change.

Egyptian art is glyptic, that is, carved or engraved. It is based on the incised edge, which I identify as the Apollonian element in western culture. Stone is obdurate, unregenerate nature. The incised edge is the line drawn between nature and culture. It is the steely autograph of the western will. We will find the sharp Apollonian contour in psychology as well as art. Western personality is hard, impermeable, intractable. Spengler says "the brilliant *polish* of the stone in Egyptian art" makes the eye "glide" along the statue surface.[34] The west's armoured ego begins in the shiny stone idealizations of Old Kingdom Pharaohs, *objets d'art* and *objets de culte*. The green diorite statue of enthroned Cheph-ren from Giza is a masterpiece of smooth, glossy, Apollonian definitive-ness. Its hardness of surface repels the eye. This masculine hardness is an abolition of female interiority. There are no warm womb-spaces in aristocratic Egyptian art. The body is a shaft of frozen Apollonian will. The flatness of Egyptian wall-painting and relief serves the same func-tion, obliterating woman's inner darkness. Every angle of the body is crisp, clean, and sunlit. Sagging maternal breasts of the Willendorf kind usually appear, oddly enough, only on male fertility gods like Hapi, the Nile god. Egypt is the first to glamourize small breasts. The breast as vernal adornment rather than rubbery milk sac, outline rather than volume: Apollonian Egypt made the first shift of value from femaleness to femininity, an advanced erotic art form.

Chthonian internality, as we shall see, was projected into the world of the dead. But Egypt also translated inner space into entirely social terms. Egypt invented interior décor, civilized living; it made beauty out of social life. The Egyptians were the first aesthetes. An aesthete does not necessarily dress well or collect art works: an aesthete is one who *lives by the eye.* The Egyptians had "taste." Taste is Apollonian discrimi-nation, judgment, connoisseurship; taste is the visible logic of objects. Arnold Hauser says of the Middle Kingdom, "The stiffly ceremonial forms of courtly art are absolutely new and come into prominence here for the first time in the history of human culture."[35] The Egyptians lived by ceremony; they ritualized social life. The aristocratic house was a cool, airy temple of harmony and grace; the minor arts had unparalleled quality of design. Jewelry, makeup, costume, chairs, tables, cabinets: from the moment Egyptian style was rediscovered by Napoleon's invaders, it has been the rage in Europe and America, influencing fashion, furniture, and tombstones and even producing the Washington Monument. Artifacts from other Near Eastern cultures—the golden bull's lyre from Ur, for example—seem cluttered, bulky, muscle-bound. In their cult of the eye, the Egyptians saw *edges*. Even their stylized gestures in art have a superb balletic contour. The Egyptians invented *elegance*. Elegance is reduction, simplification, condensation. It is spare, stark, sleek. Elegance is cultivated abstraction. The source of Greek and Roman classicism—clarity, order, proportion, balance—is in Egypt.

Egypt remains unabsorbed by humanistic education. Though its art and history are taught, it is taken far less seriously than Greece. The thinness of Egyptian literature keeps it out of core curricula. The superstition of Egyptian religion repels the rational, and the autocracy of Egyptian politics repels the liberal. But Egypt's power to fascinate endures, alluring poets, artists, actresses, and fanatics. Egyptian high culture was more complex and conceptual than has been acknowledged. It is underestimated because of the moralistic obsession with language that has dominated modern academic thought. Words are not the only measure of mental development. To believe that they are is a very western or Judeo-Christian illusion. It stems from our invisible God, who talks creation into existence. Words are the most removed of human inventions from things-as-they-are. The most ancient conflict in western culture, between Jew and Egyptian, continues today: Hebrew word-worship versus pagan imagism, the great unseen versus the glorified thing. The Egyptians were visionary materialists. They began the western line of Apollonian aestheticism that we see in the *Iliad*, in Pheidias, Botticelli, Spenser, Ingres, Wilde, and Hollywood cinema. Apollonian things are the cold western eye cut out of nature.

Egyptian culture flourished relatively unchanged for three thousand years, far longer than Greek culture. Stagnancy, a stultifying lack of individualism, says the humanist. But Egyptian culture lasted because it was stable and complete. It worked. The Apollonian element in Egypt is so pronounced that the idea of "classical" antiquity should be revised to contain it. Egypt and the ancient Near East were also the source of the Dionysian countercurrent in Greek culture. In Greece Apollo and Dionysus were at odds, but in Egypt they were reconciled. Egyptian culture was a fusion of the conceptual with the chthonian, the form-

making of consciousness with the shadowy flux of procreative nature.
Day and night were equally honored. Here alone in the world were sky-
cult and earth-cult yoked and harmonized.

Fertility religion always comes first in history. But as the food problem
is solved, nature's moral and aesthetic incoherence gradually becomes
apparent. Egypt evolved into the sun-worship of sky-cult without ever
losing its orientation toward the earth. This was because of the Nile,
center of the Egyptian economy. Each year the river flooded and receded, leaving a plain of rich black mud; each year the hard went soft,
earth turned liquid. John Read says alchemy probably began in Egypt,
since Khem was the ancient name of Egypt, "the country of dark soil,
the Biblical Land of Ham."[36] Metamorphosis is the chthonian magic of
shapeshifting Dionysus. The fertile muck was the primeval matrix, with
which Egyptians came into annual contact. The Apollonian is chaste
contour, borderlines: the Nile, transgressing its borders with majestic
regularity, was the triumph of mother nature. Egypt's ideology of sun
and stone rested on chthonian ooze, the swamp of generation I identify
with Dionysus. The oscillations of the Egyptian calendar produced a
fruitful duality of point of view, one of the greatest constructs of western
imagination.

Chthonian mysteries are the secret of Egypt's perennial fascination.
The gross and barbaric proliferated. A dung-beetle, the scarab, was
worshipped and worn as a gemstone. The scarab was minister of nature's decay, the bath of dissolution. Egyptian literature was undeveloped because internality was preempted by the death-cult. There
was only one ethical principle, justice (*maat*), a public virtue above
ground or below. Spirituality was projected into the afterlife. The Book
of the Dead was daemonic thought, ruminations, earth-chawings. The
mummy, swaddled like an infant, returned to nature's womb for rebirth.
The painted tomb was cave art, prayers to daemonic darkness. Egyptian
culture was both earth-tending and earth-rejecting. Herodotus reports
Egyptian men urinated like women. Egyptian gods were incompletely
emerged from prehistoric animism. They were monstrous hybrids, half
human and half animal or animal joined to animal. E. A. Wallis Budge
says the Egyptians clung to their "composite creatures" despite the
ridicule of foreigners.[37] One god had a serpent head on a leopard body,
another a hawk head on the body of a lion and horse; still another was a
crocodile with the body of a lion and hippopotamus. Chthonian energy,
like the Nile, is overflow and superfetation. The logic and rigor of the
Apollonian eye had to defeat Egypt's fuzzy tribal fetishism.

The Egyptian synthesis of chthonian and Apollonian was of enor-

4. *Stele of the Overseer of Magazine of Amon, Nib-Amun, and his wife, Huy,*
Eighteenth Dynasty.

mous consequence for western tradition. It was in the interplay between
earth and sky that idealized form began. Western personality is an
Egyptian *objet d'art*, an exclusive zone of aristocratic privilege. The
cartouche, a closed oval, surrounds a hieroglyphic name. In early Egyptian art, a *serekh* or square palace façade signified kingship. Cartouche
and *serekh* are symbols of hierarchic sequestration, a closing in of the
holy and royal to exclude the profane. They are a *temenos*, the Greek
word for the sacred precinct around a temple. The reserved space of the
cartouche is analogous to the *wedjat*, the apotropaic eye of Horus
studding so many amulets and hieroglyphic displays (fig. 4). The Egyptian eye is synonymous with western personality. Because the soul was
thought to reside there, the eye is always shown full face, flounderlike,
even when the head is in painted profile. The eye is licensed in Egypt.

That is, it is released but ritually bound. The glamourous black-tailed outline of Egyptian eye-makeup is a hieratic accent, both fish and fence. It contains and blocks out. Egypt honored the earth but also feared it. The pure, clean Apollonian contour of Egyptian art is a defense against chthonian muck and muddle. Egypt created the distance between eye and object which is a hallmark of western philosophy and aesthetics. That distance is a charged force field, a dangerous temenos. Egypt created Apollonian objects out of chthonian fear. The western line of Apollonian thing-making, from Homer's bronzed warriors to capitalist cars and cans, begins in the Egyptian caged eye.

One of the most misunderstood features of Egyptian life was the veneration of cats, whose mummified bodies have been found by the thousands. My theory is that the cat was the model for Egypt's unique synthesis of principles (fig. 5). The modern cat, the last animal domesticated by man, descends from Felis lybica, a North African wildcat. Cats are prowlers, uncanny creatures of the night. Cruelty and play are one for them. They live by and for fear, practicing being scared or spooking humans by sudden rushings and ambushes. Cats dwell in the occult, that is, the "hidden." In the Middle Ages, they were hunted and killed for their association with witches. Unfair? But the cat really *is* in league with chthonian nature, Christianity's mortal enemy. The black cat of Halloween is the lingering shadow of archaic night. Sleeping up to twenty of every twenty-four hours, cats reconstruct and inhabit the primitive night-world. The cat is telepathic—or at least thinks that it is. Many people are unnerved by its cool stare. Compared to dogs, slavishly eager to please, cats are autocrats of naked self-interest. They are both amoral and immoral, consciously breaking rules. Their "evil" look at such times is no human projection: the cat may be the only animal who savors the perverse or reflects upon it.

Thus the cat is an adept of chthonian mysteries. But it has a hieratic duality. It is *eye-intense.* The cat fuses the Gorgon eye of appetite to the detached Apollonian eye of contemplation. The cat values invisibility, comically imagining itself undetectable as it slouches across a lawn. But it also fashionably loves to see and be seen; it is a spectator of life's drama, amused, condescending. It is a narcissist, always adjusting its appearance. When it is disheveled, its spirits fall. Cats have a sense of *pictorial composition:* they station themselves symmetrically on chairs, rugs, even a sheet of paper on the floor. Cats adhere to an Apollonian metric of mathematical space. Haughty, solitary, precise, they are arbiters of elegance—that principle I find natively Egyptian.

5. *Cat Goddess with One Gold Earring*, Late Dynastic.

Cats are poseurs. They have a sense of *persona*—and become visibly embarrassed when reality punctures their dignity. Apes are more human but less beautiful: they posture but never pose. Hunkering, chattering, chest-beating, buttock-baring, apes are bumptious vulgarians lurching up the evolutionary road. The cat's sophisticated personae are masks of an advanced theatricality. Priest and god of its own cult, the cat follows a code of ritual purity, cleaning itself religiously. It makes pagan sacrifices to itself and may share its ceremonies with the elect. The day of a cat-owner often begins with the discovery of a neat pile of mole guts or mashed mouse limbs on the porch—Darwinian mementos. The cat is the least Christian inhabitant of the average home.

In Egypt the cat; in Greece the horse. The Greeks did not care for cats. They admired the horse and used it constantly in art and metaphor. The horse is an athlete, proud but serviceable. It accepts citizenship in a public system. The cat is a law unto itself. It has never lost its despotic air of Oriental luxury and indolence. It was too feminine for the male-loving Greeks. I spoke of Egypt's invention of femininity, an aesthetic of social practice removed from nature's brutal female machinery. Aristocratic Egyptian women's costume, an exquisite tunic of transparent pleated linen, must be called *slinky*, a word we still use for formfitting evening gowns. Slinkiness is the nocturnal stealth of cats.

The Egyptians admired sleekness, in greyhounds, jackals, and hawks. Sleekness is smooth Apollonian contour. But slinkiness is the sinuous craft of daemonic darkness, which the cat carries into day.

Cats have secret thoughts, a divided consciousness. No other animal is capable of *ambivalence*, those ambiguous cross-currents of feeling, as when a purring cat simultaneously buries its teeth warningly in one's arm. The inner drama of a lounging cat is telegraphed by its ears, which swerve round toward a distant rustle as its eyes rest with false adoration on ours, and secondly by its tail, which flicks menacingly even while the cat dozes. Sometimes the cat pretends to have no relation to its own tail, which it schizophrenically attacks. The twitching, thumping tail is the chthonian barometer of the cat's Apollonian world. It is the serpent in the garden, bumping and grinding with malice aforethought. The cat's ambivalent duality is dramatized in erratic mood-swings, abrupt leaps from torpor to mania, by which it checks our presumption: "Come no closer. I can never be known."

Thus the Egyptian veneration of cats was neither silly nor childish. Through the cat, Egypt defined and refined its complex aesthetic. The cat was the symbol of that fusion of chthonian and Apollonian which no other culture achieved. The west's eye-intense pagan line begins in Egypt, as does the hard persona of art and politics. Cats are exemplars of both. The crocodile, also honored in Egypt, resembles the cat in its daily passage between two realms: hefting itself between water and earth, the spiky crocodile is the west's armoured ego, sinister, hostile, and ever-watchful. The cat is a time-traveller from ancient Egypt. It returns whenever sorcery or style is in vogue. In the Decadent aestheticism of Poe and Baudelaire, the cat regains its sphinxlike prestige and magnitude. With its taste for ritual and bloody spectacle, conspiracy and exhibitionism, the cat is pure pagan pomp. Uniting nocturnal primitivism to Apollonian elegance of line, it became the living paradigm of Egyptian sensibility. The cat, fixing its swift predatory energy in poses of Apollonian stasis, was the first to enact the frozen moment of perceptual stillness that is high art.

Our second exhibit from western art is the bust of Nefertiti (figs. 6 and 7). How familiar it is, and yet how strange. Nefertiti is the opposite of the Venus of Willendorf. She is the triumph of Apollonian image over the humpiness and horror of mother earth. Everything fat, slack, and sleepy is gone. The western eye is open and alert. It has forced objects into their frozen frame. But the liberation of the eye has its price. Taut, still, and truncated, Nefertiti is western ego under glass.

6. *Nefertiti* (copy).

The radiant glamour of this supreme sexual persona comes to us from a palace-prison, the overdeveloped brain. Western culture, moving up toward Apollonian sunlight, discards one burden only to stagger under another.

The bust, found by a German expedition at Amarna in 1912, dates from the reign of Akhenaten (1375–57 B.C.). Queen Nefertiti, wife of the Pharaoh, wears a wig-crown peculiar to the eighteenth dynasty and seen elsewhere only on Akhenaten's formidable mother, Queen Tiy. The bust is painted limestone with plaster additions; the eye is inset rock crystal. The ears and uraeus, the royal serpent on the brow, are broken. Scholars have debated whether the piece is a studio model for court artists.

The Nefertiti bust is one of the most popular art works in the world. It is printed on scarves and molded in necklace pendants and coffee-table miniatures. But never in my experience is the bust exactly reproduced. The copyist softens it, feminizes and humanizes it. The actual bust is intolerably severe. It is too uncanny an object for domestic display. Even art books lie. The bust is usually posed in profile or at an angle, so that the missing left pupil is hidden or shadowed. What happened to the eye? Perhaps it was unnecessary in a model and never inserted. But the eye was often chiseled out of statues and paintings of the dead. It was a

7. *Nefertiti*, ca. 1350 B.C.

way of making a hated rival a nonperson and extinguishing his or her survival in the afterlife. Akhenaten's reign was divisive. His creation of a new capital and efforts to crush the powerful priesthood, his establishment of monotheism and innovations in artistic style were nullified under his son-in-law, Tutankhamen, the short-lived boy-king. Nefertiti may have lost her eye in the wreck of the eighteenth dynasty.

As we have it, the bust of Nefertiti is artistically and ritualistically complete, exalted, harsh, and alien. It fuses the naturalism of the Amarna period with the hieratic formalism of Egyptian tradition. But Amarna expressiveness ends in the grotesque. This is the least consoling of great art works. Its popularity is based on misunderstanding and suppression of its unique features. The proper response to the Nefertiti bust is fear. The queen is an android, a manufactured being. She is a new gorgoneion, a "bodiless head of fright." She is paralyzed and paralyzing. Like enthroned Chephren, Nefertiti is suave, urbane. She gazes toward the far distance, seeing what is best for her people. But her eyes, with their catlike rim of kohl, are cold. She is self-divinized authority. Art shows Akhenaten half-feminine, his limbs shrunken and belly bulging, possibly from birth defect or disease. This portrait shows his queen half-masculine, a vampire of political will. Her seductive force both lures in and warns away. She is western personality barricaded behind its aching, icy line of Apollonian identity.

Nefertiti's head is so massive it threatens to snap the neck like a stalk. She is like a papyrus blossom swaying on its river reed. The head is swollen to the point of deformity. She seems futuristic, with the enlarged cerebrum foreseen as the destiny of our species. The crown is filled like a funnel with a rain of hierarchic energy, flooding the fragile brain-pan and violently pushing the face forward like the prow of a ship. Nefertiti is like the Winged Victory of Samothrace, garments plastered back by the wind of history. As cargo, Nefertiti carries her own excess of thought. She is weighed down by Apollonian wakefulness, a sun that never sets. Egypt invented the pillar, which Greece would refine. With her slim aristocratic neck, Nefertiti is a pillar, a caryatid. She bears the burden of state upon her head, rafters of the temple of the sun. The golden brow-band is a ritual bridle, squeezing, constricting, limiting. Nefertiti presides from the temenos of power, a sacred precinct she can never leave.

Venus of Willendorf is all body, Nefertiti all head. Her shoulders have been cut away by radical surgery. Early in its history, Egypt invented the bust, a portrait style still in use. It may have been a robust double, the *ka* that enters and exits through false doors. The shoulders of the Nefertiti bust have shriveled to become their own pedestal. No physical force remains. The queen's body is bound and invisible, like a mummy. Her face gleams with the newness of rebirth. Tense with self-creation, she is a goddess as mother-father. The pregnancy of Venus of Willendorf is displaced upward and redefined. Willendorf is chthonian belly-magic, Nefertiti Apollonian head-magic. Thinking makes it so. Nefertiti is a royal highness, propelling herself like a jet into sky-cult. Forward thrust. Nefertiti leads with her chin. She has "great bones." She is Egyptian stone architecture, just as Venus of Willendorf is earthen ovals, woman as quivering poached egg. Nefertiti is femaleness made mathematical, femaleness sublimized by becoming harder and more concrete.

I said Egypt invented elegance, which is reduction, simplification, condensation. Mother nature is addition and multiplication, but Nefertiti is subtraction. Visually, she has been reduced to her essence. Her sleek contoured face is one step from the wizened. She is abbreviation, a symbol or pictogram, a pure idea of pagan pictorialism. One can never be too rich or too thin, decreed the Duchess of Windsor. I said the idea of beauty is based on enormous exclusions. So much is excluded from the Nefertiti bust that we can feel its silhouette straining against the charged atmosphere, a combat of Apollonian line. The name Nefertiti means "The Beautiful One Cometh." Her haughty face is carved out of the chaos of nature. Beauty is a state of war, a frigid blank zone under siege.

Nefertiti is ritualized western personality, a streamlined *thing*. She is forbiddingly clean. Her eyebrows are shaved and redrawn with male width and frown. She is as depilated as a priest. She has the face of a mannequin, static, posed, self-proffering. Her *knowingness* is both fashionable and hieratic. The modern mannequin of window or runway is an androgyne, because she is femaleness impersonalized by masculine abstraction. If a studio model, the Nefertiti bust is as much a mannequin as the royal dummy of a London tailor shop. As queen and mannequin, Nefertiti is both exposed and enclosed, a face and a mask. She is naked yet armoured, experienced yet ritually pure. She is sexually unapproachable because bodiless: her torso is gone; her full lips invite but remain firmly pressed together. Her perfection is for display, not for use. Akhenaten and his queen would greet their court from a balcony, the "window of appearance." All art is a window of appearance. Nefertiti's face is the sun of consciousness rising over a new horizon, the frame or mathematical grid of man's victory over nature. The idolatrous *thingness* of western art is a theft of authority from mother nature.

Nefertiti's mismatched eyes, deliberate or accidental, are a symbol of Egyptian duality. Like the cat, she sees in and sees out. She is frozen Apollonian poseur and Gorgonesque daemonic seer. The Greek Graiai, three old divine sisters, had one eye that they passed from hand to hand. Fontenrose connects this to the double pupil of a Lydian queen: "What she had, it seems to me, was a removable eye of wondrous power. It was an eye that could penetrate the invisible."[38] Nefertiti, the half-blind mannequin, sees more by being less. Mutilation is mystic expansion. Modern copyists suppress the missing eye because it is fatal to popular canons of beauty. Maimed eyes seem mad or spectral, as in the veiled vulture's eye of Poe's *Tell-Tale Heart*. Nefertiti is a mutant and visionary materialist, a thing that sees. In Egypt, matter is made numinous by the first electricity of mind. In the Egyptian cult of seeing, Nefertiti is thought in flight from its origins.

From Venus of Willendorf to Nefertiti: from body to face, touch to sight, love to judgment, nature to society. Nefertiti is like Athena born from the brow of Zeus, a head-heavy armoured goddess. She is beautiful but desexed. She is hieratic decorum and reserve, her head literally a reservoir of containment and curtailment, like her stunted torso. Her ponderous, ostentatious crown is the cold breeding ground of Greek categorical thought. Her tight brow-band is stringency, rigor, channeled ideas. The miasmic cloud of mother nature has lifted. Nefertiti's imperious jutting face is the cutting edge of western conceptualization and projection. In her profile, all roads lead to the eye. From the side, diagonals converge in peaking vectors of force. From the front, she rears up like a cobra head, woman as royal intimidator. She is the eye-intense west, the overenlargement and grandiosity of head-culture. The bust of Nefertiti is eye-pleasing but oppressive. It looks forward to Bellini's androgynous *Doge Loredan*, to Neapolitan silver reliquary busts, to Fifties fantasy drawings of smiling armless women in chic evening gowns. Authority, good will, aloofness, asceticism. Epiphany as a totem of vibrating passivity. With her welcoming but uncanny smile, Nefertiti is western personality in its ritual bonds. Exquisite and artificial, she is mind-made image forever caught in radiant Apollonian freezeframe.

3

Apollo and Dionysus

The Greek gods are sharp personalities, interacting in dramatic space. Their visualization was first achieved by blind Homer, in his epic arcs of cinematic light. Homer's conceptions were confirmed by Pheidias, the great sculptor of high classic Athens, from which came the cold white monoliths of Roman art and architecture.

In Egypt, sky-cult and earth-cult were harmonized, but in Greece there is a split. Greek greatness is Apollonian. The gods live on a peak touching the sky. Olympus and Parnassus are mountain shrines of creative power spurning the earth. In that swerve upward is the sublime conceptualism of western intellect and art. Egypt gave Greece the pillar and monumental sculpture, which Greece turns from Pharaoh to *kouros*, from divine king to divine boy. Hidden in these gifts lay Egypt's Apollonianism, which Greek artists so splendidly develop. The orderly mathematic of the Doric temple is an orchestration of Egyptian ideas. Pheidias brings person and building together on the Acropolis or High City, Athens' magic mountain. Egypt invented clarity of image, the essence of Apollonianism. From Old Kingdom Pharaohs to Pheidias is two thousand years but one step in the history of art. Greek sky-cult is an Egyptian colonnade of stony *things*, the hard, harsh blocks of western personality.

In Judeo-Christianity man is made in God's image, but in Greek religion God is made in man's image. The Greek gods have a higher human beauty, their flesh incorruptible yet sensual. Greece, unlike Egypt, never worshipped beast gods. Greek sky-cult kept nature in her place. The visibility of the Greek gods is intellectual, symbolizing mind's victory over matter. Art, a glorification of matter, wins its independence in the gods' perfection. We know the name of no artist before signed Archaic pottery of sixth-century Greece. The artist in Egypt was merely an anonymous artisan, which he became again in Rome and the Middle Ages. Judaism repressed art and the artist, reserving creativity for its fabricator God. The Greek gods, well-made but not making, float like golden solids in air.

Jane Harrison calls the Olympians "*objets d'art.*"[1] Their brilliant clarity and glittering chastity of form are Apollonian. In psychology, philosophy, and art, classical Greek imagination sought, in Eduard Fraenkel's words, "λόγος, *ratio* . . . the intelligible, determinate, mensurable, as opposed to the fantastic, vague, and shapeless."[2] The Apollonian, I said, is the line drawn against nature. For Harrison, the Olympian gods are patriarchal betrayers of earth-cult and mother nature. The chthonian is her test of authenticity and spiritual value. But I say there is neither person, thought, thing, nor art in the brutal chthonian. It was, ironically, the west's Apollonian line that produced the matchless Jane Harrison.

Nietzsche calls Apollo "the marvellous divine image of the *principium individuationis,*" "god of individuation and just boundaries."[3] The Apollonian borderline separates demes, districts, ideas, persons. Western individuation is Apollonian. The western ego is finite, articulated, visible. Apollo is the integrity and unity of western personality, a firm-outlined shape of sculptural definitiveness. Apollo lays down the law. W. K. C. Guthrie says, "Apollo was first and foremost the patron of the legal or statutory aspect of religion."[4] Apollo links society and religion. He is fabricated form. He is exclusion and exclusiveness. I will argue that the Olympians as *objets d'art* symbolize social order. Roger Hinks says: "Olympian religion is essentially a religion of the successful, comfortable, and healthy ruling-class. The downtrodden peasant, harassed by the necessities of keeping body and soul together in a naturally unfruitful land, crippled by debt and social injustice, asked something very different of his gods: the Olympians bore a discouraging resemblance to his oppressors."[5] Aristocracy is aboveness. The Olympians are authoritarian and repressive. What they repress is the monstrous gigantism of chthonian nature, that murky night-world from which society must be reclaimed day by day.

Greek art transformed Apollo from the virile bearded god to a beautiful young man or ephebe. He was once a wolf god: Apollo Lukeios, the Wolfish Apollo, gave his name to the academic Lyceum, literally "Place of Wolves." Apollo's wolfishness survives in his severity and austerity, his Doric plainness and rigor. The Dorians, who invaded Greece from the north in the twelfth century B.C., may have been blonde, recalled in Homer's red-haired Menelaus. I think Apollonian light turned again into blondeness, one of Europe's racist motifs, glamourized in Botticelli and the Apollonian *Faerie Queene*. Blondeness is Apollo's wolfish coldness and conceptualism. It made its mark on our century in Hitler's homoerotic Aryanism and in the icy eye-spear of black and white Apollonian cinema. By the early fifth century, Greek art purged both chthonian and single-sex elements from the major Olympians. Only the brothers Zeus and Poseidon retained their full beards and burly torsos. The ephebic androgyny of the high classic Apollo turned into effeminacy in Hellenistic art.

Apollo's latent transsexualism is partly evident in his connection to his twin sister, Artemis. Mythological twins are normally male, as in battling brothers from Egyptian Set and Osiris to Lewis Carroll's Tweedledum and Tweedledee. Apollo and Artemis represent not conflict but consonance. They are mirror images, male and female versions of one personality, a motif not returning until the incestuous brother-sister pairs of Romanticism. The fraternal androgynes Apollo and Artemis are, with Athena, the most militant of Olympians in the war against chthonian nature. Jane Harrison resents their twinship, deriving their "barren relation of sister and brother" from the early hierarchy of Great Mother over son-lover.[6]

Artemis thwarts the gross fecundities of earth-cult. Euripides' Hippolytus, her celibate devotee, is destroyed by jealous Aphrodite, who unleashes the monsters of chthonian nature. Walter Otto calls Apollo and Artemis "the most sublime of the Greek gods," distinguished by their "purity and holiness," the root meaning of the name Phoebus: "In both deities there is something mysterious and unapproachable, something that commands an awed distance. As archers they shoot unerringly and unseen from afar."[7] The coldness of Apollo and Artemis is so intense it burns like fire. Apollo's amours are late fables. At his most characteristic, as on the temple pediment at Olympia, he stands alone (fig. 8). Artemis is pre-Christian chastity, overlooked by those who stereotyped paganism as sexual license. Her supposed infatuation with Endymion belongs to the moon goddess Selene, with whom she was falsely identified in the Hellenistic era. Moon worship is Near Eastern, not Greek. Like her twin, Artemis is a beam of blinding Apollonian daylight.

The Greeks popularly connected Artemis' name, which has no apparent Greek root, with *artamos*, "slaughterer, butcher." Early Artemis was Potnia Theron, the dread Mistress of the Beasts, as the *Iliad* calls her. Archaic art shows her standing between heraldic animals, which she strangles with each hand. She rules them and she slays them. A remnant of Proto-Artemis survived in the Ephesian Artemis, whose temple in Asia Minor was one of the seven wonders of the ancient world (fig. 9).

8. *Apollo and the Combat of Centaurs and Lapiths* (detail), from the west pediment of the Temple of Zeus at Olympia, 465–457 B.C.

It was to the great port of Ephesus that St. Paul travelled with Mary, who died there. The Madonna is a spiritual correction of Ephesian Artemis, symbol of animal nature. A copy of the idol was brought to Rome to stand in the Temple of Diana on the Aventine Hill. Its mummiform torso is covered with bull testicles or breasts in canine profusion. Ephesian Artemis is the swarming hive of mother nature, that heavy apple tree foaming with fruit which I found, in human terms, so repellent.

9. *Ephesian Artemis.* Imperial
Roman statue of Hellenistic design.

The descent of Artemis the huntress from the Great Mother accounts
for the puzzling fact that she, a virgin, rules over childbirth and is
invoked by women in labor. The Greek Artemis substitutes androgynous twinship for the Asian Artemis' androgynous fecundity. Hellenistic art gradually merged the faces and genders of brother and sister. The
Greek Artemis is a sexual persona, a projected personality. The nar-
rowest of the major Olympians, she is a condensation of their Apollonian character. She is rigidly visible. Artemis' mystique of virginity is
very western. Indeed, her sexual absolutism makes her one of the most
western of personae, for which there is no counterpart in other cultures.
Chastity *is* visibility in Artemis. Her superb authority as a female per-

sona comes from her resistance to nature's sexual flux. Her cleanliness of contour is the bold line of pagan pictorialism.

Artemis is the Amazon of Olympus. Amazon legends were pre-Homeric. Theseus, it was said, drove off an Amazon invasion from Athens, with the Areopagus the site of victory and the women's encampment afterward called the Amazonium. The battle of Greeks and Amazons was one of the great themes of Greek art, as on the western metope of the Parthenon. The Amazonomachia, or Amazon contest, symbolized the struggle of civilization against barbarism. It was used as a metaphor for the Persian Wars, rarely otherwise documented in surviving monuments. Perhaps there was malicious humor in portraying the effete Persians as masculine women. The Amazons may have been beardless Asian males with braided hair who from a distance appeared to be women. The Amazon homeland was Scythia, the Black Sea region of southern Russia later linked with sexually ambiguous shamans. Until the fifth century B.C., when they donned the short tunic of runner and huntress, Amazons appeared in Greek art in Scythian trousers, boots, and Phrygian cap.

Controversy continues about whether the Amazons were historical or mythical. Bodies of women in armour have been unearthed in Germany and Russia, but there is still no evidence of autonomous female military units. The Greeks derived the name Amazon from *amazos*, "breastless." The Amazon was said to cut or pinch off her right breast to draw the bowstring. This etymology may have been invented to explain a word which was in fact *amaza*, "without barley bread" (cognate with "matzoh," unleavened bread). The persistent motif of the amputated breast may be connected to breast-amputation in rites of the great goddesses of Asia Minor. One theory about Ephesian Artemis was that she was strung with garlands of sacrificed breasts. Amazons were the legendary founders of both the city and temple of Ephesus.

Many have wondered why Greek art never shows the Amazon with breast cut off. My answer is that deformity or mutilation of any kind was contrary to the idealizing classical imagination and the hyperdeveloped Greek sense of form. True or false, the tale illustrates the Greek view of the Amazon as an androgyne. Breast-amputation, as in Lady Macbeth's desire to "unsex" herself, is equivalent to male castration. The Amazon's torso is half male, half female. The same idea appears in depictions of the Amazon with one breast bared. The great Greek sculptors competitively tackled the theme *Dying Amazon*, where the warrior lifts one arm above her chest wound. Vergil's Amazon Camilla is slain by a javelin beneath the exposed breast. The Amazonian motif recurs in

Delacroix's *Liberty Leading the People*, where a flag-waving citizeness
with one breast bare leaps the barricades. Amazonian exposure of the
breast paradoxically desexualizes.

Greek epithets illustrate the Amazon's ferocity. She is called *mega-
thumos*, dauntless, fearless; *mnesimache*, war-lustful; *anandros*, living
without men; *styganor*, man-hating; *androdamas*, man-subduing; *kreo-
botos*, flesh-devouring; *androdaiktos*, *androktonos*, *deianeira*, man-
murdering. Amazons are at eternal war with men. Their defeat prefigured the absolute power of husband over wife in classical Athens,
where women had no civil rights. Greek art never shows the Amazon as
a hulking Gorgon. She gained grace and dramatic dignity through the
code of *arete*, the Greek quest for honor and fame. The Amazon was
later vulgarized by sex. Ovid makes her a woman of fanatical sexual
refusal laid low by man's phallic sword. Pope uses the idea in *The Rape
of the Lock*, where spiteful Amazons make a drawing-room charge on a
pack of foppish beaux. The Amazon's sole moment of real distinction
after Greek art is in Renaissance epic, in the woman warriors of Boiardo, Ariosto, Tasso, and Spenser. But as we shall see, the English
Renaissance too subdued the Amazon to social frames of reference.

The Amazon is woman in groups, a myth of female bonding. Artemis
is the Amazonian will in solitary self-communing. She is pure Apollonian ego, glinting with the hostile separatism of western personae. She
is assertion and aggression, followed by withdrawal and purification
through self-sequestration. Artemis needs an Apollonian imagination
like Spenser's to do her justice. Like the Amazon, she sank into erotic
formula and lost her severity and coldness. Judeo-Christianity has
nothing like her except Joan of Arc. Our sense of ancient Artemis
sculptures comes from the *Diana of Versailles*, a Roman copy. Striding
forward, bow in hand, the goddess glances over her shoulder as she
draws an arrow from her quiver. She wears the huntress' short chiton
and buskins, acquired in fifth-century Greece. Artemis stalks through
western space, piercing and dominating it.

Postclassical art feminizes and pacifies Artemis. Kenneth Clark can
lament the decline in nobility of a god while overlooking the same thing
in his twin: depictions of Apollo lost their "feeling of dread," turning
him into "the complacent bore of classicism."[8] Dread is the proper
response to beings of hieratic purity. Major western painters have been
inhospitable to the Artemis idea. In *Diana and Actaeon*, for example,
Titian makes the goddess an awkward, rump-heavy matron. Rembrandt's *Diana* is homely and middle-aged, breasts and belly sagging.
Rembrandt's *Bellona* gives the Roman war-goddess a stunted body and

porky face. French Renaissance art has many Dianas, inspired by Diane de Poitiers, mistress of Henry II. Because of their residual Gothicism, these works of the Fontainebleau school are persuasively slim, small-breasted, and emotionally cold, but they are unmistakable conflations of Diana and Venus. Goujon's marble *Diana of Anet* and even Boucher's later *The Bath of Diana* retain Artemis' clarity of outline, but they are both too chic for the fierce goddess of the woods.

The true Artemis is remote and intimidating, offering nothing for fantasy. As an independent female impulse, she seems to have triggered a persistent negativity among male artists, who turn her swift and sudden action into fleshy passivity. Louis XIV ordered the muscles of the classical *Venus of Arles* planed down to conform to an acceptable canon of femininity. Sexual reduction is also apparent in Saint-Gaudens' colossal gold *Diana*, which stood upon the turret of the old Madison Square Garden (1891) and now commands the grand staircase of the Philadelphia Museum of Art. The goddess has a magnificent heroic bow, but as she draws back the string, no muscular tension ripples through her arms or empty upper back. There is no passion for the chase or "feeling of dread" in this nubile nymph. The true Artemis is taut in body and mind.

Artemis is overshadowed by Clark's Vegetable Aphrodite, woman as opulent organic form. Fruitfulness is the metaphor of times of famine, physical or spiritual. The first completely nude female in monumental sculpture appears at the dawn of the Hellenistic era, Praxiteles' *Aphrodite of Knidos* (ca. 350 B.C.). Greek art had been full of vigorous male nudes for two hundred years. The buxom *Knidian Aphrodite* marks a shift from the homosexuality of classic Athens. It starts a tradition of female posture, transmitted to Botticelli's Venus through the Roman *Venus Pudica*, modestly stooping, knees pressed together. We saw this in the Venus of Willendorf, where procreative woman is bound down by her own abundance, hormonal ropes of flab. I spoke of the knock-knees of the wide-hipped woman that inhibit running. Because of their narrow hips, men can move their legs efficiently, like pistons. The best women runners have lean male bodies. Big-breasted, wide-hipped women excel at few sports. The intimacy between fat and fertility is demonstrated by menstruation halting in woman athletes whose body fat falls below a certain biological level. Artemis is a cancellation of the Vegetable Aphrodite. She rejects anatomy as destiny. Rover and ravener, she is the woman runner who is always first. Nefertiti reverses Venus of Willendorf by displacing energy into the head. Artemis, living in and for the body, streamlines the female form by her implacable male will. She is one of the Greeks' greatest Apollonian ideas, pitiless and frigid.

Artemis exists alone. Her Amazonism is directed toward women as well as men. As with Apollo, her sexual duality is in her self-completion. No one before the Roman poet-pornographers attributed aberrant tastes to her. Boucher illustrates the lesbian salaciousness in an episode from Ovid, *Zeus as Artemis, wooing Callisto.* But Artemis and Athena are incapable of lesbianism, since their mythic identity is predicated on militant chasity. This chastity is a metaphor for power, freedom, and audacity. It descends from the Great Mother's renewable virginity, signifying independence from males. The postclassical era has personified chastity in softer, more ingratiating forms—modest maidens, silent nuns, or blushing children, like Dickens' Little Dorritt. Judeo-Christian chastity is devout self-sacrifice. But the Greeks saw chastity as an armed goddess of brazen ego.

An Orphic hymn calls Artemis *arsenomorphe,* "masculine in form or look." I will use this adjective for Katharine Hepburn in *The Philadelphia Story,* which is structured around a Diana myth. Hepburn is the only true Artemis in western art after Spenser's Belphoebe, the female warrior who swerves from all touch. Artemis is velocity and splendor. She is woman imperiously eluding the world and definitions of men. The sole male she honors is her brother, her double. Like Athena, she is resolution and action. But in Athena, action takes place in and for society: she is the helpmeet. Artemis is solitude and action joined. She is selfish, but she pushes selfhood to the limits of western possibility. She inhabits a purely physical realm. Spengler says, "Apollo and Athene have no souls."[9] Artemis is pre-Christian purity without spirituality. Like Nefertiti, she is a visionary materialist. She is western personality as *thing,* matter cleansed of the chthonian.

As a woman, Artemis has a heroic glamour. She has nerve, fire, arrogance, force. She belongs to the warlike Age of Aries, preceding Christian charity. She is blood lust, bloody-mindedness. Worldwide, she is the female persona of maximum aggression, expressed in the hunt by pursuit, speed, defiance, risk. Her Apollonian arrow is the western eye and the western will. Like an athlete, she is for victory and glory. Artemis is uncomplex. She has no contradictions because she has no inner life. Her Amazonism is in her polished armoured ego. She is incapable of relaxation or relenting. As a character type, she is an arrested adolescent. Her figure is boyish, her breasts undeveloped. She cannot be psychologically, much less physically, invaded. Artemis is unfeminine because uninfluenced by the environment, which she sur-

mounts. She is pristine. She never learns. In her blankness and coldness, she is a perfect selfhood, a sublime energy. Seeking parallels, one
thinks of Greta Garbo, with her reclusiveness and frosty emptiness, but
not of Marlene Dietrich, who has the stunning physical brilliance of Artemis but also an irony gained from a worldly experience of which Artemis can know nothing. Artemis the runner, connecting only through
her arrows of domination, is woman darting away into western epic
space. She puts into divine perpetual motion the burden of woman's
chthonian body.

In the revival of pagan culture from the Renaissance on,
Apollo was hailed as the supreme creation of classical mythology. As
patron of poetry he appealed to artists, and as a beautiful young man he
appealed to homosexuals. Athena has received far less attention. But
she dominates the *Odyssey*, and she was the patron of classical Athens,
which she surveyed from two colossal statues on the Acropolis. Amazon
goddesses, a brilliant pagan idea, have won no popularity contests in
Christian times.

Athena, I would argue, is Apollo's equal. She has no parallels or
descendants. Though she is the most cinematic of the Greek gods, film
has never reproduced her. She is massive yet mobile, overwhelming by
both mental and physical force. She is icon-laden, a power lifter overdetermined by duty (fig. 10). Gilbert Murray says, "Athena is an ideal,
an ideal and a mystery; the ideal of wisdom, of incessant labor, of almost
terrifying purity."[10] Otto says: "The modern, and particularly the north-
erner, must accustom himself to the lightning clarity of her form gradually. Her brightness breaks into our foggy atmosphere with almost
terrifying harshness."[11] Athena is a beam of hard white light, a cold
pagan sunburst. She has a dangerous luminosity. Tugged by the hair,
Homer's Achilles recognizes her immediately, "so terrible was the bril-
lance of her eyes."[12] The Apollonian Olympians are eye-gods, living,
warning, and ruling by the aggressive western eye.

Athena has a complex sexual duality, beginning with her bizarre
birth. Hesiod says Zeus, warned that his pregnant first wife Metis will
bear a son stronger than his father, swallows her whole. Athena then
springs from Zeus' brow, her exit facilitated in some accounts by the
hammer blow of Hephaestus or Prometheus. Metis' role was probably
invented to explain the older legend of Athena's birth from the head of
Zeus. Perhaps androgynous Athena is a collapsing of Metis into her
male fetus. Athena is born of aggression. She must fight her way out.
The hammer blow is *her* power too, like a fist pounding a table. We

10. *Athena Parthenos.* The
Varvakeion statuette. Roman marble
copy, first century A.D., of ivory and
gold colossus by Pheidias in the
Parthenon, ca. 447–439 B.C.

speak of being "struck" by a thought or, in Sixties slang, of having a
"flash" of insight. Athena is Zeus ponderously thinking, treading by
dread giant steps of primitive induction. Zeus too is hermaphrodite: he
has the power of self-insemination and procreation or conception,
which in English as in Latin has a double meaning of pregnancy and
comprehension. Egyptian Khepera, the masturbatory First Mover, is
shown coiled in an uroboros-like circle, feet touching head, from which
leaps a tiny human figure. So perhaps Zeus too is a primal masturbator,
loving himself as he would next love his sister Hera. Amazon Athena is a
brazen spume of divine self-love. Gregory Zilboorg compares Athena's
birth to the ritual couvade, where a father, after delivery of a baby,
jealously takes to bed and is attended as if he were in labor. Citing
schizophrenic fantasies of a baby issuing from head or penis, Zilboorg
concludes that the myths of Athena's and Dionysus' birth come from

"woman-envy," male envy of female powers, which he thinks earlier and "psychogenetically older and therefore more fundamental" than Freud's penis-envy.[13]

Athena's sexual duality is also expressed in her masculine armour. The Athenians incorrectly understood her title Pallas to mean Brandisher of Weapons (*pallo*, "I wield or brandish"). In the *Iliad* she vanquishes the god of war by knocking him down with a boulder. Zeus loans her his own arms, including the "huge heavy spear" and panic-spreading aegis, which she wears like a shawl. A goatskin ringed with serpents, the aegis is a vestige of chthonian violence. It may represent a storm cloud split by snaky thunderbolts. I see the aegis as Olympian but not yet Apollonian. That is, it descends from earliest sky-cult, when heaven was primitive, occult, opaque rather than rational and transparent—when it was purple-black rather than blue-white. The sacred animal of the Acropolis, the great serpent of Erechtheus, legendary king of Athens, coils behind Athena's shield. Sometimes she is shown casting a snake like a spear. The serpent may be her male alter ego, a phallic projection. It clings to her images as a remnant of her early character as a Minoan vegetation goddess.

Becoming Apollonian, Artemis throws off all sign of her chthonian origins. Athena, on the other hand, bristles with barbaric badges, notably the Gorgon's head on breast and shield. Freud says this "symbol of horror" makes her "a woman who is unapproachable and repels all sexual desires—since she displays the terrifying genitals of the Mother."[14] Serene virginity symbolized by chthonian ugliness: Milton resolves this incongruity in defining Minerva's "snaky-headed *Gorgon* shield" as the goddess' "rigid looks of Chaste austerity" (*Comus* 447–50). A rigid look is phallic ocular aggression.

In Athena's elaborate iconography, so unlike the emblematic simplicity of the other Olympians, resides her uncanniness, her sex-surpassing power. Scholarship has shown relatively little interest in her transvestite armour. There is universal acceptance of Martin Nilsson's theory that Athena was a pre-Hellenic deity who became palace goddess of the Mycenaean warlords. Hence she donned her armour as defender of the citadel. But etiology does not explain persistence. The armed Athena lingered on more than five hundred years after the end of Mycenaean culture. As Thucydides notes, the Athenians were the first people to go about without weapons. C. J. Herington describes two different versions of Athena worshipped on the Acropolis: the goddess of the Erechtheum was a peaceful fertility goddess, shown seated and unarmed; Athena Parthenos, the virgin goddess of the Parthenon ("Virgin Temple"), was a standing or striding warrior in battle armour. These presumably correspond to her incarnations as Athena Ergane, patron of handicrafts and weaving, and Athena Promachos, champion of the fighting line. She appeared as the latter in Pheidias' two colossi, the ivory and gold statue inside the Parthenon and its outdoor companion, whose glinting helmet could be seen by ships at sea as far as Cape Sunium.

Thus, far from the Mycenaeans permanently fixing Athena in their own martial image, her Minoan prototype remained available for metaphorical development until the high classic period. We must explain why the armed Athena prevailed in Athens, for whom she meant far more than military might. As Herington remarks, "When we reach the age of Pericles and Pheidias it will be *she* who is chosen to express the highest beliefs of that age."[15] Athens' mirror image was a solar androgyne, perfect in body, mind, and eye. Athena's sexual hybridism is already evident in Homer, who makes her descents a sexual masquerade. In the *Iliad*, Athena appears on earth four times as a male, once as a vulture, and six times in her own form. In the *Odyssey*, she appears eight times as a male, twice as a human girl, six times as herself. She is sometimes aged Mentor or Phoenix, sometimes a beautiful shepherd or "sturdy spearman" in arms. One of Homer's most magical motifs is this busy flying about of Athena-energy. Only once does another deity take cross-sexual form, when Iris appears to Priam as his son Polites. Hera never appears as a man, since she lacks the masculine component that would enable her to do so. Vergil adopts the transsexual motif somewhat mechanically: Juturna, Turnus' sister, appears once as a warrior and twice as a charioteer. But this is because the *Aeneid* has absorbed and lavishly reimagined Homer's Amazon theme in the glamourous and willful tragic heroines, Dido and Camilla.

What does Athena's androgyny mean? Jane Harrison says patriarchy turned "the local Kore of Athens" into "a sexless thing, neither man nor woman": "To the end she remains manufactured, unreal, and never convinces us. . . . We cannot love a goddess who on principle forgets the Earth from which she sprang."[16] Harrison acknowledges Athena's androgyny but finds it distasteful. The indignation in her long indictment comes from her mistaken belief in a Mediterranean matriarchy, overthrown by men. Athena is therefore a collaborator with the oppressor. She is sexually inauthentic because of her abandonment of the chthonian, the analysis of which is the permanent distinction of Harrison's wonderful body of work. Harrison has influenced me heavily, but my theory of the chthonian is darker and less trusting. I see too much

Wordsworth in her nineteenth-century view of nature. I follow Sade and Coleridge.

My refutation of Harrison's view begins with her assertion, "The strange denaturalized birth of Athene from the brain of Zeus is a dark, desperate effort to make *thought* the basis of being and reality."[17] But Athena never did represent pure thought. Metis, the name of her supposed mother, means "counsel, wisdom, skill, cunning, craft." Even *sophia* is first "cleverness, skill, cunning, shrewdness" and only secondly "scientific knowledge, wisdom, philosophy." Athena is *techne* ("art, skill") rather than *nous* ("mind"). Thus her patronage of the crafts. Her special favorites are men of action, especially Odysseus, Homer's "man of many wiles." The virtues she gives are listed by a suitor praising Penelope—"the matchless gifts that she owes to Athene, her skill in fine handicraft, her excellent brain, and that genius she has for getting her way."[18] Both Odysseus and Penelope are tricksters and master strategists. Life for him is a performance art. He brings down Troy by a ruse, where brute force has failed. He can make a boat from scratch or carve a bed from a living tree. He escapes Cyclops' cave by improvising a cruel log tool and mimicking the Trojan horse by riding out under a ram. Homeric mind is ingenuity, practical intelligence. There is no Rodin-like deep thinking, no mathematical or philosophical speculation. That comes much later in history. Odysseus thinks with his hands. He is athlete, gambler, engineer. Athena rules technological man, the Greek heir to Egyptian constructionism.

Here, I propose, is the answer to Athena's androgyny. She appears in more disguises and crosses sexual borderlines more often than any other Greek god because she symbolizes the resourceful, adaptive mind, the ability to invent, plan, conspire, cope, and survive. The mind as *techne*, pragmatic design, was hermaphroditic for the ancients, much as the psyche is hermaphroditic for Jung in an era when selfhood expands to include the unconscious. Athena personifies only the waking ego, daylight energies. Premodern psychology externalized daemonic powers that we locate in the soul. Thus the Gorgon is on Athena's breast but not in her heart. Athena as the transsexual contriving mind exploits situation and opportunity, subduing circumstance to will and desire. Here for the first time we see the androgyne as a cultural symbol of mind. The Renaissance recasts the androgyne in alchemical terms to represent intuition and the spiritualization of matter. Romanticism uses the androgyne to symbolize imagination, the creative process, and poetry itself.

All-male Ares is the battle frenzy, a rabid half-animal state. But androgynous Athena mentalizes war. Among her inventions are the war harness, the trumpet, and the Pyrrhic dance in armour. She is goddess of battle music and the battle shout. In a Futurist Manifesto, Marinetti speaks of "an aesthetics of war." Athena turns war into an art form: calculated resolute action is the historical crisscrossing of western space. Harrison's association of Athena with pure thought belongs to the Hellenistic era, when the goddess increasingly personified sober, solitary wisdom.

As presiding deity of the *Odyssey*, Athena is a projected displacement of the mercurial consciousness of cagey Odysseus, the dexterous escape artist. The connection between Athena's adventurous transsexualism and the machinations of the subtle mind is demonstrated in a scene where she changes sex before our eyes. Waking on the foggy shore of Ithaca, the goal toward which he has struggled for ten years, Odysseus sees a young shepherd with a javelin, Athena in disguise. Odysseus spins a long spurious saga of woe.

> The bright-eyed goddess smiled at Odysseus' tale and caressed him with her hand. Her appearance altered, and now she looked like a woman, tall, beautiful, and accomplished. . . .
>
> "And so my stubborn friend, Odysseus the arch-deceiver, with his craving for intrigue, does not propose even in his own country to drop his sharp practice and the lying tales that he loves from the bottom of his heart. But no more of this: we are both adepts in chicane. For in the world of men you have no rival as a statesman and orator, while I am preeminent among the gods for invention and resource."[19]

Thus Homer's first scene after the hero achieves his *nostos* or homecoming takes ritualistic form: one of Odysseus' shrewd stratagems is enclosed within, like a set of heraldic parentheses, Athena male and Athena female. The dreamlike sex-transformation is a masquelike reenactment of the central false speech. Smiling with pleasure, Athena says in effect, "What a marvelous liar you are!" Lies are legal Bronze Age piracy. Here as at the Phaeacian banquet, Odysseus the storyteller stands proxy for Homer the bard. Homeric cinema: the sex-change episode theatrically synchronizes word and image. The link between Athena's technical skills and Odysseus' lies is perfectly conveyed in our word "fabrication." Sexually mobile Athena literally *is* the shifting, shifty powers of human intelligence. Sexual personae are the jumpy primal nerve-chemistry of impulse and choice.

To Harrison's complaint, then, that Athena has forgotten "the earth from which she sprang," I reply that Athena is divorced from earth because she represents the man-made. As patron of the crafts and cultivated olive, she gives man control over capricious nature. For Harrison, Athena's virginity is sterile because unfertile in the chthonian sense. But virginity is perfect autonomy. Jackson Knight says, "The maidenhood of city goddesses seems to have been in some magical sympathy with the unbroken defence of a city."[20] Athena as patron of Athens is the wall that shuts the enemy out, the enemy nature as well as the enemy man. Her virginity is her stable Apollonian self, the intractable will behind her hermaphrodite changes. She is fortitude and pressing forward, a job to do. She is the fanatical purposiveness of the west, limited but all-achieving.

Aphrodite and Hermes illustrate the gradual purgation of chthonian elements from the Olympians. Neither became completely Apollonian, as I define it. But they provide models for two of my sexual personae.

Aphrodite, a Near Eastern fertility goddess, was one of the last additions to the Olympian pantheon. She began as potent All-Mother and ended up in late antiquity as a sentimental literary convention, patron of love and beauty. In some places, her cult retained traces of her original bisexual character. Hesiod is the source of the story of her birth from sea foam splashed up by the fall of Uranus' mutilated genitals. Though this savage tale may be another fanciful etymology (*aphros*, "foam, froth"), it suggests something sexually problematic in the goddess, for newborn Aphrodite is a transubstantiation of Uranus' virility. Athena bursts from a divine brain, Aphrodite from divine balls. The goddesses of mutant birth are to be victors over males in separate realms.

On her native Cyprus, Aphrodite was worshipped as the Venus Barbata, the Bearded Venus. Her image wore female clothing but had a beard and male genitals. Ritual sacrifices were conducted by men and women in transvestite dress. Elsewhere, as the Venus Calva or Bald Venus, Aphrodite was shown with a man's bald head, like priests of Isis. Aristophanes calls her Aphroditos, a Cypriot male name. Aphrodite appeared in battle armour in Sparta, which may have borrowed the custom from Cythera. The Venus Armata or Armed Venus became a Renaissance convention, partly because of the appearance of Vergil's Venus as Diana. I adopt the names Venus Barbata and Venus Calva, the Bearded and Bald Venus, for certain highly aggressive, corrosively verbal movie stars like Bette Davis and Elizabeth Taylor.

Early Hermes was indistinguishable from the piles of stones and phallic monuments called "herms" that marked Greek boundary lines. When he attains human shape, it is as a mature bearded man, Psycho-pompos, escorter of souls to the underworld. The two centuries from Archaic to Hellenistic art change him into a beautiful beardless youth, like Apollo. Masculine agrarian vigor becomes androgynous urbanity. Late Hermes influences Roman Mercury, to whom Vergil gives "blonde hair and graceful young limbs" (*Aen.* IV.559). The development from Hermes to Mercury is from crude earth-centered monolith to earth-defying air-swimmer—from the chthonian to the Apollonian. Late Hermes appears in Giambologna's sleek bronze of Mercury in flight, a logo of American florists.

Our idea of the mercurial comes from the swiftness of wing-footed Mercury. Hermes is patron of magic and theft. His epithets are "crafty," "deceiving," "ingenious." Otto speaks of his "nimbleness and subtle cunning," his "wonderful deftness" and "mischievousness."[21] In real life, I observe, a volatile mingling of masculine and feminine accompanies this constellation of irrepressible, unscrupulous traits. Free movement among mood states automatically opens one to multiple sexual personae. Though he has Hermes' cunning, Odysseus' persona is ruggedly masculine, like early Hermes. The sexual duality latent in Odysseus' strategic personae resides in his androgynous patron, Athena. Mercurius, Latin for the god, planet, and quicksilver, is the allegorical hermaphrodite of medieval alchemy. I adopt the name Mercurius for a crazed, witty, restless, elusive, sexually ambiguous creature. Examples are Shakespeare's Rosalind and Ariel, Goethe's Mignon, Tolstoy's Natasha, and Patrick Dennis' Auntie Mame.

Hermes carries either a magic herald's staff or the caduceus, a winged rod wrapped by two serpents, a symbol of healing. The caduceus may have a bisexual meaning, like the Egyptian uraeus, Cretan labrys or double ax, and our Thanksgiving cornucopia, which is both a phallic bull's horn and an overflowing, abundant womb. The circular uroboros is similarly bisexual. Neumann calls it "the serpent which at once bears, begets, and devours." An alchemic text, cited by Jung, says, "The dragon slays itself, weds itself, impregnates itself."[22] Bisexuality, in symbol or persona, recreates the plenum of primitive cosmogony.

Dionysus, Apollo's antagonist and rival, is not among Homer's Olympians, though he is the son of Zeus. The Apollonian Olympians, I said, are eye-gods. Dionysus represents obliteration of the western eye. Heir to the Great Mother of chthonian nature, he is, with

Osiris, the greatest of the dying gods of mystery religion. Out of his worship came two rituals of enormous impact on western culture, tragic drama and Christian liturgy.

Dionysus' androgyny, like Athena's, begins in a sexually irregular birth. When his pregnant mother, Semele, demands her lover prove he is Zeus, she is burnt to a crisp. Zeus plucks his son from her womb, makes a slit in his own thigh, and sews up the fetus till it comes to term. In the *Bacchae*, Euripides imagines Zeus summoning Dionysus to "enter this my male womb" (526–27). Zeus's artificial womb resembles Adonis' tusk-torn thigh, a symbol for the castration of the mother-cults. Zeus's Dionysian pregnancy makes the symbolic equation of child with penis that Freud finds in the maternal psyche. The analogy is supported by a Greek pun on the words for grapevine and scrotum (ὤσχη and ὄσχη), honored at the Athenian Oschophoria, harvest festival of Dionysus the wine god.

The Greeks inaccurately read Dionysus' double birth in his epithet Dithyrambos, the name also of his ritual song: *di* + *thura* = "double door." The god is born through two doors, one female, one male. Jane Harrison says of puberty rites of passage, "With the savage, to be twice born is the rule, not the exception." And elsewhere: "The birth from the male womb is to rid the child from the infection of its mother—to turn him from a woman-thing into a man-thing."[23] At the opening of the *Odyssey*, Telemachus, inspired by male-born Athena, searches for his father by turning against his mother. Jesus too publicly spurns his mother to be about his father's business. Male adulthood begins with the breaking of female chains. But Dionysus reverses loyalties. He remains the son of his mother, wearing her clothes and loitering with bands of women (fig. 11).

Dionysus' transvestism is more complete than Athena's. She adds male armour to a female tunic, but he retains nothing male except a beard. Archaic vases show him in a woman's tunic, saffron veil, and hairnet. His name Bassareus comes from the Thracian *bassara*, a woman's fox-skin mantle. He is called Pseudanor, the Fake Man. Ritual transvestism was fairly common in Greek cult. The procession of the Oschophoria was led by two boys dressed as girls. Performers of Dionysus' ritual dance, the Ithyphallos, appeared in the costume of the opposite sex. In the Hybristika and Hysteria, Aphrodite's festival at Argos, men wore women's veils and women wore male dress. In the festival of Hera on Samos, men wore women's robes and adorned themselves with bracelets, necklaces, and golden hairnets. On wedding nights at Cos, the bridegroom wore women's robes. At Sparta, the bride,

11. *Dionysus and Maenads.* Attic red-figured amphora by the Kleophrades
Painter, ca. 500 B.C.

head shaved, wore men's garments and boots. At Argos, the bride
donned a false beard.

Several Greek hero sagas have transvestite interludes. Supermascu-
line Hercules is enslaved by the Amazon Omphale, who makes him
wear women's clothing and spin wool. The tale was reenacted in the
Hercules cult at Cos, where his priest wore female dress. Arriving in
Athens, young Theseus was mistaken for a girl and mocked by a crowd
of laborers. Nothing changes in the construction trade! The hero re-
sponded by hurling a chariot over a rooftop. Achilles, the supreme
Greek warrior, began his career in drag. The story of his exposure by
Odysseus, who found him among the women on Scyros, may recall
tribal initiations where a band of men invades the women's quarters to
kidnap a boy into adult life. Polygnotus painted the transvestite Achilles
in the Propylaea of the Acropolis, and Euripides devoted a lost play to
the subject, *The Scyrians.*

Ritual transvestism, then and now, is a drama of female dominance.
There are religious meanings to all female impersonation, in nightclub
or bedroom. A woman putting on men's clothes merely steals social
power. But a man putting on women's clothes is searching for God. He
memorializes his mother, whom he watched at the boudoir ritual of her

mirror. Mothers and fathers are not in the same cosmic league. Fatherhood is short, motherhood long, for earth is a mother of ever-changing
costume, green to brown and back. The Bible condemns tranvestism as
bag and baggage of the Asiatic mother-cults. Yet the pagan tradition
survives in Rio de Janeiro at Carnival, in New Orleans at Mardi Gras, in
Philadelphia on New Year's Day, and everywhere on Halloween. Halloween masquerade is apotropaic, mimicking the dead on their night of
nights in order to drive off their ghosts. Ancient transvestism could be
similarly propitiatory. What is sexually grotesque or criminal in our
culture may have symbolic significance elsewhere. Frazer says of a
tribal custom in north New Guinea, where the genitals of a murdered
man were eaten by an old woman and the genitals of a murdered
woman eaten by an old man, "Perhaps the intention is to unsex and
disarm the dangerous ghost."[24] In primitive life, sex is religion and vice
versa. Christianity has never shut down the ritual theater of sex.

Dionysus' transvestism, then, symbolizes his radical identification
with mothers. I connect this to his association with water, milk, blood,
sap, honey, and wine. The Roman and Renaissance Bacchus is no more
than a wine god. But Greek Dionysus rules what Plutarch calls the
hygra physis, wet or liquid nature. Dionysus is, as Farnell puts it, "the
liquid principle in things."[25] Dionysian liquidity is the invisible sea of
organic life, flooding our cells and uniting us to plants and animals. Our
bodies are Ferenczi's primeval ocean, surging and rippling. I interpret
Plutarch's *hygra physis* as not free-flowing but contained water, fluids
which ooze, drip, or hang in tissues or fleshy sacs. The *hygra physis* is the
mature female body, which I declare a prison of gender. Female experience is submerged in the world of fluids, dramatically demonstrated in
menstruation, childbirth, and lactation. Edema, water-retention, that
female curse, is Dionysus' leaden embrace. Male tumescence is an
assertion of the separateness of objects. An erection is architectural,
sky-pointing. Female tumescence, through blood or water, is slow, gravitational, amorphous. In the war for human identity, male tumescence
is an instrument, female tumescence an obstruction. The fatty female
body is a sponge. At peak menstrual and natal moments, it is locked
passively in place, suffering wave after wave of Dionysian power.

There are male initiates into female experience. The white circus
clown, for example, is an androgyne of female fatness. In silhouette, he
is pregnant. Stumbling, tumbling, buffeted, he is a tumescence which
cannot act but is only acted upon. The morbidly obese man, my next
example, loses virility because he is paralyzed by passive engorgement.
The fat man as hollow female vessel appears in Prince Hal's satire of

Falstaff as "that trunk of humors, . . . that swoll'n parcel of dropsies, that huge bombard of sack, that stuffed cloakbag of guts" (*I Hen IV* II.iv.454–57). In *Emblems* (1635), Francis Quarles expands these images to nature, rebuking the fat man, "Thy skin's a bladder blown with watry tumours; / Thy flesh a trembling bog, a quagmire full of humours" (I.xii.4). Bog and quagmire are my chthonian swamp, that dank primal brew of earth and water that I identify with the female body. Fatness is fluidity, the Dionysian master principle. Karl Stern diagnoses as "a caricature of femininity" the self-thwarting of neurotic men "whose attitude toward life was one of hoarding and retentiveness, with a tendency to unproductive accumulation, a kind of unending pregnancy of material inflation which never came to creativeness or 'birth'." He calls this syndrome "accumulation without issue."[26] It is a diseased male pregnancy, a stagnant fatness of mind rather than body. It may be an occupational hazard of academe, typified by the disappointed mythographer Casaubon of George Eliot's *Middlemarch*.

Dionysus' female chthonian swamp is inhabited by silent, swarming invertebrates. I proposed that the taboo attached to women is justified and that the infamous "uncleanness" of menstruation is due not to blood but to uterine jellies in that blood. The primal swamp is choked with menstrual albumen, the lukewarm matrix of nature, teeming with algae and bacteria. We have a food that symbolizes this swamp: raw clams on the half-shell. Twenty years ago, I noticed the strong emotions roused by this delicacy, to which few are indifferent. Common reactions range from ecstasy to revulsion. Why? The clam is a microcosm of the female *hygra physis*. It is as aesthetically and psychologically disturbing as menstrual albumen. The primitive shapelessness of raw clams offers sensuous access to some archaic swamp-experience.

Botticelli's Venus coasts to shore on the half-shell. Sexual love is a deep-sea diving into the timeless and elemental. G. Wilson Knight says, "Life rose from the sea. Our bodies are three parts water and our minds compacted of salty lusts."[27] Woman's body reeks of the sea. Ferenczi says, "The genital secretion of the female among the higher mammals and in man . . . possesses a distinctly fishy odor (odor of herring brine), according to the description of all physiologists; this odor of the vagina comes from the same substance (trimethylamine) as the decomposition of fish gives rise to."[28] Raw clams, I am convinced, have a latently cunnilingual character that many find repugnant. Eating a clam, fresh-killed, barely dead, is a barbarous, amorous plunging into mother nature's cold salt sea.

Scatology and graffiti, in their perennial folk wisdom, rudely acknowledge woman's marine character. Slang calls female genitals "the bearded clam." Bawdy t-shirts and bumper stickers link fish-consumption with virility. Ivy League students recently traded the following ripostes, scratched in different hands on the wall of a library study stall: "Women smell like fish! Men smell like shit! Do women like to smell fish? Do fish smell like women? Do fish like to smell women?"

Dionysus, god of fluids, rules a murky no man's land of matter half-turned to liquid. Neumann notes the linguistic connection in German between *Mutter*, mother; *Moder*, bog; *Moor*, fen; *Marsch*, marsh; and *Meer*, ocean.[29] A chthonian miasma hangs over woman, like the polluted cloud raining pestilence on Oedipus' Thebes. The miasma is woman's procreative fate, linking her to the primeval. Artemis is woman on the run, breaking out of her cloud into Apollonian sunlight. Artemis' radiance is a militant self-hardening, a refusal of menarche. Dionysus, endorsing woman, also keeps her in the chthonian swamp. Sartre speaks of the mucoid or slimy, *le visqueux*, "a substance in between two states," "a moist and feminine sucking," "a liquid seen in a nightmare,"[30] Sartre's slime is Dionysus' swamp, the fleshy muck of the generative matrix. There is no vision because there are no eyes. Apollo's solar torch is put out; the heart of creation is blind. In nature's female womb-world, there are no objects and no art.

Dionysus is the all-embracing totality of mother-cult. Nothing disgusts him, since he contains everything that is. Disgust is an Apollonian response, an aesthetic judgment. Disgust always indicates some misalignment toward or swerving away from the maternal. Huysmans speaks of "the humid horror" of woman's unclean body.[31] I will argue that nineteenth-century aestheticism, a vision of a glittering crystalline world, is a flight from the chthonian swamp into which nature-loving Wordsworth inadvertently led Romanticism. Aestheticism insists on the Apollonian line, separating objects from each other and from nature. Disgust is Apollonian fear at a melting borderline. Ernest Jones says Hamlet's denunciation of his mother shows "that almost physical disgust which is so characteristic a manifestation of intensely 'repressed' sexual feeling."[32] Yes, Hamlet struggles against the lure of Oedipal incest. But we all commit incest with the nature mother. Hamlet rails against the "reechy kisses" of "the bloat King" (III.iv.183–85). A bloated male is my pregnant paralyzed clown. Or it is a ripe corpse in a garden, the thrifty baked meat of the royal wedding table. Hamlet, as all sons of all mothers, is bloated with "this too too solid flesh." His first soliloquy is a strange chain of associations with a hidden chthonian logic: it moves from suicidal self-disgust to thoughts of the world as "an unweeded garden," overgrown by "things rank and gross in nature," and ends in lurid visualization of his mother's sex life amid rumpled "incestuous sheets," sweaty soiled rags, both swaddlings and shroud, mother nature's bindings of birth and death (I.ii.129–59). The play is filled with bad smells. The stench is from an unavenged corpse but also from the female *prima materia*, the humid base of organic life, which Hamlet resists in decadent revulsion.

Another female closet, another swamp of sex and filth: Jonathan Swift's odd poem, *The Lady's Dressing Room*. Another male as lover, hater, voyeur, forcing his way into the squalid womb-world from which we came. It is slippery with refuse, poison, and magic ointments. Swift rejects his protagonist's disgust: "Should I the Queen of Love refuse, / Because she rose from stinking Ooze?" Venus skims into town on a sewer. Swift confirms my identification of shellfish and swamp. The hearty poet will eat the clam, while his protagonist gags with Sartre's nausea. Swift's boudoir mire may come from Milton's *Comus*, where a virgin is stuck to her enchanted chair, "smear'd with gums of glutinous heat." These are piney Dionysian resins, fishy female jellies, the dead weight of Medusan paralysis. Sex locks us in place. The virgin is released from the mucoid swamp by a water-nymph from under "the glassy cool, translucent wave," an Apollonian realm of purity, clarity, and vision. Milton's chastity is "clad in complete steel," "a quiver'd Nymph with Arrows keen," like Spenser's Amazons.[33] Chastity is always a triumph of Apollo over Dionysus. It is the sanctity of the object reclaimed from the dank, clingy liquidity of chthonian nature. Scylla or Charybdis: woman's lubricious lubrications are the easy road to Lear's hell, where both sexes are lost.

The Dionysian was trivialized by Sixties polemicists, who turned it into play and protest. Pot on the picketline. Sex in the romper room. Benign regression. But the great god Dionysus is the barbarism and brutality of mother nature. Comparing the Orphic to Olympian strains in Greek religion, Gilbert Murray says, "These things are Gods or forms of God: not fabulous immortal men, but 'Things which Are', things utterly non-human and non-moral, which bring man bliss or tear his life to shreds without a break in their own serenity."[34] Dionysus liberates by destroying. He is not pleasure but pleasure-pain, the tormenting bondage of our life in the body. For each gift he exacts a price. Dionysian orgy ended in mutilation and dismemberment. The Maenads' frenzy was bathed in blood. True Dionysian dance is a rupturing extremity of torsion. The harsh percussive accents of Stravinsky, Martha Graham, and rock music are cosmic concussions upon the human, volleys of pure force. Dionysian nature is cataclysmic. Our bodies are pagan temples, heathen holdouts against Judeo-Christian soul or mind. A modern overimbiber, kneeling, moaning, and compulsively vomiting, is said to be "worshipping at the porcelain god." When the body's chthonian spasms take over, we are invaded by Dionysus. The uterine contractions of menstruation and childbirth are Dionysus' fist clenching in our bowels. Birth is expulsion, a rocky cascade of spasms kicking us out in a river of blood. We are skin drums which nature beats. Invitation to Dionysian dance is a binding contract of enslavement to nature.

The violent principle of Dionysian cult is *sparagmos*, which in Greek means "a rending, tearing, mangling" and secondly "a convulsion, spasm." The body of the god, or a human or animal substitute, is torn to pieces, which are eaten or scattered like seed. Omophagy, ritual eating of raw flesh, is the assimilation and internalization of godhead. Ancient mystery religion was posited on the worshipper's imitation of the god. Cannibalism was impersonation, a primitive theater. You are what you eat. The body parts of dismembered Osiris, scattered across the earth, were collected by Isis, who founded a shrine at each site. Before his arrest, Jesus tears the Passover bread for his disciples: "Take, eat; this is my body" (Mt. 26:26). At every Christian service, wafers and wine are changed into Christ's body and blood, consumed by the worshipper. In Catholicism, this is not symbolic but literal. Transubstantiation *is* cannibalism. Dionysian sparagmos was an ecstasy of sexual excitation and superhuman strength. Try disjointing a grocery chicken with your bare hands!—much less a living goat or heifer. The scattering of sparagmos inseminated the earth. Hence swallowing the god's parts was an act of physical love. There may be an element of omophagy in all oral sex, a mystic ritual, reverent and sadistic. Nature lives by sparagmos, no literary abstraction. She is forever tearing apart in order to remake: a witness of a recent air crash, where 131 died when a wind shear slapped the plane to the ground, told reporters, "It was like arms and legs separated and burning." Accidents and disasters are a religious spectacle. The sensationalizing media give us the grotesque truth about reality.

Meditating on Apollo and Dionysus, Plutarch says dismemberment is a metaphor for Dionysus' metamorphoses "into winds and water, earth and stars, and into the generations of plants and animals."[35] Dionysus, like Proteus, shifts through all forms of being, high to low. Human, animal, plant, mineral: none has special status. All are equalized and sacralized in the continuum of natural energy. Dionysus, leveling the great chain of being, respects no hierarchy. Plutarch says "riddles and fabulous tales" about Dionysus "construct destructions and disappearances, followed by returns to life and regenerations." Mystery religions offered initiates eternal life. Promise of resurrection was and is a major reason for Christianity's spread. Olympian cult had no such lure: the visible separatism of the sharp-edged Apollonian gods applied also to their relations with worshippers. Jane Harrison says of the birth of tragedy in Dionysian ritual, "Athene and Zeus and Poseidon have no drama because no one, in his wildest moments, believed he could become and be Athene or Zeus or Poseidon."[36] Mystery religion's impersonation and theatricality linger in Christian liturgy, where celebrant and laity replay the Last Supper and blood-sacrifice of the Crucifixion. The Imitation of Christ suffuses prayer and ritual, as in the fourteen Stations of the Cross or the stigmata, Christ's bleeding wounds miraculously appearing on hands and feet of the devout. Our word enthusiasm comes from Dionysian *enthousiasmos*, a wild state of holy inspiration. The devotee was *entheos*, "full of the god." Man and god were fused: Frazer says, "Every dead Egyptian was identified with Osiris and bore his name."[37] Mystery religion is a communion, a union of human and divine, surging through the world with all-conquering force. Mystery religion is a vibration, a tremor or temblor reducing the visible to the tangible, a brute laying on of hands.

The Apollonian and Dionysian, two great western principles, govern sexual personae in life and art. My theory is this: Dionysus is identification, Apollo objectification. Dionysus is the empathic, the sympathetic emotion transporting us into other people, other places, other times. Apollo is the hard, cold separatism of western personality and categorical thought. Dionysus is energy, ecstasy, hysteria, promiscuity, emotionalism—heedless indiscriminateness of idea or practice. Apollo is obsessiveness, voyeurism, idolatry, fascism—frigidity and aggression of the eye, petrifaction of objects. Human imagination rolls through the world seeking cathexis. Here, there, everywhere, it invests itself in perishable things of flesh, silk, marble, and metal, materializations of desire. Words themselves the west makes into objects. Complete harmony is impossible. Our brains are split, and brain is split from body. The quarrel between Apollo and Dionysus is the quarrel between the higher cortex and the older limbic and reptilian brains. Art reflects on and resolves the eternal human dilemma of order versus energy. In the west, Apollo and Dionysus strive for victory. Apollo makes the boundary lines that are civilization but that lead to convention, constraint, oppression. Dionysus is energy unbound, mad, callous, destructive, wasteful. Apollo is law, history, tradition, the dignity and safety of custom and form. Dionysus is the *new*, exhilarating but rude, sweeping all away to begin again. Apollo is a tyrant, Dionysus a vandal. Every excess breeds its counterreaction. So western culture swings from point to point on its complex cycle, pouring forth its lavish tributes of art, word, and deed. We have littered the world with grandiose achievements. Our story is vast, lurid, and unending.

Now to translate these principles into psychology and politics. Plutarch calls Apollo the One, "denying the Many and abjuring multiplicity."[38] The Apollonian is aristocratic, monarchist, and reactionary. Volatile, mobile Dionysus is *hoi polloi*, the Many. He is rabble and rubble, both democratic mob-rule and the slurry of uncountable objects rumbling through nature. Harrison says, "Apollo is the principle of simplicity, unity and purity, Dionysos of manifold change and metamorphosis."[39] Greek artists, says Plutarch, attribute to Apollo "uniformity, orderliness, and unadulterated seriousness" but to Dionysus "variability," "playfulness, wantonness, and frenzy." Dionysus is a masquer and improviser; he is daemonic energy and plural identity. Dodds states: "He is Lusios, 'the Liberator'—the god who by very simple means, or by other means not so simple, enables you for a short time to *stop being yourself*, and thereby set you free. . . . The aim of his cult was *ecstasis*—which could mean anything from 'taking you out of yourself' to a profound alteration of personality."[40] *Ecstasis* ("standing outside of") is trancelike self-removal, schizoid or shamanistic. Dionysus' amorality cuts both ways. He is god of theater, masked balls, and free love—but also of anarchy, gang rape, and mass murder. Playfulness and criminality are first cousins, flouting the norm. Frosty Apollo has a sculptural coherence and clarity. The Apollonian "One," strict, rigid, and contained, is western personality as work of art, haughty and elegant.

Dionysian sparagmos and Dionysian liquidity are analogous. Sparagmos denies the identity of objects. It is nature grinding down and dissolving matter to energy. Ernst Cassirer speaks of the "instability" and "law of metamorphosis" of the mythical world, which is "at a much more fluid and fluctuating stage than our theoretical world of things and properties."[41] Dionysian fluidity is the plenum of the dank female swamp. Dionysian metamorphoses are the scintillations of nature's high-energy perpetual-motion machine. Sparagmos and metamorphosis, sex and violence flood our dream life, where objects and persons flicker and merge. Dreams are Dionysian magic in the sensory inflammation of sleep. Sleep is a cavern to which we nightly descend, our bed a musty burrow of primeval hibernation. There we go into trance, drooling and twitching. Dionysus is our body's automatic reflexes and involuntary functions, the serpentine peristalsis of the archaic. Apollo freezes, Dionysus dissolves. Apollo says, "Stop!" Dionysus says, "Move!" Apollo binds together and battens down against the storm of nature.

G. Wilson Knight remarks, "The Apollonian is the created ideal, forms of visionary beauty that can be seen, sight rather than sound, intellectually clear to us."[42] We contemplate the Apollonian from an aesthetic distance. In Dionysian identification, space is collapsed. The eye cannot maintain *point of view*. Dionysus can't see the forest for the trees. The wet dream of Dionysian liquidity takes the hard edges off things. Objects and ideas are fuzzy, misty—that mistiness Johnny Mathis sings of in love. Dionysian empathy is Dionysian dissolution. Sparagmos is *sharing*, breaking bread or body together. Dionysian identification is fellow feeling, extended or enlarged identity. It passed into Christianity, which tried to separate Dionysian love from Dionysian nature. But as I said, there is no agape or caritas without eros. The continuum of empathy and emotion leads to sex. Failure to realize that was the Christian error. The continuum of sex leads to sadomasochism. Failure to realize that was the error of the Dionysian Sixties. Dionysus expands identity but crushes individuals. There is no liberal dignity of the person in the Dionysian. The god gives latitude but no civil rights. In nature we are convicted without appeal.

4

Pagan Beauty

The competing Apollonian and Dionysian elements in Greek culture remained unresolved. Egypt alone was able to synthesize sunlit clarity of form with daemonic earth-cult: it honored both the eye and the labyrinth of biology. Egyptian state religion, with its mystic obscurantism yet soaring clear geometries, unified the classes in one system of belief. In Greece there may have been a split, with aristocrats following Olympian sky-cult, while farmers, nominally Olympian, cautiously continued to honor primeval spirits of the soil. Fifth-century Athenian culture was supremely Apollonian. Indeed, classic style is always a defeat of Dionysus by Apollo. It is form rescued from mother earth's oceanic dissolutions.

High classic moments, as at the Renaissance, are short. The artist speaks for his nation and is buoyed by a rush of collective confidence. This was the Shakespeare of the Elizabethan 1590s or the Michelangelo of the *David* and *Creation of Man*. But politics spiral out of control. David turns into Goliath. The idealist on the throne is followed by the cynic. Out of the morass of Byzantine court politics came the Jacobean Shakespeare of *Hamlet* and the problem plays and the Mannerist Michelangelo of the stormy *Last Judgment* and Medici Chapel nudes. High classic art is simple, serene, balanced. Late-phase art is accomplished but anxious. Composition is crowded or overwrought; color is lurid. The Hellenistic *Laocoön* shows the theatrical perversity of late style: heroic male athleticism strained and bursting, strangled by serpents. Beautiful and grotesque conjoin. Late-phase art defiles high classic form with mother nature's sex and violence. Dionysus, bound down by Apollo, always escapes and returns with a vengeance.

The movement from Dionysus to Apollo and back is illustrated in two landmarks of Greek drama, Aeschylus' *Oresteia* (458 B.C.) and Euripides' *Bacchae* (407 B.C.), which stand at either end of classical Athens. From Aeschylus' generation, exhilarated by its defeat of the Persian

invaders, came the formal perfection of classic art and architecture—
the beauty and freedom of male sculpture, the grand yet humanistic
proportions of the Parthenon. The *Oresteia* proclaims Apollo's triumph
over chthonian nature. Fifty years later, after Athens' decline and fall,
Euripides answers each of Aeschylus' Apollonian assertions. The *Bacchae* is a point-by-point refutation of the *Oresteia*. The Apollonian
house that Athens built is demolished by a wave of chthonian super-
power. Dionysus, the invader from the east, succeeds where the Persians failed. Sky-cult topples back into the earth-cult.

Aeschylus makes the ancient legend of the House of Atreus a metaphor for the birth of civilization out of barbarism. For him, history is
progress; in this respect, he is the first liberal. Unfortunately for women,
the ideal of Athenian democracy celebrated by the *Oresteia* requires a
defeat of female power. Modern readers may not catch the chutzpah in
Aeschylus' local boosterism: his steering of a Homeric saga toward his
hometown (a mere hamlet in the *Iliad*) is like an American poet making
the Knights of the Round Table emigrate to New York. But Aeschylus
was right. The coming decades were to be a peak moment in world
history, a burst of creativity accompanied by institutionalized misogyny.
Women played no part in Athenian high culture. They could not vote,
attend the theater, or walk in the stoa talking philosophy. But the male
orientation of classical Athens was inseparable from its genius. Athens
became great not despite but because of its misogyny. Male homosexuality played a similar catalytic role in Renaissance Florence and Elizabethan London. At such moments, male bonding enjoys an amorous
intensity of self-assurance, a transient conviction of victory over
mothers and nature. For 2,500 years, western culture has fed itself on
the enormous achievements of homosexual hybris, small bands of men
attaining visionary heights in a few concentrated years of exaltation and
defiance.

The *Oresteia* recapitulates history, moving from nature to society,
from chaos to order, from emotion to reason, from revenge to justice,
from female to male. Father kills daughter; wife kills husband; son kills
mother. Who is guilty, who innocent? The competing claims, weighed
by an Athenian tribunal, produce a tie vote. It is broken by Athena,
the warrior-androgyne, who unexpectedly endorses male rule on the
grounds that she is motherless, born from her father alone. Athens'
patron is the armoured woman, a female hard-body, without chthonian
interiority. Athena seals up the womb-space of mother nature. She
closes the *Oresteia* in two senses, just as Clytemnestra opens it. Athena
is the Apollonian answer to the problem of woman dogging every man.

The first words of male-willed Clytemnestra evoke the ancient power of fertile "mother night" (*Ag.* 265). She stands for female rights, the priority of mother over son and wife over husband. Unlike Homer, Aeschylus makes Aegisthus a gigolo, lesser consort of a goddess-queen. The Furies, Clytemnestra's hellhound avengers, are daemonic spirits of earth-cult, black as their mother night. They are ugly. They *offend the eye.* The Furies are snake-crowned hags, eyes dripping pus. Apollo and his priestess cannot stand to look at them: he banishes them to their home of "beheadings, torn-out eyes, cut throats, castration, mutilation, stoning, and impalement" (*Eum.* 186–90). The Furies come from the realm of Dionysian sparagmos or ritual dismemberment. The chthonian annihilates form and obliterates the eye. The Furies complain of lack of respect from the Olympian "whelps," young gods wet behind the ears. History stirs from nature's grasp. Apollo, the solar eye, has broken free of mother night.

The *Oresteia* shows that society is a defense against nature. Everything intelligible—institutions, objects, persons, ideas—is the result of Apollonian clarification, adjudication, and action. Western politics, science, psychology, and art are creations of arrogant Apollo. Through every century, winning or losing, western mind has struggled to keep nature at bay. The *Oresteia*'s sexist transition from matriarchy to patriarchy records the rebellion every imagination must make against nature. Without that rebellion, we as a species are condemned to regression or stasis. Even rebelling, we cannot get far. But all vying with fate is godlike.

The *Oresteia*'s sexism was the first shock wave of Greek conceptualism. Art and architecture had near to hand the Egyptian formalism of stone column and sculpture, which had been slowly developing through the Archaic era. Philosophy suddenly emerged from pre-Socratic physics. Aeschylus' Apollonian trilogy inaugurated the golden age of classicism. Greek tragedy is a conceptual cage in which Dionysus, founder of theater, is caught. A play is an anxiety-formation freezing his barbaric Protean energy. At the end of the *Oresteia* the Furies, cleansed of the chthonian, become Eumenides, "Kindly Ones," Athens' benevolent guardians. Greek tragedy is an Apollonian prayer, stifling nature's amoral appetite. It works only while society coheres. When the center does not hold, tragedy disintegrates. Dionysus is the mist slipping through society's cracks.

After 431 B.C., Athens was humiliated by plague, the failed Sicilian expedition, and defeat by Sparta in the Peloponnesian War. Idealism and sense of mission were gone. Apollonian clarity and perfection were no longer possible. Euripides' *Bacchae,* emerging from the city's self-doubt and self-criticism, satirically reverses the *Oresteia:* chthonian nature, which Aeschylus defeats, rebounds with terrible force. Dionysus makes landfall at Thebes, site of Sophocles' greatest play. Euripides rewrites his precursors' central statements. Teiresias, who in Sophocles warns Oedipus to seek Apollonian illumination, now warns Pentheus the other way. Again, Teiresias is the sexual track along which the protagonist moves to destruction. Oedipus' twenty-four-hour transformation from hypermasculine hero to maimed sufferer is echoed by Pentheus' transformation from strutting young buck to drag queen to shredded corpse.

The *Oresteia* begins with a signal fire bouncing from summit to summit, Troy to Argos. Clytemnestra's device to learn of Troy's fall, it is the flame of rage passing from that war to this. It is the murderous chain of causality, the bloodline of three generations of the House of Atreus, like the red carpet trod by Agamemnon, the stream of his own blood. The flare is also the poetic flame passing from Homer to Aeschylus, a cultural shift of genres from epic to tragedy. The third play of the *Oresteia* opens by mirroring the first. Transmission over time: Apollo's priestess, the Pythoness, recites Delphi's ownership from Mother Earth to Apollo, earth-cult to sky-cult, prefiguring the Olympians' neutralization of the Furies. Aeschylus' brilliant movements, lofty, systematic, and historical, are parodied by the *Bacchae.* Greece again catches fire from Asia, but for apocalypse, not evolution. History moves backwards, civilization relapsing into nature. Dionysus leads barbarian hordes of marauders: Thebes is first, with all of Greece ahead. Teiresias prophesies, flouting Aeschylus' Pythoness, that Dionysus will leap the crags at Delphi. The *Bacchae* is a demolition derby, a catastrophe saga. And all fall down. Dionysus the invader is plague, fire, and flood, the titan of nature unbound.

The *Oresteia* is Freudian psychodrama. Orestes, young ego, is swamped by the id of the Furies, until superego Apollo puts them in their place. Aeschylus makes an analogy between society and personality. The *Bacchae* disfigures society's Apollonian constructions. Dionysus is nature's raw sex and violence. He is drugs, drink, dance—the dance of death. My generation of the Sixties may be the first since antiquity to have had so direct an experience of Dionysus. The *Bacchae* is our story, a panorama of intoxication, delusion, and self-destruction. Rock music is the naked power of Dionysus as Bromios, "the Thunderer." In the *Bacchae,* Apollonian sky-cult and political authority are bankrupt. Society is in its late or decadent phase. The ruling hierarchy consists of the senile and the adolescent. Pentheus is like Homer's callow suitors, a lost generation of pampered dandies unseasoned by war and adventure. Heir rather than founder, he is bully and braggart. Thebes is a moral vacuum into which Dionysus surges. He is a return of the repressed, the id of Aeschylus' Furies bursting from bondage.

Chronicling the birth of a religion out of the collapse of the old, the *Bacchae* strangely prefigures the New Testament. Four hundred years before Christ, Euripides depicts the conflict between armed authority and a popular cult. A long-haired nonconformist, claiming to be the son of God by a human woman, arrives at the capital city with a mob of scruffy disciples, outlandish provincials. Are the palms of Jesus' march on Jerusalem a version of Dionysian thyrsi, potent pine wands? The demigod is arrested, interrogated, mocked, imprisoned. He offers no resistance, mildly yielding to his persecutors. His followers, like St. Peter, escape when their chains magically fall off. A ritual victim, symbolizing the god, is lofted onto a tree, then slaughtered and his body torn to bits. An earthquake levels the royal palace, like the earthquake during Jesus' crucifixion that tears the Temple veil, symbol of the old order. Both gods are beloved of women and expand their rights. The play identifies transvestite Dionysus with the mother goddesses Cybele and Demeter. He avenges his mother's defamation by maddening her sister Agave into infanticide. Agave, cavorting onstage with her bloody trophy, cradles the severed head of her son Pentheus in a grisly mock-pietà. Against her will, she mimes murderous mother nature.

Euripides shows what is excluded from the supposed universality of Athenian tragedy. Dionysus' eerie smile, playful and cruel, gives the lie to tragedy's high seriousness. The salacious voyeurism into which Dionysus lures Pentheus may be Euripides' comment on the moral evasions of theater—the perverse voyeurism of the audience, the residue of untransformed barbarism in tragedy's deaths and disasters. The *Bacchae*'s messenger speeches are crammed with grotesque and miraculous detail. Wild Maenads, girt with writhing snakes, give suck to wolves and gazelles. Water, wine, and milk pour from the soil. Women tear cattle to bits with bare hands. Snakes lick splattered blood from cheeks. Dismembering Pentheus, the Maenads play ball with his arms, feet, and ribs. Agave, foaming at the mouth, impales his head on her wand. In these savage, sportive speeches we look directly into daemonic fantasy, the hellish nightscape of dream and creative imagination. Shapeshifting Dionysus, who is bull, snake, lion, dissolves the Apollonian borderlines between objects and beings. He is ample, indiscriminate, all-engulfing.

The *Bacchae* deconstructs western personality. Pentheus, brought onstage in parts on a stretcher, has gone to pieces. He is shattered. He has lost his head. We speak of falling apart, having a breakdown, getting on top of things, getting it all together. Only in the west is there such conviction of the Apollonian unity of personality, hierarchically tidy and task-oriented. Turning Pentheus from a warrior calling for his armour to a drag queen primping with her hem, Dionysus melts the west's armoured ego in moral and sexual ambivalence. The *Bacchae* returns drama to its severe ritual origins. What Aeschylus seized for Apollo, Euripides returns, bloodstained, to Dionysus.

Tragedy springs from the clash between Apollo and Dionysus. Apollonian order, harmony, and light make a clear space in nature where the individual voice can be heard. Apollo is a lawgiver; Dionysus is beyond the law. Tragedy fades to melodrama when the individual becomes greater than the state. Lyric, invented earlier by the Greeks, is the genre of private experience. When lyric invades tragedy, a public mode, tragedy is over. Tragedy makes *sightlines*, a mathematic of social space. Greek theater formalizes the eye-relations of group or polis: it captures and distances Dionysus, binding down nature to be *looked at* and therefore cleansed. The extreme visibility of the elegant Parthenon, poised on the crest of the Acropolis, hovers above the ritual visibilities of the Theater of Dionysus, carved from the cliffside below. The Parthenon and the *Oresteia* were born simultaneously as Apollonian ideas. To see, and to conquer by seeing. The rites of Dionysus, as depicted in the *Bacchae*, were participatory and free-form, to the point of chaos. The conversion of bacchanal into liturgy happened at Athens. The Greek drive for Apollonian conceptualization made program and structure out of the spring fertility festival of Dionysus. Greek theater was an *exercise of the eye*. The audience, sitting and looking, was strengthening the cultural suppression of chthonian nature. It was intensifying eye and mind in their war with the body.

Apollo is the western eye victorious. Dionysus, I noted, is visceral and spasmodic: he is eating and feeling. Sparagmos is nature chewing, reducing objects to the soupy primeval swamp. On the temple pediment at Olympia, Apollo flings out his arm to quell the roiling centaurs, a wedding party broken into riot and rape. This fascist gesture is also made by the *Apollo Belvedere*, following his arrow with his eye. Apollo's outstretched arm is *the horizon line* of sky-cult. It is the piercing sight-line of the aggressive western eye, the straight line invented by Egypt as a correction of mother nature's sexy curves. At Olympia, the Apollonian straight arm suppresses the tacky tumult of chthonian nature. Apollo is superego grandly subduing the libidinous id, as in the *Oresteia*. The centaurs are man's animal impulses, controlled by social form. Half horse, they symbolize Dionysian metamorphosis.

Dionysus charges matter with motion and energy: objects are alive, and people are bestial. Apollo freezes the living into objects of art or contemplation. Apollonian objectification is fascist but sublime, enlarging human power against the tyranny of nature. Apollo's western eye gives us identity by making us visible. His outstretched arm reappears in Renaissance court ritual, preserved in classical ballet. Extension of the arm, needed to escort a woman in a hoop skirt, is *activation of the upper body*. It is literally courtly; that is, it creates a visible, hierarchic social space, the artistic arena in which ballet still moves. The Caucasian "line" of the dancer's body is Apollo's hard incised edge. His outflung arm represents head and upper body rebelling against chthonian pelvicism. Remember the hip-heavy Venus of Willendorf's shrivelled arms. Dionysus, with his Maenadic night rites, is the body as internal womb-space, tunneled for eating and procreating. Apollo, haughty, severe, and judgmental, makes the plane of the eye by which we rise above our murky bodies.

Apollonian form was derived from Egypt but perfected in Greece. Coleridge says, "The Greeks idolized the finite," while Northern Europeans have "a tendency to the infinite."[1] Spengler similarly identifies the modern "Faustian soul" with "pure and limitless space." Following Nietzsche, he calls the Apollonian "the principle of *visible limits*" and applies it to the Greek city-state: "All that lay beyond the visual range of this political atom was alien." The Greek statue, "the empirical visible body," symbolizes classical reality: "the material, the optically definite, the comprehensible, the immediately present."[2] The Greeks were, in my phrase, visionary materialists. They saw things and persons hard and glittery, radiant with Apollonian glamour. We know the Maenadic Dionysus mainly through the impressionistic medium of Archaic vase painting. He appears in statue form only when he loses his beard and female garb and turns ephebic Olympian, in the fifth century and after. High classic Athenian culture is based on Apollonian definitiveness and externality. "The whole tendency of Greek philosophy after Plato," remarks Gilbert Murray, "was away from the outer world towards the world of the soul."[3] The shift of Greek thought from outer to inner parallels the shift in art from the male to the female nude, from homosexual to heterosexual taste. Spengler says of Greek society, "What was far away, invisible, was *ipso facto* 'not there'."[4] I cited Karen Horney's observation that a woman cannot see her own genitals. The Greek world-view was predicated on the model of absolute outwardness of male sex organs. Athenian culture flourished in externalities, the open air of the agora and the nudity of the palestra. There are no female nudes in major fifth-century art because female sexuality was imaginatively "not there," buried like the Furies turned Eumenides. To the old complaint that the Greeks gave their statues the genitals of little boys, one could reply that the male nude offers the whole body as a projected genital. The modestly stooping *Knidian Aphrodite* marks the turn toward spiritual and sexual internality. It is the end of Apollo.

Kalokagathia, the beautiful and (or as) the good, was implicit in the Greek world-view from the start. Apollonian idealization of form was already present in Homer, while the visual arts were still groping toward a style. Homer's cinematic pictorialism put armoured western personality on the literary map. Jane Harrison suggestively refers, without elaboration, to "the Homeric horror of formlessness."[5] I find this horror in the *Iliad*'s epic battle between Achilles and the river Scamander, a strange episode which oscillates surreally between terror and comedy. The river is in a fluid half-state of identity, a personification dilating and contracting at will. It thinks and speaks like a demigod, then diffuses into the immensity of natural force, beyond human scale. Greek Archaic art tucked sprightly river or wind gods into the corner of temple pediments. They are gleeful twisty creatures, a man's face and torso ending in a blue corkscrew. Homer's Scamander is good-natured but easily provoked. It protests its defilement with blood and gore by ravening Achilles. There is a long test of wills. Weapons are useless against the "foaming cataracts" and "black wall of water." Achilles is buried in a "mighty billow," the earth swept from beneath his feet.[6] The episode passes in nightmare slow motion. Human size, human strength are not enough. Achilles survives only because Hephaestus intervenes, scalding the river with fire and turning it to steam. It is a war of the elements. Only nature can fight nature. The scene switches to Olympus, where the gods are in a rumpus. Ares, Athena, Aphrodite, Artemis, and Hera fling insults and cuff each other about, while Zeus laughs in delight. This book of the *Iliad* is an allegorical tableau in which formlessness opposes form. It recapitulates the birth of object and person out of the capricious flux of nature. Identity is imperiled but fights its way to visibility and freedom. The Olympian gods, with their radiant specificity, culminate the evolution of form. Sharp words, sharp blows: the gods are hard; they wear the body-armour of Apollonian contour. Fright turns to laughter.

The war of man and nature ends in the charm of sky-cult. Homer brings form out of the flood of chthonian darkness.

The moral principle of Greek paganism, I propose, was reverence for the integrity of the human form. About to bestow immortality upon her favorite, Tydeus, Athena was repulsed by his brutish death: in his last agony, he broke open the skull of his enemy, Melanippus, and devoured his brains. Apollonianism *is* unity and purity of form. Through her many disguises, Athena has a pristine persona, an untouched Apollonian cell of self to which she always returns. Dionysus, on the other hand, is truly Protean, the sum of his tumbling roles. In Homer, Athena may zestfully zip about, but in Athens she stands still. The two colossi of the Acropolis showed her in regal Apollonian stasis. Even her hand, perch of a winged Victory, rested on a pedestal. High classic figures have a serene equilibrium of face and posture. Their Apollonian contour keeps personality in and nature out.

Euripides, shrewd charter of Greek decline, shows Homer's chthonian river in new flood. Like the *Bacchae*, *Medea* uses Greek legend to symbolize the fall of Apollonian Athens. Within a year of its production, the city was ravaged by a plague that put the ugliness, vulgarity, and passivity of the human body on public display. Thus ended, I say, Athens' Apollonian idealizations. Ephebic male beauty had an Achilles heel, where the hand of mother nature grips us. An amazing passage in *Medea* prophetically depicts profanation of the human form by repressed forces beneath and beyond Greek culture. Foreign Medea, spurned by Jason, sends poisoned wedding gifts to his bride, daughter of the king of Corinth. The death of princess and king is one of the most horrifying scenes in literature. A messenger describes the girl receiving and donning the fancy robes and diadem. She smugly pats her hair, smiling in the mirror; she parades through her chambers, looking herself up and down. Suddenly, she trembles and staggers.

A double plague assailed her. The golden diadem on her head emitted a strange flow of devouring fire, while the fine robes were eating up the poor girl's white flesh. All aflame, she jumps from her seat and flees, shaking her head and hair this way and that, trying to throw off the crown. But the golden band held firmly, and after she had shaken her hair more violently, the fire began to blaze twice as fiercely. Overcome by the agony she falls on the ground, and none but her father could have recognized her. The position of her eyes could not be distinguished, nor the beauty of her face. The blood, clotted with fire, dripped from the crown of her head, and

the flesh melted from her bones, like resin from a pine tree, as the
poisons ate their unseen way. It was a fearful sight. All were afraid
to touch the corpse, taught by what had happened to her.

The king rushes in. Weeping and lamenting, he throws himself on his
daughter's body, embracing and kissing her. When he tries to stand up:

He stuck to the fine robes, like ivy to a laurel bush. His struggles
were horrible. He would try to free a leg, but the girl's body stuck to
his. And if he pulled violently, he tore his shrunken flesh off his
bones. At last his life went out; doomed, he gave up the ghost. Side
by side lie the two bodies, daughter and old father.[7]

We listen to the messenger's eloquent formal speech with a stunned
combination of admiration and physical revulsion. It is a daemonic aria,
a flight of decadent imagination. The princess is simply a cipher. Nameless, she never appears in the play. But Euripides has particularized her
execution with terrible and uncanny detail, threatening our sympathy
for his plaintiff protagonist. Medea, gifted niece of the sorceress Circe,
is a vehicle of chthonian disorder. She is a metamorphosist who can
change gold to dross, joy to horror.

The scene prefigures the transition in Greek art from high classicism
to Hellenistic style. Father tangled with daughter is like Laocoön dying
with his strangled sons. The Apollonian borders of the body are burst
through. The passage's emotional power comes from the brutal contrast
between the princess's smirking vanity and the sudden melting of her
features beyond recognition. Holocaust and apocalypse. She stands at
ground zero, incinerated by a distant invader. Primping princess is
sister to primping Pentheus, self-intoxicated in the electric moment
before lightning strikes. Mirror, crown, palace: the princess is Apollonian selfhood and social hierarchy. For the feminist Euripides, looking
backward at Pheidian Athens as Aeschylus looked forward, Greek
sexual personae are shallow and conventional. Fatuous Jason, like the
segregated Athenian audience, makes rigid definitions of male and
female. The clotheshorse princess falls victim to chthonian overflow.
The Apollonian *principium individuationis* of father and daughter are
abolished. Tossing her flaming head, the princess is goaded into a
Maenadic dance of death. Her flesh melts "like resin from a pine tree":
she runs with Dionysian fluids. The princess dies by the sedition of her
own body, upon which her father is crucified, like Pentheus on the fir
tree. Flesh torn in sparagmos, they lie scorched by ecstasy and annihilation.

Euripides makes two planes of reality collide. Into the world of glittering Apollonian appearances springs a form-dissolving fountain of chthonian force, erupting from primeval chaos. The intelligible momentarily loses to the irrational, manifested as a fiery lava flow cruelly generated by the human body itself. The king, trapped by his tar-baby daughter, turns into the gummy log of Hamlet senior, a crusted corpse in a garden. Euripides destroys the *Oresteia*'s psychodrama: when the princess as young ego is swamped by id, no Apollo rides to the rescue. The chthonian triumphs in *Medea*, as in the later *Bacchae*. The two plays are symmetrical: citizenship is denied to a sexually ambiguous, magic-working alien, who vengefully debases and liquidates society's arrogant hierarchs.

Euripides savors the sexually grotesque. King and blinded princess cleave together in a parody of union, a reply to Sophocles' incest-drama. Male-willed Medea, who slaughters her children, dismembers her brother, and dupes Pelias' daughters into killing their father, spreads perversion like a plague. As a Scythian witch, she can violate the unconscious of her victims. In this tour de force of sadomasochistic description, Euripides shows Greek culture in mental and physical breakdown. Spengler says, " 'Soul' for the real Hellene was in last analysis the form of his body."[8] The princess' meltdown of face and flesh dissolves what neurologists call the proprioceptive sense, by which we know ourselves in the concrete world. Personality is palpable and visible, an Apollonian self-projection. Zevedei Barbu says of schizophrenics, "The disintegration of the self seems to be related to the deterioration of the perception of form."[9] In *Medea*, body-image disintegrates as society self-destructs. Form is created by the Apollonian eye: King Creon's lament over his mutilated daughter is therefore an elegy for Athenian high classicism.

The Athenian cult of beauty had a supreme theme: the beautiful boy. Euripides, the first decadent artist, substitutes a bloody moon for the golden Apollonian sun. Medea is Athens' worst nightmare about women. She is nature's revenge, Euripides' dark answer to the beautiful boy.

Though the homosexuality of Greek high culture has been perfectly obvious since Winckelmann, the facts have been suppressed or magnified, depending on period and point of view. Late nineteenth-century aestheticism, for example, was full of heady effusions about "Greek love." Yet Harvard's green and red Loeb Library translations of classical literature, published early this century, are heavily censored. The pen-

dulum has now swung toward realism. In *Greek Homosexuality* (1978),
K. J. Dover wittily reconstructs from the evidence of vase painting the
actual mechanics of sexual practice. But I depart from sociological
rationales for Greek love. For me, aesthetics are primary. The Athenian
turn away from women toward boys was a brilliant act of conceptualization. Unjust and ultimately self-thwarting, it was nevertheless a crucial
movement in the formation of western culture and identity.

The Greek beautiful boy, as I remarked earlier, is one of the west's
great sexual personae. Like Artemis, he has no exact equivalent in other
cultures. His cult returns whenever Apollonianism rebounds, as in
Italian Renaissance art. The beautiful boy is an androgyne, luminously
masculine and feminine. He has male muscle structure but a dewy
girlishness. In Greece he inhabited the world of hard masculine action.
His body was on view, striving nude in the palestra. Greek athletics, like
Greek law, were theater, a public agon. They imposed mathematics on
nature: how fast? how far? how strong? The beautiful boy was the focus
of Apollonian space. All eyes were on him. His broad-shouldered,
narrow-waisted body was a masterwork of Apollonian articulation,
every muscle group edged and contoured. There was even a ropy new
muscle, looping the hips and genitals. Classic Athens found the fatty
female body unbeautiful, because it was not a visible instrument of
action. The beautiful boy is Adonis, the Great Mother's son-lover, now
removed from nature and cleansed of the chthonian. Like Athena, he is
reborn through males and clad in the Apollonian armour of his own
hard body.

Major Greek art begins in the late seventh century B.C. with the
Archaic *kouros* ("youth"), a more than life-size nude statue of a victorious athlete (fig. 12). He is monumental human assertion, imagined
in Apollonian stillness. He stands like Pharaoh, fists clenched and one
foot forward. But Greek artists wanted their work to breathe and move.
What was unchanged for thousands of years in Egypt leaps to life in a
single century. The muscles curve and swell; the heavy wiglike hair
curls and tufts. The smiling kouros is the first fully free-standing sculpture in art. Strict Egyptian symmetry was preserved until the early
classic *Kritios Boy*, who looks one way while shifting his weight to the
opposite leg (fig. 13). In the broken record of Greek artifacts, the *Kritios
Boy* is the last kouros. He is not a type but a real boy, serious and regal.
His smooth, shapely body has a white sensuality. The Archaic kouros
was always callipygian, the large buttocks more stressed and valued
than the face. But the buttocks of the *Kritios Boy* have a feminine
refinement, as erotic as breasts in Venetian painting. The contrapposto

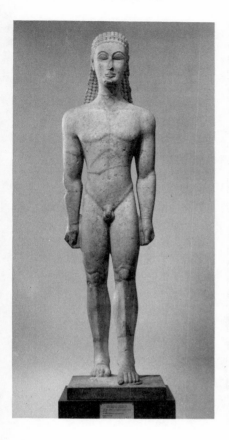

12. *New York Kouros*, ca. 600 B.C.

flexes one buttock and relaxes the other. The artist imagines them as apple and pear, glowing and compact.

For three hundred years, Greek art is filled with beautiful boys, in stone and bronze. We know the name of none of them. The old-fashioned generic term, "Apollo," had a certain wisdom, for the solitary, self-supporting kouros was an Apollonian idea, a liberation of the eye. His nudity was polemical. The Archaic *kore* ("maiden") was always clothed and utilitarian, one hand proffering a votive plate. The kouros stands heroically bare in Apollonian externality and visibility. Unlike two-dimensional pharaonic sculptures, he invites the strolling spectator to admire him in the round. He is not king or god but human youth. Divinity and stardom fall upon the beautiful boy. Epiphany is secularized and personality ritualized. The kouros records the first cult of personality in western history. It is an icon of the worship of beauty, a hierarchism self-generated rather than dynastic.

The kouros bore strange fruit. From its bold clarity and unity of

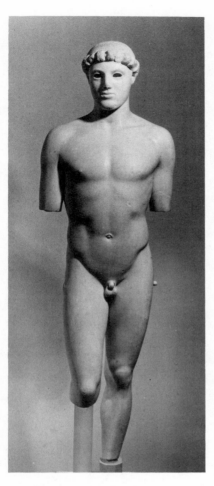

13. *The Kritios Boy*, ca. 480 B.C.

design came all major Greek sculpture, by the fourth century female as well as male. Hellenic art spread throughout the eastern Mediterranean as Hellenistic art. From that grew medieval Byzantine art in Greece, Turkey, and Italy, with its dour mosaic icons of Christ, Virgin, and saint (fig. 14). The Italian Renaissance begins in the Byzantine style. Thus there is a direct artistic line from Archaic Greek *kouroi* to the standing saints of Italian altarpieces and the stained-glass windows of Gothic cathedrals. Homoerotic iconicism goes full circle in the popular Italian theme, St. Sebastian, a beautiful seminude youth pierced by phallic arrows (fig. 15). Those arrows are glances of the aggressive western eye, solar shafts of Apollo the archer. The Greek kouros, inheriting Egypt's cold Apollonian eye, created the great western fusion of sex, power, and personality.

14. *Byzantine Saints, 1138–1148.*

15. Sandro Botticelli,
St. Sebastian, 1474.

In Greece the beautiful boy was always beardless, frozen in time. At manhood, he became a lover of boys himself. The Greek boy, like the Christian saint, was a martyr, victim of nature's tyranny. His beauty could not last and so was caught full-flower by Apollonian sculpture. There are hundreds of pots, shards, and graffiti hailing so-and-so *kalos*, "the beautiful," flirtatious public praise of males by males. Dover demonstrates the criteria governing depiction of male genitalia, opposite to ours: a small thin penis was fashionable, a large penis vulgar and animalistic. Even brawny Hercules was shown with boy's genitals.

Therefore, despite its political patriarchy, Athens cannot be considered—horrid word—a phallocracy. On the contrary, the Greek penis was edited down from an exclamation point to a dash. The beautiful boy was desired but not desiring. He occupied a presexual or suprasexual dimension, the Greek aesthetic ideal. In convention, his adult admirer could seek orgasm, while he remained unaroused.

The beautiful boy was an adolescent, hovering between a female past and male future. J. H. Van den Berg claims the eighteenth century invented adolescence.[10] It is true children once passed more directly into adult responsibilities than they do now. In Catholicism, for example, seven is the dawn of moral consciousness. After one's First Communion, it's hell or high water. Brooding identity crises were indeed the Romantic creations of Rousseau and Goethe. But Van den Berg is wrong to make adolescence entirely modern. The Greeks saw it and formalized it in art. Greek pederasty honored the erotic magnetism of male adolescents in a way that today brings the police to the door. Children are more conscious and perverse than parents like to think. I agree with Bruce Benderson that children can and do choose. The adolescent male, one step over puberty, is dreamy and removed, oscillating between vigor and languor. He is a girl-boy, masculinity shimmering and blurred, as if seen through a cloudy fragment of ancient glass. J. Z. Eglinton cites images of youthful "bloom" in Greek poetry: "The adolescent in bloom is a synthesis of male and female beauties."[11] The slightly older ephebos gained in gravity but retained a half-feminine glamour. We see it in the pedimental Apollo, the Delphic Charioteer, the bronze Apollo at Chatsworth, the white-lekythos Eretrian warrior seated before a gravestone. These youths have a distinctly ancient Greek face: high brow, strong straight nose, girlishly fleshy cheeks, full petulant mouth, and short upper lip. It is the face of Elvis Presley, Lord Byron, and Bronzino's glossy Mannerist blue boy. Freud saw the androgyny in the Greek adolescent: "Among the Greeks, where the most manly men were found among inverts, it is quite obvious that it was not the masculine character of the boy which kindled the love of man; it was his physical resemblance to woman as well as his feminine psychic qualities, such as shyness, demureness, and the need of instruction and help."[12] Certain boys, especially blondes, seem to carry adolescent beauty into adulthood. They form an enduring class of homosexual taste that I call the Billy Budd topos, fresh, active, and ephebic.

The beautiful boy is the Greek angel, a celestial visitor from the Apollonian realm. His purity is inadvertently revealed in Joseph Campbell's negative critique of fifth-century Athens: "Everything that we read of it has a wonderful adolescent atmosphere of opalescent, time-less skies—untouched by the vulgar seriousness of a heterosexual commitment to mere life. The art, too, of the lovely standing nude, for all its grace and charm, is finally neuter—like the voice of a singing boy." Campbell quotes Heinrich Zimmer's praise of the "heterosexual flavor" and yogic awareness of Hindu sculpture: "Greek art was derived from experiences of the eye; Hindu from those of the circulation of the blood."[13] Campbell's "neuter" is a blank, a moral nothing. But the beautiful boy's androgyny is visionary and exalted. Let us take Campbell's own example, "the voice of a singing boy." In a Seraphim recording of Fauré's *Requiem* that substitutes the King's College choir for the usual women, the treble parts are taken by boys from eight to thirteen. Alec Robertson's review seeks a tonality of emotion for which our only language is religious: boys' voices "add an unforgettable radiance and serenity to their part, impossible to sopranos, however good"; the soloist's singing has "an ethereal beauty that no words can describe."[14] The rosy English or Austrian choirboy, disciplined, reserved, and heart-stoppingly beautiful, is a symbol of spiritual and sexual illumination, fused in the idealizing Greek manner. We see the same thing in Botticelli's exquisite long-haired boy-angels. These days, especially in America, boy-love is not only scandalous and criminal but somehow in bad taste. On the evening news, one sees handcuffed teachers, priests, or Boy Scout leaders hustled into police vans. Therapists call them maladjusted, emotionally immature. But beauty has its own laws, inconsistent with Christian morality. As a woman, I feel free to protest that men today are pilloried for something that was rational and honorable in Greece at the height of civilization.

The Greek beautiful boy was a living idol of the Apollonian eye. As a sexual persona, the kouros represents that tense relation betweeen eye and object that I saw in Nefertiti and that was absent in the Venus of Willendorf, with her easy, forgiving, spongy female amplitude. Zimmer correctly opposes heterosexual Hindu "circulation of the blood" to Greek aesthetics of the eye. The beautiful boy is a rebuke to mother nature, an escape from the labyrinth of the body, with its murky womb and bowels. Woman is the Dionysian miasma, the world of fluids, the chthonian swamp of generation. Athens, says Campbell, was "untouched by the vulgar seriousness of a heterosexual commitment to mere life." Yes, mere life is indeed rejected by the idealizing Apollonian mode. It is the divine human privilege to make ideas greater than nature. We are born into the indignities of the body, with its relentless inner movements pushing us moment by moment toward death. Greek

Apollonianism, freezing the human form into absolute male externality, is a triumph of mind over matter. Apollo, slaying the Python at Delphi, the navel of the world, halts the flood of time, for the coiled serpent we carry in our abdomen is the eternal wave-motion of female fluidity. Every beautiful boy is an Icarus seeking the Apollonian sun. He escapes the labyrinth only to fall into nature's sea of dissolution.

Cults of beauty have been persistently homosexual from antiquity to today's hair salons and houses of couture. Professional beautification of women by homosexual men is a systematic reconceptualizing of the brute facts of female nature. As at the nineteenth-century fin de siècle, the aesthete is always male, never female. There is no lesbian parallel to Greek worship of the adolescent. The great Sappho may have fallen in love with girls, but to all evidence she internalized rather than externalized her passions. Her most famous poem invents the hostile distance between sexual personae that will have so long a history in western love poetry. Gazing across a room at her beloved sitting with a man, she suffers a physical convulsion of jealousy, humiliation, and helpless resignation. This separation is not the aesthetic distance of Apollonian Athens but a desert of emotional deprivation. It is a gap that can be closed—as Aphrodite laughingly promises Sappho in another poem. Lascivious delectation of the eye is conspicuously missing in female eroticism. Visionary idealism is a male art form. The lesbian aesthete does not exist. But if there were one, she would have learned from the perverse male mind. The eye-intense pursuit of beauty is an Apollonian correction of life in our mother-born bodies.

The beautiful boy, suspended in time, is physicality without physiology. He does not eat, drink, or reproduce. Dionysus is deeply immersed in time—rhythm, music, dance, drunkenness, gluttony, orgy. The beautiful boy as angel floats above the turmoil of nature. Angels, in Judaism too, defy chthonian femaleness. This is why the angel, though sexless, is always a youthful male. Eastern religion does not have our angels of incorporeal purity, for two reasons. A "messenger" (*angelos*) or mediator between the divine and human is unnecessary, since the two realms are coexistent. Second, eastern femaleness is symbolically equivalent to and harmonious with maleness—though this has never improved real women's social status.

The pink-cheeked beautiful boy is emotional vernality, spring only. He is a partial statement about reality. He is exclusive, a product of aristocratic taste. He flees the superfluity of matter, the womb of female nature devouring and spewing out creatures. Dionysus, we noted, is "the Many," all-inclusive and ever-changing. Life's totality is summer *and* winter, floridity and devastation. The Great Mother is both seasons in her benevolent and malevolent halves. If the beautiful boy is pink and white, she is the red and purple of her labial maw. The beautiful boy represents a hopeless attempt to separate imagination from death and decay. He is form seceding from form-making, *natura naturata* dreaming itself free of *natura naturans*. As an epiphany, eye-created, he binds up the many into a transient vision of the one, like art itself.

Besides the *Kritios Boy*, the preeminent examples of this persona are the bronze *Benevento Boy* of the Louvre (fig. 16), the Antinous sculptures commissioned by the emperor Hadrian (fig. 17), Donatello's *David*, and Thomas Mann's Tadzio in *Death in Venice*. The Apollonian is a mode of silence, suppressing rhythm to focus the eye. The beautiful boy, sexually self-complete, is sealed in silence, behind a wall of aristocratic disdain. The adolescent dreaminess of the Antinous sculptures is not true inwardness but a melancholy premonition of death. Antinous drowned, like Icarus. The beautiful boy dreams but neither thinks nor feels. His eyes fix on nothing. His face is a pale oval upon which nothing is written. A real person could not remain at this stage without decadence and mummification. The beautiful boy is cruel in his indifference, remoteness, and serene self-containment. We rarely see these things in a girl, but when we do, as in the magnificent portrait photographs of the young Virginia Woolf, we sense catatonia and autism. Narcissistic beauty in a postadolescent (like Hitchcock's Marnie) may mean malice and ruthlessness, a psychopathic amorality. There is danger in beauty.

The beautiful boy has flowing or richly textured hyacinthine hair, the only luxuriance in this chastity. Long male hair, sometimes wrapped round the head, was an aristocratic fashion in Athens. Antinous' thick hair is crisply layered, as in Van Dyck's silky princes or Seventies rock stars. In its artful negligence and allure, the hair traps the beholder's eye. It is a nimbus, a pre-Christian halo, scintillating with fiery flakes of stars. The beautiful boy, glittering with charisma, is matter transformed, penetrated by Apollonian light. Greek visionary materialism makes hard crystal of our gross fleshiness. The beautiful boy is without motive force or deed; hence he is not a hero. Because of his emotional detachment, he is not a heroine. He occupies an ideal space between male and female, effect and affect. Like the Olympians, he is an *objet d'art*, which also affects without acting or being acted upon. The beautiful boy is the product of chance or destiny, a sport thrown up by the universe. He is, I suggested, a secular saint. Light makes beautiful boys incandescent. Divinity swoops down to ennoble them, like the eagle falling upon

16. *The Benevento Boy.* Roman copy from the Augustan period, first century B.C., of a Greek work of the fifth century B.C. Found at Herculaneum. Remnants of two sprays of wild olive, the victor's crown at Olympia. Acquired by Count Tyskiewicz in the 1860s from a Naples dealer, who had bought it in nearby Benevento.

17. *Antinous.* Hadrianic Roman sculpture in the Greek style, second century A.D. Museo Nazionale, Naples.

Ganymede, who is kidnapped to Olympus, unlike the pack of female lovers like Leda whom Zeus casually abandons as types of the generative mother.

In the *Phaedrus*, Plato sets forth Greek homosexuality's ritualization of the eye. Socrates says the man who gazes upon "a god-like countenance or physical form," a copy of "true beauty," is overcome by a shudder of awe, "an unusual fever and perspiration": "Beholding it, he reverences it as he would a god; and if he were not afraid of being accounted stark mad, he would offer sacrifice to the beloved as to a holy image of divinity."[15] Beauty is the first step of a ladder leading to God. Writing in the fourth century about memories of the fifth, Plato is already postclassical. He is suspicious of art, which he banishes from his ideal republic. Visionary materialism has failed. In the *Phaedrus*, however, we still see the aesthetic distance vibrating between Greek personae. Plato has Sappho's fever, but it is cooled by the dominating and dominated western eye. In Greece, beauty was sacred and ugliness or deformity hateful. When Odysseus bludgeons Thersites, a lame, hunchback commoner, Homer's heroes laugh. Christ's ministry to the lepers was unthinkable in Greek terms. In the Greek cult of beauty, there was mystical elevation and hierarchical submission, but significantly without moral obligation.

The Greek principle of domination by the beautiful person as work of art is implicit in western culture, rising to view at charged historical moments. I see it in Dante and Beatrice and in Petrarch and Laura. There must be distance, of space or time. The eye elects a narcissistic personality as galvanizing object and formalizes the relation in art. The artist imposes a hieratic sexual character on the beloved, making himself the receptor (or more feminine receptacle) of the beloved's mana. The structure is sadomasochistic. Western sexual personae are hostile with dramatic tension. Naturalistically, Beatrice's expansion into a gigantic heavenly body is grandiose and even absurd, but she achieves her preeminence through the poet's sexually hierarchizing western imagination. The aesthetic distance between personae is like a vacuum between poles, discharging electric tension by a bolt of lightning. Little is known of the real Beatrice and Laura. But I think they resembled the beautiful boy of homosexual tradition: they were dreamy, remote, autistic, lost in a world of androgynous self-completion. Beatrice, after all, was barely eight when Dante fell in love with her in her crimson dress. Laura's impenetrability inspired the "fire and ice" metaphor of Petrarch's sonnets, which revolutionized European poetry. "Fire and ice" is western alchemy. It is the chills and fever of Sappho's and Plato's uncanny love experience. Agonized ambivalence of body and mind was Sappho's contribution to poetry, imitated by Catullus and transmitted to us through folk ballads and pop torch songs. Western love, Denis de Rougemont shows, is unhappy or death-ridden. In Dante and Petrarch, self-frustrating love is not neurotic but ritualistic and conceptualizing. The west makes art and thought out of the cold manipulation of our hard sexual personae.

Domination by the beautiful personality is central to Romanticism, specifically in its dark Coleridgean line passing through Poe and Baudelaire to Wilde. The Pre-Raphaelite Dante Gabriel Rossetti, imitating his namesake, invented his own Beatrice, the sickly Elizabeth Siddal, who obsessively appears throughout his work. That Siddal, like Beatrice and Laura, was a female version of the beautiful boy is suggested by the speed with which her face turned into the face of beautiful young men in the paintings of Rossetti's disciple, Edward Burne-Jones. The beautiful boy's narcissistic remoteness and latent autism became somnambulism in Rossetti's pensive Muse. Antinous, Beatrice, Laura, and Elizabeth Siddal passed with ease into art because in their cool, untouchable impersonality they already had the abstract removal of an objet d'art. Transcendance of sexual identity is the key.

The bungling brooder, John Hinckley, infatuated with the boyish Jodie Foster, replicates Dante's submission to distant Beatrice. Dante's love was just as preposterous, but he made poetry out of it. The untalented literalist, failing to recognize the aggression already inherent in the western eye, picks up a gun instead of a pen. The sexual ambiguity of Jodie Foster's onscreen persona supports my point about Beatrice. The absence of moral obligation in this sexual religiosity explains the amorality of aestheticism. Oscar Wilde believed the beautiful person has absolute rights to commit any act. Beauty replaces morality as the divine order. As Cocteau said, following Wilde, "The privileges of beauty are enormous."

The beautiful boy, the object of all eyes, looks downward or away or keeps his eyes in soft focus because he does not recognize the reality of other persons or things. By making the glamourous Alcibiades burst drunk into the *Symposium*, ending the intellectual debate, Plato is commenting in retrospect on the political damage done to Athens by its fascination with beauty. Spoiled, captivating Alcibiades was to betray his city and end in exile and disgrace. When the beautiful boy leaves the realm of contemplation for the realm of action, the result is chaos and crime. Wilde's Alcibiades, Dorian Gray, makes a science of corruption. Refusing to accept the early death that preserved the beauty of Adonis and Antinous, Dorian compacts with a fellow art object, his portrait, projecting human mutability onto it. The ephebic Dorian is serene and heartless, the beautiful boy as destroyer. In *Death in Venice*, Mann's homage to Wilde, the beautiful boy does not even have to act to destroy. His blinding Apollonian light is a radiation disintegrating the moral world.

The beautiful boy is the representational paradigm of high classic

Athens. He is pure Apollonian objectification, a public sex object. His lucid contour and hardness originate in Egypt's monumental architectonics and in Homer's gleaming Olympian sky-cult. The Apollonian beautiful boy dramatizes the special horror of dissolved form to Pheidian Athens, with its passionate vision of the sunlit human figure. Unity of image and unity of personality were the Athenian norm, satirized by Euripides in his chthonian dismemberments, symbol of fragmentation and multiplicity. The androgynous beautiful boy has an androgynous sponsor, the male-born Uranian Aphrodite whom Plato identifies with homosexual love. While the Archaic kouros is vigorously masculine, the early and high classic beautiful boy perfectly harmonizes masculine and feminine. With the Hellenistic tilt toward women, prefigured by Euripides, the beautiful boy slides toward the feminine, a symptom of decadence.

Praxiteles registers this shift in his ephebic *Hermes* (ca. 350 B.C.), which misaligns the elegance of classic contrapposto. Hermes awkwardly leans away from the engaged leg rather than toward it, curving his hips in a peculiar swish. His arm, supporting infant Dionysus, rests heavily on a stump. Farnell says of the Praxitelean "languor," "Even the gods are becoming fatigued."[16] Kenneth Clark finds in high classic Greek art a perfect "physical balance of strength and grace."[17] In the Hellenistic beautiful boy, grace drains strength. Rhys Carpenter sees Praxiteles' *Knidian Aphrodite* as a sexual degeneration of Polycleitus' canonical fifth-century *Doryphoros*, a "languid devitalization of the male victor-athlete into an equivalent feminine canon."[18] Hauser says of the *Hermes* and Lysippus' *Apoxyomenos*, "They give the impression of being dancers rather than athletes."[19] Jane Harrison denounces Praxiteles' Hermes on the grounds that as *Kourotrophos* ("boy-rearer") he "usurps the function of the mother": "The man doing woman's work has all the inherent futility and something of the ugly dissonance of the man masquerading in woman's clothes."[20] Again, Harrison recognizes sexual duality but finds it repugnant. Clark points out that wherever contrapposto appears in world art, it shows Greek influence, even in India, to which it was carried by Alexander. Originally a male motif, it entered female iconography to become "a vivid symbol of desire."[21] What seems overlooked is that contrapposto was erotic from the start, in the dignified exhibitionism of the early classic kouros. Hellenistic ephebes use a more extreme hip-shot pose, ripe with sexual solicitation. It is the street stance of harlot and drag queen, ancient or modern. Male contrapposto with hand on hip, as in Donatello's *David*, is provocative and epicene.

Portraits of Dionysus illustrate the sensual feminization of male personae in Greek art. The Archaic transvestite Dionysus fuses a bearded
adult man with a sexually mature woman. In the fifth century, he loses
his beard and becomes indistinguishable from the ephebic Apollo of the
Parthenon frieze. The Hellenistic Dionysus is a voluptuously appealing
beautiful boy. A third-century head at Thasos could be mistaken for a
woman, a movie queen, with thick shoulder-length hair and expectant
parted lips. Scholars have generally been repelled by these beautiful
objects, with their overt homoeroticism. Even Marie Delcourt, in her
excellent study, *Hermaphrodite*, attacks the "effeminacy" of the Hellenistic Dionysus, which "pandered" to Greek homosexual desire.[22] But it
was the Hellenistic Dionysus and Apollo who were the androgynous
models for the exquisite Antinous sculptures.

The long, decentralized Hellenistic era was like our own time, lively,
anxious, and sensationalistic. Hellenistic art teems with sex and violence. High classic Greek art honors ideal youth, while Hellenistic art is
full of babies, brutes, and drunks. Athenian eroticism is pornographic
in kitchen and tavern pottery but sublime and restrained in major
sculpture. Hellenistic sculpture, on the other hand, likes large-scale
wrestling and rapine—massacre, pugilism, and priapism. Hellenistic
sex is in such free flow that the gender of shattered statues can be
doubtful. Misidentifications have been common.

Dover speaks of the change in homosexual taste in Athens from the
fifth century, which glorified athletic physiques, to the fourth, when
softer, passive minions came into vogue. It is in the fourth century that
the hermaphrodite first appears in classical art. The plush creature with
female breasts manages to expose its male genitals, either by a slipping
cloak or a tunic boldly raised in ritual exhibitionism. The *Sleeping
Hermaphrodite* influenced later art, like eighteenth-century reclining
female nudes. From one side, the drowsy figure displays ambiguously
smooth buttocks and the half-swell of a breast; from the other, female
breast and male genitals pop out clear as day. I found the Villa Borghese
copy prudently pushed against the wall to discourage inspection! The
decorative popularity of hermaphrodites is paradoxical, for everywhere
in antiquity the birth of a real hermaphrodite was greeted with horror.
This condition, hypospadias, may be examined *ad stuporem* in the
hundreds of photographs of Hugh Hampton Young's pioneering text,
Genital Abnormalities, Hermaphroditism, and Related Adrenal Diseases
(1937). Since a hermaphrodite birth was a bad omen presaging war,
disaster, or pestilence, the infant was usually destroyed or left to die by
exposure. As late as Paracelsus, hermaphroditic children were thought

"monstrous signs of secret sins in the parents."[23] The annalist Diodorus Siculus, in the Roman era, records a case where an Arabian girl's tumor burst open to reveal male genitals. She then changed her name, donned men's clothes, and joined the calvary.[24]

The source of the Hermaphrodite legend is unknown. It may be a vestige of the sexual duality of early fertility deities of Asia Minor. Later stories improvised upon the name to claim he/she was the child of Hermes and Aphrodite. Ovid started a mythographic muddle with his version in the *Metamorphoses*, possibly based on a lost Alexandrian romance. The amorous nymph Salmacis traps the beautiful boy Hermaphroditus in her forest pool, entwining him with her arms and legs, until the gods grant her prayer to unite them into one being, like Plato's primeval androgynes. The tale may have begun as a folk legend about a cursed pool sapping the virility of men who bathed in it.

Greek androgyny evolved from chthonian to Apollonian and back: vitalistic energy to godlike charisma to loss of manhood. I do not agree with the disparagement of the later androgyne by Jane Harrison and Marie Delcourt. Effeminate men have suffered a bad press the world over. I accept decadence as a complex historical mode. In late phases, maleness is always in retreat. Women have ironically enjoyed a greater symbolic, if not practical freedom. Thus it is that male and not female homosexuality has usually been harshly punished by law. A debater in Lucian declares, "Far better that a woman, in the madness of her lust, should usurp the nature of man, than that man's noble nature should be so degraded as to play the woman."[25] Similarly today, lesbian interludes are a staple of heterosexual pornography. Ever since man emerged from the dominance of nature, masculinity has been the most fragile and problematic of psychic states.

Greek culture has come to us mainly through Rome. Greek Apollonianism appealed to the highly ritualistic Romans, with their solemn formalism of religion, law, and politics. Rome returned Apollonianism to its Egyptian roots. Like Egypt, Rome was centered on a cult of the state; hierarchy and history were the means of national identity. The Apollonian is always reactionary. For its own propaganda, Rome made Greek style monolithic. Gracious human scale yielded to officialism, governmental overstatement. Kouros became colossus. Columns swelled and towered. Rome imitated not the plain, vigorous Doric pillar of the Parthenon nor the sleek, elegant Ionic pillar of the Erechtheum and Propylaea but the gigantic, frilly Corinthian pillar of the temple of Zeus on the plain below the Acropolis. Our cold white Federal architecture is Roman. Banks and government buildings are vast temples of state, tombs and fortresses. No Greek temple looks like a tomb. Rome rediscovered the hieratic Egyptian funeralism latent in Greek Apollonian style. The Greeks were not interested in the dead. But Egypt and Rome defined themselves by death-rituals of preparation or commemoration. Roman ancestors were eternal male presences. Their portraits, the *imagines*, first wax death masks and then stone busts, were kept in a household shrine and paraded at funerals. Roman identity was condensed into discrete units of personality carried down the linear track of dynasty and history. Clan, tribalism, still so strong in Italian culture, framed ethics and society. Sculptural western personae began in Egypt but were given their definitive stamp by Apollonian Rome. Rome made the roster of western selves, names engraved in stone.

Rome inherited Greek style in the Hellenicization of the Mediterranean world in the centuries before Christ. But the Roman mind was neither speculative nor idealist. A Greek temple is solid, rare marble. A Roman temple is usually brick faced with marble. Economy and practicality outweigh abstract aesthetics. The pedimental Parthenon sculptures are finely carved front and back, even though tiny crimps of drapery would be hidden from the ground. But the back of a Roman statue in a niche could be left relatively rough. Egyptian and Greek Apollonianism was a metaphysic of the eye, an aristocratic aestheticism making spiritual order of the visible and concrete. The Romans, except for Hellenophiles like Hadrian, were not aesthetes. Rome took the eroticism and dreamy obliqueness out of Greek iconic sculpture. The great Prima Porta statue of Augustus, for example, is kouros turned suave, sober diplomat. Law and custom became sacred ends in themselves. The Roman persona was a public construction: it had severity, weight, density. The Greeks were peripatetic, walking and talking. Argument was mobile and improvisatory. But the Romans were declamatory, oratorical. They took stage and held it. The Roman persona was the stable prow of an ancient ship of state. Indeed, a "rostrum" *is* a ship's prow, the trophy-hung speaker's platform of the Forum.

Roman personality was equivalent to Greek epic, a repository of racial history. The group was paramount. The hero legends of early Rome, Marcus Curtius, Mucius Scaevola, Horatius Cocles, Lucius Brutus, teach self sacrificed to state. The Roman legion, much larger than the Greek phalanx, was an extrapolation of Rome's political will: fortitude, resolution, victory. Rome began in combat against its Italic neighbors and finally reduced the known world to servitude. Its growth was a martial clash of identities, celebrated in the lavish triumph, another procession miming the linearity of history. Roman art was documentary, while Greek art treated contemporary history as allegory. Gisela Richter remarks: "We have not a single representation of the battles of Thermopylai or Salamis, of the Peloponnesian war, of the great plague, of the Sicilian expedition. . . . How different the Romans or the Egyptians and Assyrians with their endless friezes recording their triumphs over their enemies."[26] Roman art used facts to magnify reality; Greek art transformed reality by avoiding facts. Roman architecture was equally pragmatic, excelling in brilliant engineering, colossal public works like baths, aqueducts, and a far-flung network of paved roads, so sturdy they are still in use. Greek Apollonianism was a sublime projection, mind made radiant matter. But Roman Apollonianism was a power play, a proclamation of national grandeur. The hard Roman persona ultimately descended from pharaonic self-conceptualization, the Old Kingdom's foursquare enthronements. State and self were monuments carved by Apollonian borderline.

What of Apollo's rival? Roman Bacchus is not Dionysus' peer. He is merely a rowdy wine god, a tippler and mirthmaker. Dionysus was so strong in Greece because of the dominance of Apollonian conceptualism. The combat between Apollo and Dionysus, never resolved, produced the rich diversity of Greek culture. Dionysus was unnecessary in Rome because of the ancient chthonianism of Italian religion. Buying Greek prestige wholesale, the Romans identified their gods willy-nilly with the Olympians, an imperfect match-up in the case of rough Diana. The *manes*, the deified dead, occupied a sepulchral chthonian realm. Ancestor-worship is also ancestor-fear. Roman memoriousness was part celebration, part propitiation. At the Parentalia in February, the family dead were honored for a week. At the Lemuria in May, wandering ghosts were driven out of the family house. The dead pressed upon the dutiful consciousness of the living.

To this day, relatives in my mother's village near Rome visit the cemetery every Sunday to lay flowers on the graves. It is a kind of picnic. I remember childhood feelings of chill and awe at the candle kept burning by my grandmother before a photograph of her dead daughter Lenora, the small, round yellow flame flickering in the darkened room. A sense of the mystic and uncanny has pervaded Italian culture for thousands of years, a pagan hieraticism flowering again in Catholicism, with its polychrome statues of martyred saints, its holy elbows and jawbones sealed in altarstones, and its mummified corpses on illuminated display. In a chapel in Naples, I recently counted 112 gold and glass caskets of musty saints' bones stacked as a transparent wall from floor to ceiling. In another church, I found a painting of the public disembowelling of a patient saint, his intestines being methodically wound up on a large machine like a pasta roller. Nailed like schools of fish to church walls are hundreds of tiny silver ears, noses, hearts, breasts, legs, feet, and other body parts, votive offerings by parishioners seeking a cure. Old-style Italian Catholicism, now shunned by middle-class WASP-aspiring descendants of immigrants, was full of the chthonian poetry of paganism. The Italian imagination is darkly archaic. It hears the voices of the dead and identifies the passions and torments of the body with the slumbering spirits of mother earth. A ritual fragment survives from a southern Italian mystery-cult: "I have entered into the lap of the queen of the underworld." I believe I understand this with every atavistic fiber of my being—its pagan conflation of longing, lust, fright, ecstasy, resignation, and repose. It is the daemonic sublime.

If there is an Apollonian-Dionysian dialectic in Rome, it is in the tension between individual and group. This is the theme of the first four books of Vergil's *Aeneid*, symbolized by red and gold. Carnal red is emotion, sex, life in the body here and now. Imperial gold is the Roman future, harsh and glorious. Dutiful Aeneas must harden and limit himself. He carries ancestors and posterity on his back. Apollonian gold wins over Dionysian red, flaming up in Dido's funeral pyre. In Homer as in Vergil, woman is an obstacle to the heroic quest. The epic journey must free itself from female chains and delays. The Trojan women burn the ships, and Dido makes Aeneas her consort.

Half of Aeneas' destiny, says the opening of the poem, is to find the true wife Lavinia, his passage into Italian bloodlines. But Lavinia, no Penelope, shrinks as the poem goes on. Vergil oddly gives his imaginative sympathies to Amazon enemies of Rome. Carthage, founded by a Phoenician queen, is a transplant of Near East autocracy and goddess cult. Woman is in mythic ascendancy. Venus, appearing as Diana to her son Aeneas, says her huntress's quiver and high red boots are the Carthaginian female style. Aeneas inspects murals of the Trojan War in the rising temple of savage Juno. When he comes to "Penthesilea furens," Dido enters the poem. She is the Amazon of the first half of the *Aeneid*, just as Camilla is the Amazon of the second. Aeneas falls under her sway, and the male will is stymied. He builds her city instead of his own.

Venus armed is Aeneas' lesson. Carthage is both the pleasure principle and the Orient from which he uproots himself. East yields to west, Asia to Europe. The Italian tribes think Aeneas effeminate. Turnus calls him a "half-man": "Let me foul in the dust that hair crimped with curling-tongs and oiled with myrrh!" Dido's suitor Iarbas calls him "this second Paris, wearing a Phrygian bonnet to tie up his chin and cover his oily hair, and attended by a train of she-men."[27] Aeneas must purify his masculinity, creating the simplicity and gravity of Roman personality. The Volscian warrior Camilla, apparently Vergil's invention, is a new burst of female furor that must be quelled for Rome to be born. The *Aeneid* is remarkably attracted to the glamourous androgynes, Dido and Camilla, who steal the thunder of pallid Lavinia. The poem follows its hero through a war of sexual personae. Female deviance, losing to decorous femininity, takes the poetry with it. The twin viragos win in defeat.

Vergil writes at the borderline between republic and empire. In under a century, Rome accelerated in size and ambition. The new cosmopolitan sexual personae broke with tradition. There was a shift from Apollonian unity and narrowness to Dionysian pluralism, uncontrolled and eventually decadent. Granting universal citizenship, Rome brought civilization to the world but diluted itself. Eight hundred years intervene between Homer and Vergil. When Vergil picks up the epic genre, it no longer obeys poetic command. Epic plot, the male trajectory of history, is the weakest thing in the *Aeneid*. Homer's great rhetorical rhythms are missing. The *Iliad* and *Odyssey* were all-day performance art, recited to live audiences by a professional bard of athletic stamina. The *Aeneid* is closet drama. Vergil was melancholic, reclusive, possibly homosexual. His nickname Parthenias, "the maidenly man," is a pun on Vergil/*virgo* and Parthenope, a poetic name for Naples, near which his villa was located.

Vergil, unlike Homer, knew urban coteries of aristocratic refinement, a court milieu of febrile worldliness. This experience affects the *Aeneid* in unsuspected ways. Its sexual personae have undergone the same transformation as its epic gifts. Homer's heroes exchange iron cauldrons and tripods, functional ware of high Bronze Age value. Vergil's gifts are objets d'art, gold and silver and studded with jewels. Alexandrian museum consciousness has come into being. Vergil's detachment and connoisseurship, so damaging to epic's male pyrotechnics, intensify the erotic aura around persons and things. There is an intricate psychological meshing between poet and poem not present in Homer. Vergil is "involved" with Dido. Her obsession, suffering, and passion of love-hate are the grandest things in literature since Euripides' *Medea*. Vergil's identification with her is as palpable as Flaubert's with Madame Bovary or Tolstoy's with Anna Karenina. The suicide of a male-willed heroine, in all three cases, may be a rite of exorcism, objectifying and terminating a male artist's spiritual transsexualism. Falling on Aeneas' sword, Dido cries, "Sic, sic iuvat ire sub umbras" ("Thus, thus is it pleasing to go beneath the shades"). The liquid Latin is thrillingly, hypnotically autoerotic, like honey and dark wine. The shadowy tongue tapping in our mouth is as private and phallic as the fetishistic sword.

Little else in the *Aeneid* approaches the brilliance of the Carthaginian books. The poet probably knew it, as he ordered the unfinished poem burnt after his death—like self-immolating Dido. Vergil is a decadent poet, a virtuoso of destruction. His fall of Troy is a cinematic apocalypse, flames filling the night sky as violation and profanation swirl below. His characteristic imagery is sinuous, writhing, glistering, phosphorescent. The only translation that captures the *Aeneid*'s uncanny daemonism is by W. F. Jackson Knight, in prose. In this poem, Roman ritualism falls to forces of the irrational, so long kept in check. Vergil, an admirer of Augustus, shows the costs of political destiny—most recently, the suicide of another Oriental queen, Cleopatra, Dido's model. Epic plot in the *Aeneid* is failed self-containment, a male scheme to bridle transsexual reverie. Vergil's relation to his own poem is perverse. At a historical crisis in sexual personae, he turns to epic to stop it and stop himself. Spenser reproduces this conservative but deeply conflicted strategy in *The Faerie Queene*. Sexual personae are vampires on plot in the *Aeneid*, a phenomenon I find in Coleridge's *Christabel* and call psychoiconicism.

The Roman republic made the persona, Greek theater's wooden mask, a legal entity, sharp-contoured in the Apollonian way. The Roman decadence, ingenious in pleasures and cruelties, was a reaction against and satiric commentary on the austerity of republican personae, a profanation of ancestor cult. Republic to empire was like high classic to Hellenistic, unity to multiplicity. Roman religion's chthonian reverence turned into Dionysian orgy, now removed from fertile nature. Maenadism was un-Roman. There was no Asiatic wildness in Roman cult, with its priestly hierarchy, as in Egypt but not Greece. There was program, formula, decorum, even in the honoring of omen-filled nature. The Roman priest was an interpreter who kept his wits about him. He did not go into trance like the Delphic oracle.

True Greek orgy meant mystic loss of self. But in imperial Roman orgy, persona continued. The Roman decadent kept the observing Apollonian eye awake during Dionysian revel. More Alexandrian connoisseurship, here applied to the fashionable self. Eye plus orgy equals

decadence. Salaciousness, lewdness, lasciviousness: such interesting
hyperstates are produced by a superimposition of mind on erotic action.
The west has pioneered in this charred crimson territory. Without
strong personality of the western kind, serious decadence is impossible.
Sin is a form of cinema, seen from a distance. The Romans, pragmat-
ically adapting Greek ideas, made engineering out of eroticism too. The
heir of Greek theater was not Roman theater but Roman sex. The
Roman decadence has never been matched in scale because other
places and times have lacked the great mass of classical forms to corrupt. Rome made daemonic music of gluttony and lust from the Dionysian body. The Maenadism absent from Roman cult became imperial
ecstasy, mechanized greed.

Roman literature's sexual personae are in hectic perpetual motion.
Greek aristocratic athleticism split in two in Rome: vulgar gladiatorship
by ruffians and slaves, and leisure-class sexual adventurism, a sporting
life then as now. As the republic ends, Catullus records the jazzy promiscuity of Rome's chic set. Patrician women loitering on dark streets,
giving themselves to common passers-by. Half-clad men molested by
their mothers and sisters. Effeminates soft as a rabbit and "languid as a
limp penis." A sodomite waking with battered buttocks and "red lips
like snow," mouth rimmed with last night's pasty spoils. The strolling
poet, finding a boy and girl copulating, falls upon the boy from behind,
piercing and driving him to his task. Public sex, it is fair to say, is
decadent. Oh, those happy pagan days, romping in green meadows: one
still encounters this sentimental notion, half-baked Keats. It is quite
wrong. Catullus, like Baudelaire, savors imagery of squalor and filth.
His moral assumptions remain those of republican Rome, which he
jovially pollutes with degeneration and disease. His poetry is a torch-lit
descent into a gloomy underworld, where we survey the contamination
and collapse of Roman personae. Men and women are suddenly free,
but freedom is a flood of superfluous energy, a vicious circle of agitation,
quest, satiation, exhaustion, ennui. Moral codes are always obstructive,
relative, and man-made. Yet they have been of enormous profit to
civilization. They *are* civilization. Without them, we are invaded by the
chaotic barbarism of sex, nature's tyranny, turning day into night and
love into obsession and lust.

Catullus, an admirer of Sappho, turns her emotional ambivalence
into sadomasochism. Her chills and fever become his "odi et amo," "I
hate and I love." Her beloved maidens, fresh as orange flowers, become
his cynical Lesbia, adulteress and dominatrix, vampiristically "draining
the strength of all." The urban femme fatale dons the primitive mask of

mother nature. Lesbia, the wellborn Clodia, introduces to Rome a depraved sexual persona that had been current, according to aggrieved comment of the Old Testament, for a thousand years in Babylon. Female receptivity becomes a sinkhole of vice, the vagina a collector of pestilence to poison Roman nobility and bring it to an end.

Catullus is a cartographer of sexual personae. His lament for the dying god Attis (Carmen 63) is an extraordinary improvisation on gender. Castrating himself for Cybele, Attis enters a sexual twilight zone. Grammatically, the poem refers to him as feminine. "I a woman, I a man, I a youth, I a boy": in this litany of haunting memory, Attis floats through a shamanistically expanded present tense of gender, all things and nothing. Like imperial Rome, he has been pitched into an ecstatic free fall of personae. Suspension of sexual conventions brings melancholy, not joy. He is artistically detached from ordinary life but feels "sterile." Attis is the poet himself, mutating through gender in a strange, new, manic world.

Ovid, born forty years later, is the first psychoanalyst of sex. His masterpiece is aptly called *Metamorphoses:* as Rome changes, Ovid plunders Greek and Roman legend for magic transformations—man and god to animal and plant, male to female and back. Identity is liquid. Nature is under Dionysian spell; Apollo's contours do not hold. The world becomes a projected psyche, played upon by amoral vagaries of sexual desire. Ovid's encyclopedic attentiveness to erotic perversity will not recur until Spenser's *Faerie Queene*, directly influenced by him. His successors are Sade, Balzac, Proust, Krafft-Ebing, and Freud.

The *Metamorphoses* is a handbook of sexual problematics. There is Iphis, a girl raised as a boy who falls in love with another girl and is relieved of her suffering by being changed into a man. Or Caeneus, once the girl Caenis, who rejects marriage and is raped by Neptune. As compensation, she is changed into a man invulnerable to wounds, martial and sexual. According to the Homeric scholiast, Caeneus set up his spear as a phallic totem in the marketplace, prayed and sacrificed to it, and commanded people hail it as a god, angering Zeus. In Vergil's underworld, Aeneas sees Caeneus as a woman, the morphological ghost of her femaleness reasserting itself. Ovid's complications of violation and fetishism are theory, not titillation. The theme is our "double nature," his term for the centaurs who smother impenetrable Caeneus after a horrifying orgy of Maenadic pulverizations. Like Freud, Ovid constructs hypothetical models of narcissism and the will-to-power. His point of view comes from his position between eras. Sexual personae, in flux, allow him to bring cool Apollonian study to bear upon roiling Dionysian process.

In his lesser works, Ovid lightens Catullus' bitter sex war into parlor politics. In *The Art of Love*, he says the seducer must be shrewd and changeable as Proteus. This is the Roman Dionysus, metamorphic Greek nature reduced to erotic opportunism. Sex-change is a foxy game: the wise adulteress, counsels Ovid, transsexualizes her letters, turning "he" to "she." The empire diverted Roman conceptual energy into sex. So specialized is Martial's sexual vocabulary that it influenced modern medical terminology. Latin, an exact but narrow language, became startlingly precise about sexual activity. The Latinist Fred Nichols tells me that a verb in Martial, used in poetry for the first time by Catullus, describes the fluttering movement of the buttocks of the passive partner in sodomy. There were, in fact, two forms of this verb: one for males and another for females.

Classical Athens, exalting masculine athleticism, had no conspicuous sexual sadomasochists and street transvestites. The Roman empire, on the other hand, if we believe the satirists, was overrun by epicene creatures. Ovid warns women to beware of elegant men with coiffures "sleek with liquid nard"—they may be out to steal your dress! "What can a woman do when her lover is smoother than she, and may have more boyfriends?"[28] Ausonius tells a sodomist with depilated anus and buttocks, "You are a woman behind, a man in front." Girlish boys and long-haired male prostitutes appear in Horace, Petronius, and Martial. Gaius Julius Phaedrus blames homosexuals of both sexes on drunken Prometheus, who attached the wrong genitalia to human figures he was molding. Lesbianism, infrequent in Greek literature, makes a splash in Rome. Martial and Horace record real-life tribads, Balba, Philaenis, and Folia of Arminum, with her "masculine libidinousness." There are lesbian innuendos about the all-woman rites of the Bona Dea, crashed by Publius Clodius in drag. Lucian's debater condemns lesbian acts as "androgynous passions" and calls dildos "infamous instruments of lust, an unholy imitation of a fruitless union."[29] Rome's sexual disorientation was great theater, but it led to the collapse of paganism.

Pursuit of pleasure belongs on the party circuit, not in the centers of power. Today too, one might like playfulness and spontaneity in a friend, lover, or star, but one wants a different character in people with professional or political authority. The more regular, unimaginative, and boring the daily lives of presidents, surgeons, and airline pilots, the better for us, thank you very much. Hierarchic ministry should be ascetic and focused. It does not profit from identity crises, the province of art. Rome had a genius for organization. Its administrative structure was absorbed by the Catholic Church, which turned an esoteric Palestinian sect into a world religion. Roman imperial bureaucracy, an extension of republican legalism, was a superb machine, rolling over other nations with brutal force. Two thousand years later, we are still feeling the consequences of its destruction of Judaea and dispersion of the fractious Jews, who refused to become Roman. We know from Hollywood movies what that machine sounded like, its thunderous, relentless marching drums pushing Roman destiny across the world and through history. But when the masters of the machine turned to idleness and frivolity, Roman moral force vanished.

The Roman annalists give us the riveting gossip. Sodomy was reported of the emperors Tiberius, Nero, Galba, Otho, Commodus, Trajan, and Elagabalus. Even Julius Caesar was rumored to be bisexual. Hadrian fell in love with the beautiful Antinous, deified him after his death, and spread his image everywhere. Caligula had a taste for extravagant robes and women's clothes. He dressed his wife Caesonia in armour and paraded her before the troops. He loved impersonations, appearing in wig and costume as singer, dancer, charioteer, gladiator, virgin huntress, wife. He posed as all the male and female gods. As Jupiter, he seduced many women, including his sisters. Cassius Dio tartly remarks, "He was eager to appear to be anything rather than a human being and an emperor."[30]

Nero chose the roles of bard, athlete, and charioteer. He dressed as a tragedian to watch Rome burn. Onstage he played heroes and heroines, gods and goddesses. He pretended to be a runaway slave, a blind man, a madman, a pregnant woman, a woman in labor. He wore the mask of his wife Poppaea Sabina, who had died, it was said, after he kicked her in her pregnant belly. Nero was a clever architect of sexual spectacle. He built riverbank brothels and installed patrician women to solicit him from doorways. Tying young male and female victims to stakes, he draped himself in animal skins and leapt out from a den to attack their genitals. Nero devised two homosexual parodies of marriage. He castrated the boy Sporus, who resembled dead Poppaea, dressed him in women's clothes, and married him before the court, treating him afterward as wife and empress. In the second male marriage, with a youth whom Tacitus calls Pythagoras and Suetonius Doryphorus, sex roles were reversed: the emperor was bride. "On the wedding night," reports

Suetonius, "he imitated the screams and moans of a girl being de-flowered."[31]

Commodus gave his mother's name to a concubine, making his sex life an Oedipal drama. He appeared as Mercury and transvestite Her-cules. He was called Amazonius, because he dressed his concubine Marcia as an Amazon and wanted to appear as an Amazon himself in the arena. Elagabalus, Caracalla's cousin, brought the sexually freakish customs of Asia Minor to imperial Rome. He scandalized the army with his silks, jewelry, and dancing. His short reign was giddy with plays, pageants, and parlor games. Lampridius says, "He got himself up as a confectioner, a perfumer, a cook, a shopkeeper, or a procurer, and he even practiced all these occupations in his own house continually."[32] Elagabalus' lordly ease of access to plebeian roles was social mobility in reverse. Like Nero, he practiced "class transvestism," David Reisman's phrase for the modern bluejeans fad.[33]

Elagabalus' life passion was his longing for womanhood. Wearing a wig, he prostituted himself in real Roman brothels. Cassius Dio reports:

> He set aside a room in the palace and there committed his indecen-cies, always standing nude at the door of the room, as the harlots do, and shaking the curtain which hung from gold rings, while in a soft and melting voice he solicited the passers-by. There were, of course, men who had been specially instructed to play their part. . . . He would collect money from his patrons and give himself airs over his gains; he would also dispute with his associates in this shameful occupation, claiming that he had more lovers than they and took in more money.

Miming an adulteress caught in the act and beaten by her husband, the emperor cherished black eyes as a souvenir. He summoned to court a man notorious for enormous genitals and greeted him with "a ravishing feminine pose," saying, "Call me not Lord, for I am a Lady." He impersonated the Great Mother in a lion-drawn chariot and publicly posed as the *Venus Pudica*, dropping to his knees with buttocks thrust before a male partner. Finally, Elagabalus' transvestite fantasies led to a desire to change sex. He had to be dissuaded from castrating himself, reluctantly accepting circumcision as a compromise. Dio says, "He asked the physicians to contrive a woman's vagina in his body by means of an incision, promising them large sums for doing so."[34] Science, which only recently perfected this operation, is clearly laggard upon the sexual imagination.

Absolute power is a door into dreaming. The Roman emperors made living theater of their turbulent world. There was no gap between wish and realization; fantasy leapt into instant visibility. Roman imperial masque: charades, inquisition, horseplay. The emperors made sexual personae an artistic medium, plastic as clay. Nero, setting live Christians afire for a night banquet, played with reality. Roman copies of Greek statues are a bit dull and coarse. So too with Rome's sexual literalization of Greek drama. The emperors, acting to provoke, torture, or arouse, removed the poetry and philosophy from theater. The vomitoria of Roman villas are troughs for vomiting the last six courses before starting on the next. Vomitoria is also the name for the exits of Roman amphitheaters, through which the mob poured. Imperial Rome, heir to sprawling Hellenistic culture, suffered from too-muchness, the hallmark of decadence. Too much mind, too much body; too many people, too many facts. The mind of the king is a perverse mirror of the time. Having no cinema, Nero made his own. In Athens, the beautiful boy was an idealized *objet de culte*. In Rome, persons were stage machinery, mannequins, décor. The lives of the wastrel emperors demonstrate the inadequacy of our modern myth of personal freedom. Here were men who were free and who were sickened by that freedom. Sexual liberation, our deceitful mirage, ends in lassitude and inertness. An emperor's day was androgyny-in-action. But was he happier than his republican ancestors, with their rigid sex roles? Repression makes meaning and purpose.

The more moral an emperor, the less he was drawn to theater. Dio says of Trajan's empress: "When Plotina, his wife, first entered the palace, she turned round so as to face the stairway and the populace and said: 'I enter here such a person as I wish to be when I depart.' And she conducted herself during the entire reign in such manner as to incur no censure."[35] With old Roman integrity, Plotina rejects random metamorphosis of personality. The moral man has one persona, firmly fixed in the great chain of being. Plato dismisses myths about the gods changing shape: "Is not the best always least liable to change or alteration by an external cause? . . . Every god is as perfect and as good as possible, and remains in his own form without variation for ever."[36] Virtue and divinity are unitary, homogeneous, Apollonian. Thus the empress Plotina resists the self-division of worldly experience. Multiplicity of persona is anarchic. Hermes is a thief. Hence the neoclassic eighteenth century, unlike the Renaissance, rejects the androgyne: Pope assails epicene Lord Hervey, whom he casts as Nero's catamite Sporus, for defying the great chain of being. Sporus refuses to confine himself to one social or sexual role, transgressing the borders of male and female, mammal and reptile, even animal and mineral.[37] For Pope, a man knows his own place and his own face. There are no masks.

Theatrical self-transformation, a seductive principle of our time, can never be reconciled with morality. From antiquity on, professional theater has been under a moral cloud. Autocrat, artist, actor: freedom of persona is magical but destabilizing. An emperor's appearance onstage was shocking, since actors were déclassé, barred from Roman citizenship. St. Augustine denounces "the voluptuous madness of stage-plays" and "the foul plague-spot" of the theater.[38] Tertullian complains of theater's immorality and its frequenting by prostitutes, who even took to the stage to advertise themselves. The first English actresses, in the late seventeenth century, were notorious for promiscuity. In 1969, the New York Social Register still dropped the name of a man who married a movie star. The Puritans, who managed to close the theaters for eighteen years, equated fiction with deceit. They were right. Art remains an avenue of escape from morality. Actors live in illusion; they are skittish shamans, drenched in being. Crafty fabricators of mood and gesture, they slip along the edges of convention. Actor and artist are the first to register historical change. They write the sibylline leaves of western sexual personae.

Roman decadence was the final skirmish between the Apollonian and Dionysian elements in pagan culture. The strength and vigor of the Roman republic came from its synthesis of an Apollonian cult of the state with archaic chthonian ritualism. Major early Roman gods were male, with subordinate fertility goddesses. Although worship of the Great Mother had been introduced in 204 B.C. and had always been an option of the aristocracy, her popularity during the empire was a significant departure from Rome's first principles. She came from the eastern Mediterranean, where nature is less hospitable and more absolute. Was this turn toward female divinity a cultural advance or retreat? Then and now, worship of the Great Mother in an urban era is decadent. Imperial Romans no longer lived in and by the cycle of nature. The Great Mother went from fertile life force to sadomasochistic sexual persona. She was the ultimate dominatrix. In late Rome, men were passive to history. Decadence is the juxtaposition of primitivism with sophistication, a circling back of history on itself. The Roman Great Mother, with her multiple names and symbols, was heavy with the past. Her pregnancy was curatorial, another Alexandrian museum.

The Great Mother was the focus of new anxieties and spiritual longings that would not be satisfied until the consolidation of Christianity.

The Church Fathers recognized the Great Mother as the enemy of Christ. St. Augustine, writing at a turning point in western culture (ca. 415 A.D.), calls the rites of Cybele "obscene," "shameful," "filthy," "the mad and abominable revelry of effeminates and mutilated men": "If these are sacred rites, what is sacrilege? If this is purification, what is pollution? . . . The Great Mother has surpassed all her sons, not in greatness of deity, but of crime." Cybele is a "monster," imposing a "deformity of cruelty" on her castrated priests. Even Jupiter sinned less: "He, with all his seductions of women, only disgraced heaven with one Ganymede; she, with so many avowed and public effeminates, has both defiled the earth and outraged heaven."[39] The Great Mother, like Rome herself, is the Whore of Babylon.

Christianity could not tolerate the pagan integration of sex, cruelty, and divinity. It thrust chthonian nature into the nether realm, to be infested by medieval witches. Daemonism became demonism, a conspiracy against God. Love, tenderness, pity became the new virtues, soft qualities of the Palestinian martyr. The pagan veneration of force had turned politics into a bloodbath. Late Rome oscillated between fatigue and brutality. Flagellation and castration in the mother-cults was a sacrificial symbol of human dependency on nature. In the empire, however, whipping got kinky, and castrates went professional. Packs of them, in wigs, makeup, and garish female dress, roamed the towns and highways clinking cymbals and begging for alms. Apuleius describes them "squeaking for delight in their splintering harsh womanish voices."[40] Eunuchs had a high profile in the empire. Church leaders despised them. Christian strictness about sex roles dates from this period of crass, flamboyant personae. The Great Mother's castrate devotees, turning ritual orgy into street carnival, put the effeminate or homosexual male into permanent ill repute. When woman resurfaces in the Christian pantheon, she will be the mild Virgin without animal taint. Banished by Augustine, the Great Mother disappears for over a thousand years. But she returns in all her glory in Romanticism, that historical wave of the archetypal.

Though it destroyed the outward forms of paganism, Christianity has never interrupted the pagan continuity of sexual personae, latent in our language, ideas, and images. Christianity inherited Judaism's suspicion of image-making, but in its centuries of expansion, it began to use pictures as a didactic tool. The earliest Christians were an illiterate underclass. Christian pictures were first rudimentary scrawls, a new cave art in Roman catacombs; then they sailed upward into Byzantine domes, where they copied Greek iconic posture and hard-edged Apollonian style: Christian saints are reborn pagan personae. Martin Luther correctly diagnosed a loss of aboriginal Christianity in the Italian Church. The Romanism in Catholicism is splendidly, enduringly pagan, spilling out in Renaissance, Counter-Reformation, and beyond.

Paganism is pictorialism plus the will-to-power. It is ritualism, grandiosity, colossalism, sensationalism. All theater is pagan showiness, the brazen pomp of sexual personae. Judaism's campaign to make divinity invisible has never fully succeeded. Images are always eluding moral control, creating the brilliant western art tradition. Idolatry is fascism of the eye. The western eye will be served, with or without the consent of conscience. Images are archaic projection, earlier than words and morals. Greco-Roman personality is itself a visual image, shapely and concrete. The sexual and psychological deficiencies of Judeo-Christianity have become blatant in our own time. Popular culture is the new Babylon, into which so much art and intellect now flow. It is our imperial sex theater, supreme temple of the western eye. We live in the age of idols. The pagan past, never dead, flames again in our mystic hierarchies of stardom.

5

Renaissance Form

Italian Art

The Renaissance, a rebirth of pagan image and form, was an explosion of sexual personae. Recent scholarship has followed a Christianizing tendency, smoothing the rough edges off the Renaissance and giving it an anachronistic moral tone. Specialists have slowly redefined Renaissance humanism in their own image, patient and prudent. Yet the disciples of saintly Raphael could plot the murder of a rival artist in the street. The sudden intellectual and geographical expansion of culture inaugurated three centuries of psychological turbulence. Renaissance style was spectacle and display, a pagan ostentation. The Renaissance liberated the western eye, repressed by the Christian Middle Ages. In that eye, sex and aggression are amorally fused.

The great chain of being, a master principle of western culture from classical antiquity to the Enlightenment, sees the universe as hierarchical: mineral, plant, animal, man, angel, God. The Renaissance was politically unstable. Shakespeare's Ulysses grounds politics in the great chain of being: disrespect for authority is like misaligned planets causing earthquake and storm (*Troilus and Cressida* I.iii.83–126). From the tension between sexual personae and public order came an abundance of Renaissance literature and art. Celebrations of the beauty and necessity of order are a reflex of the nearness of disorder.

The medieval great chain of being suffered a climactic trauma: the Black Death of 1348, a bubonic plague that killed up to 40 percent of Europe's population. Boccaccio describes the breakdown of law and government, the desertion of child by parent and husband by wife. A wellborn woman who fell ill was nursed by a male servant: "Nor did she have any scruples about showing him every part of her body as freely as she would have displayed it to a woman . . . ; and this explains why those women who recovered were possibly less chaste in the period that followed."[1] The Black Death weakened social controls. It had a polar effect, pushing some toward debauchery and others, like the flagellants, toward religiosity.

The Athenian plague, I argued, brought high classicism to an end. The Black Death worked in reverse, giving birth to the Renaissance by destroying the Middle Ages. Philip Ziegler says, "Modern man was forged in the crucible of the Black Death."[2] Christianity's failure to protect the good damaged Church authority and opened the way for the Reformation. I think the grossness and squalor of plague broke the Christian taboo on display of the body. Pagan nudity reappeared in its anguished Hellenistic form of torture, massacre, and decay. By reducing persons to bodies, the plague put personality into a purely physical or secular dimension. I begin Renaissance art with the shock of the Black Death. Public ugliness and exhibitionism unmoralized the body and prepared it for its reidealization in painting and sculpture. Boccaccio's plague-framed *Decameron*, the first work of Renaissance literature, is an epic of cultural disintegration and renewal.

At the Renaissance, says Jacob Burckhardt, there was an "awakening of personality."[3] Renaissance art teems with personalities, arrogant, seductive, vivacious. Italy restores the pagan theatricality of western identity. There is a craze for cosmetics, hairstyles, costumes. What would have been vanity and sybaritism in the Middle Ages becomes the public language of personae. Architecture takes vivid hue. The white marble of the Florentine Duomo (completed in the early Renaissance) is crossed with red and green, hallucinatory vibrations in the Italian sun. This burst of multiple color is like coming to Vergil after Caesar and Cicero. The *Aeneid*'s new artistic palette—rose, violet, purple— signals the manic proliferation of imperial personae. So too in the Renaissance, as in the psychedelic Sixties. Colors and personae are in dynamic relation. By the late Renaissance, architecture dissolves in color or is buried under ornamentation. Bernini uses twenty colored marbles for the Cornaro Chapel. In that outbreak of pagan sex and violence which is the Bernini Baroque, the liberated eye finally drifts into a sea of sensual excitation.

The Renaissance infatuation with sexual personae is reflected in Castiglione's *Book of the Courtier* (1528), which had enormous influence all over Europe. It is a program for theatricality. The man with a talent, says Castiglione, should "adroitly seek the occasion for displaying it."[4] Social life is a stage and each man a dramatist. Castiglione set high standards of taste for dress and deportment. The courtier is an artifact, a work of self-sculpture. He is also an androgyne: he has "a special sweetness," a "grace" and "beauty." Two of his primary qualities, *sprezzatura* and *disinvoltura* ("nonchalance" and "ease"), are hermaphroditizing. That is, by making speech and movement seem effortless, they disguise or efface masculine action. Woman is central to the *Book of the Courtier:* the dialogue takes place in the apartments of the Duchess of Mantua while the Duke sleeps, and woman literally has the last word. The Castiglione woman is purely feminine. Castiglione opposes the double-sexed Petrarchan model of womanhood, with its proud, killing cold. The courtier's sweetness and grace seep into him from contact with women. Male education is Castiglione's theme as much as Plato's, but woman has now captured the symbolic high ground of spiritual value. In Castiglione, all women are Diotimas.

The courtier quests for a sexual persona perfectly balancing masculine and feminine. Castiglione warns against effeminacy, excessive feminization. The courtier's face should have "something manly about it":

> I would have our Courtier's face be such, not so soft and feminine as many attempt to have who not only curl their hair and pluck their eyebrows, but preen themselves in all those ways that the most wanton and dissolute women in the world adopt; and in walking, in posture, and in every act, appear so tender and languid that their limbs seem to be on the verge of falling apart; and utter their words so limply that it seems they are about to expire on the spot; and the more they find themselves in the company of men of rank, the more they make a show of such manners. These, since nature did not make them women as they clearly wish to appear and be, should be treated not as good women, but as public harlots, and driven not only from the courts of great lords but from the society of all noble men.[5]

Is this merely an attack on open homosexuality? Castiglione implies that effeminacy is somehow inspired by the presence of authority figures. The issue is the moral welfare of court and sovereign.

We come now to history's most repellent androgyne, completely overlooked by feminist promoters of androgyny. I call it the "court hermaphrodite." Renaissance high culture was organized around the courts of duke and king, upon whom artists and intellectuals depended for patronage. Art was a tool of competitive display, by which a ruler maintained his prestige. Power always generates sycophancy. Enid Welsford says, "The blasphemous flattering of princes, which was such a disagreeable characteristic of Renaissance literature and revelling, was not a mere fashion of speech but a sign that the state was being regarded as an end in itself."[6] A prince, one step from God, reproduced the great chain of being in his court hierarchy. Flattery was secular prayer, worship of the sacred order. But the insincere flatterer was leech and opportunist, a polluter of language. In Castiglione's detestation of the type, we see the moral dangers of Renaissance theatricality.

The court hermaphrodite appears wherever there is wealth, power, and fame. He is in governments, corporations, university departments, and the book and art world. We know the professional sycophant from the Hollywood flack or yes-man. He is the celebrity hairdresser, the boudoir confidant and lounge lizard, the glossy escort. Ava Gardner said of an unctuous gossip columnist, "He's either at your feet or at your throat." Flattery and malice come from the same forked tongue. The sycophant is an androgyne because of his pliability and servility. He is a deformation of Castiglione's courtier: self-sculpture becomes slavish plasticity to the ruler's whim and will. Identity is self-evacuated. The flatterer opens himself like a glove to the royal hand. Castiglione's male "harlots" are, or seem to be, homosexual because sycophancy is political sodomy. We call a flatterer a brown-nose, an ass-licker, sucking up, grovelling, supine. His shameless self-abasement is unmanly, elevating bum over head. Lloyd George said Lord Derby was "a cushion who always bore the impress of the last man who sat on him." Like Milton's "fawning" Satan, the smooth flatterer crawls on his belly, twisting and turning with changing circumstance. He is purely reactive, a parody of femininity, each word and deed a cloying mime of the ruler's desire. This phenomenon may be a perversion of male bonding, a social spectacle of dominance and submission.

Shakespeare's Richard II is rebuked by his lords for the "thousand flatterers" who sway his judgment (II.i.100). Flattery poisoning the court world of *Hamlet* is one cause of the hero's chronic nausea. Polonius and the young courtier Osric agree like annoying echoes with each of the exasperated Hamlet's nonsensical assertions. The court hermaphrodite has no gender because he has no real self or moral substance. Most painful to Hamlet is the betrayal of his childhood friends, Rosencrantz and Guildenstern, who turn spy for the king. Hamlet calls Rosencrantz a "sponge . . . that soaks up the king's countenance, his rewards, his authorities" (IV.ii.12–21). Goethe's Wilhelm Meister rejects a proposal to combine the two men into one: there ought to be "at least a dozen" of them, for "they are society itself."[7] Shakespeare's dramatic doubling of Rosencrantz and Guildenstern is the court hermaphrodite sterilely cloning itself. Inseparable and indistinguishable, they hover in floating passivity. Pope's ambitious dunces dive into London sewage: sycophancy was a foul byproduct of Renaissance secularism. John Donne alludes to "painted courtiers" and "strange Hermaphrodits" (*Epithalamion made at Lincolnes Inne*). In Ben Jonson's *Volpone*, the "parasite" Mosca is cunning household sycophant to a nobleman whose entourage includes a eunuch, Castrone, and a hermaphrodite, Androgyno. Pleased with Mosca's services, Volpone cries, "My witty mischief, / Let me embrace thee. O that I could now / Transform thee to a Venus!" (V.i.) Flattery *is* sexual subordination. Hierarchy is conceptualized eroticism, which is why, as homely Henry Kissinger said, power is the ultimate aphrodisiac. The Renaissance court aesthetic is still thriving in the eighteenth century, when Pope denounces Lord Hervey as a cynical court hermaphrodite and Mirabeau calls Marie Antoinette "the only man at court." Two cinema court hermaphrodites are Katharine Hepburn's nervy, epicene secretary Gerald in *Woman of the Year* and the odious eunuch Photinus, Pharaoh's lord chamberlain in the Elizabeth Taylor *Cleopatra*.

Renaissance hierarchies are dramatized in the noisy climax of Benvenuto Cellini's *Autobiography* (1562). The artist is one of the great sexual personae of the Renaissance, a culture hero and worker of marvels. Before this, sculptor and painter, as manual laborers, were always inferior to the poet. Everywhere except Greece, they were simply artisans, like today's carpenter and plumber. Cellini's bronze *Perseus* is forged in a Wagnerian storm of western will. The artist attacks by earth, air, water, and fire. He piles on wood, brick, iron, copper; he digs a pit; he hauls ropes. He shapes his hero out of clay and wax. He exerts superhuman energies, until he is struck down by fever. Cellini takes to bed in ritual couvade, while *Perseus* strains to be born. The metal curdles and must be resurrected from the dead. Finally, the shouting, cursing artist, transfigured by creative ecstasy, defeats all obstacles and brings *Perseus* into the world in an explosion, "a tremendous flash of flame" like a thunderbolt. Cellini has made "miracles," triumphing by a godlike blend of male and female power.[8]

Now *Perseus* is placed in Florence's public square (fig. 18). At its unveiling, the crowd sends up "a shout of boundless enthusiasm." Dozens of sonnets are nailed up, panegyrics by university scholars. The Duke sits for hours hidden in a palace window, listening to citizens acclaim the statue. This thrilling episode demonstrates the potential for collectivity at certain privileged moments in history. The Renaissance made public art, uniting the social classes in a common emotion. A

18. Benvenuto Cellini, *Perseus with the Head of Medusa*, ca. 1550.

figure on a platform; the mingling of nobles, intellectuals, plebeians: one thinks of the broad audience of Shakespeare's Globe Theatre. It is impossible to imagine a modern art work provoking a shout from a socially mixed crowd. Our sole equivalent is cinema, as at the Atlanta premiere of *Gone with the Wind*. Cellini illustrates the national differences in Renaissance form: in Italy, the objet d'art; in England, drama.

Whether Cellini lies or exaggerates is irrelevant. His autobiography (dictated to a scribe) is compulsively western in its hierarchical vision. Little in the East corresponds to this epiphanic theatricality of the art object, this concentration of affect upon a single point, the apex of a perceptual pyramid. The *Perseus* is an Apollonian idol of the aggressive western eye. It is partly Cellini's victorious superself and partly a homoerotic glamourization of the beautiful boy, a Greco-Roman theme revived in the Renaissance. Western personality is raised on a pedestal, in Florence or in Nuremberg. Leni Riefenstahl did for Hitler what the neoclassic David did for Napoleon. Personality is ritualized by the fascism of the western eye. Cellini, by divine force of genius, raises his *Perseus* to a summit presided over by an invisible godlike Duke. *Agon* and revelation: western religion, art, and politics use the same dramaturgy of form, because they are all emanations of cold hierarchical mind.

Perseus was Cellini's answer to the heroic marble *David* made by Michelangelo forty years earlier for the same public square. Both statues descend from Donatello's bronze *David*, the first beautiful nude and the first truly free-standing sculpture since the fall of Rome. Blatantly homosexual in inspiration, it shows David standing victorious over the severed head of Goliath, which he tramples underfoot (fig. 19). The story of David and Goliath, like that of Judith and Holofernes, would become a political symbol of Florentine resistance to tyranny. Donatello's David is astonishingly young, even younger than the *Kritios Boy*. David's contrapposto is languorously Hellenistic. The hand on hip and cocked knee create an air of sexual solicitation. From the side, one is struck by the peachy buttocks, bony shoulderblades, and petulantly protruding boy-belly. The combination of child's physique with female body language is perverse and pederastic. Michelangelo is to adopt this erotic formula for his more athletic nudes, where it becomes overtly sadomasochistic.

For H. W. Janson, Donatello's David is "strangely androgynous," "*le beau garçon sans merci*, conscious only of his own sensuous beauty." There may be a connection to Beccadelli's poetry collection, *Hermaphroditus*.[9] David has long feminine locks of hair, tangled with ribbons,

19. Donatello, *David*,
ca. 1430–32.

and a splendidly raffish wreathed hat, a version of the traveller's hat of Hermes Psychopompos. But here is no traveller's cloak, only exquisitely etched leather buskins. A pornographic trope: the half-dressed is more erotic than the totally nude. The feathery wing of Goliath's helmet, like an escaping thought, climbs ticklishly up the inside of David's thigh, pointing toward the genitals. Roman putti often display their genitals or mischievously urinate, a motif adopted for Renaissance fountains. Donatello poeticizes the *ostentatio genitalium*, a pagan showing. The hoary head of a monster conquered is a familiar iconographic detail, but here it vomits a wreathlike flood of blood ringing the statue. The stream is the giant's, and the artist's, own desire. David, plunging his massive sword to the center, has stolen the adult penis, as he has stolen hearts. The gushing blood, wing-topped, is a carnal cloud, Zeus as a maimed eagle bearing up Ganymede.

I think Donatello's *David*, even more than the ancient *Venus Pudica*, was the true model for Botticelli's *Venus*. David, fusing Venus and Mars, skims into view on a swirl of the dreaming artist's fantasy, half spasmodic release, half rising sigh. The *David*'s shimmery, slithery bronze is a frozen wet dream, an Apollonian petrifaction. It is also a portrait of the artist, whose oppressed face appears like a signature at the bottom, another homoerotic motif borrowed by Michelangelo. The armed boy bursts like Athena from the artist's imprisoned brain.

The glamourous Apollonianism of Italian Renaissance art begins with Donatello, who frees sculpture from its medieval subordination to architecture. From his *St. George* (1417), stepping from its niche, to *David*: stone knight to bronze kouros. Medieval armour is the pagan exoskeleton of western personality. Hard, shiny, absolutist, it is a product of that radiant Apollonian thing-making which passes from Egypt to Greece and Rome and resurfaces in the High Middle Ages as military design. The bronze *David* is *St. George*'s suit of armour turned inside out. David's brazen nudity is the impermeability of western personality. His compact frame is supercondensed by the aggressive western eye. He is personality as sex and power.

The beautiful boy is homosexuality's greatest contribution to western culture. Un-Christian and anti-Christian, he is an iconic formalization of the relation between the eye and reality. Repeated in a thousand forms in Italian painting and sculpture, he is the ultimate symbol of Renaissance art. He is St. Sebastian, the Christian Adonis pierced by arrows, or ephebic St. Michael, whom the Renaissance took out of his Byzantine tunic and clad in silver armour. The Northern European Renaissance has few beautiful boys and no Apollonian grandeur. Figures (portraits excepted) rarely fill the pictorial plane. They are modest, fluttery, and to my Mediterranean eye dry and insipid. They allow space to press upon them. Italian art makes personality and gesture florid and theatrical, in the fascist Apollonian manner. Donatello's *David* stands on its own because it has rejected northern Gothicism for southern paganism. Its hardness and domination of space come from the artist's rediscovery of the authentically western will, inflexible and amoral. Art has rearmed itself with the pagan glorification of matter.

Donatello's youths are always sexually ambiguous. His marble, clothed *David* (1409) has a graceful, feminine hand and girlishly delicate face with a small, pretty mouth. The statue was apparently based on an Etruscan goddess in the Medici collection.[10] The unfinished marble *David* in Washington has fleshy cheeks in classic Greek style. The bust of a youth in Florence has a sensitive face and sweet smile and a provocatively swelling throat and breast. With longer hair, he could pass as a woman. In his harrowing late period, Donatello abandons his ephebic dreams and banishes pagan eroticism from his art. The emaciated wooden *John the Baptist* and *Mary Magdalene* are withered by guilt and atonement. *David*'s glossy Apollonian surface is scored and slashed, the flesh already bored by worms. Such self-laceration is typical of Mediterranean Catholicism, with the ecstatic mortifications of its pagan heritage.

The morally and sexually ambiguous smile of Donatello's *David* has a long subsequent history. It goes directly to Michelangelo's *Victory* after passing through Verrocchio to Leonardo, where it ends up on the *Mona Lisa*. Finally, we see it on Bernini's androgynous angel impishly piercing St. Teresa. David's smile is dreamy and solipsistic. He is the beautiful boy as destroyer, triumphing over his admirers. He is western armoured ego as sex object, free-standing because separatist. Despite his beguiling insouciance, David's Apollonian hardness, mental and material, is evident when we compare him to Caravaggio's beautiful boys. Here, by the richness of oil paint, the Dionysian mouth intrudes on the Apollonian eye. Caravaggio's cardinal metaphor of fruit is written all over his street urchins' inviting nudity. Subtly, despite ourselves, we salivate. In high classic dignity, Donatello's David, unlike Caravaggio's bolder boys, does not meet our eyes. His sword keeps us at a distance. He has true Apollonian iconicism. While entranced by his eroticism, we look *up* to him and leave him in his temenos of sacred beauty. Like Nefertiti, he is a hierarch of the western eye.

In my history of sexual personae, Botticelli is Donatello's heir. I see Donatello's androgynous *David* in every face in Botticelli. It is the same

elaboration of a single face into a whole universe of sexual ambiguity
and muted color tones that happens from Rossetti to Burne-Jones.
Botticelli turns Gothic's wavy slimness and height into sophisticated
Apollonian linearity. He shares with Pollaiuolo and Mantegna the
sharp Byzantine outline that, thanks to Donatello, survived Masaccio's
new shadowed contours. Pollaiuolo's anatomies are busy and strained,
but Botticelli's, in his best work, have a high classic unity and repose.
Even in the segmented *Primavera*, personality is in the foreground,
literally and figuratively. Botticelli thinks in terms of sexual personae,
swelling with innate authority. I spoke of the descent of Byzantine icons,
with their sharp edges and static frontality, from the Greek kouros.
Botticelli resurrects the paganism in the Byzantine line. Inspired by
Donatello's free-standing *David*, he restores Apollonian iconicism to
the painted figure. Botticelli's clarity of outline is the same armouring of
western personality we first saw in the enthroned Pharaoh Chephren.
The hardness of the Botticellian body is, I venture, a subliminally
homosexual motif, like the closing off of female internality in Greek
sculpture. It will become the *Panzerhaft* or glazed armouring of Mannerist figures in Pontormo and Bronzino. By deduction, therefore, Mannerist hardness is the ultimate result of Donatello's momentous step
from marble to bronze, from stone armour to armed nudity.

In *The Birth of Venus*, Botticelli reimagines a chthonian goddess as
Apollonian personality (fig. 20). She scuds to shore on a metallic scallop
shell, the heraldic shield of woman's marine origins. On her face is the
pensive smile of Donatello's dreamy *David*, and around her winds, as a
heavy rope of strawberry-blonde hair, the ruddy wish-stream of Donatello's bleeding Goliath. *The Birth of Venus*, thirteen feet wide, is a
pagan altarpiece. The goddess's monumentality and proud separatism
come from sculpture. In this cultic epiphany, Venus dominates the eye,
as she dominates the picture plane. She rises from the starburst shell (a
trumpeting petrifaction of her splashing foam) to stand in Apollonian
sunlight. She is sex and love washed clean of mystery and danger. The
freshest of breezes skips across the scene, a dewy spume blown from the
lips of a libidinous zephyr into a handmaiden's billowing cloak. The
shallow composition is Byzantine, as is the sharpness of line. Botticelli's
Venus is Kenneth Clark's Crystalline Aphrodite. She is a springtime
goddess, showered with flowers of mathematical articulation. There is
no chthonian tangle or brooding pregnancy in this nature. Every tendril
and herb has a fine Apollonian identity. The sea itself has no murky
depth. Botticelli's revised Venus is an Apollonian idea. Female secrecy

20. Sandro Botticelli, *The Birth of Venus*, 1485.

and entrapment are abolished in her frank, yet decorous nudity, her perfect visibility. An air-blown or aerated womanliness: Raphael takes this from Botticelli for his genial *Galatea*. I find it again in the modern *Galatea*, the *Life* magazine pin-up of Rita Hayworth.

The Birth of Venus is Botticelli's cinematic resolution of the unsettling sexual complexities of his *Primavera*, another large, imposing painting (fig. 21). The *Primavera* is a black egg cracked open by *The Birth of Venus*. The transfer of tapestry design into paint in the *Primavera* produces a sinister claustrophobia unacknowledged by scholarship. Because of its enclosed space and atomized placement of figures, I classify the painting as decadent—the last gasp of Gothicism. The umbrella pine is Botticelli's favorite symbol of contracted omnipotent nature, overhanging human thought. In the *Primavera*, the dark grove is an emanation of Spring's bulging womb, at the picture's exact center. Why do we not rejoice with the promise of fertility? We seem to be in elegy, not pastoral. The spindly trunks, ashy leaves, and metallic fruit belong to Dante. There is a sunless sky we cannot reach. The trees are a spiritual stockade. The figures are separated by invisible barriers. Each is locked in an allegorical cell, oblivious to the others. Even the three dancing Graces avert their eyes. Mercury turns his back on the whole scene, in superb indifference. He will pluck his own fruit, and of his own kind. This beautiful boy is Donatello's David two years later. Puberty is

21. Sandro Botticelli, *Primavera*, 1478.

fleshing him out. His hat, like his attitude, is haughtier and more warlike. Like the Graces' impenetrable female circle, androgynous Mercury is narcissistic and self-complete.

Across the way, Flora casts petals from her brimming, self-fecundated lap. What of her strange face framed by cropped male hair? After years of puzzling over my Uffizi copy, I realized Botticelli has joined two faces together, as in the dream sequence of Bergman's *Persona*. One half belongs to a female aristocrat, cool, chaste, and self-possessed. The other belongs to a coarse gutter waif, roguish and lewd. Love for sale. Botticelli has condensed the extremes of sex and caste in an unsettling fusion of Renaissance personae. Flora, as much as Mercury, makes love to herself. The energies of the *Primavera* are boxed or, to use a term from English poetry, embowered. The zephyr so freely blowing in *The Birth of Venus* is caught in the trees here, his wings tangled and his stopped cheeks bursting. His impure thoughts dribble in leafy syllables from the lips of an anxious nymph. The allegory of the *Primavera*, however it may be worked out, cannot explain away the picture's chilling atmospherics, its decadent precision of bleakness and elegance.

Botticelli's pictures have *mood*. This was something new in the history of painting. I say it came from the sexual aura of Donatello's *David*, the Apollonian corona which warns us away. Hauser speaks of Botticelli's "effeminate melancholy."[11] Eroticized melancholy is everywhere in Botticelli, in angels, Madonnas, saints, boys, nymphs. It is extruded as subtle tints of rose, sepia, grey, pale blue. Similar color values in Piero della Francesca do not have the same perverse effect. Why? Because Botticelli, unlike Piero, is a poet of sexual personae. Botticelli's personalities have a fixity and dreamy apartness. They offer themselves to the eye and yet rebuff our intimacy. Within their nervous carved lines, they have a heaviness or density of consciousness. Their dispassionate faces are like the barred backdrop of the *Primavera*, a cultivated closure.

Donatello and Botticelli's rediscovery of the Apollonian iconicism in western personality comes to them as a homosexual conceptualization, as in Greek high classicism. The Apollonian borderline, I said, is a turning away and a shutting out. The sharp Botticellian line is part of the self-definition of Renaissance personality, its withdrawal from medieval Christianity and its reorientation in secular space. Botticelli's unity of tone is produced by his figures' awakened yet entranced eyes. His personae, unreachable, contemplative, hover in a dream vision. They have the materiality of pagan pictorialism. Their pale smooth flesh glitters with the aristocracy of Apollonian beauty, an artistic dynasty founded in Egypt.

This theatrical compounding of sexual personae with moody ambiance, sober and ascetic in Botticelli, is reproduced and darkened by Leonardo da Vinci. Botticelli's subtle atmospherics are so transparent they are easy to miss. But in Leonardo a thundercloud of chiaroscuro is gathering. Leonardo, who melts the Apollonian line in shadow, is linked to Botticelli by the motif of an obsessively repeated face, used for both sexes. Leonardo and Michelangelo, solitary and depressive, created the persona of the artist as spiritual quester, as much a man of ideas as any philosopher. For both men, art, science, and construction were intellectual substitutes for sex—not sublimation but undisguised aggression, a hostile domination of nature. Their celibacy and ill temper were correlated, rational responses to our outrageous extension in these tyrannous bodies, branded with gender by mother nature. Leonardo dissected and anatomized the body to remove its female mysteries, unstringing muscles, detaching bones, even opening a womb to draw the huddled fetus. In his inventions, from flying machines to engines of war, the laws of dynamics were captured by the mathematical male mind. Michelangelo, by titanic masculine athleticism, tried to hammer matter into servitude. After the breakup of the ordered medieval cosmos, both men turned anxiety into megalomania, a fanatical expansion of the will. But Leonardo painted little. Even his finished works had a

22. Leonardo da Vinci,
Mona Lisa, 1503.

self-destruct quotient, like *The Last Supper*, with its experimental technique, which made the paint almost immediately begin to peel off the
refectory wall.

Leonardo's *Mona Lisa* is the premiere sexual persona of western art
(fig. 22). She is the Renaissance Nefertiti, eternally watching. She is
unnervingly placid. The most beautiful woman, making herself a perfect stillness, will always turn Gorgon. I spoke of the *Mona Lisa* as
Leonardo's apotropaion, his household charm of warding-off. She is an
ambassador from primeval times, when earth was a desert inhospitable
to man. She presides over a landscape of raw rock and water. The
distant river's snaky meander is the elusiveness of her cold daemonic
heart. Her figure is a stable female delta, a perceptual pyramid topped
with the mystic eye. But the background is deceptive and incoherent.
The mismatched horizon lines, which one rarely notices at first, are
subliminally disorienting. They are the unbalanced scales of an archetypal world without law or justice. Mona Lisa's famous smile is a thin
mouth receding into shadow. Her expression, like her puffy eyes, is
hooded. The egglike head with its enormous plucked brow seems to
pillow on the abundant, self-embraced Italian bosom. What is Mona
Lisa thinking? Nothing, of course. Her blankness is her menace and
our fear. She is Zeus, Leda, and egg rolled into one, another hermaphrodite deity pleasuring herself in mere being. Walter Pater is to

23. Leonardo da Vinci, *Virgin and Child with St. Anne*, 1508–10.

call her a "vampire," coasting through history on her secret tasks. Despite many satires, the *Mona Lisa* will remain the world's most famous painting. Supreme western works of art, like *Oedipus Rex* and *Hamlet*, preserve their indeterminacy through all interpretation. They are morally ungraspable. Even the *Venus de Milo* gained everything by losing her arms. Mona Lisa looks through us and passively accepts our admiration as her due. Some say she is pregnant. If so, she radiates the solipsism of woman gloating over her own creation. The picture combines fleshy amplitude, emotional obliqueness, and earthly devastation. Leonardo has drawn mother nature from life.

In his major female paintings, Leonardo recloses the bright open space of *The Birth of Venus*, the temporary reprieve Botticelli's Apollonian metric won against the entanglements of procreative nature. Leonardo's *sfumato*, or smokiness, is a chthonian leakage, a spreading miasma. *The Madonna of the Rocks* (1483–90) is backed by a looming cavern and a forest of ancient stalagmites, brute ziggurats or phallic totems. The women of the *Virgin and Child with St. Anne* totter at the edge of a stony cliff, harsh and barren (fig. 23). In the distance is a ghostly moonscape, like blasted Gothic cathedrals. These peaceful scenes of mother and child have a chthonian undertow, threatening to suck us back to earth-cult. Mona Lisa's ambiguous smile is a hieroglyph symbolizing the link between Leonardo's sexual personae and their enshrouding atmosphere, a strange light which is their own stormy inner weather. The same smile appears on *Leda* and both women of *The Virgin with St. Anne* and even on two male figures, *St. John the Baptist* and its twin *Bacchus*, where smile and pointing finger turn seductive and depraved. So Leonardo's smile is androgynous, a sexual hex sign. It is beginning to bud on the lips of the gesturing angel of *The Madonna of the Rocks*, a male so feminine that students seeing the picture for the first time insist he is a woman.

Freud traces the mysterious smile to Leonardo's buried memory of the lost biological mother preceding his adoptive mother, the two women of *The Virgin with St. Anne*. Freud connects the painting to Leonardo's childhood dream of a bird of prey, the hermaphroditic Egyptian vulture goddess, Mut. Meyer Schapiro rejects Freud's reasoning and claims the source of the Leonardo smile is in his master Verrocchio. The grouping of the two women was traditional, says Schapiro, their oddly close ages signifying "the theological idealization of Anne as the double of her daughter Mary."[12] But there is nothing sinister or disturbing in the gentle Verrocchio. I trace the smile all the way back through Botticelli to Donatello and find it amoral, solipsistic, and gender-crossing from the start. Leonardo injected Verrocchio with his own perversity: one of his earliest works is the androgynous angel he painted as an apprentice in Verrocchio's *Baptism of Christ* (1472).

Freud rightly senses uncanniness in Leonardo's doubling of St. Anne and the Virgin. Mary seems not so much sitting on Anne's lap as slipping off it. The figures are like photographic superimpositions, two images seen simultaneously, eerie and hallucinatory. Yes, the women are doubles, just like Demeter and Persephone. Both Farnell and Frazer comment on Greek depictions of divine mother and daughter as "twin-sisters," their "identity of substance" symbolizing the stages of vegetable growth.[13] In Leonardo's charcoal cartoon (1499) and finished panel, St. Anne's magnetic attentiveness to her companion seems menacingly or lasciviously intense. Anne's blocky fist of a gesture in the cartoon turns into a mannish, piratical hand on hip in the painting. Love in Leonardo is never normal. His mystic doubling of Anne and Mary, their uncertain spatial placement and ambiguous smiles, and the bleached landscape give the painting an archetypal power found nowhere else in Renaissance art except in Michelangelo. St. Anne and the Virgin are joined in autocratic nature-rule. These divine twin sisters are one archaic personality that has parthenogenetically cloned itself. Life is an endless series of self-replicating females. Leonardo reverses Genesis, so it is maleness, in the chubby infant Jesus, that is successive and subordinate to femaleness. But as the grotesque landscape shows, this is no celebration of female power. Like Michelangelo, Leonardo finds the condition of male servitude intolerable, and rightly so.

I give the name "allegorical repletion" to the doubling of *The Virgin with St. Anne*. The term describes a redundant proliferation of homologous identities in a matrix of sexual ambiguity. Allegorical repletion is present in the Hymen episode ending Shakespeare's *As You Like It*; in the incestuous mirroring of characters and family names of Emily Brontë's *Wuthering Heights*; and in two surreal Rossetti paintings, *Astarte Syriaca* and *The Bower Meadow*, which contain ominously multiple versions of a single melancholy female face. Leonardo's suffocating doubling of figures in *The Virgin with St. Anne* is another version of *Mona Lisa*'s stolid, self-contained hermaphroditism. We now know what a pregnant *Mona Lisa* carries within her: her fetal twin. The theme of Leonardo's two paintings is the same: the male eye and psyche flooded by female power. Leonardo's neatest composition is *The Last Supper* (1495–98). Is there a connection between the all-male Passover party and the regular, rational mathematical design of the room, with its perspective lines converging behind Christ's head? Male space makes sense in Leonardo. But female space is crowded, murky, eccentric, destabilizing. Leonardo's paintings may be so few in number because the journey from idea to rectangular picture plane was beset with female daemons. Science and engineering, then as now, are Apollonian havens from the vertigo of gender.

Both Leonardo and Michelangelo are commonly classified as homosexual, but whatever sex they may have had was surely rare and anomalous. The monastic strain runs deep in the Italian temper. Freud observes that it is emotional attraction, not physical activity which proves sexual orientation. In their private lives, Leonardo and Michelangelo were evidently interested only in male beauty. Of course, they had no real private lives apart from art and intellect. They were half-mad visionaries, as misanthropic as hermit saints. Their ritualistic cultism was a natural flowering of Mediterranean paganism: extremism, militancy, and hieraticism are always near at hand for the Italian Catholic. Leonardo and Michelangelo's homosexuality was part of their angry quest for autonomy of imagination, against everyone and everything— parents, teachers, friends, rivals, society, nature, religion, God. The western dynamic of conflict and combat is crystal-clear in them. They have no Christian charity or generosity, only pagan hunger to conquer, surpass, subdue by force. We too are their subjects. Their dominance demands our submission. The two geniuses of the High Renaissance remake art by making art aggressive. Homosexuality in Leonardo and Michelangelo was intellectual as well as erotic, in the western way. It was a resistance to the grossest of human dependencies, our enslavement by nature.

Why was Michelangelo so productive as an artist and Leonardo so frustrated? Michelangelo's total output was staggering, a virtuosity in sculpture, painting, and architecture unparalleled in the history of the arts. The vigor and vitality of the Renaissance flowed into him, as into Shakespeare. Why did Leonardo complete so little? My answer is that his technique and theme were at odds. Style and sexual personae sabotage each other. The smokiness of *sfumato* is Dionysian mistiness, the fog hanging over the chthonian swamp. Decadent Euripides, we saw, uses Dionysian liquidity to destroy Apollonian Aeschylus. But Leonardo is a high classicist, an archon of the mathematical mind. He wants to subdue mother nature, but in depicting her, he allows her to dictate his style. *Sfumato* is her game. The more he plays it, the less he can paint. Even the self-dissolving *Last Supper* is infected by her.

Michelangelo, on the other hand, an athlete stonecutter, began with sculpture and retained its Apollonian laws in painting, which the pope forced on him in the Sistine Chapel. Oil painting and color, said Michelangelo, are for "women and the lazy." His sharp-edged Apollonian style is the only way to beat back mother nature. It is the hieratic signature of the western will. This is why Leonardo's sketches and private notebooks, with their Apollonian pen line, are so voluminous. But there is never a final victory in fighting nature. Michelangelo was locked into a pattern of endlessly renewed anxiety. Again and again and again. To the end of his long life, Michelangelo leapt from labor to labor, piling up the man-mountain of his stunning achievement. He converted a quest for freedom into another enslavement, sweat-stained, day blurring into night. His bequest is the most brilliant series of Apollonian images since Athens' revival of Egypt's royal glamour.

Michelangelo's huge *David* (1501–04) is companion to *Mona Lisa* in the star chart of Renaissance sexual personae. The original, removed in 1873 from the weather, is enshrined in a simple temple of pagan design. It is a true kouros, Donatello's *David* as teenaged athlete, a sinewy boy-man. We see him before action rather than after. He glares toward Goliath along a plane of the aggressive western eye. His body is half-resolute, half-apprehensive, the left leg shrinking away but sending its energy into the hand-held stone, about to rise to the slingshot. In its monumentality and armoured hardness, *David* is an apotheosis of the male body as Apollonian perfection. The tension of male will has contracted the torso, so head and hands seem overlarge. This contraction is a sexual condensation, a homoerotic defeat of female murk and interiority. The *David* overwhelms the pilgrim viewer by its blazing solar radiation, its defiant domination of space. The very air around it seems as impenetrable as the body itself. David, like Michelangelo, fends us off..The dreaminess of Donatello's charmer is gone. Michelangelo's David is awakened western consciousness, studying the enemy in the cold hostile light of Apollonian day.

Michelangelo's obsessive theme is glorified maleness. *Moses* (1513–15) Hellenizes another Biblical persona. It is an astonishing improvisation on pagan images. The rippling *Belvedere Torso* swells Moses' bulging biceps. The serpentine undulations of the just-excavated *Laocoön* spill through the long beard, trapping Moses' index finger, his own halted motivation. Massed Greek draperies hang on the powerful leg like a shroud. The Hebraic lawgiver, letting slip the stone tablets, breaks his own code. Like David, he glares furiously to the left. He sees the golden idol of his fickle people. But the artist raises Moses as a new idol, Zeus-Jehovah, a theatrical amalgam of intellectual and physical force. Moses makes God in his own image. And Michelangelo creates as an entrancing father-figure the one sexual persona more virile than he.

The *Moses'* maleness is absolute. It drives femaleness out of existence. There are no mothers in this cosmos. Only monumental Assyrian relief has such propagandistic machismo. We come to the limit of sexual representation. The female body can never attain such grandiosity of assertion. *Moses* is an idealization, but its exaggerations are of normal physical contours produced in men by male hormone. This definitive articulation and massiness of muscle and joint are unavailable to women except through automedication with steroids. John Addington Symonds says that "the superiority of male beauty" consists in "the complete organization of the body as the supreme instrument of vital energy."[14] I agree. When admiring the sleek body of a woman athlete, I see androgyny, not femaleness. I honor her capture of a male mode. *Moses* is specifically western in its masculinity. Nothing in the art of other cultures resembles it in stature or abundant facial hair. Michelangelo's electrifying icon of the Hebrew iconoclast is a racist paradigm of Greek physical culture. The Apollonian, I said, is a Dorian and therefore Aryan aesthetic. *Moses* challenges modern liberal pieties on every front. It is beauty as power, beyond ethics.

Michelangelo's exaltation of maleness deforms his depiction of women. Like many Renaissance artists, he used male models for female figures, since a woman posing nude was scandalous. But from the evidence of his surviving drawings, Michelangelo never sketched any woman from life, dressed or not. Furthermore, the cross-sexual origin of his female figures has left a strong visual residue. The best examples are the Sibyls of the Sistine Chapel ceiling. The early drawing for the Libyan Sibyl is obviously of a male model, whose athletic physique survives in the final figure. The Delphic and Eritrean Sibyls have start-lingly heavy male arms. The old Cumaean Sibyl is one of the most fantastic sexual personae in art (fig. 24). She has grim wizened features yet bursting breasts, fat as pumpkins. Her lumbering shoulder and arm are brawny beyond human maleness. She is witch, hag, wet nurse. She is Michelangelo's *Mona Lisa*, mother nature in the flesh, old as time but teeming with coarse fertility.

Cousins to the Sibyls are the reclining female nudes of the Medici Chapel (1520–34), products of Michelangelo's Mannerist late phase. No one knows what these figures mean or even what they should be called. Anxious *Dawn*, lifting a listless hand, flexes her male bicep. *Night* bares a hammy haunch as she twists in restless half-sleep, her abdomen ridged like a washboard (fig. 25). The women's breasts are knobby protuberances stuck to male torsos. Clark calls them "humiliat-ing appendages."[15] *Night*'s choppy nipples are angry and puckered. Who would care to suck such sour pippins? Among Renaissance per-sonae, Michelangelo's massive females, including *Leda* and the muscu-lar Madonna of the *Doni Tondo*, belong to a sexual cabal. I classify them as viragos, uniquely blending male and female. With *Night* as my model, I define the virago as a fusion of Great Mother and Amazon, but without the fecundity of the former or free movement of the latter. Like Artemis, the Amazon has an adolescent body type. But the virago is large-breasted, sexually mature, her body heavy and inert. She is spir-itually imprisoned and poisoned. Jeanne Duval, Baudelaire's bisexual harlot Muse, was such a sterile virago, indolent and self-thwarting. Baudelaire in fact wrote a verse about Michelangelo's *Night* ("The Ideal"). The virago is one of our darkest androgynes. The Medici Chapel nudes, perched uncomfortably on their slippery, too-small tombs, labor and bring forth nothing. *Night* is a Gorgon *Mona Lisa* who has devoured her own rocky landscape. The virago is self-enclosed, paralyzed, and dyspeptic.

In art, monumentality or abstraction impersonalizes and therefore masculinizes women. This principle applies to Michelangelo, the Nef-ertiti bust, and Assyrian relief, with its beefy muscle-bound goddesses. Michelangelo's women are not all androgynes. There is winsome Eve peeking brightly from the crook of God's arm in the *Creation of Man*.

24. Michelangelo, *Cumaean Sibyl*, 1508–12.

And there is the pure, tranquil Virgin of the Rome *Pietà*. But in both cases, the female body is largely concealed. Eve and Mary's appealing femininity is made possible for Michelangelo by suppression of their bodies. Moreover, the women appear with two of his most magnificent male nudes, who absorb his imagination. Eve and Mary are hand-maidens of a sublime but enervated masculinity, without which Michel-

25. Michelangelo, *Night*, 1525–31.

angelo would never dream of bringing them into being. Adrian Stokes
calls the Sistine God's flaring, creature-packed cloak a "uterine mantle."[16] So Eve is just a particle subdivided from a hermaphrodite male
deity. The medieval Madonna Misericordia, tenting humanity beneath
her wings, has been robbed of her garment by the aggressive Sistine
God.

Michelangelo's life work is an epic in which femininity plays little
part. His lyric poetry resembles Shakespeare's sonnets in its dual inspiration: a beautiful boy, Tommaso Cavalieri, and a potent woman,
Vittoria Colonna, who combines the sexes. I cited, apropos of the Delphic oracle, Michelangelo's salute to Colonna as "a man, a god rather,
inside a woman." This makes mythologically intelligible his depiction
of the Sibyls as half-male viragos. Michelangelo's late admiration for
the pious Colonna, who took to a convent after her husband's death, has
been misunderstood as romance by many commentators. She became
one of Michelangelo's sexual personae, but she inspired no eroticism.
She was a hermaphrodite Muse, a voice of judgment, appealing to his
admiration for hierarchic force. She did not exist as a body. She was an
invisible mother-father, hovering like the Sistine Sibyls midway between heaven and earth.

Michelangelo, we have seen, invested his imaginative energies nearly exclusively in masculinity. But an occult rule of his art is that the masculine is in constant danger of melting into the feminine. Consider as a sexual persona the Medici Chapel's idealized portrait of Giuliano de' Medici, Duke of Nemours (fig. 26). This statue repeats the pose of the awesome *Moses*, but it is hemmed in its narrow niche in Mannerist closure, the imprisonment of late-phase art. Michelangelo packs Donatello's free male figure back into its Gothic pen. Despite its vigorous athleticism, the *Giuliano* has a wonderful half-female glamour. The neck supporting the *Apollo Belvedere* head is sinuous, swanlike, and feminine. The torso is suggestively explicit. First, the breasts are excessively developed for a male. Second, the torso is a brilliant fantasia on the *cuirasse esthetique*, the molding of a Roman leather or bronze breastplate to the personal imprint of the chest. Vasari says of the *Giuliano*, "The very buskins and cuirass seem not of this world."[17] The chest and abdominal muscles are fluent, tactile, sensual. Michelangelo so persuasively reproduces human skin folds on the cuirass's caul-like transparency that the metal shoulder clamps seem to be biting into living flesh. I always think of the nipple-piercing pins in sadomasochistic sex shops. Surely this lurid motif has come to Michelangelo from the Capitoline bust of the emperor Commodus draped in Hercules' lionskin, open jaws capping his head and claws resting on his chest. But Michelangelo perversely sexualizes it. Unlike his pensive brother Lorenzo, sitting across the chapel in an ordinary cuirass, Giuliano is exquisitely autoerotic.

Michelangelo likes to stress the male chest. Of examples like the mighty Christ of *The Last Judgment*, Clark speaks of "that strange compulsion which made him thicken a torso till it is almost square," "almost a deformation."[18] Giuliano's chest has erotic delicacy and the intelligence and sensibility one normally expects of a face. John Pope-Hennessy says Michelangelo was "deeply uninterested" in portraiture.[19] Michelangelo's only portrait, as Vasari exclaims, is of the beautiful Tommaso Cavalieri. I propose that the luxurious chest of *Giuliano de' Medici* is the second of Michelangelo's homosexual portraits. It is analogous to the glossy buttocks of the *Kritios Boy*, which borrow artistic energy from the still, sober, high classic face. *Giuliano's* flesh-piercing ornaments are subliminally sodomitic. They are an iron pen filling the blank page of the torso with flowing erotic script. The male torso is Michelangelo's landscape, the broad stage of human experience and action. *Giuliano's* mounded breasts are forbidden Cities of the Plain.

26. Michelangelo, *Giuliano de' Medici*, 1531–34.

Giuliano de' Medici belongs to a category of Renaissance androgyne separate from that of the beautiful boy. I call it "Epicoene, or the man of beauty," after Ben Jonson's transvestite play, *Epicoene, or The Silent Woman*. The man of beauty has an active, athletic adult maleness. But in insolent narcissism, he retains an ephebic transsexual quality, expressed in a feminine alabaster skin, here arising from the dazzling white marble. Three other examples of my Epicoene category are George Villiers, first Duke of Buckingham, Lord Byron, and Elvis Presley, all dangerous men of notorious charisma.

Gender in the *Giuliano* is barely held in balance by the male military regalia. The foursquare male chest of resolute western will is disordered by the serpentine disengagement of the curvy neck. A feminine masochism is beginning to encroach upon the statue through the limp flipped wrist and pierced breasts. The theme of masochistic sensuality is already present in the so-called *Dying Slave*, one of a series of "Captives" for the uncompleted tomb of Julius II (fig. 27). The huge statue (height 7' 6½") is usually explained in Neoplatonic terms as a symbol of the soul's struggle against the body. But the theory leaves too much emotional overflow. Leg flexed, the languid *Dying Slave* poses like a beauty queen, voluptuously postorgasmic. The cross-sexual element comes partly from the statue's Greek models, both female: a wounded Niobid and the *Dying Amazon*, with raised arm. The *Dying Slave* is a sexual reversal of Michelangelo's alertly masculine *David*, whose leg placement it parodies. A phantasmic band of cloth winds the eroticized chest, touched by dainty fingers of onanistic tenderness, a gesture borrowed from Donatello's early marble *David*. The combination of athletic male physique with female mood and body language is perverse. It turns the milder flaunting of Donatello's bronze *David* into decadent sexual cultism, an ecstasy of sadomasochistic bondage. The *Dying Slave*, backed by the lurking ape of bestial instinct, is a pagan crucifix. This is a gratified St. Sebastian who has swallowed his tormentors' shafts. He drifts in his own perfect fantasy. When as a youngster I saw a picture of this statue, I was fascinated by its blatant eroticism, which scholarship, in its quick escape to allegory, studiously ignores.

The *Victory* (1532–34) is another of Michelangelo's provocative works of sexualized theater: a beautiful youth with cruelly blank Donatello face crushes his knee upon a hogtied older man, whose bearded face resembles Michelangelo's. Is the defeated elder the Old Adam of experience? Yawn. Sexual personae are the red flame of Renaissance imagination. *Victory* is a homage to Donatello's *David*, who treads the grizzled head of Goliath. In the psychic force-field of the aggressive

27. Michelangelo, *Dying Slave*, 1513–16.

western eye, beauty dominates the observer. All-dominating Michelangelo is undone and humiliated by his own homosexual eye. The beautiful boy, with his beckoning feminine hand, is an angel-vampire leaping
up with Michelangelo's repressed energy, the burden of his jailed self. I
cannot be convinced that great artists are moralists. Art is first appearances, then meaning. The *Dying Slave* and *Victory*, as well as the
twenty exhibitionistically self-twining *ignudi* or nude youths of the
Sistine ceiling, are complex pagan sex objects. These works resemble
Spenser's *Faerie Queene* in the way that moral allegory has wandered
into prurient sexual naturalism.

Michelangelo's primary principle is the quest for Apollonian form.

His figures must exert enormous pressure to keep their shape. Our and
the artist's eye must remain vigilant and aggressive. The dialectic between definitiveness and dissolution is evident as early as *Bacchus*
(1497). "Androgynous and seductive," in Robert Liebert's phrase, Michelangelo's boyish wine-god careens unsteadily, offering us his lifted
cup.[20] But the seduction is more than sexual. Major western sculpture, I
said, is Apollonian. Therefore *Bacchus* staggering is Apollonian form
seduced by the chthonian, deliquescing. Mother earth calls. Michelangelo never has to use Bacchus overtly again, since his figures artistically
assimilate the Dionysian theme. Clark speaks of "a feeling of thundery
oppression" in Michelangelo's torsos. Stokes sees in the sculpture and
painting "a state of uneasy passivity, known to us in terms of an oppressive weight."[21] What is it that oppresses Michelangelo's figures? His
terribilità ("awesomeness" or "fearfulness") is the malign gravitation of
mother nature, who dissolves all forms in her cycle of change and
remaking. The Apollonian line asserts the identity of objects. Sculptural
contour is so emphatic in Michelangelo because of the danger of feminine surrender to nature.

Like Greek artists indifferent to landscape, Michelangelo makes the
male figure the field of combat. His resistance to nature is like William
Blake's: both men are obsessed with the dream of a world generated
and sustained by masculinity alone. To materialize that world, the
choleric Michelangelo drove himself with remorseless athleticism, a
hyperbolic titanism. But a wholly masculine cosmos is untenable. It
cannot last even when erected by a genius. Consequently, Michelangelo's male figures are exhausted with their effort and helplessly infected by femininity, which shimmies upward from a spiritually opaque
gravitational center. The pornographic fluorescence of the *Dying Slave*
comes from its will-lessness, its sensually engorged surrender. The
ruggedly masculine Michelangelo, like Ernest Hemingway, required
rituals of male inflation to fight off the lure of transsexual submission.
Mother nature turns us all to eunuchs.

Nearly everything in Michelangelo has some sexually disturbing undercurrent. Effeminates cavort behind the Holy Family of the *Doni
Tondo*, pagan desire escaping Christian control. The Sistine *ignudi*
seem like castrates, ritually tormented initiates of an unknown cult.
Even the great *Pietà*, surely partly inspired by Botticelli's *Venus and
Mars*, is a tableau of female immortality and perishable manhood. In
archetypal terms, has the Holy Mother not drained her son? *Mor-
bidezza*, the *Pietà*'s softness or delicacy of modelling, also means "effeminacy" in Italian. Perhaps the Medici Chapel nudes are less mas-

culine women than men being transformed, as in a nightmare, into women. Michelangelo's sexual ambiguities are apotropaic formulas, repeating what is feared in order to drive it off.

Intransigent Michelangelo is the best example of the western aesthetic of perceptual control. The art object, in its Apollonian unity and clarity, is a protest against the too-muchness of nature. Late in Michelangelo's career, the multiplicity of objects rebounds, breaking back into the Mannerist *Last Judgment* (1536–41) and filling it with a dithery mass of churning bodies. But by this point the artist is starting to flag in his Apollonian enterprise. Turning, like Donatello and Botticelli, back to the church, he portrays himself as a shapeless flayed skin in St. Bartholomew's grasp and leaves his mammoth figures half-buried in stone. Apollonian form deflates or aborts. Matter has won.

Renaissance Apollonianism originated in Florence and spread to Rome. Its emphatic sharp edge, descending through Byzantine style from the Greek kouros, was initially a homosexual idea, a line drawn against female nature. It then passed into general artistic usage and lost its secret polemicism. Florentine intellectuality and Florentine homosexuality were linked phenomena. Beautiful boys, everywhere in Florentine art, rarely appear in Venetian painting, which is full of luscious female nudes. Mercantile Venice did not seethe with philosophers and crackpots, like Florence. In art, fleshy Venetian women, half-Oriental odalisques, relax in cordial landscapes—a far cry from Leonardo's abandoned rock quarries. Venetian personae and Venetian landscape are equally heterosexual. Venice's appreciation of female beauty allowed acceptance of rather than resistance toward nature. Was this not the result of the city's unique physical character? Venice, veined by water, is in placid relation to marine nature. Its people and artists imaginatively internalized female fluidity, the prime chthonian principle. The Renaissance City of Art, a triumph of architectural ingenuity, was its own balance of Apollonian and Dionysian and did not need to explore these ideas in painting. That balance was eventually disrupted by the ubiquity and omnipotence of Venetian water. The city rotted, flooded, and began to sink. Mann records its modern degeneration in *Death in Venice.*

Hard-bodied boy-form is implicit in Florentine aesthetics. It surely influenced the Florentine female nude, like Botticelli's Venus, with her small breasts and tall, slim build. Procreativeness was neither a Florentine nor an Athenian value. The luxuriance savored by Venice in female curves was projected by Florentine artists into men's flowing hair, one of the most mesmerizing themes of Renaissance art. Like Michelangelo's muscle-man *Moses*, this is a natively western mode. Only Caucasians, a motley blend of ethnic types, have such a variety of hair colors and consistencies. Portrait art has made European hair a gorgeous palette of sexual personae. In the Renaissance as now, a pretty boy with a long, fine head of hair has a drop-dead androgynous allure. All those dashing Italian Renaissance angels are crowned with pagan physicality.

Raphael of Urbino, youngest of the three High Renaissance geniuses, diverted Florence's homoerotic glamour back toward the procreative female. He created the Christmas-card persona of the warm Madonna, a simple peasant girl of open face and arms. Raphael was heavily influenced by Leonardo and Michelangelo, who enabled him to break from his master Perugino, with his spare, bland, small-figured Northern European style. But Raphael takes the sexual ambiguity and psychological conflict out of Leonardo and Michelangelo. He does to them what Keats does to Coleridge, sweetening and purifying the daemonic, making the maternal a blessing rather than a curse. Raphael subtly corrects his teachers. His matchless glow of color, a half-liquid envelope of feminine emotion, is a clarification of Leonardo's louring atmosphere. From the surviving portraits and self-portraits of all three artists, Raphael seems the most feminine in manner and appearance. His turn toward woman prefigures the sexual shift of late-Renaissance art.

In Mannerism and Baroque, as in Hellenistic art, the sexes repolarize. Cellini's Perseus, with whom we began, holds his scimitar at crotch level to punctuate his victory over the femme fatale, whose dripping head he brandishes aloft. Bernini's David, a self-portrait, is stoutly masculine and in mad motion. The androgyny and Apollonian apartness of the first Renaissance Davids have been redefined in late-phase terms. Bernini's Apollo pursues a nymph melting into a bristling tree. Metamorphosis is the Dionysian principle of Baroque illusionism. Bernini even stations four giant, undulating, brazen pagan serpents to hold up the canopy over the main altar of Christendom. The supreme Baroque work, his *St. Teresa in Ecstasy*, a sex-parody of Renaissance Annunciations, makes the armed androgyne merely a titillating boudoir provocateur. The orgasmic victim is in full sail on a Dionysian cloud. Woman, with all her vibrating internality, takes center stage.

6

Spenser and Apollo

The Faerie Queene

English literature is one of the supreme constructions in the history of art. It is both music and philosophy, a sensory stream of thought feeding each generation of writers from the Middle Ages to modernism. English literary distinction begins in the Renaissance and is the creation of one man, Edmund Spenser. His epic poem, *The Faerie Queene* (1590, 1596), does for the English Renaissance what painting and sculpture did for the Italian. Spenser is Botticelli's heir. By his intuitive grasp of the hard-edged Apollonian line, Spenser puts English literature into the ancient dynasty of western sexual personae. The arts, except for portraiture, were weak in the English Renaissance, partly because of Henry VIII's destruction of Catholic images. Spenser recreates English pictorialism in poetic form. His influence upon later writers, beginning with Shakespeare, was incalculable. It was through Spenser's quarrel with himself that English literature gained its amazing complexity. Romantic poetry's chthonian daemonism, for example, is a flowering of the secret repressions of *The Faerie Queene*. We will see it pass from Coleridge to Poe to Baudelaire and beyond. Spenser invented the artistic vocabulary of English poetry, which he turned into a meditation on nature and society, on sex, art, and power.

At the moment, *The Faerie Queene* is a great beached whale, marooned on the desert shores of English departments. Spenser is a hostage of his own critics, who have thrown up a thicket of unreadable commentary around him. Renaissance studies are woefully overspecialized; a lurid era has been reduced to a jumble of multilingual footnotes. Efforts to draw different arts or nations into one frame of reference are resisted. Even Spenser and Shakespeare are rarely discussed together. *The Faerie Queene* has been ruined for many students

by the numbingly moralistic way it is taught. Spenser spoke to other
poets as a bard, not a preacher. And when bards summon the Muse,
they themselves may not always know what they speak.

Scholars begin English literature with Chaucer and list Spenser as his
disciple. But English literature would have remained merely national if
it had really followed Chaucer. I would argue that Spenser made English literature world-class only by abandoning Chaucer and erad-
icating his influence. There is a huge shift of style between the Chaucerian *Shepheardes Calendar* (1579), which made Spenser's name, and
The Faerie Queene, begun the same year. Pastoral eclogue was a pagan
genre, adopted by apprentice Vergil, but *The Shepheardes Calendar* is
medieval Christian in tone and detail.

Through his friendship with Sir Philip Sidney, an advocate of Castiglione's aristocratic ideals, and through his devotion to the queen, to
whom he dedicated *The Faerie Queene*, Spenser reawoke the mystic
hieraticism of power latent in western sexual personae. The mass glorification of Elizabeth I revived the radiant laws of Apollonian beauty.
Her portraits are Byzantine icons, stiffly ceremonial and encrusted with
jewels. I spoke of the origins of Botticelli's hard edge in Byzantine art
and Donatello's sculpture. We know Spenser was familiar with some
Botticelli: that he modelled a major sex scene in *The Faerie Queene* on
Botticelli's *Venus and Mars* was one of the earliest observations of
Spenser criticism. Copies of Italian art came to England largely in the
form of engravings, a new technique that would intensify hard Apollonian contours and add them even when absent in the original. *The
Faerie Queene* has an Apollonian brilliance found nowhere in Spenser's
medieval or Renaissance sources, including Ariosto, who lacks his as-
perity and iconicism, his concentration and hard edge.

The Faerie Queene turns to pagan style to defeat Christian Chaucer.
My theory of comedy puts Oscar Wilde in the same haughty Apollonian
line as Spenser. Chaucer's comic persona resembles that of Charlie
Chaplin's Little Tramp, whom I seem to be alone in loathing. Chaucer's
humanism is predicated on the common man, on our shared foibles and
frailties, our daily muddle. He absolves his admirers of guilt. There is
no fear and trembling in his theology. Chaucer's conviviality is full of
winks, chuckles, and nudges. The hearty warmth of it all makes my skin
crawl. Chaucer is a populist, while Spenser is a hierarchist. *The Faerie
Queene*, like Wilde's *The Importance of Being Earnest*, is aristocratic in
form and content. Chaucer, and here is his continuing appeal, *accepts
the flesh*. But the Apollonian resists nature by its hostile eye-drawn line.
For me, reading Chaucer is like fighting through cattails while being

worried by midges. There are *too many words*, Gothic flutters and
curlicues. Portraiture in *The Canterbury Tales* has a scratchy, rustling
detail coming, like Northern European painting, from manuscript illumination. In Greco-Roman terms, it is a coy, labored style. Wise
Chaucer, putting roses in the cheeks of medieval asceticism, opposes
absolutism and extremism in all things. But the idealizing Apollonian
mode is absolutist and extremist from the first architectural overstate-
ments of Old Kingdom Egypt. Western greatness is unwise, mad, inhuman.

Revolutionary Spenser puts the eye into English poetry. Horace's
theory that a poem should be like a picture was much discussed in the
Renaissance. But Spenser goes far beyond this. Image, A. C. Hamilton
rightly insists, is as crucial as allegory.[1] The aggressive eye is the conceptualizing power of *The Faerie Queene* and the master of its largest
ideas. Spenser is history's first theorist of aggression, anticipating
Hobbes, Sade, Darwin, Nietzsche, and Freud. Only Leonardo and
Michelangelo before him had struggled with the moral problem of the
awakened eye. Spenser's pagan eye burns cozy Chaucer right out of
English poetry. Not since Homer had there been so cinematic a poet.
Spenser's long blazing sightlines prefigure the epic sweep of film and
the probing light-beam of the projector. The opening up of secular
space in Italian painting through perspective is paralleled in the vast
distances of *The Faerie Queene*. Spenser's typical moment is the glancing of light off the armour of a faraway knight. Who or what is it? We
never hear a name until the scene is nearly over. Spenser, as much as
Donatello, understands the meaning of medieval armour as a vehicle of
western pagan identity. Spenser is an Apollonian thing-maker in the
tradition linking stony Pharaoh Chephren to modern metal cans and
cars.

Personality in Spenser is armoured, an artifact of aggressive forging.
The theme of *The Faerie Queene* is the same one I found in Michelangelo, a conflict between definitiveness and dissolution of self. In the
Renaissance, sex has a dangerous freedom. That barbaric power consigned to the medieval Hell now waits in every glade, returned to its old
place in nature. The western eye, creator of the sharp boundaries of
selfhood, is sucked into will-lessness by the lure of sensual beauty. To
preserve its autonomy, the Spenserian eye suspends itself in voyeurism,
a tactic of defense that turns into perversion. Judaism had avoided this
dilemma by elevating the word and banishing the eye. But Christianity,
assimilating pagan art, was divided against itself from the moment it
left Palestine. Spenser's profound study of the amoral dynamics of the

western eye makes *The Faerie Queene* the supreme work of Renaissance literature until *Hamlet,* which uses Spenserian voyeurism in virtually every scene.

The Apollonian line to which *The Faerie Queene* belongs began in Egypt and Greece and passes through Donatello, Botticelli, Michelangelo, Blake, and Shelley to the Pre-Raphaelite painters and Oscar Wilde. It then reappears in cinema, which was implicit in western art and thought from the start. *The Faerie Queene* makes cinema out of the west's primary principle: to see is to know; to know is to control. The Spenserian eye cuts, wounds, rapes. Since Vasari, artists have been divided into draughtsmen and colorists, practitioners of Wölfflin's painterly style. The argument flares in the nineteenth century, when Blake rejects chiaroscuro as mud and when rough-brushed Delacroix opposes clean-lined Ingres. Spenser uses the incising draughtsman's pen. Direct contact with Botticelli was unnecessary, since the Apollonian style was latent in medieval armour, in which Spenser clothes so many characters. Spenserian armour is western personality imagined as discrete and indissoluble, cohesive and luminous.

The sex and glamour of the armour-infatuated *Faerie Queene* separate it from a more faithfully Protestant work like its descendant, *Pilgrim's Progress* (1678). Upstairs, downstairs: Bunyan's kitchen Spenser returns allegory to its legible medieval form, as in the morality plays. *Pilgrim's Progress* makes a charmingly direct path between simple image and simple message, which the Bible allows us to decode. But in the tricky *Faerie Queene,* Protestant individualism has been usurped by a pagan aesthetic. In Spenser, as nowhere in Bunyan, we constantly contemplate the ritual visibility of fabricated personality, a Greco-Roman idea. Armour is the Spenserian language of moral beauty, signifying Apollonian finitude and self-containment.

Spenser's questing knights, isolated against empty panoramas, replay Apollo's hostility to nature. The west has always made Apollonian art objects out of arms of war (fig. 28). The bronze carapace of Homer's heroes is a male exoskeleton, the hardness of western will, a theme to return in a discussion of American football in my next book. In Odysseus' Ithaca, weapons are kept on display in the banquet hall. In the Middle Ages, a shield hung on the wall, as a painting would be in the Renaissance, was a badge of clan identity. The heraldic crest is another Egyptian cartouche, a privileged sacred space.

Western culture has always been obsessed with severe burnished surfaces. The elegant Corinthian Greek war helmet, for example, with its flat cheek-guards and keyhole eyes, is an eerie superself, smooth

28. *Homogeneous Tilting Armour,*
German, 1580. Maker: Anton
Peffenhauser, Augsburg.

as a staring skull (fig. 29). Eastern armour, in contrast, is squat, sinuous, and bushy. Asian art is based on the female curve, not the rigid
male line. Eastern armour uses organic shapes, while western armour
insists on technological insulation from nature. The western soldier is a
steely marching machine. The Japanese Samurai is bristly and rotund;
his armour seems pregnant, overgrown by vegetation. He is half-
camouflaged, relapsing into female nature, like *The Faerie Queene*'s
leafy knight Artegall, who is in a spiritually unreconstructed condition.

Compare the imperial tombs of Egypt and China. The Pharaohs'
mummiform granite sarcophagi or Tut's fitted gold coffins are heavy
and solid, fused from head to foot. But the gleaming jade burial suits of
Han princes are faceted and stitched like fish scales. Western Apollonianism is ungiving, impermeable, adamantine. It is an aesthetic of
closure. Donald Keene says Japanese sentences "trail off into thin
smoke," a vapor of hanging participles.[2] In other words, Japanese sen-

29. *Greek Helmet.* Corinthian type, late seventh to early sixth centuries B.C. Border of wave pattern.

tences avoid closure. Even the sword blade, in the west a harsh phallic totem, is given an interior by Japanese connoisseurs, who project poetic landscapes into its hundred folded layers. Western armour is separatist, dividing self from self and self from nature. Spenser's armour is the symbol of Apollonian externality, of strife and solar wakefulness. It ensures permanent visibility, personae hardened against their own sexual impulses. In *The Faerie Queene,* nature lurks everywhere with her seductive dissolutions of surrender and repose.

Arms and armour in *The Faerie Queene* symbolize male fortitude and self-assertion. We expect these qualities from heroes. But Spenser extends them to heroines, in a way that speaks directly to our time. His armed Amazons, Belphoebe and Britomart, are among the most potent women in literature. Spenser removes the usual archetypal basis of female force, the daemonic, and imagines his heroines as Apollonian angels. This had not been done since Greek Artemis. Spenser creates the new Renaissance cult of married love. As C. S. Lewis observes, Spenser's "romance of marriage" replaces the "romance of adultery" of medieval courtly love.[3] Before the Renaissance, poets sang of their mistresses but not of their wives. Marriage was a utilitarian affair, having nothing to do with art. Elizabeth, the Virgin Queen, was urged to marry throughout her reign, to ensure a peaceful succession. *The Faerie Queene* moves toward marriage but never reaches it (the poem is a mere fragment of Spenser's ambitious plan). The female knight Britomart is to wed Artegall and start the dynasty leading to Elizabeth and England's greatness.

Britomart's maternal destiny introduces an image foreign to the Renaissance as a whole: a benevolent Great Mother, whom Spenser calls Great Dame Nature. We saw how the androgynes of Italian art are usually beautiful boys and how dominatrixes, like Leonardo's *Mona Lisa* or Michelangelo's *Night,* tend to be sinister or sterile. In Shakespeare too, with his staggering range of sexual personae, references to creative chthonian females are rare. Spenser's attraction to the Great Mother is anomalous. He exalts her, where Cellini, decorating *Perseus'* pedestal with Ephesian Artemis, defeats her. Britomart reverses Artemis' evolution: she begins as the adolescent Apollonian androgyne and ends as the primeval mother goddess. Spenser's Great Mother, like her ancient precursors, is always double-sexed. In Venus' Temple, the idol, serpent-twined like Roman statues of Atargatis or Dea Syria, exhibits the genitalia of both sexes. She is "both male and female," "sire and mother," begetting and conceiving by herself alone (IV.x.41).[4]

Spenser's recasting of sexual mythology is daring, original, and perhaps unsupportable. The grandest epic quest of *The Faerie Queene* is his own. He wants to cleanse the procreative of its daemonic taint. Spenser's Renaissance ideal of marriage cooperates with genre in his two famous epithalamia. But now in epic, with its more aggressive sexual personae, nature is not so easily contained. *The Faerie Queene* tries to repair splits in Spenser's own imagination. It tries to turn the foul cup of the Whore of Babylon into a Holy Grail.

Spenser's most militant instrument of Apollonian definition is chastity, a self-armouring of personality. St. Augustine calls continence "unity of self."[5] Virtue in *The Faerie Queene* means holding to one's visible shape. In the human realm, formlessness or wanton metamorphosis is amoral. Only evil characters (Archimago, Duessa, Guyle, Proteus) change shape. The heroic Prince Arthur can transform other things but never alters himself. Hybrid beings (part dog, fox, dragon, hag) are always bad. This is the reason, I think, that Spenser was troubled by the five "Hermaphrodite stanzas," which he mysteriously dropped from the poem after its first edition. Amoret and Sir Scudamour, embracing, melt into one another until they seem a Roman Hermaphrodite statue. Spenser may have cancelled these stanzas because they violate his own Apollonian laws, trespassing the boundaries of form. In *The Faerie Queene,* mutilation is horrific. Words like "misshapen" and "deformitee" recur. The human form is paradigmatic, as in the anatomical architecture of the House of Temperance (II.ix). Belphoebe and Britomart, personified chastity, express their radical autonomy in a blaze of self-generated light, the same light that pours from the

Olympian gods as patrons of aristocratic order. The body in Spenser is a social integer. Apollonian illumination and integrity of form are art, politics, and morality all in one. Clarity of eye is purity of being.

The Elizabeth-inspired Amazons, Belphoebe and Britomart, are the greatest sexual personae of *The Faerie Queene.* They flood the verse with a strange golden light. St. Thomas Aquinas makes "brightness or clarity" a prime quality of beauty.[6] Eliade says of Vishnu, "Mystically perfect beings are radiant."[7] Burckhardt remarks that blonde was the ideal hair color of the Italian Renaissance. But Spenserian blondeness is a moral, not a cosmetic principle. Belphoebe and Britomart's heraldic blondeness is analogous to their upper-class hermaphroditism. Dorian and authoritarian Apollo, I said, is ice-blonde. Belphoebe's Apollonian blondeness is a transparency, hard and clear. The whole *Faerie Queene* is a "world of glass," a construct of visionary materialism (III.ii.19).

Light seems to penetrate blonde forms, so they seem midway between matter and spirit. St. Gregory the Great, seeing fair-haired British boy slaves in Rome, exclaimed, "They are not Angles but angels" (*Non Angli sed angeli*). In body type, Belphoebe and Britomart are the Crystalline Aphrodite, like Botticelli's Venus. All angels are ectomorphic. Spenser's female angels, suppressing the maternal silhouette, approach the sexually indeterminate. The blondeness of his heroines is a prism through which light is intensified and projected. The radiance of the Olympian gods as objets d'art is identical to the glamour of Hollywood publicity in which Kenneth Burke sees "a hierarchic motive."[8] Movie stars of the Thirties and Forties, photographed in halos of shimmering light, had Spenserian glamour. They were aristocrats of a dark era of economic chaos and war. The camera's idealizing eye gave them Apollonian power and perfection. The Amazons of *The Faerie Queene* shed light because they too are produced by an instinct for hierarchy. This poem, like most English Renaissance literature, is inspired by a reverence for social order.

Spenser and Shakespeare star beautiful female androgynes in their galaxy of personae. Here the English Renaissance strongly departs from the Italian: there were willful educated women like Caterina Sforza and Isabella d'Este, but they were not the focus of Italian imagination. Perusing the stunning Italian portraits crammed into museums and palazzi, one is struck by the disparity between male and female representation. Italian men and boys are vivacious, ravishing; but the women seem placid, stolid, even stupid. The feminine conventions of shaved eyebrows and bulbous forehead don't help. The divergence is extreme in double facing portraits like Piero della Francesca's of the

Duke and Duchess of Urbino or Raphael's of Angelo and Maddalena
Doni: the men are fully developed personalities, while their wives seem
static and bland. Not only could respectable women not pose at leisure,
but there was the Plotina effect: a lady confines herself to one persona.
Decorum means expressionlessness.

Spenser and Shakespeare throw all this out the window. They love
imperious, volatile women. England was governed by a charismatic
spinster who boxed the ears of her nobles and bashed ale flagons into
tabletops. Her chief minister Lord Burghley said the queen was "more
than a man and (in truth) sometimes less than a woman." Not until
Mannerism do aggressive real-life women finally make it into Italian
art. Bronzino, for example, captures the mannish profile of poetess
Laura Battiferri, whom he calls, punning on her name, "all iron within,
ice without." As for England, appreciation of fierce females did not
survive the Renaissance, thanks to the upsurge of Puritanism. Early
eighteenth-century portraits of noblewomen are as frigid and formulaic
as those of the Italian Renaissance. But Amazons were to stage a
comeback in the Augustan salon, as we know from *The Rape of the
Lock*.

So the liberated woman is the symbol of the English Renaissance, as
the beautiful boy is the symbol of the Italian. In *The Faerie Queene*, we
see her in free movement. I speak, of course, of artistic projection and
not of the life of real British women. But art is what transcends and
survives. Of all truths, it is the finest. Belphoebe bursts into *The Faerie
Queene* like a divine epiphany. Spenser gives her one of the most
dazzling theatrical entrances in art. Narrative action stops dead, while
ten long sianzas minutely describe her appearance. The Apollonian eye
is locked in place. It is a privileged moment of hieratic stillness and
silence, as if a frame of film were frozen before us.

Belphoebe, a huntress and solitary forest-dweller, recalls Venus disguised as Diana in the *Aeneid*. She resembles Penthesilea, "Queene of
Amazons." She carries "a sharpe boar-spear" and a bow and quiver
"stuft with steele-headed darts." Her face is the "heavenly portrait" of a
"bright Angel," rose-red and lily-white. She has an ivory brow. Her eyes
dart "fiery beames," full of "dread Majestie," that quell lust. Her long,
loose yellow hair, "crisped like golden wire," is lifted by the wind and
flecked with falling flowers—which suggests Spenser had also seen
copies of Botticelli's *Primavera* or *Birth of Venus* or both. Belphoebe
wears a pleated white silk tunic, sprinkled with golden ornaments like
twinkling stars. Her skirt has a gold fringe. Her gilt buskins are deco-

rated with gold, enamel, and jewels. Her legs are like "marble pillars" supporting "the temple of the Gods" (II.iii.21–31).

Belphoebe seems like a work of sculpture embedded in the text. Spenser's lavish description, far longer than anything in Boiardo, Ariosto, or Tasso, has the stylization and high specificity of a Byzantine icon. Belphoebe is the Byzantine Elizabeth. But she also has a high classic symmetry and mass, a mathematical measure. With her white and gold Amazonian splendor, she is like the chryselephantine colossus of Athena in the Parthenon. Every detail and edge is deeply incised, because Spenserian personality must be forcibly carved out of obdurate nature and defended against the erosion and lassitude of fatigue or hedonism. The intricacies of Belphoebe's golden hair and costume correspond to the categories and subsets of the great chain of being, ascending Apollonian order. Belphoebe's hypervisibility is our own Apollonian consciousness, our aggressive pagan eye. She is a masterpiece of western objectification, the sex object that leaps from the brain and repels all touch.

Belphoebe appears and disappears, like a dream vision. Not till a full book later does Spenser disclose her birth and education. In Book Two, she is formal and abstract, a sudden manifestation of hierarchic power. With her grace, dignity, and *arete*, she may be a living illustration of the golden mean, the parable of Medina and her sisters in the prior canto. Belphoebe mediates between the extremes of art and nature, masculinity and femininity. Her name means "beautiful Diana." She carries "deadly tooles," her male weapons (II.iii.37). We usually see her caught up in bloodlust, fast on the red trail of fleeing prey. A woman of "Heroick mind," she intimidates by her monomania, evasion of physical contact, and want of ordinary homely emotion. Discovering the injured Timias, she is touched for the first time by pity, "soft passion and unwonted smart" (III.v.55, 30). Even binding his wounds, she remains austere and remote. She is impenetrable, like the frosty, unknowable Garbo, in whom Roland Barthes sees an archetypal impersonality.

Belphoebe's chastity is a form of hierarchic sequestration. Proclus says, "The peculiarity of purity is to keep more excellent natures exempt from such as are subordinate."[9] The Apollonian universe of domination and submission permits no emotional involvement. Cold and self-complete, the Apollonian androgyne is isolated behind a wall of silence or muteness. I find this narcissistic phenomenon in the Greek beautiful boy, Mann's enigmatic Tadzio, and Melville's stammering Billy Budd. Compare Belphoebe's odd habit of dashing off in the middle of sentences. Exaltation of the Apollonian mode in *The Faerie Queene* tends to make the virtuous characters somewhat slow-witted! Belphoebe, for example, is given to rather dull speeches. Eloquence belongs to evil characters, like seductively musical Despair (I.ix.38–47). Spenser invented the word "blatant," meaning talk as noisy babbling. In the first canto, the pictorial *Faerie Queene* vomits its own words. Belphoebe's later adventures with Timias show her naturalistically: she has a reduced power, unlike the glory of her presence at first entrance. Spenser no longer shows Apollonian radiance emanating from her because, with the advent of pity into her heart, Belphoebe has forfeited her Amazonian autonomy. She descends to the realm of human hurts from the empty zone of her Olympian mind.

Self-sequestered Belphoebe stands apart from the main action of *The Faerie Queene*. But her Apollonian peer, Britomart, is one of the central protagonists, with a whole book and more devoted to her. She is chastity with an enchanted spear, the poem's only invincible knight. We first see her through the hostile eyes of Prince Arthur and Guyon, who think her a man. They see her as a mirror image of themselves, a warrior in full armour. During the ensuing skirmish, Spenser calls Britomart "he," deceiving us as well. Then he reveals her sex to us in an aside and switches to "she" for the rest of the joust, which we now watch with quickened attention (III.i). He uses this transsexual trick of perspective twice more, when Britomart approaches Malbecco's house and when she challenges and defeats Artegall (III.ix.12; IV.iv.43). Spenser's sleight of hand with grammatical gender, like his withholding of characters' names, seems to be part of his prescient insight into the problematic nature of perception and identity.

Trouncing the poem's leading men, Britomart is a paragon of knightly prowess. Spenser summarizes her double sexual nature: "For she was full of amiable grace, / And manly terrour mixed therewithall" (III.i.46). She inspires both love and fear, appealing to the eye but subduing the spirit. This is a pagan synthesis. Like Belphoebe, Britomart throws off a dazzling angel light. We see her only when she disarms, a sudden revelation the more overwhelming. "Her golden locks," falling to her heels, are "like sunny beames" bursting from a cloud, "golden gleames" shooting "azure streames" through the air (III.ix.20). Later, doffing her "glistring helmet," she lets her golden hair fall "like a silken veile" about her body. It is like "the shining sky in summer's night," the day's "scorching heat" now "crested all with lines of fiery light, / That it prodigious seemes in common people's sight" (IV.i.13). Britomart is Apollonian supernature, moon and sun, cold and hot. She is Virgin and

Lion, summertime constellations shot with sparkling meteor showers. People look up and marvel. But they are seeing Babylonian and not Christian gods.

This kind of glittering feminine beauty in Spenser always has a masculine component. Tasso's Amazon, the warrior Clorinda, never gives off the Apollonian light of *The Faerie Queene*, but there are precedents for the above passages in Ariosto. What Spenser adds to Ariosto is the quality of *strangeness*, of uncanny hierarchical excitation. Spenser senses the conceptualism and hieraticism in the aggressive western eye. He pushes vision into forbidden celestial space. Seraphic light unnerves and paralyzes the mortal viewer. Lascivious Malecasta, stealing upon sleeping Britomart, shrieks in fear. Her household finds her swooning at the feet of the wrathful knight:

> they saw the warlike Maid
> All in her snow-white smocke, with locks unbownd,
> Threatning the point of her avenging blade.
>
> Wherewith enrag'd she fiercely at them flew,
> And with her flaming sword about her layd. [III.i.63, 66]

Britomart, affronted chastity, is a pillar of fire. She is the archangel at Eden's gate, driving off sin from her holy sequestered self, a virgin circle. Belphoebe similarly recoils from the lustful advances of Braggadocchio, a Chaucerian lunk: "With that she swarving backe, her Javelin bright / Against him bent, and fiercely did menace" (II.iii.42). Spenser's female androgynes of Apollonian radiance assert their self-preserving masculine will by explosive extrusions of phallic projectiles. These javelins, swords, and darts are contained in western light. They are solar beams, killing glances of our omnipotent eye.

Britomart is motherless, like Athena, Atalanta, and Camilla. We hear only of a royal father and an old nurse, Glauce. There is a peculiarly physical scene between Britomart and the nurse, who revives her from love-sickness caused by a glimpse of her future betrothed in a crystal ball. Glauce rubs her charge all over the body and kisses her eyes and "alabaster brest" (III.ii.34, 42). These intimacies are maternal and then some. Spenser habitually complicates even innocent exchanges by some eroticizing adjective, usually describing inviting white flesh. Britomart's relation with Glauce corresponds to Rosalind and Celia's childhood union in Shakespeare's *As You Like It*, a proto-lesbianism, the prepubescent female matrix from which the sexually ambiguous heroine emerges into heterosexuality.

A lesbian suggestiveness of a different kind occurs in the prior canto in Castle Joyeous, where Malecasta, thinking Britomart a man, is consumed by desire. "Panting soft, and trembling every joint," she prowls the corridors like Diderot's obsessed lesbian mother superior and finally takes the masculine initiative by invading Britomart's bed (i.60). Malecasta has only seen Britomart's face through her open visor—a face we know to be quite feminine; hence her attraction to Britomart is subtly homoerotic. This is clear when one compares the episode to its source in Ariosto, where the Princess Fiordispina falls in love with the female warrior Bradamante. The tone is completely different. Fiordispina's impossible plight has an affecting pathos; there is nothing decadent about it. Malecasta is a jaded sophisticate and chatelaine, not an ingénue. Her sexual aggressiveness turns things kinky, a word that applies to Spenser but never to Ariosto. Kinky is a mental twist, top-spin on the eyeball. Malecasta's "wanton eyes" that "roll too lightly" are hostile western perception on the loose (41).

Though Britomart, feeling an intruder under the covers, leaps up outraged, Spenser persists in putting her in compromising quasi-lesbian situations. Later she kisses, embraces, and sleeps with Amoret, Belphoebe's feminine sister. Refusing to accept the False Florimell as her paramour, Britomart treats "her owne Amoret" as if she were actually Amoret's male champion (IV.v.20). Indeed, before Amoret knows her identity, the distracted Britomart pursues her male impersonation beyond the strictly necessary. Amoret becomes fearful of Britomart's "doubtfull" behavior, a lovemaking and "lustfulnesse" that threaten "some excesse" (IV.i.7).

These homosexual touches are part of Spenser's grand plan for Britomart. Her character has extraordinary amplitude, covering the full range of human experience, from masculine achievement to maternal generation. Britomart is one of the sexually most complex women in literature. Like Belphoebe, she is a dazzling Apollonian androgyne, with the figure of an adolescent boy. But unlike Belphoebe, she will renounce athleticism and militancy for motherhood. Even her inspired name is one of the Cretan titles of the Great Mother (Britomartis) and not, as one first thinks, Spenser's fusion of "British" and "martial." One of Britomart's missions, peculiar in a supposedly Christian poem, is her pilgrimage to the shrine of Isis. There she has "a wondrous vision" where she is robed and mitred as a male priest, then transformed into the pregnant goddess (V.vii). This sex change, paralleling the finale of As You Like It, is Britomart's life pattern. She traverses the vast landscape of sexual personae, progressing from solitary knightly quester to obedient wife and mother.

Britomart's encounters with her future mate are full of comic ironies. Artegall, to whom she must cede sovereignty in marriage, is repeatedly crushed by her in hand-to-hand combat. *The Faerie Queene* follows Artegall's education and training. He must earn his wife. At the moment, he falls dismally short of Britomart's daydreams, where he is "wise, warlike, personable, curteous, and kind" (III.iv.5). He enters the poem in an untidy state of rude strength, his armour covered with moss and weeds. His steed has oak leaves for trappings. The motto on his ragged shield is *"Salvagesse sans finesse,"* savagery without refinement (IV.iv.39). Artegall must be tempered from this extreme of brutish masculinity to become more androgynous. Spenser's letter to Sir Walter Raleigh says of Prince Arthur that the poem will "fashion a gentleman or noble person in virtuous and gentle discipline." Spenser praises Sir Calidore, hero of the Book of Courtesy, for his "gentlenesse of spright and manners mylde" (VI.i.2). Castiglione, we recall, gives the ideal Courtier "a special sweetness" and "grace." The accomplished gentleman has a feminine sensitivity to the social moment. Good manners are tentative and accommodating. The man passing from battlefield to court must be devirilized.

In journeying toward his feminine pole, however, Artegall goes too far. Falling beneath the sway of Radigund, the Amazon queen, he becomes effeminate. With Radigund, that strange glittering light returns to the poem after an absence of a book and a half. It is the radiance of the Spenserian androgynous. Under her coat of mail, Radigund wears a purple silk tunic woven with silver and quilted on milk-white satin. She has painted buskins "basted with bends of gold." Her scimitar hangs from an embroidered belt, and her jewelled shield shines like the moon (V.v.2–3). The description deliberately recalls Belphoebe. But Radigund, "halfe like a man," is a bully. In her solitary self-communing, Belphoebe does not affront the freedom of others. Radigund is a new Omphale, dressing captive knights in women's clothes and making them sew and wash to earn their supper (V.iv.36, 31).

Artegall makes two errors of judgment. First he promises, if defeated, to obey Radigund's law (Britomart later refuses to agree to such terms). Second, after he knocks Radigund cold, he is undone by her beauty, like Achilles over Penthesilea, and rashly flings away his sword. Thus he emasculates himself: "So was he overcome, not overcome, / But to her yeelded of his owne accord" (V.v.17). Radigund breaks Artegall's sword as a symbol of castration and hustles him into drag. "So hard it is to be a woman's slave," Spenser remarks, warning that all women except queens were born to obey men (V.v.23, 25). The great chain of being governs Spenser's definition of sexual order, perfected in marriage. In the Book of Justice, Artegall offends that principle by upsetting the sexual balance of power. The Renaissance thought men's political supremacy over women was based in natural law.

Britomart rides to the rescue. She must restore Artegall to manhood in order, paradoxically, to surrender to him. Chivalric sex roles are reversed. Britomart is the white knight and Artegall the damsel in distress. Catching sight of her intended in female dress, Britomart turns her head aside in embarrassment. Challenging Radigund to combat, she suffers a shock. For the first and only time in the poem, she loses. It takes one hermaphrodite to beat another. We see a contest between two womanly androgynies, as if to prove the truer or higher type. Britomart, who significantly has just come from Isis' Church, where she surveyed her maternal future, recovers and kills the Amazon outright. She destroys Radigund's revolutionary kingdom, repealing "the liberty of women" and restoring them to "men's subjection" (V.vii.42).

As the end of *As You Like It* also demonstrates, the Renaissance, despite its humanistic expansion of the rights of women, could not permit Amazonism to flourish within the social world. But Spenser's sexual personae play mischief with his official doctrine. Britomart has more force and common sense than her husband-to-be. She, not Artegall, is Spenser's epic hero. Britomart carries the blood of noble Trojan refugees, which will pass from her into the royal British line to raise the third Troy of Elizabethan London. Thus she is the real Aeneas of the poem. I elsewhere note her other sexual ambiguities.[10]

Britomart's martial superiority is no modern freak. Spenser laments its present rarity. Long ago, in "Antique glory," women fought battles and inspired poets to verse. Let great female deeds awake again, he proclaims (III.iv.1–2). In *The Faerie Queene*, helpless, retiring femininity is a spiritually deficient persona. Fleeing, ever-receding Florimell, brainwashed by the literary conventions of the love-game, is a caricature of hysterical vulnerability. Terrified by the sound of leaves, she runs even from admirers and rescuers. Spenser values courage and confrontation. Florimell's timidity and irrational fear are a defect of will. Belphoebe and Britomart's arms signify readiness to engage in spiritual combat. For male and female alike in *The Faerie Queene*, the psychological energy of aspiration and achievement is masculine. Life is rigor; no rest is possible. Seductive Phaedria tries to dissuade her suitor knights from conflict, but it is only by the clashing strife of contraries that Temperance or the temperate golden mean is achieved. *The Faerie Queene*'s androgyny theme belongs to this classical tradition of the *coincidentia oppositorum* or fruitful synthesis of opposites.

Female arms and armour are the panoply of sex war. One of the cardinal events of *The Faerie Queene* is rape, which occurs in dozens of forms, some real, some fabricated. The maidens Una, Belphoebe, Florimell, Amoret, Samient, and Serena are attacked once or repeatedly by rapists. Children born of rape include the sorcerer Merlin, the knights Satyrane and Marinell, and the chivalric triplets Triamond, Priamond, and Diamond. Males too fall victim to rape, kidnapped by the giantess Argante, her brother Ollyphant, and Jove himself. Even avarice is imagined as rape, the sacrilegious wounding of earth's "quiet wombe" for tinselly silver and gold (II.vii.17). The rape cycle of *The Faerie Queene* is the most advanced rhetorical structure in Renaissance poetry, surpassed only by Milton's freezing of epic plot into oratory in *Paradise Lost*. The masculine hurls itself at the feminine in an eternal circle of pursuit and flight.

The rapes of *The Faerie Queene* come from Ovid's *Metamorphoses*, the most imitated book of the Renaissance. But rape in Ovid, as in Hellenistic and Baroque art, is a bit of a jamboree, a romp of popping male muscles and bursting female globes. Spenser intellectualizes the Ovidian motif. Rape is his metaphor for biology, for the surges of aggression in nature. The sex war of *The Faerie Queene* is a Darwinian spectacle of nature red in tooth and claw, of the eaters and the eaten. Bestial Lust and his agents, like the hyena monster stalking Florimell, literally feed on women's flesh, devouring their bodies. Woman is meat, and the penis, symbolized in oak logs brandished by Lust and Orgoglio, is a thing, a weapon. The theme culminates in Book Six, where Serena is stripped and appreciatively manhandled by slavering cannibals and where Pastorella, lusted after by brigands, is embraced and entangled in a heap of corpses, the gross triumph of matter.

The rabid struggle for sexual dominance in *The Faerie Queene* is love debased to the will-to-power. Christian ethics are assailed on every side by pagan instinct. Spenser is the first to sense the identity of sex and power, the permeation of eroticism by aggression. Here he looks forward to Blake, Sade, Nietzsche, and Freud. Lust is the medium by which each sex tries to enslave the other. Spenser personifies it in numerous forms: as Lechery riding a goat in the procession of vices; as Sansloy, the lawless knight; as enemies of Temperance besieging the sense of touch; and as the grotesque predator Lust, all fangs, nose, and pouchy ears, a walking phallic symbol. As a state into which the virtuous characters may fall, lust is allegorically projected as a series of felons, cads, and sybarites who use force, fraud, or magic to have their way. The Spenserian rapist is a savage, churl, or knight who is not "curteous" or "gentle," who has not, in other words, undergone the feminizing refinement of social life. Due to his failure to incorporate a feminine component, he pursues fleeing, malleable femininity with a headlong ferocity that is a hunger for self-completion. His lust is a semantic error, a self-misinterpretation, a confession of psychic inadequacy. But on the other hand, weakness inspires attack. Vulnerability generates its own entrapments, creating a maelstrom of voracity around itself. Nature abhors a vacuum. Into the spiritual emptiness of pure femininity in Spenser rush a storm of masculine forces. Florimell, for example, is a professional victim. In her mad flight, she is called a "Hynd," the deer whom fierce Belphoebe pursues at her first entrance. Florimell's narrow escapes from disaster are sheer melodrama; they are not self-won or spiritually paid for. She remains novice and ward, living off the dole.

In *The Faerie Queene*, the ability to fend off rape is a prerequisite of the ideal female psyche. We saw how spectacularly Belphoebe and Britomart turn their weapons against lechers male and female. Amoret's inability to defend herself shows she is incomplete. Assaulted by Lust, she shrieks, in a striking display of lack of animal energy, too "feebly" to wake the sleeping Britomart (IV.vii.4). And Amoret is grotesquely defenseless against the sorcerer Busyrane, who binds her to a pillar, slashes open her naked breast, and extracts from "that wide orifice her trembling heart," laying it in a silver basin (III.xii.20–21). This episode, one of the most decadent in *The Faerie Queene*, is a formal spectacle of eroticized masochism. The genital symbolism is lurid and unconcealed. Spenser intensifies the moral ambiguity by using a poetry so deliciously beautiful that the reader is attracted to and emotionally implicated in Busyrane's sadism. Ivory, gold, silver, "skin all snowy cleene" dyed "sanguine red"; fainting tremors, despoiling hands. Amoret, due to her spiritual limitations, may have invoked this morbid scene of martyrdom as an imaginative projection. But the gravest seduction is of our own sensibilities. Spenser, making exquisite aestheticism out of torture and rape, arouses us through the aggressive pagan eye. Amoret's "wide wound" is her passivity but our probing and delectation. Western sex as mental surgery.

Feminine and unarmed, Florimell and Amoret are flagrant targets for attack. Sadism and masochism engender one another in dizzy oscillation. Caught on the swing of the sexual dialectic, the rapist vainly strives to obliterate his opposite. *The Faerie Queene*'s savage circular world of rape is transcended by the higher characters, who internally subsume the chastened extremes of masculine and feminine. Florimell's unmixed femininity makes her unfit for quest. It is her impoverished lack of sexual complexity that allows a knock-off copy of her to be so easily fabricated. The witch-hag makes a "snowy" False Florimell and animates it with an epicene, possibly homosexual evil spirit skilled in female impersonation (III.viii.8). Because of her psychologically embryonic state, Florimell's identity is quickly invaded and occupied by a daemonic hermaphrodite. This too is the knife of Busyrane, the sensual self-wounding of femininity. Spenser's naive rape victims turn up again in Coleridge's *Christabel,* one of the nineteenth century's most influential poems. And they are everywhere in that autoerotic sadist, Emily Dickinson. Neither of these far-reaching effects of Spenserian sex crime has been noted before.

I have been speaking of assaults of male on female. But some of *The Faerie Queene*'s boldest sexual aggressors are the licentious femmes fatales: genitally deformed Duessa (a version of the Whore of Babylon), Acrasia, Phaedria, Malecasta, Hellenore. Manipulative and exploitative, they seek humiliating sexual victory over men. Their greatest power is in womblike closed spaces, in bedchambers, groves, and caves like the leafy grotto of Homer's Calypso, where the male is captured, seduced, and infantilized. Spenser's great word for such places is "bower," both garden and burrow. Embowerment is one of *The Faerie Queene*'s primary processes, a psychological convolution of entrancement, turning the linearity of quest into the uroboros of solipsism.

The Bower of Bliss, wrathfully destroyed by Sir Guyon, is the most lavishly depicted of these female zones, which express the invitation and yet archetypal danger of sex. At the gate, Excess, a "comely dame" in disordered clothes, crushes scrotal grape clusters (a Dionysiac symbol) into a vaginal cup of gold, the male squeezed dry for female pleasure (II.xii.55–56). At the damp heart of the dusky Bower lies Acrasia, hungrily hovering over the dozing knight Verdant, who sprawls enervated and depleted, his weapons abandoned and defaced. Acrasia is a Circean sorceress and vampire: she "through his humid eyes did sucke his spright" (73). This sultry postcoital scene is based on Botticelli's *Venus and Mars,* whose long narrow design signifies the triumph of mother nature's horizontals over the verticals of spiritual ascent (fig. 30).

Spenser's femmes fatales tempt their male victims and paramours away from the pursuit of chivalric honor into "lewd sloth"—languid indolence and passivity (III.v.1) *The Faerie Queene* represents this moral

30. Sandro Botticelli, *Venus and Mars*, 1485–86.

degeneration as dissolution of Apollonian contour. Sinister fogs blanket
the landscape, a Dionysian miasma. Lying down to rest in pretty glades,
Spenser's knights feel their strength flowing away. In *The Faerie Queene*,
the hard Botticellian edge of heroic male will is constantly fighting off
the blurring of female *sfumato*. Spenser is the anatomist of an economy
of sex, of physiological laws of pressure and control, embodied in
images of binding and loosing. The Bower of Bliss is the chthonian
swamp, the matrix of liquid nature. It is inert and opaque, slippery with
onanistic spillage. The bower is an erotic capsulization, a pocketing of
the eye. Apollo's chariot is mired in Dionysian deliquescence. Images
shimmer in our self-generated heat. The Spenserian bower is our libidinous mother-born body, matriarchal property in perpetuity. The rule
of *The Faerie Queene* is: keep moving and stay out of the shade. The
penalty is embowerment, sterile self-thwarting, a limbo of lush pleasures but stultifying passivity.

   The Faerie Queene is the most extended and extensive meditation on
sex in the history of poetry. It charts the entire erotic spectrum, a great
chain of being rising from matter to spirit, from the coarsest lust to
chastity and romantic idealism. The poem's themes of sex and politics
are parallel: the psyche, like society, must be disciplined by good government. Spenser agrees with classical and Christian philosophers on
the primacy of reason over animal appetite. He looks forward to the
Romantic poets, however, in the way that he shows the sex impulse as
innately daemonic and barbaric, breeding witches and sorcerers of evil
allure. Like the *Odyssey*, *The Faerie Queene* is a heroic epic in which the
masculine must evade female traps or delays. But two millennia of rising and falling urban culture intervene since Homer. Spenser ponders
how love is affected by worldly manners, how it is embellished or
distorted by the artificiality of courts. Hence sex in *The Faerie Queene*

reaches extremes of decadent sophistication not present in literature since Roman satire and never in the genre of epic. Marriage is the social regulation and placement of sexual energies, which for Spenser otherwise fall back into the anarchy of nature, ruled by the will-to-power and survival of the fittest. Marriage is the sanctified link between nature and society. Sex in Spenser must always have a social goal.

Spenser's theory of sex is a continuum from the normative to the aberrant. Chastity and fruitful marriage occupy one pole, after which the modalities of eroticism darken toward the perverse and monstrous. First in blame is what we would call recreational sex, heterosexual impulses hedonistically squandered. I elsewhere enumerate incidences of other illicit practices, which make *The Faerie Queene* an encyclopedic catalog of perversions, like Krafft-Ebing's *Psychopathia Sexualis*: not only rape and homosexuality but priapism, nymphomania, exhibitionism, incest, bestiality, necrophilia, fetishism, transvestism, and transsexualism.[11] Above all is a recurrent motif of sadomasochistic sexual bondage. Captivity and enslavement, chains and snares, love as a sickness or wound: Spenser diagnoses these Petrarchan stereotypes as themselves diseased. Literary convention led lovers to confuse sex with self-immolation. Love was corrupted by Freud's death-instinct.

Sexual bondage in *The Faerie Queene* belongs to the larger theme of politics. Hierarchy and ceremony, radiations of the great chain of being and master principles of Renaissance culture, are criminalized in the sexual realm. Bondage is a daemonic antimasque, the uncontrolled sexual fantasy of morally secessionist authoritarians. Another pathological category is flight from sex, either sexual fear or frigidity, which Spenser incorporates in a theory of narcissism that is psychoanalytically pioneering. Dainty self-withholding turns into autoeroticism, a stagnant psychic pool. Personality becomes a prison. On her throne in the House of Pride, Lucifera raptly gazes at herself in a hand-mirror, "And in her selfe-lov'd semblance tooke delight." (I.iv.10). In her rudderless boat, Phaedria eerily laughs and sings to herself, "Making sweet solace to her selfe alone" (II.vi.3). Narcissism is "idleness," a big word in Spenser. In self-love there is no energy of duality and therefore no spiritual progression. Autoeroticism, self-abuse literally and figuratively, inhibits the enlargement and multiplication of emotion in marriage and therefore the investment of psychic energy in the public structures of history.

Voyeurism or scopophilia is one of the most characteristic moods of *The Faerie Queene*. An observer is posted by chance or choice at the perimeter of a voluptuous sexual scene, to which he plays peeping Tom.

Voyeuristic elements are present in the episodes of Phedon and Phi-lemon, where a squire is made to watch a sexual charade defaming his bride (II.iv.). They are rampant in the Bower of Bliss, where Cymochles peruses a bevy of half-naked damsels, ogling them through deceptively half-closed lids; where bathing lady wrestlers expose themselves to the distinctly interested Guyon; and where flimsily clad Acrasia fastens "her false eyes" on drowsy Verdant, a scene repeated in the tapestry of Venus and Adonis in Castle Joyous (II.v.32–34, xii.73; III.i.34–37). At Malbecco's banquet, Hellenore and Paridell arouse each other by bra-zen eye contact and a lewd sexual theater of spilled wine, a voyeurism to resurface in their host's plight as a hidden spectator at the debauchment of his wife, who is pleasurably mounted by a satyr nine times in one night (III.ix, x). Sleeping Serena is inspected by a tribe of cannibals, who seat themselves like an audience and judiciously weigh the merits of each appetizing part of her body (VI.viii). On Mount Acidale, Sir Cal-idore stumbles on the dazzling scene of a hundred naked maidens dancing in a ring, Spenser's supreme symbol for the harmony of nature and art (VI.x). In the *Cantos of Mutabilitie*, Faunus is punished for witnessing Diana at her bath (VII.vi.42–55). Cumulatively, these epi-sodes in Spenser surely inspired the voyeuristic spying of Milton's Satan on Adam and Eve in the Garden of Eden, a detail not in the Bible (*P.L.* IV, IX).

The voyeurism of *The Faerie Queene*, endangering the poem itself, arises from the problem of sensuous beauty, which can lead the soul toward good or evil. C. S. Lewis was the first to apply the term "skep-tophilia" (his spelling) to Spenser's Bower of Bliss, but criticism did not follow it up.[12] G. Wilson Knight rightly calls the poem "perilously near decadence": "*The Faerie Queene* is itself one vast Bower of Bliss."[13] I would go even further: the poetically strongest and most fully realized material in *The Faerie Queene* is pornographic. Spenser, like Blake's Milton, may be of the devil's party without knowing it. In a paradox cherished by Sade and Baudelaire, the presence of moral law or taboo intensifies the pleasure of sexual transgression and the luxury of evil. A great poet always has profound ambivalences and obscurities of motiva-tion, which criticism has scarcely begun to study in this case.

The Faerie Queene is didactic but also self-pleasuring. In the midst of dissipation and atrocity, we hear a voice saying "Ain't it awful!" Scholar-ship's major error, incredible in this century of the New Critical doctrine of persona, has been to identify that voice with the poet. *The Faerie Queene* is contrapuntal. There is an ethical voice and a wanton voice, dissolving the other into lust by its delicacy and splendor, its hypnotic appeals to the untamed pagan eye. Voyeurism is the relation of this poet to this poem. It is the relation of every reader to every novel, of every spectator to every painting, play, and film. It is present in our study of biography and history, and even in our conversations about others.

Voyeurism is the amoral aesthetic of the aggressive western eye. It is the cloud of contemplation that enwraps us as sexual personae, transporting us unseen across space and time. Christianity, far from putting out the pagan eye, merely expanded its power. Christianity's vast tracts of the forbidden are virgin territory for the pagan eye to penetrate and defile. *The Faerie Queene* is a massively original analysis of these tensions in western culture. Criticism assumes that what Spenser says is what he means. But a poet is not always master of his own poem, for imagination can overwhelm moral intention. This is what happens in Coleridge's *Christabel.* But I think Spenser far more cunning and conscious of his teasing ambiguities. His favorite erotic trope is half-revealed white female flesh, glimpsed through ripped or parted garments. *The Faerie Queene* often becomes what it condemns, nowhere more overtly than in its voyeurism, in which both poet and reader are deeply implicated.

The Faerie Queene's decadent aesthetics reflect the Apollonian hierarchism of the Renaissance court world. Spenserian pornography is always sexual spectacle, a ceremonial tableau or procession. Formality creates perversity. Before Amoret slashed by Busyrane, there is the suicide Amavia, whom Guyon finds still-conscious with a knife in her riven "white alabaster brest." "Purple gore" stains her garments, the "grassy ground" and "cleane waves" of a bubbling fountain, and finally the cruelly playing hands of "a lovely babe." Beside her is the corpse of the knight Mortdant, bloody but smiling and, according to the poem, still sexually irresistible (II.i.39–41). Proud Mirabella, having tormented her admirers and laughed at their sufferings and death, is now punished by being whipped along by Scorn, who laughs in turn at her cries (VI.vii). Artegall finds a headless lady, murdered by her knight Sir Sanglier, who is now forced to carry her dead head as a penalty (V.i). The iron man, Talus, chops off and nails up the gold hands and silver feet of beautiful Munera or self-worshipping money (V.ii). As in Michelangelo's "Captives" and *ignudi,* allegory has gone to hell.

Such combinations in Spenser of beauty, laughter, sex, torture, mutilation, and death are emotionally startling and ethically problematic. I find but one precedent: Boccaccio's tale of Nastagio degli Onesti in the *Decameron.* A haughty woman rejects and gloats over her suffering lover, who commits suicide. For eternity, they are condemned to pursuit and flight. Whenever he catches her, he kills her. He slits her back, tears out her "hard, cold heart," and feeds it and her entrails to dogs. Then she springs to life, and the chase resumes. Nastagio, courting his own proud maiden, lays a banquet in a pine grove, so that the guests and his callous beloved may witness "the massacre of the cruel lady."[14] Bon appétit! Botticelli's workshop painted this savage, salacious tale, presumably to his design. A black knight on a black steed waves his rapier at a nude woman, who in weirdly conflated scenes runs through the forest and lies on her face, her back being sliced open. A second panel shows the festive banqueters witnessing the bloody capture, as the lady's white buttock and thigh are seized at table height by toothy mastiffs. The Spenserian decadence in Boccaccio's tale is produced by the coolness and casualness of the detached eye, which treats sex and violence like art. Eye and object are positioned precisely as in modern cinema.

Spenserian cinema is ritualized sexual perception. We feel the poet's own connoisseurship everywhere in *The Faerie Queene*. It is probably the source of the erotic overtones in Glauce's bedroom massage of Britomart and in Princess Claribell's bizarre reunion with her long-lost Pastorella, where mother jumps daughter and rips her bodice open (VI.xii.19). Connoisseurship, as we will see in nineteenth-century aestheticism and Decadence, is the dominance of the intellectualized eye. *The Faerie Queene* is like a stunt film substituting a satirical soundtrack for the real one. A sermonizing voice earnestly comments on disturbing or pornographic images. But the eye in Spenser always wins.

The Faerie Queene is pulled in two directions, one Protestant, one pagan. Spenser wants good to come out of noble action. But sexual personae have a will of their own. The spectral sex signs of western art are vaunting creatures of hostility and egotism. *The Faerie Queene*'s harsh clangor of combat is our native music. Spenser's contradictions are uneasiest in his nature theory. He glorifies woman, but her body is a morass in which action is lost. Spenser is poetry's first master of daemonic image. The ambivalent bower theme that he bequeathed to his successors would make English literature supreme. It makes all the difference, for example, between Rousseau and Wordsworth. Spenser asks of fertile nature, should we resist or yield to it? *The Faerie Queene* opposes the armoured to the embowered woman. Spenser's myth of benevolent fertility ties him to Keats. But in his broodings upon the secrets of nature, paralleled in the Renaissance only by Leonardo, he is disquieted and indecisive. His Gardens of Adonis, a creative womb-world with female mount and odorous dripping boughs, are another male prison.

Britomart's shiny armour and Belphoebe's Byzantine glitter are attempts to polish and perfect the eye and keep it free. Spenser longs for an Apollonian woman. To make everything visible: we saw that ambition in homosexual Greek classicism. The long cinematic sightlines of *The Faerie Queene* create a clear, articulate pagan space. Spenser turns medieval allegory into pagan ostentation. Scheduled moral meanings barely survive this apotheosis of the pagan eye. Spenser's pictorialism is a compulsive Apollonian thing-making. And the most glamourous of these made things is the female warrior, who combats fallen nature, where the vampire drains maleness and the rapist annihilates femaleness. Spenser's aristocratic Amazons, Belphoebe and Britomart, renouncing dominance in the boudoir and masochistic vulnerability in the field, carry the western eye to Apollonian victory.

7

Shakespeare and Dionysus

As You Like It and Antony and Cleopatra

Spenser's initial heavy impact upon English literature was in the 1590s, just when Shakespeare was developing his style. Shakespeare's two early long poems, *Venus and Adonis* and *The Rape of Lucrece* (1592, 1593-94) are homages to Spenser. The first is about sensual embowerment in female nature, its legend of dominant goddess and kidnapped pretty boy borrowed straight from *The Faerie Queene*. The second is a lurid account of a politically pivotal rape from early Roman history. Shakespeare slows down the sexual cinema of Spenser's rape cycle to an arousing frame-by-frame inspection of the assailant's invasion of bedroom, bed, and white body. Spenser's sophisticated amalgam of prurience and moralism is adroitly duplicated. But Shakespeare had to throw off Spenser in order to get on with his own creative mission. His struggle against Spenser produced, I would argue, the titanism of the greatest plays, in which Shakespeare pushes into new ground beyond Spenser's reach. I see *Titus Andronicus* (1592-94), long thought Shakespeare's weakest play, as a devastating parody of Spenser. It has usually been misread (though not by A. C. Hamilton) as slipshod bad taste. But this Roman drama of rape and mutilation turns the Spenserian rape cycle into slapstick comedy. It is hilariously, intentionally funny. The ravished Lavinia doggedly persists in waving her "stumps" about like a windmill. Like Wilde's Apollonian *The Importance of Being Earnest*, *Titus Andronicus* should be played by romping drag queens, so that its outrageous mannerisms clearly emerge. This play is Shakespeare's taunting farewell to Spenser. He is about to launch his own original explorations of love and gender. In *Titus Andronicus* Shakespeare tries to fix and reduce Spenser, in order to pin him down and get past him. Lavinia's endlessly stressed amputated tongue and hands are Atalanta's balls, blood-red herrings tossed along the racetrack of the Muses.

Spenser is an iconicist, Shakespeare a dramaturge. Spenser is ruled by the eye, Shakespeare by the ear. Spenser is an Apollonian, presenting his personae in a linear series of epiphanies, carved out by the Botticellian hard edge. He makes tableaux, episodic vignettes, so loosely connected by plot that no one can ever remember what happens when. I see *The Faerie Queene*'s processional technique of short dramatic tableaux of high-colored sexual personae repeated in D. H. Lawrence's *Women in Love*, with its overt Apollonian-Dionysian theme. Shakespeare is a metamorphosist and therefore closer to Dionysus than to Apollo. He shows *process*, not objects. Everything is in flux—thought, language, identity, action. He enormously expands the inner life of his personae and sets them into the huge fateful rhythm which is his plot, an overwhelming force entering the play from beyond society. Shakespeare's elemental energy comes from nature itself. I think this remark by G. Wilson Knight the most brilliant thing ever said about Shakespeare's plays: "In such poetry we are aware less of any surface than of a turbulent power, a heave and swell, from deeps beyond verbal definition; and, as the thing progresses, a gathering of power, a ninth wave of passion, an increase in tempo and intensity."[1] The sea, Dionysian liquid nature, is the master image in Shakespeare's plays. It is the wave-motion within Shakespearean speech which transfixes the audience even when we don't understand a word of it.

Spenser's medieval language is archaic, backward-looking. By reversing contemporary changes in language, he means to halt the giddy changes in Renaissance personae. His Apollonian personalities are historically retrograde. Epic is always a genre of nostalgia. Spenser, like Vergil, turns to epic at a moment of sudden anarchic multiplication of sexual personae. We will see Blake similarly responding to the psychological crisis which is Romanticism. Multiplicity of persona, random role-experimentation, is always evil in *The Faerie Queene*. Positive Spenserian hermaphroditism is never fluid and improvisational, as it is in Shakespeare, but rather formalized, frozen, and emblematic, as in Britomart's phallic spear or the Isis idol's "long white slender wand" (V.vii.7). Shakespeare responds to Spenser's archaism with dynamic futurism. The sixteenth century transformed Middle English into modern English. Grammar was up for grabs. People made up vocabulary and syntax as they went along. Not until the eighteenth century would rules of English usage appear. Shakespearean language is a bizarre super-tongue, alien and plastic, twisting, turning, and forever escaping.

It is untranslatable, since it knocks Anglo-Saxon root words against Norman and Greco-Roman importations sweetly or harshly, kicking us up and down rhetorical levels with witty abruptness. No one in real life ever spoke like Shakespeare's characters. His language does not "make sense," especially in the greatest plays. Anywhere from a third to a half of every Shakespearean play, I conservatively estimate, will always remain under an interpretative cloud. Unfortunately, this fact is obscured by the encrustations of footnotes in modern texts, which imply to the poor cowed student that if only he knew what the savants do, all would be clear as day. Every time I open *Hamlet*, I am stunned by its hostile virtuosity, its elusiveness and impenetrability. Shakespeare uses language to darken. He mesmerizes by disorienting us. He suspends the traditional compass-points of rhetoric, still quite firm in Marlowe, normally regarded as Shakespeare's main influence. Shakespeare's words have "aura." This he got from Spenser, not Marlowe. Spenser's daemonic imagery turns into turmoil and hallucination in Shakespeare. Shakespeare's language hovers at the very threshold of dreaming. It is shaped by the irrational. Shakespearean characters are controlled by rather than controlling their speech. They are like Michelangelo's Mannerist sculptures, restive under night visitations. Consciousness in Shakespeare is soaked in primal compulsion.

Language and personae mirror each other in both Spenser and Shakespeare. The archaizing language of *The Faerie Queene* is analogous to the Apollonian unity of its armoured personalities. Belphoebe and Britomart have one line of thought, as they have one line of action. They are not besieged by fantasy or mood, by the rising torrent of imagination surging through Shakespeare's major characters. The cool, tensionless consistency of identity of Spenser's godly Una ("Accept therefore my simple selfe"; I.viii.27) appears in Shakespeare only in helpless maidens like Ophelia, Cordelia, and Desdemona, who are destroyed by their plays. In *Antony and Cleopatra*, the Una-like Octavia comes off as a party-pooper and stick-in-the-mud compared to Shakespeare's loquacious firebrand heroine. Octavia's reticence and feminine whispers affront the genre of drama, which is all voice. But in *The Faerie Queene*, we saw, epiphanic Apollonian silence rules. Language is truncated or abbreviated for virtue's sake. In Spenser, action speaks louder than words. Significantly, the decadent Bower of Bliss is cacophonous, a confusion of "birds, voices, instruments, winds, waters" (II.xii.70). This resembles Plutarch's description of the wheeling nature-metamorphoses of Dionysus.

That proteanism is evil in *The Faerie Queene* accounts for Spenser's puzzling portrayal of Proteus as a cruel tyrant and rapist.[2] Shakespeare, on the other hand, is proteanism personified. Coleridge calls him "the one Proteus of the fire and the flood."[3] Multiplicity of personae, afflicting Hamlet but magnifying Rosalind and Cleopatra, is a major principle in his plays, just as multiplicity of language is his poetic style. Voice is so primary in Shakespeare that costumes and time-schemes may be radically altered, as they are in modern productions, without affecting the higher meanings of the drama. But strict authenticity of costume is crucial to Spenser's iconistic personae. Put Belphoebe in a tennis dress or Regency chemise, and all is lost. Apollonian armature is not the rotating wheel of fashion. It is hard and eternal. In Spenser, I showed, chastity *is* integrity of form. But Shakespeare's characters are forever changing their clothes, especially in the comedies. Shakespeare takes the inherited theme of mistaken identity, as old as Menander and Plautus, and turns it into a meditation on Renaissance role-playing. He is the first to reflect upon the fluid nature of modern gender and identity.

Accordingly, Shakespeare is impatient with objets d'art, unlike the eye-obsessed pictorialist, Spenser. We see this as early as *Venus and Adonis*, where Shakespeare's goddess speaks of sullen Adonis as a "lifeless picture, cold and senseless stone, / Well-painted idol, image dull and dead, / Statue contenting but the eye alone" (211–13). Wherever art works appear in Shakespeare—Viola grieving like "Patience on a monument," Octavia as "a statue rather than a breather," Hermione as a statue brought to life—they are usually symptoms of some emotional lapse or deficiency, of the callous abandonment of good, usually by blameworthy males. Cold objectification is lofty in Spenser, but in Shakespeare it is an obstruction to the free flow of psychic energy. Shakespeare's resculptured rapee, Lavinia, may be the ultimate Spenserian mute. Shakespeare rejects Spenserian hieraticism. Stasis is a danger on stage, where it slows the propulsiveness of dramatic plot. Every slighting reference to the visual arts in Shakespeare is a pointed rebuke to Spenser. Spenserian aesthetics are cunningly evoked at odd moments, as in Macbeth's gorgeous description of the murdered king, "his silver skin laced with his golden blood" (II.iii.112). Shakespeare puts Spenser's glittering Byzantine iconicism into a traitor's mouth. The essence of Shakespeare is not the objet d'art but the metaphor. Metaphors are the key to character, the imaginative center of every speech. They spill from line to line, abundant, florid, illogical. They are Shakespeare's dream-vehicle of Dionysian metamorphosis. The teeming metaphors are the objects of the medieval great chain of being suddenly unstacked and released into vitalistic free movement. Shakespeare's metaphors, like his sexual personae, flicker through a rolling stream of development and process. Nothing in Shakespeare stays the same for long.

If Spenser is a pictorialist, Shakespeare is an alchemist. In his treatment of sex and personality, Shakespeare is a shape-shifter and master of transformations. He returns dramatic impersonation to its ritual origins in the cult of Dionysus, where masks were magic. Shakespeare recognizes that western identity, in its long pagan line, *is* impersonation. Kenneth Burke calls role in drama "salvation via change or purification of identity (purification in either the moral or chemical sense)."[4] The pattern of chemical breakdown, remixture of elements, and composition of new personality is clear in *King Lear*, where the protagonist is set to the boil on a stormy heath. Alchemy, which began in Hellenistic Egypt, entered the Middle Ages through Arabic texts and remained influential throughout the Renaissance. Its esoteric symbolism was a matter of literate common knowledge down to the seventeenth century, when science took over its terms and techniques. There is debate about how much alchemical lore survived the Renaissance and was transmitted to the founders of Romanticism. That Coleridge was influenced by German commentary on the subject seems certain.

Alchemy, like astrology, has been stigmatized at its worst rather than remembered at its best. It was not just a mercenary scrabble for a formula to turn lead to gold. It was a philosophical quest for the creative secrets of nature. Mind and matter were linked, in the pagan way. Alchemy is pagan naturism. Titus Burckhardt says alchemy's spiritual aim was "the achievement of 'inward silver' or 'inward gold'—in their immutable purity and luminosity."[5] Jung speaks of alchemy as not only "the mother of chemistry" but "the forerunner of our modern psychology of the unconscious."[6] Jack Lindsay sees alchemy prefiguring all scientific and anthropological "concepts of development and evolution."[7] The alchemical process sought to transform the *prima materia*, or chaos of mutable substances, into the eternal and incorruptible "Philosopher's Stone." This perfected entity was depicted as an androgyne, a *rebis* ("double thing"). Both the primal matrix and the finished product were hermaphroditic, because they contained all four basic elements, earth, water, air, and fire. The self-contained magnum opus of alchemical process was symbolized by the uroboros, the self-begetting, self-devouring serpent. The synthesis of contraries in the watery "bath" of the *opus* was a *hierosgamos* or *coniunctio* ("sacred marriage" or "union"), a "chymical wedding" of male and female. This pair appeared as brother and sister in incestuous intercourse. The terminology of incest is everywhere in alchemy, betraying its implicit pagan character. Romanticism's incest themes may bear this ancient history.

The alchemists gave the name "Mercurius" to an allegorical hermaphrodite constituting all or part of the process. Mercurius, the god and planet, is liquid mercury or quicksilver, the elixir of transformations. Arthur Edward Waite says, "*Universal Mercury* is the animating spirit diffused throughout the universe."[8] Mercurius is my name for one of the most fascinating and restless western sexual personae. We earlier traced the idea of the "mercurial" to crafty, wing-footed Hermes. My Mercurius, first conceived by Shakespeare, is the androgynous spirit of impersonation, the living embodiment of multiplicity of persona. Mercurius possesses verbal and therefore mental power. Shakespeare's great Mercurius androgyne is the transvestite Rosalind and after her the male-willed Cleopatra. The main characteristic is an electric wit, dazzling, triumphant, euphoric, combined with rapid alternations of persona. Lesser examples are Goethe's Mignon, Jane Austen's Emma, and Tolstoy's Natasha. Lady Caroline Lamb, Byron's tempestuous mistress, will be our real-life example of the negative or afflicted Mercurius. At their most stagy and manipulative, Katharine Hepburn as Tracy Lord in *The Philadelphia Story* and Vivien Leigh as Scarlett O'Hara in *Gone with the Wind* are the riveting Mercurius. Above all is Patrick Dennis' breezy Auntie Mame, lavish practitioner of multiple personae, whose cult status among male homosexuals is the unmistakable sign of her cross-sexual character.

Shakespeare is the most prolific single contributor to that parade of sexual personae which is western art. The liberated woman, I said, is the symbol of the English Renaissance, as the beautiful boy is of the Italian. In Shakespeare, liberated woman speaks, irrepressibly. Wit, as Jacob Burckhardt suggests, is a concomitant of the new "free personality" of the Renaissance.[9] Western wit, culminating in Oscar Wilde, is aggressive and competitive. It is an aristocratic language of social maneuvering and sexual display. The English and the French jointly created this hard style, for which there are few parallels in the Far East, where cultivated humor tends to be mild and diffuse. *The Faerie Queene*'s arms and armour turn into wit in Shakespeare's Renaissance Amazons. Rosalind, the young heroine of *As You Like It* (1599–1600), is one of the most original characters of Renaissance literature, capsulizing the era's psychological changes. The play's source is Thomas Lodge's prose romance, *Rosalynde or Euphues' Golden Legacy* (1590), which contains most of the plot. But Shakespeare makes the story a fantasia upon western personality. He enlarges and complicates Rosalind's character by giving her wit, audacity, and masculine force. Rosalind is Shakespeare's answer to Spenser's Belphoebe and Britomart, whom he spins into verbal and psychological motion. Rosalind is kinetic rather than iconistic. She too is a virgin. Indeed, her exhilarating freshness depends on that virginity. But Shakespeare removes Amazonian virginity from its holy self-sequestration and puts it into social engagement. Rosalind, unlike the high-minded Belphoebe and Britomart, has fun. She inhabits newly reclaimed secular space.

In her transvestite adventure, Rosalind seems to resemble Viola of Shakespeare's *Twelfth Night*, but temperamentally, the two women are completely unalike. In her authority over the other characters, Rosalind surpasses all of Shakespeare's comic heroines. Productions of *As You Like It* rarely show this. Intrepid Rosalind is usually reduced to Viola, and both parts are marred by summer-camp pastoral sentimentality. Rosalind's whole meaning is lyricism of personality *without* sentimentality. These roles, written for boy actors, have ambiguities of tone which modern actresses suppress. The androgynous Rosalind is prettified and demasculinized. Shakespeare's Portia is momentarily transvestite in *The Merchant of Venice*, where she wears a lawyer's robe for one act. But Portia's is not a complete sexual persona; that is, the play's other characters do not respond to him/her erotically. Rosalind and Viola are sexual instigators, the cause of irksome romantic errors. In many tales available to Shakespeare, a disguised woman inspires another woman's unhappy love. Most such stories were Italian, influenced by classical models, like Ovid's Iphis. The Italian tales, like their English prose counterparts, imitate the droll Ovidian manner of sexual innuendo. *As You Like It* and *Twelfth Night* depart from their sources in avoiding bedchamber intrigue. Shakespeare is interested in psychology, not pornography.

Both Rosalind and Viola adopt male clothing in crisis, but Viola's predicament is grimmer. She is orphaned and shipwrecked. Rosalind, on the other hand, banished by her usurper uncle, elects a male persona as whim and escapade. Both heroines choose sexually ambiguous alter egos. Viola is Cesario, a eunuch, and Rosalind Ganymede (as in Lodge), the beautiful boy kidnapped by Zeus. Rosalind is brasher than Viola from the start, arming herself with swashbuckling cutlass and boar-spear. Viola, with her frail court rapier. makes a girlish and delicate boy at best. She is timid and easily terrorized. Rosalind relishes trouble and even creates it, as in her malicious meddling in the Sylvius-Phebe romance. When Olivia falls in love with her, Viola feels compassion toward this victim of her sexual illusion. But Rosalind is incapable of compassion where her own direct interest is not at stake. She can be hard, disdainful. Rosalind's lack of conventional feminine tenderness is part of her lofty power as a sexual persona. There is intimidation in her, uncaught by modern productions. Unlike Viola, Rosalind acts and conspires and laughs at the consequences.

Twelfth Night's plot resolution depends on the mechanistic device of twins. Viola surrenders her uncomfortable male role to a convenient brother, who uncomplainingly steps into her place in Olivia's affections. *As You Like It*, however, is centered on the more ambiguous Rosalind, who subsumes both twins within her nature. Viola is melancholy, recessive, but Rosalind is exuberant and egotistical, with a flamboyant instinct for center stage. The difference is clearest at play's end. Viola falls into long silence, keeping the joy of reunion to herself. Her decorous self-removal is the opposite of Rosalind's lordly capture of the finale of *As You Like It*. Dominating her play better than her father has dominated his own realm, Rosalind asserts her innate aristocratic authority.

Shakespeare rings his double-sexed heroines with rippling circles of sexual ambiguity. Olivia's infatuation with Viola/Cesario is as suspicious as that of Spenser's Malecasta with Britomart, for the disguised Viola strikes everyone as feminine in voice and appearance. *Twelfth Night* begins with Duke Orsino savoring his sexual submission to the indifferent Olivia, whom he describes with outmoded Petrarchan metaphors of coldness and cruelty. Since the narcissistic Orsino is of dubious masculinity, Viola's ardor for him is problematic. In both *Twelfth Night* and *As You Like It*, the transvestite heroines fall for men far inferior to them. Even feminine Viola has sexual peculiarities. L. G. Salingar says of Viola and her precursors in the play's Roman and Italian sources, she is "the only one to fall in love *after* assuming her disguise."[10] So Viola falls in love not as a woman but as an androgyne. That she senses and esteems Orsino's half-feminine state is suggested in a covert confession of love where she casts him fleetingly as a woman (II.iv.23–28). Conveying Orsino's masochistic endearments to the arrogant Olivia, Viola is an androgyne bearing a hermaphroditic message from one androgyne to another. Violas transports Orsino's residual maleness before Olivia, where it radiates as an amatory promise seeming to come from Viola herself. Thus Viola's official mission further masculinizes her. Richard Bernheimer speaks of personality as a vehicle of representation by diplomats and attorneys: in "the fascination of his presence," deputy may eclipse employer.[11] The fetching Viola is a conflation of sexual representations. She represents Orsino but also, as Cesario, she represents a male. *Twelfth Night* relativizes gender and identity by this masque-like succession of representations. The principal characters become androgynous echoes of one another.

Like his counterpart in *Twelfth Night*, the male lead of *As You Like It* has severe dramatic shortcomings. Orlando, with whom Rosalind instantly falls in love, is adolescent-looking, barely bearded. Shakespeare undercuts his athletic prowess by making him the butt of constant jokes. The slow-witted Orlando is an unimpressive exponent of his sex in a play ruled by a vigorous heroine. Bertrand Evans calls him "only a sturdy booby."[12] Like Orsino, Orlando is more manipulated than manipulating. There may be a homoerotic element in his prompt consent to Rosalind/Ganymede's transsexual game. In *As You Like It*, Shakespeare reduces the Renaissance prestige of male authority to maximize his heroine's princely potency. Rosalind is intellectually and emotionally superior, sweeping all the characters into her sexual orbit. There is a lesbian suggestiveness in Phebe's infatuation with the disguised Rosalind, whose prettiness she dwells on and savors (III.v.113–23). Rosalind as a boy is, in Oliver's words, "fair, of female favor" (IV.iii.86–87). Her maleness is glamourously half-female.

The childhood liaison of Rosalind and Celia is also homoerotic. Shakespeare puts the girls into emotional alignment from the first moment Rosalind is mentioned and before she has even appeared. "Never two ladies loved as they do"; they have been "coupled and inseparable," even sleeping together (I.i.109, iii.71–74). This amorously exclusive friendship functions in the first act as a structural counterpoise to the adult marriages of the last act, which ends in a vision of the wedding god. In an essay on the use of "you" and "thou" in *As You Like It*, Angus McIntosh remarks that "you" often carries "an overtone of disgust and annoyance." After they encounter Orlando in the Forest of Arden, Celia, with "a note of huffiness," begins to "you" Rosalind, indicating "the intrusion of Orlando into the cosiness of their hitherto undisturbed relationship."[13] I find evidence of Celia's jealousy even in the first act, when Rosalind hangs back to compliment Orlando and Celia says sharply, "Will you go, coz?" (I.ii.245). In the forest, Rosalind tries to get Celia to play the priest and marry her to the duped Orlando. "I cannot say the words," Celia replies (IV.i.121). She must be prodded three times before she can bring herself to give away the bride. That Shakespeare intends this subtext of sexual tension seems proved by the fact that in his source in Lodge it is the Celia character who merrily invents and urges on the sham wedding ceremony.

Because of the premodern prestige of virginity, the union of Rosalind and Celia is surely emotional and not overtly sexual. Their intimacy is that female matrix I found in Britomart's bond to her nurse. In *As You Like It* the matrix is an early stage of primary narcissism from which emerge the adult heterosexual commitments of the finale. Midway through the play, Rosalind exclaims, "But what talk we of fathers when there is such a man as Orlando?" (III.iv.35–36). Family and childhood alliances must yield to the new world of marriage. This is a characteristic English Renaissance movement: exogamy reinforces the social structure. Rosalind undergoes a process of increasing sexual differentiation. She splits from Celia by psychic mitosis. Their friendship is an all-in-all of gender, a solace for that motherlessness which Shakespeare curiously imposes on his maidens, leaving them defenseless in *Hamlet* and *Othello*. At the end of *As You Like It*, Rosalind and Celia sacrifice their relationship to take up the fixed sex roles of marriage. A choice is made, not necessarily inevitable. Hugh Richmond was, to my knowledge, the first critic to freely admit Rosalind's "capacity for bisexuality."[14] Unlike Viola, Rosalind is borderline. She could go either way. One of the unnoticed themes of *As You Like It* is Rosalind's temptation toward her outlaw male extreme and her overcoming of it to enter the larger social order. She is distinctly flirtatious in her prank with Phebe. Rosalind as Ganymede pretends to be a rakish lady-killer and, at her assumption of that sexual persona, actually becomes one. A superb language of arrogant command suddenly flows from her (III.v.35ff.). She is all sex and power. It is a complex psychological response to erotic opportunity, which she may or may not consciously recognize. In the scene in Spenser where she romances the dismayed Amoret, Britomart's actions are divorced from her thoughts, which are on her future husband. So Spenser and Shakespeare prefigure the modern theory of the unconscious, which Freud said was invented by the Romantic poets. Britomart and Rosalind drift into an involuntary realm of lesbian courtship. Male disguise elicits wayward impulses from the socially repressed side of their sexual nature.

Are there any fixed coordinates for masculinity and femininity in Shakespeare's transvestite comedies? Commentary on sex-differences can be fatuous, as in Orsino's pontifications. Rosalind's maxims on the sexes are usually satirical. In these plays, clothes make the man. By fixing the social persona, costume transforms thought, behavior, and gender. The one distinction between male and female seems to be combat ability. Viola is afraid to duel, and Rosalind faints at the sight of blood. Viola's twin, Sebastian, on the other hand, is hot-tempered and slaps people around. So Shakespeare gives men a physical genius that will out. Aside from this, Shakespeare seems to view masculinity and femininity as masks to put on and take off. He makes remarkably few allusions to sexual anatomy here: in the two plays I find one explicit remark and two or three puns. Viola, quailing at a duel, cries, "A little thing would make me tell them how much I lack of a man" (III.iv.313–15). Man minus "little thing" equals woman. Rosalind's resolve to "suit me all points like a man" hints at the obvious qualification that one male point isn't ordinarily available to army supply (I.iii.114). A clown parodies Orlando's love verse: "He that sweetest rose will find / Must find love's prick, and Rosalind" (III.ii.111–12) To consummate his love for Rosalind, the moping Orlando must recover his manly autonomy. Like Artegall in drag, he must straighten up and take charge. Second, Rosalind as rose is both flower and thorn. Disguised as an armed male, she has dual sexual attributes, the phallic "love's prick" as well as the female genital "rose." One expects more bawdiness in cross-dressing Renaissance imbroglios. In a source of *Twelfth Night*, Barnabe Rich's *Of Apolonius and Silla* (1581), Silvio, Viola's precursor, reveals her sex at the end by "loosing his garments down to his stomach," showing "his breasts and pretty teats." An arresting moment in boudoir reading, ill fit for the stage! Shakespeare's treatment of sexual ambiguity is remarkably chaste.

Shakespeare's characters often fail to read the correct sex of their colleagues or even to recognize their own lovers onstage. The motif of twins mistaken for one another comes from Plautus and Terence, who took it from Greek New Comedy. But in classical drama, the twins are the same sex. The Renaissance, with its attraction for the androgynous, altered the theme to opposite-sex twins. As if sparked by the zeitgeist, Shakespeare managed to father boy-and-girl twins. The use of virtuoso boy actors in all female roles conditioned Elizabethan playgoers to a suspension of sexual disbelief. The textual ambiguities of the transvestite comedies would be heightened by the presence of boys in the lead roles. The epilogue to *As You Like It*, which some think not by Shakespeare, demands audience recognition of the theatrical transsexualism. The actor playing Rosalind comes forward in female dress and addresses the audience: "If I were a woman, I would kiss as many of you as had beards that pleased me." A touch of male homosexual coquetry. At the end of performance, modern female impersonators similarly step out from the dramatic frame, revealing their real sex by tearing off wig and brassiere or emerging in tuxedo. Male portrayal of female roles in Elizabethan theater was inherently more homoerotic than the same custom in Greece or Japan. Greek actors wore wooden masks; Japanese Kabuki employs heavy schematic makeup. Greek and Japanese actors could be any age. But Elizabethan theater used beardless boys, probably with wigs and some makeup. But there were no masks. A boy had to be facially feminine enough to pass as a woman. The erotic piquancy must surely have led to claques of groupies, like those dogging the castrati of Italian opera.

Earlier, I spoke of the androgynous beauty of adolescent boys and the religious purity of their singing voices. The boy-angel inhabiting the stage Rosalind added his own hermaphroditism to an already sexually complex role. *As You Like It* and *Twelfth Night* played by boys would be shimmering spectacles of the mystery of gender. The quality of spectacle is evident in the last act of *Twelfth Night*, where the twins protract the traditional recognition scene to hypnotic length, a technique of cinematic slow motion I found in Shakespeare's *Rape of Lucrece*. London's National Theatre attempted an all-male production of *As You Like It* in 1967, the costumes Sixties mod. The director sought "an atmosphere of spiritual purity."[15] The episode where Rosalind as Ganymede induces Orlando to mock-woo her would specially benefit from such idealizing treatment, for it is a dazzling series of impersonations: we see a boy playing a girl playing a boy playing a girl. A reviewer said this production was "as simple, stylised and, in fact, as cold as a Noh play." Still, these actors were young adults, not boys. Roger Baker claims boys as Rosalind and Viola would be "really unnerving": "Boys can act with a natural gravity and grace."[16] Transvestite boys, we saw, led the Greek sacred procession of the Dionysian Oschophoria. Their unmasked presence on the Elizabethan stage reproduced the archaic ritualism and cultism of early drama.

Like Michelangelo's poetry, Shakespeare's sonnets are addressed to two love-objects, a baffling forceful woman and a beautiful boy. The unidentified fair youth was evidently highly androgynous in appearance. Shakespeare calls him "angel," "sweet boy," "beauteous and lovely youth" (144, 108, 54). Most blatant is Sonnet 20, where Shakespeare calls the youth his "master mistress" and says he has "a woman's face" and "a woman's gentle heart." Meaning him to be a woman, Nature "fell a-doting" and mistakenly added a penis. This is like Phaedrus' drunken Prometheus getting human genitals wrong. Sonnet 20 anticipates modern hormonal theory, where a fetus with male genitalia may retain female brain chemistry, producing an inner conviction of womanhood and a longing to change sex. The youth of Sonnet 20 is a hermaphrodite, facially and emotionally female but with the sexual superfluity of a penis—from which Shakespeare explicitly abstains. I suspect Shakespeare, like Michelangelo, was a Greek homosexual idealist who did not necessarily seek physical relations with men. G. Wilson Knight says Shakespeare's sonnets express "the recognition in his adored boy of a bisexual strength-with-grace" and identifies this view with Plato's, calling it "the seraphic intuition." Knight writes brilliantly about erotic idealism, which transforms libidinal energy into aesthetic vision, "a flooded consciousness": "You must have a maximum of ardour with a minimum of possible accomplishment, so that desire is forced into eye and mind to create."[17]

The beautiful boy belongs to the sonnets and must remain there. He cannot enter the plays. Rosalind is the beautiful boy reimagined in social terms. References to homosexuality are rare in Shakespeare's plays. There may be homosexual overtones to Iago's behavior in *Othello* and Leontes' in *The Winter's Tale* or to Antonio's devotion to Sebastian in *Twelfth Night* and Patroclus' to Achilles in *Troilus and Cressida*. But Shakespeare never dwells on homosexuality or constructs a play or major character around it like his contemporary Marlowe, who opens *Dido, Queen of Carthage* with Jupiter "dandling Ganymede upon his knee" and *Edward the Second* with the king's male lover reading a mash note in the street. That play ends with the anal execution of the homosexual king with a red-hot poker.

I see in Shakespeare a segregation by genre, which diverts homosexuality into lyric and keeps it out of drama. I spoke of the Greek-invented beautiful boy as an Apollonian androgyne, silent and solipsistic. He is an objet d'art, brought into being by the admirer's reverent eye. Silence is a threat to drama, which thrives by voice. Northrop Frye speaks of "the self-enclosed world of the unproductive and narcissistic beautiful youth of Shakespeare's sonnets, a 'liquid prisoner pent in walls of glass'."[18] Frye is using an alchemical image from Sonnet 5, where summer flowers are distilled into an alembic of perfume, like love and beauty transformed into art. The beautiful boy of the sonnets is asocial, self-absorbed. Shakespeare exhorts him to marry and beget heirs lest his patrician line end (Sonnets 1–17). Ironically, as I see it, if the youth were to make the social commitment of marriage, he would immediately lose his glamourous narcissistic beauty, which is produced by his removal from time and community. I have stressed that the Apollonian mode is harsh, absolutist, and separatist. Apollonian beings are incapable of Dionysian participation: they cannot "take part," since Apollonianism is coldly unitary, indivisible. The transvestite Rosalind inherits the marriage obligation of the fair youth, whose refusal of social integration confines him to the sonnets. A beautiful boy in the plays would seem shallow and small. In Shakespeare's drama, the only Ganymede is a woman. In Rosalind, the beautiful boy makes the choice for others rather than self.

Shakespeare's reflections upon androgynous personae were inspired by the Renaissance ferment in sex roles, which hit England later than Italy. The distance between these national phases of the Renaissance is illustrated by the fact that Shakespeare and Marlowe were born the same year Michelangelo died at age eighty-nine. Puritan preachers of the Elizabethan and Jacobean period inveighed against effeminate men and masculine women wearing men's clothes. Thus Shakespeare's transvestite comedies address a public issue and take a liberal position on it. Unlike Botticelli, who allowed Savonarola to destroy his pagan style, Shakespeare never yielded to Puritan pressure. In fact there is a turn toward decadence rather than away from it in his Jacobean plays. Shakespeare continued to believe in sexual personae as a mode of self-definition. This theme is treated in different ways in his two principal genres. His sonnets circulated in manuscript among an aristocratic coterie of Apollonian exclusiveness. But the plays were for the mixed social classes of the Globe Theatre, the democratic "Many" whom Plutarch identifies with Dionysus. Hence the psychic metamorphoses of Shakespeare's androgynes were in analogy to the rowdy pluralism of his audience.

That boy actors played girls is consistent with *As You Like It*'s claim that boys and women are emotionally alike. Rosalind as Ganymede claims she cured a man of love by pretending to be his beloved: "At which time would I, being but a moonish youth, grieve, be effeminate, changeable, longing and liking, proud, fantastical, apish, shallow, inconstant, full of tears, full of smiles; for every passion something and for no passion truly anything, as boys and women are for the most part cattle of this color" (III.ii.400–06). There are intimations here of the charming vexations of pederasty. Vergil's Mercury says, "Woman is forever various and changeable" (*Aen.* IV.569–70). Verdi's duke agrees: "La donna è mobile." Woman is mobile, changeable, fickle. Boys are moonish, as Rosalind puts it, because their mercurial inconstancy of mind resembles the ever-altering phases of the feminine moon, ruler of women's lives. Shakespeare is speaking of adolescents, more proof that Van den Berg is wrong to say adolescence was never noticed and therefore did not exist before the Enlightenment. Rosalind's speech is a catalog of rapid shifts of persona, that giddy free movement among mood-states which I identify with the fun-loving but deceitful Hermes/

Mercury. Are boys and women volatile by hormonal alchemy? Some male artists and writers have the nervous sensibility and delicate trembling fingers of women. Sensitivity begins in the body, which mind and vocation follow.

Shakespeare elsewhere broadens his model of androgynous volatility to include special men or men in special situations. "The lunatic, the lover, and the poet / Are of imagination all compact": artists and lovers are like lunatics, literally moon-men (*Midsummer* V.i.7–8). To love "is to be all made of fantasy." The true lover is "unstaid and skittish in all motions" save the beloved's image. The lover should wear "changeable taffeta," for his mind is "a very opal" (*AYLI* V.ii.93; *Twelfth* II.iv.17–20, 73–75). Love dematerializes masculinity. Things are glimmering, wavering, liquefied. Art and love dissolve social habit and form, a Dionysian fluidity. Shakespeare's clowns also inhabit a déclassé world of androgynous freedom. The medieval fool or jester had licensed access to satiric commentary and multiple personae. In *King Lear* Shakespeare gives the asexual fool Zen-like maxims of ultimate truth, toward which the pompous king makes his painful way. In *Romeo and Juliet* the jester role is played by the ill-starred nobleman Mercutio, named for his unruly mercurial temperament. His speech is a mad rush of images, metaphors, puns. Woman, boy, lunatic, lover, poet, fool: Shakespeare unites them emotionally and psychologically. They share the same fantastical quickness and variability. They are in moonlike psychic flux, which becomes manic-depressive instability in the frantic Mercutio. As a poet, Shakespeare belongs to this invisible fraternity of mixed sex. Inwardly, he too is a mercurial androgyne. Sonnet 29 charts one of his crushing mood-swings—low, lower, then up and away with the lark of sunrise.

Rosalind, the alchemical Mercurius, symbolizes comic mastery of multiple personae. Viola and Rosalind discipline their feelings, while the minor characters are full of excess and self-indulgence. Both women patiently maintain their male disguise in situations crying out for revelation. They differ, however, in their speech. Viola is discreet and solicitous, Rosalind aggressive, mischievous, bantering, railing. Riffling through her endless personae with mystical ease, Rosalind seems conscious of the fictiveness of personality. She theatricalizes her inner life. She stands mentally outside her role and all roles. Rosalind's characteristic tone is roguish self-satire: "Make the doors upon a woman's wit, and it will out at the casement; shut that, and 'twill out at the keyhole; stop that, 'twill fly with the smoke out at the chimney" (IV.i.154–57). Her own darting wit is this gusty draft in the closed household of

Renaissance womanhood. Rosalind turns words to smoke, a spiritualis-
tic emanation of her restless motility of thought. Her performance in
drag is high camp—a useful if passé homosexual term. The essence of
camp is manner, not décor. Rosalind fulfills Christopher Isherwood's
definition of camp: she mocks something, her love for Orlando, which
she takes seriously. Her supreme moment of high camp is the wooing
scene, where she pretends to be what she really is—Rosalind.

The Mercurius androgyne has the reckless dash and spontaneity of
youth. Despite our racy modern bias, if Rosalind were to keep her male
disguise, she would cease to grow as a character. Shakespeare's plays, I
said, esteem development and process, Dionysian transformation. Rosalind transforms herself by going to the forest, but she would stagnate
if she stayed there. Her valiant Amazon personality would be diminished and trivialized. She would turn into Shakespeare's other mercurial androgyne, the cavorting sky-spirit Ariel, who is all shape-shifting
and speed, changing himself to Harpy and sea-nymph. Ariel, the trickster Till Eulenspiegel, and J. M. Barrie's Peter Pan (a boy played by an
actress), demonstrate the feminizing effects of psychic mutability on
males. This reverses the principle I found in Michelangelo, where
monumentality masculinizes women. Rosalind must put an end to her
proteanism and rejoin the Renaissance social order. Modern productions completely miss the severe pattern of ritualistic renunciation in *As
You Like It*. Rosalind is not Peter Pan, nor is she Virginia Woolf's
reckless, cigar-smoking Sally Seton. Rosalind is never madcap or flippant. Behind her playfulness of language and personae is a pressure of
magisterial will. Multiplicity of mood tends toward anarchy. Shakespeare's Renaissance wisdom subordinates that multiplicity to social
structure, containing its exuberant energies in marriage. In the Renaissance as now, play must be part of a dialectic of work, or it becomes
decadent.

At the climax of *As You Like It*, Rosalind constructs a ceremony of
farewell to her androgynous self. It is her moment of maximum wit or
creative intelligence. The play's romantic entanglements are in total
confusion. Rosalind proclaims that by "magic" she will deliver to each
person his or her heart's desire. The revelation of her own identity and
gender is the key: *As You Like It* ends in an alchemical experiment
where Rosalind, as the hermaphroditic Mercurius, transmutes the
play's characters and destinies, including her own. The magnum opus
begins with a chant, a spell or litany of erotic fixation and frustration.
The lines go round and round in circle magic, rings of the alchemical
uroboros (V.ii.82–118, iv.116–24). The play proposes a riddle, as

snarled as the Gordian knot. Rosalind's personality, self-displayed, resolves these dismaying intricacies. When she appears undisguised,
Rosalind is the surprise conclusion to an elegant sexual syllogism. Her
shamanistic epiphany reorders the erotic chaos of the play. This Sphinx
answers her own riddle. Oedipus' reply, "Man," works again, for Rosalind is the *anthropos* or perfected man of alchemy.

Rosalind's hybrid gender and perpetual transformations are the
quicksilver of the alchemical Mercurius, who had the rainbow colors of
the peacock's tail. Jung says Mercurius as quicksilver symbolizes "the
'fluid', i.e., mobile, intellect." Mercurius, like Rosalind, is "both material and spiritual."[19] Rosalind's spirituality is her purity, purpose, and
romantic fidelity; her materiality is her realism and mordant pragmatism. An alchemical treatise of the early seventeenth century is called
Atalanta Fugiens, "Atalanta in flight." It makes the swift huntress a
metaphor for "the strength of the volatile Mercury."[20] *As You Like It*
compares Rosalind to Atalanta and identifies wit with speed: "All
thoughts ... are winged" (III.ii.147; IV.i.135; III.ii.273–74). In her
emotional reserve and verbal agility, Rosalind is an Atalanta *fugiens*.
The Philosopher's Stone or hermaphroditic *rebis* of alchemy often has
wings, which Jung interprets as "intuition or spiritual (winged) potentiality."[21] Both masculine and feminine, Rosalind is a Mercurius of
swift, sovereign intelligence. Speed as hermaphroditic transcendance:
we see this in Vergil's Amazon Camilla and Giambologna's ephebic
Mercury in ecstatic flight.

Rosalind is the catalyst of *As You Like It*, the magic elixir transmuting
base into noble metals. The editor of *Atalanta Fugiens* remarks, "Mercurius is the mercury in which the metals have to be dissolved, reduced
to the primary matter before they can become gold."[22] The *rebis*, we
noted, is often shown as incestuous brother and sister. Shakespeare
alters the forest roles of Lodge's Rosalynde and Aliena (Celia) from
page and mistress to brother and sister, as if to facilitate an alchemical
analogy. This change does not preclude eroticism, in view of the lesbian
tinge to Rosalind and Celia's friendship. As first cousins, they too risk
incest. The primary transactions undertaken by Shakespeare's Mercurius are the Sylvius-Phebe romance (which turns triangle) and the
bamboozling of the lovelorn Orlando. These alchemical experiments, in
the closed glass retort of the play, succeed. Like Nero, Rosalind experiments with person and place. But hers is white rather than black magic,
leading to love and marriage rather than debauchery and death.
Lodge's Rosalynde claims to have a friend "deeply experienced in
necromancy and magic," but Shakespeare's Rosalind boldly arrogates

these occult powers to herself. Rosalind is both producer and star of the finale. Her hierarchically most commanding moment is paradoxically the one where she ritually lays aside her hermaphroditism to take up the socialized persona of obedient wife to Orlando. Her incantatory speech in female dress ceremonially restores heterosexual normality to the play. In it she names and cleanses her major social relationships, then reifies them. A new social structure is being constructed, with her father reinvested with his ducal authority. "Ducdame, ducdame, ducdame," sings Jaques in the forest, a nonsense word bemusing scholars (II.v.49). I say, the duke is a dame. Rosalind, as much as her uncle, has usurped her father's manhood. Now she surrenders what is not hers to reclaim her own sex.

Rosalind's magic is real, for she produces Hymen, the marriage spirit who enters with her in the last scene. Hymen is a prominent figure in court masque, but he is conspicuously out of place in a Shakespeare play. He is an embarrassment to modern commentators on the play, who ignore him whenever possible. Why this allegorical invasion of the naturalistic *As You Like It?* First of all, Hymen symbolizes the mass marriages which end Shakespearean comedy. He is reconciliation and social harmony, knitting the classes and leading the banished characters back to the redeemed city. But Hymen is also a by-product of the play's psychoalchemy. The alchemical operation had two parts: distillation and sublimation. Hymen, traditionally depicted as a beautiful young man, is a sexual sublimate. He is the emanation or double of Rosalind herself. He is the ghost of her maleness, exorcised but lingering on to preside over the exit from Arden. Shakespeare's technique here is allegorical repletion, the term I invented for Leonardo's *The Virgin with St. Anne*. Hymen's odd doubling of Rosalind is like Leonardo's awkward photographic superimposition of two female figures. Sexual personae flood the eye. The characters of *As You Like It* stand startled. Hymen is their collectively projected mental image of the transvestite Rosalind, now only a memory. Hymen is a visible distillation of her transsexual experience. In her romantic conspiracies, Rosalind has impersonated Hymen and hence evoked his presence. As the Mercurius who overcomes sexual duality and perfects base materials, she possesses the magnetic power of concord, ensuring the integrity of Renaissance social order.

Rosalind is, to borrow a phrase from Paracelsus, "a fiery and perfect Mercury extracted by Nature and Art."[23] She reinterprets the classical Amazon, making physical prowess intellectual. Rosalind is Shakespeare's version of Spenser's glamourous androgynes. Britomart's flash-

ing armour and flaming sword become Rosalind's unanswerable wit.
Shakespeare's transvestite heroine has masculine pride, verve, and cool
aristocratic control—scarcely to be found in today's simplistic, innocuous Rosalinds. The ideal Rosalind must have both lyricism and force.
There must be intelligence, depth, spontaneity, something quick and
vivacious, with a hint of the wild and uncontrolled. The girl-boy Rosalind is in Atalanta-flight from mood to mood, an adolescent skittishness.
The closest thing I have ever seen to Shakespeare's authentic Rosalind is
Patricia Charbonneau's spirited performance as a coltish Reno cowgirl
in Donna Deitch's film *Desert Hearts* (1985), based on a lesbian love
story by Jane Rule.

Rosalind as Mercurius has a quick smile and mobile eye. Shakespeare's view of woman is revolutionary. Unlike Belphoebe or Britomart, Rosalind has a jovial inner landscape. It is not Spenser's grim
arena of virtue's battle with vice. This landscape is airy and pleasant,
full of charm and surprise. Rosalind's self-pleasuring is not like Mona
Lisa's. No daemonic fog of solipsism hangs over her. Rosalind has an
invigorating alertness. She is not smugly half-asleep, like Leonardo's
Renaissance woman. Mona Lisa still has the baleful Gorgon eye of
archaic archetype. She burns us with her glance. The daemonic eye sees
nothing but its prey. It seeks power, the fascism of nature. But Rosalind's
socialized eye *moves to see*. It takes things in. Hers are not the lustful
rolling eyes of Spenser's femmes fatales, which slither, pierce, and
possess. Rosalind's eye honors the integrity of objects and persons. Its
mobility signals a mental processing of information, the visible sign of
western intelligence. In Spenser, we saw, the virtuous eye is rigidly
controlled. Until our century, a respectable woman kept her eyes modestly averted. Shakespeare legitimizes bold mobility of the female eye
and identifies it with imagination. Rosalind's eye is truly perceptive: it
both sees and understands. Shakespeare's great heroine unites multiplicity of gender, persona, word, eye, and thought.

Despite his love for the glamourous personality of multiple moods and masks, Shakespeare subordinates all his characters to
the public good. The great chain of being reasserts itself at the end of his
plays. The psycho-alchemic pattern of Shakespeare's comedies is release, remelting, and reincorporation in society. So Dionysian fluidity
and metamorphoses move toward a final Apollonian ordering, a Renaissance moral value in which Shakespeare rejoins Spenser. In *Antony
and Cleopatra* (1606–07) Shakespeare amplifies the psychology of his
transvestite comedies. *Antony and Cleopatra* shows us what happens

when sexual personae refuse reincorporation in society and insist on remaining in nature, the realm of perpetual transformations. This play confirms that the price of Rosalind's remaining an androgyne in the Forest of Arden would be spiritual death.

Antony and Cleopatra, long thought technically flawed, may be the favorite Shakespeare play of my generation of critics. Unlike older scholars, some of us find *King Lear* boring and obvious, and we dread having to teach it to resentful students. *Antony and Cleopatra* has come into its own. Its choppy multitude of scenes, flying about the ancient Mediterranean, do not irritate sensibilities schooled on cinema. Here again is Shakespeare's mobile eye. Spenser's camera is the obsessive zoom lens, concentrated and iconistic. But Shakespeare's hand-held camera takes to the air, dominating western space. *Antony and Cleopatra* closely follows its source in Plutarch. But as usual, Shakespeare adds his own metamorphic metaphors and pyrotechnic personae. I see this play as the most thorough of Shakespeare's replies to Spenser. The Egypt of *Antony and Cleopatra* is Spenser's Bower of Bliss, fertile stamping ground of the femme fatale. But Shakespeare, the Dionysian alchemist, is determined to rescue nature from its daemonic taint. He will show it at its rawest and most brutal, then defend it. Yet Renaissance order must have the last word.

Over the past century, Shakespeare's Cleopatra has undergone a radical change in critical fortunes. She used to be the lowest of the low among Shakespeare's protagonists. Her sexual libertinism and volatility led to Victorian and post-Victorian vilification. Her sharp mood-changes were thought moral duplicity. In scholarly literature before the feminist 1970s, rare indeed is a comment like A. C. Bradley's: "Many unpleasant things can be said of Cleopatra; and the more that are said the more wonderful she appears."[24] Perhaps apocryphally, a Victorian theatergoer leaving a production of *Antony and Cleopatra* remarked, "How different from the domestic life of our own dear Queen." Since then, there has been a huge shift in sexual assumptions about women, from which Cleopatra has profited. The Victorians admired Cordelia, Lear's one honest daughter, as the saintly perfection of femininity. To me, probably as time-bound as they, Cordelia seems a vapid nincompoop, self-righteous and self-thwarting. Even for her most generous apologists, Cleopatra presents interpretative problems. Her temperamental excesses make people uneasy. She is, in my terms, Shakespeare's most uncontrolled and uncontrollable Dionysian androgyne, the metamorphosing Mercurius who obeys no law but her own. Hence she cannot survive her play.

Spenser makes England's fierce Virgin Queen an ivory Diana. Shakespeare makes her an umber Venus. *Antony and Cleopatra* is a Baroque *Venus and Mars*, bursting Spenser's chaste Botticellian line. Shakespeare repeats *The Faerie Queene*'s psychological dialectic of definitiveness and dissolution, but he reverses its meanings. Apollonian social order again opposes Dionysian energy and wins. But Shakespeare, unlike Spenser, gives his imaginative sympathies to the Dionysian extremists. The traditional persona of republican Rome, we saw, was fixed to the point of rigidity. *Antony and Cleopatra* takes place at a great transition in history, when empire replaces republic, creating the era of international peace in which Christianity would spread. The old masculine Roman virtues are suddenly passé. Only Antony, the sexually most unstable male in Shakespeare's play, extols machismo. His contempt for Octavius Caesar, the politician who refuses to meet him in hand-to-hand combat, strikes even us as faintly anachronistic, and his challenge is dismissed as absurd by the gruff Enobarbus, the lone Roman who has not yet smoothed his blunt speech into the glib diplomacy of the dawning age of empire.

In *Antony and Cleopatra* Rome follows a conservative republican psychology. Roman personality is strictly delimited, preserving the bounds of ego. At the news of Antony's death, Caesar declares, "The breaking of so great a thing should make a greater crack" (V.i.14–15). He means the announcing of so important an event should make a louder noise, like a thunderclap. But Caesar also envisions Antony's death as the toppling and shattering of a statue, a colossus. Throughout the play, Roman personality is static and brittle, like stone. Caesar defines identity and kinship in legalistic terms. The abstract and public take precedence over the concrete, emotional, and sensuous (III.vi.6). The Romans constantly condemn Antony for abandoning the former for the latter. Roman social order is hierarchically inflexible, as Ventidius shrewdly sees. Rome's voice is the bleak reality principle of political expediency. In Egypt, on the other hand, energy pours into self-expression. Antony and Cleopatra's Alexandrian revels are an endless round of feasts and games. Enobarbus saw the panting Cleopatra "hop forty paces through the public street" (II.ii.235). Dionysian beings are playful and democratic. As queen, Cleopatra is indifferent to decorum. Her hilarity contrasts with Caesar's puritanical sobriety. Caesar stands on ceremony. He is driven by a single purpose, consolidation of the Mediterranean under Roman rule. He has no personal life. He completely identifies private with public interest. Hence he is unstoppable. Such men can be political geniuses or monsters.

Roman time and Roman space also obey Apollonian laws. Caesar sees time as a linear strip, a Roman triumph, the chronicle of civic history (V.i.65–66). Cleopatra blurs time in the eternal now of imagination. Narrated memories in Egypt have such emotional immediacy they seem more vivid than events before us. Enobarbus, a Roman in Rome, is overcome by Egyptian memory when he describes Cleopatra on her royal barge. Caesar remembers only for duty or revenge. Throughout the play, Roman space is defined by images of closure, contrasting with Antony and Cleopatra's expansive "new heaven, new earth" of love (I.i.17). Space is cut up like urban districts, the Apollonian borderlines of Greek demes and tracts. The Romans speak of hoops, edges, fences, stalls, pillars, the rigid language of public architecture and Apollonian containment.

Antony and Cleopatra respect no boundaries. Antony's infatuation "o'erflows the measure." He sends "his bounty overplus" even to defectors. His heart and chest burst his buckles. The heart of dead Cleopatra strains to blow free. Caesar places Antony's old legions in the vanguard "that Antony may seem to spend his fury upon himself" (I.i.2.; IV.vi.22; IV.vi.10–11). Even his archenemy acknowledges Antony's transpersonal extensiveness of identity. Everything in Egypt is abundance, profligacy, Dionysian too-muchness: "Eight wild boars roasted whole at a breakfast, and but twelve persons there" (II.ii.185–86). Caesar tries to channel and subdue the flood of emotion and sensation which is Egyptian experience. His victory is signalled when Cleopatra is "confined" to her tomb, the "frame" of his own Apollonian will (V.i.52–56). Like Blake's tyrant Urizen, Caesar lays the cold compass of Apollonian measure upon Cleopatra's "infinite variety" (II.ii.242).

Caesar's Roman world-view is a desiccated or devivified Apollonianism: hierarchical order and dignity, intellectual categorization, the sharp-edged unitary ego, separation from sexuality and the sensory. Caesar's patron is, to use Nietzsche's phrase, "Apollo, the founder of states."[25] Cleopatra's world-view is promiscuously Dionysian: abolition of limits and boundaries, multiple personae, eating and drinking, sex, anarchic energy, natural fecundity. Caesar and his retinue call Antony effeminate, yet Antony is more masculine than Caesar in the usual sense. Caesar, a bland managerial type, is sexually neuter. He is an Apollonian androgyne. The dominant sexual persona of Spenser's *Faerie Queene* has completely lost its glamour in Shakespeare's Dionysian genre. In *Antony and Cleopatra*, Apollonianism is merely officiousness, the spite and banality of small minds.

Cleopatra's Dionysian multiplicity is richly illustrated throughout the play. For example, when she hears of Antony's marriage to Octavia, Cleopatra swerves back and forth between extreme emotions five times in ten lines (II.v.109–19). Each mood-swing, toward and away from Antony, has its own operatic tone, gesture, and posture. Critics used to wonder which is the "real" Cleopatra, or where is she? The secondary selves must be cunning stratagems. Worse, the issue of Octavia's height and hair color, interwoven with Cleopatra's lamentations and faintings, make the queen seem silly and superficial in academic eyes. How like a woman! But Cleopatra is an actress, and as we shall see, theatricality is the model of human psychology in *Antony and Cleopatra*. Cleopatra is the sum of her masks.

Cleopatra's Dionysianism dissolves male into female. The fruitful female principle is so dominant in Shakespeare's Egyptian Bower of Bliss that male power is dwarfed and stymied. Cleopatra is surrounded by eunuchs, disdained by the Romans. The historical Antony was already a notorious drinker and carouser before he met Cleopatra, but in the play he is charged with Egyptian degeneration after a nobly stoic Roman past. For the Romans, Antony suffers a reduction of identity through his feminizing association with Cleopatra. But Shakespeare sees it as an aggrandizement of identity which Antony, unlike Rosalind, is unable to control. Cleopatra recalls a transvestite game where she decked Antony in her robes and headdress while she strapped on his battle sword (II.v.22–23). This detail is not in Plutarch, though everything else in the passage is. Surely Shakespeare is directly addressing Spenser here. He takes Artegall's transvestite enslavement to the Amazon queen and recasts it with Dionysian dramatic energy. What is shameful and depressing in Spenser becomes playful and mirthful. Artegall is at a dead end. But Shakespeare's transvestite Antony and Cleopatra give the impression of vitality, of identity opening and multiplying. Exchange of clothing is a paradigm for the emotional union of love. Antony and Cleopatra so interpenetrate that they are mistaken for one another (I.ii.80).

Even before she absorbs Antony's identity, Cleopatra is robustly half-masculine. Rivalled only by Rosalind, Cleopatra appropriates the powers and prerogatives of both sexes more lavishly than any other character in literature. Her sexual personae are energized by stormy infusions of Dionysian nature-force. Here Rosalind is more limited because more civilized. Cleopatra is psychically immersed in the irrational and barbaric. She is voluptuously female, a rarity in Shakespeare. Her sexuality is so potent in European terms that the Romans are always calling her whore, strumpet, trull. As the "serpent of old Nile," she is the archetypal femme fatale (I.v.25). Cleopatra appears costumed as Isis, whom as queen she literally embodies. Her main distinction from the mocking Rosalind is her maternalism, which makes her cradle the asp like "my baby at my breast" (V.ii.309). The mother is one of Cleopatra's many personae, but Rosalind and Spenser's Britomart will become mothers only outside the frame of their works. This is because the archetype behind Rosalind is the chaste beautiful boy. Cleopatra is a virago, the androgynous type I found in Michelangelo's Medici Chapel nudes, with their thrusting breasts. Rosalind inhabits the crisp Forest of Arden, the Northern European green world. But Cleopatra belongs to the heat-enervated Orient, whose oppressiveness hangs over Michelangelo's women. Cleopatra is not more feminine than Rosalind, but she is far more female. Cleopatra greets the messenger: "Ram thou thy fruitful tidings in mine ears" (II.v.24). A pagan Annunciation. Physically craving the absent Antony, Cleopatra is a sexual vessel forcibly filled. Yet the penetrating force is hers; she invokes it by command. Her overwrought metaphor incidentally implies a touch of homosexual perversion in the murder-by-ear of Hamlet Senior in his drowsy Spenserian bower.

Cleopatra's male persona is equally strong. As queen of Egypt, Cleopatra, like Hatshepsut, is an impersonation of a royal male. Janet Adelman suggests that Cleopatra wearing Antony's sword is a Renaissance *Venus armata* and that for battle at Actium she would appear in male dress.[26] Psychologically, Cleopatra is always armed. She has a fiery belligerence. She threatens to bloody her maid's teeth; she even threatens Antony, using a pun which advertises her penis-envy (I.iii.40–41; ii.58–61). When the messenger arrives with news of Antony's marriage, Cleopatra passes beyond threats to actual assault and battery, hitting him, hauling him up and down, and pulling a knife. Such scenes caused the long critical resistance to Cleopatra. By modern middle-class standards, they require defense. Shakespeare gives Cleopatra an intemperate flair for masculine violence unique in the sympathetic portrayal of women in literature. The violence of Medea or Lady Macbeth is transient, either male-inspired or deflected through a male's action. In Cleopatra violence is constantly present as a potential male persona. It is the raging warfare of her hermaphrodite character. For parallels we must go to villainesses like Lear's daughters or outside social literature to mythic horrors like Scylla. Into Cleopatra as Isis flows the untransformed energy of nature, sheer sex and violence.

Is it unseemly for queens to brawl? Dionysian beings instinctively subvert the hierarchical. As an Italian, I have little problem reconciling violence with culture. Rousseau drove the wedge between aggression and culture, so colorfully united in the Renaissance. Cleopatra's pugilistic energy is matched by her sadistic imagination and flights of daemonic metaphor, where eyeballs are punted like footballs and whipped bodies steeped in pickle brine (II.v.63–66). Shakespeare shows us the turbulent emotion-in-action of the Dionysian androgyne. Language seethes like boiling oil. Cleopatra's rabid speeches sound more shocking to Anglo-American than to Mediterranean ears. A savage vehemence of speech is common among southern peoples, due to the nearness of agriculture and the survival of pagan intensity. Those who live on and by the land recognize nature's terrible amorality. Cleopatra's sadistic images are normal in Italian terms. My immigrant relatives used to say, "May you be killed!" or "May you be eaten by a cat!" Common Italian-American expressions, according to my father, took the form "Che te possono" (May such and such be done to you). For example, "May your eyes be torn out," "May you drag your tongue along the ground," "May they squeeze your testicles," "May they sew up your anus." The similarity to Cleopatra's rhetorical style is obvious. Torture and homicide are immediately accessible to the Mediterranean imagination.

I called Dionysian impulses sadistic, but the proper term is sadomasochistic, both active and passive. Provoked, Cleopatra is off on runaway flights of masochistic vision. It is the psychic countercurrent to her aggression, what Heracleitus calls *enantiodromia*, "running to its opposite." When Antony calls her "cold-hearted," she blurts out a surreal fantasy of poison hail, blighted wombs, and unburied bodies covered with flies and gnats (III.xiii.158–67). Taken prisoner, she storms that, preferable to jeers in Rome, let her naked corpse be thrown into the mud and swelled up by waterflies—or hung in chains on a pyramid (V.ii.55–62). Cleopatra's sadomasochistic imagination makes Dionysian leaps through nature. Her body is the earth mother torn by the strife of the elements in the cycle of birth and death. Ugliness, pain, abortion, and decay are nature's reality. Cleopatra's rough speech has a daemonic eloquence. Shakespeare opens a window into the unconscious, where we see the sex and violence we carry within us. There is the grinding dreamwork, spewing out metaphors which appall us. Cleopatra's images tumble out with bruising force, like the boulders tossed like chaff in Coleridge's underground river.

The passionately active Cleopatra contrasts with feminine, retiring Octavia. Chaste Octavia is a "swan's-down feather" on the tide: she is will-less, the pawn of larger forces. She is of "a holy, cold, and still conversation," a model Roman matron. She moves so primly "She shows a body rather than a life, / A statue than a breather" (III.ii.48; II.vi.122–23; III.iii.23–24). Like brother, like sister. In Shakespeare, iconic Apollonian statues are dead wood. Cleopatra's Dionysian prote- anism and velocity take Shakespeare's eye. He makes Octavia's virtue seem torpid. Octavia is matter and Cleopatra energy. Cleopatra is scourge, not feather. Her dominion over gender is dramatized in ath- letic transformations of dizzying speed. "I am pale, Charmian," she murmurs—and a line later leaps at the messenger and slugs him to the floor (II.v.59–61). Cleopatra vaults from one sexual extreme to the other, barely taking breath. The delicate Lady of the Camellias switch- hits with burly Ajax. The genders so indiscriminately mingle in Cleo- patra that she makes transsexual word errors under stress (II.v.40–41, 116, 45). Cleopatra has a Dionysian all-inclusiveness. She breaks through social restraints to plunge into the sensual, orgiastic pleasure of pure feeling.

Cleopatra embodies the Dionysian principle of theatricality. Shake- speare often makes analogies between personality and stagecraft but never, save in *Hamlet,* so systematically as he does in *Antony and Cleopatra.* From first scene to last, public and private behavior is cri- tiqued in terms of performance. Politics itself is stage-managed. Antony and Cleopatra are always going in and out of their legendary roles as Antony and Cleopatra. For Cleopatra, life is theater. She is a master propagandist. Truth is inconsequential; dramatic values are supreme. Cleopatra shamelessly manipulates others' emotions like clay. Once her cleverness misfires, when she sends word she is dead and Antony kills himself. Cleopatra resembles Rosalind in the gleeful way she throws herself into a role. This is so even at her lowest moment, when she scripts her suicide. Like Rosalind, Cleopatra is producer and star of play's end. She makes a masque-like tableau of her own death. Shake- speare presses Renaissance theatricality beyond moral norms. Meta- morphoses are horrific for both Spenser and Dante, who consigns impersonation to one of the lowest circles of the *Inferno:* incestuous Myrrha, "falsifying herself in another's form," is classed with liars and counterfeiters (XXX.41). Puritan hostility to theater was justified. Secu- lar theater is Greco-Roman and therefore pagan. Shakespeare makes Cleopatra his accomplice and advocate for dramatic impersonation.

Cleopatra has a sensational flair for improvisation and melodrama. Her vamping and camping are more extreme than Rosalind's as Ganymede. Cleopatra's postures of romantic martrydom are as self- parodying as a drag queen's. Self-parody is always sex-parody. The virtuoso tone of Cleopatra's theatrics recurs in Wilde's *The Importance of Being Earnest,* where it clearly springs from wholesale desexualization of the characters. Cleopatra's moment of maximum consciousness of persona is when she sets aside both feminine swooning and masculine intimidation for a briskly efficient interrogation of the messenger. She extorts intelligence on Octavia's age, height, voice, hair, and face shape (III.iii). I consider this neglected scene one of the classic moments in all drama. A game of personae is being played. Cleopatra is mentally auditioning Octavia, cattily revising her virtues downward, always with her rival's theatrical impact on Antony in mind. Cleopatra is gracious and queenly, but we tangibly feel her sense of her persona, as well as her maid Charmian's sense of it. Charmian, like a church deacon, keeps piping up the required response, in ritual antiphony. Shakespeare makes us see Cleopatra's detachment from her masks and yet her complete identification with them. Her showy self-representations have both intellectual duality and hierarchic authority. Cleopatra is Shakespeare's despotic Muse of drama.

The only character in literature whose theatrical personae rival Cleopatra's is Auntie Mame. Patrick Dennis' *Auntie Mame* (1955) is the American *Alice in Wonderland* and in my view more interesting and important than any "serious" novel after World War II. The original book is far sharper than the wonderful play and movie (1958), starring the great Rosalind Russell. The subsequent musical and Lucille Ball movie (1974) are of little worth, turning the regal Auntie Mame into trivial spunk and cuddles. I mentioned Auntie Mame as a type of the Mercurius androgyne. She is an archaeologist of persona. Each event, each phase of life is registered in a change of costume and interior décor. Style and substance are one, in the Wildean manner. When the story opens in the Twenties, Auntie Mame is in her Chinese period, her Beekman Place apartment as exotic as Shakespeare's Egypt. Like Cleopatra, Auntie Mame stands for a flamboyant, extravagant, wine-drenched, ethnically diverse world threatened by a rationalist Apollonian prude, the WASP banker Mr. Babcock, Mame's Caesar-like chief antagonist. Like Cleopatra, Mame is attended by androgynes—a giggling eunuch-like Japanese houseboy, a virago confidante (the actress and drunk, Vera Charles), and epicene party-guests (a "woman-man and man-woman"). Like Cleopatra, Mame is bossy, peremptory, and given to "a little half-hour show of histrionics," "her lifetime habit." Like Cleopatra, she has so many feminine personae that, mysteriously, she ends up ceasing to seem female at all. My Hermes/Mercury principle: a multitude of personae suspends gender. One remembers Mame's long green lacquered fingernails and sweeping bamboo cigarette holder, her Oriental robe of embroidered golden silk, her black satin sheets and bed jacket of pink ostrich feathers. Panic and crisis: how does one dress for Scarsdale? "Any discussion of clothing always won Auntie Mame's undivided attention." Trying to avoid a Georgia fox hunt, Mame "powdered herself dead white" and put on "an unbecoming shade of green."[27] *Auntie Mame* is a study of multiple impersonations, the theatrical principle of western selfhood. Emotion is instantly objectified. Costume, speech, and manner are a public pagan language of the inner life.

Expiring with emotion upon learning of her new rival, Cleopatra manages to convey to her envoy, "Let him not leave out the color of her hair." Like Auntie Mame, Cleopatra, a creature of theater, sees persona as a mirror of soul. The pagan folk sciences, astrology, palmistry, and phrenology, have never forgotten that externals are truth. Beauty is only skin-deep; you can't tell a book by its cover: these pious axioms come from a contràry moral tradition. The aesthete, who lives in a world of surfaces, and the male homosexual, who lives in a world of masks, believe in the absoluteness of externals. That is why Auntie Mame was a diva of homosexuals. Cleopatra's multiple personae are far from feminine fickleness. She represents a radical theatricality in which the inner world is completely transformed into the outer.

Did Shakespeare base Cleopatra on an Italian model? A. L. Rowse thinks the Dark Lady of the sonnets was the half-Italian Emilia Bassanio. Luigi Barzini describes "the importance of spectacle" in Italian culture, with its public staging of emotional scenes. He speaks of "the transparency of Italian faces," which allows conversations to be followed at a distance: "Undisguised emotions, some sincere and some feigned, follow each other on an Italian's face as swiftly as the shadows of clouds over a meadow on a windy day in spring."[28] Shakespeare's self-dramatizing Cleopatra has a fluid Italian expressiveness. In her amoral dissimulations, she confirms the negative Northern European view of Italian and papist character in the Renaissance. Renaissance England was more flamboyant than modern England but less so than Renaissance Italy. Hence in the spiritual geography of *Antony and Cleopatra*, Egypt is to Rome as Renaissance Italy was to Renaissance England. Cleopatra belongs to an emotional and sexual southland. But Shakespeare is well aware of the anarchic danger in a life of impersonations. Caesar wins in *Antony and Cleopatra* because he represents political order, the dream of the fractured, fractious Renaissance. *Antony and Cleopatra*'s reactionary political premise is borne out by Italian history, where theatrical individualism weakened centralized authority, aiding the rise of the tribal Mafia. Since World War II, nearly fifty governments have come and gone in Rome. Restless change is the rule.

We turn now to the ultimate question of Shakespeare's play. If Cleopatra contains all emotional modes and all powers of male and female, why is she defeated by the world? Why is she not a perfected image of man? Cleopatra dies, while Rosalind triumphantly survives, because Cleopatra is an incomplete Mercurius and as such cannot advance her play toward the goal of English Renaissance art: social and hierarchical consolidation. An important image pattern in *Antony and Cleopatra* has aroused little or no comment. Astrology, even more than alchemy, was one of the great symbol systems of the Renaissance. Its iconography pervaded Renaissance art, book illustration, and interior décor. The formidable combined forces of Judeo-Christianity and modern science have never succeeded in wiping out pagan astrology, nor will they ever. Astrology supplies what is missing in the west's official moral and intellectual codes. Astrology is the oldest organized art form of sexual personae. Waging war on astrology, the medieval and Renaisssance Church promulgated the distortion that astrology is fatalism, a flouting of God's Providence and the necessity for moral struggle. But the predictive part of astrology is less important than its psychology, which three thousand years of continuous practice have given a phenomenal subtlety. Astrology does insist upon self-discipline and self-transformation. Judging astrology by those vague sun-sign columns in the daily paper is like judging Christianity by a smudged shop window of black-velvet day-glo paintings of the Good Shepherd. The idea that the stars literally influence men (by a falling fluid, an *influenza*) is plainly untenable. But that the movements of the constellations are a clock by which earthly changes can be measured is less easy to dismiss. I subscribe to what Jung calls synchronicity. Things happen in complex patterns of apparent coincidence, noticed by the keen eyes of the artist. Astrology links man to nature, its major point of departure from Judeo-Christianity. The Greek word zodiac means circle of animals. Most birth signs are symbolized by animals, whose character astrology identifies with human types. Our behaviorist age is generally resistant to the idea of genetic traits, for individuals, sexes, or races. But ask any mother of a large family whether personality is innate or learned. She senses a child's inborn shyness or aggression from earliest infancy. People who dismiss astrology do so out of either ignorance or rationalism. Rationalists have their place, but their limited assumptions and methods must be kept out of the arts. Interpretation of poem, dream, or person requires intuition and divination, not science.

The Renaissance embraced astrology as part of its infatuation with sexual personae. *Antony and Cleopatra*, Shakespeare's greatest drama of sexual personae, makes astrological metaphors crucial to its psychological design. Each sign of the zodiac is associated with one of the four elements, named by the pre-Socratic philosopher Empedocles. From long study, I summarize the astrological meaning of the elements as follows. Fire is will, originality, boldness, the amoral life force. Air is language, wit, balance, humane perspective. Water is intuition, sympathy, deep feeling, mystical oneness, and prophecy. Earth is order, method, precision, realism, materialism. Modern science discarded the four elements in favor of finer terminology. From the late Renaissance on, more and more basic elements were discovered, now approaching one hundred. John Anthony West claims, however, that the four principal elements of modern organic chemistry, hydrogen, carbon, oxygen, and nitrogen, closely correspond in function to fire, earth, air, and water.[29] Northrop Frye says, "Earth, air, water, and fire are still the four elements of imaginative experience, and always will be."[30] A person's natal horoscope sometimes lacks one of the four elements, a disturbing imbalance which can and should be compensated for through self-analysis and vigilant effort. My theory is that Shakespeare has cast for Cleopatra a horoscope lacking the element of earth and that this psychic incompletion, with her refusal to correct it, dooms both herself and Antony.

The most poetic speech in the play, by normally curt Enobarbus, is a gorgeous dreamlike memory of Cleopatra's arrival at Tarsus to meet Antony: "The barge she sat in, like a burnished throne, / Burned on the water" (II.ii.197–98). Cleopatra is Venus in motion, a Dionysian epiphany. Shakespeare is answering the frozen iconic entrance of Spenser's Belphoebe, the Apollonian Diana. With its gold deck and purple sails, the barge is the Amazon sanctuary of Phoenician Dido, whom Vergil decks with red and gold. Cleopatra carries her own bower with her, getting it out of the swampy Spenserian glade onto the brisk high seas. Shakespeare's motion picture has its own soundtrack, flute music and the beating of silver oars. Air and water swirl toward the barge, which exudes "a strange invisible perfume." A magnetism or suction pulls people out of the marketplace toward the wharves. Cleopatra as Venus is the power of physical attraction among the elements, which Empedocles attributes to Aphrodite. She is in heat: Shakespeare carefully

adds fire to his tableau. That the barge "burns" is his addition to
Plutarch's description. Cleopatra is Venus born from the sea. In Enobarbus' speech, she commands three elements: water, air, and fire.
Earth is pointedly excluded. In fact, earth is evacuated, denuded of its
properties by the rush of citizens shoreward. Shakespeare's Cleopatra is
the free play of sovereign imagination, hostile to the steadfastness and
stability of earth.

The climax of *Antony and Cleopatra* is the battle of Actium, a turning
point in western history. Antony's loss is Caesar's gain and the beginning of Roman empire, united under one man. Shakespeare stunningly
mythologizes Plutarch's account, without loss of factual accuracy. He
introduces elemental metaphors effecting a poetic transformation of
history. Antony's fateful decision to fight by sea ruins him. Commander
of infantrymen and master of land warfare, he foolishly allows Cleopatra to dictate his battle plan. The Egyptians are seafarers. Cleopatra
insists the ultimate contest with Caesar be by navy, not army. Antony's
seasoned soldiers passionately appeal to him, but blinded by love, he
waves them away. In agreeing to fight by sea, Antony repudiates the
element of earth, the foundation of his illustrious career. At the same
time, he shrugs off common sense and practicality, qualities astrologi-
cally symbolized by earth. In imposing the element of water upon her
lover, Cleopatra destroys him. Shakespeare weaves the elemental imagery into the play from the start, so that the words "land" and "sea"
chime ominously in the deliberations at Actium.

The scene where Antony blithely severs his connection with earth
ends with the naming of Caesar's lieutenant, Taurus (III.vii.78). The
next scene, just a few lines long, begins with Caesar calling out to
Taurus, who answers and departs, his sole appearance in the play.
Shakespeare has plucked this name from Plutarch's roster of military
officers at Actium. A Renaissance audience, familiar with simple astrology, would immediately recognize that Taurus is the first of the three
earth signs of the zodiac. Taurus was also Shakespeare's birth sign. This
is what Maynard Mack would call "the emblematic entrance and exit"
in Shakespeare's plays.[31] Caesar's deputy is an earth-spirit because
Antony and Cleopatra identifies Caesar with the astrological qualities of
earth—patience, pragmatism, emotional reserve, discipline, applica-
tion. Caesar is the reality principle, *Realpolitik*. He represents what
Antony and Cleopatra have rejected, and because drama must take
place in human space and human time, he defeats them. Psychic fixity
overcomes psychic volatility. The historical Caesar was himself ruled by
an earth sign. Suetonius reports that Augustus Caesar commemorated

an astrological prediction of his rise to power by ordering struck "a silver coin stamped with Capricorn, the sign under which he had been born."[32] In *Antony and Cleopatra* Caesar consolidates his Capricornian earth-power by binding Taurus to him, taking away the heart of Antony's military identity.

Ancient and modern historians have been puzzled by Cleopatra's sudden flight from the battle of Actium, and even more by Antony's shameful abandonment of his troops and ships to follow her. As Shakespeare presents it, Cleopatra and the Antony whom she has infected veer off from the theater of war because of a lack of the tenacity and resolution that earth contributes to a horoscope. Cleopatra is the "fire and air" of imagination afloat upon the sea of perpetual transformations. Fire is her fierce or fiery character of aggression and violence. Air is her verbal energy and poetic power of image-making. Water is her uncontainable surges of emotion and her mercurial shifts of mood. Cleopatra's personae are in constant, uncontrollable change because earth is not present to stabilize or set a single persona. The sea she chooses at Actium is Dionysian "liquid nature," a phrase from elsewhere in Plutarch. This is the watery chthonian which separates her from Rosalind.

Cleopatra is Egypt, and Egypt is the Nile. In the Renaissance way, Cleopatra is addressed by the name of her realm, even by Antony. In *Antony and Cleopatra*, dry Egyptian earth has no inherent value. Fertility comes only when earth is subdued by water, turned to "slime and ooze" by the flooding Nile (II.vii.22). This muck is the primal swamp of Dionysian metamorphosis. The Egyptian serpent (already identified with Cleopatra) is bred from mud by the fiery sun (II.vii.26–27; I.iii.68–69). Cleopatra as Isis is Great Mother to her people. But Antony, in entering the humid Bower of Bliss of her liquid realm, loses his sense of self. He is not just a private person but a leader upon whom thousands depend. A leader cannot live by love alone. Antony betrays his men, and he betrays himself. The lovers' indifference to public concerns and their exaltation of emotion over duty are prefigured from the start in metaphors which inundate land with water. Antony declares, "Let Rome in Tiber melt, and the wide arch / Of the ranged empire fall!"—unadmirable sentiments for a Roman triumvir (I.i.33–34). Cleopatra angrily cries, "Sink Rome!" and "Melt Egypt into Nile!" (III.vii.15; II.v.78, 94). Antony and Cleopatra, obliterating earth in the waters of emotion, cannot resist the steady, inexorable pressure of earth's representative, Caesar.

The Renaissance Shakespeare knows Antony and Cleopatra are morally in the wrong, yet he projects into them the liquefied proteanism of his own artistic self. Antony, once the "pillar" of the Roman world, sees himself turning into shifting clouds, shapes of horse, bear, lion, citadel, cliff, mountain (IV.xiv.2–14). Cleopatra has dissolved and naturalized him. Jane Harrison says of the Greek Orphics, with their persistent cloud metaphors, "Their theogony, their cosmogony, is full of vague nature-impersonations, of air and ether and Erebos and Chaos, and the whirlpool of things unborn."[33] Orphism is anti-Olympian and hence anti-Apollonian. In *Antony and Cleopatra*, Apollonian Rome, with its statutory limits, sets up rational barriers to the chaotic flux of sensory experience. Antony is alchemized by Cleopatra, queen of Dionysian nature. He is hermaphroditized by his dissolution in watery Egypt. Mars drowns in Venus. At his darkest moment, Antony says to Cleopatra, "Love, I am full of lead" (III.xi.72). This is the play's nadir, before the transformation begins into spiritual gold.

Magic and prophecies are efficacious throughout. After his death, Cleopatra sees Antony as the astrological cosmic man, his eyes the sun and moon (V.ii.80). The hermaphrodite *rebis* of alchemy was often shown as a union of Sol and Luna, sun and moon. Both Antony and Cleopatra reach perfection in death. As the incomplete Mercurius, Cleopatra must achieve her magnum opus outside of life rather than in it. Before her suicide, she says, "Now from head to foot / I am marble-constant: now the fleeting moon / No planet is of mine" (239–41). Cleopatra is renouncing what Shakespeare elsewhere calls "the wat'ry moon," the symbol of emotional volatility we found in *As You Like It* (*Midsummer* II.1.162). At last she acquires that stony fixity of will which the play ascribes to Roman personality. Her ceaseless transformations end in the immobility of death—immutable as the Philosopher's Stone. Death is already in her lips when she says, "I am fire, and air; my other elements / I give to baser life" (289–90). Actually, she has finally mastered her too-combustible fire and air and achieved a spiritual integration of all four elements. With the addition of "marble-constant" earth, the coldness of death, Cleopatra is now the complete Mercurius, enshrined upon her altar-like bier. "Husband, I come," she says to the dead Antony. The medieval alchemic process was called both marriage bed and funeral bier. Those who have sought a redemptive pattern in *Antony and Cleopatra* are correct, but Christian it is not. Shakespeare ends his play with the alchemic purification of pagan personality.

The symbolic marriage of Antony and Cleopatra, enacted at the moment of death, removes the lovers from the social order. Their hedonism and self-involvement have damaged their nations and their

cause. Eight boars for breakfast is no recipe for political success. Cleopatra was the last of the Ptolemies, a three-hundred-year-old Macedo-
nian dynasty. After her death, Egypt was annexed as subject state to
Rome and never regained its former glory. *Antony and Cleopatra* demonstrates that life cannot be lived as a series of perpetual self-transformations without violating social and ethical principles. My generation
learned this the hard way, going down in sexual disease and drug
overdoses. *Antony and Cleopatra* takes a double point of view: Shakespeare acknowledges the eternal authority of beauty and imagination,
but he renders unto Caesar the things that are Caesar's. Social order
and stability were primary English Renaissance values. This is why
Rosalind, unlike Cleopatra, is the perfected Mercurius. At the end of
her play, Rosalind demonstrates the subordination of personality to
society by relinquishing her theatrical androgyny and metamorphoses
for obedience in marriage. Hierarchy is restored, in home and palace.

If Rosalind is a role difficult to play, Shakespeare's Cleopatra is even
more so. A bad Rosalind is simply simpering or flat. But a bad Cleopatra
is ludicrous. No one fits the part—except Tina Turner, Kent Christensen's superb suggestion to me. In the video of "What's Love Got To
Do With It?" Tina Turner is Shakespeare's "tawny" Cleopatra in all her
moods, regal, raffish, masculine, maternal, strolling among her people
in the city streets. Cleopatra's fiery sexual expressionism is Shakespeare's reply to the cool introversion of Spenser's chaste heroines.
Cleopatra is Amazon and mother but also chatterbox. The silent pictorial iconicism of *The Faerie Queene* is part of the poem's search for self-
definition. Spenser turns the hard Apollonian line against his own
plush pornographic impulses. Shakespeare bases language in the Dionysian body. In all his mature plays, speech is sensory and muscular.
Stage gesture and movement are implicit in the zigzagging syntax.
Every major Shakespeare character unites sexual personae with blooming language, while Spenser divides them. Nothing in literature is more
majestic than the sound of a true king speaking in Shakespeare. The
enormous assertion of that voice and the internal stability in the verse
are functions of Renaissance hierarchy, overflows of the great chain of
being. Unfortunately, the heroic Shakespearean sound is muffled these
days for scaled-down television performance or productions by liberal
directors with antifascist axes to grind. But Shakespeare's aristocratic
voice must be heard. It is a moral ideal. Rosalind and Cleopatra, we
have seen, strain at the limits of the Renaissance hierarchic code.
Shakespeare dramatizes the Renaissance tension between sexual personae and social order, one of his profoundest concerns. The major

theme of Shakespeare's plays is personality-in-history, the heart of western identity.

Spenser, Shakespeare, and Freud are the three greatest sexual psychologists in literature, continuing a tradition begun by Euripides and Ovid. Freud has no rivals among his successors because they think he wrote science, when in fact he wrote art. Spenser, the Apollonian pictorialist, and Shakespeare, the Dionysian alchemist, compete for artistic control of the English Renaissance. Shakespeare unlooses his metamorphic flood of words and personae to escape Spenser's rigorous binding. Luckily, he had drama to flourish in. In this genre he could be free of Spenser's strictures. The contrast between Shakespeare and Spenser is replayed in Metaphysical poetry, the next important literary movement. John Donne is Shakespeare's heir, muscular, theatrical, and metaphor-ridden. Donne fills even devout religious poems with flamboyant sexual personae and eccentric transpositions of gender. George Herbert is Spenser's heir. The exquisite aestheticism of *The Faerie Queene* turns into feminine homoeroticism in Herbert. The silvery sweetness of Herbert's simple style is exactly like Sappho's. If you want to know how Sappho sounds in Greek, don't read her pedestrian translators; read Herbert. Herbert discourages anything abrupt or emphatic—that is, masculine. Climactic speech is often ignored, restrained, or expelled. Herbert's world of contemplative serenity and whispery intimacies is androgynous. Its divine male presences have internalized femininity, so that real women are unnecessary and *de trop*. Though his poems seem disarmingly open and transparent, Herbert is psychologically embowered. He is alone, under Spenserian glass.

Shakespeare managed to evade Spenser, but Milton as epic poet had to meet Spenser on his own turf. *Paradise Lost* (1660) staggers under the burden of *The Faerie Queene*. If Spenser is the English Botticelli, Milton is its Bernini. *Paradise Lost* is a Baroque Laocoön, strangling itself with its own stately ornateness. Though Milton uses Shakespeare's over-spilling line, Shakespeare's speed is gone. The best things in *Paradise Lost* are pagan developments of Spenser. The worst things are humorless Protestant sermonizing, which has imprisoned this poem in parochial nationalism. Milton can only be read in English. Translated, he withers. The pagan Spenser corrupts the Puritan Milton. Milton tries, vainly, to correct Spenser morally. But Italian pictorialism, coming partly through *The Faerie Queene* and partly through the most decadent passages of the *Aeneid*, swamps Milton's Protestant iconoclasm. Spenser's radiant Apollonian armouring becomes Milton's louring metallic daemonism, militant and misogynistic. Satan's legions gleam with hard

Spenserian light. Milton sinks when he sings of the foggy formlessness of good. His God is poetically impotent. But his noisy, thrashing Spenserian serpents and monsters; his lush Spenserian embowered Paradise; his evil, envious Spenserian voyeurism: these are immortal. Milton tries to defeat Spenser by wordiness, Judaic word-fetishism, tangling the Apollonian eye in the labyrinth of etymology. Shakespeare succeeded here by joining words to pagan sexual personae. But the Christian Milton is mastered by Spenser, who bounds over him and through him to Romanticism.

8

Return of the Great Mother

Rousseau versus Sade

Romanticism is the forge of modern gender. Two Renaissance principles reemerge: flamboyant androgynous sex roles and the idea of divinely inspired artistic genius. The Renaissance, we saw, revived the Apollonian element in Greco-Roman paganism. In Renaissance art, even Dionysian beings, like Shakespeare's Cleopatra, are subordinated to social and moral order. Romanticism swings toward Apollo's rival, Dionysus, who appears in a great wave of the chthonian. The Enlightenment, developing Renaissance innovations in science and technology, was ruled by the Apollonian mind. Not since Greek high classicism had clarity and logic been so promoted as intellectual and moral values, determining the mathematical form of poetry, art, architecture, and music. "ORDER is Heav'n's first law," says Pope, from the cold beauty of Descartes and Newton's mechanical universe (*Essay on Man*, IV.49). The Enlightenment, as Peter Gay asserts, used pagan scientism to free European culture from Judeo-Christian theology.[1] Reason, not faith created the modern world. But overstress of any faculty causes a rebound to the other extreme. The Apollonian Enlightenment produced the counterreaction of irrationalism and daemonism which is Romanticism.

Romanticism makes a regression to the primeval, the archaic nightworld defeated and repressed by Aeschylus' *Oresteia*. It brings a return of the Great Mother, the dark nature-goddess whom St. Augustine condemns as the most formidable enemy of Christianity. Turning from society toward nature, Rousseau creates the Romantic world-view. Though he allows authority to the state for public good, his most enduring bequest is the flamingly antiestablishment stance of radicals from Blake and Marx to the Rolling Stones. Rousseau makes freedom a western watchword. Like the Renaissance, the Enlightenment glamourized hierarchy, the great chain of being swept away by Romanticism. For Rousseau, the Swiss Protestant reformer, no hierarchy comes from nature. Politics can be reshaped by human will, for human benefit. Romanticism regards hierarchy as a repressive social fiction. But man is biologically a hierarchical animal. When one hierarchy is removed, another automatically springs up to take its place. The great irony of Romanticism is that a movement predicated on freedom will compulsively reenslave itself to imaginative orders even more fixed.

Nature, hailed by Rousseau and Wordsworth as a benevolent mother, is a dangerous guest. The ancient cult-followers of Dionysus knew that subordination to nature is a crucifixion and dismemberment. Human identity is obliterated in the Dionysian conversion of matter to energy, a theme of Euripides' *Bacchae*. Romanticism, like the Rousseauist Swinging Sixties, misunderstands the Dionysian as the pleasure principle, when it is in fact the gross continuum of pleasure-pain. Worshipping nature and seeking political and sexual freedom, Romanticism ends in imaginative entrammelment of every kind. Perfect freedom is intolerable and therefore impossible.

Romanticism's overexpanded superself immediately subjects itself to artificial restraints as a chastening *ascesis*, a discipline and punishment. First of all, Romantic poetry invents an archaic ritual form, implicitly pagan. Second, it steeps itself in sadomasochistic eroticism, never fully acknowledged by scholars. The sadomasochism becomes blatant in Decadent Late Romanticism, which defies Rousseau and Wordsworth by rejecting chthonian nature for Apollonian aestheticism. I view nineteenth-century Decadence as a Mannerist convolution of High Romanticism and date it unusually early—1830. The themes I find in High and Late Romanticism—cruelty, sexual ambiguity, narcissism, fascination, obsession, vampirism, seduction, violation—are all the still-uncharted psychodynamics of erotic, artistic, and theatrical cathexis. I define American Romanticism as Decadent Late Romanticism, in the French manner. Decadence is a counterreaction within Romanticism, correcting its tilt toward Dionysus. This ambivalent pattern is there from the start. Rousseau is savagely answered by the decadent Marquis de Sade, who stands half in the Enlightenment, half in Romanticism. Blake, Sade's British brother, answers himself, his voices of experience devouring his voices of innocence. And Wordsworth is secretly answered and undermined by his colleague Coleridge, who through Byron and Poe turns Romanticism into Decadence in English, American, and French literature and art.

Rousseau and Wordsworth, loving female nature, open the door of a closet St. Augustine locked. Out pop vampires and spirits of the night, who still stalk our time. We remain in the Romantic cycle initiated by Rousseau: liberal idealism cancelled by violence, barbarism, disillusion, cynicism. The French Revolution, degenerating into the bloody Reign of Terror and ending in the restoration of monarchy in imperial Napoleon, was the first failed Rousseauist experiment. Rousseau believes man naturally good. Evil springs from negative environmental conditioning. Rousseau's saintly child, marred by society, is opposed by Freud's aggressive, egomaniacal infant—whom I hear and see everywhere. But Rousseauism flourishes among today's social workers and childcare experts, whose smooth, sunny voices too often exude piety and paternalism.

In *The Confessions*, modelled on Augustine's, Rousseau says a childhood incident formed his adult sexual tastes. He is eight, beaten and inadvertently aroused by a woman of thirty. Since then, his desires have been masochistic: "To fall on my knees before a masterful mistress, to obey her commands, to have to beg for her forgiveness, have been to me the most delicate of pleasures." In love, he is passive; women must make the first move.[2] Rousseau ends the sexual scheme of the great chain of being, where male was sovereign over female. In Romanticism, unlike the Renaissance, Amazons retain their power. Rousseau wants it both ways. Idolizing woman is natural and right, a cosmic law. On the other hand, male recessiveness is blamed on female coercion. Either way, sadomasochistic dominance and submission are inherent in Rousseauism from the start.

Rousseau feminizes the European male persona. The late eighteenth century, the Age of Sensibility, gives the ideal man a womanlike sensitivity. He is Castiglione's courtier without athleticism or social savvy. He looks to nature and beauty with misty emotion. Rousseau makes sensibility a prelude to Romanticism. The Petrarchan lover fancied himself deliciously powerless vis-à-vis one charismatic ice-queen. The man of feminized sensibility lacks an erotic focus. He is sufficient unto himself, savoring his own thoughts and feelings. His narcissism evolves into Romantic solipsism, doubt about the reality of things outside the self.

For Rousseau and the Romantics, the female principle is absolute. Man is a satellite in woman's sexual orbit. Rousseau calls his first patron, Madame de Warens, "Mamma," and she calls him "Little one." Stendhal's heroes will replay Rousseau's erotics of maternalism. Rousseau says of his sexual initiation by De Warens, "I felt as if I had committed incest." She later "compells" him to put on her dressing gown: he is transvestite priest to a goddess. Rousseau attends the Venetian carnival as a masked lady, then adopts Armenian robes as daily dress and busies himself making laces: "I took my cushion round with me on visits, or worked at my door, like the women."[3] Rousseau absorbs femininity from women, but they cannot reciprocate. They must remain female. He is repulsed by the flat chest of intellectual Madame d'Épinay. But the voluptuous female figure is enhanced by transvestism: Madame d'Houdetot, model for his *Nouvelle Héloise*, conquers Rousseau when she arrives on horseback in men's clothes.

Rousseau's nature-theory is grounded in sex. Worshipping nature means worshipping woman. She is a mysterious superior force. Late in life, Rousseau likes to let his boat drift in a Swiss lake (a scene paralleled in Wordsworth's *Prelude*): "Sometimes I cried out with emotion: 'O Nature! O my mother! I am here under your sole protection. Here there is no cunning and rascally man to thrust himself between us'."[4] The son-lover of the Great Mother spurns his sibling rivals. For all his talk of tenderness and fraternity, Rousseau was notoriously quarrelsome, finding conspiracy and persecution everywhere. He constantly fought with male friends, including his benefactor, British philosopher David Hume. Rousseau's flights from city to nature were pilgrimages purifying him of masculine contamination. He started a fashion. Once Rousseau lauded the Alps, Van den Berg says, people's desire to see Switzerland spread through Europe "like an epidemic": "It was then that the Alps became a tourist attraction."[5]

Through power of imaginative projection, Rousseau imprinted European culture with his peculiar constellation of sexual personae. The man who created modern autobiography made political science autobiographical. He was the first to claim what we call a sexual identity. Before the late eighteenth century, identity was determined internally by moral consciousness and externally by family and social class. Rousseau anticipates Freud in inserting sex into the childhood drama of character development. How striking a departure this was is clear when we compare Rousseau to his self-analytic French precursors. In his *Essays* (1580), Montaigne lists his sexual habits as casually as his menus or bowel movements. Sex for Montaigne is office schedule and flow chart: how often and at what times of day does he lie with his wife? The sex act is rhetorically equivalent to his taste in wines or reluctance to use silverware (an effete Italian import). Montaigne's identity is not shaped by sex. He is discursive intellect musing on social custom. Pascal's *Pensées* (1670) strip away Montaigne's cheerful intimacies. Pascal says Montaigne talks too much of himself. In the transition from Renaissance to seventeenth century, identity has become barer and more anxious. Pascal never reflects upon his sexual identity. The supreme question is the soul's relation to God, or, more fearfully, the soul's relation to a universe without God. Sex is merely part of the earthliness impeding man's spiritual struggles.

Rousseau makes sex a master principle of western character. Psychic fluidity and ambiguity, themes of Shakespeare's transvestite comedies, enter the mainstream of thought and behavior. Autobiography becomes apologia. *The Confessions* are a romance of self. Rousseau is the first to trace adult perversity to childhood trauma. The Christian quest for salvation is recast in erotic terms. Rousseau's guiding female spirits are apparitions, angels, and demons. He is a pagan Moses, climbing the Alps to meet his god. Adrift in the lake, he floats in the womb of liquid nature. The sexual revolution he wrought is evident in the emergence of homosexuality as a formal category. From antiquity, there were homosexual acts, honorable or dissolute depending on culture and time. Since the late nineteenth century, there is homosexuality, a condition of being entered after searching or "questioning," a Rousseauist identity crisis. Modern psychology, following Rousseau, pessimistically roots sex deeper than does Judeo-Christianity, which subordinates sex to moral will. Our sexual "freedom" is a new enslavement to ancient Necessity.

Rousseau's philosophizing of sex originates in the failure of social and moral hierarchies in the late eighteenth century. Before the Enlightenment, rigid class stratification, however stultifying, provided a sense of community. Now identity, suddenly expanding, must find other means of definition. But sex is no substitute for metaphysics. Pascal says, "The tendency should be towards the general, and the bias towards self is the beginning of all disorder, in war, politics, economics, in man's individual body."[6] Sex was central to ancient mystery religions, but they had a coherent view of omnipotent nature, both violent and benign. Rousseau, the first fabricator of sexual identity, seeks freedom by banishing social hierarchies and worshipping a uniformly benevolent nature. My theory: when political and religious authority weakens, hierarchy reasserts itself in sex, as the archaizing phenomenon of sadomasochism. Freedom makes new prisons. We cannot escape our life in these fascist bodies. Rousseau's masochistic subordination to women comes from his overidealization of nature and emotion. Making honey, he stings himself.

One cause of Rousseau's simplistic nature-theory: there was no *Faerie Queene* in French literature to show the dangers of nature. Consequently, Sade arose, with all his horrors, to check Rousseau's happy hopes. Rousseau and Sade together equal the totality of Spenser. Spenser and Sade see the daemonism in sex and nature. The Marquis de Sade (1740–1814) is a great writer and philosopher whose absence from university curricula illustrates the timidity and hypocrisy of the liberal humanities. No education in the western tradition is complete without Sade. He must be confronted, in all his ugliness. Properly read, he is funny. Satirizing Rousseau, point by point, he prefigures the theories of aggression in Darwin, Nietzsche, and Freud. Sade was prosecuted by both conservative and liberal governments and spent twenty-seven years in prison. His books were banned at publication, but rare private editions influenced avant-garde French and English writers throughout the nineteenth century. Sade's complete surviving works were finally published in reliable form after World War II. French intellectuals embraced him as a poet-criminal in the style of Jean Genet, homosexual thief and jailbird. But Sade has made barely a dent on American adacemic consciousness. It is his violence far more than his sex which is so hard for liberals to accept. For Sade, sex *is* violence. Violence is the authentic spirit of mother nature.

Sade is a transitional figure. His aristocratic libertines belong to the eighteenth-century novel of worldliness, like Laclos' *Les Liaisons dangereuses* (1782). But Sade's emphasis upon energy, instinct, and imagination puts him squarely in Romanticism. He is writing in the same decade as Blake, Wordsworth, and Coleridge. Extending Rousseau's idea of sexual identity, Sade makes sex a theater of pagan action. He drives a wedge between sex and emotion. Force, not love is the law of the universe, the highest pagan truth. Sade's daemonic mother nature is the bloodiest goddess since Asiatic Cybele. Rousseau revives the Great Mother, but Sade restores her true ferocity. She is Darwin's nature, red in tooth and claw. Simply follow nature, Rousseau declares. Sade laughing, grimly agrees. "Cruelty is natural," he says in *Philosophy in the Bedroom* (1795). In *Justine* (1791), he calls nature our "common mother." Sade's world is ruled by a female titan: "No, there is no God,

Nature sufficeth unto herself; in no wise hath she need of an author."[7]
The Great Mother, Sade's supreme female character, begins and ends
all.

In Sade's sacred rites, libertines flagellate, rape, and castrate their
victims, then devour their bodies and drink their blood. Like Aztec
priests, they vivisect, extracting the living heart. A product of the elegant
French aristocracy, Sade primitivizes his own culture and makes it
decadent. He mingles sex acts with assault and mutilation to show the
latent brutality of sex. As in Freud, the sex instinct is amoral and
egotistical. In *Juliette* (1797), answering Rousseau's *Julie*, Sade says of
lust, "It demands, it militates, it tyrannizes." Sex is power. Sex and
aggression so fuse that not only is sex murderous but murder is sexual.
A woman declares: "Murder is a branch of erotic activity, one of its
extravagances. The human being reaches the final paroxysm of delight
only through an access of rage." The orgasm is a burst of violence, "a
kind of fury" showing nature's intention that "behavior during copulation be the same as behavior in anger."[8] Freud says the infant witnessing the primal scene of parental intercourse thinks male is wounding
female. Sade corrects Rousseau's map of the past: Rousseau's eroticism
was shaped by Sadean subordination, not Rousseauist tenderness. The
flagellated eight-year-old was an initiate into Sadean cult.

Sade meshes his case against Rousseau with his case against Christianity. Like Nietzsche, whom he clearly influenced, Sade attacks
Christianity's bias for the weak and outcast. By preserving the lowly,
Christian pity "disrupts the natural order and perverts the natural law."
Dominance is the right of the strong. Against Christ and Rousseau,
Sade says benevolence and "what fools call humaneness" have "nothing to do with Nature" but are "the fruit of civilization and fear." The
founder of Christianity was "some feeble individual," "some puny
wretch." Sade dismisses Christian charity and Rousseau's equality and
fraternity as sentimental delusions. There are no social or moral obliga-
tions for the philosopher: "He is alone in the universe."[9] Because of his
Romantic concentration on self, Sade's libertines never permit love or
friendship to survive. Loyalty is a temporary pact among criminal co-
conspirators.

Humanity has no special status in the universe. Sade asks: "What is
man? and what difference is there between him and other plants,
between him and all the other animals of the world? None, obviously."
This is a classically Dionysian view of man's immersion in organic
nature. Judeo-Christianity elevates man above nature, but Sade, like
Darwin, assigns him to the animal kingdom, subject to natural force.

Vegetable too: man is soulless, "an absolutely material plant." And
mineral: Juliette says, "Man is in no wise Nature's dependent; he is not
even her child; he is her froth, her precipitated residue."[10] Rousseau's
mother nature is Christian Madonna, lovingly enfolding her infant son.
Sade's mother nature is pagan cannibal, her dragon jaws dripping
sperm and spittle.

Since man has no privileges in Sade's universe, human acts are
"neither good nor bad intrinsically." From nature's point of view, marital sex is no different from rape. To prove human benevolence a utopian
theory contradicted by reality, Sade assembles a catalog of atrocities
committed by every culture in history, often in the name of religion. His
anthropological syncretism, anticipating Frazer's, demonstrates the relativism of sexual and criminal codes. Surprisingly, Sade's abolition of
civil and divine law does not lead to anarchy. The libertines establish
their own rigorous structures, the natural hierarchy of strong and weak,
master and slave. Whether *Juliette*'s Sodality of the Friends of Crime or
the vast School for Libertinage in *120 Days of Sodom,* Sade's libertines
organize themselves into autonomous social units. They issue prospec-
tuses and statutes, design formal architectural environments, and herd
their victims into erotic classes and subsets. Like colonies of ants, they
secrete systems. These things in Sade come from the Apollonian Enlightenment. As a Dionysian sexualist, Sade abolishes the great chain of
being, sinking man into the continuum of nature, but he cannot shake
off the intellectual hierarchism of his age. The libertines' identity precedes their cooperative clustering for debauchery. Personality in Sade is
hard and impermeable—that is, Apollonian. There are no mysteries or
ambiguities because nothing is left in the unconscious, whose most
perverse fantasies empty into the cold light of consciousness. In Sade,
Apollonian personality is plunged into Dionysian sewage but emerges
clean and intact.

Sade's libertines are often double-sexed. Soft-figured males crave
passive sodomy. Dolmancé belongs to a third sex: with his "feminine
manias," the sodomite was created by nature to "diminish or minimize
propagation." Sade's heroines are among the most potent women in
literature, sister to Shakespeare's bare-knuckles Cleopatra. Madame de
Clairwil of *Juliette* and Madame de Saint-Ange of *Philosophy in the
Bedroom* have extraordinary self-command and aristocratic presence.
They match the male libertines in erudition and intellectual force.
Clairwil (Apollonian "clear will") combines "Minerva" with "Venus."
Her keen glance is "too fiery to withstand." Juliette herself, through her
voluminous adventures (1,193 pages), has a captivating freshness, re-

silience, and masculine willfulness. Sade's female aggressors have Cleopatra's power of intimidation and attack, but they enact what Cleopatra only imagines. Clairwil remarks, "Torturing males is still my favorite pastime." Juliette admires Clairwil at play, "when I saw her daubing her cheeks with the victim's blood, tasting it, drinking it, when I saw her bite into his flesh and tear it away with her teeth; when I saw her rub her clitoris on the bleeding wounds she opened in the wretch." Another exploit: "The fierce creature opens the abdomen of the boy who has been entrusted to her, she tears out his heart and thrusts it hot into her cunt. . . . Clairwil sent up a howl of pleasure. 'Juliette,' she gasped, 'Try it, Juliette, try it, there's nothing to equal the sensation'."[11] Not since the *Bacchae* had there been so direct a transcription of daemonic experience. Sade recreates the agony and ecstasy of ancient mystery religion. His female libertines are high priestesses of savage nature, doing her work day and night.

Juliette calls herself "manlike in my tastes as in my thinking." For her first crime, sexual assault upon and murder of a woman pedestrian, she dons men's clothing, the sign of her burgeoning male will. She turns Rosalind's transvestism into an executioner's masked ball. Noirceuil enlists Juliette for transvestite double marriages, surpassing Nero's. Dressed as a woman, Noirceuil marries a man; then dressed as a man, he marries a catamite dressed as a girl. Juliette, meanwhile, dresses as a man and marries a lesbian; then dressed as a woman, she marries a lesbian dressed as a man. A sexual maze.

The masculinity of Sade's women can be anatomical. Madame de Champville of *120 Days of Sodom* and the beautiful nun Madame de Volmar of *Juliette* have three-inch clitorises. Madame Durand has an obstructed vagina and a clitoris "as long as a finger," with which she forces sodomy on women and boys. In these ruthless penetrators, Sade creates a freakish new sexual persona: the female active sodomite. Sade and Baudelaire like lesbianism for its aura of the unnatural. The female squanders her reproductive energy upon herself. Sade finds lesbians superior to other women, "more original, more intelligent, more agreeable." His lesbian couplings go on constantly all over Europe. The lesbian heroines imitate the "ceaseless flux and action" of nature. Plucky Juliette contrasts with her goody-goody sister Justine, much as Cleopatra does with shy Octavia. Every disaster and outrage comically befall patient, humble Justine. Virtue fails; vice prospers. I think that Justine is Rousseau and that Juliette is Sade. Virtue is "inert and passive," but nature is "motion," "active agitation."[12] In Sade as in Spenser, pure femininity is a vacuum into which nature's energy violently rushes. Nature finally strikes Justine dead with a bolt of lightning. In Sade as in Blake, energy is male. Hence Sade's great heroines are masculinized by their criminal vitality.

Sade's libertines retain Apollonian intellect in nature's surging Dionysian flux. Though Sade thinks men no different from plants, his characters contradict him by their long unplantlike speeches. In fact, they never stop talking. Learned disquisitions go on amid orgies, as in *Philosophy in the Bedroom*, with its rapid seesaw between theory and praxis. Cleopatra's stormy speeches came from Dionysus' link to language—hence the logophilia of Sade's copulators. But there is no Dionysian self-abandonment in Sade. Moderate delirium may occur at orgasm (Madame de Saint-Ange: "Aië! aië! aië!"), but words generally sail on through ejaculation. Sade's sexual dissenters seek Dionysian lawlessness and abandon themselves to Dionysian fluids. Physiologic squalor, theme of Swift's *The Lady's Dressing Room*, is minutely detailed in *120 Days of Sodom*. Here are more excremental interludes than in any other Sade novel, not only coprophagy but lapping up of the most obscure bodily secretions. As in Whitman, identity is expanded and redefined by taking in life's debris. To be sexually aroused by something eccentric, insignificant, or disgusting is a victory of imagination. Sade demonstrates Dionysus' promiscuous all-inclusiveness. He makes licking and sucking mental acts. Without the great chain of being, there is no hierarchic dignity or decorum. Sade's libertines freely wallow in filth and find no humiliation in being flogged or sodomized in public. The excretory voiding of one person into the mouth of another is Dionysian monologue, a pagan oratory.

Sade consigns the human body to the realm of Dionysian dismemberments, scorned by Aeschylus' Apollo as chthonian home of the Furies. The tortures invented by the libertines are of the form-pulverizing kind I found in Homer and Euripides. The libertines eagerly obliterate the body's formal contours, tearing, piercing, scraping, gouging, maiming, slicing, shredding, burning, melting. Readers' tolerance for Sade's barbaric fantasies will vary. Even I cannot stand many passages, despite my long study of the chthonian and, possibly more germane, a college summer as ward secretary of a downtown hospital emergency room. Don't read Sade before lunch! Sade is subjecting the body to Dionysian process, reducing the human to raw matter and feeding it back to rapacious nature.

Plutarch calls Dionysus "the Many." Sadean sex is not democratic, but it always occurs in groups. Private rooms annex the sexual arena of *120 Days of Sodom* but seem merely ornamental. The libertines prefer mob-frenzy, a Bacchic rout. Dionysus' metamorphoses are in Sade's roiling sex-action, inventing sexual personae and molding the body into new shapes. Men take masochistic roles and women rape and torture in order to destroy traditional sexual hierarchy. Paganism is restored and the hermaphroditic world of Roman orgy recreated. Sade wants to create an androgyne as perfect monster, combining as many perverse identities as possible. Sodomized as she rapes her mother, the ingénue Eugénie cheerfully cries, "Here I am: at one stroke incestuous, adulteress, sodomite, and all that in a girl who only lost her maidenhead today!" Fornicating with her brother, Madame de Saint-Ange is sodomized by Dolmancé, who in turn is being sodomized by the gardener. She declares to Eugénie, "Behold, my love, behold all that I simultaneously do: scandal, seduction, bad example, incest, adultery, sodomy!" Eugénie, an initiate into pagan mysteries, is catechized by her preceptress, satirizing Rousseau's progressivist theory of education. Sade concocts roles and experiences with Romantic audacity. In *120 Days of Sodom*, the President de Curval explores another variation: "In order to combine incest, adultery, sodomy, and sacrilege, he embuggers his married daughter with a Host." Sade stirs affronts to the sacred into his stew. Again: "A notorious sodomist, in order to commit that crime with those of incest, murder, rape, sacrilege, and adultery, first inserts a Host in his ass, then has himself embuggered by his own son, rapes his married daughter, and kills his niece."[13] The Sadean orgiast is intellectual and contortionist, a Laocoön entwined by his proliferating desires.

Sade's sexual conglomerations are like answers to a riddle: what is black and white and red all over? He produces them a posteriori (!) in response to the question, how may I outrage as many conventions as possible? They are prison puzzles worked out by ingenious wit, as in the ritualistic finale of *As You Like It*, where Rosalind makes herself the solution to a sexual conundrum. But note the difference between Renaissance and Romantic imagination. Rosalind simplifies her superimposed sexual identities to ensure social consolidation and progress. Sade crushes identity upon identity to demolish social structure. Romantic incest, we will see, is a contraction of relationships. Incestuous inbreeding rules Sade's sexual conglomerates.

At a Naples revel, Juliette enjoys receiving "three pricks simultaneously, two in the cunt, one in the ass":

> There were several times when everybody forgathered upon a single woman. Thrice did I withstand the weight of that general assault. I was lying upon one man who was embuggering me; Elise,

squatting over my face, gave me her pretty little cunt to suck; another man embuggered her above me, while frigging my cunt; and Raimonde was stimulating that man's asshole with her tongue. Within reach of my two hands were Olympia to one side, on all fours, Clairwil to the other side: I introduced a prick into the asshole of each, and each of them sucked a prick belonging to the fifth and sixth man. The six valets, after having discharged eight times each, were finally received without difficulty.[14]

We see a gigantic complex sexual molecule with a female center. It is the writhing octopus of mother nature. Sade's multisexed hybrid is like Scylla or Hydra or other chthonian horrors of Greek myth. Such grotesques in Spenser and Blake are always negative. But not in Sade, who substitutes sexual for social relations. His libertines swarm together in mutually exploitative units, then break apart into hostile atomies. Multiplication, addition, division: Sade perverts the Enlightenment's Apollonian mathematic. A schoolmaster's voice: if six valets discharge eight times each, how many valets does it take to . . . ?

One of Sade's most outlandish conjunctions occurs in a convent in Bologna. Juliette makes the unforgettable remark, "The Bolognese nun possesses the art of cunt-sucking in a higher degree than any other female on the European continent." Sade parodies Diderot's magisterial style, investigating, comparing, concluding.

Delicious creatures! I shall ever sing your memory. . . . It was there, my friends, that I executed what Italian women call the *rosary:* all fitted out with dildoes and gathered in a great hall, we would thread ourselves one to the next, there would be a hundred on the chain; through those who were tall it ran by the cunt, by the ass through those who were short; an elder was placed at each novena, they were the paternoster beads and had the right to speak: they gave the signal for discharges, directed the movements and evolutions, and presided in general over the order of those unusual orgies.[15]

A hundred nuns linked by dildos! The style of Busby Berkeley or the Radio City Rockettes. The holy rosary becomes the primeval uroboros, a vicious circle. Human connectedness is sexually literalized. The orgiast nuns are like a polysyllabic Greek or German noun, spawning prefixes and suffixes and hyphenated by dildos. As a man of the Enlightenment, Sade organizes Dionysian experience into Apollonian patterns, punctuated by hierarchical speech.

Sade's Dionysian modes are multiplicity and metamorphosis. Dolmancé urges Eugénie "to multiply those excesses even to beyond the
possible," a Romantic formulation. An abbess tells Juliette, "Variety,
multiplicity are the two most powerful vehicles of lust." Madame de
Saint-Ange explains the boudoir's many mirrors: "By repeating our
attitudes and postures in a thousand different ways, they infinitely
multiply those same pleasures for the persons seated here upon this
ottoman. Thus everything is visible, no part of the body can remain
hidden: everything must be seen." Madame de Saint-Ange is voyeur
and cubist, dividing the body into parts spread across a single screen of
vision. In Sade, the aggressive Apollonian eye never loses its power. He
creates a night of morality but never of sight. Noirceuil, echoing Ovid,
counsels wives, "Metamorphose yourselves, assume many roles, play at
this sex and that."[16]

Dionysian metamorphosis is obvious in the transvestite and transsexual episodes. A roué wants to be spanked by "a man got up as a girl," a
"masculine flagellatrice" called "she." The Duc de Blangis, kissing a
boy, is suddenly sodomized: "Virtually without noticing it, he changed
sex." Transsexual operations are brutally improvised: "After having
sheared off the boy's prick and balls, using a red-hot iron he hollows out
a cunt in the place formerly occupied by his genitals; the iron makes the
hole and cauterizes simultaneously: he fucks the patient's new orifice
and strangles him with his hands upon discharging." The libertines
practice daemonic medicine. Another transsexual experiment, with
organ transplants: "A sodomist: rips the intestines from a young boy and
a young girl, puts the boy's into the girl, inserts the girl's into the boy's
body, stitches up the incisions, ties them back to back to a pillar which
supports them both, and he watches them perish."[17] Remember, these
are ideas, not acts. Sade isolates the aggression in the western scientific
mind. And he demonstrates (my constant theme) the sexual character
of western seeing. Sade plays Darwinian mother nature, mutating gender and cross-fertilizing with heavy hands. Like her, he makes manure
and loam out of humanity.

So identity in Sade, as in Romanticism, comes not from society but
from the daemonized self. But Sade differs from the more passive
Romantics (except Blake) in making identity arise from action, for
libertine and victim alike. One originates an act, and the other suffers it.
The context of Sadean identity is dramaturgical. There are always
"tableaux" and "dramatic spectacles" of interlaced bodies, of which
people make witty aesthetic judgments. Theatricality is blatant in modern sadomasochism, with its costumes, stage props, and scripts. Sado-

masochism, I suggested, is a symptom of cultural thirst for hierarchy. Religion is misguided when it relaxes its ritualism. The imagination longs for subordination and will seek it elsewhere. Sade, a *philosophe* casting the church out of his universe, ends by making sex a new religion. His lavish sexual ritualism dramatizes the natural hierarchism of sex—a hierarchism having nothing to do with social custom, for women can be masters and men slaves. Sadomasochism is coldly formal, a condensed expression of the biologic structure of sex-experience. In every orgasm there is domination or surrender, open at all times to both sexes, in groups, pairs, or alone. Richard Tristman remarked to me, "All sexuality entails some degree of theater." Sex contains an element of the abstract and transpersonal, which only sadomasochism forthrightly acknowledges. Tristman continued: "All sexual relations involve relations of dominance. The desire for equality in women is probably an attenuated expression of the desire to dominate." Hailed in the Sixties as a sexual liberator, Sade is actually the most scholarly documenter of sex's subjection to hierarchical orders.

The theatricality of Sade's libertines comes from their clarity of consciousness. Daydreaming or introspection is unneeded in a world where realization immediately follows desire. The libertines are like Roman emperors in wealth and power, two things, as Sade observes, which give absolute sexual control over others. Like Blake, Sade exalts Romantic imagination, the source of wish and therefore fulfillment: "The imagination's fire must set the furnace of the senses alight." Free imagination is able "to forge, to weave, to create new fantasies." Juliette declares, "The imagination is the only cradle where pleasures are born." Without it, "all that remains is the physical act, dull, gross, and brutish."[18] Sade's biggest erogenous zone is the mind. His works, like Genet's, are autoerotic prison dreams creating a perverse universe of new sensations and sexes. Sade is the cosmogonic Khepera, eternally renewing his lust. Masturbation is his motivating principle.

In *120 Days of Sodom,* with its *Decameron*-like format, the compulsion to find fresh sexual rituals to stimulate orgasm appears in the numbered lists of the final sections, still in draft when the manuscript disappeared in the storming of the Bastille. Sade invents an astonishing series of short sexual scripts isolating the drama of subordination, fantasies stripped down to their skeletal hierarchical structure. Each has a date and number. The lists are part journal, saints' calendar, epic catalog, Apollonian calculus.

We may sense the eroticism in this, even if we fail to share its appeal: "The 22nd of December. 109. He rubs a naked girl with honey, then binds her to a column and releases upon her a swarm of large flies." St. Sebastian becomes the seething hive of Ephesian mother nature. Other scenarios are more puzzling. "Has her run naked about a garden at night, the season is winter, the weather freezing; here and there are stretched cords upon which she trips and falls." Or: "He holds the girl by the ears and walks her around the room, discharging as he parades with her." The imagery is of malice and sabotage, hunt and trophy. The girl is a flayed coney run to earth. Sade's scripts can be disarmingly mild: "Has a woman with beautiful hair brought to him, saying he simply wishes to examine her hair; but he cuts if off very traitorously and discharges upon seeing her melt into tears and bewail her misfortune, at which he laughs immoderately."[19] This is Spenserian masque, a public spectacle eroticized by juxtaposing feminine vulnerability with icy, lustful hierarchic power.

Sade's precision gives his fantasies a comic gratuitousness: "He pulls out her teeth and scratches her gums with needles. Sometimes he heats the needles." Hot needles are the least of her problems. Sade's self-satirizing decadent style belongs to an eighteenth-century fin de siècle. There are Swiftian sallies: "The 17th of February. 90. A bugger cooks up a little girl in a double boiler." The pot gleams with recipe-like professionalism. My favorite recalls Alice introduced to the plum pudding: "He binds the girl belly down upon a dining table and eats a piping hot omelette served upon her buttocks. He uses an exceedingly sharp fork."[20] Heated needles, double boiler, ticklish tines: the eye is drawn in by increasing specificity of detail until we find ourselves poring over a grotesque scene with scientific absorption. Sade's epicene wit allies him with Lewis Carroll and Oscar Wilde. The lists of *120 Days of Sodom* are like a roster of outrageous Wildean epigrams.

The theater director of *120 Days of Sodom* is male, but in Sade's work as a whole, females are not more abused than males. Sade and Blake grant women the sexual freedom of men. Though he honors his great female libertines, Sade detests procreative woman. Pregnant women are tortured, forced to abort, or crushed together on iron wheels. Madame de Saint-Ange tells Eugénie, "I declare to you, I hold generation in such horror I should cease to be your friend the instant you were to become pregnant." Madame Delbène urges Juliette, "Do not breed." A statute of the Sodality of the Friends of Crime is, "True libertinage abhors progeniture." The three major figures of *Philosophy in the Bedroom* detest their mothers. The novella ends in a ritualistic assault upon a mother, Madame de Mistival, who comes to rescue her daughter

Eugénie from her corrupters. Instead, Mistival is raped, flogged, and infected vaginally and anally by a syphilitic valet. Then vagina and rectum are sewn up with "a heavy red waxed thread."[21] Needlework torture occurs elsewhere in Sade, but nowhere so emphatically. Only here is the thread red, hinting at the arterial and umbilical. The scene looks forward to Huysmans' archetypal dream of mother nature, where female genitalia turn into syphilitic flower.

Sade is seeking a female equivalent to castration. How does one desex a woman without dismembering and therefore killing her? In *120 Days of Sodom* the Duc de Blangis attempts such an operation, disordering a woman's entrails by piercing the vaginal, intestinal, and gastric walls. But in *Philosophy in the Bedroom* Sade wants to androgynize the procreative female and send her back into the world in humiliating sterility. Similar symbolic action was at work in Jack the Ripper's extraction and public nailing up of the uterus of his victims. I suspect Sade is a bit vague about female sexual anatomy; otherwise, he would surely have splattered such impromptu hysterectomies all over his work. Mutilation of female genitals, reported to this day throughout the world, descends from ancient perceptions of the uncanniness of female fertility. Jung says, "Occasionally it still happens that the natives in the bush kill a woman and take out her uterus, in order to make use of this organ in magical rites."[22] Such things arise not from social prejudice but from legitimate fear of woman's alliance with chthonian nature.

The female body is often ridiculed in Sade. Two effeminate homosexual minions strip Justine and laugh uproariously at her genitals: "Nothing nastier than that hole." A man in *Juliette* calls female genitals an "unclean, fetid gulf." The female bosom is lustfully admired by Sade's lesbians, but it leaves many males cold. In *120 Days of Sodom* a priapic gentleman rebukes Madame Duclos: " 'Devil take those damned tits of yours,' he cried; 'who asked you for tits? That's what I can't bear about these creatures, every single impudent one of them is wild to show you her miserable bubs'."[23] Breasts often appear only to be flailed and cut to ribbons—or in one case severed and fried on a griddle. But before we condemn Sade, think of Tiepolo's painting, *The Martyrdom of Saint Agatha* (1750). The saint ecstatically expires, eyes raised to heaven, while her bloody amputated breasts are collected for us by an insouciant pageboy hefting a silver platter. Are we expected to vomit or eat? For two thousand years, the torture of martyred saints, as well as of Christ, has filled western imagination with sadomasochistic reverie. Adolescent Yukio Mishima had his first orgasm upon seeing a copy of Guido Reni's

St. Sebastian. The sex and violence in Christian iconography are an eruption of pagan mystery religion, of which Christianity is a development.

Sade believes the female body less beautiful than the male. Compare a naked man and woman: "You will be obliged to conclude that woman is simply man in an extraordinarily degraded form."[24] Like Michelangelo, Sade admires muscular articulation, the Blakean correlate of his Romantic energy. De Beauvoir and Barthes connect Sade's devaluation of the female body to his homosexual craving for sodomy.[25] But sexual symbolism is greater than private habits. Sodomy is Sade's rational protest against relentlessly overabundant procreative nature. Dog-style heterosexual copulation, a staple of current pornography, represents the animality and impersonality of sex-experience. When face is averted from face, emotion and society are annihilated. Remember the masked face of the Venus of Willendorf. The zippered leather mask of modern sadomasochistic gear covers the whole head and primitivizes the personality. Sodomy's ritual significance appears in a myth recorded by Clement of Alexandria. As a reward for directions to the underworld, Dionysus promises to sodomize Proshymnos. But when the god returns, Proshymnos is dead. To fulfill his vow, Dionysus anally penetrates the corpse with a branch carved like a penis. Sodomy is imagined as ritual entrance to the underworld, symbolized by man's bowels.

The ritual sex acts of ancient earth-cult were meant to stimulate nature's fertility. Sodomy in Sade blocks the procreative. Like Blake, Sade brings the Great Mother into being as an act of hostility. The campaign against Madame de Mistival begins with Dolmancé's proclamation, "We owe absolutely nothing to our mothers." After Harold Bloom's study of male poetic strife in *The Anxiety of Influence*, it is impossible to read such a statement without hearing its real meaning: "We owe absolutely everything to our mothers." Sade's works ritualize sex on a gigantic scale. If a ritual relieves anxiety, Sade's sadomasochistic inventions are modes of distancing by which male imagination tries to free itself from female origins. Again, there are parallels with Blake. Jane Harrison says, "Man cannot escape being born of woman, but he can, and if he is wise, will, as soon as he comes to manhood, perform ceremonies of riddance and purgation."[26] Sade's obsessive sodomy is a ritual of riddance to evade maternal power.

Hence Sade alternately celebrates and reviles woman. He gives his intellectual female libertines another male prerogative, in defiance of reality: the passion for sexual atrocities. Anyone can see, just by reading the newspaper, that men commit sex-crimes and women do not. The feminist idea that sexual violence is caused by the social denigration of women is disproved by the many cases of homosexual torture and rape-murder of boys by the dozen. Sex-crimes arise less from environmental conditioning than from a failure of socialization. Mutilating crimes by women are extremely rare. There are the Papin sisters, whose massacre of their employers inspired Genet's *The Maids*. After that we are at a loss, driven as far back as ax-wielding Lizzie Borden, who may have gotten a raw deal. As for what Sade calls "lust-murder" or "venereal murder"—homicide that stimulates orgasm or is a substitute for it—I beg for female nominees. One of history's most intriguing women, Hungarian Countess Erzsebet Bathory (1560–1614), the prototypical lesbian vampire of horror films, may have been sexually aroused in her torture and murder of 610 maidens, but rumor reports only that she bathed in their blood to preserve her youth. As Freud says, "Women show little need to degrade the sexual object."[27]

Serial or sex murder, like fetishism, is a perversion of male intelligence. It is a criminal abstraction, masculine in its deranged egotism and orderliness. It is the asocial equivalent of philosophy, mathematics, and music. There is no female Mozart because there is no female Jack the Ripper. Sade has spectacularly enlarged female character. The barbarism of Madame de Clairwil, orgasmically rending her victims limb from limb, is the sign of her greater *conceptual* power. Sade's female sex-criminals are Belles Dames Sans Merci of early Romanticism. The Romantic femmes fatales will be silent, nocturnal, lit by their own daemonic animal eye. But Sade's women, inveterate talkers, retain the clear Apollonian solar eye of western intellect.

Sade's enormous influence upon Decadent Late Romanticism has not been fully studied. His importance is demonstrated by Mario Praz in "The Shadow of the Divine Marquis" in *The Romantic Agony* (1933), a major book shunned by most critics as simplistic and sensational. Baudelaire and Swinburne stress their debt to Sade, who prefigures Decadent sensibility in several ways. He finds beauty in the horrible and revolting. Like the Roman emperors, he juxtaposes artificiality and sophistication with chthonian barbarism. His libertines are "indifferent to everything simple and commonplace," a Decadent phrase.[28] The libertines are always self-immured, a Decadent claustrophobia. We will find a parallel in the imprisoned spaces of the Gothic novel, which reach the Decadence through Poe. Sade's corpse-strewn sexual arenas resemble the Gothic morgue. These heaps of rotting matter are the accumulated objects of nature and society which I see oppressing Romantic imagination.

9

Amazons, Mothers, Ghosts

Goethe to Gothic

The young Goethe, a disciple of Rousseau, begins German literary self-consciousness in a welter of sexual ambiguities. Like Sade, Goethe is a transitional figure, half classic, half Romantic. A new Renaissance man, he sought mastery of all arts and sciences. By the end of his long life he was the cultural leader of Europe, as Voltaire had been in the eighteenth century. Biography long ago established Goethe's sexual eccentricities and amoral titanism of will. But too much of the vast scholarship on Goethe's poems, plays, and novels is stultifyingly dull, paralyzed by reverence. No other writer of this rank suffers so gaping a rift between biography and criticism.

Goethe's novella *The Sorrows of Young Werther* (1774) gave the *Sturm und Drang* school, with its Rousseauist sensibility, an international impact. Werther, to whom Goethe gives his own birthday, is Rousseau's emotional feminized male, pale, melancholy, tearful. He is the moody double-sexed adolescent first documented by Shakespeare. Romantic adolescence has spiritual superiority. For Werther, childhood is beautiful and pure, while masculine adulthood is sordid and debased; so refusing to grow up is noble. Werther clings to his feminine mood-states to defeat time and gender.

The Sorrows of Young Werther ends in the hero's suicide, which started a vogue for real suicides throughout Europe. This was the first salvo of Romantic youth-cult, to return in our own frenetic 1960s. I attribute these suicides to the shift in sexual personae at the close of the eighteenth century. Theodore Faithfull says in another context, "Dreams of self-destruction, and probably many cases of suicide, are desires or attempts on the part of narcissistic individuals to give themselves a new birth by sexually attacking themselves and thus bringing about self-fertilization."[1] Werther-style suicide had an aggressive autoeroticism, glamourizing an act that the Church condemns as the gravest sin. Werther's Rousseauist emotionalism is self-dissolving: "My powers of expression are weak and everything is so hazy in my mind that all contours seem to elude me."[2] The Enlightenment's sharp Apollonian lines disappear in Dionysian mist. Werther is like Shakespeare's suicidal Antony, whose identity shifts like clouds. *The Sorrows of Young Werther* demonstrates how Rousseauist sensibility acted as an alchemic bath, hermaphrodizing the European male persona in emotional fluidity. Like Rousseau, Werther worships the earth mother, in whose lap he dies. His suicide is strongly ritualistic: the pistols must pass through the daemonizing hands of Lotte, a pleasant maiden whom Werther turns into a Romantic femme fatale. Goethe said the novel came from "the decision to let my inner self rule me at will" and to let outside events "penetrate."[3] In Romantic creativity, the male waits in spiritual passivity, acted upon by internal and external forces. The feminized inner self is the Muse who becomes increasingly ferocious as Romanticism goes on.

Wilhelm Meister's Apprenticeship (1796) is a tangle of sexual problematics. Goethe's novel begins the tradition of the *Bildungsroman* or novel of education, the story of a young man's development, modelled on Rousseau's *Confessions*. A feminized male is the center of *The Sorrows of Young Werther*, but *Wilhelm Meister* is dominated by masculine women. The novel opens with transvestism: an actress steps offstage in male military dress, with sword. She refuses to change clothes, since she has a rendezvous with Wilhelm Meister, whom Goethe called his "dramatic likeness." Like Balzac's Sarrasine and Wilde's Dorian Gray, Wilhelm has fallen in love with a stage persona, whose red uniform he clasps with fetishistic "rapture."[4] Female transvestism is everywhere in *Wilhelm Meister*, from Tasso's warrior Clorinda to women disguising themselves as pages and hunter-boys.

The novel has a mysterious "Amazon" who finds Wilhelm lying wounded by bandits. The shape of the radiant "angel" is concealed by a man's white great coat, which she ritualistically lays upon him. This light-shedding Apollonian androgyne, suddenly appearing in a forest, resembles Spenser's Amazon huntress Belphoebe, whose roots are in Ariosto and Tasso. Wilhelm becomes obsessed with her, replaying her epiphany in his dreams. When she becomes a real and intelligent person at novel's end, the Amazon loses her glamour. This pattern of declension is common in works with sexually ambiguous themes, like Virginia Woolf's *Orlando* and *Mrs. Dalloway*. The Amazon's magnetism comes only from her mystical androgyny. *Wilhelm Meister*'s transvestism is so pronounced that the hero mistakes a real soldier for a woman. Another actress carries a dagger, the "faithful friend" which is her totemic male self. She kisses it and tucks it in her bosom or whips it around, cutting Wilhelm. Wilhelm Meister is not as feminine as Werther, but Goethe swamps him sexually by surrounding him with viragos and transvestites. Wilhelm speaks for his creator in saying that "the novel-hero" must suffer, while the dramatic hero should act and achieve.[5] Even in action, like Werther's suicide, Goethe's novel-heroes seek self-subordination. Goethe hastens the evolution of Rousseauist sensibility into Romantic masochism.

The star transvestite of *Wilhelm Meister* is Mignon, whom Georg Lukács calls "the very embodiment of the romantic spirit" and Victor Lange the "most exquisite embodiment of Romantic lyricism."[6] When Wilhelm first sees her, the adolescent Mignon is in male dress, and he cannot guess her gender. She is an "enigma" with a magical fascination for him. Her name has erotic associations: the French "mignon," whence our "minion," means "favorite" or "darling" in female prostitution and male homosexuality. Although she is in the novel's earliest manuscript, Mignon resembles a boyish Venetian acrobat whom Goethe saw in Italy in 1790. "Neither male nor female," Mignon is fanatical about her transvestism. She passionately rejects female clothing: "I am a boy, I will be no girl!"[7] After playing an angel in a pageant, she refuses to surrender her seraph's robe. Two dozen pages later, she is dead, after becoming more and more attenuated and etherealized as a character: she loses vital energy when she abandons male clothing. At the funeral, her body is laid out in her winged angel's costume. The service is a masque, with recitations by boys in Apollonian azure and silver.

Mignon conforms to two categories of the androgyne. She is the beautiful boy, the Apollonian angel, but she is also a negative or afflicted Mercurius, the volatile shape-shifter. Mignon's early death is foreshadowed in her unnatural excitation. When Wilhelm meets her, she "darted like lightning through the door": "She never walked up or down the stairs, but jumped. She would spring along by the railing, and before you were aware, would be sitting quietly above upon the landing." She dances "lightly, nimbly, quickly." Mignon sounds like Shakespeare's antic Ariel, but there is something disturbingly pathological in her energy. She has palpitations and fits, a worsening "spasmodic vivacity" or "restless stillness." She constantly twists or chews thread, napkins, paper, as if to drain "some inward violent commotion." She is alarmingly "frantic with gayety"; hair flying, she raves and capers like a

"Maenad."[8] Mignon finally falls dead from a heart spasm. The Dionysian Mercurius dances herself to death.

In her emotional purity and intensity, Mignon is an early version of
Faust's Euphorion, the symbol of poetry modelled on Byron. Euphorion
too is agitated and volatile, but Mignon is more feverish and hysterical. I
call her Goethe's Euphoria, after the uncontrollable "up" phase of
manic-depression. Shakespeare's Rosalind is the perfected Mercurius
of mercurial wit and multiple personae. The afflicted Mercurius is like
Byron's mistress, Lady Caroline Lamb. Sometimes appearing in pageboy or other male dress, Lady Caroline was notorious for her mad
nervous energy and exhibitionistic pranks. She smashed china in her
rages; she was publicly self-destructive, as when, jealous of Byron, she
shattered a wineglass in her hands. Byron called her "Little Mania."
Dangerous to herself and others, she died prematurely, like Mignon.
Lady Caroline was androgynous in her willfulness, transvestism, and
adolescent body-type. Her excessive thinness went against contemporary fashion: besieged by her after his ardor had cooled, Byron declared,
"I am haunted by a skeleton."

Though Mignon is more innocent than the calculating Lady Caroline
Lamb, the two have the same hyperactivity and spasmodic tension. In
her mobile charm, Mignon is like Tolstoy's mischievous Natasha, who
appears once in *War and Peace* in a mustache. In Rosalind as Mercurius, language is developed to its maximum. But Mignon is a Mercurius of silence: "Often for the whole day she was mute."[9] Even from
childhood, "she could not express herself" with words. This muteness is
Mignon's Apollonian side, which she shares with Spenser's Belphoebe,
with her broken sentences, Melville's stammering Billy Budd, and
Thomas Mann's dreamy Tadzio. Another afflicted Mercurius: Edie
Sedgwick, the short-lived blonde socialite and Andy Warhol superstar
who, like Lady Caroline, was childish, boyish, angelic, monstrous, and
self-destructive, constantly dancing or setting her bed and hotel afire.
Next, the affected aspiring actress Gloria (Barbara Steele) in Fellini's
8½, wearing out her aging lover by her madcap dancing, poetic raptures, and hysterical mood-swings.

Not until the end of *Wilhelm Meister* do we learn that Mignon was
born of the incest of brother and sister. Incest, defended here, is to
become the paradigm of Romantic sexuality. Mignon's parents mentally deteriorate. An "Apparition" appears, "a beautiful boy standing at
the foot of their bed and holding a bare knife."[10] This avenging angel of
the guilt-ridden unconscious prefigures the doomed transvestite Mig-

non. Stationed at the bed of sin, the boy-spirit is like Rosalind's double, Hymen, the hovering marriage-idea. Mignon's death is analogous to the Amazon's loss of glamour when she regains her social identity. Like *As You Like It* and *Twelfth Night*, *Wilhelm Meister* consigns the romance of transvestism to spiritual adolescence. Wilhelm enters maturity by renouncing the theater, arena of impersonations. For Wilhelm to advance from apprentice to master of life, the novel must sacrifice his inseparable companion, Mignon. She is an externalization of his double-sexed adolescence. Her death is equivalent to Rosalind and Viola killing off Ganymede and Cesario, the transvestite heroines' male alter egos. Wilhelm's new concern for permanence and continuity comes from Goethe's neoclassic side. Wilhelm becomes "father" and "citizen." Like Empress Plotina, he rejects multiple personae for the stable, unitary persona that is the basis of civic order. Like Shakespeare's transvestite comedies (surely Goethe's inspiration), *Wilheim Meister* ends with the setting aside of masquerades and the rediverting of psychic energy into society.

Goethe's Mignon had a long and unacknowledged influence on nineteenth-century literature. I think she is the source, ultimately forgotten, of a series of Romantic and Late Romantic androgynes. An untranslated and now obscure work, Henri de Latouche's *Fragoletta* (1829), takes up *Wilhelm Meister*'s motif of female transvestism and transmits it to two writers strongly influenced by la Touche, Balzac and Gautier. Gautier's *Mademoiselle de Maupin*, inspired by *Fragoletta*, becomes the first bible of the French and English Decadence. In the manuscript of *Wilhelm Meister's Apprenticeship*, found early this century, Mignon's sexual ambiguity went beyond transvestism. Goethe calls her sometimes "she," sometimes "he," a witty subtlety suppressed in earlier editions (including Thomas Carlyle's still-sold translation) because it was thought an error. In the sequel, *Wilhelm Meister's Travels*, Goethe calls Mignon "boy-girl" and "pseudo-boy." Mignon should be credited to Shakespeare's enduring continental influence. Gautier rejoins the female transvestite to her source in *As You Like It*, performed by his characters as a mime of their own gender confusion.

In the *Venetian Epigrams*, ancestor of Mann's *Death in Venice*, Goethe celebrates the Mignon-like acrobat, Bettina. He accepts as his own his novel-heroes' fascination with the perverse. Goethe sees Bettina as an incarnation of the beautiful boys or "cherubim" of Italian Renaissance painting (Epigram 36). He compares her to Ganymede, whom he as king of the gods covets (38). Performing, Bettina plunges the admiring observer into dreamlike uncertainty and doubt: "Everything hovers in space in unstable form. / So Bettina confuses us, twisting her beautiful limbs" (41).[11] Bettina is sexually and morphologically ambiguous. Her acrobatic dexterity makes Goethe question her species: she is mollusk, fish, reptile, bird, human, angel (37). Mobile Bettina represents both Apollonian ideal beauty and Dionysian metamorphosis. She violates all categories.

One of the *Venetian Epigrams* suppressed because of their frank sexual content is about Bettina: "What worries me most is that Bettina grows always more skillful, / Always more supple becomes every joint in her frame; / At last she'll bring her little tongue into her dainty slit; / She'll play with her charming self, lose all interest in men" (34).[12] Goethe the voyeur imagines Bettina acrobatically masturbating, like Catullus' autofellating sleazebag, Gellius. Bettina becomes a Romantic circle of incest and narcissism. She is the uroboros devouring itself or the Egyptian sky goddess arching backwards. She is sexually complete and self-embowered, like Blake's autoerotic "Sick Rose." Visually, she resembles Blake's engravings of solipsistically contorted figures. Goethe invents an autonomous, rapacious female sexuality. He is merely a spectator at a pagan ritual. Man is on the periphery, woman at the center. In the next epigram, Goethe predicts Bettina's first lover will find her acrobatics have torn her hymen. She has, in other words, the masculine power to deflower herself. Bettina is hardier and uncannier than Mignon. Her serpentine limbs slink into and bind Goethe's strange sexual imagination. In her flaunting exhibitionism, she is like baby mother nature at play.

Faust, Goethe's contribution to world literature, joins the Renaissance to Romanticism. Not since *Hamlet,* which influenced this play, had there been so searching an analysis of the moral and sexual ambiguities of western consciousness. The historical Doctor Faustus was an unscrupulous magician denounced by his contemporary, Martin Luther. The first *Faustbook* (1587), condemning Faust for his intellectual hybris, shows Protestantism awakened against the dangers of Renaissance paganism. Goethe expands the sexual commentary in the *Faust* story. The western mind is seen as sex and power, striving against God and nature. Don Juan and Faust are the most characteristic myths of the postclassical west. They represent dominance, aggression, the will-to-power, all the imperial ambitions of paganism that Christianity has never been able to defeat.

Faust is Goethe, the artist as magus, just as Mephistopheles is Goethe, the artist as enemy of God. As a Renaissance alchemist, Faust seeks the secrets of nature. What Goethe has added to the story is the seduction theme, borrowed from Don Juan and Casanova. In Marlowe's *Doctor Faustus* (1593), Helen of Troy, summoned for Faust's delectation, is a majestic love goddess. Goethe's Ophelia-like Gretchen, on the other hand, is the humble handmaiden in a saga of lust, violation. guilt, and remorse. Goethe makes an analogy between the exploitation of women by men and the exploitation of nature by the self-infatuated western mind. Here Goethe parallels Blake, who is the first to protest against the industrial corruption and pollution of green England.

Faust shows sex as a mode of western knowledge and control. Gretchen, the lamblike feminine innocent, is physically and morally ruined, ending in infanticide. Her illicit intercourse with Faust implants her with western aggression. Seduction is an intellectual game. It is the invasion of one hierarchy by another. By creating sacred spaces apart from nature, the west invites their despoilment. Like Spenser's Florimell, Gretchen induces destruction by her own passivity and defenselessness. Goethe exalts the feminine principle and makes Gretchen a redeemed martyr, but like all great artists he is ambivalent toward his own moral constructions. Faust in league with Mephistopheles is Goethe yielding to his own cannibal impulses.

The west's will-to-power has created our perverse dynamics of willing. The rapist says, she wanted it, she asked for it. This conviction is produced by the separation and tension between sexual personae. She who may or may not ask for it is a real person, with a sharp identity. The defeat of her will is part of the thrill of seduction or rape. Coercion requires free will, in both homosexual and heterosexual acts. Faust's seduction of Gretchen is intrusion, trespass, criminal entry into posted space. This is one of the west's premiere sexual tropes, intensified by our categorizations and hierarchic rankings. In classical antiquity, immoderate lust was priapism, which was, like drunkenness, the fault of fools and satyrs. Christianity's animus against sex and its stark polarity of good versus evil intellectualized lust and raised its significance. Lust is a crossing of the gap between western sexual personae. Lust sharpens the aggressive, predatory western eye, making it prelude and coda of touch. Faust and Mephistopheles, watching, are voyeurs at Gretchen's stalking, capture, soiling, and imprisonment.

Faust, a play with an alchemist hero, has a diffuse alchemical form. It has two parts, a multitude of episodes, and a crowd of minor characters. It combines classical with Christian culture. It mixes tragedy with comedy, epic with lyric, ideal beauty with the grotesque and obscene. Gretchen is naive sentiment, Mephistopheles cynical sophistication.

Faust is caught in the middle, like all mankind. *Faust* has a variety of sexual personae, more than any other work of major literature. Goethe inserts Romantic androgynes into the traditional Faust story. Faust's acquisitive western intellect is invaded by hybrid sexual forms, bursting out of the alchemic unconscious. All of *Faust* is a *Walpurgisnacht*, a return of the occult. The witch-revel episode, Goethe's addition, is a pagan encroachment upon a Christian drama. Goethe identified imagination with the daemonic: he repeatedly spoke of daemonic assaults upon gifted men. *Faust* is structurally amorphous because it is daemon-haunted. The play itself suffers Dionysian fluctuations: metamorphosis was the master principle of Goethe's speculations in science and art. Critics comment on his inability or refusal to finish anything. All Goethe's stories, even *Werther* and *Wilhelm Meister*, were to continue in sequels. As a drama, *Faust* breaks Aristotle's and Racine's Apollonian rules. It is restless, volatile, glutted with magic epiphanies and contradictory emotional textures.

The two characters in *Faust* symbolizing poetry are double-sexed. The girlish Boy Charioteer is fancily decked out with jewels and tinsel. Euphorion, Faust and Helen's son, is a classic beautiful boy, part Apollo, part Icarus. He wears feminine adornments of Asiatic opulence. Like Homer's Athena, he is the androgyne as symbol of human intelligence. Poetry, Goethe implies, attains universality by a fusion of genders. To be transsexual in appeal, art must be bisexual in origin. Euphorion is short-lived because he represents Romantic lyricism, which burns hot and fast. Goethe joins the vernality of the Greek beautiful boy to the true facts of English Romanticism, whose second generation of poets died glamourously young.

The Adonis-like Paris is a maturer Euphorion. Goethe's Paris is even more effeminate than Homer's. Goethe suggests that femininity in a male alienates men but arouses women. Thus the unmanly Paris won the most beautiful woman in the world. Other examples of the languid boudoir manner are Byron's Don Juan and George Hamilton, Hollywood's most popular escort of famous women. The man discreetly attending women becomes a misty mirror of their femininity.

There are two sex changes in *Faust*. Mephistopheles slips into the shape of female Phorkyas. Now a smooth courtier, Mephistopheles can call on chthonian metamorphosis at will—the realm he came from when he began his interventionist career as a serpent trailing after a woman. The second example occurs at a carnival, where the Scraggy One, a parodic Teiresias, identifies himself as a miser whose sex has waned from female to male. Like Dante and Spenser, Goethe identifies the female principle with emotional generosity. The Scraggy One is a gargoyle, spiritually contracted, the androgyne as moral monstrosity.

An alchemical experiment is performed in the second part of *Faust*. Homunculus, a fabricated being, hovers in its glass retort, a self-propelled bubble. Goethe considered giving Homunculus a Homuncula as a mate, but his efforts to bring them together failed. Presumably Homunculus, as double-sexed as the alchemic *rebis*, rebuffed a wife as redundant. *Faust* shows the creative process as alchemic. The glass jar is the lucid self-contained world of art, harboring both beauty and deformity. As a creative symbol, Homunculus is goblin-twin to Euphorion and the Boy Charioteer. As a specimen of bioengineering, Homunculus anticipates Mary Shelley's creature in *Frankenstein* and her husband's Hermaphrodite in *The Witch of Atlas*. Manufacture becomes a metaphor for the aggressions of Romantic imagination.

Faust's most imposing androgynes occupy an eerie netherworld beyond space and time. Mephistopheles, uneasy, calls them "the Mothers." They are blind goddesses in a murky barren zone lit by a glowing Delphic tripod. The Mothers are Greek Fates combined with Plato's eternal forms: "Formation, Transformation, / Eternal Mind's eternal recreation."[13] Mephistopheles takes Faust to the omphalos of the universe, a female heart of darkness. The Mothers are nature's brute force of metamorphosis. Their creative solipsism is a daemonized version of Bettina's autoerotic circularity. *Faust*'s descent to the underworld shows past, present, and future. The realm of the Mothers is repressed pagan nature, which Enlightenment science failed to illuminate. Romanticism reverses the moral values of day and night. Mephistopheles himself hails from "Mother Night," Clytemnestra's home.

Certain Cretan nymphs were called "the mothers," mentioned by Diodorus Siculus as "the Cretan nurses of Zeus."[14] Goethe's familiarity with classical arcana is shown by his use of the name Baubo for one of *Faust*'s witches: Baubo is an ancient totem of ritual exhibitionism, raising her skirt to show her genitals. Goethe's goddesses are the Great Mother cloning herself, as profuse as the many breasts of Ephesian Artemis or the thousand names of Isis. The Mothers' multiplicity is sinister and suffocating. They flock like Sirens or Harpies, but they are far vaster in power. Goethe's maternal limbo is unparalleled, though it takes its tone from the witch scenes of *Macbeth*. In modern times, even when the Great Mother is treated sympathetically, as she is by Joyce and Woolf, she controls only green nature, not this gloomy Stygian cavern with which western myth associates swarthy male hierarchs. Emptiness and barrenness are usually produced by a flight from the maternal, as in the refusal to mourn the dead mother in Camus' *The Stranger* or in the horror of the mucoid object-world in Sartre's *Nausea*. Wasteland vision denies or suppresses the mother. In *Faust*, however, barrenness and fertility are creepily simultaneous. Goethe honors female power, but he sees it blocking everything. All roads lead to maternal darkness.

The Mothers appear in *Faust* when the hero tries to materialize the spirit of Helen. Adult love is overshadowed by maternal claims to priority. The male struggles through his sexual stages, returning to the mother even when he thinks himself most free of her. Faust finds his way to the Mothers with a key that phallically swells. When key and tripod touch, they stick. Now Faust is able to conjure up alluring Helen. If the mother-realm is the unconscious, key and vulval tripod are the self-fecundation of imagination. The Mothers as eternal forms ("*Gestalten*") are the archetypes tapped by the artist in his quest for ideal beauty, the elusive Helen. The male artist descending to the Mothers makes a journey to *terra incognita*, his own repressed feminine side, where his mother still dwells.

In key drawn to tripod, Goethe shows the ambivalent compulsions of sexual intercourse. Every male copulating with a woman returns to his origins in the womb. Goethe postponed intercourse until he was forty. This must be related to his self-imposed distance from his forceful mother. To refuse phallic penetration is to refuse surrender to the female matrix. Goethe was at least seventy-two when he wrote the Mothers episode. Therefore it represents a confrontation and perhaps reconciliation with a mode of experience he had cast out of his youthful imaginative life. Faust shudders at the Mothers' name. They are uncanny, archaic, and inescapable. Freud says that the uncanny (*unheimlich*) is really the familiar, the homely (*heimlich*) which one cannot bear to recognize. The strangeness of Goethe's Mothers comes from their perpetual proximity. We live with them. The simplistic sexual pattern of Part One of *Faust*, where the virile hero feeds upon the fragile femininity of Gretchen, is an evasion of the grosser truths faced by Part Two in the Mothers. Faust has an appetite for quivering Gretchen. But the Mothers have an appetite for quivering Faust. He is Everyman frozen before his maker.

Faust's angelic and infernal androgynes were produced by an imagination both fascinated and repelled by the mystery of sex. In his study of biological morphology, Goethe says the scientist must remain "just as mobile and pliant" as nature herself. Goethe counsels receptivity and subordination but finds them intolerable. After a sickly childhood, he undertook a vigorous exercise program to increase his strength: he

seized masculinity by force of will. Goethe's energy in old age was
legendary. Deceased contemporaries were the subject of condescending
remarks. Goethe seemed to feel he had a superhuman power to hold
death at bay. Thomas Mann says there was something "brutal" and
"heathenish" in "the arrogant way Goethe sometimes boasted of his vitality, his indestructibility."[15] Goethe turned his vulnerability to mother
and nature into imperious mastery of knowledge and other men. His
principal relationship was with his sister Cornelia, a year younger and
his only real childhood friend. His imaginative connection to her was
like Tennessee Williams' to his mad sister, Rose. In his memoirs, Goethe speaks of Cornelia as his twin. She was his Romantic alter ego, what
Jung would call his *anima*, a sister-Muse. Cornelia died at twenty-six,
soon after her marriage. Did she fail after separation from her twin?
Goethe's sister-fixation is evident throughout his love affairs. In letters
and poems he uses the word "sister" for lover or wife. Goethe's many
androgynes may represent a condensed incestuous twinship.

A sister is a woman who is not the mother. Goethe would not allow his
mother's name to be spoken in his presence. He avoided her. He refused
to answer questions about the episode of the Mothers. Goethe's mother
was too strong a personality. He feared to come near her lest he be
reabsorbed into her gravitational field and returned to childhood dependency. Goethe's biographer says, "Most of his relations with women
ended in sexual renunciation."[16] Heterosexuality for men will always
carry the danger of loss of identity. Goethe, unlike Antaeus, gained
strength by *not* touching mother earth.

Wilhelm Meister's transvestism echoes an incident just before Goethe
began *The Sorrows of Young Werther*. The source of this story is his own
mother. Goethe invited her and her friends to watch him skate on a
frozen river. His mother wore a long red fur cloak trimmed with gold.
Goethe demanded the garment, put it on, and skated away—leaving
her astonished and bewildered. Old engravings of the scene appear in
popular articles about Goethe. K. R. Eissler says: "It is most remarkable
that the greatest German poet, one week before he set out to write his
greatest novel, felt the impulse on the spur of the moment to exhibit
himself to his mother and a large crowd dressed in a conspicuous piece
of female clothing."[17] Theft and expropriation. Artists take what they
want and need. Goethe plays rude Baubo with the Great Mother. He
makes aggression and mockery an open-air pagan theater.

Freud thinks the fetishist's fur and velvet are symbolic substitutes for
the mother's pubic hair.[18] Masoch's *Venus in Furs* (1870) seems to
support this. Goethe lures his mother into an arena of hierarchic as-

sault. The frozen river is his own unnatural coldness to her: this ice is Dante's pit, where fathers eat their children. Generations are at war, striving for dominance. Like Prometheus, Goethe steals the red flame of the old order. He wrests the vatic mantle from his mother, claiming for himself the Delphic power to give birth to *Werther*. Harold Bloom says, "A strong poet . . . must divine or invent himself, and so attempt the impossibility of *originating himself.*"[19] Goethe forces a public ritual of self-origination. Jesus' career begins at Cana, where he harshly tells Mary, "Woman, what have I to do with thee? mine hour is not yet come" (John 2:4). Goethe on the frozen river says to his mother, my hour is come, and I take from you what I need to give birth to myself. The midwives stand gaping on the banks, spurned and useless. Remus, leaping his brother Romulus' wall, meant to break its magic, as by rape. Plutarch reports that Julius Caesar, the night before he crossed the Rubicon, dreamed he had sexual relations with this mother. Goethe too crosses a river and rapes his motherland. Attack and retreat: a declaration of imaginative independence. Henceforth, Goethe will be defiantly separate from his formidable mother. He steals the Palladium, the cultic Athena, which brings down Troy. Formerly under his mother's aegis, he now wears it. He is transvestite son to a vanquished Amazon goddess. For another artist, turning from the mother might mean a withering of feeling, a creative stunting. But Goethe instinctively reoriented himself toward his sister-spirit, borrowing her purified femininity. Together they would rule his new inner world, twin Ptolemies of self-orphaning Romanticism.

Goethe used transsexual analogies to describe his creative process, referring to himself as a pregnant woman. He spoke of being "suddenly overwhelmed" by his poems, which forced themselves upon him fully formed. Artistically, he felt feminine and passive toward a superior power, an idea we will find in Wordsworth, Shelley, and Keats. Recollections of Goethe often use sexually ambiguous terminology. Schiller, for example, said, "I look on him as a haughty prudish woman whom one wants to get with child." Goethe called his intimacy with Karl August, Duke of Weimar a "marriage." The two even slept in the same room. In the period of his Bettina poetry, Goethe admits to homosexual feelings. A suppressed Venetian epigram declares, "I'm fairly fond of boys, but my preference is girls; / When I have enough of a girl, she serves me still as a boy" (40).[20] Sodomy unexpectedly rears its head at the end of *Faust*, when the hero's soul escapes because Mephistopheles is distracted by the angels' physical attractions. Are *Wilhelm Meister*'s female transvestites and girl-boy Mignon sexually transformed males?

Goethe, who repeatedly compared himself to Voltaire's Mambre, eunuch philosopher to Pharaoh, was a castrate priest declining to worship his goddess. The ice upon which he tauntingly skated hardened and externalized the chthonian swampiness of sex and mother love. Late in life he said, "The sexual act destroys beauty, but nothing is more beautiful than what precedes this moment. Only in ancient art is eternal youth captured and depicted. And what does eternal youth mean other than never to have known a man or a woman."[21] Sex destroys beauty: Dionysus subverts the Apollonian eye. Romantic Goethe continually seduced classical Goethe. In the Wincklemann way, Goethe thought the male body more beautiful than the female. There may be less homosexuality in this than Apollonian idealization, the high articulation of the eye, often accompanied by chastity. Goethe was heroically self-contained and self-sufficient. Like Beethoven, he married himself.

Goethe's androgynes are fitting symbols for his life work, with its titanic all-inclusiveness. Sex for Goethe is a gathering in, not a dissemination. He claimed there was no vice or crime of which he could not find a trace in himself. Romantic art is self-exploratory, self-arousing, self-maiming. Goethe said, "Geniuses experience a second adolescence, whereas other people are only young once." Goethe retained his access to both sexes by renewing and prolonging puberty, in which gender fluctuates. Romanticism once seemed to make large simple gestures of rebellion. But we barely begin to understand its charged sexual complexities and archaic pagan ritualism.

Decadence is inherent in Romanticism. Sadomasochism, we have seen, is already present in Romantic eroticism from its first formulation by Rousseau. As the historical rhythm of Romanticism moves forward, the organic logic of artistic style takes over. The late phase of Romantic style is luridly Hellenistic or Mannerist: distortion of form, sadomasochistic fantasy, and psychological closure. Our first example is Heinrich von Kleist (1777–1811), a poet of the late phase of German Romanticism. What Goethe dreamed about through Werther, Kleist put into action. Kleist obsessively meditated upon and ritualistically planned his suicide, which he succeeded in at age thirty-four. Goethe had made suicide poetic and erotic. Kleist, the perfect masochist, allowed dominant Goethe to write a grisly life-poem through him.

Kleist's play, *Penthesilea* (1808), illustrates the daemonic sensationalism of German Late Romanticism. It reverses the hierarchy of sexual personae in the Greek legend of Achilles and Penthesilea. Instead of Achilles killing the Amazon queen, she kills him. Kleist's militant Amazons have tremendous chthonian ferocity. Epic similes compare Penthesilea to a she-wolf, a raging torrent, a storm wind, a thunderbolt. When the normally Apollonian Amazon enters drama, there is an eruption of Dionysian violence. Spenser defeats the surly Amazon Radigund, but Kleist exalts her. In Romanticism, nature, not society rules. In *Penthesilea* woman, as conduit of the natural, obliterates manhood and history.

The design of Kleist's play is sadomasochistic oscillation. Achilles and Penthesilea try to dominate each other physically and psychologically. Each surge of assertion is followed by relapse, a hypnotic longing for sexual submission. Achilles and Penthesilea manage to capture each other a ludicrous number of times: Kleist's anarchic plot line reflects the ambiguities and contradictions in heterosexuality. Sadistic Penthesilea is aroused by masochistic fantasies in which her dead body is battered, degraded, and discarded. I hear the influence of Shakespeare's *Antony and Cleopatra* here, as also in Kleist's images of land submerged in water, the public persona drowned in erotic obsession.

Kleist's Achilles, unlike Homer's, wants to lose. Three times he casts away sword and shield. He walks to his death in somnambulistic trance, seeking enslavement to Penthesilea, who falls upon him with her dogs. The play suddenly ascribes a feminine softness to Achilles. As he turns his neck, it is pierced by Penthesilea's arrow. Neck-turning or neck-exposing is a classically feminine gesture, with parallels of animal surrender. I find it in Michelangelo's Giuliano de' Medici, portraits of Byron, Flaubert's Madame Bovary, and George Eliot's vain Rosamond Lydgate. In Kleist, Achilles' feminine neck is his Achilles' heel, phallically penetrated by the Amazon. She and her dogs go into chthonian furor, savagely ripping off Achilles' armour and sinking their teeth into his chest. Penthesilea locks onto his left breast, blood dripping from her mouth. Later she laments she "ravaged" Achilles by breaking through the "snow-white alabaster wall" of his breast.[22] Her assault is masculine violation of feminine virginity. The rape focuses on breasts rather than genitals. Achilles seems to give suck to his beloved and her dogs, his breasts flowing with gore rather than milk. Kleist invents a gruesome version of the androgyne I call Teiresias, the nurturant male. He is injecting Sade's nature into Rousseau's tender mother-relations.

Penthesilea, a Romantic vampire, drains her victim, body and soul. Is Achilles' pierced breast an example of Freud's "displacement upwards" from the genitals? So Penthesilea castrates. The rape-like devouring of a penis disguised as a breast appears in Bob Dylan's brilliant invective, "Ballad of a Thin Man," where a sadistic voice attacks the naive Mr.

Jones with the homosexual demand, "You're a cow! Give me some milk or else go home!" Kleist's Achilles and Dylan's Mr. Jones enter and misread a menacing sexual scene. Both are punished for their misreading by compulsory feminization. Teiresias too turns female after stumbling on a chthonian scene. Voracious Penthesilea sinks to the level of her dogs. Dogs suckling a human breast reverse the image of Romulus and Remus nursed by the she-wolf (for which Eliade finds parallels in Central Asia). Multiple nursing is usually animalistic, an exception being Daumier's allegorical *The Republic*. Achilles' death is a primitive, barbaric spectacle. Michelangelo's Giuliano similarly combines a feminine neck with sadistically pierced breasts. In Kleist, however, there is a thrashing violence, Hellenistic storm and stress. Amazon and dogs in feeding frenzy fuse with and hybridize Achilles' body, a horrific mutilation-through-accretion recalling the grotesque deaths of Euripides' *Medea*, where princess and king stick and burn like tar. Late-phase art disfigures the human form.

Phallus as breast: one explanation, as we saw, for the penile or canine breasts of the Ephesian Artemis was that Amazons hung the idol with gift strings of their amputated breasts. Attacking Achilles' chest, Penthesilea is not only desexing him but *making him an Amazon,* a version of herself. She is a sadistic erotic mastectomist. All Romantic femmes fatales are avatars of daemonic mother nature. Kleist's Amazon is a hermaphrodite deity rewriting Genesis. She hurls Adam's rib back through his Adam's apple, then mutilates his rib cage without healing it. Like Jehovah, she makes man in her own image. The dying Achilles is now her twin, her Romantic sister-spirit.

Kleist dwells on the Amazons' amputated breasts throughout the play. Greek artists, we saw, never showed the Amazon's body as maimed. The Late Romantic Kleist, on the other hand, makes the detail central. Nowhere else in literature or art, not even in Sade, is so much made of breast amputation. Kleist's hero is fetishistically aroused by a woman's mutilating masculinization. He presses his face to Penthesilea's breast with a rush of endearments. Decadence is a style of excess and extravagance which approaches self-parody. It operaticizes by overliteralizing. Hence one laughs even when shocked or repelled, as in Sade. Kleist's stage directions are also parodic. This one, for example, rivals Shakespeare's "Exit, pursued by a bear": "Penthesilea looks round as if for a chair. The Amazons roll up a stone."[23] It was presumably the decadent elements in *Penthesilea* that led Goethe to condemn it as "unplayable."

As a classical saga of the erotic destruction of male by female, *Penthesilea* prefigures Swinburne's verse-play *Atalanta in Calydon.* Kleist and Swinburne identify kissing with biting, sex with appetite and cannibalism. Achilles' macabre murder resembles the narrated climax of Tennessee Williams' *Suddenly Last Summer*, where the epicene Sebastian Venable is torn to pieces and eaten by a mob of boys he has solicited. Penthesilea's maniacal ecstasy comes from Euripides' Agave, who dismembers her son in the *Bacchae*. Penthesilea raves, foams at the mouth, hurls boulders, tears Achilles' body limb from limb. She longs to root up sky and planets, to drag down the sun "by his flaming golden hair," to pile mountain on mountain. Dionysian vision is disordering and anti-hierarchical. In "Voodoo Child," Jimi Hendrix aspires with drug-induced titanism: "I stand up next to a mountain, and I chop it down with the edge of my hand." Shamanistic peaking is aggressive and self-destructive. Space is traversed, transcended, exploded. Penthesilea's expansion of self through the influx of primeval force is so overwhelming that she begins to devour all other selves. Kleist reshapes classical legend into a parable of Romantic solipsism. *Penthesilea's* ritualistic oscillations between sadism and masochism are unique in Romanticism. In Poe, for example, the sadomasochistic relations of male and female personae are relatively stable and mappable. But *Penthesilea* is a swirling vortex of sadomasochistic passions, each savagely devouring the next. Welcome to Late Romantic nature, created by Rousseau's benign overidealizations. *Penthesilea* can be read allegorically, as a descent into the poet's unconscious, where two parts of the psyche, masculine and feminine, fight for supremacy.

The play's sexual personae have indeterminate boundaries, which are corrected and hardened by emotional, physical, and sexual assault. Penthesilea's dangerous expansion of self has historical causes. The failure of traditional hierarchies in the late eighteenth century removed social and philosophical limitations essential for happiness, security, and self-knowledge. Without external restrictions, there can be no self-definition. The dissolution of hierarchical orders permitted personality to expand so suddenly that it went into a free fall of anxiety. Hence the self had to be chastened, its boundaries redefined, even by pain. The self must be *reduced in size*. This is the ultimate meaning of *Penthesilea's* erotics of mastectomy. Romanticism, swelling, contracts itself in Decadence. Mutilations and amputations belong to an aesthetics of subtraction, a pathological metaphysic in which the imagination reorients itself to the world by a surgical reduction of self. Sadomasochism will always appear in the freest times, in imperial Rome or the late twentieth century. It is a pagan ritual of riddance, stilling anxiety and fear.

Kleist's Achilles, lying in streams of blood under a pack of dogs, is glamourous with masochistic ecstasy. Dying, he touches Penthesilea's cheek: "O my bride, is this / The festival of roses that you promised?" (To which she should reply, if she could get her teeth out of his chest, "I never promised you a rose garden.") Late Romantics love the climactic pietà, starring what I call the male heroine. Woman cradles the victim, but only after she has batted him down and crushed him. The romance of the male heroine is a dream of disordered receptivity, in which there is a transsexual impulse. I find a parallel symbolism in a fringe-group homosexual practice that appeared in the 1970s: "fist-fucking," whose devotees crave anal penetration by a male arm, greased by Crisco, up to the elbow. Proctologists warned about internal damage they were re-pairing, first sign of the cycle of excess that led to AIDS. Ten years ago, I was deeply impressed by an early pornographic film I saw of these activities. It had the solemnity and gloom of a pagan ritual, like the tableaux of Pompeii's Villa of the Mysteries. Sex as crucifixion and torture. Fist-fucking, in its starkly depersonalized conflation of volun-tary rape and primitive exploratory surgery, dramatizes the daemonism of the sexual imagination, untouched by five thousand years of civiliza-tion. My amazement never ceases at the biological conceptualism in male sexuality. What woman could invent such compulsive structures? What woman, unpaid, would live and love in so hellish an underworld?

The life of Heinrich von Kleist reveals the sexual conflicts that in-spired *Penthesilea*. Kleist's failure to follow family military tradition was severely censured. Literature was an unsuitable and unserious voca-tion. Kleist's suicide, by pistol in the mouth (like Hemingway's shot-gun), expresses his martyrdom to Teutonic masculinity. Guns in the mouth may also suggest something not immediately apparent in *Pen-thesilea*: repressed and therefore destructive homosexual desire. Kleist tried to persuade his friends to a double suicide pact, and one finally agreed. Kleist spoke erotically of the anticipated event as "the most glorious and sensual of deaths."[24]

A Romantic solipsist is in inevitable intimacy with a sister, in this case Kleist's half-sister Ulrike, who he said had "nothing of her sex but the hips." He longed to live with her, in Romantic union. Is she the model for Penthesilea? Many scholars note the recurrence of ideas, images, and phraseology in Kleist's work. Walter Silz says, "Kleist is the most persistent self-plagiarist in German literature."[25] Self-plagiarism is in-cest and autoeroticism, the uroboros of Goethe's Bettina. It is the self-devouring style of the sadomasochistic *Penthesilea*. Kleist's turn toward his sister was toward his missing sexual component, but he was femi-nine and she masculine. She was the *he* which he needed. Kleist's

Romantic family romance produced the defiant Amazon manifesto of *Penthesilea*, which rings with modernity. Women have rarely spoken so boldly for themselves as Kleist speaks for them here.

Sade's reaction against Rousseau was sweeping and systematic, but it was censored and thus not absorbed into French literature until long afterward. The English reaction against Rousseau took assimilable form: the Gothic novel. Because English literature had the archetypal precedents of *The Faerie Queene* and *Paradise Lost*, English Romanticism from the start had a daemonic intensity that French Romanticism took forty more years to acquire. English Gothicism of the 1790s is equivalent to the medieval alchemy and occultism in *Faust*, which Goethe was working on at the time. Gothic darkness and roughness oppose the Apollonian Enlightenment's light, contour, and symmetry. Protestant rationalism is defeated by Gothic's return to the ritualism and mysticism of medieval Catholicism, with its residual paganism. Art withdraws into caverns, castles, prison-cells, tombs, coffins. Gothic is a style of claustrophobic sensuality. Its closed spaces are daemonic wombs. The Gothic novel is sexually archaic: it withdraws into chthonian darkness, the realm of Goethe's Mothers. Mother night pervades Romanticism, from Coleridge and Keats to Poe and Chopin with his brooding nocturnes. The ghosts released by Gothic will stalk through the nineteenth century as spiritualism, whose séances continue today in Great Britain.

The Gothic tradition was begun by Ann Radcliffe, a rare example of a woman creating an artistic style. The Gothic novel with the greatest impact on Romanticism, however, was Matthew G. Lewis' *The Monk* (1796). Lewis, a friend of Byron, influenced all the English Romantic poets as well as Hoffmann, Scott, Poe, Hawthorne, and Emily Brontë. *The Monk*'s medieval monastery is a sequestered Christian space which Lewis, like Sade, defiles with pagan eroticism. As we saw in Spenser, illicitness increases the pleasure of sexual transgression. Reviewing *The Monk*, Coleridge praised its "libidinous minuteness."[26] Lewis' hero, the abbot Ambrosio, discovers his fellow monk Rosario is actually Matilda, a woman in disguise. Lewis withholds Matilda's identity in the Spenserian manner, speaking of her up to this point as "he." Matilda tears open her habit and rests a dagger on her left breast, lit by moonbeams. Fin-de-siècle Gothic has a decadent sensationalism. Lewis' erotic chiaroscuro juxtaposes lust with chastity, exhibitionism with voyeurism. Does Matilda point with the dagger to inflame or mutilate herself? to direct and sharpen our aggressive western eye? Her transvestism is the mildest of her perversities. Only Coleridge's *Christabel* surpasses *The Monk* in its pornographic exploitation of Christian moralism.

Matilda is sexually divided. She insists on retaining her male name as an erotic aid. After she seduces the monk, she oddly becomes more masculine instead of more feminine. She seems to grow in mental power, prefiguring Poe's Ligeia. Lewis implies Matilda's gender is in flux: a self-adjusting mechanism maintains her hermaphroditism, like water seeking its own level. Ambrosio's homoerotic longing for the vanished Rosario shows his preference for a feminine pseudo-male over a sexually available masculine woman. But the startling last pages of *The Monk* force us to reread. Lucifer, come to claim Ambrosio's soul, reveals Matilda is a male demon sent to corrupt him. This is from Spenser: a male spirit masques as the False Florimell. Matilda's postcoital "manliness" is therefore the flaunting sashaying of a triumphant drag-queen demon. Our first and psychologically primary reading of the novel has been in complete error. The meltingly delicious sex between Ambrosio and Matilda—all pantings, twinings, and obscure refinements—has been homosexual and daemonic, not heterosexual. Our own sexual perceptions have been seduced. Sensuality aglow in Gothic gloom: surely Keats has normalized Lewis' carnal scene for *The Eve of Saint Agnes*, with its bedchamber show of lush sweetmeats.

Matilda's male identity is not the only surprise at the end of *The Monk*. Lucifer reveals that Ambrosio has unwittingly committed incest and matricide: "Antonia and Elvira perished by your hand. That Antonia whom you violated, was your sister! that Elvira whom you murdered, gave you birth!"[27] Here again is the riddling sound of impacted sexual psychodrama, which I found in Shakespeare's *As You Like It* and Sade's *120 Days of Sodom*. *The Monk* turns out to be a festering family romance. Lucifer's incantation, unlike Rosalind's, looks toward the past. It is like a curtain drawn back from a Mannerist panorama, where we see the sweeping diagonal of Ambrosio's spiritual history in a glare of lurid light. Ambrosio is the first haunted hero of Romantic sex-crime. *As You Like It* ends with the reknitting of Renaissance community, but *The Monk* ends in terrible primeval isolation. Lucifer drops Ambrosio onto a rocky nightmare landscape, like *Mona Lisa*'s lunar lawn. He is "bruised and mangled," his limbs "broken and dislocated." The sun scorches him, insects devour him, eagles tear his flesh and dig out his eyeballs: Lewis, like Sade, has a Darwinian vision of amoral apocalyptic nature. The Gothic novel rebuts Rousseau: *The Monk* redaemonizes sex, linking it to sin, suffering, and natural brutality. Ambrosio's incest demonstrates the occult compulsiveness of sex. He is magnetically

drawn to his unknown mother and sister by unconscious fatality. I
suspect Balzac borrowed this detail for *The Girl with the Golden Eyes*.
The Romantic prestige of incest springs from its reversal of history and
its collapsing of psychic energies into the overenlarged self. Incest is
part of the sexually archaic material released into society whenever
hierarchies weaken.

Satan is the severe pagan god of *The Monk*. At the end, Lucifer shows
his true chthonian form: "blasted limbs," taloned hands and feet, snaky
Medusan hair. But his first appearance is as an Apollonian angel, meant
to dupe the homosexual-tending Ambrosio. Lucifer is a dazzling naked
ephebe with fiery long hair and crimson wings. He wears a star on his
forehead and diamond bracelets on his arms and ankles. He carries a
silver myrtle branch. Romanticism returns to the Renaissance style of
epiphanic sexual personae. In art, self-display is meaning, more than
criticism has understood. I have shown this iconicism going back to
Egypt and Greece. Lewis' Lucifer aestheticizes and sexualizes a Biblical seraph, a Babylonian not a Hebraic style. He may be influenced by
Spenser's Byzantine Belphoebe, who also halts narrative action. Lewis'
Lucifer is again the "light-bearer," but he is hard and crystalline. His
silver branch is a golden bough, the wand with which art freezes and
transcends vegetative nature. Appearing in a rose-colored cloud, Lucifer fills the monk's "cavern" with air and light. Nietzsche sees the
German mind in "clouds and everything that is unclear." Spengler
identifies occult Magian experience with the "world-cavern."[28] The
Apollonianism of Lewis' androgyne propels sunlit Mediterranean formalism into the daemonic murk of the Gothic novel. His seraph may be
in *Faust*'s Euphorion, in Balzac's Seraphita, and in the ghost of Bloom's
son in Joyce's *Ulysses*, a "fairy boy" whose diamond and ruby buttons
and violet colors recall the seraph's diamonds and rose light.

There is latent eroticism in the entire tradition of the
"novel of terror," which began in late eighteenth-century Gothicism
and became the modern horror film. Freud says "the sexually exciting
influence of some painful affects, such as fear, shuddering, and horror, . . . explains why so many seek opportunities to experience such
sensations" in books or the theater.[29] The thrill of terror is passive,
masochistic, and implicitly feminine. It is imaginative submission to
overwhelming superior force. The vast audience of the Gothic novel
was and is female. Men who cultivate the novel or film of terror seek
sex-crossing sensations. Horror films are most popular among adolescents, whose screams are Dionysian signals of sexual awakening. Re-

viewers often wonder why the packed audiences of bloody slasher films are sedate couples on weekend dates. Shared fear is a physically stimulating sexual transaction. Freud's use of the word "shuddering" shows the common area between fear and orgasmic pleasure. In Yeats's "Leda and the Swan," the "shudder in the loins" is both the rapist's climax and the victim's fright.

Violent horror films, of the splattering kind now so common, seem to me a most pedestrian taste. A classy genre of vampire film follows a style I call psychological high Gothic. It begins in Coleridge's medieval *Christabel* and its descendants, Poe's *Ligeia* and James's *The Turn of the Screw*. A good example is *Daughters of Darkness* (1971), starring Delphine Seyrig as an elegant lesbian vampire. High Gothic is abstract and ceremonious. Evil has become world-weary, hierarchical glamour. There is no bestiality. The theme is eroticized western power, the burden of history. *The Hunger* (1983) comes close to being a masterpiece of this genre but is ruined by horrendous errors, as when the regal Catherine Deneuve is made to crawl around on all fours, slavering over cut throats. Please. Butchery is not the point of vampirism. Sex—domination and submission—is. Gothic horror must be moderated by Apollonian discipline, or it turns into gross buffoonery. The run-of-the-mill horror film is anti-aesthetic and anti-idealizing. Its theme is sparagmos, the form-pulverizing energies of Dionysus. Horror films unleash the forces repressed by Christianity—evil and the barbarism of nature. Horror films are rituals of pagan worship. There western man obsessively confronts what Christianity has never been able to bury or explain away. Horror stories ending in the victory of good are no more numerous than those ending in the threat of evil's return. Nature, like the vampire, will not stay in its grave.

Vulgar horror films awash in red slop or grungy decay reflect a Northern European sensibility, the self-soiling of too-clean Protestantism. Undignified abuse of the body is analogous to medieval gargoyles or fairy tales' dwarves and trolls, whom I find impossible to take seriously, even in Wagner. The Mediterranean rightly identifies chthonian deformations with impressive female monsters, like Scylla. Northern European male trolls are an evasion of the harsh reality of female nature. Horror films dwell on Dionysian mutilations of or encrustations upon the human figure—scabs, scars, swellings. Movie monsters seem covered with moss or fungus. They are as gnarled and lumpish as tree stumps. G. Wilson Knight says, "Much of our horror at death is, at bottom, a physical repulsion."[30] The horror film uses rot as a primary material, part of the Christian west's secret craving for Dionysian truths.

The horror film blunders about, seeking, without realizing it, the chthonian swamp of generation, the female matrix. There is dissolution in nature, but there is also fecundity and cosmic grandeur. The horror film is philosophically incomplete, because Christianity is incomplete. Classical paganism had a far more comprehensive view of sex and nature. Like Fifties science-fiction films, Seventies disaster films, such as *The Towering Inferno*, have been blamed on international political tensions and anxieties. I disagree. Dreams of disaster will always appear when benevolent Rousseauism is in the air. The liberal Sixties, identifying sex and nature with love and peace, produced the Sadean counterreaction of Seventies catastrophism. The present preoccupation with nuclear apocalypse is also crypto-religious. Fear of world holocaust is another self-haunting, a way to subordinate the self to the cosmos in an era of easy, all-forgiving therapies and faiths.

The eighteenth-century novel of terror inherited the emotional complex of sublimity. The idea of the sublime came to the Augustans from Roman Longinus and culminated in Edmund Burke's *Philosophical Enquiry into the Origin of our Ideas of the Sublime and Beautiful* (1757). Burke sees "a mode of terror, or of pain" as the cause of the sublime. Burke anticipates Freud's idea of the sexual excitation in fear: "Terror is a passion which always produces delight when it does not press too close."[31] Lionel Trilling wrongly connects Burke's sublime with masculinity: "The experience of terror stimulates an energy of aggression and dominance."[32] But Burke's locutions clearly demonstrate the passive self-subordination of male devotees of the sublime. In Shelley's "Mont Blanc," nature overwhelms male imagination with chilling fascistic force. The sexual element is already apparent in early theories of the sublime. John Dennis' essay on Longinus (1704) says the sublime "ravishes and transports us." It is "an invincible Force, which commits a pleasing Rape upon the very Soul of the Reader." Schiller too, following Burke, sees a "paroxysm" or "shudder" in the sublime, a joy turning to "rapture."[33] The sublime, a mode of pagan vision, is one of the first historical signs of the Romantic withdrawal from masculine action. In sublimity and Gothic terror, western emotion opens itself directly to nature, with its ghostly flood of archaic night.

10

Sex Bound and Unbound

Blake

William Blake is the British Sade, as Emily Dickinson is the American Sade. Directly inspired by *The Faerie Queene* and its incomplete response in *Paradise Lost*, Blake makes sex war the first theatrical conflict of English Romanticism. The daemonic wombs of the Gothic novel are too confined for Blake's cosmic drama. In the same decade as Sade, Blake turns sex and psyche into a Darwinian cycle of turbulent natural energies, fleeing, chasing, devouring. The postwar critics who rescued Romantic poetry from low esteem tended to ignore or downplay troublesome sexual and moral ambiguities. For example, Northrop Frye's pioneering study of Blake, *Fearful Symmetry* (1947), optimistically promotes sexual liberation in a way that seems, a weary generation later, simplistic and naive. How much was hoped from sex. How little sex can deliver. Blake's writing is split by a terrible contradiction: Blake wants to free sex from its social and religious constraints, but he also wants to escape the domination of the Great Mother of chthonian nature. Alas, with every turn toward sex, we run right back into mother nature's dark embrace. Blake's tireless productivity as poet and draughtsman came from the intolerable entrapments male imagination finds itself in when reflecting on nature. Blake's poetry is sexual grand opera of instability, anguish, and resentment.

Prophet and radical, Blake denounces all social forms. He takes Rousseau's hostility to civilization farther than Rousseau himself. For Blake, sexual personae, which belong to the social realm of role-playing, are artificial and false. He differs from the other English Romantics on several points. All believe love is primal energy. But Blake is the only one to oppose androgyny as a solution to rigid sex roles. Blake condemns androgyny as solipsism. His hermaphrodites are monstrous.

Romantic solipsism, a self-communing and self-fructification, becomes sterile in Blake. Why? Because Blake, though he follows and extends Rousseau's politics, sees nature with Sade's eyes. In Blake, Rousseau's tender nature mother makes a fin-de-siècle leap into daemonic monumentality. Brother to Sade, whom he could not have known or read, Blake revives the bloodthirsty goddess of ancient mystery religion, sensational with Asiatic barbarism. He longs to defeat her. But by attacking her, he creates her and confirms her power. Ironically, he becomes her slave and emissary, a voice crying in the wilderness. Nowhere else in literature is the Great Mother as massively, violently eloquent as she is in Blake.

Blake, following Spenser, constructs a complex symbolic psychology not yet fully understood. One of Blake's basic patterns is that of warring contraries through which spiritual progress is pursued, as in *The Faerie Queene*. As his poetry develops, Blake's principal combat is between male and female, metaphors for the tension between humanity and nature. In the early *Songs of Innocence* (1789), sex war is not yet an issue, but it is prefigured in the theme of tyrannical power relations, toward which Blake takes Rousseau's view but Sade's tone. Blake is interested in coercion, repetition-compulsion, spiritual rape. He sees sadism and vampirism in male authority figures. The child speakers of "The Chimney Sweeper" and "The Little Black Boy" are physically exploited and psychologically manipulated. They are the invisible slaves or houris of a corrupt new industrial society. Their minds have been invaded by a daemonic compact of church and state. "So if all do their duty, they need not fear harm": adult voices come from their mouths in evil ventriloquism. The sexual element in this brainwashing is evident in "Holy Thursday," where grey-haired beadles with "wands as white as snow" herd a stream of children into St. Paul's Cathedral. The wands are Spenser's phallic white rods, here symbolizing wintry devitalization. The beadles are perverts, voyeurs, decadents. They freeze the children's river of life.

In *Songs of Innocence* white is the color of desexing. The white hair of the lamblike chimney sweep, little Tom Dacre, expresses his premature adult experience. The child-slaves advance from childhood to old age without passing through adult virility. As in the penalty card of capitalist Monopoly: "Go directly to Jail. Do not pass Go. Do not collect $200." Elsewhere in Blake, sexual jealousy cripples human energy. In *Songs of Innocence*, male authority is an impotent Herod, massacring the innocents while ravishing them with eye and mind. Society operates by vicious pederasty. In 1789, both sexes still powdered their hair or wore

wigs. The eigthteenth century honored age and tradition, overthrown by
Romanticism in its youth-cult. Blake's white-haired chimney sweep is
ritual victim of an unnatural regime. The high stylization of eighteenth-
century wigs—we hear of women unable to pass through doorways, of
towering arrangements of fruit, foliage, and birds' nests—was a symptom of decadence. Powdered hair is a perverse fantasy of frost and angel
dust, worldliness masquerading as innocence. Blake's artificially whit-
ened children are overexperienced and knowledgeable. An unsettling
analogy can be found in a Roman imperial sarcophagus decorated with
leering obese putti, fetid with adult sensuality. Blake's cherubs are
depraved by adult tyranny. Henry James takes up Blake's theme in *The
Turn of the Screw*, where an obsessed hierarch, the governess, projects
sexual sophistication upon a boy who dies an exhausted prisoner of her
febrile imagination. Blake's white-haired chimney sweep represents the
class of all exploited persons. The white hair is sexually universalizing,
because the exploited are humiliatingly feminized by amoral political
power. Erich Fromm says, "For the authoritarian character there exist,
so to speak, two sexes: the powerful ones and the powerless ones."[1]
Sexual personae in *Songs of Innocence* are imagined as generations
cannibalizing each other. Blake's innocent children are precursors of his
male victims emasculated by cruel women.

"Infant Joy" is Blake's most neglected major poem. Harold Bloom
devotes one sentence to it in his book on Blake, and he and Lionel
Trilling omit it from the *Oxford Anthology* of Romantic literature. "Infant Joy" has a deceptive simplicity:

> I have no name
> I am but two days old.—
> What shall I call thee?
> I happy am
> Joy is my name,—
> Sweet joy befall thee!
>
> Pretty joy!
> Sweet joy but two days old.
> Sweet joy I call thee:
> Thou dost smile.
> I sing the while
> Sweet joy befall thee.

We have regressed to the infancy of consciousness. We see Rousseau's
saintly child as it crosses the border into being. What do we find there?
Tenderness and innocence threatened on all sides. I learned to read

poetry from Milton Kessler, whose brilliant remarks on "Infant Joy" I reconstruct from my college notes:

> "Infant Joy" is a flawless physical caress which induces weeping. The metaphor for this poem is taking the child in one's hands. But an adult taking up a newborn is suddenly, involuntarily conscious of the ease with which he could crush it to pieces. In "Infant Joy" there is a sense of the enormous proximity, the closeness and intimacy of the speaker. The child has no voice of its own yet. It is given an identity by some great coercive power. There are certain forms of sadistic tenderness more intimate than the psyche will allow. "Infant Joy" is like Theodore Roethke's "Elegy for Jane," where the bearlike poet, with his terrifying and roaring energy, approaches a delicate being in dangerous nearness. The elegy begins: "I remember the neckcurls, limp and damp as tendrils."

"Infant Joy" exposes the authoritarianism in Rousseauist "concern," "caring," and "understanding," today's self-righteous liberal values. In the poem's eerie dialogue I hear George Herbert's homoerotic intensities. In its blank encapsulization I feel claustrophobic Spenserian embowerment. "Infant Joy" comes from the rape cycle of *The Faerie Queene*. It is the provocative vulnerability of the fleeing Florimell, the purity that sucks filth into its wake. "Infant Joy" is a Rousseauist vacuum into which Sadean nature is about to rush.

Blake's infant has no name, no persona. It is barely individuated. Infant joy is what Blake later calls a "state," a condition of being. We feel rawness, sensitivity, defenseless passivity. Rousseauist childhood is no blessing. Sensory experience is the avenue of sadomasochism. "Infant Joy" recreates the dumb muscle state of our physicality, the readiness which converts into sex, or rather the surging power that is sex. George Eliot says, "If we had a keen vision and feeling of all ordinary human life, it would be like hearing the grass grow and the squirrel's heart beat, and we should die of that roar which lies on the other side of silence. As it is, the quickest of us walk about well wadded with stupidity."[2] "Infant Joy" removes the buffering between persons and beings. Eliot imagines a perfect perceptual openness and a sensory flood into a receptacle too small to contain it. The egoless softness of the poem awakes in us Kessler's sensation of overwhelming power, which we unconsciously check. Sharpening the senses inflames them—and here comes sadism. Rousseauist responsiveness and nurturance automatically flip over into their opposites.

"Infant Joy" has the moral emptiness of Spenser's femininity, a space cleared in nature. It is like the still heart of a geode, rimmed with crystalline teeth. In "Infant Joy" a devouring presence waits, a Blakean tiger: the reader. This is one of the uncanniest poems in literature. Seemingly so slight and transparent, it harbors something sinister and maniacal. "Infant Joy" is strongly ritualistic. Kessler calls it a "caress." The poem's hypnotic repetitions are a series of soothing gestures, like rubbing a lantern to make a genie appear. The poem is a spell materializing a dark power, latent in the reader. "Infant Joy" is a daemonizing poem: it daemonizes the reader, drawing him into the rapacious cycle of natural process. By making the reader a sadist, it subverts his complacent trust in his own morality and benevolence. Blake was contemptuous of "Mercy, Pity, Peace." "Infant Joy" is a parodistic critique of Rousseauism. As much as Blake's chimney-sweep poems, it indicts the oppressive paternalism of society's self-appointed guardians. Every gesture of love is an assertion of power. There is no selflessness or self-sacrifice, only refinements of domination.

The psychosexual design of "Infant Joy" is *hovering*. Hovering is the relation of speaker to infant, reader to poem. The evil droning menace in such proximity is shown in Blake's watercolor, *God Creating Adam* (fig. 31). Winged Urizen, Blake's tyrant Jehovah, hovers with a smothering weight above corpselike Adam, stretched flat as if crucified. God is a vampire snatching back man's Promethean fire. The picture seems to show an unnatural sex act, homosexual and sadomasochistic. Criticism is squeamish about admitting these perversities in Blake. Hovering is always emotionally and sexually problematic. It is everywhere in the Late Romantic voyeur, Walt Whitman, who imagines himself wandering all night, "swiftly and noiselessly stepping and stopping." He bends "with open eyes over the shut eyes of sleepers"; he listens to the quiet breathing of children; he passes his hands "soothingly to and fro" over the suffering and restless. Elsewhere, lifting the gauze over a cradle, he stares "a long time" at the infant and "silently" brushes away flies (*The Sleepers; Song of Myself,* 8). When Wordsworth looks out from Westminster Bridge, the city's sleepers are only inferred. Whitman's sleepers are warm, sensuous bodies. Whitman's all-embracing Rousseauist love is Romantic vampirism, scopophiliac tyranny. The poet's eye is omnipotent, while its objects are passive and defenseless, without thought or identity. The nearness with which Whitman approaches the sleepers is predicated on their unconsciousness. He makes them feminine objects of his godlike delectation. Romantic love—all love—is sex and power. In nearness we enter each other's animal aura. There is magic there, both black and white.

31. William Blake, *God Creating Adam*, 1795.

Violating the psychic space of his sleepers, Whitman rapes them. Wordsworth too remembers his boyhood "merciless ravage" of a nut grove, a "virgin scene" that he left a Spenserian "mutilated bower" ("Nutting"). Trespass is always subliminally erotic. Piercing a temenos—a sacred space of mind, body, bedchamber, or nature—is always a domination and defilement. Blake's "Infant Joy" evokes an impulse toward criminal trespass. Reading it, we hover at the edge of a forbidden locus of experience. We hold our breath. We uneasily sense the aesthetic contrast between our adult grossness and the infant's delicacy, eroticized by the poem's implied touching. The infant exists in Blake's Beulah state of blissful passivity, the numb groping of polymorphous perversity. The infant is blind. But we aggressively see. Along the track of our seeing skids our unbrakeable will.

The same dialectic of blind whiteness and aggressive eye occurs in *The Faerie Queene*, where the boisterous cannibals hang over sleeping Serena to study her "dainty flesh," which the poet gives a silky sheen (VI. viii. 36–43). Is this the source of Blake's poem? The violation in "Infant Joy" is the exposure of something private, unprotected, quivering, and moist. An infant two days old is barely sexually differentiated.

It is still muzzy from the womb. "Infant Joy" brings us face to face with the biologically fundamental. The preconscious simplicity of Blake's infant is almost cellular. In fact, the poem *is* a cell, one simple cell of protoplasmic life. "Infant Joy" unveils a physiological mystery. We have penetrated into a female realm, as Melville does in *Tartarus of Maids* or Leonardo in his drawing of a fetus. This is proved by Blake's drawing of the poem, where an infant lies in the lap of a hovering mother and both are swallowed up in the flamelike maw of a giant flower, Blake's rapacious nature (fig. 32). Thus the infant's powerlessness is a version of the chimney sweeps' enslavement. The womblike "Infant Joy" is a surgical opening up of a female body, nature's organic machine. "Infant Joy" is the secret sex-crime of a ravisher-poet. It looks forward to Blake's overtly sadistic *Mental Traveller*, where the "Babe" of humanity is handed over to old mother nature, surgeon and torturer. *The Mental Traveller* literalizes the authoritarian manipulations of "Infant Joy." Blake corrects Rousseau: man is born into his chains, the mother-born body binding us to creature comfort, sex, and pain.

In *Songs of Experience* (1794), "Infant Joy" advances to sexual maturity. Blake's response to "Infant Joy" is not "Infant Sorrow" but "The Sick Rose." Here the Spenserian embowerment of Blake's newborn shifts from Rousseau to Sade:

> O Rose thou art sick.
> The invisible worm,
> That flies in the night
> In the howling storm:
>
> Has found out thy bed
> Of crimson joy:
> And his dark secret love
> Does thy life destroy.

"The Sick Rose" is Spenser's Bower of Bliss destroyed by sex war. The literary convention of female flight and male pursuit, satirized by Spenser in the ever-fleeing Florimell, reveals its innate hostility. Woman's flirtatious arts of self-concealment mean man's approach must take the form of rape. The phallus becomes the conquerer worm, death's agent. Withdrawal and concealment are always negative in Blake. Here they provoke sadistic attack, partly a hallucination by the reclusive rose. The rose is a narcissistically convoluted psyche. Female genitals are traditionally symbolized by the queen of flowers, from the medieval Mystic Rose of Mary to the rock classic, "Sally, Go Round the Roses." Blake sees solipsism as the danger in female sexuality. The rose's exclusive-

32. William Blake, *Infant Joy*, from *Songs of Innocence and of Experience*, 1794.

ness blends fear, shame, and pride. Its layered petals are a form of self-population. That the rose's "bed of crimson joy" suggests masturbatory pleasure is well accepted by critics. For Blake the rose's self-completion is perverse and sterile. The rose is a sexual schismatic, making division where there should be wholeness and unity in nature. It is thus an early version of the solipsistic hermaphrodites of Blake's prophetic books.

Blake's masturbatory rose belongs to the tradition begun in Egypt where autoeroticism is a method of cosmogony. Blake sees a sexually private world as a prison cell. The rose is sick because, she thinks, the communion of sex drains and obliterates her identity. Blake's own ambivalence toward sex produces the cryptic duality of the poem. Male fear of woman's self-containment is written all over mythology and culture. It is male, not female identity that is annihilated in the night-storm of nature. The fascination of woman's autonomy is plain in Ingres' *The Turkish Bath*, a witty parallel to Blake's rose poem (fig. 33). Ingres' painting is oddly round, a rose window or Madonna tondo turned pagan peephole, through which we spy the plump nude bodies of a dozen women amorously entwined, like lesbian flower petals. It is a snaky Medusa head, steamy with Asiatic lewdness. Trying to liberate sex from society, Blake keeps running back into the cul-de-sac of female sexuality. Courtly convention alone did not make woman "the hidden."

33. Jean-Auguste-Dominique Ingres, *The Turkish Bath*, 1862.

Nature makes woman's body a cavern of the unseen, divined by sado-masochistic mystery religion.

The ambiguous "Sick Rose" qualifies the sexual assertions of Blake's earlier *The Book of Thel* (1789). A cloud tells the virgin Thel she is "the food of worms": "Every thing that lives, / Lives not alone, nor for itself." Nature as harmonious interrelationship: this Buddhist perception is not sustained in Blake, who is too conflicted about the dominance of female nature. In "The Sick Rose," Thel's worms are phallic heavenly messengers, miming the growth cycle. Blake thinks the being living alone and for itself is sick because it rejects the strife of contraries by which energy evolves. Thel's book ends in hysterical retreat, as she jumps from her seat and dashes shrieking back to her native valleys. Blake combines the seat-stuck virgin of Milton's *Comus* with Spenser's fleeing Florimell and Belphoebe, who disappears mid-sentence. Blake regards virginity as a perverse fetish. He wants to believe Thel's rejection of sexuality is childish, a swerve from menarche and fruitfulness. Thus Blake's chastity is diametrically opposite to that of Spenser and Shakespeare, for whom it signifies spiritual integrity and force. Like Sade, Blake sees chastity as unnatural, energy-killing. But in urging Thel, a sick rose, to cure herself by surrendering to communion, Blake is closer to Shakespeare of the comedies, where all are given in marriage, than he is to his fellow Romantic poets, for whom solitude is imaginative perfection. Shakespeare, subordinating sex to society, makes a Renaissance escape from the problem confronting Blake. Trying to eliminate society but redeem sex, Blake keeps finding himself in Leonardo's rockscape. Every inch he saves for sex is lost in the desolate mile of mother nature.

Blake's "London," like Emily Dickinson's "Our journey had advanced," is one of those rare lyric poems that achieve epic sweep. The Hebrew prophet wanders through modern Babylon, which he denounces with the voice of Rousseau. In "London," institutions, symbolized by church and palace, oppress individuals. Their impersonal walls are deaf to the chimney sweep's cry and soldier's sigh. For Blake, buildings are society's face, abstract, mechanical, lifeless. "London" has a radical new way of seeing grand works of urban architecture as blank, sinister monoliths. Blake prefigures Baudelaire and Kafka in his vision of the dead night-world of the modern city, today an arid grid of glass and concrete. Society's indifference to the suffering poor paints it black. Blake's church is a whited sepulchre stained with vice, the soot that will not out. From the sky falls a plague of red rain, the dying soldier's last breath wafted from a foreign battlefield and turning from breeze to drizzle over foggy London. The nameless massacred innocents leave their mark in red writing on the royal wall, their blood but also Pharaoh's, French terror leaping to England. The city weeps but does not recognize its own tears. Church and palace are a frozen or petrified face. Emotionless stone walls are what Blake's prophetic books call "the limit of contraction." If the palace face or façade runs with the blood of sacrificial lambs, then the poem is a Veronica's veil, imprinted with the face of suffering. The trickling blood is Christ's, for industrial society is un-Christian. George Herbert tells death, "Our Saviour's death did put some blood / Into thy face." Modern London, drained of Christian compassion, is spiritually dead.

Blake's cold-walled city-faces are obviously sexless. They are sexless personae, looking forward to Emily Dickinson's pitiless clock faces, whose rule of time is enforced by church, state, father, and death.

Blake's church and palace walls are self-armouring calcifications. His "Human Form Divine" is obliterated in the magnification of persons into institutions, coarse insensate colossi. City buildings are manufactured objects, a Romantic mode of androgyne. "London" logically ends in the syphilitic streetwalker, since she bears the displaced sexuality of respectable society. She is diseased because her sex is both secret and commercial. Blake's harlot is nature, exiled from the city and therefore returning under cover of night to stalk and prey.

One of Blake's remarks about whores: "In a wife I would desire / What in whores is always found / The lineaments of Gratified desire." Stone tablets, stony face. Blake thinks religious repression of sex makes misery and hypocrisy. Lower-class whores, then and now, sop up the male run-off from "decent" middle-class marriage. Men chase by night those they will not greet by day. For Blake, the whore is another victim or scapegoat, like exploited children and soldiers. She is the third emblematic oppressed individual of "London." But in another way, she is the poem's third institution. Outcast and vagrant, she will extrude her own housey shell in the nineteenth century, era of the courtesan. Blake is the first artist to recognize the whore as a kindred spirit. In Paris, artists and whores will dwell together in creative mass marriage for over a century. In Zola's *Nana* (1880), the courtesan presides from the apex of public hierarchy. Church, palace, harlot: Blake's sequence recalls the ritual temple prostitution of the Asiatic Great Mother, whom he normally despises. Is his harlot "youthful" because she is a vampire drunk with the male blood of the prior stanza? The "midnight streets" of "London" are the labyrinthine bowels of the earth mother, from which Icaran imagination tries to escape. The poem joins ancient archetype to a modernist panorama of hostile architecture. The combination recurs in Kafka, where the bureaucratic labyrinth of the tyrant father is dreamily one with the womblike rooms of the abandoning mother. Blake's "Marriage hearse," from which Emily Dickinson will write one of her greatest poems, is the mobile carriage of our own death-tending bodies. The earth mother, both womb and tomb, has the last word in Blake's poem, as she does everywhere and at all times.

In *The Mental Traveller*, Blake moves the epic conflicts of "London" into the open air of stormy nature. Institutions, once his Rousseauist concern, fade into irrelevance. *The Mental Traveller* is Blake's recognition of the insuperable problem of nature, which he once tried to tame into a romance of mutually rewarding sex. I think the sadomasochism of this poem comes from Blake's reading of *The Faerie*

Queene, whose decadent brutalities he understood as no modern critic has. *The Mental Traveller* is Sade made poetry. The acrid clarity of language is sharply modern or Late Romantic. Blake is way beyond Rousseau. He answers himself, as Coleridge will answer and correct Wordsworth. Bloom says of *The Mental Traveller:* "All the males in the poem are one man, humanity, men and women together. All the females are nature, the confinements of the human."[3] *The Mental Traveller* is a Sadean critique of love and sex. I insist that the genders of Blake's sexual personae must be accepted as dramatically authoritative in their own right.

The Mental Traveller is a cycle of sexual cannibalism enacted by a male and a female figure, who attack and retreat in obsessive rhythms of victory and defeat. A boy babe is given to "a Woman Old," who nails him down upon a rock, binds iron thorns around his head, pierces his hands and feet, and cuts his heart out "to make it feel both cold & heat." "Her fingers number every Nerve." She lives on his "shrieks & cries" and "grows young as he grows old." Now the cycle reverses: "he rends up his Manacles / And binds her down for his delight." The poem moves by systaltic throbbing of the heart. Blake's oscillations between power and weakness are vortices moving in opposite directions—the source of Yeats's theory of historical gyres. Each sadistic act by Blake's female is a portent of her future torment and indeed the occult ritual which invokes it. The entire poem is a ritual. Its systematic cataloguing of atrocities resembles the itemizations of Sade's *120 Days of Sodom.* Like Sade, Blake foreshadows Frazer's anthropological syncretism. *The Mental Traveller* recreates the bloody rites of the Great Mother. Nature, not society, is humanity's ultimate arena. *The Mental Traveller* has renewed life in one of rock's major lyrics, a song it surely influenced, the Rolling Stones' "Jumpin' Jack Flash."

Blake's newborn babe goes straight to his crucifixion. Innocence is ravaged by experience, a Madonna turned hag. Rebel Orc always ages into tyrant Urizen. Blake has learned from the moral decay of the French Revolution, whose sadism betrayed its patron, Rousseau. The babe's tortures recall the legends of Prometheus, Jesus, and Loki. Blake daringly superimposes classical, Christian, and Norse mythologies without giving Christianity its usual preeminence. Masochistic male sufferers, whom we saw in Rousseau, Goethe, and Kleist, are profuse in Romanticism. Here the babe is handed over to a grim tutor for his education, as Achilles is given to the centaur. The witch of *The Mental Traveller* is the first malign governess of nineteenth-century literature. The babe's training or *Bildung* is harshly physical. Blake anticipates

Freud in grounding intellect in the body. In his earlier "To Tirzah,"
witch and mother are one: "Thou Mother of my Mortal part / With
cruelty didst mould my Heart, / And with false self-deceiving tears, /
Didst bind my Nostrils Eyes & Ears." Nature, weaving the tissues of the
body, wraps us at birth in her shroud.

Nailing the babe down by his five senses, the witch "catches his
shrieks in cups of gold." A gold cup is chillingly archetypal. It is virginal,
vaginal, eucharistic. Thel's golden bowl is her selfish self-preservation.
It is the organic morally petrified, like "London"'s walls. The witch's
miserly gold cups are her infatuated self-regard and self-divinization,
the sexual solipsism of the sick rose. A poisoned cup: the Whore of
Babylon holds a gold cup scummy with fornications; Loki's wife cups up
the venom of a serpent hung above his bound body. Blake's witch is a
vampire catching spurts of infant blood in order to drink them. We saw
in "London" how Blake magically turns sound to sight, sighs and cries
into running blood. The gold cups of *The Mental Traveller* are its own
stanzas brimming with the agonies of humanity.

At the start of *The Mental Traveller,* the dominance of female over
male seems so complete as to be insuperable. The babe is inert matter
manipulated by a female First Mover. She knows him through sadistic
touching. Normally, female bodies are the stringed instrument plucked
by males. Here mother nature is a master harpist making dark music to
herself. By his torments, the male gains his identity, still missing in the
newborn of "Infant Joy." His gender is reinforced by nature's biological
authoritarianism. *The Mental Traveller* proceeds by sexual peripeties.
The first is a pietà, where the old witch becomes a virgin with her
"bleeding youth." The Great Mother, mourning her son-lover, is wrestled down and bound in turn. Now male exults in woman's masochistic
vulnerability. Service has switched on the Sadean tennis court. Gender
flames and fades in *The Mental Traveller.* Dominance and submission,
nature's law, compulsively structures the poem. We saw a similar pattern in Kleist's *Penthesilea. The Mental Traveller* has a choreographic
ritualism. It's like a parody of ballroom dancing where the lady keeps
trying to lead. At the end, we are sent back to the start of the poem to
read it again—a trope Joyce adopts for *Finnegans Wake. The Mental
Traveller* is a uroboros mimicking the circularity of natural process.
Each sex devours the other.

Blake's *Mental Traveller* shows sex as a barbaric ritual drama where
the performers periodically exchange masks. The poem is energized by
explosive returns of the repressed. Woman's provocative flight recurs
late in the poem. She is a stag fleeing through her own self-planted

thicket of fear, images straight from *The Faerie Queene*. She is the sick rose wrapped in menacing pubic thorns. Her coquettish "arts of Love & Hate" come from the poetry of courtly love. We are born into sex war but learn to prolong it. The thicket is the theatrical personae of Petrarchan love, intellectualizing desire. For Blake, multiple personae are sterile rusing deceptions.

The first scene of *The Mental Traveller*, with its sadomasochistic bondage, has a clashing industrial character. The hag performs her ghastly tasks with businesslike efficiency and managerial zeal. The rock is a torture rack or anvil, an image in other Blake poems. We are all on the anvil, hammered by mother nature. Nature is a factory, a satanic mill which turns men into robots. The infant, his heart cut out, is crowned with iron thorns, reminiscent not only of Christ but of Spenser's robot Talus, "the iron man." In his painting of *The Faerie Queene*, Blake shows Talus with a burr of metal spikes about his head. Heart and brain aborted, his maleness crushed by enforced passivity, the babe is an unsexed manufactured object.

The frightful opening of *The Mental Traveller* is a brazen incantation of female triumph of the will. I find nothing in the poem suggesting that the sexual cycle can be ended or transcended. Criticism has over-philosophized *The Mental Traveller* and made it moralistic and didactic, rarely Romantic aims. The poem has overwhelming power as ferocious psychodrama. Its technique is surreal sexual cinema. *The Mental Traveller* is a ritual of riddance, an externalization of conflict. Blake sets the brute sex cycle going, like a perpetual motion machine, then lets it spin off into space to devour itself. The poem is circle magic. But the externalization did not work, for Blake had to return to the same theme again and again. His poems got longer and longer, as if epic scale could finally fix the matter. The unfixable theme is universal female power. Sade and Blake's sadomasochistic systems are rebuttals of Rousseau's maternal naturism. The awful energy of Blake's sinister females is equivalent to the eerie stillness of Goethe's brooding Mothers. Nineteenth-century Romantic literature and art are dominated by the femme fatale. Blake feels this coming and tries to stop it. Ironically, in grappling with mother nature, Blake has not so much laid her ghost as raised and immortalized it. Our movements against nature lock us to her. Blake's daemonized poetry gathers a storm cloud over sex that will never clear.

Like *The Mental Traveller*, "The Crystal Cabinet" was not published until 1863. Thus it could not have influenced Keats's "La Belle Dame Sans Merci," which it so resembles in dramatic form that

the two poems must reveal a deep structure of Romantic sexual imagination. "The Crystal Cabinet" is narrated by a male victim of female
entrapment. A maiden catches him dancing in the wild. She puts him
into her "Cabinet" and locks him up with "a golden Key." The cabinet,
made of gold, pearl, and crystal, contains "a World" under "a little
lovely Moony Night." Gold cup, gold bowl, gold cabinet. The prison is
the vagina. The key is the male's own penis, which woman steals to
make herself hermaphroditically complete. Sexual keys appear in Milton's *Comus*, as well as Goethe's *Faust*. Blake's golden key is a golden
bough, Vergil's passport to a chthonian underworld. Gold is also the
male's own narcissism. Blake elsewhere compares the phallus to "a
pompous High Priest" entering the Holy of Holies or secret shrine of
the vagina (*Jerusalem* 69:44).

"The Crystal Cabinet" opens on the male's carefree childhood, when
he lives in the body without ambivalence or fear. But sexual initiation
ends his trusting view of nature. His *rite de passage* is into containment,
luxurious but humiliating. The maiden trapping him like bird or butterfly is a collector, a connoisseur with a museum of sexual specimens.
She is like Circe with her stable of swine or Omphale with her male
domestics. The maiden's calculation is decadent. She is like the lordly
Late Romantic collectors of Sade, Poe, and Huysmans. The crystal
cabinet is a reliquary storing hosts or saints' bones. It is like Donne's
"well wrought urne," both poem and funeral vase mingling the ashes of
canonized lovers. But Blake's ashes are far more bitter. The male is
martyred, a lamb led to slaughter. The vagina is a sexual crematorium.
The crystal cabinet destroys by miniaturizing (cutting an erection down
to size). It contains another world and another maiden: "Translucent
lovely shining clear / Threefold each in the other closd / O what a
pleasant trembling fear." Microcosms are dangerous in Blake because
they are separatist and solipsistic. The crystal cabinet is like Spenser's
"world of glass," both mirror and crystal ball. The pregnant tear of
Donne's "Valediction: of weeping" contains the beloved's reflection and
also "a globe" of the world. In Blake, the male enters a looking-glass
world of sexual anti-matter. His pleasant fear is his masochistic delectation at female dominance. The male willfully prolonging his sexual
subordination makes his own hell.

The crystal cabinet requires man's voluptuous self-surrender. When
he asserts himself, the illusion falls to pieces. The cabinet bursts, and he
is "a weeping Babe upon the wild." Near him reclines a "Weeping
Woman pale." The cabinet is Spenser's torpid Bower of Bliss, here
accidentally destroyed by a devotee. Like the erotic idylls of Keats's

"Lamia" and "La Belle Dame Sans Merci," Blake's poem ends in cold, shame-filled awakening. A movement toward the illicit produces a violent movement outward into desolation. The primary model is Adam and Eve's expulsion from the garden. We see the same pattern in the finale of *Moby-Dick*, where Ahab's attempt to pierce the heart of nature by harpooning the white whale ends in catastrophe and vast, empty silence. "The Crystal Cabinet" says there is no way to understand nature. Every son is expelled from every mother. The more he searches for her through sex, the more she recedes from him. Bloom places the cabinet's daemonically threefold hostess in "a carnival of mirrors."[4] I think of the climax of Orson Welles's *The Lady from Shanghai* (1948), where Rita Hayworth as the siren of the labyrinth appears in dizzying profusion, until the hall of mirrors, like the crystal cabinet, is shattered by her angry male pursuer. Blake's threefold maiden is triple Hecate, ominous and nocturnal. In Blake, any numerical multiple is diseased. Unity is paradigmatic. The maiden's "threefold Smile," like Kali's many arms, represents nature's metamorphoses. But it is also multiple sexual personae, for Blake always artificial and mendacious. Hybrid forms in Blake are wanton trick lenses, suggesting vain self-contemplation. The maiden of "The Crystal Cabinet" overpopulates herself, like the sick rose. Unlike Shakespeare of the transvestite comedies, Blake opposes psychic diversification as decadent. God may say, "Be fruitful, and multiply," but Blake says, "Multiply, and be fruitless."

The male narrator of "The Crystal Cabinet" believes he has entered sexual maturity. But as he tries to claim adult authority, he is propelled back to infancy. He is the helpless babe starting *The Mental Traveller*. The weeping woman is the mother of his Nativity and Lamentation. "The Crystal Cabinet" ends like Giorgione's *The Tempest* (1505), where a nude woman nurses a child under a thundery sky. Blake's cycle is replayed by D. H. Lawrence in *Women in Love*, where Gerald's violent intercourse with Gudrun strangely transforms him into "an infant . . . at its mother's breast."[5] Restored to the landscape where he was found, the male of "The Crystal Cabinet" undergoes a melancholy reabsorption into biology, symbolized by a pale woman half-dead from labor pains. Sex pleasure, sex torture: it's all the same to mother nature.

The crystal cabinet is a razed Temple of sex, from which the faithful are dispersed into the wilderness. Architecturally, Blake's cabinet is unique. Primitive depiction of female genitals is stark and unadorned. Fertility religion makes pubic deltas or ridged ovoids. Literature and art follow the medieval Venusberg tradition of the Tannhäuser saga, where the *mons veneris* echoes earth's rounded hills. Western depiction of

male genitals tends to use fabricated rather than natural shapes—
swords, spears, guns, herms, even (in Melville) a chimney. Whether
Amazon or Hedda Gabler, the woman taking up a man's weapon hermaphroditizes herself. Western masculinity defies female nature.

A phallic totem is easily made and rather impressive. But how to
achieve a female sex symbolism of equal dignity? Melville's *Tartarus of
Maids*, for example, though sympathetic to women's plight, is a somewhat nauseating tour of the physiological waterworks. Woman as civilization rather than nature must be represented by her secondary rather
than primary sex organs. As I noted of Egyptian art, the female breast as
shapely adornment rather than saggy bladder accompanies the invention of femininity, sign of advancing culture. After prehistory, the breast
takes over western female symbolism. Remarkably, Blake's crystal cabinet imagines female genitals at a high degree of artifice. There are few
parallels. Female genitalia are not beautiful by any aesthetic standard.
In fact, as I argued earlier, the idea of beauty is a defensive swerve from
the ugliness of sex and nature. Female genitals are literally grotesque.
That is, they are of the grotto, earth fissures leading to the chthonian
cavern of the womb. Italians have a special feeling for grottos and are
constantly building them behind homes or churches. It is part of our
pagan heritage, our ancestral memory of earth-cult. Female genitals
inspire in the observer, depending upon sexual orientation, that stirring
in the bowels which is either disgust or lust. "The Crystal Cabinet"
shows lust flipping over to disgust. Blake's golden female genitals are a
work of art—but here that is evil. His radical revision of traditional
iconography is produced by his distrust of society. For him, literature
and art reinforce the hostile game-playing of love; courtly convention
traps the free energy of sex. But archetype thwarts Blake's intention.
The male, thrusting into the cabinet's sexual center, sees where he came
from and is horrified. I reject criticism's tidy assessment of Blake's sex
theory, where redeemed imagination opposes and reconciles civilization and nature. Poetry is written and read with emotion, not mind.
Emotionally, Blake's world is out of control.

Blake and Lawrence have reputations as sexual revolutionaries. But
both were agitated by the threat of female dominance, which their
works prove rather than disprove. Blake is our greatest poet of sexual
anxiety. Bloom rightly says of "The Crystal Cabinet," "The speaker has
suffered only loss, through seeking in sexual experience a finality it
cannot afford anyone."[6] Bloom's pessimistic realism is truer to Blake
than Northrop Frye's dreams of sexual harmony. My generation has
seen the workings of sexual freedom not in an imagined future but a

chaotic present. Hence I value Blake not as a prophet of sexual liberation but as a magus who has studied the secrets of nature and seen the
outrageous enslavements of our life in the body. *The Mental Traveller*
and "The Crystal Cabinet" dramatize the limitations of sex. There is no
sex without yielding to nature. And nature is a female domain. Blake's
dreadful fate was to see the abyss from which most men shrink: the
infantilism in all male heterosexuality. Criticism's disregard of Blake's
blatant sadomasochism has censored him. Like Spenser, he left a message that remains unread.

Blake's long prophetic poems have a curious psychologi-
cal system. Bear with me for a synopsis hacked out of the jungle of Blake
scholarship, much of it frustratingly contradictory.

Human beings suffer division in the fallen realm of Experience,
which is marked by the dramatic interaction of entities called Emanation and Spectre. The Emanation is projected cathexis, a cinema of the
unquiet mind. It is desire longing for realization. Emanations can be of
either sex, but the most important ones are female. In Innocence, the
female Emanation is integrated within the self. In Experience, the
Emanation must migrate outward (i.e., emanate). A self which imprisons its Emanation becomes solipsistic and hermaphroditic. Once
the Emanation achieves outwardness, it must not escape so far as to
become alienated from the self. This would be the erotic perversity of
female flight and concealment, by which woman dominates man. Spiritual health is the correct positioning of self to Emanation, in loving
marriage. The archenemy of happy union between self and Emanation
is the Spectre, whom Blake identifies with rationalism. One may be
turned into a Spectre by the desertion of one's Emanation. But just as
often, the Spectre pursues and haunts the self. Blake's Spectre is always
male. Hence it is an early example of the nineteenth-century doppelgänger, like the stern double tracking Poe's William Wilson. When
dominated by the Spectre, the self becomes a hermaphroditic Selfhood,
whom Blake calls Satan or Death. In this state, the created world is at its
most remote and densely material or contracted.

Until commentary becomes simpler and more persuasive, Blake's
long poems will languish unread, known only by Blake specialists, the
same parochialization suffered by Spenser. It should be immediately
evident—though nowhere pointed out in central Blake studies—that
Blake's Spectres and Emanations are equivalent to the ghosts of the
contemporaneous Gothic novel. The late eighteenth century was the
end of something and the beginning of something. The disintegration

of the Apollonian Enlightenment produced a psychic fragmentation or splintering. In the static psychology of the early eighteenth century, character was constructed of building blocks of fixed "qualities." A century earlier, Donne illustrated the rational unity and simplicity of the Christian model of personality in "Holy Sonnet I," where the soul is tugged up toward heaven and down toward hell, while the poet looks forward toward death and backward toward his sinful life. Directions are resolutely foursquare, like a compass. The moral universe is geometrically coherent and intelligible. In Blake, however, there is no up or down. Tracks of emotional force are not rectangular but spiral: Mannerist images of the "Vortex" recur. The Spectre veers off at an eccentric angle from the self. Blake's fluid world is full of disjunctions of scale, gross expansions and stifling diminutions. It has the spongy relativism of modern physics.

In Blake the soul has split, so that the prophetic poems ask what is the "true" self. This is a new question in history, more sweeping than the multiple impersonations of the Renaissance, where social order was still a moral value. In Blake, territorial war is waged among parts of the self. His characters are in identity crisis, Rousseau's invention. In his Spectres and Emanations, Blake is doing allegorically what the nineteenth-century novel will do naturalistically, documenting the modulations of emotion. Blake rejects Judeo-Christian morality. Nevertheless, he wants to integrate sexuality with right action. But sex, which Christianity correctly assigns to the daemonic realm, always escapes moral control. The paradoxes of Blake's eerie Gothic psychodrama of Spectre and Emanation arise from the impossibility of his mission: to redeem sex from its miring in mother nature.

Fallen Experience constantly generates phantom selves which cloud perception. Parodic pregnancies abound in Blake. The failure to emanate is like a perversely prolonged pregnancy, where being is choked. Blake's psychodrama takes the form of unnatural sex acts of bizarre surrealism. Blake is Sade's peer in sexual imagination. Take, for example, Los's capture of his fleeing Emanation, Enitharmon: "Eternity shudder'd when they saw, / Man begetting his likeness, / On his own divided image" (*Urizen* 19:14–16). I am impatient with critical over-stress of the allegory here, where Los is time and Enitharmon space. On the primary emotional level of poetry, we see a violent public sex act, from which the horrified universe cannot avert its eyes. Incestuous self-insemination: the grappling duo is a new Khepera, the masturbatory Egyptian cosmos-maker. Actors and audience are a sexual octopus of many legs and many eyes.

The contest between male Spectre and female Emanation is archaic ritual combat. I find homosexual overtones in the betrayal of the self into a queasy spectral world ruled by dark, deceiving male figures. Note the elegance with which Blake's Spectre theory fits Shakespeare's *Othello*. A conspiratorial Spectre, Iago, is homoerotically obsessed with splitting Othello, through jealous fears, from his Emanation, Desdemona. (Jealousy and fear are the Spectres' regular weapons.) Othello, cleaving to his Spectre instead of casting him off, destroys himself. He ends by killing not his Spectre but his Emanation. Another example is Joseph Losey's film, *The Servant* (1963, screenplay by Harold Pinter from a novel by Robin Maugham). An upper-class bachelor is dominated by a homosexually insinuating male Spectre, his housekeeper and valet (Dirk Bogarde), who coolly and systematically drives away the master's fiancée. The fiancée, Blake's Emanation, is the master's link with reality. Severed from her, he sinks beneath the Spectre's power into enervation and decadence, Blake's solipsism. In Blake, the self must choose between joyous heterosexual marriage with a female Emanation or evil homosexual bonding with a male Spectre. Homosexuality is negative and narcissistic for Blake because it evades the fruitful opposition of sexual contraries.

Blake's fallen world is full of delusive personae, like swindling "bubble" speculations of the nineteenth century. Vala, for example, is a taxidermic decoy, like Spenser's False Florimell. She vampiristically captures and absorbs Albion's libidinal energy. The self must make its way past frauds and extortionists who lure the psyche into committing spiritual capital to unsound investments. Blake sees sexual personae as false advertisement. As a moralist, Blake is a spiritualist. As a sexualist, he is a materialist. Never the twain shall meet. Arguments with one's self make art. Blake's poetry is border strife, communiqués from the endless guerrilla war between sex and good intentions.

The "Hermaphrodites" of Blake's prophetic poems may be the most shrilly negative androgynes in literature and art. Blake's attitude toward sexually dual figures is mixed, since he thinks of prelapsarian man as androgynous. Crabb Robinson reported a "rambling" conversation with Blake about life before and after the Fall: the poet spoke of "a union of sexes in man as in Ovid, an androgynous state, in which I could not follow him." For Blake, the sexes should be fused only in the unfallen world. Albion, like the Kabbalistic Adam Kadmon, contains both sexes because he precedes history. When history stops, Albion will regain his dual gender.

Though he may allude to a primeval hermaphrodite, Blake puts little stress on it in his poetry. Of far more import are the monstrous hermaphrodites of Experience. The hermaphroditic Satan, "black & opake," hides the male within him "as in a Tabernacle Abominable Deadly" (*Four Zoas* 101, II:33–37). Tabernacles and arks, like crystal cabinets, are evil because Blake opposes everything hidden or set aside in special holiness. Satan is a mutation of the Great Mother. He is "unformd & vast," like the chaos of archaic night before the birth of the eye. Blake's hermaphrodites are negative for the same reason they are positive for the French and English Decadence: their imperious self-containment. The hermaphrodite's inability to mate and its incapacity for emotional opening are moral defects for Blake, who says, "The most sublime act is to set another before you" (*Marriage of Heaven and Hell*). The hermaphrodite is severe sexual closure. Satan is a black hole of super-dense matter, a spiralling convolution of psyche. He is spiritually blocked.

Blake's war at Jerusalem's Gate is a vast "aggregate" hermaphrodite or "Polypus," heaving like an earthquake (*Four Zoas* 104, II:19–21, 56:14–16). This Wagnerian passage is a great epiphany of the Dionysian androgyne. Chthonian spasms give birth to the "monstrous" deformity, Satan. Swirling, swarming mobs are a single writhing being. Baudelaire uses a similar effect in "A Carcass," where seething maggots rise and fall like a wave. Blake's surreal warpings of perspective resemble Vergil's in his grotesque Rumor, tyrant of city life. Hermaphrodite war and hermaphroditic Satan, spawned by daemonic parthenogenesis, belong to the category of androgyne I call the moral monstrosity.

A reverse image of Satan's birth occurs in *Milton*, where the poet-hero returns from Eden to become his own hermaphrodite Shadow. There are labor pains of ingress, as dead Milton forces the ribbon of time to run backwards so he may revise his life work. Milton, as if in masquerade, assumes hermaphrodite costume to recover his Emanation, Ololon. He is like Odysseus disguised as a beggar to free his Emanation, Penelope, from captivity in their house usurped by Spectres. Milton faces the Blakean sexual crux, a choice between a blissful bride and a male double (Satan). Milton's quest for his Emanation requires separating her from her own tendency toward hermaphroditism. She is at a sexual crossroads, like the Greek fork where Oedipus slew Laius. Milton must capture his Emanation before she takes the road to Delphi, where she will become, like Alice, an omnipotent queen. Hermaphrodite Milton is tempted by orgiastic apparitions sent by the malevolent nature goddesses, Rahab and Tirzah. These hermaphrodites, "Double-sexed; / The Female-male & the Male-female," have an Apollonian beauty glowing against chthonian darkness, like Lucifer in *The Monk* (19:32–33). They flash with the neon luridness of urban prostitution, homosexual and heterosexual. Milton is being confronted with his ambivalence about sex.

In *Jerusalem*, in one of the most daring assaults upon the masculine in all of Blake, Vala denounces Los: "The Human is but a Worm, & thou O Male: Thou art / Thyself Female, a Male: a breeder of Seed: a Son & Husband: & Lo. / The Human Divine is Womans Shadow, a Vapor in the summers heat. ... O Woman-born / And Woman-nourishd & Woman-educated & Woman-scorn'd!" (64:12–17). A giant hermaphrodite suddenly forms, and the colors of crimson wrath, green jealousy, and purple frustration vibrate in the heavy air. The united beings loom over the Thames like a colossus, a toxic mushroom cloud. Vala as nature denies the male exists as a separate sex. He is merely a subset to woman. Nature shrinks man to her adolescent son-lover. Vala's torrent of abuse resembles the hectoring verbal attacks of female upon cowering male in Lawrence's *Women in Love* and the films *All About Eve* and *Who's Afraid of Virginia Woolf?* I invent a special category of the androgyne, the Venus Barbata, for such strident termagants.

One of Los's tasks in *Jerusalem* is to break apart false hermaphrodite forms to release their male and female energy. He pounds them on his anvil, asserting the aggression of masculine will. Los has to halt the careening orgy of the Daughters of Albion, who "divide & unite at will" as, "naked & drunk," they pour through the London streets (58:1–2). The Daughters of Albion seem to clone themselves and make love to their own mirror images. Lesbianism is also implied in the physical intimacy of Jerusalem and Vala, surely illustrated in the introductory plate to the second chapter, which speaks of "unnatural consanguinities and friendships" (19:40–41, 28:7). Los's hammer blows are the harsh metrical accents of poetry, imagination escaping and defeating nature's organic rhythms. His beats are the renewed strife of contraries, the source of Blakean energy stunted by premature hermaphrodite fusings. Malevolent nature tries to reduce all objects to sameness, the infancy of history.

Commentary on Blake's hermaphrodites is scanty and confusing. The received interpretations are theories, not proven solutions. In his *Blake Dictionary*, J. Foster Damon, following Milton O. Percival, makes a distinction between hermaphrodite and androgyne that makes no sense whatever to me. Damon and Percival believe the sexes are equal in the androgyne but that the female dominates in the hermaphrodite.[7]

But the latter idea comes from Ovid's embroidered tale of Salmacis and Hermaphroditus, extremely late in mythological tradition. The words hermaphrodite and androgyne should be virtually synonymous. The only distinction might be to see the hermaphrodite as genitally dual but the androgyne as sexually ambiguous in face, hair, frame, clothes, manner, or spirit. But even this is an unnecessary split.

Why are androgynes horrific in Blake's poetry? Of the English Romantics, Blake is the most oriented toward the patriarchal Old Testament, which purges femaleness out of God. Like Dante and Spenser, Blake sees metamorphic hermaphroditism as evil. His loathsome hermaphrodites may be a tweaking of Milton's and Swedenborg's noses. In Milton's heaven, angels change gender and have sex in perfect purity, their soft bodies "dilated or condens't" at will (*P.L.* I.423–31, VIII.615–29). But Blake denies there can be happiness in a realm that devalues the sexual body as grossly material. Blake's hermaphrodites make Miltonic couplings, clotting and splitting at staccato pace. Their solipsism may be a satire on Milton's angels, whom Blake views as passive, sterile jellies. In Milton's heaven, like unites with like, for Blake a dead end of narcissism.

What Blake most abhors in Milton's angelic intercourse is its dissolution of outline, as the boneless entities meet and merge. This I see as the main reason for his hostility to hermaphrodites. Blake is the only major poet who is also an artist. The central reference point of his poetry and drawings is "the Human Form Divine," specifically the male form, with which Blake identifies human imagination struggling to free itself from female nature. Like Michelangelo, Blake gives female figures a masculine musculature. Because Blake knew Michelangelo's work only from engravings, his Michelangelo-inspired modelling has a sinewy hardness, like Signorelli's. Blake blames Venetian and Flemish painting for "losing the outlines." There must be "firm and determinate outline": "The great and golden rule of art, as well as of life, is this: That the more distinct, sharp, and wiry the bounding line, the more perfect the work of art; and the less keen and sharp, the greater is the evidence of weak imitation, plagiarism, and bungling. . . . How do we distinguish the oak from the beech, the horse from the ox, but by the bounding outline? How do we distinguish one face or countenance from another, but by the bounding line and its infinite inflexions and movements?"[8]

Blake's "hard and wiry line of rectitude" is the sharp Apollonian contour I have traced to the incised edges of Egyptian art. It is Blake's barrier against nature, a perceptual device by which objects and persons gain their identity. Spenser too identifies virtue with sharp-edged personality, and sloth and vice with melting dissolution of form. Blake condemns "blotting and blurring" in art, "broken lines, broken masses, and broken colours." He calls chiaroscuro, originating in Leonardo's ambiguous *sfumato*, "that infernal machine," cranking out the murk of hell.[9]

The androgyne seemed benign to Blake the less clearly he thought about it: hence his obscure "rambling" to Robinson. As soon as Blake actually visualized the androgyne, it became a horror. Explicitly hermaphroditic figures are repugnant to him for the same reason they were to high classic Greek artists, who avoided depicting mutilations or monstrosities. For Blake the hermaphrodite offends against the virtuous optical integrity of the human form. The same zeal moved Spenser to cancel his "Hermaphrodite stanzas." Blake abandoned the few drawings he attempted of the hermaphrodite, and he has his own rejected hermaphrodite stanzas, two fragments about Tharmas and his Emanation which were never included in *The Four Zoas*. Thus Blake's hostility to the hermaphrodite has two sources, ethical and aesthetic. Male and female as principles of energy must not lose their autonomy in torpid self-absorption. Second, the visionary clarity of the unitary human form must not be defiled by grotesque hybridization.

Blake's art theory extends to his view of personality. We can distinguish one face from another. Blake says, only by the bounding borderline, without which "all is chaos again." There is an undertow in nature, sucking phenomena back to primeval nondifferentiation. Personality maintains its discreteness by an act of will. Otherwise one person will flow helplessly into another. Both Spenser and Blake hate the amorphous. But Blake's anxiety is obsession. His insistence on the bounding line is like Dr. Johnson's compulsion to touch fence posts as he walked. Blake says, "Nature has no Outline" ("The Ghost of Abel"). Bloom speaks of Blake's Rahab as "mother of the indefinite, queen of the abyss of objects without contour, lines without clear outline."[10] Looking at a smoky, coloristic painting, Blake feels he is looking into Rahab's abyss.

Blake says chiaroscuro makes a painting "all blocked up with brown shadows." Though Rubens' "original conception was all fire and animation, he loads it with hellish brownness, and blocks up all its gates of light." Blake uses "clear colours unmudded by oil." Mud, hellish brownness: excrement. Blake confirms this association elsewhere when he calls Rubens' coloring "most Contemptible": "His Shadows are of a Filthy Brown somewhat of the Colour of Excrement."[11] Hellish brownness is the belly and bowels of mother nature, the labyrinth where the

Apollonian eye is lost. Blake's mud is primal ooze, the chthonian swamp
of generation. In Spenser and Blake, the self must be constructed and
sustained against demoralizing relaxations (laxness of line). Personality
is architectonic. Without virile force, the self slips back into the dissolution of swampy female nature.

Blake says a weak bounding line is evidence of plagiarism. Bloom's
anxiety of influence: by firmness of line, one defends oneself against an
overwhelming precursor. Who is the ultimate precursor? The Great
Original, mother nature, who delegates her authority to our individual
mothers. Blake's bounding line expresses a gnawing need for self-
origination. It is a territorial strategy, by which the male separates
himself from his female source. Like Jesus, Blake defies his mother:
"Then what have I to do with thee?" ("To Tirzah"). When Blake says
faces are indistinguishable without the bounding line, the two faces
threatening to collapse into each other, as in the dream climax of
Bergman's *Persona*, are those of mother and son.

Blake's scorn for chiaroscuro is related to his resentment of the
hidden and secret. He boldly calls for an end to shame about the
genitals; he wants them flooded in the light of *Glad Day*, with its
exuberant nudity. Alas, sexual openness applies only to men. A man can
walk vigorously free on the earth, exposing his genitals without self-
consciousness or guilt. But a woman's genitals are not visible when she
stands or walks. To expose herself, she must lie on her back or squat
over the observer's face! In other words, she must take a position of
submission or dominance, as in a primitive statuette or cult act. Man is
either gynecologist or supine asphyxiate. The female body can never be
made completely visible; it will always be a dark, secret place. I applied
Karen Horney's remark on woman's inability to see her genitals to my
theory of the Greek male nude, which I interpret as a projected genital.
Embodying every emotion in titanic human form, Blake's long poems
are a psychic gigantism, a compulsive externalization inspired by the
desire to abolish the secrecy of woman's reproductive matrix. Gigantism is distinctively masculine, as in Michelangelo and Goethe. Gigantism in a woman is transsexualizing, transmuting the female self by
male potency. The desire to turn male is latent in two examples of
female gigantism, Emily Brontë's Heathcliff and Rosa Bonheur's vast,
muscular painting, *Horse Fair*.

Blake's supreme desire is to free sex from the tyrannical nature
mother. One of my central theses is that sex and parturition occur in the
liquid realm. Art is a flight from liquidity in its manufacture of discrete
objects defying their origins. Blake's extraordinary rhetorical energy

and enormity of assertion come from his revulsion from the female-ruled liquid condition of physical life. The Greek beautiful boy, I said, is imagination freed from nature, but his freedom is attained through sexual renunciation, chastity. Blake desires free imagination, but he exalts eroticism and makes chastity a perversion. This is impossible. There can be no active sexuality without surrender to nature and to liquidity, the realm of the mother. Blake wants nature bound but sex unbound. Sex is chthonian, but as artist and man Blake seeks the Apollonian. Before the symbolism of his prophetic books was analyzed, Blake used to be called "mad." This was obviously wrong. Yet in the long poems there is a hysteria or excess unacknowledged by criticism. Art is born of stress, not repose. Art is always a swerve from primary experience. Blake's long poems are full of knots, breaches, and strains. They are held together by force of will, like an ancient monument (the Porch of the Maidens) sutured by iron rods. Blake's lack of complete intelligibility comes from his philosophical discontinuities. His hopeless but heroic task, to redeem sex from nature, is a western epic saga.

Translating him into moral terms, criticism is at odds with how Blake's poetry feels. Bloom presents Blake as a man of peace who hates war. But Blake's prophetic poetry *is* war, violent, terrible. His long poems seethe with hostility, of which his obsession with mother nature is but one example. As I read the accumulated criticism, I keep asking, why is Blake a poet rather than a philosopher, if everything he wrote reduces so neatly to these manifest ideas? Blake scholarship denies there is a latent content. In life as in art, moral flag-waving may conceal a repressed attraction to what is being denounced.

Blake's treatment of women is full of ambivalences. Here is his model of the future: "In Eternity Woman is the Emanation of Man she has No Will of her own There is no such thing in Eternity as a Female Will" (*A Vision of the Last Judgment*). It is not enough to say all Blake's females are nature and all his males are man and woman together. Whenever gender is symbolized, we must ask why. As long as imagination is formed by culture, it may be impossible to free the sexes from their inherited meanings in art. I am not particularly vexed by Blake's negative female symbols, since I am too aware of a contradictory latent content breaking through. So stunning a vision of nature as *The Mental Traveller* is not produced by someone secure in the triumph of male imagination. In *A Room of One's Own*, Virginia Woolf satirically describes her perplexity at the bulging card catalog of the British Museum: why, she asks, are there so many books written by men about women but none by women about men? The answer to her question is that from the beginning of time men have been struggling with the threat of woman's dominance. The flood of books was prompted not by woman's weakness but by her strength, her complexity and impenetrability, her dreadful omnipresence. No man has yet been born, even Jesus himself, who was not spun from a pitiful speck of plasma to a conscious being on the secret loom within a woman's body. That body is the cradle and soft pillow of woman's love, but it is also the torture rack of nature.

Blake seems to be the one Romantic who denies the femme fatale's power over him. But this is his propaganda, not reality. Even Los's activity is the hammering heart of sex fear. In one of the most spectacular passages in Blake's poetry, the naked Daughters of Albion perform a grim ritual of nature cult. They hunker on a stone altar, the rock landscape of *The Mental Traveller*. With a flint knife, castration tool of the Great Mother, they gash the howling male victim. His blood stains their white bodies. They thrust their fingers in his heart; they pour cold water on his brain and lid his eyes. "Glowing with beauty & cruelty: / They obscure the sun & the moon; no eye can look upon them." One drinks the blood of her "panting Victim." He pants because he is a deer caught by an eerily unwinded Diana. The sex act has drained him. Woman soaks up male energy for her insatiable pleasure and pride (*Jer* 66:16–34, 68:11–12).

The Daughters of Albion are so superbly glamourous and the whole terrifying scene so astoundingly visualized that we must ask whether such things in Blake really come from militant resistance to the femme fatale. I fail to see significant differences between this passage and the erotic vampire poems of Baudelaire. Surely there is secret delectation in Blake's vivid detailing of each step of the prostrate male's torture. This is a great flight of sadomasochistic poetry. I feel very strongly in it Blake's shiver of voluptuous identification with the humiliated victim. It prefigures Whitman's keening sexual litanies. The manifest content of the passage is that nature is pitiless and tyrannical. The latent content is that Blake's excess of opposition to the "Female Will" springs from his attraction to her and from the danger of his imminent surrender.

Blake's sexual vulnerability is only to chthonian androgynes, the Great Mother and her subset, the vampire. The Amazon figure severed from sexuality offers no archetypal danger to him; hence his stern rejection of her is uncomplicated. Blake's virginity is a haughty, solitary Artemis, like Spenser's Belphoebe. Apollonian Elynittria, "the silver bowed queen," has a "terrible" light and "immortal beauty," driving off trespassers with her silver arrows (*Eur* 8:4; *Mil* 12:1, 11:37–38). Blake finds immature the self-sequestration of Spenserian virginity. Significantly, his crowded painting of *The Faerie Queene* omits both Belphoebe and Britomart. Blake has a nightmare vision of Amazon legions on the move, modelled on Milton's demon army. Thousands of women march over "burning wastes of Sand," as blazing lightning strikes their armoured shoulders (*Four Zoas* 70:21–23). Virginity, burning with repressed desire, is a hot thin soil where nothing grows. Blake's war against female hegemony extends even to his Muse. He claimed he took dictation from the spirit of his dead brother, who died at nineteen. Thus Blake has a male Muse, an extraordinary aberration in the history of poetry. Milton bizarrely descends into Blake's foot in his garden—poetic destiny transmitted from one male to another, without the Muse's mediation. Blake will not let femaleness touch him on any side.

Blake, unlike Wordsworth, is chock-full of characters, who are the very stuff of his poetry. But he is not concerned with personality as such. His characters are generalized and typological. Blake is interested in universal, not idiosyncratic experience. In the huge corpus of his art work, there are few portraits, and these are usually caricatures or grotesques. Blake resembles Michelangelo in his indifference to the portrait mode, a medium of social personae. Manners are rituals, which Blake opposes in society or religion as mechanical formulas imposed on the spontaneous and organic. Ironically, in dispensing with social ritualism, Blake left himself open to the far more brutal sadomasochistic ritualism of sex and nature, which became his favorite poetic style. Like D. H. Lawrence, Blake wants sex to transcend social names and identities. Also like Lawrence, he desires a return to naturalness without succumbing to nature. In Blake's world, the mere appearance of a persona is a sign of disease. A mask is a moral husk.

Blake attacks all hierarchies. There is no great chain of being in his poetry; nothing is holier than anything else. But Blake's bounding line is an Apollonian and hence hierarchical principle. I noted that Blake is against dissolution of form, the Dionysian force destroying hierarchy in Euripides' *Medea* and *Bacchae*. Despite his bounding line, Blake opposes centripetal identity as solipsistic. Urizen, for example, is "self-closd, all-repelling" (*Urizen* 3:3). Here the bounds of self are *too* firm. Blake's most famous drawing is the centrifugal *Glad Day*, athletic Albion with arms flung wide, a symbol of the free energy Blake loves. Free energy is Dionysian. One cannot be simultaneously for contour and for sexuality, since sexuality by its very nature is an abridgement of contour. Two people making love are the beast with two backs. The

most perfectly contoured personalities in literature and art are those
Apollonian angels of chastity whom Blake despises for their coldness
and exclusivity.

These irreconcilable contradictions arise from Blake's violent yoking
together of two opposing systems, the Bible and the visual arts. As a
graphic artist, Blake is already beyond Old Testament Judaism, which
condemns image-making as idolatry. The Ten Commandments forbid
pictures of all kinds—of animals, fish, or gods. This is a Hebrew strategy against pagan fertility cults, which saw divinity in nature. Yahweh's
injunction diverted Jewish creative energy away from the visual arts
into theology, philosophy, literature, law, and science, by which the Jews
have made a stunning impact on world culture, far outweighing their
small numbers. Blake's eccentric psychology comes from the fact that
he is a strange combination of artist and Hebrew prophet.

Blake rejects Greco-Roman literature and exalts the Bible, whose
psychology he adopts. There are no sexual personae in the Bible, except
among harlots. Biblical character is unitary and homogeneous. Psychic
splits are of the "whited sepulcher" kind, where the self is cleanly
divided into visible and invisible halves. Multiplicity is just the moral
duality of a fair face concealing a foul heart. The self breaks down no
finer than this. Metamorphosis is reserved for seraphs; God and demons make marvels, turning into a pillar of fire or bouncing into a pig.
There is no suggestion of the turbulent welter of impulses in Euripides'
Medea. The Bible is unconcerned with mystery of motivation. Pharaoh's hardness of heart is stupidity and self-destructiveness, the donkey
halting in its track. Saul's envy is an exception—but perhaps a chunk of
the story has vanished along the way.

Classical personality, in contrast, is a theatrical projection of self. A
tremendous amount of imaginative energy was invested in the construction of persona. It is in the persona that honor resides, and offenses
against honor require revenge, a principle still colorfully operative
among the Mafia. Classical psychology, revived in the Renaissance,
lingers on in Italian culture, where persona is called *figura* (as in "cutting a figure"). In the Bible, individuals are inseparable from their acts.
Matthew Arnold says, "The uppermost idea with Hebraism is conduct
and obedience."[12] That Biblical personality exists in and for moral
action makes sense inasmuch as the Bible is a chronicle, the record of a
chosen people moving through history. While action is important in
classical culture, the persona is separate from and greater than acts. No
value inheres in an action unless one is seen performing it. The Greek
gods certainly don't give a fig, unless their personal vanity is involved.

Hence the act is merely instrumental, common clay in the sculpting of persona, which is a public work of art. Blake seeks out the Hebrew roots of character and tries to throw off the classical theatrical persona. But the Hebrew view of personality as moral content creates a tension in his poetry with the Greek view of personality as visible formal contour, to which Blake is drawn despite himself, because of his artist's eye. In his indictment of the Great Mother, Blake writes like St. Augustine, as if she were an immediate threat. Thus his poetry recreates the historical situation in which the Jews warred with Egypt, Babylon, and Rome.

Despite his apparent radicalism, Blake is deeply conservative about personality. He is obsessed with the subject, because he stands on the threshold of one of the great leaps in western culture in number and volatility of sexual personae. The last had been at the Renaissance. With the intuition of genius, Blake feels the forces at work in the late eighteenth century which will produce the chaotic proliferation of modern personalities. Like Spenser, Blake tries to halt the breakdown into multiplicity of personae. With the Apollonian bounding line, he wants to bind up the self into honesty, to ban all psychic fictions. But as Blake pursues his moral quest, the principal tools which come to hand are feverishly propagating Spectres and Emanations. Their thronging presence in his riven poetry makes it symptomatic in literary history of the very fragmentation it condemns.

11

Marriage to Mother Nature

Wordsworth

William Wordsworth, not William Blake, defined nature for nineteenth-century culture. Visiting France in the early 1790s, Wordsworth read and admired Rousseau. Disillusioned by the French Revolution's moral degeneration, he turned away from politics toward nature, the focus of his hopes. Nature's inability to sustain him emotionally becomes one of Wordsworth's sad themes. From first to last, he sees nature with Rousseau's eyes. Wordsworth's refusal to acknowledge the sex or cruelty in nature is one source of the palpable repression in his poetry, which constricts and weighs it down. This repression, approaching depressiveness, accounts for Wordsworth's lack of appeal to young readers, who are drawn to energy, not to mention lust. Wordsworth's sexlessness is not neurotic failing but conceptual strategy. He must renounce sex in order not to see or feel nature's sadism. Blake wants sex without nature. Wordsworth wants nature without sex. As Rousseau is answered by Sade, so is Wordsworth answered—by his friend and colleague, Coleridge. There is a harsh sexual symbiosis between the two men: Wordsworth displaces onto Coleridge what he himself cannot acknowledge in nature. From Coleridge comes the savage line of nineteenth-century pornographic daemonism, Poe and Hawthorne to Baudelaire, Wilde, and James. The bitter war between Wordsworth and Coleridge goes on for a hundred years.

Wordsworth's first principle is "wise passiveness," a feminine receptivity opening us to nature. In "Expostulation and Reply," from Wordsworth and Coleridge's revolutionary *Lyrical Ballads* (1798), a friend chides the poet for dreaming his time away. Wordsworth replies that the eye sees, the ear hears, and our bodies feel "against or with our will." Unknown "Powers" play upon us. These powers are chthonian, but

Wordsworth severs them from their ancient connection to sex and barbarism. Reality is active, the poet contemplative, dominated by nature. The poem is a manifesto of sexual dissent, a withdrawal from the traditional masculine sphere of action and achievement. It starts a movement in modern literature leading to Melville's self-entombed Bartleby ("I would prefer not to") and Kafka's crippled cockroach, Gregor Samsa. Wordsworth forfeits maleness for spiritual union with mother nature: wholeness through self-mutilation. His poetry revives the ritualism of the Asiatic mother-cults, whose priests castrated themselves for the goddess.

In a companion poem, Wordsworth denies we can learn anything from books, that is, from the words of other men. Instead, "Let Nature be your teacher." Intellect "mis-shapes" beauty: "We murder to dissect." All you need is a heart that "watches and receives" ("The Tables Turned"). As in Dante, reason cannot lead us to ultimate truth. Wordsworth's reason is brutal and uncreative. Murder by dissection means analysis is masculine, penetrating and killing. Intellect is too aggressive. The heart "receives" knowledge as a bride opens to her husband. The poet's sex reversal is unmistakable: his shadowy Powers appear here as female nature. The male perfects himself by shamanistic sacrifice of virility. When he is completely passive, nature showers him with gifts. He is holy newborn and she Madonna and Magi. There is nothing negative in the teacher. Thus there can be nothing negative in the lesson. This was Wordsworth's major error.

The Rousseauist family romance of mother and child is explicit throughout Wordsworth. In *The Recluse* he calls himself a "nursling of the mountains" tamed by female nature, who turns him from "Warrior's Schemes" and tells him, "Be mild, and cleave to gentle things" (726–45). Enlightenment means androgyny. Nature is man's model. Since she is female, he must become feminine. This internalization of femininity is celebrated in the last book of *The Prelude*, where the heart of the spiritually evolved male is "tender as a nursing mother's heart" and his life full of "female softness," "humble cares and delicate desires, / Mild interests and gentlest sympathies" (XIV.225–31). A man reaches the height of moral understanding through psychic transsexualism. His inner life is colonized by feminine emotions and experiences. Intuitive vision is trancelike removal from the active body. Wordsworth calls it "that serene and blessed mood," a yogic suspension of breath and blood: "We are laid asleep / In body, and become a living soul." The aggressive western eye is "made quiet" as "We see into the life of things" (*Tintern Abbey*). There is no gender in pure contemplativeness, since there is no gender-defining body, now neutralized and transcended.

Wordsworth systematically suppresses the body, the medium of masculine action. When *Peter Bell*'s hardhearted protagonist reforms, his joy turns to tears, melting "his nerves, his sinews": "Through all his iron frame was felt / A gentle, a relaxing, power!" Fibers weakened, he is helpless, "mild and gentle as an infant child." The iron frame of masculine architecture is dissolved by feminine emotion, restoring childhood innocence. Like Goethe's Werther, Wordsworth identifies masculinity with corrupt adulthood. He is amending and reversing *The Faerie Queene*. Wordsworth welcomes melting relaxation for the same reason Spenser abhors it: because it is a feminizing deconstruction of the male will. Wordsworth's ideal is a Bower of Bliss in overhanging nature. He seeks Dionysian deliquescence without sex. Wordsworth wants to prolong childhood emotional purity into genderless adulthood. Is this a Puritan bequest? Emotion without eroticism is impossible.

The poet is a "gentle creature" with a female mind, happiest when sitting "brooding" like a "mother dove." At Cambridge, Wordsworth was as "sensitive" to nature's changes as waters to the sky. He was "obedient as a lute" waiting for "the touches of the wind" (*Pre* I.135–41, III.138–39). Wordsworth often calls river or sea a female "bosom" or "breast." So if he is water, he is female, as in ancient cosmogonies which imagine female earth inseminated by male sky. Erotic passivity is implicit in Romanticism's favorite topos of the Aeolian wind-harp, here a lute symbolizing the artist's subordination to nature's inspiring power.

Wordsworth's descriptions of mental processes are sexually tinged. The mind is "lord and master"; the senses are "obedient servant of her will" (*Pre* XII.222–23). Mind is a dominatrix. The poet's inner life is womblike: "*Caverns* there were within my mind which sun / Could never penetrate" (III.246–47). Wordsworth uses "pregnancy" and "impregnation" in nonsexual contexts. The cavern image appears in two of *The Prelude*'s major passages. Crossing the Alps, Wordsworth thinks of imagination as an "awful Power" that "rose from the mind's abyss / Like an unfathered vapour" (VI.594–95). Geoffrey Hartman says imagination is unfathered because "self-begotten."[1] The mind in its abyss is a double-sexed earth mother, fertilizing herself without male help. Imagination is unfathered because it shuns the pricking stimulus of male reason; its sole parent is female intuition. The poet is like the Delphic oracle maddened by vapors. Wordsworth reverts to matriarchal consciousness, receiving signals from earth and heart, rather than sky and brain. Hartman finds "sexual or birth-channel implications" in

Wordsworth's images of "narrow chasm," "gloomy strait," and "dark deep thoroughfare."[2] Ascending Mount Snowdon, Wordsworth sees a mind feeding upon infinity, brooding over "the dark abyss" (XIV.70–72). The mind as mother dove broods upon its own inner cavern. *Paradise Lost* opens with God sitting "brooding on the vast Abyss" to make it "pregnant" (I.21–22). Wordsworth's maternal poetic consciousness takes over God's powers and privileges.

Eye and ear, Wordsworth says in *Tintern Abbey*, not only "perceive" but "half create." There should be "balance" and harmony between "the objects seen, and eye that sees." Wordsworth wants to blunt the aggressive western eye without darkening it in solipsism. He scorns as "passive minds" those failing to see the "affinities" and "brotherhood" between men and natural things (*Pre* XIII.375–78, II.384–86). This negative use of "passive" is unexpected. Wordsworth assails "Presumption, folly, madness, in the men / Who thrust themselves upon the passive world / As Rulers of the world" (*Pre* XIII.66–68). As Hitler said, the masses are feminine. Wordsworth's thrusting, self-erected rulers rape the people. "One maternal spirit" fills the world, except where man is unjustly made "a tool or implement, a passive thing" (*The Excursion* IX.111–16). Bad government is against nature. In Wordsworth's play, *The Borderers*, "the tyranny of the world's masters" lives only "in the torpid acquiescence of emasculated souls" (III.354–57). Dominance requires submission. Political power is sadomasochistic sex. In a sonnet of 1803, Wordsworth urges England to "wean" its heart from "its emasculating food." England is on its knees, sucking from the wrong sex and the wrong spigot.

Wordsworth's negative, emasculated passivity occurs when men subordinate themselves not to maternal female nature but to other men. Acceptance of political tyranny is a betrayal of divine mother love. Modern social man is a moral catamite, like Pope's court-enamoured Sporus. Hence Wordsworth, like Blake, has his own sexual crux. A man may choose emasculation in the service of the state, stultifying his imagination, or he may choose marriage with a mother goddess. But who is the bride, who the groom? Wordsworth, son and spouse, is self-eunuchized. Male-defending Blake would denounce this marriage and be ejected from the church.

Wordsworth exalts suffering, as well as perception. "Action is transitory," merely "the motion of a muscle," while "Suffering is permanent, obscure, and dark, / And shares the nature of infinity" (*Bor* III.405–10). Through suffering one enters Wordsworth's dark abyss. Suffering is an Eleusinian mystery, a chthonian cavern. Action is masculine, suffering feminine. Men's acts are "transitory," but the travails of women and woman-identified males are "permanent." Wordsworth's sexuality is in dreams of self-immolation.

Reviewing the sexual personae of his collected works, we discover Wordsworth's radical exclusion of one human type: the adult man of active virility. His poems are filled with children, women, old men, and animals. But a stone in the road arouses more fellow-feeling in Wordsworth than does a masculine man. Exiles from society automatically win his Rousseauist respect. Since Wordsworth identifies society with masculinity, the masculine male, smug victor of the social sweepstakes, is barred from the poetry. For Blake the Man is everything; for Wordsworth he is nothing, a moral zero. Though Wordsworth's compassion seems ideologically all-inclusive, it is not. The more glaring art's omissions, the bigger the imaginative swerve. Wordsworth burns with aversion toward virile males.

For Wordsworth's emotion to flow toward him, a male must suffer some curtailment of virility. We meet a sailor in "Incidents upon Salisbury Plain," but he is old and impoverished. His feet are half bare, his red military coat faded, patched, and torn. He is a murderer and thus, like Cain, doomed to solitary wandering. In *The Prelude* Wordsworth meets a tall man in military dress with "a lean and wasted arm": "a more meagre man / Was never seen before by night or day" (IV.387ff.). Sailor and soldier have been expelled from social hierarchies. They are the detritus of a civilization moving obliviously through history. It is for their obsolescence and "desolation" that Wordsworth admires them. Another sailor appears in "The Waggoner," which starts to follow his adventures in a surprisingly straightforward way. Can this be a Wordsworthian virile male? No, a hundred lines later: "Up springs the Sailor from his chair— / Limps (for I might have told before / That he was lame) across the floor" (II.102–04). Men must be mutilated to get into Wordsworth's poetry. Wordsworth is so used to impairing his males physically or spiritually that he elides the sailor's lameness at first entrance, leaving the affliction understood as a traumatic assumption of his poetic world. Or perhaps he conceives of the sailor as virile but then finds his imagination stiffened by the presence of so strange and sexually obtrusive a being. He must jump backward to cancel the disturbing implication of maleness. Only after the sailor is hastily lamed in an awkward parenthesis can the poem proceed.

An attractive American youth appears in "Elegiac Stanzas" (1820)—but only because he has drowned in the lake at Zurich. In "Vaudracour and Julia," a young man violently pursues his love, then retires to a forest to raise his illegitimate child. The children die because of a mysterious error by the father, who degenerates into imbecile muteness. Moral: virility slaloms downhill into squalor. In "Michael," an eighteen-year-old youth cuts a handsome figure. But the implacable Wordsworth destines him for disaster in "dissolute" London: "ignominy and shame" drive him overseas. The city is Babylon, tempting men to sexual and automatically fallen experience. In "Hart-Leap Well," a knight builds a "pleasure-house" where he kills a stag and will play with his "Paramour." The poem equates killing and sex: as in *Faust*, domination of nature is domination of woman. In the second part, the mansion has vanished, and the spot is "curst," the trees "lifeless stumps." Phallicism is sterile, an affront to nature.

In "The Two April Mornings" and its companion poem, "The Fountain," a seventy-two-year-old schoolmaster recalls his adulthood as "a vigorous man." Virility is documented only when lost. It is distanced at several narrative removes, memory within memory: the first poem ends with Wordsworth remembering the schoolmaster remembering. Virility is contemplated through the bleared lens of age. In "The Last of the Flock," we meet "a healthy man, a man full grown." But he is weeping in the road! Once rich, he has sold his fifty sheep to buy food for his children. Wordsworth turns the flock's diminishing into a litany of dwindling manhood: fifty, ten, five, three, two, one, none. Wordsworth's arithmetic charts the shrinking of patriarchal domain. As his property shrivels to the borders of his body, the protagonist, like Odysseus or Lear, will soon be nobody. His Wordsworthian decline is like Kleist's male mastectomy in *Penthesilea*, a surgical reduction of self. Wordsworth empathizes with the virile male of "The Last of the Flock" because he is suffering and because his masculine identity is fast approaching the vanishing point. For Wordsworth, a man becomes greater as he becomes less. Self-sacrifice and public martyrdom canonize him in the cult of female nature.

In "Character of the Happy Warrior," Wordsworth asks, "Who is the happy Warrior? Who is he / That every man in arms should wish to be?" This is virtually the last we hear about arms, since it turns out that the best warrior "makes his moral being his prime care." The poem is a series of precepts more applicable to philosopher than soldier. In "The Happy Warrior" there is no glamour in action, only in quality of being. Late in his career, Wordsworth added a preface revealing the poem had been inspired by Lord Nelson: "But his public life was stained with one great crime, so that . . . I have not been able to connect his name with the poem as I could wish." The crime was Nelson's affair with Emma,

Lady Hamilton. The open but by no means promiscuous sexuality of England's naval hero caused his name to be struck from the honor roll of Wordsworth's poetry. What Byron would praise, Wordsworth condemns. Wordsworth adds that the virtues of the happy warrior were found in his own brother, a ship's commander, who died in a wreck at sea in 1805. This masculine brother appears by name in Wordsworth's poetry—but naturally only in "Elegiac Verses" after his death.

There is a striking epiphany of virility in *The Prelude*, a vision coming to the youthful Wordsworth near Stonehenge. He hears primitive tribes at war and sees "A single Briton clothed in wolf-skin vest, / With shield and stone-axe," a figure of "barbaric majesty (XIII.312–26). For the first and only time, Wordsworth's imagination is kindled by a masculine male. But again virility enters the poetry only as a memory thrust backward in time. The older Wordsworth remembers the young Wordsworth having a racial memory. The fierce Briton belongs to prehistory. He is man-in-nature, outside and prior to contemporary society, the focus of Wordsworth's hostility. Another example from *The Prelude* completes our sex survey. In the sunny fresh air, Wordsworth sees a brawny laborer caressing a "sickly babe" on his knee (VII.602–18). Like Praxiteles' Hermes with infant Dionysus, Wordsworth's laborer is *kourotrophos*, the child-rearer. He is a male mother, the category of androgyne I call Teiresias. Unconsciously, the laborer has modelled himself upon nature's maternal spirit. The babe softens his gender and makes it tolerable for the poet.

Thus Wordsworth's emotion is never invested in figures of active virility, unless that virility is qualified by suffering or feminine feeling or unless it is seen through the distancing perspective of memory. Since femaleness suffuses the created world, the pure male is cast out. He has no right to life. In order to matriculate in Wordsworth's green campus, one must undergo a punishing series of entrance exams. Under a special admissions program, women, children, and old men have privileged status, as disadvantaged minorities in patriarchal society. Males hoping for acceptance must undergo a perilous *rite de passage*. They must suffer deeply, even die, or they must become mothers. Each option is sexually transformative. Etymologically, to matriculate means to enter the realm of womb and mother. Wordsworth is the iron chancellor of spiritual matriculation, soaking his beings with tenderizing mother-emotion.

What of Wordsworth's other sexual personae? I conclude that the more emotionally remote a person is to Wordsworth, the more pictorially detailed. The more emotionally central, the vaguer and more numinous. The poet calls his future wife, Mary Hutchinson, "a Phantom of delight," "a lovely Apparition." She is "a dancing Shape, an Image gay," "a Spirit, yet a Woman too," bright with "angelic light." The poem begins and ends with Mary as an angel of dissolving gender. In *The Prelude* Wordsworth again calls Mary "phantom" and "spirit" (XIV.268–70). The mysterious Lucy dies into formal indeterminacy, "Rolled round in earth's diurnal course, / With rocks, and stones, and trees" ("A Slumber Did My Spirit Seal"). Beyond personality, Lucy is submerged in nature's Dionysian metamorphoses—possibly a detail from the climax of Lewis' *The Monk*. The angelic Mary moves upward in the chain of being, while Lucy moves downward. But both suffer the same Wordsworthian fate: their bodies are dematerialized and desexed. Reduced to matter, Lucy loses her gender and human identity.

Wordsworth uses the same indeterminacy of form for his sister, Dorothy, by far the most important person in his life, as he was in hers. After his break with Wordsworth, Coleridge tartly called her (in Greek) "the sister-brother-worshipper" or "-slave." In Wordsworth's poetry, Dorothy is bodiless and sexless. No matter how many times one reads *Tintern Abbey*, Dorothy's appearance at the end is always startling. Self-absorbed Wordsworth seems so utterly alone in his reflections and memories. Dorothy suddenly materializes, like a spirit. At first, her gender is unclear: "thou my dearest Friend, / My dear, dear Friend"—the same abstract honorific Wordsworth uses for Coleridge throughout *The Prelude*. Only after eight long lines do we get any information about the friend's sex or identity. Yet Wordsworth is listening to the friend's voice and looking into "the shooting lights" of the friend's eyes. For eight lines we are left helplessly free-floating, in sexual suspension. We are asked to hear a voice and look into the eyes of a being of unfixed gender.

Dorothy is bodiless and sexless in *Tintern Abbey* because she is Wordsworth's Jungian *anima*, an internal aspect of self momentarily projected. Hence her suddenness of appearance, since for most of the poem's interior monologue, she has not really been external to her brother. When Wordsworth hears in Dorothy's voice "the language of my former heart" and sees his "former pleasures" in her eyes, he seems to be contemplating his twin or double. Bloom calls Dorothy "an incarnation of his earlier self."[3] Gazing into Dorothy's face, Wordsworth is looking into a magic mirror and seeing his past self. He is like Spenser's Britomart glimpsing in the crystal ball or mirror her future self in sexually transmuted form. Coleridge speaks of a looking-glass as a "Sister Mirror." Seeing himself in Dorothy's eyes, Wordsworth is like

Donne's lover seeing her reflection mirrored in the poet's tears. Words-worth's eight sexually suspended lines are a moment of psychic parturi-tion in which the sister-spirit emerges from her brother's male double. The passage records her systematic coalescence of gender and identity, as she pulls away from coextensiveness with her brother, like the moon tearing itself from primeval earth.

Dorothy hovers at Wordworth's side like a tutelary spirit maintaining discreet silence until summoned. She is ritualistically invoked because Wordsworth needs her to quell a sudden anxiety. He has just completed a history of his relation with nature since childhood. Now he reaffirms he is still "A lover of the meadows and the woods, / And mountains." But something has changed. Addressing Dorothy, Wordsworth adds parenthetically, "Knowing that Nature never did betray / The heart that loved her." This knowing is hope under duress. Dorothy's materializa-tion is Wordsworth's strategy to keep despair at bay. She is a visible symbol of relatedness, stilling Wordsworth's fear at the death of his tranquil relation with nature. Proteus changed shape to elude pursuers, until he was finally wrestled to the ground. Proteus' transformations are the flux of Wordsworth's emotion, agitating him until he forces it into one human shape, his sister. The poet mentally grasps his externalized sister to prevent his vision of union with nature from slipping away. "Knowing that Nature never did betray": material of overwhelming emotional importance is consigned to a participial phrase. Virginia Woolf does the same thing in *To the Lighthouse*, where Mrs. Ramsay's death is casually announced in a participial phrase. Mrs. Ramsay is Woolf's charismatic mother, whose premature death caused the novel-ist's first mental breakdown and was the determining catastrophe of her life. These participles are a ritual formalization and distancing of intol-erable emotion. Wordsworth's mother died when he was eight. He says of her in *The Prelude*, "She left us destitute" (V.259). Mothers do betray. Nature is Wordsworth's second abandoning mother.

So the sister-spirit abruptly appears in *Tintern Abbey* because Words-worth is troubled by a new destitution, the departure of loving maternal nature. Perhaps the *anima* is always externalized at moments of spir-itual crisis. Addressing the nation the morning he left the White House after his resignation, Richard Nixon was overcome by reminiscences of his mother. Tears in his eyes, he said, "She was a saint." Media derision of this as Nixonian calculation surprised me: Italians do not find it ridiculous to speak of one's mother at peak dramatic moments. Italian soldiers lying wounded on the battlefield in the two world wars called upon not wives or sweethearts but "Mamma, Mamma." At his moment of cataclysmic loss, a dissolution of the politically supreme male persona, Nixon underwent a voyage of Proustian memory from a sordid, self-befouled present into a mythical lost paradise of childhood. In the process, he summoned his mother, who was, I submit, powerfully evoked. She really did hover at his side as his projected *anima*, visible to the eye of imagination. Athletes whooping it up on the sidelines after a personal triumph look into the camera and say, "Hi, Mom!" It's rarely "Hi, Dad," because the father figure can never serve, as do mothers, sisters, and beautiful youths, as emblem of passage from one imaginative realm to the next. Father and brother are society; mother and sister are emotion.

In *The Prelude* Dorothy is the Muse confirming Wordsworth in his poetic vocation. She is a marriage broker or Psychopompos guiding him through the Orphic underworld of emotion toward his "true self." Her "sweet influence" drew him away from the severity and "terror" of Milton's masculine style: "Thou didst soften down / This over-sternness." Her femininity flowed into and tempered him (XI.333–48, XIV.237–50). Wordsworth's spiritual identity with his sister was so intense we must classify it as Romantic incest. Some suggest the two were sexually involved, which I think unlikely. The one Romantic who may actually have committed incest was Byron, and that did not last long. Wordsworth and his sister transformed incest into a spiritual principle. Here and in Shelley's *Epipsychidion*, Romantic incest is a metaphor for supersaturation of identity. It is an archaic device to propel history backwards, enabling the poet to return to primal sources of inspiration.

In his culminating reference to Dorothy in *The Prelude*, Wordsworth says the highest condition of the man of imagination is "singleness" (XIV.211). A spouse is superfluous, since the superior man contains both sexes married within his own psyche. G. Wilson Knight calls this Wordsworth's "higher integration": it is a "wholeness beyond normality," "an androgynous state."[4] Bloom says of all artists, "The poet-in-a-poet *cannot marry*, whatever the person-in-a-poet chooses to have done."[5] In *The Prelude* there is a direct chain of connection, over seventeen lines, from Wordsworth's "singleness" to the heart "tender as a nursing mother's." Wordsworth internalizes the feminine world and makes it his bride-state. Now he thinks of the angelic messenger who impregnated him with her female power, Dorothy, "Sister of my soul!" (232). The sister is the feminine half of the soul allowing the poet to remain superbly alone, a magus contemplating reality but not subordinated to it.

Wordsworth's poetry represents the three women closest to him as

physically porous. In other words, Wordsworth's high affect blurs female contour. The women characters of Wordsworth's anecdotal story-
poems are far more definitive as physical presences. The less a woman
is loved by Wordsworth, the more clearly she is *seen*. Oddly for a poet of
nature, Wordsworth's ardor dematerializes or seraphicizes the beloved.
She ceases to be an object, much less a sex object. Does Wordsworth
fear his own aggressive eye? Compare this generalizing style to Wordsworth's pictorial technique for his most characteristic figure, the aged
male solitary. The old Cumberland beggar, for example, eats scraps of
food out of "a bag all white with flour." Showers of crumbs fall from "his
palsied hand." His body is "bow-bent." As he "creeps" along, the wind
beats "his grey locks against his withered face." The leech-gatherer of
"Resolution and Independence" is a "decrepit Man," with a body "bent
double." He seems the oldest man "that ever wore grey hairs." He props
himself, "limbs, body, and pale face," on "a long grey staff of shaven
wood." These detailed figures are vastly more individuated than Dorothy, Lucy, or Mary. They have the lugubrious specificity of muckraking
photojournalism.

Wordsworth's male solitaries are found objects, art works made by
buffeting nature. Survivors of some wreck of civilization, they are
weathered like driftwood. Their Giacometti-like thinness is a withering
by pitiless experience. External forces devour the human until it is close
to absorption by nature. The solitaries are dignified but paralyzed. They
exist in a melancholy state of contraction from which there is no escape
through action. Only passive responses are possible: fortitude and endurance. The thinness of Wordsworth's solitaries is another reduction
of self. Wordsworth said, in the classic maxim of Romantic solipsism, "I
was often unable to think of external things as having external existence." The specificity and density of the male solitaries come from the
poet's attempt to externalize them, to pin and fix them as temporary foci
of perception. But a forbidding open space surrounds them, an agoraphobic wasteland. As in Edvard Munch's *The Scream*, Wordsworth's
male figures are simultaneously abandoned in dreadful isolation and
assaulted by malicious waves of natural force. Descartes, Bloom says,
created "the dumbfoundering abyss between ourselves and the object."[6] The estranged western space between persons is crossed by
Wordsworth's eye. He throws his vision out like a harpoon drawing its
line after it, a harpoon not so much piercing its target as casting about it
an encapsulating sac of sympathetic emotion, an aura protecting it
momentarily from the elements. But the force pressing so fiercely on
these old men is Wordsworth's "love," a love that desiccates their flesh

and crushes them to skeletal scarcity of being. Like Blake in "Infant Joy," Wordsworth demonstrates the secret aggression in Rousseauist sympathy.

Wordsworth's poetry makes an apparently generous extension of significance into the most minute and commonplace details of nature, benevolent "nurse" of humanity. But in the poems of aged male solitaries and in such scenes of "visionary dreariness" as the one in *The Prelude* (XII.251–61) where a girl bearing a pitcher on her head is battered by the wind, a different emotional physics obtains. Instead of spiritual expansion, there are stark disproportions, terrifying vacancies, energy clusters burst and abraded—sudden sacralizations followed by intolerable desolation. The solitaries express Wordsworth's secret fear. They are what is left when mother nature is done with man, dry bones she has picked over. Romantic consciousness is unlimited, but the image of the self, the body-image, has gotten smaller. In Wordsworth it is a tottering old man with palsied hands. The liberated Rousseauist self fails to fill the space vacated by religion and society. It has shrunk from its role in the great theater of the Christian cosmos. The star has become only an extra. Extra means on the very verge of the human, nudged out of consciousness into the brute inarticulateness of object-life. Gender disappears in Wordsworth not simply because personality is devalued, as in Blake, but because human experience is under sentence of extinction. Arguing that nature is benign, Wordsworth is haunted by a spectre of isolation, his own repressed dread of mother nature's cruelty.

The aged and infirm male is Wordsworth's most powerful self-identification. Contracted body-image is his psychomorphic topos. The solitaries are a nightmare other self, and Wordsworth's dialogues with them are daemonic communion with a doppelgänger. On the terrace of his villa shortly before his death, Shelley encountered his double, a phantom who demanded, "How long do you mean to be content?" Wordsworth's double has a contrary message. The leech-gatherer, with his soothing sibylline smile, is an oracle telling his story, then receding like a shade in the underworld. He assures the poet that rueful contentment is still possible amid universal desolation. The confrontation with the infirm doppelgänger is a script that Wordsworth writes over and over. His poetry is filled with ritualistic returns of this cadaverous spectre, who appears in different places and under different names. The Wordsworthian solitary is like Donatello's late-phase sculptures, scored, tormented figures of Gothic leanness and angularity. In their stony decrepitude, Wordsworth's old men are like stalagmites or dolmens, picturesque artifacts of affliction. They are highly specific, yet typologi-

cal. Their omnipresence in Wordsworth's poetry is part of his exclusion
of virile males. Goethe says, "Thought expands, but lames; Action
animates, but narrows."[7] Wordsworth's contracted male bodies have
been produced by the modern fall of the western hero. The Wordsworthian solitary is sexually composite. He is a male heroine, a passive male
sufferer. For the poet, both solitary and soul-mate sister are modes of the
self in half-feminine form.

If his imagination seeks to pass beyond itself through mental intercourse with reality, Wordsworth can only be aroused by incarnations of
nature-inspired femaleness. Perhaps no one spouse is sufficient. Perhaps the slow succession of protagonists, male and female, in Wordsworth's story-poems are nominees, candidates who are scrutinized and
rejected. Only nature, the all-mother, can satisfy the marriage-hunger
of Wordsworthian imagination. My belief that Wordsworth's character
is sexually dual contradicts Coleridge's assertion: "Of all men I ever
knew, Wordsworth has the least femininity in his mind. He is *all* man.
He is a man of whom it might have been said, 'It is good for him to be
alone'."[8] There is reason to question this subliminally homoerotic statement, as we will see when we examine Coleridge's anguished character.
Coleridge said in conversation, "A great mind must be androgynous," a
remark paraphrased by Virginia Woolf in *A Room of One's Own*. She
goes on to describe major male writers in sexual terms: Shakespeare
was "androgynous," Shelley "sexless"; Milton, Wordsworth, and Tolstoy had "a dash too much of the male," Proust "a little too much of a
woman."[9] As the years pass, this arresting passage seems more and
more meaningless to me. One could defend each writer against Woolf's
charges, but let's stick with Wordsworth. Throughout her work, Woolf
makes the androgyne superior to ordinary virile men, an attitude I find
mean and parochial. The androgyne is a great creative symbol, but it
should not usurp the authority of all other sexual personae.

That Wordsworth is too male is the reverse of the truth. Bloom says,
"It is true that Wordsworth is almost too masculine a poet."[10] But is
there any poem or passage in Wordsworth about which we could say,
this is too masculine? The most masculine passages in Wordsworth are
the most Miltonic. But these are among his greatest, for example, the
ascent of Mount Snowdon. Wordsworth's sister-spirit helped liberate
him from Milton's style, with its ponderous, declamatory Latinism and
syntactic inversions, which do appear in *The Prelude*. Later in his
career, Bloom demonstrated how heavily Milton's precedent fell upon
"belated" English poets, who had to struggle against him. In my view, to
say Wordsworth is "almost too masculine" is to say he is too much in the

grip of Milton. Too-masculine Wordsworth is a slave, hopelessly swallowed up in his great precursor. So paradoxically, when Wordsworth is most masculine, he is poetically most passive! In poetic terms, much has come to us by Milton speaking through Wordsworth. In psychobiographical terms, Wordsworth's efforts to find a personal voice were sexually swamped by Milton. The sadomasochism in this process will be directly felt by Wordsworth's colleague, Coleridge.

Wordsworth is never too masculine. The real danger in him is the too feminine. Wordsworth has several voices. The most male is the Miltonic sublime. The most female is the languishing pathos of the story-poems, where the sufferings of women, children, and animals are dwelt upon at excruciating length. Wordsworth created Victorian sentimentalism. Modernism's cool revolt against Wordsworthian sentiment is typified by Oscar Wilde's cynical resumé of a teary Dickens novel: "One must have a heart of stone to read the death of Little Nell without laughing." Lewis Carroll's wacky verses, like "The Aged Aged Man," mock Wordsworth's solemn solitaries. That Wordsworthian pathos lends itself so easily to parody suggests there is some real excess in it. The palsied hands of the old Cumberland beggar, the grey hairs (significant plural) "worn" by the leech-gatherer are grotesque details confining and limiting emotion instead of freeing and deepening it. Unlike melodrama, high tragedy never depends on overdetermined externals. The leech-gatherer, with his sparse grey hairs, reminds me of Woolf's father, Sir Leslie Stephen, who as a morose widower was overheard loudly moaning as he trudged up the stairs, "Why won't my whiskers grow? Why won't my whiskers grow?" In the sentimental mode, too little is asked to bear too much. Wordsworth's story-poems are self-dramatizations of excessive pathos, the ever-present trap in Wordsworth's world. The story of Margaret, for example, a beautiful extract from *The Excursion* called "The Ruined Cottage": can empathy really be sustained in perfect integrity for as long as this woeful tale demands? In fact, is Wordsworth himself capable of so prolonged a habitation in the sorrows of another? Such sentimental narratives are disguised dramas of Wordsworth's feminine self. F. W. Bateson says: "Wordsworth had experienced most of Margaret's miseries. In a sense he *was* Margaret."[11] That a writer may enter his own fiction as a less developed version of himself is a principle we saw operating in Goethe's Werther and Wilhelm Meister.

Wordsworth's poetry is weakened when his identification with a suffering character is too extreme. Empathy degenerates into sentimentality, which I interpret as self-pity, since the protagonists are self-projections. Wordsworth's best moments are when he achieves a balance between his male and female voices. This he does in *Tintern Abbey*, which has perfect pitch. It is lean, supple, and majestic. There is only one misstep: at the end, Wordsworth recalls "the sneers of selfish men." These are obviously virile males! The poet's voice turns strident. His sneering men are like a row of desperados noisily taking snuff. *Tintern Abbey* maintains emotional balance because of its ritualistic externalization of the sister-spirit. Wordsworth's address to the numinous Dorothy functions as a correct positioning of the female part of the self to the male, like that fine-tuning necessary for Blake's mobile Emanations. Wordsworth turns to his sister and rejoices in her companionship. He sees her as separate, even as he simultaneously acknowledges her as his mirror-image. His female self-identification is purified and strengthened by consciousness. It is candid, not covert. It is in the covert self-identifications that Wordsworth falls into sentimental excess.

Coleridge thought Wordsworth's unknown Lucy was Dorothy—whom De Quincey described as having an "unsexual" stride. Commenting on "the curious sexlessness" of the Lucy poems, Bateson theorizes that Wordsworth's crisis of 1798 was the increasing threat of incest with Dorothy: Lucy's premature death is Wordsworth's subconscious termination of his "horrible" attraction to Dorothy "by killing her off symbolically."[12] But no Romantic poet except Blake resists incestuous fantasies. Far from struggling against incest, Wordsworth elegantly assimilates it into his imaginative life. Lucy's death is like the deaths of Dido, Madame Bovary, and Anna Karenina, the ritualistic slaying of an unmanageably feminine element in a male artist. Lucy and Dorothy are the female half of the soul. But Lucy is Dorothy escaping control by the male half. This is why Lucy is represented as lost, at a distance, elusive. Wordsworth searches for her, but it is important he not find her. She is the Blakean Emanation who flees in order to dominate. What is symbolically killed off is not incest but sentimentality, the greatest temptation and danger to Wordsworth's poetry. Wordsworth's pathetic story-poems are languid Spenserian bowers where the female half of the soul lures the male half into drowsy ecstasies of passive surrender. Michelangelo, a far more masculine man than Wordsworth, was fascinated by similar dreams of voluptuous passivity.

"What is a Poet?" Wordsworth asks in the preface to *Lyrical Ballads*. "He is a man speaking to men." But how does a man speak when finally free of tradition and form? Wordsworth is bedeviled by male and female impulses, which he struggles to harmonize in a single style. Hartman says the "I" of Wordsworth's *Prelude* does not indicate "a persona-consciousness": "An inner confidence allows him to meet nature, or his own emotions, without a persona."[13] But Wordsworth's persona is one of the strongest, fiercest, and falsest in all poetry. As the intensely persona-conscious Wilde said, "To be natural is such a very difficult pose to keep up." There can be no speech, no man speaking to men without persona. Words are contaminated with personality. Even in journalism, history, or science, there are no words without point of view. Wordsworth is under tremendous self-imposed pressure to find a persona, for that is the voice he needs to justify the ways of nature to men. "I do," Wordsworth says to the nature-mother, but he cannot allow himself to see her clearly. Censoring out the negativity and savagery in nature, he puts his own voice in a bind. Wordsworth is the first humorless liberal. Even Rousseau is more self-analytical and aware of his quirky perversities. Sade, laughing, sees comedy in cruelty and knows there is cruelty in all comedy. Eighteenth-century wit, imitated by Wilde, was the most aggressive of rhetorical forms. Renouncing wit and repressing nature's sadism, Wordsworth made bathos his slough of despond. The chthonian miasma made a new swamp for her blind son to fall into.

Shelley may have been the first to charge Wordsworth with inhibited sexuality. In his satire, "Peter Bell the Third," Shelley calls Wordsworth a "moral eunuch," "a male prude," "a solemn and unsexual man," "a male Molly." Knight says, *"The Prelude* is peculiarly non-sexual. The silence in so general a statement is remarkable."[14] Trilling declares, "There can be no doubt about it, Wordsworth, at the extreme or perversion of himself, carries the element of quietude to the point of the denial of sexuality."[15] Hartman protests this critical current and insists the great themes of Wordsworth's poetry must not be "profaned by such partial analysis."[16] What is partial and reductive in most Freudian interpretations of art is that they focus on sex without realizing that sex is a subset of nature. Joining Frazer to Freud, as I try to do, solves this problem. Everything sexual or unsexual in art carries world-view and nature theory with it. The sex in Wordsworth is in the eroticized female emotions, which wrap Wordsworth in a numinous cloud whenever he descends from the masculine Miltonic sublime. Wordsworth hopes for happiness through pure feeling, but the happiest things in his poetry are daffodils. His devotions to mother nature simply produce frightful hallucinations of parched, mute spectres, his starved self. Wordsworth cannot admit that the hand that will not feed is closed in a fist. Wordsworth's sexlessness is his capitulation to mother nature. She lives for him. The prison of society or the prison of nature: leaving one, Wordsworth enters the other. Hence the strange stillness of his poetry, the quietude that is really immobility. Energy, sought by Blake, is shunned by Wordsworth. Through energy to sex to cruelty: Wordsworth, pursuing Rousseau's mother nature, embraces a deceiving ghost.

12

The Daemon as Lesbian Vampire

Coleridge

Coleridge, unlike Wordsworth, finds nature. Or rather, she finds him. Wordworth spent a lifetime editing out of his poetry the brute reality that Coleridge frankly faces: the daemonism of nature. In *Christabel*, inspired by the rape cycle of *The Faerie Queene*, Coleridge destroys Wordsworth's Rousseauist world of feminine tenderness. *Christabel* is one of the most misread poems in literature. Critics have projected a Christian moralism upon it. Coleridge himself could not bear what he had written, and he tried to revise and reinterpret long afterward. *Christabel* is a splendid case study of the tension between imagination and morality. Through it, we follow a great poet into his excess of daemonic vision and then out again into the social realm of humane good wishes, where the visionary is beset by doubt, anxiety, and guilt. *Christabel* shows the birth of poetry in evil, hostility, and crime.

To arrive at *Christabel*, we must tour Coleridge's other major poems to demonstrate their eccentric sexual character. His favorite proverb was "Extremes meet." He calls imagination "that synthetic and magical power," producing "the balance or reconciliation of opposite or discordant qualities."[1] In *Christabel*, opposites come together so powerfully that Coleridge could not shape the poem according to his stated intention. It is no coincidence that his supreme works are dream poems. Freud says dreams disregard "the category of contraries and contradictions": " 'No' seems not to exist so far as dreams are concerned."[2] No, says the Decalogue, thou shalt not. Much of Coleridge's conscious life was devoted to defenses of Christianity. In the poetry welling up from his dream life, however, the Judeo-Christian no is obliterated by sexually dual daemonic powers. "Grant me a nature having two contrary forces," he once wrote. M. H. Abrams sees influence here from the

Cabalists, Bruno, Boehme, and Swedenborg.[3] The synthesis of contraries comes to Coleridge from outside orthodox Christianity. He is drawing on the underground current in western culture, that promiscuous pagan mixture of Hermeticism, alchemy, and astrology. His essay on alchemists (1818) is less crucial than the dream poems themselves, morally unstable concoctions boiling over with daemonic energy.

Coleridge's "primary Imagination" is "the infinite I AM."[4] The self-divinizing Romantic poet displaces Jehovah. His "I AM" is cosmos-devouring. It confers upon the artist that inalienable right to self-assertion we see in the Decadent Late Romantic cult of self. In Wilde, for example, Coleridge's theory turns into the ideal of personality as a work of art and of the life as superior to the work. Wilde says, "The true artist is a man who believes absolutely in himself, because he is absolutely himself."[5] Poetic identity as infinite ego: we will see this at work at the opening of *Christabel*, where Geraldine wills herself into existence out of the darkness.

Coleridge contrasts true imagination with uninspired "Fancy," merely "a mode of Memory" playing with "fixities and definites." If we extend this distinction psychologically, fancy's fixities become rigid sex roles inherited from the past. Coleridge says of "secondary Imagination," "It dissolves, diffuses, dissipates, in order to re-create." His dream poems are metamorphoses of psyche where primary imagination uses secondary imagination to dissolve sexual personae. The poems are an alchemic bath of swirling Dionysian liquidity. From the dissolution of morality and history comes daemonic re-creation, a synthetic Homunculus. Over all Coleridge's great poems hovers a strange androgyne, a fabricated superself.

Coleridge's sexual ambiguities are already evident in "The Eolian Harp" (1795), a far stranger poem than scholars admit. It is nearly schizophrenic in its argument with itself. Sara, the wife named again and again, is merely a symbol of the social and moral, with which Coleridge never managed to achieve correct relation. Husband, citizen, pious Christian: these were chimeras that taunted the poet; these were personae that he strove toward and never won. Criticism sees "The Eolian Harp" as a hymn to marital bliss. But what the poem shows is a sexual turbulence that will erupt two years later in the mystery poems.

The wind-harp of the title begins a High Romantic tradition, reaching its peak in Shelley's "Ode to the West Wind." It is a vehicle of sexual self-transformation. The poet is a passive instrument played upon by the masculine Muse-force of nature. Coleridge openly eroticizes the metaphor from the start: the harp is "by the desultory breeze caress'd, /

Like some coy maid half yielding to her lover." Scholars, sexually normalizing the poem, identify Sara with the coy maid. But Sara is imaginatively peripheral. Coleridge addresses her only to remind himself who or what he should be. Every allusion to Sara is tense and frenetic.

Romantic poems are radically solipsistic. Coleridge, not Sara, is the coy maid. His ecstatic self-projections are always feminine: "Full many a thought uncall'd and undetain'd, / And many idle flitting phantasies, / Traverse my indolent and passive brain." For Coleridge, like Wordsworth and Keats, indolence is creative, a drowsy dream state into which the unconscious releases images uncensored by intellect. The indolent male has a female receptivity. This passage, deceptively pleasant and airy, becomes cruelly darker when read in the light of the later mystery poems. By the time we get to *Christabel*, "idle flitting phantasies" will not just traverse but rape the poet's brain. Femininity is dangerous. What enables the poet to speak here will stop all speech later.

In "The Eolian Harp," Coleridge swerves back and forth between his sense of social and religious duty and his longing for erotic and creative passivity. To get these things together at one moment would seem impossible. Yet that is what happens the night Coleridge listens to Wordsworth recite *The Prelude*, which he celebrates in a peculiar poem, "To William Wordsworth" (1807). Here it is clear that, for Coleridge, spiritual exaltation means sexual self-immolation. Roll, Jordan, roll: Wordsworth's voice sweeps over Coleridge in wave after wave of bardic power: "In silence listening, like a devout child, / My soul lay passive, by thy various strain / Driven as in surges now beneath the stars." He feels like "a tranquil sea, / Outspread and bright, yet swelling to the moon." Coleridge is a wind-harp vibrating to someone else's music. Wordsworth speaks for nature and crushes Coleridge by the enormity of his achievement. There is no dialogue, only monologue, an intercourse of brute assertion and thrilling receptivity. The scene is distinctly erotic. The swelling sea-soul echoes Wordsworth's sonnet of the prior year, "The World Is Too Much With Us," where the sea "bares her bosom to the moon." Wordsworth and Coleridge were locked in a sadomasochistic marriage of minds, where Wordsworth kept the hierarchical advantage and Coleridge surrendered himself to ritualistic self-abasement.

Coleridge, we saw, curiously said of Wordsworth, "He is *all* man." Not only is this not true of Wordsworth, but it rings with homoerotic infatuation. Tortured, inconstant Coleridge saw in Wordsworth's cold composure a kind of masculine resoluteness. Wordsworth needed Coleridge as much as Coleridge needed Wordsworth. I argued that when

Wordsworth's voice is at its most masculine (significantly, in *The Pre-lude*,) it is in poetic terms at its most passive because most Miltonic. The night reading of *The Prelude* is a spectacle of shamanistic black magic. Wordsworth, dominated by Milton, dominates Coleridge. Poetic iden-tity, gelling and melting, streams down a cascade of hierarchical levels, a sexual feudalism of master-slave relationships. Let us recall it is Coleridge whom *The Prelude* most continually addresses. Coleridge's submissiveness allows Wordsworth to emerge intact from his flooding by Milton in that poem. Coleridge, listening to it, is Danae impregnated by Zeus's golden shower. Coleridge puns on the idea of spiritual insem-ination in the second line, where he says of *The Prelude*, "Into my heart have I received that Lay." He is penetrated and filled by Wordsworth, to whom he abandons himself. Sex is poetry; poetry is sex.

Coleridge did his best work under Wordsworth's influence. After they separated, Coleridge languished poetically and never matched his early achievements. The nature of their collaboration was this: Wordsworth was a father/lover who absorbed Coleridge's self-punishing superego and allowed his turbulent dream life to spill directly into his poetry. The supreme irony, as we shall see, is that everything that is great in Cole-ridge is a negation of Wordsworth. This is the son's ultimate revenge upon the father. Wordsworth's leading moral idea of nature's benev-olence is annihilated in Coleridge. Coleridge sees the chthonian horror in nature that Wordsworth could not acknowledge. The vampires of *Christabel* and *The Rime of the Ancient Mariner* are the true nature-mother. Wordsworth reawakened sleeping pagan nature-cult, then flew from the spectres he had roused. How easily Wordsworth was assimi-lated into bourgeois nineteenth-century culture. His Protestant moral-ism was his barrier against the daemonic. It is pagan Coleridge, not Protestant Wordsworth, who is the begetter of nineteenth-century ar-chetypal vision. The Decadent Late Romantic line of Poe, Baudelaire, Moreau, Rossetti, Burne-Jones, Swinburne, Pater, Huysmans, Beards-ley, and Wilde descends directly from Coleridge's mystery poems. By his pregnant servitude to Wordsworth, Coleridge bore monstrous chil-dren who would destroy their father.

Tutelary relationships are filled with sexual ambiguities. Coleridge calls Wordsworth "O Friend! my comforter and guide! / Strong in thy-self, and powerful to give strength!" But perhaps the teacher is never strong except in teaching. Perhaps teaching is a kind of vampirism in which mesmerizing assertions of authority drink the energy they arouse. I find two parallels to the alliance between Wordsworth and Coleridge. In Jane Austen, Emma's intimacy with the docile Harriet, upon whom she imposes calamitous pretensions, arises from her own narcissistic oscillations of sexual identity. In Virginia Woolf, ugly, clumsy Doris Kilman binds the beautiful young Elizabeth Dalloway to her by a domineering authority hiding doubt and self-contempt. In all three cases, teaching is an erotic transaction. A submissive companion becomes the audience toward whom a hierarchic persona is theatrically projected.

Performance and audience are multiply present at the end of "To William Wordsworth." "Round us both / That happy vision of belovéd faces": this ring of eyes is one of Coleridge's persistent motifs. Wordsworth as "comforter and guide" is Beatrice and Vergil combined; the faces of family and friends are celestial circles of the mystic rose. Rising, in the final line, to find himself "in prayer," Coleridge appeals not to God but to Wordsworth. And what he prays for is more poetry—his own. The universe has become a theater of sex and poetry. Wordsworth, performing, is watched by Coleridge. But Coleridge, seduced and inseminated by Wordsworth, is watched by the ring of eyes. The poem dissolves into a magic circle that is primal scene and family romance. In similar passages in Whitman and Swinburne, the erotic ecstasy of a masochistic male heroine is strongly stimulated by a ring of attentive eyes. "To William Wordsworth" is a luridly pagan poem. Incantation by a god-priest in a cult of personality leads to ritual public intercourse. Climax is epiphany and transfiguration. Sexual exhibitionism and voyeurism are at the heart of art. Here as in *Christabel*, the hunger for conversion is expressed as a hunger for rape.

Literature's most influential male heroine is the protagonist of *The Rime of the Ancient Mariner*. Wordsworth was the first to notice the Mariner's passive suffering. In the 1800 edition of *Lyrical Ballads*, Wordsworth lists the "great defects" of the poem: "first, that the principal person has no distinct character . . . secondly, that he does not act, but is continually acted upon." Bloom speaks of the Mariner's "extraordinary passivity." Graham Hough equates the ship's motionlessness with "complete paralysis of the will." George Whalley goes further: "The Mariner's passivity is Coleridge's too."[6] My reading of *The Ancient Mariner* makes this passivity the central psychological fact of the poem. I reject moral interpretations, typified by Robert Penn Warren's canonical essay. Edward E. Bostetter argues against Warren point by point: "The poem is the morbidly self-obsessed account of a man who through his act has become the center of universal attention."[7] Two hundred sailors, dying, stare dolefully at the Mariner. The

male heroine, by operatic self-dramatization, is a prima donna triumphing through exquisite public suffering. The eyes of the universe
are fixed on him. Coleridge's ring of eyes is part paranoiac reproach,
part eroticizing adoration. Eyes crucify his protagonists, pinning them
in immobilized passivity, an uncanny world fear.

Sagas of the male heroine are always artistically endangered by the
serpentine dynamic of self-identification. The Mariner, with his "long
grey beard" and "skinny hand," recalls those Wordsworthian solitaries
of "grey hairs" and "palsied hand" in whom I see a self-identification by
the poet so extreme as to debilitate the text by sentimentality. Parts of
The Ancient Mariner are ill-written to the point of Lewis Carroll parody:
" 'Hold off! unhand me, grey-beard loon!' / Eftsoons his hand dropt he."
"The Wedding-Guest here beat his breast, / For he heard the loud
bassoon." "Four times fifty living men . . . With heavy thump, a lifeless
lump, / They dropped down one by one." Rhyme is merely ritualistic
chiming, the darkening cloud of fate. Stanzas fall into slapstick and
heedlessly sail on. *The Ancient Mariner* is one of the greatest poems in
English, yet what it achieves is almost in defiance of language. Vision
and execution often wildly diverge. Coleridge's sober "conversation
poems" are in better taste; but they are minor works in literary history,
belonging to the age of sensibility, and would never have made the
poet's fame. The same disjunction of form and content afflicts Poe,
Coleridge's heir. The French accused America of slighting her greatest
poet in Poe, who may sound better in Baudelaire's translation than in
English. Poe, like Coleridge, is a giant of imagination, and imagination
has its own laws. In Poe's tales and Coleridge's mystery poems, the
daemonic expresses itself nakedly. Dionysus always shakes off rules of
Apollonian form.

Coleridge and Poe are seized by visions that transcend language, that
belong to the dream experience beyond language. Psychoanalysis, I
said, overestimates the linguistic character of the unconscious. Dreaming is a pagan cinema. The wit of dreams comes from treating words as
if they were objects. Coleridge and Poe have written works of cinema.
Had film been available as a medium, perhaps that is the form they
would have chosen, for language here is only an obstruction to vision.
Evaluating the language of *The Ancient Mariner* by Renaissance or
Augustan standards would be depressing. There are a few great lines in
it; for example, "And ice, mast-high, came floating by, / As green as
emerald." I maintain that all such wonderful moments in *The Ancient
Mariner* look forward to *Christabel*, that *Christabel*, with its cold green
snake, is struggling to be born throughout this poem. The rhetorical

weaknesses in Coleridge and Poe have been produced by a warp of self-identification. Vision drives with such force from the unconscious that the craftsmanlike shape-making of consciousness lags behind.

The Ancient Mariner, a rhapsody of the male heroine, is filled with piercing arias: "Alone, alone, all, all alone, / Alone on a wide wide sea! / And never a saint took pity on / My soul in agony." Emotional expressionism of this kind is possible in Italian but not in English. At his maudlin fall, Shakespeare's Richard II cries, "My large kingdom for a little grave, / A little, little grave, an obscure grave" (III.iii.152–53). Intensified littleness gives you a cartoon pinpoint of dancing dwarves. Coleridge's intoning "alones" overpopulate themselves, baying like a canine chorus. Sheer velocity of identification makes him miss the infelicity of rhyming "thump" with "lump." There is too much agrarian comedy latent in our Anglo-Saxon monosyllables. The principle at work in *The Ancient Mariner*, as in "To William Wordsworth," is pagan sexual exhibitionism. Self-pity in *The Ancient Mariner* is like the self-flagellation of the ancient goddess-cults. It is neither callow nor sick. It is a ritual device to facilitate daemonic vision. The Romantic male heroine is a self-emasculating devotee of chthonian nature.

Personae in *The Ancient Mariner* form a sexual allegory. The poem begins with the Mariner stopping the Wedding-Guest as he enters a marriage banquet. The scene's deep structure is exactly the same as at the opening of *Christabel:* a stranger with a "glittering eye" puts a spell on an innocent, who falls under daemonic compulsion. The Mariner detains the guest with his tale of woe, which takes up the whole poem. At the end, the guest gloomily turns away from the Bridegroom's door and departs. The merry feast goes on without him. My theory is this: Bridegroom, Wedding-Guest, and Mariner are all aspects of Coleridge. The Bridegroom is a masculine persona, the self comfortably integrated in society. This virile alter ego is always perceived longingly and at a distance, through an open door through which come bursts of happy laughter. The Wedding-Guest, "next of kin" to the Bridegroom, is an adolescent supplicant aspiring to sexual fulfillment and collective joy. To achieve this, the Wedding-Guest must merge with the Bridegroom. But he is always prevented from doing so by the appearance of a spectre self, the Mariner, the male heroine or hermaphroditic self who luxuriates in passive suffering. It's a case of always the bridesmaid and never the bride. The Wedding-Guest turns away at the end because once more the hieratically wounded self has won. The Guest will never be the Bridegroom. As many times as he attempts to pass through the door to the place of festivity, the Mariner will materialize and paralyze him with

his seductive tale. This doorway is the obsessive scene of the Coleridgean sexual crux. Ostracism and casting out are the Romantic road
to identity. Will that doorway ever be breached? Yes, in *Christabel*. And
only by the most bizarre strategy of perversity and transsexualism.

The apparently pivotal event in the Mariner's tale is the killing of the
albatross, from which follow all his sufferings. From the moment I read
the poem in high school, I thought the albatross a superficial appen-
dage, a kind of pin the tail on the donkey, and I found the stress on it by
teachers and critics unconvincing and moralistic. Long afterward, I
learned it was Wordsworth who suggested the idea of the albatross to
Coleridge, which proves my point. This albatross is the biggest red
herring in poetry. Its only significance is as a vehicle of transgression.
The Mariner commits an obscure crime and becomes the focus of
cosmic wrath. But he is as blameless as the shadow heroes of Kafka,
who are hauled before faceless courts of law. In the world of *The Ancient
Mariner*, any action is immediately punished. Masculine assertion is
rebuked and humanity condemned to passive suffering.

Blake's "Crystal Cabinet" contains the same dramatic crisis: the
moment the male acts, he is expelled into the wilderness. Blake's male
is changed to a weeping babe in infantile dependency on a weeping
woman. Coleridge's Mariner is also propelled backward to a maternal
world. The ship is becalmed: "The very deep did rot: O Christ! / That
ever this should be! / Yea, slimy things did crawl with legs / Upon the
slimy sea." Stasis, slime. This is a vision of primal nondifferentiation,
the chthonian swamp of generation. The universe has returned to one
big womb, claustrophobic, airless, teeming with monstrous prehuman
mud creatures. The Mariner's appeal to Christ is the opposite of what it
seems. It shows that Coleridge, despite his conscious assent to Christianity, understands with the intuition of a great poet that the swamp-
world of the Great Mother precedes the world of Christ and is ready at
any moment to engulf it. Two remarks prove that Coleridge literally visualized a chthonian swamp: he once spoke of the "Sands and Swamps
of Evil" and elsewhere of lust as "the reek of the Marsh."

The Ancient Mariner is one of Romantic poetry's great regressions to
the daemonic and primeval. Every man makes a marine voyage out of
the cell of archaic ocean that is the sac of womb-waters. We all emerge
covered with slime and gasping for life. "The many men, so beautiful! /
And they all dead did lie: / And a thousand thousand slimy things /
Lived on; and so did I." All hopes for beauty and manhood lie dead.
Male power can never surpass female power. We live in the slime of our
bodies, which hold imagination hostage. Our mother-born bodies are

unregenerate nature, beyond God's redemption. The "slimy sea" of chthonian nature nullifies the words of Christ. Coleridge is over-whelmed by a pagan vision coming to him from below and beyond his own ethics. *The Ancient Mariner* transports its Gothic tale out of the historical world of castles and abbeys into the sublime theater of a desolate nature. But expansion of space is just another cul-de-sac. Coleridge brilliantly converts the open sea into a rotting sepulchre, which I called the daemonic womb of Gothic. This is one black hole from which Christ will never rise. *The Ancient Mariner* is the source of Poe's *The Narrative of Arthur Gordon Pym,* with its disastrous voyage in a womb-tomb ship. Evolution and motion are an illusion in the dank prison space of chthonian nature. Hence the male heroine's crushing passivity. Mankind staggers under the burden of mother nature.

Language, I said, is mutilated for vision in *The Ancient Mariner.* Thus the appeal to good has a backlash effect, sparking the birth of evil. Invo-cation of Christ's name fails to release the Mariner from his imprison-ment in ocean's nightmare womb. When a sail appears on the horizon, there is a moment of hope and joy. The Mariner attempts a new prayer: "Heaven's Mother send us grace!" But sacred language is profaned by daemonic revelation. On the ship is the grossest female apparition:

> *Her* lips were red, *her* looks were free,
> Her locks were yellow as gold:
> Her skin was as white as leprosy,
> The Night-mare LIFE-IN-DEATH was she,
> Who thicks man's blood with cold.

Appeals to sky-cult are useless. As if irritated by references to her benign successor, the tender Madonna, the ur-mother makes her sen-sational appearance. She is the Whore of Babylon, the daemon un-bound. Her lips are red with provocation and the blood of her victims. She is all health and all disease. She is a masque of the red death, a Medusa who turns men to stone but also the mother who stirs the blood pudding of her sons till their bodies congeal in her womb. To give life is to kill. This *is* heaven's mother, who comes when called. She is the vampire who haunts men's dreams. Aubrey Beardsley depicts a Cole-ridgean epiphany of the vampire Madonna in *The Ascension of St. Rose of Lima.* Mary, lasciviously embracing St. Rose, hovers in the air like a poison black cloud. Another monstrous epiphany occurs in Ingmar Bergman's *Through a Glass Darkly* (1961), where a mad girl sees God as a sexually aggressive spider.

The Ancient Mariner surges forward on its wave of daemonic vision

from Parts I through IV, but then something happens. Parts V through
VII are a muddle. The poem recovers only when the Mariner's tale
ceases and the narrative frame resumes, where the Mariner delays the
Wedding-Guest at the Bridegroom's door. *The Ancient Mariner* drags
on pointlessly for too long, and I think I know where and why it goes
wrong. As Part IV ends, the Mariner sees water-snakes in the sea:
"Blue, glossy green, and velvet black, / They coiled and swam; and
every track / Was a flash of golden fire." This is one of the great
moments in Romantic poetry. We are back at the dawn of time. Firma-
ment has not yet separated from the waters. The sun is only a yolky
yellow in the albuminous jelly of the mother-stuff. Primeval ocean
swarms with slimy life. But the water is also man's body shot with veins.
These serpents, writhing with Vergilian opalescence, are the chains that
bind us, our physical life. Man is a Laocoön bedeviled by serpents. We
all struggle in the toils of our mother-born body. Why are the sea-
snakes veins? Because, as I said, all great lines in *The Ancient Mariner*
look forward to *Christabel*, where the vampire has exquisite "blue-
veined feet." Geraldine, the green snake who strangles the dove, is the
daemon of chthonian nature, trampling man in her triumph of the will.

Coleridge has penetrated far into the daemonic realm. Too far, for
there is an immediate retreat into conventional emotion. Vision fails,
and the poem begins to drift. Why? What have the sea-snakes roused
that Coleridge cannot face? The Mariner's response to them is embarrassingly simplistic. "A spring of love" gushes from his heart, and he
blesses them. The moment he can pray, the albatross falls from his neck
and into the sea. How dreadful to see our shaman-poet unmasked,
cranking the bellows of afflatus like a stagehand. Coleridge is overcome by anxiety and surrenders to Wordsworth and to Christianity.
Love and prayer are a ludicrously inadequate response to the chthonian horror that Coleridge has summoned from the dark heart of
existence. The roiling sea-snakes are the barbaric energy of matter, the
undulating spiral of birth and death. What is the proper response to this
ecstatic hallucination? Coleridge is hemmed in. His protagonist, the
Mariner, is insufficiently advanced as a sexual persona. The male heroine will need to be revised if daemonic vision is to be sustained. *Christabel* is a rewriting of *The Ancient Mariner* in new and more daring terms.
There, as we shall see, when the protagonist meets the serpent face of
nature, there will be no swerving away. The poet, disguised so that
Wordsworth can no longer find him, will hurl himself into the chthonian abyss.

The problem with moral or Christian readings of *The Ancient Mari-*

ner is that they can make no sense of the compulsive or delusional frame of the poem. If the "spring of love" felt by the Mariner were imaginatively efficacious, the poem should be able to conclude. Or at the very least, it should permit the Mariner to be redeemed. But the falling off of the albatross is followed by three more parts. And even at the end of the poem, the Mariner is still forced to wander the world, repeating his "ghastly tale" again and again. Having introduced a benevolent emotion into his daemonic poem, Coleridge is at a loss how to proceed. A new cast of characters is hustled in—seraphs, a Pilot, a Hermit. There is confused dialogue, a fuzzy twisting and turning. Here is the point: the moment the Mariner prays, the moment good rather than evil triumphs, the poem falls apart. At the end of Part IV, Coleridge is overwhelmed with fear at what he has written and vainly attempts to turn his poem in a redemptive direction. The superego acts to obscure what has come from the amoral id. Nineteen years later, Coleridge added the marginal glosses still adorning the poem. These dithery festoons are afterthoughts, revisions that often depart crucially in tone from the text they "explain." We hear in them the Christian Coleridge trying to soften the daemonic Coleridge, exactly as the older, Urizenic Wordsworth "corrected" his early nature poetry. By rationalization and moralization, Coleridge strove to put out the daemonic fires of his own imagination.

The poetic discordancies are blatant in the conclusion. The Mariner says, "O Wedding-Guest! this soul hath been / Alone on a wide wide sea: / So lonely 'twas, that God himself / Scarce seeméd there to be." This is the truth. In the cosmos of *The Ancient Mariner,* Jehovah has been obliterated by the vampire mother who rises from the slime of nature. But the Christian Coleridge keeps stitching the veil he has rent. The Mariner illogically goes on to celebrate communal churchgoing under the kind gaze of the "great Father" and ends his message: "He prayeth best, who loveth best / All things both great and small; / For the dear God who loveth us, / He made and loveth all." What a frail twig to cling to in the maelstrom of chthonian nature. This is like Blake's ironic moral tags, evasive distortions of the severity of experience depicted in his poems: "So if all do their duty, they need not fear harm"; "Then cherish pity, lest you drive an angel from your door." The Mariner's farewell stanzas are a poetic non sequitur. They contradict everything that is great in the poem. Coleridge himself seems to have sensed this, for long afterward he remarked that *The Ancient Mariner* had "too much" of a moral in it: "The only or chief fault, if I might say so, was the obtrusion of the moral sentiment so openly on the reader."

Imagination has the last word anyhow in *The Ancient Mariner.* Here
are the closing lines, as the Wedding-Guest turns away from the Bridegroom's door: "He went like one that hath been stunned, / And is of
sense forlorn: / A sadder and a wiser man, / He rose the morrow morn."
If one accepts the Christian interpretation of the poem, how explain
this peculiar reaction? The Wedding-Guest is not morally strengthened
by the Mariner's exhortations. He is plunged into gloom and severed
from society. The Mariner counsels Christian love, but the Wedding-
Guest walks away as if the Mariner has said, "There is no God, and
nature is a hell of appetite and force." But this is the secret message that
the Wedding-Guest has divined, the message that has slipped past
Coleridge despite his vigorous efforts to steer the poem in a morally
acceptable direction. The guest arises the next day "a sadder and a
wiser man," because through the smokescreen of the Christian finale
has come the terrible revelation of Coleridge's daemonic dream vision.

Now to consider "Kubla Khan" in terms of sexual personae. The poem's poet-hero is both omnipotent emperor and mad
prophet and outcast. He dwells in magic circles—domes and ritual
precincts, the sacred spaces of art. His power comes from below, the
hell of chthonian nature that erupts in *The Ancient Mariner.* From
earth's still womblike caverns come phallic geysers of force, tossing
boulders like hail. Nature pants in sexualized spasms of creation. The
poet from his light-flooded dome of imagination surveys nature's savage enormity, prehuman and premoral. He cannot control it, but he is
its voice. Art synthesizes glassy Apollonian form with coarse Dionysian
flux. The dome is state and skull, riding the serpent desires of bowels
and belly.
     Coleridge's protagonists are always sexually dual. Contraries meet in
the poet of "Kubla Khan":

> And all should cry, Beware! Beware!
> His flashing eyes, his floating hair!
> Weave a circle round him thrice,
> And close your eyes with holy dread,
> For he on honey-dew hath fed,
> And drunk the milk of Paradise.

The Mariner has become a mental traveller. He is a prisoner of perception. Voluptuary and ascetic, he feasts by fasting. The food of the gods
makes him less and more than a man. Bloom says he is "the youth as
virile poet."[8] But there is no virility here. He is an androgyne tied to the

stake. Celibate and solitary, he is the Wedding-Guest who cannot be Bridegroom. A thousand doors are closed to him. He is the gift-bringer as beggar, the alien who can never cross the threshold.

The poet is a beautiful youth in the Hellenistic style, an ephebic kouros of female emotionalism. His flashing eyes and floating hair combine masculine power with feminine beauty. Flashing eyes may command and pierce, but they can also be inviting without ambivalence, as in vivacious maidens whose eyes dance with light. A poet's eye flashes in this second sense; it is like a movie screen flickering with spectral images. The poet is feminine because passive to his own vision. He is arresting because arrested. His senses are a house of detention. His eyes are the barred window of poetry.

Floating hair normally belongs to the female canon of beauty. One thinks of Botticelli's Venus, Rita Hayworth, Hedy Lamarr. But during the late 1790s, when "Kubla Khan" was written, long unpowdered hair symbolized youth, vitality, and nonconformity. Coleridge's flashing eyes and floating hair appear in portraits of Napoleon, like Gros's *Bonaparte at Arcole* or David's *Napoleon Crossing the Alps*, where the hero's long hair flares in the wind of destiny. In "Kubla Khan," the poet's hair lifts by lyric afflatus; he is an Aeolian lyre played by the wind. I said the hyacinthine hair of the beautiful boy erotically entangles the observer's eye. Even in Napoleon's streaming hair there is something cross-sexual. It was the feminine element in Napoleon's charisma, a principle I think always sexually dual. Napoleon wore long hair only while he was young and lean, an aspiring outsider. His cropped Caesar-style hair belongs mainly to the imperial period, when he tended toward corpulence. What was earlier expressed by his hair now resided in the female fleshiness we see in David's *Napoleon in His Study*, where the emperor, burning the midnight oil, caresses his own belly.

The poet of "Kubla Khan" is also a gaunt outsider of cometlike charisma. His floating hair is his hermaphrodite banner, taunting and narcissistic. Long hair is the badge of many warrior cultures, Spartan to Sikh. But in the main line of western sexual personae, long hair has been and will remain the language of feminine eros. A long-haired male is, consciously or unconsciously, calling attention to something feminine in him. He makes himself a sex object passive to the probing eye. This was clearly the case with the seventeenth-century Cavaliers, whose portraits have a stunning epicene glamour. The west has persistently and probably correctly associated long male hair with a dangerous because entrancing and self-entranced egotism. We see this as early as the Biblical tale of Absalom, with his Alcibiades-like career of beauty and sedition. The long, unkempt hair of Coleridge's poet is sexually, socially, and morally defiant. It is natural because informal, but it is perverse because self-divinizing and autoerotic.

Dangerous: the poet of "Kubla Khan" is enclosed in a zone of "holy dread." He is an untouchable, a carrier of charisma kept under quarantine. He has an eerie sexual iridescence. Masculine and feminine dilate about him like a solar corona. People cry, "Beware! Beware!" But not because he is virile. He is not a man who acts but a man who sees. He can induce hallucinations in others as well as himself. "Kubla Khan" follows archaic ritual rules. Frazer says, "Holiness, magical virtue, taboo, or whatever we may call that mysterious quality which is supposed to pervade sacred or tabooed persons, is conceived by the primitive philosopher as a physical substance or fluid, with which the sacred man is charged just as a Leyden jar is charged with electricity." Elsewhere he says, "The primitive mind seems to conceive of holiness as a sort of dangerous virus, which a prudent man will shun as far as possible, and of which, if he should chance to be infected by it, he will carefully disinfect himself by some sort of ceremonial purification."9 A Maypole circle is woven around Coleridge's poet to contain his excess of mana. Magic against magic: society uses all its defenses against the dangerous radiance of art.

"Kubla Khan" ends in double ceremonies, as the poet soars into trance and as society salts the ground he stands on. This is scorched earth, a temenos where nothing will grow again. The poet is gifted but cursed, condemned to social exclusion. Coleridge chillingly closes the eyes of humanity to his poet—that is, to himself. It is a real-life game of blindman's bluff. At this mystic moment, all eyes are sealed. Artist and audience are at war. The poet is a nonperson, subject to mass shunning. He suffers "the Silence," the ostracism imposed by military cadets on one who has broken the honor code. We must remember this for *Christabel*, where the heroine is cruelly shunned after her election by the daemonic and where she is imprisoned in her own silence. The poet is a visionary who sees too much and is tortured by his visions. He is a scapegoat fed on delicacies, like Aztec victims before their slaughter or like Roman volunteers in army camps who enjoyed every sensual indulgence before being ritually executed. The poet is blind, maimed, lame. His imagination is free, but his body is bound in ritual limitation. He is a daemonic Apollo, an oracle maddened by intoxicants, here sap and milk, fluids of Dionysus. As a sexual persona, Coleridge's poet is a suffering hermaphrodite, a sacred monster, breeding genies from the sterile air.

      Christabel is the destination to which the Coleridgean line of sexual ambiguity runs. Destination as epic goal and as tragic fate or fatality. Destination is termination in *Christabel*. Poetry falls under sentence of death. Trance ends in paralysis and language in silence. In this poem, Coleridge created a daemonic plenum from which he could not escape. Wordsworth is annihilated, and Coleridge is free. But his freedom has been purchased by sexual and metaphysical enslavement, a shamanistic transformation so complete that the poet became invisible to readers, even though he is standing squarely before them.

    Christabel has an odd history. Its two parts were written in 1797 and 1800. Coleridge withheld it from publication, but it circulated privately in manuscript. Its release in 1816 was at the urging of Byron, who loved it and called it the source of all of Sir Walter Scott's verse tales. Coleridge never regarded *Christabel* as done and claimed plans for three more parts. His mind returned fretfully to the poem for years, and his inability to finish it was an abiding disappointment. For a century, critics have advanced various theories to account for this. The corpus of commentary on *Christabel* is very small. Probably no poem in literary history has been so abused by moralistic Christian readings. Its blatant lesbian pornography has been ignored or blandly argued away.

    The Christian interpretation of *Christabel* found ample justification in Coleridge's remark to his friend Gillman that the theme of the final poem would be "that the virtuous of this world save the wicked." The contradictions between Christian sentiment and poetic vision are even more radical in *Christabel* than in *The Ancient Mariner*. Little here supports what Coleridge declared his moral program. Piety is blasted by a night wind. Heaven is conquered by hell. Virtue does not and cannot redeem in the poem. The greatness of *Christabel* comes from its lurid pagan pictorialism. It is an epiphany of evil. Mother nature returns to retake what she lost. *Christabel* is a daemonic screenplay, a script for an apocalyptic comeback. Behold the star: the lesbian vampire Geraldine is the chthonian reawakened from its earthy grave.

    That daemonic vision is the true heart of *Christabel* is demonstrated by Shelley's reaction at first hearing. When in Geneva Byron recited some memorized passages, Shelley shrieked and rushed from the room. He was found trembling and bathed in sweat. During the description of Geraldine, he saw eyes in the nipples of Mary Godwin, his future wife. This is reported by Polidori, who was present, and confirmed in a letter of Byron. Shelley's vision of the archetypal phallic woman shows that the poem's amoral essence was instantaneously transmitted from one great poet to another. Coleridge's imagination is invested not in "the virtuous of this world" but in daemonic personae of hermaphrodite force. *Christabel* is a psychologically archaizing poem. Far from proving Christian truth, it abolishes Christianity and returns the psyche to a primitive world of malignant spirit-presences. Coleridge the Christian was the first misreader of Coleridge the poet.

Christabel rewrites *The Ancient Mariner* by reversing its movement. Daemonic revelation occurs not on the high seas but in the citadel of state. Evil invades the secret cells of body and mind. *Christabel* is a boudoir epic. Sex, the point of intersection between man and nature, is contaminated. The poem opens with the lady Christabel leaving her father's castle at midnight to pray for her betrothed knight. As at the start of *The Ancient Mariner,* there is an impulse toward conventional marriage that will be defeated. Christabel is an innocent who believes love and virtue go together. Her mission of heterosexual piety will be grotesquely defiled by the poem. Sex will turn and sting the Christian will. Christabel's maiden voyage into archaic night is foolish and possibly provocative. She summons the very evil she hopes to quell. Neither Christianity nor Wordsworthian nature can defend her. A bleak, decadent sterility has turned the green leaves grey. Persephone in the meadow is about to be raped, but her assailant is the earth-mother and her dark prison her own home.

Even as Christabel kneels in prayer, the daemonic drama begins. "It" has moaned, the brute sexless, sexfull thing, the stirring form of pagan nature waking from its long sleep. The poet's voice interjects: "Hush, beating heart of Christabel! / Jesu, Maria, shield her well!" We recall another appeal to heaven in *The Ancient Mariner,* an appeal answered by a leprous vampire. The Coleridgean moral inversion operates again. Christian prayer produces pagan epiphany. Heaven is either deaf or sadistic. The materialization of the vampires in *Christabel* and *The Ancient Mariner* perversely awaits the invocation of a divine name. It is as if daemonic power is intensified by Christian assertion. A lust for profanation hangs in the air like a shadow-mist. It suddenly takes brilliant shape. In a burst of luminous, numinous cinema, the vampire Geraldine appears in all her white beauty. "Mary mother, save me now!" says Christabel, pressed by that harsh Coleridgean irony. The Madonna becomes the serpent in the garden. In her embrace, Christabel will fall; her touch will be the mark of Cain exiling Christabel from her race. Christabel's trust and good will are a blank spot of tender passivity in nature, as in Blake's Spenserian "Infant Joy." The benign is devoured by its context, hungry black flames of daemonic energy.

Geraldine gives birth to herself by "the infinite I AM" of Coleridgean imagination. She is poetry leaping full-armed from the unconscious, a hermaphrodite Muse. The voices of art in Coleridge prophesy not peace but war. Art is conflict, turbulence, negation. And art mirrors nature, from which Wordsworth has finally been driven. The vampire Muse makes poetry in *Christabel* by seduction and corruption. Poisoned words will lead to poisoned sex. She lies in order to lay. "Stretch forth thy hand, and have no fear!" Geraldine says to Christabel. After a long falsehood, the invitation is repeated, this time successfully. Geraldine seems to evoke the unconscious complicity of her prey. Bloom rightly calls Christabel a "half-willing victim."[10]

The vampire's satanic temptations are garnished by spurious sex-romance. She assumes the frailest feminine persona. Five warriors have kidnapped her from her father's house and abandoned her: "Me, even me, a maid forlorn." The irony of Geraldine's tale of rape is that she is herself a rapist. What Christabel hears is what is to be done to her. Psychologically, the tale translates to: men are brutes! This is how Geraldine severs Christabel's mental connection with her betrothed knight and induces her to give her hand. The daemonic mother lures the bride backward, away from menarche into the womb of regression. In Coleridge's plan for the conclusion, Geraldine was to impersonate Christabel's fiancé, by transsexual ruse. In Part I, we see that Geraldine has already replaced him. Once Geraldine has won her first victory, she has won everything. She has made her first penetration of Christabel's psyche and now manipulates her thoughts. It is Christabel who introduces the idea of "stealth" and who proposes they share the same bed. From such covertness come erotic intensity, trespass, and shame.

Geraldine's strategies are modelled on Spenser. Her woeful tale echoes the one told by duplicitous Duessa to the Redcrosse Knight in the first book of *The Faerie Queene*. In the forest Geraldine recalls Belphoebe and in the castle Malecasta. *Christabel*'s sexual style, its combination of cool medieval beauty with voluptuous embowered evil, is uniquely Spenserian. Coleridge, like Blake, senses the decadent perversity in Spenser. *Christabel*'s rape theme comes from the rape-infested *Faerie Queene*. But virginity has lost its Christian militancy. No armour defends Coleridge's heroine against sexual predators. Christabel's simple femininity is her undoing. Daemonic rapacity surges into her and obliterates her maidenhood. She is no match for hermaphrodite aggression. There is no longer a working Christian scheme to divert lust into sublimation. The Spenserian bower where Christabel is lost is her own.

Invitation to the rape: from Christabel's hospitable gesture to her actual seduction there are 140 lines. A long distance must be traversed. The Mariner's epic voyage is internalized. But "the moat" is crossed at the moment of Christabel's assent. This is her Rubicon, from which there is no turning back. The 140 lines are a dreamlike sarabande, both funeral and wedding march. In stages drawn from Shakespeare's *Rape of Lucrece*, the poem follows each step of Geraldine's invasion of gate, court, hall, chamber. The castle of Christabel's father resembles the metaphorical ruined castle of Goethe's *Werther.* In Coleridge, the male castle of society and history is entered and disordered by the chthonian. But the castle is also Christabel's body, which is systematically possessed by Geraldine. The "little door" unlocked by Christabel's key is her own chastity.

At the gate, Geraldine sinks down, and Christabel must carry her through it. Bloom says, "Geraldine cannot cross the threshold, which probably is charmed against her."[11] In old Scandinavia, an ax was buried beneath the threshold to guard a house against lightning—and to prevent a witch from entering. Similarly, ancient cities were protected by founders' bones entombed in the gate lintel. Jackson Knight, we saw, shows that virgin goddesses were patrons of cities because the integrity of walls was imagined as a virgin's hymen. Hence the Trojan horse brought down Troy: as it passed the gate, it broke the magic spell protecting the city. Taboos governing the sanctity of walls were so strict that a Roman soldier who leapt the camp wall instead of leaving by the gate was executed, for he had broken the defenses; this appears to be why Romulus kills Remus for jumping his new wall. Thus in *Christabel,* Geraldine's passage through the iron gate from which an "army in battle array" has marched is a Trojan subterfuge. Hidden in Christabel's arms, she simultaneously overthrows male power and penetrates the virgin's body. She is the cunning sacker of cities, dangling from the lamb's wool.

Christabel's breached gate is the doorway which could not be crossed in *The Ancient Mariner.* The Wedding-Guest has finally become the Bridegroom. Christabel lifting Geraldine over the threshold is the groom with her bride. She has begun her daemonic marriage to Geraldine, from which there can be no divorce. Geraldine is "a weary weight," the terrible burden of our physical life. Christabel staggers under the tree of nature upon which Blake sees us crucified. The doorway is Coleridge's sexual crux, his *via crucis*. Geraldine's advance through the castle will be recast by Poe in *The Masque of the Red Death*, where bloody biology triumphs over all. Geraldine too is a masquer, mother nature who uses her Wordsworthian mask of beauty to hide her chthonian brutality. In Poe the midnight chamber holds a clock, in Coleridge a bed. Both are epiphanies of maternal power. Geraldine and Christabel's slow passage has an abstract formality, a religious solemnity. Seduction ("leading astray") becomes induction, initiation into daemonic mysteries. The poem's eroticism is generated by this methodical movement, which inflames by anticipation and suspense. Darkness, seclusion, and silence accentuate Christabel's tantalizing sexual vulnerability.

The procession moves through the castle as if through a church, nave to chancel to altar, the bed of seduction. No guard or hierarch rises to block the queen's sweep of the board. The presiding male, Sir Leoline, is ill and asleep. The watchdog, with animal instinct, moans but does not wake. Only in the bedchamber does Geraldine meet resistance, from the ghost of Christabel's mother, a guardian spirit springing out like the sacristan of the sanctuary. The mother died at the hour of Christabel's birth, vowing she would hear the castle bell strike twelve on her daughter's wedding day. The poem begins with the tolling of midnight. So this is Christabel's wedding day, and she is about to consummate her perverse nuptials. In this poem, good strangles itself; birth leads to death: pregnancy is a terminal disease. The wine made by Christabel's mother from wildflowers—presumably Wordsworth's daffodils!—serves only to energize the vampire in her territorial war. Geraldine grapples with the ghost and repels her: "Off, wandering mother! . . . this hour is mine. . . . 'tis given to me." Given by whom? God and fate take the side of evil. Archaic night makes her inexorable return.

After her mother's defeat, Christabel is completely at Geraldine's mercy. The triumph of the daemonic is signified by Christabel kneeling at her side. Geraldine has subdued the cosmos of the poem, and she is now its deity. Christabel obeys without question Geraldine's command to unrobe herself: "So let it be!" In other words, "I do." They are married. She lies down in bed to await her master. Like the poet of "Kubla Khan," Christabel is a sacrificial victim, whom we actually see led to the altar and laying herself down nude upon it. Christabel is Iphigenia meekly awaiting the stroke of the knife. Geraldine is the high priest praying before her bloody task—but she prays to herself, the daemonic will. Murder here is sexual intercourse, for sex is how mother nature kills us, that is, how she enslaves the imagination. Nature draws first blood, of virgins, of us. Like "To William Wordsworth," the poem climaxes in a pagan ritual sex act. *Christabel*'s ceremonialism continues in the deliberate preparations for bed, a sexual mime. This is one of the points the Christian Coleridge tried to fudge. Twenty years after writing the poem, he inserted seven lines (255–61) in which Geraldine "seeks delay" before laying down with Christabel and taking her in her arms. The reader must never be misled by the attempts of Coleridge the anxious reviser to cover the work of Coleridge the visionary. Vampire and conscience are mutually exclusive. The poem in its fine original inspiration presents a Geraldine who never hesitates, who cannot hesitate, who is implacable.

There is a mystery when Geraldine undresses. "Behold! her bosom and half her side— / A sight to dream of, not to tell! / O shield her! shield sweet Christabel!" What is revealed by the daemon's unveiling? G. Wilson Knight speaks of "some sort of sexual desecration, some expressly physical horror."[12] In Part II, Christabel has a chilling flashback: "Again she saw that bosom old, / Again she felt that bosom cold." Scholars immediately recognized this as a detail from *The Faerie Queene:* when beautiful Duessa is stripped, she has "dried dugs, like bladders lacking wind" (I.viii.47). Waking the next morning, Christabel sees her companion's "heaving breasts." Geraldine must be a classic vampire of great age, her breast withered only when she hungers. After she has sated herself, whether by drinking blood or somehow draining her victim's life-energy, her breasts recover sensual fullness. In Part II, Christabel remembers "the touch and pain," so something surgical has definitely occurred!

Whatever is repellent about Geraldine's bosom, it is the identifying mark of a witch. In her study of European witch-cult, Margaret Murray describes another mark, the "little Teat," which appeared on odd parts of the body and "was said to secrete milk and to give suck to the familiars, both human and animal." Supernumerary breasts or nipples are a medical anomaly found on chest, abdomen, shoulder, buttock, or thigh.[13] A withered bosom, misplaced nipples, multiple breasts: the witch's body is a perversion or parody of the maternal. It is fitting, therefore, that Geraldine's sole opponent is Christabel's benevolent mother, and it is a severe truth about the poem that this power is crushed and expelled. The witch, with her animal teats, is virtually a third sex. She is the ugliness of procreative nature. She is the chthonian mother who eats her children.

A third sex: how does Geraldine sexually violate Christabel? Coleridge says of the two as they lie together:

> A star hath set, a star hath risen,
> O Geraldine! since arms of thine
> Have been the lovely lady's prison.
> O Geraldine! one hour was thine—
> Thou'st had thy will!

The star which has set is Jesus'. The star which has risen is the ancient sign of the daemon, the sexual scorpion. The prison is the embrace of mother nature, from which Jesus cannot redeem us. Geraldine has had her "will" of Christabel. This locution belongs exclusively to male experience. It is not used of a woman anywhere else in major literature. The sole analogy I find is in the journal of Victoria Sackville-West, who describes carrying off her lover Violet Trefusis to a French hotel two days after the latter's wedding: "I treated her savagely, I made love to her, I had her, I didn't care."[14] "I had her": how strange the language of masculine possession sounds in a female context. In Coleridge, female sexual receptivity is mysteriously transformed into the power to rape. What happens? If there is draining of blood, it must occur with mentalized orgasmic excitement, like the cloudy feverishness of *Carmilla*, J. Sheridan Le Fanu's Victorian tale of a lesbian vampire obviously inspired by *Christabel*.

Can there be a phallic subtext to this daemonic intercourse? There is an ambiguity about the body of Spenser's Duessa. Fradubio surprises her at her bath: "Her nether parts misshappen, monstrous, / Were hid in water, that I could not see, / But they did seeme more foule and hideous, / Than womans shape man would beleeve to be" (I.ii.41). This is inconclusive, but when Duessa is unmasked, the poet speaks in his own voice: "Her nether parts, the shame of all her kind, / My chaster Muse for shame doth blush to write" (viii.48) He seems to give the most depraved female evil a penis. A modern British woman reported that as she and the female medium sat nude at a London séance, an icy "phantom penis" left the medium's genitals, crossed the space between them, and entered her.

Rising from her bed next morning, Christabel says, "Sure I have sinn'd!" She remembers nothing, but her sense of lost innocence is acute, for the witch has entered her, body and mind. Geraldine sleeps satisfied like a man, the triumphant seducer, while the violated girl weeps in shame. She is humanity after the fall. Her eyes are open. She

knows we are naked, defenseless against nature. Wordsworthian illusions about mother nature are over. Incest and cannibalism are the
lovemaking of man's family romance. Christabel has been impregnated by the Muse and bears the burden of fear and suffering. "The
vision of fear, the touch and pain": her sexual crucifixion is a spectacle
of sadomasochistic bondage. Her pain may be from the vampire's bite
or from deviant penetration. In medieval covens, the Devil performed
ritual public intercourse with a forked penis, entering his devotees
through two orifices. Initiation into ancient nature-cults always involved some abuse of the body, from flagellation to castration. In *Christabel*'s pagan epiphany, the daemon returns in an orgy of Dionysian
pleasure-pain. Vampire and poem are a raptor-rapture of monstrosity.

Geraldine's daemonic aggression resides in her eye. Vampires have a
phallic eye, probing, penetrating, riveting. In the hallway, the hearth
fire flames, "And Christabel saw the lady's eye, / And nothing else saw
she thereby." She is obsessed, subjugated. At her moment of maximum
power in the bedchamber, Geraldine rises to her full "lofty" height, an
erection fueled by her dominance of the mother-spirit, Christabel's
submission and genuflection, and the wine she changes into Christabel's blood. This is the full moon of the vampire eye: "Her fair large
eyes 'gan glitter bright." Bloom says Geraldine, like the Ancient Mariner, is "a hypnotist or mesmerist."[15] Christabel's seduction is a sexual
hypnotism. Freud says the "blind obedience" of hypnosis comes from
an "unconscious fixation of the libido on the person of the hypno-
tizer."[16] Thus Christabel spiritually participates in her own defloration.

Christabel's hypnotism theme will recur in the mesmerism of Hawthorne's *The Blithedale Romance*. The lesbian tension between feminine Priscilla and willful Zenobia comes from the liaison of Christabel
and Geraldine:

> As yet, the girl had not stirred. She stood near the door, fixing a
> pair of large, brown, melancholy eyes upon Zenobia,—only upon
> Zenobia!—she evidently saw nothing else in the room, save that
> bright, fair, rosy, beautiful woman. It was the strangest look I ever
> witnessed; long a mystery to me, and forever a memory. . . . She
> dropped down upon her knees, clasped her hands, and gazed
> piteously into Zenobia's face. Meeting no kindly reception, her
> head fell on her bosom.[17]

"And nothing else saw she thereby." The look blotting out all else; the
kneeling and dominance and submission: Hawthorne's decadent eroticism is a homage to Coleridge. Poe also recasts Geraldine as the fierce

Ligeia and toothsome Berenice, phallic fixators and revenants of the daemonic graveyard. And Coleridge's lesbian couple will end up, by way of Hawthorne, in Henry James's *The Bostonians*, where Perseus rescues Andromeda from the seacoast hoard of the feminist vampire.

The phallic optics of Coleridge's mystery poems arises from the war between vision and language that disrupts *The Ancient Mariner*. In Shelley's sex vision, menacing female eyes signify the omnipotence and ubiquity of procreative nature. The daemonic turns man to stone. Jane Harrison calls the Gorgon an "incarnate Evil Eye": "The monster was tricked out with cruel tusks and snakes, but it slew by the eye, it *fascinated*."[18] Fascination is the black magic of art, love, and politics. Kenneth Burke remarks: "The theme of fascination in Coleridge's 'Mystery Poems' is that of an ambivalent power. He gives us, as it were, a poetic thesaurus dictionary of terms ranging from thoroughly 'good' fascination to thoroughly 'bad' fascination."[19] Fascination is ambivalent because love is ambivalent. The Latin *fascinare*, "to enchant, bewitch, charm," is related to the Greek *baskainein*, "to use ill words" as in slander but also "to bewitch by spells or by means of an evil eye." *Fascinare* and *baskainein* are linguistically connected to words of speaking, Latin *farari* and Greek *phaskein*, "to say." As she lies down with Christabel, Geraldine says, "In the touch of this bosom there worketh a spell, / Which is lord of thy utterance, Christabel!" Next morning, Christabel cannot tell her pain or appeal for help. Evil eye and magic spell: daemonic sorcery deprives its victim of speech, hurtling them backward through history to the animal realm. Thus Circe's most sadistic torture is stopping the mouths of Odysseus' men. Minds acute in their swine bodies, they can only grunt. *Christabel*'s heroine is plunged into muteness. Her "vision of fear" obliterates language.

The vampire's power to fascinate derives from the snake's legendary ability to immobilize its prey by fixing its eyes upon it. The fear freezing an animal in its tracks and the fear paralyzing a person beneath the vampire's gaze are one and the same. It is an emanation of the cruel hierarchy of biology. The Gorgon who petrifies and the vampire who seduces achieve their ends by *sudden hierarchic assertion*. That the penis is power is one of the social lies men tell themselves to overcome their fear of the daemonism of sex. That woman can drain and paralyze is part of the latent vampirism in female physiology. The archetype of the femme fatale began in prehistory and will live forever.

The vampire's authority is a form of charisma, the power enabling a leader to suspend the will of his followers and induce them to sacrifice themselves for his personal vision. Hitler, we noted, called the masses feminine: the ability to entrance and focus the minds of a nation is a form of sexual seduction. Politics and theater were interrelated long before the age of mass media. An actor with stage presence, innate authority, masters the audience. A "spellbinding" orator literally casts a spell. He "captures" attention. An audience is "captivated" or "enthralled," meaning enslaved (a thrall is a slave or bondman), when no one stirs restlessly or chatters to his neighbor, when it's "so quiet you could hear a pin drop." Metaphors of sex and power abound in political and artistic performance. The speaker dominates the plane of eye contact. All eyes are fixed on him, as if hypnotized. The audience is propelled into *immobilization* and *muteness*, ancient prerogatives of the daemon. Actor and fiction operate on an audience by subduing the rebellious body and fixing the mind on one spirit-governing focal point. Fascination is *becalming*, that condition of erotic passivity in which the Ancient Mariner sees the vampire of nature at sea. Vision, silence, castration. We are approaching the sexual center of Coleridge's mystery poems.

Fascination is both the theme and genesis of *Christabel*. Part I ends with Christabel still in Geraldine's arms. I will argue that this encompasses the totality of Coleridge's vision and that the second part written three years later, as well as his rough plan for three more parts, was born of fear at what he had already created. *Christabel* remained unfinished because, try as he might, Coleridge could not turn his daemonic saga into a parable of Christian redemption. Even Part II ends with Christabel's father abandoning her and allying himself with false Geraldine. Coleridge's conscious mind wills the victory of virtue. But his unconscious replies: evil is older and will endure. Part I, ending, says of Christabel, "But this she knows, in joys and woes, / That saints will aid if men will call: / For the blue sky bends over all!" Christian interpreters have missed the terrible irony of these lines. For Coleridge, we saw, calling heavenly powers brings disaster. Christabel suffers from the pathos of rationalization of Blake's exploited chimney sweeps. She is like the rape victims of *The Faerie Queene*, whose femininity invites disaster, or the heroine of Sade's *Justine, or Good Conduct Well Chastised* (originally called *The Misfortunes of Virtue*). Good is actually a titillation to lust and provokes the vampire's assault. Paganism stakes its claim in the virgin heart of Christian virtue.

The transition from Part I to Part II is jarring. We pass from sinister dreaminess to farce. The poem goes flat. Unimportant people pop up and down ringing bells and telling beads. We meet Christabel's father, Sir Leoline, whom the poet should have left snoring. Scholars have noticed the sudden loss of mythic intensity but have neither explored nor explained it. Humphrey House, for example, says, "The two parts differ so much from each other, that they scarcely seem to belong to the same poem."[20] I must amend my critique: there are two fine passages in Part II. The first depicts Geraldine and Christabel waking together in the bedchamber (360–86). The second records the bard Bracy's ominous vision of a "bright green snake" coiled about a dove's body (547–56). But both these passages reinvoke the sexual intercourse of Part I. In other words, the best poetry of Part II has been produced by daemonic infection from Part I, a contagion of vice.

Why is Part I so much stronger? The poem's greatness resides in the seductive vampirism of Geraldine. It was inspired by a vision of a female persona of overwhelming force. Everything in the poem is subordinated to Geraldine. Coleridge manipulates character, time, and place to form an admiring circle about her, from which she radiates her cold hieratic glamour like a sun king. *Christabel* is structured by an archaic technique of ornamental display, a ritual exhibitionism. Gods descend when man is in crisis, but the daemon ascends from her bed of ghostly loam. Heterosexuality has failed: maternalism is weak and masculinity in decay, the father's armour a musty relic. Art can see but not act: the bard warns but is not believed. Father spurns daughter in Lear-like disloyalty.

The world of *Christabel* has run down and is ripe for apocalypse. Into this vacuum steps the lesbian vampire, dazzlingly beautiful, relentlessly masculine. Like *As You Like It*, *Christabel* is an alchemic experiment whose main event is the crystallization of a *rebis* or hermaphroditic personality. The poem is an alembic of superheated psyche. Energy is released and rebonded. Vampires make vampires: Christabel, "hissing," has been genetically altered, irradiated by the daemonic. Fascination, capture, possession, transfiguration.

Christabel is Coleridge dreaming aloud. Kathleen Coburn thinks Coleridge could not finish the poem "because it was too closely a representation of his own experience." She connects Geraldine's advances to the poet's nightmares, "in which one gathers he was frequently pursued by unpleasing female figures": "Geraldine is a malignity out of Coleridge's own dreams."[21] Here, from his notebooks, are two such dreams:

a most frightful Dream of a Woman whose features were blended with darkness catching hold of my right eye & attempting to pull it out—I caught hold of her arm fast—a horrid feel—Wordsworth cried out aloud to me hearing my scream—

> I was followed up & down by a frightful pale woman who, I
> thought, wanted to kiss me, & had the property of giving me a
> shameful Disease by breathing in the face
> &️ again I dreamt that a figure of a woman of a gigantic Height,
> dim & indefinite & smokelike appeared—& that I was forced to
> run up toward it—[22]

Coleridge records many dreams of sexual assault, some by males. Once
he feels a man "leaping on me, & grasping my Scrotum." Bostetter sees
the similarity between Geraldine and Coleridge's nightmare woman,
whose size Norman Fruman connects to that of the "tall" and "lofty"
Geraldine.[23] If Geraldine is the imposing figure who pursues Coleridge
in his dreams, then we must logically infer some element of self-
identification in Christabel. Coburn says Christabel is "significantly
one side of his own nature." But these insights, which should have been
so consequential for interpretation of the mystery poems, are left undeveloped, tottering on the edge of the sexually problematic but not
plunging into it.

Christabel contains one of the greatest transsexual self-transformations in literature. I spoke of the drama of the male heroine in *The
Ancient Mariner*, a complex of self-identification sliding into sentimentality. In *Christabel*, the residual maleness of the male heroine is gone,
and gender has shifted completely to the female. Christabel is Coleridge, a poet condemned to fascination by the daemonic. The poem
begins a peculiar nineteenth-century tradition in which a sexually ambivalent poet paints a scene of intense lesbian eroticism in order to
identify himself, by a daring warp of imaginative gender, with the
passive partner. Balzac's Byronic (and therefore Coleridgean) *The Girl
with the Golden Eyes* starts the French version of this theme, which
produces Baudelaire's *Delphine and Hippolyte*, from which in turn
come Swinburne's *Anactoria* and Verlaine's and Pierre Louÿs' Sapphic
idylls. *Christabel* is a ritual of surrender to pagan corruption. Its heroine
is entranced, morally drugged, powerless to flee from an irresistible
power. The vampire Geraldine, an enlargement of the sea-witch of *The
Ancient Mariner*, is the dominatrix of Coleridge's psychic and poetic life.
She is cruel mother nature, whose second coming lays Wordsworth to
rest. She will take Coleridge beyond rescue, to the entombed inner
place where Wordsworth cannot hear his night cry.

Clues within the poem corroborate the identification of Coleridge
with Christabel. The bard dreams of Sir Leoline's pet dove, named for
Christabel, lost in the forest, "a bright green snake / Coiled around its

wings and neck": "With the dove it heaves and stirs, / Swelling its neck as she swelled hers!" He wakes as the clock strikes twelve. It is the hour of Christabel's marriage, now being consummated: dove and snake, locked together, heave, stir, and swell in spasms of pain and ecstasy. Coleridge was drawn to this hybrid image. In "Dejection" (1802), he declares: "Hence, viper thoughts, that coil around my mind, / Reality's dark dream!" His opium addiction, he once said, was a way of "escaping from pains that coiled round my mental powers as a serpent around the body and wings of an eagle!" Thus this metaphor, where he is a bird in the grip of a snake, abode with the poet. Man's body is the mortal coil, and imagination is the serpent-stung bird that cannot fly. Man lies in chains of sex and nature.

Next is the curse laid by Geraldine on Christabel's power of speech, keeping her from informing her father of the rape. This detail must come from the ancient tale of Philomela, a rape victim whose tongue is cut out to ensure her silence. Coleridge mentions her in "The Nightingale" (1798). "O'er-mastered by the mighty spell," Christabel can utter only a single sentence. Her hermaphrodite spouse is "lord of her utterance." Christabel is like Melville's Billy Budd, an innocent ensnared by a homosexual conspirator and undone by a speech impediment. Christabel struggling to speak is a prophetic self-portrait of Coleridge the poet, whose achievement was abortive. By modern standards, Coleridge left an enormous body of work of vast scope. But he died under the burden of great expectations, his own and others'. His masterpiece evaded him. Poetry came to him only in fragments. Hence his apologia, needless to us, for "Kubla Khan," with its spurious knock on the door. Toward the end of life, Coleridge wrote in his notebooks, "From my earliest recollection I have had a consciousness of Power without Strength—a perception, an experience, of more than ordinary power with an inward sense of weaknesse." Hazlitt said of him, "His nose, the rudder of the face, the index of the will, was small, feeble, nothing—like what he has done."[24] Coleridge thought he had "a *feeble*, unmanly face": "The exceeding *weakness*, strengthlessness, in my face, was ever painful to me." After first meeting him, Carlyle said, "His cardinal sin is that he wants *will*. He has no resolution."

Christabel mute is Coleridge irresolute. Her truncated speech is like Lewis Carroll's stammer, which appeared in the challenging company of adults, never children. Carroll portrays himself in *Alice* as the earthbound, dowagerlike Dodo bird, whose name is how Charles Dodgson would have stammered his own last name. Christabel's inability to speak is Coleridge stammering. It represents within the poem the poet's

inability to complete the poem itself. Thus the spell laid upon Christabel is also laid upon Coleridge. It is his struggle with language, his fear
of betrayal by and helpless alienation from language. The inability to
speak is a dark spot in the poem, a melanoma that may spread and stop
all poetry. The danger is that Coleridge will become a Philomela with
her tongue torn out. Kiss but don't tell. The dark spot is a place of
dangerous vision where words have not coalesced. It is a magic circle of
frail tissue where there should be bone, like the soft spot on a baby's
head. I think of the first great script of Rod Serling's *Twilight Zone*,
"Little Girl Lost," where a hole in a bedroom wall sucks a child into
another dimension. So in the boudoir-dominated *Christabel*, the failure
of speech is a zone of desolation that may draw Coleridge's poetry into
nonbeing. The vampire Muse of *Christabel* is a Sphinx, the Greek
"Strangler." She is the riddle of nature that the poet cannot solve. She
brings vision but steals speech. Geraldine is the mother of lies. The
serpent in the garden is a suave forked tongue, eating and entering the
sanctified body of innocence.

Thus Coleridge as Christabel is a tongueless male heroine who is no
longer identifiably male. He is the "coy maid half yielding to her lover"
in "The Eolian Harp" and the "woman wailing for her demon-lover" in
"Kubla Khan." Christabel in the vampire's arms is a lyre sadistically
played upon by daemonic nature. But her music is silence. The story of
nature cannot be told, for she will always betray the heart that loves her.
By land and by sea: the Ancient Mariner's compulsive storytelling is an
early, lesser version of Christabel's muteness. The Mariner tries to solve
by excess of words the mystery that silences Christabel. *Christabel* (Part
I) is the profounder poem. It is not marred by *The Ancient Mariner*'s
sentimentality; its language is dignified, seamless. Why? The Wedding-
Guest cannot get through the doorway of *The Ancient Mariner* because
he is still male. The marriage may go on, but he will not see it. In
Christabel, the doorway is breached and the marriage occurs because
the poet has jettisoned his gender. He disappears into his heroine and
marries his Muse, who will speak for him. Geraldine is a ventriloquist.
She writes the poem, and Christabel suffers it. Coleridge at his sexually
most self-abased is at his poetically most potent. Art transfigures by
self-mutilation.

Extremes meet in *Christabel*: vice and virtue, male and female, nature and society. All is dominated by the daemon. There is no more of
the Ancient Mariner's self-pity, only moral, emotional, and sexual extremity. *Christabel* is a perfection of extremity. It is a hierosgamos, an
unholy marriage, and the boudoir is a mountaintop of vision, where the

poet is mounted by the Muse. As in "To William Wordsworth," it is an epiphany, a peak experience. Geraldine is the poetic will, pure primeval id. As in "Kubla Khan," those struck by prophecy are trapped in taboo. Christabel is shunned, persecuted. Touched, touching, untouchable. Elected by the daemonic, she is *made*, that is both violated and initiated. Like Clodius in drag, Coleridge penetrates the ancient mysteries. Paganism sweeps back into culture. A new phase of history is kicked off by rape. *Christabel*, I think, is one source of Yeats's "Leda and the Swan." Geraldine is the brute god who stuns, rapes, and abandons.

The poem's Christian theme has been completely misread. Christabel is the Christian Coleridge, the hopeful moralist perpetually defeated by the daemonic. The she-that-is-he will never emerge from her enslavement. In *Christabel*, Christianity is abolished by a return of the chthonian. The "love and charity" ending Part I are the epitaph of the Christian Coleridge. Virtue is invoked only to increase the Sadean perversity of transgression. The rape is more passionate, more evil because of the borderlines set up for it to overcome. Christabel, the beautiful Christ, meets her ruin in the barbaric ugliness of mother nature, the old, cold bosom where every man is born and buried.

Christabel is a sexual apocalypse in which Coleridge no longer sees the hermaphrodite god through a glass darkly but face to face. His fascination by Geraldine has made her the autocratic *tyrannos* of the poem, to the detriment of everything in Part II. She illustrates a principle I call psychoiconicism: it governs literary works whose primary inspiration is an experimental, charismatic persona, appearing epiphanically, in iconic frontality. The figure is invested with so much psychic power that other characters lose fictive energy and fade into the background. Sir Leoline, for example, is merely a sketch, part of the décor. Psychoiconicism resembles the register method of Egyptian wall art, where the hierarchically central figure is three times larger than lesser mortals. Psychoiconicism is produced by the west's obsessive ritualization of personality. Spenser's Amazonian Belphoebe is psychoiconistic. Her scale of representation is startlingly disproportionate to that of characters around her, with whom her dramatic interaction is awkward and stilted. Psychoiconicism accounts for the inequality between Rosalind and her admirers in *As You Like It* and for the expository patchiness of Woolf's transsexual *Orlando*. Hermaphrodite visions have a life of their own. They are vampires upon their own texts.

Geraldine is one of the greatest androgynes of art. She has a refined feminine beauty but a masculine spirit. She is like the narcissistic witch-queen of *Snow White*, the wicked stepmother of fairy tales who is a projection of the repressed negativity of and toward the real mother. Christabel protests her father's alliance with Geraldine like a child refusing to accept a widower's new wife. The poem's lesbianism is paralleled by the family romance of *Snow White*, in which Bloom sees traces of mother-daughter incest. Walt Disney's *Snow White*, which I saw at three, had the same stunning effect on me that *Christabel* did on Shelley. The witch-queen is a persona lying utterly outside the moral universe of Christianity. It is a pre-Christian form of the malevolent nature mother.

In *Christabel*, pagan imagism triumphs over the Judeo-Christian word. It is fitting, therefore, that the only modern parallels to Geraldine occur in cinema, our machine of the aggressive eye. Marlene Dietrich in *Morocco*, Maria Casarès in *Orphée* and *Les Dames du Bois de Boulogne*, Lauren Bacall in *Young Man with a Horn*, Stéphane Audran in *Les Biches:* elegance, sophistication, composure, cold lesbian will. The vampire eye penetrates space and time. *Christabel*'s voyeurism, like that of *The Faerie Queene*, reflects the unacknowledged voyeurism of western art. The vampire, as we see from the replay from Geraldine's point of view in the Conclusion to Part I, has been watching all along, and most evilly, she makes the defeated mother watch the rape of her own daughter. The thousand hungry eyes of daemonic nature wait in the forest of the night.

Christabel is a pornographic parable of western sex and power. It is the English *Faust*. Domination and seduction are at the center of western knowing. Coleridge's self-immolating male heroines descend through Poe and Dostoyevsky to Kafka, whose crucified cockroach is a comic version of mute Christabel. Defloration in *Christabel* is Wordsworth despoiled, his happy flowering fields stripped to reveal nature's brute chthonian substratum. *Christabel* shows the conflict, hostility, and ambivalence in love and poetry. It rebukes the liberal idealizers of emotion. Coleridge's lifelong desire to "finish" the poem was misconceived. His additions to it, like the nervous marginalia of *The Ancient Mariner*, are a form of self-thwarting, another stammering. They are a blatant deflection of the poem's authentic inspiration, where the vampire has an authoritarian glamour and supernatural self-assurance. Geraldine is the daemonic spirit of archaic night, and in Coleridge's original and truer conception, her power has no beginning and no end.

13

Speed and Space

Byron

The second generation of English Romantic poets inherited the achievement of the first. Byron, Shelley, and Keats read and absorbed Wordsworth and Coleridge's poems and gave them new form. The younger men created the myth of the doomed Romantic artist. All three went into exile and died young, in pagan Italy and Greece. Publicity and fashion made them sex-heroes of European high society: they were real-life sexual personae, as Blake, Wordsworth, and Coleridge were not. The poems of Byron, Shelley, and Keats are theatrical gestures of self-definition. The first Romantic generation released the psychic energy in which the second swam and sometimes drowned. Achieving freedom is one problem, surviving freedom another. The early deaths of Byron, Shelley, and Keats demonstrate the intolerable pressures in the Romantic and liberal world-view. Blake and Wordsworth wanted identity without personality: but personality is ultimate western reality. Byron, Shelley, and Keats had a love-hate relationship with personality, their own and others'.

Lord Byron makes Romantic incest stunningly explicit. I see *Manfred* (1817) as a cross-fertilization of Goethe's *Faust* with Wordsworth's *Tintern Abbey*. Byron's passionate hero is tormented by guilt for some mysterious crime. He is obsessed with his dead sister Astarte, his twin in eyes, face, and voice. Byron relishes sexual criminality. Forbidden love makes his characters superhuman. Rejecting all social relationships, Manfred seeks only himself in sexually transmuted form. Wordsworth's sister allows him to remain alone, sex-free, but Astarte (Phoenician Venus) lures Manfred into the vertigo of sex.

The sister-spirit appears in *Manfred* at exactly the point where she materializes in *Tintern Abbey*. Astarte died in Manfred's tower when her heart "wither'd" while gazing on his. She has no tomb. What happened? Where is she? Manfred's western lust for knowledge annihilates his sister, like Faust with Gretchen. Oscar Wilde reimagines the scene in the climax of *The Picture of Dorian Gray*, where two doubles, a man and his portrait, confront each other in a locked attic room. The man is found dead, hideously "withered"—Byron's word.[1] Astarte, gazing at her brother's heart as if into a mirror, dies of daemonic narcissism. Brother and sister trespass the borderlines of western identity and exchange personality. Manfred merges too fiercely with his sister. He assimilates her. How else explain the disappearance of her body?

Manfred's union with his sister is a solipsistic sex-experiment that fails. His restlessness and remorse are symptoms of his engorgement by her. Like Thyestes, Manfred has eaten his own flesh; like Kronos, he must vomit it out. Because real sexual relations have occurred between Manfred and his double, the physical world becomes intolerable to him. Byron's poem is surrealistically expanded in Poe's *The Fall of the House of Usher*, where the sister, entombed in the skull-like house, returns as a bloody apparition to stalk her hysterical brother. In Byron, the sister-spirit's materialization promises psychic relief. Manfred appeals to her to speak, so she can regain her autonomy and *stay* externalized. But she only prophesies her brother's death and disappears. I say sister collapses back into brother, renewing his sufferings.

In *Tintern Abbey*, Wordsworth's sister does not need to speak. She is the *anima* in correct relation to the poet. The intercourse of brother and sister is spiritual, not physical. In *Manfred*, fraternal intercourse is violent and voracious. Blood is shed, which Manfred hallucinates on a wine cup. He has ruptured his sister's virginity. The blood-rimmed cup from which he cannot drink is a nightmare vision of the locus of violation. It is also his bloody mind and bloody tongue, thinking and speaking against nature.

Like Coleridge's *Christabel, Manfred* centers on a ritual sex act defying social and moral law. In the poem's pagan cult of self-worship, matrimony, communion, and last rites are simultaneous. The ritual victim is torn by the phallic knife and her flesh consumed. Astarte is tombless because she has been perversely absorbed, body and soul, by her brother. As in Poe's *The Tell-Tale Heart,* Manfred is tormented by the internal presence of another being, illegitimately enwombed like a daemonic fetus. Manfred is the Romantic solipsist who has devoured the universe, but it sickens within him. Amputation or self-gorging? Kleist's Achilles makes one choice, Byron's Manfred another. The self is out of sync with the object-world, which floods in or cruelly withdraws, marooning Wordsworth's puckered solitaries. In *Manfred* Byron makes illicit sex the lists of combat. Romantic sexual personae scratch and claw in attraction and repulsion.

Rumor said Byron committed incest with his half-sister, Augusta Leigh. True or false, the story added to his fame. Incest obsessively recurs in Byron's poems. *Cain* turns the issue into legal conundrum. God allows incest for mankind's second generation, who must marry their siblings. The poem dwells on the mutual love of Cain and his twin sister, incredulous at the prohibition of fraternal sexuality to their own children. In "Parisina," the Phaedra-like incest is between wife and stepson, an exception to Byron's favorite brother-sister pattern. Originally, Byron's central characters in "The Bride of Abydos" were brother and sister in love. In the final version, they are first cousins. But their infatuation dates from childhood, and the girl still believes the boy her brother when, feverishly kissing him, she rejects an arranged marriage. Byron says, "Great is their love who love in sin and fear" ("Heaven and Earth"). Incest is sexual dissent. Its value is in impurity. Byron would spurn Blakean innocence. He takes the Sadean approach to sex and psyche: make a line, so I can cross it. Unlike Blake or Wordsworth, Byron wants to reinforce the boundaries of self. In incest, libido moves out and back, making a uroboros-circle of regression and dynastic exclusiveness.

Romanticism's feminization of the male persona becomes effeminacy in Byron. The unmanly hero of "The Bride of Abydos" is stranded among women. Incestuous feeling is incubated in an Oriental haze. "The Corsair" introduces seductive Gulnare, to appear transvestite in a sequel. Gulnare's relations with the corsair are like Kleist's Penthesilea with Achilles, a dancelike exchange of strength and weakness. There are heroic rescues, then capture, humiliation, and recovery. Byron ritualistically elaborates each stage of assertion and passivity, making the narrative a slow masque of sexual personae.

Until the end of "Lara," Byron teasingly implies that the effeminate pageboy, Kaled, is homosexually attached to the chieftain Lara. The truth outs when Lara is killed and the boy faints. Bystanders reviving him loosen his garments and discover Kaled is the woman Gulnare, in love with the corsair Lara. Byron's rippling poetry makes sexual metamorphosis happen before our eyes. First we are admiring "the glossy tendrils" of a beautiful boy's "raven hair." Suddenly, he swoons into sensuous passivity. Now we join the voyeuristic marvelling at public exposure of a woman's breasts, as she lies unconscious. Homosexual and heterosexual responses have been successively induced or extorted from the reader. The blink-of-an-eye sex change recalls Spenser's switch of sexual perspective, but Byron retains his woman's male name to prolong her sexual ambiguity. Surely Gautier imitates this scene in *Mademoiselle de Maupin*, when a page is knocked unconscious from his horse and his shirt parted to reveal a girl's "very white bosom." I think it all ends up in *National Velvet* (1944, from Enid Bagnold's novel), where a fallen jockey, played by the young Elizabeth Taylor, is carried unconscious from the race course. The motif is now safely sanitized: a doctor, not titillated passersby, undrapes the succulent bosom.

"Lara"'s sex games echo Byron's own. After leaving Cambridge, Byron had an affair with a girl whom he dressed as a boy and called his brother. G. Wilson Knight suggests Lady Caroline Lamb masqueraded as a pageboy to rekindle the poet's fading passion.[2] Byron probably models Kaled's service to Lord Lara on that of transvestite Viola to Duke Orsino in *Twelfth Night*. Byron's responses are as bisexual as Shakespeare's. He is equally and even simultaneously aroused by an effeminate boy and a bold cross-dressing woman. Byron's last poems are addressed to a handsome Greek youth with whom he was unhappily infatuated. His early poems to "Thyrza" were inspired by a Cambridge choirboy, probably John Edleston. The boy has a female name partly because the poems could not have been published otherwise. But this is also an example of my principle of sexual metathesis, a shift in gender producing a special eroticism. We feel it in Byron's lascivious delight in "Lara"'s open-air spectacle of sexual unmasking—the topos of de-blousing, recreating the mood of the naughty Italian romances purified by Shakespeare.

In *Sardanapalus* (1821), Byron vies directly with Shakespeare. The poem recasts *Antony and Cleopatra*—with the hero as Antony *and* Cleopatra. In a prefatory note, Byron claims he got the story from Diodorus Siculus. The Greek Sardanapalus bore little resemblance to the Assyrian king and general, Assurbanipal. Delacroix's crimson tableau shows Byron's Sardanapalus amid the decadent conflagration of empire. Byron begins his poem as Shakespeare begins his play: a hostile bystander scorns the sexual degeneracy of the protagonist, who enters for our inspection. In Shakespeare, the cynical commentary is contradicted by Antony and Cleopatra's love. Byron's Sardanapalus, however, is just as unmanly as foretold. He sweeps onstage crowned with flowers and "effeminately dressed," followed by a train of women and young slaves. Sardanapalus is Euripides' Dionysus with his Maenads—but now Dionysus is king. We are in Shakespeare's Egypt, a liquid realm of

woman, music, and perfume. Maleness dissolves. The king's companions include eunuchs, "beings less than women." Sardanapalus'
brother-in-law calls him "the grandson of Semiramis, the man-queen."
Who's the queen, Semiramis or Sardanapalus? Calling his hero a "she-
king," a "*she* Sardanapalus," Byron develops an entire character out of
Antony's transvestite game. Sardanapalus denies he is a soldier and
denounces the word and all who identify with it. Byron tries to argue
that Sardanapalus' manhood is more comprehensive than the ordinary.
But morality is not the Romantic strong suit. Byron quickly flits off into
sexual caprice, his best manner. Sardanapalus' feminized masculinity is
far from efficacious. His kingdom is destroyed, and he with it.

Sardanapalus is an experiment in personae: how far can a male
protagonist be shifted toward the female extreme without total loss of
masculinity? The enervation in *Sardanapalus* is more extreme than
anything in *Antony and Cleopatra*, which bursts with Renaissance energy. In his journal Byron speaks of the delightful "calm nothingness of
languour" and elsewhere describes a "voluptuous state, / At once Ely-
sian and effeminate" ("The Island"). This floating condition sabotages
Sardanapalus. The king laments the heaviness of objects, as if his
muscles have atrophied. Sardanapalus is western personality submerged in Dionysian flux. When military crisis forces him into the
social world, reality seems stubbornly dense.

Sardanapalus' most masculine moment is his arming for battle, prefigured in Shakespeare when Cleopatra acts as Antony's arms-bearer.
Sardanapalus calls for his cuirass, baldric, helmet, spear—and mirror.
He flings away his helmet because it doesn't look good. The king of
Assyria, who should be psyching himself up for battle, seems more like
a lady trying on hats. Shakespeare's hero is attended by his lover. In
Byron, the lover becomes a mirror. Sardanapalus is the complete Romantic hero, in love with his mirror-image. He is his own audience and
critic, a projected eye. Byron nullifies Sardanapalus' manhood with
feminine narcissism. We saw this pattern in Lewis' *The Monk*, where
each sexual movement immediately swings in the opposite direction.
Sardanapalus risks his life by fighting bare-headed, apparently because
he wants to show off "his flowing hair." This hair belongs to the poet of
Coleridge's "Kubla Khan," whose sexual ambiguity Byron divines. Byron attaches Coleridge's whole line to the king's Amazon slave, Myrrha
(Dante's incestuous sinner), who strides into battle with "her floating
hair and flashing eyes." Poets, unlike critics, sense the sex and decadence in art.

As a program for androgyny, *Sardanapalus* is unconvincing. I find the poem more ominous than does Knight, who praises the "poet-like" hero for "joining man's reason to woman's emotional depth."[3] Sardanapalus seems too vain and whimsical to lead a nation, or even produce art. The brawling Cleopatra gets more done. The effeminacy of Byron's hero is perverse, not ideal. *Sardanapalus'* richness of Shakespearean reference raises an interesting question. Byron always spoke negatively of Shakespeare. Lady Blessington concluded Byron must be feigning animosity, since he knew so much Shakespeare by heart. Bloom's anxiety of influence would suggest that Byron owed Shakespeare too much and was determined to deny it, even to himself.

In *Don Juan* (1819–24), his longest and greatest poem, Byron invents another sexually unconventional hero. The seducer Don Juan, a Renaissance Spaniard, is one of the west's unique sexual personae. In contrast to Mozart's Don Giovanni, Byron's Don Juan is smaller, shyer, more "feminine." He is "a most beauteous boy," "slight and slim, / Blushing and beardless," perfect as "one of the seraphim" (VIII.52; IX.53, 47). Juan is partly Byron and partly what Byron likes in boys. Knight, Frye, and Bloom comment on the hero's sexual passivity toward dominant women.[4] When Juan is sold as a slave in Constantinople, a eunuch forces him into female clothing, supplemented by makeup and judicious tweezing. Juan has caught the sultana's eye. By transvestism he can be smuggled into the harem for her pleasure. Byron's sensual, self-enclosed harem world is like Blake's rose, femaleness multiplied and condensed in a small humid circle.

The sultana Gulbeyaz is one of Romanticism's most potent women. *Don Juan* continues *Sardanapalus'* maneuvering of an effeminate male along the sexual spectrum. Juan's tenuous manhood is near-obliterated by female drag. Now Byron shoves him next to an Amazon dominatrix. Juan in petticoats is a trembling pawn upon whom the raging queen bears down. Gulbeyaz is the Cleopatra missing from *Sardanapalus.* She is the androgyne as virago, luxuriously female in body but harshly male in spirit. Gulbeyaz has Cleopatra's vigorous duality: her "large eyes" show "half-voluptuousness and half-command." She is "imperial, or imperious," with a haughty smile of "self-will." Her eyes "flash'd always fire," blending "passion and power" (V.108, 110–11, 134, 116). Gulbeyaz wears a male poniard at her waist. Byron's sultana will end up as a smouldering Spanish marquise in Balzac's *The Girl with the Golden Eyes*, where that poniard is drawn and dreadfully used.

Gulbeyaz's entrance into the poem overwhelms Don Juan's residual masculinity. Introduced as a girl to sultan and harem, he blushes and shakes. Byron chooses not to defend his hero's virility and mischie-

vously absents himself to take the sexually external point of view. Poor
Juan is now simply "she" and "her." Even Spenser, after briefing the
reader, allows his transvestites their proper pronoun. In the next canto,
Byron allows "he" intermittent return. But it is rudely jostled by the
harem's unflagging attention to the newcomer: "Her shape, her hair,
her air, her everything" (VI.35). Gossip, admiration, envy: Juan's female
alter ego is fixed by and projected to a captive audience. Asked his
name, Juan replies "Juanna." And Juanna he is called for the rest of the
Turkish episode, even by Byron himself. This sex transformation of his
own name is a sign of Juan's developing sexual complicity, like Coleridge's Christabel lifting the vampire over the threshold. Apologizing
for calling his hero Juanna, Byron wantonly stresses the sexual equivo-
cal: "I say *her* because, / The gender still was epicene" (58). Even at his
most perverse, Spenser is never this coy. Byron is flirting with the reader,
something new in literature.

Logically, a young man spirited into a harem, like a fox in a hen-
house, should soon profit from his access to, as Byron puts it, "a thousand bosoms there / Beating for love" (26). But this is a Romantic and
not a Renaissance poem, and in a Romantic poem, as should now be
clear, virility is granted no privileges. Juan becomes the object of desire
not because he is male but because he is thought female. The harem
women fight over who is to sleep with Juanna, and more than sleep is on
their minds: "Lolah's eyes sparkled at the proposition" (82). Gulbeyaz is
included in this steamy stuff. The sultan is "always so polite" as to
announce his conjugal visits in advance, "especially at night." Since the
harem is marked by "the absence of all men," the sultan would presumably not be surprised to find Gulbeyaz in bed with her own women
(V.146; VI.32) *Don Juan*'s lesbian innuendos frustrate conventional
sexual expectation. How does one defeat the virility of a man at happy
liberty in a harem? The Romantic poem, with cross-sexual virtuosity,
blithely replies: why, by turning him into a transvestite and making him
the object of lesbian lust!

The rest of *Don Juan* is a series of sexcapades across Asia and Europe.
The unfinished poem ends in female transvestism, a scene probably
inspired by *The Monk:* Juan's bedchamber is invaded by a ghostly,
hooded friar, whom the closing words reveal to be a "voluptuous"
woman. The best things in *Don Juan* take place in the Near East, which
Napoleon's expedition to Egypt in 1798 had made a subject of European interest. Knight says "Byron is saturated in oriental sympathies."[5]
Byron's Orient, like Shakespeare's, is an emotionally expansive realm
liquefying European sexual personae. Genders proliferate: Byron calls

eunuchs and castrati "the third sex." We cannot comprehend the mysteries of love, he says, until we imitate "wise Tiresias" and sample "the
several sexes." *Don Juan*'s teeming eunuchs—the sultan's eunuch train
is "a quarter of a mile" long—are extreme versions of its androgynous
hero. Transvestite Juan subject to Gulbeyaz is like a castrate priest of
Cybele. The Byronic Orient is matriarchal. *Don Juan*'s seraglio, a "labyrinth of females," is a drowsy Spenserian bower, the womb-tomb of the
male will. As in *Antony and Cleopatra*, the Orient also stands for liberated imagination. It is the anarchic unconscious, a dream-world of
unstable sex and identity where objects cannot hold their Apollonian
shape.

Don Juan's free and easy style is difficult to analyze. Style reflects
poet. Spengler says western history demands "contrapuntally strong
accents—wars or big personalities—at the decisive points."[6] The huge
influence of Byron's personality on the nineteenth century is still incompletely assessed. His early poems of brooding defiance, like *Cain*
and *Manfred*, conform to the popular image of Byronism, but *Don Juan*
actually captures the poet's essential spirit. *Don Juan* is emotionally
various and comprehensive. Bloom says, "The last word in a discussion
of *Don Juan* ought not to be 'irony' but 'mobility', one of Byron's favorite
terms."[7] Byron defined mobility as "an excessive susceptibility of immediate impressions." The mobile male is receptive and half-feminine. I
myself hit upon "mobility" to describe the psychic volatility of Shakespeare's boys and women, whom his plays class with lovers, lunatics,
and poets. The many moods of *Don Juan*'s omniscient narrator make
him a Mercurius of multiple personae. The poem explores the emotional tonalities available to a poetic voice speaking for itself and not
through projected characters. It is analogous to Chopin's development
of the lyric potential of the piano. In *Don Juan* Byron takes himself for
subject nearly as forthrightly as Wordsworth does in *The Prelude*.

Byron's dedication to *Don Juan* attacks Wordsworth, Coleridge, and
Southey for "a narrowness . . . which makes me wish you'd change your
lakes for ocean." A lake is enclosed and trapped by the conventional and
known. No one point of view can do justice to ocean, vast and metamorphic. Byronic energy overflows Wordsworthian decorum. Impa-
tiently, Byron overlooks the sexual ambivalences in Wordsworth and
daemonic Coleridge. He charges them with parochialism, with dam-
ming up the waters of emotion in stagnant spiritual ponds. The English
are traditionally a seafaring people. Their location on an island amidst a
turbulent northern ocean contributed to the outpouring poetic vitality of

the English Renaissance. By the early nineteenth century, the psychic fluidity of Shakespeare's England was long gone. Like Shelley, Byron, the most mobile of poets, fled the resentments of a closed society. The English had become emotionally and sexually landlocked. Frazer links ancient Egypt's stability and conservatism to its desert geography. Agriculture's "monotonous routine" gives the farmer "a settled phlegmatic habit of mind very different from the mobility, the alertness, the pliability of character which the hazards and uncertainties of commerce and the sea foster in the merchant and the sailor," with their "mercurial spirit."[8] In *Don Juan*, Byron takes English imagination back to sea. As Juan is tossed and turned by adventure, the narrator's shifting voice recreates the ceaseless sea change of sex and emotion.

Like *Childe Harold's Pilgrimage*, which made Byron famous, *Don Juan* is structured by the archetypal journey theme. But *Don Juan*'s journeying has *speed*. Alvin Kernan speaks of an "onward rush" in the poem, "a vital forceful onward movement."[9] From locomotive to jet plane, speed has transformed modern life. The Renaissance reeled from its sudden expansion of space, as the known world doubled and tripled. Speed is western domination of space, a linear track of the aggressive will. Modern speed alters perception. As late as 1910, E. M. Forster's heroine in *Howards End* resists the new speed of the motorcar, which makes her lose "all sense of space." Mr. Wilcox sings out, "There's a pretty church—oh, you aren't sharp enough." Margaret's premodern eye moves sluggishly: "She looked at the scenery. It heaved and merged like porridge. Presently it congealed. They had arrived."[10] Speed melts the object-world without remaking it. Revolutionary Byron senses an imminent change in the nature of space, which he did not live to see. *Don Juan* marks the first appearance in art of modern speed.

Critics sometimes speak of the "swiftness" of Shelley's poetry. But Shelley's movement is upward. He seeks rhapsodic exaltation (*exaltare* means "to lift up"). Byron is never exalted. His movement is secular and vehicular. Byron's space was created by the Renaissance Age of Discovery and measured by the Enlightenment. Speaking of Milton, Don Cameron Allen says Judeo-Christianity urges man "to abandon the horizontal movement of human history for the vertical motion of the spiritual life."[11] Shelley is spiritual verticality, Byron earthly horizontality. Shelley is always subverting horizontals: the Witch of Atlas' boat defies gravity and sails upstream, or the procession of "The Triumph of Time" shows life as a leaden line of slaves. Shelley's objects, as we shall see, are weightless and porous, penetrated by vision. Byron's concrete objects are firmly fixed in space and time. Shelley's imagination moves, but what moves in Byron is the body. Byron is a Greek athlete, challenging and surpassing. Objects are his counters and stepping stones.

Shelley's and Byron's speed are energized by different principles of sex-transcendance. *Don Juan*'s speed is a skimming, like Raphael's Galatea flying in her chariot across the sea. But Galatea is drawn by porpoises. Byron's speed is *self-motivating*. All self-motivating speed is hermaphroditic—in angels, Vergil's Camilla, or Giambologna's Mercury. Pope's Camilla "skims along the Main" (*An Essay on Criticism*, 373). Byron actually compares the dancing Don Juan to Vergil's Amazon: "Like swift Camilla, he scarce skimm'd the ground" (XIV.39). Don Juan the character and *Don Juan* the poem are world-skimmers. The skimming is in both style and content. Byron's poetry is not "finished," that is, finely crafted and polished. Sir Walter Scott saw in Byron "the careless and negligent ease of a man of quality." Calling him "slovenly, slipshod," Matthew Arnold rebuked Byron for "negligence" and "want of art, in his workmanship as a poet."[12] But this slapdash freedom gives Byron his relentless forward propulsion. Since the lines are not crisply formed, each tips into the next with breathless haste. Shakespeare's spilling lines are weightier, his diction craggier. I said vision in Coleridge and Poe often overpowers language, leaving it rude or weak: words run hot and cold, gorgeous splotches followed by shabby scrabble. But Byron's poetry has evenness of texture, a liquid fluency. Byron greatly admired the Augustan poets, but though his aristocratic satire is Augustan, his style is not. There is no braking midline caesura, nor is there Pope's massy orotundity. Byron cultivates a sensation of linearity. His verse is like a clear, rapid stream. Byron's objects have a friendly exactitude. His moods and objects are tumbled like smooth pebbles in the stream of his poetry. Love and hate, male and female, lobster salad and champagne: this is Byron's object-world in genial rolling flux. All come together in his poetry to make us feel we are skimming a surface.

Poetry began as music, and music began as dance. Shelley's movements are like those of classical ballet, which takes place in abstract space. Ballet ideologically defies gravity. Great male dancers are applauded for their ability to hover at the crest of their leaps, as if momentarily breaking their tie to earth. Female dancers mutilate their feet to remain inhumanly on point, keeping their contact with earth to the absolute minimum. The arms extended from the body, a gesture originating in the Baroque court, suggest wings, contempt for the earth's surface. Ballet is the body rising. Ballet is ceremonial and hieratic. Its disdain for the commonplace material world is the source of its authority and glamour. Ballet is Apollonian. Martha Graham invented or rather reinvented chthonian dance. Modern dance is primitivistic and pelvic. It slaps bare feet on mother earth and contracts with her spasms. The dance of Byron's poetry is neither Apollonian nor chthonian. Byron is attuned neither to sky nor to earth's bowels. He skims earth's surface, midway between realms. *Don Juan*'s Byronic style is found in only one dancer: Fred Astaire. Astaire's supple dancing is a silvery gliding along hard polished surfaces. There is no balletic aspiration in Astaire. He is the here and now, a sophisticate moving in cosmopolitan space. Even when springing up on chairs or climbing the walls, Astaire is exploring the dimensions of our common life. Rudolf Nureyev is a haughty Lucifer shut out from heaven, which he tries to reach in angry leaps. Nureyev is early Byron, tense and defiant. Astaire (and his admirer, Mikhail Baryshnikov) is late Byron. Astaire is a suave reed bending to the wind. He has Byron's "ease," the well-bred manners and gentle smiling irony. Astaire is as elegantly elongated as Giambologna's Mercury. With his smooth head and slim body, he is ageless and androgynous. He is a gracious host or guide, like Milton's Raphael, "the sociable Spirit" or "affable Arch-angel." Astaire's fluid grace is Byron's mobility, skimming across the world.

Byron knew both his speed and his space. His dedication to *Don Juan* proclaims to rival poets that, "wandering with pedestrian Muses," he will not contend with them "on the wingèd steed." He is not Nureyev, making Pegasus-like skyward leaps, but Astaire, spiralling across the earth's dance floor with merry carnal Muses (Ginger Rogers, Rita Hayworth). An eternal "wandering" or surface-skimming: like all picaresque works, Byron's travel poems have no necessary ending and could go on and on. I call *Don Juan*'s lightness and quickness *breeziness*. A connection to Camilla: Jackson Knight says the idea of a fleet figure running atop the grain stalks may have originated in Volscian belief in "the presence of some spirit of the corn."[13] So the meadows' wavelike motion is the wind's invisible steps. The breeziness of *Don Juan* is the freshness of a spring breeze, a new spirit entering and aerating history. The breeze emanating from Byron—literally, his emanation—is the spirit of youth, which was to have enormous impact upon European and American culture. Rousseau invented the modern cult of childhood; Goethe popularized Rousseau's moody adolescent. But Byron created the glamourous sexy youth of brash, defiant energy, *the new* embodied in a charismatic sexual persona. Hence Byron senses the dawn of the age of speed. Youth is swiftness in emotionally *transient* form. Transience, from the Latin *transeo*, contains the ideas both of travel and of the short-lived. Byron, portrayed by Goethe as the androgynous, self-thwarted Euphorion, died in 1824. The first passenger locomotive appeared in 1825. Byron's spirit seems to have transmigrated into the engine of speed.

Surveys show that two advertising words rivet our attention: "free" and "new." We still live in the age of Romanticism. When novelty is worshipped, nothing can last. Byronic youth-culture flourishes in rock music, the ubiquitous American art form. *Don Juan*'s emotional and poetic style is replicated in a classic American experience: driving flat-out on a highway, radio blaring. Driving is the American sublime, for which there is no perfect parallel in Europe. Ten miles outside any American city, the frontier is wide open. Our long, straight super-highways crisscross vast space. Mercury and Camilla's self-motivating speed: the modern automobile, plentifully panelled with glass, is so quick, smooth, and discreet, it seems an extension of the body. To traverse or *skim* the American landscape in such a vehicle is to feel the speed and aerated space of *Don Juan*. Rock music pulsing on the radio is the car's heartbeat. European radio stations are few and mostly state-controlled. But American radio-bands teem with music and voices, like the many moods of Byron's poem. Driving through upstate New York, horizontally slashed by six hours of straight-as-the-crow-flies Thruway, one hears music from Illinois, Kentucky, North Carolina, as distant as Italy is from England. Twirling the radio dial while travelling the open road, the American driver flies along on a continuous surface of music, with a sublime sense of huge space surveyed and subsumed.

Rock music is normally a darkly daemonic mode. The Rolling Stones, the greatest rock band, are heirs of stormy Coleridge. But rock has an Apollonian daylight style as well, a combination of sun and speed: the Beach Boys. *Don Juan* and the Beach Boys combine youth, androgyny, aeration, and speed. Lillian Roxon calls the Beach Boys' first album "a celebration of airiness and speed, speed on the water or the road."[14] The romance of motion survives in the Beach Boys' soaring harmonies and chugging sound, like the chuff-chuff-chuff of a locomotive or steamboat. The Beach Boys made the California surfer a new American archetype, like the cowboy. Surfing, of course, is *skimming* in its purest form.

The Beach Boys use a falsetto lead voice set against a boyish chorale; their sound is effeminate and yet enthusiastically heterosexual, as in the immortal "California Girls." We find the same odd combination in Byron. Byron may have been partly or even primarily homosexual, but his poetry affects a distinctive eroticism of effeminate heterosexuality. The

Beach Boys' seraphic boy voice gives an unexpected beauty and religiosity to their trivial high-school themes. The tone is Byronic: sympathy and satire, without cynicism. In their exuberance, hedonism, and mannered irrelevance, the Beach Boys epitomize the self-sustaining and annoyingly self-congratulatory modern youth culture that Byron began. The American teenager in a souped-up car bursts the confines of adult space.

Why did Byron's poetry turn to skimming? Bernard Blackstone remarks, "We know how much Byron objected to seeing his wife eating, and while this may have something to do with his own horror of obesity and recollections of his mother's gormandising, there were probably moments at which Byron saw himself as an homunculus between the steady munch, munch of Annabella's upper and lower jaws."[15] Byron had a weight problem and struggled to keep thin, even by starving himself. Fat is femaleness, nature's abundance, symbolized in the bulging Venus of Willendorf. Femaleness, I argued, is primitive and archaic, while femininity is social and aesthetic. Byron courts femininity but flees femaleness. His fear of fat is his fear of engorgement by mother and wife. Woman gets under his skin. Skimming is keeping the fat off, in soup or milk. *Don Juan*'s skimming is a defense mechanism, a compromise between earth's primitive chthonianism and sky's repressive Apollonianism. Byron keeps moving, reclaiming space from mother nature. Byron's Sardanapalus eliminates and supplants Cleopatra because Byron fears the femme fatale and female stasis. Even fierce Gulbeyaz is trapped in a male world, the sultan's prisoner.

Byron loved water and was so expert a swimmer that he wondered if he had been a merman in a previous life. He chose a mermaid for his carriage crest. Is the mermaid androgynous Byron—or archetypal woman closed to penetration? Swimming was club-footed Byron's freest motion. One of his feats was swimming the Hellespont: Byron honored liquidity but sought to dominate it, athletically. As much as Wordsworth, he wanted nature without chthonian danger. The clarity of Byron's late style is a denial of the murk of woman and water. Female fluids are opaque, resistant; fat, the wateriest part of our body, is mother nature's grip on the human will. Like Blake, Byron refuses to yield to Jehovah *or* Cybele. "Run, run, run," say a dozen classic rock songs. To grow, a plant must put down roots. So keep young and die. Byron's restless animal motion defeats his female vegetable flesh. *Don Juan* does not stop because Byron cannot stop.

A contemporary spoke of Byron's "magical influence" on people. Mary Shelley said of him, "There was something enchanting in his

34. Thomas Phillips, *Lord Byron*, 1814.

manner, his voice, his smile—a fascination in them."[16] Byron had pure charisma, a power of personality divorced from the conceptual or moral. Charisma is electromagnetism, a scintillating fusion of masculine and feminine. Lady Blessington said Byron's "voice and accent are peculiarly agreeable, but effeminate." His friend Moore saw "a feminine cast of character" in "his caprices, fits of weeping, sudden affections and dislikes."[17] Byron belongs to the category of androgyne I invented for Michelangelo's *Giuliano de' Medici*: Epicoene, or the man of beauty, an athlete of alabaster skin. Jane Porter found Byron's complexion "softly brilliant," with a "moonlight paleness." Lady Blessington called his face "peculiarly pale," set off by curling hair of "very dark brown": "He

35. *Elvis Presley* in the film
Speedway, 1968.

uses a good deal of oil in it, which makes it look still darker."[18] White
skin, dark oiled hair: Elvis Presley. In homage to singer Roy Orbison,
Presley dyed his brown-blonde hair black and continued to do so to the
end, despite friends' urging to let the natural color return. Presley, a
myth-maker, understood the essence of his archetypal beauty.

Byron and Elvis Presley look alike, especially in strong-nosed Greek
profile (figs. 34 and 35). In *Glenarvon*, a roman à clef about her affair
with Byron, Caroline Lamb says of her heroine's first glimpse of him,
"The proud curl of the upper lip expressed haughtiness and bitter
contempt."[19] Presley's sneer was so emblematic that he joked about it.
In a 1968 television special, he twitched his mouth and murmured, to
audience laughter, "I've got something on my lip." The Romantic curling lip is aristocratic disdain: Presley is still called "the King," testimony to the ritual needs of a democratic populace. As revolutionary
sexual personae, Byron and Presley had early and late styles: brooding
menace, then urbane magnanimity. Their everyday manners were
manly and gentle. Presley had a captivating soft-spoken charm. The
Byronic hero, says Peter Thorslev, is "invariably courteous toward

women."[20] Byron and Presley were world-shapers, conduits of titanic force, yet they were deeply emotional and sentimental in a feminine sense.

Both had late Orientalizing periods. Byron, drawn to oriental themes, went off to fight the Turks in the Greek war of independence and died of a mysterious illness at Missolonghi. A portrait shows him in silk turban and embroidered Albanian dress. The costume style of Presley's last decade was nearly Mithraic: jewel-encrusted silk jumpsuits, huge studded belts, rings, chains, sashes, scarves. This resembles Napoleon's late phase, as in Ingres' portrait of the emperor enthroned in Byzantine splendor, weighed down in velvet, ermine, and jewels. Napoleon, Byron, and Presley began in simplicity as flaming assertions of youthful male will, and all three ended as ornate *objets de culte*. British legend envisions a "westering" of culture: Troy to Rome to London. But there is also an eastering of culture. We are far from our historical roots in Mesopotamia and Asia Minor; yet again and again, collective emotion swelling about a charismatic European personality instinctively returns him or her to the east. Elizabeth I also ended as a glittering Byzantine icon.

Another parallel: Byron and Presley were renowned for athletic vigor, yet both suffered chronic ailments that somehow never marred their glossy complexions or robust beauty. Both constantly fought off corpulence, Presley losing toward the end. Both died prematurely, Byron at thirty-six, Presley at forty-two. Byron's autopsy revealed an enlarged heart, degenerated liver and gall bladder, cerebral inflammation, and obliteration of the skull sutures.[21] Presley suffered an enlarged heart and degenerated colon and liver. In both cases, tremendous physical energy was oddly fused with internal disorder, a revolt of the organism. Presley's drugs were symptom, not cause. Psychogenetically, Byron and Presley practiced the secret art of feminine self-impairment.

Discussing Michelangelo's *Giuliano*, I noted the statue's swanlike neck, strangely contrasting with the massive knees and calves. Countess Albrizzi said of Byron, "His neck, which he was in the habit of keeping uncovered as much as the usages of society permitted, seemed to have been formed in a mould, and was very white." (Shelley also appeared with "his white throat unfettered.") Most of Byron's portraits emphasize the neck. Narcissistically turning his feminine neck, the man of beauty offers his profile for our admiration. The feminine meaning of an exposed neck is plain in Flaubert's *Madame Bovary* when Emma flirts with her future husband by tossing off a liqueur and, head back, licking the bottom of the glass. I find similar provocative body language in

Lucretius' Mars, Ingres' Thetis, Girodet's Endymion, Kleist's Achilles, George Eliot's Rosamond, and Tilly Losch as the vain Chinese dancer in *The Good Earth* (1937). One of the hallmarks of Elvis Presley's late Orientalizing period was his architectural stiff standing collar, elongating the neck and revealing the throat in a plunging V to the chest. In his Las Vegas shows, Presley ritualistically draped scarves about his neck and cast them into the audience—self-distribution as formulaic neck-remembrance. Do this in memory of me.

Where does charisma belong? Where should it stay? Byron was full of political ideas, which led him to sacrifice his life in the cause of liberty. But he was an Alcibiades whose glamour was too intense for his own society. England could not tolerate Byron's presence and convulsively expelled him. Perfect narcissism is fascinating and therefore demoralizing. Byron's narcissism released the archaic and asocial phenomenon of incest. What if Lord Byron had entered English politics? We have the precedent of another man of beauty, George Villiers, first Duke of Buckingham, favorite of James I and Charles I. Wandering through the Palazzo Pitti twenty years ago, I was electrified by an ill-lit, unmarked portrait of stunning androgynous beauty. It turned out to be Rubens' painting of Buckingham. Playing Buckingham in Richard Lester's *The Three Musketeers* (1974), Simon Gray is wonderfully made up to resemble Rubens' portrait. David Harris Willson says:

> Buckingham was a seductive young man, with something of the allurements of both sexes. He was esteemed one of the handsomest men in the whole world. Tall, comely, and beautifully proportioned, he had great physical vigour and skill in bodily sports . . . The antiquarian and diarist, D'Ewes, recorded: "I saw everything in him full of delicacy and handsome features, yea, his hands and face seemed to me especially effeminate and curious."[22]

As the man of beauty, Buckingham combined athleticism with feminine charm. Once again we find the contrast of dark hair and fine complexion. The political consequences of Buckingham's extraordinary beauty were severe and longlasting. Perez Zagorin states:

> He rose to the meridian of power, there to shine in blazing splendour until the knife of an assassin extinguished his light. . . . A golden shower of wealth and offices descended on him. . . . Buckingham's domination formed an epoch of critical importance in the pre-history of the revolution. It deformed the workings of the King's government and the patronage system. It sowed disaffection

in the Court and was a prime cause of enmity on the political scene. It brought the royal regime into hatred and contempt. To the favourite's ascendancy must be ascribed in no small measure the decline of the crown's moral authority—an authority indispensable to government which, once lost, can hardly ever be recovered.

With all his sway over affairs, Buckingham had no real policy or extended aims. Unlike his contemporary ministers, Richelieu and Olivares, his predominant purpose in the use of power was to aggrandize himself and his dependents.[23]

Alcibiades helped bring down the Athenian empire. Buckingham hastened England's regicidal revolution. Excess charisma is dangerous, to self and others.

Byron, the Romantic exile, did England a favor. Energy and beauty together are burning, godlike, destructive. Byron created the youth-cult that would sweep Elvis Presley to uncomfortable fame. In our affluent commercial culture, this man of beauty was able to ignore politics and build his empire elsewhere. A ritual function of contemporary popular culture: to parallel and purify government. The modern charismatic personality has access to movies, television, and music, with their enormous reach. Mass media act as a barrier protecting politics, which would otherwise be unbalanced by the entrance of men of epochal narcissistic glamour. Today's Byronic man of beauty is a Presley who dominates the imagination, not a Buckingham who disorders a state.

14

Light and Heat

Shelley and Keats

Fathers earn and sons spend. Entrepreneurs in business or art fight their way to identity, amassing fortunes that they leave to their heirs. The son, having it all, has nothing to press against, except the father. So many sons of famous fathers are alcoholics, drug addicts, dilettantes. The first generation of Romantic poets forcefully created themselves out of the declining eighteenth century. Their personalities were conflicted and contradictory, grand even in disarray. The second generation, beginning on the assumptions of the first, was breezier but lacked stamina. Byron, Shelley, and Keats lyricize reality. Lyric, a Greek genre, is based on simple parallelism between nature and emotion. In antiquity, lyric was supplemented by the other genres, which taken as a whole give a complete picture of the universe. Lyric cannot stand alone as a genre. Dante, Spenser, Shakespeare, and Milton subordinated lyric to larger statements. So did Blake and Wordsworth, and so did Coleridge, who turned to philosophy to escape his lyric agonies. Byron, Shelley, and Keats expanded the lyric to extraordinary length. But length did not protect them from the torment implicit in lyric emotion, when unframed by stable social structure. All three fled south, as if to recharge lyric at its source. The first Romantic to make lyric survive the northern winter was Emily Dickinson—and that was because she stayed put and used Spenser and Blake to confront nature's sadism. The second Romantic generation tried to argue away the daemonism which the first had uncovered in sex and nature.

Imagination for Shelley is "the principle of synthesis," uniting "all irreconcilable things."[1] Like Coleridge, he extends the synthesis of contraries to sexual personae. He is the first Romantic to use the overt Hermaphrodite positively. In the elegy *Adonais* (1821), Shelley portrays

Keats as a half-feminine Adonis, treacherously slain. His preface attributes Keats's tubercular death to "the savage criticism" of "Endymion," Keats's version of the myth of beautiful youth and moon-goddess. "These wretched men" of the *Quarterly Review* had "the most violent effect on his susceptible mind." Later rave reviews "were ineffectual to heal the wound thus wantonly inflicted." Adonis' goring by the boar's tusk becomes a poet's goring by hostile critics. The poet as beautiful boy ritually slain by society recalls Thomas Chatterton, mentioned in *Adonais.* Chatterton, a frustrated poet who killed himself at seventeen in 1770, became a Romantic archetype of tragic youth. Shelley's unscrupulous critics are like Wordsworth's sneering "selfish men." Society is controlled by virile males who abuse the feminine poet. Shelley says "the poisoned shaft" of "their insults and their slanders" is fatal when landing on a heart "like Keats's composed of more penetrable stuff." The arrow is a tusk, the heart a groin. Susceptible Keats is penetrable as a woman. Shelley is remembering Shakespeare's sadomasochistic eroticism in *Venus and Adonis:* "Nuzzling in his flank, the loving swine / Sheathed unaware the tusk in his soft groin" (115–16). Critics, of course, are unloving swine.

For Shelley and all Romantics except Blake, the poet is a passive sufferer. Shelley's major use of the theme is in *Prometheus Unbound,* where youthful Prometheus says "Pain is my element" (I.477). The Promethean poet steals the divine fire of imagination, but in Romantic terms, his punishment is for any attempt at assertive action. The poem opens on the sadomasochistic spectacle of Prometheus helplessly pinned down, pierced by ice spears and the beak of a marauding bird. All male artists have Keats's penetrable body and heart. Like Blake's *God Creating Adam, Prometheus Unbound* is male sex war. The oppressor is virile and therefore unjust. Shelley revises classical myth and *Paradise Lost* by driving Jupiter from heaven. As "the supreme Tyrant" sinks, his power drains away. The vengeful poet castrates in turn.

Shelley's "Ozymandias" charts another male fall. Pharaoh, probably Rameses II, noisily pumps himself up but is defeated by time. Again, tyranny and virility "sneer." The artist, a nobody, sees all. Ozymandias' "shattered visage" is the western male persona, riven with cracks. The poem is an iconoclasm, a breaking of the image. Patient, persistent nature topples the male idol of sex and politics. Political power is built on sand, but art lasts. How true of Rameses II: we remember him only through Abu Simbel, the Book of Exodus, and *The Ten Commandments,* where he is brilliantly played by Yul Brynner. Nature's revenge: today Rameses II makes the news as a tiny mummy infested by parasites and shipped air freight to Paris for gas treatment. In Shelley's sonnet, gas is Pharaoh's problem.

The two main figures of *The Witch of Atlas* (1820) are androgynes. The witch is born fully potent in a "chamber of gray rock." Like Athena, she has no childhood; like Circe, she is a metamorphosist and daughter of the Sun. The witch represents the magic of art. Her birthplace, "the enwombèd rocks," are Wordsworth's chthonian caverns of the mind. She is a secretion, an earth-thought. Shelley echoes "Kubla Khan," turning Coleridge's ostracized poet into a Spenserian femme fatale. But there is no Spenserian sex. The witch is "a sexless bee" (Pindar's Delphic oracle), "a lovely lady garmented in light." One of Shelley's favorite strategies is to use Apollonian light to temper or sweeten chthonian mysteries. In its dynamics of art-making, *The Witch of Atlas* denies that creation must come out of destruction.

The clairvoyant witch enters human consciousness, watching the movements of social and erotic life. "Her own thoughts were each a minister": she has an inner male court. Self-populated, she needs no mate or friend. She shows emotion only once, when she weeps at the futility of cultivating sea-nymphs or tree-spirits, since they are mortal and she is not. Leaving her mountain solitude for some sightseeing, the witch invents a mechanical companion to power her spirit-boat. Out of "fire and snow" she makes Hermaphroditus, "a sexless thing" with the "grace" of both genders. It has "gentleness and strength," a swelling bosom and angel's wings. Its fire and snow belong to Spenser's False Florimell, a male spirit skilled in female impersonation. The Hermaphrodite breaks natural law by propelling the boat upstream. As an art work, it personifies its own text, a poem-within-a-poem.

The sexless witch models her creature on herself. I see the Hermaphrodite as a self-portrait, an extrapolation of her sexual duality. Its fabrication is a Romantic materialization of the double, like those in Wordsworth's *Tintern Abbey* and Byron's *Manfred*. In Wordsworth, the double is silent but alert. In Byron, the double hesitates but finally speaks. In Shelley, the double is mute and even autistic. It lies with "unawakened eyes" in the boat, "busy dreams" playing over its face. It smiles, cries, sighs, murmurs to itself. Arguing against Knight's view that the Hermaphrodite is "the evolutionary or transcendental goal of mankind," Bloom rightly says it is "only a robot."[2] The Hermaphrodite is comatose, catatonic. Like Goethe's Homunculus, it is the androgyne as nineteenth-century manufactured object.

I call this type of torpid, glacial androgyne the android, a futuristic entity. The classic modern android was the high-fashion model of the

Fifties to Seventies, with her haughty masklike face. Anthony Burgess reports a friend's rendezvous with "the ideal mannequin, all legs and no breasts": "It was like going to bed with a bicycle."[3] David Bowie used the mannequin style in his transvestite period, when his skull-like face seemed coldly artificial. An android female, reviled by D. H. Lawrence, appeared in the Twenties. Parker Tyler calls studio-era stars like Garbo "somnambules."[4] I class as affectless movie zombies Gene Tierney in *Leave Her to Heaven* (1945), Joan Greenwood in *The Importance of Being Earnest* (1952), Kim Novak in *Vertigo* (1958), and Catherine Deneuve in *Repulsion* (1965) and *Belle de Jour* (1966). Emotional life-lessness is psychological abstraction, a masculine impersonality. Other somnambulistic androids are Wilde's entranced, robotlike Salomé and Lawrence's slow-moving, "scarcely conscious" Hermione Roddice, with her "drugged" face.[5]

The hermaphroditic manufactured object predates the Industrial Revolution. Vergil calls the Trojan Horse a "womb" filled with soldiers, a "fatal machine pregnant with arms." Built with the "divine art" of androgynous Athena, the Trojan Horse is hermaphroditic because of its soulless fecundity: artificial insemination breeds monstrous mechanical parturition (*Aen.* II.20, 52, 237–38, 15). Spenser's daemonic False Florimell is an android, as is the bust of Nefertiti, who shares her one bad eye with David Bowie. I spoke of Nefertiti's advanced cerebral development and surgically truncated shoulders. We are still untangling the legal and moral problems caused by the invention of a new sex, the transsexual, produced by chemical and surgical manipulation of the body. The transsexual is a technological androgyne whom we are happy to call "she" out of the courtesy owed to all inspired makers of fiction. Close to transsexual is my favorite technological androgyne, Luciana Avedon, formerly the Princess Pignatelli, who radically resculpted face and body in her quest for beauty. Avedon's first book begins:

> A few times every century, a great natural beauty is born. I am not one of them. But what nature skipped, I supplied—so much so that sometimes I cannot remember what is real and what is fake. More important, neither can anyone else.[6]

The android is nether male nor female because it is a machine made of synthetic materials. In a wonderful commercial for Camay soap, the radiantly amiable Luciana Avedon turned her surgically altered face to the camera and addressed the viewer in a slow robot voice that stretched the phrase "coconut-enriched lather" to impossible hypnotic length.

Transsexual Renée Richards shows the same odd combination of facial flat affect with elongated somnambulistic speech, a mechanical drone.

Insofar as it is an android, therefore, Shelley's Hermaphrodite cannot be regarded as a model for human life. It is one of the most solipsistic and emotionally dissociated beings in Romantic poetry. The Hermaphrodite descends from Talus, Spenser's "iron man" who does Artegall's bidding. Talus is originally the servant of immortal Astraea, who rears Artegall in a cave looking forward to the cave of the Witch of Atlas. Shelley's poem may be a reply to his wife's *Frankenstein*, published two years earlier. The Hermaphrodite is his version of an experimental automaton, an Apollonian angel of emotional detachment and aesthetic perfection. Some competition or debate was clearly going on between the Shelleys, for in her "Note on the *Witch of Atlas*," Mary recalls urging her husband to "increase his popularity by adopting subjects that would more suit the popular taste than a poem conceived in the abstract and dreamy spirit of the *Witch of Atlas*," which lacks "human interest and passion." Shelley counters with six stanzas defending the "visionary" quality of his poetry. The merely human is not his concern. Romantics aim higher and lower.

Shelley wrote *The Witch of Atlas* near Pisa in August 1820. Three months later, Mary Shelley and Claire Clairmont met Emilia Viviani, the nineteen-year-old daughter of the governor of Pisa, who was packing her off into an arranged marriage. Emilia was the inspiration for *Epipsychidion*, which Shelley began in January 1821. My theory is that from the moment he laid eyes on her, Shelley saw Emilia Viviani as a stunning materialization of the Hermaphrodite of his just-completed *Witch of Atlas*. In the first poem, the Hermaphrodite is seen through an artist-intermediary, the witch. In the second, the poet himself confronts the Hermaphrodite. *Epipsychidion*, a major poem, is ill-understood. It attempts to convert Romanticism, a daemonic and chthonian mode, into the Apollonian. It combines androgyny with incest, already present in the first words of *The Witch of Atlas*, which describe the incestuous birth of twins.

Epipsychidion has been completely misread as a polemical defense of adultery. The friendship between the Shelleys and Emilia Viviani was short but intense. Early commentators speculated endlessly on Mary Shelley's attitude toward her husband's intimacy with Emilia. In her roman à clef, *Lodore* (1835), Mary depicts the relation as platonic, which some think a whitewash. I feel, however, that the platonic connection is perfectly clear in *Epipsychidion* and that it is central to interpretation of the poem. *Epipsychidion* imagines a new kind of relationship, eroticized but nongenital, where both partners are of wavering gender.

The first line of *Epipsychidion* addresses Emilia as "Spirit" and "Sister," the poem's governing ideas. "Sister-spirit," one of my favorite Romantic phrases, comes from cancelled stanzas. The poet longs to be Emilia's twin, born of one mother. Not only is Emilia to be Shelley's sister, but his wife is to be *her* sister (45–48). In other words, Shelley makes his own wife his sister. For the Romantic poet, every relation contracts to family romance. Emilia's letters to the Shelleys (theirs to her were apparently destroyed) show familial language was explicit among them. Emilia calls Shelley her brother and Mary her sister.

Shelley's longing for twinship is a desire for genetic identity within a heterosexual coupling. In the essay *On Love*, Shelley says something in us from birth "thirsts after its likeness." As Emilia's twin, the poet would be united with his likeness and escape human anxieties of separation and incompletion. Incest's asociality is brilliantly embodied in his idea of twins whose incestuous relation precedes their social identities. Incest is older than and prior to civilization. The poet leaps backward to the dawn of time.

That Shelley may be thinking of incestuous intercourse between twins in the womb cannot be dismissed, since it occurs in *The Faerie Queene*. The twin giants Argante and Ollyphant, themselves the product of incest, mingle "in fleshly lust" before birth and emerge clasped in the "monstrous" act (III.vii.48). The Renaissance poet condemns what the Romantic poet celebrates. Prenatal sex is an old idea: Plutarch reports Isis and Osiris copulated in the womb. Mind, not body, is the issue in *Epipsychidion*. Shelley seeks a form of knowledge prior to the rational. He and his twin make a joint expedition to the origins of human consciousness.

Shelley hails Emilia as "Seraph of Heaven," "Veiled Glory," "Spouse! Sister! Angel!" The seraphic imagery of *Epipsychidion* is unparalleled in English literature. Like Wordsworth, Shelley seraphicizes the beloved woman, giving her a numinous glamour. Flooded by Apollonian light, Emilia is desexualized and dematerialized. She becomes a shimmering presence of unfixed gender. In an omitted fragment, Shelley records different views of Emilia. Some call her a familiar, some a woman. Others "swear you're a Hermaphrodite," "that sweet marble monster of both sexes." So Emilia's gender and identity were a matter of public dispute in Pisa. A Roman Hermaphrodite statue also appears in Spenser's cancelled "Hermaphrodite stanzas." Did Shelley write his own Hermaphrodite stanza in order to cancel it, in homage to Spenser? Or is a parallel aesthetic simply at work? *Epipsychidion* and *The Faerie Queene* follow Apollonian laws. The Hermaphrodite statue, with its anatomic blatancies, is too gravity-bound for the world of Apollonian radiance. The poetic energy of *Epipsychidion* is in the weightless verticals of spiritual ascent.

Shelley's second draft for the preface contains a peculiar fantasy. *Epipsychidion*, it claims, was found in the personal effects of "a young Englishman, who died on his passage from Leghorn to the Levant." He was accompanied by "a lady who might have been supposed to be his wife" and by "an effeminate looking youth," who turned out to be a woman in disguise. He had bought a Greek island with a Saracenic castle, where he intended to "dedicate the remainder of his life to undisturbed intercourse with his companions." *Epipsychidion* clearly emerged from a matrix of perverse fantasy. Shelley's preface is Byronic: the Englishman is travelling to the east; the effeminate youth is like Byron's pageboy Kaled, the transvestite woman who dies of grief at Lara's death. Shelley seems to be imagining himself accompanied by his wife and by Emilia Viviani in boy's clothing. Byron must have told his friends the Shelleys about his erotic adventures with a girl dressed as a boy. But Shelley revises Byron's caprice into a *ménage à trois*, as exotic as a Shakespearean acting company on tour. What is the wife's relation to the girl-boy—tolerance or independent erotic interest? Because of *Epipsychidion*'s incest theme, it is possible that the lady "who might have been supposed to be his wife" might instead be the Englishman's sister, with whom he is romantically involved.

In another fragment Shelley tells Emilia: "If any should be curious to discover / Whether to you I am a friend or lover, / Let them read Shakespeare's sonnets, taking thence / A whetstone for their dull intelligence." This is a direct challenge to the reader. Shelley is saying we must guess whether Emilia is the Italian Dark Lady of the sonnets—or the beautiful boy. He doubts "the presumptuous pedagogues of Earth" can "tell the riddle offered here." The riddle Emilia is like Goethe's "enigma," the transvestite Mignon. Androgynous Emilia looks backward to transvestite Rosalind, with her riddling circle magic, and forward to Balzac's ambiguous Seraphita. *Epipsychidion* is an Apollonian cinema where Shelley invents image after image to answer the riddle of Emilia's identity.

Shelley declares Emilia the embodiment of a dazzling figure he has dreamed of since youth. This "veiled Divinity" recalls Spenser's veiled hermaphrodite Venus. Like Coleridge's *Christabel*, *Epipsychidion* is a sexual apocalyse in which the hermaphrodite god is seen face to face. Critics agree that Shelley's long-sought image is the "epipsyche" of the title, a word translated as "a soul within the soul." Carlos Baker speaks of Shelley's "psyche-epipsyche strategy": "The mind (psyche) imaginatively creates or envisions what it does not have (epipsyche), and then seeks to possess epipsyche, to move towards it as a goal."[7] This excellent formulation would be accurate about Blake but not about Shelley. The femininity of Shelley's epipsyche is not what his psyche does not have, since he is already half-feminine—shown by the wealth of details in *Epipsychidion* stressing his passivity. The epipsyche may be an aspect of self projected and pursued. But it is not a repressed feminine component, since in Romanticism after Blake, femininity is never repressed. If the Romantics repress anything, it is masculinity. I revise Baker's statement: Shelley's feminine psyche pursues what it does not have—masculinity, which it embodies in a female epipsyche. Pursuer and pursued are hermaphrodites.

Shelley enjoyed subordination to female power. He told Elizabeth Hitchener, "You are as my better genius." A letter to his future wife declares: "Your thoughts alone can waken mine to energy. . . . My understanding becomes undisciplined without you." This persona of ritual dependency is a characteristic Romantic mask. John Stuart Mill similarly idolized Harriet Taylor, whom he calls a genius and his intellectual superior, source of those achievements for which the world mistakenly honors him alone. Gertrude Himmelfarb, among others, shows this to be a patent falsification.[8] However, Mill's *imagining* Harriet as superior may genuinely have energized him. Creativity flows from an archaic repositioning of sexual personae. In some way, Harriet as Diotima or dominatrix stilled guilt. Oddly, the one person Mill compares Harriet to in his autobiography is Shelley himself—only to find Shelley wanting. Harriet resembled Shelley "in thought and intellect" and everything else, but Shelley "was but a child compared with what she ultimately became."[9] Alas, the unremarkable Harriet cannot survive so cruel a test.

Shelley wears his persona of elected passivity throughout *Epipsychidion*. He is "a dizzy moth" seeking "a radiant death" in the flame of his angelic dream-image. The poem's midsection chronicles his erotic history, as he sought the image "in many mortal forms." The three major women in his life, Claire, Mary, and Emilia, become comet, moon, and sun, exerting their power upon him, "this passive Earth." Shelley is making an astrological and therefore pagan revision of Dante's tutelage by the Madonna, St. Lucy, and Beatrice. He repeats in four different ways Coleridge's metaphor of the poet as feminine sea played upon by larger forces. Shelley's first encounter with Emilia combines Dante and Spenser: "Into the obscure Forest" came his "Vision," who "flashed from her motion splendour like the Morn's." Dante's pilgrim meets Spenser's Belphoebe, the glittering Apollonian huntress. Emilia, an "Incarnation of the Sun," is "penetrating me with living light." The poet is "a hunted deer," pierced by her raylike solar arrows. (Earlier, imagination shoots "many a sun-like arrow".) So Shelley is the female deer wounded by Belphoebe at her entrance into *The Faerie Queene.* A few months later, in *Adonais,* he again describes himself as a "deer struck by the hunter's dart." Emilia is penetrator, Shelley penetrated.

Sometimes Emilia is a gentle sister or "poor captive bird," her real-life phrase for herself (her father had put her in a convent for her schooling). At other times she is imperiously Amazonian: "Thou Wonder, and thou Beauty, and thou Terror!" Echoing the Song of Songs (6:4), Shelley gives woman a masculine militancy. In a poem on Leonardo's *Medusa* he says, "Its horror and its beauty are divine." The painting, with its "Gorgonian eyes," has "the tempestuous loveliness of terror." Medusa is Apollonian Emilia's chthonian twin. Beauty and terror together in a person of either sex are prima facie hermaphroditic. We see them in Coleridge's longhaired poet, who makes people cry "Beware! Beware!"

In *Epipsychidion,* therefore, a passive poet glorifies a woman who is alternately an incestuous twin, a genderless spirit, and an Amazon. The third and final section of the poem prophesies their future relationship. The poet's summons to Emilia is usually dismissed as a sentimental elopement fantasy. But Emilia will be "a bride" to the poet's spirit and "a vestal sister" to his body. Vestal means virgin: this is a no-sex marriage. Shelley imagines their voyage to an idyllic Greek island with fountains and streams "as clear as elemental diamond," under "the roof of blue Ionian weather." I suspect the wording and décor influenced Baudelaire's gorgeous "Invitation to the Voyage," with its dreamy appeal to the Romantic sister-spirit.

Shelley's Greek imagery establishes his theme of eroticized chastity in exclusively formal terms. Bloom strongly resists scholars' ascription of Platonism to Shelley's poetry. Platonism is of little use in reading poetry; its historical meanings are too broad. However, I substitute the term Apollonian for Shelley's idealizations. He is a Greek visionary of the visible world, with its eye-dominated Apollonian radiance. Homer's white-armed Nausikaa, Sappho's maidens, and the Athenian *Kritios Boy* are in the high Greek style of simplicity, clarity, purity, and beauty. Shelley's purity would be no less Greek were his imaginary island off Scotland. He is having "an antenatal dream": the island's "calm circumference of bliss" is life in the womb, where the incestuous twins unite. *Epipsychidion's* voyage is into not the future but the past.

Shelley and his sister-spirit finally reach an ancient cavern filled with "the moonlight of the expired night." There they come together:

> Our breath shall intermix, our bosoms bound,
> And our veins beat together; and our lips
> With other eloquence than words, eclipse
> The soul that burns between them, and the wells
> Which boil under our being's inmost cells,
> The fountains of our deepest life, shall be
> Confused in Passion's golden purity

The passage continues to a blazing height, from which the poet falls back abruptly. Vision fails him, because the union, the most radical seraphicization in poetry, veers in an unexpected direction. Social personae recede. Shelley the dramatic character falls silent, while Shelley the choral commentator continues as long as he can. Words cease, since prenatal incest precedes culture.

Shelley describes his union with Emilia in multiple metaphors drawn from the Hermaphrodite myths in Plato, Ovid, and Milton. The intermixture of breaths and binding of bosoms have led many scholars to misread the poem as a defense of free love. Kissing and embracing prove no genital connection, in view of Emilia Viviani's letters speaking of her ardent desire to kiss and embrace *Mary* Shelley. Something physical is going on in *Epipsychidion*, but it is not normal sexual intercourse. The boiling wells, fountains, and springs refer to Ovid's forest pool of the nymph Salmacis, who fuses with the youth Hermaphroditus. In Shelley's version, Emilia's body disappears into his. Gender is eradicated and biology defied. Life begins again. Shelley and Emilia are to be *reborn as one person*. *Epipsychidion* leads to the womb, the body-warmed sac of waters. The poem boils like an alembic on the Delphic tripod. Its cavern is the Witch of Atlas' birth chamber of "enwombèd rocks." *The Witch of Atlas* begins where *Epipsychidion* ends. Shelley's two Hermaphrodite poems make a single continuous movement. Like Coleridge's pornographic *Christabel*, *Epipsychidion* is a superheated psychoalchemic experiment, releasing and rebonding sexual energy. In *Epipsychidion*, an Apollonian poem with a chthonian climax, orgasmic sexuality is vanquished and transcended. Body is consumed in the flames of imagination, which light and heat the poem.

But *Epipsychidion* implodes. The search for a new identity based on gender-free eroticism ends in the extinction of *all* identity. The unity of incestuous twinship collapses into nondifferentiation. Incest restores primeval chaos. Shelley sinks into dispiriting density, like the swamp mud of the Great Mother. The poem is reclaimed by the chthonian. *Epipsychidion* attempts the impossible task of reconciling regression to the womb with Apollonian seraphicization, a burning away and ascent of the gender-limited body. But the Apollonian angel is by definition anti-chthonian, a flight from the mother-ruled labyrinth of sex, body, and nature. At the moment the poet thinks himself victorious over matter, the earth exerts her malign gravitation and plummets him downward to her embrace. Shelley awakened her power early in the poem when he opened himself to the womb-state: "Would we two had been twins of the same mother!" Summoned, the archaic mother appears.

Shelley's parting from Emilia Viviani was not cordial, though there seems to have been no one provoking incident. Newman Ivey White describes it as a "revulsion" from her, similar to "several other sudden revulsions" in Shelley's history.[10] The poet ended by suppressing *Epipsychidion*. In a letter just before his death the next year, Shelley said of his estrangement from Emilia: "I think one is always in love with something or other; the error . . . consists in seeking in a mortal image the likeness of what is perhaps eternal." This is the disease of western love. Shelley's letter describes psychological heliotropism, my term for susceptibility to the glamour of charismatic personality. The person is intensely visualized: in *Epipsychidion*, Shelley cries, "See where she stands!" The western cinematic eye is directed, fixed, inflamed. But the person invested with so much hieratic energy is coldly discarded when he or she proves humanly frail. The idealizing lover surrenders himself to dramatic illusion, the power of persona. I think Shelley's disillusionment came when Emilia, then nineteen years old and at the very borderline of adolescent bloom ("A Metaphor of Spring and Youth and Morning; / A Vision like incarnate April"), suddenly crossed over and looked like a woman instead of an androgyne. The first time I read *Epipsychidion*, I knew what Emilia Viviani looked like: Hadrian's Antinous. The poem's brilliant glamour could only have been inspired by a person of extraordinary androgynous beauty. Thus it was no surprise when I learned Emilia had "faultlessly regular Greek features."

Shelley's final preface to *Epipsychidion* compares it, without explanation, to Dante's *Vita Nuova*. Bloom rejects this: Shelley's parallel is "hardly justified" and "does not help us to comprehend anything of value in the poem."[11] But the allusion to Dante is exactly right: *Epipsychidion* is Shelley's *Vita Nuova*. I argued that Dante's Beatrice was a narcissistic personality, a girl-boy to whom the obsessed poet ritually subjected himself. Only Knight seems also to have noticed Beatrice's "youthful presexual perfection."[12] Glancing over the fragments and drafts connected with *Epipsychidion*, we see how easily Shelley's mind moved from the Roman Hermaphrodite statue to a transvestite girl as beautiful boy to the *Vita Nuova*, with its charismatic adolescent Beatrice. *Epipsychidion* and the *Vita Nuova* are classic texts of western erotic perversity, which gives enormous hierarchic stature to self-enclosed Apollonian personality, a living objet d'art. I think the exclamatory style of *Epipsychidion* partly comes from the aggressive force needed to break into the near-autistic consciousness of this kind of glamourous androgyne, with his or her dreamy apartness. Remember the Witch of Atlas' Hermaphrodite: all that buzzing and murmuring, that labial self-love. The girl as beautiful boy is a silver automaton hearkening to its own inner music. Narcissists receive callers without opening the door.

Shelley's revulsion from Emilia Viviani was an aesthetic swerve. It happened like this: Emilia's seraphically transparent flesh suddenly appeared heavy and coarsely female. I have seen with my own eyes the humiliating changes life works on the personality of high glamour. The luminous complexion turns muddy; the aura vanishes. Glamour is a gift under no one's control. In women it may peak and ebb with the menstrual cycle. A Shelleyan declension from idealization to disillusion occurs in D. H. Lawrence's *The Rainbow*, in Ursula's infatuation with her teacher, Winifred Inger. It begins in Apollonian radiance and Greek archetype and ends, like *Epipsychidion*, in a sad fall into earthliness. "Firm-bodied as Diana," dressed in a tunic "like a Greek girl's," Inger is "proud and free as a man, yet exquisite as a woman." Ursula thinks: "Ah, the beauty of the firm, white, cool flesh! Ah, the wonderful firm limbs. . . . The whole body was defined, firm and magnificent." But after the two become intimate, Ursula experiences the Shelleyan revulsion. She feels "a sort of nausea," "a heavy, clogged sense of deadness." Inger is "ugly, clayey": "Her female hips seemed big and earthy."[13] Ursula is evolving from lesbianism to heterosexuality, continued in the sequel, *Women in Love*. Ursula's vision of her teacher is like Shelley's of Emilia Viviani. The Apollonian androgyne of radiant Greek beauty degenerates into matter without contour. The poet moved on and left the shell of his vision behind.

Shelley said in a letter, "Incest is, like many other incorrect things, a very poetical circumstance." Poetry and incest coexist outside the norm. Romantic incest is a closed internal world. St. Augustine finds the prohibition against incest rationally justified for "the multiplying of relationships": " 'Father' and 'father-in-law' are the names of two relationships. When, therefore, a man has one person for his father, another for his father-in-law, friendship extends itself to a larger number. But Adam in his single person was obliged to hold both relations to his sons and daughters, for brothers and sisters were united in marriage."[14] Incest closes society down by regressing to prehistory. In Poe's clannish, incestuous Ushers, desire shrinks from contact with aliens. Incest in antiquity had an aristocratic elitism. Ovid's Byblis, lusting for her twin brother, argues: "Yet surely gods have married their sisters? . . . But the gods have their own laws."[15] Byron's incest with his half-sister (if it occurred) was self-hierarchizing: the gods have their own laws, and I am a god. Like the Greek Ptolemies in Egypt, kings intermarry to preserve dynastic purity. The Romantic poet marrying his sister founds a new hierarchy. He belongs to a privileged caste, the visionary or magus. Catullus says the Persian magus must be born of the incest of mother and son (90). Magian poetic vision transcends space and time by violating social and natural law.

Remarkably, *Epipsychidion*, Romanticism's most operatic incestromance, has nothing to do with a real brother and sister. Shelley perversely imposes sisterhood on Emilia Viviani. He materializes it by magian imagination, then violates it with incest. Shelley's fictive brotherhood is emotional and sexual dialogue with one's double, whose features alter, as in a magic mirror, to those of the opposite sex. We saw how Byron changes Shakespeare's Cleopatra into Sardanapalus' mirror. The knight whom Spenser's Britomart sees in the mirror is simultaneously herself and her future husband. The Renaissance double matures into the social other, while Romantic doubles often lock and die. This happens with Byron's Manfred and Astarte, Poe's Roderick and Madeline Usher, and Wilde's Dorian Gray and his portrait. It also happens at the climax of *Epipsychidion*, when the poet and sister-spirit convulse into "one annihilation." Earlier, Shelley actually calls Emilia "Thou Mirror." In *The Cenci*, Shelley's Count uses a mirror metaphor to curse Beatrice, the daughter whom he forces into incest: may her child be "A hideous likeness of herself, that as / From a distorting mirror, she may see / Her image mixed with what she most abhors, / Smiling upon her from her nursing breast" (IV.i.145–49). Beatrice looks into a living mirror and sees her monstrous double, stuck to her like a tumor. The nursing baby born of incest is her daemonic self-portrait, like the picture of Dorian Gray. It combines her face with her hated father's, female mixed with male. Count Cenci, perverter of the paternal, makes his daughter a Medusan Madonna.

Knight, who calls *Epipsychidion* "autoerotic," declares, "Both homosexuality and incest may be symptoms of a state which approaches self-sufficiency and integration, and so looks for affection less to an opposite than to a replica."[16] Otto Fenichel says the male transvestite may fantasize that "the masculine element in his nature can have intercourse with the feminine (i.e. with himself)."[17] Is there a secret connection between Byron's incest and Don Juan's transvestism? Freud speaks of masturbatory fantasies where a person "pictures himself both as the man and as the woman in an imagined situation." He observed a hysterical attack where "the patient pressed her dress to her body with one hand (as the woman) while trying to tear it off with the other (as the man)."[18] Romantic incest-romance makes poetry of this psychodrama. No one has completely explained the romantic fascination with incest. M. H. Abrams traces it to the underground alchemic tradition, with its pervasive incest symbols.[19] I feel that most Romantic incest is free of alchemic influence and that it is produced by the late eighteenth-century crisis in sex roles.

One of the great Romantic metaphors, the Aeolian lyre, has a latent sexual ambiguity unnoted by major criticism. In "The Correspondent Breeze," a central Romantic study, Abrams discusses the Aeolian lyre in erudite detail without taking slightest notice of the fact that the male poet identifying with a wind harp makes himself feminine toward inspiring power.[20] Shelley says poetry cannot be composed by an act of will: "the mind in creation is as a fading coal, which some invisible influence, like an inconstant wind, awakens to transitory brightness."[21] The wind rouses the fading coal just as it plays upon the lyre. The poet waits like an odalisque, a Giorgione nude asleep in a meadow. Shelley's "invisible influence" recalls Blake's phallic "invisible worm" flying in a storm-wind toward the rose; a flower metaphor in fact appears in the next sentence. Like Wordsworth, Shelley elevates intuition over "reasoning," aggressive tool of *Adonais'* slanderous Keats-killers. Keats's friend Haydon uses the lyre metaphor to describe the poet reciting from "Endymion" to a curt and unresponsive Wordsworth: "It was rather ill-bred to hurt a youth, at such a moment when he actually trembled, like the String of a Lyre, when it has been touched."[22] As with Coleridge and the night recital of *The Prelude:* watch out for Wordsworth one-on-one. Rousseauist Wordsworth could play by Sade's rules. No love is lost between artists claiming the same turf.

The sexual conventionalism of so much twentieth-century criticism was especially damaging to Romanticism, with its intrinsic perversities. I find Douglas Bush's hostile remarks about Shelley from 1937 more accurate about the poet than much of the commentary by admirers during the postwar Romantic revival. Bush rejects Shelley's "sentimentality": "His heroes and martyrs are all alike, all physically weak and spiritually lonely, pale youths who perish, or are ready to perish, unupbraiding. They are all variations on the portrait of himself as an effeminate romantic idealist."[23] Fifty years ago, these words were meant to produce a shudder of distaste in the manly reader, but time and the revolution in sex roles have now made Bush's prosecutorial judgment sound value-free. Bush derides Shelley's language in *Prometheus Unbound:* "pale feet," "pale wound-worn limbs," "soft and flowing limbs / And passion-parted lips." Shelley's sensual sex-crossing images seemed uncomfortably homoerotic. Bush's attitude reflects the modern reaction against Swinburne, who borrowed from Shelley, and it also falls in the shadow of the disgraced Wilde. I suspect Shelley modelled his canon of effeminate beauty on Michelangelo's *Pietà* and androgynous Hellenistic sculpture in Rome, where *Prometheus Unbound* was partly composed.

The sexual passivity Abrams fails to note in the metaphor of the Aeolian lyre is crucial to Shelley's "Ode to the West Wind." To overlook or ignore this element is to misread the poem. The poet is the lyre through which wild nature makes music. The "ashes and sparks" of his thoughts fly from the inflamed fading coal. The poet is a "dead leaf," like *Epipsychidion*'s incinerated moth. The "uncontrollable" west wind's tremendous masculine force exaggerates the poet's frailty or creative reactivity. His "dead thoughts," scattered across the universe "to quicken a new birth," are seeds of insemination. But while the torpid seed is Shelley's, the ejaculation is the wind's. Astonishingly, the poet is a *passive inseminator.* Man is half-loved, half-raped by nature. Poetry is panting sex speech, wrung from slaves on a long invisible leash. The poet as ocean "wave" again recalls Coleridge's feminine sea spread beneath Wordsworth's power. But Coleridge's wave swells languorously, while Shelley's peaks with feverish sexual excitement. The "Ode to the West Wind" is a spiritual sex drama of vast proportions. The poem's greatness, its electrifying expansive rush, resides precisely in the poet's ability to project himself and us into the sensation of passive surrender to titanic power. Shelley's ecstasy comes from convention-defying sex experience. He is erotically joined, body and soul, to the wind as masculine ravisher. "Ode to the West Wind" is a tour de force of sex-crossing Romantic imagination. I view it as a sexualized revision of the magnificent "Mont Blanc," where Shelley contemplates the stunning enormity of nature, a bleak geologic panorama without sexual personae.

The Aeolian lyre expresses not just the passivity but the compulsive-ness of Romantic creativity. Achievement drives from the unknown part of self. Nietzsche thinks artists undersexed: "Their vampire, their talent, grudges them as a rule that squandering of force which one calls passion. If one has a talent, one is also its victim; one lives under the vampirism of one's talent."[24] This is true of anyone pursuing an obsessive project, which steals years and drains love. Yeats reformulates the metaphor of passive poet-as-lyre: "We who are poets and artists . . . live but for the moment when vision comes to our weariness like terrible lightning, in the humility of the brutes."[25] We saw the protracted birth-agony of Cellini's *Perseus*. Shelley says, "A great statue or picture grows under the power of the artist as a child in the mother's womb."[26] Male artists have Erik Erikson's female "inner space." Giving the artist a male womb (like Euripides' Zeus), Shelley radically alters masculine body-image. Nature makes woman's body a humid bower, model for Spenser's Bower of Bliss. The body is first sculptor of imagination. Male homosexuality, for example, is not aesthetically or emotionally equivalent to heterosexuality. The man who is anally penetrated or who takes another's penis in his mouth is making his body a female bower.

Shelley claims the poet is "more delicately organized than other men, and sensible to pain and pleasure, both his own and that of others, in a degree unknown to them."[27] The nervous, impressionable poet has a feminine sensitivity. He is a stranger exiled among virile men. The price for the Romantic poet's appropriation of female powers is mutilation, which Erich Neumann calls "the condition of all creation."[28] Western literature begins with a blind bard. The head of the poet Orpheus, torn to pieces by Maenads, floated to Lesbos, implanting that island with the first flowering of Greek lyric genius.

Romantic mutilation is ritual self-limitation. With the failure of hi-erarchies at the close of the Enlightenment, consciousness became stronger, but it did not become more masculine. Paradoxically, the more it asserted, the more it had to fear. We saw in Kleist's *Penthesilea* that unlimited expansion of self produces paralyzing anxiety. There was an excess of phenomena no longer ordered by social structures, phenomena flooding consciousness in an exhausting plenum. The femininity of the Romantic artist partly expresses his passivity toward this oppressive multiplicity. The artist sacrifices his virility as a propitiation of unknown gods. The problem of evil had an assigned place in all-inclusive Christian theology. But as religion weakened, evil sprang free. The evil of chthonian nature is far less rational and explicable than the evil of an envious master demon. Romantic imagination faced evil without the organized certitudes of church and state. The power to punish was taken over by the self. Hence the nineteenth-century abundance of daemonic epiphanies of the double. The self ambushes, harasses, flails itself. Romanticism's most terrifying encounter with the double was ironically by the atheist Shelley. Making himself feminine, the poet was under the fascist rod of what he had repressed.

Keats, Shelley's slain Adonis, supplements and corrects Wordsworth. Keats's nature welcomes rather than abandons, because he restores to it the sensuality and eroticism that Wordsworth removed. But Keats, as much as Wordsworth, cannot bear the daemonism Coleridge sees in sex and nature. Reviving the femmes fatales of *The Faerie Queene*, Keats revises the unpalatable facts of female power. His poetry is a *Eumenides*, a renaming and palliation. Keats turns every Fury into a "Kindly One." His clear, simple style is as much a defense mechanism as Blake's in the stormy, opaque prophetic books. Keats's sexual anxiety, suppressed in the poems, is perfectly apparent in his letters.

Keats's theory of creativity comes from Wordsworth's "wise passiveness." Like Byron, Keats esteems a happy "Laziness" or fainting "languour," "a state of effeminacy." Nature visits us with thoughts: "let us open our leaves like a flower and be passive and receptive." Indolence, theme of an ode, is waking sleep. Sleep for Keats is a mode of vision, putting masculine power into feminine suspension. "Negative Capability" gives a man the ability to remain "in uncertainties, Mysteries, doubts, without any irritable reaching after fact & reason." Great men, "especially in Literature" and Shakespeare above all, possess negative capability, which is female waiting, a refusal to intervene, impose, or dominate.[29]

"The camelion Poet," says Keats, is "every thing and nothing":

He has no Identity—he is continually in for—and filling some other Body. . . . When I am in a room with People if I ever am free

from speculating on creations of my own brain, then not myself
goes home to myself: but the identity of every one in the room
begins to press upon me that I am in a very little time annihilated—

The receptive poet is in metamorphosis, dissolving into multiple identities. Other beings pass through him as if he were a wraith. The poet is
like Plutarch's Dionysus, who turns into winds, water, earth, stars,
plants, animals. Keats's Dionysian self-transformations are clear in
"Bright Star," where by sympathetic identification he projects himself
into star, sea, and shore. The identity-free poet is a feminine receptacle
into which pour the Many of nature. Keats says of all "Men of Genius,"
"they have not any individuality, any determined Character."[30] Geniuses nullify their own western personalities. The Keatsian man of
vision is a transsexual shaman like Empedocles, who claimed that in
former lives he was a boy, a girl, a bush, a bird, and a fish.

Organic life floods into Keats's imagery like a green tide. Things have
vivid sensory presence. The delicacies Porphyro sets before his sleeping
beloved in *The Eve of St. Agnes* are so individuated, so uncannily
materialized that one expects them to stand up and demand to be
introduced. The great ode "To Autumn" is a series of lush holograms.
By a cinema of kinesthesia, the Dionysian feelies, Keats reproduces the
harvest fruits as they "swell" and "plump" with mouth-filling fatness.
Words bubble with nascence. Language itself is in advanced pregnancy.
"To Autumn" internalizes the nature mother at her fleshiest. Keats's
indolence slows the male body to the fecund rhythms of natural process,
that creeping, interminable cycle in which women live. Keats says of
women he loved, "My mind was a soft nest in which some one of them
slept though she knew it not."[31] Wordsworth speaks of Coleridgean
"caverns" of the mind, Shelley of the artist's "womb." In Keats, the mind
is warm bed and amniotic sac, fetally encapsulating the beloved and
suspending her in honey. She lives in the poet's imagination. But she
lives most vividly by *sleeping*. She is removed from the social arena of
action and returned to embryonic innocence. Think of the sleeping
heroine of *The Eve of St. Agnes*: is her sleep nature's sacralization—or
Keats's neutralization of woman's sexual danger?

Keats speaks of the heart as "the teat from which the Mind or intelligence sucks its identity."[32] He gives primacy to emotional life, identified as feminine. If the heart is breastlike, the poet is a shaman with
female breasts. Even read conservatively, the metaphor forces us to see
a feminine heart-breast hovering just inside the male chest wall. Keats
is the Teiresias androgyne, the nurturant male, whom I also find in

Egyptian Hapi, the Nile god with female dugs, and in Roman personifications of the Nile and Father Tiber, a burly, bearded nude reclining
under a swarm of rollicking infants. The Teiresias androgyne rules *The
Eve of St. Agnes:* the most brilliantly written part of the poem is when the
male reverses sexual convention and feeds the female. Keats's language
suddenly intensifies into a sensual cascade of ripe nouns and adjectives.
The poem turns cornucopia.

Lionel Trilling says: "We are ambivalent in our conception of the
moral status of eating and drinking. . . . But with Keats the ingestive
imagery is pervasive and extreme."[33] Trilling is wonderful on Keats's
appetitiveness and its connection to the maternal, but his essay has a
psychological inconsistency approaching incoherence. Trilling insists
on Keats's "manliness" or "mature masculinity," when all the evidence
he presents contradicts it. Food language in *The Eve of St. Agnes* has a
stunning virtuosity. Porphyro lays out "a heap / Of candied apple,
quince, and plum, and gourd; / With jellies soother than the creamy
curd, / And lucent syrops, tinct with cinnamon." Keats's ingestive imagery invokes the sense of taste for one reason: to induce liquidity. The
quick, short consonants and oozing vowels subvert the reader's detachment from and control over the poem, artfully compelling him to salivate. I call this passage mouth-embowering. It replicates in the reader's
skull the poem's embowered bed-scene, with its luxurious ritual of male
nurturance. A contemporary said Keats had a "capacious mouth." We
will return to the idea of a capacious skull. Of all male artists, there is in
Keats the least flight from liquidity. Sartre's *Nausea* is the most passionate protest against the mother-ruled realm of the moist, a gluey "mucoid." Keats seems the most reverent and affectionate of nature-sons,
finding in the moist not annihilated consciousness but enhanced imagination, a new paradise garden.

But great literature and art are never affirmative. Or rather, affirmation is always a swerve from the negative. We celebrate in order to win
victory over something else, something uncontrolled. Of major western
artists, Raphael and Keats are closest to the all-benign. But both were in
competition with an older generation of brooding titans, their artistic
fathers. Did Raphael and Keats choose masquing sexual personae?
They eluded by seeming too generous to confront. Take "Lamia,"
Keats's poem about a snake-vampire imprisoning a male in a house of
illusion. Imagination is perilous, yet reason, embodied in Apollonius, is
too rigid. Critics identify Apollonius as the Alexandrian philosopher of
Burton's *Anatomy of Melancholy.* But in the poem's latent mythology,
Apollonius is Apollo, who slays the female Python at Delphi. "Lamia"

recapitulates the *Oresteia*, where Apollo triumphs—as he can never do in Romanticism. Bush recognizes Coleridge's *Christabel* as the main influence on the poem. There is a tremendous alteration of tone between *Christabel* and "Lamia." Chthonian menace and horror yield to geniality and melodiousness. "Lamia" is polemical and propitiatory; it turns the archetypal female into a "Kindly One." Her daemonism is honored but distanced, repositioned in safe relation to the psyche. Lamia, a sexual fiend and man-killer, is beautifully reimagined until she improbably glows like a Raphael Madonna. Keatsian charm is her aura, the soft nest of the poet's best wishes.

Keats's letters to Fanny Brawne as he was composing "Lamia," partly inspired by her, plainly reveal the turbulence expressed in *Christabel* but concealed or transformed in "Lamia." Walter Jackson Bate's biography of Keats (1963) is one of the great books of our time, with the force and sweep of a nineteenth-century novel. But Bate's commentary, so movingly truthful for five hundred pages, comes apart when it deals with Keats's letters to Fanny Brawne. This is Keats's most fertile period. Yet his letters seethe with jealousy, hostility, obsession. Bate does not know what to do with Keats's jealousy and suggests he is affecting it. Keats's benevolence had become such a scholarly convention it was impossible to think anything else. There is an abyss in Bate's study between Keats's emotional and creative lives. Keats tells Woodhouse "he does not want ladies to read his poetry: that he writes for men." He bitterly assails contemporary women writers and intellectuals. To his friend Bailey:

> I am certain I have not a right feeling towards Women—at this moment I am striving to be just to them but I cannot—Is it because they fall so far beneath my Boyish imagination? . . . When among Men I have no evil thoughts, no malice, no spleen—I feel free to speak or to be silent—I can listen and from every one I can learn— my hands are in my pockets I am free from all suspicion and comfortable. When I am among Women I have evil thoughts, malice spleen—I cannot speak or be silent—I am full of Suspicions and therefore listen to no thing—I am in a hurry to be gone—

Faced with this amazing passage, Bate eloquently argues that Keats suffers such feelings because his mind is "strongly empathic or sympathetic," "habituated to identifying itself with what it conceives," and with women "such an identification is lacking."[34] This is credible only if one holds the Trilling view of Keats's "manliness." Probably the first to apply the word "manly" to Keats was Bailey himself. As with Coleridge calling Wordsworth "*all* man," it tells us less about Keats than about Bailey. "Manliness" is an utterly inappropriate word for a poet who extolls the imaginative virtues of passivity and effeminacy. Far from being unable to identify with women, as Bate claims, Keats in women's company ran the risk of *over*identification, loss of psychic autonomy. I adapt from the letter on the chameleon poet: woman's overfull identity "begins to press upon" Keats, so that he is "in a very little time annihilated." My theory seems confirmed by Keats's complaint to Fanny Brawne: "You have absorb'd me." Keats flees the company of women to escape being swallowed up by them. Their hunger is infinite.

The idealized view of Keats leaves us at a loss with "La Belle Dame Sans Merci," one of the supreme Romantic poems. Its heroine is a Circean sexual predator. Robert Graves sees her as his White Goddess, which Bloom calls a "misreading."[35] I too think it a misreading, but for different reasons. I follow in the Italian sado-baroque line of Mario Praz: I think that the sexual level of "La Belle Dame Sans Merci" is primary and that any allegory is supplemental and diversionary. Graves's hieratic White Goddess is wrong, since Keats's charmer is mysteriously undaunting: "I met a lady in the meads, / Full beautiful—a faery's child, / Her hair was long, her foot was light, / And her eyes were wild." The poem's sexual personae puzzled me for a decade. Representationally, Keats's "beautiful woman without mercy," destroying warriors, princes, and kings, is nonhierarchic. How does this disarming androgyne exert her masculine power?—a power manifest only a posteriori, never a priori in the persona she presents to human eyes. She is springtime nature tricking us into the winter of our discontent. Still, there is theater. What is her mask? I finally found an analogue to Keats's Belle Dame: the ruthless Lady Caroline Lamb, whom I compared to Goethe's Mignon and Warhol's Edie Sedgwick. This is the negative Mercurius androgyne, elfin, gamine, manic with nervous energy. Proof can be found in Keats's description of Fanny Brawne, model for his Belle Dame. It could serve as a portrait of Lady Caroline. Fanny is "beautiful and elegant, graceful, silly, fashionable and strange." Her face is "pale and thin." She is "monstrous in her behaviour flying out in all directions, calling people such names." Bate says other accounts of Fanny Brawne convey "her quick liveliness of manner and movement" and "general vivacity."[36] Mercurius is electric with hidden shocks. Keats lyricizes woman but cannot defeat her.

Keats's low opinion of women intellectuals is part of his antipathy to the trendy literary world. But it also relates to his poems of sexual danger, from *Endymion* through "Lamia" to "La Belle Dame Sans

Merci." Scholars who fail to see anxiety in Keats's sex poems readily acknowledge it in the *Hyperion* sequence, where the coloration is cool, grave, and desolate. Warmth for Keats is like light for Shelley. Appetite, tactility, body heat: when these gutter out, we are left with Dantesque grey. Keats's *Hyperion* and *The Fall of Hyperion* are *rite-de-passage* poems, perhaps the most striking in literature. In the first, Apollo moves from one psychic stage to the next. In the second, it is Keats himself. For Bloom, these poems record crises of poetic belatedness. But in the poems' deep structure, men are overpowered by female titans. *Hyperion* opens on a tableau of male impotence and is set into motion by infusions of female energy. This sexual double vision may have inaugurated the entire *Hyperion* sequence: a humiliating panorama of female domination and broken manhood.

Taking place at the transition from one generation of gods to the next, *Hyperion* begins in a masculine vacuum. The Muse-like females are connecting historical links. The third book repeats the poem's opening cycle. We find the poet Apollo weeping and inert. The titaness Mnemosyne, his invisible guardian, comes to his aid. Mnemosyne (Memory) fills him with "names, deeds, grey legends," pouring them into "the wide hollows" of his brain. This is one of the classic moments of Romantic sex-reversal. A dominatrix inseminates the passive poet with a torrent of knowledge, which Yeats borrows and sexually normalizes for "Leda and the Swan." Keats's female fecundator forces herself into the poet's vaginal skull, an image Keats repeats in *The Fall of Hyperion*, where Moneta's "hollow brain" is "enwombed." Apollo's brain-womb brims over through spiritual intercourse with nature and history.

Keats's Apollo has an elegant androgynous beauty—undulating "golden tresses" and limbs of "immortal fairness." He is a Hellenistic Apollo melting into Aphrodite. His "white melodious throat" is an Adonis motif I have defined as cross-sexual in a male. Apollo's sensuous "white soft temples" magically appear at the poem's most violent moment. Keats feminizes the head of all poets. Apollo is self-embowered in moody adolescence, which Mnemosyne forcibly terminates. The ephebic poet is raped by a female colossus, who injects him with a rushing sense of the reality of things outside himself. Like the vampire with Christabel, she speaks through the poet by invading his personality. Can she really make him a god? Hartman compares Apollo's paroxysm to the pangs of "childbirth or sexual climax."[37] Apollo gives birth to himself out of his own head, Zeus and Athena in one. His "wild commotions" are vatic spasms, prefiguring those of his oracle. In *The Fall of*

Hyperion, Keats himself shouts "with a Pythia's spleen." *Hyperion* ends in poetic couvade, with Apollo shrieking in pain.

Just before we see what Apollo brings to birth, *Hyperion* breaks off midsentence, leaving a row of asterisks. Scholars try to explain this puzzling truncation, with no agreement. The end of *Hyperion* belongs to my Apollonian category of muteness, stammering, and broken speech. *Hyperion* is self-frustrated because it attempts to transform the Apollo-poet from androgyne into potent male. Since it is a Romantic poem, it cannot do this. It meets a sexual barrier which Romantic imagination cannot pass and from which it falls back in defeat. Like *Christabel*, *Hyperion* is inspired by the poet's vision of sexual subordination to a supernatural female hierarch. Keats cannot finish *Hyperion* for the same reason Coleridge cannot finish *Christabel*: the entrancing hermaphroditic psychodrama is complete and will brook no sequel.

In *The Fall of Hyperion*, a reconstruction of *Hyperion*, Keats takes over Apollo's role. The saga comes nearer. In the mysterious sanctuary of his dream, the poet sees a distant image with features huge as a cloud. It is a statue of defeated Saturn, but for most of the poem, its gender is indeterminate. The only competence in the *Hyperion* poems belongs to spectral female superpowers, who oppress even as they liberate. Moneta is silent, terrific, uncanny. The poet swoons again and again: "I had a terror of her robes, / And chiefly of the veils." The ghostly veils "curtain'd her in mysteries," constricting the poet's heart. Moneta's veils are from the house of Spenserian couture. Is she the veiled hermaphrodite Venus of *The Faerie Queene?* If so, she is all-knowing, ever-secret mother nature. In Keats, she is the true threat to poetry. Moneta is "the veiled shadow" or "the tall shade"—desexing locutions like Shelley's numinous dematerializations. Keats's towering women are androgynes, monumental totems of world-force. Cloudy Saturn may be only a displacement or psychic split of veiled Moneta. When he appears in the second poem, he is much weaker than in the first. Moneta has overwhelmed him poetically. When Saturn rises painfully and starts to walk, the poem breaks off. He is now an anemic shade, drained of fictive energy.

Hyperion's Mnemosyne is more maternal than *The Fall of Hyperion*'s severe, sepulchral Moneta. Moneta makes the second poem palpably more anxious than the first. This anxiety is not just about poetic vocation but about sex and identity. The Greeks, says Farnell, tried "to avoid the mention, wherever possible, of the personal names of the chthonian powers and to substitute for them appellatives which were generally

euphemistic."[38] Keats's poetry treats the chthonian with ritual euphemism. His "Ode on a Grecian Urn" becomes darker if one accepts my
principle that the western objet d'art is an Apollonian protest against the
chthonian. If Keats's monumental females are sober versions of the
Great Mother, then his ambivalence toward them must reflect a latent
ambivalence toward biologic process. His vivid sensory imagery and
capacious vaginal skull bring the body to birth by pure imagination,
dramatized in Apollo's painful self-extrusion. Is this hostile usurpation
of female power? Keats goes around sex directly to the *prima materia*—
evading the mother. Like Blake and Wordsworth, he tries to abolish
sexual personae. But he is haunted by daemonic hierarchic females. By
becoming the identity-free chameleon poet, Keats eliminates gender.
Dissolution of identity also abolishes the female sex. In "To Autumn,"
woman is unneeded, for she has been internalized by the poet, with his
capacious, fecund, and self-irrigating imagination. The feminized male
self becomes all-encompassing and self-sufficient. Keats's poems, opening the reader to nature, close off the poet in his own rigorous ritual
precinct.

15

Cults of Sex and Beauty

Balzac

Decadence is the Mannerist late phase of Romantic style. Romantic imagination broke through all limits. Decadence, burdened by freedom, invents harsh new limits, psychosexual and artistic. It is a process of objectification and fixation, disciplining and intensifying the rogue western eye. High Romanticism valued energy, room to breathe. Decadent Late Romanticism shuts the doors and locks self and eye in pagan cultism. Its nature theory follows Sade and Coleridge, who see nature's cruelty and excess. Art supplants nature. The objet d'art becomes the center of fetishistic connoisseurship. Person is transformed into beautiful thing, beyond the law. Decadence takes western sexual personae to their ultimate point of hardness and artificiality. It is drenched in sex, but sex as thought rather than action. Decadence is an Apollonian raid on the Dionysian, the aggressive eye pinning and freezing nature's roiling objects.

France pioneered in modern sophistication. The arrogant, urbane French manner began in the court world of the *ancien régime*. Imitated by Oscar Wilde, it became what I call the English epicene, transplanted to America as male-homosexual manners. French sophistication is an excess of wordly knowledge, a cynicism born of turbulence and reaction. From its self-devouring revolution to the Nazi occupation, France seemed destined to a cycle of extravagant pride and humiliation. English Romanticism, unchecked by national disasters, projected its optimism into nineteenth-century popular culture. But French Romanticism, buffeted by politics, quickly turned into Decadence. The century's first completely Decadent work is Balzac's *Sarrasine* (1830), which was written four months after the July Revolution and rise to the throne of Louis Philippe, the Citizen King. The same year saw the first noisy avant-garde debut, when Victor Hugo's *Hernani* opened to a jeering, cheering audience. The French polarization of artist and bourgeois, fiercest in the struggle between painter and Academy, helped formalize the public ritualism of Decadence.

Behind *Sarrasine* is *Fragoletta* (1829), a forgotten novel by Balzac's friend, Henri de Latouche, which also influenced Gautier's *Mademoiselle de Maupin* (1835), a central text of French and English Decadence to the end of the century. Latouche's heroine, Camille, nicknamed Fragoletta ("little strawberry"), is a transvestite adolescent surely inspired by Goethe's boyish Mignon. But while Mignon dies before sexual maturity, Camille lives on. As in *The Monk*, novel's end forces us to reread. Camille turns out to be the same person as her twin brother, a callous despoiler of girls. The lesbian theme reappears at the luxurious court of Naples, where the queen seduces Emma, Lady Hamilton, wife of the English ambassador. Camille's self-transformation into an invented male twin is prefigured by the "Sleeping Hermaphrodite" that she and her companions inspect in Naples. Latouche calls the statue a "fabulous reverie" expressing man's "double nature," words echoed in a Gautier poem. The visitors are "poor northerners" who are "lost in the labyrinth of thought" and unable to comprehend the Hermaphrodite. Italians, on the other hand, "continue antiquity" by their worship of beauty, a theme Gautier expands in *Maupin*.[1] Latouche is, to my knowledge, the first writer to join the androgyne to the amoral cult of beauty, a Decadent staple. Camille, denying she is of the human species, already suffers from Decadent alienation. Though it begins the androgyne's Decadent career as a symbol of damnation, *Fragoletta* as a whole has an airiness and robustness we see again only in *Maupin*. The ominous closed spaces of the Decadence are created by *Sarrasine*.

Normally classed as a social novelist, Balzac also belongs to the history of nineteenth-century Decadence. Many of his major characters are double-sexed. The social novel is the literary genre least hospitable to the androgyne, for reasons I will address. Balzac, like Goethe, is dual. As a novelist, he is documentary and analytic. As a Romantic, he is perverse and occult. It is from sex-crossing Romantic imagination that his androgynes come. In *The Human Comedy*, as in *Faust*, the androgyne symbolizes the all-inclusiveness of the text itself, subsuming opposites of sex, mood, and style.

In *Sarrasine*, a pivotal work in the shift from High to Late Romanticism, Balzac reimagines the Italian adventures of Latouche's transvestite heroine in Decadent terms. Visiting Rome in 1758, Sarrasine, a French sculptor, falls madly in love with a prima donna, La Zambinella.

The singer embodies the "ideal beauty" celibate Sarrasine has vainly sought in real life, the model for which were "the rich, sweet creations of ancient Greece."[2] Only after a rendezvous with Zambinella does Sarrasine learn, to his public humiliation, that she is a male, a castrato. Again, a sexual revelation forces us to reread. Zambinella's first appearance onstage becomes a sacred epiphany, ravishing Sarrasine with a vision of hermaphrodite perfection. Ideal beauty has eluded him because ordinary mortals have one gender, while Zambinella is sexually composite, in the Greek way. Sarrasine's susceptibility comes from his artistic self-absorption. He has no sexual needs because he is already half-feminine. Barthes points out, in a muddled commentary, that the name Sarrasine connotes "femininity"; the usual French form would be Sarrazin.[3] Hence the androgyne Sarrasine can be emotionally subjugated only by another androgyne. He dies a virgin, assassinated by order of Zambinella's patron, a homosexual cardinal.

Romantic poetry, I noted, grants virility no privileges. *Sarrasine,* a Late Romantic fiction, eradicates virility altogether by making a castrate its premiere sexual persona. Eunuchs in Byron's *Don Juan* are merely decorative accessories. Now the eunuch is hierarchized as an idol inspiring love and lust. Romanticism evades sexuality through its withdrawal from masculine action, but Balzac frustrates sex by deforming nature. Sarrasine reviles Zambinella: "Monster! You who can give life to nothing!" Seceding from nature, Decadence wipes Rousseau out of Romanticism. Sade, we saw, combats Rousseau by daemonizing nature and descending into its turbulence. Decadence turns from energy toward stasis. Romantic creative passivity becomes Decadent aestheticism, contemplativeness toward precious things sealed off from nature. Balzac's Zambinella is the first Decadent art object. The transsexual castrato is an artificial sex, product of biology manipulated for art. Zambinella *does* give birth—to other art objects. First is Sarrasine's statue of him/her; then a marble copy commissioned by the cardinal; next a painting of Adonis based on the copy; finally, Girodet's sensuous painting of effeminate sleeping Endymion, inspired, Balzac claims, by Zambinella as Adonis. The sterile castrato, propagating itself through other art works, is an example of my technological androgyne, the manufactured object. Like Vergil's Trojan Horse, he/she teems with inorganic seed.

Like Coleridge's poet, Zambinella is privileged but cursed. Her castration is the shamanistic sacrifice of virility accompanying a special gift in antiquity. Showered with acclaim, she suffers harsh removal from normal life. She hates humanity: "For me, the world is a desert. I am an accursed creature." The androgyne's lonely isolation looks backward toward *Fragoletta* and forward toward Baudelaire's "Delphine and Hippolyte," which borrows Balzac's words. Zambinella inhabits an uncanny temenos, a sequestered zone created by her hieratic power. When Sarrasine first sees her, she is protected by the theatrical frame, through which no one can step. Visiting her mansion, he is led through a moonlit "labyrinth" of halls and stairs to the innermost sanctum, a sumptuous "mysterious room." Zambinella is kept, in effect, in a seraglio, a motif Balzac reuses in *The Girl with the Golden Eyes*. The physical and psychological imprisonment is Decadent. *Sarrasine*'s pitiless hierarch, the shadowy cardinal, keeps Zambinella in bondage. She is a prized art object lent for guarded public display. Hovering in detached omniscience, the cardinal is like Cellini's hidden Duke listening to the crowd's adulation of *Perseus*. The work is under jealous watch, amorous and despotic.

In Shelley's *Epipsychidion* I found psychological heliotropism, the western pattern of erotic submission to a personality as art object. The Decadence turns this into obsession and enslavement, shown by Sarrasine's first reaction to Zambinella: "Fame, knowledge, future, existence, laurels, everything collapsed." His personality is invaded and his artistic autonomy overthrown. When the dream-woman proves fake, he plots revenge, but as a Romantic male he cannot act. Instead of killing, he is killed. The story's ritual pattern is an Actaeon myth: Sarrasine is slain for having seen something forbidden. All Rome knows Zambinella's status, but Sarrasine is a stranger blundering into a domain of ritual conventions and proscriptions. He profanes a religious mystery. The cardinal is a vengeful high priest spilling the blood of an impious trespasser. Discussing Blake, I called the female body a veil and concealment, a series of inner sanctuaries, like a temple. *Sarrasine* is a process of uncovering a body never actually seen naked. It records the discovery of gender, or rather of nongender. Moving through successive closed spaces, the story takes its form because the castrato, by posing as a woman, makes it mimic the hiddenness of female anatomy. Room by room, Sarrasine advances to the cella of the hermaphrodite god, veiled like Spenser's Venus. Balzac gathers these penetrated spaces within a final border, the narrative present in which Zambinella's past is recreated for an appalled confidante.

The novella brilliantly depicts Zambinella's radiant glamour, luring Sarrasine into an intrigue that closes about him. Remember the sexual errors of Shakespeare's transvestite comedies. Despairing, Sarrasine demands of Zambinella: "Have you any sisters who resemble you?

Then die!" This is not the Renaissance, where a lucky twin steps forward to deflect homoerotic impulses into marriage. Sarrasine's sexual
error ends in his death. He is a Decadent victim to art, a new religion
craving martyrs. What is modern about *Sarrasine* is its central question
of sexual identity, Rousseau's invention. Balzac shows sexuality as
something incomprehensible and deranging. The Renaissance transvestites guide their admirers back to social integration. But Zambinella,
odalisque and artistic solipsist in one, is a Decadent androgyne indifferent to her suitor's fate. His annihilation reflects her own sexual self-
cancellations.

Zambinella's glamour connects the Italian castrati to modern film
stars, the most glamourous creatures since the Greco-Roman gods.
Angus Heriot speaks of early opera's "international star-system": "The
great singers of the eighteenth century were in a sense the precursors of
Clark Gable and Marilyn Monroe."[4] Glamour and charisma are hermaphroditic principles. Balzac captures the decadence inherent in the
Catholic castrati. Heriot calls ecclesiastic policy "absurdly inconsistent": even accomplices in the act of castration could be excommunicated, yet every Italian church had castrato singers, even the Vatican. St.
Paul's injunction that women keep silent in church kept them out of
choirs until the seventeenth century and later. Hence high parts were
taken by boys or eunuchs. Like English chimney sweeps, children were
sold into castration by impoverished parents. Protestants like Lady
Mary Wortley Montagu condemned the practice as barbaric.[5] In Rome
in 1745, Casanova makes Sarrasine's sexual error. An attractive person
enters a café: "At the appearance of his hips, I took him for a girl in
disguise, and I said so to the abbé Gama; but the latter told me that it
was Bepino della Mamana, a famous castrato. The abbé called him
over, and told him, laughing, that I had taken him for a girl. The
impudent creature, looking fixedly at me, told me that if I liked he
would prove that I was right, or that I was wrong." Casanova says of
papal toleration of the castrati, "Rome the holy city ... in this way
forces every man to become a pederast."[6] The castrati system was
another illustration of Roman Catholicism's vestigial paganism.

Opera's star castrato inspired bisexual ardor. There were hot claques
of groupies, a frenzied eroticism like the homosexual hysteria at Judy
Garland performances, which I compared to orgiastic rites of the Great
Mother. The star always has a transsexual and hierarchic significance.
He or she is a creator of cults. Balzac's description of Sarrasine's passionate reaction to and conversion by Zambinella is, I conclude, the first
analysis of the psychodynamics of popular culture. We see the actual

moment of cathexis when eroticism is transferred from spectator to sexual persona in performance. Sarrasine is the thunderstruck modern movie fan.

Queen Christina, Napoleon, Goethe, and Wagner sponsored or praised castrati. The castrate voice had a strange power not duplicated by soprano or countertenor. Schopenhauer called it "supernaturally beautiful," with a "silver purity" yet "indescribable power." Singer Emma Calvé called it "strange, sexless, superhuman, uncanny."[7] The castrato voice had more gravity and authority than a boy's voice. The music of these mutilated creatures, irreparably indentured into artistic servitude, paradoxically attained a seraphic freedom and dignity. Like stars of the Hollywood studio, the castrati were both slaves and hierarchs. Though several lived to the end of the nineteenth century, their great era was over by the 1820s. Their influence is still felt in the transvestite breeches roles or pants parts now filled by women, such as Cherubino in Mozart's *Marriage of Figaro* and Octavian in Strauss's *Der Rosenkavalier*. Europe's increasing liberalism would no longer tolerate the castration of boys; so the disappearance of the castrati paralleled the resistance to slavery and child labor. But there was also a change in artistic fashion: the epicene castrato voice belonged to the courtly *ancien régime*.

The Girl with the Golden Eyes (written March 1834–April 1835) is the second of Balzac's Decadent fictions. Structurally, it resembles *Sarrasine:* a mysterious woman is followed into a dangerous labyrinth and private prison. Both sexual adventures end in death, but now it is not the passionate pursuer but the sequestered sex-object who is slain. The dandy Henri de Marsay, hero of *The Girl with the Golden Eyes*, is one of Balzac's recurring characters, later rising to Prime Minister. At the Opéra in *Lost Illusions*, where he crushes provincial Lucien de Rubempré with patrician snobbery, De Marsay has "a kind of girlish beauty: beauty of a languid, effeminate kind."[8] His androgyny causes all the trouble of *The Girl with the Golden Eyes*.

Idle and spoiled, De Marsay holds no ethical or political beliefs whatever. The English Regency dandy was a final flowering of eighteenth-century epicene style, as embodied in that slippery court hermaphrodite, Lord Hervey. De Marsay is based on contemporary Parisian dandies like the Duc de Morny, with his "effeminate charm."[9] De Marsay must take his name from the Comte d'Orsay, the bewitching "Dandy or Exquisite" whom Lady Blessington scandalously added to her entourage. Byron called him "a beauty."[10] *The New Yorker*'s supercilious, monocled Eustace Tilley is a dandy of the D'Orsay type.[11]

The Girl with the Golden Eyes is dedicated to Delacroix, whose Oriental luxury and barbarism came from Byron. De Marsay is the illegitimate son of a French marquise and the English libertine Lord Dudley, based on Byron. Like Byron, Dudley flees England in 1816 "to escape from English justice, which gives its protection to nothing exotic except merchandise." Spotting De Marsay in Paris, Dudley asks who "the beautiful young man" is: "On hearing his name he said: 'Ah! He's my son. What a pity!' "[12] Like Byron, therefore, Dudley is both bisexual and negligent. He created a "second masterpiece," a daughter sired upon a Spanish lady. None of his many bastards knows the others.

Balzac's long prelude is a Dantean survey of the "inferno" of amoral Paris. The city is ruled by two forces, "gold and pleasure," images to be fused in the girl with the golden eyes. Meeting De Marsay in a garden, Paquita Valdes is overcome by a "paralysing shock," which the young man attributes to the "animal magnetism" of "elective affinities." These affinities come from the fact that Paquita lives in sexual bondage to a Spanish lesbian, the Marquise de San-Real, who turns out to be De Marsay's half-sister and hence his Byronic Romantic double. Paquita's gold eyes signify her material value as a sensual and artistic object. She is a victim of the cold acquisitiveness of Byron's aristocratic children. Smuggled in as an alien, Paquita becomes a hapless symbol of Paris and its vices.

De Marsay smugly assumes that the heavily guarded girl is the marquis' mistress: "He was about to act the eternally old, eternally new comedy with three characters," an old man, a girl, and a suitor. But De Marsay is in sexual error. The drama has one man and two women, and it will be tragedy, not comedy. At his first rendezvous, De Marsay is blindfolded and driven endlessly through the streets, an estranging device which makes his native city a sexual labyrinth. Balzac achieved the same effect in *Sarrasine* by transporting his hero from Paris to Rome. De Marsay reaches Paquita as Sarrasine does Zambinella in her palazzo, by ritualistic passage through a series of darkened rooms.

De Marsay finds himself in a secret chamber, an opulent boudoir hung with red fabric and adorned with silver and gold. It is the first elaborate aesthetic environment of the Decadence, looking forward to Baudelaire's real-life salon and Huysmans' mansion in *A Rebours*. Gautier says Balzac occupied an identical salon while writing *The Girl with the Golden Eyes*, but it is unclear which room influenced the other.[13]

Balzac's description of the boudoir is long, painterly, and deeply influenced by Delacroix. The lesbian marquise, constructing a seraglio for a one-woman harem, is a female aesthete and hence the first Decadent architect. She is a Sadean libertine, her citadel, with its soundproofed walls, shutting out society and law. Her sexual arena is a kind of tomb. Again we are in the claustrophobic space of the Decadence. Every detail of décor is meant to "incite to voluptuousness." Eros is intensified by captivity, a black-box theater of sexual personae. The boudoir is a Spenserian Bower of Bliss or Blakean crystal cabinet, dedicated to the self-enjoyment of the female principle. Its asymmetrical design, half curved, half rectangular, reflects the marquise's divided nature: female organicism joined to male geometry, a psychic hermaphroditism. The color scheme—red, white, and pink—gives the boudoir a vaginal character, crucial to the shocking finale.

De Marsay's first sex with the girl is transvestite: she puts him in a red velvet gown and woman's cap and shawl. His pleasure is unsurpassed. Is it due to Paquita's virtuosity—or his female drag? Next day, he is furious: "Everything showed him that he had posed for another person." Yet when he returns to the boudoir for a final rendezvous, he initiates the transvestism. His femininity is surfacing. At climax, he is stunned by "the first mortification" of his pampered life: Paquita deliriously calls out a woman's name. He looks for a dagger to kill her, as if sudden action could remedy the affront to manhood. Paquita is clearly imagining her lover as the marquise, a transposition I call sexual metathesis. De Marsay has been drafted into a sexual theater: he exists only to phallicize an absent woman lover. The girl with the golden eyes has exploited his virility for her own perverse purposes.

De Marsay vows revenge. To kill Paquita, he and his friends assault the mansion, oddly meeting no resistance. In the boudoir, De Marsay finds the marquise returned from London:

> The girl with the golden eyes lay dying, bathed in her own blood. . . . The white boudoir, in which the crimson of blood stood out so coldly, showed that a prolonged struggle had taken place. Paquita's blood-stained hands were imprinted on the cushions. . . . Whole strips of the fluted hangings had been torn down by bleeding hands which doubtless had put up a long struggle. Paquita must even have tried to scramble up the wall. There were the marks of her feet along the back of the divan, along which she had no doubt run in her flight. Her whole body, slashed by the dagger-thrusts of her executioner, showed how fiercely she had fought . . .

She was stretched out on the floor and, in her dying throes, had bitten through the muscles of Madame de San-Real's instep. The marquise was still holding her blood-stained dagger, her hair had been torn out in handfuls, she was covered with bites, several of which were still bleeding, and her tattered robe revealed her half-naked form and her lacerated breasts. She was a tragic picture.

She had the face of a fury avid for and redolent of blood. She was panting, with her mouth half-open, and her breath came too quickly for her to take the air in through her nostrils.

Decadent eros, I said, treats the beloved as an objet d'art. Balzac demonstrates the Decadent transformation of person into object in this horrifying scene, where the girl with the golden eyes is torn to shreds by her pitiless mistress. The fanatically preserved art work is dashed to pieces. The profusion of wounds is a brutal iteration of the murder's provocation, the girl's phallic defilement by De Marsay. Unlike the Ephesian Artemis, with her many penises, the hermaphrodite Marquise has one honed penis, the dagger, which makes many vaginas. Her abuse of her lover's body dramatizes Paquita's femaleness, her sexual facticity or objecthood.

The violence is intensified by the bloody devastation of the aesthetic boudoir. Acrasia's Bower of Bliss is razed not by the white knight Guyon but by the witch herself. The marquise enacts a phallic rupture of the vaginal cell. Panting in frenzy and bleeding from her own wounds, she experiences a macro-orgasm through her rape-murder of both girl and room. Balzac stages a savage Sadean orgy, a return of Medea. The ransacked boudoir is a panorama of civilization disordered by the chthonian. The scene seems to be an apocalypse of Romantic energy. But no: we do not witness the murder, even by flashback or messenger speech. Like De Marsay, we meet it when it is already a memory and the boudoir is in archaeological ruins. Balzac is interested in the murder not as act but as Apollonian tableau, a frozen Decadent glyph.

Visually, the murder scene is surely modelled on Delacroix's *Death of Sardanapalus*, with its tumult of destruction (fig. 36). The marquise combines Byron's cold-eyed effeminate emperor with the straining guard plunging his knife into the throat of a nude odalisque, caught and sexually pinned from behind. The marquise, with her "moorish complexion," is also Byron's sultana Gulbeyaz, who wears a poniard and here uses it. Balzac's marquise is the first ferocious chthonian female of the Decadence, prefiguring Cleopatra, Herodias, and Salomé. She is the virago androgyne, plushly female but mentally masculine. She is

36. Eugène Delacroix, *Death of Sardanapalus*, 1826.

Dionysian because of her furor (she does not see De Marsay) and her form-obliterating style of murder, a choppy Dionysian signature. A parallel with *Sarrasine:* the marquise, like the cardinal, is the jealous hierarch avenging profanation of a sequestered possession. But the cardinal sends emissaries armed with daggers, while the marquise, as an oriental Amazon, wields the murder weapon herself. A parallel with Coleridge's *Christabel:* a sex crime occurs in a palace nominally ruled by an aged, impotent male. Meanwhile, the house is being turned upside down by lesbianism and blood sports.

We wait in suspense for Paquita's unknown guardian, until the daemonic epiphany of the final pages. The marquise arrives like a medieval king returning from war to avenge a dishonored spouse. She left her bride in a chastity belt: Paquita laments "the ring of bronze drawn round between myself and creation." Bronze ring, gold eyes, crowded circles of the Parisian inferno. Female sex-experience, centering upon the boudoir's solipsistic Blakean rose, has a primitive intractability and exclusivity. The true hierarch shows up in this story, as he does not in *Sarrasine.* How does Balzac depict it? The eagerly awaited person appears first as a foot! When De Marsay bursts into the boudoir, we look through his eyes at the dying Paquita and ravaged room, minutely described. Then we glance up Paquita's prone body to find her teeth sunk in the marquise's foot. The novella now abandons the girl and transfers its attention to the marquise, with whom it remains to the end. Balzac's technique is astonishingly prophetic of cinematic style. His eye is camera and spotlight. He pans the boudoir, zooms in on a foot, then slowly rises to take in the statuesque marquise. The bitten foot belongs to a Decadent aesthetic. Havelock Ellis says of Decadent art, "The whole is subordinated to the parts."[14] Overall design is atomized, as in Mannerism. Balzac's marquise appears not just as a foot but as part of a foot, an instep, and even as part of that, the muscles of an instep. The human is reduced to the bestial, as with Dante's skull-gnawing Ugolino. But Dante's women never sink so low. Balzac uses his romance of the fixed foot as a narrative *rite de passage*, turning the track of the story toward a new character. In this singular moment, French literary imagination veers toward Decadence.

The finale of *The Girl with the Golden Eyes* anticipates a classic moment of cinema. Paquita is not just killed but slaughtered, butchered, as in the murder scene of Alfred Hitchcock's *Psycho* (1960). In Hitchcock as in Balzac, a knife-wielding hermaphrodite (the transvestite Norman Bates, played by Anthony Perkins) compulsively slashes the body of a beautiful woman enclosed in a female bower (Janet Leigh as Marion Crane, ecstatically soaping herself in a gleaming white shower). The horror of the two scenes comes from the mutilation of a sensuous female body around which an erotic aura has been painstakingly built up, in Balzac by the stressing of Paquita's "luminous" beauty and in Hitchcock by the voyeuristic display of half-naked Janet Leigh, who models lingerie from the first scene on. Until her unfortunate shower, Marion tends to appear in imposing Fifties brassieres, white then black, in accord with her changing moral mood. Is she vulnerable to attack only when she removes her Amazonian armature? Dying Paquita rips down the drapes, and dying Marion rips down the shower curtain. Tearing of a veil signifies destruction of the bower of the female body. Balzac and Hitchcock turn the beautiful woman into an object. Marion's blood flows indifferently with the bathwater down the drain. Her body falls awkwardly over the edge of the tub. Her cheek is deformed by the tile floor. And the last we see of her is her dead *eye*, lingered over by the camera until it has the iconicism of Paquita's golden eyes. Cold and marmoreal but still glittering with beauty, Marion's eye belongs to a fallen statue, an art object vandalized and abandoned. Balzac and Hitchcock record symbolic sex acts by megalomaniacal but phallically impotent cultists. Norman Bates, like the marquise, has his own sequestered ritual love-object—the body of his mummified mother!

We left the marquise standing distracted over Paquita's body. When she finally sees De Marsay, she rushes at him with raised dagger. He seizes her by the arm, and for a long moment they stand trembling, staring at each other in cold shock: "The two Menaechmi could not have been more alike. In one breath they asked the same question: 'Is not Lord Dudley your father?' " Pointing to Paquita, De Marsay says, "She remained true to the blood." This is the story's second frozen tableau. The Romantic fraternal doubles come together in a great recognition scene. Their terror is from confronting an uncanny mirror-image. The desire in Shelley's *Epipsychidion* to enter into deep emotional or sexual dialogue with one's double is fulfilled in *The Girl with the Golden Eyes*. Though brother and sister are strangers, they irresistibly meet through the magnetism of their identical soul-substance, a gravitation at work in *The Monk*, where incest is inadvertently committed. Byron's incest, I said, may be a dream of copulating with oneself in sexually transmuted form, something that nearly happens in Balzac: De Marsay grabs and kisses the marquise, who pulls away. A displaced incest has in fact occurred, for both brother and sister lust for and enjoy the same sexual object. Gang rape by army platoons or fraternity brothers may conceal subliminal homosexual impulses. Similarly, the marquise and De Marsay meet in the body of Paquita, whom they both inseminate. They flood her with their superior force, sweeping her away.

Brother and sister have "the same voice." Both are aesthetes, sensualists, murderers. Balzac makes half-feminine Byron the progenitor of twin androgynes. In this *Twelfth Night*, Viola is fiercer than Sebastian. De Marsay is an epicene Hellenistic Apollo, and his twin is Artemis as Mistress of the Beasts. Before and after the murder, the marquise too is a Decadent. She leaves bound for a Spanish convent, a typical Decadent pattern: the voluptuary ends in the church, stepping easily from perversion to celibacy, simply exchanging one ritualized excess for another. In the convent, will the marquise undertake an impious memorialization of dead Paquita? Or will she replay the lesbian caprices of Diderot's *The Nun*? The marquise imports archaic Mediterranean barbarism into modern Paris, just as Cleopatra threatens to do to Rome. De Marsay's passage through city labyrinth to secret boudoir is thus a regression through history, where, as always in Romanticism, incest waits as a spiritual destination.

De Marsay calls Paquita "the most adorably feminine woman I have ever met." As in Spenser, Blake, and Sade, femininity is an invitation to disaster. This is obvious when De Marsay and friends invade the mansion. Mythologically, the men should be liberators, like Perseus rescuing Andromeda from the monster (the lesbian marquise). Instead, in a Decadent reversal, the men come to slay the maiden. Hence feminine Paquita is crushed between opposing forces. She is killed both for insulting the masculine principle and for yielding to it. The illiterate girl knows nothing but sex, Sadean philosophy of the boudoir. She practices a sexual alchemy, discovering and reinforcing the twinship of the marquise and De Marsay by imposing a rusing sexual persona upon him. Like Shelley's Witch, she fabricates a servant Hermaphrodite, a male mannequin of the marquise. Simultaneously, she intensifies the androgyny of the marquise, whose jealousy shifts her radically toward the masculine extreme. Submitting in fantasy to the woman with a penis, Paquita creates her, for the marquise seizes the phallic dagger to slay her. Balzac confirms Spenser's and Blake's intuition of the erotic perversity of unqualified femininity: flirting with De Marsay, Paquita induces her own rape-murder.

Naturalistically, De Marsay deputizes his friends to overcome the mansion's guards, who melt away by their arrival. But archetypally, De Marsay needs male companions to retain his own gender in a hallucinatory female environment. If the marquise is Byron's Gulbeyaz, the mansion is *Don Juan*'s seraglio, where virility is yoked and mocked. De Marsay's transvestism is thus Don Juan's as Juanna. Like Byron's seraglio, the boudoir is a matriarchate guarded by eunuchs—here the sinister African Christemio, foreshadowing the ghoulish eunuch-executioner of Gustave Moreau's *Salomé*. Paquita has polluted a female sanctuary. For her sacrilege of admitting a male, like Publius Clodius transvestized at rites of the Bona Dea, she is slain and the temple destroyed. The marquise murders Paquita as a holocaust to an angry goddess. Since this is a Romantic fiction, the sanctuary harbors a cult of the self: the marquise is that goddess.

Late Romantic Balzac extends Rousseau's and Sade's philosophizing of sex. In *The Girl with the Golden Eyes*, brother and sister prove kinship through intercourse with the same woman. A sex act is the ritual medium of identity. Functioning abstractly, stripped of emotion, the act is a western instrument of self-knowledge. The girl with the golden eyes is only a boundary herm where two nationals meet. The knowledge gained by the fraternal doubles from their collaborative sex-experience benefits no one. It is ethically dissipated by the Romantic separation of self from society. Unlike Shakespeare's twins, these doubles do not affiliate but immediately diverge: sister flatly tells brother, "We shall never meet again." Each returns to amoral Sadean solitude. The Renaissance twins arouse and satisfy multiple erotic responses, but the Romantic twins solipsistically focus on and obliterate the same girl, in an incestuous cul-de-sac.

For their mutual recognition, brother and sister return to their poetic origins in the Byronic seraglio, a Delphic omphalos-spot. Byron is the progenitor of *The Girl with the Golden Eyes* both inside and outside the text. I suspect, in fact, that the marquise sojourns in London for most of the story because she is taking transfusions from English Romantic imagination. Her lesbianism comes from Byron's sultana, Latouche's Camille, and notorious sophisticates like George Sand. The story ends with the new Decadent cynicism, a revival of eighteenth-century libertinage. De Marsay, promenading, dismisses a query about the girl with the golden eyes: she is dead, he says, of "a chest ailment." In other words, she had a heart. Rousseau's erotic lyricism is gone. The blood-drenched boudoir of *The Girl with the Golden Eyes* encapsulates the turn from High to Late Romanticism, with its artificiality, enslavement, and corruption.

Balzac began writing *Seraphita* (December 1833–November 1835) before completing *The Girl with the Golden Eyes*. I view the two as morally opposite halves of a single sexual idea. One is the Inferno of *The Human Comedy*, the other the Paradiso. *Seraphita* is unusual for Balzac in taking place outside France, in Scandinavia, home of the Swedish mystic Emanuel Swedenborg, whose ideas overwhelm the narrative. Norway's icy whiteness allows Balzac to achieve dazzling Apollonian effects like Spenser's. Probably due to its occultism, *Seraphita* was Yeats's favorite Balzac work.

A man and woman, Wilfrid and Minna, fall in love with Seraphita, whom he perceives as female and she as male. The indeterminacy of gender is sustained throughout the novella. Seraphita belongs to my category of androgyne as Apollonian angel. Like Wordsworth and Shelley, Balzac attempts a Romantic seraphicization, the most elaborate in literature. Wilfrid and Minna will witness Seraphita's transfiguration into a real seraph, welcomed by celestial hosts. *Seraphita* is the French *Epipsychidion*.

In Part One, "Seraphitus," we see the angel in his masculine phase. He is an adolescent ephebe of "brilliant splendor," his eyes blazing with

solar fire. His northland is a visionary realm glittering with "flashes of
the ephemeral diamonds produced by the crystallized surface of the
snow and ice."[15] Character and climate are saturated with Apollonian
light. Descending the mountain to reenter society, Seraphitus turns into
Seraphita. Spiritual retraction, sexual transformation: the figure softens; the voice turns treble. Spenser's switch of sexual perspective is a
quick jump-cut, but Balzac's is a long gliding declension, an Ovidian
metamorphosis, slow and magical. Balzac cleverly anchors the novella
to a homely group of sometimes tedious humans. Minna, for example,
like Goethe's Charlotte, is of conspicuously average intelligence. These
people function as rhetorical lightning rods, absorbing the electric
charge generated by charismatic Seraphita. They stabilize the naturalism of the text and prevent it from turning into allegory.

Seraphitus rejects Minna's advances: sex is "too gross" or material.
Like Latouche's Camille, he calls himself monster and exile, a Romantic outcast. The hermaphrodite, too complete, is imprisoned in solitude.
Like Spenser's Belphoebe, he/she flees the contamination of lesser
beings. Nine-year-old Seraphita could sit in church only when separated from others: "If this space is not left about her, she is ill." Like
Goethe's Mignon, Seraphita has an excess of nervous intensity. She is
self-sequestered in the magic circle of ritual purity, a shamanistic quarantine. Like Byron's Manfred, Seraphitus declares, "I live by myself
and for myself." Late Romantic knowledge presses on him: "Like the
debauched Emperors of Pagan Rome, I am disgusted with all things."
He has the paradoxical Decadent conflation of satiety with virginity.

In Part One we saw Seraphitus from the point of view of enamoured
Minna. In Part Two, "Seraphita," we take the point of view of enamoured Wilfrid, who thinks the angel female. Seraphitus denied he was a
man. Now Seraphita denies she is a woman. Seraphita always positions
herself to the other side of whatever gender is projected onto her. These
are the chaste evasions of the Apollonian androgyne, like Belphoebe
"swerving back" from lustful clutches. Beloved, like Rosalind, by both
man and woman, Seraphita finds a unique Romantic solution. She
declares Wilfrid and Minna "one being," simultaneously "a brother or
a sister" to her. So let this brother and sister marry each other! The story
ends with the union of the two, so little acquainted that up to this point
they have addressed each other with the formal *vous*. Their marriage is a
Romantic coalescence of doubles, the pattern of Byron's *Manfred* and
Sardanapalus. Seraphita plays Shakespeare's Hymen, a numinous nup-
tial spirit. The finale is an ascension of a god, leaving his disciples

behind to perpetuate his cult. Wilfrid and Minna as "one being" are divided halves of a Platonic androgyne. Like Shelley's Witch, Seraphita makes a mirror-image, a hermaphrodite self-portrait. To marry off her admirers is to fuse two sexual views of one personality. Seraphita performs a daring perceptual experiment and reassembles herself in human form. She replays *Epipsychidion* by creating her own incestuous twin.

"Who and what are you?" asks Minna, like Shelley pondering Emilia Viviani's ontological status. Wilfrid compares Seraphita to gases, half material, half spiritual. Occult beings "work magic" on "hapless victims," reducing them to "wretched serfdom" by "the weight and magnificent sway of a superior nature." "Penetrated" by Seraphita, Wilfrid suffers Decadent enslavement: "I love her and I hate her!" Her sexual duality plunges him into Catullus' emotional ambivalence. He has Decadent visions of phosphorescence and narcosis. Seraphita is like opium or the torpedo fish "which electrifies and numbs the fisherman." The charismatic personality is a vampire, oblivious to human suffering.

Part Three, "Seraphita-Seraphitus," fills in the angel's genealogy. She seems "conceived by the union of sun and ice," like the Spenserian "fire and snow" of Shelley's Hermaphrodite. As the child of Swedenborg's cousin and "most zealous disciple," Baron Seraphitz, Seraphita is an emanation of Swedenborg's thought. Swedenborg's relation to *Seraphita* is like Byron's to *The Girl with the Golden Eyes*: both men are eccentric trendsetters and progenitors of androgynes. Young Balzac, says Félix Longaud, "nourished himself" upon his mother's Swedenborg collection.[16] *Seraphita* treats Swedenborg half seriously, half comically. A pastor describes Swedenborg's work as a "torrent of celestial illumination": "As you read, you must either lose your wits or become a seer."

Seraphita's most modern theme is the relativity of perception, also addressed by Emily Brontë's *Wuthering Heights*. In a ritual triangulation of the eye, three people in a castle courtyard gaze in at Seraphita through the window. She stands enraptured in a glamourous mist, a cult object in a crystal cabinet. Each visitor makes a different sexual interpretation: Minna sees a man; Wilfrid and the pastor see a woman. Enigmatic Seraphita is personality at the vanishing point. No speaker seems to hear another, as in Virginia Woolf's *The Waves*. By the end, bitter dispute about Seraphita's gender breaks into the open. The story starts to oscillate surreally, line by line. The sole analogy is Catullus' litany to castrated Attis. Balzac's manipulations of gender are the most complex in literature. Even Woolf's *Orlando*, with its midpoint sex-change, treats its androgyne with schematic simplicity, compared to *Seraphita*'s flamelike interweaving of objective and subjective gender. Much is lost in translation, since Balzac exploits the grammatical ambiguity of Romance languages: English must choose *his* or *her* in pronouns, while French can avoid committing itself. Seraphita's gender wavers, so that Wilfrid and Minna misunderstand each other as they dream aloud about their entrancing angel.

At death and transfiguration, Seraphita becomes "*Il*"—he or it. She is now a male seraph and angel ("le Séraphin," "[le] ange"). The story is organized by verticals which Minna and Wilfrid cannot follow, like Shelley falling back from afflatus. Talky Seraphita passes into Apollonian silence, beyond language. Dematerializing, she sublimates self and text. I think her frailty and terminal etherealization come from Goethe's Mignon, who turns angel and dies. Balzac's heroine takes to her bed to give birth to herself. She clones a perfect androgyne, her artistic superself, as in Cellini's couvade. The *Perseus* is a Renaissance triumph of aggressive practicality, matter subdued to will. Seraphita advances by Romantic purification of consciousness. Cellini's saga ends with artist and art work separated by social distance. But Balzac's Romantic saga ends with self and work united. The self is the work of art, another Romantic coalescence of doubles.

Seraphita as symbol of perfected man may be influenced by social theorists like Ballanche and Saint-Simon, who identified the androgyne with liberal reform and universal brotherhood.[17] The optimistic androgyne is the only nineteenth-century example of the public (rather than personalistic) androgyne of the Renaissance kind. Setting his tale in 1800, Balzac (born 1799) suggests that his era breaks with the past through Seraphita's sexual revelation. This is like Freud's postdating the first edition of *The Interpretation of Dreams* to inaugurate the twentieth century and give it a revolutionary Freudian character.

The Girl with the Golden Eyes and *Seraphita* answer each other, inverting their hermaphrodite stars. In the amoral *Girl*, with its Decadent closure, two androgynes are murderously aligned toward a conventional center. In the moral *Seraphita*, with its space and height, two conventional genders are lovingly aligned toward a median hermaphrodite. *The Girl with the Golden Eyes* is infused with southern sexual passion, recreated in the marquise's opulent boudoir. *Seraphita* chills sex and gender on Nordic ice. Body vs. mind, sensuality vs. abstraction: like D. H. Lawrence, Balzac diagrams the European cultural schizophrenia. Nature is in bondage to the seraph. The ice cracks and nature revives only when Seraphita weakens and dies. Balzac's two tales check and correct each other in a circular pattern of sex and geography.

Androgynous personae appear everywhere in *The Human Comedy*. In Balzac's major character triad, the girlishly beautiful Eugène de Rastignac and Lucien de Rubempré are enslaved by the Machiavellian master criminal, Vautrin. The transsexual similes applied to Eugène are like a violet tincture making his feminine narcissism visible to the reader's eye. Lucien apes the dandy De Marsay, just as Wilde's Dorian Gray will ape Lord Henry Wotton, whose moral seduction of Dorian recalls Vautrin's of Lucien. Lucien has womanly hands, feet, and hips, a Greek profile, cheeks of "silky down" and "golden-white temples" of "Olympian suavity."[18] "Diabolic" Vautrin is a masculine hierarch attended by two effeminate angels. By homoerotic magnetism, he draws Eugène and Lucien into the intimate sanctum of his amoral consciousness, where is spread the delusive satanic banquet of wealth and power.

One of Balzac's major female androgynes, based on George Sand, is the novelist Félicité des Touches, whom Balzac calls "the illustrious hermaphrodite" because of her masculine genius.[19] Her pen name, Camille Maupin, is a coalition of respectful references to Latouche and Gautier. The heroine of *Cousin Bette* (1846) is an androgyne in a different mode, the chthonian. She is "a primitive peasant" with a "masculine stiff temperament," energized by her emotional proximity to nature. Her favorite moods are "hate and vengeance uncompromising, as they are known in Italy, Spain, and the East," regions "bathed by the sun."[20] Hence Bette is savage sister to the Spanish marquise of *The Girl with the Golden Eyes*. Celibate Bette has a touch of the marquise's lesbianism. Her "love of power" is awakened by a weak-willed Polish artist, Count Wenceslas Steinbock, "a pale, fair young man." "Nature had made a mistake," says Balzac, "in assigning their sexes." Their relation of dominance and submission is modelled on George Sand's affairs with the delicate Chopin and Alfred de Musset.

Bette turns "dictatorial" Muse, making the dreamy artist productive. When he marries and becomes sexually active, his work fails and halts. Balzac thought celibacy crucial for artistic and intellectual achievement, and he remained celibate for most of the years of work on the gargantuan *Human Comedy*. Bette's primitivistic materiality jolts her protégé. She fructifies him and makes him potent as an artist, but only by inhibiting him sexually. When he exchanges sadomasochistic servi-

tude for personal happiness, he loses his artistic identity. Like Keats's
Apollo, he is roused from melancholic torpor by a brute female titan.
Bette's mental and physical force comes from her virginity, which gives
her "a diabolical strength or the black magic of the Will." Her hardness
of personality is like that of Spenser's radiant characters of sharp Apollonian contour. Chastity is normally an anti-chthonian strategy, but
Balzac strangely combines it with chthonian power. Bette becomes "a
black diamond," "a Byzantine Virgin" whose "erect hieratic carriage"
recalls the gods of Egyptian sculpture. She is "walking granite, basalt,
porphyry." Condensing herself into an Apollonian objet d'art, she mimics society in order to penetrate and derange it. *Seraphita*'s Apollonian
ice-crystals become *Cousin Bette*'s amoral black diamond. Bette's primal aggression darkens the conceptual western eye. Though she belongs to a social novel, she resonates with the archetypal, because she is
a willful Romantic androgyne.

Balzac aspired to aristocracy, ennobling himself by adding a "de" to
his name. There may be wishful identification in his Henri de Marsay,
debonair arbiter of Parisian fashion. We should group De Marsay with
Eugène and Lucien as sexual personae. Balzac's charismatic half-
feminine *epheboi* represent what the Apollonian Amazons Belphoebe
and Britomart did for Spenser. They are visionary ideograms of aristocracy, of the cold beauty of rank and breeding. Balzac, a centaurian
mesomorph, projects these elegant ectomorphs as creatures of a hierarchic dream. The ill-fated Lucien and Wenceslas seem to have the
"artistic" temperament, sensitive and impressionable. But they are not
Balzacian. Ironically, Balzac's coarse female androgynes are closer to
him in body and mind. Cousin Bette has his muscular force and tenacity, and to her he gives his real-life theory of conservation of energy
through sexual renunciation. Hence these many androgynes are Balzac's self-portraits, mirroring each other like the perceptual halves of
Seraphitus/Seraphita. The male androgyne is fantasy, the female androgyne reality.

16

Cults of Sex and Beauty

Gautier, Baudelaire, and Huysmans

The begetter of French and English Decadence is Théophile Gautier, who started his career as a painter. He creates aestheticism, the neopagan worship of beauty. Gautier's liberation and ritualization of the eye turn Romanticism from chthonian to Apollonian, putting it in the main line of western hierarchism beginning in Egypt and Greece. Gautier deeply influenced, by their own admission, Baudelaire, Flaubert, Mallarmé, and Swinburne and is therefore powerfully present in Walter Pater and Oscar Wilde. As the librettist of *Giselle* and *The Spectre of the Rose,* he also contributed to dance history. Criticism's neglect of Gautier may be due to prudery after the fall of Wilde, but it also reflects indifference to the sensuality of art. Analysis of style is still an imperfect science. Style, primary in Gautier, is the music of sexual personae.

Gautier's masterpiece is *Mademoiselle de Maupin* (1835), for Sainte-Beuve a "Bible" of Romanticism. It was Balzac's favorite book during an important creative period. Baudelaire called it a "hymn to Beauty" and said he had a "nervous convulsion" upon encountering Gautier's "undulating and glossy" style.[1] *Maupin* is ruled by a new Rosalind. Not since the Renaissance Amazons had there been a bolder, more athletic or charismatic heroine.

Piqued by a magazine article, Gautier undertook a historical romance on Madeleine de Maupin d'Aubigny, a bisexual actress and transvestite of the seventeenth century. However, says René Jasinski, Maupin's eyes, hair, figure, and "virile spirit" belong to George Sand.[2] In sexual structure, the novel resembles *Seraphita:* a man and woman are enamoured of an androgyne, who rejects both admirers and, before disappearing forever, commands them to unite in his/her name. But the two works were written simultaneously (1833–35), and neither could have influenced the other. Balzac and Gautier did not meet until after the publication of *Mademoiselle de Maupin*, which so impressed Balzac that he sought an introduction to its author, the start of a lifelong friendship. The mysterious similarity is due to the stories' indebtedness to Latouche's *Fragoletta* and to the historical shift from High to Late Romanticism.

Though the first part, epistolary musings by a melancholy Romantic male, may have been written earlier, *Maupin* is unified by its sexual problematics and the new theme of aestheticism. A male androgyne, the aesthete D'Albert, is destined to be obsessed by a great female androgyne. His opening monologue provides the psychosexual context from which Maupin forcibly emerges, sweeping up the novel in a fictive energy that does not flag till the end. Like *Faust*, *Maupin* experiments with genres. Reacting to its ambiguous multiplicity, Baudelaire speaks of it as novel, tale, tableau, reverie. Prose rises dreamily to poetry, something increasingly evident in Gautier's later work. John Porter Houston calls *Maupin* the ancestor of the modern lyrical novel.[3] It incorporates letters, narrative, dramatic dialogue, even an essay—the infamous preface, first manifesto of aestheticism. Gautier attacks bourgeois values and asserts art has neither social utility nor moral content. Beauty alone is art's mission. The preface is not, as often claimed, disconnected from the story. The novel sets forth the premise of beauty, absent from modern culture, then illustrates it in the dazzling form of Mademoiselle de Maupin. Gautier, with Latouche, forges the Decadent fusion between sexual ambiguity and the aesthetic which will hold through Pre-Raphaelitism, Art Nouveau, and Symbolism all the way to Art Deco and Erté.

Depressed D'Albert is a sensitive sufferer like Chateaubriand's René, who caught his *mal du siècle* from Goethe's Werther. But D'Albert has the first fully developed Late Romantic consciousness. I spoke of High Romanticism's oppressive self-consciousness, of which Shelley's confrontation with his spectre is a masque or allegory. Late Romanticism relieves this oppressiveness by a strategy of sophistication. D'Albert's Romantic travails have a new air of detachment. There is a witty *commenting* upon the self, as if from a spectator's distance. High Romantic solipsism becomes Late Romantic sequestration, not of the object (as in Balzac) but of the subject. Late Romantic consciousness, severed from nature, makes art and therefore the eye its sole mode of knowledge. This connoisseurship of self-cultivation is alien to all High Romantics except Byron. Byron's aristocratic irony may be a primary

source of French Late Romanticism. His breezy humor is everywhere in
Gautier.

D'Albert is Rousseau's man of sensibility, but Rousseau's disciples did
not court the eyes of a public theater. D'Albert is a dandy, dawdling and
blasé. He wears rich fabrics (like Gautier) and curls his hair to antago-
nize the conventional, who calls him effeminate. As with Goethe's
epicene Paris, women may be attracted by what disgusts men: Balzac's
preening De Marsay says, "Women love fops."[4] Maupin complains
about men's coarseness and clumsiness, erotic disabilities. For Gautier
and the Decadents, masculinity is unaesthetic. The male must be hermaphrodized for love. In Spenser's rude Artegall, similarly transformed, Renaissance action is made moral. But in the aesthete, action is
disarmed to become beautiful.

D'Albert is "more like an actor than a man," escaping the prison of
sex through a mummery of personae. He fantasizes about changing sex,
like Teiresias. Finally, he embarks on a Platonic quest. Like Shelley,
D'Albert dreams of and then brings into being an "imaginary woman,"
the embodiment of "abstract beauty." The High Romantic master principle is imagination, a dynamic process by which the mind plays upon
reality. The French Late Romantic principle is art, largely as static
painting and sculpture. Prerevolutionary French aristocratic and religious art was far more ornate than anything in England. French
Romanticism revived the austerity of Gothic, to which Gautier was
hostile. D'Albert makes a countermovement toward Greek classicism,
the Apollonian assumptions of Italian Renaissance art followed by
Jacques-Louis David. He subscribes to Greek idealism: "I worship
beauty of form above all things; beauty is to me visible divinity."[5] As
in Plato, the beautiful person is a god. Gautier told the Goncourts,
"My whole distinction is that I am a man for whom the visible world
exists."

Mademoiselle de Maupin demonstrates how the aesthete's infatuation
with the visible is at the expense of the invisible or ethical. The aesthete
is an immoralist. D'Albert rejects "the mortification of matter which is
the essence of Christianity." He says, "It is a real torture to me to see
ugly things or ugly persons." Since externals are all-important, he
avoids old people, "because they are wrinkled and deformed." Here are
the origins of Wilde's aesthetic, with its arrogant exclusiveness. The old
or ugly are valueless to the poet of the visible world. D'Albert makes the
high Greek claim, "What is physically beautiful is good, all that is ugly
is evil."[6] The Apollonian is always cruel. Only Dionysus gives empathy.
Aestheticism invests in art objects the affect withdrawn from persons.

D'Albert judges women as if they were statues and loves statues as if they were women. Emotion is ritualized and objectified.

Condescending toward real women because of their fleshly imperfections, D'Albert is stunned by Mademoiselle de Maupin, who breaks all rules. She is disguised as a cavalier, so beautiful to him that he thinks he is turning homosexual. For the first time, he experiences electrifying erotic submission to a living person, fulfillment of his aesthetic prophecy. The same thing happens to Balzac's Sarrasine. Maupin is a materialization of Gautier's theory of ideal beauty, just as Balzac's Seraphita is an emanation of Swedenborg's thought.

Gautier begins to play games with the reader. In Spenser's switch of sexual perspective, Maupin's true sex would be revealed once we saw her from the public point of view. But Gautier, like Balzac, is interested in Romantic ambiguity for its own sake. He pretends to know as little as we about the cavalier's gender. Maupin enters as "he" and remains "he" for many chapters. Her relations with her page, another girl in disguise, are physically affectionate. Gautier seduces the reader into a strange twilit bower of sexual uncertainty. As in *The Faerie Queene*, there's lots of smooth white flesh half-seen through disarrayed garments. The reader is being manipulated and aroused, his or her own ordinary sexual responses confused. Maupin herself sways back and forth. When Rosette, D'Albert's mistress, confesses her passion for her, Maupin replies, "I have often wished to be able to love you, at least in the way that you would like; but there is an insurmountable obstacle between us which I cannot explain to you."[7] Note Gautier's alteration of Shakespeare: the transvestite woman does not merely discourage the advances of her female admirer but for the first time admits to crossing in imagination over the sexual barrier. Gautier, post-Rousseau, gives his heroine a naturalistic sexual identity, fluctuating unpredictably with changing circumstance.

When the page is knocked cold from his horse, Rosette opens his coat and shirt. This imitates Byron's scene of discovery in "Lara," where the bosom of swooning Gulnare, disguised as a boy, is exposed by bystanders. Gautier dwells on and elongates the moment of seeing. Rosette is unhappy with what she finds, "a round, polished ivory bosom . . . delicious to see, and more delicious to kiss."[8] Gautier's arch tone has that connoisseurship which I identify as distinctively Late Romantic. The sensuous is scrupulously observed but never possessed. Aesthetic distance is ingeniously preserved between eye and object. Eroticism is inflamed by the voyeuristic succession of observers: gazing at the unconscious, seminude object are the astonished Rosette, behind her the lascivious Gautier, and behind him the Peeping Tom reader. Gautier creates ritual and theology of the new religion of art. The passive person turned art work is invaded and possessed by the aggressive western eye. The eye has all rights, the object none. As in Sade, the dominant knower makes enormous hierarchic claims. Western seeing, I maintain, is innately fascistic and amoral.

Each narrative shift in *Maupin* brings further erotic complication. Disturbingly attracted to the cavalier, D'Albert defends homosexuality with ancient precedents. Roman poetry is a "monstrous seraglio" of beautiful boys, repugnant to Christianity. He declares, "Christ has not come for me; I am as much pagan as were Alcibiades and Phidias." He has a sharp-edged Apollonian vision of Athens: "Never mist or vapour, never anything uncertain or wavering. My sky has no clouds, or if there be any, they are solid chisel-carved clouds, formed with the marble fragments fallen from the statue of Jupiter." The mountains have "sharp-cut ridges," every contour fine and clear. "There is no room for the softness and dreaming of Christian art. . . . Christ has wrapped the world in his shroud. . . . The palpable world is dead."[9] The Greek eye, sculpting the world with high Apollonian articulation, opposes the clouds of Christian inwardness, northern Europe's gloomy fogs. Like Balzac, Gautier takes the sunlit Mediterranean point of view. D'Albert says, "Correctness of form is virtue"—which could serve as an epigraph to the Apollonian *Faerie Queene*. Gautier's dialectic of pagan visualization vs. misty Christian emotionalism is surely the distant source, via Pater, of Yeats's depiction of Christianity as "a fabulous, formless darkness" ("Two Songs from a Play"). Condemning Christian hostility to physical beauty, Gautier invents aestheticism's radical exaltation of outer over inner, the literalization of which is to bring down Oscar Wilde.

D'Albert argues that the Madonna symbolizes the Christian love of woman, who supplants the Greco-Roman androgyne. He celebrates homosexual Athens' idealization of "adolescent beauty." The Hermaphrodite, Maupin's precursor, was "one of the sweetest creations of Pagan genius":

> To an exclusive worshipper of form, can there be a more delightful uncertainty than that into which you are thrown by the sight of the back, the ambiguous loins, and the strong, delicate legs, which you are doubtful whether to attribute to Mercury ready to take his flight or to Diana coming forth from the bath? . . . In the whole habit of the body there is something cloudy and undecided which it is

impossible to describe, and which possesses quite a peculiar attraction.[10]

Gautier has broken his own rules. Hastily joining two phases of Greek art, he reverses himself. Idealized adolescence was a high classic theme; the overt Hermaphrodite flourished in the sensationalistic Hellenistic era. This chapter of *Maupin* asserts the Apollonian and then refutes it in the Hermaphrodite, whom Gautier has surely taken from the Naples Museum episode of *Fragoletta*. He admires the classical for lacking "anything uncertain and wavering" yet admires the Hermaphrodite for being "cloudy and undecided." He is caught unaware in a contradiction which Spenser, equally loyal to Apollonian contour, detected in *The Faerie Queene* and fixed by cancelling the "Hermaphrodite stanzas." Surrendering to the Romantic love of ambiguity, Gautier strays from his Greek ideals.

Gautier's poem, "Contralto" (1849), opens with a description of the "Sleeping Hermaphrodite." Ten stanzas pass before we realize the statue is a vision overwhelming the poet as he listens spellbound to a woman singer with a husky contralto voice, midway between male and female. The poem was inspired by Ernesta Grisi, Gautier's companion and mother of his children. The "enigmatic statue" has a "disturbing beauty." "Is it a young man? is it a woman?" Gautier asks Rousseau's question of sexual identity. Hanging back in fascinated suspension, the spectators need Keats's negative capability. Gender is conundrum and public spectacle. Men think one thing, women another, as in *Seraphita*'s relativity of sexual perception.

The Hermaphrodite, an "ardent chimera" or "charming monster" of "accursed beauty," is alienated from the multitude, like Coleridge's poet. Both provocative and reclusive, it is a ritual cult-object to which gifts are brought. The Hermaphrodite is separated from society and nature. It is a Late Romantic freak, symbol of the impossible. "Dream of poet and artist," "supreme effort of art and pleasure," it is an artificial sex. Its "multiple beauty" unites the art object's sexual duality with the multiplicity of response art generates in its audience. Art forms transpose, sculpture changing to music; reverie evaporates matter to sound. Gautier calls the contralto both Romeo and Juliet and compares her to Byron's transvestite Gulnare and virile epic heroes. She is autoerotic, with the power of self-fecundation. Transfixed by a singing androgyne, the poet is like Sarrasine before Zambinella. In Ernesta Grisi, Gautier seems to have procured his own resident castrato. Stars like Marlene Dietrich, Barbara Stanwyck, and Lauren Bacall demonstrate the eerie-ness of the beautiful woman with an alto voice, charismatically attracting both sexes.

D'Albert's ode to the Hermaphrodite establishes Maupin's status as a living art object discovered by a Late Romantic connoisseur. Now we enter her mind and hear her voice. No longer a remote archetype, she becomes a modern woman sick of "conventional masks, conventional opinions and conventional modes of speech," antagonizing the sexes.[11] The historical Maupin was an expert fencer who killed many men.[12] Gautier's athletic heroine adopts male costume to study social reality up close. As a wandering female transvestite, she is influenced by both Rosalind and Mignon. Goethe's characters perform *Hamlet* at the climax of their novel; Gautier's characters perform *As You Like It*, their ultimate Renaissance source. At the rehearsal, where Maupin appears as Rosalind in woman's clothes, the novel for the first time stops calling its heroine "he." Lit by a mysterious radiance, she appears in a doorway and holds position, framed like a painting. The others cry out and applaud. Like "Contralto"'s Hermaphrodite, she is the art object on public display, fusing genres. D'Albert's Platonic quest for ideal beauty is ceremonially consummated. Maupin's transfiguring "floods of white light" are the by-product of her alteration of gender-states. Her Apollonian glamour is Gautier's version of Shakespeare's ghostly Hymen. Her entrance is an epiphany of hermaphrodite authority. She stuns the other characters by sudden hierarchic assertion, dominating the plane of eye-contact and subordinating the audience to her will.

Sexual confusion is not resolved by Maupin publicly acknowledging her true gender. Instead we double backward to hear her spiritual autobiography, recorded in letters. Her lesbian flirtation is far more blatant than Rosalind's. Gautier stages feverish boudoir scenes where Rosette throws herself at the disguised Maupin, their bodies voluptuously intertwining like Salmacis and Hermaphroditus. Unlike Rosalind, Maupin is in real doubt about her gender. She claims she belongs to "a third, distinct sex, which as yet has no name," an idea to return in the homosexual polemicists John Addington Symonds and Radclyffe Hall. In the third sex, "the sex of the soul does not at all correspond with that of the body."[13] So nature has erred. Maupin's abnormality is not relative but absolute. No society could satisfy her. Following Rousseau, she ponders her sexual identity. Like "Contralto"'s Hermaphrodite, she has an accursed beauty alienating her from both sexes. She must remain alone, Romantically autonomous.

Like Balzac's marquise, Maupin is a female aesthete, drawn to women as "the possessors of beauty." Gautier maliciously vilifies his own sex. Men, says Maupin, are smelly, misshapen, bestial. Masculinity is grossly material. Hence the pursuit of beauty is always a flight from the masculine. Forced, during one of Rosette's assaults, to contemplate the female bosom at close quarters, Maupin makes silent aesthetic judgments, in which mischievous Gautier clearly concurs. Rosette's rounded "satin flesh" is "enchantingly delicate and transparent in tone," and so on.[14] Here again is Gautier's ritualized voyeurism, that series of attentive observers, of which we are the last in line. He creates the Late Romantic eye, erotic, aggressive, and knowledgeable but ever-distant.

Maupin preserves the artist's detachment from primary experience. She samples but will not commit. In this modern transvestite comedy, overt sex replaces the Renaissance wedding scene. The novel ends with the virgin warrior Maupin tasting heterosexuality and homosexuality in a single night, passing noncommittally from D'Albert's bed to Rosette's and then disappearing at dawn. She leaves instructions, like Seraphita, for her male and female admirers to mate with each other as a rite of memory in her name. Sexual initiation shows her the banality of the ideal made real. She is overcome by disillusion, a major theme of nineteenth-century novels. Maupin's recoil from sex is Decadent, though the novel is High Romantic in tone. There is no Decadent closure, for example. The heroine can still ride off into the woods at the end of the story. Though art is preferred to nature, nature remains airy and lyrical. Unlike Rosalind, Maupin makes a choice for self rather than community and preserves her androgyny beyond the narrative frame. She marries herself, withdrawing her energy from society and reinvesting it in her own imagination. The abrupt finale is unique: an autoerotic elopement.

Mademoiselle de Maupin is one of the last literary examples of the woman disguised in men's clothing, a Renaissance motif fading in the nineteenth century, as women leave home to work in factory and office. When film picks up the theme, the transvestism is merely titillating. The practicality of Rosalind and Maupin's male dress is gone. The perilous world of adventure dwindles to the stage of a Berlin cabaret. Dietrich's transvestism in Josef von Sternberg's Thirties films is a Hollywood transplant of Weimar perversity, a survival of fin-de-siècle Decadence. Few transvestite films address serious psychological and artistic issues. In Robert Aldrich's *The Legend of Lylah Clare* (1968), an actress (Kim Novak) is possessed by a dead, Dietrich-like movie queen. As in *Maupin*, transvestism causes sexual error. A fatal accident is shown three different ways, until we see that the raffish hoodlum manhandling Lylah Clare (herself surreally speaking and laughing in a male voice) is a lesbian in disguise. The film demonstrates the contraction of the transvestite theme since the Renaissance. Now cross-dressing is just an aphrodisiac game in a tawdry urban milieu. Hollywood is as full of predators as the Forest of Arden (the film ends allegorically, with a dog-food commercial degenerating into wolfish chaos), but the transvestism is not imagined as a defense against them.

The more picaresque the genre, the more utilitarian the female transvestism. Hence Katharine Hepburn's boy-disguises in the strident *Sylvia Scarlett* (1936). There is always an erotic tinge to a woman dressed as a man. A man in female clothing is usually shown as comic or neurotic, because of his deviance from the masculine. This reverses the facts of transvestism in real life. Female transvestism in its strict sense, says Robert J. Stoller, is "a condition that may not exist." As for butch lesbians dressing in men's clothing, "Neither they nor other women have a fetishistic relationship to male apparel: they do not become sexually excited by such objects."[15] Male transvestites are not only sexually stimulated by female clothing but may require it for orgasm, as with the surprising number of heterosexual men who secretly dress up in their wives' lingerie. Women are not sexual conceptualizers, just as they are not lust-murderers. For women, male clothing means social freedom and authority. For men, female clothing is religious or cultic. It is the costume of the mother, with whom the son unites by ritual impersonation, like priests of Cybele. The female transvestite seeks merely to pass. Do not gaze at her too long, for her disguise is fragile. But the male transvestite is his own best voyeur, exploiting his internalized eye for maximum excitement. The female transvestite arouses others, not herself. Semitransvestism is a musical comedy convention: Dietrich, Judy Garland, and Shirley MacLaine combine high heels and net stockings with top hat and tails. The style is nineteenth-century, probably originating in the theatrical personae of sadomasochistic prostitution, a specialty of English taste satisfied in Paris. Its element of hierarchical formality is crucial.

A film of *Mademoiselle de Maupin* should have been made in the Thirties, the one decade that could have caught its sexual mystery and glamour. Parker Tyler had "an uncommunicated obsession" that Garbo play Maupin.[16] The transvestite *Queen Christina*, which she commissioned, shows that Garbo had the tall, commanding figure and cold reserve for the role. Diana Rigg, in her *Avengers* period, would have been the ideal Maupin. Rigg has Maupin's verbal energy, unlike the morose, laconic Garbo. Gautier's novel was the first detailed analysis of irresolution of gender. The hermaphrodite had appeared throughout literature and art since antiquity, but this was the first time it was given a turbulent inner life. Is Maupin, for all her force and vitality, an ideal female persona? She is a transition from the High Romantic to the Decadent androgyne, glaringly absent from feminist apologias for androgyny. Would universal androgyny really improve relations between the sexes? *Mademoiselle de Maupin* demonstrates the facile optimism of such a view. Gautier correctly shows hermaphroditism as asocial, because autarchic. His physically and spiritually perfect heroine secedes from human relationships and collective values. Sex itself is dispensed with. Vanishing into the distance, Maupin defiantly returns to that chastity symbolizing her uncompromising definitiveness of personality.

Gautier's artistic development capsulizes the shift from High to Late Romanticism. His story *A Night with Cleopatra* follows *Mademoiselle de Maupin* by only three years, yet there has been a stunning transformation in style and sexual personae. The aesthete Gautier has become a Decadent. He must by now have read Balzac's *The Girl with the Golden Eyes*. Had he also read Sade? Gautier's ruling androgyne is no longer virginal Rosalind of the greenwood but an Oriental despot, cruel and sensual. Cleopatra, bored and dangerous, is the first exotic heterosexual femme fatale of the Decadence. The androgyne has changed because nature has changed.

The air is still and dead. The noon sun discharges "leaden arrows." A dazzling "hard light" streams down "in torrents of flame," producing "a blazing reddish haze." Cleopatra complains:

> This Egypt destroys and crushes me. . . . Never a cloud! never a shadow, and for ever this red, dripping sun which stares like the eye of a Cyclops! . . . From the enflamed eyeball of this sky of bronze has never yet fallen a single tear on the desolation of the earth; it is a huge tombstone, a dome of a necropolis, a sky dead and dried up like the mummies it covers! it weighs on my shoulders like a too heavy coat! it irks me and distresses me; it seems to me as if I could not rise to my full height without bruising my forehead against it. . . . Imagination here produces nothing but monstrous chimaeras and inordinate monuments; this sort of architecture and art terrifies me; these colossi, whose limbs fixed in stone condemn them to rest eternally seated with their hands on their knees, tire me with their stupid immobility; they obsess my eyes and my horizon.[17]

This is one of the supreme examples of Decadent closure. The sky is no longer the gate of the Romantic infinite but a bronze dome sealing up space. The world is a desert, seared by the glaring, hostile sun. Architecture is menacing and surreal, anticipating Baudelaire's night Paris. Movement is impossible, yet everyone is exhausted because the object-world presses so heavily. Making "a mighty effort" in her "enormous fatigue," Cleopatra manages to walk thirty steps to her bath. Byron and Delacroix's Orient has lost its energy because the human is cut off from nature, from which Rousseau and Wordsworth expected so much. Shakespeare's fertile Egypt is now a stone tomb heaped with frozen art objects. This Egypt is the imprisoner, not the liberator of European imagination.

Thus *Maupin*'s airy High Romantic nature has become louring Late Romantic nature. The androgyne shifts modes: enslaved by nature, Cleopatra becomes a Sadean sexual enslaver. Gautier's new style is also an enslaver, violently subordinating literature to the visual arts. In long, endless sentences, person or panorama is described in crisp pictorial detail, an avalanche of sensory images which astonish but, like Egyptian nature, finally oppress. Gautier's descriptions, dismissed as trivial or lifeless, may have been chief cause of his loss of reputation. But by them he creates Decadent nature, an inorganic realm of art works rather than vegetation.

In *A Night with Cleopatra*, the painter Gautier seeks a literary language for color. The Nile banks are "salmon," with "greenish clay, reddish ochre, tufa rock of a floury white." There are slopes of "rose-colored marble," gaping with "black mouths" of quarries. An Egyptian sunset is violet, azure, lilac, blue, rose, red, pale lemon, turquoise. Gautier constantly halts the story for scrutiny of form, surface, ornament. His frustration of plot is a development of Romanticism's withdrawal from masculine action. It looks forward to modern avant-garde narrative, where it is quite permissible and even desirable for nothing whatever to happen. But we sense in Gautier the cold immobility of the object so meticulously dissected, as if by autopsy. Since he dwells so much on the external, there is no one to identify with. The treatment of persons as art objects is present as an ambition in *Maupin* but is not technically realized until *A Night with Cleopatra*. The admirer of Gautier is not repelled by his dehumanizations but entranced by his poetic virtuosity of ritualized description. His delicate modulations of color are Late Romantic ideas, replacing High Romantic emotion.

Cleopatra, subjected to Gautier's description, disintegrates. There goes a nostril, a lip, an eyebrow, a chin! We are too close, like Gulliver straddling the nipple of the giantess. Gautier's eye is invasive, disrupting point of view. The Petrarchan blazon similarly dismembered the beloved. Gautier invents the Decadent blazon or anatomy, a catalog of exquisitely documented parts dissolving the whole. Literary energy is absorbed by nouns and their adjectives, multiplied like ceremonial epithets. There are few verbs in Gautier. Everything floats in apposition. This is the source of Pater's style, which radically deactivates the verb. Gautier formalizes Romantic passivity, laying the world flat against a picture plane. In *A Night with Cleopatra*, the eye sees *everything*. The eye becomes its own prison. The heavy domed sky *is* the eye, choking upon its own excess of perception.

Decadence is a disease of the western eye. It is an intensification of the voyeurism latent in all art. The pictorial itemizations of *A Night with Cleopatra* coerce the eye and make the reader a connoisseur, forced to assist in a despiritualization of reality. Gautier is the progenitor of Roger Fry's art theory of "significant form." The Decadent exaltation of the part follows from the rejection of moral content, for are not ethics the subordination of selfish part to social whole? Remember the Decadent climax of *The Girl with the Golden Eyes*, where the murderous marquise appears first as a foot, a part, and even as part of that, an instep. I think Gautier absorbed this detail and expanded it into an entire story, *The Mummy's Foot* (1840).

Browsing in an antiquities shop, an aesthete purchases a mummy's foot to use as a paperweight. The foot, minutely described, is artistically so perfect that he first mistakes it for a fragment of a statue. That night, Pharaoh's daughter turns up to reclaim her foot, which proves unexpectedly churlish. It leaps about to elude her and carries on an animated dialogue with her, insisting in ancient Coptic that it is no longer her property. After the aesthete reconciles the disputants, the foot consents to be rejoined, and princess and foot fly back through time to their homeland. I omit the chorus, where mummified cats mew, ibises flap their wings, and African nations chant, "The Princess Hermonthis has found her foot again."[18]

What is the real meaning of this story? The body is treated as an art object, as form stripped of human meaning. Hawked in a shop, the foot is a mere artifact, a detail of décor. *The Mummy's Foot* is a parable of Decadent aestheticism in which a part declares itself independent of the whole. In Gogol's *The Nose* (1835), it is the protagonist who suffers a humiliating reduction of appendages, but in Gautier it is the art object, the erotically projected image. Gogol's tale looks forward to Kafka's *Metamorphosis* as a nightmare of self-incapacitated male will. Gautier, however, is concerned with the new autonomy of art. The distance between eye and object is so vast that the artist is severed from his own work, form severed from content, and part severed from whole. In the Renaissance, the *Moses* will not walk, despite even Michelangelo's command. But in Late Romanticism, the art object has so broken down into richly observed parts that a foot, turgid with its own imaginative authority, can flounce away and rudely decline to return to its owner.

The Late Romantic eye is a tyrant, and the act of seeing is erotically inflamed. This may lead to paranoia, as in Cleopatra's staring eye of the sun. Sexual voyeurism, sporadic in *Maupin*, is at the center of Gautier's *King Candaules* (1844), a long story based on Herodotus. Nyssia, the Lydian queen, is rumored to have a double pupil enabling her to see through walls. But strangely, she who sees *is* seen. The boastful king arranges for his wife to be seen by another man, Gyges. Outraged, she will plot Candaules' murder. The queen senses Gyges' eyes upon her by a "lively magnetic susceptibility" of her skin. Feeling contaminated, she orders ewers of water poured on her, as if by this "lustral ablution" she could "efface the stain due to the glances of Gyges." She rubs herself frantically: "She wished she could have torn away the skin on which the rays of his burning eyes seemed to her to have left traces. . . . 'Oh, that glance! that glance! It clings to me, enfolds, envelops, and burns me like the poisoned robe of Nessus; I feel it under my vestments like a flaming tissue which nothing can detach from my body.' "[19]

Before and after this compulsive, Lady-Macbeth-like ritual, Nyssia is called a "statue" of perfect beauty. Candaules mistakenly treats as an objet d'art a femme fatale of uncanny occult power. Nyssia has the archaic daemonic eye which penetrates and paralyzes. The power of sight is sexual and aggressive. To see is to possess; to be seen is to be raped. Made involuntarily passive beneath another's gaze, Nyssia is driven to blood revenge. Unlike Balzac's girl with the golden eyes, she can and must recover from a state of erotic facticity. In this story, seeing even alters what it touches, lingering like a wraith. Gautier knows western eye-contact is just that, a sensory assault by the questing imperialistic mind.

Why this obsession with visual relations in Gautier? High Romanticism, thinking imagination alone can sustain the universe, is riven with anxieties. An excess of phenomena, no longer ordered by society or religion, floods consciousness. Late Romantic imagination contracts in fatigue, protecting itself by motifs of closure. The world collapses into a heap of objects, honored by the Decadence for their morbid decay. Gautier invents aestheticism as a mode of perceptual control. The

lavish, plot-halting passages of *A Night with Cleopatra* are a ritualization of the eye-object relation. A fixed aesthetic distance stems the
obliterating influx of phenomena. In Gautier, to see means *to keep at a
distance.* Art structures everything in him, sexual and metaphysical.
Gautier creates Decadent style, freezing word to image to propitiate the
pagan eye.

     Baudelaire's *Flowers of Evil* (1857) is dedicated to his
"master," Gautier. Baudelaire translated Poe and hailed him as his
second self. Poe's spiritual father was the Coleridge of the mystery
poems. Thus Coleridge, coming through Poe to Baudelaire, daemonizes Gautier, with his Byronic breeziness. Baudelaire's new Decadent
tone is haughty and hieratic. His poems are ritualistic confrontations
with the horror of sex and nature, which he analyzes with Sade's cutting
rhetoric. The chthonian is his epic theme.
     Baudelaire grants mother nature neither Rousseau's benevolence nor
Sade's vitality. Poe's Coleridgean nature is hostile but still sublime, a
vast swirling seascape. But Baudelaire is a city poet for whom there are
no more adventures. He adopts Cleopatra's Late Romantic fatigue.
Baudelaire makes ennui hip, an avant-garde pose. Ennui certifies the
sophisticate's excess of experience: one has seen and done everything.
Unlike Poe, Baudelaire invents no secondary male personae for himself. His subject is the self as artificial enclave, like the citadel of Poe's
Masque of the Red Death, which nature secretly enters and disorders.
Baudelaire is the first poet of mental and physical disease.
     For Baudelaire, sex is limitation, not liberation. Desire, normally a
spur to masculine action, makes the male passive toward his mother-
born body. He is betrayed by the body, delivered into female hands
through sexual weakness. Nature's power is wielded by pitiless vampires, the most numerous personae of Baudelaire's poetry. As in Poe,
woman is always superior. Poe likes to dream of domestic bliss with a
mother-bride. But Baudelaire's women are rigid and uncompanion-
able. In his one maternal scene, "The Giantess," he lives with a primeval titaness at "her terrible games." He climbs her "enormous knees"
and, "like a quiet hamlet," sleeps "in the shadow of her breasts." The
female body is curvy geography, as in the Venus of Willendorf. Sexual
connection is patently out of the question, for the male is no bigger than
a trained flea. The playful, sunny tone, uncharacteristic for Baudelaire's
erotica, is possible because the scene is archaic rather than modern—
like Salisbury Plain, which prompted Wordsworth to make a similar
sexual exception for his prehistoric warrior.

Baudelaire's women are intimidating. The "impure woman" is a "blind and deaf machine, fertile in cruelties," "drinker of the blood of the world." Beauty is "a sphinx" against whose stone breast every man bruises himself; she has a "heart of snow" and never weeps or laughs. She is a "monster enormous, frightful." The sphinx Jeanne Duval, Baudelaire's obsession, is like "the bleak sand and blue sky of deserts, insensible to human suffering." She is nothing but "gold, steel, light and diamonds." With "the cold majesty of the sterile woman," she shines "like a useless star." Duval has a "beautiful body polished like copper." She is a glistening serpent with eyes like "two cold jewels in which gold mingles with iron." She is a "beast implacable and cruel"; her cold cat gaze "cuts and splits like a dart." She is an "inhuman Amazon," a "great angel of the bronze brow," a "charming poniard" leaping from its sheath. Marie Daubrun, another of the poet's favorites, is a ship with jutting prow. Her breasts are shields "armed with rose points." Her muscular arms, like those of infant Hercules, are "the solid rivals of glossy boa constrictors," made to squeeze her lover and imprint him on her heart.[20] The apocalyptic whore of "The Metamorphoses of the Vampire" brazenly boasts, "I replace, for him who sees me nude and without veils, the moon, the sun, the sky and the stars!" Sucking the marrow from her victim's bones, she turns into a bag of pus and a rattling skeleton screeching in his bed. The vampire is ever-changing mother nature, whose embrace is rape and ecstasy, death and decay.

Baudelaire's daemonic females renounce Rousseau's tenderness. They have a Sadean sterility, divorcing the chthonian from fecundity. They are inorganic monoliths of steel and stone, their only living associations feline or reptilian. Their mineral hardness comes from their barren habitat, an urban wasteland of "metal, marble, and water" petrifying the flesh ("Parisian Dream"). Like Blake's Harlot, they are city-goddesses of polluted terrain. Gautier says of Baudelaire's mythic women, "To none can a name be given. They are types rather than persons."[21] Impersonality always masculinizes a woman. Baudelaire's female personae are hermaphroditic because of their blank indifference to the human. Sterility and emotional torpidity in a heavy-breasted woman constitute my category of androgyne as virago. Baudelaire's viragos resemble Michelangelo's in the Mannerist Medici Chapel, a parallel the poet notes ("The Ideal"). Baudelaire is uninterested in boy-girls or transvestites. His androgynes must be voluptuously female in body contour. In women he seeks only hierarchic assertion. They have no other use for him, since they are stripped of their sexual and procreative functions.

What of the male who inhabits this woman-ravaged universe? We meet him in "A Voyage to Cythera," for me one of the poems of the century. A ship is in full sail. The poet's heart flies joyfully round the rigging like a bird in the cloudless sky. Suddenly a black stony island appears—Cythera, once-happy birthplace of Venus. On a three-branched gallows hangs the poet's image, a corpse ravaged by birds, who peck out the eyes and eat the genitals. A prowling pack of wolves wait for the leavings. Cythera is the world of sexual experience, into which the poet presses toward a horrifying revelation. Structurally, the poem echoes Poe's *Masque of the Red Death*, with its climactic phantom in a bloody burial shroud. Baudelaire represents Decadent closure in entirely perceptual terms. The poem opens in space and fresh, free motion, then shuts down to a solitary image, the poet's double, upon whom the eye obsessively fixes. Nature dwindles to the contracted self.

"A Voyage to Cythera" moves from innocence to experience and from High to Late Romanticism. Its first illusion is about nature, which seems benign. The poet, misled by Rousseau, thinks of green myrtle and blooming flowers. But nature's reality is Sadean, red in tooth and claw. Odysseus, tied to the mast, sees piles of moldering skeletons littering the island of the Sirens. Baudelaire's lustful priestess, wandering a temple grove, belongs to the pagan era, which integrated sex with religion. Christianity, on the other hand, afflicts humanity with chronic guilt. The gallows is the crucifix, desolating the sexual world. It is also the tree of nature, a black cypress against the sky. Man is crucified upon his own body. Nature is a Decadent tree loaded with rotten fruit, a "ripe" corpse bursting its skin and dribbling foul matter.

Baudelaire's double is an androgyne, the male heroine, a Romantic martyr. The passive male is attacked by drill-beaked birds, lacerating sexual desires. Venus' doves turn Harpy. The victim is castrated and his body reshaped in parodic femaleness: his eyes are holes, and his belly spills out its bowels. Like Poe's Morella, he gives birth to a lesser version of himself at the moment of death. The rotten sausage of his hanging intestines mocks his vanished genitals. Vital organs are ransacked because the human body is a house divided against itself, undone by physical needs. Nature coerces man into sexual activity, then punishes him with syphilis, venereal because the gift of Venus. "To make a voyage to Cythera" was French slang for sexual intercourse.[22] Baudelaire, inspired by Nerval, may be sardonically revising Watteau's exuberant painting, *Embarkation for Cythera* (1717). He says in another poem, "I am the wound and the knife!" He is simultaneously female masochist and male sadist, in agonizing psychic coitus, a Decadent self-abuse. In

"A Voyage to Cythera," the overexpanded High Romantic self is firmly dealt with by a public ritual of Late Romantic enslavement.

The passivity of all humanity toward rapacious nature is brilliantly dramatized in "A Carcass." Strolling one summer morning, the poet and his beloved stumble on an animal carcass: "Legs in the air, like a lewd woman, / Burning and oozing poisons," it opens its putrid belly to the sky. "The sun was shining on that rottenness, / In order to cook it to a turn, / And to render a hundredfold to great Nature / All that she had joined together." The carcass "bloomed like a flower," its perfume an overpowering stench. Flies buzz, and maggots rise and fall like a sparkling wave. The carcass gives out "a strange music," like water and wind or grain in the winnower's basket. Its form is dreamily wavering and dissolving. A hungry female dog skulks, furious at the interruption. The poet tenderly informs his beloved, "You will be like that filth, that horrible infection, star of my eyes!" When she mildews among the bones, vermin like his "decomposed loves" will devour her with kisses. Decadent romance, sweet and sour.

"A Voyage to Cythera" is a portrait of the artist as ritual victim where the poet confronts his physically degenerated double, as Dorian Gray is to do with his corroded portrait. In "A Carcass," Baudelaire forces his beloved to confront her own double, a putrefying animal carcass, which omnipotent nature exploits to feed her microbes, parasites, and beasts. The poem is a kind of *déjeuner sur l'herbe:* nature is dining at home! The animal's gender and identity and even its integrity as an object are receding. It is being reduced to primary materials, much as Sade's victims are rent and abraded into subhuman particles. The teeming maggots are a prophetic vision of inanimate nature-process or matter in molecular wave-motion. Baudelaire's "strange music" is also heard in Melville's *Moby-Dick*, where a tropical grove hums like the loom of vegetable nature.

Nature's dichotomy of sunniness and cannibalism is mirrored in the poem's polished classic form and gross content, beauty and repulsiveness joined. Baudelaire ironically brings love poetry's exalted endearments to bear upon nature's brute physicality, to which they are hopelessly unsuited. "A Carcass" is in the *carpe diem* tradition: Renaissance poems also dwell on the future death and decay of a too-virginal beloved. But note Baudelaire's Late Romantic innovation: he no longer uses mortality as an argument to extort sexual favors, for the Decadence always swerves from sexual experience. Intercourse is far from his thoughts. In fact, if there is any eroticism in the poem—and he ostentatiously introduces it by comparing the carcass to a spread-eagled whore—it arises from his imagining the female body undergoing future Decadent disintegration. In Decadent beauty, I said, part triumphs over whole. In "A Carcass," embryogeny is reversed. Death, forcing the beloved to imitate the animal's deconstruction, will make her surrender gender, identity, and coherence. It is this primitive spectacle of degeneration that arouses the poet—an a priori necrophilia. The proud beloved will be raped by dominatrix mother nature, the jealous fanged bitch waiting in the shadows.

So woman in Baudelaire is unsexed by being a vampire, a corpse, or, as we shall now see, a lesbian. The first title of *Flowers of Evil*, advertised by the publisher in 1846, was *The Lesbians*. Martin Turnell says, "Baudelaire's interest in Lesbianism is something of a mystery and no one has yet accounted satisfactorily for the prominence given to it in his poetry."[23] Proust, according to Gide, thought the theme proved Baudelaire's homosexuality.[24] I doubt this, for Baudelaire rarely savors male beauty. The solution to the mystery is my principle of sexual metathesis, an artistic sex-change.

Most lavish of the lesbian poems is "Damned Women: Delphine and Hippolyte." In a dim curtained chamber, young Hippolyte lies weeping on perfumed cushions. Delphine, like a tigress, gloats at her feet. Their first sex together has just occurred. Women's kisses, says Delphine, are light and delicate, while men are heavy-hooved oxen, making ruts in women's bodies with their wagons or "lacerating plowshares." Yokels and lummoxes! Hippolyte appreciates Delphine's erotic tutelage (like Sade's Eugénie with Madame de Saint-Ange) but feels anxious and dyspeptic, as if she has eaten too rich a night meal. Black phantoms rush at her, leading her along roads closed by "a bloody horizon." Have they sinned? "But I feel my mouth move toward you," the magnetism of Romantic compulsion. Shaking her mane of hair, Delphine goes into a snit and curses the stupid "useless dreamer" who first mixed morality with love. Hippolyte, drained, longs for annihilation in Delphine's bosom. The poet's doleful voice suddenly intervenes: "Descend, descend, lamentable victims, descend the road of eternal hell!" The lesbians will burn forever in their insatiable passion. They will wander the desert as scorched exiles of cities of the plain, fleeing the infinity in their souls.

Baudelaire owes this long, impressive poem to Balzac. Delphine and Hippolyte are the Marquise de San-Real and Paquita Valdes, and we are in the boudoir of *The Girl with the Golden Eyes*. The psychodrama is identical: a fiery sexual aggressor imprisons a fragile innocent in an opulent, claustrophobic retreat. Balzac never nears the moment of lesbian union, which only appears once removed in De Marsay's transvestite rendezvous. In "Delphine and Hippolyte," however, we ourselves are so close to the characters *post coitum* that our invisible presence inflames the already oppressive atmosphere. The palpable voyeurism of poet and reader comes from Gautier's *Mademoiselle de Maupin.* Hippolyte's "bloody horizon," opening her sexually but sealing up earthly space, is from Gautier's *A Night with Cleopatra.* Baudelaire recasts the sexual realm in entirely female terms. Woman is self-entombed in a perverse cell of sexual solipsism. Delphine repeats Maupin's aesthetic judgments: women are erotically refined, while men are clumsy brutes.

Lesbianism is a breach in procreative nature, which Baudelaire is always eager to insult. The lesbian is therefore another sterile woman, like his metallic city-vampires. Baudelaire thinks homosexuality, as an unnatural practice, can never be fully satisfied. It is a noble pursuit of "the impossible" that attracts Gautier. In a shorter poem also called "Damned Women," Baudelaire hails lesbians, of "unquenched thirsts," as "Virgins, demons, monsters, martyrs, / Great spirits contemptuous of reality, / Seekers of the infinite." Lesbians are great because they defy society, religion, and nature. Baudelaire's celebration of lesbianism must not be mistaken for sexual libertarianism. He would not picket for gay rights. Walter Benjamin remarks, "To him, social ostracism was inseparable from the heroic nature of this passion."[25] Hence the huge metaphysical background of the climax of "Delphine and Hippolyte." The poem cinematically opens the boudoir's languid, upholstered intimacy into a vast wasteland, the moral geography of lesbianism. Like Dante, Baudelaire sees the damned buffeted by winds and flames of desire.

In this poem a sex act is destiny, just as it is fraternal identity in *The Girl with the Golden Eyes.* Baudelaire's two women have Greek names and may even be citizens of Lesbos, but the poem's world-view is Christian. Hippolyte is overcome by guilt, and Delphine denounces Jesus (the "useless dreamer") for worsening the "insoluble problem" of sex. Christianity may be the antagonist, but it is also Christianity that gives lesbianism its moral or rather immoral stature. Baudelaire says, "The supreme voluptuous delight of love lies in the certainty of doing *evil.*" Like Sade, he needs the fixities of organized religion to give his outrages an ethical significance and therefore erotic charge. He constantly seeks, as Colin Wilson notes, the gratuitous violation of taboo.[26] The original shock of "Delphine and Hippolyte" is largely lost to our more tolerant time. Today, nothing sexual can appear quite so evil, unless amplified by violence. Sexuality, by winning the war with religion, has been diminished in scale.

"Delphine and Hippolyte" is highly unusual for Baudelaire in having an entirely feminine woman, victim of lesbian seduction. Who is Hippolyte? I say she is Baudelaire himself, who has, by the same daring warp of imaginative gender we saw in Coleridge's *Christabel*, identified himself with the passive partner of a lesbian couple. Baudelaire, as always, is hierarchically subordinate to his ferocious vampire. I found images elsewhere in Coleridge confirming his projection into his heroine's trauma. There is a parallel between "Delphine and Hippolyte" and "A Voyage to Cythera." Hippolyte, like the poet's hanged double, is attacked by swooping black creatures, phantoms in one poem and crows in the other. Baudelaire gives Jeanne Duval, "bizarre deity," the name of a notorious Roman lesbian: "I am not able, libertine Megaera, to break your courage and keep you at bay, to become Proserpine in the hell of your bed!" ("Sed non satiata"). Baudelaire regrets he cannot do in real life what he elegantly achieves in "Delphine and Hippolyte": to turn himself into a woman to seize the attention of a lesbian dominatrix. If he is the maiden Persephone, Duval is the raptor Pluto, god of the underworld, here a whore's rank crowded bed. In the shorter "Damned Women," the obsessed lesbians are the poet's "poor sisters." Elsewhere he calls the "hypocrite reader" his "double" and "brother." So Baudelaire's lesbian sisters are also his doubles. The title *The Lesbians* was self-characterizing. Orpheus' head, torn off by Maenads, floated to Lesbos from Thrace: Orphic, woman-persecuted Baudelaire is a lesbian both as poet and sexual persona. The premiere lesbian poet was an androgyne: Baudelaire, echoing Horace, calls her "the male Sappho, the lover and the poet" ("Lesbos"). She is male not only because she desires women like a man but because she is "*le* poëte."

Baudelaire's lesbian poems are complex psychic mechanisms. First, the lesbian aggressor usurps the male privilege of defloration. Second, the poet's gender change intensifies the erotic passivity of his usual subjection to women. Third, women sexually occupied with each other automatically suspend masculine obligation. Man enjoys sexual amnesty from humiliating fears of impotence. Fourth, a lesbian's erotic life is a locked room which man cannot penetrate. Thus lesbianism preserves the mystery of the Great Mother for a poet who finds nature's processes otiose. By becoming a lesbian, the poet wins momentary right of entry into a sexual heart of darkness. Fifth, lesbian self-sterilization thwarts the relentless fertility of nature, for Baudelaire just a mass of "sanctified vegetables" that cannot move him.[27] Hence the increasing frequency of lesbianism, which the poet eagerly records, signals nature's degeneration or apocalyptic decadence.

The sex poems of *Flowers of Evil* caused a scandal, and the book's proofs were seized. Baudelaire and his publisher were tried and fined. Six poems, declared an "offense against morality and decency," were condemned and censored, an official ban not revoked until 1949. These included "Delphine and Hippolyte," "Lesbos," and "The Metamorphoses of the Vampire." "Delphine and Hippolyte" had diverse progeny during the next decade. Courbet's *The Sleepers* (1866) is surely indebted to Baudelaire and Balzac. Two women, blonde and brunette, lie nude and sensuously intertwined, broken pearls and hair comb cast about the mussed bed as erotic evidence of haste and tumult. The background is a heavy drape of dark blue velvet, ominous cloud of a Baudelairean night sky. Two poetic redramatizations of "Delphine and Hippolyte": Swinburne's *Anactoria* in *Poems and Ballads* (1866) and Verlaine's *The Girlfriends: Scenes of Sapphic Love* (1867). The self-projections of both these poets were demonstrably masochistic. Proust's theory that Baudelaire's lesbian themes prove homosexuality would better fit the openly homosexual Verlaine. Proust, like everyone else, overlooks lesbianism's symbolic meaning in nineteenth-century nature-theory. He has in fact transferred to Baudelaire his own homosexual use of sexual metathesis in *Remembrance of Things Past:* the secret transformation of bewitching Alfred Agostinelli into the lesbian Albertine is a virtuoso act of Late Romantic imagination. Albertine, a mysterious prisoner of love descending from the girl with the golden eyes, did not slip into her new gender without arousing the skepticism of knowledgeable Parisians.[28]

Baudelaire's prose contains a theory of the ideal male persona. *The Painter of Modern Life* (1863) makes the dandy the epitome of personal style. Baudelaire is partly drawing on Barbey d'Aurevilly's essay on dandyism (1845), which descends from Castiglione. Baudelaire calls dandyism a Romantic "cult of the self" arising from "the burning need" to create "a personal originality." High Romantic politics were populist and democratic, but Late Romantic ones are reactionary. Dandyism is "a new kind of aristocracy," a "haughty and exclusive" sect resisting "the rising tide of democracy, which invades and levels everything."[29] Late Romanticism is arrogantly elitist, a point that must be remembered for Oscar Wilde, whose political views have been sentimentalized by modern admirers. Baudelaire loathes the new mass culture, which he identifies with mediocrity. He equally rejects

reformers and do-gooders. Gautier says, "Baudelaire abhorred philan-
thropists, progressists, utilitarians, humanitarians, utopists."[30] In other
words, Baudelaire condemned Rousseauism in all its forms. Today,
Rousseauism has so triumphed that the arts and the avant-garde are
synonymous with liberalism, an error reinforced by literature teachers,
with their humanist bias. I follow the Decadents in trying to drive
Rousseauist benevolence out of discourse on art and nature. The Decadents satirized the liberal faith in progress with sizzling prophecies of
catastrophe and cultural collapse.

Baudelaire's dandy is an Apollonian androgyne, drawing a sharp line
between himself and reality. The dandy, with "aristocratic superiority of
mind," aims for "*distinction* above all things." Distinction is aboveness
and apartness. The dandy's vocation is elegance, incarnating the Platonic "idea of beauty" in his own person. He is an artificial personality.
The self, sculpted by imperious Apollonian contour, has become an
object or objet d'art. In Late Romanticism, the expansive High Romantic self, ecstatically open to nature like Shelley with the West Wind,
undergoes hieratic sequestration. Baudelaire was the first artist to live
as an aesthete, putting into practice what Poe only imagined. Sartre says
Baudelaire turned the English dandy's virile athleticism into "feminine
coquettishness."[31] But Barbey already calls dandies "the Androgynes of
History," belonging to "an indecisive intellectual sex," combining grace
with power.[32] There was nothing athletic in the languid Baudelaire,
who had, says Gautier, a neck of "feminine elegance and whiteness."[33]
Gautier calls him a cat, that favorite animal of aesthetes and Decadents.
The cat too is a dandy, cold, elegant, and narcissistic, importing hierarchic Egyptian style into modern life.

In Greek and Renaissance art, the Apollonian androgyne represented
social order and public values. But Baudelaire's Apollonian dandy represents art divorced from society. No laws are recognized except aesthetic ones. Late Romantic personality is debilitated by its own absolutism. After Baudelaire's generation comes a sexual persona I call the
depraved Decadent aesthete, like the court hermaphrodite repellent for
its narrow egotism. Baudelaire's languor, the fatigue of one cut off from
nature, remains with the aesthete to the fin de siècle. We see it in
Wilde's Lord Henry Wotton, with his opium-tainted cigarettes. But
Wotton, robustly English, is immune to the occupational disease of the
depraved aesthete, a neurasthenic sickliness covered by ghastly cosmetics. Examples are Huysmans' Des Esseintes, Mann's Aschenbach,
and Proust's Charlus. In real life there were the Satanist Aleister Crow-
ley and Count Robert de Montesquiou, model for Des Esseintes and

Charlus. In our century, an international class of aging male homosexual conforms to this type, with epicene manners and aesthetic pretensions. The voice is waspish, the figure thin and fluttery; the pallid,
puffy face seems boneless, like that of Miss Havisham, Dickens' rouged
crone. Homosexual fashion has passed the type by in America, but he
still flourishes in Latin countries. The dilettante aesthete is a decayed
Apollonian androgyne.

Another chapter of *The Painter of Modern Life* considers the female
persona, for whom Baudelaire espouses extremism in cosmetics. In an
inimitably French locution, he scornfully dismisses the idea that rouge
should be used sparingly to enhance nature: "Who would dare to
assign to art the sterile function of imitating Nature?" Rousseau and
Wordsworth shrink into their foxhole. Cosmetics are pure artifice,
meant to hide nature's insulting blemishes and to create "an abstract
unity in the color and texture of the skin." The face is a mask, a canvas
on which to paint. Cosmetics must seem unnatural, theatrical. Woman
is "an idol," obliged to appear "magical and supernatural." All fashion
is "a sublime deformation of nature."[34] Actress Stéphane Audran in *Les
Biches* is for me the most stunning exemplar of Baudelairean cosmetics.
As usual, Baudelaire makes woman into an *objet de culte* with a hard,
metallic surface. To emphasize woman's surface is to deny her internal
space, her murky womb-world. The heavily rouged woman—in the
nineteenth century a whore (*Gone with the Wind*'s hot-pink Belle
Watling)—is another symbol of Baudelairean sterility.

Elsewhere Baudelaire says: "Woman is the opposite of the dandy.
Therefore she must inspire horror. . . . Woman is *natural*, that is to say
abominable."[35] Why horror?—an oddly intense word in the context of
the dandy. The answer is that the mineral flesh of Baudelaire's vampires
restricts and confines nature's chthonian liquidity. Woman is the dandy's opposite because she lacks spiritual contour and inhabits the procreative realm of fluids where objects dissolve. All art, as a cult of the
autonomous object, is a flight from liquidity. The Decadent swerve from
sexual experience is identical with the Decadent creation of a world of
glittering art objects. Both are responses to the horror of the female
liquid realm. The Baudelairean woman is mentally and physically impenetrable. The hideous bag of pus of "Metamorphoses of the Vampire"
hardens to stone, into which the poet cannot be sucked. Baudelaire's
pagan poems seal up female internality, the maw of rapacious nature.

Joris-Karl Huysmans' novel *A Rebours* (1884) expands the
Decadent innovations of Balzac, Gautier, Poe, and Baudelaire. The title

means "against nature" or "against the grain." Des Esseintes, the epicene hero, is product of an incest-degenerated aristocratic line, like
Poe's Usher. Romantic solipsism contracts to its ultimate Decadent
closure. Renouncing social relationships, Des Esseintes withdraws into
the self-embowered world of his ornate mansion. Surrounded by curios
and art works, he is like a Pharaoh entombed with his possessions. He is
both priest and idol of his own cult. But his dream of perfect freedom is
defeated by humiliating dependency on others—servants, doctors, den-
tists, horticulturists. *A Rebours* contains its own ironic self-deflation.
Like *Madame Bovary*, it shows reality comically frustrating the lofty
ideals of an author-identified protagonist. Des Esseintes wants life
entirely artistic and artificial. But nature takes her revenge, tormenting
him with toothache, nauseating him with his rare perfumes, disordering his delicacy-sated stomach. Unable to eat, Des Esseintes is fed by
enema, "the ultimate deviation from the norm" which he relishes as "a
happy affront against nature": "What a slap in the face for old Mother
Nature!"[36] The novel ends with the ailing aesthete forced to return to
society and nature. So the Decadent enterprise fails.

A Rebours is a novel without a plot, consistent with the Romantic
withdrawal from action. It is spiritual autobiography, recording a journey not through space but through modes of perception and experience.
The chapters, containing few events, are meditations on *things:* books,
flowers, antiques. Persons are also things. Des Esseintes performs a
botched Sadean experiment on a boy by trying to turn him into a
criminal. Des Esseintes has the Decadent sexual recessiveness. He
trifles, with poor results, with two masculine women he hopes will give
him a new sensation. Miss Urania, an American acrobat with boy's hair
and "arms of iron," is really an automaton, slow and witless. When her
oscillating gender turns feminine, Des Esseintes drops her like a hot
potato. Reality always falls short of imagination. Miss Urania is all
muscle and no mystique. She exasperatingly refuses to take charge.
Without Baudelairean sexual subordination, Des Esseintes is impotent
(apparently like Huysmans himself). But potency belongs to the realm
of vulgar acts. Decadent eroticism is perceptual or cerebral.

Unlike Poe, Baudelaire, and Swinburne, Huysmans has no *anima* or
projected female spirit. Even Roderick Usher is immured with a sister.
Des Esseintes' lavish mansion may be Huysmans' attempt to construct a
male house, a mental space excluding the female. But the repressed
always returns with redoubled force. The aesthete's buried affect toward women produces the horrors of Chapter Eight, a spectacular flight
of imagination. Over ten astonishing pages, woman appears in stages of

increasing sexual clarity. It is Huysmans' metamorphoses of the vampire. The process begins as another exercise in Decadent connoisseurship. Des Esseintes has been a collector of artificial flowers that look real, nature of course being inadequate: "Nature, he used to say, has had her day; she has finally and utterly exhausted the patience of sensitive observers by the revolting uniformity of her landscapes and skyscapes." But Chapter Eight advances past this Baudelairean position into new Decadent terrain: "Tired of artificial flowers aping real ones, he wanted some natural flowers that would look like fakes."[37] He will force nature into art's frame.

Des Esseintes inspects cartloads of hothouse specimens, lurid flowers of evil. There are Caladiums with "swollen, hairy stems" and "huge heart-shaped leaves." Aurora Borealis with "leaves the colour of raw meat." Echinopsis with "ghastly pink blossoms" like "the stumps of amputated limbs." Nidularium, with "sword-shaped petals" and "gaping flesh-wounds." Cypripedium like a diseased, bent-back "human tongue" in a medical text. Some flowers seem "ravaged by syphilis or leprosy," others "blistered by burns" or "pitted with ulcers." To make these "monstrosities," nature borrows tints of rotting flesh and the "hideous splendours" of gangrene. Muses Des Esseintes, "It all comes down to syphilis in the end."[38]

Huysmans' fantastic catalog is a meditation on Romantic nature. It is an anti-Rousseauist polemic, where not society but nature is shown as deeply corrupt. Organic life is in advanced disease, clotted with mutilations insulting beauty and form. We seem to be in a brand-new genre, science fiction, transporting us to a Venusian jungle of half-animal plant creatures. This is Huysmans' voyage to Cythera, Venus' isle. Baudelaire's syphilitic hanged man is infected by Huysmans' noxious blooms, the ulcerated genitals of mother nature. Syphilis, which Des Esseintes sees devastating every generation "since the beginning of the world," is like Poe's red death invading the prince's castle and annihilating humanity. The flowers are a Trojan Horse bringing deadly freight into Des Esseintes' walled city: the daemonic female of chthonian nature.

Adam in the primeval garden falls asleep for the birth of woman. Exhausted, Des Esseintes dreams a series of weird female androgynes, first a tall, thin woman in Prussian soldier's boots, then a haggard "sexless creature" on horseback, her green skin studded with pustules. He recognizes her as "the Pox," a female version of Poe's ghoulish masquer. The dream shifts to "a hideous mineral landscape," surely Baudelaire's rocky Cythera. Here Des Esseintes has one of the most horrifying archetypal experiences in literature. Something stirs on the ground, "an ashen-faced woman, naked but for a pair of green silk stockings." Nepenthes pitchers hang from her ears; "tints of boiled veal" show in her flaring nostrils. As she calls to him, her eyes glow, her lips redden, and her nipples shine like "two red peppers." He recoils in horror from her spotted skin.

> But the woman's eyes fascinated him, and he went slowly towards her, trying to dig his heels into the ground to hold himself back, and falling over deliberately, only to pick himself up again and go on. He was almost touching her when black Amorphophalli sprang up on every side and stabbed at her belly, which was rising and falling like a sea. He thrust them aside and pushed them back, utterly nauseated by the sight of these hot, firm stems twisting and turning between his fingers.

Her arms reach toward him. He panics as her eyes turn a terrible "clear, cold blue." "He made a superhuman effort to free himself from her embrace, but with an irresistible movement she clutched him and held him, and pale with horror, he saw the savage Nidularium blossoming between her uplifted thighs, with its swordblades gaping open to expose the bloody depths." Just before he touches the plant's "hideous flesh-wound," he wakes up, choking with fear. " 'Thank God,' he sobbed, 'it was only a dream.' "[39]

Thus Chapter Eight ends, with Des Esseintes having escaped, like Poe's hero in the maelstrom, from a forcible return to female origins, sucked into the womb of the rapacious all-mother. The woman in green stockings is a syphilitic whore, like Blake's Harlot. Her earrings of carnivorous plants symbolize her command over nature. The boiled veal of her nostrils is the fetid grossness of biology, to which the female always resummons the male. Her nipples are red peppers because they scald the lips of every infant and perforate the chest of every man. Her eyes fascinate because she is the vampire hypnotizing by eye-contact. Des Esseintes is magnetically drawn to her even in his terror because she exerts earth's malign gravitation, which we saw at work in Michelangelo.

Amorphophallus is, incredibly, a real flowering plant of great height; the name means "shapeless" or "misshapen penises." The black fronds springing up and stabbing at the woman's belly are her self-generated male organs, by which she pleasures and fecundates herself. Her belly "rising and falling like a sea" contracts in orgasm and labor: she is Baudelaire's parkside carcass billowing with maggots. The swordblades ringing her vulval "bloody depths" reproduce mythology's vagina dentata. Female genitals perceived as a wound are a commonplace of psychoanalytic literature. That they can be a diseased flower we know from Blake's "Sick Rose." Tennessee Williams told Elizabeth Ashley about being taken to a brothel for his "initiation into manhood." A prostitute forced him to look between her legs: " 'All I could see was somethin' that looked like a dyin' orchid. Consequently I have never been comfortable either with orchids or women.' "[40] In *A Rebours,* female genitalia are flower and wound, because this is the place where man is born and from which he must tear himself away. Des Esseintes builds a palace of art against nature, but in his dreams nature comes to reclaim and devour him.

Huysmans' poisonous genital flowers are botanic androgynes, like Lewis Carroll's shrewish rose and tiger-lily. "Androgynous" is actually a scientific term for plants with staminate and pistillate flowers in one cluster. The female vegetation of *A Rebours* relates to some amazingly misogynous remarks Huysmans made about Degas' paintings of bathing women. He speaks of "the humid horror of a body which no washing can purify."[41] Humid horror: here is that inescapable connection I find between female physiology and the chthonian liquid realm. Certain male celibates or homosexuals express their phobic attitude toward the female body in a nervous fastidiousness, a compulsive cleanliness manifested in small well-scrubbed hands, punctilious dress, and aridity of manner and speech. In the old days, such men were the petty tyrants of musty midlevel civic, bank, and library bureaucracies. The female, with her dark, dank inwardness, is visually unintelligible. Medusa's pubic head is the plant world of writhing stems and vines; she is artistic disorder, the breakdown of form. Liquidity plus vegetative overgrowth equals the chthonian swamp of female nature. The male homosexual, the most active dissenter from female dominance, rebels against the marshy organicism of the female pudendum and the cushy softness of the female body, which he perceives as irresolution of silhouette. This is one reason why, in America, so many gay men are reed-thin, while so many gay women are fat. When women stop trying to please the harsh male eye, the female body just drifts right back to oceanic nature. In *A Rebours,* written by an idealizing celibate, the connoisseur Des Esseintes creates a ritual cult of sharply defined objets d'art, because Decadent aestheticism is the most comprehensive system of aversion to female nature devised by western culture.

Tennessee Williams' memory of his traumatic initiation confirms my chthonian reading of *Suddenly Last Summer.* The play originally appeared with another in *Garden District* (1958), a New Orleans place name that Williams makes a metaphor of rapacious nature. The brilliant movie of *Suddenly Last Summer* (1960), directed by Joseph L. Mankiewicz with a screenplay by Gore Vidal, was a critical disaster. It shows mother nature as a Sadean and Darwinian vortex where the weak are devoured by the strong. In an incantatory scene of expressionistic horror, straining at the emotional limits of film, Katharine Hepburn as Violet Venable narrates the annual assault of birds of the Encantadas on newborn turtles as they race for the sea.

Suddenly Last Summer is *A Rebours* turned inside out. Instead of a chthonian cubicle (Huysmans' horticultural Chapter Eight) inside an aesthetic domain, there is an aesthetic cubicle inside a chthonian domain. Williams' aesthetic cubicle is a votive shrine preserved by a despotic *mater dolorosa* in honor of her son/lover, the homosexual aesthete Sebastian Venable, who produced one perfect poem per year, in a fancy private edition worthy of Des Esseintes. Wealthy mother and son were "a famous couple," touring fashionable Europe. In the inseparable Violet and Sebastian, Williams sexually updates Shakespeare's hermaphrodite twins, Viola and Sebastian. Modernization here, as in Picasso, means a return to primitive archetype. Violet and Sebastian are the Great Mother and her ritually slain son. He is killed by a pack of predatory beggar boys, who hack and eat his flesh in ritual sparagmos. She cultivates insectivorous plants in a steaming "jungle-garden," which the play describes with language straight from *A Rebours*.[42] The sinister garden is cinema's most potent evocation of the primeval swamp-world, rivalled only by the dinosaur saga of Disney's *Fantasia*. Mankiewicz' film is sophisticated and learned: hanging in the son's chamber is a Renaissance painting of St. Sebastian, the bleeding beautiful boy. Sebastian Venable belongs to the tradition of homoerotic martyr, to which Oscar Wilde contributed by taking the name Sebastian Melmoth after his release from prison.

Des Esseintes' aesthetic ambition is to discriminate, to use Pater's word, every thing and every experience. This scholarly process secures the identity of objects against nature. Ironically, in *A Rebours* discrimination collapses back into nondifferentiation. All the aesthete's exotic fragrances begin to smell disgustingly alike. Language alone retains its Decadent separateness. Gautier says imperial late Latin was "an ingenious, complex, learned style," which Baudelaire drew upon for inspiration, since "the fourteen hundred words in Racine's vocabulary" are inadequate for complex modern ideas.[43] Hugo's *Hernani*, whose defense Gautier led, defied the Racinian canon with its eccentric locutions in the Shakespearean manner. *A Rebours* culminates this movement to broaden the rationalist French language. Huysmans' rich, bizarre vocabulary is both antiquarian and futurist. Symons said, "He could describe the inside of a cow hanging in a butcher's shop as beautifully as if it were a casket of jewels."[44]

The diversification of Huysmans' language is a psychic and therefore sexual self-development. *A Rebours* has few characters, for words substitute for persons. Des Esseintes admires imperial Latin because "it was rotten through and through and hung like a decaying carcass, losing its limbs, oozing pus, barely keeping, in the general corruption of its body, a few sound parts."[45] Language becomes Baudelaire's crucified corpse. I said the body in Spenser is a social integer. The paradigm in Baudelaire is the alienated body: each poem is a corrupted object, a mirror of the self. Baudelaire made lyric a reliquary of decay. In Huysmans, with his glut of rare words, language generates dense new personae. *A Rebours* (originally called *Alone*) is Romantically self-contained, its linguistic energy invested in internal sexual differentiation. Its words are thronging multiples, spores of competitive identity. The whole, subdividing into fractious parts, makes love to itself.

Two minor writers of the late nineteenth century also depict sexual personae in Decadent enslavement and closure. In *Venus in Furs* (1870), Leopold von Sacher-Masoch, who gave his name to masochism, creates a theatrical world of female dominance. Like Baudelaire and Swinburne, Masoch hails "the tyranny and cruelty that constitute woman's essence and her beauty." Severin, his hero, imposes a ritual role on Wanda, whom he drapes in furs and arms with a whip. She is a sexual totem, bristling with symbols. Severin says, "It is possible to love really only that which stands above us."[46] Here one clearly sees that masochism is not an illness but a hierarchical dream, a conceptual realignment of sexual orders. Eros parodies or recapitulates the sacred because, as I suggested, sexuality, even at its most perverse, is implicitly religious. Sex is the ritual link between man and nature. Masoch's obsession with furs is, in Freudian terms, a fetishistic longing for the mother's pubic hair. But Anthony Storr calls fetishism "a triumph of human imagination": the fetishist's desire is moved "from a sensation to an idea."[47] I view Masoch's furs as chthonian. Wanda casts them around Severin like Aeschylus' female net, the harness of Necessity, an image Masoch actually cites. The furs are "electric," like Zeus's thundercloud and Athena's aegis. Wanda is "the cruel northern Venus in Furs," half chthonian, half Apollonian, fusing emotional and cultural opposites. The novel's imaginative center is a series of stunning cinematic stills of Wanda in epiphany. She appears in glamourous hieratic attitudes blazing with light, an Apollonian icon in a private cult. Narrative halts, as we contemplate the androgyne in the Apollonian mode, a work of visual art temporarily dominating its own text. Hierarchic assertions of tremendous force are needed to lock the aggressive western eye into perceptual submission.

The Decadent is usually male, since decadence, literally a "falling off," requires renunciation of a cultural burden, abandonment of a public persona or duty. Rachilde, wife of Arthur Vallette, founder of *Le Mercure de France*, produced a huge volume of work in her long life, but her most notorious book was *Monsieur Vénus* (1884), one of the oddest things ever written by a woman. George Sand had been granted the honorific "man of letters," which Rachilde took for her calling card. She was to be called Paris' "androgyne of letters." In *Venus in Furs*, sadism is induced from a normal woman by a masochistic male. In *Monsieur Vénus*, masochism is induced from a delicate male by a sadistic woman.

The title alludes to both the soft youth, Jacques Silvert, and his lordly master-mistress, Raoule de Vénérande, a corrupted matronymic indicating her descent from Venus in the century of syphilis. Like Maupin, Raoule is an Amazon and expert fencer. But her desires are more sensual and perverse. She discovers Jacques, a maker of artificial flowers, exactly as Cousin Bette unearths the feminine Polish sculptor. Raoule installs her acquisition in a luxurious boudoir, a love prison modelled on *The Girl with the Golden Eyes*. She systematically eradicates Jacques's residual maleness. Adonis becomes an odalisque, his gender dissolving in the boudoir's shimmering liquid realm. Raoule indignantly denies she is lesbian. This vice, deliciously scandalous fifty years before, has already become banal, "the crime of boarding-school teachers and the fault of the prostitute." Like Gautier's D'Albert, Raoule craves "the *impossible*": she wants to be "in love like a man with a man."[48] The sole parallel I find is in an Olympia Press sex novel, where someone says of a butch lesbian, "She was so queer she had finally come around to men, *as a faggot!*"[49] Visiting Jacques, Raoule begins to wear male evening dress and refer to him as "she." She forces "various degradations" on him: "They were more and more united in a common thought: the destruction of their sex." The distance from *Mademoiselle de Maupin* is enormous. Maupin's quest for a man's freedom becomes Raoule's campaign to reduce a male to servitude, like Hercules under Omphale.

Raoule seeks something transcendental from sex experience, but her technique is Decadent enslavement. When Jacques begins to drift from control, she coolly arranges for his execution. Adonis, ritually slain, will be ritually mourned by his patron goddess. *Monsieur Vénus* ends in a shocking spectacle of Decadent closure. In a secret chamber, Raoule builds a shrine to her dead lover. A wax and rubber effigy lies in state on the bed, a Venus seashell. Hair, lashes, teeth, and nails are all real, "torn from a corpse," as endorsed by Poe. In sometimes male, sometimes female dress, Raoule kisses the statue's mouth, which moves by "a hidden spring." Decadent objectification, begun by the High Romantic turn toward art, reaches its final grotesque point. A person has literally become a thing. The beautiful boy as Adonis, who enters the novel hung with garlands of satin roses, is turned into the androgyne as manufactured object, a frigid android. Raoule is like Balzac's marquise, killing her lover in order to memorialize her. But the marquise then leaves the boudoir behind. Raoule de Vénérande, at the height of the Decadence, walls up her sanctuary even more willfully. She remains alone, married to herself and a work of sexual sculpture. All other objects of the visible world, annihilated by their Decadent profusion, have sunk to nothingness.

17

Romantic Shadows

Emily Brontë

English Romanticism in the nineteenth century had two choices: Wordsworth or Coleridge? Their argument between benevolent and daemonic nature is continued by Emily Brontë in *Wuthering Heights* (1847). Romanticism's amorality and pagan power are concentrated in its Byronic hero, Heathcliff, product of a stunning sex change. Heathcliff is Emily Brontë, a woman who pressed at the limits of gender and, failing to find satisfaction in art, died. After epic, the social novel is the genre most hostile to the androgyne. But *Wuthering Heights* is not a social novel, like those of Jane Austen and George Eliot. It is a Romantic prose-poem, belonging like Hawthorne's eerie tales to the tradition of romance, which, as Northrop Frye says, "radiates a glow of subjective intensity."[1] The covert subjectivity of *Wuthering Heights* produces its sexual ambiguities. In the novel's secret psychodrama, hermaphrodite Emily Brontë clashes with society, law, fate.

Before arriving at *Wuthering Heights*, we must briefly consider the social novel. Nineteenth-century literature embraces ordinariness, the routine minutiae of daily life. The rise of the Romantic objet d'art is paralleled by the social novel's documentation of objects, rare in eighteenth-century fiction. Balzac opens *Père Goriot* with a slow, photographic inspection of a squalid rooming house. Character in the social novel, a child of Rousseau, is formed by environment. George Eliot says she seeks "as full a vision of the medium in which a character moves as of the character itself." She records "the hampering threadlike pressure of small social conditions, and their frustrating complexity."[2] Context rivals character. The English, French, and Russian nineteenth-century novel contains a Shakespearean profusion of personalities, each with a private code of speech and gesture. Yet there are few androgynes. Why?

A good example is Eliot's *Middlemarch* (1871–72), which traps its characters in a web of interdependence. Chief victim is the intelligent, womanly heroine, Dorothea Brooke. Because it is concerned with wholes, the interaction of groups and subgroups, the social novel subjects sexual personae to the discipline of *limitation. Middlemarch* bridles its two nascent androgynes, Rosamond Lydgate and Will Ladislaw. Frivolous Rosamond, saboteur of her husband's career, paralyzes by "torpedo contact." F. R. Leavis sees in her narcissistic turn of the neck "a sinister hint of the snake."[3] She is the archetypal fatal woman, but the social novel curbs and reduces her in scale. The fearful and barbarous become the shallow and silly. Eliot gives the vampire's psychopathic moral blankness clever new form: "In poor Rosamond's mind there was not room enough for luxuries to look small in."[4] The vampire is half-modern, half-archaic, a *bourgeoise* and dinosaur with the brain of a pea.

Everyone agrees that Will Ladislaw, with whom Dorothea inexplicably falls in love, is, as Arnold Kettle puts it, Eliot's most glaring "artistic failure."[5] My explanation: the flitting Ladislaw suffers from the social novel's antipathy to the androgyne. How has a Pole turned up in an English country town anyway? I think he is Balzac's effeminate Polish artist, the Chopin-inspired Wenceslas, whom potent Bette takes under her wing. Eliot tries to make Ladislaw charismatic: "When he turned his head quickly his hair seemed to shake out light." He has a "preternatural quickness and glibness" of speech, hardly the reliable style of "solid Englishmen."[6] Mercurial or puckish speed always diminishes the masculine. Ladislaw is a Shakespearean androgyne of verbal mobility, but the nineteenth century denies him his Renaissance authority. Ladislaw's aura of light winks feebly on and off because the social novel, in its devotion to the whole, opposes the hieratically self-isolating charismatic personality. Note the way Tolstoy portrays Napoleon, one of the most charismatic men in history, as a small man with small hands and a small smile. By its reality principle of limitation, *Middlemarch* confines the androgynes Rosamond and Ladislaw to the diurnal and prosaic, truncating their affective power. Rosamond is a ninny and Ladislaw a *flâneur.* Eliot says her heroine's pulses of emotion "tremble off and are dispersed among hindrances."[7] Dispersion also rules dominant personae like the androgyne: the social novel's fictive energy, distributed throughout the minor characters and environment, is rarely concentrated in a node of high glamour.

The frigidity of the Apollonian androgyne in a social novel is a social crime, for withholding of emotion frustrates community and compromise. Egoism is the androgyne's raison d'être. Self-complete beings need no one and nothing. Jane Austen's *Emma* (1816) illustrates the social novel's association of androgyny with selfish privatism. Edmund Wilson first pointed out the delicate touch of sexual ambivalence in the beautiful and witty Emma Woodhouse: she is "relatively indifferent to men" and "inclined to infatuations with women." Marvin Mudrick says, "Emma prefers the company of women, more particularly of women whom she can master and direct; . . . this preference is intrinsic to her whole dominating and uncommitting personality." Andrew H. Wright speaks of Emma's "supreme self-confidence and serene delusion" and Douglas Bush of her "managerial vanity and arrogance."[8] Emma's autocracy and lesbian flirtation are a single phenomenon, a hermaphroditic hierarchism which the social novel cannot tolerate. Stuart M. Tave brilliantly says of Emma, "What really defeats her, it seems, is the ordered form and truth of the plot which, from start to finish, meets her at every turn as it maintains its beautiful and inevitable course."[9] In other words, the novel itself, in its formal essence, rises up to check the pretensions of the charismatic personality, humanizing and normalizing it for marriage, foundation of the social order. There is a parallel with English Renaissance literature, where the Amazon sacrifices her androgyny for the public good.

Emma, like Dorian Gray, enchants by a double-sexed charm, to which not all readers are susceptible. But it is the mysterious iridescence of Emma's half-repellent character that has evoked from commentators on the novel a body of criticism unusual in its fineness. *Emma* is a reactionary work of Augustan assumptions, and its heroine presides from a tribunal of privilege. Emma's well-bred aggression becomes crasser in Rebecca Sharp, the upwardly mobile adventuress of Thackeray's *Vanity Fair* (1847–48). Becky has Emma's manipulativeness and Cousin Bette's cold male will. Her masculine force of personality upstages the nominal heroine, placid, feminine Amelia Sedley. Nevertheless, *Vanity Fair*, as a social novel, maintains its opposition to glamour, which appears as an amoral hardness.

Becky's rare visits to her neglected son Rawdon are in the radiant style of Apollonian epiphany. She glitters with jewels and high fashion, superb, "unearthly," unreachable. She bursts upon the eye like Spenser's Belphoebe in the forest—an episode based on another maternal epiphany, the appearance of Vergil's armed Venus to Aeneas. But now the assumptions are different. Thackeray laments: "Oh, thou poor lonely little benighted boy! Mother is the name for God in the lips and hearts of little children; and here was one who was worshipping a

stone!"[10] Stony Becky Sharp, self-sculpted by sharp Apollonian contour, descends on her son as a goddess, a meteorite Palladium. Becky's
moral fault is her evasion of ordinariness, of simple homely emotion.
The social novel differs from Renaissance and Romantic literature in its
resistance to the mystically transcendent personality. Apollonian glamour always occurs at the expense of the ethical. We see this in Balzac's
dandy De Marsay snubbing Lucien at the Opéra or in Proust's Duch-
esse de Guermantes turning her back on the dying Swann to hurry to
her carriage on the way to a dinner party, in that cruel and pivotal
moment, modelled on a similar scene in Balzac, which is exactly midway through *Remembrance of Things Past*.

The Apollonian hierarch is a narcissist, frozen in moral adolescence.
Hence Artemis' and Belphoebe's boyish body type. Apollonian perfection and fixity are foreign to the social novel, which endorses a develop-
mental model of personality. Developmentalism comes from Rousseau,
dramatized in his autobiography. Personality in the social novel must be
in evolutionary change, not the same thing as Dionysian metamorphosis. The high-energy Dionysian androgyne alters spontaneously, for
no climax of maturation. Personality change in the social novel may
come through petty, grinding humiliations, unlike the sudden turns of
Fortune's wheel bringing down the hero of Renaissance drama. Renaissance personality is immanent. Similarly, Romantic personality is primary and absolute, a flame of imagination lit by the gods. A Renaissance aristocrat has quality of blood, wondrously manifested in fine
complexion, manner, and speech, even in a kidnapped prince reared in
a hovel. In the social novel, an aristocrat is simply a social type. His is a
chance supremacy, evolutionary and not innate. He is like a boulder left
on a summit by a vanished glacier.

The purer the social novel, the more negative it is to the androgyne.
The greater the influx of Romantic consciousness, as in Virginia Woolf,
the greater the frequency of hermaphroditic personae. Dickens, for
example, disagrees with George Eliot on several basic issues. His social
structures are not educative, leading from self-involvement to community, but oppressive and labyrinthine, emotion-killing. His novels descend from Blake's protest poems on exploited chimney sweeps. The
child is Dickens' ideal type, uncorrupted, as in Rousseau and Wordsworth, by civilization. His virtuous characters retain the unitary qualities of childhood: innocence, purity, simplicity. His veneration of the
presexual child makes him receptive to male androgynes of benevolent
eccentricity, like quirky Mr. Micawber, holy lunatics of untainted mind.
Dickens' novels retain elements of the parable or morality play. Thus

when he turns to allegory, the androgyne immediately appears, as in the three sexless or sexually dual apparitions of *A Christmas Carol.*

Androgynes are more common in the French novel, where they enjoy thematic centrality. The hero is usually a half-feminine *ingénu*, as in Stendhal's *The Red and the Black* (1830) and *The Charterhouse of Parma* (1839). Women are older or of higher rank, following Rousseau and Goethe. Stendhal's androgyny is adolescent malleability or naiveté, ripe for disillusion. His pretty phrases for Julien Sorel are adopted by Balzac for the girlish Eugène de Rastignac. A line of transmission is clear to Flaubert's *The Sentimental Education* (written 1843–45), where one feels the impact of Decadent Late Romanticism. Flaubert's Frédéric Moreau has a homoerotic intimacy and a perverse attraction to a Diana-like dominatrix, a woman in military dress. The culminating sexual debacle of Frédéric's flight from a brothel confirms Flaubert's definition of androgyny as arrested adolescence. The story goes full circle in returning the hero from his adventures among women to his primary but socially regressive union with a male friend.

The French novel's adolescent androgyne is not the ideal persona of High Romanticism, where sexual duality signifies imaginative range and power. Julien and Frédéric have sensibility but not imagination. They achieve nothing permanent. They contemplate neither their own souls nor the great realities of nature and culture. Once again, the laws of the social novel consign hermaphroditism to a realm of limitation, where it represents only weakness and inefficacy, potentiality falling short of realization. The English social novel, mastered by so many women writers, is less concerned with the adolescent male as a character type and less indulgent toward his misapprehensions and disappointments. Stendhal's and Flaubert's self-projection into their unlucky heroes is tinged with satire, like Byron's ironic affection for his fresh-faced Don Juan.

Flaubert said of the heroine of his best novel (1857), "Madame Bovary, c'est moi!" She contains his spiritual struggles and sexual contradictions. Baudelaire felt "a virile spirit" still present in "this bizarre androgyne," who "remains a man."[11] The motherless Emma sketches Minerva (a self-portrait?), wears masculine accessories, dresses as a man at a ball. Gaston Bachelard says, "The literary creation of a woman by a man or of a man by a woman are burning creations."[12] Madame Bovary carries Flaubert's adolescent Romantic dreams. She is one of the social novel's great misinterpreters of reality, demanding life's slow, bland routine yield a fantasia of ecstasy and sensation. Reality, never excluded for long in this genre, must finally close about her. *Anna*

Karenina (1873–76), Tolstoy's version of *Madame Bovary*, pits another willful adulteress against social constraint. Emma's latent masculinity survives in Anna's severe black-velvet ball dress and in the tendency of women to fall "in love with" or "lose their hearts" to her.[13] Society wins; the heroines are defeated. The suicides of Emma, Anna, and Vergil's Dido may function as an exorcistic divorce of the writer's adult male persona from the mesmerizing female persona of his inner life, a shadow of mother and memory.

All these themes of sexual duality and deviance are gathered together in Emile Zola's *Nana* (1880). Just as Becky Sharp is a brasher Emma Woodhouse, so is Nana a more perverse Bovary and Karenina. The sexual outlaw has graduated from adultery to prostitution. Nana is queen of Parisian courtesans. She is a Venus, an Amazon, a "man-eater," a monster resting her feet on "human skulls." Nana intensifies the ambivalences of the earlier nineteenth-century heroines. She takes a jealous lesbian lover, picks up girls, and dons male disguise to visit brothels to "watch scenes of debauchery to relieve her boredom." Zola imagines his great androgyne as the enemy of civilization. She is "a force of nature, a ferment of destruction, unwittingly corrupting and disorganizing Paris between her snow-white thighs." He sees her "dominating the city" from "the horizon of vice."[14] *Nana* has Decadent elements from Baudelaire, Huysmans, and Moreau, but as a social novel it must redeem the social order from its enslavement to this titanic hermaphrodite, high priestess of mother nature. Like St. Augustine, Zola condemns the Great Mother as the Whore of Babylon. The book ends with a tour de force of Decadent description, a nearly geological analysis of the loathsome face of Nana's corpse suppurating with small-pox, nature undoing its consummate creation.

Thus even in the French novel, where nineteenth-century society is banal and conformist, the androgyne is always disciplined for the social whole. Compare the vampire hierarchs of *Nana* and *Christabel*. Zola's voracious femme fatale is destroyed by the very archetypal forces she invokes. But Coleridge's malign Geraldine, a High Romantic androgyne, gets out of her poem intact. In fact, when we part from the unfinished *Christabel*, Geraldine is still gaining in power. And nothing can check the Late Romantic vampires of Baudelaire and Huysmans. In its negativity toward the archetypal female, the social novel agrees with epic: androgyny destabilizes the public structures of history.

The first novels of Emily and Charlotte Brontë, published the same year, revived out-of-fashion Gothic style. They share rugged, brooding heroes and a wild atmosphere of mystery and gloom. But the books belong to different genres. Despite sex-reversing moments, Charlotte's *Jane Eyre* is a social novel governed by public principles of intelligibility. It records the worldly progress of an ingénue from childhood to maturity, culminating in marriage. Emily's *Wuthering Heights*, on the other hand, is High Romantic, its sources of energy outside society and its sex and emotion incestuous and solipsistic. The two Brontë novels differ dramatically in their crossing lines of identification. Charlotte palpably projects herself into her underprivileged but finally triumphant heroine, while Emily leaps across the borderline of gender into her savage hero.

Critics have disagreed about nearly everything in *Wuthering Heights*. The story is set in receding frames, pictures within pictures, darkening panes of relativity. Brontë's jump-cuts from present to past were prophetic of later developments in the novel but irritated and confused many contemporary readers, who thought the book disorganized. *Jane Eyre*, in contrast, is content with traditional chronological narration. Are there psychological reasons for Emily Brontë's formal innovations?

Wuthering Heights' central problem is the passionate attraction between Catherine Earnshaw and rough Heathcliff, with his "half-civilized ferocity."[15] This celebrated love story contains curious gaps of sexual affect, which the popular audience has bridged on its own. Emotion is a flash flood of turbulence, glutting the personae with amoral energies. There is tremendous emphasis on cruelty, brutality, and violence, which few critics manage to integrate into a balanced view of the novel. Most ignore the subject altogether, since sadism is incompatible with academic humanitarianism.

Q. D. Leavis, for example, admits the presence of a violent "Lear-world" in *Wuthering Heights* but dismisses it as "due not to sadism or perversion in the novelist ... but to the Shakespearian intention."[16] David Cecil thinks the "fierceness and ruthlessness" of Brontë's characters express "the vitality of nature": "Like the adherents of some primitive religion we watch the Earth God stiffen in the death of winter; rise with youth mysteriously renewed to blossom in the spring."[17] Nature does stand behind the novel, but it is nature as stormy masculine force, not as fertility or renewal. Dorothy van Ghent speaks of "the impulse to destruction" and "the inhuman excess" of Heathcliff and Catherine's passion, "an excess everywhere present in language—in verbs and modifiers and metaphors that seethe with a brute fury."[18] Virginia Woolf says, "There is love, but it is not the love of men and women."[19] Cecil calls Catherine's love "sexless," "as devoid of sensuality as the

attraction that draws the tide to the moon, the steel to the magnet."
Cecil's word "sexless" persists in commentary on the novel but has so
many possible meanings that critics misunderstand one another.

Catherine tells her puzzled housekeeper, Nelly Dean, that she will
marry Edgar, not Heathcliff, because she and Heathcliff are too alike:
"He's more myself than I am. . . . Nelly, I *am* Heathcliff."[20] Such love,
arising from a sense of identity rather than difference, is beyond gender.
The resemblances between Heathcliff and Catherine are literal. She is
as violent and vengeful as he. A hoyden of "fiery temper" who demands
a whip as a gift, she is always attacking people and knocking them
about. Catherine and Heathcliff suffer emotion as physical paroxysms.
Both grind their teeth in fits of temper and dash their heads against hard
objects. In one of her episodes of "maniac's fury," Catherine tears up a
pillow with her teeth, scattering feathers like a fox shaking a chicken.
One of the novel's first sympathetic commentators, Emile Montégut,
declares, "He and she are, so to speak, but a single person; together they
form a hybrid monster, twin-sexed and twin-souled; he is the male soul
of the monster, she the female."[21] The metaphor comes from French
Decadent Late Romanticism; a High Romantic one might be better.
Claire Rosenfield says, "Cathy and Heathcliff are themselves exact
Doubles differing in sex alone."[22] This love affair is Emily Brontë's
Romantic coalescence of the doubles.

As a sexual persona, Heathcliff is modelled on Byron and specifically
on Byron's Manfred, tormented with love for his sister. *Wuthering
Heights'* incest theme has been long recognized but only sporadically
discussed. Catherine and the orphaned Heathcliff grow up in the intimacy of brother and sister. Heathcliff could even be Earnshaw's bastard
son and hence Catherine's half-brother. But critics have gotten the
incest theme backwards by rationalizing it without regard for its High
Romantic sources. Heathcliff and Catherine cannot marry, some claim,
because of an implicit incest taboo. Yet as we have seen, incest is so
indispensable to Romantic consciousness that even when a sibling does
not exist, as in Shelley, he or she *must be invented.* Incest is not a danger
to be shunned but a royal empowerment of imagination.

Heathcliff and Catherine's love is inflamed, not checked by their
fraternal twinship. Their love can be called sexless, since carnal intercourse is not desired. Romantic union is a conflation of soul-images,
mirrored self-love. In *Manfred*, genital contact is an error, a demeaning
literalization. It is their mad striving for an impossible union which
makes Heathcliff and Catherine's last meeting, on the day of her death,
so astonishing a moment in fiction. The two embrace with wild, bruis-

ing convulsions. The scene is less love than ritual combat. H. J. Rose says the arousal of excitement in ancient ceremonies was to create magical energy or power. Heathcliff and Catherine are like the *Oresteia*'s brother and sister, rhythmically working themselves into a hyperstate of love-hate. Behind Emily Brontë's long thrilling scene I feel Shelley's fusion with his sister-spirit at the climax of *Epipsychidion*. There the fictive siblings beat, burn, and boil in a mystic welter of water and fire. Shelley calls the poem "an antenatal dream," regressing through history. But the Apollonian *Epipsychidion* swerves from the gross facts of primitive experience. It is Emily Brontë who completes the High Romantic quest for incest. *Wuthering Heights* recreates the daemonism of the primeval incest-realm. Hence the book's universal sadism.

The cluttered family romance of *Wuthering Heights* is predicated on Romantic history-reversal. Eric Solomon correctly sees that "Emily Brontë casts a vague incestuous aura" over the whole story: "Heathcliff marries his lost love's sister-in-law; his wife's son marries her brother's daughter; Cathy's daughter marries *her* brother's son."[23] Major criticism overlooks the novel's atmosphere of sexual claustrophobia, the vast turns of cathexis back upon itself from one generation to the next. The incestuous introversion is reinforced by repetition of names or echoes of names: Heathcliff, Hindley, Hareton, Linton, There is an elder and younger Catherine and an elder and younger Linton (surname and first name). C. P. Sanger's oft-reproduced genealogical chart (1926) may mislead by implying there is a clarity of characterization in *Wuthering Heights* accessible to any diligent reader. Family identity is fluid in Romantic literature. Hindley, Hareton, Linton: the rabbity names breed and slide into each other, helplessly retracting to an embryonic state. The generations do not really progress in *Wuthering Heights*. They are irresistibly called back to their origins, for in Romantic sex and emotion, the future is only a misty emanation of the past.

One of *Wuthering Heights'* most powerful achievements is its surging matrix of genetically homologous identities. Only the heart of the book is in psychosexual flux. The guardians of the narrative frame, pragmatic Nelly Dean and fatuous Lockwood, are sharply delineated characters. I gave the name allegorical repletion to this style of representation, which I see in Leonardo's *The Virgin and Child with St. Anne* and Rossetti's *Bower Meadow* and *Astarte Syriaca*. Allegorical repletion is the *filling up* of fictive space with a single identity appearing simultaneously in different forms, juxtaposed like facets of a jewel. In allegorical repletion, a dominating personality is extended through psychological space.

Heathcliff and Catherine seek sadomasochistic annihilation of their separate identities. Their desire to collapse into one another produces a gigantic spirit-body in the text, preventing other family members from attaining normal size. A social novel progresses systematically toward character differentiation. The personae of *Jane Eyre*, for example, become increasingly distinct as they develop or reveal a secret past. But *Wuthering Heights* moves the other way. As a Romantic work, it blurs even generational differences at its core, toward which personae and events sink back by centripetal compulsion.

Heathcliff and Catherine's incestuous alliance does not, as might be expected, compete with a normal marriage. *Wuthering Heights* has a dark and a light hero, an unusual "male version," Frye observes, of the nineteenth-century motif of dark and light heroines in Scott, Poe, Hawthorne, and Melville.[24] Femininity lingers in Edgar Linton, swarthy Heathcliff's timid blonde rival. Edgar is "the soft thing," with a sweet "soft-featured face" and "too graceful" a figure.[25] As a wife, Catherine is dominant; her will is law. Heathcliff and Catherine's hermaphrodite doubling is therefore opposed by Edgar and Catherine's hermaphrodite marriage, where sex roles are reversed.

Wuthering Heights follows the psychosexual geography of Shakespeare's *Antony and Cleopatra*. Thrushcross Grange, the Linton estate, is like Caesar's Rome, a respectable world of static social personae. The Earnshaws' Wuthering Heights, like Cleopatra's Egypt, is a realm of raw natural energy and uncontrolled metamorphoses. Romantic heights are sublime, exalted, extreme. A grange is nature managed, contained, agrarian, aptly symbolized by a crossing thrush, a pretty unpredatory bird. In Shakespeare, the hero must choose between two opposed worlds, but in Brontë it is the heroine. Returning from her stay at Thrushcross Grange, Catherine is the street-reveller Cleopatra turned into sedate Octavia: "Instead of a wild, hatless little savage jumping into the house, and rushing to squeeze us all breathless, there lighted from a handsome black pony a very dignified person, with brown ringlets falling from the cover of a feathered beaver, and a long cloth habit which she was obliged to hold up with both hands that she might sail in." Her decorous new persona is gained at great loss of vitality. Emblem of the Grange is what Heathcliff calls "the vacant blue eyes of the Lintons."[26] The Lintons are blonde sky-gods representing, like Shakespeare's Caesar, a stolid, arid Apollonianism. Their eyes are vacant because blind to the dark, roiling realm of Heathcliff's Dionysian nature-force. The Grange is sheltered from the storms that blast and flatten vegetation on the Heights. This hostile landscape of "bleak winds and bitter northern skies" is the novel's master stroke. Winter at Wuthering Heights invades and surmounts summer. Here is Brontë's most significant departure from High Romanticism, where nature even at its most tumultuous is usually an inexhaustible well of fertility. For her, nature is primarily force, not nurturance. She creates, in other words, *a nature without a mother.*

Wuthering Heights systematically revises its Romantic sources. It transfers *Epipsychidion*'s incestuous meeting of twin-souls from contemplative to active and from spiritual to material. Shelley's Emilia is a cloudy "Angel" or "Seraph of Heaven," but Catherine, who identifies her love for Heathcliff with "the eternal rocks," dreams happily of being expelled from heaven by the angels. *Wuthering Heights* is *Epipsychidion* with nature written in. Brontë treats Byron similarly, by rerooting him— or rather his famed persona of glamourous will—more deeply in the natural. In Heathcliff there is now a direct passage between Byronism and natural power, for in Byron's poetry, nature serves largely as lyrical background. With his "sharp cannibal teeth" and "the expression of a vicious cur," Heathcliff stands at the border of the human. Birds build their nest near him, mistaking him for "a piece of timber."[27] Brontë's sharpest correction is of Wordsworth. *Wuthering Heights*, written at the zenith of Victorian nature-worship, envisions a cosmos of Coleridgean cruelty. Brontë barbarizes Wordsworth, transforming his serene, majestic testimony of moral cooperation between man and nature into a harsh prose ode heaving with subterranean disturbances. The novel is a sadomasochistic swirl of primitive noise and motion, the rending and tearing of Dionysian sparagmos, which is only made tolerable or even intelligible by the brilliant distancing device of the nesting narrative frames.

Wuthering Heights is a catalog of chthonian horrors, each a Coleridgean affront to Wordsworthian benevolence. It is full of outbreaks of violence and lurid imaginings of death and torture. We witness or hear of whipping, slapping, thrashing, cuffing, wrenching, pinching, scratching, hair-pulling, gouging, kicking, trampling, and the hanging of dogs. Hindley hopes his horse will "kick out" Heathcliff's brains. Catherine, bitten by a dog, would not cry out even "if she had been spitted on the horns of a mad cow." Isabella shrieks "as if witches were running red-hot needles into her." Heathcliff ponders "flinging Joseph off the highest gable, and painting the housefront with Hindley's blood." He throws a tureen of hot applesauce in Edgar's face. Hindley shoves a carving knife between Nelly's teeth and threatens to push it down her throat. Nelly fears Heathcliff "smashing Hareton's skull on the steps." Heathcliff says of Edgar, "I'll crush his ribs in like a rotten hazel-nut!" The moment Catherine ceased loving Edgar, "I would have torn his heart out, and drunk his blood!" "I have no pity!" Heathcliff cries. "The more the worms writhe, the more I yearn to crush out their entrails!" Isabella says Heathcliff is adept at "pulling out the nerves with red hot pincers"; he seized her heart, "pinched it to death," and flung it back to her. He hurls a dinner knife at her, cutting open her neck. Discovering Hindley's body, he says, "Flaying and scalping would not have wakened him." On and on. The reader may feel, with Catherine, "A thousand smiths' hammers are beating in my head!"[28]

Virtuosity of sadistic speech pours from all the characters, not just Heathcliff. Even affable Nelly Dean speaks this primitive language. The novel's sadistic eloquence ultimately belongs to Emily Brontë herself, who may have learned her cascading curses from raging Cleopatra. Sometimes the cruelty is quite subtle. When Catherine falls ill with fever, Mrs. Linton visits Wuthering Heights to nurse her, then insists on taking her to Thrushcross Grange to convalesce. Nelly recalls: "But the poor dame had reason to repent of her kindness; she, and her husband, both took the fever, and died within a few days of each other."[29] The sudden exit of the elder Lintons always inspires me with admiring laughter. They die so fast we nearly hear their bodies hitting the floor, like Coleridge's sailors dropping to the deck. We are meant to notice Catherine's spoiled self-absorption, thoughtlessly leaving ruin in her wake, like Cleopatra veering off from Actium. But the two deaths also demonstrate the fatality of the liaison of Heathcliff and Catherine, who give off a kind of chthonian miasma, infecting and devastating the social world. This is one of the blatantly anti-Wordsworthian moments in *Wuthering Heights*. The Lintons' generosity, hospitality, and humane emotion are harshly answered by Emily Brontë's nature-as-destroyer. It is the author as sniper, playfully cutting down her characters from an invisible height. She is Artemis Hecaerge, "the far-shooter," "she who works from afar."

From the least to the most obvious cruelty: Lockwood's terrible dream of Catherine's ghost. Oddly, it is rarely discussed. Yet it is the psychologically most central thing in the novel, coming directly from Brontë's earliest inspiration. Rummaging through mildewed books at Wuthering Heights, Lockwood drifts off to sleep. He is disturbed by the rattling of a fir-bough against the window:

"I must stop it, nevertheless!" I muttered, knocking my knuckles through the glass, and stretching an arm out to seize the importunate branch: instead of which, my fingers closed on the fingers of a little ice-cold hand!

The intense horror of nightmare came over me; I tried to draw back my arm, but the hand clung to it, and a most melancholy voice sobbed,

"Let me in—let me in!"

"Who are you?" I asked, struggling, meanwhile, to disengage myself.

"Catherine Linton," it replied shiveringly (why did I think of *Linton?* I had read *Earnshaw* twenty times for Linton), "I'm come home, I'd lost my way on the moor!"

As it spoke, I discerned, obscurely, a child's face looking through the window—terror made me cruel; and, finding it useless to attempt shaking the creature off, I pulled its wrist on to the broken pane, and rubbed it to and fro till the blood ran down and soaked the bedclothes: still it wailed, "Let me in!" and maintained its tenacious gripe, almost maddening with fear.

"How can I!" I said at length. "Let *me* go, if you want me to let you in!"

The fingers relaxed, I snatched mine through the hole, hurriedly piled the books up in a pyramid against it, and stopped my ears to exclude the lamentable prayer.

I seemed to keep them closed above a quarter of an hour, yet the instant I listened, again, there was the doleful cry moaning on!

"Begone!" I shouted, "I'll never let you in, not if you beg for twenty years."

"It's twenty years," mourned the voice, "twenty years, I've been a waif for twenty years!"[30]

The wrist rubbed on broken glass is one of the most frightful images in literature, for it involves the torture of a child. Coleridgean-Byronic Emily Brontë is settling Wordsworth's hash. By drafting the pedestrian Lockwood into this bloody pagan spectacle, she demonstrates the innateness of sadism. The dreamer's primitive instinct for self-preservation bursts through the mask of good manners and social custom. A man who would normally tenderly clasp or kiss a lady's hand tries to hack it off. The traveller Lockwood makes a Wordsworthian journey back to nature and finds himself in his own daemonic heart of darkness, containing not compassion but barbarism. The scene has a wonderful dream-logic. For example, the ghost's arm is a fir-bough because wild Catherine has been reabsorbed into nature. Self-destructive in life, she is a speaking tree from Dante's wood of the suicides. Lockwood therefore runs her wrist across jagged glass because he is *sawing a branch*.

Why does Catherine appear as a child, yet give her married name of Linton? Mark Kinkead-Weekes suggests, "Cathy and Heathcliff are fixed in a mode of being forged in childhood."[31] Incest, I said, is regression through history back to nature. The spool of time is rewound. The ghost of the emotionally undeveloped Catherine takes prepubescent form and lingers at a window symbolizing the borderline between childhood and adulthood. "A child's face looking through the window": Lockwood sees Catherine eternally reliving her last moment of perfect union with Heathcliff, as they peer into the Lintons' window at plush Thrushcross Grange, after which she disappears into that world and comes back changed forever. Her daughter is also named Catherine Linton. Therefore the elder Catherine, who dies in childbirth, is usurping the identity of her own child, like Poe's vampiristic Morella.

Why does the ghost want to come in? Shrewd Emily Brontë anticipates her Victorian audience's misreading of this passage, into which it would project a Blakean and Dickensian pathos. The ghost must be a tattered orphan begging for shelter. But the sadistic passions of *Wuthering Heights* shake this humanitarian complacency. Lockwood understands the ghost's desire better even than modern readers. He later tells Heathcliff, "If the little fiend had got in at the window, she probably would have strangled me!"[32] Archaic religious ritual mollified the roving spirits of the dead. Ancestor worship is really ancestor propitiation, a "warding off." A ghost wants to enter in order to drink the blood of the living. Catherine's ghost seizes Lockwood's hand to live again at his expense. Pugnacious Catherine Earnshaw, at the age assumed by her ghost, was never so defenseless and pitiable a child. Therefore we must conclude that the ghost has adopted *a rusing persona*, like Coleridge's vampire Geraldine, who pretends to faint in order to win entrance to Christabel's castle. Brontë's primal dream-scene, with its blood-soaked bedclothes, is an exercise in Coleridgean seduction. Marriage to nature is once again rape and defloration. We, as much as Lockwood, are raped and lose our innocence here. Brontë revises every Wordsworthian assumption into daemonic sex and violence. All this is true even if the ghost is a dream rather than a supernatural visitation, for Catherine has invaded Lockwood's mind, materializing herself in his dream-life through Ligeia-like force of will. The books that Lockwood piles against her are the barrier of rationalism. But in *Wuthering Heights*, as in Emily Brontë's short life, daemonic divination prevails.

   In Romanticism, we have seen, the masculine is always qualified or impaired, a principle applying to *Wuthering Heights* for new and startling reasons. The difference between Heathcliff and Edgar first seems, in street terms, the difference between a real man and a sissy. But Heathcliff, a force of nature beginning with his craggy name, is strangely infertile. His marriage to Edgar's sister produces no vigorous offspring. Quite the opposite, the weak blood of the Lintons surmounts his, resulting in "a pale, delicate, effeminate boy," feeble and sickly, "more a lass than a lad." Heathcliff contemptuously rebukes his son: "Thou art thy mother's child, entirely! Where is *my* share in thee, puling chicken?"[33] There is some impediment to the transmission of virile energy in Heathcliff. He is *seminally vitiated.* His power flows not into heterosexual generation but into incestuous passion for his double. Sadomasochism cuts two ways, aggression moving out and in. Like Byron and Elvis Presley, Heathcliff suffers internal self-impairment. Appearances and reputation to the contrary, Heathcliff as a sexual persona is not conventionally masculine. Another law of Romanticism is that it is a mode of self-projection. Every Romantic work is organized by a shadowy speculative persona, through whom the artist searches for a new alignment of nature and psyche. Popular sentiment would link Emily Brontë with Catherine Earnshaw, enamoured of the dark Byronic hero who is the author's wish-fulfillment fantasy. Major criticism never indulges in such reveries, partly because of the textual absolutism of the now-old New Criticism. But the reluctance to ask biographical questions about *Wuthering Heights* produced the present impasse, with many moral and sexual issues unresolved.

   My theory is this: Heathcliff is one of the great hermaphrodite sexual personae of Romanticism, a dream-representation of Emily Brontë as naturalized Byron. The Brontë Gothic novels intersect, for Charlotte retains her gender in her story while Emily, like Coleridge in *Christabel*, abandons hers. Much commentary advances the traditional but preposterous thesis that Heathcliff is modelled on Branwell Brontë, only male of six siblings at Haworth Parsonage. Walter L. Reed, for example, declares, "That there was some connection between Branwell and the figure of Heathcliff is evident."[34] But this has been a mistaken idea from the start. In terms of sexual personae, Branwell was the complete antithesis of the active, vehement, imperious Heathcliff. Physically stunted, self-indulgent, finally dying an opium addict, Branwell belonged to the category of dreamy, vacillating, degenerated manhood typified by the real-life Coleridge and by Poe's Usher.

Branwell is a distracting superfluity to any discussion of the genesis of *Wuthering Heights*, for Emily Brontë herself, by overwhelming evidence, possessed all the masculinity necessary for the creation of her great hero. Charlotte Brontë calls her dead sister "stronger than a man, simpler than a child." She had "a secret power and fire that might have informed the brain and kindled the veins of a hero": "Her temper was magnanimous, but warm and sudden; her spirit altogether unbending."[35] Elsewhere, Charlotte speaks of "a certain harshness in her powerful and peculiar character." Branwell was barely five feet tall, while Emily was the tallest family member aside from her father. Haworth townsfolk said Emily was "more like a boy than a girl." She looked "loose and boyish when she slouched over the moors, whistling to her dogs, and taking long strides." The word "masculine" recurs in local memories of Emily. Her family nickname was "the Major." Monsieur Héger, the Brussels professor, said, "She should have been a man." Charlotte said of George Eliot's lover, "Lewes' face almost moves me to tears, it is so wonderfully like Emily's." But George Henry Lewes was called "the ugliest man in England"! In a mushy, fictionalized biography (1936) suggesting a connection between Emily and Heathcliff, Virginia Moore finds Emily's "self-identification with men" even in the family Gondal games, where her sister Anne chose feminine roles.[36]

We are confronted here, as in the case of Emily Dickinson, with the paradox of a woman of Romantic genius. We saw that the Romantic poet, finding the western male persona too limited, hermaphroditizes himself to seize the Delphic powers of feminine receptivity. But a female artist, sexually advantaged by birth, must extend her imperial reach in the other direction, toward the masculine. I noted that gigantism in a female artist is self-masculinizing. My examples are *Wuthering Heights* and Rosa Bonheur's vast painting *Horse Fair* (1853–55), which abolishes female internality in a surging tableau of hard animal dynamism. Heathcliff has *Horse Fair*'s polemical muscularity. Charlotte Brontë calls Heathcliff "colossal," for he is charged with an excess of sex-crossing aspiration. Two other great women writers, alluding to *Wuthering Heights*, independently think of the word "gigantic." Emily Dickinson hails "gigantic Emily Brontë," and Virginia Woolf says Brontë's "gigantic ambition is to be felt throughout the novel."[37] Gigantism is overreaching, a fascist claim to universal power. Gigantism is the self-electrifying strategy of a woman defying the insulting dictatorship of gender.

Heathcliff's seminal weakness betrays his transsexual origins. He is a woman with a man's energy but without a man's potency. By denying her Byronic hero a consummate virility, Emily Brontë shows that she sees through Lord Byron's seducer's mask and discerns his Romantic hermaphroditism. An artist's intuition: Goethe and Balzac similarly show Byron as half-feminine Euphorion and bisexual Lord Dudley, progenitor of androgynes. Yet Byron's international reputation for grand machismo persisted until G. Wilson Knight's modern studies.

Emily Brontë's Romantic self-portrait as Byron is an example of my principle of sexual metathesis, an artistic sex change. Examples are Byron's transformation of choirboy John Edleston into Thyrza, Proust's of Alfred Agostinelli into Albertine, and Virginia Woolf's of Victoria Sackville-West into Orlando. It would be vulgar to reduce sexual meta-thesis to fear of homosexual scandal. An ampler spiritual economy is at work. Sexual metathesis is a metaphysical advance, an expansion of identity through a mentally prolonged erotic sensation. The real-life original is like a sexual word translated into new imaginative language. The sexual metathesis operating in *Wuthering Heights*, like that in Coleridge's *Christabel*, is directed toward the self rather than a charismatic other. It arises from the artist's desire to vivify and eternalize his or her essential but socially forbidden identity. Sackville-West participated in both modes of sexual metathesis. In her novel *Challenge* (1924), she is the hero Julian Davenant, the same persona she assumed to wander the Paris streets in male dress with her lover, Violet Trefusis.

Wuthering Heights falls stylistically into two parts. John Berryman remarks, "What you remember as the book is only the first half of the book." V. S. Pritchett calls the last part "unevenly felt."[38] I think the novel suffers tremendous loss of intensity, and I see a parallel to *Christabel* and *Orlando*, which fall off in power because of what I call psycho-iconicism. All three works are ruled by a "fascination" of personality, which crowds the narrative space and dwarfs the other personae. *Orlando*'s fictive energy comes from Woolf imagining Victoria Sackville-West as a man. When, halfway through, Orlando turns into a woman— that is, when Vita becomes simply herself—the life goes out of the book. We know from her diary that, after beginning in a feverish "rapture" of inspiration, Woolf lost interest in *Orlando* and had to struggle "list-lessly" to complete it.[39] And frankly, the book's brilliant idea, of a hermaphrodite time-traveller embodying each great phase of English

literature, is poorly executed. It may have been Woolf's scorn for masculine intellectual history that crippled her and made what should have
been the wittiest of her books into one of the most tedious.

Hermaphroditic declension produces the weak second half of *Wuthering Heights* and *Orlando.* I found the pattern twice in Goethe's
Wilhelm Meister: when the Amazon gains a social name, her glamour
fades; when Mignon abandons male dress, she weakens and dies.
Wuthering Heights declines with the diminution of Heathcliff's archetypal force. He becomes a naturalistic character, a country squire and
tyrannical paterfamilias. He loses his aura of glamour, the uncanny
scintillation of the author's identification. Emily Brontë has absented
herself. She dutifully finishes the scheme she has designed, but it is like
Vasari painting over Leonardo's battle mural. *Wuthering Heights* flattens into a social novel and leaves its lurid Romantic irrationalism
behind.

Why the sudden reduction of scale and style? Emily Brontë's sexual
metathesis into Heathcliff is inseparable from the incestuous-twin
theme. Heathcliff is conceived as one end of an erotic polarity. If Brontë
enters her novel as a man, then her feeling for the vanished Catherine is
homosexual. Moore points out that Emily left home for three months to
study at a girls' school, then abruptly returned to write passionate love
poems full of treachery and revenge. Moore suggests there could have
been no opportunity at so sequestered a Victorian institution to fall in
love with anyone except another girl. I find in many of Brontë's lyrics a
delicate lesbian eroticism focusing on the night approach of angelic
female spirits with long silken hair. There is persistent imagery of
smoothness and softness, of enamoured watching and hushed, eerie
nearness.[40] Like Christina Rossetti's strange dream-poem *Goblin Market* (1862), with its embowered sister-sensuality and lush, fruity dangers, Brontë's poetry may reflect a premodern sexual state, inflamed but
celibate. Visionary nuns have lived in this exalted condition for a thousand years. Emily Brontë seeks clairvoyance, not orgasm, a burning
vapor of ghostly cathexis.

Wuthering Heights' lapse in energy is virtually simultaneous with
Catherine's death. As in *Christabel,* the second half quickens only when
the erotic connection of the first half is reinvoked as memory. That the
novel begins with such force is surely due to Catherine's spectral epiphany before terrified Lockwood. Heathcliff himself, throwing open
the window and sobbing into the night, is denied this vision. If Heathcliff is Brontë, then Catherine is a woman from whom there has been an
irrevocable separation. The mysterious inspirer of ardor at the girls'

school is relatively inconsequential. That person was merely the shadow of another. Family romance shapes all our erotic lives, but for the Romantic, family romance is artistic destiny. Haworth townsfolk said Emily and Anne were "like twins, inseparable companions," publicly intertwined. But the crucial sibling was Maria. Of the ghost's complaint that she has been "a waif for twenty years," David Daiches asks: "Is it relevant that Maria, the precocious eldest of the Brontë sisters who had taken over the guidance of her little brother and sisters on her mother's death when she was barely eight years old, had died twenty years before Emily wrote this chapter? We know how the memory of this devoted elder sister, who had died at the age of twelve, haunted both Emily and Charlotte Brontë."[41] Branwell claimed he heard Maria's voice crying outside the windows at night. But note this places Branwell in the position of simpering Lockwood, not Heathcliff, who frantically longs to hear the voice but cannot. We must believe, therefore, that Catherine contains some aspect of Maria, erotically transformed.

In *Wuthering Heights*, Maria becomes the incestuous Romantic sister-spirit to Emily's male poetic genius. Byron's life and work are recreated. His homosexual liaisons and incest with his half-sister are fused in Brontë's submerged lesbian incest. Then *Manfred*, with its half-mad incestuous recluse mourning for a dead sister, is reproduced in Emily-as-Heathcliff convulsively mourning for Maria-as-Catherine. The sister's phantom makes a terrifying appearance in both *Manfred* and *Wuthering Heights*. Brontë even reimagines the cup upon whose brim Manfred hallucinates his sister's blood. For what is the jagged windowpane rubbing Catherine's wrist if not *a bloody rim*? Both grisly images suggest symbolic sexual injury. Maria is Emily's sacrificial Muse. The Muse or *anima*, the soul's repressed and projected feminine half, is *she who comes from outside*. Emily Brontë, stern, sudden, and austere, is masculine in relation to a hovering female fructification. The ghost tapping at the window, whether lost lesbian beloved or lamented late sister, is a girl who is a haunting memory, who presses at the portals of consciousness. Lockwood fears the ghost as a strangler (the root-meaning of "Sphinx"). The ghost is therefore a vampire-spirit like lesbian Geraldine, who makes a night visit to Coleridge-Christabel and seals her lips in silence. Love and fear, desire and hostility: sexual metathesis is Brontë's self-healing pagan magic.

Emily Brontë suffered three abandonments by women, each an echo of the others. First her mother, who died when Emily was three. Next Maria, who died when Emily was seven. Finally, Miss X, the teen siren, who, if one can extrapolate from Emily's already fixed emotional pattern of loss, was probably a cool customer. The family romance of Haworth Parsonage was structured by ritualized sexual exchange. Unlike Wordsworth and Woolf, Emily Brontë did not respond to a mother's death with a compensatory Cybele-myth of creative natural process. On the contrary, she strips Wordsworthian maternalism from nature because of her own alienation from the procreative, which she purges from her body through her self-desexualization as Heathcliff. In other words, the nature without a mother in *Wuthering Heights* is *a swerve from the self.* The novel promulgates a nature-cult without a goddess. Frazer says the high priest of Cybele "drew blood from his arms" as an offering to the goddess; then the assisting priests, whirling about "with waggling heads and streaming hair" and "rapt into a frenzy of excitement and insensible to pain," slashed their bodies with potsherds and knives "in order to bespatter the altar and the sacred tree with their flowing blood."[42] This resembles the slitting of the ghost's wrist (on pottery-like glass shards) and the "splashes of blood about the bark of the tree" against which Heathcliff dashes his head.[43] Catherine and Heathcliff are self-maiming priests of a pagan cult of unmaternal stormy nature.

It strains credulity to suppose the ineffectual, weak-willed Branwell Brontë had any part in the formulation of this severe world-view, which was the product of Emily Brontë's uncompromising half-male imagination. Branwell's position in Haworth family romance was far less impressive. He was the spoiled baby and runt of the litter. If there was a symbiotic twin-connection between him and Emily, it may have resided in her sense that she had somehow stolen her brother's masculinity, an embezzlement of funds from one account to another in the same genetic bank. Emily caught cold at Branwell's funeral, refused rest and medical aid, and died shortly thereafter, a sequence suggesting a rite of guilt and atonement. Did she feel her supreme imaginative success had been at her brother's expense, that she had usurped his gender for her own amoral purposes? Her behavior is exactly like Heathcliff's when, to unite with Catherine beyond the grave, he wills his death by spurning food and sleep. Thus Emily Brontë merged with her mighty hero, taking his *ascesis* for her own. Her final days spoke her hostility to the body. In *Epipsychidion,* as in the *Symposium,* love's feverish battle is a quest for primeval unity. But *Wuthering Heights,* with its buffeting embraces, contains a more perverse psychodrama: the body as the basis of gender is an affront to imagination and emotion, which in Emily Brontë is homosexual-tending. It is this body, an obscuring material veil, that is torn by the novel's sadomasochism.

I submit that the formal innovations of *Wuthering Heights* came from Brontë's own displacements of identity. The mediation through two limited narrators and the shifts of time and point of view are layers of intercession between a real and fictive self. Brontë's apparent self-removal from *Wuthering Heights* conceals her enormous centrality to it, her projection into Heathcliff, produced by her self-removal from gender. If Rousseau is the first to assign himself a sexual identity, Emily Brontë is the first to treat her sexual identity as an abstraction dwelling apart in another dimension of space and time. The brilliant narrative frame came into being because Brontë was so distantly self-regarding. Nelly Dean and Lockwood represent the social norm, contemplating Heathcliff with impatience or incomprehension. These lesser observers show Brontë's maturely measured sense of herself and her projected persona. She is in double relation to her hermaphrodite hero, in whom she is simultaneously present and absent. *Wuthering Heights* goads the reader with questions: "Is Mr. Heathcliff a man? If so, is he mad? And if not, is he a devil?" "Is he a ghoul, or a vampire?" These partial opinions have an eerie incandescence in sexual terms: "I did not feel as if I were in the company of a creature of my own species." "He's a lying fiend, a monster, and not a human being!" "He's only half a man—not so much."[44] Heathcliff, toward whom we are moved by these unjust exclamations, *is* a monster and not a man insofar as he is a woman transfigured into a hero.

Coalescing with her Romantic double, Emily Brontë died the year after *Wuthering Heights* was published and poorly received. Art was not enough. Like her Romantic precursors, Brontë is not a social historian but the writer of one great poem, that is, one body of self-referential work. It is possible, therefore, that *Wuthering Heights*, because of its fully realized hermaphroditic inner action, would have had no sequel. Its extremism may have been career-ending. The novel's internal decline is Brontë's own. In the second half, the monumentality of Heathcliff/Catherine dwindles to a thin pale light in which voices are heard as if from a distance. Romanticism is yielding to Victorianism, the pleasant, ordered present in which Emily Brontë refuses to dwell. Extending and revising High Romanticism, she follows Byron, Shelley, and Keats in electing to die young, at the height of imagination.

18

Romantic Shadows

Swinburne and Pater

In Swinburne's poetry, the paganism of Romanticism becomes totally overt. Swinburne creates English Late Romanticism by using French Decadence to reinforce Coleridge against Wordsworth. An admirer of Sade, Gautier, and Baudelaire, Swinburne restored to English literature the sexual frankness it lost after the eighteenth century. Though he had enormous influence on English literature, he has virtually disappeared from the curriculum. Even Victorian poetry courses tend to exclude his most lurid and to me most central poems. But Baudelaire too is censored in French classes in American colleges. The reason is that there is no accepted theory of Decadent art, a gap I am trying to fill. The revolt against Swinburne after the fall of Wilde was part of the modernist defection from classical tradition, which T. S. Eliot's *The Waste Land* wrongly shows in disarray. Swinburne demonstrates the great continuity of western culture, that brazen union of pagan antiquity with imperial Hollywood. Swinburne is a Hollywood poet. His pagan sexual personae, Dolores and Faustine, are blazing projections of Decadent cinematics. Through his voice, the sensational female superstar dominates space and time.

Swinburne was a Decadent but not an aesthete. Unkempt and dishevelled, he had no taste whatever in the major or minor arts. The first English aesthete was Walter Pater, whose publishing career began a year after Swinburne's scandalous *Poems and Ballads* (1866). Swinburne prepared the way for Pater in two ways. First, Swinburne's poetry dissolves the Saxon solidity of English syntax by Decadent moral suspension and French linearity, that glossy accentless flow which Baudelaire makes a sinister murmur of entrancement. Second, Swinburne's Late Romantic imagery daemonizes Shelley into a degenerate classicism. In other words, Swinburne uses Coleridge to corrupt Shelley. Swinburne's paganism is Hellenistic and neo-primitive. It is not the radiant idealism Shelley takes from Apollonian Athens. French Late Romanticism, I said, is predicated on worship of objets d'art, thanks to the pioneering Gautier's transfer of perceptual relations from the visual to the sexual realm. English Decadence is less concerned with *objets*, than with *style*, the self-consciously beautiful mode of discourse of an epicene male persona.

Swinburne sets Baudelaire's Decadent vampires in Sade's violent nature. Swinburne's world surges with natural power, because English high culture was and is incapable of continental contempt for nature. Even when defining it as negative and destructive, the English artist, unlike the French, opens himself to nature, a pattern we see in Coleridge, Emily Brontë, and Swinburne. Swinburne's poetry demolishes Victorian society and plants matriarchy amid patriarchy. Swinburne is a female monarchist. The title of his first published work, *The Queen-Mother* (1861), boldly fuses sex and hierarchy. Recreating the archaic mother-religions, Swinburne sweeps Christianity away, as Coleridge did in *Christabel.* Now earth-cult is given a new liturgy and body of prayer. Hence Swinburne's peculiar incantatory style, parodied from the moment it appeared. I would defend that style, admired by so many young Englishmen, by arguing that in Swinburne the ritual origins of art are recovered and restored. Swinburne's poetry shows paganism as it really was, not idleness and frolic but a severe code of ritual limitation, curbing the dangerous daemonism of sex and nature.

Dolores, long and serpent-shot, demonstrates the cultic character of Swinburne's poetry and its magnetic orientation toward female power. The poem begins: "Cold eyelids that hide like a jewel / Hard eyes that grow soft for an hour; / The heavy white limbs, and the cruel / Red mouth like a venomous flower." Cold, hard jewel eyes: Dolores is Baudelaire's mineral and reptilian vampire. She is ritualistically visualized by the Decadent catalog, that itemizing/atomizing style Gautier invented in *A Night with Cleopatra.* The erotic object disintegrates into parts. Dolores' "heavy white limbs" float surreally into view between eyes and red mouth, as if she were a broken statue. We are in a dead city, a forest of fallen columns overrun by lizards and poison poppies. This opening sequence of cold luminous images recalls Shelley's *Epipsychidion:* aggression of the poet's eye leads to dissolution of the object and emotional dissociation of the perceiver.

"O mystic and sombre Dolores, / Our Lady of Pain": this blasphemous epithet ends stanza after stanza. In form, *Dolores* is surely inspired by Baudelaire's "Litanies of Satan." Like Baudelaire, Swinburne appeals to hell rather than heaven, but his goal is more radical. He removes himself from the Christian world altogether by invoking an omnipotent goddess. Like Aubrey Beardsley's Swinburnian *Saint Rose of Lima, Dolores* daemonizes the Virgin Mary, dispatching her into the past to meet her ancient precursors, from whom sexuality was not yet divorced. Before American Catholicism snobbishly purged itself of ethnic traces, one of its splendors was the evening devotion and Litany of the Blessed Mother. As the priest intoned each line in the dusky church, the congregation answered with the muttered phrase "Pray for us," a rumbling antiphony of gloomy majesty. In this hypnotic night ritual, one heard the buried pagan voice of Italian Catholicism. *Dolores* systematically inverts the sacred epithets, creating an Anti-Mary, as Baudelaire's Satan is Antichrist. Dolores is the Whore of Babylon: "O garden where all men may dwell, / O tower not of ivory, but builded / By hands that reach heaven from hell; / O mystical rose of the mire." Medieval Mary, the chaste walled garden, becomes the plundered bower of an urban brothel. Dolores is the arrogant tower, a self-made colossus rising from primeval mud to tear down heaven's gate.

In Swinburne as in Baudelaire, sex is not pleasure but torment. The Christian Madonna is a Mater Dolorosa because she grieves for her martyred son. But Swinburne's "fierce and luxurious" Dolores is Our Lady of Pain not because she suffers but because she brings suffering to male victims. She is "our Lady of Torture," whose "prophet, preacher, and poet" is the Marquis de Sade. The mild, merciful Virgin, the intercessor God cannot refuse, disappears into the Great Mother of the savage animal world. Dolores is "my sister, my spouse, and my mother." Swinburne revises Shelley, steering him from Apollonian to chthonian by adding the mother to the incest-romance. Swinburne's Great Mother, an incestuous triad or matriarchal trinity, is no longer fecund. The "splendid and sterile Dolores" enjoys "barren delights," "things monstrous and fruitless." Like Sade's murderous mother nature and Baudelaire's stony idols, Swinburne's Dolores frustrates the procreative, her solipsistic sensuality turning phenomena back upon themselves.

Dolores is vaster in scale than Baudelaire's vampire poems. Dolores is transtemporal: she is an eternal principle of evil and disorder, defiling history. Her power over the historical comes from Swinburne's malice toward High Victorian culture, with its imposing Roman synthesis of intellect and imperialism. The poem's last half is a brilliant exercise in sexual syncretism, the favorite backwash of late phases of culture. Swinburne identifies Dolores with rulers and gods, male and female, from ancient chronicles. She is wrathful Jehovah, scourging mankind. She is Nero, lighting his garden with live Christian torches. She is Cybele, Astarte, Cotytto, Aphrodite, Venus. Dolores is like Isis, of whom Frazer says, "Her attributes and epithets were so numerous that in the hieroglyphics she is called 'the many-named,' 'the thousand-named,' and in Greek inscriptions, 'the myriad-named.' "[1] Swinburne's thousand-named Dolores is a daemonic Cosmic Woman, trampling male history beneath her feet. Her metamorphic identity seeps inexorably into place, mind, and word, contaminating both language and action.

Faustine is another dark litany. In his defense of *Poems and Ballads*, Swinburne says *Faustine* records "the transmigration of a single soul, doomed as though by accident from the first to all evil and no good, through many ages and forms, but clad always in the same type of fleshly beauty."[2] Faustine is the vampire who cannot die, and her poem has an insomniac obsessiveness. She is "A queen whose kingdom ebbs and shifts / Each week." She has "bright heavy brows," "white gloss and sheen." Wine and poison, milk and blood mix in her lips, ever since "the devil threw dice with God" for her. She loves games where men die, "As though the slain man's blood and breath / Revived Faustine." She vacations in late Rome: "All round the foul fat furrows reeked, / Where blood sank in; / The circus splashed and seethed and shrieked / All round Faustine."

Faustine is the goddess Fortuna gambling with dead men's bones. She rules flux and change because she is an early version of Swinburne's ocean mother. Like all his Decadent centerfolds, she is not nymph but dowager, a Belle Dame Sans Merci of ripe midlife heft. Her brow weighs like a thundercloud, bulging with omniscience. Venom runs in her veins. Under her régime, love and death are gaping hungry mouths. Faustine is nature's womb and tomb, the playground of sex war. "Nets caught the pike, pikes tore the net": mothers, sons, and lovers clash like gladiators, their mismatched genitals the tools of shredding and capture. *Faustine* is Swinburne's *Masque of the Red Death:* man's life drains with every breath, leaking from every pore. The earth is a sand pit of carnage, drinking up human blood to fertilize the insatiable all-mother. Like Dolores, Faustine is another Nero, a jaded Fate turning thumbs down on man for her own amusement. Death in the afternoon as the Queen Mother's high tea.

The name Faustine, closing each stanza, is repeated forty-one times, a malignant refrain. Swinburne's speaker is a Late Romantic imprisoned consciousness. The poem shows thought perpetually circling back to one sexual focal point. Each stanza is a paradigm of decadence, a decline or "falling away," for the lines rise up only to fall back with fatigue, like Sisyphus in his no-win labors. Language is a burden taken up and dropped again and again. All things return mechanically, compulsively to one female center, primary and corrupt. Faustine is a mass of female matter blocking the movement of mind, so that each stanza is an irrevocable *nostos*, a forced-march coming home. Carroll's Alice repeatedly tries to strike out through the garden, only to have the path seem to shake itself and fling her back toward the house. In *Faustine* a monstrous apparition awaits us at the door. Mario Praz says of Swinburne's women, "They have a good deal of the idol about them—in fact of the εἴδωλον, the phantom of the mind rather than of the real human being."[3] In *Faustine*, mind too is a phantom, subdued and vaporized by the brute obduracy of the mother-stuff, the muddy morass from which all life has sprung.

Faustine is the most incantatory of Swinburne's poems and therefore the most overtly ritualistic. The lines are short and the meter harsh and relentless. *Faustine* provides a stylistic rationale for Swinburne's notorious and oft-derided alliterations. The most famous is from *Dolores:* "The lilies and languors of virtue / For the raptures and roses of vice." Swinburne's alliterations dramatize his repetition-compulsion, by which he constructs a vast world of female force. In *Faustine*, a terrible and uncanny poem, poetry returns to its origins in religious ritual. Few things in literature provide so intense a replication of primitive experience. Modern readers, eyeing *Faustine*'s somewhat sleazy locutions, may doubt this—until we try to read the poem aloud. The forty-one thudding returns of Faustine are literally unbearable. Even Poe's Ligeia returns only once!

Swinburne's vampires inherit the promiscuous lesbianism of Baudelaire's Jeanne Duval, all the more atrocious for an English audience unprepared for such aberrations by a Balzac or Gautier. The women's plural sexuality comes from their multiple identities, flooding history. Dolores has lesbian adventures in Greek shadows of sexual ambiguity. "Stray breaths of Sapphic song" blow through Faustine, shaking her "fierce quivering blood." She seeks "sterile growths of sexless root or epicene," "kisses without fruit of love." She is "a thing that hinges hold, / A love-machine / With clockwork joints of supple gold." Ambisexual Faustine is drawn to lesbianism for its Baudelairean sterility, by which nature is self-devastated. Swinburne transforms Sapphism into the inorganic, a necrophiliac compost heap. Faustine as love-machine is another androgyne as nineteenth-century manufactured object, like Shelley's Hermaphrodite. *Faustine*'s tyrannically mechanical meter is therefore form's response to content. The poem itself is an automaton driven by a robotlike female despot. Faustine is Faust, Mephistopheles, and Homunculus all in one, a barren bone mill whirring with daemonic internal transactions.

Dolores and *Faustine* are titanic projections of female hierarchic authority. Swinburne's few transient males merely illustrate a sensual embowered passivity. A typical sex-reversal from *Dolores:* "O lips full of lust and of laughter, / Curled snakes that are fed from my breast, / Bite hard, lest remembrance come after / And press with new lips where you pressed." In a grisly Mannerist metaphor, Dolores' cruelly laughing lips are curled snakes, disconnected from her face by Decadent fission. The snake-lips are attacking a male breast. Swinburne is the doomed Cleopatra (subject of another poem) giving suck to her asps, phallically generated by potent Dolores. The passage may be a perverse daemonization of Keats's remark about the heart as "the teat from which the Mind or intelligence sucks its identity." Swinburne becomes the Teiresias androgyne, a nurturant male. He assumes the Great Mother's parturient powers where she has abandoned them. But his nursling is a vampire, draining blood rather than milk. Male breasts are eternally dry, an archetypal curse. Man is no Muse. Swinburne emulates Kleist's Achilles, whose breasts are gnawed by the Amazon and her dogs. The victim invites Dolores' abuse in order to sink into oblivion. Sexual pain is a ritual to drive off the mental. Conscience is merely an aspiring leech. Swinburne evades both Christian guilt and Romantic self-consciousness by a historical detour, surrender to the primeval dominatrix.

In *Laus Veneris* ("Praise of Venus"), Swinburne's version of the Tannhäuser legend, the sexual world is female terrain where man lies chained. Tannhäuser is imprisoned in Venus' bower, both the garden of mother nature and the genital womb-world of every female. Men are many and dispensable: "Their blood runs round the roots of time like rain: / She casts them forth and gathers them again; / With nerve and bone she weaves and multiplies / Exceeding pleasure out of extreme pain." The hero finds wound round his neck "the hands that stifle and the hair that stings." Medusan Venus has hissing serpent-hair. She sheds her lovers' blood to irrigate the seasons. Like Cadmus sowing dragon's teeth, she plants her victims' corpses and harvests fresh crops of men. Like the Fates or Homeric sorceresses, she weaves at a mysterious loom, the pregnant female body. Binding Adonis by a "chain" of "flesh and blood," she divides him "vein by vein." Spenser's boyish demigod becomes Blake's prisoner humanity of *The Mental Traveller*,

dissected by the maternal sadist condemning him to sexual life. Swinburne's frequent word "divide" suggests life is torn by warring contraries, united only by death. "Daemonic," Bloom notes, descends from the
Greek *daiein, meaning to divide or distribute.[4] Thus Swinburne's
world of daemonic female power is predicated on male division, a black
marriage of heaven and hell.

Stanza after stanza, *Laus Veneris* depicts humiliating sexual compulsion. The male, in moral darkness, moves outward with infant "blind
lips" (eroticizing Milton's "blind mouths") into a sexual trap. Like Poe's
sailor in *A Descent into the Maelström*, he is reabsorbed into a churning
female matrix. Swinburne studiously gathers for his poetry all the
iconography of classic femmes fatales. He arms his vicious personae
with every biological weapon. Venus is a sexual aggressor: "Yea, she laid
hold upon me, and her mouth / Clove unto mine as soul to body doth."
The succubus is demiurge, mother, bride, and Muse. The hero says, "I
dare not always touch her, lest the kiss / Leave my lips charred." The
poet making poetry is the maiden Semele in a trance of Blakean love-
fear, while Venus is a golden idol burning with supernatural fire. The
profane is sacred.

Swinburne's reputation was made by the verse-play *Atalanta in Calydon*. A year before *Poems and Ballads*, it displays his
signature cast of sexual personae, all androgynes. There is Atalanta, the
Amazon runner; Althaea, a vengeful omnipotent mother; and her son,
Meleager, in whom action melts into erotic passivity. Meleager is scis-
sored between lines of female force. *Atalanta in Calydon* has a cru-
ciform pattern, with man the scapegoat. Will is in decline. The Greek
hero can no longer defeat the Sphinx.

Atalanta in Calydon cascades with magnificent archetypal imagery.
Love is storm and strife. Season devours season. Earth turns to ocean.
There is little characterization: everyone speaks the same Swinburnian
language. Character is forged through opposition, the clash of sexual
personae. The play is Decadent family romance. *Atalanta in Calydon*
combines chthonian intuition with Greek visionary aestheticism. The
play is more authentically Greek in phrase and feeling than the
Fitzgerald translations of Homer now enshrined as standard texts in
American universities. Swinburne uses the Meleager legend to revise
Aeschylus: *Atalanta in Calydon* is the *Oresteia* recast in Late Romantic
terms, with Apollo replaced by his twin sister. In his study of Greek
cults, Farnell says, "Atalanta is Artemis under another name."[5] Althaea
combines Clytemnestra and Furies. Now Orestes loses: the tormented

son, Meleager, is destroyed by an impossible choice between mother
and lover. Woman smothers all options. Fatherhood does not exist. In
Swinburne's *Oresteia*, Apollonian and chthonian war, but neither gains
the upper hand. Apollonian Atalanta's first words are "Sun, and clear
light among green hills." Sky-cult and earth-cult joust for power, with
man as the prize. But after the game, the gods simply go back to their
pleasures.

Atalanta was celebrated for her swiftness or masculine mobility.
Swinburne's version of her legend is inspired by Ovid but influenced by
Spenser. "Arcadian Atalanta, snowy-souled," is frosty with Apollonian
chastity. Artemis' favorite, she rejects spouse and children and haugh-
tily affirms her own "forest holiness, / Fame, and this armed and iron
maidenhood." Atalanta is Spenser's huntress Belphoebe, who flees all
touch. Meleager, fascinated by Atalanta's androgyny, calls her "Most
fair and fearful, feminine, a god, / Faultless." The chorus sees Atalanta
as "a maiden clean, / Pure iron, fashioned for a sword; and man / She
loves not." Atalanta invades the male horde and makes division. At the
hunt, Meleager's uncle insults him: "Why, if she ride among us for a
man, / Sit thou for her and spin." Anatomy and destiny change hands:
woman will rove, while man sits bound by self-spun cords. Meleager
becomes Spenser's transvestite Artegall, doing woman's work in the
Amazon household. Woman's advance means man's regression.

Meleager's mother denounces Atalanta in social terms: "A woman
armed makes war upon herself, / Unwomanlike, and treads down use
and wont." But this is camouflage in sex war. Althaea's resentments are
deeper. For her, motherhood is possession, and possession is ten-tenths
of the law. Later, she concedes Atalanta's sexual uncanniness, calling
her "She the strange woman, she the flower, the sword, / Red from spilt
blood, a mortal flower to men, / Adorable, detestable." These vivid
images are partly self-projections from Althaea's own chthonian nature.
Atalanta is flower and sword, the angel blocking the way to the garden.
The genital duality of flower/sword recalls transvestite Rosalind, who is
both rose and prick. Althaea reshapes Atalanta in her own image, a
carnivorous flower like Huysmans' bloody vaginal blooms.

Thus *Atalanta in Calydon* subordinates its hero to Apollonian and
chthonian androgynes, cornering him in a sexual cul-de-sac. Neither
earth-cult nor sky-cult spares the supplicant. In Greek legend, Meleager's mother guards his life term, magically residing in a brand
plucked from the fire. Swinburne makes the brand man's helpless
sexual nature, burning but numbed. Hercules' phallic club is a toy in
woman's hands. The Fates gave Althaea control over the brand: she

declares, "The gods are many about me; I am one." Motherhood and godhead are in league, a cosmic conspiracy. When Althaea bitterly rebukes him for loving someone other than her, Meleager laments the ambivalence of the mother-relation: "For there is nothing terribler to men / Than the sweet face of mothers, and the might." Love is the mask; power is the reality. The mother is met at every turn of life's path, multiplied in a hundred hidden forms.

When she kills her son by flinging the brand into the fire, Althaea makes an audacious proclamation of maternal priority:

> Fate is made mine for ever; he is my son,
> My bedfellow, my brother. You strong gods,
> Give place unto me; I am as any of you,
> To give life and to take life. Thou, old earth,
> That has made man and unmade; thou whose mouth
> Looks red from the eaten fruits of thine own womb;
> Behold me with what lips upon what food
> I feed and fill my body; even with flesh
> Made of my body.

The speech vibrates with biblical and classical allusions. The mother gathers into herself the whole of cultural history. Like Clytemnestra, slaughtering Agamemnon for sacrificing their daughter, Althaea insists all legal and moral rights must yield to maternity. In Swinburne, husband and child are one, marked for death. Romantic incest collapses human relationships into primeval unity. Family romance is destiny. Althaea claims, as a mother, that she is greater than the gods: we are back in Aeschylus, where the *Eumenides* opens with the oracle reciting the successive owners of Delphi, from ancient Earth (Ge) to the upstart Olympians. In Swinburne, Earth, with whom Althaea allies herself, returns to drive away Apollo and retake control. Earth is Sadean nature, her mouth red from feasting on her own children—one of the most frightful images in nineteenth-century poetry. She is Goya's parental Titan, mutilating her prey. Althaea impudently fuses Eucharist with Thyestean banquet: she repossesses the body of her beloved son, whom she cooks and consumes in the cauldron of her womb. The family of man is a House of Atreus where all communing is a bloody last supper.

The climax of *Atalanta in Calydon* is a spectacle of Greek lamentation and ritual exhibitionism. Meleager is carried onstage and just lies there, expiring. Perfunctory in the original myth, the scene is amazingly protracted. Though Swinburne calls his play a tragedy, Aristotle's pity and terror are Romantically revised. All affect is so imperiously internalized by the dying hero that the audience is left high and dry. *Atalanta in Calydon* ends in a mass pietà—with Christ still talking. As in Wordsworth's melancholy story poems, Swinburne's secret script is the ecstasy of the male heroine, a central Romantic androgyne. Martyred Meleager is at exquisite stage center, rimmed by that erotic ring of eyes first appearing in Coleridge's *Ancient Mariner*. Like Goethe's Werther, Swinburne daydreams his pathetic death, a displaced sex act or necrophiliac self-wounding. Late Romantic vision stains its own white radiance. In *Atalanta in Calydon*, dramatic and sexual climax coincide, with the male in radical recession.

I suspect Walt Whitman's influence on Swinburne here. The finale of *Atalanta in Calydon* parallels an interlude in *Song of Myself* where Whitman casts himself as the male heroine: "I am the mash'd fireman with breast-bone broken, / Tumbling walls buried me in their debris." The victim hears his comrades' shouts and "the distant click of their picks and shovels": "they tenderly lift me forth." Now he lies in the hushed night air: "White and beautiful are the faces around me, the heads are bared of their fire-caps, / The kneeling crowd fades with the light of the torches" (33). Body annihilated but senses sharp, the male heroine is the dramatic focus of a public arena, part theater, part church. He is handled by reverent attendants and knelt to by a silent crowd. The gaze of "beautiful" male faces brings a tingling arousal. The male heroine is a self-made fallen idol of pagan flaunting.

Whitman's eroticism requires the nearness of those manly firemen, half gravediggers, half midwives, who canonize the martyr by labors both heroic and delicate. But Swinburne's eroticism comes from the symmetrical heraldry of female androgynes, who pin the male in a fatal double bind. Only grand opera has death scenes as emotionally overextended as the one in *Atalanta*. Music is the proper analogy, for Swinburne is pushing language beyond the rational. Even Dickens' Little Nell doesn't sing her own elegy. *Atalanta in Calydon* is both a celebration of and protest against the omnipotence of female nature. Meleager's farewell to his mother, delivered as he lies glamourously prone, like an odalisque, is a stunning archetypal flight:

> Thou too, the bitter mother and mother-plague
> Of this my weary body—thou too, queen,
> The source and end, the sower and the scythe,
> The rain that ripens and the drought that slays,
> The sand that swallows and the spring that feeds,
> To make me and unmake me—

Althaea is Cybele reclaiming the epiphenomenon of her son. We are no longer in Greece but in the ancient Near East. Swinburne's gorgeous biblical metaphors demonstrate his transformation of Baudelaire. Nature's operations are ever-near, however much its destructive late phase is stressed. Althaea as vegetative cycle descends from the great body of Spenser-inspired English High Romantic poetry, which France never came close to rivalling.

Meleager's funeral oration ends with an intricate appeal: he asks Atalanta to touch him with her "rose-like" hands, fasten up his eyelids with her mouth, cover his body with her veil and clothing, and finally lie on top of him. Let no man say he was "slain through female fingers in his woof of life." The fabric of life is spun and torn by the fingers of female Fates, both phallic and fickle: the sower as sewer. Meleager demands a ceremony of investiture: the bride as bridler. Atalanta's veil becomes Aeschylus' net, a shroud to wrap her wooer. Her covering gesture is transvestite, as when the Amazon spreads her coat on Goethe's wounded Wilhem Meister. What of Meleager's bizarre wish that Atalanta recline upon him as he dies? Consummation by suffocation: the road runner as steamroller. As in Poe, physical contact is possible only when one lover is dead or dying. In Late Romanticism, the deathbed is the only bed.

The intense, sublimated eroticism of Swinburne's finale is based on hieratic manipulation of the body induced by male from female—induced but not achieved, since Atalanta rejects the list of requests and rushes offstage, like Spenser's Belphoebe. Meleager longs for deft, soothing touches, as if he were a patient being operated on. The universe of the male heroine is a medical amphitheater in which his passive body is the subject of rapt study and visual caresses. Similarly, our soap opera, originally a feminine genre, teems with doctors and hospitals. Female sexual experience is based on physiologic receptivity and expectancy; hence it gives rise to an eroticism of visual and tactile manipulation by groups of admiring others. By the end, Meleager the boar-slayer becomes a quivering membrane of sexual stasis, a jelly adrift in a female sea. Shifting his hero into the female condition, Swinburne finds a language that is a triumph of passive aggression. Poetry flames with astonishing vitality, but it is always the burning brand on the verge of extinction.

Swinburne's favorite metaphor of female dominance is the nature-mother as man-engulfing sea. It was an early obsession, reinforced by Whitman. The ode of invocation in *The Triumph of Time* personifies the sea with incestuous ardor. "I will go back to the great sweet mother, / Mother and lover of men, the sea. / I will go down to her, I and none other, / Close with her, kiss her and mix her with me." The sea "fed with the lives of men" is "subtle and cruel of heart": "Thou art full of thy dead, and cold as they." She is "older than earth": "From the first thou wert; in the end thou art." Swinburne's sea is the primeval matrix, site of distant human origins, where birth and death coincide. Dissolution is rape and purification, an eternal cycle of daemonic redemption. Sexual union is impersonal, obliterating human identity. Begging the sea, "Find me one grave of thy thousand graves," Swinburne eroticizes death-by-drowning, a *Liebestod* or English love-death. As in Freud, the death instinct propels us toward the inert material past. As in Ferenczi, ocean is "that prototype of everything maternal," the womb-world to which we are sexually called back.[6] In Swinburne, men go down to the sea without ships.

The ocean stanzas of *The Triumph of Time* are a chthonian Nicene Creed, a prayer to the mother goddess returning to conquer her younger rivals. She, not Jehovah, is Alpha and Omega. She is the liquid base of physical life. In Swinburne there is no swerve whatever from physiologic liquidity, because he is the least ambivalent of poets toward female dominance. The sea has shaped the alliterative, reiterative form of his poetry. Ian Fletcher finds a "rhythm of tumescence and detumescence that flows and ebbs" in Swinburne's major poems.[7] But Swinburne is without phallic aspiration. We should speak of edema rather than tumescence, for Swinburne's engorgement is by water, not by blood. His latent rhythms are female, lunar pulls and tugs, surges of exaltation and subsidence rather than peaks of assertion or propulsion.

T. S. Eliot says of Swinburne's verse, "The object has ceased to exist, because the meaning is merely the hallucination of meaning, because language, uprooted, has adapted itself to an independent life of atmospheric nourishment."[8] I cited Swinburne's lack of aestheticism, unique among Late Romantic artists. The object does not exist in Swinburne's poetry for the same reason the objet d'art did not exist in his life: because he is unconflicted toward female liquidity and does not require the objet d'art as a perceptual defense against it. Swinburne's uprooting of language is characteristic of Late Romanticism, particularly as influenced by Gautier. Detached from social and moral systems, the image becomes form without content. Swinburne's images, separated by daring syntactic distances, are particles rising and falling in waves, like the seething maggots of Baudelaire's "A Carcass." So nature's force operates on the smallest technical details of Swinburne's poetry. This partly accounts for the deranged metric of *Faustine*. Not only is the name Faustine so repeated that word is reduced to thing, but mind is acted upon as if it too were matter. It is swept into rhythmic pulses, symbolizing the cruelty and coercion of natural cycle.

The theme of male subordination to female authority is more consciously developed in Swinburne than in any other major artist. As with the Marquis de Sade, life and work dovetail, for Swinburne was apparently a masochist in its strict sense. That is, he liked to be whipped by women and visited brothels for this purpose. I resist the general perception that sadists and masochists are maladjusted. Like drag queens, they see through the sexual masks of society. Unlike drag queens, they quest for archaic nature. Swinburne's masochism had a metaphysical meaning. His recreational whippings were connected to his poetic cosmology, which restores the Great Mother to power. Self-flagellation was intrinsic to the ancient mother-cults. Flagellation, flogging, thrashing: threshing grain with a flail (from the Latin *flagrum* or *flagellum*, "a whip, scourge"). Swinburne's ritual flagellation mimicked the public operations of agriculture. Sadomasochism is perverse nature-cult. Surrendering himself to whipping, Swinburne theatrically formalized the hierarchical sexual relations of a universe activated by female force. Mind and body, pleasure and pain, mother and son were reunited in archaic sexual ceremony.

Thus the hierarchy of female over male is the spiritual principle of Swinburne's poetry. What then shall we say about the all-woman *Anactoria*?—a poem that would prove Swinburne's indebtedness to Baudelaire even if we did not have his celebratory essay on his Decadent precursor. Nominally, *Anactoria* is an elaboration of Sappho's two longest surviving poems, the Aphrodite ode and "He seems to me a god." But it is actually, as has not to my knowledge been observed, a reworking of Baudelaire's condemned poem, "Delphine and Hippolyte," whose structure it imitates: a claustrophobic lesbian scene suddenly widens to an enormous wasteland world. Only two people are present, the fierce Sappho and her young lover Anactoria, a name from the Sapphic fragments. In *Anactoria*, Swinburne claims, he has identified himself with Sappho: "I have striven to cast my spirit into the mould of hers, to express and represent not the poem but the poet."[9] But never trust a Romantic poet talking about his own work—particularly when self-identification is involved.

Anactoria is a victim of Rousseauist literary studies, which censor in the name of liberalism: the poem rarely appears in college curricula or

Victorian literary histories. *Anactoria* is not only Swinburne's greatest poem but a supreme poem of the century. Its language is grave and ceremonious, its ideas complex and extensive. Baudelaire's sexual scenario is philosophically enriched by Swinburne's reading of Sade, who gives Sappho the authority of his mordant analyses of society, nature, and God. *Anactoria* is the most overwhelming female monologue in literature. Swinburne gives Sappho towering emotional and intellectual passion. She combines Cleopatra's steamy volatility with Madame de Clairwil's late-Enlightenment high I.Q. In *Anactoria* the female voice has stupendous hermaphroditic power. We hear Horace's "mascula Sappho" and Baudelaire's "la mâle Sapho," male by force of genius and Promethean will. Hubris, the prestigious male sin, for the first time falls within a woman's grasp. And Swinburne's Sappho, unlike Brontë's Heathcliff, dominates without shifting her gender.

Like "Delphine and Hippolyte," *Anactoria* has a pagan setting but a Judeo-Christian God. We are accustomed to female deities in Swinburne. Ordinarily, the only male god is an effeminate Jesus, as in "Hymn to Proserpine": "Thou hast conquered, O pale Galilean; the world has grown grey from thy breath." This follows, I suspect, from Gautier's "Christ has wrapped the world in his shroud."[10] But in *Anactoria*, though Aphrodite is Sappho's patron, God is intensely masculine, a Shelleyan tyrant and oppressor. Swinburne gives him this masculinity so that Sappho can be *more* masculine in her defiance and sedition.

Anactoria has three parts. The first is a love poem of lesbian sadism. The second is a portrait of God as a sadist and of the universe as a cold mechanism of sadistic force. The third is a manifesto of Sappho's immortality as a poet, by which she will defeat God's power. From the first line, "My life is bitter with thy love," love is shown as deeply ambivalent. Sappho chides Anactoria for toying with "lesser loves," but the issue is not jealousy but sexual philosophy. The sex impulse, driving from nature, unites Eros and Thanatos. Sappho's love-talk is suffused with death imagery: "I would my love could kill thee." She longs to impose "amorous agonies" and "superflux of pain." She would press her lips "To the bruised blossom of thy scourged white breast" and taste the blood dripping from the "sweet small wounds." She would drink Anactoria's veins like wine and eat her breasts like honey, so that her body is "abolished and consumed" and "in my flesh thy very flesh entombed." Alarming sentiments in a boudoir! Love is caged animal energy, and consummation is conspicuous consumption.

Criticism has understandably shrunk from Sappho's Swinburnian endearments. Love in Swinburne leads not to emotional union and

social bonding, as in Shakespeare, but to renewed distance. Hence the
hypnotic lure of death-by-drowning: Swinburne's sea reduces phenomena to tranquil primeval unity, swallowing up social personae in the
faceless nature-mother. Love in *Anactoria* makes painfully palpable the
estranged distance between identities, a gap bridged by cannibalism.
Sappho conquers division by inflicting pain and then murdering and
devouring the beloved, literally assimilating her identity, as Byron's
Manfred does with his sister. Sappho is a priestess on daemonic mission, herding objects back to the primeval fold. In Baudelaire, homosexuality is insatiable because of anatomical misalignment. But to say
that Sappho hates because she cannot conventionally consummate her
love would be quite wrong, for in Swinburne even male and female
disdain sexual connection.

Sappho's hostility springs from a second, more esoteric source. *Anactoria* departs from Swinburne's other poems in its Late Romantic concern with eye-object relations. "All thy beauty sickens me with love":
Sappho protests her subordination to Anactoria's beauty. One reason for
the male aesthete's effeminacy is his submission or enslavement to the
objet d'art and to the beautiful person who is the objet d'art. Wilde says,
"The work of art is to dominate the spectator."[11] *The Picture of Dorian
Gray* is based on this idea. Swinburne's Sappho, like the lesbian marquise of Balzac's *The Girl with the Golden Eyes*, is a female hierarch
who cannot bear such subordination and, rather than yield to it, will
destroy the love-object. Beauty is an encroachment upon autonomy.

A third source of Sappho's hostility is a sexual principle I found in
Spenser, Blake, Sade, and Balzac: pure femininity automatically en-
genders its voracious opposite. Anactoria's lamblike innocence and
defenselessness ("Thy shoulders whiter than a fleece of white, / And
flower-sweet fingers, good to bruise or bite") are lacunae in nature's
fabric, where nature has nodded at her labors. Sadistically assaulting
Anactoria, Sappho therefore acts as nature's representative, spreading
rapacity throughout the physical world. Blake's *Songs of Innocence*
taught Swinburne how to show tender proximity giving rise to a lust for
violation. The daemon rushes in where angels seem to tread. *Anactoria*
devours in imagination what remains untouched in reality. Sappho is an
imperialist of aggressive orality, an amoral champion of pure poetic
voice. For her, to speak is to eat is to make love. Swinburne makes
poetry into the brute will-to-power, a Sadean rather than Rousseauist
art form.

Anactoria's sensuous vulnerability inspires her lover with a virtuosity
of sadomasochistic language. Sappho envisions "pain made perfect" in

her victim. She will "Strike pang from pang as note is struck from note, / Catch the sob's middle music in thy throat, / Take thy limbs living, and new-mould with these / A lyre of many faultless agonies." Unlike Sade, Swinburne wants to retain affect in his primal scene of sexual atrocities. Sade exalts the orgasm, while Swinburne, ideologically more feminine, relishes *suffering*. Anactoria's body is an Orphic lyre played by the Lesbian poet, who makes music from her sobs and poetry from her pain. Swinburne brings art and sex into astonishing simultaneity. The word "perfect" recurs. Perfection was the goal of the ancient Mysteries, with their stages of ritual initiation. For Swinburne, sexual experience is spiritual striving and religious illumination. Because it is pain rather than pleasure, his sex is overtly ascetic. The body is tested to the limit of endurance and the dominatrix satisfied only by ideas—by contemplative self-removal from the sex act, which she voyeuristically observes from an Olympus of hierarchic mastery.

Since Romanticism, sexuality has been asked to bear a burden for which it is ill-equipped. Swinburne's poetry is one of the most comprehensive modern attempts to turn sex into epistemology. His sense of quest is shown in *Dolores*, which speaks of sins still to "discover" and of tortures "undreamt of, unheard of, unwritten, unknown." Surfeited by its Enlightenment adventurism and the High Romantic magnification of self, mind yields to the flesh, melancholy object of the Late Romantic age of discovery. Action and experience shrink to the parameters of the body, fawningly titillated by the sense-experiments of Huysmans' Des Esseintes and fixed and defined by agonized sensation in *Anactoria*. Dolores is like the sexual preceptress of Kundalini yoga, except that Swinburne's universe is ruled by negation. Love is terminal surgery, illicit knowledge that kills.

The modern era, which I date from the late eighteenth century, detached sex from society, so that sex no longer required institutional validation for meaning. The unhappy result of this liberation is evident in Baudelaire and Swinburne, for whom sex is a tormenting affliction visited upon us by God and nature. The scorched sexual landscape of Baudelaire's Venusian Cythera becomes the nightmare cosmos of *Anactoria*, which shows the God-ordained "mystery of the cruelty of things." In Swinburne's great flight of Decadent poetry (based on Ulysses' speech on "degree" in Shakespeare), the mind's eye moves outward from earthen snaky graves to the "flamelike foam of the sea's closing lips," to the "wind-blown hair of comets" and "disastrous stars," the "sorrow of labouring moons" and "travail of the planets of the night." *Anactoria*, Praz says, shows "sadism permeating the whole universe."[12]

This daemonic nature, lit by "the sterile sun," is ruled by a sadist God who oppresses his creation, a spectral Blakean tiger with "hidden face and iron feet." *Anactoria*'s poetry is turbulent with Vulcanian clangings. It shows a world convulsed with death trauma, an infernal plain grey under an ashy firefall. We see a sunless Burne-Jones landscape blasted by the fiery breath of God.

Sappho's perverse imagination both mirrors and resists this cruel enormity. Her Late Romantic fatigue comes partly from physical laws: "I am sick with time," she declares. Life is infected with death from the start. But Sappho is also weary from her contention with God, whom she challenges and insults. *Anactoria* is a war of hierarchic orders: female power vies with male. The third and final part is a meditation of the Romantic self upon itself. It is to Swinburne's honor that he gives this task to an imperious female artist. "I Sappho," she boldly declares, in a thrilling assertion of poetic vocation. *Anactoria* shows both the Romantic insistence upon personal identity and the Late Romantic weariness with it, a longing for repose turning into a longing for death. Identity is inflamed in Sappho: it is a ring of fire within which she contemptuously isolates herself. In her scornful parting shot at Anactoria, Sappho says in effect, "You will die, because you are not a poet." Genius is Sappho's means of evading God's authority: "Of me the high God hath not all his will." God's power affects only her body, which is passive toward natural law. Therefore her femaleness is marked for dissolution, while her maleness, invested in her self-created poetic identity, triumphantly escapes into eternal life, a hermaphroditic transfiguration.

Sappho's most implacable assertion of her maleness is at the end, where she speaks of future generations who will preserve her fame:

> and they shall praise me, and say
> "She hath all time as all we have our day,
> Shall she not live and have her will"—even I?
> Yea, though thou diest, I say I shall not die.
> For these shall give me of their souls, shall give
> Life, and the days and loves wherewith I live,
> Shall quicken me with loving, fill with breath,
> Save me and serve me, strive for me with death.

Artistic immortality is the artist's devouring of the life of reader or spectator. Sappho is another of Swinburne's vampires, now conquering the conceptual as well as chthonian realms. Her remarks are directed toward *us*. Swinburne means us to feel a tremor of apprehension as his belligerent female persona approaches the fictive borderline and begins to violate the space between poem and reader. The breath with which we read *Anactoria* is the breath which Sappho will snatch from us! That there is a sexual element in this is obvious. Consider Swinburne's line, "Shall she not live and have her will?" This is a memory of the vampire Geraldine, whom Coleridge addresses after her rape of virgin Christabel: "O Geraldine! one hour was thine— / Thou'st had thy will!" Here as in Coleridge, it is eerie to find the masculine locution "having one's will of" in a female context. At the climax of *Anactoria*, Swinburne's vampire Sappho has her will of posterity, male and female, whom she spiritually and sexually invades, gorging herself on our life-energy in order to defeat God and time. Swinburne's Sappho rejoins Balzac's and Baudelaire's lesbian vampires to their ultimate source in Coleridge, who entered French Late Romanticism via his artistic heirs, Byron and Poe.

Returning to the sexual personae of *Anactoria*, the issue with which we began, we see it is out of the question that Swinburne has identified himself with Sappho. She is too despotic a hierarch to harbor any important aspect of his ritually self-abasing character. Shared poetic vocation is irrelevant, for surely Swinburne would cite antiquity's abundant testimony to prove that Sappho, the "Tenth Muse," was a much greater poet than he. The etiology of *Anactoria* may have been in Swinburne's increasing sense of his poetry becoming uncomfortably strong. Therefore he revives Sappho *in propria persona* in order to be crushed yet again beneath female superiority, this time in the sanctuary of his art. *Anactoria* is a device to give lyric poetry, like nature, purely female origins, thus enabling Swinburne to blot out the entire intervening masculine tradition. There is nothing now between Sappho and him. She is his daemonic progenitor.

Anactoria is the most sensuously finished and intellectually developed of Swinburne's poems. Its oratory is dignified and restrained, with none of the shrillness sometimes marring the poems in a male voice. I say *Anactoria*'s power comes from sexual metathesis, that is, from Swinburne's transsexual transformation into Anactoria, passive receptor of Sappho's savage advances. Swinburne achieves a formal poetic perfection through his unconditional surrender of gender. When Sappho, like the raging Cleopatra, leaps from one sadistic fancy to the next, the vividness and vigor of language arise from the fact that it is Swinburne's own body that is being mentally manipulated by the dominatrix. Sappho's metaphor of Anactoria's body as "a lyre of many faultless agonies" is telling. This is the seminal High Romantic topos of the Aeolian lyre or wind-harp, here played by cruel Sappho as nature's representative.

Anactoria is a lyre because she is the Romantic Swinburne in transsexual disguise. While Shelley invokes a male West Wind to blow through
him, Swinburne invokes Coleridge's evil lesbian daemon. This passage
is at the heart of Swinburne's poetry. It is an allegory of his creative
process: we see his innermost soul-action, the pain-music of his poetry
being wrung from him through the occult mediumship or Muse-like
control of a female hierarch. Swinburne, a mutilated Orpheus marooned on Lesbos, paints as his self-portrait the most wonderfully
perverse Aeolian lyre in Romanticism. For why is the poem called
Anactoria rather then *Sappho?* Though she is probably present, like
Baudelaire's girlish Hippolyte, Anactoria is invisible. She never speaks
and is never even named. She is as mute as Christabel under the
vampire's spell. My principle of sexual metathesis solves this problem.
Anactoria takes its title from Swinburne's own sex-crossing persona.
Author, author! The poet stands veiled at center stage.

     Unlike Baudelaire, Swinburne was fascinated by modes
of hermaphroditic beauty other than the chthonian. "Fragoletta" is
addressed to Henri de Latouche's bisexual and transvestite heroine.
"Sexless" Fragoletta embodies the mystery of gender. Like Cupid, she
is "sightless," first because her double nature depersonalizes her and
second because it risks cruelty and solipsism. The poem's interrogatory
form comes from Gautier's "Contralto." Swinburne savors Fragoletta's
piquant boyishness: "Thy sweet low bosom, thy close hair, / Thy strait
soft flanks and slenderer feet, / Thy virginal strange air." This androgyne is far from Swinburne's marmoreal virago Faustine, like Michelangelo's massy, writhing "Night." Fragoletta is a perverse adolescent, mute, passive, and sensually blank. She has the languid petulance
of an autistic child. Her debilitation belongs to civilization in its apathetic late phase.

"Hermaphroditus," a companion piece to "Fragoletta," was written
in the Louvre. Like "Contralto," it meditates on a Hellenistic statue of
the "Sleeping Hermaphrodite": "Two loves at either blossom of thy
breast / Strive until one be under and one above." Swinburne injects
Gautier's genial Hermaphrodite with Baudelaire's sterility. Fragoletta
has a "barren bosom"; Hermaphroditus, with its "fruitless" breasts,
turns "the fruitful feud of hers and his / To the waste wedlock of a sterile
kiss." Gautier's poem is still High Romantic in its easy, far-ranging
metaphors of heaven and earth. But Swinburne's Hermaphrodite poems suffer a Late Romantic introversion or self-stifling. His Hermaphrodite is spiritually impacted, a pod straining with imprisoned abun-

dance. Nature's phases of germination and efflorescence have stalled
and halted. The Hermaphrodite is dormant, multi-aspected but half-
born. In Swinburne, English epithalamia are the Thames run backward.

Like Coleridge, Swinburne made prose defenses of his poetry, moral
revisions obscuring his original intentions. Art and rationalization come
from different parts of the mind. A poet without his Muse is as dull as
anyone else. Discussing "Hermaphroditus," Swinburne praises the
symbolism of barrenness, nimbly having his Decadent cake and eating
it too:

> There is nothing lovelier, as there is nothing more famous, in later
> Hellenic art, than the statue of Hermaphroditus. No one would
> compare it with the greatest works of Greek sculpture. No one
> would lift Keats on a level with Shakespeare. . . . At Paris, at Flor-
> ence, at Naples, the delicate divinity of this work has always drawn
> towards it the eyes of artists and poets. [A note quotes a Her-
> maphrodite stanza from Shelley's *Witch of Atlas.*] . . . Perfection
> once attained on all sides is a thing thenceforward barren of use or
> fruit; whereas the divided beauty of separate woman and man—a
> thing inferior and imperfect—can serve all turns of life. Ideal
> beauty, like ideal genius, dwells apart, as though by compulsion;
> supremacy is solitude.[13]

"Nothing lovelier" than the statue of Hermaphroditus? Only primitives
and sophisticates find beauty in the grotesque. The first and last of
history meet in Decadence. Swinburne sees, as Gautier does not, that
Hermaphrodite statues belong to the late phase of Greek art, a period of
excess, confusion, and frustrated rather than heroic action. Multiple
sexual possibilities cancel each other out, and being lies paralyzed. Like
Huysmans and Pater, Swinburne celebrates a late classicism of too-
muchness. Supersaturation of opportunity and experience ends in self-
lacerating asceticism.

Swinburne's critique of heterosexuality is clever and disarming. Heterosexuality is the measure of all things but common as household dust.
Representing "ideal beauty" for him as for Gautier, the Hermaphrodite
is like arrogantly separatist Sappho, withdrawing from society and
nature. Barrenness is now a spiritual privilege. Male and female are
"inferior" because they follow reality too closely. About to be slain for
her illicit sexual duality, Latouche's heroine cries she is not of the
human species. Thus Swinburne's Hermaphrodite, exiled from social
dialogue by its static doubleness, broods in self-thwarting estrange-

ment. Love means never having to unpack your bags. The honeymoon is a swollen orb of psyche hanging low over a never-gathered harvest. ˙

Swinburne's androgynes are Romantic shadows of evolutionary nostalgia, of being longing for nonbeing. As Victorian personae, they are insolently anti-historical. One reaction to highly polarized Victorian sex roles came after the fact in Bloomsbury's polemical androgynism, a revolt of sons and daughters against fathers. But the first reaction was contemporary: Swinburne's poetry is a sexual heterocosm, an insurrection of language as well as personae. Like Baudelaire, Swinburne is anti-utopian and anti-progressivist. That is, he asserts the primitive and daemonic character of emotion, sex, and nature. Sade and Swinburne show that sexual sadomasochism is always subliminally archaizing. Through ritual flagellation Swinburne returned his imagination to the barbaric human past. Nineteenth-century liberalism, in politics and psychology, was predicated on the western concept of free will. The future would bring a social millennium. Swinburne is a Decadent because of his contrary conviction of and longing for decline. In his poetry, psyche is pulled back to nature, a sinking movement like that of Michelangelo's swooning, matter-bound athletes.

For free will Swinburne substitutes compulsion, one of his greatest themes. Even Sappho, his most self-assertive voice, must constantly defend her freedom against overpowering enslavements—to beauty, to nature, to God. The idea of criminal compulsion was invented by Poe: the deranged speaker of *The Tell-Tale Heart*, irrationally driven to murder, bequeaths his experience to Dostoyevsky's Raskolnikov, who takes up the matricidal ax in a motiveless trance. But it is Swinburne who invents the idea of *sexual* compulsion, a Decadent enslavement. Karl Stern says all sexual perversion contains "an eschatological dread."[14] In its ritual repetitions and subordination to female hierarchs, Swinburne's poetry recreates the primitive world where culture had not yet risen as a defense against nature and where human life was dictated by brute rhythms of the chthonian. The confident Victorian alliance of society and heaven, wedded by Christian assumptions of love and charity, cannot withstand the force of Swinburne's pagan poems, once the imagination is caught up in their daemonic metric. For Swinburne remakes man in nature's image, sending him back to his origins in a world of hostility and fear.

Like Swinburne, Walter Pater emerged from the Pre-Raphaelite milieu at Oxford. He spent most of his reclusive life in the university, influencing a generation of students through his writings on art. Pater adopts Gautier's ideal of literary style as Romantic persona. Through style, he shows how to see. Swinburne, I noted, separates and suspends the units of English syntax. Pater takes Swinburne's suspension to a Decadent extreme. His long sentences have an errant, eccentric grace. Gautier needs his polemical preface to do what Pater does through style alone: to neutralize all social and moral limitations on art. Swinburne is ruled by sexual hierarchies, and his poetry is energized by daemonic nature. But there is no energy in Pater; his writing is the ultimate in Decadent lassitude and closure. There is no sex or even emotion in him. Nothing exists but the perceiving self. Pater perfects Romantic solipsism. The male persona projected by his prose is the most passive in western literature. Language too is radically deactivated. Heracleitus, his hero, gives Pater his vision of life as an ever-changing river. But Pater wants fluidity and flow, Dionysian principles, without passion, participation, or self-surrender. He wants dreaminess without chthonian night. Pater's contradictions appear in the attack upon his writing by what he has repressed: daemonic mother nature, who appears once and once only.

Studies in the History of the Renaissance (1873) is the first classic of English aestheticism. Pater's disciple, Oscar Wilde, called it "my golden book" and "the very flower of decadence."[15] Pater's homage to Renaissance painters refutes Ruskin, for whom medieval Venice is a Virgin and Renaissance Venice a whore. His "Conclusion" caused such a scandal that Pater withdrew it from the second edition. The "Conclusion" was the first thing I ever admired for style alone. When I stumbled on it as a schoolgirl, it seemed to express everything missing from the drowsy Victorian 1950s.

"To burn always with this hard, gemlike flame, to maintain this ecstasy, is success in life."[16] Pater's hypnotic, seductive sentences are a Romantic spell, drawing the reader into a strange passionless state of contemplativeness. They make perception the ultimate creative act. For Pater, not even creation is as creative as perception. The aesthete is not artist but connoisseur. Pater abolishes morality by frustrating the ability to act: this he does by sabotaging the verb and purging it of energy. Pater's verbs are passive or static. "Is," his favorite, does nothing. In *Marius the Epicurean* (1885), Pater speaks of seeing as superior to having or doing and of vision as a condition of being.[17] Pater's "is," therefore, is the verb of perfect seeing and being. In Gautier's Decadent catalog, verbs are suppressed to favor nouns, which gain vividness and substantiveness through color, mass, and form. But in Pater, the noun does not wax as the verb wanes. We struggle to halt his nouns to inspect them more closely, but they slip by on the eddying stream of his prose. Infinitives and participles, in disorienting positions, usurp the verb's active function. Pater diverts and dissipates syntactic energy into tributaries of clauses, which drain authority from the conventional English marriage of noun and verb. Pater follows the Romantic archpattern of regression by making Heracleitus' river run backwards. His sentences, seeming to take everything in, actually make movements of self-divestiture and self-cancellation.

The "Conclusion" had tremendous impact upon the 1890s, the Mauve Decade. Pater said of the suppressed "Conclusion," "I conceived it might possibly mislead some of those young men into whose hands it might fall." The misleading was into sexual hedonism, specifically homosexuality. Pater complained his pagan hedonism was misunderstood: he followed ascetic Epicurus, not the sensual Cyrenaics. But was immorality the real reason for his self-censoring? Pater urges refinement of consciousness, not masculine achievement in a materialistic imperialist culture. There are Buddhist parallels: the Zen master too seeks to be rather than to strive. But the analogy breaks down when we compare Pater's writing to the closest British equivalent to Buddhist mysticism, the *Centuries* of Thomas Traherne, a seventeenth-century divine whose emotion is simple and buoyant. In Pater we find emotional repression and inhibited movement, a subtle torsion or Mannerist sinuosity in the sentences, and finally an obscuring of the visible just when we eagerly turn toward it.

I think Pater's distress at misreadings of the "Conclusion" came from his horror of action, sexual or otherwise. He withdrew the chapter to preserve his spiritual identity, which resided in superpassivity of persona. An act connects person to person, or self to world. But for Pater neither the world nor other people can defeat "that thick wall of personality through which no real voice has ever pierced on its way to us." Reality is merely a series of "impressions unstable, flickering, inconsistent." The mind of each isolated individual keeps as "a solitary prisoner its own dream of a world."[18] Action is illusion in a realm where, as Heracleitus says in Pater's epigraph, "all things flow." Logically, Pater cannot exalt direct, unmediated experience and also insist on the imprisoned self. The "Conclusion" celebrates aesthetic perception in an affectless chain of images beginning with "strange dyes, strange colours" and ending with "the face of one's friend." This face, certainly male and faintly erotic, is merely an object among objects. It is a pale fading oval, like the Cheshire Cat. Traherne extends significance to the

lowly, turning dust and pebbles to gold, but Pater finally drains significance from everything. The pursuit of beauty leads him into a Bower of
Bliss that is a life sentence, solitary confinement without parole. He is
like Rachilde's Raoule, the necrophiliac aesthete in a self-made tomb.

Such limitations upon a self thinking itself free of tradition are another Decadent enslavement. We feel this enslavement when surrendering ourselves to Pater's prose, whose fluidity moves in an oppressive
silent vacuum. His young contemporaries found cultural liberation in
that prose. Its exquisite languor was a vapor or miasma clouding the
masculine icons of duty and deed. Pater's prose transsexualizes the
male reader by shifting consciousness into an Oriental floating world.
Though the senses are enhanced, the body has vanished. Nothing is left
to which gender can be assigned.

Like Byron, Pater values "susceptibility," a feminine receptivity. Consciousness is totally reflective, like Coleridge's sea. The self is as passive
as a barometer. Though Pater makes it the standard of aesthetic judgment, the self seems oddly undefined. "What is this song or picture, this
engaging personality presented in life or in a book, to *me?* What effect
does it really produce on me?" It: person and art work are equivalent
and interchangeable, as in *The Picture of Dorian Gray.* Pater's critic
needs only "a certain kind of temperament, the power of being deeply
moved by the presence of beautiful objects."[19] Personal response is
everything. But personality is only a temperament, a shimmering watery wraith. Pater's temperament is another Late Romantic Aeolian
lyre, played upon by external forces. Now art, not nature does the
playing. And the lyre is no longer obliged to sing. The Decadent exults
in *feeling* more intensely than others, a talent conveniently inaccessible
to proof. He is excused by aristocratic detachment from organizing
these feelings into the new symbolic structures of art.

Pater's religion is a cultic code of Decadent connoisseurship. His
influence would fall more heavily on men than women, who have no
public role to abandon. Rejecting Ruskin's evangelical view of the
morality of art, Pater argues that form takes precedence over content.
Art can have no content whatever: "All art constantly aspires towards
the condition of music."[20] Morality is excess baggage on the winged
steed. Pater's prose is musical: his clean, clear, chastened sentences are
flutelike. Pater's impressionism is paralleled by French Impressionism
of the 1890s: Debussy, Fauré, Ravel, Chausson, and Roussel have a fin-
de-siècle elegance, suavity, and coolness. There is no exertion or, in
Paterian terms, no action. Debussy's experiments with the whole-tone
scale were inspired by Javanese music he heard at the 1889 Paris

Exposition. Pater's Orientalism is in the sliding meanders and glancing syncopation, a subversion of western measure. Spengler says: "To the Chinese all the music of the West without distinction is *march-music*. Such is the impression that the rhythmic dynamic of our life makes upon the accentless Tao of the Chinese soul."[21] Pater and Debussy lure imagination away from western action toward eastern contemplativeness. Pater's disciple George Moore also noticed the analogy: "If he had lived to hear *L'après-midi d'un faune*, he could not have done else but think that he was listening to his own prose changed into music."[22] What is not Oriental in the French Impressionist composers is their delicate perversity. Each tone has equal emphasis, leading to a dreamy moral and sexual ambiguity. Twenty years ago, I was surprised at how many heterosexual men detested Debussy and Ravel, to whom male homosexuals at the time seemed instinctively drawn. Debussy has an epicene glamour to which rationalists refuse to yield. A similar division of opinion still surprisingly affects Virginia Woolf, whom David Cecil calls "the final exquisite flower of Pater's 'doctrine."[23] Pater, Debussy, Woolf, and Proust launch male consciousness upon an undulating stream, bright and melancholy.

Pater's fluidity is an apparent anomaly in aestheticism. The aesthete, I said, honors sharply contoured Apollonian objets d'art as a protest against the chthonian liquid realm of female nature. Heracleitus' free-flowing water is not Dionysian liquidity. Dionysus represents opaque liquids that ooze, drip, or swell in organic sacs. This distinction is evident in Woolf, who loves fluid imaginative movement but is nauseated by all physiology. As aesthete and art critic, Pater manages to make externals not more but less real to his readers. Objects do not really exist in him; they merely appear. In *Marius*, Pater says we have "a false impression of permanence or fixity in things, which have really changed their nature in the very moment in which we see and touch them." We create out of our "fluid impressions" an imaginary world of "firmly outlined objects," so that we think "stark and dead what is in reality full of animation, of vigour, of the fire of life."[24] Out of context, these remarks sound persuasive. But they occur in a novel whose style contradicts them. If Heracleitus' fluid vision opens the authentic world to Pater, where is the animation, vigor, and fire? *Marius* completely lacks energy. It is overpoweringly effete—beautiful, grave, and austere, but Decadent with enervation. Pater's contemporaries felt this immediately. Max Beerbohm recalls his student reaction to Pater: "Even then I was angry that he should treat English as a dead language, bored by that sedulous ritual wherewith he laid out every sentence as in a shroud."[25]

Moore says that language in *Marius* lies in state. So Pater makes English a Decadent corpse to make love to. Something is amiss between Paterian theory and practice.

What are Pater's mechanics of perception? "Experience seems to bury us under a flood of external objects, pressing upon us with a sharp and importunate reality." But reflection magically dissolves the Apollonian "cohesive force" of things: "Each object is loosed into a group of impressions—colour, odour, texture—in the mind of the observer."[26] In his ritualized perceptual relations, Gautier distances the modern world's excess phenomena by seeing, fixing, and recording an astonishing exactitude of detail. But Pater's loosed impressions are a Decadent disintegration. He wants to make objects transparent and weightless, like serum. His Heracleitean theory of universal mobility is actually a defense against the opacity of things, specifically the chthonian opacity of female nature. Even as he declares objects aerated or liquefied by perception, their weight is so great that he is immobilized. Hence the total passivity of his rhetorical persona. This invisible weight is what vexed Pater's first readers into metaphors of shroud and funeral. Pater both refines the eye and blurs its focus. An aesthete, I said, is one who lives by the eye, a process of Apollonian objectification begun in Egypt. Pater is trapped in an uncomfortable intermediate state. His Apollonian transformation of nature is incomplete. Taking refuge in Heracleitus does not solve his metaphysical problem. If all things flow, the self cannot be a prison. Pater's persona is as static as Baudelaire's, but Baudelaire correctly and consistently projects petrifaction, not fluidity as the optimal condition of the aesthete's universe.

In Pater, aesthetic perception is at war with its archenemy, female nature. The Apollonian eye of the male connoisseur is under siege from the baleful Gorgon eye that Coleridge unshutters in his triumphant daemon, the lesbian vampire Geraldine. That Pater's Heracleitean aestheticism stems from an anxiety about nature is proved by his meditation in *The Renaissance* on Leonardo's *Mona Lisa*. By far the most powerful passage in his writing, it is a spectacular vision of Decadent Dame Nature. Mona Lisa is a "presence" rising beside the waters. Her eyelids are "a little weary." Her beauty is "the deposit, little cell by cell, of strange thoughts and fantastic reveries and exquisite passions." In her face appear ancient lust, medieval reverie, and Renaissance sins, "the return of the Pagan world." She is a "vampire," "older than the rocks among which she sits." She was Leda, mother of Helen of Troy, and St. Anne, mother of Mary. She has "perpetual life, sweeping together ten thousand experiences."[27]

Pater's Mona Lisa is mother nature as perceptual oppression, blocking the object-world with her exhausting omnipresence. She squats like a grimacing Gorgon over space and time. She is that "permanence or fixity in things" which Pater tries to make our "false impression" of reality. Mona Lisa is everything Pater fears and represses. This notorious patch of purple prose is both invocation and exorcism. It is Pater's ritual confinement of mother nature to a strict temenos within his writings. By compressing and containing her, he defends his identity as an aesthete, a master of the eye. But even as we gaze at her, she freezes us with her evil animal eye. Like Byron's transvestite Don Juan dragged before the virago, we meet her while we are in sexual declension. We are clothed only in Pater's effetely passive prose. It is a moment of dreamlike paralysis, as in Huysmans' flower nightmare. We are dangerously exposed, sexually vulnerable. Appealing to Heracleitus, Pater wants perception without a frame, in the eastern way. But here he tries to frame Mona Lisa in a moment of hermaphrodite epiphany. She will not stay still. Within this frame she twists and turns, snaking through history.

Pater's hymn to Mona Lisa stems from Gautier's essay on Leonardo. Gautier detects "a certain fatigue" in Mona Lisa, with her "sinuous, serpentine mouth." We see her "violet shadows" through "a black gauze"; we hear voices whispering "languorous secrets" and "repressed desires."[28] Pater fuses Gautier's Mona Lisa with Swinburne's Dolores and Faustine, criminal voluptuaries metamorphosing like Baudelaire's vampire from era to era. Pater's Mona Lisa is a sexual catchall, civilization's storm-sewer, a prowling promiscuous Clodia. She gluttonously appropriates "all modes of thought and life." As Bloom says, "She incarnates too much, both for her own good and for ours."[29] Mona Lisa swells with Decadent too-muchness. Only Blake's cruel nature goddesses are this vast.

Unlike Baudelaire and Swinburne, Pater has no erotic interest in his titanic vampire. His sublimated tastes are exclusively male. The only sexual or crypto-sexual event I find in his writing is the climax of *Marius*, where the hero, in an ecstasy of sharpened consciousness, sacrifices his life for a male friend. The scene is surely modelled on the agon of the male heroine in Swinburne's *Atalanta in Calydon*. Pater sees "a touch of something sinister" in Mona Lisa's "unfathomable smile." She smiles because she commands vision, knowledge, and experience. The male can no more avoid her or find a place where she is not than he can bring himself into existence. She is the weight and burden of biology.

Following Gautier, Pater turns prose into poetry. He challenges Ruskin's medieval morality by making a corrupt High Renaissance objet d'art culturally primary. Yeats endorsed Pater's lyricism by excerpting the *Mona Lisa* section and printing it as the first modern poem in the *Oxford Book of Modern Verse* (1936). Unfortunately, he broke the sentences into lame free verse, destroying their discreet rhythm. His preface says the passage "dominated a generation."[30] Yeats, who claimed he grew up "in all things Pre-Raphaelite," owed a great deal to Pater.[31] Adopting the sexual syncretism of Swinburne's vampires, Pater makes Mona Lisa both Leda and St. Anne (Mary's weird double in Leonardo). Pater's mother daemon thus kicks off both the classical and Christian historical cycles, an idea Yeats borrows for Leda in "Leda and the Swan" and for Mary in "Two Songs from a Play." But Yeats makes a crucial sexual revision, inspired by his own anxieties. His Leda is raped and impregnated by a harshly masculine Zeus. Pater's Mona Lisa needs no partner: she gives birth to phenomena by parthenogenesis. So "Leda and the Swan," the premiere twentieth-century poem, was itself a ritual of exorcism by which Yeats freed himself from Pater, fin-de-siècle Decadence, and his own lingering Swinburnian dreams of sexual servitude.

As a "presence" rising beside the primeval womb-waters, Mona Lisa is shapeless and genderless, only secondarily taking human form. This apparition is "older than the rocks" because she created them. Pater imagines her at the Darwinian dawn of species. Like Baudelaire's vampires, Mona Lisa inhabits a cold mineral realm. Her beauty too is mineralized, the cell deposit of her perverse thoughts. She fabricates herself by coral accretion, an incrementation of Decadent parts. Her dreamy autoeroticism is like that of Blake's impacted "Sick Rose." The slow gathering of "strange thoughts" and "maladies" of the soul into her face will reappear in Wilde's corroded picture of ageless Dorian Gray. Like Swinburne's Dolores, Pater's Mona Lisa is simultaneously primeval and Decadent, Alpha and Omega. She sets the world into motion and also registers the fatigue of its late phase in her sultry eyelids. These eyelids, like the eyebrow of Gautier's Cleopatra, are a supreme example of Decadent partition, the aesthete's detachment of the part for clinical inspection.

Transmigrating Mona Lisa has been a male merchant of "strange webs" and a male "diver in deep seas," whose sunset light clings to her. These far-flung vocations are her inquisitional way of demonstrating her divine immanence. Like Prometheus and Jehovah, she too is a workman god. But why a diver? I suspect Pater is recalling Gautier's

King Candaules, where the king muses at length about diving into "the green depths" to find his wife, mystic-eyed Nyssia, "a perfect pearl, incomparable in brilliancy and purity."[32] Is this pearl of great price the daemonic vampire eye that Mona Lisa wears? Or is she, like Swinburne's bisexual Dolores and Faustine, a lesbian adventuress diving into genital shadows for a slippery female pearl? (Cf. the slang term "muff-diving.") Mona Lisa works under cover, a travelling jack-of-all-trades. Like the playacting Roman emperors, she is a queen on plebeian patrol.

There are just two sexual personae in Pater: the passive male aesthete and his cosmic antagonist, mother nature. She is summoned only once in his writing because her ultimate threat is more perceptual than sexual to celibate Pater. The passage on Mona Lisa is in Swinburne's Hollywood style. The star makes a personal appearance, fearfully in the flesh. She is a cast of thousands played by one. He-e-ere's Mona! The longest running show in history. Pater is a crucial figure in the eye-intense western tradition. Perceptual relations are his whole arena of quest and struggle. He demonstrates the monasticism and religiosity in aestheticism and Decadence, once dismissed as affectation or libertinage. Pater uses Heracleitus to dissolve the too-too solid flesh of his archaic Venus. By Decadent connoisseurship, he will clarify and purify the murky chthonianism of nature. High and Late Romantic vampires are not just the mossy paraphernalia of diverting ghost stories. Romanticism, in radically expanding identity, also generated stalking predators upon identity. The vampire is usurpation of identity by daemonic nature. Swinburne propitiates his vampire, while Pater ritually wards her off. By discrimination of the eye, Pater means to reclaim objects from their oppressive progenitor. But Heracleitus' river, relieving him of mass, keeps him in flux. Like Keats, Pater writes his name in water. Name your poison. Mother nature, mistress of change, wins at all our war games of land and sea.

19

Apollo Daemonized

Decadent Art

In the last decades of the nineteenth century, Decadent sexual personae crowd literature and art. An 1893 poem by Albert Samain proclaims "the era of the Androgyne," who mushrooms over culture like an antichrist. The sex-repelling Decadent androgyne is Apollonian because of its opposition to nature and its high mentalization, a western specialty. It is louring and enervated rather than radiant. Colette calls this type of androgyne "anxious and veiled," eternally sad, trailing "its seraphic suffering, its glimmering tears."[1] Similarly, Jung sees in the feminine head from Ostia of Mithras or Attis "sentimental resignation," passive self-pity.[2] Androgyny is not, as some feminists imply, the solution to all human ills. In *The Time Machine* (1895), H. G. Wells foresees the dangers of collective androgyny. Society has polarized into a worker class, the ugly subterranean Morlocks, and a leisure class, the effeminate Eloi, beautiful, weak, and apathetic. The Eloi, or Upper-Worlders, are Apollonian aesthete-parasites exiled from the productive chthonian realm, run by scuzzy utilitarians. Wells's time-traveller first admires the Eloi's androgyny but is then repelled by their Decadent degeneration. The modern androgyne, seeking only self-realization, forfeits the Spenserian energy of opposition and conflict.

Decadent art suffered the same fate as academic painting of the Salon, swept away by the triumph of the avant-garde and modernism. The last twenty years have seen an international revival of figurative painting. Museums are dusting off the discards in their cellars. What is now needed is a revision of art history that would acknowledge how much avant-garde art really was Decadent Late Romantic: much of Whistler and Manet, all of Toulouse-Lautrec, Munch, and Gaudí, and even Seurat's *La Grande Jatte*, with its Decadent immobility and claustrophobia.

Decadent art is ritualistic and epiphanic. Its content: Romantic sexual personae, the hierarchs, idolators, and victims of daemonic nature. Even depicting episodes from poetry, Decadent art is never mere illustration. It dramatizes dominant western image and sexual subordination of the aggressive eye. Decadent art makes hostile claims on the viewer. Its style is pagan spectacle and pagan flaunting. Behind the trashiest Decadent painting are complex Romantic assumptions about nature and society overlooked by textbook accounts of nineteenth-century art. Modernist culture-heroes like Cézanne are overemphasized. Cézanne's plainness and "honesty," homely Protestant values, are in the Rousseauist-Wordsworthian line. Decadent art, like Counter-Reformation Baroque, tells big lies. Dante Gabriel Rossetti, Edward Burne-Jones, Gustave Moreau, and Aubrey Beardsley must be given higher rank. Despite brief popularity in the 1960s, Beardsley, a major graphic artist, is shockingly absent from American university curricula and slide collections. Like Sade, he has been censored by the liberal humanities.

The Pre-Raphaelite Brotherhood, founded in 1848, lasted only five years, but its style was absorbed by late nineteenth-century art and design across the continent. Inspired by Ruskin, the Pre-Raphaelites sought to recover medieval simplicity and purity lost in the pagan luxury of High Renaissance art, typified, they oddly felt, by Raphael. Unlike their Decadent descendants, they professed collective social values. The only member of the Brotherhood whom I identify as already Decadent is Rossetti, whose Italian blood would out. But in all Pre-Raphaelite painting there is an unsettling tension between form and moral content.

Pre-Raphaelite painting begins with Keatsian ardor for the minutiae of organic nature. But instead of High Romantic energy or dynamic process, we get Late Romantic stasis. Pre-Raphaelite art, like Mannerism, disturbingly avoids pictorial focus. Our eye is not automatically guided to the human figures but is forced to wander over the microscopic detail. Color is unshaded and applied in separate cells, as in Byzantine mosaic or Gautier's gorgeous color units. Flowers and blades of grass are brilliantly lapidary, the paint surface so richly worked that there is only a single step from Pre-Raphaelite naturism to Gustave Moreau's Decadent jewelled artifice. Everything in Pre-Raphaelite painting is seen *too clearly*. The eye is invited but coerced. Part triumphs over whole, exerting an uncomfortable pressure on the viewer. Landscape has *an unnatural stillness*, making it a Decadent frozen tableau.

Sunlit panoramas are locked in Decadent closure, a Spenserian embowerment. Pre-Raphaelite painting deadens even as it celebrates.
Persons and things are candied, mummified, miniaturized.

The Pre-Raphaelites revived Blake, who had died unknown. Swinburne promoted Blake's daemonic poetry, and Rossetti promoted his
art. In 1847 Rossetti bought the notebook where Blake attacks chiaroscuro and praises "the hard and wiry line of rectitude," that Apollonian contour I traced from Egypt and Greece to Botticelli and Spenser.
Ruskin too condemns Renaissance chiaroscuro. So Pre-Raphaelite
sharpness of detail is polemically Apollonian. Pre-Raphaelite mummification is Apollonian objectification and fixation, which Rossetti
makes his master principle of sexual personae. Rossetti, unlike the
others, had trouble painting landscape from nature and sometimes had
to recreate it imaginatively from the Decadent ritual solitude of a black-
velvet-draped chamber.

As his career progressed or, some said, degenerated, Rossetti's paintings obsessively returned to a single subject, a woman of somnambulistic languor (fig. 37). The Rossetti woman rebels against Victorian convention, her unpinned hair and unstructured medieval gown flowing
with lyrical freedom. The heavy head sways on a serpentine neck. Her
long thick hair is the Belle Dame Sans Merci's net of entrapment. Her
swollen lips are to become a universal motif of Decadent art, thanks to
Burne-Jones and Beardsley. The Rossetti vampire mouth cannot speak,
but it has a life of its own. It is gorged with the blood of victims. Like
Blake's sick rose, the Rossetti woman is blanketed in silence and humid,
private pleasures.

Rossetti ritually commemorated the face of Elizabeth Siddal, a melancholic consumptive who died of a laudanum overdose shortly after he
married her. Seven years later, he exhumed her corpse to rescue the
sheaf of poems that, in a Romantic fit, he had buried with her. He
constantly drew and painted Siddal before and after her death. His
friend Ford Madox Brown wrote in a diary, "It is like a monomania with
him."[3] Rossetti's brother said John Everett Millais' *Ophelia* (1852) was
the most faithful likeness of Siddal. Guess what: Siddal herself didn't
look in the least like a Rossetti painting! It is as if the artist were in
bondage to Poe's Ligeia, whose image vanquishes all living women.
Like Leonardo, Rossetti was under enchantment by some archetypal
original, probably a Romantic shadow of the mother. William Holman
Hunt said of his treatment of later models: "Rossetti's tendency in
sketching a face was to convert the features of his sitter to his favourite
ideal type, and if he finished on these lines, the drawing was extremely

37. Dante Gabriel Rossetti, *The Lady Lilith*, 1868. Adam's sinister first wife. The flowers, including magic foxglove on the vanity table, normally bloom at different times of year. So this is mythological woman, queen of nature.

charming, even if you had to make-believe a good deal to see the likeness, while if the sitter's features would not lend themselves to the pre-ordained form, he went through a stage of reluctant twisting of lines and quantities to make the drawing satisfactory."[4] Obsession is psychic closure, a Decadent deforming of reality. What in Siddal evoked Rossetti's fanatical devotion? Her frailty seemed feminine to others. Rossetti saw, as his namesake Dante did in Beatrice, the hermaphrodite remoteness of the beautiful boy, the cruel perfection of solipsistic beauty. From the brooding girl-boy Elizabeth Siddal came the definitive sexual persona of all Decadent art.

Italian Catholicism's vestigial paganism resurfaces in Rossetti through the impact on him of High Romantic poetry. His painting begins to drift from the Pre-Raphaelite Middle Ages toward the pagan past, a Romantic regression. Symons sees the sinister transformation of Rossetti's women into "idols": Venus grows "more and more Asiatic"; his dreams are "lunar, spectral, a dark and unintelligible menace."5 Moving back toward Cybele, Rossetti daemonizes the medieval veneration of woman and changes English Romanticism from High to Late. He and Swinburne agree about female omnipotence. The sleepy vampires of his late paintings are chillingly oblivious to the masculine, upon which they have already fed. Rossetti gradually fleshes out skinny Elizabeth Siddal with post-Raphaelite Baroque massiness. He compensates for Romanticism's lack of sculpture by giving his female personae a sculptural density, expressing the hidden oppressions in Pre-Raphaelite nature. The most blatant of his *objets de culte* is *Astarte Syriaca* (fig. 38). The somber goddess and two vamping angels all have the same face, a combination of Siddal with Jane Morris, who according to photographs had a mannish hardness. Chiaroscuro, banished from early Pre-Raphaelitism, has returned to cloud heart and mind.

Rossetti and his disciple Burne-Jones practice allegorical repletion, my term for Leonardo's *The Virgin and Child with St. Anne*. Doubled female faces always signify an incestuous collapsing of identities, a chthonian undertow. In *The Bower Meadow*, which I think is Rossetti's version of Botticelli's imprisoned *Primavera*, the same woman appears in uncanny quadruplicate, changing only hair color and style, like a molting bird (fig. 39). The four women sing and dance with averted faces. Emotionally disconnected, they float down crossing planes of vision into distant space. Van den Berg says the nineteenth-century self came apart or "pluralized."6 In *Astarte Syriaca* and *The Bower Meadow*, psyche fragments into female plurals, the masochistic self-haunting of a Romantic sister-spirit. These alienated twins exert their ominous power across a dead space of Late Romantic materiality. Rossetti repeats the same face thrice in *Rosa Triplex* and *La Ghirlandata*. Is she Blake's witchy threefold maiden? In *The Blessed Damozel*, one face appears at different ages. Spooked lovers stare at their doubles in *How They Met Themselves*. Rossetti dramatizes the too-muchness of Romantic identity. He names the Spenserian arena of Romantic crisis: nature as a bower meadow, both open and closed, eternal threshing floor of birth and death.

38. Dante Gabriel Rossetti,
Astarte Syriaca, 1877.

Burne-Jones inherited Rossetti's perversities. Martin Harrison and
Bill Waters trace the hermaphroditism in Burne-Jones' painting to
Swinburne and Simeon Solomon: "This ambiguous interpretation of
the sexes is not present in any form in the art of Rossetti."[7] But all
of Rossetti's women are hermaphrodites. Take *Beata Beatrix* (1863),
where dead Elizabeth Siddal, a clairvoyant Beatrice, prays to the divinized idea of herself with closed eyes. She is like Shelley's android
Hermaphrodite, murmuring and smiling to itself with sealed eyes. As I
said of Nefertiti, impersonality or emotional lifelessness in a woman is a
masculinizing abstraction. Siddal's Decadent androgyny resided in her
solipsistic self-embowerment, her eerie aura. Decadence is about dead
ends. The one medievalism Rossetti retains in his late period is Dante's
grandiose cultism of dead Beatrice. In the sexual hierarchy of the *Vita
Nuova*, Dante subordinates himself to a coolly narcissistic female adolescent, who I'll bet no one else in Florence thought was anything
special. The latent sadomasochism in this becomes overt in Rossetti, of
whom Burne-Jones said, "Gabriel was half a woman." Western artists
ritualize sex, because western art ritualizes nature.

39. Dante Gabriel Rossetti, *The Bower Meadow*, 1872.

Burne-Jones subtly corrupts Pre-Raphaelite medievalism with Italian Renaissance style, specifically Mantegna's Donatello-derived Apollonian hardness. All his personae, male and female, have Elizabeth
Siddal's face. He is invaded and saturated by Rossetti's monomania.
Burne-Jones' pensive Sir Galahad (ca. 1857), for example, is obviously
Siddal as equestrian knight. Victorious St. George is so feminine one
may mistake him for Joan of Arc. In *Perseus and the Graiae* (1892), the
girlish hero is less masculine than the archetypal women he boldly

deceives. The youth of *Pygmalion* has the same face as the girl of *Danaë*. The two lovers of *Cupid and Psyche* are mirror-images. Octave Mirbeau said of Burne-Jones' faces: "The rings under the eyes . . . are unique in the whole history of art; it is impossible to tell whether they are the result of masturbation, lesbianism, normal love-making or tuberculosis."[8] These harrowing black eyes come from the sickly Siddal. Cosmetically applied to the great heroes of western saga, they drain masculine motivation and action at their source. Burne-Jones' knights are obsessed insomniacs watching over the decline of culture.

Burne-Jones' transsexual world is populated by one incestuously self-propagating being. We are in another Late Romantic bower, shadowless under a grey sky. The ritual limitation on his sexual personae is a Decadent closure, denying our eye right of access to other human types. *The Golden Stairs* (1880) expands Rossetti's triplets and quadruplets. We drown in a shower of identical women, eighteen in all, cloning themselves and assaulting the eye. Beauty in excess makes Decadent dyspepsia. The sadomasochistic tableau of *The Wheel of Fortune* multiplies the male. Giant Fortuna turns her torture wheel, chaining a row of beautiful young men, male odalisques in Michelangelo's troubled late style. Each seems languid twin of the next, limbs stretched in sensual suffering.

Burne-Jones' embowered nature begat Art Nouveau, which flourished from the 1880s to World War I. Then modern machine culture geometrized Art Nouveau's organic patterns into Art Deco. So Spenser's dynasty, extending through High and Late Romanticism, unexpectedly ends in the Chrysler Building and Radio City Music Hall. Burne-Jones' serpentine line comes from Blake, whose rapacious flamelike flowers reveal the covert sexual meaning of Art Nouveau's arabesques. The copious histories of Art Nouveau lack psychological insight. Twenty years ago, I was struck by Art Nouveau's popularity among male homosexual aesthetes, for whom neither it nor Beardsley had to be revived, since they had never been forgotten. In every star, style, or art work celebrated by these Alexandrian homosexuals, there is always a secret hermaphroditism. So with Art Nouveau, the most epicene style since Mannerism.

Art Nouveau, unlike Islamic pattern, is not value-neutral. But then, nothing in art is value-neutral. Style is always a shadowy emanation of assumptions about nature and society. Art Nouveau subliminally expresses the Decadent world-view. Rooms or buildings undulate with curvy rhythms, sexual subversions of western will, which since Egypt has based its public monuments on the stable, foursquare directionals of the male chest. Mainline western architecture has a rational organization unshared by Hindu temples, with their mazelike warrens and swarming surfaces. Gaudí's Art Nouveau rooms and caves are archaic with female swellings. Art Nouveau is active but sterile. The leaves and vines slithering up gates, grills, lamps, panes, and bookbindings are a garden of moral darkness, a jungle reclaiming the works of men. Like Huysmans' *A Rebours*, Art Nouveau shows nature at her stupidest and most unspiritual, a primeval tangle of insinuating plant-motion. Art Nouveau is *growth without fruitfulness*. Keatsian plumpness withers and contracts. Art Nouveau is a harvest of spines and thorns. It shows the modern city as a Sodom in black flames. It shows nature as cold biology writhing in final spasms. Art Nouveau combines the primitive with the sophisticated, a decadent technique invented by Hellenistic art and turned into cruel fun and games by the Roman emperors.

Critics disparage Burne-Jones' painting as too "mannered." But this is the elegant self-consciousness of Mannerism. Even Whistler's suave Japanese interiors have a Mannerist linearity; his clean, uncluttered line carries an anatomical message. House and body have been in analogy since the birth of architecture. The stout, bosomy Victorian *grande dame* is an upholstered sofa. The tall, flat-chested Pre-Raphaelite New Woman, typified by bisexual Sarah Bernhardt, is a bony Mackintosh chair: tea and sympathy on a Scottish torture rack. Mannerist Art Nouveau denies female mass and internality. Its iron spirals of flash-frozen vegetation nullify nature's fecund liquidity. Its whiplash, a sado-masochistic trope, stings the eye. Art Nouveau combats the chthonian, mimicking in order to petrify it in art. Art Nouveau is a Late Romantic Apollonian style, turning nature's perpetual motion to perceptual stasis.

Burne-Jones, the progenitor of Art Nouveau, shows the Medusa-head of nature in all its suffocating disorder. The pretty knights of *The Briar Wood* sprawl comatose outside Sleeping Beauty's castle (fig. 40). Scattered armour lies twisted in a bramble thicket of stunning density, Botticelli's prison-bar pines restored to medieval tapestry. We see the triumph of mother nature over the masculine. In *The Doom Fulfilled*, Burne-Jones' greatest painting, Perseus is Laocoön in the grip of coiling nature (fig. 41). The design recalls the illuminated letters of the Book of Kells, because Romanticism is the sacred text of nature-cult. Perseus is thrust into the hungry maw of a Blakean flower. The picture proves that Art Nouveau's running vines are an abstract version of daemonic nature, come to aggressive life to trap and strangle the human. Burne-Jones' brassy serpent is a scroll of Art Nouveau ironwork. The organic is invincibly metallic, while Perseus wears a visionary armour of leafy

40. Sir Edward Burne-Jones, *The Briar Wood*, 1870–90.

vegetation. A Greek hero becomes Spenser's weedy knight Artegall, who keeps relapsing into nature. So we must ask of Burne-Jones' picture: has the touch of the chthonian serpent contaminated Perseus? Is nature one instant from turning the male back into herself? Legend says Perseus wins. But the painting depicts the archetypal moment of doubt in which we are all caught in our daily battle with nature.

Other Pre-Raphaelites were less interested in problems of sex and nature. Holman Hunt illustrates a necrophiliac Keats poem in *Isabella and the Pot of Basil* (1867), where a mourning maiden waters her lover's severed head with her tears. William Morris adapts Elizabeth Siddal's face, swollen lips, and flowing hair for *The Archangel Gabriel* (1862). Simeon Solomon recasts her for *Until the Day Breaks* (1869), whose ivory-fleshed, androgynous brother and sister anticipate Jean Cocteau's homoerotic ephebes. Their dreamy incestuous intimacy is learnedly reproduced in the entranced sailor twins embracing in Madonna's superb peep-show video, "Open Your Heart" (1986), which confirms many of my ideas about the symbiosis of art and pornography.

Rossetti's continental ally is Gustave Moreau, born two years earlier. Moreau does to Byronic Delacroix what the Pre-Raphaelites do to Keats: he turns warmth and energy into fixation and closure. Moreau's static, lapidary Orientalism comes from Flaubert, who got it from Gautier. The jewelled incrustations of his murky paintings are Paterian deposits of age and weary experience. The gangrenous surfaces are flecked with soul-particles, Decadent atomizations. Moreau's substitution of inorganic for organic things illustrates aestheticism's flight from liquidity. His ornate Byzantine style is like Balzac's "black diamond,"

41. Sir Edward Burne-Jones, *The Doom Fulfilled*, 1885.

Cousin Bette, an Apollonian crystal clotted with chthonian darkness. The high decorativeness of late-phase art is a relief from social tensions of role and gender. Surface is beyond body and beyond sex. Hence Moreau's primary persona is logically the androgyne. Huysmans drafted the reluctant painter into the Decadent tradition in *A Rebours*, where Des Esseintes praises and purchases two of the *Salomé* pictures that were to produce Wilde's play and Strauss's opera.

Moreau's supreme theme is the femme fatale—Judith, Delilah, Helen, Cleopatra, Messalina, Theban Sphinx. My favorite Moreau is the draft in brilliant oils of *Helen at the Scaean Gate* (fig. 42). The rough, rapid brush strokes make it prophetically abstract expressionist. Stroll-

42. Gustave Moreau, *Helen at the Scaean Gate*, ca. 1880.

ing along the high wall of Troy, gigantic Helen seems to dwarf the city.
She has a blank mannequin's face. Her robes are smeared with crimson
stains. Far below, the Trojan plain is covered with shapeless red heaps
and smoking funeral pyres. Helen promenades like a chic lady of the
boulevards, averting her gaze from the wreck of civilization she has
caused. Huysmans, who elsewhere speaks of the "spiritual onanism" of
Moreau's women, says of the Helen of the final version: "She stands out
against a terrible horizon spattered with phosphorus and striped with
blood, clothed in a dress incrusted with jewels like a shrine; . . . the
large eyes are open, fixed, in a cataleptic stare."[9] Moreau's Helen is a
cruel idol of pagan nature.

Moreau is fond of males of Burne-Jones androgyny. His Jason has a
girl's soft, white, hairless body and shoulder-length hair as long as
Medea's. Poets like Orpheus and Hesiod have feminine face and hair
and smooth adolescent chest. Most astonishing of the series is *The Poet
and Nature* (1894), where an androgynous beautiful boy slumps, stu-
pefied, in a pool of water. Above him stands titanic mother nature, her
face in a demented stare. She grips the poet's head like a bowling ball,
both killing and inspiring him. She wears only a long, overgrown man-
tilla of lichens. Leonardo is the weatherman of Moreau's thundery sky.
This dreadful allegory takes place in my chthonian swamp, a primeval

marsh hung with Spanish moss and streaky, melting undersea vegetation.

Moreau uses hermaphrodite symbolism to revise his French precursors. His rigid, virile Jacob fights an insouciant, long-haired angel with jewelled tunic and blazing halo who, like Delacroix's Sardanapalus, leans his elbow on a rock and stares languidly into space. The visionary and hermaphroditic triumph over the moral and masculine. Does this fancy angel come from Balzac's *Seraphita?* In *The Suitors*, taut, vengeful Odysseus, drawing his great bow, slaughters the young upstarts, whose sleek corpses are an androgynous version of Sardanapalus' murdered odalisques. Hovering in the air, in a starburst medallion like a Byzantine halo, is Odysseus' patron Athena. She seems borne upward by the great serpent of Erechtheus, phallically protruding from her body. *Jupiter and Semele* (fig. 43) recasts Ingres' *Jupiter and Thetis* (1811). The massive, bearded father god becomes a bedizened Hindu effeminate, cross-eyed in solipsistic ecstasy. Jupiter is a Hellenistic Apollo hallucinating over his lyre. Michelangelo, shaving Christ's beard for the Second Coming, makes up for it by giving him a thick chest and heroic energy. Moreau's god, dripping jewels and pearls, is a longhaired houri. Semele's horror, as her tiny figure slips from the god's lap, comes from her recognition of woman's irrelevance to so perfect a divine hermaphroditism. Suffusing the painting is a morally ambiguous undersea light, like Pater's "fallen day."

Beautiful boys for their own sake are relatively rare in Decadent art. In Jean Delville's *Orpheus* (1893), the poet's head, trimmed by Maenads, floats on a lyre toward Lesbos. His effeminate face, orgasmically misted by a sanctifying moonglow, is based on that of the painter's wife. His long, voluptuously exposed throat recalls the alabaster neck of Michelangelo's Giuliano, one of my hermaphrodite tropes. Note the Romantic reversal of a Renaissance theme: now the hero is not decapitator but decapitated. Decadent art's main mission is to record the modes of female power. Its theme is hierarchic assertion, pure charismatic presence. Because of its mute iconicism, painting is more efficient than literature for this purpose. Decadent art's daemonic epiphanies are a response to the moral overestimation of woman in nineteenth-century culture, produced by Rousseau's utopian psychology. So woman becomes the enforcer of violent, primitive Sadean nature. Most such works are technically not Decadent in composition; that is, they are monadic, ruled by a single subject. Decadent painting is one of the most obsessively ritualistic styles in the history of art.

Decadent Symbolism flourished on the continent in the 1890s. Franz

43. Gustave Moreau, *Jupiter and Semele*, 1869.

44. Franz von Stuck, *Sin*, 1893.

von Stuck's *Sin*, a portrait of Eve, smiles ironically at the viewer (fig. 44).
We return her stare, until we suddenly notice, amid the masses of thick
black hair framing her white breasts and belly, an enormous boa constrictor fixing us with malevolent eyes. Eve is the modern Medusa,
wearing a boa like a boa. Von Stuck divines the serpentine menace in
Rossetti's motif of long female hair. His *Sphinx* is equally lurid: a fierce,

naked woman stretches like a panther, belly down on a rug. Her hand-some, aggressively intelligent head and opulent torso imitate the alert posture of the male Great Sphinx. Behind her is Leonardo's barren landscape of rocks and water. In *The Kiss of the Sphinx*, a full-breasted half-animal woman bends a kneeling male helplessly backward, pene-trating his mouth with hers. Von Stuck's hermaphrodite visions preserve woman's ravishing physical beauty, denied by the impurity-haunted Huysmans. Fernand Khnopff also continues the Sphinx tradition begun by Baudelaire and Moreau. His Oedipus has a feminine Burne-Jones face and rosebud mouth. Khnopff's women are modelled on his sister, in a Romantic incest-relation reminiscent of Kleist's.

The style of Gustave Klimt, another Decadent Symbolist, is pre-figured in Khnopff's *The Offering* (1891), with its surreal elongations and displacements of depth. Klimt's dazzling Byzantine surfaces de-scend from Moreau. He ingeniously mixes flat mosaic work with fleshy naturalism. In other words, he jams together different phases of art history, a Decadent syncretism, learned and claustrophobic. Klimt shows personae stuck in the object-world, half-born, half-swallowed. Nature and art wrestle for control. His nude *Salomé* (1909) takes her hard sophisticated face from Von Stuck's reclining Sphinx. At the bot-tom, half-hidden, is John the Baptist's severed head. The male is a setting sun eclipsed by the full moon of female fatality. *Judith* repeats this sexual design. The Jewish heroine of Florentine art is now a cynical demimondaine with a cold, worldly Joan Crawford face. Smiling, she runs her fingers through dead Holofernes' hair, parodying romantic tenderness. Her white expanse of breast and belly and taunting direct-ness of gaze come from Von Stuck's *Eve*. Klimt's *Pallas Athene* (1898) is one of the few postclassical works retaining the militant androgyny of an Amazon goddess. Her great spear at her side, Athena wears a mask-like bronze helmet through which her eyes glitter impassively. On her breast is her barbaric soul-image, the archaic Gorgon with out-thrust tongue. Her chain-mail aegis is tumbling gold coins, Zeus's sex gift to Danaë. Klimt's dominatrix Athena is the materialistic city-goddess of frothy fin-de-siècle Vienna.

Whistler was an ostentatious international promoter of aestheti-cism, baiting Ruskin head-on. His *The Little White Girl* (1863) is Pre-Raphaelite in mood and style, a Romantic apparition hovering in a Victorian salon. Ironically, his most famous painting is a supposedly minor work, *Arrangement in Gray and Black* (1872), which popular imagination dubbed *Whistler's Mother*. I nominate her as another Late

Romantic vampire, created a year before Pater's *Mona Lisa*. There is good reason for the picture's staying power: the eternal mother imago. Whistler's mother is chilly, half-dead, averting her face from her progeny. She is a Sphinx sitting in solid squares like stony Pharaoh, entombed in a sparse throne room of Decadent stasis. She is as mummified by dry Victorian decorum as the taxidermic mother of *Psycho*. Enduring popularity of art works always reveals the secret poetry of archetype. This is Whistler's *Mona Lisa*. His bland, witty title seeks to objectify the mother and curb her emotional power. But in vain. The daemonic bursts every Apollonian confinement.

Edvard Munch is wrongly classed with the coming Expressionists rather than the contemporary Decadents. His work addresses Late Romantic themes of sexual menace, as in *The Vampire*. His nude *Madonna* recalls Von Stuck's Eve in its shameless self-display of serene female power. The male is a timid, starved fetus shivering at the bottom. Along the borders, a line of sperm race without hope of entry. I wonder if *Madonna* was inspired by a speech in Strindberg: "I believe all you women are my enemies. My mother did not want me to come into the world because my birth would give her pain. She was my enemy. She robbed my embryo of nourishment, so I was born incomplete."[10] Munch's fetus oppressed by female magnitude reappears in the agoraphobic paranoid of *The Scream* (1895). Frozen on the bridge of history over the abyss of nature, the deranged Pierrot is a hairless hermaphrodite, mentally and physically stunted. Beardsley also uses the fetus as a sexual persona: he says of one of his drawings, "The little creature handing hats is *not* an infant but an unstrangled abortion."[11] A fetus is the ultimate Romantic regression. Shelley gives himself the happy company of an incestuous twin for his prenatal dreams, but Munch's desexed fetus suffers in frigid modern solitude.

Beardsley, the supreme Decadent artist, symbolizes the 1890s, the Mauve Decade. Spengler says in another context, "Violet, a red succumbing to blue, is the colour of women no longer fruitful and of priests living in celibacy."[12] Celibate, reclusive Beardsley was a monastic pornographer, reducing mother nature's colors and volumes to unfruitful black and white. Like Keats, he caught tuberculosis, dying at twenty-five. His works are amazingly voluminous, rivalling the two *Fausts* in variety of androgynes: angels, beautiful boys, ephebes, eunuchs, Amazons, viragos, vampires, earth mothers. He creates a vast self-enclosed realm of esoteric sexual personae. Rousseau's self-reflexiveness reaches a painful extremity in Beardsley's erotic mentalizations. Like Whitman and Genet, Beardsley vivifies his sexual universe by the masturbatory principle of Khepera, the Egyptian First Mover. The compulsive self-population of art usurps nature's powers.

Too much is made of Beardsley's debt to French rococo. He began as a disciple of the Pre-Raphaelites. From Burne-Jones he takes the Spenserian thicket of embowered nature, which he redramatizes as elegant conjunctions of perverse sexual personae. Rococo is vernal, lyrical. Beardsley's sharp line is harsh and Blakean; he inherits Art Nouveau's daemonized Apollonianism. Chthonian danger is ever-near in him, as it never is in rococo. Elizabeth Siddal's face appears on both sexes throughout Beardsley, in homage to Rossetti and Burne-Jones. She gives her lips to his early bosomy Hermaphroditus; she is Venus on the title page of the Swinburnian *Venus and Tannhäuser*; she becomes three longhaired pageboys in the first *Toilette of Salomé*. Something odd: Siddal as Venus looks exactly like Jacqueline Kennedy Onassis. So, like all living myths, one of the most famous women of our time evokes the hermaphrodite. Cecil Beaton confirms this, recording Jackie's "suspicion of a mustache" and her "big boyish hands and feet."[13]

Gender in Beardsley is constantly in doubt. Men and women in the *Salomé* series have indistinguishable faces. Homosexual couples fade toward the feminine. *The Woman in the Moon* is jowly Oscar Wilde. Gautier's D'Albert is more feminine than the rakish cavalier, Mademoiselle de Maupin. *Earl Lavender*'s half-clad lady stylishly flips her whip at the bare back of a kneeler whose head is coyly cut by the picture edge, the sex of the passive communicant remaining, as they used to say in television schedules, to be announced. Brigid Brophy asks if Beardsley's women transvestites are "female fops," "female effeminates," or "male hoydens, male tomboys, boy butches."[14] Beardsley's monstrosities are gnomes, dwarves, embryos, pasty-faced chinless eunuchs, sycophantic court hermaphrodites of a dead régime. His androgynes are malignant sports of history and heredity. Like Huysmans' venereal blossoms, they are the tainted flora of late phases of culture.

Closest to Beardsley himself are his effete courtiers and soliciting ephebic sodomites. A self-portrait shows him as a leering elf flaunting the phallic javelin of his ink-pen. He is as neutered as extraterrestrial David Bowie. Beardsley said of himself, "Once a eunuch always a eunuch." He likes phallicized women. Two versions of Swinburne's flat-chested Atalanta give her an artificial penis, a hunter's bow or leaping hound, inspired, I think, by Moreau's serpent-sexed Athena rampant. Salomé has a war-crown of tusks, thorns, and lunar crescents. She seems half porcupine, half randy ram butting heads with the Baptist, who shrinks from this hectoring apparition. She is the Venus Barbata, my term for a nagging harridan of the type played by Bette Davis in *All About Eve* and Elizabeth Taylor in *Who's Afraid of Virginia Woolf?*

Beardsley's hermaphrodite homunculi are not always identifiable. One recurrent persona is a pear-shaped male with bulging hips, buttocks, and thighs. The Abbé of *Under the Hill* is a haughty, muff-toting dandy in a knock-kneed, pouter-pigeon stance. The male's female fleshiness may be accentuated by extreme costume, as in *Lady Gold's Escort*, with its phalanx of Russian decadents in zoot-suit pantaloons. The only analogue I find is a metaphor by Shakespeare's Thersites: "the devil Luxury, with his fat rump and potato finger" (*T.C.* V.ii.53–54). Beardsley's callipygian males resemble the Venus of Willendorf, with her spindly legs and ballooning midriff. It is as if the Great Mother has fused with her son/lover. The son adopts her silhouette as an act of sympathetic identification, like Cybele's castrated priests donning her robes. That this swelling male anatomy is based on a female original is confirmed by Beardsley's bookplate: the nude, book-browsing hermaphrodite has a large butt and tiny vestigial udders.

Paradoxically, whenever she herself appears, Beardsley's Great Mother is usually repulsive. Herodias, for example, is a pig-eyed, slit-nosed dowager pugnaciously pushing her bosom before her like the prow of a Roman galley. Her breasts are straining bladders scored with veins. Dancing Salomé thrusts her shapeless stomach forward, so that we are forced to contemplate what looks like a deformed withering of the abdomen into the pudendum. Her nipples protrude like diamond studs. Her veil, twisting up from between her thighs in a phallic spire, spumes with bubbles of orgasmic fantasy. In *John and Salomé*, Salomé's nipples are angry blossoms, her black navel vulval, tendrilous, vaguely insectimorphic. The empress Messalina is a big-rumped British fish-wife storming, fists clenched, up the stairs. Her peevish breasts lead the charge with spiked nipples. In *The Fat Woman*, a satire on Whistler's wife, a huge bosom, propped against a café table like a sack of wheat, suffocates the viewer with its blank expanse. Wagner's *Erda* is a weary, dull-witted earth mother encumbered with a smothering black mantle of hair, flowing heavily into the muddy soil. *The Wagnerites* is Beardsley's Medici Chapel: an audience of viragos with broad shoulders and manly biceps pack a claustrophobic temple of art.

Beardsley identifies the mature female with a nauseating superfluity of flesh. Woman is mass, primeval matter. His Byzantine flatness forces the procreative female into two dimensions, which she still disorders with her unstable inflations. Beardsley's precious line is one of the most fluid in art history. This is a Paterian fluidity, streaming across a depth-less surface which shuts up female internality. Once again aestheticism ingeniously escapes the spongy volumes of the chthonian liquid realm. In *The Black Cape*, which illustrates nothing in Wilde's *Salomé* except its sexual hierarchy, the female body is completely eliminated. This lady with her tumescent beehive wig is a vampire bat, a Queen of the Night in strange timeless costume. Is it Swinburne's transhistorical Dolores on a night out? Her complicated, close-fitting dress, with its ziggurat of epaulets and flowing "pancake" train, seems quite capable of taking to the air on its own. Its audacity of form is gender-concealing. A man could wear this dress to equal effect, for it is a kind of body-mask. There is a covert transvestism in Beardsley's striking designs. The goddess of the *Venus and Tannhäuser* frontispiece lacks breasts. Her elegant strapless gown reveals her shoulders, slightly too wide for a woman. Like Botticelli's Flora, this may be a youth cross-dressing for a masquerade ball.

Transvestism is far more common among men, I noted, because it originates in the primary relation of mother and son. Before the recent shift in sex roles, it was a female hierarch in female dress who lingered at the end of the mental tunnel of every child. *A Child at Its Mother's Bed* may be the only pathetic thing in coolly cynical Beardsley. Dressed as a clown, the boy with a cloud of Blakean white hair approaches his sleeping mother, who has one of Beardsley's malformed female faces—smudged eyes, double chin, a boxer's broken nose. This boudoir is the shrine of a mother goddess, its altar visible in the background: a long mirror flanked by two tall church candles on vanity tables. Is this Beardsley's version of the prayerful devotion of Thackeray's young son to supercilious Becky Sharp? Beardsley's pale child, a portrait of the artist, is small, flat, and weightless. But the mother, with her black carapace of heavy hair, is a node of suppurating materiality. Nowhere is it more evident that Beardsley's flat graphic style is a purgation of oppressive female volumes.

Beardsley's view of breasts as aggressive arms of war is part of his critique of the eternal megalomania of female power. We recall the shield-point nipples of Baudelaire's virago or the nipples changed to piercing vampire eyes on Shelley's future wife. Beardsley uses the many-breasted Ephesian Artemis, borrowed from Moreau, to symbolize the animalism of procreative woman. His ambivalence toward the mother is obvious in his Swinburnian Madonnas. The seductive Virgin of *The Ascension of St. Rose of Lima* is no alma mater (fig. 45). Her spiked Spanish Baroque crown makes her bristle like a black cat. Her

45. Aubrey Beardsley, *The Ascension of St. Rose of Lima.*

46. Aubrey Beardsley, *Portrait of Himself*, from *The Yellow Book*, Volume 3.

obscene gesture, propositioning nuzzling St. Rose, comes from Leonardo. The eagerly consensual saint is a lesbian Ganymede. The white innocent is swept toward heaven by the Virgin's great black cape, billowing voraciously in the wind. Beardsley repeats the pattern on terra firma in *A Christmas Card*: a Black Madonna, sporting her informal at-home spiked crown, dandles a white infant on her lap. The whole picture is nightmarishly black, from the imprisoning forest, in which Botticelli's pines suffer a population explosion, to the Virgin's funereal robe, an ermine-bordered black-velvet tapestry with silver-filigree flowers. The drowning white child is a frail Persephone in the bowels of hell.

Now we can interpret Beardsley's curious self-portrait, from *The Yellow Book*, of himself in bed (fig. 46). I see it as a sophisticated abstract version of his Madonna pictures. A boy in an invalid's white turban peers over the edge of his coverlet. He is swallowed up in a towering black canopy scattered with embroidered roses. The design is surely from Piero della Francesca's *Dream of Constantine*, where the emperor sleeps in his field tent, a white fez on his head. Woman's only overt appearance in Beardsley's picture is as a slatternly animal-hoofed caryatid on the bedpost. But the tent housing the boy-artist is the black body of maternal nature, adorned with decapitated blossoms and bound with tasseled umbilical ropes. This is Beardsley's descent into the maelstrom, the womb of archaic night. Man, infantilized, is entombed in mother nature's bower, the ultimate Decadent closure. Nature gives and nature takes away, letting her curtain fall upon her tubercular son.

20

The Beautiful Boy as Destroyer

Wilde's *The Picture of Dorian Gray*

Oscar Wilde, a master of mass media, projected himself internationally as the ultimate aesthete. He synthesizes a half century of French and English Decadent Late Romanticism and joins it to the great tradition of English comedy. Wilde criticism is cautious and oddly solemn. One reason is that a male academic specializing in Wilde still risks being judged both queer and frivolous. Thus critics drift toward apologia, tediously extolling Wilde's humanity or morality, things utterly nonexistent in his best work. The time is past when it was necessary to defend a homosexual genius. As an advocate of aestheticism and Decadence, I feel no need to disguise Wilde's cruelty and immoralism.

Wilde is an Apollonian conceptualizer in the line we have followed from Egypt and Greece through Botticelli and Spenser to Blake, Gautier, and Rossetti. In him we see that brilliant fusion of the aggressive western eye with aristocratic hierarchism, created by the Old Kingdom Pharaohs. Wilde was not a liberal, as his modern admirers think. He was a cold Late Romantic elitist, in the Baudelairean manner. Arrogantly turning life into public theater, Wilde became drama's ancient ritual scapegoat. Apollonianism is objectification, a radical pagan materialism. Wilde uncannily, compulsively literalized or materialized his own ideas, bringing about his spectacular tragic fall.

Wilde's two supreme works, a novel and a play, are energized by the western dynamic of competitive sexual personae. *The Picture of Dorian Gray* (1890–91) is the fullest study of the Decadent erotic principle: the transformation of person into objet d'art. Wilde shows the strange symbiosis between a beautiful boy and a painting, that is, between a charismatic androgyne and his portrait. I noted that the artist's hierarchic submission to a glamourous personality is characteristically western, as illustrated by Dante and Beatrice, Petrarch and Laura, Shelley and Emilia Viviani. In Wilde, as in Baudelaire and Rossetti, the relation is a Decadent ritual of sadomasochistic enslavement. The artist Basil Hallward is "dominated" by Dorian Gray. But Dorian himself is to be dominated by his own entrancing mirror-image, the art work recording Basil's imaginative submission.

Dorian Gray opens with a perceptual pyramid, like the public unveiling of Cellini's *Perseus*. Basil and Lord Henry Wotton sit looking up at "the full-length portrait of a young man of extraordinary personal beauty."[1] This triangulated scene dramatizes the new nineteenth-century authority of art, with its coterie audience. Romanticism freed art from society and Christianity; photography freed it from realism. By the late nineteenth century, the art work was more separate and elevated than it had ever been. The picture of Dorian Gray stands alone in its hierarchic command. It is imperious as a Byzantine icon but divorced from any collective value system. Wilde's painting, beginning in a position of spiritual preeminence, actually increases in power as the novel goes on. We see the art work steadily escaping into independent mastery. What Gautier undertakes as an amusing fantasy in *The Mummy's Foot*, with its rude, refractory object-life, becomes Wilde's nightmare vision of matter avenging itself on imagination. Basil's painting, like Balzac's boudoir a masterpiece of civilized artifice, will generate the most savage barbarities. The artist himself will be butchered at its feet, his body dismembered and dissolved in acid.

Wilde systematically charts the painting's ritual sequestration. Basil refuses to exhibit it. Dorian accepts it as a gift but, as it starts to change, conceals it behind a screen, then a drapery, and finally in a locked attic room. The painting becomes holier and holier as it becomes more and more daemonic. The novel proceeds by a daemonization of the Apollonian, my principle of Decadent art. The painting is the precious monstrance of a cult of the beautiful boy, modelled on pagan prototypes. Wilde compares Dorian to Adonis, Narcissus, Paris, Antinous. With his "crisp gold hair" and Greek name, Wilde's hero represents the Aryan absolutism of the Dorian invaders, whose blondeness I found in Spenser's Amazons. He belongs to the Billy Budd category of ephebic androgyne, retaining the adolescent bloom into adulthood. Dorian is half-feminine, with "finely-curved scarlet lips" and a "delicate bloom and loveliness." He has a "rose-red youth" and "rose-white boyhood," like a fairy-tale maiden. Lord Henry tells him, "You really must not allow yourself to become sunburnt. It would be unbecoming"—as if Dorian were Scarlett O'Hara forgetting her parasol. Images of flowers support

Dorian's identification with Adonis. The novel opens with "the rich odour of roses," followed by a hypnotic Paterian description of a blooming garden.[2] I suspect *Monsieur Vénus* is a source of *Dorian Gray:* Wilde introduces his Adonis as Rachilde does hers, as a beautiful youth shut up in an urban bower of roses.

I said of Greek art that the narcissistic beautiful boy is emotionally undeveloped and self-contained to the point of autism. His senses are solipsistically sealed. It is the apprehender, the aggressive eye, who brings him into existence. Dorian Gray is unconscious of his beauty, even while it is being painted. Lord Henry, the serpent in the garden, infects him with self-consciousness. *Dorian Gray* is unique in permitting the beautiful boy to develop an inner life, which is immediately deflected onto his copy. The novel's major premise is Dorian's repudiation of the Christian inner world for the pagan outer world. By a ritual of riddance, he detaches himself from his postclassical soul and projects it onto his portrait. The ancient beautiful boy remained beautiful by dying young. Dorian is the first beautiful boy with a will of his own. He rejects his archetypal fate. He envies and usurps the formal permanence of a work of art. But the beautiful boy, or the girl who is a beautiful boy, is already a work of art and can remain at this stage of adolescent glamour only at the price of perversion, decadence, and mummification. The novel's last lines bring this mummy literally before us: Dorian's "withered, wrinkled" corpse sprawling under the painting. As a sexual persona, the beautiful boy, by his blonde transparency, tries to purge the female murkiness of chthonian nature. But in Wilde's denouement of Decadent closure, Dorian, entombed in a chamber so tightly sealed that his rescuers must break through the windows, is the material world shrunken to Spenserian deformity. A hideous heap, he is identified only by his rings, as if he were charred in a holocaust. As in Poe's *Masque of the Red Death* and Huysmans' *A Rebours*, nature surges back into the palace of art. *Dorian Gray* begins and ends in a Spenserian bower. And here, as in *The Faerie Queene*, we see master and slave, vampire and victim: the beautiful witch Acrasia "hanging" over a drowsy youth has become Wilde's perfect painting hanging victorious over its dead double.

Lord Henry, following Gautier and Pater, asserts the Decadent principle of person as objet d'art: "Now and then a complex personality took the place and assumed the office of art; was indeed, in its way, a real work of art, Life having its elaborate masterpieces, just as poetry has, or sculpture, or painting." Since art works, as objects, are removed from the realm of choice and act, the person as art work is outside the law.

Dorian makes a career of ruining others. The beautiful boy's moral obliviousness is shown by his dreamily casting his eyes downward, as in the Antinous sculptures and Donatello's *David*. The beautiful boy's cruelty appears in the Sibyl Vane episode, where Dorian courts and brutally spurns a young actress, causing her suicide. Like Alcibiades turning on Athens, he is merely following the destiny of type. I said the beautiful boy straying into the social world is a destroyer, serene in his Apollonian indifference to the suffering of others. Wilde later called the "terrible moral" of the ending "an artistic error," "the only error in the book."[3] This is like Coleridge regretting the tidy moral finale of *The Ancient Mariner*. In Decadent Late Romantic terms, Dorian has a perfect right to his cruelty, through the Nietzschean privilege conferred by beauty. Lord Henry calls beauty "a form of Genius," one of "the great facts of the world, like sunlight": "It cannot be questioned. It has its divine right of sovereignty. It makes princes of those who have it."[4] Beauty, appealing to the pagan eye, is Apollonian hierarchy, Greek divinity.

Dorian Gray makes complicated use of the western idea of hierarchies. Beautiful persons are *aristoi*, "the best." They are Dostoyevsky's "extraordinary men," who have the Sadean "right to commit any crime."[5] The ugly belong to a lower order of being. Gautier's D'Albert, we saw, avoids old people, since it is "torture" to see "ugly things or ugly persons."[6] Wilde said in conversation, "I consider ugliness a kind of malady, and illness and suffering always inspire me with revulsion."[7] In prison, he retreated from this anti-Christian position. But Wilde became humane only when he was already ruined as an artist and thinker. Decadent aestheticism is a visionary idealism, asserting the primacy of beauty over all modes of experience. Wilde was one of the last theorists before modernism to insist on the inseparability of art and beauty. Modernist art, with its distortions and dissonances, adopted Gautier's idea of the autonomy of art but left his worship of beauty behind. Since World War I, only homosexual aesthetes have carried on the Gautier-Wilde philosophy, applying it to antiques, opera, and movies. The witty persona Wilde bequeathed to modern homosexuals contains, like a box of ready-to-assemble furniture, the whole frame of reference of Decadent connoisseurship.

Beauty is intemperate in its exclusiveness, leading the devotee into astounding utterances. For example, Wilde says, "If the poor only had profiles there would be no difficulty in solving the problem of poverty."[8] This is Wilde's true Apollonian voice, callous and definitive. Does he mean that the squalor of the poor is an emanation of their lack of

physical beauty? Is beauty spiritually transformative? Or would it simply enable the poor to survive by soliciting or posing for paintings? To
base value on profiles is a class arrogance bordering on racism. Wilde's
defense would be, as he says in *The Critic as Artist*, "Aesthetics are
higher than ethics."[9] Higher than: the aesthete, a Paterian discrimina-
tor of things, persons, and moments, is a conceptualizing hierarchist.

Another example of Wilde's amoral aesthetics: in *The Decay of Lying*,
his spokesman calls Japan "a pure invention" and the Japanese people
"simply a mode of style, an exquisite fancy of art."[10] As in Gautier and
Pater, art structures our perception of the world. Wilde contemplates
the Japanese from the far distance with his coldly formalist eye. Lord
Henry's wife declares, "You have never been to any of my parties, have
you, Mr. Gray? You must come. I can't afford orchids, but I spare no
expense in foreigners. They make one's rooms look so picturesque."[11]
Aliens as interior décor. In the Sixties, Andy Warhol "rented" members
of his decadent underground for display at chic Manhattan parties. The
poet Gerard Malanga, sexily bare-chested and sporting glossy red-
leather pants, was photographed hung like a painting on the wall, a
strap round his waist. In a letter from Paris after his release from prison,
Wilde describes a theater outing with his lover, Lord Alfred Douglas:
"Bosie was seated next a *German* who exhaled in strange gusts the most
extraordinary odours, some of them racial (it is smell that differentiates
races)."[12] I notice that the Wildean-style homosexual still speaks of race
and class with the same breezy daring. Oppressed groups tend to oppress other subgroups. But lesbians do not talk this way. On the contrary, lesbians, in my experience, are relentlessly populist—possibly a
function of their repressed maternalism. Male homosexuals have an
instinct for hierarchy unparalleled in contemporary culture, outside of
Roman Catholicism. Hierarchism explains their cult of the Hollywood
star, in whom so many are dazzlingly learned.

Hierarchy, the secret subject of *Dorian Gray*, comes from Wilde's
Apollonian vocation as a poet of the visible. He said, "Like Gautier I
have always been one of those *pour qui le monde visible existe*."[13] A
hierarch by virtue of his beauty, Dorian is himself subject to Lord
Henry's "influence." Henry follows Balzac's master criminal Vautrin in
subduing a glamourous ephebe to his will. He begins the first internalization of a beautiful boy by invading his Apollonian autonomy with
words, to which Apollonian androgynes are resistant. Like Wilde himself, Henry cites and misinterprets Pater, twisting Pater's monastic contemplativeness toward praxis: "The only way to get rid of a temptation is
to yield to it. . . . A new Hedonism—that is what our century wants."

Pater snobbishly complained, "I wish they would not call me a hedonist. It gives such a wrong impression to those who do not know Greek." Pater espoused perceptual refinement, not sexual action. Wilde's ruin was to come from his materialization of his master's doctrine. The effect on Dorian of Lord Henry's long monologue is immediate: " 'Stop!' faltered Dorian Gray, 'stop! you bewilder me.' " He calls both "music" and "words" troubling, "terrible." Since words and music are Dionysian phenomena, Dorian experiences them as foreign intrusions. Words mar the Apollonian androgyne's glacial unity with internality. Henry's flattery makes Dorian mentally part from himself for the first time: "The sense of his own beauty came on him like a revelation. He had never felt it before." This self-division produces his Faustian compact: he sees his portrait from the new distance enabling him to see himself. "I would give my soul" for the picture to grow old and he remain young.[14] Dorian gives away what, as an Apollonian beautiful boy, he never had until a moment ago.

Lord Henry's practice on Dorian is subliminally sexual. Mulling over his evening with Dorian, he echoes but revises Pater's great sentence from the "Conclusion" to *The Renaissance:*

> And how charming he had been at dinner the night before, as, with startled eyes and lips parted in frightened pleasure, he had sat opposite to him at the club, the red candleshades staining to a richer rose the wakening wonder of his face. Talking to him was like playing upon an exquisite violin. He answered to every touch and thrill of the bow. . . . There was something terribly enthralling in the exercise of influence. No other activity was like it. To project one's soul into some gracious form, and let it tarry there for a moment; to hear one's own intellectual views echoed back to one with all the added music of passion and youth; to convey one's temperament into another as though it were a subtle fluid or a strange perfume; there was a real joy in that. . . . Yes; he would try to be to Dorian Gray what, without knowing it, the lad was to the painter who had fashioned the wonderful portrait. He would seek to dominate him—had already, indeed, half done so.[15]

Pater's list of beautiful things, ending with "the face of one's friend," is homoerotically intensified. We are no longer in the cloistered university but out on the town, in fashionable London society. Pater's passive, prayerful perception becomes hierarchic aggression, mental intercourse. The pale oval of the friend's face reddens with an indecorous sexual flush. In this candlelit moment of public intimacy, Wilde creates a male boudoir or bower. Lord Henry plays upon Dorian, lips girlishly parted, as if he were a stringed instrument, to which Europe gives hourglass female shapes. Dorian is the last great Romantic wind-harp. Like Anactoria, he is stroked and probed by amoral words. But while Swinburne's Sappho speaks for stormy nature, Lord Henry makes a Late Romantic chamber music. Dorian is an acquisition of Decadent connoisseurship, suavely inspected like a jewel held up to the light. Lord Henry, like the aristocratic seducer of *Les Liaisons dangereuses*, takes mentalized sex-pleasure in deflowering Dorian's rosy innocence. In this classic moment of Decadent eroticism, an aesthetic distance, as usual, is preserved between personae, a charged space crossed by the libidinous eye. Henry projects his "temperament" (Pater's word) into Dorian as if it were "a subtle fluid or a strange perfume" (Pater again). Late Romantic consciousness is the seminal agent, a mobile, insinuating, ghostly vapor. Henry's mind-control is prefigured by Seraphita's electromagnetic domination of her admirer in Balzac.

Lord Henry experiments with a male vampirism, transplanting his temperament into Dorian, who is possessed by him in both the sexual and daemonic sense. Basil is increasingly dismayed by Dorian's adoption of Henry's cynicism, style, and sophisticated epigrams. The Apollonian androgyne has no voice of its own; therefore, once its impermeability is breached, it begins to speak with the voice of another. Dorian, like the Delphic oracle, is under the mediumship of a hidden god. In his review of the book, Pater calls the portrait Dorian's "Döppelgänger."[16] I see a second doppelgänger pattern in Henry's relation with his protégé: Dorian *becomes* Lord Henry, the beautiful boy turned Decadent aesthete. The transformation is complete when Wilde attaches the word "languidly" to Dorian, Henry's emblematic epithet from his first appearance.[17] An act of homosexual generation has occurred, a hermaphroditic cloning of sexual personae. Teaching again as an erotic transaction: we see the candlelit courtship, the sexual initiation and insemination, and the Decadent fruition. Dominant Lord Henry spawns the remade Dorian from his cold ivory brow.

Dorian himself dominates Basil, by the artist's own admission. Basil recalls the origin of his subordination, at a crowded London soirée. It resembles the moment of cathexis when Balzac's Sarrasine falls under the spell of the singing castrato.

> I suddenly became conscious that someone was looking at me. I turned halfway round, and saw Dorian Gray for the first time. When our eyes met, I felt that I was growing pale. A curious

sensation of terror came over me. I knew that I had come face to face with someone whose mere personality was so fascinating that, if I allowed it to do so, it would absorb my whole nature, my whole soul, my very art itself.

Homosexuals, now as then, recognize each other by a mysterious hard meeting of the eyes, a trope of western aggression. The source of this passage is in Plato's *Phaedrus*. Basil's paleness and terror are the "shudder," "awe," and "fever and perspiration" afflicting the philosopher who encounters a human embodiment of "true beauty": "Beholding it, he reverences it as he would a god."[18] Homoerotic Platonism is overt in Basil's later confession:

> Dorian, from the moment I met you, your personality had the most extraordinary influence over me. I was dominated, soul, brain, and power by you. You became to me the visible incarnation of that unseen ideal whose memory haunts us artists like an exquisite dream. I worshipped you. . . . I hardly understood it myself. I only knew that I had seen perfection face to face.[19]

Ordinary sexual desire is not the issue. Greek idealism is a glorification of the eye, not a glut of the senses. Apollo lives by day, Dionysus by night. Basil seeks not to sleep with Dorian but to paint his picture. The portrait is not sublimation but conceptual perfection. Painting, an iconic Apollonian mode, preserves Dorian's hierarchic command and the aesthetic distance symbolizing the Late Romantic's contemplative submission to the eroticized object. Subordination to the person as objet d'art explains the androgyny of all aesthetes. Such subordination is intolerable, we saw, to Swinburne's masculine Sappho, whose admiration of Anactoria's beauty escalates into sadism.

Basil and Dorian's first meeting also invokes one of the primary Romantic principles, vampirism. In the middle of a party, Basil senses someone looking at him. Dorian's gaze is palpable, like the one Gautier's Queen Nyssia tries to wash from her body. It has an eerie extrasensory effect on Basil, because it is an expression of sudden hierarchic assertion, casually exercised by an agent still unconscious of his powers. When their eyes meet, Basil feels Dorian is "so fascinating" as to "absorb" him. At this moment of visual fixation, Dorian, like a vampire, dominates the plane of eye-contact. Basil, mesmerized, actually grows "pale," like the vampire's bled victim. But Wilde gives the daemonic an Apollonian setting. Basil somehow grasps Dorian's "personality" without a word being spoken. He only sees Dorian; he does not hear him.

There is an unpleasant intensification of ambient sound in the room. Enlightened consciousness flows into the visual. Basil's revelation occurs in a temenos of muteness, into which noise can pierce only by becoming more grating. We witness one of English literature's great Apollonian epiphanies. The Apollonian is a mode of silence: Dorian's personality, like Belphoebe's at her glittering entrance into *The Faerie Queene*, is conveyed by entirely physical, visual means. This is a representational law of pagan sexual personae.

Wilde calls Basil's painting a "portrait of a young man of extraordinary personal beauty." Personal: what other kind of human beauty could there be? This homoerotic locution means Dorian has beauty of personality, but not personality as normally understood. At his first trial, Wilde sparred with his cross-examiner, who read aloud from Basil's confession to Dorian:

> *Edward Carson:* Do you mean to say that that passage describes the natural feeling of one man towards another?
> *Wilde:* It would be the influence produced by a beautiful personality.
> *Carson:* A beautiful person?
> *Wilde:* I said "a beautiful personality." You can describe it as you like. Dorian Gray's was a most remarkable personality.[20]

Carson's formulation, "a beautiful person," has a moral inflection that Wilde is quick to correct. His own phrase, "a beautiful personality," is morally indifferent. For Wilde, personality is a fact, a given. It is not character, shaped by education or ethics. Personality for him is immanent, belonging to a preordained rank in the great chain of being of authority and glamour. It is a visual construct. I spoke of the externality and theatricality of the Greco-Roman persona, a public projection, metaphorically visual. Wilde, the most self-dramatizing of English writers, makes this metaphor literal. Joining Greek idealism to Late Romantic connoisseurship, he imagines personality as a radiant icon of Apollonian materiality, the godlike summation of the visible world.

Personality is central to Wilde's literary theory, where it is the measure of both artist and critic. He says: "It is only by intensifying his own personality that the critic can interpret the personality and work of others. . . . As art springs from personality, so it is only to personality that it can be revealed."[21] The idea comes from Pater. But there is a great difference between Pater's "temperament" and Wilde's "personality": the first is misty and receptive, the second hard and dominant. *The Importance of Being Earnest* is a spectacle of this hardness of

Wildean personality. *Dorian Gray* makes personality hierarchic in the Greek way, but it also promotes a Romantic view of the mystery of sex and power. Only Coleridge's *Christabel* surpasses *Dorian Gray* as an analysis of the occult operations of fascination.

No word appears more often in *Dorian Gray* than "fascinating." It refers to a person, an experience, a drug, a book (*A Rebours*, by which Dorian is "poisoned"). The fascination theme belongs to the novel's romance of hierarchy. An unanswered question of history is how one individual can control masses of people. Freud speaks of the "fascination" of very beautiful, narcissistic women: narcissism has "a great attraction" for others because of that "self-sufficiency and inaccessibility" shared by children and cats.[22] Narcissistic politicians induce the investment of mass emotion by a process of fascination.

I compared the charisma of Lord Byron and Elvis Presley to that of the opportunistic first Duke of Buckingham. Max Weber sees charisma as "an extraordinary, supernatural, divine power" that must be manifested by a warlord in heroic deeds or by a prophet in miracles.[23] I question this definition insofar as it makes charisma dependent upon acts or external effects. Early Christianity first uses the Greek word *charisma* ("gift, favor, grace") for the gift of healing or speaking in tongues. But I view charisma as completely pre-Christian. Athena gives charisma to Achilles when she sheds "a golden mist around his head" and makes his body emit "a blaze of light." She gives charisma to Odysseus on Phaeacia: he becomes "taller and sturdier"; his hair thickens like "the hyacinth in bloom"; he is "radiant with comeliness and grace."[24] Xenophon says the beauty of a victorious athlete, like "the sudden glow of a light at night," "compelled everyone to look at him": "Beauty is in its essence something regal."[25] Charisma in classical antiquity meant exactly what it does in the pagan mass media: glamour, a Scottish word signifying, as Kenneth Burke points out, a magic "haze in the air" around persons or things.[26] Charisma is the numinous aura around a narcissistic personality. It flows outward from a simplicity or unity of being and a composure and controlled vitality. There is gracious accommodation, yet commanding impersonality. Charisma is the radiance produced by the interaction of male and female elements in a gifted personality. The charismatic woman has a masculine force and severity. The charismatic man has an entrancing female beauty. Both are hot and cold, glowing with presexual self-love.

Wilde gives Dorian Gray pure charisma. Dorian is a natural hierarch who dominates by his "fascinating" beauty, drawing both sexes toward him and paralyzing the moral will. The narcissism of this beautiful boy has disastrous consequences: suicide, murder, vice. Dorian excites a mesmeric followership among his well-born companions, but one directed toward no public aim, not even tyranny. Basil demands:

> Why is your friendship so fatal to young men? . . . You have filled them with a madness for pleasure. They have gone down into the depths. You led them there. Yes: you led them there, and yet you can smile, as you are smiling now. . . . They say that you corrupt everyone with whom you become intimate, and that it is quite sufficient for you to enter a house, for shame of some kind to follow after.

Seduction literally means "leading astray." Paterian influence has become entrancement and compulsion. Dorian daemonizes his followers, deconstructing the social order. He is a Late Romantic rather than Renaissance androgyne, bound by the public good. As a homosexual Alcibiades, Dorian frustrates dynastic continuity. He is ostracized by the elder archons, who formally demonstrate their displeasure by leaving the room of a club whenever Dorian enters it. He creates a seditious heterocosm within society, a colony of pagan idolatry. Wilde says of one of Dorian's ill-fated admirers, "To him, as to many others, Dorian Gray was the type of everything that is wonderful and fascinating in life."[27] Extreme male beauty, like a siren song, lures toward destruction.

Dorian effects these multiple cathexes by pagan magic. In the London netherworld, he is called "Prince Charming," a cliché we are meant to hear in its oldest occult sense. Hierarch as sorcerer, Dorian has a "strange and dangerous charm." He enchants not by words but by visible charisma. Mr. Hubbard, the "celebrated frame-maker," comes instantly at his bidding: "As a rule, he never left his shop. He waited for people to come to him. But he always made an exception in favour of Dorian Gray. There was something about Dorian that charmed everybody. It was a pleasure even to see him." The young shop assistant reacts similarly: "[He] glanced back at Dorian with a look of shy wonder in his rough, uncomely face. He had never seen anyone so marvellous." Like the star of film or popular music, Dorian draws heterosexuals into bisexual responses. Depressed, he wanders into Covent Garden: "A white-smocked carter offered him some cherries. He thanked him, and wondered why he refused to accept any money for them, and began to eat them listlessly."[28] The man makes a mute pagan offering to Dorian's remarkable beauty, stirred by an emotion he could not explain.

Dorian is attractive, in the original meaning of the word. He aligns the imagination of others toward himself by inborn magnetic power.

Wilde told a fable to Richard Le Gallienne, ostensibly about the problem of free will, in which a magnet infiltrates the consciousness of a group of talkative steel filings, who are mysteriously swept toward it. Wilde often speaks of the "attraction" of personality. For example: "Wickedness is a myth invented by good people to account for the curious attractiveness of others." He means that the good are ruled by abstract systems, ethical and social, while the not-good are ruled by personality alone, their "intensification of personality," as he puts it elsewhere, generating a seductive glamour.[29] This is clear in the original script of *The Importance of Being Earnest:*

> *Miss Prism.* I highly disapprove of Mr. Ernest Worthing. He is a
> thoroughly bad young man.
> *Cecily.* I fear he must be. It is the only explanation I can find of
> his strange attractiveness.[30]

Elsewhere Wilde remarks: "All charming people are spoiled. It is the secret of their attraction."[31] They are spoiled because their altar is heaped with spoils, the gifts of the multitude. Divine charisma separates the hierarch from communality by a zone of privilege. Lord Henry says of Dorian: "I never interfere with what charming people do. If a personality fascinates me, whatever mode of expression that personality selects is absolutely delightful to me." The narcissistic personality, like the psychotic, lives by its own laws. As Basil murmurs uneasily, "Dorian's whims are laws to everybody, except himself."[32]

The Picture of Dorian Gray departs from its Greek sources in this perilous pattern of Late Romantic fascination. Submission to the beautiful personality leads to degradation and death. In Plato's and Shelley's hierarchic relationships, there is no sadomasochistic pleasure in suffering. On the contrary, the imagination is exalted, perfecting and purifying itself in Apollonian contemplation. Remember the speed with which Shelley dumped Emilia Viviani when she no longer served his artistic purposes. In Decadent Late Romanticism, however, eroticism is terminally obsessive. Basil, admitting to Dorian, "I worshipped you too much," is slain before his masterpiece, the symbol of his Decadent enslavement.[33] *Dorian Gray* is also Late Romantic in having a male rather than female fascinator. Since the beautiful boy is anti-chthonian and since aestheticism is predicated on a swerve from nature, the female impinges only weakly on the emotional world of Wilde's novel. No goddess loves this Adonis. Sibyl Vane is a sentimental, ill-drawn caricature. My principle of psychoiconicism: feminine Sibyl and her mother, like *Christabel*'s Sir Leoline, lose their fictive energy to the dominant androgyne. Wilde's writing, like Pater's, has but one cruel chthonian woman, Salomé. *Dorian Gray* is governed by triumvir. The three male leads tolerate the feminine only as a component of their own hermaphroditism.

One frequently encounters the misperception that Dorian Gray was modelled on Wilde's lover, the boyishly handsome Lord Alfred Douglas. But Wilde did not meet Douglas until after *The Picture of Dorian Gray* was published. Dorian was conceived a priori. He is the beautiful boy of antiquity given complex modern form. Wilde writes to Douglas of "the soul of the artist who found his ideal in you, of the lover of beauty to whom you appeared as being flawless and perfect."[34] Therefore Wilde's first encounter with Douglas after the release of *Dorian Gray* was a Platonic fulfillment, exactly like Shelley's with Emilia Viviani, stunning incarnation of the Hermaphrodite of his just-completed *Witch of Atlas*. But Shelley wrote a greater poem afterward, *Epipsychidion*, for there were *no sexual relations* between himself and his self-foretold hermaphrodite deity. Wilde, forgetting the abstinence of Socrates with Alcibiades, made the fatal error of copulating with his representational ideal. Byron's crazed Manfred leaps into the same demeaning literalization. In *Dorian Gray*, Wilde correctly portrays the beautiful boy as a destroyer. Douglas drew Wilde into Late Romantic infatuation and fascination, disordering his mature judgment and ending his career at the height of his fame and artistic power. Wilde later wrote to him, "The basis of character is will-power, and my will-power became absolutely subject to yours."[35] Douglas childishly goaded Wilde to file an ill-advised lawsuit for libel against his father, the Marquess of Queensberry, first of a rapid series of events leading to Wilde's conviction and imprisonment for homosexuality, from which he never recovered. He died prematurely three years later, at forty-six. Wilde was already guilty of a sensual materialization of Paterian doctrine in Lord Henry's swerve from contemplative to active. His affair with Douglas was the gravest of his materializations, for which he was forced to undergo in painful, public reality that apocalypse prophesied for half a century by Late Romantic catastrophe theory. Wilde's fall in 1895 ended aestheticism and Decadence.

The beautiful boy is never deeply moved by the disasters he brings on his admirers, since he is scarcely aware of anything outside himself. His ruthlessness is an Apollonian *apatheia*, Stoic emotionlessness. In a long, bitter letter to Douglas from prison, later expurgated and synopsized as *De Profundis*, Wilde dismisses as preposterous the charge that he was a bad influence on an impressionable youth. He asks: "What was there, as a mere matter of fact, in you that I could influence? Your brain? It was undeveloped. Your imagination? It was dead. Your heart? It was not yet born."[36] Why, it might be asked, was Wilde ever drawn to so contemptible a man? The true aesthete is always a lover of narcissistic beauty. Wilde's list of Douglas' defects is neither strident nor rhetorical. It is absolutely consistent with the long western history of the beautiful boy, who is a thing, an objet d'art. Wilde, seething in prison, has simply switched perspective on the same unchanging fact.

After Basil's confession of adoration, Dorian Gray drifts into thought, wondering "if he himself would ever be so dominated by the personality of a friend": "Would there ever be someone who would fill him with a strange idolatry?" As the oblivious beautiful boy, he can fall in love with no one—except himself. What fills him with "a strange idolatry" is his own mirror-image. Dorian falls into erotic subordination to Basil's painting. Seeing it finished, he declares, "I am in love with it." The autoeroticism is blatant: he later kisses the "painted lips," like Narcissus "almost enamoured of it." As the painting degenerates, "He grew more and more enamoured of his own beauty."[37] The picture of Dorian Gray is the fetish of a Romantic cult of self-love.

Magic pictures are a traditional romance motif. In Poe's *The Oval Portrait*, an artist's paint drains the vitality of his bride, who dies the instant her portrait is completed. But never is there the fanatical intensity of connection Dorian has with his portrait. High Romantic harmony of man and nature has become Late Romantic enslavement of man by art work. The picture of Dorian Gray resembles *Snow White*'s magic mirror, which the witch-queen, like Dorian, constantly consults. Dorian in fact calls the painting "the most magical of mirrors." But *Snow White*'s mirror has a personality quite distinct from that of its owner, to whom it makes bold and unpleasing remarks. There is a "horrible sympathy" between Dorian and his portrait, "atom calling to atom in secret love of strange affinity."[38] Man and painting are bound by Dorian's self-divinizing autoeroticism. The phrase "secret love" is from Blake's "Sick Rose," whose hermaphrodite convolutions Dorian enacts: he stands with a mirror before his painting in the locked room, looking from one face to the other in solitary self-absorption. The three sequestered Dorians recall the triple females of Blake's Crystal Cabinet, complacently self-propagating. The tableau also recalls the dialogue of Byron's effeminate Sardanapalus with his mirror. Elsewhere, Wilde says, "To love oneself is the beginning of a life-long romance."[39] In his secret pagan cult, Dorian is god, priest, and devotee, worshipping at his own graven image.

The iconicism of the art work is far more developed in Wilde than in Poe. The picture of Dorian Gray is an idol, heavy with mana. Relieved at its departure from his studio, Basil remembers "the intolerable fascination of its presence." The painting is a sinister vampire-object, invading the consciousness of its human servants. Basil's premonition that Dorian's personality will vampirically "absorb" him is redramatized in Dorian's relation to his portrait. The picture absorbs Dorian's mental energy to the point of obsession. He cannot stop thinking about it. It interferes even in his pleasures: at his country house, "he would suddenly leave his guests and rush back to town to see that the door had not been tampered with, and that the picture was still there."[40] The portrait literally captivates Dorian, controlling him by a magnetism mimicking his glamourous magnetism over others. Like a jealous parent or lover, it summons him back from the outside world to its airless cell. And Dorian is never tranquil except when there. Between him and his portrait is a ghostly umbilical link, like the incestuous bond between Romantic twins.

Late in the novel, Dorian complains, "My own personality has become a burden to me." He has so intensified his personality in the Wildean manner that he has animated his mirror-image. Now his double, drunk with power, tries to usurp the identity of its human original. The painting feeds on Dorian, until in desperation he murders Basil, a propitiatory blood-sacrifice before an *objet de culte*, from whose bondage he fights to be free. But the painting will be satisfied with no other victim but Dorian. The finale is one of the uncanniest moments in literature. Killing Dorian, the painting achieves its ultimate vampirism, triumphantly regaining "all the wonder of [its] exquisite youth and beauty."[41] The painting finds the elixir of eternal youth by shedding Dorian's blood.

A peculiar mystical act occurs. Dorian stabs the painting but is found with a knife in his heart. One recalls Balzac's Sarrasine, who attacks a living art work only to be slain himself; or Balzac's marquise, who succeeds in her knife assault upon the sequestered precious object because she is a female androgyne of chthonian force. Or Poe's William Wilson, who traps his antagonist in a small room and skewers him, only to find he has murdered his "mirror" likeness and therefore his moral self. How does Dorian's knife end up in his own heart? We do not ordinarily ask naturalistic questions of magical fictions. Dorian's death is simultaneous with the blow he strikes. But if we were to expand that point of time into a cinematic sequence—and Wilde's novel encourages the deformation of time by imagination—I think we would see the portrait standing like a cruel, laughing god, plucking the knife from its body like an arrow caught in midflight, and hurling it back into the heart of its impious assailant. *The Picture of Dorian Gray* ends in a spectacle of perverse animism.

Many admirers have felt *Dorian Gray*'s punitive finale uncharacteristic of Wilde and an evasion of the decadence of the whole. In a letter to the editor defending the book against scandalized reviewers, Wilde says, "Dorian Gray, having led a life of mere sensation and pleasure, tries to kill conscience, and at that moment kills himself." His qualification that this moral is "an artistic error" exempts us from taking him seriously on the question of conscience. But if he believed what he said, the man who wrote that letter did not understand what he had written in *Dorian Gray*. No great work of Romantic imagination has anything to do with conscience. *Dorian Gray* is a web of Romantic fascination, a force field of Apollonian and daemonic charisma, heir to *Christabel* in its dark vision of sex and power. We need no moral axioms to interpret it. Dorian commits certain forbidden acts and is punished for them. But he operates under ritual rather than ethical proscriptions. The Bible, for example, begins the human story by granting access to all trees of Eden but *one*. The mystery of divine law appears throughout the world in arbitrary rituals of prohibition or avoidance. By his hubristic defiance of time, Dorian wanders into an infrahuman realm where he is at the mercy of pitiless daemonic agents. He is *devoted* to his portrait: I use the word as in classical Latin, where "devotus" means bewitched, enchanted, cursed, consecrated, dedicated to divine service, and *marked for slaughter*. *Dorian Gray* is about not morality but taboo. The ending shows not the victory of conscience but the destruction of person by art work. Dorian says: "There is something fatal about a portrait. It has a life of its own."[42] The painting, like all hierarchs, makes its own laws and subordinates reality to its will. Pater speaks of "the fatality which seems to haunt any signal beauty, whether moral or physical, as if it were in itself something illicit and isolating."[43] *Dorian Gray* is about the amorality of beauty and the fascism of the western objet d'art. It is about the magic of art in the magic of person.

Dorian Gray is like the ritual scapegoat of Aztec festival. Frazer says a young man, chosen for "his personal beauty," served as the double of the god Tezcatlipoca. For a year, the youth was "apparelled in gorgeous attire" and "trained to comport himself like a gentleman of the first quality, to speak correctly and elegantly, to play the flute, to smoke cigars and to snuff at flowers with a dandified air." When he walked through the city, people flocked to see and honor him. At the end of his time, "this bejewelled exquisite" was butchered on the temple steps, his breast sliced open and his heart torn out.[44] Dorian Gray, in "the wanton luxury and gorgeous splendour of his mode of life," is also a dandy, a connoisseur, a man of leisure smoking Lord Henry's cigarettes, a charismatic beauty attracting attention and veneration in the streets.[45] Like the Aztec scapegoat, he is privileged but doomed, destined for execution at the feet of an idol, his heart pierced by a knife. The painting is his divine double, the god who allows him to live like a prince but, thirsting for blood, demands his sacrifice.

Another anthropological parallel: the picture of Dorian Gray is like Meleager's brand in that a man's life term resides in an enchanted object. I examined Swinburne's play on this subject. In Wilde's version, there is no longer a nature-identified female custodian of the precious relic, since the novel's women are few and puny. The ancient Meleager legend belongs to a complex of primitive beliefs about the soul. Frazer says the savage thinks of life as "a concrete material thing of a definite bulk, capable of being seen and handled, kept in a box or jar, and liable to be bruised, fractured, or smashed in pieces." This entity can be removed from a man's body yet "still continue to animate him by virtue of a sort of sympathy or action at a distance." If it is destroyed, he dies. Totemistic cultures believe in "the possibility of permanently depositing the soul in some external object—animal, plant, or what not—, . . . just as people deposit their money with a banker rather than carry it on their persons."[46] In *Dorian Gray*, Romanticism's tidal dynamic of regression makes art revert to primitivism. Aestheticism concretizes the invisible world, allowing Dorian to deposit his soul in an external object, which affects him, in Frazer's words, by "sympathy or action at a distance." When Dorian tries to destroy it, he dies. In *Dorian Gray*, a malevolent totem lures a sophisticate into an act of savagery, Basil's grisly murder. The novel supports my definition of decadence as sophistication without humaneness or humanism.

Wilde's assumptions are normally Apollonian. In *The Critic as Artist* he says: "Form is everything. It is the secret of life. . . . Start with the worship of form, and there is no secret in art that will not be revealed to you."[47] Praising Pre-Raphaelite painting, he condemns Impressionism as "mud and blur."[48] He follows Blake in preferring the clarity of the Apollonian incised edge. Even in Monet's studies of flickering light, western painting is Apollonian in its stasis, fixity, and sharp outer borders. What is odd about the picture of Dorian Gray is that it is in Dionysian metamorphosis. The changing painting insults beauty and form: Dorian calls it "the misshapen shadow," "the hideous painted thing," "this monstrous soul-life." Nature and art war for supremacy in it. Painting is invaded by a daemonic form-altering power, because Wilde has tried to make nature surrender her authority. He opens *The Decay of Lying:* "The more we study Art, the less we care for Nature. What Art really reveals to us is Nature's lack of design, her curious crudities, her extraordinary monotony, her absolutely unfinished condition."[49] Wilde has gotten this from Baudelaire via Huysmans. But in assigning a superior value to art, Baudelaire never disguises nature's violent power. And Huysmans' dreaming hero is terrified by primeval nature's choking abundance. In Wilde, however, nature lacks archetypal force. His few nature descriptions are pretty and minor. In *Dorian Gray,* nature, denied entry, seeps into the portrait-double and corrodes it from inside out: "It was from within, apparently, that the foulness and horror had come. Through some strange quickening of inner life the leprosies of sin were slowly eating the thing away. The rotting of a corpse in a watery grave was not so fearful."[50] Internality, liquidity, chthonian murk. Apollonian painting is dissolving and putrefying in Dionysian fluidity.

The locked attic room, Dorian's bower of art, recalls the tower where the incestuous doubles meet in Byron and the turret where the maiden poses for her artist-husband in Poe. The room is also a mausoleum, for it is the dusty playroom of Dorian's boyhood, preserved like Miss Havisham's bridal hall in Dickens. Hence Dorian's portrait is like the *ka* or double of the deceased in Egyptian tombs, heaped with toys and furniture. The horrified discoverers breaking into the chamber are like archaeologists finding the king's mummy thrown on the floor by grave robbers. Becoming a corpse, Dorian reaches his ultimate objectification. As the novel opens, the painting is still incomplete. Basil finishes it as Dorian begins to change, contaminated by Lord Henry. After Sibyl's maltreatment, the painting never stops changing until the end. Dorian has assumed Basil's role as his own portraitist, working on the painting by telekinesis. The painting finally achieves permanent form only with the death of its model, whose beauty it reclaims for itself. Hence *Dorian Gray* is like Woolf's *To the Lighthouse,* which I suspect it influenced, in the way that a painting and a novel are coterminous, developing in tandem, with the last brush strokes applied to the canvas in the last paragraphs.

As a self-portraitist, Dorian is a Neronian life-artist, making perverse autobiography out of the sufferings of others. The first maxim of Wilde's preface to *Dorian Gray,* imitating Gautier's polemical preface, is, "The artist is the creator of beautiful things." But Dorian, who makes life into a work of art, is a creator of ugly things: his hideous self-portrait and then Basil's corpse, a "thing" with a "grotesque misshapen shadow," a "humped back, and long fantastic arms." In artistic style, Dorian is prophetically Expressionist. The brutality of Basil's murder is in deliberate contrast to Dorian's exquisite connoisseurship. It is as if Dorian is overcome by a paroxysm of daemonic force, erupting into the Apollonian world of perfect form. We saw a similar effect in Euripides' *Medea*, where princess and king sink beneath a tarry wave of fire. The morning after the murder, Dorian must reconstruct his Apollonian persona by Paterian rituals of discrimination. He dresses "with even more than his usual care, giving a good deal of attention to the choice of his necktie and scarf-pin, and changing his rings more than once." Selecting Gautier's *Enamels and Cameos*, he admires the binding of "citron-green leather, with a design of gilt trellis-work and dotted pomegranates."[51] Returned from his descent to Hades, the barbaric chthonian realm, Dorian restores himself to normality by focusing on the Apollonian separateness of objects in the aesthete's visible world, numbering them by cognitive palpation.

Wilde constantly talks about "Art," but his actual commentary on the visual arts is sparse and inert. I think that, as a primarily verbal intelligence, he had little feeling for painting. Whistler made some tart remarks about Wilde's trespass into his territory. Wilde's stage directions to *An Ideal Husband* are full of allusions to art, comparing the characters to paintings by Van Dyck, Watteau, Lawrence. There is a chatty superficiality or name-dropping: "Watteau would have loved to paint them."[52] Paintings are being seen vaguely and generically. But Wilde's only novel is a supreme artifact of aestheticism, taking a painting for theme. The most potent art work in all literature belongs to the age of photography, which allowed painting to shift toward the strange and irrational. It is to Wilde's credit that he sensed and exploited this. The objet d'art resumes its archaic religious function. Wilde, without real knowledge of the visual arts, creates a great book about a painting because of his duality of vision: he is Apollonian in his worship of form but Romantic in his instinct for the daemonic. Together, these principles produce the despotic art work of *Dorian Gray*. Nature and art, in their ritual combat in the painting, duel to a draw and separate, leaving the marred beautiful boy as their Late Romantic victim.

21

The English Epicene

Wilde's *The Importance of Being Earnest*

Lord Henry Wotton is the link between Wilde's two best works. With his "languid voice" and "pale, fine-pointed fingers,"[1] he is first of all the Decadent aesthete—Wilde's own pose in real life. He symbolizes the aristocracy toward which the middle-class Wilde, like Balzac, aspired. Wilde admires "the great aristocratic art of doing absolutely nothing"; he declares "cultivated leisure" to be "the aim of man." His target is partly the century's bustling work ethic: "Work is the curse of the drinking classes." But more importantly, he continues the Romantic withdrawal from masculine action: "Action! What is action? It dies at the moment of its energy. . . . It is to do nothing that the elect exist. Action is limited and relative." The elect: pagan predestination. We "become perfect by the rejection of energy."[2] High Romanticism was able to hold androgyny and energy together in one synthesis. Late Romanticism, because of its divorce from nature, makes energy antithetical. Weary Lord Henry, like Wilde, is inconsistent about sensual indulgence, obviously a form of action. The Decadent aesthete is in the ambiguous position of having to be inactive yet also glutted by worldly experience. Sexually, he *has* acted or *will* act, but he must never be *seen* to be acting. It's like the White Queen's rule, "Jam tomorrow and jam yesterday—but never jam today."

Lord Henry, with the four young lovers of *The Importance of Being Earnest*, belongs to a category of sexual personae that I call the androgyne of manners, one of the most western of types. The androgyne of manners inhabits the world of the drawing room and recreates that world wherever it goes, through manner and speech. The salon is an abstract circle where male and female, like mathematical ciphers, are equal and interchangeable. Personality becomes a sexually undifferentiated formal mask. Rousseau says of the eighteenth-century salon, "Every woman at Paris gathers in her apartment a harem of men more womanish than she."[3] The salon is politics by coterie, a city-state or gated forum run on a barter economy of gender exchange.

Elegance, the ruling principle of the salon, dictates that all speech must be wit, in symmetrical pulses of repartee, a malicious stichomythia. Pope complained that Lady Mary Wortley Montagu and the epicene Lord Hervey had "too much wit" for him. He sensed the icy cruelty of the beau monde, to whom moral discourse is alien because it elevates the inner world over the outer. Sartre says of Genet, "Elegance: the quality of conduct which transforms the greatest quantity of being into *appearing*."[4] The salon, like the petrified object-world venerated by the aesthete, is a spectacle of dazzling surfaces. Words, faces, and gestures are exhibited in a blaze of hard glamour. Though he toys with the idea of spiritual hermaphroditism, Pope loathes the androgyne of manners, whom he satirizes as the Amazonian belles and effeminate beaux of *The Rape of the Lock*. The salon is populated by sophisticates of a classical literacy, but its speed of dialogue and worship of the ephemeral inhibit deliberation and reflection, recklessly breaking with the past. Pope might have said, had the word been available, that the salon was too chic. The androgyne of manners—the male feminine in his careless, lounging passivity, the female masculine in her brilliant, aggressive wit—has the profane sleekness of chic.

Before his career abruptly ended, Wilde was moving toward an Art Nouveau aesthetics. Art Nouveau, then at its height of decorative popularity, is a late phase in the history of style, analogous to Italian Mannerism. Kenneth Clark says of Cellini's and Giambologna's streamlined Mannerist figures:

> The goddess of mannerism is the eternal feminine of the fashion plate. A sociologist could no doubt give ready answers why embodiments of elegance should take this somewhat ridiculous shape— feet and hands too fine for honest work, bodies too thin for child-bearing, and heads too small to contain a single thought. But elegant proportions may be found in many objects that are exempt from these materialist explanations—in architecture, pottery, or even handwriting. The human body is not the basis of these rhythms but their victim. Where the sense of chic originates, how it is controlled, by what inner pattern we unfailingly recognize it—all these are questions too large and too subtle for a parenthesis. One thing is certain. Chic is not natural. Congreve's Millamant or

Baudelaire's dandy warn us how hateful, to serious votaries of chic, is everything that is implied by the word "nature."[5]

Smoothness and elongation: the Mannerist figure is a chain of polished ovoids hung on a mannequin's frame. Like Spenser's aristocrats, Lord Henry Wotton, with his "long nervous fingers," is an ectomorph, an undulating ribbon of Mannerist Art Nouveau. The ectomorphic line is a suave vertical, repudiating nature by resisting gravity. But the Mannerist figure, overcome by worldly fatigue, sinks back toward earth in languorous torsion. The androgyne of manners can be seen in effete collapse in Henry Lamb's painting of Lytton Strachey turning his back to a window, his long denatured limbs draped over an armchair like wet noodles. Because of its swift verbal genius, the androgyne of manners is best represented as sleekness and speed. Count Robert de Montesquiou, model for Huysmans' Des Esseintes and Proust's Charlus, was called a "greyhound in evening dress," a perfect phrase for Lord Henry.

Sleekness in a male is usually a hermaphroditic motif. Cinema evokes this theme in its topos of the well-bred English "gentleman," a word that cannot be perfectly translated into any other language. The English gentleman shows the influence of Castiglione's theory of courtesy as late as the eighteenth century. Movies from the Thirties through the Fifties used actors of this kind to illustrate a singular male beauty, witty and polished, uniting sensitivity of response to intense heterosexual glamour: Leslie Howard, Rex Harrison, Cary Grant, Fred Astaire, David Niven, Michael Wilding, George Hamilton. The idiomatic qualities are *smoothness and elongation:* smooth both in manner and appearance, long in ectomorphic height and Nordic cranial contour. I think, for instance, of the astounding narrowness of Cary Grant's shiny black evening pumps in *Indiscreet* (1958). The smoothness and elongation of figure are best shown off by a gleaming tuxedo, signifying a renunciation of masculine hirsutism. The debonair cinematic gentleman is usually prematurely balding, with hair swept back at the temples. His receding hairline is sexually expressive, suggesting hermaphroditic gentility, a grace of intellect and emotion. The flowing hyacinthine hair of the beautiful boy traps the beholder's eye, a portent of future enslavement. But the sleek head of the cinematic gentleman is a promise of candor and courtesy, of eroticism without ambivalence or suffering. Smoothness is always social in meaning: it is nature subdued by the civil made second nature.

In *The Importance of Being Earnest*, the English gentleman, in whom the masculine has been moderated by courtesy, may be seen turning into the androgyne of manners, in whom smoothness has become the cold glossiness of a bronze surface, like the *Panzerhaft* or "armoured look" of Bronzino's Mannerist portraits. Meeting and mating with their counterparts, the play's Art Nouveau androgynes speak Wilde's characteristic language, the epicene witticism, analogous to their personae in its hardness, smoothness, and elongation. The Wildean epigram, like a Giambologna bronze, is immediately identifiable by a slim spareness, an imperious separateness, and a perverse elegance. Wilde makes speech as hard and glittering as possible. Speech follows Wildean personality into the visual realm. Literature normally is visual through pictorialism or metaphor. But there are few metaphors in Wilde and no complex syntactic units. Vocabulary and sentence structure are amazingly simple, arising from the vernacular of the professional raconteur. Yet Wilde's bons mots are so condensed they become *things*, artifacts. Without metaphor, his language leaps into concreteness.

Language in Wilde aspires to an Apollonian hierarchism. His epigrams turn language from the Dionysian "Many" into the Apollonian "One," for as aphorism and conversation-stopper the epigram thwarts real dialogue. Cutting itself off from a past and future in its immediate social context, it glories in self-created aristocratic solitude. The epigram is the language of the Apollonian lawgiver, arbitrarily imposing form, proportion, and measure on life's fluidity. A character in Wilde's *An Ideal Husband* declares, "Women are never disarmed by compliments. Men always are. That is the difference between the sexes."[6] The iron rod of classification is thrust before us—even if it does not fall where expected! In form and content, the Wildean epigram is a triumph of rhetorical self-containment. No one in English, or probably any modern language, has produced a series of utterances more mysteriously delimited. The Renaissance and eighteenth-century epigram was a poem ending in sententious or sharply ironic verses. But the *epigramma* of classical antiquity was an inscription, as on a tombstone. Thus Wilde restores the epigram to its original representational character. His language has a hieroglyphic exactitude and cold rhetorical stoniness, separating itself from its social background by the Apollonian incised edge.

In *The Importance of Being Earnest*, the courtship of youth and maiden, at the traditional heart of comedy, loses its emotional color in the Wildean transformation of content into form, soul into surface. Jack Worthing and Algernon Moncrieff, idle gentlemen about town, and Gwendolen Fairfax and Cecily Cardew, their well-bred beloveds, are all androgynes of manners. They have no sex because they have no real sexual feelings. Wilde's play is governed by the formalities of social life, which emerge with dancelike ritualism. The key phrase of the English fin de siècle was Lionel Johnson's maxim, "Life must be a ritual."[7] In *Dorian Gray*, Wilde says, "The canons of good society are, or should be, the same as the canons of art. Form is absolutely essential to it. It should have the dignity of a ceremony, as well as its unreality."[8] In *Earnest*, the ceremony of social form is stronger than gender, shaping personae to its public purpose and turning the internal world into the external.

The play's supreme enforcer of form is the matriarch Lady Bracknell. She too is an androgyne, a "Gorgon" with (in the original script) a "masculine mind."[9] She remarks with satisfaction, "We live, I regret to say, in an age of surfaces."[10] In another play, Wilde praises a butler's Sphinx-like "impassivity": "He is a mask with a manner. Of his intellectual or emotional life, history knows nothing. He represents the dominance of form."[11] An optimal performance of *Earnest* would be a romance of surfaces, male and female alike wearing masks of superb impassivity. The Anthony Asquith film (1952), though it shortens and censors the text, comes close to achieving this. Joan Greenwood's entranced, somnambulistic performance as Gwendolen—slow, stately, and ceremonious—is the brilliant realization of the Wildean aesthetic. But the effort to make Dorothy Tutin's Cecily sympathetic at Gwendolen's expense is sentimentally intrusive, a misreading of the play disordering the symmetry between the women, twin androgynes who fight each other to a standoff.

Productions of *Earnest* are often weakened by flights of Forest of Arden lyricism, which turn what is sexually ambiguous in Wilde into the conventionally heterosexual. The play's hieratic purity could best be appreciated if all the women's roles were taken by female impersonators. Language, personality, and behavior should be so hard that the play becomes a spectacle of visionary coldness. The faces should be like glass, without gender or humanity. *The Importance of Being Earnest* takes place in Spenser's Apollonian "world of glass," a realm of glittering, sharp-edged objects. Chapman says of the goddess Ceremony, "all her bodie was / Cleere and transparent as the purest glasse."[12] Gwendolen and Cecily are the goddess Ceremony conversing with herself, her body transparent because she lacks an inner life. That Wilde may have thought of his characters in such terms is suggested in *Dorian Gray*, where Lord Henry longs for "a mask of glass" to shield him from the chthonian "sulphurous fumes" of life.[13]

Gwendolen is the first of the women to enact a drama of form. Goading Jack to propose to her, she announces in advance that she will accept him but still insists that her bewildered suitor scrupulously perform the traditional ritual, on his knees. Gwendolen's thoughts never stray from the world of appearances. At the climax of their romantic interlude, she tells Jack, "I hope you will always look at me just like that, especially when there are other people present." This voyeuristic series of observers is a psychosexual topos of Decadent Late Romanticism, which I first identified in Gautier's *Mademoiselle de Maupin.* Gwendolen imagines Jack looking at her, while she looks at others looking at *them.* As a worshipper of form, Gwendolen craves not emotion but display, the theater of social life.

Cecily exhibits Gwendolen's self-observing detachment in the same situation, a marriage proposal. To Algernon's confession of love, Cecily replies, "If you will allow me, I will copy your remarks into my diary." Emotion is immediately deflected into a self-reflexive Mannerist torsion. Moving to her writing table, Cecily exhorts her suitor to continue his wooing: "I delight in taking down from dictation." Intimacy swells into oratory, and poor Algernon is like Alice grown suddenly too big for the White Rabbit's house. Despite their impending marriage, Cecily forbids him to see her diary. But it is "meant for publication": "When it appears in volume form I hope you will order a copy." The Sibylline archivist, with professional impartiality, grants no special privileges to her sources of data.

Never for a moment are Gwendolen and Cecily persuasively "female." They are creatures of indeterminate sex who take up the mask of femininity to play a new and provocative role. The dandified Algernon and Jack are simply supporting actors whom the women boldly stage manage. Gwendolen and Cecily are adepts of a dramaturgical alchemy. They are Cerberuses on guard to defend the play against encroachment by the internal, which they magically transform into the external. *Earnest* is a long process of crystallization of the immaterial into the material, of emotion into self-conscious personae. In Shakespeare's volatile Rosalind and Cleopatra, automanipulation of personae originates in a Renaissance abundance of emotion, overflowing into multiple dramatic forms. But Wilde's Gwendolen and Cecily inhabit a far more stringently demarcated world, the salon of the androgyne of manners. Their personae are radically despiritualized, efflorescences not of psyche but of couture.

Lady Bracknell also ruthlessly subordinates persons to form. If Algernon does not come to dinner, "It would put my table completely out," and Lord Bracknell will be banished upstairs. Apollonian symmetry is the law, at home or abroad. She rebukes Jack for being an orphan: "To lose one parent, Mr. Worthing, may be regarded as a misfortune; to lose both looks like carelessness." Matters of form are uppermost, in life and death. Emotion is nothing, the public impression everything. Once again note the Late Romantic stress on visual cognition: "may be *regarded* as a misfortune"; "*looks* like carelessness." Every event occurs with naked visibility on a vast, flat plain. Life is a play scrutinized by a ring of eyes. *Dorian Gray* contains a major Wildean principle: "To become the spectator of one's own life is to escape the suffering of life."[14] Late Romantic spectatorship is an escape from suffering because affect is transferred from the emotional and tangible into the visual. No wounds can pierce the glassy body of the Wildean androgyne. The autonomous self lacks biologic or historical identity. A parent is merely a detail of social heraldry. To lose both parents, therefore, is not tragedy but negligence, like tipping the tea service into the trash bin.

The religion of form, in which Lady Bracknell as high priestess catechizes her daughter Gwendolen, has a liturgy fixed by fashion. Its bible is any one of "the more expensive monthly magazines." Lady Bracknell declares: "Style largely depends on the way the chin is worn. They are worn very high, just at present." The chin is arrogantly "worn" like a piece of clothing because the human figure is merely decorative, like the mummy's foot used as a paperweight in Gautier. There is a latent surrealism here, for once the chin, like the perfect eyebrow of Gautier's Cleopatra, has been detached from the body by Decadent partition, it can be worn elsewhere—on the shoulder, perhaps, or hip! Gwendolen, asking Cecily's permission to examine her through a lorgnette (Cecily graciously makes the Late Romantic reply, "I am very fond of being looked at"), boasts that her mother "has brought me up to be extremely short-sighted." In the salon, the body is self-sculpted at the whim of fashion. Gwendolen's lorgnette is the dandy's disdainful monocle, his myopia signifying his hieratic self-absorption.

At the tea table, Gwendolen "superciliously" declines Cecily's offer of sugar: "No, thank you. Sugar is not fashionable any more." To the choice of cake or bread and butter, she replies "in a bored manner": "Bread and butter, please. Cake is rarely seen at the best houses nowadays." Tastiness is irrelevant, since the body has no needs in the Apollonian world of form. Cake and sugar are items of décor, marks of caste by which a group separates itself from a lower group. Personal preference is renounced for hierarchic conformity. Note that cake is "rarely *seen*," not eaten: its status is visual, not gustatory. Gwendolen is the androgyne of manners rapidly approaching the android. She is as preprogrammed as a machine, seeing myopically by maternal edict, eating, drinking, hearing, thinking, speaking solely by the book. Mallarmé says Fashion ("la Mode") is "the goddess of appearances." Fashion is the deity of the Wildean world of form, which Lady Bracknell and Gwendolen uphold with apostolic fervor.

The term "high comedy" is too loosely applied to any comedy without physical or broadly jokey humor. I would argue that the most advanced high comedy is a mannered "presentation of self," the ceremonial style of *The Importance of Being Earnest*, as splendidly embodied in Gwendolen. Indeed, in Gwendolen Fairfax, Wilde has reached the outer limit of high comedy. Her haughty self-hierarchization is so extreme that other characters are virtually dispensable. But without at least two characters, drama dies. When Gwendolen speaks, it is as much to herself or to an abstract choir of celestial observers. Like the picture of Dorian Gray, which will not stay in its assigned place and rejects its entelechy, she seems ready to abandon drama for some unknown destination.

Here is Wilde's greatest departure from the Restoration dramatists, for he detaches the witticism from repartee, that is, from social relationship. The Wildean witticism is a Romantic phenomenon in its proud isolationism. In this mode of high comedy, there is an elaborate ritual display of the persona, indeed a brandishing of it, like Athena's Gorgonian aegis. I am thinking of Cellini's Mannerist Perseus, holding aloft the head of Medusa. The practitioner is in a double relation to the self, acting but also observing. A Late Romantic connoisseurship: the self is the subject of Decadent studiousness and scholarship. Modern androgynes of manners of this type are Edna May Oliver as Hildegarde Withers, Margaret Rutherford as Miss Marple, Nancy Kulp as Miss Jane on *The Beverly Hillbillies*, and Hermione Gingold as herself. With their fussy Decadent pedantry of word and gesture, Miss Withers, Miss Marple, and Miss Jane are the androgyne of manners in a century without a salon. Solitary, sexless, and batty, they may seem closer to the frumpy White Queen than to Wilde's glamourous Gwendolen, but all three are first cousins in the dynastic descent of English high comedy.

Let us examine several of Gwendolen's incomparable utterances, with their unyielding uniformity of tone. Late in the play she says, "I never change, except in my affections." This could be a satiric caption to Pater's *Mona Lisa!* Gwendolen means she is rigidly punctilious in formal, external matters, while emotions are beneath notice, aimless flotsam and jetsam. Note the way she brandishes her personality, flaunting her faults with triumphant self-love, a pagan ostentation. Her speech always has a hard, even, relentless, and rhetorically circumscribed character, as in her first words in the play:

Algernon [*to Gwendolen*]: Dear me, you are smart!
Gwendolen: I am always smart! Am I not, Mr. Worthing?
Jack: You are quite perfect, Miss Fairfax.
Gwendolen: Oh! I hope I am not that. It would leave no room for
    developments, and I intend to develop in many directions.

If we were to speak of a psychodramatic music, then in this last half-sentence we are hearing the monody of a Gautierian contralto, the husky self-pleasuring of hermaphrodite autonomy. Identical intonations are present in two other of Gwendolen's remarks. At one point she gratuitously informs her suitor, "In fact, I am never wrong." And in the last act, as Jack struggles to regain her affections, she says, "I have the gravest doubts upon the subject. But I intend to crush them." Such lines must be properly read—with slow, resonant measure—in order to appreciate their intractable severity. "I intend to develop in many directions": in upper-class British diction, this is flat, formal, and sonorous, forbidding with self-command. The phonology is monochromatic, the consonants sharp and vowels hooded. Its nasality is close to a sneer. Note the way personality is *distributed* throughout the sentence, filling the narrow channel of its syntax with a dense, silvery fluid, acrid and opaque. Gwendolen's willful, elegantly linear sentences fit her like a glove. Smooth with Mannerist spareness, they carry not an extra ounce of rhetorical avoirdupois. There is no Paterian mistiness in Gwendolen. She overtly relishes her personality, caressing its hard edges, echoed in the brazen contours of her sentences. In this half-male doyenne of Art Nouveau worldliness, Wilde has created a definitively modern selfhood, exposed, limited, and unsentimental, cold as urban geometry.

Wilde charges Gwendolen, above all his characters, with the mission of creating an Apollonian dramatic language. Her speech, like his own epicene witticisms, has a metallic, self-enclosed terseness. She spends her words with haughty frugality for the same reason that Spenser's Belphoebe dashes off in the middle of sentences: the Apollonian is a mode of hieratic self-sequestration. The bon mot, prizing brevity, is always jealous of its means. It is a sacramental display, baring the self in epiphanic flashes, like the winking of a camera shutter. The bon mot's spasms of delimitation are attempts to defy the temporal character of speech, turning sequences of words into discrete objets. Ideas are never developed in the Apollonian style because of its hostility to internality. The maliciously witty androgyne of manners uses language confrontationally, as a distancing weapon, like Britomart's flaming sword. Gwendolen's self-exhibiting utterances follow the principle of *frontality*, intrinsic, as Hauser observes, to "all courtly and courteous art."[15] Spurning the modesty of the unmarried maiden, potent Gwendolen turns herself full-face to her suitor, bathing him with a rain of hierarchic emissions.

Admiration of *The Importance of Being Earnest* is universal, but discussion of the play is scarce and slight. Critics seem to have accepted Wilde's own description of it—"exquisitely trivial, a delicate bubble of fancy." Scholarship has never been able to analyze this kind of high comedy, with its elusive sophistication. Frye-style myth criticism, for example, can do little with *Earnest*. From my view of Decadent Late Romanticism, however, every line in the play is rich with implications.

We will take two examples. Disputing with Cecily, Gwendolen declares, "I never travel without my diary. One should always have something sensational to read in the train." The second sentence comes as a surprise, for ordinarily one travels with a diary not to read but to write in. Gwendolen, however, as an Apollonian androgyne, does not keep a journal for self-examination—inwardness being distasteful—but for self-display. To read one's diary as if it were a novel is to regard one's life as spectacle, which Wilde advocates. Gwendolen contemplates her life with appreciative detachment, acting both as objet d'art and Late Romantic connoisseur. Reading normally means personal expansion: one reads to learn what one does not know. But here reading is an act of Romantic solipsism. Gwendolen reads not to enlarge but to condense herself. A book, far from Emily Dickinson's mobile frigate, has become a mirror in which one sees only one's own face. The diary is a self-portrait. Hence Gwendolen reading her diary in a train compartment is exactly like Dorian Gray standing before his picture in the locked room. Both are performing their devotions to the hierarchized self.

The life recorded by her diary is, says Gwendolen, "sensational," a source of public scandal and eroticized fascination. To find one's life sensational is to be aroused by oneself. The eyes, as always in Late Romanticism, are sexual agents. Gwendolen reading her diary is lost in autoerotic skopophilia, titillation of the eye. If books can corrupt, and we know from *Dorian Gray* that they can, then one can be corrupted by one's own diary. To be corrupted by oneself is sexually solipsistic, as with Goethe's twisting acrobat Bettina, self-pleasuring and self-devirginizing. Gwendolen is an uroboros of amorous self-study, an Art Nouveau serpent devouring herself. Train reading is casual reading, passing time with minimal effort. The life recorded and contemplated in the diary is therefore trivialized. It is just a series of sensational incidents without moral meaning.

Reading one's diary like a novel implies one has forgotten what is in it. It demonstrates a lack of moral memory typical of Decadents. In Wilde's *A Woman of No Importance*, Lord Illingworth declares, "No woman should have a memory. Memory in a woman is the beginning of dowdiness." The internal erodes the Apollonian perfection of surfaces. In *An Ideal Husband*, someone says of his antagonist, "She looks like a woman with a past," to which a lord replies, "Most pretty women do."[16] But as we see from Gwendolen's relations with her diary, the person with a past has no past. The self is a tabula rasa open only to sensationalized impressions. There is no moral incrementation. Experience corrupts but does not instruct. Lord Henry Wotton reflects, "Experience was of no ethical value. It was merely the name men gave to their mistakes."[17] Reading one's diary is a diversion of late phases of culture. Memory is inhibited because one has done *too much*, like Pater's Mona Lisa. Her information-retrieval system blocked by sensory overload, the robotlike Gwendolen is a stranger to herself, a stranger-lover.

Gwendolen never travels without her diary because it is her familiar, the inseparable escort enabling her to remain in a state of Wildean externalization. This is one of many traits she shares with Cecily, who uses her diary similarly, as we saw in the proposal scene, where Cecily instantly petrifies Algernon's sentiments midair, as if engraving them on stone tablets. Gwendolen's diary, again like the picture of Dorian Gray, is a repository of the soul that she carries about with her like a hatbox, preserving her soulless Apollonian purity. The diary is a chronicle, the holy testament of Gwendolen's cult of the self. A Romantic's diary is a personal cosmogony, a book of first and last things.

Thus we see that Wilde's witticisms contain a wealth of unsuspected meaning. Even his apparently nonsensical *boutades* are Late Romantic gestures. Lady Bracknell tries to terminate the stormy scene at the Manor House by declaring to Gwendolen, "Come, dear, we have already missed five, if not six, trains. To miss any more might expose us to comment on the platform." I have read these lines a hundred times and never cease to marvel at their bizarre genius. They have that air of lunatic certitude we know from Lewis Carroll, who I think strongly influenced Wilde. What is Lady Bracknell saying? Missing a train, even "five, if not six" (a Decadent precision), normally has only private and not public consequences. In the Looking-Glass world of form, however, failure to adhere to plan is an affront to natural law, bringing murmurs of complaint from passersby. But how do others learn of one's deviation

from a train schedule? Since everything is visible in this landscape of
externals and since the mental life of these androgynes, like their
bodies, has a glassy transparency, their intentions must precede them,
like a town crier, alerting the populace to their tardiness. In its visionary
materialism, *The Importance of Being Earnest* reverts to the Homeric
world of allegorized psychic phenomena, where enraged Achilles feels
Athena tugging at his hair. If we analyzed Lady Bracknell's remark in
naturalistic terms, we would have to speak of a megalomaniacal paranoia. She imagines a general consciousness of their every move; everyone knows what they are doing and thinking. But this is a logical
development of aristocratic worldliness. Fashionable life, as Proust
attests, does indeed take place before the unblinking eyes of *le tout Paris*.

"To miss any more might expose us to comment on the platform":
Lady Bracknell exists in a force field of visual sightlines. Like Gautier's
Queen Nyssia, tainted by another's gaze, Lady Bracknell fears being
"exposed" to infection, here an infection of words. Barthes says of
Sade's novels: "The master is he who speaks . . . ; the object is he who is
silent."[18] Lady Bracknell will lose caste if she is subject to public "com-
ment." Her hierarchic dominance will drain from her like divine ichor.
The scene of shame she envisions on the railway platform is one of
ritual exposure, like Hawthorne's Hester Prynne on the town scaffold.
In Wilde's world, of course, crime is not sin but *bad form*.

The Importance of Being Earnest was the last thing Wilde wrote
before his fall. Its opening night coincided with the start of Queensberry's worst campaign against him, and the play continued to be
performed, to great acclaim, during his two trials. Now it is a strange
fact that Wilde's passage to prison was a terrible fulfillment of this
remark by Lady Bracknell. He recalls:

> On November 13th 1895 I was brought down here from London.
> From two o'clock till half-past two on that day I had to stand on the
> centre platform of Clapham Junction in convict dress and hand-
> cuffed, for the world to look at. . . . When people saw me they
> laughed. Each train as it came up swelled the audience. Nothing
> could exceed their amusement. That was of course before they
> knew who I was. As soon as they had been informed, they laughed
> still more. For half an hour I stood there in the grey November rain
> surrounded by a jeering mob. For a year after that was done to me I
> wept every day at the same hour and for the same space of time.[19]

Lady Bracknell's railway platform was to be the site of Wilde's greatest
humiliation. Who can doubt imagination can shape reality to its will?

Emerson says, "The soul contains the event that shall befall it; for the event is only the actualization of its thoughts."[20] So similar are these scenes of ritual exposure that I wonder if Wilde's memory of Clapham Junction was not a hallucination, a variation on an artistic theme in the solitude and squalor of prison. But granting its truth, it is yet another example of his shamanistic power to bring his own ideas into being. Publication of *Dorian Gray* produced Lord Alfred Douglas, the beautiful boy as destroyer, who brought Wilde down. Clapham Junction came as the agonizing materialization of Wilde's principle of life as spectacle. The whole Late Romantic tradition of concentrated visual experience reaches a disastrous climax on that railway platform, and it ends there, with Wilde the dizzy center of the visible world, like the Ancient Mariner the focus of cosmic wrath, here taking the unbearable form of laughter. The comedian, losing control of his genre, is devoured by the audience.

The epicene witticism has received little attention, partly because it fits no critical categories. Thus Wilde's plays are deemed worthy of explication, while his conversation is not. But the androgyne of manners, typified by Wilde himself, makes an art of the spoken word, which we can examine only when preserved by a Boswell-like amanuensis. Wilde, with his radical formalism, created an original language I call the *monologue extérieur.* I believe that the modern epicene, spoken by male homosexuals, is a survival of Late Romanticism and that it constitutes an unacknowledged lost poetry.

Wilde's epigrams resemble the one-liners of American stand-up comedy, developed out of vaudeville by Jewish entertainers. Woody Allen uses the axiomatic style as an acerbic trope: "What if everything is an illusion and nothing exists? In that case, I definitely overpaid for my carpet."[21] Where Wilde and Allen differ is in their persona-construction. The Jewish witticism can be just as harsh as the Wildean, but it always contains a residue of suffering or victimization. A Brooklyn grandmother said of a neighbor, "She's had so many operations, her stomach is like the map of Jerusalem." The Jewish witticism reflects the social history of its people in imagining persons as passive to harrowing external circumstance. The persona latent in Woody Allen's comedy is the male heroine or schlemiel, a clumsy bumbler. The persona latent in the Wildean witticism is a hierarch, the androgyne as social despot.

The epicene witticism is a rhetorical bonding of masculine and feminine. Geoffrey Hartman says Wordsworth's simple "pointless" style helped liberate modern poetry from "the tyranny of the witty style," the

Augustan forte. Dr. Johnson's definition of literary "point" is "a sting of an epigram; a sentence terminated with some remarkable turn of words or thought."[22] That Wordsworth avoids epigrammatic thrust (a subliminally phallic word) is logical, since he is a poet who qualifies intellect with feminine tenderness. The salon dialogue of the androgyne of manners is a duel of "cutting" remarks. Language is used aggressively as a tool of masculine warfare to slash, stab, pierce, and penetrate. Dorian Gray says to Lord Henry, "You cut life to pieces with your epigrams."[23] It is no coincidence that terms describing a witty exchange—thrust, parry, riposte, repartee—come from swordplay. The interrelation of language and martial combat in western culture is demonstrated by fencing parlance that speaks of a "conversation" or "phrase" of action. Thus we see how a woman of the salon who commands this sharp, challenging rhetoric is masculinized into an androgyne of manners. The male androgyne of manners combines aggressive language with a feminine manner, graceful, languid, and archly flirtatious. The persona of Wilde's epicene witticisms conflates masculine intimidation and attack with feminine seduction and allure.

To "cut" someone is to wound him, but it is also to sever social connections with him. Carroll puns on this duality, when Alice is introduced to the leg of mutton:

> "May I give you a slice?" she said, taking up the knife and fork, and looking from one Queen to the other.
> "Certainly not," the Red Queen said, very decidedly: "it isn't etiquette to cut any one you've been introduced to. Remove the joint!"[24]

Wilde's witticisms operate by systematic "cutting," separating the self from communality and withdrawing it into aristocratic sequestration. Language in *The Importance of Being Earnest* is a mode of hierarchical placement. It is a series of psychodramatic gestures, each remark asserting a caste location vis-à-vis some other person or class of person. The speakers are constantly *positioning* themselves at fixed distances from others. This even occurs, as we saw, in the marriage proposals, where the heroines befuddle the heroes by ceremonial demarcations, bulletins of incipient intimacy, which they narrate like play-by-play sportscasters. To paraphrase: "We will shortly be intimate"; "We are now being intimate"; "Pray continue to be intimate." The Wildean heroine is a hierarchical commentator, plotting the relations of personae on a mental map.

Wilde's use of language as signs of placement is overt in the tea-table clash. Cecily says, "When I see a spade I call it a spade." Gwendolen replies, "I am glad to say that I have never seen a spade. It is obvious that our social spheres have been widely different." This literalized metaphor, a Wildean materialization, makes a spade, like sugar or cake, a calibrator of caste. Gwendolen glories in her self-expanded hierarchical distance from Cecily. The play opens with Algernon playing the piano: "I don't play accurately—anyone can play accurately—but I play with wonderful expression." Anyone can play accurately: this false, self-absolving premise, like a ladder leaned against a wall, stretches a great chain of being before us, with Algernon exulting over the masses from a top rung of aesthetical "sensibility." Wilde uses the technique everywhere. His spokesman in *The Critic as Artist* says, "When people agree with me I always feel that I must be wrong." A character in *An Ideal Husband* says, "Only dull people are brilliant at breakfast."[25] Rhetorical energy is devoted to social differentiation and segregation. Wilde's Apollonian goal was to create hierarchy through wit, ennobling himself, like self-naming Balzac, through a magisterial persona-construction.

Hence the epicene witticism is a language of hierarchic command in sexually aberrant or rather sexually denatured form. Wilde's pointed style descends from the eighteenth century and particularly from Pope, whose poetry he vociferously disliked. Brigid Brophy thinks Wilde's epigram "an adaptation of the logical axiom and the scientific definition," owing something to "the Irish—perhaps originally the theological—habit of paradox."[26] Wilde's epigrams, which so obstruct the quickness of Restoration repartee, acquire their substantiveness from Enlightenment generalization. It is his intellectual power of generalization that gives Wilde's writing its permanent distinction. A modern play in the Wildean manner, Noel Coward's *Private Lives* (1930), has only one true Wildean line: "Certain women should be struck regularly, like gongs."[27] And even this generalization vulgarizes Wilde, in whom contemplativeness is never distorted by action.

Pope was the first to make poetic beauty out of philosophy, devising an elegant discursive style of Apollonian containment and high finish. Pope's social and rhetorical assumptions were transmitted to Wilde, apparently against his will, by the conservative Jane Austen, in whom we first detect Wilde's distinctive voice, tart, bantering, and lucid. Consider, for example, the great opening sentence of Austen's *Emma*: "Emma Woodhouse, handsome, clever, and rich, with a comfortable home and happy disposition, seemed to unite some of the best blessings of existence; and had lived nearly twenty-one years in the world with very little to distress or vex her."[28] There is a delicate play of modern irony about the psychological perimeter of this sentence that is almost impossible to arrest and define. It is an atmospheric rippling, an undulating vocal convection. The sentence contains the whole novel. Rhetorically, it is a glissando from eighteenth-century to nineteenth-century style. The grand public oratory of "handsome, clever, and rich" sinks down to the small, homely "vex," the thorn that will prick the bubble of Emma's pride. As the sentence ends, we hear the new obliqueness of modern writing and almost see the author's hidden smile. Philosophically, Austen's novels, though contemporaneous with High Romanticism, affirm the eighteenth-century world-view, with its neoclassic endorsement of the sexually normative. Only in *Emma* is there anything sexually ambivalent (Emma's infatuation with Harriet), and even there it is slight and discreet.

Wilde diverts Jane Austen's comedy into the epicene through his own identity as a Decadent. Augustan wit is aligned with divinely ordered nature, from which Wilde makes a Late Romantic swerve. This anti-naturism helps him eliminate the pornography of Restoration comedy. Human lusts no longer exist in *The Importance of Being Earnest*. Even Algernon's perpetual hunger is an angelic appetite, for the characters feed on things insubstantial as manna: bread and butter, cucumber sandwiches, muffins, crumpets, and tea cake. They are like the Bread-and-butter-fly of *Through the Looking-Glass*, whose head is a lump of sugar and who lives on weak tea with cream. Wilde uses Jane Austen to *clarify* high comedy, stripping away the broad and farcical elements present in it since Shakespeare. There are no longer any low-comic or crudely dialectal interludes. Even *Earnest*'s secondary characters are erudite verbalists. (*Miss Prism:* "I spoke horticulturally. My metaphor was drawn from fruits.") Wilde prunes and simplifies high comedy by Augustan standards of taste, decorum, and correctness.

There is a second influence in Wilde's epicene transformation of Jane Austen. He is aided by the one wit who stands between himself and her: Lewis Carroll. Carroll detaches English comedy from the ethical (present even in Restoration drama, with its virtuous finales) and prepares it for its definitive amoralization by Wilde. After Wilde, this genre of glittering high comedy is confined to the epicene and can be practiced only by sex-crossing imaginations—Ronald Firbank, Noel Coward, Cole Porter. Carroll's sexual ambiguity is not textually overt, but it is quite obvious in his life. His friends and biographers speak of his long hair and "curiously womanish face," his fascination with little girls, his dislike of boys, which his nephew described as "an aversion, almost amounting to terror." Carroll said of boys, "To me they are not an attractive race of beings." And another time: "Boys are not in my line: I think they are a mistake."[29] Carroll's spiritual identity was thoroughly feminine.

Dramatically, the *Alice* books are supported by the stability of Victorian social structure. Alice is an imperialist of custom. Thrust into an irrational dream-world, she remains serene and self-assured, a model of well-bred composure. In her firm sense of appropriate behavior, she is twin to that snappish menagerie of potentates, human and animal, who chide her for transgressions of mysterious local codes of conduct. There is even a surprising cultural kinship between Alice and her chief critic, the fierce Red Queen, whom Carroll elsewhere describes as "formal and strict, . . . the concentrated essence of all governesses."[30] But the Red Queeen is a governess only insofar as the governess is the first representative of the hierarchical in the lives of English children, ruling as a regent in the name of society.

Carroll did not, I contend, hold the Romantic or modern view that social laws are artificial and false. On the contrary, he took an Apollonian pleasure in them, admiring and cherishing them as he did the theorems and equations he manipulated as an academic mathematician. One of his first published pieces as a young man at Oxford was "Hints for Etiquette; or, Dining Out Made Easy":

I

In proceeding to the dining-room, the gentleman gives one arm to the lady he escorts—it is unusual to offer both.

III

To use a fork with your soup, intimating at the same time to your hostess that you are reserving the spoon for the beefsteaks, is a practice wholly exploded.

VII

We do not recommend the practice of eating cheese with a knife and fork in one hand, and a spoon and wine-glass in the other; there is a kind of awkwardness in the action which no amount of practice can entirely dispel.

VIII

As a general rule, do not kick the shins of the opposite gentleman under the table, if personally unacquainted with him; your pleasantry is liable to be misunderstood—a circumstance at all times unpleasant.[31]

It would be a typically modern error to assume that this is an essay in "debunking," that Carroll is reducing manners to the absurd to demonstrate the fictiveness of social custom. But everything shows him to have been an inflexible advocate of order. A contemporary speaks of Carroll's "rigid rule of his own life," his fixed daily routine. Another says he was "austere, shy, precise, . . . watchfully tenacious of his dignity, stiffly conservative in political, theological, social theory, his life mapped out in squares like Alice's landscape." Phyllis Greenacre calls him "a compulsive indexer," ceaselessly filing and documenting his possessions.[32]

The evidence suggests that rules and manners in "Hints for Etiquette" and the *Alice* books draw their force from Lewis Carroll's faith in their tradition-consecrated, a priori character. His comedy arises from a natively English love of formality and ceremony. There is a tonality of wit in Carroll that is unparalleled in premodern literature but that appears throughout Virginia Woolf. Note the similarities of voice between his "Hints for Etiquette" and this letter to Victoria Sackville-West, in which Woolf reviews the comments roused by her newly bobbed hair:

> 1. Virginia is completely spoilt by her shingle.
> 2. Virginia is completely made by her shingle.
> 3. Virginia's shingle is quite unnoticeable.
>   These are the three schools of thought on this important subject.
> I have bought a coil of hair, which I attach by a hook. It falls into the soup, and is fished out on a fork.[33]

This sophisticated comic style is produced in England by an unexplored interaction between language and persona.

Woolf's mealtime falling coil descends from the courtly mutton, peevish pudding, and talking soup tureen of Alice's banquet. The deep structure of such passages: an excessive or unexpected event occurs within the strict confines of convention. The dining table is a favorite locus of display, as the arena of daily ritual. But the incident evokes *no reaction*, or only a muted one. All personae remain in dignified flat affect, preserving the rule of normality. The highest English comedy is predicated on Wildean impassivity, the proverbial stiff upper lip. Woolf's letter, in fact, allows three diverse reactions to cancel each other out, cleverly effecting a return to stasis. The energy deflected from reaction flows into the moment's social structure, which is felt with architectural solidity, vibrating with public power.

Woolf's shingle saga is really about British impersonality and detachment. Person is detached from person; mind is detached from body; the coil is literally detached before plunging into the soup. Woolf speaks of herself in the impersonal third person: the public self-who-is-seen is detached from the invisible self-who-writes. The letter parodies Bloomsbury art criticism, the bequest of Pater and Wilde. Person is objet d'art. Therefore we hear three views, three peremptory, mutually contradictory voices in heated debate before a painting or sculpture. "Virginia" is a neo-primitif found object. She is like a mannequin gussied up and trundled out for display. The coil of hair is attached as clinically as one would screw in a lightbulb, and it seems to tumble soupward by the accumulation of received opinions. The only things the mandarin Woolf does are consent to the shingle and buy the coil. Everything else is experienced passively: the commentary by others, the fall of the coil. Even the rescue of coil from soup may not be hers. The coil "*is* fished out," as if it were a regular event, ritually dealt with by the forks of all. Is this satire of Cambridge anthropology? In English discourse, the self is an amused observer of life. The self is public yet somehow isolated, presiding with unflappable aplomb from a temenos of reserve and decorum.

Carroll's *Alice* books introduced an epicene element into English discourse that, consolidated by Wilde, flourishes to this day. Development of the English epicene was facilitated by the cultural availability of the persona of the gentleman. English society is also noted for a toleration of eccentricity, a taste for sadomasochistic erotica, and a high incidence of male homosexuality, stimulated by the monasticism of public-school and university life. Goethe exclaimed at the youthful verve of the dashing Englishmen who visited Weimar and made the ladies swoon.[34] From at least the eighteenth century, we can identify as a distinct sexual persona the exuberant English aristocrat, positive, active, and amusing. The English have a maturity of manner in youth and a youthfulness in maturity; hence they achieve an ideal age, the aesthetic balance sought by high classic Greek art.

Carroll synthesized several potent forces in English high culture: wit, hierarchy, and spiritual hermaphroditism. After Carroll, English comedy, in literature and educated speech, tends toward the absurd and incongruous, in which there is always a shadow of the epicene. The upper-class English taste for flights of fluty affectation originates, I am convinced, in the *Alice* books. An example from E. M. Forster's *Howards End* (1910):

Then the door opened, and "Mr. Wilcox, Miss Wilcox" entered, preceded by two prancing puppies.

"Oh, the dears! Oh, Evie, how too impossibly sweet!" screamed Helen, falling on her hands and knees.[35]

The comedy comes from the context of British formality. The impassive Wildean butler, invisible guardian of decorum, is the palace wall against which Helen's screechy zaniness caroms like a tennis ball. Formality is the key to high comedy, a principle escaping today's inept Hollywood directors. *I Love Lucy*, for example, profits from its grounding in strict Fifties social conventions. Thus when Lucy sits on Charles Boyer's hat, squirts him with ink, rips his coat, and hits his head with the door, it's hilarious—not because of slapstick but because of the breach of Boyer's hierarchic decorum. Only the British can still create high comedy of this kind, because of their culture's lingering formality. In Forster, Helen's excess of response, sparked by the unschooled pups, explodes from the repressed energy of the social norm. She speaks a heightened, hieratic, nonsensical language. What is an impossible sweetness? And what is the *too* impossible? We must turn back in defeat. Helen is darting into the linguistic infinite on a jet of the English epicene.

Next an example from Frederick Raphael's Oscar-winning screenplay for *Darling* (1965). The animated Diana (Julie Christie), recalling her meteoric rise, says, "Suddenly, one felt madly *in!*" Like Helen's outburst, this rush of British effervescence has a pointed epigrammatic structure, climaxing in a Johnsonian sting. Note the sense of caste groupings and the detached British impersonality of "one felt" (instead of "I felt"), jostling the slangy Sixties trendiness of "in." The sentence's Apollonian limitations of form and content barely contain the abandoned "madly," with its hectic social whirl. "Madly" has the epicene extravagance of fashionable discourse. A contributor to Nancy Mitford's analysis of "U" or upper-class British culture says, "As in the eighteenth century, U-conversation is larded with vehement and extreme adjectives (*ghastly, frightful, disastrous, nauseating*), but they are no more intended to be taken *au pied de la lettre* than the unprintable epithets so freely used by soldiers."[36] In the salon, all emotions are sensationalized. Language carries more in order to mean less. The final irony of "one felt madly *in*" is that "in" has tauntingly reversed its meaning, turning itself into an ecstatic pinpoint of worldly externalization. To be "in" is paradoxically to have leapt into total hierarchic visibility.

Books and films about Hollywood stars gravitate toward an epicene style, because a star's career is based on *image*, on hierarchic display and a conflation of sightlines, the eyes of a vast, admiring audience. Thus Joseph L. Mankiewicz' *All About Eve* (1950), with its rising and falling stars, automatically adopts the Wildean wit of the English epicene. In the edgy party scene, Bette Davis as Margo Channing finds her husband tittering with her unscrupulous protégé. He says amiably, "I was just telling Eve about the time I looked into the wrong end of a camera finder." Davis furiously snaps back, in a great Carrollian sally, "Remind *me* to tell *you* about the time I looked into the heart of an artichoke!" At a cocktail party, only the artichokes have hearts. Fidelity or emotion has no claims upon the externalized world of socialite and star. The soul has shrunk to the new Vitruvian proportions of an hors d'oeuvre. *All About Eve*'s artichoke heart is Pope's "A trifling head, and a contracted heart," dollhouse *bibelots* of the salon (*Dunciad* IV, 504). The envy-green book of the heart irately scrutinized by Bette Davis is like the engraved cigarette case rudely "read" by Wilde's Algernon, bronzed leaves of denatured sophistication.

Darling is another adventure in modern image: Julie Christie plays a commercial model whose picture is plastered all over London. The script follows its star into a Wildean externalization. Her disillusioned lover (Laurence Harvey) says to her disdainfully, "Put away your Penguin Freud, Diana." He is accusing the faithless Diana of simplistic psychologizing, as if from an elementary primer, a popularized Penguin edition. He implies a star cannot possibly make emotional judgments, because of her perfect soullessness. Such lines demonstrate the ease with which the English epicene shifts into allegory because of its Wildean materialism. As in Dante, multiple levels operate simultaneously. As the real Julie Christie listens to Harvey speak, the allegorical Julie Christie may be seen on the next level up, as on the mezzanine of a department store, an open paperback in her hand!

The English epicene, jointly created by Carroll and Wilde, can be found in many places: Sir Frederick Ashton's sleek choreography for the Royal Ballet; the television series *The Avengers;* and John Lennon's punning witticisms, moralistically stripped from him by his Japanese wife, Yoko Ono, in her misunderstanding of the fertile western fusion between aggression and intellect. What Carroll did, first of all, was to invent a non-chthonian animism: he gives Romantic nature a social voice. The *Alice* books are a din of creatures, speaking as uncompromising social hierarchs. There is no tenderness in Carroll's characters, save in the bumbling and ineffectual, like the senile White Knight. All are sharp, forceful personalities, nodes of aggressive selfhood. The *Alice* books, like *Earnest,* are glutted with rules of behavior, which pop up at improbable moments, as when Alice tries to cut a slice of the protesting plum pudding: " 'Make a remark', said the Red Queen: 'it's ridiculous to leave all the conversation to the pudding!' "[37] Carroll's Red Queen will become Lady Bracknell, just as his Ugly Duchess, tossing her baby about like a bladderball, will become Miss Prism, "a female of repellent aspect" who mislays an infant in a handbag.

Formality is Carroll's preeminent principle, governing not only the narrative design (a pack of cards structuring the first book and a chessboard the second), but the characters' psychodramatic style, a punctilious ritualism like Carroll's own. The noisiest examples are the ritual combats of Tweedledum and Tweedledee and the Lion and the Unicorn, which erupt again and again. Carroll's characters follow compulsive cycles of speech and behavior, which Alice inspects as if moving from one museum diorama to the next. Each is a celebrant of personal ceremony, pagan priest of a pastoral shrine. The Red Queen's draconian championship of good manners is merely the most blatant of the ritual formulas of Carroll's animistic world. Manners are the public language of hierarchy. Thorstein Veblen calls manners "symbolical and conventionalised survivals representing former acts of dominance or of personal service": "They are an expression of the relation of status,—a symbolic pantomime of mastery on the one hand and of subservience on the other."[38]

The ancient history of manners as power energizes Gwendolen and Cecily's climactic confrontation, the center not only of *Earnest* but, in my view, of Wilde's entire oeuvre. In one of the few things on Wilde worth reading, Mary McCarthy, as a Thirties leftist, is oblivious to this, speaking of the scene's "tedium" and "exhausting triviality."[39] Yet her satirical novel, *The Group* (1963), is a triumph of the English epicene style. In a tableau of brilliant formal beauty, Wilde makes a tea table the arena of a ferocious war game, with manners the medium of ritual advance and retreat. Gwendolen and Cecily manipulate their personae with chill virtuosity. Nowhere is it clearer that the gender of the androgyne of manners is purely artificial, that femininity in the salon is simply a principle of decorum shared by male and female.

The women's escalating emotion is completely absorbed by the ceremonial framework and by the formality of their social masks.

Cecily [rather shy and confidingly]: Dearest Gwendolen, there is
no reason why I should make a secret of it to you. Our little

county newspaper is sure to chronicle the fact next week. Mr.
Ernest Worthing and I are engaged to be married.

Gwendolen [*quite politely, rising*]: My darling Cecily, I think there
must be some slight error. Mr. Ernest Worthing is engaged to
me. The announcement will appear in the *Morning Post* on
Saturday at the latest.

Cecily [*very politely, rising*]: I am afraid you must be under some
misconception. Ernest proposed to me exactly ten minutes ago.
[*Shows diary.*]

Gwendolen [*examines diary through her lorgnette carefully*]: It is
very curious, for he asked me to be his wife yesterday
afternoon at 5:30. If you would care to verify the incident, pray
do so. [*Produces diary of her own.*]

Each gesture, each rhetorical movement is answered by a symmetrical
countermovement of balletic grandeur. Language becomes increasingly elaborate, in baroque convolutions of ironic restraint: "It would
distress me more than I can tell you, dear Gwendolen, if it caused you
any mental or physical anguish, but I feel bound to point out that since
Ernest proposed to you he clearly has changed his mind." There is no
hysteria, or even excitement. The women's immovable wills press so
fiercely against the social limits of the moment that the hierarchical
structure of manners leaps into *visibility*, another Wildean materialization. Stylization and ritualism approach the Oriental. The scene is a
Japanese tea ceremony where gracious self-removal yields to naked
Achillean strife—with the bone of contention a chimeric fiancé. Gwendolen and Cecily, negotiating with frosty British efficiency, are heavenly
bodies circling an earthly clod. They seek power and territoriality, not
romance.

Lewis Carroll made this great episode possible. In Carroll, manners
and social laws are disconnected from humane or "civilizing" values.
They have a mathematical beauty but no moral meaning: they are
absurd. But this absurdity is predicated not on a democratic notion of
their relativism but on their arbitrary, divine incomprehensibility. In the
Alice books, manners are meaningless but still retain their hierarchical
force. They are Veblen's "pantomime" of mastery and subservience.
Wilde sets Carroll's view of the mechanisms of social power into a
larger system of aristocratic assumptions, derived partly from his identity as a Baudelairean Decadent Late Romantic (always reactionary and
anti-liberal) and partly from his reading of English drama, in which
aristocracy is a moral idea. The leading interpreter of this aspect of

English literature is G. Wilson Knight, who speaks of kingship in Shakespeare as "a dramatic intensification of personality," the "objectified super-self" or "Eros-music" of each citizen.[40] The English have invested extraordinary imagination in the institution of aristocracy, ceremonial symbol of the nation's history.

In a century of middle-class values, to which even the queen subscribed, Wilde reaffirms aristocratic *virtù*, fabricating it out of its accumulated meanings in English literature. *The Importance of Being Earnest* is a reactionary political poem that makes aristocratic style the supreme embodiment of life as art. Through its masquelike use of manners as social spectacle, the play seeks out the crystallized idea or Platonic form of aristocracy, which resides in rank, the ascending great chain of being. Wilde's bons mots are the Logos of his Apollonian cosmos. Language and ceremony unite to take hierarchy to its farthest dazzling point, until it becomes form without content, like the lacy latticework of a snowflake. Thus the play's characters have abnormal attitudes, reactions, and customs and embark upon sequences of apparently irrational thought, for they are a strange hierarchic race, the *aristoi*.

Earnest is inspired by the glamour of aristocracy alone, divorced from social function. Here it departs from Augustan literature, which celebrates Anne's wise and stable rule. In Wilde, no collective benefits flow from throne or court, where the upper class is at perpetual play. No contemporary régime is eulogized, no past one nostalgically commemorated. Society is divorced from practical reality. Class structure in Wilde exists as art, as pure form. In *Earnest*, unlike the speech on "degree" by Shakespeare's Ulysses, order is admired not because it is right or just but because it is *beautiful*. In fact, order here makes no intellectual sense at all. In Carrollian terms, it is *absurd*. Hence it is an error, and a common one, to say that Wilde is "satirizing" Lady Bracknell, making her ridiculous in her haughty presumptions. Lady Bracknell is beautiful *because* she is absurd. Aristocracy in *Earnest* satisfies aesthetic and not moral demands. The world of the play is *kosmios*, well-ordered and comely. And that it is ruled by the chic makes sense, since this word's descent resembles that of "cosmetic" from "cosmos": the French "chic" is apparently a version of the German *Schick*, meaning taste, elegance, and *order*.

Outside his art, Wilde found himself in the same quandary as Coleridge and Swinburne, anxiously attempting apologia and moral revision of their daemonic poems. Thus he says in *The Soul of Man Under Socialism:* "All authority is quite degrading. It degrades those who exercise it, and degrades those over whom it is exercised."[41] Wilde was torn between his instinctive hierarchism as an Apollonian idealist and the liberalism toward which he was impelled by the miseries of being homosexual in a Christian society. This led him into glaring self-contradictions. For example, at his first trial, Wilde was questioned about his relations with working-class youths.

Carson. Did you know that one, Parker, was a gentleman's valet, and the other a groom?

Wilde. I did not know it, but if I had I should not have cared. I don't care twopence what they were. I liked them. I have a passion to civilize the community.

Carson. What enjoyment was it to you to entertain grooms and coachmen?

Wilde. The pleasure to me was being with those who are young, bright, happy, careless, and free. I do not like the sensible and I do not like the old.

. . . .

Carson. What was there in common between this young man and yourself? What attraction had he for you?

Wilde. I delight in the society of people much younger than myself. I like those who may be called idle and careless. I recognize no social distinctions at all of any kind; and to me youth, the mere fact of youth, is so wonderful that I would sooner talk to a young man for half-an-hour than be—well, cross-examined in Court!

Carson. Do I understand that even a young boy you might pick up in the street would be a pleasing companion?

Wilde. I would talk to a street arab, with pleasure.

Carson. You would talk to a street arab?

Wilde. Yes, with pleasure. If he would talk to me.[42]

In these responses, Wilde is in *mauvaise foi*. It is patently untrue that he "recognized no social distinctions at all of any kind." Like Proust, he was vain of his traffic with the rich and titled. Of great English writers after the eighteenth century, Wilde is the most guilty of snobbery. His pleasure in the company of the déclassé, which he defends as liberal broad-mindedness, must be translated into the terms of *Dorian Gray*. What Wilde on the witness stand calls "youth, the mere fact of youth" is really *beauty*, and specifically male beauty. The apparent absence of "social distinctions" conceals dogmatic faith in another hierarchical system, Plato's cult of divine beauty in human form.

The Wildean epicene unites English drama's theme of aristocracy with Late Romanticism. First, Wilde severs Jane Austen's eighteenth-century hierarchical values from the idea of commonweal: he treats society simply as an ornate objet d'art or cotillion ball. Second, he sexually volatizes English wit. The charming banter of the celibate Austen and Carroll becomes epicene in Wilde because of his sexual experience, which shifts him into Decadence. Since, as Richard Ellmann long ago observed, Wilde did his best work after turning homosexual, art for him was inextricably linked with criminality. Perhaps the society glorified by a homosexual wit can be no larger than the salon. Wilde demonstrates the congruities between high society and the male-homosexual world. One, already mentioned, is image, a tyranny of the visual. Two others are scandal and gossip. Gwendolen, we saw, calls her diary "sensational." To say or do something scandalous is to create a sensation, literally an erotic *frisson* of shock. Arousal is generated at physical remove, over that aesthetic distance I perceive in Apollonian phenomena.

The salon is a western drama of *seeing* and *saying*. Works of epicene wit are therefore always dominated by gossip. In Clare Boothe Luce's *The Women* (1939), a cult film among male homosexuals, Rosalind Russell plays a gossip-drunk matron in a constant frenzy of discovery and disclosure. Like Vergil's Rumor, she has multiple eyes: grotesque Gorgonian eye-brooches pinned all over her bodice. The Countess (Mary Boland), the film's Wildean hierarch, murmurs "L'amour, l'amour" as her epithet, altering it at the boisterous climax to "La publicité!" Love in the salon is only publicity. Gossip as a form of erotic displacement is also evident in Jessica Walter's superb performance as a frigid opportunist in the film of *The Group* (1966). Mirror-gazing Libby is a sensationalizing telephone monologuist, substituting words for sexual action. Someone speaks of "that red scar she calls a mouth." As usual, western culture fuses eroticism with verbal aggression. Libby's lushly painted lips are the duelling scar of a Wildean despot of febrile, worldly wit.

There is no scandal or gossip in the *Alice* books because they have no sexual "free energy." Carroll is an annalist of aggression but not of eroticism. In Wilde, however, gossip intensifies the aura of glamour that signifies prestige in the salon. Algernon says of a widow, "I hear her hair has turned quite gold from grief." A character in *A Woman of No Importance* remarks, "It is said, of course, that she ran away twice before she was married. But you know how unfair people often are. I myself don't believe she ran away more than once." A lord declares, "It is perfectly monstrous the way people go about, nowadays, saying things against one behind one's back that are absolutely and entirely true." The morning after Sibyl's suicide in *Dorian Gray*, Lord Henry callously says, "Things like that make a man fashionable in Paris. But in London people are so prejudiced."[43] The gossip "item" of Paris or Hollywood is like the chin that Lady Bracknell turns into a detached item of Wildean décor. Both are heraldic accretions to persona. The erotic excitation of scandal and gossip leads to the volatility of Wildean wit. Words cast off their moral meanings and escape into the sexually transcendental, leaving only vapor trails of flirtation and frivolity.

Oscar Wilde was the formulator of personal style for the modern male homosexual. Thus, for most of this century, the male-homosexual world replicated the salon, even in dingy bars in provincial cities. In the Twenties, while touring with a road show of female impersonators, Mae West was asked why she consorted only with male and never female homosexuals. She replied, "Lesbians are not humorous persons." From Wilde's life and work came the aesthetic of high camp, an Apollonian mode of comedy and connoisseurship. As Mae attests, lesbians as a group have never been either camp or comic. The male homosexual, by his Wildean self-conceptualization, carries on the work of western imagination. Even today, as camp has faded, part of the male-homosexual world still follows a vanished aristocratic code: class consciousness, racial stratification, amoral veneration of youth, beauty, and glamour, love of scandal and gossip, and use of the stinging bon mot and theatrical persona of the androgyne of manners. Thus Wilde's English epicene has secretly transmitted British hierarchism to other lands and other times.

The caste system of *The Importance of Being Earnest* is ruled by Lady Bracknell, with her head-on Gorgonian confrontationalism. She even rings doorbells in a "Wagnerian manner." Her domineering pronouncements have an exalted, trumpetlike sound. In the film, Dame Edith Evans, the definitive Lady Bracknell, sits in the train bound for the Manor House accompanied by blasts of loud, imposing music. She serenely faces us in courtly frontality, like a dynastic totem. The shot prefigures Diane Arbus' photograph, "Woman with a Veil on Fifth Avenue" (1968), where a dowager's turbaned head shows the same masculine massiveness. Elsewhere Wilde says, "Twenty years of romance make a woman look like a ruin; but twenty years of marriage make her something like a public building."[44] Lady Bracknell's function as stern guardian of social convention has given her an architectural character. She is masculinized by the principle of hierarchic abstraction I saw at work in Egyptian monumentality.

The one mother of Wilde's play is far from indulgent toward emotion or romance. As champion of public form, Lady Bracknell insists on arranged marriages. Like a Roman matron, she is contemptuous of illness or weakness. She resembles Henry James's grandes dames or the Marx Brothers' high-society hostess, played by Margaret Dumont, whose wide face, ample bosom, and statuesque height symbolize the solidity and stolidity of institutions. What is Wildean in Dumont is her vacancy. Brilliant smiles and withering glances alternate in her face with daffy regularity. All emotions are transient, because no emotion goes very deep. Like Wilde's androgynes, she has no memory, starting each moment fresh, no matter what insult she suffers from the delirious, Dionysian Marx Brothers. Lady Bracknell has more control over her fictive world. Her self-assertions are flashes of mesmerizing female power. Male homosexuals have made "bitchiness," applied to dominant women, a peculiar positive. "She's such a bitch," they say approvingly of egotists like Barbra Streisand. I identify the locution as another hierarchism. Lady Bracknell is a bitch of this kind, unjust, immoderate, dictatorial.

Of the play's heroes, Algernon is more the effeminate aesthete. Like Lord Henry Wotton, he speaks "languidly" and is "always overdressed"; his flat is "luxuriously and artistically furnished." In the original script, he cries, "Exercise! Good God! No gentleman ever takes exercise. You don't seem to understand what a gentleman is."[45] Algernon holds the Late Romantic view of the vulgar inauthenticity of action. When Jack rebukes him for "calmly eating muffins" during a crisis, he replies, "Well, I can't eat muffins in an agitated manner. The butter would probably get on my cuffs." Muffin-eating is the only action he is guilty of. Energy is merely agitation, a Dionysian centrifuge spraying butter about the room, besmirching the burnished world of surfaces. Jack can also be epicene: he finds both town and country life "excessively boring"; he accepts Lady Bracknell's definition of his smoking as a worthy fulltime "occupation." In performance, the differences between Jack and Algernon should not be significant. They are Romantic doubles who drift fatefully together. The play resembles Balzac's *The Girl with the Golden Eyes* in the way that siblings separated at birth locate each other by telepathic magnetism. Furthermore, Jack and Algernon, like undergraduates packing a telephone booth, try to crowd into the same identity, that of the make-believe Ernest.

The symmetry between Wilde's suitors corresponds to the far fuller symmetry between the two women, which the film spoils by fomenting populist antagonism against the elitist Gwendolen. The greatness of the tea-table scene is lost if the audience is lured into siding with Cecily. Its beauty depends on Apollonian balance, military parity between ferocious opponents. Gwendolen and Cecily are like Rossetti's duplex females, dancing in the bower meadow. Their Romantic twinning is obvious in those two moments when they have *simultaneous thoughts* and chant aloud in uncannily synchronized sentences. Wilde's female twins have fused into a single hierarchic personality. They differ only in aristocratic style, of which Gwendolen is a consummate master. She fulfills Goethe's definition of the nobleman: "A certain stately grace in common things, a sort of gay elegance in earnest and important ones." Asking "What is *noble?*" Nietzsche replies as if to describe Gwendolen: "Apparent frivolity in word, dress, bearing, through which a stoic severity and self-constraint protects itself against all immodest inquisitiveness. Slowness of gesture, and of glance." She is like Veblen's gentleman of the "highest leisure class," who has "a divine assurance and an imperious complaisance, as of one habituated to require subservience and to take no thought for the morrow."[46] Cecily has not reached this level of sophistication, because of her rural life. But once wed in London, she will surely make rapid progress in the school of Wildean worldliness. Lady Bracknell forecasts this when she says to Cecily, "Pretty child! your dress is sadly simple, and your hair seems almost as Nature might have left it. But we can soon alter all that. A thoroughly experienced French maid produces a really marvellous result in a very brief space of time." French maids, ambassadors from Baudelaire's Paris, are naughty necromancers turning nature into art.

Cecily is no naive ingénue. In fact, her romantic behavior is even more perverse than Gwendolen's. Reversing the habit of love stories, Wilde gives his women a rhetoric more "experienced" than their male suitors'. For example, Gwendolen, with Decadent erudition, dismisses as "metaphysical speculation" Jack's plaintive question about whether she would continue to love him if his name turned out not to be Ernest. She later remarks, "The simplicity of your character makes you exquisitely incomprehensible to me." Woman is complex, man simple. Even when Gwendolen says "I adore you," there is a glacial tinge of satiric self-dramatization. *Earnest*'s maiden androgynes have a strange precocity, a way of surprising the conversation from unexpected angles and defeating the wits of their suitors. The men love and are loved, but they are *dealt with* by the women, who predict their every move. The women dictate the structure and pace of relationship. The men think they act on their own, but they are always preceded and foreseen, not by a daemonic vampire of the continental Decadence but by the pert English girl of literary tradition. The women are eager to marry— probably in order to dominate! In marriage, as defined by Lady Bracknell, the male is recessive. Gwendolen says of her cowed father, "The home seems to me to be the proper sphere for the man."

One of the remarkable things in *Earnest* is its female anticipation of male volition. Nothing the men do surprises the women, because the latter survey the play from a mount of Delphic omniscience. That Wilde assigns Cecily the more effeminate fiancé suggests something sexually problematic in her. Jaded Algernon is infuriatingly smug—until he meets Cecily. She immediately takes the offensive, turning his greeting against him and seizing control of the conversation. Despite her innocent appearance, virtue is not what she seeks in a suitor. If Algernon is not "wicked," as advertised, he is useless. The proposal scene is an astonishing performance. Although they have just met, Cecily claims she and Algernon have been engaged for months. He stands dazed, as she unveils a long saga of courtship, alienation, and reconciliation, recorded in diary and letter. Algernon protests, "My letters! But, my own sweet Cecily, I have never written you any letters." She replies, "You need hardly remind me of that, Ernest. I remember only too well that I was forced to write your letters for you. I wrote always three times a week, and sometimes oftener." Cecily has *imagined* Algernon before he has had any opportunity to act on his own. Like Poe's William Wilson, he meets his other self, a doppelgänger projected by Cecily. She creates a past for him, a prefabricated set of memories. He is as passive as the waxy Hermaphrodite of Shelley's Witch of Atlas, another clever rural recluse. Algernon is half-delighted, half-horrified. The game sways dizzily back and forth from illusion to reality. The episode is a development of Rosalind's wooing scene with the tutored Orlando, where a suitor is enveloped in the imagination of a female androgyne. In both cases, romantic union is plotted in advance by an ingenious virgin dramatist. Wilson Knight warns, "We regularly let ourselves be born from a woman of whom we know nothing."[47] Algernon, in a condition of masculine nescience, lets himself become engaged to a woman of whom he knows nothing. Thus Cecily's witty manipulation of her suitor is more invasive of male autonomy than Gwendolen and Lady Bracknell's bossier maneuvers.

The wonderful airiness of *The Importance of Being Earnest* comes from the way it diverts potentially sinister sexual relations into comedy. Mating is accomplished with dreamlike ease. Chthonian danger and murk are transmuted into glittering Apollonian words and gestures. I call woman "the hidden." Wilde's epicene formalism and visionary materialism bring everything hidden and internal into dazzling visibility. Sexual turbulence never disturbs the play's smooth, urbane surface. And yet it is a drama of Blake's rapacious "female will." Both Gwendolen and Cecily want to marry a man named Ernest: men are to be earnest, where women are not. Wilde says, "In all important matters, style, not sincerity, is the essential." And elsewhere: "What people call insincerity is simply a method by which we can multiply our personalities."[48] By forcing their suitors to be earnest or sincere, the women psychodramatically circumscribe them. In other words, they bind the men by ritual limitations prior to marriage. The women, meanwhile, parade their own lack of earnestness, as in the tea-table scene, where they sabotage and reverse field on each other with blithe indifference to truth or logic.

Why do the men dash off to be rechristened "Ernest"? They abandon their identities and undertake a Romantic regression to be born again in the image of female desire. The women profess admiring astonishment: "For my sake you are prepared to do this terrible thing?" "To please me you are ready to face this fearful ordeal?" Christening, a passive, unrisky event, becomes a harrowing *rite de passage*. The play parodies literary conventions: for example, Jack, like the archetypal hero, has a mysterious birth—in a railway station. As in *The Rape of the Lock*, comedy is produced by a diminution of the scale of epic conflict. At the peak of hostilities, Gwendolen solemnly informs Cecily, "You have filled my tea with lumps of sugar, and though I asked most distinctly for bread and butter, you have given me cake." This line (perfectly, mournfully read by Joan Greenwood) imitates outbursts from poetic drama like, "You befoul God and nation by your wanton, heinous act!" But in psychological terms, Gwendolen and Cecily's pleasure in the men's will-to-christen translates to, "For me you are willing *to revert to infancy?*" The women are Procrustean linguists, chopping their suitors' identities and lifelines. The play's reconciliation between the sexes is therefore much more complicated than it seems. The male "self-sacrifice" (Gwendolen's word) making it possible is induced by female coercion, nascent maternal tyranny. *Earnest*'s great achievement is that none of these emotional ambivalences is felt by the audience, so beautifully has the sexual anxiety been redirected and absorbed. But our exhilaration at the finale comes partly from our subliminal sense of many dangers present that have not been allowed to develop. Wilde's epicene wit keeps female chthonian power in check by turning all four principals into the glass-bodied androgyne of manners, who escapes and transcends physiology.

The Importance of Being Earnest is a ritual purification of Wilde's earlier works, *Dorian Gray* and *Salomé*. It dispels the anxiety of two critical relationships, each a Romantic marriage of sexual personae. The first is between a man and his double. In *Dorian Gray*, the portrait-double is victorious, regaining eternal beauty by killing its human model. In *Earnest*, John Worthing creates a double identity for himself: he is Jack in the country but a fictive Ernest in the city. His friend Algernon assumes this false self to invade the country house as Ernest Worthing. At that moment, Jack, dressed in black, arrives to announce the death of his brother Ernest. Jack is shocked to learn that, far from being dead, the nonexistent Ernest is sitting in the dining room. As in *Dorian Gray*, the double has come to unpleasant life, escaped from its master's control. Since *Earnest* is a comedy, the double cannot exert the daemonic oppression it has in Wilde's novel. Jack is furious with vexation, but he is not terrified. This is one of those moments where we see Wilde using the Apollonian epicene to neutralize his literary antecedents. Here he discharges the unstable occultism from the Romantic theme of the double. *Earnest* ends with that coalescence of the doubles I identify as a master motif of Romanticism. In the play's last moments, Jack, to his astonishment, turns out to be named Ernest after all. Thus he fuses with his alter ego. Furthermore, Algernon turns out to be his long-lost brother. That is, the person who poses as an invented brother *becomes* that brother. The coalescence of the doubles on the last page of *Dorian Gray* means leprous contamination and death. But *Earnest* ends in fraternal concord and joy. Wilde takes the negativity out of the ominous Romantic theme of the shadowy second self by switching genres into comedy, with its classical and Renaissance tradition of the missing twin.

The second relationship *Earnest* purifies is between man and chthonian woman. This is the subject of *Salomé* (1893), which capsulizes the French Decadent tradition of the femme fatale. Wilde wrote it in French, the language of Decadent prestige. Its uneven translation is by Lord Alfred Douglas. Fifty years later, another alienated Irishman was to use French for his best play, *Waiting for Godot*. *Salomé* contains Wilde's only chthonian woman. French is his strategy of linguistic distancing, laying an impassable moat or English Channel between the homosexual aesthete and the femme fatale. For the idealizing Wilde, the chthonian is literally an alien realm. He consigns *Salomé* to French to keep his native tongue in a state of Apollonian purity. Its translation by his lover is therefore an ephebic rerouting of the text, a decontamination of its female dangers.

Salomé sounds better in French, since English prose, as shown by the painful failure of Woolf's *The Waves*, cannot sustain an incantatory style. *Salomé* is full of hieratic repetitions and theatrical Decadent excesses. For example, Salomé and Jokanaan (John the Baptist) are deep in tense conversation, when the young Syrian infatuated with her suddenly kills himself and falls between them. Neither one takes the slightest notice of this unusual interruption, which is like a sack of laundry flung down on the floor. *Salomé* inevitably turned itself into an opera, under the hand of Richard Strauss (1905). I said Gwendolen's epicene language is not so much communication as hierarchic self-sequestration. Similarly, speech in *Salomé* is self-directed and self-hypnotizing. The characters are catatonic somnambules, virtually every one an androgyne of my android type. Words are subordinated to seeing, along harsh planes of eye-contact or eye-evasion. Wilde brings to an obsessive extreme the Decadent eroticization of visual experience begun by Gautier. Salomé stares at John, while Herod and the Syrian stare at her. Sex hovers in a static, sterile trance state. Salomé is a Late Romantic vampire, fixing John with her aggressive Medusa-eye and driving him into the terminal passivity of death. Wilde wrote at a time when respectable ladies avoided too "free" an eye, the mark of a whore—a rule of moral deportment missing from today's sloppy films on premodern times.

Huysmans makes Salomé "woman virginal and lubricious," thinking everything but doing nothing. Ortega y Gasset says, "Salomé fantasizes in a masculine manner."[49] Cecily Cardew, I submit, is Wilde's revision of his own fantasizing Salomé. Salomé and Cecily cast their imaginations around a man, as Clytemnestra casts her net around Agamemnon. In *Salomé* as in *Dorian Gray*, a man sits for his portrait: John's head is literally drawn from life. Salomé creates a Decadent work of art: the severed head is male destiny sculpted by the female will. Wilde's incredible stage direction: "A huge black arm, the arm of the Executioner, comes forth from the cistern, bearing on a silver shield the head of Jokanaan."[50] This grotesque erection—the only erection possible in a Decadent work—may be a memory of Baudelaire's black tree of nature, hoisting aloft the crucified poet. Salomé seizes the head and kisses and soliloquizes to it, like Hamlet in the graveyard. Like Rachilde's Raoule, she makes love to the dead. Like Dorian Gray, she kisses her own portrait, a point captured by Beardsley in *The Climax*, where male and female seem Medusan mirror-images (fig. 47). In *The Dancer's Reward*,

47. Aubrey Beardsley, *The Climax*, from *Salomé*, 1894.

Beardsley turns head and shield on black arm into macabre sculpture on a pedestal. Unfortunately, his Salomé, fondling the saint's long hair, looks a bit like a cook trussing the dinner roast.

At the end, the femme fatale is apparently defeated, crushed beneath the shields of the palace guard. I interpret this bizarre method of execution as a symbol of Salomé's loss of perceptual control. She is buried beneath the multiplied objects of the material world. This was the obscure fear of Gautier's suffocating Cleopatra, which I think Wilde adapts. But the vampire has a thousand lives and is not so easily mastered. In *Earnest*, Wilde tries again and this time succeeds. Like *Salomé*, *Earnest* deals with the theme of female dominance. As an apotropaic construction, it absorbs the sexual anxiety expressed but not resolved in *Salomé*. *Earnest* purifies woman of her chthonian taint by turning her into the crystalline androgyne of manners. Now woman's vampire-command of the plane of eye-contact is an instrument not of sexual obsession and enslavement but of pursuit of the chic. Wilde's female hierarchs rule the salon of Apollonian sunlight, not the dark womb-world of objects without contour.

Mythologically, says Frye, comedy moves toward "the rebirth and renewal of the powers of nature."[51] *The Importance of Being Earnest* is the least natural comedy in major literature. Its primary inspiration is Decadent hostility to nature. Drama is a mode of Dionysian vocalism, while Apollonian works are characterized by silence and visual clarity. *Earnest*, with its Apollonian formality and delimited language, is an attempt to cut off the Dionysian roots of drama and create an Apollonian theater, as coldly outlined as an objet d'art. The play is the last skirmish in the Late Romantic campaign against nature. In *The Decay of Lying*, Wilde asks: "For what is Nature? Nature is no great mother who has borne us. She is our creation. It is in our brain that she quickens to life." Wilde's nature is like Aeschylus' Athena, born of a male god. Taking Baudelaire's tone, Wilde declares, "Art is our spirited protest, our gallant attempt to teach Nature her proper place."[52] But Baudelaire's nature is still chthonian, in all her cruelty and barbarism. Wilde, trying to remove the chthonianism from nature, trivializes her, an error for which he will later suffer.

Baudelaire, thanks to Sade, is ultimately writing against Rousseau. Wilde, battling Victorian culture, is ultimately writing against Rousseau's disciple, Wordsworth. My theory is this: Coleridge is the only way to defeat Wordsworth. The Apollonian Wilde, unable to take Coleridge's daemonic view of nature, loses to Wordsworth and, amazingly, flips back into him. At the end of his career, Wilde becomes Words-

worth, just as Dorian Gray becomes Lord Henry Wotton. One of
Wilde's anti-Wordsworthian precepts: "The first duty in life is to be as
artificial as possible." He rejects Wordsworth's analogy between imagination and nature: the only "function of Art" is to awaken "exquisite
sterile emotions." His spokesman in *The Decay of Lying* refuses to lie on
the grass and talk: "But Nature is so uncomfortable. Grass is hard and
lumpy and damp, and full of dreadful black insects."[53] This riposte,
denying man can be at ease in nature, is very amusing—until one
recalls that Baudelaire created a great work of art on this theme, "A
Carcass," where inhospitable nature teems with maggots. Wilde seems
to be fighting for imagination's freedom, but his flippant remarks about
nature underestimate her power. I think at this period he was going to
too many chic parties, a practice fatal to serious writing. Fellini's *La
Dolce Vita* (1959) ends with a spent troop of decadent partygoers strag-
gling out onto a bleak beach at dawn. There they see, marooned, a
monstrosity of primeval nature, the apparition of what they have repressed and therefore become.

Taken in its own terms, Wilde's wicked satire of Wordsworth can be
delicious. Wilde is, of course, indifferent to the sublime: Niagara Falls is
"simply a vast unnecessary amount of water going the wrong way and
then falling over unnecessary rocks." He said of the Mississippi in angry
flood, "No well-behaved river ought to act that way." He is invoking
Apollonian principles: nature has both no form and bad form. My high-
school favorite of the epigrams: "People who count their chickens before they are hatched act very wisely: because chickens run about so absurdly that it is almost impossible to count them accurately."[54] Wilde's
frantic chickens are Wordsworth's daffodils, "Tossing their heads in
sprightly dance." Nature's vital energy has become silly tumult. The
uncountable chickens are a Maenadic band surveyed and scorned by an
Apollonian spectator, peering through his dandy's monocle. Are these
chickens woman as brooder/breeder? Wilde sees nature as mindless
proletarian sprawl.

Earnest is full of jabs against Wordsworth. Lady Bracknell asks, "You
have a town house, I hope? A girl with a simple, unspoiled nature, like
Gwendolen, could hardly be expected to reside in the country." Gwendolen, glancing at the garden, remarks, "I had no idea there were any
flowers in the country." For Wilde, the city is the center of value. He said
in conversation, "Town life nourishes and perfects all the more civilized
elements in man." And: "A gentleman never looks out of the window."[55]
When, pressed by his producer, Wilde hastily cut *Earnest* down to three
acts, he made several regrettable changes of venue. The tea-table scene

was originally in the drawing room, not the garden. The drawing room, its proper place, is the eighteenth-century salon of the androgyne of manners. The revisions also destroyed one of the most sardonic stage directions in English drama. The play's war between the sexes originally began with the women's decampment: "They retire into the garden with scornful looks."[56] This brilliant line extends Wilde's anti-naturism past his immediate target, Wordsworth, to take in the whole of English poetry, going back to the maidens and gardens of Spenser, Donne, and Marvell. Spenser's two fair sister-nymphs stamp off with furrowed brow into a suddenly less idyllic mead. The stage direction now reads, "They retire into the house with scornful looks"—from which there has been a tremendous loss of reference.

The High Romantic revolt against neoclassicism comes full circle in the Late Romantic Wilde. Like the neoclassics, he exalts society over raw nature, aristocracy over democracy, artificiality over simplicity, wit over emotion, Apollonian limitation over Dionysian limitlessness. Wilde confirms Rousseau's and Wordsworth's belief that following nature makes man tender and benevolent: swerving from High Romantic nature, Wilde becomes cruel. He insults the Victorian taste for pathos, as when he says of a Dickens tear-jerker, "One must have a heart of stone to read the death of Little Nell without laughing." Like Sade and Freud, Wilde sees altruism as covert egotism. Lord Henry Wotton says, "I can sympathize with everything, except suffering," and "Philanthropic people lose all sense of humanity. It is their distinguishing characteristic." Wilde's primary principle is aesthetic perfection of persona, beyond morality. Lord Henry tells Dorian, "To be good is to be in harmony with one's self. Discord is to be forced to be in harmony with others." At his trial Wilde said, "I think that the realization of oneself is the prime aim of life." He echoes Lord Henry: "The aim of life is self-development. To realize one's nature perfectly—that is what each of us is here for."[57] This is the pagan voice of the Hellenophile Wilde. Complete self-realization: was this not sought by Nero? Attila the Hun? Hitler? Late Romanticism's extremism remains uncomfortably avant-garde.

Wilde was incapable of sympathy or collective emotion because of his Apollonian opposition to the Dionysian, the mode of the "Many" and of what I call the empathic. In his fall, his Apollonian system was overturned and demolished. It all began with a self-deceiving literalization. *Earnest*'s glittering great chain of being is a visionary construction and not the actual social world of law, finance, or aristocracy. Wilde knew this. But intoxicated by his supreme artistic success, which had brought

Dorian Gray into being as Lord Alfred Douglas, he sought to turn institutional power to his own selfish ends. Enraged against Queensberry, Wilde stepped over the line from fiction into reality, from which he never returned:

> The one disgraceful, unpardonable, and to all time contemptible action of my life was my allowing myself to be forced into appealing to Society for help and protection. . . . Of course once I had put into motion the forces of Society, Society turned on me and said, "Have you been living all this time in defiance of my laws, and do you now appeal to those laws for protection? You shall have those laws exercised to the full. You shall abide by what you have appealed to." The result is I am in gaol.[58]

The daemon hubristically conjured up by an Apollonian Late Romantic is society itself, a genie that will not go back into its bottle.

Crushed by conviction and imprisonment, Wilde undergoes a revolution of principles. *De Profundis* contains one of the most extraordinary recantations in the history of art. The pitiless sophisticate now embraces suffering as the highest human experience:

> I used to live entirely for pleasure. I shunned sorrow and suffering of every kind. I hated both. I resolved to ignore them as far as possible, to treat them, that is to say, as modes of imperfection. They were not part of my scheme of life. They had no place in my philosophy.

His mother often quoted Goethe's lines about weeping through "the midnight hours": "I absolutely declined to accept or admit the enormous truth hidden in them. I could not understand it." But a year of weeping in prison has changed his mind:

> Clergymen, and people who use phrases without wisdom, sometimes talk of suffering as a mystery. It is really a revelation. One discerns things that one never discerned before. One approaches the whole of history from a different standpoint. . . . I now see that sorrow, being the supreme emotion of which man is capable, is at once the type and test of all great Art.[59]

Maternal woman was central to the nature cult of Dionysus, who wears her robes and snood in art. The ephebic male was the model for the Apollonian Olympians, whose obliviousness to emotion is explicit in *De Profundis:* Wilde speaks of the cruelty of Apollo and Athena, with the "steel shields" of her pitiless eyes.[60]

In prison, the amoral worshipper of beauty passes from Apollonian cruelty, at its height in his ephebic Dorian Gray, to Dionysian empathy, province of the mature heterosexual woman, his own potent mother. Woman is internality, both procreative and emotional. *De Profundis* ("from the depths") was written in tears and at the midnight hour, not in Apollonian sunlight. It descends into the murky, fluid female world of brooding invisibility, which *Earnest* combats. *The Decay of Lying* denies nature's priority: "Nature is no great mother who has borne us." But *De Profundis* declares, "The Earth is mother to us all." By the bitterest of ironies, the Apollonian Wilde was thrown back into the arms of maternal nature. His words at the end of *De Profundis* echo Swinburne's ode to the ocean-mother: "I have a strange longing for the great simple primeval things, such as the Sea, to me no less of a mother than the Earth. It seems to me that we all look at Nature too much, and live with her too little. . . . I feel sure that in elemental forces there is purification, and I want to go back to them and live in their presence."[61] Wilde's Decadent biography fulfilled Huysmans' prophetic pattern: the man warring against mother nature suffers ignominious defeat and must surrender himself to her for healing and detoxification.

Like Swinburne's poetry, *De Profundis* charts a regression to prehistoric matriarchy, before the invention of male society and even before the birth of objects. Readers have missed the primitivizing impulse in it because it contains so much distracting talk of Christ. The Christian references mean no more than they do in Coleridge's mystery poems: Christ is the ultimate male heroine, the passive public sufferer. Wilde depicts "the crucifixion of the Innocent One before the eyes of his mother and of the disciple whom he loved."[62] We are meant to see Wilde pilloried—and at the foot of the cross, the uneasy duo of Lady Wilde and Douglas. The long disquisition on Christ is lugubrious and self-indulgent. But as in *The Ancient Mariner*, self-pity is the Romantic male heroine's mesmerizing litany and *modus operandi.*

Wilde's new idea that sorrow is "the supreme emotion" and "the type and test of all great Art" merges Hellenistic emotionalism with Victorian pathos. Despite the cynicism of his epigrams, he was always vulnerable to sentimentality. He himself saw a connection between the two: "Remember that the sentimentalist is always a cynic at heart. Indeed sentimentality is merely the bank holiday of cynicism." Wilde's weakness is embarrassingly obvious in *Dorian Gray*'s dreadful Sibyl Vane episode and in his plays' melodramatic treatment of unlucky women. Reviewing his career in *De Profundis*, he grossly overestimates his accomplishments in drama and poetry: "Whatever I touched I made beautiful in a new mode of beauty."[63] But it is just when he tries to be "beautiful" that he is most sentimental. Although he made a great show of being a poet, not one of his tepid poems would have preserved his name beyond his lifetime. The "poetic" passages in his essays, compared to parallel moments in Baudelaire, are watery and bathetic. *Dorian Gray*'s catalogue of priceless objets d'art is borrowed from Huysmans and written in an English not nearly so fine as Robert Baldick's superb translation of *A Rebours*. Unlike Gautier, Wilde had few powers of luxurious or lyric description. His efforts to be beautiful seem puerile or, more precisely, *girlish*.

Though Wilde was Wordsworth's most merciless antagonist, the two possessed virtually identical creative psychologies. The principal danger to imagination in both Wilde and Wordsworth arose from an uncontrolled feminine element of sentimental pathos. The weak in Wilde's writing, everywhere intermingled with the strong, is the result of an emergence or disinterment of this feminine persona, which is born, as in Wordsworth, from complexities of identification with a *mater dolorosa*. This may have contributed to Wilde's downfall. Aside from the misjudgment of his libel suit, he had ample opportunity to leave the country between his first and second trials. As Ellmann says, "He enticed the age to crucify him, and of course it was as acquiescent in such matters as other ages."[64] His reluctance to flee was part of his public ritual of abasement of the will. In Wilde and Wordsworth, men must be hermaphroditized by disaster.

Wilde had developed his personality to so high a degree of tension that all of nature and culture pressed intolerably on the bounds of self. High comic repartee is sometimes called "brittle," suggesting its glittering, crystalline character. The brittleness of worldly wit comes from its tightness and narrowness, its willful condensation and contraction. It may break from *what is excluded*. Wilde's epicene epigrams belong to the Botticellian tradition of the incised edge, used for the same purpose by Spenser and Blake. His Apollonian delimitations are attempts to separate language from archetypal nature. Aestheticism is predicated on nature's exclusion. But Wilde was undone by his simplistic view of nature, whose chthonian ferocity he never imaginatively grasped. The repulsiveness of procreative nature is the crucial first principle of Decadent beauty. The gorgeous lapidary surfaces of Moreau and Huysmans, the exquisite scintillations of imagery in late Gautier and Baudelaire were made possible by the hostile power these artists saw in nature. Nature's formlessness and liquidity energize the aesthetic reaction, producing a rigorous art of crystalline hardness. Wilde, by blinding himself to the chthonian, severed himself from the primal sources of Decadent beauty. Thus his poetry and prose-poems are weak and inconsequential.

The reason Wilde did his best work after turning homosexual is that women simply reinforced his own feminine sentimentality. He had no gift for lyric, since lyric is based on simple, "natural" emotion. Wilde's writing must be hierarchical in order to be beautiful. He has to kill emotion with Apollonian cruelty. Heterosexuality inhibited his imagination because woman is physically and psychologically internal. Wilde says, following Gautier: "To the aesthetic temperament the vague is always repellent. The Greeks were a nation of artists, because they were spared the sense of the infinite."[65] For the infinite, substitute the invisible, that dark realm of the female body toward which Hellenistic art turns, paralleling the inward movement of Greek philosophy. Wilde's conversion to the homosexual worship of beauty provided him with the master image of the articulated male body, with its radical sexual externality. The beautiful boy, because of his lack of an inner life, became Wilde's emancipator of imagination.

In *The Importance of Being Earnest*, the failed poet created a magnificent new poetry, one that even he did not recognize. Wilde's play, after Spenser's *Faerie Queene* and Shelley's *Epipsychidion*, is the most dazzling burst of Apollonian poetry in English literature. It was made possible by a hermaphroditic transformation, the strangest I have ever studied. The desirable male body was efficacious for Wilde by its fixing of visible limits. Ordinarily, the epicene is synonymous with effeminacy. But the epicene made Wilde *more masculine* by giving him the aggressive power of Apollonian delimitation, which I found everywhere in the language, manners, and aristocratic social order of *The Importance of Being Earnest*. The epicene gave Wilde the discipline of conceptual form that he most lacked as a sentimental lyricist. When, through his own self-thwartings, he was forced by tomblike imprisonment to abandon the amoral Greek worship of the visible world, his sentimentality returned, flooding back into the empathic *De Profundis* and bringing woman with it.

22

American Decadents

Poe, Hawthorne, Melville

In America, English Romanticism fuses with a debilitated Puritanism. American Romanticism is really Decadent Late Romanticism, a style of sexual perversity, closure, and fragmentation or decay. Poe, Coleridge's heir, shows Wordsworthian nature as a dead end. His Gothic entombments shut down the American frontier and repeal the ideal of progress. Poe moves Romanticism into its Mannerist late phase. From 1830 on, American and French Romanticism develop on parallel tracks. French Decadence, we saw, was hastened along by Coleridge coming through Byron to Delacroix, Balzac, and Gautier and by Coleridge coming through Poe to Baudelaire. Now we will examine sexual ambiguities and obsessions that critics have ignored or minimized in major American writers. Decadent Late Romanticism was America's first internal critique of its optimistic overidealizations, a bequest of the Apollonian Enlightenment.

Classic American literature suffers from a sex problem. Genitality is evaded, or woman is excluded to facilitate what Leslie Fiedler calls "the holy marriage of males."[1] America's origins in sectarian Protestantism produced a circumscription of personae like that of republican Rome. Puritan personality, unitary and sharply bounded, was formed by the "rectitude" of acts, a masculine straightmeasure. Hawthorne shows patriarchal will waning in *The House of the Seven Gables*, with its decadent relics of shabby mansion and inherited curse.

America's sex problem began with the banishment of the maternal principle from Protestant cosmology. Medieval Mariolatry was and is a pagan survival that Protestantism, faithful to early Christianity, correctly opposes. But the absence of the mother from pioneer American values imaginatively limited a people living intimately with nature. A society enamored of the future sweeps away the mother, because she is the past, the state of remaining. As I said of Byronism, America is a land of transients and transience, of movement *to* and *across*. In its Enlightenment self-fabrication, America rejected the archaic, leaving a symbolic vacuum partly filled by Indian and Negro. English Romanticism, a neo-pagan cult of the sexual archetypal, arrived as a second revolution, daemonizing American literature. The first artist to register this fully is Poe, who introduces the numinous woman to America. His best tales are redramatizations of Coleridge's *Ancient Mariner* and *Christabel,* which was inspired by Spenser's *Faerie Queene.* So what we will be tracing in the American Decadents is the action-at-a-distance of Italian Renaissance paganism, a style exploited by Emily Dickinson in her wanton Catholic corruptions of her family's New England Protestantism.

Poe's tales are Romantic rather than Gothic, because of the intense identification between himself and his narrators. His women have many names, but there is only one narrator, one voice. Poe's persona or Magister Ludi is the Romantic male heroine of passive suffering. His major women, Berenice, Ligeia, and Morella, tall, beautiful, and strangely erudite, are all versions of Coleridge's vampire Geraldine, who comes to fainting Christabel out of the night. But there is no sexual metathesis and hence no lesbian fantasy. Unlike Coleridge, Balzac, Baudelaire, and Swinburne, Poe keeps his heroes to their own gender. He demands overt male subjection to female power. His women are hermaphrodite divinities, multiple faces of the black Venus. Huysmans, with French intuition, calls Poe's women "unsexed": they have "the inert, boyish breasts of angels."[2]

There is no sex instinct per se in Poe. His eroticism is in the paroxysms of suffering, the ecstatic, self-inflaming surrender to tyrant mothers. The narrator of *Ligeia* is a "child" beneath the tutelage and "infinite supremacy" of the heroine (named, I presume, after a Homeric Siren in Milton). Like Shelley and Mill, Poe dreams of male eclipse by a Muse-like female mind. Ligeia mysteriously lacks a "paternal name," because woman is parthenogenetic, conceived and conceiving without male aid.[3] The narrator cannot remember when or where he met her: she is the mother-shadow at the door of infant memory.

The sexual laws of Poe's world are so strict that a normal, feminine woman cannot survive in it. The narrator's second wife, blonde Lady Rowena, must be exterminated to restore the proper hierarchy of female over male. Raven-haired Ligeia, overcoming death by brute willpower, returns from the grave to invade the body of her successor. I say

Poe is rewriting Geraldine's rape of Christabel. He turns Coleridge's ritual scene back toward heterosexuality, as he does again in *Morella*, where a dead woman returns to obliterate her daughter. *Ligeia* ends in daemonic epiphany, a "hideous drama of revivification," as the narrator shrieks with joy and fear. There is a horrible burst of "huge masses of long and dishevelled hair ... *blacker than the wings of the midnight.*"[4] Ligeia is mother nature and archaic night, an eruption of the pagan chthonian. She defies God's law of mortality because she, not he, is the resurrection and the life. Through the cataract of Medusan hair slowly open, robotlike, Ligeia's "cold, dead eyes"—the eyes by which Geraldine hypnotizes Christabel. What happens next? The story self-destructs. Poe's narrator is turned to stone by the Gorgon eye of nature, vomiting its coarse tangle of serpent-growth from the black soil.

In *Berenice* (1835), written three years earlier, the sudden hierarchic assertion occurs at the start rather than end of the psychodrama. Incest again: Berenice and the narrator are cousins. She dominates him with her catatonic "glassy stare." He anxiously studies her "thin and shrunken lips," which part in a strange smile to reveal *"the teeth."*[5] Coleridge's vampire bares her fangs. The vagina dentata, which sucks in Huysmans' hero, is a kind of beacon in Poe: his vampire Muse guides, leads, eats. Face to face with nature, Poe sees not Wordsworth's benevolent mother but Darwin's cannibal, the Mistress of the Beasts. Berenice is literally long in the tooth, older than time. Poe's vampire tales are religious literature, like Donne's Holy Sonnets. They confront ultimate realities, shocking and unconsoling.

Berenice's teeth are an example of Decadent partition. Like Gautier's mummy's foot, they secede from the whole and greedily swell with power. They invade and rape what the narrator calls "the disordered chamber of my brain," modelled on the vaginal skull of Keats's Apollo.

> The teeth!—the teeth!—they were here, and there, and every where, and visibly and palpably before me; long, narrow, and excessively white, with the pale lips writhing about them. . . . In the multiplied objects of the external world I had no thoughts but for the teeth. . . . They—they alone were present to the mental eye, and they, in their sole individuality, became the essence of my mental life.[6]

Here, there, and everywhere: Berenice has gotten her teeth from Coleridge's red-lipped Nightmare Life-in-Death, scudding along on water, water everywhere, poison to body and mind. Poe's narrator is crucified on the phallic teeth, which doom him to Decadent fixation and contraction. The teeth absorb his consciousness, condensing the universe to one totemic symbol. A task of the Late Romantic artist, I said, is to order the excess of phenomena pressing at the close of High Romanticism. Hence the narrator's fixation on the teeth paradoxically frees him from enslavement to "the multiplied objects of the external world." Late Romantic sexual obsession is a metaphysical strategy, a formula of perceptual control. Poe and Gautier simultaneously develop ritualized eye-object relations out of the collapse of High Romanticism. Berenice's teeth attract and secure the imagination, reducing the world to tolerable proportions. When she dies or seems to die, the narrator pursues her to the grave and tears out her teeth, which he fetishistically preserves like saints' relics or magic talismans. The teeth are now his guardians of identity. *Berenice*'s "dental surgery" is like Kleist's mastectomies: mutilation and reduction of the body are a ritual ascesis of overexpanded modern imagination.

The story's climax, the surgical assault on Berenice's body, is a perverse sex act, like the knife-rape of Balzac's girl with the golden eyes (written the same year). In Poe, woman can be sexually approached only if dead. Person becomes object, in the Decadent manner. The narrator farms and harvests Berenice, as if she were an oyster and her teeth pearls. Sexual desire is diverted from animal flesh toward calcified mineral deposits, those antique enamels we carry in our mouth. The narrator can act only in a trance of self-removal. He is passive to his own extreme emotion, from which he is further separated by a memory lapse. Action is compulsive. The narrator would probably insist, with justice, that he is under criminal compulsion by Berenice herself, who lures him into barbarism by her chthonian force. Love leads to sadism. The Hellenistic Berenice was an Egyptian queen from whom a lock of hair was shorn. Poe's hermaphrodite Berenice, stripped of her "sentient" teeth, is symbolically castrated. But she still lives. The vampire of nature will not stay in her grave. In Poe, sex is ritual combat, a hundred engagements with one outcome: female victory.

Poe, following Coleridge, is always revising Wordsworth. His most spectacular Coleridgean nature-saga is *A Descent into the Maelström* (1841), with its hurricane and whirlpool. The male is sucked into nature's maw, a titanic funnel with "an appalling voice, half shriek, half roar," a bisexual clamor.[7] He spirals down to its nadir, the zero or ninth circle of a female inferno, the nothingness of primeval origins. Sinking, he surveys "the wide waste of liquid ebony," a stunning phrase that combines nature's vast desolation with its flux of dark liquidity. In one day, the sailor's hair turns white. To tell his tale, like Coleridge's Mari-

ner, he climbs the highest peak. Like Moses, he has seen God. But
Moses descends from his encounter with the sky-god, while Poe's hero
must ascend from the bowels of the earth-mother, who parts the waves
of her own Red Sea. *Maelström* contains the cosmology of Poe's vampire
tales. Ligeia, Berenice, and Morella are nature's sexual personae. Poe,
like Sade, sets sex into the sinister continuum of savage nature.

Nature speaks again at the finale of *The Fall of the House of Usher*
(1839), where a mansion is swallowed up by the "black and lurid tarn,"
another liquid ebony: "There was a long tumultuous shouting sound
like the voice of a thousand waters." This tarn, with its "pestilent and
mystic vapor, dull, sluggish, . . . and leaden-hued," is the primeval
swamp of generation. *Usher*, like Gautier's simultaneous *A Night with
Cleopatra*, is a maturely Decadent fiction, exuding an atmosphere of
"extensive decay."[8] History has shrunk to an effete aesthete and his
Byronic sister-double, sealed in a crumbling mansion covered with
fungi. Nature creeps and crawls but will win with a bang. The story ends
like Balzac's *Girl with the Golden Eyes* in a panorama of civilization
overwhelmed by the chthonian. The tarn is Poe's maelstrom in hibernation. Its stagnant morass is mother nature's mouth in fetid repose. At the
violent climax, brother and sister fuse in a sadistic love-death, like the
fiery cleaving of Euripides' princess and father. Incest is Romantic
regression. The cracked house of Usher, an Apollonian head fractured
by madness, surrenders to the Dionysian, the murky womb-world of the
primeval abyss.

Palace, apocalypse: Poe repeats this *Bacchae*-like pattern in *The
Masque of the Red Death* (1842), a masterpiece of amazing brevity.
Prince Prospero tries to defy and shut out nature, which finally crushes
him—a plot echoed by Huysmans. The donnée is from Boccaccio's
Decameron, where a party of Florentine gentry flee to the countryside to
escape the Black Death. But Poe's Red Death is biology-as-pestilence,
"the redness and the horror of blood." Prospero constructs a temple of
art, a corridor of lavish chambers of blue, purple, green, orange, white,
and violet. The seventh chamber reveals the discontinuities of Decadent aestheticism. It is the only one where the color of tapestries, carpet,
and stained-glass windows fails to match: the fabrics are black, but the
glass is "scarlet—a deep blood color."[9] This chamber, where prince and
spectre meet, is the womb, light piercing the membrane in a ruddy
stream. Masoch, probably imitating Poe, adds a similar room to *Venus
in Furs:* "a red streak, like blood," lights up "a dark, dank, subterranean" cell, where the hero is cut free from umbilical ropes.[10] The ebony
clock of Poe's seventh chamber is the ominous heartbeat of the mater-

nal body. Since the Red Death is life itself, the clock is the passing bell that tolls for every man.

The Masque of the Red Death has two rhetorical peculiarities. First, its protagonist is masculine. Second, it is written in impersonal third-person narration, rare in Poe. The two are one: as a male heroine, Poe, like Wordsworth, cannot project himself into a masculine persona. This is the most apocalyptic of his tales, ending with the unforgettable sentence, "And Darkness and Decay and the Red Death held illimitable dominion over all." *Maelström* and *Usher* are less absolute, for at least the narrators escape to tell their tales (a device Melville borrows for the finale of *Moby-Dick*). But *The Red Death* ends with the annihilation of all humanity. Psychosexually, Prospero has produced this through his own vaunting masculinity, for unlike Poe's tremulous first-person narrators, he never subordinates himself to hierarchic female personae, who are excluded from his mad revels. Hence the greater the show of masculinity in Poe, the more catastrophic the punishing reversal. The Red Death, the ghoulish vampire masquer, shadows Prospero as his bodiless, genderless double, liquidating him in the black chamber. Scornfully vanishing into thin air, the Red Death is nature's ungraspable mystery.

Prospero's seventh chamber has a whole story devoted to itself in *The Pit and the Pendulum*, written the same year. The narrator is trapped in a strangely mobile room with "fiery walls," closing upon him in spasms of contraction. This is a body-warmed womb-world: the floor is "moist and slippery," "treacherous with slime," suggesting female secretions. The narrator is caught between a circular pit, a dank "abyss" like Lear's female hell, and the razor-sharp pendulum of time, to which men are condemned at birth. The story takes us into "the red walls" of the vagina dentata. It is as if we were in Berenice's mouth, watching the portcullis of her teeth descending. Poe is obsessed with closure, from *The Premature Burial* to *The Cask of Amontillado*, with its murder by walling-up. In *Maelström*, Charybdis to *The Pit*'s Scylla, he even converts the flat sea into a vacuum-vortex of female internality. Poe's closed spaces are always vaguely anatomical. They are literally living rooms. In *Ligeia*, for example, mechanical wind behind the draperies gives the bridal chamber "a hideous and uneasy animation."[11] Architecture in *The Tell-Tale Heart* is distinctly anthropomorphic, for in hiding the dismembered body beneath the floorboards, the guilty narrator seems to have devoured his eye-intense father-victim, whose heart beats in him like that of a daemonic fetus.

Characters are buried alive in Poe because he sees nature as a hostile womb from which humanity can never be fully born. His master image is like the Mycenaean *tholos*, the subterranean beehive womb-tomb. His stories are Late Romantic *tholoi* fusing the traumas of birth and death. His world suffers an interminable, festering pregnancy. The graveyard soil in which his imagination burrows is the High Romantic landscape, which, once vivified, almost immediately sank into the Late Romantic mass of decaying object-life. The "Many" of created nature, deftly inspirited by Keats, lie in squalid heaps that Late Romanticism is too fatigued to make intelligible. Hence Poe's suffocation and claustrophobia. His narrator's voice never changes because he is writing the same story over and over. Poe personalizes the Gothic novel's daemonic wombs by adding the Coleridgean "I AM." Gothic atmosphere becomes psychology or rather psychopathology, stormy inner weather. Poe's tales are developments of High Romantic lyric. They are *short* stories rather than novels, because they are like the skeletal sexual scripts of Sade's *120 Days of Sodom*. Narrative detail is stripped away to reveal the hierarchic framework in cold clarity. Poe's tales are pagan odes of invocation, realigning male imagination toward omnipotent female nature.

Had he been French, Poe would have been, with Gautier, a founder of aestheticism. He is full of aesthetic yearnings. But his attempts at aristocratic environments of objets d'art usually fizzle, due to the poverty of American culture in his day. There was nothing here to cultivate his taste, no European galleries, mansions, cathedrals. Balzac, Gautier, and Baudelaire, on the other hand, partied and promenaded with avant-garde painters. Talk about art filled the air. *Ligeia*'s elaborate bridal chamber is to Poe what the ornate boudoir is to Balzac. But alas, Poe has tackily plopped "a gigantic sarcophagus of black granite" in each corner of the room. His gilded style of décor is like that of William Randolph Hearst's San Simeon, a muddle of priceless but incongruous objects. Similarly, Poe's language is too often ho-hum journalese, peppered with bathos. Coleridge and Poe have cinematic minds. They are masters of emotional extremity and archetypal visualization. But in his Baudelairean quest for a theory of art, Poe was ill-served by his nation, with its lingering Puritan hostility to beauty and pleasure.

In the detective story, invented by Poe, the Apollonian male mind breaks free of sex and nature. Only *The Murders in the Rue Morgue* (1841) is Decadent. There, nature again invades the inmost chamber, Poe's temenos of archetypal encounter. But now nature is an ape in brutal masculine action, on the rampage against female power. Woman, who binds us into materiality, is battered and mutilated to plug up the chimney hole or maelstrom through which she steals from men in order to give birth.

Poe's essays are similarly sexualized. *The Imp of the Perverse*, prefiguring Freud's theory of the unconscious, sees humanity as vulnerable to amoral impulses. The vampire tales show the genesis of this idea, which is another version of male passivity. In *The Philosophy of Composition*, Poe declares, "The death of a beautiful woman is, unquestionably, the most poetical topic in the world."[12] This looks like run-of-the-mill nineteenth-century sentimentalism. But the glamourous Poe woman is not feminine but masculine. Hence the death of the *masculine* principle is poetical, because it unites male and female, aggression and passivity, appearance and disappearance. In Poe as in Coleridge, poetry is a synthesis of contraries.

The mother banished from Protestantism makes her American debut at the climax of Poe's *The Narrative of A. Gordon Pym* (1837). This novella, in a specially bound private edition, appears in *A Rebours*, exactly as a copy of *A Rebours* appears in *Dorian Gray*. *Pym* is an archetypal journey to the heart of creation. Its hero, the transformed Poe (Pym = pseudonym), witnesses a tremendous return of the repressed, for which the price is death.

As the polar sea around his drifting boat turns warm and "milky," Pym goes numb with "a dreaminess of sensation." White ashy powder rains down, like the flakes of fire Dante compares to Alpine snow (*Inf.* XIV, 28–30). A huge cataract curtained in vapor falls silently into the sea, lit by "a luminous glare." The boat rushes "into the embraces of the cataract, where a chasm threw itself open to receive us." A titan rises, skin white as snow. Here the story ends.[13]

Who or what is the apparition? Our reading must be imagistically consistent with Poe's other tales. Pym meets the nature mother, into whom he is reabsorbed. She is shrouded, like Spenser's Venus, because she is hermaphroditic. This is a chthonian epiphany, muffled and eyeless. We enter the Dionysian realm of formlessness and dissolution. Poe borrows the chasm, "mighty fountain," "lifeless ocean," and "milk of Paradise" from "Kubla Khan" and joins them to *Epipsychidion*'s dream of prenatal incest. The white curtain over life's mystery parts, and the frail soul-boat plunges into the birth canal. At degree zero, a seminal torrent rushes eternally into the womb of matter. The smothering white shower is phenomena sinking back to primeval origins. White noise, white hole, the birth and death of stars: this spectacle of soundless sensory deprivation is a Romantic triumph. All hysteria resolves into oppressive calm.

At almost the same moment, Nathaniel Hawthorne too was thinking of the goddess mother and her veils. *The Minister's Black Veil* (1836) is a bizarre exercise in transvestism. The Reverend Mr. Hooper greets his congregation with his face hidden by "a simple black veil, such as any woman might wear on her bonnet." People are perplexed or terrified. The minister stays in costume for the rest of his life. Assumption by critics that the veil is the burden of original sin unpersuasively imposes the moral and rational on the compulsive and uncanny. Hooper diagnoses the sexual incompleteness of Protestantism and remedies it by automedication. He does not seek concrete sexual experience. On the contrary, his refusal to remove the veil drives away his fiancée, whose loss he accepts with a coy smile. The gender-blurring veil is like the goddess' robe donned by male initiates of the Eleusinian Mysteries. Devotee merges with nature mother by transsexual impersonation. The story acknowledges its pagan inspiration when Hooper, spooked by his veiled face in the mirror, rushes into the night: "The Earth, too, had on her Black Veil."[14] So the minister's black veil is the female shadow of archaic night.

Hawthorne's tales ponder Christianity's uneasy relation to woman and nature. In *The Birthmark*, a scientist destroys his bride by trying to remove "the bloody hand" imprinted by nature on her cheek. In *Rappaccini's Daughter*, a sequestered girl is turned into a poison flower by her harsh father, an Apollonian Jehovah playing dirty tricks in Eden. In *The May-Pole of Merry Mount*, Puritans squelch a town's pagan revels in the woods. In *The Scarlet Letter*, Hawthorne puts the mother at center stage. The adulteress Hester Prynne, infant at her bosom, is "the image of Divine Maternity," which only "a Papist among the crowd of Puritans would recognize."[15] In other words, Hester is the Catholic Madonna drummed out of Protestantism. That the mother theme of *The Scarlet Letter* had something to do with Hawthorne's own mother is clear from the chronology of composition. After his mother's death on 31 July 1849, he fell ill from a "brain fever," from which recovery was slow. There is a gap in his notebooks from 30 July to 5 September, during which he began work on *The Scarlet Letter*. The book was completed the next February and published that year.

In "The Custom-House," the semiautobiographical preface, Hawthorne introduces his antagonist persona, a Puritan patriarch, "that first ancestor" of his family who "still haunts me": "this grave, bearded, sable-cloaked, and steeple-crowned progenitor,—who came so early, with his Bible and his sword."[16] In *The Scarlet Letter*, the exiled sexual persona of the saintly natural mother will defeat Hawthorne's despotic male progenitor, who carries a church on and in his head. Both preface and novella are twice their optimal length. *The Scarlet Letter* is over-written. Its secret preoccupation is embedded, hidden, layered with anxious afterthought. The story is as obsessively embroidered as the red letter itself.

Hawthorne's tale of adultery is not like *Madame Bovary* and *Anna Karenina*, social novels. *The Scarlet Letter* is a Late Romantic dream poem, stirred by inner turbulence. Fiedler says "the carnal act" of adultery is "deprived of reality by being displaced in time" and is thus, "in the psychologist's sense, prehistoric."[17] There is a striking diversion of affect away from Hester toward a homoerotic male dominator, "mis-shapen" Roger Chillingworth. Why did Hawthorne drag in this super-fluous Mephisto character? Chillingworth's presence is a psychological necessity. By binding him to the alleged adulterer Arthur Dimmesdale (they are together "sleeping and waking"), Hawthorne leaves Hester and her daughter Pearl in a "magic circle" or "circle of seclusion," an archetypal female temenos no man can enter.[18] Old Chillingworth is the cold, paralyzing hand of Hawthorne's father and forefathers. Hester is his divinized mother, half Virgin, half Magdalene. Adultery is the son's jealous charge against a mother abandoning him for his father. Hester is Antigone standing against the town, while Dimmesdale is Oedipus ruined by incest.

Hester is a wandering goddess still bearing the mark of her Asiatic origins. She has "a rich, voluptuous, Oriental characteristic,—a taste for the gorgeously beautiful," expressed in needlework. The scarlet letter, standing for adultery but also for the Alpha and Omega of divinity, is adorned with "elaborate embroidery and fantastic flourishes of gold thread." A Byzantine Madonna or Renaissance queen, Hester exposes the multiple repressions of Puritanism: beauty, sex, imagina-tion, art. Hawthorne's Gretchen has expanded in power, while Faust has shrunk. Like the veiled minister, Dimmesdale is a man of God who seeks the goddess. His virility is as dim as his name. With his breathless tremors and "childish weakness," the "passive" Dimmesdale is a Ro-mantic male heroine, more son than lover. Even if one accepts the adultery as a given, the sex act has permanently crippled the male, a drone stunned by the queen bee. Hester must exhort Dimmesdale, "Preach! Write! Act!"[19] She has energy because she is Romantic nature, while Puritan patriarchy is in decadent decline.

The climax is Dimmesdale's night ascent of the public platform of ritual exposure to stand with Hester and her daughter. As they hold hands, "a tumultuous rush of new life," "a torrent" of "vital warmth" pours through him: "The three formed an electric chain."[20] The minister's acceptance of moral responsibility?—worthless in my view if not in the day. I see the scene as a tableau of matrilineage staged on the pagan altar of archaic night. The male joins himself to the electric chain of femaleness. Rejuvenated by a surge of female force, he declares, in effect, "I too am born of woman!"

As in *The Minister's Black Veil*, a covert transsexualism is at work. In his early twenties, before secluding himself in his mother's house for twelve years, Hawthorne added a *w* to the family name Hathorne. This *w* prefigures the scarlet letter that, in "The Custom-House," he tries to fix to his breast but drops on the floor when he feels it burning with ghostly mana. "Hawthorne" is his father's name blasphemously hermaphroditized. The *w*, I think, is for *woman*, whom Hawthorne injects into his patrimony, just as he is to restore the mother to the Puritan seventeenth century in *The Scarlet Letter*. The Romantic idea of a hermaphroditic surname may have come to him from the fact that his mother's maiden name was *Man*ning.

The hypnotic or somnambulistic liaison between the men of *The Scarlet Letter* anticipates the one between the women of *The Blithedale Romance* (1852). As I showed, Geraldine's seduction of Christabel is Hawthorne's model for the fiery Zenobia's mesmeric domination of feminine Priscilla. Henry James will redramatize *The Blithedale Romance* in *The Bostonians*, where Coleridge's lesbian theme boldly resurfaces. Coleridge and Hawthorne share a fascism of the eye. Criticism fails to notice that major nineteenth-century American literature has as perverse a visual eroticism as anything in Decadent Paris. Hester, warning the palpitating Dimmesdale of Chillingworth's "evil eye," tries to break the spell by "fixing her deep eyes on the minister's, and instinctively exercising a magnetic power" over him.[21] In Romantic vampirism, ocular fascination accompanies monstrous soul-divisions. One gender may split into a warring pair, autoerotic and self-tormenting. Dimmesdale is tied to Hester by guilt and dependency but not by sexual cathexis. His real lover is Chillingworth, to whom he is locked in sterile sadomasochistic marriage.

The bareness of Puritan plain style and the absence of inherited art works starved the American eye and aggravated the dangerous power of the visual when it arrived via Romanticism. Asceticism, fearing the eye, actually sharpens it. Hawthorne illustrates the sexual problematics of the visual when Hester is brought before the multitude: "The unhappy culprit sustained herself as best a woman might, under the heavy weight of a thousand unrelenting eyes, all fastened upon her, and concentred at her bosom. It was almost intolerable to be borne."[22] Hester as scapegoat is the focus of projected eroticism. The thousand eyes obsessively fixed on the scarlet letter are "concentred at her bosom" because the mother's flowing breasts have been expelled from Puritan consciousness. There is a mass voyeurism of attraction and repulsion. Let us follow Hawthorne's language into all its strange implications. Hester bears the intolerably "heavy weight" of eyes "fastened upon her." Surreally, the thousand eyes are attached to her bosom, sacs of engorged significance. Standing on the platform that is the scene of western hierarchic assertion for Cellini's *Perseus*, the picture of Dorian Gray, and Hitler at Nuremberg, Hester is the Ephesian Artemis on her pedestal, the Asiatic mother-idol of a hundred animal breasts. Shelley saw vampire eyes in female breasts. Hester, like Vergil's adultery-spurred Rumor, is spangled with multiple staring eyes. At this cardinal moment, Hawthorne's grotesque superornamentation of style is as Decadent as Gustave Moreau's.

An archetypal reading of *The Scarlet Letter* removes its Americanism, its sense of place. It also suppresses the plot. But the American elements in the Late Romantic *Scarlet Letter* are relatively superficial. Prerevolutionary New England is simply "the ancestral" in the shorthand of local dialect. It is no more authentic than the creaky medievalism of a Gothic novel. Plot is always negligible in Romanticism. Plot is history, cause and effect rationally unfolding in time, but in Romantic poetry, history is irrationally propelled backward toward the primeval. The plot proffered by Coleridge's *Ancient Mariner* is false. The same with *The Scarlet Letter*, which can be read for plot only if one ignores huge emotional and sexual gaps. *The Scarlet Letter* is an archetypal vision of persecuted woman moving serenely in the magic circle of her sexual nature. Dimmesdale is a son-lover who longs to merge with the mother but cannot. Pearl is the infant son purged of his divisive maleness. Hester clones her in the stress of solitude. Time has ground down the adulteress' stones to sand, around which forms a perfect pearl. For Hawthorne-as-Dimmesdale, the mother is both too near and too far. *The Scarlet Letter* formalizes Hawthorne's ambivalent adult relation to his mother, who must be thrust into the mental distance for imagination's survival.

Herman Melville's composition of *Moby-Dick*, a dawdling, on-and-off affair, was galvanized by his reading Hawthorne's work and meeting with him in August 1850, shortly after publication of *The Scarlet Letter. Moby-Dick* took its present form in a burst of activity from that August to the next. The book, dedicated to Hawthorne, was published in the fall. What artistic dynamic was at work between Melville and Hawthorne? I see *Moby-Dick* as a sexual reply to *The Scarlet Letter*. Both books correct a sexual exclusion, but *Moby-Dick*'s worldview is vaster. Melville drowns Protestant rationalism and Wordsworthian benevolence in a storm of barbaric nature-force. Behind *Moby-Dick* is Coleridge's *Ancient Mariner* and Poe's *Maelström* and *Pym*. Hawthorne symbolizes Protestant defects in an excommunicated woman. But Melville, for his own reasons, cannot idealize woman. *Moby-Dick*, a chthonian epic, refuses to acknowledge the maternal as primary. Thus the novel sways back and forth between High Romanticism and Decadent Late Romanticism, between celebration of mighty nature and contorted resistance to it, in the florid manner of Huysmans.

Moby-Dick rejects male sexual destiny, which Romanticism portrays as servitude to female power. Melville declares: I shall revive the chthonian but in masculine form. The novel subtly hermaphroditizes the great whale without genuinely diluting his masculinity. Moby-Dick steals his "uncommon magnitude" from mother nature. Like *Pym*, the book honors a subterranean or submarine deity, a mute, amoral counterconception to talkative, lawgiving Jehovah. The whale inhabits the primeval realm, from which he makes capricious epiphanies.

The novel's nonfiction sections, surveying the whale and its species, have two purposes. *Moby-Dick* aspires to epistemology, organizing the known, if only to dramatize what cannot be known. Melville plumbs and dissects his whale, measuring and naming each part. But his epic catalogs are *feignings of inclusiveness*. They give every name to the great whale but one: mother. The novel's cognitive data are fragments shored against male ruin. Again and again, Melville elevates the masculine principle above the feminine, driving back and limiting female power. This book, which takes the whiteness or blankness of nonmeaning as its premiere symbol and which is the first novel to acknowledge "the heartless voids and immensities of the universe," should logically take a depersonalized view of nature.[23] But Melville's treatment of nature is amazingly inconsistent, full of the swerves of sexual anxiety.

Moby-Dick is a lavish portrait of rapacious Sadean nature, "the universal cannibalism of the sea" and the "horrible vulturism of earth." Melville rejects Christian and Wordsworthian tenderness: "We are all killers, on land and on sea." "Butchers we are" of "sharkish" will. Like Baudelaire, he challenges the hypocrite reader: "Go to the meat-market of a Saturday night and see the crowds of live bipeds staring up at the long rows of dead quadrupeds. . . . Cannibals? who is not a cannibal?" Humanism and liberalism are daytime masks. Night releases our animal appetites. One of the novel's supreme moments is its archetypal vision of the great squid:

> A vast pulpy mass, furlongs in length and breadth, of a glancing cream-color, lay floating on the water, innumerable long arms radiating from its centre, and curling and twisting like a nest of anacondas, as if blindly to clutch at any hapless object within reach. No perceptible face or front did it have; no conceivable token of either sensation or instinct; but undulated there on the billows, an unearthly, formless, chance-like apparition of life.[24]

This is the snaky Medusa-head of nature, swampy and inert, a Burne-Jones thicket at sea. The squid is faceless, but is it sexless? We will see this "pulpy mass" again in Melville's story *The Paradise of Bachelors and The Tartarus of Maids*, where it represents woman's nonstop fertility.

The squid is what Melville will not let his whale become. It is the female grossness of matter, a sticky, viscous web. He later revises the squid into the magnificent loom of vegetable nature, humming in its lush South Seas "bower." Bowers, as bequeathed by Spenser through Milton to the Romantics, are the secret cells of female power. Melville does not simply drop the bower's traditional gender for a scientific inspection of nature's machinery, which would be understandable. He strenuously personalizes and resexualizes his bower in the opposite direction. The loom is run by a "weaver-god" called "he."[25] This god is surprisingly like the Christian deity whom *Moby-Dick* is otherwise eager to belittle and defame. Melville cannot bear to leave his loom gender-neutral, despite its appropriateness to his coldly stringent cosmology. Why? He feels too strongly *the presence of female power* in his Romantic spectacle of seething greenery. The ultimate weaver of world mythology is woman, and the loom is her body. Here Melville follows Blake in refusing to concede female control over procreation.

I suspect the heart of *Moby-Dick* was generated by Melville's ambivalent reaction to Hawthorne's female-centered work. Running through the novel's bulky midsection is a chain of improvised sexual images reflecting, I theorize, a process of association from Melville's dream life. The weaver-god chapter is a sexual cancellation of an earlier chapter, "The Grand Armada," where a whaleboat is drawn into the eye of a whale herd moving in concentric circles. The boat rests in the "enchanted calm" of an "exceedingly transparent" lake. Far below float pregnant and nursing whales. At first disturbance, everything vanishes. The episode has been compared to the *Paradiso*, where rings of angels form a mystic rose of light. So this is Melville's chthonian substitute for the Christian sublime. But there are no ambivalences in Dante's vision. Midchapter, Melville compares the stillness to the "mute calm" amid "the tornadoed Atlantic of my being." Man's inner life is female, in the Romantic way. *Billy Budd* calls the heart "sometimes the feminine in man," like a "piteous woman" appealing to a judge for mercy.[26] But at this unearthly moment in *Moby-Dick*, Melville's axiom is too calculated and sententious. As with Coleridge glossing his *Mariner*, the fearful and impersonal are rationalized and weakened. The first Grand Armada threatened America's motherland, ruled by a queen. Who or what is menaced by Melville's armada?

That the whaleboat is "becalmed" in the maternal lake should alert us. Everything else in *Moby-Dick* champions the driven and stormy over the quiet and sheltered, that "lee shore" with which Melville identifies the "treacherous, slavish" complacencies of society and religion. D. H. Lawrence says Melville's sea voyages were flights from "HOME and MOTHER": "The two things that were his damnation."[27] The becalmed whale-boat is in a fallen, not a redeemed state. Masculine movement and action are paralyzed by straying too near a magnetic omphalos-spot. This contemplative bliss is experienced by men who have turned to stone. Through the glassy uterine waters, mother and child are seen united and in repose, but achingly across space and time, for their peaceful uncomplexity of relation belongs to infancy. Man can regain this paradise state only by shrinking to a captive minnow, a genie in a female bottle.

"The Grand Armada" is a spectacle of uncanny luminosity with hidden dangers. Melville adds a strange footnote, an afterthought betraying his ambivalences. He says of the breasts of female whales: "When by chance these precious parts in a nursing whale are cut by the hunter's lance, the mother's pouring milk and blood rivallingly discolor the sea for rods. The milk is very sweet and rich; it has been tasted by man; it might do well with strawberries." Welcome to one of Huysmans' grotesque banquets, Coleridge's milk of paradise served bloody rare. Melville sensualizes the blood and water of Christ's spear wound. Milk and blood aggressively compete with each other and with the stained sea. Mother and hunter are enemies. Archetypally, the hunter cuts her to escape from her. The attraction and repulsion and the sequence of images are Decadent. The vivid strawberries, which follow rather than more humanely precede the spilled blood, are fleshy mammaries or red corpuscles forcing the bittersweet brew of milk and blood into the reader's mouth. Behind this footnote is surely the strawberry mark on the face of Hawthorne's heroine in *The Birthmark*. It too is red on white, "a crimson stain upon the snow."[28] Hawthorne's "bloody hand" sym-bolizes mother nature's supremacy, which male science rejects. In Mel-ville as in Hawthorne, the female is maimed to limit her power. But Hawthorne takes woman's side, while Melville, despite himself, takes the hunter's.

The chapters following "The Grand Armada" withdraw step by step from its already qualified vision of female origins. On the next page, we are asked to admire the vast size of the male whale, an "Ottoman" among smaller, "delicate," self-sacrificing "concubines." Twenty pages later comes the first mention of the male weaver, when a castaway loses his wits and sees "God's foot upon the treadle of the loom." Next page, the narrator Ishmael and his shipmates knead tubs of spermaceti: "Squeeze! squeeze! squeeze!" The men clasp hands in the goo and exchange sentimental looks. "Would that I could keep squeezing that sperm for ever! . . . In visions of the night, I saw long rows of angels in paradise, each with his hands in a jar of spermaceti." This is Melville's real heaven, an all-male platoon, each with his hand in someone else's pocket. The circle jerk is another Romantic uroboros. Melville's spermy male hands are a joyous dream-substitution for Hawthorne's "bloody hand" of female nature. Turn another page, and we are in *Moby-Dick*'s most totemic chapter, which focuses on the whale's penis, a "gran-dissimus" so heavy it takes three men to carry it. This "very strange, enigmatical object" or "unaccountable cone" is the "idol" of a male nature cult. Melville is practicing representational gigantism, the style I found in Michelangelo and Blake and defined as a defense against female power. To mince blubber, a sailor dons the whale's tough penis skin like a priest's cassock.[29] This chapter is funny, but for the wrong reasons. Ithyphallos/ichthyphallos: Greek comedy's erections turn sod-den and lugubrious in Melville. The whale has become a cartoon kingpin.

Thus by a series of linked passages, in which the female is minimized in size and temper and the male maximized in member and function, Melville in less than fifty pages inverts the maternal dominion of "The

Grand Armada" into male control of the loom of vegetable nature. Mythologically, there never has been a purely masculine vegetation deity. Melville demotes the female to a lower order of being. I called *Moby-Dick*'s nature Sadean, but it is really Coleridgean. The great squid, for example, is a version of *The Ancient Mariner*'s undulating sea snakes. Melville wants Coleridge's nature without Coleridge's vampire queen, the Nightmare Life-in-Death. Hence he exaggerates his whale into the male "Titanism of power." He indulgently dwells on the whale's massive penis to give masculinity integrity and visibility in the female sea of dissolution that is "Queen Nature." He names Michelangelo as a fellow admirer of the "robustness" and "brawniness" of true divinity, which "the soft, curled, hermaphroditical Italian pictures" fail to show. Whenever he gives his whale some feminine trait, Melville immediately cancels it by a masculine afterthought—of violence or rape.[30] Masculinity struggles for dominance throughout *Moby-Dick*. The great whale's "mighty mildness" is a homoerotic tenderness, part of the longing for comradeship that Melville shares with Whitman, Lawrence, and Forster.

Moby-Dick begins with a ritual of male bonding. Ishmael and Queequeg are tied by "matrimonial" language and bedroom embraces. The first chapters record the assembly and knitting together of men before they launch out onto nature's turbulent bosom. Even the ship is an androgyne, with "bearded" bows. The "ship's navel" is a gold doubloon, the badge of men not born of women or of men who have struck out their female origins. The first mate laments he must "sail with such a heathen crew that have small touch of human mothers in them." Woman enters *Moby-Dick* only as displaced chthonian force. Her sexual allure is never acknowledged, except in bawdy banter among three foreign sailors on watch. Woman's allure is diverted into "the pagan harpooneers," delegates of the races. Each bears some hermaphroditic sign: Tashtego and Fedallah have long hair; Daggoo wears gold ear hoops; Queequeg's body is adorned with tattoos that burn with "Satanic blue flames." Melville's Byronic harpooneers tower with imaginative authority. "Tawny features" set off by the "barbaric brilliancy" of their teeth, they are a lustrous coalescence of the ugly and the beautiful.[31] The harpooneers are daemonic archangels, tanned by hellfire. I view their multiracialism as a sexual transposition. As Romantic sexual personae, silent, solitary, and proudly self-complete, they have stolen their dark glittering glamour from repressed woman.

Masculinity's quest for dominance in *Moby-Dick* is struggling against a major Romantic principle, impairment of the masculine. The novel ingeniously evades this rule by half-surrender. Its climax is the most devastating reversal of male will in Romanticism, as the ship, smashed by the whale, sinks in the infernal "vortex" of Poe's maelstrom. But only *human* masculinity suffers this crushing subordination, the penalty for its hubris of assertion. Its chastiser is not female nature but a brute male dominator, perfect in unintelligible force. The tax laid upon masculinity in *Moby-Dick* is evident in the burden of sexual symbolism borne by Captain Ahab, the Romantic outlaw. He stands upon the "dead stump" of an amputated leg, a sexual injury consistent with his one-night-stand marriage. His artificial leg nearly pierces his groin, leaving an incurable wound: he is thigh-torn Adonis, severed from mother nature by his "unsurrenderable wilfulness." A missing limb lingers as a "pricking" phantom memory. Therefore the harpoon Ahab darts at Moby-Dick is a phallic mental projection, born of frustrated desire. During his wildest speech, the harpoon lies "firmly lashed in its conspicuous crotch," a disturbingly suggestive phrase.[32]

The scar running down Ahab's face and body is "a birth-mark," the mark of Cain. Ahab seems "made of solid bronze, . . . like Cellini's cast Perseus," that western paradigm. Bronze is the Apollonian strategy of a man hardening himself against nature. Ahab's scar is his birthmark because he has no navel. It is from his golden body that the ship's doubloon has been struck. He hails the pagan lightning as his divine sire and, like Athena, claims to know no mother. He usurps motherhood into his own overbearing will: "The queenly personality lives in me, and feels her royal rights." It is Actium, and transsexualized Ahab is Cleopatra defeated at sea.

Ahab commandeers ship and crew in his lust for unconditional freedom. But like liberal Romanticism itself, the worshipper of autonomy is under internal and external compulsion. Ahab is driven by a "hidden lord and master, and cruel, remorseless emperor": "I act under orders." Melville declares: "All men live enveloped in whale-lines. All are born with halters round their necks." This umbilical halter, the harpoon line that will strangle Ahab, is Aeschylus' "harness of Necessity." It is Clytemnestra's net, the femme fatale of nature symbolized in the writhing great squid. Earlier, Melville speaks of "that immaculate manliness we feel within ourselves" that remains "intact" through all disaster.[33] The innermost self is a *virgo intacta* ravished by life's physical indignities. Immaculate manliness belongs to those untouched by the humiliating "bloody hand" of Hawthorne's female nature, which thrusts us into the world. Whipsawed between paradoxes, Melville forces his own sexual resolution on his Romantic materials. In *Moby-Dick*, his attempt to suppress the indebtedness of male to female has produced a stunning sadomasochistic spectacle of male subdued to male.

For perfect consistency, the great whale should be sexually neuter, its "appalling" whiteness an obliteration of person, gender, and meaning. But acrid, Late Romantic family romance intrudes upon a High Romantic epic of raw Dionysian energy. Why is *Moby-Dick* staggeringly greater than anything else Melville wrote? The novel's operatic gigantism comes from its force of *sexual protest*. Its storminess is a reaction against the paralyzing bliss of female stasis, glimpsed in "The Grand Armada." Man searching for the secrets of nature is like "an Ohio honey-hunter, who seeking honey in the crotch of a hollow tree, found such exceeding store of it, that leaning too far over, it sucked him in, so that he died embalmed." On the same page, Queequeg plays "obstetrics" in rescuing Tashtego from a sinking whale's head. The head is the prison of male intellect, says Melville, immediately revising his hollow tree into "Plato's honey head," in which so many have perished.[34] But this head is another of Melville's inflated male members, a hoaxing subterfuge. The real honeyed crotch in which we all drown is the womb-tomb of mother nature.

My view of the repressed sexual subject of *Moby-Dick* is confirmed by an odd story Melville wrote in the next several years, *The Paradise of Bachelors and The Tartarus of Maids* (published April 1855), which compares the sexual experiences of men and women. The first part is naturalistic, while the second is grotesque with biomorphic allegories. Is the story really liberal and reformist? I say it shows Melville's social conscience arguing unsuccessfully against his daemonic fear of woman and nature.

Tartarus of Maids is a descent into a sexual underworld, both inferno and Venusberg. We are seeing the dark underbelly of High Romantic landscape. Melville surely takes his genital topography from Poe: Pym enters "a narrow gorge" with an "excessively slippery" cleft.[35] Melville's gorge contracts into a clitoral "Black Notch," then expands into a labial purple hollow amid "shaggy" pubic mountains. From vaginal "Devil's Dungeon" springs menstrual "Blood River," boiling like Coleridge's Alph amid huge boulders. In Melville as in Poe, a polar zone turns ominously warm. The traveller of *Tartarus of Maids* tours a paper mill "stifling with a strange, blood-like abdominal heat." The factory parodies procreation. "The dark colossal water-wheel, grim with its one immutable purpose," is woman's inexorable monthly calendar. Rows of girls, like "mares haltered to the rack," shred fabric on a "long, glittering scythe," tearing things apart to remake them. The scythe is Poe's pendulum, here a phallic tool of father time. Next, in a messy "bespattered place," are two great vats full of "a white, wet, woolly-looking stuff, not unlike the albuminous part of an egg, soft-boiled." The vats are ovaries glutted with the mucoid, the swampy morass I identify with female physiology and Dionysus. This is another detail from *Pym*, with its gummy purple water, a placenta shot with many-colored "veins" (cf. Coleridge's sea-snakes).[36] We have already seen *Tartarus'* eggy batter in the "vast pulpy mass" of *Moby-Dick*'s "cream-colored" squid. Thus we know the squid's secret gender.

I found in Blake's indictment of woman-as-vampire a negative manifest content masking a latent content of impermissible attraction. Another split between aim and affect occurs in *Tartarus*, but in reverse. Melville shows women enslaved by their sexual destinies and exploited by a managerial class of carousing bachelors. But humanitarianism is the story's first level of meaning only. The frostbite numbing the narrator's cheeks is sexual fear and loathing. "Redly and demoniacally boiled Blood River," declares Melville in a moment of unguarded vision.[37] Woman is in league with the irrational. Nature, more than society, is her true oppressor. Menstruation and childbirth, which we long to regard as "normal" and "natural," are surges of barbarism. Melville's traveller, society's emissary, stands speechless before the industrial titanism of female nature.

A sample of the story's ambiguous duality: "At rows of blank-looking counters sat rows of blank-looking girls, with blank, white folders in their blank hands, all blankly folding blank paper." Here is the boredom of mass production, the meaninglessness of modern labor alienating Melville's self-entombed Bartleby, another paper pusher. But in *Tartarus*, there is no pity without terror. The blank girls with blank pages are white goddesses creasing the tabula rasa of man's soul. They are blind, impassive Fates or Graiai. The narrator, whose boy Vergil is named Cupid, shudders at the teeming circles of this hell. But his relation to the damned is far more ambivalent than Blake's or Dickens' to their abused waifs. The inescapable fact is that Melville represents female physiology as grossly spiritless, brute biological process.

A huge machine stands in a corner, its piston hammering a heavy wood block. A pale girl feeds it rose paper, upon which it stamps a wreath of roses. The mill's great paper-making machine is an "inflexible iron animal," at which the narrator gazes in awe. Heavy machinery of this kind strikes "strange dread into the human heart, as some living, panting Behemoth might." What is "so specially terrible" is "the metallic necessity, the unbudging fatality." "The thin gauzy vail of pulp" marches on "in unvarying docility to the autocratic cunning of the machine." The narrator stands "spell-bound": "A fascination fastened on me."[38]

The wreath of roses is love poetry's naively cheerful commentary on sex experience. But men are not the villains. Like Baudelaire's "A Carcass," *Tartarus* exposes the gap between literary convention and nature's reality to evoke horror rather than empathy. The narrator, spellbound by Romantic fascination, is paralyzed before the Medusa-head of vegetable nature. The phallic piston itself is driven by the machine. *Tartarus* contains *Moby-Dick*'s true loom. The tyrant machine is the female body, grinding and milling the pulp of matter, the gluten of human flesh.

The narrator asks the proprietor why female workers are "indiscriminately called girls, never women."[39] Melville anticipates feminist complaint on this argot, which shrinks women to children. Mythologically, however, the girls of *Tartarus* are virgin *kore* figures. They are Persephones whose mother Demeter is too monstrous to take human form, for *she is the machine.* Note the link to *Moby-Dick:* Melville calls the machine a living "Behemoth"; the girls' blankness is the great whale's "appalling" (literally, pale-making) whiteness. Moby-Dick, who should be gender-neutral, is so fiercely masculine in order to keep him from *turning into a female.* In other words, the whale's hyper-masculinity defensively obscures the femaleness of nature. The maternal peace and beauty of Melville's "Grand Armada" are a poignant sexual dream, for *Tartarus* reveals the horror of what must be repressed. I repeatedly call woman "the hidden." *Tartarus of Maids* makes the invisible visible. We see the hydrodynamics of female engineering articulated into rational clarity. To see, to know, to sympathize. But a daemonic energy wells up from below Melville's consciousness to deform the female organs into disgusting *disjecta membra* at surreal cubist angles. *Tartarus* contains the marine descent eluded by the lone survivor of *Moby-Dick.* In its quest to give masculinity cosmic dominance, Melville's epic novel has had to smother nature's chthonian plumbing.

The Tartarus of Maids, a nightmare condensation of *Moby-Dick*'s chthonian theme, is the reverse image of Melville's last story, *Billy Budd, Sailor,* which he left in draft at his death in 1891. *Tartarus'* ugly, turgid procreative realm is opposed by *Billy Budd*'s daylit Apollonian realm of beauty, clarity, and charisma. *Billy Budd* is the supreme Apollonian work of American literature, to which visionary idealism is foreign because of the cultural bias toward pragmatism. In Melville's oeuvre, *Billy Budd* is to *Tartarus* as Balzac's *Seraphita* is to *The Girl with the Golden Eyes:* the celestial seraphic supplants the hell of female barbarism. *Billy Budd* was made possible by Melville's descent to and escape from the female miasma.

Billy Budd belongs to the glamourous company of beautiful boys we have traced from the Athenian *Kritios Boy* to Donatello's *David*, Shakespeare's fair youth, and Wilde's Dorian Gray. In the first manuscript (1886), he was much older. The story is dedicated to Jack Chase, an Englishman who also inspired *White-Jacket* (1850). Citing Melville's admiration of an Antinous sculpture in Rome during his travels of 1856–57, Fiedler calls Billy Budd "Jack Chase recast in the image of Antinoüs."[40] My own theory is that *The Picture of Dorian Gray* affected *Billy Budd*, in which I hear echoes of Wilde's language. A year before its release in book form, *Dorian Gray* appeared in the July 1890 issue of *Lippincott's Monthly* (Philadelphia and London). Scholars cannot tell when Billy Budd regressed from adult to ephebe.[41] I suspect *Dorian Gray* revived Melville's memories of Antinous and produced the final story's more androgynous hero.

Billy Budd has a springtime freshness. Though twenty-one, he has "a lingering adolescent expression" and smooth "feminine" complexion. He has "yellow curls" and "welkin eyes"—literally, sky eyes. He is an "Apollo," a purebred product of "the Saxon strain": his blonde Apollonian radiance is the Dorian or Aryan element in European culture. He is "an angel," like "Fra Angelico's seraphs," who have "the faint rosebud complexion of the more beautiful English girls." Transsexual similes compare Billy to "a rustic beauty" or "vestal priestess." In his single defect, he is "like the beautiful woman in one of Hawthorne's minor tales"—that is, *The Birthmark*. His unknown mother is visible in his curved mouth, small ear, and arched foot. The crew call him "Beauty," like a fairy-tale maiden. His "masculine beauty" is an androgynous combination of "strength and beauty," "comeliness and power," like the duality of Gautier's contralto.[42]

Like *Dorian Gray, Billy Budd* is structured by Apollonian hierarchy. Billy belongs to the class of "Handsome Sailor," a "superior figure" of "natural regality." His peers, "the lesser lights of his constellation," make him a star and offer him "spontaneous homage." The love child clearly shows "noble descent": he is a half-divine hero with a mysterious birth. Like Dorian, Billy is an exemplar of pure charisma. His shipmates make him gifts, "do his washing, darn his old trousers": "Anybody will do anything for Billy Budd."[43] The crew are vassals offering tokens of feudal subordination. Billy crystallizes hierarchy around himself, an Apollonian vertical cutting the sea's horizontals.

Billy Budd's catastrophe is a clash of hierarchic orders. The Iago-like master-at-arms, John Claggart, drifts into strange enmity toward Billy. Melville plainly specifies "what it was that had first moved him against Billy, namely, his significant personal beauty"—a phrase straight out of Wilde. Claggart's "monomania" is an erotic and aesthetic obsession. He is oppressed and enslaved by Billy's beauty, a western pattern invented by Sappho and revived by Petrarch. "Magnetically" drawn to Billy against his will, Claggart protests his subordination by the sodomitic baton tap he gives Billy from behind. It is provoked by spilled soup, which Claggart subconsciously experiences as chthonian contamination. "He was about to ejaculate something hasty at the sailor, but checked himself": Claggart simmers with self-poisoned desire. He is a brooding skeptic who converts the visionary and seraphic into a nauseated sense of violation by Billy's mental image. Claggart's "official" tap aggressively restores conventional hierarchy. He tries this again in the accusation scene, where he "mesmerically" stares at Billy, a daemonic eye-intercourse Melville borrows from Hawthorne.[44]

Billy is a "peacemaker" who transforms the crew's quarters from "a rat-pit of quarrels." The merchant captain says, "Not that he preached to them or said or did anything in particular; but a virtue went out of him, sugaring the sour ones." This virtue is aesthetic rather than moral. It is virtù, the beautiful or rare. Billy's beauty induces mass cathexis, quelling the competitive many into contemplative unity. But his charismatic personal hierarchy is at odds with public hierarchy. Obliviously, he makes his own cult, which must be suppressed by Caesar. Billy Budd follows in the line of the beautiful boy as destroyer by *causing disorder* in the social realm. W. H. Auden says, "It is not an accident that many homosexuals should show a special preference for sailors, for the sailor on shore is symbolically the innocent god from the sea who is not bound by the law of the land and can therefore do anything without guilt."[45] The law of the land is administered by Captain Vere, who reluctantly sentences Billy to death for killing an officer. *Because of* and not despite his fascinating glamour, Billy must die for the collective good. Strung up from the main yard, he is the ancient hanging god, an Adonis ritually slain in the flower of youth. Richard Chase calls him "the hermaphrodite Christ."[46] Like Christ, Billy poses an internal threat to an empire at war. They're right to hang him.

As a beautiful boy, Billy Budd is not cruel, but he is narcissistic—the primary narcissism of the child. The beautiful boy's solipsism is in

Billy's stutter, the "vocal infirmity" halting his speech under stress. The Apollonian, as always, is a mode of silence or muteness. Billy lacks "self-consciousness": his "simple nature" is the unitary Apollonian character, internally undeveloped. He is "illiterate," unlettered because the Apollonian androgyne has no words. When Claggart lies, Billy struggles to reply but, frustrated, fells his accuser with one blow. He is Phoebus (the Pure), avenging profanation by expelling the invader from his immaculate psychic space. After Billy's death, the surgeon is asked why there was no movement in the body, since a hanged man is usually convulsed by a "mechanical spasm."[47] Billy dies the ever-virgin, un-defiled by orgasm. Another Apollonian principle: the beautiful boy rejects orgasm because of Apollo's flight from the temporal. There is no motion because there is no Dionysian rhythm, only crystalline stasis.

Billy Budd inverts *The Tartarus of Maids*. This all-male saga shuts out chthonian female power. We last see Billy "ascending" into the rosy dawn: the rising seraph opposes Melville's descent to the gloomy realm of Goethe's Mothers. Philosophically, the beautiful boy abolishes the density of female matter (*mater* and *materia* have the same root). Apol-lonian androgynes make the visible world vibrate with spiritual il-lumination. Like *Moby-Dick*, *Billy Budd* defies Hawthorne by stealing sexual authority from woman. Melville gives purified femininity to the beautiful boy, shimmering with Apollonian light.

Billy Budd was not published until 1924, so it could not have influenced Thomas Mann's *Death in Venice* (1911), which is deeply indebted to *The Picture of Dorian Gray*. *Death in Venice* is a late flower of the fin de siècle. Civilization is in decay: Venice, the city of art, is "diseased," "filled with the smell of things rotting." The writer Gustav von Aschenbach arrives in Venice to find, like Goethe in the *Venetian Epigrams* and Hofmannsthal in *The Death of Titian* (1892), that it harbors a fascinating adolescent androgyne. What Melville polarizes in the antithesis *Billy Budd/Tartarus of Maids* Mann condenses in one tale. Aschenbach has a vision of primeval nature, clearly inspired by Huysmans: "a tropical swampland under a heavy murky sky, damp, lux-uriant and enormous, a kind of prehistoric wilderness . . . sluggish with mud," "hairy shafts of palms rising out of a rank lecherous thicket," "fat, swollen" plant life rooted in green "stagnant pools."[48] This is the female swamp of generation, the chthonian miasma against which the beautiful boy dreamily protests, his dazzling formal perfection a rebuke to nature's indiscriminateness and fluidity. The swampland of *Death in Venice* corresponds to *Tartarus'* pulpy "albuminous" matrix.

Aschenbach, the man of words, is captivated by an image of the Apollonian visual arts. An "absolutely beautiful," longhaired fourteen-year-old boy, straight out of "Greek sculpture," appears in an epiphany of Apollonian stillness. Surrounded by women—a governess, imposing mother, and three "nunlike sisters"—Tadzio is a sequestered god doomed to die young. Arriving near May Day, Mann's vernal androgyne is an Adonis, the privileged son-lover of a mother goddess. I suspect this cool, dignified woman wandering alone with her children was inspired by Hawthorne's mother-of-Pearl, Hester Prynne. She wears a simple gray dress strangely oramented with "priceless" jewelry and pearls, a "fantastically lavish" effect—reminiscent of Hester's plain Puritan dress and sumptuous scarlet letter, embroidered in "Oriental" style.[49]

Tadzio has the Apollonian attributes of "aristocratic distinction" and vocal impediment. Because the boy is Polish, "Aschenbach did not understand a word he said"; the writer sees him "smiling, with something half muttered in his soft vague tongue." Tadzio's Delphic utterances, like Billy Budd's stutter and Belphoebe's broken sentences, are another Apollonian muteness. Tadzio has a radical visibility. Each of his appearances is literally spectacular, as in his theophanic emergence from the sea. He steps from the waves not because he is *of* the sea but because he renounces the fluid realm, the seraph transcending foam-born Venus. "Astonished, terrified" by Tadzio's "godlike beauty," Aschenbach is as hierarchically subordinated as Basil Hallward to Dorian Gray or Claggart to Billy Budd. *Death in Venice* explicitly incorporates the references to Plato's *Phaedrus* I found implicit in *Dorian Gray*: Aschenbach experiences "the hot terror which the initiates suffer when their eyes light on an image of the eternal beauty."[50]

Like Basil, Aschenbach is an artist destroyed by a beautiful boy, who dresses in an "English sailor suit," a period style that may be an allusion to Wilde. Mythologically, Tadzio's sailor suit belongs to Saxon Billy Budd. But Mann's beautiful boy is more solipsistic than Melville's, his fatality literalized by the epidemic claiming his admirer's life. Though their eyes sometimes meet, the boy does not really see Aschenbach: "It was the smile of Narcissus bent over the reflecting water, that deep, fascinated, magnetic smile with which he stretches out his arms to the image of his own beauty."[51] Aschenbach's eyes are mirrors in which Tadzio sees nothing but himself. Obsessed, the writer imagines invitation where there is only autism. The beautiful boy, iconically isolated, is a mirage of the inflamed eye. As part of its Decadence, *Death in Venice* makes a Florentine beautiful boy a symbol of heterosexual Venice in its degenerate late phase.

Even at the height of hallucination, Aschenbach does not desire sex. It trivializes *Death in Venice* to reduce it, as has been done, to a homosexual chronicle of coming out of the closet. The beautiful boy is never contaminated by touch, for the Apollonian recedes with every step taken toward it. Stalking Tadzio through the streets, Aschenbach carefully preserves the critical aesthetic distance. He has become the deranged fan of the star-god. The beautiful boy, always fatal to his admirers, leads Aschenbach from dynastic and professional dignity toward self-immolation in the pre-Hellenic past. Like Euripides' Pentheus, Aschenbach is transvestized and Orientalized: decked with jewels, he uses perfume, dye, mascara, rouge. The western analytic mind is reabsorbed into its sultry Asiatic origins. Mann calls the Byzantine basilica of San Marco, into which Aschenbach pursues Tadzio, an "Oriental temple"; Aschenbach is felled by "Asiatic cholera," "hatched in the warm swamps of the Ganges delta."[52] If we step back from the naturalistic surface of *Death in Venice* and look at it mythologically, we will see that it contains, internalized, Melville's female Tartarus. A jealous mother goddess envelops her son's admirer in her chthonian miasma, for it is she who brings the pestilence into the city of art.

23

American Decadents

Emerson, Whitman, James

Ralph Waldo Emerson, whose father and forefathers were ministers, was caught in the clash between American Protestantism and English Romanticism. As a transcendentalist, he sought to open imagination to nature, in the Wordsworthian way. Emerson thought of himself as a poet, and although lectures and essays made his fame, controversy over the essays' vague structure was almost immediate. No Romantic work need conform to Apollonian logic. But are there psychological reasons for Emerson's eccentricities of style?

The essays are a treasure-trove of idea and maxim. Linguistically, Emerson's style occupies a magic convergence point, the crux of European languages. He reads as Plato, Augustine, and Nietzsche translate: an exalted clarity, the words orotund yet translucent, qualities that seem to belong to the typescript itself. But never has there been a prose more magnificent in pieces and more oppressive as a whole. Emerson's voice has an unnatural sameness, a phlegmatic flat affect. He lacks music—dynamics, melody, variation. We are feeling the burden of Protestant moralism, which Emerson never could shake off.

Emerson calls poets "liberating gods": "They are free, and they make free." Symbol-making means "emancipation and exhilaration": "We seem to be touched by a wand which makes us dance and run about happily, like children."[1] Emerson exhilarated? The joyful, spontaneous poet is what he longs to be but is not. Though his best lyrics are tense and muscular, they are hampered by excessive shortness of line. This gives speed, but speed is not Emerson's strong suit. He has a slower, graver mind of Wordsworthian deliberativeness. The poetry is far less realized than the essays, which swarm with brilliant Romantic images.

The principal charge against the essays is disorganization. The problem, as I see it, is that Emerson constantly interrupts or reverses his line of thought, leaving each set of ideas languishing in a solitary cell. Circularity has its symbolic uses, as in George Herbert's "A Wreath," whose verses intertwine in a perfect solar circle. Emerson's *Circles* follows this contemplative tradition: "The eye is the first circle; the horizon which it forms is the second."[2] But his wandering essay style does not always seem premeditated. I think it arises from some stoppage at the deepest generative level of language. From the archaic cave of the unconscious, wraithlike morphological wholes emerge to incarnate themselves in words. Image, rhythm, emotion are first; words are later.

Before Romanticism, literary style is shared discourse. After Romanticism, style is persona. Emerson may be the first whose style tells us so much. The monotony of his prose is ultimately a limitation on internalized personae, for each of our moods is the shadow of a persona. His essays, as adventures in voice, are struggles against the masculine Puritan past, which traps him in the sharp-bounded ethical ego. Transcendentalism seeks unity with nature by rejecting codes and institutions. But in Emerson the self itself, paralyzed by its own cultivation, is the obstacle to unity.

Emerson's conflicts are evident in his notorious eyeball metaphor: "Standing on the bare ground,—my head bathed by the blithe air and uplifted into infinite space,—all mean egotism vanishes. I become a transparent eyeball; I am nothing; I see all; the currents of the Universal Being circulate through me; I am part or parcel of God."[3] High Romantic aspiration; Late Romantic eye. Barbara Packer says, "Emerson's Eyeball has provoked scorn ever since its unsettling appearance in the first edition of *Nature*." The eyeball, she notes, is a later addition to the original passage in the journals.[4] Emerson is trying to remove the barriers between man and nature. His eyeball is a version of the Romantic Aeolian lyre: the "currents" circulating through him recall the West Wind sweeping through Shelley. Emerson intensifies the lyre's androgyny, to ill effect. Passive to the life force, he no longer sings but only sees. Seeing without doing, I demonstrated, is a primary principle of Decadent Late Romanticism. Emerson envies the eastern eye of mystic vision, but he cannot escape the history-heavy solidity of European personae.

Emerson's eyeball has the two properties I found in his prose: *orotundity* and *translucence*. The eyeball is ponderous, a dirigible his afflatus is not quite able to lift. The "bare ground" is naked, bald like his "bathed" or baptized infant head. The eyeball is concrete and monumental, a frozen colossus ventilated by the dawn breeze. Emerson longs to merge but cannot. The eyeball in which nothing can befall him is a uterine sac, a glass alembic through which he peers like Goethe's Homunculus. He is locked "In the belly of the grape" of his poem "Bacchus." The eyeball is the uncrushed grape of separation, the Apollonian skull of intellectual and connoisseur.

The transparent eyeball is significantly an afterthought—a self-betraying pattern I found in Melville. The image's lateness is its mark of Decadent perversity. Packer says, " 'Eye' is a neutral word, but 'eyeball' has something grotesque about it; it smacks too much of the dissecting room."[5] We have a new item for our lurid list of nineteenth-century amputations: Berenice's teeth, Balzac's instep, Gautier's foot, Cleopatra's lip, Gogol's nose, Wilde's chin, Emerson's eyeball. Emerson's detached retina is gross and shocking because it is a swollen Late Romantic member: the part exalted over the whole, an immobile and isolated *looking*. This globe of extracted tissue quivers with infirmity. It is Plato's circle-androgyne stripped of its limbs and abandoned. Emerson's apparent escape from egotism is another Romantic uroboros, the circular track on which the self meets the self. In his journals he says, "Man is insular, and cannot be touched. Every man is an infinitely repellent orb."[6] The self's untouchable orb repels invaders, like a citadel, but it also repels or repulses in the aesthetic sense. The repellent eyeball is a Decadent self-portrait, like the grisly picture of Dorian Gray. Emerson-as-eyeball says he is "part or parcel of God." Pack up our Decadent parts with golden twine, but this parcel is too heavy for air mail.

Transparency, I have shown, is an Apollonian phenomenon: it is the density of female matter pierced and vanquished by the aggressive western eye. So what is a bulky ophthalmic transparency doing in the middle of a celebration of nature? We are close to the contradictions at the heart of Emerson's work. He seems to take a Dionysian view of reality: "Metamorphosis is the law of the universe. All forms are fluent." He speaks of the "evanescence and lubricity of all objects": "All things swim and glitter." This could be a defense of his wandering prose style: "The quality of the imagination is to flow, and not to freeze."[7] He would prefer Dionysian process to Apollonian contour and stasis. The essays fragment because he suspends Apollonian master control: there is no hierarchical ascent or progress of argumentation. The prose lies in multiples, a Dionysian "Many." Unfortunately, this multiplicity is also Decadent decay and too-muchness, which clot Emerson's essays into unreadability.

But it is poetry that Emerson yearned for, not the essay. What inhibitions did he suffer when he took up the poet's mask? I described the transparent eyeball as a bald fetal androgyne. It is a projected self purged of gender and even extension in the body. Romantic poets are always self-consciously hermaphroditic; thus Emerson calls the "highly endowed man" a "Man-woman" who needs no wife. He sees the great man as a feminine receptor of historical force, his "impressionable brain" prophetically vibrating to the future. But the transsexual theme is only fleetingly present. We usually get the opposite. In *Nature*, for example, Emerson says of "Spirit" as "Creator": "Man in all ages and countries embodies it in his language as the FATHER."[8] This garish battery of capitals, blinking like a factory sign, is an irregular emphasis for Emerson, and the benign father-god whom it enshrines has no business in a Romantic work. At this moment, Emerson has surrendered to his Protestant forefathers. His imperialistic headline is apotropaic, guarding *Nature* against a contrary sexual force.

Emerson rarely mentions women, from whom Romanticism normally draws its power. His principal poems feature males: "Uriel," "Merlin," "Bacchus," "Brahma." The few archetypal females are quickly cited. "Maia," the veil of illusion, has just one stanza. "The Sphinx" is long and juicy but ends in the outwitting of the Sphinx and the defeat of female power: "Through a thousand voices / Spoke the universal dame; / 'Who telleth one of my meanings / Is master of all I am.' " This is what is wished, not what is. No man, no poet, not even the greatest of archimagi, is master of female nature. Emerson's imagination is hopelessly split: he dons Blakean armour on a Wordsworthian quest.

Woman appears so little in Emerson that when she does she has enormous force. He says in *Fate:* "Men are what their mothers made them. . . . When each comes forth from his mother's womb, the gate of gifts closes behind him."[9] This stunning indebtedness of man to woman is the pessimistic truth. Emerson's doctrine of self-reliance, by which America declared independence of European culture, is also a rejection of a female past. As a poet, Emerson is stuck. English Romanticism enables him to turn away from his rationalist heritage toward nature. But the absence of an American mother imago prevents him from activating the other crucial component of Romantic consciousness, the sexual archetypal, without which no Romantic poem can be written.

The Sphinx is everything Emerson's poetry has refused to internalize. "Bacchus," for example, stubbornly avoids the chthonian, which should be intrinsic to its theme of mystic union. The poem's quickness and excitement may come from its energy of evasion. Its short, hasty lines are Decadent *terminations,* self-severings, a boundary line drawn just before the poet is entered by female force, with its blurring dissolutions. Emerson's incomplete hermaphrodization as a Romantic poet obstructs the organic form of essay and poem, flattens mood and tone, and inserts an Apollonian eyeball into an ode to nature. As a Romantic sexual persona, Emerson's "I" is half-born.

American poetry's opening toward woman was achieved by Emerson's admirer, Walt Whitman, whose long untidy poetic line takes in everything Emerson excludes. The Dionysian, which Emerson wrongly envisions in discrete images, is a torrent into which Whitman eagerly plunges.

Whitman invents the American nature-mother, a heaving cycle of birth and death gorged with objects and persons. She is "the ocean of life," "the fierce old mother." She is voluptuous darkness, archaic night: "Press close bare-bosom'd night—press close magnetic nourishing night!" Whitman corrects Wordsworth's benign maternalism without resorting to Coleridge's horrific vampirism. By bardic instinct rather than learning, he revives the cosmology of the ancient mother cults. He imagines a turbulent world-pregnancy: "Urge and urge and urge, / Always the procreant urge of the world . . . always substance and in-crease, always sex." He hears "Voices . . . of the threads that connect the stars, and of wombs and of the father-stuff."[10] The all-mother encom-passing this propagating universe is sexually dual. Whitman is son-lover and priest of the hermaphrodite goddess, with whom he unites through impersonation. He wants to assimilate all being into the self, imagined as a capacious sac. The epic catalogs of *Leaves of Grass* are the poet's gluttonous self-fecundation or female swelling, a portrait of the artist as Great Mother, a Universal Man-Woman.

Whitman solicits sexualized intrusions into his psyche. His technique is identification, the Dionysian empathic: "Of every hue and caste am I, of every rank and religion, / A farmer, mechanic, artist, gentleman, sailor, quaker, / Prisoner, fancy-man, rowdy, lawyer, physician, priest." These multiple personae, from pimp to priest, level the great chain of being. "Maternal as well as paternal," Whitman makes transsexual projections: "I am the actor, the actress" or "the sleepless widow" or a girl primping for her gentleman-caller. The poetry takes in all of earth's creatures. One sequence lists three dozen animals, insects, fish, and plants, from panther to crab to persimmon. "My lovers suffocate me," says Whitman; they call his name "from flower-beds, vines, tangled underbrush." Like Keats, he imitates Dionysus' extension throughout the ripe "Many" of the world. He bursts every barrier: "Unscrew the locks from the doors! / Unscrew the doors themselves from their jambs!" There must be no Apollonian sequestration: privacy or purity are sterile patches, seceding from wholeness. *Leaves of Grass* has a promiscuous all-inclusiveness. Democratic Dionysus broadens significance to refuse, chips and scraps: "the deform'd, trivial, flat, foolish, despised"; "Chaff, straw, splinters of wood, weeds, and the sea-gluten, / Scum, scales from shining rocks, leaves of salt-lettuce, left by the tide." Judeo-Christian man rules this world, but Dionysian man is ruled by it. Whitman synthesizes contraries: "Do I contradict myself? . . . I am large, I contain multitudes."[11] Dionysus' polymorphous perversity breaks down Apollonian categorization and hierarchy.

Emerson's prophecy of the poet as liberator was fulfilled by Whitman, whose revolutionary free verse, like Antony in Egypt, "o'erflows the measure." It sets all things into motion in nature's flux. In its freewheeling structure and perpetual metamorphoses, *Leaves of Grass* is literature's most perfectly Dionysian poetry. It descends from ancient chants naming the attributes, fruits, crops, and animals of the earth-mother to awaken and stimulate her fertility. Whitman's weaknesses also come from his Dionysianism, which offends Apollonian form and decorum. At his best, he has the sublimity of Pindar; at his worst, he is screechy and cornball, like a carnival barker. But remember the unhappy precedent of Emerson, who could not become Dionysus Lusios (the Liberator) because of his intellectual refinement.

Like Baudelaire, Whitman seeks to scandalize the Christian and bourgeois. He is the conduit of "forbidden voices, / Voices of sexes and lusts . . . Voices indecent by me clarified and transfigur'd." He makes another swerve from the Protestant past. Puritanism, an austere cult of the inner life, honored acts but not objects. The pagan *Leaves of Grass*, sweeping a jumble of reborn objects into itself, removes the ethical dimension from acts, which are now merely *experiences*. The Puritan will, lulled in a Turkish bath of female relaxation, drops its confrontationalism. Whitman speaks of "Winds whose soft-tickling genitals rub against me." Or he sees "the young men float on their backs, their white bellies bulge to the sun."[12] There are no erections in this world. Penises are pollen-flecked fruit stirred by the breeze, or glossy tubers lapped in water. There is no tension or discipline, because *Leaves of Grass* makes languorous female realities supreme.

Whitman's Dionysian multiplicities are a pagan syncretism, as shown by his Emerson-inspired appeals to "Osiris, Isis, Belus, Brahma, Buddha."[13] D. H. Lawrence complains that Whitman's greedy "song of myself" turns the self into "a mush," "a hotch-potch," "the awful pudding of One Identity."[14] Like the Hinduism of Forster's *A Passage to India* (the title of Whitman's last poem), the zeal to honor and absorb everything courts a collapse into nondifferentiation. But Whitman, who portrays himself as a Madonna della Misericordia, a hundred figures wrapped in her compassionate cloak, never fully succeeds in his Dionysian drive toward one expanded identity. Like Emerson with his heavy eyeball, Whitman finds the will-to-merge blocked by a veil of flesh, his troublesome self. *Leaves of Grass* asserts unity but proves separateness. Its genial song of "Embraceable You" draws reality in to fill a gnawing emptiness. This apparently generous poetry is marred by moral ambiguities, of which the most lurid is a Decadent voyeurism. Like *Moby-Dick*, *Leaves of Grass* is a High Romantic work bedeviled by Late Romantic impulses.

Whitman loves to linger in imagination by the beds of the sleeping and sick, a taste he later put into action in Civil War hospitals. *The Sleepers*, which I compared to Blake's "Infant Joy," is a rhapsody on this subject: "I wander all night in my vision, / Stepping with light feet, swiftly and noiselessly stepping and stopping, / Bending with open eyes over the shut eyes of sleepers." He stands in the dark, passing his hands "soothingly to and fro a few inches from them." He goes "from bedside to bedside," visiting children, corpses, drunks, onanists, idiots, spouses, sisters, everyone asleep or dead.

In class, Milton Kessler spoke of *The Sleepers*' "ghoulishness" and "prurience." The poet makes "a magical godlike gesture" over the sleepers, who are "like fetuses": "He creates them. They are all helpless before him." Whitman's sympathy and identification are based on aggression and invasion. The poem has a skopophiliac tyranny: the omnipotent eye forces passivity on its objects, denying them personal consciousness. Whitman, normally the Dionysian enemy of hierarchy, spreads all mankind before him from horizon to horizon, in abject postures of subordination. The sleepers are matter awaiting the impress of his mind. His criminal trespass, a violation of their dreams as well as bedrooms, has a hushed erotic excitement. The poem is a psychosexual breaking and entering, and Whitman is the vampire who walks by night.

Like Blake, Whitman claims to shatter false laws, banishing sexual secrecy and shame. But his jovial exhibitionism is a mask. *The Sleepers* shows the scope of his self-concealment. As in "Kubla Khan," the eyes of the crowd are closed to the poet, but now it is the poet who closes them. *The Sleepers* is a nocturnal patrol through the city of the dead. Whitman's relation to people is tense. He does not genuinely celebrate their otherness, their multiple identities, for these condemn him to solitude. Hence he "infolds" them in archaic night, drowning them in the democracy of dissolution. His taut self-curtailments are a Decadent closure. Whitman has a Late Romantic sister-spirit in American literature. His Decadent voyeurism looks forward to the lubricious death-connoisseurship of Emily Dickinson. Unexpectedly, the hobo sexual iconoclast and the spinster recluse share the same perverse sensibility.

Whitman's sexual prowess is also not what it seems. Unable to trust his poetry's hermaphroditic message, he spent a lot of time advertising a virility that has since proved to be false. He wonderfully describes himself as "hankering, gross, mystical, nude," "Turbulent, fleshy, sensual, eating, drinking and breeding." He spurns "neuters and geldings" in favor of "men and women fully equipt."[15] This is not biography but psychography. That is, such fictive assertions constitute the masculine personae of the bisexual *Leaves of Grass*. In fact, the hermaphroditic all-mother is so potent a conception that the individual male is unnecessary. Like Balzac's avenger gathering an armed retinue to enter the female realm of the Oriental boudoir, Whitman must overemphasize his maleness to retain his own sex in the surging female nature of his poetry.

Because of his identification with the Great Mother, masculinity is the feeblest of Whitman's personae. His pseudomale would pop like a birthday balloon. Swinburne, whose sensuous ocean mother was inspired by Whitman's, has no sexual anxiety in the same situation. He welcomes male subordination to woman, probably because he has the authority of Sade and Baudelaire behind him. Upper-class Swinburne comes to poetry from the salon world of manners, but Whitman cannot escape his proletarian past, where a man is a man by labor and robustness. Hence *Leaves of Grass* makes us listen to the tiresome rattling of an imaginary saber.

Although lust for women is merely mimed, Whitman is not at all misogynistic: "I say it is as great to be a woman as to be a man, / And I say there is nothing greater than the mother of men." He honors even the machinery of procreation, which unlike Melville he anatomizes with ardor: "The womb, the teats, nipples, breast-milk, tears, laughter." Like Keats, Whitman speaks of "the udder of my heart," from which his poetry drinks. Heterosexual desire is another matter. The real eroticism of *Leaves of Grass* goes toward athletic males in Iliadic spectacles of pleasure-pain: "I see a beautiful gigantic swimmer swimming naked

through the eddies of the sea. . . . I see his white body, I see his un-
daunted eyes." He is dashed on the rocks, "baffled, bang'd, bruis'd."
The waves are spotted with his blood: "They roll him, swing him, turn
him, / His beautiful body is borne in the circling eddies. . . . Swiftly and
out of sight is borne the brave corpse."[16] Voyeuristic Whitman, a hovering gull, luxuriates in the red rents made in a white male beauty. The
scene combines Achilles' combat with the River Scamander with Odysseus' battering against the sea cliff. But Homer's heroes survive. Whitman prefers a Late Romantic sexual script, sensuously sadomasochistic
and terminated by martyrdom at nature's hands.

For Whitman, homosexual action and gratification are as inconceivable as any other. His eroticism remains in Decadent voyeuristic suspension. When he enters his sexual scenes, rather than hanging back in
spectral aloofness, he is passive to displaced sex acts. He remembers
"How you settled your head athwart my hips and gently turn'd over
upon me, / And parted the shirt from my bosom-bone, and plunged
your tongue to my bare-stript heart, / And reach'd till you felt my beard,
and reach'd till you held my feet." Unlike Christabel, whose tongue is
stolen by homosexual rape, Whitman gains another, which snakes
through him and incites him to ecstasies of language. The companion
passage is the fantasy of the male heroine I cited vis-à-vis Swinburne: "I
am the mash'd fireman with breast-bone broken, / Tumbling walls
buried me in their debris."[17] This is the bosom-bone broken by the male
tongue, a homosexual defloration. The fireman is mashed by an imploded womb, like Poe's flexing "fiery walls." "My comrades . . . tenderly lift me forth": like Queequeg delivering Tashtego from the whale
head, Whitman's firemen pull the poet from the cul-de-sac of the
maternal body. The scene is a Late Romantic pietà, with Whitman the
ritually slain son of the all-mother.

Desire is homosexual in *Leaves of Grass* for the same reason the penis
stays soft: the physical impossibility of mating with the Great Mother,
mountainous as Baudelaire's giantess. The male body is swallowed up
in nature's enormity. Thus the futility of Whitman's muscleman shams:
the masculine persona he covets is dwarfed to insignificance in his
hermaphroditic cosmos, with its abundance and immensity. As in Swinburne, union is not genital but oral. Whitman consumes his object-
world, just as he is consumed by it. His poetic style is sexual litany, long
pulses of invocation readying the self for invasion by the world-mother
who is the world-matter. In form and content, *Leaves of Grass* has the
fluidity of womanly Dionysus. "You sea!" the poet cries, "Dash me with
amorous wet." Or in a vision worthy of the *Bacchae:* "Seas of bright juice

suffuse heaven."[18] But Whitman is incapable of Maenadic community. His poetry is far more populated than Wordsworth's, yet he suffers the same anguished apartness. Like Swinburne's melancholy Hermaphrodite, he is trapped in sexual solitude. His own androgyny, a privilege and a curse, keeps him from union with lovers male or female. There is no true intimacy in Whitman. His poetry is a substitute for intimacy and a record of the swerve *from* it.

As a sexual persona, solitary, cosmos-creating Whitman is the androgyne I call Khepera, the masturbatory Egyptian First Mover, who also symbolizes the monkish, sexually ambiguous worlds of Aubrey Beardsley and Jean Genet. Sartre could be describing Whitman when he says, "Genet *is* in all his characters, and they are by turns a rose, a dog, a cat, a clematis. He makes himself all of man and all of nature."[19] These three artists are a perverse paradox of fertility and negation. In each, autoerotic imagination flourishes in the prison of the modern self.

Henry James, normally considered a social novelist, is a Decadent Late Romantic, which gives his writing its unique and aggravating character. James criticism is too adulatory. The result, as with Spenser and Goethe, is the academic censoring of a fantastically perverse imagination. James's last novels, published early this century, belong like *Death in Venice* to the fin de siècle. No other English fiction is so encumbered with Alexandrian ornamentation, the sign of a "late" style. The English social novel, I noted, has few androgynes. James's sex reversals are a symptom of his covert Romanticism.

The most passive James hero appears in *The Ambassadors* (1903). Lambert Strether, with his spindly, dithery name, is the timid male cowed by dominant women. Thinking of his fiancée, Mrs. Newsome, he recalls the time "when he had held out his small thirsty cup to the spout of her pail." She is full, he empty. Mrs. Newsome, a New England grande dame, is a garrulous Muse or bloated teapot, a great gushing force of phallic personality cascading into his littleness. Strether calls consciousness "a helpless jelly" poured into the "tin mould" of life.[20] Such rueful thoughts in James occur only to men.

James's figures of speech can be queerly ominous. Talking with friends, Strether feels like "the laundress bringing home the triumphs of the mangle." Woman as wringer: even the laundry is an arena of female triumph of the will. In *The Death of the Lion*, in which two novelists take transsexual pen names, the relation between Mrs. Wimbush and Neil Paraday parallels that between Mrs. Newsome and Strether. "A blind, violent force," she is "constructed of steel and

leather." He, on the other hand, is of "india-rubber." Mrs. Wimbush is a
brazen totem, a locomotive flattening a doll. She resembles Mrs. Lowder of *The Wings of the Dove* (1902), who is "a projectile, of great size,
loaded and ready for use." Even Mrs. Lowder's furniture is "so almost
abnormally affirmative, so aggressively erect." She is "the car of Jugger-
naut," bristling with "the strange idols, the mystic excrescences" of her
massive furniture. The Jamesian dowager is a slow, crushing diesel,
leading with a bosomy prow of grappling hooks. Mrs. Lowder directs
dinner conversation as if steering a boat, resuming, "with a splash of her
screw, her cruise among the islands."21 Manhandling her phallic pro-
peller, the hostess gets under weigh on a floating torture rack—the
dinner table as *Raft of the Medusa*.

Women in James have innate authority, while men are in retreat.
Merton Densher, the shrinking violet of *Wings of the Dove*, reflects, "He
had thought, no doubt, from the day he was born, much more than he
had acted." Too much thought blurs the male's definitiveness of self.
Densher is subject both to Mrs. Lowder and her bold niece, Kate Croy,
to whom he offers "his pure passivity." He enjoys "mere spectatorship,"
while Kate is "the faultless soldier on parade." He says of her rel-
ishingly, "Ah, she's very masterful." The wishy-washy James hero is
always making obsequious verbal genuflections towards his master-
mistress. Densher to Kate: " 'You're prodigious!' 'Of course I'm prodigious!' "22 Such moments border on the distasteful because of their
flagrant affect, ill-hid by a veil of irony. It's like a hedgehog rooting
about under a doily. Wilde is more honest in allowing Lady Bracknell
and Gwendolen to dominate spunky male opponents. James, maneuvering his insipid heroes into reverential attitudes, makes himself a
court hermaphrodite, an unctuous flatterer at the queen's court. His
slavishness is another version of the cultic reverence of Poe, Baudelaire,
and Swinburne for their Romantic vampires.

As a sexual persona, the passive male predates James's Decadent late
phase. Sickly Ralph Touchett of *The Portrait of a Lady* (1881) is genetically half-feminine: his father was "the more motherly" and his mother
"paternal," even "gubernatorial." He is "an accidental cohesion of
related angles": "He shambled, and stumbled, and shuffled, in a manner that denoted great physical helplessness." This maladroit mar-
ionette says of his subservience to the plucky heroine: "Isabel Archer
has acted on me—yes; she acts on every one. But I have been absolutely
passive."23 The Jamesian male puts himself *under the influence* of female power, like a patient submitting to a hypnotist. He glows only in
reflection, the male moon to a female sun. In his late work, James drops

invalidism as an excuse for his heroes' inertia. The protagonist of *The Beast in the Jungle* (1903) does not marry simply because, like Melville's Bartleby, he would prefer not to. His virginal modesty is a modern abulia. The Jamesian male, with his urban pallor, is a Bartleby with a bank account. Avoiding marriage, he is the opposite of the English Renaissance androgynes, who stampede toward the altar. Like Mademoiselle de Maupin, he remains alone to protect his androgyny, but unlike Maupin, he chooses passivity and stasis, female waiting.

James's sadomasochistic scheme also has female victims. Three novels join the theme of lesbian enthrallment to the humiliation of an unworldly young woman. James has gotten this from Hawthorne's *The Blithedale Romance*, whose ancestor is Coleridge's *Christabel*. Thus Romanticism flows directly into the plotting of his major novels. Masterful Isabel Archer is herself mastered by the clever and fascinating Madame Merle, with whom she has a faintly erotic relationship. Merle urges her "to get used to" men in order to "despise them." *The Portrait of a Lady* has two theatrical moments of domination and submission, based on the vampire epiphanies of Romanticism. First Isabel, entering a drawing room, finds Merle standing and the aesthetical Gilbert Osmond seated, looking up at her. This is a breach of decorum: no gentleman sits while a lady stands. Madame Merle is in command, outside the social frame. The second incident is the novel's climactic revelation, where Isabel repeats the subordinate posture.

> "Who are you—what are you?" Isabel murmured. "What have you to do with my husband? . . . What have you to do with me?" . . .
>
> Madame Merle slowly got up, stroking her muff, but not removing her eyes from Isabel's face.
>
> "Everything!" she answered.
>
> Isabel sat there looking up at her, without rising; her face was almost a prayer to be enlightened. But the light of her visitor's eyes seemed only a darkness.
>
> "Oh, misery!" she murmured at last; and she fell back, covering her face with her hands. It had come over her like a high-surging wave that Mrs. Touchett was right. Madame Merle had married her![24]

Merle, via Hawthorne, is the vampire Geraldine transfixing the eyes and overcoming the will of kneeling Christabel. Even the suggestive muff-stroking evokes Coleridge's scene of seduction. "Madame Merle had married her": in period parlance, this means Merle secretly arranged Isabel's marriage, married her off. But in a perverse ambiguity, it also means Merle has made Isabel her own lesbian bride. Their union is on the conspiratorial level of daemonic mentalization, where the vampire triumphs. "Who are you—what are you?" Merle ("blackbird" in French) is an emanation of animal night, a Romantic intrusion into a social novel.

A similar shadowy design governs *The Wings of the Dove.* Artless Milly Theale is bewitched by her "wondrous" victimizer, Kate Croy, who seems like "a breezy boy." Milly is preoccupied with Kate's charismatic beauty. Fending off a proposal from Lord Mark, she suggests he marry Kate instead: "Because she's the handsomest and cleverest and most charming creature I ever saw, and because if I were a man I should simply adore her. In fact I do as it is."[25] So Mark is to act as Milly's proxy in possessing Kate. Or is Kate to usurp Milly's identity by doubling for her in her adult roles?—exactly what Coleridge's vampire does the morning after the seduction.

The most blatant of James's plots of lesbian bonding and entrapment is *The Bostonians* (1886), whose debt to *The Blithedale Romance* is well recognized. Hawthorne's willful Zenobia has become domineering Olive Chancellor, a feminist spinster. Her protegée, Verena Tarrant, is the daughter of a mesmerist, another detail from Hawthorne. Like Merle, Olive is hostile to men, "the brutal, blood-stained, ravening race." It is in Verena's nature "to be easily submissive, to like being overborne." She is the psychologically undefended woman of pure femininity whom we have met in Spenser, Sade, Blake, Coleridge, and Balzac. Her sexual simplicity is an emptiness attracting predators, male and female. I suspect *The Bostonians'* power struggle between a rich lesbian and an egotistical lady's man for a feminine girl comes from Balzac's *The Girl with the Golden Eyes.* As in Balzac, the lesbian is a fierce androgyne, her gender in question: "What sex was it, great heaven?"[26]

Hawthorne is to James as Poe is to Baudelaire, the transmitter of Coleridge's daemonic psychology of sex and power. In no other way could James, a social novelist, have come into deep imaginative contact with Coleridge. The social novel, I argued, is predicated on control or exclusion of the sexual archetypal, a source of public and private disorder. The sequence Coleridge, Hawthorne, James parallels the sequence Balzac, Baudelaire, Swinburne as a line of descent of lesbian erotica. One lesbian couple is refracted into three beams of identity. The sexually ambivalent artist projects himself into the passive girl, corrupted by a dominatrix. Edmund Wilson sees transsexual identification in all James's heroines: James's interest in "immature girls who are objects of desire or defilement" came from a polarization with his brother William in "an opposition of feminine and masculine": "There was always in Henry James an innocent little girl whom he cherished and loved and protected and yet whom he later tried to violate, whom he even tried to kill."27 What is perverse in James is the obsessive *repetition* of this psychodrama. Like Poe, he writes the same story over and over again. Repetition, imperfect individuation: as in *Wuthering Heights*, such blurring of characterization signals the presence of Romanticism.

Like Poe's *Red Death*, *The Bostonians* is unique among James's works in having a virile hero. The pushy Basil Ransom is no Jamesian milquetoast. The lesbianism is also more explicit than in any other novel. The two things are related. Masculinity emerges unimpaired in *The Bostonians* because of the completeness with which James has fused with passive Verena. Olive's unmasked lesbian ardor holds him in his transsexual state, without risk of contamination by maleness. Hence Basil, left to himself, can expand to the limit of his gender. My archetypal analysis of *The Scarlet Letter* and *The Minister's Black Veil* would suggest that in *The Blithedale Romance* Hawthorne has similarly projected himself, by sexual metathesis, into the meek maiden who is the object of lesbian domination. Thus he penetrates into the female magic circle denied him in *The Scarlet Letter*. Borrowing Hawthorne's motif for a social novel, James revises it. In *The Blithedale Romance*, society-constructing energies fail, and suicidal Zenobia returns to nature, absorbed into the "Black River of Death" with its "weedy and slimy" heart.28 But Olive Chancellor is only an irritable political ideologue whose summery Cape Cod has no connection to dangerous chthonian nature. James's transfer of Hawthorne's lesbian couple into a social novel is exactly like Wilde's ritual purification of *Salomé* by turning its vampire into the mannered twin androgynes Gwendolen and Cecily. My theory again: high comedy is always a defeat of the chthonian. *The Bostonians* is *The Blithedale Romance* dedaemonized. It demonstrates that James's comedy of manners is a strategy of resistance to the perverse Romantic undercurrent in American literature.

No James story better shows *what must be kept out* than *The Turn of the Screw* (1898). Its literary gamesmanship: Charlotte Brontë's governess invades the Arcadia of a Jane Austen country house, which she disorders with Poe's obsessive eroticism. As we shall see, James's immediate target is *The Importance of Being Earnest*, staged three years earlier. Tending a boy and girl of "angelic beauty," the governess falls under the sway of two daemons of Blakean opacity, who menace the children's Apollonian transparency. Peter Quint and Miss Jessel are homosexual "fiends" returned from the dead, servants turned master in a Saturnalian or rather Saturnian reversal. They exert a leaden, obstructive pressure on the story.[29]

The Turn of the Screw is brilliantly poised between the reality and unreality of its ghosts. Kenneth Burke says: "The governess' struggle with the ghosts of her predecessors for the possession of the children is not sexual, as judged by literal tests of sexual appetite. But it is ambiguously sexual, a sexuality surrounded at every point by *mystification.*" We see "one class struggling to possess the soul of another class," adult vs. children, "a classification 'prior' to sex, and leading into the mysteries of ancestor worship."[30] Ancestors are worshipped to keep their ghosts from encroaching on the living. Quint and Jessel are Harpies, "Snatchers." The evil into which they threaten to abduct the children is more potent for its vagueness. Their lust is for homosexual capture, not contact. They entice their victims into a world of sexual anti-matter. Geoffrey Hartman speaks of James's "superstitious response to spirit of place."[31] Quint and Jessel are malign *genii loci,* guardians of a territory one may enter but never leave. By cohabitation rather than blood, they construct an Unholy Family, a house outside the law. It is a more sinister version of the unsavory four-branched ménage into which the densely Jessel-like Madame Merle draws Isabel Archer.

The governess, regent of a realm from which the owner absents himself in godlike indifference, is a Late Romantic imaginist who creates a psychodrama of enslavement. As usual in Decadence, the medium of domination is the visual. In the first apparition, Quint stands on the crenellated tower, gazing at the governess with "a bold hard stare," too free to belong to a gentleman. In the second, he stands outside the window looking in, staring at her with a look "deep and hard." In the third, "a woman in black, pale and dreadful," stands across the lake gazing at little Flora (a Botticellian name). She "fixed" the child with "awful eyes," "with a kind of fury of intention."[32] Jessel's ocular fixation belongs to Coleridge's vampire. Her gaze is a paralytic intervention in nature, fixing Flora in eerily prolonged childhood, sexually aging her mind while halting maturation of her body. The vampire, by sudden hierarchic assertion, projects the white leprosy of time.

The Turn of the Screw's great planes of eye-contact are one of the most sensational examples of the tyranny of the visual in French, English, and American Late Romanticism. Quint and Jessel exist not as characters, in a novelistic sense, but as *nodes of visibility.* They are hieratic personae in a cult of the western eye. The womb-tombs of the Gothic tale of terror empty themselves into the story's appalling open spaces, with their violent, piercing sightlines. James demonstrates the aggression in the act of western seeing, an iron chain binding person to person in Euclidean triangles. Quint and Jessel's opacity comes from their intensity of seeing and being seen, which withers them like Words-worth's solitaries or Baudelaire's crucified poet. They are points of negative cathexis, reverse images of the entrancing art-object hierarchs of *Sarrasine* and *Dorian Gray*. What is Decadent in Quint and Jessel is their visual concentration and immobility, their horrifying stillness. They are Coleridgean saboteurs in Wordsworthian nature. They have the gravity of Emerson's eyeball and the density of Balzac's black dia-mond. They are moral anthracite embedded, like Moreau's gems, in James's canvas.

Eroticism in *The Turn of the Screw* takes the frigid form of voyeur-ism. Quint and Jessel practice shamanistic transportation of conscious-ness, a *hovering* at the edge of thought. This is a modern magic, pro-duced by Rousseau's unstable fusion of sexuality and identity. We saw the same hovering in Blake's sadomasochistic *God Creating Adam* and "Infant Joy." We saw it in the vampire's hovering outside Christabel's castle and in Whitman's hovering at the bedsides of sleepers. We shall see it again in the ponderous hovering of James's late style.

The voyeuristic tension of *The Turn of the Screw* makes sex *men-talized*, in the fanatical western way. The governess whose psychic space is invaded by eye-potent spectres is the oppressed turned oppressor, hovering in a Gothic cloud over her charges. She imposes a Man-ichaean duality on the children, who are torn between heaven and hell. The governess is another Khepera, a cosmogonic hermaphrodite excit-ing herself into autoerotic action. The ghosts may be emanations of her own double-sexed imagination, schizophrenically alienated: rejecting marriage, male and female separate for a homosexual spree. Juxtapos-ing these hard dark stars with the children, with "their more than earthly beauty, their absolutely unnatural goodness," the governess is a Decadent artist, joining moral and aesthetic extremes, evil with beauty, a Beardsleyesque black and white. Her one theme is the *fleur du mal* of her "endless obsession."[33] Like Blake's beadles with their frozen wands, she kills in order to save, enveloping the children in her morti-fying fiction. A headstrong hermaphrodite lost in self-pleasuring fan-tasy at the country house of an uncle-guardian absent in the city: we have already met James's governess in Wilde's Cecily Cardew, whose tutor Miss Prism becomes the housekeeper Mrs. Grose. Cecily is Sa-lomé purified of the chthonian. *The Turn of the Screw* redaemonizes her.[34]

What of the screw of the title? Unwound, it belongs to a spinster with a screw loose. Tightened, it is the nail of excess mental control, splintering society's hierarchical frame, which the governess rigidly reinforces with her sadomasochistic reverie. We know from the aggressive Mrs. Lowder that James's screw is a phallic tool of torture. Turning her screw in a vortex or maelstrom of pleasure-pain, the governess as deranged Khepera makes love to and fertilizes herself. As in Blake's *Mental Traveller*, the rack on which the dominatrix tortures her children is her own body. Interrogating Flora, the governess goes dizzy with nerves, gripping her "with a spasm that, wonderfully, she submitted to without a cry or a sign of fright." But the governess' supreme achievement is the death-by-imagination of the terrorized boy-child Miles, who expires in her imprisoning arms.[35] Like the witch-queen of *Snow White*, she is the stepmother of fatal embrace. Miles's Late Romantic love-death comes from Poe: Usher's heart stops when his dying sister collapses on him. But in James, woman triumphs, dandling the dead male in her personal pietà.

The Turn of the Screw is rich in Romantic archetypes. Quint at the window may recall Catherine's ghost at the window in *Wuthering Heights*. The ghost who can't get in in Brontë and James finally steps cheerily into the room in Saki's *The Open Window*, whose malicious fantasist is James's Flora, now adolescent and practicing what she learned from her governess. Quint on the tower is a crow-black rook—a castle in chess—who glides from post to post. Jessel is the black queen surveying the board across sweeping distances. Is this Lewis Carroll's influence? Black rook and queen, stalking the white pawns, pollute the pieties of Romantic childhood. Jessel is always poised by a lake of placid female waters. The two fiends subdue both nature and culture.

In their icy composure, Quint and Jessel both descend from Coleridge's Geraldine. "She wants Flora," says the governess of Jessel. This lesbian predator is "wonderfully handsome" but "infamous." She is "dark as midnight in her black dress, her haggard beauty." Like Geraldine, she is haggard with *watching*. In her uncanniest moment, "she rose erect," a "pale and ravenous demon," by the lake. Jessel is Poe's self-erected Ligeia, who returns in a shroud of hair "blacker than the wings of the midnight." James is also activating another of Geraldine's doubles. The governess says of Quint, "He's a horror," and of Jessel, "The woman's a horror of horrors."[36] In *The Blithedale Romance*, the corpse of Hawthorne's raven-haired Zenobia is pulled from the river with this ironic eulogy: "Six hours before, how beautiful! At midnight, what a horror!"[37] Jessel stands by a lake because she is the resurrected

Zenobia, emerging by Ligeian willpower from waters she has quelled to stillness.

The Bostonians dedaemonized *The Blithedale Romance.* But *The Turn of the Screw* is a great rebirth of the archaic, returning Hawthorne to his Coleridgean source by infusions of charismatic Late Romantic evil. Published in 1898, it just precedes James's late style, exemplified by the three major novels of 1902–04. My theory: the late style's complexity and impenetrability are a defense against the dangerous outbreak of the daemonic in *Turn of the Screw.* In this story, the middle-class country house, the sphere of experience opened by Jane Austen, is swamped by the Romantic and irrational. James's vocation as a social novelist was under secret attack by forces of the perverse. He tried to dismiss *The Turn of the Screw* as a "pot-boiler," a metaphor that betrays his troubled sense of its nakedness, its lurid psychic overflow.

Now for the late novels. I find the first commentaries on James truer in tone than the more recent, reverent academic analyses. For example, in 1916 Rebecca West says, "With sentences vast as the granite blocks of the Pyramids and a scene that would have made a site for a capital he set about constructing a story the size of a hen-house." She speaks of "those great sentences which sprawl over the pages of *The Golden Bowl* with such an effect of rank vegetable growth that one feels that if one took cuttings of them one could raise a library in the garden."[38]

Here is a sample cutting from *The Golden Bowl* (1904). Prince Amerigo is thinking about Charlotte Stant: "Nothing in her definitely placed her; she was a rare, a special product. Her singleness, her solitude, her want of means, that is her want of ramifications and other advantages, contributed to enrich her somehow with an odd, precious neutrality, to constitute for her, so detached yet so aware, a sort of small social capital."[39] Nothing definitely: we are in limbo. Social novels normally chart social relationships. But James wants Charlotte *without* relation. Detached, neutral, unramified, she floats free. James disorients the reader by dimming the spatial and psychological premises of perception. The character set before us becomes more, not less nebulous, an apparition that we strain to bring into focus but that eludes three-dimensional resolution. Syntax is equally perverse. The prose is self-interrupted by hedging clauses, endless qualifications of Decadent precision, a pedantry numbing by overabstraction.

James has a baffling style. That is, he sets the prose as a baffle or barrier between the reader and the thing described. In conversations, what is not said presses upon what is. In the late novels, the prose itself exerts this pressure, forcing the reader into submission. There is a taunting obscurantism. For example, Strether asks someone, "For what do you suggest that I suppose her to take you?"[40] This busy mound of supposition, with its stately rotation of points of view, is like an anthill we gingerly step around. It is three times removed from emotion.

People who dislike James are not simpletons impatient with complexity. His claim to explore every mental nuance is false. There is good reason to be repelled by James's duplicity and guile, for line by line we are being deflected from what we really want to know. His web of qualification is a ruse. Like Penelope, he weaves and unweaves to delude us. We try to enter his world but are checked by an invisible force. The turgidity of the prose is a buzzing background noise or scrim of chalky powder, covering even the print on the page. The self-concealing technique reverses that of Blake's "Infant Joy," which sucks the daemonized reader into a burrow or vacuum. *The Turn of the Screw* is "Infant Joy" writ large: it is a dream of the ease and horror of psychological invasion. In the late novels, therefore, James's systematic exclusion of the reader is crucial to his defense against the daemonic.

James has a reputation as a psychologist. Yes, he records internal events, but his psychological insights are not particularly abundant. James is monotonous. His characters' inner lives are poorly personalized. There is only one consciousness, his own. Saying James has "a very short list of characters," Forster makes the kind of remark I value from early commentary: "Maimed creatures can alone breathe in Henry James's pages—maimed yet specialized. They remind one of the exquisite deformities who haunted Egyptian art in the reign of Akhenaton—huge heads and tiny legs, but nevertheless charming."[41] James's world is populated by a small nuclear family in claustrophobic proximity. Even travel to Europe is another closure. Open any novel at random: who is being talked about? We grope about, at a loss. Names are rare. James likes luxurious misty rowings through he, she, you, I. As in Emerson, there is a limitation on personae. James's novels are Romantic family romance. His internal world is a compromise between social reality and the preconscious realm of imagination and archetype into which Romanticism descends.

James describes states of *waiting*. He seeks fullness, retention, rumination in the bovine sense. The unexpressed is an edemic engorgement, a male pregnancy without issue. Wilde, who did not even live to see the final novels, said, "Mr. Henry James writes fiction as if it were a painful duty."[42] Reading late James is like swimming upstream. The prose resists us with its weight and opacity, its "dizzying, smothering welter" (a phrase from *The Golden Bowl*).[43] In his Romantic withdrawal from masculinity, James wraps each act or remark in an immobilizing sheath of excess words. He sadistically imposes a sense of frustration and entrammelment on the reader. The prose is the medium but not the message. It reproduces the density of ambiguous circumstance in which the characters are caught. It is a large, humming, *hovering* mass.

Not everything in James is artistically intelligible. As a stream-of-consciousness writer, he is quite unlike Proust or Woolf in the vague *menace* we feel in his situations. He has a Late Romantic disease of unease. The cumbersome tapestry of his writing is fouled with catches or snarls. When her father refers to her "duty," Kate Croy's "tired smile watched the word as if it had taken on a small grotesque visibility."[44] I will argue that grotesque visibility is one of James's primary techniques. The dense swaying mass of his prose rouses itself into tottering apexes of metaphor, in the late novels increasingly bizarre and sensational. I called the ghosts of *Turn of the Screw* nodes of visibility. The metaphors are the same thing in new form.

James's grotesque metaphors are Decadent tropes of moral and sexual ambiguity. Milly Theale thinks of her relation to her doctor as "something done up in the softest silk and tucked away under the arm of memory." Memory, hardly likely to be parading about with silkstuffs under her arm, is a recumbent goddess—a Decadent corpse laid out in lavender. Milly thinks of pity holding up "its tell-tale face like a head on a pike, in a French revolution, bobbing before a window."[45] We are to imagine some sleepy Parisian stay-at-home looking up from a book to see a guillotined head dancing outside. Pity, paternalized, is hostile, an evil portent. It is a grinning jack-in-the-box, a grisly *fleur du mal* of phallic elasticity. We have seen this head at the window before. By her sadomasochistic reverie, mild Milly Theale revives the stalking daemon Peter Quint of *The Turn of the Screw*.

Kate Croy's father declares, "If I offer you to efface myself, it's for the final, fatal sponge that I ask, well saturated and well applied."[46] Fatal sponges are refugees from horror films. Croy is seeing himself as a self-cleaning blackboard. But the sponge "applied" to him sounds like a sticky poultice or leech. He seems to be inviting the obliterating contact of his daughter's slavering lips!—a filial kiss of death. He is the crucified one to whom bystanders extend a sour, unnourishing sponge. "Final, fatal sponge" also echoes the formula "final, fatal plunge" by which tabloids picture the defenestration of suicides. The comic Jamesian metaphor is a studded conglomerate of sadomasochistic meanings.

An exchange between Madame de Vionnet and Strether: "The gold-en nail she had then driven in pierced a good inch deeper." The worldly Vionnet is both an inquisitor of the crucified male heroine and a guest dignitary punctuating the rabble-made railroad with its final golden spike. Conversation with a dominatrix is like playing jackstraws with razors. Mrs. Newsome's daughter sums up her brother's relation to her: "Treating her handsomely buttered no parsnips; and that in fine there were moments when she felt the fixed eyes of their admirable absent mother fairly screw into the flat of her back."[47] Parsnips make language an indigestible lump, intensifying the concreteness of the second meta-phor, where a matriarch again operates her hermaphroditic screw— here an arrowlike auger launched from the eerily "fixed eyes" of a telepathic goddess.

The Golden Bowl likes fowl metaphors. Birds bruise themselves against glass or flutter in traps improbably set in roads. There are visual puns: "A scruple in Maggie raised its crest." The scruple is both army flag and cock's comb. In stress, Maggie's emotions undergo internal erection. *The Golden Bowl*, befitting its title, uses metaphors of contain-ment. Of Fanny Assingham and the Prince: "She found his eloquence precious; there was not a drop of it that she didn't, in a manner, catch, as it came, for immediate bottling, for future preservation. The crystal flask of her innermost attention really received it on the spot, and she had even already the vision of how, in the snug laboratory of her afterthought, she should be able chemically to analyze it."[48] Here we see how James purifies Romantic archetypes by rationalizing or over-literalizing them. The passage dedaemonizes Blake's *Mental Traveller.* Fanny's crystal flask is the gold cup in which the vampire catches the shrieks of her male victim. (The novel's biblical title occurs in Blake's *Book of Thel.*) The femme fatale becomes a scientist and bottler of mineral waters. But in the laboratory of her consciousness, as on Blake's anvil of nature, she is a sexual dissecter, subdividing male matter. She is also a Decadent cultist, for her flask is like a consecrated vial holding *lacrimae Christi,* the Prince's "precious" falling words.

The nesting female cubicles of flask and laboratory recur in Maggie's uncomfortable sense of her husband and stepmother's attitude toward her: "They had built her in with their purpose—which was why, above her, a vault seemed more heavily to arch; so that she sat there, in the solid chamber of her helplessness, as in a bath of benevolence artfully prepared for her, over the brim of which she could but just manage to see by stretching her neck."[49] Roman landmarks are fatal to James heroines, in *Daisy Miller* the Colosseum and here the Baths of Caracalla. Sunk in a sarcophaguslike tub, Maggie is trapped in a Piranesi prison. She is part Aida, part Poe's bricked-up Fortunato. James's metaphors are mini-tableaux of Late Romantic torture. The bath, like Fanny's flask, is a mental vessel brimming with the waters of consciousness. In James, the inner life is feminine because liquid and malleable. Thus it makes sense that his thought-stymied heroes are androgynous. The gelatins of consciousness usually elude male control. Mrs. Lowder is a master chef: " 'Why' was the trivial seasoning-substance, the vanilla or the nutmeg, omittable from the nutritive pudding without spoiling it."[50] As chemist or cook, woman does the whipping.

James's grotesque metaphors are the objets or curios of his Decadent aestheticism. Like Wilde, he joins Late Romantic sexual perversity to English high comedy of Carrollian absurdity. The link between his metaphors and art-obsessed French Decadence is clear in the comparison of Maggie Verver's troubled married life to "some wonderful, beautiful, but outlandish pagoda." Its "great decorated surface" is plated with fancy porcelain and hung with silver bells.[51] The pagoda metaphor, taking up a full page, is so long and tangled that, as West tartly remarks, "one is left with a confused impression that a pagoda formed part of the furniture at Portland Place and that Maggie oddly elected to keep her husband inside it."[52] James's exercise in Orientalism is a display of Decadent connoisseurship. The pagoda is an epic simile from which nature has been banished. As an objet d'art, its antecedents are not in the social novel but in Moreau and Huysmans.

James's metaphors are points of grotesque visibility in the diffuse mass of the late style. Since so much in him is invisible and unspoken, the prickly metaphors have a violent distinctness. His mandarinism, mussing itself with buttered parsnips, scattered feathers, and fatal sponges, plunges up and down, in radical rhetorical shifts. The metaphors are tiny psychodramas of *sexual fall*. The celibate James plays with sensations of seduction and surrender. The metaphors symbolize his own abasement before female power. His giddy drops from one level of decorum to another, like a speed jockey operating an elevator, are like the governess' delirious self-stimulations in *Turn of the Screw*.

James's Decadent autoeroticism is shown by his fondness for sexually suggestive names, all the lewder for the sedate context: Fanny Assingham, Ralph Touchett, Mrs. Condrip. The names, like the metaphors, have a knotty, self-isolating character. In the late novels, James tries, by subtle insinuations, to induce sexual misreadings of the text. For example, during an innocuous social exchange in *The Ambassadors*, he speaks of the "lubrication of their intercourse by levity." Milly

Theale after learning of her fatal illness: "It was as if she had had to pluck off her breast, to throw away, some friendly ornament, a familiar flower, a little old jewel, that was part of her daily dress; and to take up and shoulder as a substitute some queer defensive weapon, a musket, a spear, a battle-axe—conducive possibly in a higher degree to a striking appearance, but demanding all the effort of the military posture."[53] The soldier talk encourages us to see Milly, in a flare-up of Amazonism, tearing off her breast!—when she is just unpinning a brooch or corsage. James's late style subjects the reader to Decadent seduction and corruption. Language is perversely eroticized, then yanked back to safety by the conjurer's hand, leaving us aroused and guilty.

The grotesque metaphors are traps, decoys set to take the reader's eye. James's worst feature is his suppression of affect or smothering of reaction. He shuns cathartic release because he writes melodrama, not tragedy. His heroines never have a true *anagnorisis* because the moral fault is never in themselves, only in outside conspirators. The climactic revelations never release the accumulated tension because they too, like the metaphors, are agents of concealment. Page by page, the metaphors are sharp points of visibility that, like a matador's cape, make the reader lunge past a protected center. Their function is to pretend something is being revealed, when it is not. The metaphors are *apotropaia*, like the ugly gorgoneion hung on the oven door to ward off evil spirits. The reader, both invited guest and intruder, is lured and misled. We are pulled into a labyrinth or meander, then left in the dark. James dissolves the sexual body and diverts its materiality into the metaphors, which take on a crazy, leering exactitude. They are sexual displacements, erotic proxies. If, as Wilson thinks, James projects himself into his heroines, then anything that turns us away from the body is comprehensible: what the prose is concealing is James himself, transvestized.

The obscure late style is itself a sexual projection, for whenever I labor under its enormous constraints, I think, "*Someone is there.*" Who lingers at the periphery of narrative?—just like the daemons of *Turn of the Screw*. James says Isabel Archer's reputation for reading "hung about her like the cloudy envelope of a goddess in an epic." Bossy Mrs. Lowder also has a charismatic aura: her interlocutor's mind is filled with "a cloud of questions out of which Maud Manningham's large seated self loomed," like "an oracle."[54] Mrs. Lowder, given her Amazonian maiden name, Manningham (cf. the maiden name of Hawthorne's mother), is a Pythoness enthroned like Ingres's Jupiter. The cloud wrapping her and Isabel is an emanation of female power. It is identical to the haziness of James's late style.

That style is a *miasma*, a new version of the female swamp of generation. Social novels take place in civilized space marked off from nature.
When nature enters, it is usually in socialized form. For example,
Isabel, in a hotel in Rome, sits alone "in a wilderness of yellow uphol-
stery." This is one of the hostile environments, like Spenser's grove of
animate trees, through which the heroine must make her way. Like
Wilde, James recasts nature as interior décor. His miasma, still recog-
nizably chthonian, first appears in *Daisy Miller:* it is the fatal infection
Daisy contracts during her picturesque night in the Colosseum. The
story, to my happy surprise, actually describes the Colosseum's "historic
atmosphere" as "a villainous miasma."[55] *Daisy Miller* is one of James's
early and stylistically transparent works. The noxious swampy realm
into which the heroine wanders is, I maintain, his late style *in utero.*

James's late style is a Byzantine fabric of shuddering grandeur. Laden
with this opulent burden, reader and narrative are condemned to
slow funereal walking, the tiny steps of an Asiatic priestess—or of a
nineteenth-century matron heavy with social status and luxuriant
skirts. The mental image of one of Isabel's suitors has "a kind of
bareness and bleakness" because it lacks "the social drapery which
muffles the sharpness of human contact."[56] James's muffling social
drapery is female fabric hung between persons to *prevent* human contact. The mother's robes are materialized in his massy, ponderous style.

James's world, we have seen, is ruled by women. With a few slick
exceptions, men are limited, subordinate, or ludicrous. The mother
herself presses turgidly on the late novels, a paralyzing biographical
force whom James both resists and adores. We feel her *hovering* in his
ornate style. Donning a prose of female drapery, he unites with the
mother through ritual impersonation. The son-lover of the goddess
commits incest through his hieratic, hermaphrodized language. But
this holy marriage is full of danger. James says of Prince Amerigo and
his mistress, "The intensity both of the union and the caution became a
workable substitute for contact."[57] Everywhere in James, we feel an
unsettling caution. The writer of the late novels is like Condorcet disguised as a girl by his mother in order, according to Frazer, to foil the
evil eye. In James, the mother herself is the evil eye. She protects him
from the daemonic, loaning him her clothing, in the aegis-form of the
late style, as a defense against the spectres of *Turn of the Screw.* But she
is also the *channel* of the daemonic, through which man is crushed and
humiliated by nature. James's union with the mother is an imprisonment that we, oppressed by his style, share. She prevents him from fully
entering the world of personae. He is *detained* by her in a median state,

halfway between Romanticism and the social novel, his artistic goal. So we wait—and wait and wait. Nothing ever happens in James, because he and we are hostages caught in a crossfire.

James's repressions and evasions are many, varied, and exhausting. Why more people are not seen rushing shrieking from libraries, shredded James novels in their hands, I cannot say. I used to wonder whether enthusiasm for him was based on identification, since his passive, tentative heroes resemble many academics. Perhaps what is intolerable is his enshrinement in a soporific criticism. So much must be overlooked to crown him with laurel. But if James is understood as a Late Romantic, a Decadent in my extended sense, then his sadomasochistic perversities take coherent form, integrated with his witty aestheticism and ambiguous sexual personae. His fussy late style is Decadent because it is both fastidious and excessive. George Moore called James a self-made "eunuch," implying he was a prude and sissy.[58] This is much too simple. Sex cannot be understood apart from nature. James's rhetorical impediments and frustrations arise from a suppression of the daemonic, in which sex is included but to which sex too is subject.

24

Amherst's Madame de Sade

Emily Dickinson

American Romanticism, I have argued, is really Decadent Late Romanticism, the century-long evolution through which Coleridge finally triumphs over Wordsworth. Poe and Hawthorne are already registering Late Romantic perversities in the 1830s. Therefore the tardy dates of *Tom Sawyer* (1876) and *Huckleberry Finn* (1884) show what is wrong with Mark Twain. His Wordsworthian idylls are completely out of sync with the internal development of major American literature. The two books are bourgeois fantasies about childhood and lower-class life. As in my youth, teachers continue to inflict them on students as somehow proper reading. It took me twenty years to work out a critical theory to explain why I found Twain so hateful. His dislike of the witty Jane Austen provided the key. His rejection of her Enlightenment hierarchism is partly an unconscious rejection of the innate hierarchism of Late Romanticism. Twain is trying to turn the Romantic clock back. His folksiness and pastoralism are counterfeit, as decadent as Marie Antoinette's masquerades as a shepherdess. The gloomy negativity of Twain's later life is no puzzle to me. His Wordsworthian benevolence was always false. The hierarchical Lewis Carroll is the true poet of childhood, with its mystery, cruelty, and blatant aggressions. Twain as a fabulist? Fable is marshallow myth; it is myth stripped of chthonian realities. Scratch a fabulist, and you'll find fear of woman and fear of nature. Storytelling or yarn-spinning is what men do among men. It is a ritual of avoidance, a deflection of the psychological turbulence of men's lives with women. Twain's boy-stories are songs of innocence sixty years past their time. Romanticism is in its degenerate late phase. Dark, sexual songs of experience are the authentic Late

Romantic voice. And this leads us to Emily Dickinson, the greatest of women poets.

Less melodious than Sappho, Dickinson is conceptually vaster, for she assimilates two more millennia of western experience. No major figure in literary history has been more misunderstood. Ignored by her own time, Dickinson was sentimentalized in her renascence. After thirty years of scholarship, the modernist complexity of her high style is universally recognized. But criticism still ignores the bulk of mawkish lyrics in her collected works. There is no integration of her high and low styles. Psychoanalytic readings are slowly making their way, but the academic view of her remains too genteel. The horrifying and ruthless in her are tempered or suppressed. Emily Dickinson is the female Sade, and her poems are the prison dreams of a self-incarcerated, sadomasochistic imaginist. When she is rescued from American Studies departments and juxtaposed with Dante and Baudelaire, her barbarities and diabolical acts of will become glaringly apparent. Dickinson inherits through Blake the rape cycle of the *The Faerie Queene*. Blake and Spenser are her allies in helping pagan Coleridge defeat Protestant Wordsworth.

The primary qualities of Dickinson's style are high condensation and riddling ellipsis. Protestant hymn-measure is warped and deformed by a stupefying energy. Words are rammed into lines with such force that syntax shatters and collapses into itself. The relation of form to content is aggressive and draconian. The structure cramps and pinches the words like a vise. The poems shudder with a huge tremor of contraction. Dickinson's poetry is like the shrinking room of Poe's *The Pit and the Pendulum*, a torture chamber and arena of extremity. We are in the womb-tomb of Decadent closure.

Dickinson has two representational modes, which I call the Sadean and the Wordsworthian. The brutality of this belle of Amherst would stop a truck. She is a virtuoso of sadomasochistic surrealism: "The Brain, within its Groove / Runs evenly and true— / But let a Splinter swerve."[1] Like the Metaphysical poets, she finds metaphors among the mechanical and domestic arts—blacksmithing, carpentry, cooking, sewing. In this example, the brain, detached as Emerson's eyeball, is humming merrily along in its underground railroad of daily custom, when it is suddenly pierced by a splinter shooting off the wooden track. Analysts of emotion do not normally think of the brain as a soft mass spitted by malicious barbs. As in James, the metaphor belongs to horror films—or rotisserie cooking. It always reminds me of a breakfast-hour high-school driver-education film that made us contemplate a dead truck driver, his skull crushed against the dashboard by a load of lumber shifting forward. The analogies in art to Dickinson's wood-speared brain are pagan or Catholic: the *Iliad*'s gruesome battlefield deaths or Mantegna's St. Sebastian, transfixed by an arrow from chin to pate. In its sheer gratuitousness, the metaphor resembles the tortures of *120 Days of Sodom*, where Sade jams lethal blades, rods, and spikes into every orifice of the body.

Dickinson prefers the word "brain" to "mind": it is one of her earthy Anglo-Saxon tropes. She makes sharp Sadean comedy out of treating the brain as a thing: "The Brain is just the weight of God— / For Heft them Pound for Pound / And they will differ—if they do— / As Syllable from Sound" (632). The poet hefts the brain like a shopper picking through cabbages at the market. God has shrunk, like the embalmed head of Queequeg's totem. The poet sets him on the makeshift scales of human judgment. It's suppertime: communion or cannibalism? Bereaved, Dickinson declares, "I've dropped my Brain" (1046). Thought is paralyzed, with the brain dropped like a handkerchief. But such an object will hardly float to the floor. We hear a muffled thump, like the paperboy hitting the stoop with the evening edition.

Dickinson's brain has a will of its own: "If ever the lid gets off my head / And lets the brain away / The fellow will go where he belonged / Without a hint from me" (1727). The skull seems trepanned, like a cookie jar. The brain, as masculine intellect, escapes like a canary from a cage or a firefly from a bottle. We see a Late Romantic rebellion of part against whole, the brain boldly abandoning its master, like Gogol's nose or Gautier's mummified foot. The brain can be an empty, echoing space: "I felt a Funeral, in my Brain, / And Mourners to and fro / Kept treading—treading—till it seemed / That Sense was breaking through" (280). This parade of persons trampling up and down like noisy upstairs neighbors is a funeral procession of thoughts of wintry disillusion. It is also the beating of a Romantically self-oppressed heart. I suspect two influences here from Poe: the skull-like mansion/tomb of *The House of Usher* and the guiltily throbbing chamber of *The Tell-Tale Heart*.[2]

In "He fumbles at your Soul," probably an account of a fire-breathing sermon, the hearer's recovering brain is said "to bubble Cool" (315). So the brain has been boiling like a pot on the stove. The liquefied brain, steaming like magma in a crater, can also be the bonehead brain:

> Rearrange a "Wife's" affection!
> When they dislocate my Brain!
> Amputate my freckled Bosom!
> Make me bearded like a man!   [1737]

The brain has joints, subject to hoodlum arm-twisting. This stanza, from the marriage poems where Dickinson plays with earthly and celestial brides, is a violent fantasy of Amazonian desexing. Who are "they"? No matter what reading we choose, we are left with a spectacle of Sadean torture. The speaker is a martyred saint, St. Catherine racked by the deputies of the state.

Enough of brains. On to lungs. "A Small Leech on the Vitals— / The sliver, in the Lung— / The Bung out of an Artery— / Are scarce accounted Harms" (565). The leech is not a medical bloodsucker but a septic invader, an intestinal parasite. It is Dickinson's Sadean shorthand for a nagging anxiety, an invisible hemorrhaging wound, like a stress ulcer. Its ancestor is Prometheus' perforated liver. But the scene of suffering is domestic, not sublime. The leech is heaven's worm, cousin to Eden's serpent. The ailment of which the speaker complains, or rather declines to complain, is chronic rather than acute, a gnawing malady without High Romantic glamour.

As for the artery with its bung out, Dickinson sees the body bursting like a stoven barrel, gushing red in an apoplectic spout. The sliver in the lung is another of her bits of embedded shrapnel. It is unlikely the sliver has been inhaled—though one cannot dismiss any hallucination when reading Dickinson! Probably the sliver is a dart that has pierced the rib cage: it is one of Cupid's unlucky iron arrows, the spear in Christ's side lowered to household accident. Dickinson elsewhere says of an absent friend: "I got so I could stir the Box / In which his letters grew / Without that forcing, in my breath— / As Staples driven through" (293). Staples hammered into the thorax are her tender way of describing a catch in the breath, by which we should also understand the sliver in the lung. Returning to that stanza, we see how much irrational visual material it contains. The speaker stands with bungs out and leeches and splinters all over her body, like a human porcupine. The representational style is Asiatic. As in the platform scene of *The Scarlet Letter*, we see the Ephesian Artemis, an idol studded with grotesque sacrificial symbols.

Dickinson's sadomasochistic metaphors are usually overdetermined, in the Freudian sense; that is, they are conflations of multiple meanings. For instance, the disagreeable staple occurs elsewhere, showing its inherited associations. "They" ally once more for bouts of harassment. "They put Us far apart . . . They took away our Eyes . . . They summoned Us to die— / With sweet alacrity / We stood upon our stapled feet— / Condemned but just to see" (474). The stapled feet of the devoted couple represent their separation in space. Feet nailed to the ground, the speaker is like Odysseus bound to the mast or like a Kewpie doll stuck to a dashboard, swaying to the motion of cathexis. The scene is Inquisitional: two prisoners are slain for their fidelity. The speaker is like Oedipus, his ankles pierced by the jealous king, or like Christ nailed up with his criminal companions. The phrase "stapled feet" is purposefully reductive in making the carpenter's son victim of a satiric carpentry. Jesus as carpenter often appears in Dickinson: he is master of "the Art of Boards," or God forces him and humanity to walk the plank.[3]

Dickinson strews puncture wounds liberally through her poetry. She says of one of her heroes, "Fate . . . Impaled Him on Her fiercest stakes" (1031). Fiercest may mean sharpest, but it could also mean bluntest, to maximize pain. In this savage tableau, a cruel goddess waits with a sheaf of stationary spears, nature's phallic stockade. Elsewhere Dickinson declares, "No Rack can torture me": the soul is something "You Cannot prick with saw / Nor pierce with Scimitar" (384). These negatives are a paraleipsis: what cannot be done to the soul *can* be done to the body. Piercing with scimitars is credible swordplay (though slashing would be truer), but what of pricking with saws? Bizarre scenarios flash before the eyes: magicians tickling ladies in half; seamstresses pricking themselves with saws rather than pins; bandits setting upon travellers with saws, pricking forearms with abandon. Again one thinks of Sade's encyclopedic *120 Days of Sodom:* by Yankee ingenuity, Dickinson is determined to add to the sum total of imaginable human tortures.

Impalement is Dickinson's metaphor for mortality: "A single Screw of Flesh / Is all that pins the Soul" (263). Incarnation is torment. The soul, like the Greek winged *psyche*, is a butterfly fixed by a pin. The cruel lepidopterist, one assumes, is God. The metaphor recalls Mary's heart lanced by the swords of her seven sorrows, or St. Teresa's heart thrilled by the angel's dart. It is a Valentine's card by Beardsley, a holiday symbolism evoked when Dickinson says of a friend, "The largest Woman's Heart / Could hold an Arrow too" (309).

Dickinson's impalements are even more atrocious: "It is simple, to ache in the Bone, or the Rind— / But Gimlets among the nerve / Mangle daintier—terribler" (244). Gimlets among the nerve are stabs or twinges of pain, a spiritual neuralgia. But the metaphor demands we see boring tools, like corkscrews, rioting through and shredding the nerve fibers. It is like a butchering surgeon's scalpel or a drunken sculptor's auger. What is a dainty mangling? This Decadent juxtaposition of beauty and horror resembles Baudelaire's "hideous delicacies." It is a subliminally sexual Spenserian effect that few English poets attempt. The "rind," opposed to bone, is human skin. Normally, only fruit, cheese, or bacon has a rind. Dickinson's rind makes the body *peelable*. Apollo with a potato parer, she flays the Marsyas of humanity, exposing raw nerve. Man is a red-ribboned *écorché* in her laboratory.

The spectacles of affliction can be incoherent: "A Weight with Needles on the pounds— / To push, and pierce, besides— / That if the Flesh resist the Heft— / The puncture coolly tries" (264). Like tourists in Madame Tussaud's Chamber of Horrors, we pause puzzled before a new instrument of torture in Dickinson's mental dungeon. A weight with needles must be depression combined with anxiety. It is grief that deadens but thoughts that arouse. The metaphor makes us see a kind of meat tenderizer or serrated millstone. Perhaps it comes from *The Pit and the Pendulum:* it combines crushing with cutting, moving walls with rocking razorblade. Or it may be a version of the medieval Iron Maiden, which drove spikes into a victim's eyes and torso. There is a shadowy sexual element in Dickinson's image, a suggestion of rape, for the weight with needles is a force that both smothers and penetrates.

If she treats the body like a pincushion, Dickinson also treats pincushions like bodies. She speaks of a grief "that nestled close / As needles ladies softly press / To Cushions Cheeks— / To keep their place" (584). Women darning or embroidering stick needles into the cushions on which they rest their hands. If their sewing is like a book being read, the needle is a bookmark. Dickinson's anthropomorphism fiendishly makes cushions fat-cheeked sentient beings, like the paunchy pudding whom Alice tries to slice. The stanza clearly shows how Dickinson's sadomasochism is a perverse self-pleasuring. She turns ladies into sadists, ruthlessly running needles into cheeks. "Softly" has a morbid Spenserian delicacy, introducing a luxurious stillness and amorousness into the sequestered scene. We peer into another rounded capsule of female solipsism, as in Blake's "Sick Rose" or Ingres's *Turkish Bath.* The needles are the thorns of a closed garden of earthly delights.

A similar poem describes the rise and fall of a painted hot-air balloon:

> The Gilded Creature strains—and spins—
> Trips frantic in a Tree—
> Tears open her imperial Veins—
> And tumbles in the Sea—   [700]

By making the balloon feminine, Dickinson intensifies the masochism of its death. Its thrashings become exquisite and erotic. Beauty and pain sensually mix, as in Spenser's episode of the slashing of Amoret's white bosom. The word "gilded" gives the balloon the same aura Balzac uses in *The Girl with the Golden Eyes* to sensationalize the destruction of a human objet d'art. The balloon "strains," "spins," "trips frantic": we are watching the hopeless flight of a victim of rape-murder. Her veins are "torn" like silk, ravaged by vandals. The veins are imperial, because she is like a Roman opening her veins in the bath of the sky-blue sea. Is Dickinson reimagining Shakespeare's Spenserian *Rape of Lucrece*? The balloon's rupture is an orgasmic sigh of surrender.

Dickinson's displaced eroticism is evident even in poems without overt sexual personae: "Force Flame / And with a Blonde push / Over your impotence / Flits Steam" (854). The images have a stunning economy and toughness. She means man is helpless before nature's laws. The locution "a Blonde push" is so remote from common English speech that it seems nonverbal, something seen or felt rather than read or heard. It has sexual implications, like Yeats's inseminating "white rush" in "Leda and the Swan." We expect a blonde push in French boudoir painting or Baroque sculpture—Bernini's Apollo chasing Daphne. The passage is structured by a hierarchical pattern of strength and weakness, attack and defeat.

Another example of Dickinson sex and violence: "She dealt her pretty words like Blades— / How glittering they shone— / And every One unbared a Nerve / Or wantoned with a Bone" (479). A daunting woman—one suspects she is young and attractive—is set before us, her mouth bristling with steel cutlery, the long teeth of a talkative Berenice. She is making those cutting remarks I find symptomatic of aggressive western speech. Both coy and cruel, this composed hermaphrodite entertains herself with a round of exploratory surgery, uncovering nerves and "wantoning" with bones—an erotic word choice. Literally, to wanton with bones is to toss them about, as if mixing a salad. So we see bones sailing through the air on gusts of chat. Are we at a social circus? Juggler, knife-thrower, and lion-tamer have gotten their acts together, in impressive triplicate.

A parallel theme from the poet's point of view: "I've got an arrow here. / Loving the hand that sent it / I the dart revere" (1729). The arrow is probably a hurtful letter that has struck home. Drawing the missile from her flesh and studying it fondly, the poet is like a martyr holding her instrument of execution, like St. Lawrence leaning on his grill. Dickinson's iconography of suffering, with its sexualized pleasure-pain, Catholicizes austere American Protestantism. Imagistically, her poetry is late-phase Renaissance. Metaphysical poetry is an anti-Puritan Baroque style, Italian in its passion and theatricality. Dickinson's lurid metaphors are surprise renovations, polychrome statues and stained-glass windows added to a white New England church.

Dickinson favors emblematic postures where she holds some weapon. Rehashing "a Withdrawn Delight / Affords a Bliss like Murder— / Omnipotent—Acute." Hence "We will not drop the Dirk / Because We love the Wound / The Dirk Commemorate" (379). The dirk must be a letter, or the memory of a letter, and the withdrawn delight its cancellation of a longed-for visit. Dagger in hand, the poet contemplates the stigmata of her private cult. To "love the Wound" in solitude is patently autoerotic. The tone is French Decadent: Baudelaire too says, "I am the wound and the knife!" And what of murder as "bliss"? Dickinson is in her Sadean phase, a blood-red moon of sexual will.

The poet's heart is vulnerable to sudden attack by projectiles other than arrows. She calls springtime birdsong both sad and sweet because it reminds us of the dead: "An ear can break a human heart / As quickly as a spear, / We wish the ear had not a heart / So dangerously near" (1764). Wham! Chop! Faster than a speeding spear, the Dickinson ear demolishes a hapless heart, which is like a piece of liver hewn by the cook's cleaver. Ear and heart, spotlit, secede from the body and turn on each other. Normally passive and receptive, the ear becomes active and aggressive. Like Samson's jawbone, Dickinson's feisty ear is among history's more exotic arms of war. One pictures battalions marching on each other, brandishing ears rather than spears.

That Dickinson does imagine the heart as an extracted organ quivering on a flat surface is proved by this stanza, which she attached to a gift of fruit:

> My Heart upon a little Plate
> Her Palate to delight
> A Berry or a Bun, would be,
> Might it an Apricot!   [1027]

Wearing her heart on her sleeve would be too conventional for our poet, who slaps it on a fruit dish and sends it down the street like a phone-order pizza. Spenser again: Dickinson is remembering Amoret's heart laid in a silver basin. Obviously, the female friend honored with the poet's crimson gift is expected to nibble on it, like a chocolate heart on Valentine's Day. More Catholic iconography: Dickinson is like St. Philip Neri holding his flaming heart in his hand or St. Lucy offering us her eyeballs on a silver platter (a real statue in my baptismal church).

Dickinson indulges her taste for saintly epiphany in clever allegories that slip by the unwary reader. For example, she disdains pearls and jewels since "the Emperor / With Rubies pelteth me" (466). This is one of her tricky bride of Christ poems: the emperor is the deity whose motives are always suspect. The rubies pelting the speaker are not rich gifts but stones making her *bleed*. She is spotted with her own wounds, a pox or king's evil by which she is made royal. The emperor is Poe's Red Death. The jewels are drops of blood, which she elsewhere forces a friend to number like rosary beads ("But *He* must *count the drops—himself*"; 663). She is Danae whom God showers with her own blood and Mary Magdalene at whom he casts the first stone. Dickinson, *nouveau pauvre*, is an ostentatious flaunter of injuries. She says of sunset's red light, "I felt martial stirrings / Who once the Cockade wore" (152). The rosette of the Napoleonic veteran becomes a bandage with a bloodstain seeping through (cf. "The Soul has Bandaged moments"; 512). Dickinson's wounds and scars are military medals of honor, the price and prize of life experience.

Back to our catalog of Sadean abuses of the body. We saw brains and lungs undergoing rough treatment at Dickinson's hands, and this led to a list of impalements and ruptures. Eyes are next. I cited "They took away our Eyes," which means two persons have been forcibly separated and are now invisible to each other. But in Dickinson's eccentric dramaturgy, the authorities come knocking, seize the eyes, and carry them away, like a finance company repossessing a refrigerator. This is clear in a poem about the domestic aftermath of death, "When eyes . . . are wrenched / By Decalogues away" (485). Here the eyes may have put up a struggle, and death has had to yank them out like teeth. Like the dislocated brain, this may be another surreal joint, wrenched like an elbow. The haste with which the eyes are snatched recalls Perseus robbing the Graiai. The thief is God, author of the Ten Commandments, who decrees death as man's fate. As Dickinson puts it, however, the Decalogue seems greedy on its own behalf. Moses' tablets snap shut on the eyes like a mousetrap.

A frequent Dickinson formula is eyes being "put out," as in "Before I got my eye put out / I liked as well to see" (327). This may refer to her own vision problems or her self-sequestration in her second-floor bedroom. But it has an innuendo of criminal mischief, as if she has had her eye stomped out, like Gloucester in *Lear*. Possibly, she has been blinded by looking too long on the evil sun of life's mysteries. "I cannot live with You" has a witty variation of the trope: "Nor could I rise with You / Because Your Face / Would put out Jesus'" (640). Profane conquers sacred love, annulling hope of resurrection. The beloved's face is a blazing moon eclipsing the sun, putting out the holy eye of heaven. There is inferred violence in this blotting out of one face by another. We practically hear the concussion of a rubber stamp marked VOID! That

God's face is in permanent eclipse for Dickinson is confirmed by her remark about her family: "They are religious—except me—and address an Eclipse, every morning—whom they call their 'Father.' "[4]

In "Renunciation is a piercing Virtue," the "putting out of Eyes" again refers to the separation of two people, here by the poet's choice (745). Renunciation is piercing because it is a self-blinding, like Oedipus with the golden brooches. The freedom with which Dickinson waves sharp instruments about the face and body leads to this extraordinary metaphor about a neighbor's death: "like a Skater's Brook / The busy eyes congealed" (519). The expiring eyes congeal, like pudding or bacon fat in the frying pan, because they literally glaze over (cf. "The Eyes glaze once—and that is Death"; "Should the glee glaze / In Death's stiff stare"; 241, 338). The skaters are the movement of life, quickness in the Renaissance sense. They are darting thoughts, slowing and stopping. We feel the poignancy of the poet's self-created distance and isolation, as in the great "Because I could not stop for Death," where the speaker sees children playing in a schoolyard (712). The point of view is telescopic: a boisterous scene is elegiacally washed in sepia. Whatever the higher levels of the brook metaphor, we must notice how Dickinson boldly juxtaposes eyes and skates. Flashing blades zip over the cornea, scoring it with arabesques.

A poem describes death as "when the Film had stitched your eyes" (414). Here Dickinson inflicts injury on lids rather than eyes. The lids are sewn together, basted like a hem. The "film" comes from a sinister Mr. Sandman, who glues sleepers' lashes together. Death, says Dickinson elsewhere, "only nails the eyes" (561). The lids are tacked like a carpet or nailed like a shutter or coffin lid, surely nicking the eyes in the process. Another alarming example: "I've seen a Dying Eye / Run round and round a Room . . . And then obscure with Fog / And then be soldered down" (547). Like the detachable brain, the eye takes off on its own, charging around the room like a caged animal. It is captured and secured by being soldered down, like a loose cannon. Dickinson means dead eyes will never open again, but the metaphor makes us see a soldering iron applied to an eye, something like Odysseus blinding Cyclops with a red-hot stake. The dying eye may be desperately searching for God in the room. Ironically, therefore, compassionate Jesus appears with a soldering iron in his hand, since it is either he or death acting for him who executes this brutal operation (cf. 1123).

Soldering appears in another corpse poem: "How many times these low feet staggered / Only the soldered mouth can tell— / Try—can you stir the awful rivet— / Try—can you lift the hasps of steel!" (187). Here it is lips melded together, as dreadful a vision for a poet as Christabel's muteness. Dickinson's death has gotten carried away with enthusiasm and added on lock after lock, like a stage magician or bank manager sealing the vault. After soldering, he drives a rivet through the lips and lays on steel hasps like a gag. Mordantly, Dickinson urges the reader to test these fetters, and one imagines oneself trying to pry open the corpse's mouth like a hungry diner struggling with a tin can. As with the lidded head, the skull is a manufactured object, a constructivist sculpture of metal and nails, like Frankenstein's monster.

Dickinson relishes blood and is lavish with her red palette. "Sang from the Heart, Sire, / Dipped my Beak in it, / If the Tune drip too much / Have a tint too Red / Pardon the Cochineal— / Suffer the Vermilion—" (1059). The poet is a self-maiming pelican, tearing clots of flesh from her breast to feed her song, whose notes and bars float through the air in a red trail, a bloody skywriting. Elsewhere she taps the heart again, like a cask of burgundy: "The Mind lives on the Heart / Like any Parasite— / If that is full of Meat / The Mind is fat" (1355). The mind suckling on the nutlike heart is a barnacle or verminous borer, like canine heartworm. The hungry mind becomes Donne's bedroom flea, with Dickinson taking the parts of both male and female.

Dickinson's world is crowded with deaths, which she collects for her poetic archives. There are accidents and suicides: "[He] Caressed a Trigger absently / And wandered out of Life" (1062). There are executions of invented characters: "Grief is Tongueless—before He'll tell— / Burn Him in the Public Square" (793). There is even an elegy for rodents caught in traps: "A Rat surrendered here / A brief career of Cheer / And Fraud and Fear" (1340). But Dickinson gets her best black comedy from the graveyard: "No Passenger was known to flee / That lodged a night in memory— / That wily subterranean Inn / Contrives that none go out again" (1406). This is like the commercial for Black Flag Roach Motel, a little box tiled with insecticide glue: "Bugs check in, but they don't check out!" The Procrustean host of the subterranean inn is probably a Christ of mixed motives, avenging the No Vacancy of his infancy by keeping a perpetual open house with one-way doors.

Much of Dickinson's sadism comes from her sardonic speech, a rustic bluntness about birth and death. Victorian euphemism was a bourgeois phenomenon, and Dickinson as much as Baudelaire is anti-bourgeois. Here is a complete poem:

> A face devoid of love or grace,
> A hateful, hard, successful face,

A face with which a stone
Would feel as thoroughly at ease
As were they old acquaintances—
First time together thrown.   [1711]

No charity here. Face and stone are "thrown" or brought together by
felonious assault. The successful potentate is a social Goliath struck in
the brow by our obscure David, a persona Dickinson assumes elsewhere
(540). Note the satiric surrealism: the flinty face is also thrown, sailing
off to collide with the stone, as in a lawn game of bowls. Dickinson
shares many images and moods with Lewis Carroll, another celibate
fantasist whose principal creative years, the 1860s, were the same. This
poem is like Carroll's croquet match, with the ball whomped by the
head of a human flamingo.

Dickinson is a pioneer among women writers in renouncing genteel
good manners. She cultivates knavish insolence. The dying once went
to "God's Right Hand": "That Hand is amputated now / And God
cannot be found" (1551). Off with His hand, commands Amherst's
Queen of Hearts. The shocking amputation of God's hand symbolizes
the suddenness of the modern crisis of faith. God has vanished and left
his severed hand behind, like Constantine's colossal fragment in the
Capitoline courtyard, a favorite theme of eighteenth-century prints. All
that remains of God is the dead hand of the law, devoid of moral
substance. His hand appears elsewhere: "Of Heaven above the firmest
proof / We fundamental know / Except for its marauding Hand / It had
been Heaven below" (1205). Death-decreeing God is like Scylla on her
cliff, snatching victims from below. He is a bandit or pillager, a Scourge
of Men. By Decadent partition, the "marauding Hand" is another free
agent, a spidery beast with five fingers. Doctor Dickinson may have to
amputate because of gangrene: God suffers from rotting obsolescence.
But more likely she is judge and he is thief. She calls him a "Burglar" or
"Mighty Merchant" and accuses him of fraud: " 'Heavenly Father' . . . /
We apologize to thee / For thine own Duplicity" (49, 621, 1461). Thus
Emily Dickinson, with her love of gore, drags God to the chopping
block, hacking off his hand in one of the most daringly dissonant
images in nineteenth-century poetry.

Dickinson's humor is jarringly curt. A poem begins: "Split the Lark—
and You'll find the Music" (861). This means, take an ax to a songbird!
She splits the lark like a log or peach. It is the goose who laid the golden
egg carved for a Sadean banquet. She archly denies her vocation: "Nor
would I be a Poet. . . . What would the Dower be, / Had I the Art to stun

myself / With Bolts of Melody!" (505). One must laugh. Like Ben Franklin flying his kite in a thunderstorm, there's Emily Dickinson sitting in the yard, hitting herself in the head with lightning bolts. Zeus needs Hephaestus' hammerblow to give birth to Athena, but Dickinson needs no one. "Dower" suggests, as R. P. Blackmur observes, that the poet "marries herself."[5] Therefore these flashes of lightning are the autoerotic strokes of her conjugal duty. Her creative ecstasy is not afflatus but anvil chorus. If the Muses were to give this poet a heraldic crest, it would be an arm and hammer, as on a box of baking soda. Violence is her love song and lullaby.

Dickinson's rough speech can be impenetrable. She says of wintry thoughts, "Go manacle your icicle / Against your Tropic Bride" (1756). Heidi Jon Schmidt told me this sounds like a street insult, like "Up your nose with a rubber hose!" Approaching pornographic invective, it is an anti-Keatsian seasonal ode: winter embraces summer, hoary Hades capturing Persephone. The manacle (Blake's word) recalls Hephaestus' chain net, thrown over adulterous Ares and Aphrodite, but it has a dark Gothic ring. The icicle, probably the reader's body, resembles the cold phantom penis of witch-cult. I wonder if, in its unwieldy grossness, it was inspired by those dangerous two-story icicles that dangled from rural roofs in pre-insulation days. Dickinson's perverse metaphor has multiple suggestions of lust, force, bondage, and impotence. The icicle could be a phallic sword strapped to and Amazonizing the tropic bride. Either it gives her frostbite, or she melts it. The metaphor ends in a release of tension, a urinary *letting go*, a sudden warm drenching.

Dickinson has a zeal for indelicacy. She creates primitivistic pictorial effects, as in this description of a sunset: "Whole Gulfs of Red, and Fleets of Red / And Crews of solid Blood" (658). It is unusual, to say the least, to make the western sky a sea of coagulated blood. Dickinson's Late Romantic sunset is a Turner repainted by Delacroix. Here is her pleasant paean to a fall day:

> The name—of it—is "Autumn"—
> The hue—of it—is Blood—
> An Artery—upon the Hill—
> A Vein—along the Road—
>
> Great Globules—in the Alleys—
> And Oh, the Shower of Stain—
> When Winds—upset the Basin—
> And spill the Scarlet Rain—

It sprinkles Bonnets—far below—
It gathers ruddy Pools—
Then—eddies like a Rose—away—
Upon Vermilion Wheels—   [656]

A mass murder seems to have been committed in Amherst. The red streams and pools recall the curse upon Pharaoh, when the waters turned to blood. Dickinson may be showing Jehovah's rape-murder of pagan mother nature. Sadean reality triumphs over Wordsworth's illusions. The artery and vein decking this grisly bespattered landscape belong to Blake's Cosmic Man, dismembered in an orgy of sparagmos. Tasty morsels. Who else but Dickinson could think of autumn leaves as blood clots, "Great Globules in the Alleys"? I would reject a menstrual reading of these images. We're dealing with a woman who spent a lot of time with the help in the kitchen, so if any personal experience backs this poem, it's probably the decapitation and evisceration of chickens!

Her letters too display Dickinson's witty flouting of decorum. She writes her cousins, "No one has called so far, but one old lady to look at a house. I directed her to the cemetery to spare expense of moving." The tone is pure Vincent Price, a self-satirizing ghoulishness. It comes early to Dickinson, for she is barely fifteen when she remarks in a letter, "I have just seen a funeral procession go by of a negro baby, so if my ideas are rather dark you need not marvel." To another friend, a newspaper editor, she says: "Who writes those funny accidents, where railroads meet each other unexpectedly, and gentlemen in factories get their heads cut off quite informally? The author, too, relates them in such a sprightly way, that they are quite attractive. Vinnie was disappointed tonight, that there were not more accidents—I read the news aloud, while Vinnie was sewing."[6] The two sisters are Fates chuckling over earthly fatalities. Vinnie is like Madame Defarge knitting at the guillotine.

Dickinson's sense of vocation is full of the harrowing and cataclysmic. She tells her mentor, Thomas Wentworth Higginson, "I had no Monarch in my life, and cannot rule myself, and when I try to organize—my little Force explodes—and leaves me bare and charred." Anarchy, revolution, powder magazines blown sky-high. Dickinson is at war with her own metric. "Bare and charred," she is like a stand of Wordsworthian trees hit by Sadean forest fire. At his first visit, she told Higginson: "If I read a book [and] it makes my whole body so cold no fire ever can warm me I know *that* is poetry. If I feel physically as if the top of my head were taken off, I know *that* is poetry. These are the only way I know it. Is there any other way."[7] Poetry is assault and battery on the body. Shamanistic vision demands physical trauma. Her topless head is like an exploding boiler or a bottle of fermenting cider blowing its cap. Poetry is a kind of scalping, the pastime of ignoble savages (cf. 315). In the Arctic tropics of art, the poet's head is a coconut clipped by a machete.

Another vivid portrait of the artist occurs in Dickinson's letter to her cousins: "I noticed that Robert Browning had made another poem, and was astonished—till I remembered that I, myself, in my smaller way, sang off charnel steps." Elizabeth Barrett Browning had died three years earlier. Claiming surprise at Browning's resumption of his work, Dickinson says she too writes in the face of constant grief and loss. But notice how she depicts herself in a garish tableau of late-Renaissance theatricality, like a Bernini papal tomb: we see her standing and singing on the steps of a charnel house, a depository of corpses. This is a version of whistling past a graveyard (she told Higginson, "I sing, as the Boy does by the Burying Ground—because I am afraid").[8] But she is posing on the steps like a Dickens waif holding out her tin cup. Behind the metaphor may be *Hamlet*'s singing gravedigger or, I suspect, George Herbert's charming "Church-monuments," where the poet sends his body to school in a chapel of dusty tombs. Thus we should see Dickinson as a tiny scholar emerging from her ghastly lessons and bursting into song! It's like a *New Yorker* cartoon, a portly man with a newspaper turning away from the window to inform his wife, "Oh, it's just Emily Dickinson singing on the steps of her charnel house."

Dickinson's metaphors, based on the Metaphysical conceit, resemble James's in their Decadent overliteralization. But his metaphors are sporadic and delusive, while hers are on the epic scale and mean business. I said Swinburne's alliterations and incantatory rhythms are primitivizing devices, returning poetry to its origins in religious ritual. In Dickinson, it is not rhythm but image that is regressive. She uses metaphors more literally than anyone else in major literature. Her lurid concretization is her mode of Late Romantic materiality, that contraction from idea to thing we have followed through French and English Decadence. In her poetry, things become persons and persons things, and all press physically on each other in nature's brutal absolutism.

Thus far we have established Dickinson's unrecognized appetite for murder and mayhem, her sweet tooth for sadomasochistic horror. Her first posthumous reputation was based on her Wordsworthian roulades, her flights of fancy involving birds, butterflies, and beggar lads. Richard Chase declares, "No great poet has written so much bad verse as Emily Dickinson." He blames "the Victorian cult of 'little women'" for the fact that "two thirds of her work" is seriously flawed: "Her coy and oddly childish poems of nature and female friendship are products of a time when one of the careers open to women was perpetual childhood."[9] Dickinson's sentimental feminine poems remain neglected by embarrassed scholars. I would maintain, however, that her poetry is a closed system of sexual reference and that the mawkish poems are designed to dovetail with those of violence and suffering.

It is easy to misread the many lyrics affecting complacent Christian faith. Singsong rhythms and neat rhymes are always spurious in Dickinson, the first modernist master of syncopation and atonality. Metric regularity means naive credulity in the speaker (cf. 193). The mood may be cheerful and upbeat, as in "Tie the Strings to my Life, My Lord, / Then, I am ready to go!" (279). But the bride happily surrendering herself to celestial marriage is usually in for an unpleasant surprise. Death, not a Redeemer, waits at the top of the stairway to heaven. Dickinson is obsessed with *termination*, her Decadent variation on Christian apocalypse. In "Our journey had advanced," a rare instance of the female mind turned toward cosmology, the speaker gazing at New Jerusalem sees "God—at every Gate." Ominously proliferating like Hindu avatars, God is not welcoming humanity but blocking the way to eternal life (615). This is allegorical repletion, the filling up of fictive space with a single identity in different forms, a technique I found in Leonardo, Rossetti, and Emily Brontë.

Dickinson's chirpy newlyweds exit from their poems under suspicious circumstances: "I'm 'Wife'! Stop there!" (199). To keep abreast of Dickinson, like Alice running with the Red Queen, the reader must know where the bodies are buried. The speaker is under arrest; heaven is stasis, a permafrost of nonbeing. The bride poems are clever hoaxes that turn princesses into pumpkins, mere chunks of debris. Corpses drop into the grave with a thud. A frequent finale is a slow fade, the voice fumbling for words, as consciousness gutters out.

These poems require patient detective work, for they are intricate with sophisticated puns. Dickinson was a devoted student of her Webster's dictionary. Her wordplay is Alexandrian bookwork, Decadent erudition. But not all her sentimental poems contain hidden ironies. The ones I am most concerned with are just what they seem to be—pert, peppy trifles. What meaning did such poems have to so great and commanding a poet? She told Higginson, "When I state myself, as the Representative of the Verse—it does not mean—me—but a supposed person."[10] Dickinson's many voices are sexual personae. They fall into her two major modes, the Sadean and Wordsworthian. The sentimental poems are feminine personae, representing a primary response to nature, glad and trusting.

Dickinson's nature has two faces, savage and serene. Lightning sears saplings; volcanos eat villages for breakfast (314, 175). Nature's lips are "hissing Corals" that open and shut, as "Cities ooze away" (601). The volcano steams with the sultry sibilants of Milton's hell. Civilization liquefies at nature's touch. Erupting Etna "shows her Garnet Tooth": pirate nature, red-fanged, has a sinister crooked smile (1146). Sadean nature suffuses Dickinson's poetry in the violent metaphors. Her sentimental and sadistic personae constitute a seasonal allegory. The feminine voices are the vernal phase: they are *the pretty*, a meadow of flora and fauna, sunny and placid. The sadomasochistic poems are *the tectonic*, the slow brute contortions of the frigid mineral world. It is botany versus geology, spring destroyed by winter.

The sentimental poems continue a theme we saw in Spenser and Blake: femininity as pockets of undefended consciousness in nature. These are Dickinson's versions of Blake's chimney-sweep poems, where the poet incarnates himself without satire in a simpler consciousness. As in Spenser, femininity brings its opposite into existence, in a rush of voracity. Dickinson's brides are always rape victims, duped by the trickster lover, death. Early in this book, I traced the ancient evolution from femaleness to femininity, which I defended as an artifice of high culture. Dickinson performs a stunning operation on these terms. She accepts femininity but denies femaleness, sweeping it out of her cosmos. Her flowering world is without fructification, Keatsian pregnancies. In the 1,775 surviving poems, I find only one lush Keatsian moment, in "It will be Summer—eventually": "The Lilacs—bending many a year— / Will sway with purple load" (342). There are no other swelling images of sensual female weight and mass. Even this one is a future projection, not a present reality. The poet has "an Acorn's Breast"—hard and nubby (296). Nature's processes are erotic but not fertile. Stunting and mutilation are the rule.

We saw that because there was no American nature-mother, Romantic writers had to invent her. When dealing with a major woman artist, we must reverse our terms. One reason Dickinson so surpasses Elizabeth Barrett Browning, whom she admired, is her disturbance of sexual identification. She remarked to Higginson, while her mother was still alive: "I never had a mother. I suppose a mother is one to whom you hurry when you are troubled."[11] Male Romantic genius crosses the line of gender to create, but his opposite, already female, must divide mind from body to embrace the Muse. Dickinson, following Blake, says to her mother, "Woman, what have I to do with thee?"

Chase sees a "rococo style" in Dickinson.[12] Rococo perfectly describes her feminine personae of Wordsworthian or Emersonian credulity toward nature. I find a second representational style, used in her sadistic poems of freezing, fracture, and storm and in her great vaulting visions of mountains, planets, and stars: *monumentality.* "Ah, Teneriffe!" she hails a volcanic peak, "Clad in your Mail of ices— / Thigh of Granite—and thew of Steel" (666). I argued that monumentality, as in Egyptian and Assyrian art, is masculinizing and that gigantism in a female artist, as in Emily Brontë's Heathcliff and Rosa Bonheur's *Horse Fair,* is a technique of self-desexing. The titanic Dickinson is a disciple of Blake, the disciple of Michelangelo, who thus indirectly transmits his style from the late Italian Renaissance to late Puritan America. Feminine Dickinson follows Blake's *Songs of Innocence*; masculine Dickinson follows Blake's "The Tyger" and the clashing long poems. Her poems of colossal monumentality are the theater of her Brontëan swerve from gender, her alienation from the female body.

Dickinson's sadomasochistic metaphors are a technique of self-hermaphrodization, for as externalizations of internal events, they are an emptying out of female internality. Sexual ambiguities abound in her poetry and letters. She calls herself boy, man, bachelor, brother, uncle. "When I was a Boy," she likes to say.[13] She may be imitating Shakespeare's transvestite comedies: boyhood would correspond to Rosalind's androgynous adolescence. Dickinson's quirky boy-self signifies an early freedom from socialization, which she is able to evade as an adult only by lock-up in her house and room. "When I was a Boy" could also mean "before I married my Muse." She signs six letters to Higginson with the proud manly "Dickinson," breaking a lingering gender convention. Until twenty years ago, it was still ungallant to refer to a woman writer simply by her last name.

If "boy" is the past, Dickinson's other transsexual titles are the future. Her religious poems use a bizarre terminology of royal promotion: "I'm Czar—I'm 'Woman' now" (199). For Christ's bride, death is spiritual menarche; but speech falters, thought is sluggish, and heaven is a blur. The male honorific signifies the absolute power of immortality. Czar (derived from Caesar) applies only to males. Therefore to be czar and woman simultaneously is a chimera of gender. The source might be Shakespearean: the speaker is Caesar *and* Cleopatra. Or Byronic: Sardanapalus is the "she-king" and Semiramis the "man-queen."

Dickinson's male ranks include prince, duke, and emperor.[14] She applies her favorite title, earl, to God or death (ironically interchange-able). For example, a formally dressed corpse is "Riding to meet the Earl" (665). Her Webster's says, "*Earl* is now a mere title, unconnected with territorial jurisdiction."[15] So this is one of the poet's jokes at the expense of a diminished God. Sometimes she awards earldom to her-self: "When I'm Earl / Won't you wish you'd spoken / To that dull Girl?" She will wear an ermine gown, with imperial eagles on her belt and buckles (704, 452). She progresses from girl to earl like Alice from pawn to queen. Her projected sex change is like a fancy French royal portrait. This flirtatious and swashbuckling poem is addressed to a "Sweet" who just might be another woman, which would explain the satisfactions of future maleness.

Dickinson says of a flower: "I had rather wear her grace / Than an Earl's distinguished face— / I had rather dwell like her / Than be 'Duke of Exeter'" (138). Choosing nature over society, earth over heaven, she expresses these oppositions in sexual polarities. She could "wear" an earl's face but chooses not to. The rejected face is like an ancestor's mask hung on a hat rack by the door. She elsewhere uses the place name Exeter for heaven or the murky afterlife (373). Hence the Duke of Exeter is probably God—that is, the Exiter, dragging men off the world stage with his shepherd's crook. One of her letters, echoing Achilles in Hades, again projects the option of a future sex change: "I had rather *be* loved than to be called a king in earth, or a lord in Heaven."[16]

The poet dons her earl's face in a bridal poem opening with a boudoir flurry: she wears trinkets, cashmere, "Raiment of Pompadour"; ser-vants' fingers dress her hair "as Feudal Ladies wore." She has "Skill— to hold my Brow like an Earl" (473). The earl's brow is the coldness of her new corpselike state. We are left with the peculiar picture of a male face peering out from a bridal veil—a feature, we saw, of ancient fertility rites. This heroine is another divine bride left at the altar. The road to the church in Amherst is full of potholes. "I'm saying every day / 'If I should be a Queen, tomorrow'. . . . If it be, I wake a Bourbon" (373). Ominous intimations of immortality: to wake a Bourbon means, in Dickinson lingo, to ascend the guillotine.

Dickinson's royal titles are honorary degrees of extremity, marking advance into the afterlife. They are hermaphroditic because transcen-dental. Death makes woman an earl in the same way impersonality makes her an androgyne, by masculinizing her into abstraction. In her transsexual leaps into eternity, Dickinson is like Swinburne's Sappho, who turns male at death by sloughing off her passive female body. In some poems, the sex scheme of spiritual evolution is boy/woman/man,

conforming to Blake's traditional pattern innocence/experience/ redeemed innocence. Woman is merely the social mask of adult life.

Dickinson's stark juxtapositions of personae—czar/woman,
earl/girl—are a kind of sexual collage. She enjoys disconcerting the
reader with freakish conjunctions. In a poem about neglecting her
garden, she says, "My Cactus—splits her Beard / To show her throat"
(339). Why *her*? Why not its or his? She provocatively sexualizes the
cactus to make it a bearded lady, a circus hermaphrodite. She automatically uses language of gender to suggest the visual and tactile contrast
between cactus spines and fleshy core, exposed by the cracked stalk.
Dickinson's female cactus is grossly sensual, a vulval arroyo, a swatch of
sleekness in a trough of nettles. It pleases the poet, luxuriating in
solitude, to conjure up androgynes unknown to man. Note again the
epiphanic style: the cactus parting her beard to show her throat is like
Jesus or Mary pointing to their burning, pierced hearts or like St.
Francis displaying his stigmata. This eroticized religious exhibitionism
belongs to the Italian and Spanish Baroque, not to American Protestantism.

Dickinson can sexualize any situation, even the picking of a flower:

> So bashful when I spied her!
> So pretty—so ashamed!
> So hidden in her leaflets
> Lest anybody find—
>
> So breathless till I passed her—
> So helpless when I turned
> And bore her struggling, blushing,
> Her simple haunts beyond!   [91]

The poem, apparently light and frothy, is perverse psychodrama. Dickinson assumes the persona of male raptor, Hades bearing down on Persephone in the meadow. She is a giant among pygmies. As in her poem
about the dying balloon, a delectable eroticism is produced by feminine
flutterings of vulnerability and resistance—"bashful," "ashamed,"
"hidden," "breathless," "helpless," "struggling," "blushing." Even
Dickinson's most innocuous poems stir with dark undercurrents.

The most blatant of Dickinson's masculine self-portraits
is "My Life had stood a Loaded Gun," where she is a totem of phallic
force (754). The "Owner" or "Master" is only *he*, a pronoun. She is the
real power, without which he cannot act. Her consciousness engulfs his,
for he sleeps while she watches—as voyeuristic as Whitman in *The*

Sleepers. I find multiple sources for the poem. The woman-as-gun is like Aaron's rod turned serpent: Aaron similarly acts for Moses and at his bidding. Second, she is a modern Excalibur, the magic sword given Arthur by the Lady of the Lake. Third, she is Spenser's Talus, Artegall's robot squire, "the iron man" (*F.Q.* V.vi.16). Fourth, as her master's "Eye" and "Thumb," that is, his sight and hands, she reenacts the sadomasochistic romance of Charlotte Brontë, one of Dickinson's favorite writers: the woman-as-gun is spunky Jane Eyre finally ruling Rochester, blinded and maimed, at novel's end.

The executioner-gun is the inanimate point of contact between man and nature. Owner and Amazonian gun pursue a doe, Belphoebe's prey in *The Faerie Queene.* When the gun speaks, the mountains "reply": she is nature's Sadean voice. We have seen the "smile" of her "Vesuvian face" before, in Etna's evil garnet tooth. Woman-as-gun is predatory and annihilating: "None stir the second time / On whom I lay a Yellow Eye / Or an emphatic Thumb." To see is to slay. She has Petrarchan looks that kill. The yellow eye is the gun's smoky flame, a savage tiger's eye. Laying an eye on is a familiar locution (for example, "I've never laid eyes on him"); here it projects a target circle onto the victim, pierced by the gun's bullet-eye. The emphatic thumb is the master's trigger finger metamorphosed into sound. It is also her thumb, a crushing hammer. The metaphor reminds me of my Vermont landlord, a carpenter, nonchalantly grinding out live wasps on a windowpane with his thumb. Hence I wonder whether the eye and thumb come from Dickinson's actual observation of artisans at work, especially masons. The emphatic thumb is, finally, the thumbs down in life's bloody arena.

This poem is one of Romanticism's great transsexual self-transformations. Dickinson's self-projection into the gun is exactly like Coleridge's into ravished Christabel: the poet is reaching for the remotest extreme of sex experience. The vampire who violates Christabel symbolizes anti-Wordsworthian daemonic nature. "My Life had stood a Loaded Gun" is another Romantic vampire poem. The gun with "the power to kill, / Without the power to die" is the vampire who paralyzes by eye-contact. She is mechanical, a bride of metal who enters but cannot be entered. Unlike Jane Eyre, she does not share her master's pillow, because she is barren. The loaded gun is Dickinson as denatured vampire, a masculine maker of sadistic poetic speech. She is another androgyne as nineteenth-century manufactured object.

I view as a companion piece to this a fantastic poem where Dickinson switches sexual point of view: "In Winter in my Room / I came upon a Worm / Pink, lank and warm." She ties the worm with a string but returns to find it grown into a hissing snake: "He fathomed me— / Then to a Rhythm *Slim* / Secreted in his Form / As Patterns swim / Projected him." She flees to a distant town to write, "This was a dream" (1670). Eden's serpent as con man and shaker of faith? I see only sexual theater. Any eely creature that manages to blow itself up from "Pink, lank and warm" to a long wiener doing the hula tends to seize the attention of us moderns. After Freud, this poem would be unwritable, except by a child or psychotic. Its unself-conscious clarity is astounding.

The gun and worm poems are reverse images of each other. Aaron's serpent now refuses to resume its original shape. The menacing worm is the gun as not-self. In the first poem, the poet fuses with her masculine half; in the second, she is alienated from it. Here she is in her feminine persona, which perceives only Wordsworthian nature. The snake is unbearable because it is chthonian nature's abrogation of beauty, dignity, and hope. It is a symbol of the Sadean nature force that the poet herself spewed out upon the doe in the gun poem. The worm poem takes place in winter because nature is devastated. Remember the autumn poem drenched in crimson gore: autumn marks the year's massacre of creatures, Dickinson's "Green People" (314).

Other poems show the snake's meaning as a nature symbol for Dickinson. The wily snake lives in "the swamp" (1740). "A narrow Fellow in the Grass," he likes "a Boggy Acre, / A Floor too cool for Corn." The poet never meets him "Without a tighter breathing / And Zero at the Bone" (986). Swamp and bog are the chthonian swamp that antedates agriculture. The popular myth that snakes are slimy, when they are smooth and dry, contains an imaginative truth. The snake bears the invisible slime of the swamp of human origins. Speaking of the widespread "horror of reptiles," G. Wilson Knight claims we would prefer death by tiger to death by boa constrictor or octopus: "From such cold life we have risen, and the evolutionary thrust has a corresponding backward disgust. . . . And since we do not know what to make of tentacles mindlessly groping and distrust the clammy sea-moistures of the body, we fear especially our sex-organs with multiform inhibitions, seeing in them shameful serpentine and salty relations. And yet this fear is one with a sort of fascination."[17] Dickinson's snake poems are ritual encounters with the primitive and uncanny. She feels zero at the bone—a phallically penetrating cold—because the archaic snake nullifies evolution. Sadean nature's brute cycle swallows up individual beings and smashes the things made by man's mind and hand.

How did the worm poem, with its nervy performance of erection and ejaculation, come to a poet whom Higginson described as "that virgin recluse?"[18] Dickinson had an older brother, Austin, whose adultery has recently come to light. I suspect, however, that the penile model, common in rural Amherst, may have been a stallion. The string with which the poet binds the worm (like tying a string round one's finger) is a Wordsworthian leash or halter, unequal to the task, for the chthonian can burst any human chain.

In a poem with the same sexual pattern, "I started Early—Took my Dog," a sociable shoreline scene turns into a rape, as the sea assaults the incautious tourist. He rises up her apron and bodice and threatens to eat her. She flees; he follows: "I felt His Silver Heel / Upon my Ankle— Then my Shoes / Would overflow with Pearl" (520). The glutted vaginal shoe is a conceptual receptacle, moral and literary. It is first an inherited, internalized sexual restraint (cf. 340). The shoe is a male gift, not a prince's glass slipper but a paternal tyrant's iron boot. The image recurs in Sylvia Plath's "Daddy," where the Nazi father is a "black shoe" jailing the slug-white adult daughter. Second, the sea overflows Dickinson's "simple Shoe" because the revelation of nature's coarse reality is always a rape of sentimental illusions. In the worm and sea poems, the speaker flees to a town for safety. An ironic refutation of Wordsworth: civilization, into which the poet normally did not venture, is our only defense against nature.

Snakes have suppleness, a quality Dickinson mistrusts. She says, for example, "Death is the supple Suitor / That wins at last" (1445). Her males or male surrogates have a facility of movement or unctuous self-assurance, corresponding to men's complacent ease in their bodies in Woolf novels. In mythology, men are paralyzed by Medusan females, symbols of nature. In Dickinson, women are paralyzed by male hierarchs of heaven and earth. The worm epiphany is shocking because it is an invasion of the room of one's own, for Dickinson as for Woolf a sacred ideal, a temenos of the inner self. I would reject a reading of the worm poem that reduced it to a New England spinster's fear of sex. The error would be in dissociating the poet from the snake, when in fact it is her self-severed member. She has dropped it by autotomy, like the tail or claw of a fleeing lizard, lobster, or starfish. I see the scene as a surrealist film, like *Un Chien andalou*. The poet is like a man who drops his umbrella and suddenly finds himself in female clothes. He turns around to discover the umbrella changed into a condor, staring at him malevolently. In other words, the poet in the privacy of her room momentarily lays aside her loaded gun, her male persona. But when she returns, it is puffed and distended like Lucille Ball's bread dough ballooning out of the kitchen.

The snake is a fantasy of power escaping Dickinson's control. It is the poet's *swelling ambition,* which menaces the feminine persona by which she passes unseen through society. Why does it take reptilian form? Everyone thinks of the serpent of Genesis. But a snake in a poet's chamber could be Delphi's resident python, a symbol of prophecy. The serpent's schooling has been somewhat spotty, so when our sibylline poet is in her feminine phase, an oracle reigning on a trivet rather than a tripod, discipline is difficult. Second, woman and snake in a second-story chamber recall Shakespeare's Cleopatra and her phallic asps—with one asp driving the queen out of her monument into the streets of Alexandria. Third is the snake coiled round the dove's body in *Christabel,* a sleeping poet's vision of the maiden ensnared in her bedchamber by the vampire. In the gun poem, Dickinson *is* the vampire hunting female prey. In the worm poem, she switches roles and is the feminine dove resisting the vampire-serpent's advances. She saves herself only by dashing out of the house and skipping town. Fourth is the mysterious meeting in the tower of Byron's Manfred with his sister or female double. This is an incandescent moment in Romanticism, one of whose farflung influences, we saw, is Dorian Gray's fatal encounter with his double in the locked room at the top of the stairs.

Dickinson's worm poem is a Romantic confrontation of doubles. The snake is a materialization of her own phallic potency, her Jungian *animus* or repressed masculine half. Jung says, "Psychologically, demons are interferences from the unconscious."[19] Dickinson's snake is both demonic and daemonic. Incest in Byron, I said, may reflect a desire to copulate with the self in sexually transmuted form. In her Byronic tower, Dickinson as Wordsworthian naif refuses sexual relations with her chthonian double. But in this meeting of moral and sexual antitheses, the sadistic principal triumphs, driving its opponent from the field. The snake has intelligence ("He fathomed me," mentally and sexually) and the power of poetry ("Rhythm," "Form," "Patterns"). He is both a Sadean speaker and the *idea* of a Sadean poem. The snake is what Dickinson is and what she has made. But he is out of control, for Wordsworth can never put down a Coleridgean sedition. The snake is an archaic apparition disestablishing its mistress' social persona and filling the bourgeois home with its Delphic fumes.

The first poem has a further sexual ambiguity. The gun has "stood in Corners," dormant, until put to use by her master. Her masculine power is greater than his, but for it to take effect, he must drag her about and aim her. The gun is potent yet dependent. Aquinas says, "A body is composed of potentiality and act; and therefore it is both active and passive."[20] The loaded-gun metaphor is hermaphroditic because of its sexual metathesis (the poet's phallic self-transformation) and because of its synthesis of action and reaction.

Dickinson likes this binary trope. "He found my Being—set it up— / Adjusted it to place— / Then carved his name—upon it / And bade it to the East / Be faithful—in his absence" (603). The psychodrama is like that of the gun poem, except that limited travel has become immobility. The poet sees herself as a toppled gravestone or cromlech, claimed by a vagabond male (probably the bridegroom Jesus). That he "carves" his name into her, like a cattlebrand, is another of Dickinson's sadomasochistic adornments. She is like a tree initialed by a romantic swain. She is a marred block, a pillar turned toward the light, like Lot's incinerated wife.

Dickinson as scarred tombstone is *a passive phallic monument*, both masculine and feminine. Her "Columnar Self" stands on a "Granitic Base" (789). She is thinking of obelisks in the town cemetery: "And the livid Surprise / Cool us to Shafts of Granite— / With just an Age—and Name / And perhaps a phrase in Egyptian" (531). The variant for the latter is "latin inscription." Such metaphors illustrate Dickinson's monumentality, which I interpret as a self-masculinizing style. Her stone towers are sexual monoliths, slabs of aggressive assertion caught between potency and paralysis. Signed and sealed by the divine lover who will never return, she portrays herself architecturally as a fallen caryatid or armless Venus. Dickinson's experiments with active and passive echo those of Sade, who invents exotic conjunctions where an individual both penetrates and is penetrated. However, like Baudelaire's vampires, she seals up female inner space, compressing herself into impermeable blocks. The granite shafts are tombstones but also the corpses themselves, labeled like mummies in a museum.

Dickinson thinks of death as *enforced passivity*, agonizing impediment of movement. She dwells on the moment a person becomes a thing, as in "The last Night that She lived," where the pronoun disappears in the last stanza: "And We—We placed the Hair— / And drew the Head erect" (1100). A human has passed into the object-world. Some death poems use no personal pronoun at all: "'Twas warm—at first—like Us." It, it, it, she says of the dying one (519). Mind, body, and gender have gelatinized. Dickinson's death is a great neuter state. A dead female is a frozen phallic shaft; a dead male is a felled tree of humiliating inertness. Death is a maker of sterile androgynes. A corpse is soldered with rivets because it is a manufactured object, an android.

Dickinson's notorious preoccupation with death is thus a hermaphrodizing obsession, a Romantic motif in its Decadent late phase.

Both men and women are passive toward death, God's vizier. This
intensifies the sexuality of "Because I could not stop for Death," a
parodic "Swing Low, Sweet Chariot." The lady kidnapped by her gentleman caller feels a chill, "For only Gossamer, my Gown— / My Tippet
only Tulle" (712). Gulled into the grave, the speaker finds herself ill-
dressed. Her garments of fairy-tale delicacy are Christian illusions
about resurrection. This feminine persona is universal, symbolizing all
mankind. That is, humanity is feminine in relation to death, fate, God.
Men too wear the flimsy gown of false hope, transvestized by their own
credulity. Men too are raped by the trickster lover, God/death. This
illustrates the richness with which Dickinson invests femininity. As in
Sade and Swinburne, God condemns man to fascist oppression and
sexual subordination. Unable to advance or retreat, the dead rest in an
infinity of checkmate (615). Dickinson declares, "I saw no Way—The
Heavens were stitched." There is no entrance to the tent of the inhospitable Bedouin god (378, 243). Death's victims, like serfs fallen into peat
bogs, are sod androgynes, gelded or virilized into monuments of God
and nature's indifference.

Dickinson's poetry, as an art of sexual personae, comes
from Elizabethan and Jacobean drama. She thinks in theatrical or
masquelike terms. She writes capsule screenplays of agony and ecstasy
where someone is tortured, dying, transfigured. The poems are sexual
scripts, like Sade's. Dickinson turns Wordsworth's nature into an inferno, ring upon ring of pain. As in Spenser and Blake, personae stand
for spiritual states.

The masculine personae of savage nature have several tones. One is
that of routine, as when a jaunty bird strolls down the walk, bites a
worm in half, and eats "the fellow, raw" (328). Frost acts with the same
matter-of-fact pitilessness: "the blonde Assassin" beheads a flower at
play (1624). The frail victim represents human and vegetable nature,
conquered by the cold abstractions of natural and divine law. Sometimes a cat is the assassin, teasing a mouse, then mashing it to death
(762). Or the sea pursues seductively, before drowning its human guest:
" 'My pantry has a fish / For every palate in the Year,'— / To this
revolting bliss / The object floating at his side / Made no distinct reply"
(1749). Dickinson unreels her own *cinéma vérité*, anticipating the day
when Americans would be regaled at suppertime by newsfilms of
corpses being dragged from harbors. Nature can kill by patient ambush:

"How the Waters closed above Him / We shall never know. . . . Spreads the Pond Her Base of Lilies / Bold above the Boy / Whose unclaimed Hat and Jacket / Sum the History" (923). Glug, glug. The assassin is a dark sump, personified in the French Decadent manner as a haughty, handsome archetypal female, her "pancake" train the base of a leafy Tiffany lamp.

Dickinson's weather reports seem written by Sade: the wind is "like hungry dogs"; "yellow lightning" shines through fissures in "Volcanic cloud"; the trees hold up "Their mangled limbs / Like animals in pain" (1694). Nature is an ashy war zone of greed and suffering. Dickinson's usual style is gruesome Sadean comedy: "the Starved Maelstrom laps the Navies," as if it were a giant kitten playing with boats in its milk dish. The tiger "fasts Scarlet / Till he meet a Man / Dainty adorned with Veins and Tissues / And partakes": a Spenserian moment of exquisite gore (872). Snack time rocks around the clock in Sadean nature. Drowsy Keatsian satiety is impossible in Dickinson. She condemns her creatures to wakefulness and deprivation.

Humanity's Wordsworthian illusions about nature are always being sabotaged. Dickinson asks why birds on a summer morn "Should stab my ravished spirit / With Dirks of Melody" (1420). The poet is being raped and assaulted by a flock of warblers. She means nature's beauty is cruel because transient. But her stage set is a Wordsworthian landscape filled with Baudelaire's drill-beaked birds. Their chirps are a shower of knives falling on passersby (cf. "The Awful Cutlery"—forked lightning—dropped from "Tables in the sky"; 1173). Dickinson composes a clashing Sadean music, a Decadent cruel beauty. Another poem has a similar soundtrack: "The Man to die tomorrow / Harks for the Meadow Bird / Because its Music stirs the Axe / That clamors for his head" (294). Nature is in league with social forces of extermination. Its pretty sounds incite the ax to blood-lust. Dawn wakes the executioner, of course, and not the ax. But in Dickinson's dark vision, the nonhuman world telegraphs its Sadean signals from hill to hill. The ax rises up and avidly rings, just as the scaffold "neighs" in another poem, an eager whinny fusing by dream-logic the horse-drawn tumbril to the naying or negation of execution on the creaking platform (708).

In "I dreaded that first Robin, so," a Wordsworthian bird again agitates the poet with its thoughtless felicities: "I thought if I could only live / Till that first Shout got by— / Not all Pianos in the Woods / Had power to mangle me" (348). The pianos are trees sighing in the wind. Their branches against the sky, black keys on white, are played like an Aeolian lyre. Baudelaire too hears vocal trees, "living pillars" speaking "confused words" ("Correspondences"). Dickinson thinks of pianos, just as she thinks of an oppressive cathedral organ in "There's a certain Slant of light" (258). The word "mangle" is attractive to her for the number and devastation of its implied wounds. But what are mangling pianos?—certainly louder than duelling banjos. One imagines a victim tangled up in piano wires and lashed by felt hammers, like a farmhand caught in a thresher. That she sees many pianos is highly surreal, like a Busby Berkeley film. The poet is merely listening to the wind from her house or garden. But in her metaphor, she is in the woods running the gauntlet past rows of voracious pianos, their lids open like maws. Horror show again: Dickinson's nature is an unnerving spectacle of madly playing pianos escaped from human control. Even small things can mangle: she says of a spiritual problem, "This is the Gnat that mangles men" (1331). Making a Carrollian leap from midge to behemoth, a man-mangling gnat is what viciously waits amid Wordsworth's daffodils.

Like Swinburne in *Anactoria*, Dickinson shows sadomasochism suffusing the world: "The Sun took down his Yellow Whip / And drove the Fog away" (1190). Snow and wind are "Brooms of Steel," iron flails of the sky-god (1252). The moon is "like a Head a Guillotine / Slid carelessly away"—a constellation of decapitation (629). "The Black Berry wears a Thorn in his side": a wound for him or us? (554) The sea is "An Everywhere of Silver / With Ropes of Sand" (884). Dickinson's global equilibrium is harsher than Spenser's: the beaches are shackles, and her sea lies in bondage. A favorite word is "iodine," which she uses to describe sunset light in sky or water, as in "the Iodine upon the Cataract" (853, 673, 710). She is punning on its Greek root: *iodes* means "violet." But characteristically, she makes sky and stream running wounds daubed with carmine antiseptic. This resembles those two poems in which the fall landscape and western sky are great blood puddings—the universe as abattoir. She sees sunset as conflagration: "The largest Fire ever known / Occurs each Afternoon." It consumes "An Occidental Town, / Rebuilt another morning / To be burned down again" (1114). Disaster is nature's norm. The scarlet western hills and clouds are cities rising and falling, like ancient cities. The poet is Nero singing while Amherst burns.

Like Swinburne's Sappho, Dickinson thinks God jealous and vindictive, an attitude she got from Blake. God lures mankind into the grave with promises of a fair future, only to default on his contract. His credit history is a spree of embezzlements. He condemns man to death and loss: "Earth is short / And Anguish absolute" (301). Pleasure and pain are yoked: we pay for every ecstasy with anguish, "In keen and quivering ratio" (125). The rose's attar is "the gift of Screws" (675). Life is governed by sadomasochistic extremes: "A *Wounded* Deer leaps highest"; the "*Smitten* Rock" gushes; the "*trampled* Steel" springs (165). Nature's dynamism is an excruciating seesaw. God's sadism determines the poet's own. Her brutal metaphors record her search for a rhetoric equal to what God has wrought. A sadist woman speaker, one of the west's unique sexual personae, avenges the feminine passivity into which God thrusts mankind.

Dickinson reserves her most contemptuous witticisms for the Son who came to justify the ways of God to men. Unlike her precursors, she refuses to glamourize the primary Romantic persona of the martyred male heroine. "The Auctioneer of Parting / His 'Going, going, gone' / Shouts even from the Crucifix / And brings his Hammer down" (1612). Christ turned moneychanger is conducting a slave auction from the cross. He is selling souls to the highest bidder, the shadowy God who is death. "Ineffable Avarice of Jesus," murmurs Dickinson in a letter.[21] Christ's hammer is the gavel of the Last Judgment, already striking men with daily blows. Here the holy carpenter's nail wounds are masochistically self-inflicted. Keats says of himself, "Imaginary grievances . . . nail a man down for a sufferer, as on a cross."[22] "Going, going, gone": life's funeral train chugs into motion to Christ's ominous "All aboard" (cf. the puns on crucifix boards). His "It is finished" becomes a parodic diminuendo, fading echoes of *à Dieu.*

Dickinson's cynical surrealism is unparalleled among great women writers. For an analogy to the auctioneer poem we would have to turn to Bob Dylan's "All Along the Watchtower" (1968), the Golgothan dream-vision of a Jewish satirist who treats Christ much more sympathetically. Dickinson says, "God was penurious with me, which makes me shrewd with Him."[23] More of her sharp irreverence: "In passing Calvary," she likes "To note the fashions—of the Cross— / And how they're mostly worn— / Still fascinated to presume / That Some—are like My Own" (561). The faithful speak of death or sorrow as a cross to be borne. Dickinson compares her crosses with others', noting their shape, weight, and number. How are they "worn"? Does the condemned staggering up Calvary carry the cross on his left or right shoulder? What "fashions" does he model on the cross—a tunic? a loincloth? The poet is a by-stander at an Easter parade or a pedestrian pausing before a shop window, planning a future purchase. Perhaps her unorthodox train of thought was begun by the episode of Veronica's veil, for at that moment, Christ was adorned with a woman's chador. Dickinson's campy mix of religion and couture is like Baudelaire's and Wilde's.

Christ is in Dickinson's line of fire because his testament misrepresents his godfather's business. The poet is Little Red Ridinghood discovering a wolfish divine face hidden within the flowery fringes of Wordsworthian nature. Christ's incarnation had a bloody climax, reached by a road paved with good intentions. One of Dickinson's most brilliant metaphors: "Mine—by the Sign in the Scarlet prison— / Bars cannot conceal!" (528). The body is Poe's Red Death and shrinking torture cell. The body's netting of veins and arteries (like a bale of chicken wire) are the bars on door and window. What is "mine" is the certainty of extinction. The bright sign in the scarlet prison is mortality, which cannot be concealed by the bars or tribunals of future divine judgment. Dickinson agrees that life imitates Christ, for our extension in the body lays us on the cross of Blake's tree of nature.

Consciousness in Dickinson takes the form of a body tormented in every limb. Her sadomasochistic metaphors are Blake's Universal Man hammering on himself, like the auctioneering Jesus. Her suffering personae make up the gorged superself of Romanticism. I argued that modern sadomasochism is a limitation of the will and that for a Romantic like the mastectomy-obsessed Kleist it represents a reduction of self. A conventional feminist critique of Emily Dickinson's life would see her hemmed in on all sides by respectability and paternalism, impediments to her genius. But a study of Romanticism shows that post-Enlightenment poets are struggling with the *absence* of limits, with the gross inflation of solipsistic imagination. Hence Dickinson's most uncontrolled encounter is with the serpent of her antisocial self, who breaks out like the Aeolian winds let out of their bag.

Dickinson does wage guerrilla warfare with society. Her fractures, cripplings, impalements, and amputations are Dionysian disorderings of the stable structures of the Apollonian lawgivers. God, or the idea of God, is the "One," without whom the "Many" of nature fly apart. Hence God's death condemns the world to Decadent disintegration. Dickinson's Late Romantic love of the apocalyptic parallels Decadent European taste for salon paintings of the fall of Babylon or Rome. Her Dionysian cataclysms demolish Victorian proprieties. Like Blake, she couples the miniature and grandiose, great disjunctions of scale whose yawing swings release tremendous poetic energy.

The least palatable principle of the Dionysian, I have stressed, is not sex but violence, which Rousseau, Wordsworth, and Emerson exclude from their view of nature. Dickinson, like Sade, draws the reader into ascending degrees of complicity, from eroticism to rape, mutilation, and murder. With Emily Brontë, she uncovers the aggression repressed by humanism. Hence Dickinson is the creator of Sadean poems but also the creator of sadists, the readers whom she smears with her lamb's blood. Like the Passover angel, she stains the lintels of the bourgeois home with her bloody vision. "There's been a Death, in the Opposite House," she announces with a satisfaction completely overlooked by the Wordsworthian reader (389).

But merely because poet and modern society are in conflict does not mean art necessarily gains by "freedom." It is a sentimental error to think Emily Dickinson the victim of male obstructionism. Without her struggle with God and father, there would have been no poetry. There are two reasons for this. First, Romanticism's overexpanded self requires artificial restraints. Dickinson finds these limitations in sado-masochistic nature and reproduces them in her dual style. Without such a discipline, the Romantic poet cannot take a single step, for the sterile vastness of modern freedom is like gravity-free outer space, in which one cannot walk or run. Second, women do not rise to supreme achievement unless they are under powerful internal compulsion. Dickinson was a woman of abnormal will. Her poetry profits from the enormous disparity between that will and the feminine social persona to which she fell heir at birth. But her sadism is not anger, the a posteriori response to social injustice. It is *hostility*, an a priori Achillean intolerance for the existence of others, the female version of Romantic solipsism.

In the beautiful hypothesis of "Shakespeare's sister," Virginia Woolf imagines a girl with her brother's gifts whom society would have "thwarted and hindered" to insanity and suicide.[24] Women have been discouraged from genres such as sculpture that require studio training or expensive materials. But in philosophy, mathematics, and poetry, the only materials are pen and paper. Male conspiracy cannot explain all female failures. I am convinced that, even without restrictions, there still would have been no female Pascal, Milton, or Kant. Genius is not checked by social obstacles: it will overcome. Men's egotism, so disgusting in the talentless, is the source of their greatness as a sex. Women have a more accurate sense of reality; they are physically and spiritually more complete. Culture, I said, was invented by men, because it is by culture that they make themselves whole. Even now, with all vocations open, I marvel at the rarity of the woman driven by artistic or intellectual obsession, that self-mutilating derangement of social relationship which, in its alternate forms of crime and ideation, is the disgrace and glory of the human species.

Dickinson was one of those who convert every reverse into an impulse to create. Humiliation and disillusion were whisked into abstract structures, posted on the map of the world in her war room, with its game tokens of advance and retreat. Her premiere subject is power, psychological, natural, and divine, to which woman has free access only in eras of earth-cult. Hence her fondness for the word "electric." Her poems are thermal sensors, registering nature's surges of animating energy. But her changes are abrupt and traumatic. "A happy lip breaks sudden," she typically remarks (353). This stiff upper lip belongs to a marble statue with a hairline fracture. Matter thwarts spirit's urges. As a scientist of nature, Dickinson is a Decadent catastrophist, predicting transformation by convulsion.

Dickinson's breakage of objects signifies the collapse of meaning. She imports amputation, her favorite limiting device, from Dionysian nature into society. For example, she says of her mother's stroke, "Her Hand and Foot left her." When a neighbor died, "He had no hands."[25] Infirmity is *severance*, because Dickinson is a Late Romantic separatist practicing Decadent partition. Like the brain escaping the lidded skull, Mrs. Dickinson's hand and foot march out of the house like servants giving notice. The poet's amputations are like Kleist's mastectomies. Brutal self-reduction is a restocking of nature's organ bank.

Clinically, hypochondria takes two forms. The less serious is anxiety about internal disease; the more pathological is obsession with loss of limbs. Since they have more appendages to lose, men might be expected to suffer from the latter, but, just from common observation, this does not seem to be so. Laurence Sterne's *Tristram Shandy*, which I find utterly unfunny, may be a male hypochondriacal construction, for it is an accident series of disasters to body parts—a flattened nose, shattered knee, crushed groin bone, a penis circumcised by a falling window. Our amputational Dickinson exhibits the graver of the hypochondrias. This may be the castration-anxiety of a hermaphrodite poet. For we saw that the moment she detaches herself from her phallic *genius loci*, the pink worm, trouble begins like a rumble in the boys' lavatory.

Significantly, Dickinson shows little concern with disease. Her sado-masochistic horrors are confined to piercings, slashings, hackings, scorchings, and dislocations. Why? Poe's *Red Death*, Baudelaire's "Voyage to Cythera," and Huysmans' flower episode make disease a major Late Romantic metaphor. It is the depraved touch of female nature. Dickinson's substitution of accidents for disease is part of her extraordinary effort to wipe chthonian femaleness out of nature. Her nature, I said, has two faces: one benevolent, one hostile, turbulent with storm and volcano or dead with stone and ice. I argued that lapidary Decadent beauty, the bronzed and jewelled surfaces of Baudelaire and Moreau, are a protest against the chthonian. Like Poe, Dickinson is exiled from European objets d'art. Therefore her ice images, expressing a revulsion from nature identical to the French Decadents', are a great leap forward into modern metaphor.

One of Dickinson's stunning achievements is her prophetic vision of intergalactic nothingness. A funeral turns into a science-fiction film: "Boots of Lead" cross her soul, "Then Space began to toll, / As all the Heavens were a Bell, / And Being, but an Ear, / And I, and Silence, some strange Race / Wrecked, solitary, here." She drops "down, and down— / And hit a World, at every plunge" (280). Dickinson's glimpses of futuristic desolation, minimal in Jules Verne, precede H. G. Wells's by thirty years. What of her lead boots? Only we, her true contemporaries, can identify them, for we have seen them walk on the moon. Dickinson's lonely plunge into Pascal's abyss is the severest thought, to my knowledge, of any premodern woman writer. Even despairing Wordsworth gives himself one withered companion in his stark desert basins.

In "Safe in their Alabaster Chambers," a masterpiece, the "meek" dead wait for resurrection under their "Rafter of Satin, / And Roof of Stone":

> Grand go the Years—in the Crescent—above them—
> Worlds scoop their Arcs—
> And Firmaments—row—
> Diadems—drop—and Doges—surrender—
> Soundless as dots—on a Disc of Snow—   [216]

The alabaster chamber is the tomb and also the corpse's marble flesh, a palace turned prison. The coffin's satin coverlet is like the gossamer gown of the kidnapped maiden, a hope that will be rent. The stone roof is the sky that will never open. The meek *have* inherited the earth. The heavens revolve in great mathematical arcs; history speeds up, kings' crowns falling like snowflakes. The poem ends with a soft numbing of the tongue, as syllables sputter out into silence. The poet takes a position of visionary distance from which human life seems a speck in the cosmos. Especially brilliant is the muted movement of "Doges" into "Snow," all the colors of Venice—art, imagination, and worldly glory— vanishing into eternity.

This frigid, godless universe is a major theme of modern literature, as in Wallace Stevens' "The Snow Man" (1923). Dickinson anticipates Kafka in combining emptiness and absurdity with tyrannical authority. How amazing that this is the work of a solitary, neglected, untravelled woman. How did she make so remarkable an advance on contemporary literature? Dickinson's modern ice world is the direct result of her Brontëan swerve from gender, her refusal to accept femaleness in herself or nature. Science fiction's glacial wastes, which she is the first artist to see, are a landscape from which maternal procreation has been blasted. Her dreams of death by freezing are a poetic anorexia or willed starvation. There is no disease in her because disease is a female miasma, an infection. There are no contaminations, only mutilations, because nature is in a state of cold purity, its accidents a Newtonian collision of hard objects. The blood the poet sheds is lustral, a self-detoxifying bath. There is never any *disgust* in her, only *horror*, for disgust is a male response to female nature, which she has purged out of existence.

Dickinson projects chthonian unintelligibility onto phallic daemons, whom she flees because they would betray her into fecundity. Her sexual premises also determine her rhetorical forms. Whitman extends himself outward to be impregnated in huge, sprawling prose-poems. But Dickinson's small lyrics are a sexual closure, the cage of a self-sequestered sibyl. Whitman's poems aggregate while Dickinson's consolidate ego. She declares, "The Soul selects her own Society— / Then shuts the Door." The soul must "Choose One"—herself—"Then close the Valves of her attention / Like Stone" (303). The inflexible heart of metal spigots is a tomb-monument of the self.

Jane Austen calls her own writing "the little bit (two Inches wide) of Ivory on which I work with so fine a Brush," an allusion to the modest scope of provincial life that she took for subject.[26] But her ivory is not so small, first because the novel as a genre has social breadth and second because her work revives the English Renaissance ideal of marriage. Dickinson, on the other hand, is a monastic. She chooses *one* because the self must be sealed up and its integrity defended. Her poems are Apollonian cells of the *principium individuationis*. Baudelaire's poems, I noted, are corrupted entities, projections of a diseased body. Dickinson's major poems are bursting hermaphrodite lozenges, a small feminine body charged with a mighty masculine mind. The rhetoric itself is powerfully bisexed.

Language too is confined. Whitman and Huysmans' proliferation of vocabulary is the opposite of Dickinson's contraction of syntax. Her poems are *imploded*, their contours jagged and torn by suction. Poring over her dictionary, she introverts words, doubling them back in puns on their roots. Her ellipsis produces broken metrical accents, a queer lurching rhythm. She cites Higginson's prior criticism: "You think my gait 'spasmodic.' "[27] Dickinson has a *halt* meter, like a hobbled horse or a Chinese woman who has bound her own feet. Her harsh pressures on language are another ritual limitation, by which the Romantic self returns to governable dimensions from its monstrous immensity.

There is inherent irony in the idea of female Romantic genius, which I have examined in two cases, Emily Brontë and Emily Dickinson. Romanticism is an imaginative realignment of western male will toward female powers, which it internalizes. The reason the work of Elizabeth Barrett Browning and her fellow poetesses is so weak is that Romanticism is a sex-crossing mode which adds femaleness to maleness. Femaleness added to femaleness is a Romantic redundancy, to which the Muse will make no visitation. Brontë and Dickinson succeed as Romantics because they are women of masculine will who tend toward sadism.

I portrayed the High Romantic poet as a passive sufferer or male heroine. Dickinson unites this inherited persona with its opposite. As a woman Romantic, she must suffer *and* assert. She is male heroine *and* sex-defying Romantic hero. Both extremes must be forcefully materialized, which is why her sadistic metaphors are among the most grisly in major poetry. They are injections of synthetic male hormone into a hermaphroditic genre that resists female practitioners. I spoke of Wordsworth's shamanistic sacrifice of virility: Dickinson makes this Romantic surgery literal. Lacerating self-abuse is her ritual consecration, by which she makes her vows to art.

Dickinson's sadomasochism is most intense during her most creative decade. She says, "I felt a Cleaving in my Mind— / As if my Brain had split" (937). Her poetry is a war of personae, a clash of opposites; it is sexually, psychically, morally, and aesthetically bivalent. Over eternity, her pastoral Wordsworthian poems must yield to their daemonic counterparts. Criticism's error has been to regard the sentimental poems as indistinguishable from period *vers de société*. But Dickinson's contemporaries had no secret wells of savagery, no grand philosophical system. Her sentimental personae do not stand alone. The purest feminine poems are without internal ironies. They are acted upon by their *contexts*. Read any of her bird and butterfly poems while keeping her sadistic lyrics in mind, and you will find them magically transformed, their borders agitated by malign influences. In her Wordsworthian verses, the poet is a virgin odalisque, titillated by the pressure of erotic menace around her.

Sentimentality is one of Dickinson's major techniques. It is her sexual allure, the magnetism drawing her masculine and feminine personae together. She uses femininity to drive femaleness out of nature. Rejected by many women of our time, femininity attracts her as a poetic mask, partly because men too wear this mask in their encounters with God and death. Dickinson endorses femininity's artificial or rather unnatural character: it is both of and against nature, since spring always loses to frost and decay. Thus she treats femininity as simultaneously spurious and authentic. She exaggerates the social frivolities of her gender in order to thrust nature's force into the masculine, bypassing mythology's chthonian females.

The polarized sexual powers of Dickinson's poetry form a huge circle, an uroboros of pursuit and flight. Masculine devours feminine, as in Spenser. All personae are in motion, turning with the pagan solar year. The poet enters among her characters, the mark of Romantic as opposed to Renaissance literature. She is both Proteus and Florimell, rough rapist and coy maiden. She is like the onanist Genet, of whom Sartre says, "He is the criminal who rapes and the Saint who lets herself be raped."[28] Dickinson works by sexual polyphony. We cannot speak of her individual poems as "good" or "bad" but rather as *more or less masculine and feminine.*

Wordsworth and Rousseau posit hostility between nature and society, which they define as respectively female and male. Dickinson unexpectedly unites society with Wordsworthian nature by linking them both to femininity. Wordsworth's nature *is* chthonian and deeply female. But it isn't in Dickinson *because she got Wordsworth through Emerson,* and Emerson is in American flight from the female. Through her feminine personae, the poet pretends to be what she seems to be to the social eye. She has gone out the front door of her gender and come in the back. Sentimentality restores her poetic equilibrium. It adds representational weight to the light end of the sexual seesaw. Her feminine personae are mental calisthenics by which she dissuades herself from sadism. Already at a peak of masculine tension, she swings them about like Indian clubs or thistledown barbells, which enable her to maintain her muscle tonelessness in prison.

Wordsworth's poetic gifts come through the opening he makes to the mother. Dickinson's poetry requires separation from the mother, whom she demotes from creative authority. Here again she uses Blake against

Wordsworth. Her relations with her real mother should not be exaggerated, since in Romanticism it is imagination, not fact that is primary. But she told Higginson, "My Mother does not care for thought." She said of her sister Lavinia, while both parents were still alive, "She has no Father and Mother but me and I have no Parents but her." This is like Woolf calling herself her sister Vanessa's "firstborn."[29] Dickinson and Brontë cultivate the Romantic sister-relation, at its most incestuous a denial of ancestral indebtedness.

There are very few mothers in Dickinson's nature poetry, nearly all qualified by some irony. "Gentle" mother nature puts her "Golden finger" to her lip, willing "Silence—Everywhere" (790). Gold fingers are sunset rays, signaling sleep for man and beast. But nature's silence may be golden because it is the mineral coldness of death. When nature "smiles" at "Her eccentric Family," we should think of Leonardo, not Raphael (1085). I admire these lines: "In Ovens green our Mother bakes, / By Fires of the Sun" (1143). Believers in the mawkish Dickinson, a Shirley Temple who wakes when the genius nods, will dismiss such things as idle Victoriana: aproned mother nature bustles about, whipping up batches of cookies. But the kitchen scene has a cruel subplot. Nature is *Hansel and Gretel*'s witch, grilling her children in her German ovens. Here is the sober truth:

> But nature is a stranger yet;
> The ones that cite her most
> Have never passed her haunted house,
> Nor simplified her ghost.
>
> To pity those that know her not
> Is helped by the regret
> That those who know her, know her less
> The nearer her they get.   [1400]

Nature is no meadow of green promise but a spectral Gothic chamber that will not let history be born. All knowledge is a return to the past. Dickinson writes Higginson, "Nature is a Haunted House—but Art—a House that tries to be haunted."[30] Romantic art is daemonic: it finds the pagan spiritualism in matter.

In Dickinson's year, false spring supplants summer. She rejects fecund ripening for herself as well as her metaphors. Habitually dressed in white, she was always nun or bride, never mother. Her boy personae are also deflections of maturation, an anorexic suppression of sexual shape. Sentimentality in Dickinson, as opposed to Wordsworth and Wilde, is a road away from the mother rather than toward her. It is no coincidence that while some major female artists have married, very few have borne children. The issue is not conservation of energy but imaginative integrity. Art is its own self-swelling, proof that the mind is greater than the body.

In biology, neoteny is the protraction of juvenile traits into adulthood or the premature development of adult sexual traits in a hostile environment. Dickinson's feminine personae are neotenic. They are juveniles trying to stop the aging of the year, a delay that makes winter's sudden arrival more catastrophic. Her feminine personae are self-delectating fictions, in which a recluse toys with exhibitionism. There is an erotics of smallness in Dickinson resembling the seductive preciosity of Blake's "Infant Joy." She loves to appear frail and pitiable—but only to make more delicious her vamping between hierarchic levels. There are satiric tableaux of human subordination: "I hope the Father in the skies / Will lift his little girl— / Old fashioned—naughty—everything— / Over the stile of 'Pearl' "(70). Pearl is her word for the resurrected realm of white frost. She is a naif gamboling in the feminine glad rags of Christian trust. Here are three hierarchic levels: "Papa above! / Regard a Mouse / O'erpowered by the Cat!" (61). She sent the poem to her headstrong sister-in-law Susan—the cat in whose jaws the poet pleasurably struggles. Such superficially simple passages are cascades of hierarchical force, tiered fountains splashing with sadomasochistic refreshment.

Dickinson calls herself "Sparrow," "little Girl," "child." She refers to "my little Gypsy being," "my little sunburnt bosom."[31] The most cunning self-description occurs in a letter to Higginson, who had requested a photograph: "Could you believe me—without? I had no portrait, now, but am small, like the Wren, and my Hair is bold, like the Chestnut Bur—and my eyes, like the Sherry in the Glass, that the Guest leaves— Would this do just as well?"[32] What a psychodrama! The poet is small, mild, pathetic. Even her eye color is a tincture of abandonment. But she wrote every word of this in perfect consciousness of her secret greatness and power. She is like Cleopatra breathing, "I am pale, Charmian," one line before clobbering the messenger. The simile of the leftover sherry is a triumph of the Jewish-mother type of masochistic, guilt-inducing trope. Dickinson scholars are tone-deaf to this element in her. Italians and Jews tend to be alert to self-dramatizing gambits where force masquerades in personae of infirmity. For example, my formidable grandmother would respond to telephone inquiries by claiming she was

"Sola sola com' un' aiuch'," "Alone alone like an owl"—watching, in other words, in dismal solitude.[33] Now this Italian owl is bird of a feather with the Amherst wren and sparrow. A ferocious hierarch is practicing an adroit mime of misery.

Dickinson's sherry eyes appear to withdraw and be withdrawn from, when in fact they aggressively advance on the reader. What causes exasperation or panic in the children of Italian and Jewish matriarchs is being directed toward a genteel stranger with no suspicions of the poet's profound doubleness. Higginson is a fish whom Dickinson lures into reach by appetizing quavers of dependency. In her next letter, she tells him, "All men say 'What' to me, but I thought it a fashion."[34] She is the beggar girl banned from the common table. She is Cassandra, never believed, or Coleridge's poet isolated in his holy circle. Her plaintiveness is rich with gloating. It's clear everyone said "What?" to her because, like a guest without small talk, she had a bad habit of sinking dialogue under Delphic meteorites, great thudding conversation-stoppers. One has known persons who do this, fatiguingly. It is one of the most aggressive forms of speech, intimidation cloaked as revelation. Dickinson is Salomé dancing into her seven veils.

Many critics remark on the irony of Dickinson's veneration of Higginson, a man well-known in his day but now just a footnote in literary history. She called him "Preceptor" and signed herself "Your Scholar." He was the ambassador of the great world to the sequestered poet, who joked about her own nonentity: "I'm Nobody! Who are you?" (288). Her relation to him was like Shelley's to Mary Godwin or Mill's to Harriet Taylor, a symbolic deference where a stronger intelligence bows to a lesser. Dickinson's ritual self-abasements are nearly Swinburnian. A poem begins: "I was the slightest in the House—/ I took the smallest Room" (486). She likes lowness for its tingling sensations of hierarchic distance. She stretches and squeezes the artificial gap between superior and inferior, as if working an accordion or chest-expander, exhilarating herself with inhalations of subordination.

A diminutive friend of mine, a native Bostonian and paragon of archaic WASP decorum, has a psychodramatic stratagem under stress that never ceases to amaze me: *she appears smaller.* This conchlike spiral of spiritual and physical retraction is not in the Mediterranean arsenal. Quite the contrary, the beset southerner follows the animal principle of raised hackles, an emphatic enlargement of personality: one leaps to one's feet, waves the arms, raises the voice. Dickinson's most cherished maneuver is to appear smaller, a camouflage in society.

This compression of persona is a hallucination projected upon the unwary by a gamesman of tough will. The poet has duped and beguiled not Higginson alone but generations of her readers and critics.

Higginson recorded his first meeting with Dickinson in a long letter to his wife. We see the poet's calculated presentation of self with wonderful clarity:

> A step like a pattering child's in entry & in glided a little plain woman with two smooth bands of reddish hair & a face a little like Belle Dove's; not plainer—with no good feature—in a very plain & exquisitely clean white pique & a blue net worsted shawl. She came to me with two day lilies which she put in a sort of childlike way into my hand & said "These are my introduction" in a soft frightened breathless childlike voice—& added under her breath Forgive me if I am frightened; I never see strangers & hardly know what I say— but she talked soon & thenceforward continuously—& deferentially—sometimes stopping to ask me to talk instead of her—but readily recommencing.

Dickinson plays the child entering her own kingdom of heaven. Supposedly not knowing what to say, she manages to talk nonstop. Higginson is under attack by the Delphic priestess. The inner reality of their encounter is registered in his extraordinary closing words: "I never was with any one who drained my nerve power so much. Without touching her, she drew from me. I am glad not to live near her."[35] Higginson felt a strange spiritual oppression in her presence. Even without this lucky corroboration by an urbane witness, I contend we are able to tell from the poetry alone, with its sadomasochistic duality, that Emily Dickinson is one of the great examples of the vampirism of the artist. In a survey of vampire legends, Montague Summers speaks of the "spiritual vampire" or "psychic sponge" who has the ability to "re-energize" him or herself "by drawing upon the vitality of others": "Such types are by no means uncommon. Sensitive people will often complain of weariness and loss of spirits when they have been for long in the company of certain others."[36] Pressing the beam of her mental eye on Higginson, the poet extorts his vitality from him, in shamanistic transfusions of soul-plasm.

The vampire as artless child: as with Brontë's ghostly waif at the window or Coleridge's fainting Geraldine in her white robe, Dickinson's approach to visitor and reader alike is a cinematic mirage, a silvery vapor of entrancement. Of the century's major American writers, Dickinson is the most Decadent in religious and sexual psychology. Her fondness for corpses far exceeds the Victorian cult of bereavement. She is closest here not to Sir Thomas Browne and the Metaphysicals but to the Hamlet who casually says of dead Polonius, "I'll lug the guts into the neighbor room" (III.iv.213).

A typical Dickinson love poem begins, "If I may have it, when it's dead." To heck with warm flesh; she'll take the corpse. "Forgive me, if to stroke thy frost / Outvisions Paradise!" (577). The male is "it" because death neutralizes gender. He is sexually and emotionally tolerable only after he has been processed into passivity, patted and kneaded like a pie crust. Keats's Isabella waters her lover's severed head with her tears. But Dickinson sheds no tears. As she fondles the corpse, she flashes a dazzling smile.

Stroking corpses of both sexes is Dickinson's literary hobby (187). People used to die at home, and their bodies were laid out in the parlor. The quick trip from hospital to funeral home—curious term—was not yet invented. Suppression of the mechanics of death is a recent bourgeois phenomenon; at Italian funerals, for example, friends and relatives file past the open casket on the morning of burial and kiss the corpse's forehead. Nevertheless, Dickinson's corpse fantasies are beyond the norm. They are perverse because her intimacy requires inertness. Her consciousness exults in the unconsciousness of its objects. Twin to Whitman of *The Sleepers*, she is a phantom lover in the world of the dead. She values corpses as artifacts: personality has passed from Dionysian mutability into Apollonian perfection. But her language is always amorous: "By the dead we love to sit, / Become so wondrous dear" (88). She focuses on the deathwatch, prior to the shift of states: "Promise This—When You be Dying— / Some shall summon Me." To her belongs the last sigh and the right to "Belt" the dead eyes with her lips (648). Dickinson's erotic claim, like insurance compensation after an accident, is activated only by suffering and death. Her passionate kisses are for faces that can make no return. She is a priestess of the Mysteries, materializing just in time for the last rites.

Death, as a collision between time and eternity, has a transfiguring glamour: "To know just how He suffered—would be dear" (622). Soul and body in agony leave their psychic imprint, which the poet as sleuth ruthlessly ferrets out. She never bothered to conceal her ravenous curiosity. She is just twenty-three when she writes a complete stranger, Edward Everett Hale, to dig up data on the last hours of a childhood friend. Had she a current address, she says, she would be pumping the wife of the deceased instead.[37] Her eye longs to penetrate the inmost sanctuary, medical and marital. She dreams of exposing herself to death's radiation and joining the victim in the blaze of mortal fission.

Dickinson is a Decadent voyeur, and her corpse poems are specimens of sexual objectification, the primary principle of Decadent eroticism. She turns men into corpses, just as Poe turns Berenice into a box of teeth. The corpse poems formalize that eye-object relation which oppresses Romantic poets in their stultifying freedom. Seeing across space and time, Dickinson ritually fixes the distance between self and world, freezing it with her Medusan eye. She is that rarity, a female necrophiliac and sexual fetishist. Necrophilia was devised by the modern psyche to control and place sex after its sudden detachment from hierarchical systems. Like hysteria, necrophilia has gone out of fashion. People no longer paralyze their arms, like Breuer's Anna O., or root about in cemeteries, plucking up corpses to violate or snack on.[38] Dickinson hastens her lovers toward death to draft them into her poetry. She binds them with immobility, like turkeys dressed for the oven, to ready them for her post-mortem embraces. She is a connoisseur of death, a Decadent collector. Like the maiden of Blake's "Crystal Cabinet," she traps her lovers in dark bowers to which, she boasts, she owns the key (577). Each corpse poem is a glass coffin with the withered beloved on display. These are the trophies of the belle of Amherst, a Circe who shrinks men with a tap of her wand.

Like Rachilde's Raoule de Vénérande, Dickinson makes a mausoleum out of a bedchamber. Her men are living dolls, like Raoule's wax gigolo. They are manufactured objects, a romance of prosthetics. Death is the black paint in which the poet dips her brush, because the objet d'art lacks prestige in nineteenth-century American culture. Even wellborn James must go to Europe to procure his golden bowl, and significantly, it is ritually broken within its novel. Decadent Dickinson makes objets d'art of her loved ones, but for lack of artistic models, she turns them into ice sculptures, corpi delicti of God's crimes.

The lingering Puritan taboo on visual gratification, I noted, inflamed the eye in American Romanticism. Poe, Hawthorne, Emerson, Whitman, and Dickinson suffer fluctuations between voyeurism and paranoia. Dickinson flattens her chosen ones by her ocular force. She drops on them like a hawk, her eye sadistically glittering. Her Decadent voyeurism is abundantly clear in her letters, which increasingly become a chain of condolences. Death and calamity are the only subjects on which the poet speaks. Life is a string of black pearls.

The letters can be in questionable taste. Dickinson writes to a woman whose cousin drowned in, of all places, Walden Pond:

Dear friend,
   What a reception for you! Did she wait for your approbation?
   Her deferring to die until you came seemed to me so confiding—
as if nothing should be presumed. It can probably never be real to
you.

The poet, with her avid eye, rapturously theatricalizes the death so as to
sharpen grief rather than relieve it. Victim and rescuer seem actors
rehearsing a play. The lingering pondside death is critiqued as if it were
a summer charade in a gazebo. Here is a letter to a woman whose house
caught fire:

Dear friend,
   I congratulate you.
   Disaster endears beyond Fortune—
                    E. Dickinson

Thomas H. Johnson, Dickinson's Harvard editor, comments, "The letter does not sound as though the damage had been serious."[39] Poor
trusting man. The fire was obviously a catastrophe! Dickinson sends a
congratulations card because victimization means canonization in her
Sadean cosmos. There is maniacal glee in her sepulchral letters. She
makes strange hard jests at tender moments. To a friend whose infant
son had an operation for a congenital foot problem: "How is your little
Byron? Hope he gains his foot without losing his genius."[40] Flattery and
tartness queasily mingle. The letter raises the fleeting possibilities that
the boy will be either a brilliant clubfoot or an agile dolt. Our poet's
honeyed words have a secret sting.
   Letter after letter memorializes the deaths of friends or relatives of
the addressees, on whom are heaped strained, hieratic epigrams and
paradoxes. There is not a grain of Christian compassion in these letters.
They are a Late Romantic prose-poem, a stunning chronicle of necrophilia and voyeurism. The recluse chooses the moments to show
herself to the multitude. Bereavement is her opportunity: daily life
stops, and people are paralyzed. Dickinson as oracle and ritual mourner
injects herself into their suffering. The letters of condolence are death-
day rather than birthday gifts, handcrafted by the poet in her secret
forge.
   Dickinson tells Higginson: "A Letter always feels to me like immortality because it is the mind alone without corporeal friend. . . . There
seems a spectral power in thought that walks alone."[41] This stalking
spectre is the vampire-poet scanning the world for disasters. She imag-

ines the mourners receiving her letters. She is there, by telekinesis, suddenly appearing like Poe's raven on Pallas' head, ready with words of wisdom. The mourners' social masks are off. They are naked and at their most passive. This is when the poet *makes contact.* She unites with them as they confront elemental realities. She senses death's primitivistic energy, which excites her. She is a shark lured by spilled blood, a rustic hog snuffling out black truffles of woe. All of Dickinson's letters are archly seductive, but the letters of condolence are a sadomasochistic congress. She is like Blake's God creating Adam, smothering the bereaved while they are prostrated.

The letters of condolence are erotic, self-conscious, ritualized, and therefore Decadent. Like the governess of *Turn of the Screw,* Dickinson is a Romantic terrorist, presiding over eruptions of horror. Like the governess, she constructs a Decadent world of voyeuristic sightlines. Her eroticized lust to *see all* is combined with intense fear of the visual. Like Gautier's Queen Nyssia, Dickinson feels contaminated by others' eyes. She defends her perceptual purity by walling herself up in her Danae's tower or snowbound "Pearl Jail."[42] She dreads being seen precisely because *her* eye is so powerful and intrusive. Letters and poems allow her to be heard at a distance while remaining invisible, as if on a public-address system. Nothing is more terrible in her poetry than when her barriers are breached and the visual pours in on her uncontrollably: "Creation seemed a mighty Crack / To make me visible"; "Space stares all around" (891, 510).

These mirrorlike returns upon her of her own ocular aggression explain many of Dickinson's eccentricities. She refused to be photographed or to receive most callers; she would not address letters in her own hand, and she carried on conversations with visitors from behind a screen or from the next room. This is partly a rejection of stable social identity, the poet of many personae refusing to commit herself to one. But her ostentatious withdrawals are tactical. She drives up her market value by spiritual hoarding and taxes her friends by withholding herself. Her tarrying in the wings is frictional. Her appearances are delayed ejaculations, meant to bring her audience to a peak of frenzy. Her aggravating affectations, which would now be called passive-aggressive, evoked a memorable response from Samuel Bowles, who shouted up the stairs: "Emily, you wretch! No more of this nonsense! I've traveled all the way from Springfield to see you. Come down at once."[43] Her bluff called, the poet calmly descended.

Dickinson's manipulative letters are masterful in their subtle calibrations of conditional visibility. Here is her account, in a letter to her

Norcross cousins, of a great fire that destroyed downtown Amherst. Fire bells awoke her in the middle of the night:

> I sprang to the window, and each side of the curtain saw that awful sun. The moon was shining high at the time, and the birds singing like trumpets.
> Vinnie came soft as a moccasin, "Don't be afraid, Emily, it is only the fourth of July."
> I did not tell that I saw it, for I thought if she felt it best to deceive, it must be that it was.
> She took hold of my hand and led me into mother's room.[44]

Sensitive, childlike Emily—then forty-eight years old! The perversity is not so much in Dickinson's docile consent to her sister's deception as in the eerie reproduction of the scene for the Norcrosses, drawing them in as another audience and so tripling the poet's impersonations. Is Vinnie, "soft as a moccasin," Indian or snake, consoler or seducer? This is another scene of Spenserian ambiguities. Donning her mask of Wordsworthian femininity to turn from a Sadean spectacle, Dickinson is the soft focus of row after row of observing eyes, beginning with her own. She invites the gaze of the Norcrosses so that she can watch them watching *her*—like Wilde's Gwendolen. It is a theatrical triangulation of sadomasochistic perception, part coercion, part self-immolation. A similar complex moment occurs in Puccini's *Madame Butterfly* (1904), when Sharpless asks the geisha's half-American child his name. Butterfly herself responds, rhetorically addressing her son and putting words of rebuke in his mouth, her voice rising to an ecstatic climax: "Answer: today my name is Trouble. But tell my father when you write to him that on the day he returns *Joy, Joy* will be my name." Affect snakes through person after displaced person, with Madame Butterfly cleverly gathering all the ricocheting sightlines of pity back toward herself—the only person she does *not* mention. The analogues to Dickinson's sexual personae are usually Italian. Her antecedents are not in Puritan probity but in Baroque sensationalism.

The mild personae and endearments of Dickinson's letters are an artifice of courtship, Sunday dress. Her real attitude toward her correspondents is deeply ambivalent: "Are Friends Delight or Pain?" (1199). Everything in her world is governed by a sadomasochistic dialectic. She experiences oscillations of attraction and repulsion, toward and away from people. Like Baudelaire and Swinburne, she thinks love an affliction. Emotion enervates, a waste of psychic energy for unworthy or indifferent objects. She bitterly complains of others' inability to sustain her level of intensity: "Bind me . . . Banish . . . Slay" (1005). She would agree with Wilde, who speaks of pain as "a mode of self-realization": "Pleasure for the beautiful body, but Pain for the beautiful Soul."[45] Pain for her is mentalized sex, a Decadent specialty.

Dickinson turns Metaphysical paradox into Sadean combat, pull and counterpull. Divine love "invites—appalls" (673). Or "Hawthorne appalls, entices." Relationships are wrestling matches of domination and submission: "He was weak, and I was strong—then— / So He let me lead him in— / I was weak, and He was strong then— / So I let him lead me—Home" (190). These symmetrical reversals are like Kleist's sexual scheme in *Penthesilea*, where hero and Amazon repeatedly win and lose. A poem begins, "I rose—because He sank" (616). Dickinson sends a one-line note to her sister-in-law: "I can defeat the rest, but you defeat me, Susan." She has a pagan view of love as a hazardous sphere of primitive power. She applies antagonistic formulas to everything: "I saw two Bushes fight just now—The wind was to blame—but to see them differ was pretty as a Lawsuit."[46] Dickinson lived off her father and brother's law practice, but that lawsuits are "pretty" is something else. She applies a Wordsworthian word to Sade's wrangling nature. Like Wilde, Dickinson makes hierarchical placements, but only as a prelude to sudden inversion: "Cakes reign but a Day" (1578). Even cakes are victim to elevation and overthrow! Gwendolen, we saw, also makes cake a caste symbol. The snobbish Wildean analogy is clear in lines like, "The parasol is the umbrella's daughter / And associates with a fan" (1747). Dickinson sexualizes common objects and classifies them by gender and rank.

Because her eroticism is visual rather than sensual, Dickinson's love affairs take the form of adoration and apotheosis. Another one-line note to her sister-in-law: "Susan's Idolator keeps a Shrine for Susan." An early letter to her brother speaks of herself and Susan's sister: "Martha and I are very much together—we fill each niche of time with statues of you and Sue and in return for this, they smile beautiful smiles down from their dwelling places." These shrines and statues, along with her references to nuns and Madonnas, belong to Dickinson's heretical Catholicism. Here she is like Hawthorne, introducing Madonna and child into the Puritan *Scarlet Letter*. Her editor says of a poem composed on the fourth anniversary of Charlotte Brontë's death, "Throughout her life ED was especially sensitive to such occasions."[47] In other words, the poet had her own Calendar of Saints, holy days consecrated to deceased friends and great ones. Like the French and English Decadents, she is attracted to Catholicism for its ritualism, not its morality. She zeroes right in on Roman Catholicism's pagan heart.

Dickinson is a fan, a hero-worshipper, a creator of hierarchic preeminence even when, as with Higginson, there is none. Like Shelley in *Epipsychidion*, she falls in love with charismatic personality. Like Swinburne in *Dolores* and *Faustine*, she is a sexual cultist, electing gods and saints to whom she lights votive candles. Affect is dependent on hierarchic distance, so married intimacy with either sex is impossible. The letters sternly enforce a sense of estrangement even toward her principal favorites. A note to Susan, apparently after the latter returned from a trip: "I must wait a few Days before seeing you—You are too momentous. But remember it is idolatry, not indifference."[48] Elaborate ceremonial restrictions and demarcations. Susan and Austin lived next door: good fences make good neighbors. Dickinson hopes, in a poem to Catherine Scott Anthon, whom she may have turned away at the door, that someday her loved ones will understand "For what I shunned them so": "We shun because we prize her Face / Lest sight's ineffable disgrace / Our Adoration stain" (1410). For the Romantic, reality is always vulgar. The *idea* of the beloved is superior to actual fact. Dickinson has a curatorial relation to her gods: for them to retain their glamour, she must refuse to see them. She perpetuates the divinity of her chosen ones by imprisoning them in the cell of her mental eye, from which they cannot break free into concrete presence. Seclusion is her perceptual weapon against disillusion.

Until the publication of her complete works in 1955, Emily Dickinson was the heroine of an American romance. Disappointed in love, she languished alone, striking off poems on the birds and bees and lowering gingerbread to urchins from the window. Candidates were nominated for the mysterious heartbreaker—a minister, a married man, an invalid. To their credit, Dickinson scholars quickly discerned this as reductive. Her poetry shows that men in general did not press deeply on her imaginative life. We saw how the most vivid poems show the lover dead or *in extremis*. One heterosexual fantasy takes three stanzas to describe the bad weather before getting to the cozy domestic scene: "How pleasanter—said she / Unto the Sofa opposite— / The Sleet—than May, no Thee" (589). Enter and exit the master as a stuffed divan. The sofa is simply the usual corpse planted in the parlor like *Psycho*'s rocking-chair mummy. Man, always temporarily indisposed in Dickinson, is strapped into place like a convict in the electric chair. Quadriplegia and rigor mortis are her way of dealing with male suppleness.

Dickinson's contemporaries noticed her equivocations about marriage. She often addressed letters only to the wife and used showy euphemisms for the word "husband." The writer Helen Hunt Jackson says to her, " 'The man I live with' (I suppose you recollect designating my husband by that curiously direct phrase) is in New York." This quirk is like Lewis Carroll's pointed exclusion of husbands and brothers from dinner invitations. Dickinson aggressively elides husband into wife. One victim is Higginson, who writes his wife, "E.D. dreamed all night of *you* (not me) & next day got my letter proposing to come here!! She only knew of you through a mention in my notice of Charlotte Hawes."[49] The poet has evidently reconstituted her mentor, like frozen orange juice, in sexually more palatable form.

While they have discarded the popular image of the lovelorn Dickinson, many commentators still entertain the improbable idea that in her late forties she seriously considered marriage to Judge Otis P. Lord, a close friend of her late father. I cannot reproduce the name "Judge Lord" without smiling. The mere recitation of so imposing a conflation of hierarchisms must have provided the poet with exquisite shivers of Sadean subordination. I suspect Dickinson exploited Lord for a cinematic rematerialization of her father's forbidding presence. Her father (whom Higginson described as "thin dry & speechless") was her symbolic agent of *limitation*, by which she curbed and disciplined her overexpanded Romantic imagination. That she could or would have tolerated a single day of abridgment of her monastic autonomy is preposterous. Her letters to Lord are contrived and artificial. The voice belongs to her twittering feminine personae, whom she tucks in becoming postures of devotion. The Lord letters are completely blotted out in emotional intensity by those to the one person with whom she was passionately involved: her sister-in-law Susan. By every standard except the genital, the stormy thirty-five-year relationship between the two women must be called a love affair.

Susan Gilbert was Dickinson's best friend before marrying her brother Austin. Therefore the poet's claim upon Susan was the primary one. Austin's adultery may have been a side effect of the erotic intensities between his sister and wife. Dickinson's allusions to Susan begin in chatty, girlish Wordsworthianism and end in dark, charged ambivalence. In other words, their relationship recapitulates the movement from High Romanticism to Decadence. The young poet recalls kisses and confesses heartthrobs and fever: "I want to think of you each hour in the day. What you are saying—doing—I want to walk with you, as seeing yet unseen." As the years pass, tension grows. "Egypt—thou

knew'st," writes Dickinson, playing humiliated Antony to Susan's Cleopatra. Four years before her death: "With the exception of Shakespeare,
you have told me of more knowledge than any one living—To say that
sincerely is strange praise."[50] So Susan is also Iago to her Othello.
Susan has provided her with the full range of emotional experience,
from love to hate.

The most disturbing of the surviving messages to Susan: "For the
Woman whom I prefer, Here is Festival—Where my Hands are cut, Her
fingers will be found inside."[51] Flesh of my flesh: the women are
Romantic twins, mentally and physically one. But Susan has aggressively invaded and occupied the poet, like the vampire penetrating
Christabel. She is like a commensal crab taking up residence in a live
oyster or mussel. Here as elsewhere, Dickinson adapts the story of
doubting Thomas, who thrusts his fingers into Christ's wounds. The
self-divinizing poet advertises her love by exhibiting her cut hands, like
the statue of a Catholic martyr. Surreally, it is Susan who cuts her and
Susan who painfully probes the wounds she has made. And one cannot
avoid the hallucinatory sexuality here, where female fingers have buried themselves through a slit in another woman's flesh. This is Dickinson at her sadomasochistic best.

In *The Riddle of Emily Dickinson* (1951), Rebecca Patterson boldly
argued that the person who drove the poet into seclusion with a broken
heart was the possibly bisexual Catherine Scott Anthon, a revolutionary
theory even if it misunderstands Dickinson's monasticism. Unfortunately, the book preceded the first wave of Dickinson scholarship, so it
misreads the poems and ends up as a fuzzy, schmaltzy novelette. Patterson sees most of Dickinson's males as Anthon in disguise. I call such
literary transsexualism "sexual metathesis" and have found it in many
Romantic writers. Perhaps it is operating at unsuspected moments in
Dickinson's poetry. My feeling, however, is that she is more interested in
masculinizing herself than in masculinizing other women. The self-
projections of boy, prince, and rapist are her favorite transsexual mode.
Furthermore, her erotics of Sadean hierarchy require most of her males
to *be* male—but without any necessary heterosexual desire on her part.
At her most rigorous, Dickinson is a Wildean Apollonian aroused by
rank alone, irrespective of gender. She is one of the last scholastics of
the great chain of being.

Psychobiographers like the astute John Cody recognize Dickinson's
lesbian tendencies, but criticism has not assimilated such perceptions
into explication of the poetry. For most scholars, lesbianism is no way to
treat a lady. The long conventionalization of Dickinson is epitomized in

the early retouching of our one photograph of the homely poet, who ends up with a frilly white ruff and fluffy Jane Wyman hair. It ludicrously feminizes her uncompromising austerity. Dickinson knew she deviated from female respectability. She says, with her usual rape language: "What Soft Cherubic Creatures / These Gentlewomen are— / One would as soon assault a Plush / Or violate a Star" (401). The well-bred lady with her opulent bosom is half angel, half velvet cushion, materialism masquerading as virtue. Dickinson's niece remembered her standing in the upper hall, as women visitors departed, and saying, finger to her lips, "Listen! Hear them kiss, the traitors!"[52] In a line like "I like a look of Agony, / Because I know it's true," she is using her cheerful sadomasochism to wipe out the empty tea-table smiles of her modish sex (241). Her homoerotic flirtations were integral to her masculine poetic identity. To love like a man is a first step away from social and biologic destiny.

Robert Graves declares: "The function of poetry is religious invocation of the Muse. . . . I cannot think of any true poet from Homer onwards who has not independently recorded his experience of her." Male homosexuals, he claims, cannot write great poetry, since their indifference to women severs them from the Muse or White Goddess. Women poets are crippled for the same reason: "Woman is not a poet: she is either a Muse or she is nothing." He denies Sappho was a lesbian, blaming the idea on "the malevolent lies of the Attic comedians."[53] Addled by homophobia, Graves fails to follow his interesting theory to its necessary conclusion: Sappho is a great poet *because* she is a lesbian, which gives her erotic access to the Muse. Sappho and the homosexual-tending Emily Dickinson stand alone above women poets, because poetry's mystical energies are ruled by a hierarch requiring the sexual subordination of her petitioners. Women have achieved more as novelists than as poets because the social novel operates outside the ancient marriage of myth and eroticism.

Understanding of Dickinson has been hampered by her complex use of sexual personae. Her sentimental feminine personae are paradoxically a tool of her poetic self-masculinization. For Blake, imagination must liberate itself from female nature. For Dickinson, a rare woman Romantic, that femaleness is in herself, which she must jettison to be free. By polarizing nature's powers into masculine and feminine, a duality that ensures the destruction of undefended femininity, she expels chthonian femaleness from her world. Her Brontëan detachment from her gender makes possible some of her most brilliant innovations. "'Twas just this time, last year, I died"; "I heard a Fly buzz—when I died": these incredible first lines, like the technical experiments of *Wuthering Heights*, have been produced by a displacement of point of view coming from sexual abstraction and self-estrangement. By no coincidence, it is married or marriageable women who fascinate and enamour Dickinson. The femaleness she makes external to herself she isolates and honors in others. But she must be their only spouse and child. She makes them sterile with her own desire. Her beloved women, particularly the volatile, willful Susan Gilbert Dickinson, are the avatars of the Muse whose presence is indispensable to poetry.

Even the best critical writing on Emily Dickinson underestimates her. She is frightening. To come to her directly from Dante, Spenser, Blake, and Baudelaire is to find her sadomasochism obvious and flagrant. Birds, bees, and amputated hands are the dizzy stuff of this poetry. Dickinson is like the homosexual cultist draping himself in black leather and chains to bring the idea of masculinity into aggressive visibility. In her hidden inner life, this shy Victorian spinster was a male genius and visionary sadist, a fictive sexual persona of towering force.

Emily Dickinson and Walt Whitman, apparently so dissimilar, are Late Romantic confederates of the American Union. Both are self-ruling hermaphrodites who will not and cannot mate. Both are homosexual voyeurs gaming at sexual all-inclusiveness. Both are perverse cannibals of others' identities, Whitman in his gluttonous self-engorgements and invasions of the chambers of the sleeping and sick, Dickinson in her ritualistic condolences and lubricious death-connoisseurship. Voyeurism, vampirism, necrophilia, lesbianism, sadomasochism, sexual surrealism: Amherst's Madame de Sade still waits for her readers to know her.

Notes

CHAPTER 1. SEX AND VIOLENCE, OR NATURE AND ART

1 *The Anxiety of Influence: A Theory of Poetry* (New York, 1973), 94.
2 *Sexual Deviation* (Harmondsworth, Middlesex, 1964), 63.
3 "The Analytic Conception of the Psycho-Neuroses" (1908), in *Further Contributions to the Theory and Technique of Psycho-analysis*, ed. John Rickman, trans. Jane Isabel Suttie et al. (New York, 1926), 25.
4 *Lord Byron's Marriage* (London, 1957), 261.
5 "On the Genesis of the Castration Complex in Women," *International Journal of Psychoanalysis* 5 (1924): 53.
6 *Beyond Formalism: Literary Essays 1958–1970* (New Haven, 1970), 23.
7 *Atlantic Crossing* (London, 1936), 111.
8 *Sexuality and the Psychology of Love*, ed. Philip Rieff (New York, 1963), 76.
9 *Beyond Good and Evil*, trans. Walter Kaufmann (New York, 1966), 158.

CHAPTER 2. THE BIRTH OF THE WESTERN EYE

1 Quoted in E. A. Wallis Budge, *The Gods of the Egyptians* (London, 1904), 1:297. Budge calls the Khepera masturbation myth "gross," a "brutal example of naturalism" that "can only be the product of a people at a low level of civilization." It must be a survival of "one of the coarse habits of the predynastic Egyptians, that is to say, of one of the indigenous African tribes from which dynastic Egyptians were partly descended" (ibid.). Freud's sex theories were to shake such Eurocentric confidence.
2 *Male and Female* (New York, 1949), 183.
3 *Ulysses* (New York, 1961), 207.
4 *The Great Mother: An Analysis of the Archetype*, trans. Ralph Manheim (Princeton, 1955), 28.
5 *The Origins and History of Consciousness*, trans. R. F. C. Hull (Princeton, 1954), 52.
6 *On the Nature of the Universe*, trans. R. E. Latham (Baltimore, 1951), 178.
7 *The Golden Ass*, ed. S. Gaselee (London, 1915), 386 (VIII. 25).
8 *The Cults of the Greek States* (Oxford, 1896–1909), 5:163.
9 "The Cult and Mythology of the Magna Mater from the Standpoint of Psychoanalysis," *Psychiatry* 1 (1938): 353.
10 *A Handbook of Greek Mythology* (New York, 1959), 126.
11 *Male and Female*, 182.
12 *Cults* 3:111.
13 *The Histories*, trans. Aubrey de Sélincourt (Baltimore, 1954), 57.
14 *The Golden Bough*, 3d ed. (New York, 1935), 6:255–57.

15 *Shamanism: Archaic Techniques of Ecstasy*, trans. Willard R. Trask (New York, 1964), 149, 352.
16 Hesiod, *The Homeric Hymns and Homerica*, trans. Hugh G. Evelyn-White (London, 1914), 269.
17 *Vergil: Epic and Anthropology* (New York, 1967), 180.
18 *The Greeks and the Irrational* (Berkeley, 1968), 70–71.
19 *Great Mother*, 168.
20 *Against Nature*, trans. Robert Baldick (Baltimore, 1959), 106.
21 Thalia Feldman, "Gorgo and the Origins of Fear," *Arion* 4, no. 3 (1965): 488.
22 "Medusa's Head" (1922), in *Sexuality*, 212.
23 *Vergil*, 107.
24 *Prolegomena to the Study of Greek Religion* (1903; repr. New York, 1955), 187–88.
25 *Vergil*, 194–95.
26 *A Writer's Diary*, ed. Leonard Woolf (New York, 1968), 135.
27 *Odyssey*, trans. E. V. Rieu (Baltimore, 1946), 190.
28 *Python: A Study of Delphic Myth and Its Origins* (Berkeley, 1959), 116.
29 *Kabbalah and Criticism* (New York, 1975), 45–46. *Figures of Capable Imagination* (New York, 1976), 264.
30 *Metamorphoses*, trans. Mary Innes (Baltimore, 1955), 313.
31 *Origins*, 46–53.
32 *Golden Bough* 5:256–57.
33 *The Interpretation of Dreams*, trans. James Strachey (New York, 1965), 296.
34 *The Decline of the West*, trans. Charles Francis Atkinson (New York, 1929), 1:248n.
35 *The Social History of Art*, trans. Stanley Godman (New York, 1951), 1:37.
36 *Through Alchemy to Chemistry* (London, 1957), 12.
37 *Gods of the Egyptians* 1:61, 63.
38 *Python*, 285–86.

CHAPTER 3. APOLLO AND DIONYSUS

1 *Themis: A Study of the Social Origins of Greek Religion* (Cambridge, England, 1912), 462.
2 *Rome and Greek Culture* (Oxford, 1935), 25.
3 *The Birth of Tragedy*, trans. Francis Golffing (Garden City, N.Y., 1956), 22, 65.
4 *The Greeks and Their Gods* (Boston, 1955), 189.
5 *Myth and Allegory in Ancient Art* (London, 1939), 22.
6 *Themis*, 502.
7 *The Homeric Gods*, trans. Moses Hadas (New York, 1954), 62–63.
8 *The Nude: A Study in Ideal Form* (Garden City, N.Y., 1956), 104.
9 *Decline of the West* 1:187.
10 *Five Stages of Greek Religion* (Garden City, N.Y., 1951), 71.
11 *Homeric Gods*, 55.

12 *Iliad*, trans. E. V. Rieu (Baltimore, 1950), 28. In Greek (I.200): δεινὼ δέ οἱ ὄσσε φάανθεν.
13 "Masculine and Feminine: Some Biological and Cultural Aspects," *Psychiatry* 7 (1944): 290.
14 *Sexuality*, 212–13.
15 *Athena Parthenos and Athena Polias: A Study in the Religion of Periclean Athens* (Manchester, 1955), 47.
16 *Prolegomena*, 302–03.
17 Ibid., 648.
18 *Odyssey*, 40.
19 Ibid., 209–10.
20 *Vergil*, 237.
21 *Homeric Gods*, 104, 124.
22 Neumann, *Great Mother*, 30. Jung, *Collected Works*, trans. R. F. C. Hull (Princeton, 1967), 13:79.
23 *Ancient Art and Ritual* (New York, 1913), 104. *Themis*, 36.
24 *The Golden Bough* 3:190n.
25 Plutarch, *Moralia*, trans. F. C. Babbitt (Cambridge, 1936), 5:82, 86. Farnell, *Cults*, 5:123.
26 *The Flight from Woman* (New York, 1965), 28.
27 *Atlantic Crossing*, 103.
28 *Thalassa: A Theory of Genitality*, trans. Henry Alden Bunker (New York, 1938), 57n.
29 *Great Mother*, 260.
30 *Being and Nothingness*, trans. Hazel E. Barnes (New York, 1966), 774, 776–77.
31 *Certains* (Paris, 1889), 27.
32 *Hamlet and Oedipus* (Garden City, N.Y., 1949), 98.
33 *Comus* 917, 861, 421–22.
34 *A History of Ancient Greek Literature* (New York, 1897), 272.
35 *Moralia*, 5:223.
36 *Prolegomena*, 568.
37 *The Golden Bough*, 6:16.
38 *Moralia*, 5:247.
39 *Prolegomena*, 439.
40 *The Greeks and the Irrational*, 76–77.
41 *An Essay on Man* (New Haven, 1944), 81, 76.
42 *Poets of Action* (London, 1967), 268.

CHAPTER 4. PAGAN BEAUTY

1 *Lectures and Notes on Shakespeare*, ed. T. Ashe (London, 1908), 194. *Miscellanies*, ed. T. Ashe (London, 1892), 93.
2 *Decline of the West*, 1:183, 83, 259, 176.
3 *Five Stages of Greek Religion*, 154.
4 *Decline of the West*, 1:83.

5 *Prolegomena*, 224.

6 *Iliad*, 383ff.

7 *Ten Plays*, trans. Moses Hadas and John McLean (New York, 1960), 57–58.

8 *Decline of the West* 1:259.

9 *Problems of Historical Psychology* (New York, 1960), 30n.

10 *The Changing Nature of Man*, trans. H. F. Croes (New York, 1961), 71–72.

11 *Greek Love* (London, 1971), 147, 255. John Addington Symonds says, "In the bloom of adolescence the elements of feminine grace . . . are combined with virility to produce a perfection which is lacking to the mature and adult excellence of either sex." *A Problem of Greek Ethics* (London, 1901), 68–69.

12 *Three Contributions to the Theory of Sex*, trans. A. A. Brill (New York, 1962), 10.

13 Campbell, *The Masks of God: Occidental Mythology* (New York, 1964), 228–29. Zimmer, *The Art of Indian Asia* (1955), 1:131.

14 *The Gramophone*, March 1968, 495.

15 *Phaedrus*, trans. W. C. Helmbold and W. G. Rabinowitz (New York, 1956), 34.

16 *Cults* 4:351–52.

17 *The Nude*, 74.

18 *Greek Sculpture* (Chicago, 1960), 174.

19 *The Social History of Art* 1:92.

20 *Themis*, 495.

21 *The Nude*, 126.

22 *Hermaphrodite: Myths and Rites of the Bisexual Figure in Classical Antiquity*, trans. Jennifer Nicholson (London, 1961), 24, 27.

23 *Hermetic and Alchemical Writings*, ed. Arthur Edward White (New Hyde Park, N.Y., 1967), 1:173.

24 *Diodorus Siculus*, trans. Francis R. Walton (London, 1957), 11:447–53. See also 2:361.

25 *Amores* in *Lucian* (Athens, 1895), 190.

26 *The Sculpture and Sculptors of the Greeks* (New Haven, 1930), 33.

27 *Aeneid*, trans. W. F. Jackson Knight (Baltimore, 1956), 312, 103–04.

28 *The Art of Love and Other Poems*, trans. J. H. Mozley (Cambridge, 1962), 433.

29 "ἀνδρογύνους ἔρωτας" (*Amores*. 28). *Lucian*, 190.

30 *Dio's Roman History*, trans. Ernest Cary (London, 1927), 7:347.

31 *The Twelve Caesars*, trans. Robert Graves (Harmondsworth, 1957), 224.

32 *Scriptores Historiae Augustae*, trans. David Magie (London, 1924), 2:165.

33 Review of Bruno Bettelheim, *Symbolic Wounds*, *Psychiatry* 17 (1954): 302.

34 *Dio*, 9:463, 469, 471.

35 Ibid., 8:369. I alter the translation to better express the Greek τοιαύτη, "such a one."

36 *The Republic*, trans. H. D. P. Lee (Harmondsworth, 1955), 119.

37 See my graduate-school essay, "Lord Hervey and Pope," *Eighteenth Century Studies* 6 (Spring 1973): 348–71. Comments on it in lead article, *Times Literary Supplement*, 2 Nov. 1973. *Epistle to Arbuthnot*, 305–34.

38 *The City of God*, trans. Marcus Dods (New York, 1950), 37, 53.

39 Ibid., 43, 232–33.
40 *The Golden Ass*, trans. Jack Lindsay (Bloomington, 1962), 180–81.

CHAPTER 5. RENAISSANCE FORM: ITALIAN ART

1 *Decameron*, trans. G. H. McWilliam (Harmondsworth, 1972), 50–54.
2 *The Black Death* (New York, 1969), 278.
3 *The Civilization of the Renaissance in Italy*, trans. S. G. C. Middlemore (New York, 1958), 1:147n.
4 *The Book of the Courtier*, trans. Charles S. Singleton (Garden City, N.Y., 1959), 139.
5 Ibid., 29, 344–45, 36.
6 *The Court Masque* (Cambridge, 1927), 398–99.
7 *Wilhelm Meister's Apprenticeship*, trans. William Carlyle (New York, 1962), 282.
8 *Autobiography of Benvenuto Cellini*, trans. John Addington Symonds (Garden City, N.Y., 1961), 446–47.
9 *The Sculpture of Donatello* (Princeton, 1957), 2:85.
10 Marvin Trachtenberg, "An Antique Model for Donatello's Marble *David*," *Art Bulletin* 50 (1968): 268. I am grateful to Kristen Lippincott for bringing this to my attention.
11 *Social History of Art*, 2:37.
12 "Leonardo and Freud: An Art-Historical Study," in Paul Oskar Kristeller and Philip P. Wiener, ed., *Renaissance Essays* (New York, 1968), 319.
13 Farnell, *Cults*, 3:259. Frazer, *The Golden Bough*, 7:67–68.
14 *A Problem of Greek Ethics*, 68.
15 *The Nude*, 332.
16 *Michelangelo: A Study in the Nature of Art* (London, 1955), 89.
17 *Lives of the Artists*, ed. Betty Burroughs (New York, 1946), 273.
18 *The Nude*, 102, 99.
19 *The Portrait in the Renaissance*, The A. W. Mellon Lectures in the Fine Arts, 1963 (New York, 1966), 300.
20 *Michelangelo: A Psychoanalytic Study of His Life and Images* (New Haven, 1983), 65.
21 Clark, *The Nude*, 325. Stokes, *Michelangelo*, 87.

CHAPTER 6. SPENSER AND APOLLO: *THE FAERIE QUEENE*

1 *The Structure of Allegory in "The Faerie Queene"* (Oxford, 1961), 12.
2 *Japanese Literature* (New York, 1955), 7.
3 *The Allegory of Love* (London, 1936), 340.
4 All quotations from Spenser are from *The Works of Edmund Spenser: A Variorum Edition*, ed. Edwin Greenlaw et al. (Baltimore, 1932–57). To open Spenser to the general reader, I modernize the spelling of some words.
5 *Confessions*, trans. R. S. Pine-Coffin (Harmondsworth, 1961), 233.

6 *Summa Theologica,* in *Basic Writings,* ed. Anton C. Pegis (New York, 1945), 1:378.
7 *The Two and the One,* trans. J. M. Cohen (New York, 1965), 32–33.
8 *A Rhetoric of Motives* (New York, 1950), 210.
9 *Metaphysical Elements,* quoted in Dionysius the Areopagite, *The Mystical Theology and the Celestial Hierarchies,* trans. the Editors of the Shrine of Wisdom (Fintry, Surrey, 1949), 47n.
10 In my article, "The Apollonian Androgyne and the *Faerie Queene,*" *English Literary Renaissance* 9:1 (Winter 1979): 55–56.
11 My article, "Sex," in *The Spenser Encyclopedia,* ed. A. C. Hamilton et al. (Toronto, 1989).
12 *Allegory of Love,* 332.
13 *Poets of Action,* 12–13.
14 *Decameron,* 460–61.

CHAPTER 7. SHAKESPEARE AND DIONYSUS: *AS YOU LIKE IT* AND *ANTONY AND CLEOPATRA*

1 *Byron's Dramatic Prose,* Byron Foundation Lecture (pamphlet, University of Nottingham, 1953), 15.
2 "There is no satisfactory explanation in the traditional character of Proteus for his behavior toward Florimell." Lotspeich, *Variorum Spenser,* 3:270.
3 *Biographia Literaria,* ed. J. Shawcross (Oxford, 1907), 2:20.
4 *The Philosophy of Literary Form: Studies in Symbolic Action* (New York, 1957), 249.
5 *Alchemy,* trans. William Stoddart (London, 1967), 13.
6 *Collected Works,* trans. R. F. C. Hull (Princeton, 1967), 13:189.
7 *The Origins of Alchemy in Graeco-Roman Egypt* (New York, 1970), 258.
8 In Paracelsus, *Hermetic and Alchemical Writings,* 2:374.
9 *Civilization of the Renaissance in Italy,* 1:143, 163.
10 "The Design of *Twelfth Night,*" *Shakespeare Quarterly* 9 (1958): 121.
11 *The Nature of Representation: A Phenomenological Inquiry* (New York, 1961), 124.
12 *Shakespeare's Comedies* (Oxford, 1960), 93.
13 "*As You Like It:* A Grammatical Clue to Character," *A Review of English Literature* 4, no. 2 (1963): 74, 76–77.
14 *Shakespeare's Sexual Comedy* (New York, 1971), 137.
15 Quoted in Roger Baker, *Drag: A History of Female Impersonation on the Stage* (London, 1968), 240.
16 Ibid., 242, 240, 87.
17 *The Mutual Flame* (London, 1955), 112. *Neglected Powers* (London, 1971), 49. *Mutual Flame,* 219, 155, 139.
18 *A Study of English Romanticism* (New York, 1968), 140.
19 *Collected Works,* 12:69; 13:237.
20 Michael Maier, *Atalanta Fugiens,* ed. H. M. E. De Jong (Leiden, 1969), 316. First published 1617. The phrase appears in the epigraph on Maier's title page.

21 *Collected Works,* 12:202.

22 *Atalanta Fugiens,* 9n.

23 *Hermetic and Alchemical Writings,* 1:66.

24 *Oxford Lectures on Poetry* (London, 1909), 300.

25 *The Birth of Tragedy,* 124.

26 *The Common Liar* (New Haven, 1973), 92–93.

27 *Auntie Mame* (New York, 1955), 15, 25–26, 70. One good thing in the Lucille Ball *Mame:* Bea Arthur shrewdly plays Vera Charles like a man in drag.

28 *The Italians* (New York, 1965), 64.

29 West and Jan Gerhard Toonder, *The Case for Astrology* (Baltimore, 1970), 22.

30 Intro. to Gaston Bachelard, *The Psychoanalysis of Fire,* trans. Alan Ross (Boston, 1964), vii. G. Wilson Knight has an excellent discussion of the elements in *Antony and Cleopatra* but, unlike me, concludes "there is no allegory." *The Imperial Theme,* 227–44, 251.

31 "The Jacobean Shakespeare," in *Stratford-upon-Avon Studies I: Jacobean Theatre,* ed. John Russell Brown and Bernard Harris (New York, 1960), 28.

32 *The Twelve Caesars,* 103. I have yet to decide why Shakespeare embeds a third of the zodiac in the text of *Antony and Cleopatra.* Images of Pisces, Aries, Taurus, and Gemini appear in correct chronology: fishes (II.v.12), the ram (II.v.24; III.ii.30), Taurus (III.viii.1), twins and June (III.x.12, 14).

33 *Prolegomena,* 515.

CHAPTER 8. RETURN OF THE GREAT MOTHER:
ROUSSEAU VERSUS SADE

1 *The Enlightenment: An Interpretation* (New York, 1966). The first volume is called "The Rise of Modern Paganism." Gay seems to use "pagan" as a synonym for what I call Apollonian, only half of my theory of paganism.

2 *Confessions,* trans. J. M. Cohen (Baltimore, 1954), 25–28.

3 Ibid., 106, 189, 229, 555.

4 Ibid., 594.

5 *The Changing Nature of Man,* 233.

6 *Pensées,* trans. A. J. Krailsheimer (Baltimore, 1966), 154.

7 *Justine, Philosophy in the Bedroom, and Other Writings,* comp. and trans. Richard Seaver and Austryn Wainhouse (New York, 1965), 253, 608, 496.

8 *Juliette,* trans. Austryn Wainhouse (New York, 1968), 269, 940. *Philosophy in the Bedroom,* 345.

9 *Juliette,* 177. *Philosophy,* 360. *Justine,* 660. *Juliette,* 177. *Justine,* 607. *Juliette,* 178. *Justine,* 608.

10 *Philosophy,* 329–30. *Juliette,* 267, 923. *Juliette,* 171.

11 *Justine,* 277. *Juliette,* 273, 359, 364, 544.

12 *Juliette,* 699, 1,032, 1,147, 171, 480. *Justine,* 520.

13 *Philosophy,* 359, 272. *120 Days of Sodom and Other Writings,* comp. and trans. Austryn Wainhouse and Richard Seaver (New York, 1966), 602, 661.

14 *Juliette*, 943–44.
15 Ibid., 573–74.
16 *Justine*, 263. *Juliette*, 82. *Philosophy*, 203. *Juliette*, 223.
17 *120 Days*, 456–57, 445, 655–56, 649.
18 *Juliette*, 341, 1,127.
19 *120 Days*, 588, 589, 610, 605.
20 Ibid., 616, 647, 612.
21 *Philosophy*, 248. *Juliette*, 79, 423. *Philosophy*, 363.
22 *Psychological Types: or The Psychology of Individuation*, trans. H. Godwin Baynes (New York, 1926), 290–91.
23 *Justine*, 631. *Juliette*, 510. *120 Days*, 341.
24 *Juliette*, 511.
25 Beauvoir, "Must We Burn Sade?" in *120 Days*, 25. Barthes, *Sade Fourier Loyola*, trans. Richard Miller (New York, 1976), 124.
26 Sade, *Philosophy*, 207. Harrison, *Themis*, 36.
27 *Sexuality*, 65.
28 *Juliette*, 287.

CHAPTER 9. AMAZONS, MOTHERS, GHOSTS: GOETHE TO GOTHIC

1 *The Mystery of the Androgyne: Three Papers on the Theory and Practice of Psychoanalysis* (London: 1938), 49–50. Deceptive title: there is nothing about androgynes in the book.
2 *The Sorrows of Young Werther and Selected Writings*, trans. Catherine Hutter (New York, 1962), 53.
3 Ibid., 131.
4 *Wilhelm Meister's Apprenticeship*, trans. Thomas Carlyle (New York, 1962), 29.
5 Ibid., 219–21, 315, 245, 288–89.
6 Lukács, *Goethe: A Collection of Critical Essays*, ed. Victor Lange (Englewood Cliffs, N.J., 1968), 95. Lange: Introduction, *Wilhelm Meister*, 11.
7 *Wilhelm Meister*, 105, 202.
8 Ibid., 105, 115, 120, 250, 305.
9 Ibid., 115, 522.
10 Ibid., 525.
11 *Goethe's Roman Elegies and Venetian Epigrams: A Bilingual Text*, trans. L. R. Lind (Lawrence, Kansas, 1974), 101–03.
12 Ibid., 149. The censored German text gives "F" as first letter of the omitted word, which the editor, without translating it, identifies as "Fotze," a sexual vulgarism meaning "crack" or "slit."
13 *Faust, Part Two*, trans. Philip Wayne (Baltimore, 1959), 79.
14 Farnell, *Cults of the Greek States*, 2:479n. Diodorus, IV. 79.
15 *Essays of Three Decades*, trans. H. T. Lowe-Porter (New York, 1971), 107–08.
16 K. R. Eissler, *Goethe: A Psychoanalytic Study 1775–1786* (Detroit, 1963), 1:487.

17 Ibid., 1:105.
18 "Fetishism" (1927), in *Sexuality*, 217.
19 *Poetry and Repression* (New Haven, 1976), 7.
20 *Roman Elegies*, 151.
21 Quoted in Richard Friedenthal, *Goethe: His Life and Times* (Cleveland, 1965), 417.
22 *Five German Tragedies*, trans. F. J. Lamport (Baltimore, 1969), 419.
23 Ibid., 414.
24 Quoted in E. L. Stahl, *Heinrich von Kleist's Dramas* (Oxford, 1961), 139.
25 *Heinrich von Kleist* (Philadelphia, 1961), 88.
26 *Critical Review*, February 1797, 197.
27 *The Monk*, ed. Louis F. Peck (New York, 1952), 418, 420.
28 Ibid., 274. Nietzsche, *Beyond Good and Evil*, 179. Spengler, *Decline of the West*, 1:247.
29 *Three Contributions*, 63.
30 *Poets of Action*, 175.
31 *Philosophical Enquiry*, ed. James T. Boulton (Notre Dame, 1968), 136, 46.
32 *Sincerity and Authenticity* (Cambridge, Mass., 1971), 95.
33 Dennis: quoted in Samuel H. Monk, *The Sublime* (New York, 1935), 53. Schiller: "On the Sublime," in *Aesthetical and Philosophical Essays*, ed. Nathan Haskell Dole (Boston, 1902), 1:127.

CHAPTER 10. SEX BOUND AND UNBOUND: BLAKE

1 *Escape from Freedom* (New York, 1941), 168.
2 *Middlemarch* (Harmondsworth, 1965), 226.
3 *Blake's Apocalypse: A Study in Poetic Argument* (New York, 1960; rpt. Ithaca, 1970), 294.
4 Ibid., 300.
5 *Women in Love* (New York, 1960), 338.
6 Bloom and Trilling, ed., *Romantic Poetry and Prose, The Oxford Anthology of English Literature* (New York, 1973), 69n.
7 Damon, *A Blake Dictionary: The Ideas and Symbols of William Blake* (Providence, R.I., 1965), 182. Percival, *William Blake's Circle of Destiny* (New York, 1938), 110, 114.
8 *A Descriptive Catalogue* (1809), in *The Poetry and Prose of William Blake*, ed. David V. Erdman and Harold Bloom (Garden City, N.Y., 1970), 540.
9 Ibid., 540, 519, 529, 537.
10 *Yeats* (London, 1970), 31.
11 *Descriptive Catalogue*, 537, 538, 521. Annotations to *The Works of Sir Joshua Reynolds*, 644.
12 *Culture and Anarchy*, ed. J. Dover Wilson (Cambridge, England, 1969), 131.

CHAPTER 11. MARRIAGE TO MOTHER NATURE: WORDSWORTH

1 *Wordsworth's Poetry 1787–1814* (New Haven, 1964), 67.
2 Ibid., 122, 367n.
3 *The Visionary Company* (New York, 1961), 146.

4 *The Starlit Dome* (London, 1970), 23. *Lord Byron's Marriage*, 257.
5 *A Map of Misreading* (New York, 1975), 19.
6 *The Anxiety of Influence*, 38.
7 *Wilhelm Meister's Apprenticeship*, 492.
8 *The Table Talk and Omniana of Coleridge*, ed. T. Ashe (London, 1896), 339. The text says "femineity."
9 Coleridge, ibid., 183. Woolf, *Room* (New York, 1929), 102, 107.
10 *Visionary Company*, 199.
11 *Wordsworth: A Re-interpretation* (London, 1954), 128.
12 Ibid., 153.
13 *Wordsworth's Poetry*, 168.
14 *Starlit Dome*, 21.
15 *The Opposing Self: Nine Essays in Criticism* (New York, 1959), 135.
16 *The Unmediated Vision: An Interpretation of Wordsworth, Hopkins, Rilke, and Valéry* (New York, 1954), 181n.

CHAPTER 12. THE DAEMON AS LESBIAN VAMPIRE: COLERIDGE

1 *Biographia Literaria*, 2:12.
2 *The Interpretation of Dreams*, trans. James Strachey (New York, 1965), 353.
3 *The Mirror and the Lamp* (New York, 1953), 356n.
4 *Biographia Literaria*, 1:202.
5 *The Soul of Man Under Socialism*, in *Plays, Prose Writings, and Poems* (New York, 1972), 274.
6 Bloom, *Visionary Company*, 221. Hough, *The Romantic Poets* (New York, 1964), 61. Whalley, "The Mariner and the Albatross," in *Coleridge: A Collection of Critical Essays* ed. Kathleen Coburn, (Englewood Cliffs, N.J., 1967), 40.
7 "The Nightmare World of *The Ancient Mariner*," *Studies in Romanticism* 1 (1961–62): 250.
8 *Visionary Company*, 229.
9 *The Golden Bough*, 10:6; 8:29.
10 *Visionary Company*, 225.
11 Ibid., 226.
12 *The Starlit Dome*, 83.
13 *The Witch-Cult in Western Europe* (Oxford, 1921), 90.
14 Quoted in Nigel Nicolson, *Portrait of a Marriage* (New York, 1973), 114.
15 Coleridge, *Selected Poetry*, ed. Bloom (New York, 1972), 42n.
16 *Three Contributions to the Theory of Sex*, 15n.
17 *The Blithedale Romance* (New York, 1960), 51.
18 *Prolegomena*, 196.
19 *The Philosophy of Literary Form* (New York, 1957), 47.
20 *Coleridge* (London, 1953), 122.
21 "Coleridge and Wordsworth and 'the Supernatural,'" *University of Toronto Quarterly* 25 (1956): 128–30.
22 *The Notebooks of Samuel Taylor Coleridge*, ed. Kathleen Coburn (London, 1957), 1:848, 1252.

23 Bostetter, "*Christabel:* The Vision of Fear," *Philological Quarterly* 36, no. 2 (1957): 192. Fruman, *Coleridge: The Damaged Archangel* (New York, 1971), 376.

24 "My First Acquaintance with Poets," in *Complete Works of Hazlitt*, ed. P. P. Howe (New York, 1967), 17:109.

CHAPTER 13. SPEED AND SPACE: BYRON

1 *Picture of Dorian Gray* (Baltimore, 1949), 248.
2 *Lord Byron's Marriage*, 17.
3 *Poets of Action*, 226.
4 Knight, ibid., 246–47. Frye. *Fables of Identity* (New York, 1963), 184, 188. Bloom, *Visionary Company*, 274–75.
5 *The Starlit Dome*, 210.
6 *Decline of the West*, 1:145.
7 *Visionary Company*, 286.
8 *The Golden Bough*, 6:218.
9 *The Plot of Satire* (New Haven, 1965), 180.
10 *Howards End* (New York, 1921), 197–99.
11 "Milton and the Descent to Light," in *Milton: Modern Essays in Criticism*, ed. Arthur E. Barker (New York, 1965), 184.
12 *Essays in Criticism*, 2d ser., ed. S. R. Littlewood (New York, 1966), 104, 102, 105–06.
13 *Roman Vergil* (London, 1944), 93.
14 *Rock Encyclopedia* (New York, 1969), 24.
15 *Byron: A Survey* (London, 1975), 301.
16 Quoted in E. M. Butler, *Byron and Goethe* (London, 1956), 182. Quoted in Newman Ivey White, *Shelley* (New York, 1940), 2:337.
17 *Lady Blessington's Conversations of Lord Byron*, ed. Ernest J. Lovell, Jr. (Princeton, 1969), 6–7. Quoted in Knight, *Lord Byron: Christian Virtues* (New York, 1953), 81.
18 *Lady Blessington*, 6.
19 *Glenarvon* (London, 1816), 2:29.
20 *The Byronic Hero* (Minneapolis, 1962), 8.
21 The autopsy report is reprinted in "Lord Byron in Greece," *Westminster Review*, July 1824, 258–59. For a theory that Byron died from cerebral hemorrhage from a congenital aneurism, see John S. Chapman, *Byron and the Honourable Augusta Leigh* (New Haven, 1975), 233–43.
22 *King James VI and I* (New York, 1956), 384–85.
23 *The Court and the Country: The Beginning of the English Revolution* (New York, 1970), 58–59.

CHAPTER 14. LIGHT AND HEAT: SHELLEY AND KEATS

1 *A Defence of Poetry*, ed. John E. Jordan (Indianapolis, 1965), 26, 74.
2 Knight, *The Starlit Dome*, 228. Bloom, *Shelley's Mythmaking* (1959; Ithaca, 1969), 200.

3 New York Times Magazine, 11 Sept. 1977, 129.

4 *The Hollywood Hallucination* (New York, 1944), 74–99.

5 *Women in Love*, 9–10.

6 As told to Jeanne Molli, *The Beautiful People's Beauty Book: How to Achieve the Look and Manner of the World's Most Attractive Women* (New York, 1970), 1. "I was a lump, and everyone knew it." On having her nose done at eighteen: "The anesthesia may have been a bit strong. I slept for twelve hours and came out of it totally bewildered, with a form of amnesia. I did not know where I was. . . . My mother shrieked, 'They redid her nose and touched her brain'" (3, 7).

7 *Shelley's Major Poetry: The Fabric of Vision* (New York, 1961), 53.

8 *Victorian Minds* (New York, 1968), 132–33.

9 *Autobiography* (New York, 1964), 140.

10 *Shelley*, 2:325.

11 *Shelley's Mythmaking*, 208.

12 *The Golden Labyrinth: A Study of British Drama* (London, 1962), 26.

13 *The Rainbow* (New York, 1961), 336–43.

14 *The City of God*, 502, 500.

15 *Metamorphoses*, 216.

16 *The Starlit Dome*, 239. *Lord Byron's Marriage*, 259.

17 "The Psychology of Transvestism," *International Journal of Psychoanalysis* 11 (1930): 214.

18 *Dora: An Analysis of a Case of Hysteria*, ed. Philip Rieff (New York, 1963), 151.

19 *Natural Supernaturalism: Tradition and Revolution in Romantic Literature* (New York, 1971), 160.

20 In *English Romantic Poets*, ed. M. H. Abrams (New York, 1960), 37–52.

21 *Defence of Poetry*, 71.

22 Quoted in Walter Jackson Bate, *John Keats* (New York, 1966), 266.

23 *Mythology and the Romantic Tradition in English Poetry* (Cambridge, Mass., 1937), 158.

24 *The Will to Power*, trans. Walter Kaufmann and R. J. Hollingdale (New York, 1968), 431.

25 "Per Amica Silentia Lunae," in *Essays* (New York, 1924), 503.

26 *Defence of Poetry*, 72.

27 Ibid., 77.

28 *Origins*, 121.

29 To the George Keatses, 19 March 1819; to J. H. Reynolds, 19 Feb. 1818; to George and Tom Keats, 27 Dec. 1817. *The Letters of John Keats*, ed. Hyder Edward Rollins (Cambridge, Mass., 1958), 2:78, 1:232, 1:193.

30 To Richard Woodhouse, 27 Oct. 1818, ibid., 1:387. To Benjamin Bailey, 22 Nov. 1817, 1:184.

31 To Bailey, 18–22 July 1818, ibid., 1:341.

32 To the George Keatses, 21 April 1819, ibid., 2:103.

33 *The Opposing Self*, 16–17, 24.

34 Richard Woodhouse to John Taylor, 19–20 Sept. 1819, *Letters of Keats*, 2:163. Keats to Bailey, 18–22 July 1818, ibid., 1:341. Bate, *Keats*, 378–79.

35 *Visionary Company*, 403.

36 To the George Keatses, 16 Dec. 1818–4 Jan. 1819, *Letters*, 2:8, 13. *Keats*, 425.
37 *Beyond Formalism: Literary Essays 1958–1970* (New Haven, 1970), 369.
38 *Cults*, 3:281.

CHAPTER 15. CULTS OF SEX AND BEAUTY: BALZAC

1 (Hyacinthe Thabaud), *Fragoletta* (Paris, 1829), 1:89, 91–92; 2:328–29. My translation.
2 *Sarrasine*, in Roland Barthes, *S/Z*, trans. Richard Miller (New York, 1974), 237–38. Remaining quotations: 252, 246–47, 242, 238, 252.
3 Ibid., 17.
4 *The Castrati in Opera* (New York, 1974), 13, 25.
5 *Essays and Poems*, ed. Robert Halsband and Isobel Grundy (Oxford, 1977), 119.
6 Quoted in Heriot, *Castrati*, 54–55.
7 Ibid., 119, 22n.
8 *Lost Illusions*, trans. Herbert J. Hunt (Harmondsworth, Middlesex, 1971), 173.
9 Corentin Guyho, quoted in Félicien Marceau, *Balzac and His World*, trans. Derek Coltman (New York, 1966), 44.
10 Quoted in Introduction, *Lady Blessington's Conversations*, 13, 38.
11 Ellen Moers, *The Dandy: Brummell to Beerbohm* (New York, 1960), 148n.
12 *The Girl with the Golden Eyes*, in *History of the Thirteen*, trans. Herbert J. Hunt (Harmondsworth, Middlesex, 1974), 331. Remaining quotations: 309–11, 337–38, 346–47, 366, 376, 384, 388–89, 381, 390, 361, 338.
13 *Portraits of the Day*, in *The Works of Théophile Gautier*, trans. and ed. F. C. de Sumichrast (London, 1909), 3:71–74.
14 *Affirmations*, 2d ed. (Boston, 1915), 175.
15 *The Works of Honoré de Balzac*, trans. Clara Bell (amended by me) (Philadelphia, 1898), 28:15, 9–10. Remaining quotations: 20, 69, 21, 20, 28, 12, 39–40, 66, 54–55. Balzac's first reference to the germinating *Seraphita* compares it to *Fragoletta* (to Mme Hanska, 20–24 Nov. 1833).
16 *Dictionnaire de Balzac* (Paris, 1969), 235.
17 A. J. L. Busst, "The Image of the Androgyne in the Nineteenth Century," in *Romantic Mythologies*, Ian Fletcher, ed., (New York, 1967), 12–26.
18 *Lost Illusions*, 26–27. *Old Goriot*, trans. Marion Ayton Crawford (Harmondsworth, Middlesex, 1951), 192.
19 *Lost Illusions*, 459. Balzac says of Camille Maupin, "She is a man" (to Mme Hanska, 2 March 1838).
20 *Cousin Bette*, trans. Marion Ayton Crawford (Harmondsworth, 1965), 45, 165, 118–19. Remaining quotations: 79, 69, 118, 165.

CHAPTER 16. CULTS OF SEX AND BEAUTY: GAUTIER, BAUDELAIRE, AND HUYSMANS

1 "Théophile Gautier," in *L'Art romantique, Oeuvres Complètes*, ed. Pléiade (Paris, 1961), 683, 690.

2 *Les Années romantiques de Théophile Gautier* (Paris, 1929), 290.

3 *Fictional Technique in France 1802–1927* (Baton Rouge, 1972), 96.

4 *History of the Thirteen*, 347.

5. *Mademoiselle de Maupin*, intro. Jacques Barzun (New York, 1944), 39, 49, 21, 84.

6 Ibid., 86–87, 144.

7 Ibid., 100.

8 Ibid., 122.

9 Ibid., 135–36, 139.

10 Ibid., 146–47.

11 Ibid., 152. The citation later in the paragraph is from p. 195.

12 See "Women Duellists" in Robert Baldick, *The Duel* (New York, 1965), 171–72.

13 *Maupin*, 282, 225.

14 Ibid., 232–33.

15 *Sex and Gender: On the Development of Masculinity and Femininity* (London, 1968), 194, 196.

16 *Screening the Sexes: Homosexuality in the Movies* (Garden City, N.Y., 1972), 221.

17 *French Short Stories of the Nineteenth and Twentieth Centuries*, ed. F. C. Green, (New York, 1951), 32, 36–37. Citation later in paragraph: 52.

18 *The Works of Gautier*, 6:342.

19 Ibid., 4:344, 352.

20 My translation. "Tu mettrais l'univers," "La Beauté," "Hymne à la Beauté," "Avec ses vêtements," "Le Lethe," "Le Serpent qui danse," "Je t'adore," "Le Chat," "Duellum," "Je te donne ces vers," "Le Possédé," "Le Beau Navire."

21 *Art and Criticism*, in *Works*, 12:66.

22 Alfred Delvau, *Dictionnaire érotique moderne*, nouv. ed. (Basel, 1891), 373. Delvau died the same year as Baudelaire, so his definitions would be contemporary.

23 *Baudelaire* (New York, 1954), 204–05.

24 *The Journals of André Gide*, trans. Justin O'Brien (New York, 1948), 2:265.

25 *Charles Baudelaire*, trans. Harry Zohn (London, 1973), 93.

26 *Origins of the Sexual Impulse* (London, 1963), 228.

27 To Fernand Desnoyers (1853–54), in *Correspondance*, ed. Claude Pichois (Paris, 1973), 1:248. The wonderful phrase is "légumes sanctifiés." Earlier he says, "Je suis incapable de m'attendrir sur les végétaux."

28 Jeannette H. Foster says, "Colette in *Ces Plaisirs* pronounced his lesbians unconvincing little monsters, and Natalie Clifford Barney in *Aventures de L'Esprit* writes of warning him when his early volumes appeared of the difficulty of translating the experience of one sex into terms of the other." *Sex Variant Women in Literature* (New York, 1956), 205.

29 *The Painter of Modern Life and Other Essays*, trans. Jonathan Mayne (New York, 1965), 26–29.

30 *Art and Criticism*, in *Works*, 12:43.

31 *Baudelaire*, trans. Martin Turnell (New York, 1950), 147.

32 *The Anatomy of Dandyism*, trans. D. B. Wyndham Lewis (London 1928),

65. Though Barbey's essay is disorganized, the French advance in sociological speculation is already evident from the following two passages. Thomas Carlyle says, "A Dandy is a Clothes-wearing Man, a Man whose trade, office, and existence consists in the wearing of Clothes." But Barbey says: "Here is a veritable truth about Dandyism. The clothes matter not at all. They are hardly there" (8*n*). Carlyle, *Sartor Resartus and Selected Prose*, intro. Herbert Sussman (New York, 1970), 248.

33 *Art and Criticism*, in *Works*, 12:19.
34 "In Praise of Cosmetics," *Painter*, 33–34.
35 "Mon Coeur mis à nu," in *Oeuvres*, 1207.
36 *Against Nature*, trans. Robert Baldick (Baltimore, 1959), 208–09. This superb translation is by far the best.
37 Ibid., 36, 97.
38 Ibid., 97–101.
39 Ibid., 103–06.
40 Elizabeth Ashley, with Ross Firestone, *Actress: Postcards from the Road* (New York, 1978), 155.
41 *Certains*, 27.
42 "There are massive tree-flowers that suggest organs of a body, torn out, still glistening with undried blood." *Four Plays* (New York, 1976), 9. Williams evidently intends an opposition of Apollonian to chthonian, perhaps influenced by Lawrence's *Women in Love*. In the film, brooding, dark-haired Montgomery Clift fills a role the play calls "a young blond Doctor, all in white, glacially brilliant," a man of "icy charm"—much like Lawrence's Gerald Crich (9–10).
43 *Art and Criticism*, in *Works*, 12:39, 41.
44 *The Symbolist Movement in Literature*, intro. Richard Ellmann (New York, 1958), 81.
45 *Against Nature*, 49.
46 *Venus in Furs* (New York, 1965), 39. Remaining quotations: 45, 68.
47 *Sexual Deviation*, 55, 57.
48 *Monsieur Vénus*, trans. Madeleine Boyd (New York, 1929), 86–87, 90–91. Remaining quotations: 108, 110, 216–17.
49 Juliette and Justine Lemercier, *The Turkish Bath* (New York, 1969), 142. The pseudonyms come from Sade; the cover art is Ingres' *Turkish Bath*.

CHAPTER 17. ROMANTIC SHADOWS: EMILY BRONTË

1 *Anatomy of Criticism* (New York, 1968), 304.
2 Quoted in Joan Bennett, *George Eliot: Her Mind and Her Art* (Cambridge, 1948), 78. Eliot, *Middlemarch*, ed. W. J. Harvey (Baltimore, 1965), 210.
3 *The Great Tradition* (New York, 1967), 68.
4 *Middlemarch*, 754.
5 *An Introduction to the English Novel* (New York, 1951), 1:189.
6 *Middlemarch*, 241, 502.
7 Ibid., 26.
8 Wilson, "A Long Talk about Jane Austen" (1945), in *Jane Austen: A Collec-*

tion of Critical Essays, ed. Ian Watt (Englewood Cliffs, N.J., 1963), 39. Mudrick, *Jane Austen* (Berkeley, 1968), 192. Wright, *Jane Austen's Novels* (Harmondsworth, 1972), 135. Bush, *Jane Austen* (New York, 1975), 162.

9 *Some Words of Jane Austen* (Chicago, 1973), 248. See Robert L. Caserio, *Plot, Story, and the Novel: From Dickens and Poe to the Modern Period* (Princeton, 1979) on two different nineteenth-century traditions of narrative plotting.

10 *Vanity Fair*, ed. J. I. M. Stewart (Harmondsworth, 1968), 448–49.

11 "Madame Bovary," in *Oeuvres Complètes*, 652.

12 *The Poetics of Reverie*, trans. Daniel Russel (New York, 1969), 93.

13 *Anna Karenina*, trans. L. and A. Maude (New York, 1970), 72, 58.

14 *Nana*, trans. George Holden (Harmondsworth, 1972), 44–45, 452, 433, 221, 409.

15 *Wuthering Heights*, ed. David Daiches (Baltimore, 1965), 135.

16 *Lectures in America* (London, 1969), 89.

17 *Victorian Novelists* (Chicago, 1958), 144, 163, 146.

18 *The English Novel* (New York, 1953), 157–58.

19 *The Common Reader* (New York, 1925), 225.

20 *Wuthering Heights*, 121–22, 128, 166, 160.

21 *Revue des deux mondes* (1 July 1857), in *The Brontes: The Critical Heritage*, ed. Miriam Allott (London 1974), 377–78.

22 "The Shadow Within: The Conscious and Unconscious Use of the Double," *Daedalus* 90 (Spring 1963): 329.

23 "The Incest Theme in *Wuthering Heights*" (a three-page note on the novel), *Nineteenth Century Fiction* 14 (June 1959): 82–83.

24 *Anatomy of Criticism*, 101.

25 *Wuthering Heights*, 112, 106–07.

26 Ibid., 93, 92.

27 Ibid., 120–22, 212, 97, 202–03.

28 Ibid., 80, 90, 209, 89, 115, 154, 185, 189, 209, 221, 155. The overpraised film of *Wuthering Heights* (1939), starring Laurence Olivier and Merle Oberon, makes the novel falsely Wordsworthian: forbidding Yorkshire becomes a sunny suburban garden.

29 Ibid., 128.

30 Ibid., 66–67.

31 "The Place of Love in *Jane Eyre* and *Wuthering Heights*," in *The Brontës: A Collection of Critical Essays*, ed. Ian Gregor (Englewood Cliffs, N.J., 1970), 93.

32 *Wuthering Heights*, 69.

33 Ibid., 235, 254, 242.

34 *Meditations on the Hero: A Study of the Romantic Hero in Nineteenth-Century Fiction* (New Haven, 1974), 118.

35 "Biographical Notice" to 1850 edition, *Wuthering Heights*, 35–36.

36 *The Life and Eager Death of Emily Brontë* (London, 1936), 191–92, 133–34.

37 Charlotte Brontë, "Biographical Notice," 41. Dickinson, letter to Mrs. J. G. Holland (Dec. 1881), *Letters*, ed. Thomas H. Johnson and Theodora Ward (Cambridge, Mass., 1958), 3:721. Woolf, *The Common Reader*, 225.

38 Berryman, "Introduction," *The Monk*, 28. Pritchett, *"Wuthering Heights,"* *New Statesman* 31 (22 June 1946): 453.
39 *The Diary of Virginia Woolf*, ed. Anne Olivier Bell (London, 1980), 3:161, 175.
40 For example, poems 95, 157, 190. *The Complete Poems of Emily Jane Brontë*, ed. C. W. Hatfield (New York, 1941).
41 "Introduction," *Wuthering Heights*, 20–21.
42 *The Golden Bough*, 5:268.
43 *Wuthering Heights*, 204.
44 Ibid., 173, 359, 197, 188, 216.

CHAPTER 18. ROMANTIC SHADOWS: SWINBURNE AND PATER

1 *The Golden Bough*, 6:115.
2 *Notes on Poems and Reviews* (1886). *Poems and Ballads, Atalanta in Calydon*, ed. Morse Peckham (Indianapolis, 1970), 334.
3 *The Romantic Agony*, trans. Angus Davidson (Cleveland, 1956), 217.
4 *The Anxiety of Influence*, 100. I substitute the theoretical infinitive for the form Bloom cites.
5 *Cults*, 2:443.
6 *Thalassa*, 60.
7 *Swinburne* (London, 1973), 30.
8 *The Sacred Wood* (New York, 1950), 149.
9 *Notes on Poems and Reviews*, 329.
10 *Mademoiselle de Maupin*, 139.
11 *The Soul of Man Under Socialism*, 279.
12 *Romantic Agony*, 227.
13 *Notes on Poems and Reviews*, 336–37.
14 *The Flight from Woman* (New York, 1965), 172.
15 Quoted in William Butler Yeats, *Autobiography* (New York, 1965), 87.
16 *Selected Writings of Walter Pater*, ed. Harold Bloom (New York, 1974), 60.
17 *Marius the Epicurean*, intro. Osbert Burdett (New York, 1966), 263.
18 *Selected Writings*, 59–60.
19 "Preface" to *The Renaissance*, ibid., 17–18.
20 "The School of Giorgione," ibid., 55.
21 *Decline of the West*, 1:228.
22 *Avowals*, in *Collected Works* (New York, 1923), 9:197–98.
23 "Fin de Siècle," *Ideas and Beliefs of the Victorians* (London, 1949), 370.
24 *Marius the Epicurean*, 74.
25 *The Works of Max Beerbohm* (London, 1922), 129.
26 "Conclusion," in *Selected Writings*, 59.
27 "Leonardo da Vinci," ibid., 46–47.
28 "Leonardo da Vinci," in *Works*, 5:276–77.
29 *Selected Writings of Pater*, xx.
30 *The Oxford Book of Modern Verse 1892–1935* (New York, 1936), viii.
31 *Autobiographies* (London, 1966), 114.
32 Gautier, *Works*, 4:322–24.

CHAPTER 19. APOLLO DAEMONIZED: DECADENT ART

1 *The Pure and the Impure*, in *Earthly Paradise*, ed. Robert Phelps (New York, 1966), 384.
2 *Collected Works*, 5: frontispiece, 428.
3 Quoted in John Nicoll, *The Pre-Raphaelites* (London, 1970), 61. The definitive source for reproductions of Rossetti is Virginia Surtees, *The Paintings and Drawings of Dante Gabriel Rossetti: A Catalogue Raisonné*, 2 vols. (Oxford, 1971).
4 *Pre-Raphaelitism and the Pre-Raphaelite Brotherhood* (New York, 1914), 1:248.
5 *Dramatis Personae* (Indianapolis, 1923), 130–31.
6 *Changing Nature of Man*, 185.
7 *Burne-Jones* (New York, 1973), 67.
8 Quoted in Philippe Jullian, *Dreamers of Decadence*, trans. Robert Baldick (New York, 1971), 43.
9 *Certains*, 19. *L'Art Moderne* (Paris, 1902), 154.
10 *The Father* (1887), in *Six Plays of Strindberg*, trans. Elizabeth Sprigge (Garden City, N.Y., 1955), 54.
11 Quoted in Stanley Weintraub, *Beardsley* (New York, 1967), 131.
12 *Decline of the West*, 1:246.
13 *Self-Portrait with Friends: The Selected Diaries of Cecil Beaton*, ed. Richard Buckle (New York, 1979), 341.
14 *Black and White: A Portrait of Aubrey Beardsley* (New York, 1970), 38.

CHAPTER 20. THE BEAUTIFUL BOY AS DESTROYER: WILDE'S *THE PICTURE OF DORIAN GRAY*

1 *The Picture of Dorian Gray* (Harmondsworth, 1949), 7.
2 Ibid., 23, 103, 26, 29, 7.
3 To the Editor of the *St. James's Gazette*, 26 June 1890, *The Letters of Oscar Wilde*, ed. Rupert Hart-Davis (New York, 1962), 259.
4 *Dorian Gray*, 67, 29.
5 *Crime and Punishment*, trans. Constance Garnett (New York, 1944), 276.
6 *Mademoiselle de Maupin*, 86–87.
7 *The Wit and Humor of Oscar Wilde*, ed. Alvin Redman (1952; rept. New York, 1959), 213. The classy British title of this excellent but textually unreliable collection was *The Epigrams of Oscar Wilde*. Did the New York publisher underestimate American literacy?
8 *Phrases and Philosophies for the Use of the Young*, in *The Prose of Oscar Wilde* (New York, 1935), 305.
9 Wilde, *Selected Writings*, intro. Richard Ellmann (London, 1961), 117.
10 Ibid., 30–31.
11 *Dorian Gray*, 54–55.
12 To Robert Ross, June 1898, *Letters*, 753.
13 *De Profundis*, ibid., 509.
14 *Dorian Gray*, 25, 30, 26, 32, 33.

15 Ibid., 44–45.

16 *Selected Writings of Walter Pater,* 266.

17 *Dorian Gray,* 165.

18 *Phaedrus,* 34.

19 *Dorian Gray,* 12, 128.

20 Ibid., 7. *The Trials of Oscar Wilde,* ed. H. Montgomery Hyde (New York, 1962), 112.

21 *The Critic as Artist,* in *Selected Writings,* 78–79.

22 "On Narcissism," in *Collected Papers,* trans. Joan Riviere (London, 1956), 4:46.

23 *From Max Weber: Essays in Sociology,* ed. and trans. H. H. Gerth and C. Wright Mills (New York, 1946), 262, 249.

24 *Iliad,* 342. *Odyssey,* 108.

25 *Symposium,* in *Xenophon,* trans. O. J. Todd (Cambridge, Mass., 1968), IV:537.

26 *A Rhetoric of Motives,* 210.

27 *Dorian Gray,* 167, 184.

28 Ibid., 70, 158, 134, 138, 101.

29 *Phrases and Philosophies,* 305. *De Profundis,* 425.

30 *The Original Four-Act Version of "The Importance of Being Earnest,"* foreword by Vyvyan Holland (London, 1957), 62–63. I am grateful to Robert L. Caserio for alerting me to the discrepancies between the present three-act version of *The Importance of Being Earnest* and the four-act original, which Wilde cut down at the request of his producer to make time for a curtain-raiser.

31 *Sebastian Melmoth,* in *Prose,* 655.

32 *Dorian Gray,* 85, 23.

33 Ibid., 175.

34 May 1895, *Letters,* 397.

35 *De Profundis, Letters,* 429.

36 Ibid., 500.

37 *Dorian Gray,* 130, 35, 119, 143.

38 Ibid., 119–20.

39 *Phrases and Philosophies,* 309.

40 *Dorian Gray,* 129, 157.

41 Ibid., 226, 248.

42 Ibid., 131.

43 *Marius the Epicurean,* 53.

44 *The Golden Bough,* 9:276–78.

45 *Dorian Gray,* 157.

46 *The Golden Bough,* 11:95, 277.

47 *Selected Writings,* 109.

48 To Robert Ross, 16 April 1900, *Letters,* 820.

49 *Selected Writings,* 1.

50 *Dorian Gray,* 156, 247, 175.

51 Ibid., 176, 192, 181–82.

52 *Plays* (Harmondsworth, 1954), 153.

CHAPTER 21. THE ENGLISH EPICENE: WILDE'S *THE IMPORTANCE OF BEING EARNEST*

1 *Dorian Gray*, 28, 90. *Wit and Humor*, 214.
2 *Dorian Gray*, 39. *The Soul of Man Under Socialism*, 270. *Selected Writings*, 64, 87–88, 91.
3 *Politics and the Arts: Letter to M. D'Alembert on the Theatre*, trans. Allan Bloom (Ithaca, 1960), 101.
4 *Saint Genet*, trans. Bernard Frechtman (New York, 1963), 410.
5 *The Nude*, 197.
6 *Plays*, 220.
7 Quoted by Yeats, *Oxford Book of Modern Verse*, x.
8 *Dorian Gray*, 158.
9 *Original Four-Act*, 112.
10 All quotations from the present three-act *The Importance of Being Earnest* are from *Plays*, 253–313.
11 *An Ideal Husband*, in *Plays*, 205.
12 *Hero and Leander* (1598), III.117–18.
13 *Dorian Gray*, 66.
14 Ibid., 124.
15 *The Social History of Art*, 1:41.
16 *Plays*, 122, 187.
17 *Dorian Gray*, 68.
18 *Sade Fourier Loyola*, 31.
19 *De Profundis, Letters*, 490–91.
20 *Selections from Ralph Waldo Emerson*, ed. Stephen E. Whicher (Boston, 1957), 347.
21 *Without Feathers* (New York, 1976), 10.
22 *Beyond Formalism*, 48–49. See also Hartman, "Wordsworth, Inscriptions, and Romantic Nature Poetry," in *From Sensibility to Romanticism*, ed. Frederick W. Hilles (New York, 1965), 405.
23 *Dorian Gray*, 110.
24 *Through the Looking-Glass* (New York, 1946), 153.
25 *Selected Writings*, 112. *Plays*, 166.
26 *Black Ship to Hell* (New York, 1962), 341.
27 *Three Plays by Noel Coward*, intro. Edward Albee (New York, 1965), 240.
28 *Emma*, ed. Ronald Blythe (Harmondsworth, 1966), 37.
29 The first quotation is from Carroll's friend Isa Bowman, the second from his nephew Stuart Dodgson Collingwood. Quoted in Jean Gattegno, *Lewis Carroll: Fragments of a Looking-Glass*, trans. Rosemary Sheed (New York, 1976), 256, 283, 281–82. See also Phyllis Greenacre, *Swift and Carroll: A Psychoanalytic Study of Two Lives* (New York, 1955), 166. William Empson, *Some Versions of Pastoral* (New York, 1968), 273.
30 "*Alice* on the Stage" (1887), in *Alice in Wonderland*, ed. Donald J. Gray, Norton Critical Edition (New York, 1971), 283.
31 *The Complete Works of Lewis Carroll*, intro. Alexander Woollcott (London, 1939), 1113–14.

32 Professor Frederick York Powell and Rev. William Tuckwell, quoted in Greenacre, *Swift and Carroll*, 142, 141, 168.

33 5 April 1927. *The Letters of Virginia Woolf*, ed. Nigel Nicolson (New York, 1977), 3:360.

34 Johann Peter Eckermann, *Conversations with Goethe*, trans. John Oxenford (London, 1970), 254–55.

35 *Howards End* (New York, 1921), 141.

36 "Strix," "Posh Lingo," in *Noblesse Oblige: An Enquiry into the Identifiable Characteristics of the English Aristocracy*, ed. Nancy Mitford (New York, 1956), 130.

37 *Through the Looking-Glass*, 155.

38 *The Theory of the Leisure Class: An Economic Study of Institutions* (New York, 1934), 47.

39 "The Unimportance of Being Oscar," in *Wilde: A Collection of Critical Essays*, ed. Richard Ellmann, (Englewood Cliffs, N.J., 1969), 108.

40 *The Sovereign Flower: On Shakespeare as the Poet of Royalism* (London, 1958), 223. *Atlantic Crossing*, 330. See also *Byron and Shakespeare* (London, 1966), 338 and *The Sovereign Flower*, 270.

41 *Plays, Prose Writings, and Poems*, 267.

42 *Trials*, 127, 129–30.

43 *Plays*, 80, 85. *Dorian Gray*, 111.

44 *A Woman of No Importance*, in *Plays*, 91.

45 *Original Four-Act*, 54.

46 Goethe, *Wilhelm Meister's Apprenticeship*, 274. Nietzsche, *The Will to Power*, 496. Veblen, *Leisure Class*, 52–53.

47 *Atlantic Crossing*, 109.

48 *Phrases and Philosophies*, in *Prose*, 306. *The Critic as Artist*, in *Selected Writings*, 102.

49 *On Love: Aspects of a Single Theme*, trans. Toby Talbot (Cleveland, 1957), 162.

50 *Plays*, 346.

51 *A Natural Perspective: The Development of Shakespearean Comedy and Romance* (New York, 1965), 119.

52 *The Decay of Lying*, in *Selected Writings*, 27, 1.

53 *Phrases and Philosophies*, in *Prose*, 305. *The Critic as Artist*, in *Selected Writings*, 86. *The Decay of Lying*, ibid., 2.

54 In conversation, *Wit and Humor*, 127. *The Wit of Oscar Wilde*, comp. Sean McCann (London, 1969), 78. To Robert Ross, 31 May 1898, *Letters*, 749.

55 *Wit and Humor*, 66. *The Wit of Oscar Wilde*, 33.

56 *Complete Works of Oscar Wilde*, intro. Vyvyan Holland (London, 1948), 356. Holland elsewhere gives a different version: "Exeunt into garden with scornful looks." *Original Four-Act*, 82.

57 *Wit and Humor*, 84. *Dorian Gray*, 48, 43, 90. *Trials*, 108. *Picture*, 25.

58 *De Profundis*, *Letters*, 491–92.

59 Ibid., 472–73.

60 Ibid., 481.

61 *Selected Writings*, 27. *De Profundis*, *Letters*, 509.

62 *De Profundis, Letters*, 478.

63 Ibid., 501, 466.

64 *Selected Writings*, vii. My book was completed before the publication of Ellmann's long-awaited biography of Wilde.

65 *The Critic as Artist*, in *Selected Writings*, 88–89.

CHAPTER 22. AMERICAN DECADENTS:
POE, HAWTHORNE, MELVILLE

1 *Love and Death in the American Novel* (New York, rev. ed. 1966), 350–51.

2 *Against Nature*, 191.

3 *Great Short Works of Edgar Allan Poe*, ed. G. R. Thompson (New York, 1970), 180–81, 176. Milton, *Comus*, 880.

4 *Great Short Works of Poe*, 192–93.

5 Ibid., 158.

6 Ibid., 158–59. The following quotations: 161, 159.

7 Ibid., 317. Following quotation: 329.

8 Ibid., 217, 238, 219.

9 Ibid., 359, 361.

10 *Venus in Furs*, 104.

11 *Great Short Works of Poe*, 383, 371–72, 383–84, 186.

12 Ibid., 535.

13 *Selected Writings of Edgar Allan Poe*, ed. Edward H. Davidson (Boston, 1956), 403–05.

14 *Great Short Works of Nathaniel Hawthorne*, ed. Frederick C. Crews (New York, 1967), 288–89, 291.

15 Ibid., 301, 49.

16 Ibid., 9.

17 *Love and Death*, 230.

18 *Great Short Works of Hawthorne*, 64, 146, 201, 81.

19 Ibid., 72, 46, 136, 161, 170.

20 Ibid., 131.

21 Ibid., 168–69.

22 Ibid., 50.

23 *Moby-Dick*, ed. Harrison Hayford and Hershel Parker (New York, 1967), 155, 169.

24 Ibid., 235, 262, 125, 98, 85, 255, 237, 255.

25 Ibid., 373–74.

26 Ibid., 324–26. *Great Short Works of Melville*, ed. Warner Berthoff (New York, 1970), 486.

27 *Moby-Dick*, 97. Lawrence, *Studies in Classic American Literature* (New York, 1961), 136.

28 *Moby-Dick*, 326. *Great Short Works of Hawthorne*, 301.

29 *Moby-Dick*, 328, 347–51.

30 Ibid., 315, 426–27. Violence or rape: 316, 447.

31 Ibid., 32–34, 54, 53, 67, 363, 148, 152, 469, 416, 353.

32 Ibid., 469, 143, 385, 111, 391, 417.

33 Ibid., 110, 417, 445, 459, 241, 104.
34 Ibid., 163, 290.
35 *Selected Writings of Poe*, 379, 382.
36 *Great Short Works of Melville*, 211, 216–18. *Selected Writings of Poe*, 370.
37 *Great Short Works of Melville*, 214.
38 Ibid., 215, 221.
39 Ibid., 222.
40 *Love and Death*, 348, 362.
41 *Billy Budd, Sailor*, Reading Text and Genetic Text ed. from the Manuscript, Intro. and Notes, Harrison Hayford and Merton M. Sealts, Jr. (Chicago, 1962), 2.
42 *Great Short Works of Melville*, 436, 459, 434, 436, 478, 494–95, 436, 476, 438, 436–37, 455, 438, 430–31.
43 Ibid., 430, 437, 433.
44 Ibid., 459, 469, 459, 454, 476.
45 Ibid., 433. Auden, *The Enchafèd Flood or the Romantic Iconography of the Sea* (New York, 1950), 149n.
46 *Herman Melville: A Critical Study* (New York, 1949), 266.
47 *Great Short Works of Melville*, 463, 437, 498. Next quotation: 497.
48 *Death in Venice*, trans. Kenneth Burke (New York, 1965), 91, 114, 5.
49 Ibid., 39–42.
50 Ibid., 41, 69, 45, 72.
51 Ibid., 40, 82.
52 Ibid., 88, 103.

CHAPTER 23. AMERICAN DECADENTS: EMERSON, WHITMAN, JAMES

1 *Selections from Emerson*, 236, 235.
2 Ibid., 168.
3 Ibid., 24.
4 "Uriel's Cloud: Emerson's Rhetoric," *The Georgia Review* 31, no. 2. (Summer 1977): 327.
5 Ibid.
6 *Journals*, ed. Merton M. Sealts, Jr. (Cambridge, Mass., 1965), 5:329.
7 *Selections from Emerson*, 276, 257, 255, 237.
8 Ibid., 219, 350, 32.
9 Ibid., 334.
10 "As I Ebb'd with the Ocean of Life." *Song of Myself*, 21, 3, 24.
11 Ibid., 16; *The Sleepers; Song*, 33, 45, 24; "As I Ebb'd"; *Song*, 51.
12 *Song*, 24, 11.
13 Ibid., 41.
14 *Studies in Classic American Literature*, 165–66.
15 *Song*, 20, 24, 23.
16 Ibid., 21; "I Sing the Body Electric"; *Song*, 28; *The Sleepers*.
17 *Song*, 5, 33.
18 Ibid., 22, 24.
19 *Saint Genet*, 353.

20 *The Ambassadors*, ed. R. W. Stallman (New York, 1960), 208, 134.

21 *Ambassadors*, 305. *The Complete Tales of Henry James*, ed. Leon Edel (Philadelphia, 1964), 9:95. *The Wings of the Dove*, ed. F. W. Dupee (New York, 1964), 124, 61, 71, 118–19.

22 *Wings of the Dove*, 420, 359, 242, 241, 278, 257.

23 *The Portrait of a Lady*, ed. Oscar Cargill (New York, 1963), 34–35, 312, 111.

24 Ibid., 227, 376, 477.

25 *Wings of the Dove*, 126, 331–32.

26 *The Bostonians*, ed. Irving Howe (New York, 1956), 37, 337, 339.

27 *The Triple Thinkers* (New York, 1938), 128.

28 *The Blithedale Romance*, 274, 273.

29 *Great Short Works of Henry James*, ed. Dean Flower (New York, 1966), 356, 402.

30 *A Rhetoric of Motives*, 117.

31 *Beyond Formalism*, 53.

32 *Great Short Works of James*, 368, 370, 381, 383.

33 Ibid., 401, 416.

34 Although James was in London during the final performances of *The Importance of Being Earnest* after Wilde's arrest, Leon Edel claims James did not see it until 1909. *The Complete Notebooks of Henry James*, ed. Edel and Lyall H. Powers (New York, 1987), 308. Wilde's son, Vyvyan Holland, says the first publication of the three-act play was in a limited edition in 1899. *Original Four-Act*, xii.

35 *Great Short Works of James*, 394, 445.

36 Ibid., 414, 383, 413, 426. *Great Short Works of Poe*, 193. *James*, 372, 382.

37 *The Blithedale Romance*, 276.

38 *Henry James* (New York, 1916), 107–10.

39 *The Golden Bowl*, ed. R. P. Blackmur (New York, 1963), 50.

40 *Ambassadors*, 279.

41 *Aspects of the Novel* (New York, 1927), 160–61.

42 "The Decay of Lying," in *Selected Writings*, 6.

43 *Golden Bowl*, 299.

44 *Wings of the Dove*, 20.

45 Ibid., 166, 173.

46 Ibid., 21.

47 *Ambassadors*, 191, 274.

48 *Golden Bowl*, 441, 186.

49 Ibid., 300.

50 *Wings of the Dove*, 124.

51 *Golden Bowl*, 273.

52 *Henry James*, 112–13.

53 *Ambassadors*, 101. *Wings of the Dove*, 178. Robert L. Caserio drew the latter to my attention.

54 *Portrait*, 33. *Wings*, 298.

55 *Portrait*, 283. *Great Short Works of James*, 50.

56 *Portrait*, 448.

57 *Golden Bowl*, 230.

58 *Avowals*, 209.

CHAPTER 24. AMHERST'S MADAME DE SADE:
EMILY DICKINSON

1 556. All other poem numbers will be indicated in the text. Numbering
   follows *The Poems of Emily Dickinson*, 3 vols., ed. Thomas H. Johnson
   (Cambridge, Mass., 1955). For ease of reading, I sometimes remove dashes
   from poem lines run in with the text.
2 For Dickinson's familiarity with Poe, see Jack L. Capps, *Emily Dickinson's
   Reading 1836–1886* (Cambridge, Mass., 1966), 19, 120–21.
3 243, 1123, 1612, 488, 1433.
4 To Thomas Wentworth Higginson, 25 April 1862. *Letters*, 2:404.
5 "Emily Dickinson's Notation," in *Emily Dickinson: A Collection of Critical
   Essays*, ed. Richard B. Sewall (Englewood Cliffs, N.J., 1963), 81.
6 To Louise and Frances Norcross, 7 Oct. 1863, *Letters*, 2:427. To Abiah Root,
   12 Jan. 1846, 1:24. To Dr. and Mrs. J. G. Holland, autumn 1853, 1:264.
7 Aug. 1862, *Letters*, 2:414; 473–74.
8 To Louise and Frances Norcross, ca. 1864, *Letters*, 2:436. To Higginson,
   25 April 1862, 2:404.
9 *Emily Dickinson* (New York, 1951), 203, 93–94.
10 July 1862, *Letters*, 2:412.
11 Quoted in letter from Higginson to his wife, 17 Aug. 1870, *Letters*, 2:475.
12 *Emily Dickinson*, 226.
13 Poems: 986, 1487, 1545, 389, 689, 652, 1466, 801, 1499, 230, 312, 497.
   Letters: to Mrs. Holland, 2 March 1859, 2:350. To Louise and Frances
   Norcross, Oct. 1871, 2:491. To Mrs. Holland, March 1866, 2:449. To her
   nephew Ned Dickinson, ca. 1878, 2:622. To Mrs. Holland, Aug. 1876,
   2:561. To the unknown "Master," ca. 1861, 2:374.
14 466, 1090, 368, 980. Cf. also 683, 98.
15 Noah Webster, *An American Dictionary of the English Language*, 2 vols.
   (New York, 1828). George F. Whicher calls the 1847 edition of Webster's
   "the lexicon that she studied." *This Was a Poet: A Critical Biography of Emily
   Dickinson* (New York, 1938), 232. I am assuming that the first edition of
   1828 must also have been in her father's collection.
16 To Mrs. Holland, Aug. 1856, *Letters*, 2:330.
17 *Atlantic Crossing*, 106–07.
18 In a letter to Mabel Loomis Todd after Dickinson's death: "One poem only I
   dread a little to print—that wonderful 'Wild Nights',—lest the malignant
   read into it more than that virgin recluse ever dreamed of putting there."
   21 April 1891. Dickinson, *Poems*, 1:180.
19 *Psychological Types*, 138.
20 *Summa Theologica*, in *Basic Writings*, 1:1057.
21 To Martha Gilbert Smith, ca. 1884, *Letters*, 3:823.
22 To Charles Brown, 23 Sept. 1819, *Letters*, 2:181.
23 To the Hollands, Sept. 1859, *Letters*, 2:353.
24 *A Room of One's Own*, 51.
25 To Higginson, July 1875, *Letters*, 2:542. To Louise and Frances Norcross,
   Aug. 1876, 2:560.
26 To J. Edward Austen, 16 Dec. 1816. *Jane Austen's Letters*, ed. R. W. Chapman (London, 1952), 469.

27 To Higginson, 7 June 1862, *Letters*, 2:409.

28 *Saint Genet*, 398.

29 To Higginson, 25 April 1862, *Letters*, 2:404. To Mrs. Holland, Summer 1873, 2:508. Woolf, *Letters*, 2:312.

30 To Higginson, 1876, *Letters*, 2:554.

31 84, 237, 791, 425, 873, 874, 130, 163.

32 To Higginson, July 1862, *Letters*, 2:411.

33 The phrase, transcribed by my father from my grandmother's Ceccanese dialect, sounded like "Sola sola cómina *yuke*." Since the standard Italian word for owl is *gufo*, this bird must be the *allocco*, a bigger, stockier tawny mountain owl. Its Latin name, *Strix aluco*, seems to survive in the Ceccanese pronunciation.

34 To Higginson, Aug. 1862, *Letters*, 2:415.

35 16–17 Aug. 1870, *Letters*, 2:473, 476. Writing to his sister, Higginson jokes somewhat condescendingly about "my partially cracked poetess at Amherst." 28 Dec. 1876, 2:570.

36 *The Vampire: His Kith and Kin* (London, 1928), 133–34.

37 13 Jan. 1854, *Letters*, 1:282–83.

38 For startling examples of the fondling and delicatessenlike carving and devouring of corpses, see Richard von Krafft-Ebing, *Psychopathia Sexualis*, trans. Franklin S. Klaf (1886; New York, 1965), 78–82. Wilhelm Stekel, *Sadism and Masochism: The Psychology of Hatred and Cruelty*, trans. Louise Brink (1925; New York, 1953), 2:248–330.

39 To Abbie C. Farley, Aug. 1885, *Letters*, 3:883. To Mrs. James S. Cooper, ca. 1876, 2:556.

40 To Mrs. Holland, 1860, *Letters*, 2:369.

41 To Higginson, June 1869, *Letters*, 2:460.

42 To Mrs. Holland, early 1877, *Letters*, 2:572.

43 *Letters*, 2:589–90.

44 Early July 1879, *Letters*, 2:643.

45 *The Soul of Man Under Socialism*, in *Plays, Prose Writings, and Poems*, 287. *De Profundis, Letters*, 474.

46 On Hawthorne: to Higginson, Dec. 1879, *Letters*, 2:649. To Susan Gilbert Dickinson, ca. 1878, 2:631. Prose fragment to unidentified recipient, 3:924.

47 To Susan Gilbert Dickinson, ca. 1868, *Letters*, 2:458. To Austin Dickinson, 10 Oct. 1851, *Letters*, 1:146. Nuns and Madonnas: 648, 722, 918. Johnson, in *Poems*, 1:106.

48 Ca. 1878, *Letters*, 2:631 (complete).

49 *Letters*, 2:639; 2:473.

50 27 June 1852, *Letters*, 1:215; 27 Nov.–Dec. 1854, 1:310; ca. 1874, 2:533. From *Antony and Cleopatra* (III.xi.56–61). Ca. 1882, *Letters*, 3:733 (complete).

51 Ca. 1864, *Letters*, 2:430.

52 Emily Dickinson, *The Single Hound: Poems of a Lifetime*, intro. Martha Dickinson Bianchi (Boston, 1915), xv.

53 *The White Goddess: A Historical Grammar of Poetic Myth* (New York, 1966), 14, 24, 446–47.

Index

Abrams, M. H., 317, 378, 379
Achilles, 90, 183, 260–64, 281. *See also* Homer
Adam, 40, 52, 274, 285, 289, 377
Adelman, Janet, 217
Adonis, 52, 53, 89, 110, 122, 148, 190, 192, 194, 197, 255, 366, 381, 386, 391, 437, 438, 465, 513, 514, 523, 589, 594, 596
aegis, 83, 259, 436, 504, 538, 621. *See also* Athena
Aeneas. *See* Vergil
Aeschylus: *Oresteia*, 6, 46, 51, 99–102, 104, 108, 109, 158, 230, 239, 436, 447, 466–67, 468, 470, 565, 589
Akhenaten, 67, 68, 69, 70
alchemy, 62, 85, 88, 198–99, 206, 208, 209–11, 213, 226, 228, 254–56, 318, 341, 374
Alcibiades, 122, 330, 364, 515, 522, 524
Aldrich, Robert, 415
allegorical repletion, 157, 211, 447, 493, 638
Allen, Don Cameron, 355
Allen, Gracie, 47
Allen, Woody, 543
Amazons, 77–78, 128–29, 160, 165, 175–85 passim, 199, 209, 210, 211, 223, 227, 232, 249, 252, 259, 260–65, 286, 296–97, 351, 352, 373, 398, 399, 422, 437, 441, 444, 504, 505, 513, 620, 625–26, 635, 643. *See also* Camilla; Penthesilea
androgyne of manners, 531–35, 536, 537, 538, 539–40, 543, 544, 552, 562, 565, 567
androgyny, 21–22, 45, 70, 82, 84–86, 88, 89, 125, 136–37, 142, 169, 183–84, 198–99, 204–08, 213,

227, 249, 252, 270–71, 312, 328–29, 345, 350–52, 373, 381, 386–87, 390, 402–05, 417, 439–44, 480, 489, 494. *See also* castrati; Hermaphrodite; transsexualism; transvestism
android, 68, 367–69, 494, 537–38, 563, 647. *See also* manufactured object
Antinous, 118, 122, 124, 134, 375, 513, 515, 593
Antonelli, Lenora, 127
Aphrodite, 42, 44, 52, 74, 87, 89, 463; *of Knidos*, 106, 123, 177. *See also* Venus
Apollinaire, Guillaume, 46
Apollo, 12, 28, 30, 46, 73–74, 93, 96–97, 101, 102, 104–05, 111, 112, 115, 117, 124, 132, 215, 239, 383, 386–87, 568; *Belvedere*, 104, 163. *See also* Spenser
apotropaion: defined, 49–50
Apuleius, 43, 138
Arbus, Diane, 557
Ariosto, Ludovico, 78, 171, 179, 181, 182, 249
Aristophanes, 17
Aristotle, 6, 7, 255, 468
armour, 31, 148, 150, 172, 173–75, 192–93, 199, 211–12
Arnold, Matthew, 298, 356
Art Deco, 409, 496
Artemis, 43, 46, 74–81, 93, 106, 110, 160, 175, 176, 296, 400, 442, 450, 466, 467; *of Ephesus*, 42, 75–76, 77, 176, 244, 256, 262, 397, 508, 583, 626. *See also* Diana
Arthur, Bea, 681
Art Nouveau, 409, 496–97, 506, 532–33, 539, 540
Ashton, Sir Frederick, 551

Asquith, Anthony, 535
Astaire, Fred, 357, 533
astrology, 198, 221, 222–26, 318, 337, 681
Atalanta, 181, 195, 210, 212, 466–70, 506
Athena, 48, 71, 74, 80, 81–87, 88, 89, 96, 100, 106, 107, 148, 179, 181, 255, 366, 368, 386, 501, 504, 521, 542, 565, 568, 589, 635; Palladium, 56, 259, 442. *See also* aegis
Auden, W. H., 594
Audran, Stéphane, 346, 430
Augustine, St., 17, 137–38, 176, 230, 232, 299, 377, 444, 598
Augustus Caesar, 126, 130, 214–15, 224–25
Austen, Jane, 439, 556, 611, 615, 623, 656; *Emma*, 199, 320–21, 441, 444, 545–46
autoeroticism, 41, 82, 165, 189, 190, 243, 253, 256, 277, 330, 378, 413, 415, 496, 500, 506, 540, 582, 604, 607, 619, 635. *See also* Khepera; narcissism
Avedon, Luciana, 368–69, 686
Avengers, The, 416, 551

Bacall, Lauren, 346, 413
Bachelard, Gaston, 443
Bachofen, Johann Jakob, 42
Baker, Carlos, 372
Baker, Roger, 205
Baldick, Robert, 570, 689
Ball, Lucille, 220, 550, 645, 681
ballet, 105, 356–57, 408, 551
Balzac, Honoré de: 132, 252, 309–407, 412, 430, 439, 443, 531, 545, 572, 573; *Cousin Bette*, 406–07, 437, 440, 441, 498–99, 613; *The Girl with the Golden Eyes*, 267, 342, 352, 392, 394–402, 404, 405, 406, 410, 417, 420, 425–26, 428, 437, 438, 455, 464, 474, 477, 513, 526, 558, 575, 576, 578, 593, 600, 605, 610, 628–29; *Lost Illusions*, 406, 442, 516; *Sarrasine*, 249,

389–94, 395, 398, 411, 413, 518, 526, 613; *Seraphita*, 267, 371, 402–06, 407, 408–09, 501, 518, 593
Barbey d'Aurevilly, J.-A., 428, 429, 689
Barbu, Zevedei, 109
Baroque art, 169, 185, 214, 228, 356, 490, 493, 508, 629, 642, 667
Barthes, Roland, 179, 246, 391, 542
Baryshnikov, Mikhail, 357
Barzini, Luigi, 221
Bate, Walter Jackson, 384–85
Bateson, F. W., 313, 314
Bathory, Countess Erzsebet, 247
Baudelaire, Charles, 24, 66, 122, 131, 160, 170, 190, 238, 247, 279, 296, 300, 320, 322, 373, 395, 408, 421–30, 431–44 passim, 460–70 passim, 480, 485, 486, 487, 504, 508, 512, 513, 529, 535, 553, 559, 565, 570, 572, 578, 585, 603–10 passim, 624, 630, 633, 647, 649–56 passim, 667, 673; "A Carcass," 290, 424–25, 433, 471, 566, 592; "Delphine and Hippolyte," 342, 392, 425–28, 472–78 passim, 573; "A Voyage to Cythera," 423–24, 427, 432, 436, 475, 563, 613, 627, 649, 654
Beach Boys, 358–59
Beardsley, Aubrey, 41, 320, 325, 462, 490, 491, 496, 505–11, 563–65, 607, 613, 627
Beaton, Cecil, 506
beautiful boy, the, 32, 109–23, 136, 148–49, 162, 168, 169, 179, 205–08, 211, 250, 252, 255, 267, 295, 309, 329, 352, 371, 376, 412, 492–93, 500, 505, 512–30, 571, 593–97. *See also* kouros
Beauvoir, Simone de, 246
Beckett, Samuel, 562
Beerbohm, Max, 484
Beethoven, Ludwig von, 260
Bellini, Giovanni, 71
Benderson, Bruce, 115
Benevento Boy, The, 118, 119

Benjamin, Walter, 426
Bergman, Ingmar, 152, 294, 325
Berkeley, Busby, 241, 650
Bernhardt, Sarah, 497
Bernheimer, Richard, 201
Bernini, Giovanni Lorenzo, 141,
    149, 169, 228, 627, 629, 637
Berryman, John, 455
Beverly Hillbillies, The, 538
Black Death, the, 140–41, 576
Blackstone, Bernard, 359
Blake, William: 3, 23, 167, 173, 185,
    190, 195, 215, 231, 235–46 pas-
    sim, 253, 254, 270–99, 300, 303,
    304, 314, 316, 334, 340, 347, 349,
    359, 365, 366, 372, 381, 388, 392,
    401, 452, 476, 486, 491, 506, 508,
    512, 528, 561, 570, 585, 587, 601,
    610, 611, 624, 636, 639, 640, 642,
    648, 650, 652, 658, 666, 672, 673;
    "The Crystal Cabinet," 283–87,
    324, 396, 493, 664; *Four Zoas*,
    290, 293, 297; "Infant Joy," 272–
    76, 282, 311, 333, 474, 496, 497,
    604, 613, 616, 660; *Jerusalem*,
    291, 296, 591; "London," 279–80,
    282, 422, 433, 635; *The Mental
    Traveller*, 280–83, 285, 287, 465–
    66, 614, 618; "The Sick Rose,"
    276–78, 352, 378, 398, 434, 487,
    525, 628
Blessington, Marguerite Power,
    Countess of, 352, 360–61, 394
blondeness, 73–74, 177, 513, 593,
    629
Bloom, Harold, 4, 246, 259, 272,
    286, 294, 295, 307, 309, 310, 312,
    321, 328, 333, 334, 338, 346, 352,
    354, 367, 373, 385, 386, 486
Boccaccio, Giovanni, 140–41, 191–
    92, 243, 576
Bogarde, Dirk, 289
Boiardo, Matteo Maria, 78, 179
Boland, Mary, 556
Bonheur, Rosa, 294, 454, 640
Bostetter, Edward E., 321, 342
Botticelli, Sandro, 61, 73, 149–53,
    156, 170, 173, 195, 207, 228, 491,

512, 570; *The Birth of Venus*, 51,
    79, 92, 148, 150–51, 152, 155,
    168, 178, 329; *Primavera*, 150,
    151–52, 153, 178, 493, 497, 508,
    511, 612; *Nastagio degli Onesti*,
    191–92; *Venus and Mars*, 167, 171,
    187–88, 214
Boucher, François, 79, 80
Bowie, David, 368, 506
Boyer, Charles, 550
Bradley, A. C., 213
Breuer, Marcel, 664
Brontë, Anne, 454, 457
Brontë, Branwell, 453–54, 457, 458
Brontë, Charlotte, 444–45, 453, 454,
    457, 611, 643, 668
Brontë, Emily, 157, 265, 294, 404,
    439, 444–59, 461, 473, 611, 614,
    640, 653–62 passim, 672–73
Brontë, Maria, 457
Bronzino, Agnolo, 115, 150, 178,
    534
Brophy, Brigid, 506, 545
Browne, Sir Thomas, 663
Browning, Elizabeth Barrett, 637,
    639, 657
Browning, Robert, 637
Brynner, Yul, 366
Buckingham, George Villiers, 1st
    Duke of, 165, 363–64, 521
Budge, E. A. Wallis, 62, 675
Bunyan, John, 173
Burckhardt, Jacob, 141, 177, 199
Burckhardt, Titus, 198
Burgess, Anthony, 368
Burke, Edmund, 269
Burke, Kenneth, 177, 198, 339, 612
Burne-Jones, Edward, 122, 150, 320,
    476, 490, 491, 493, 494–99, 500,
    504, 506, 585
Bush, Douglas, 379, 384, 441
Byron, George Gordon, 6th Baron,
    115, 165, 199, 232, 251, 261, 265,
    306, 331–32, 309, 342, 347–64,
    365, 371, 378, 381, 395, 400, 404,
    409–10, 418, 421, 449–59 passim,
    477, 483, 521, 572, 573, 588; *Don
    Juan*, 352–59, 391, 397, 401, 402,

Byron, George Gordon (*cont.*)
413, 443, 486; "Lara," 349–50,
411; *Manfred*, 347–49, 354, 366,
377, 403, 446, 457, 474, 524, 529,
576, 646; *Sardanapalus*, 350–52,
377, 397, 403, 525, 640
Byzantine art, 53, 112, 113, 138,
148, 150, 168, 171, 179, 193, 197,
267, 362, 407, 490, 498, 501, 504,
507, 513, 581, 621

Caligula, 25, 134
Callas, Maria, 54
Callimachus, 46
Camilla, 77, 84, 128–29, 181, 210,
356, 357, 358. *See also* Vergil
camp, 209, 219, 557
Campbell, Joseph, 115–16
Camus, Albert, 257
capitalism, 36–37, 38
Caravaggio, Michelangelo da, 149
Carlyle, Thomas, 252, 343, 689
Carpenter, Rhys, 123
Carroll, Lewis, 74, 220, 244, 290,
313, 322, 343, 434, 464, 531, 536,
541, 544, 546–49, 551–56 passim,
614, 619, 623, 628, 634, 638, 641,
650, 670
Casanova, Giovanni, 254, 393
Casarès, Maria, 346
Caserio, Robert L., 690, 693, 698
Cassirer, Ernst, 97
Cassius Dio, 134–36
Castiglione, Baldassare, 141–43,
171, 183, 232, 428, 533
castrati, 205, 354, 391–94
castration, 23, 44, 51, 101, 138, 184,
236, 242, 245, 261, 296, 301, 340,
423, 507, 622, 654
Catherine, St., 626
Catholicism, Roman, 33, 127–28,
139, 149, 157, 393, 462, 493, 516,
573, 625, 629, 630, 668–69, 671.
See also Christianity; Italians;
Mary; Protestantism
cats, 64–66, 70, 422, 429
Catullus, 44, 121, 131–33, 253, 377,
404

Ceccano, Italy, 700
Cecil, David, 445–46, 484
Cellini, Benvenuto, 144–46, 169,
176, 380, 392, 405, 513, 532, 538,
583, 589
Cézanne, Paul, 490
Chaplin, Charlie, 171
Chapman, George, 535
Charbonneau, Patricia, 212
charisma, 329, 330, 360, 363–64,
521, 523, 593, 594. *See also* glam-
our
Chase, Richard, 637–38, 640
Chaucer, Geoffrey, 171–72, 181
Chephren, 57, 59, 60, 68, 150, 172
Chopin, Frédéric, 265, 354, 406, 440
Christ. *See* Jesus Christ
Christensen, Kent, 227
Christianity, 3–4, 8, 11, 18, 23, 25–
26, 28, 30–31, 33, 40, 72, 89, 98,
137–39, 191, 222, 236, 268–69,
331–32, 345, 410, 412, 423. *See
also* Catholicism; Jesus; Judaism;
Protestantism
Christie, Julie, 550–51
chthonian: defined, 5
cinema, 31, 32, 61, 74, 86, 131, 136,
172, 173, 177, 192, 193, 213, 267–
69, 322, 346, 371, 399, 460; *All
About Eve*, 291, 507, 551; *Auntie
Mame*, 220; *Belle de Jour*, 368; *Les
Biches*, 346, 430; *The Birds*, 51;
Chien andalou, 645; *Cleopatra*,
144; *Les Dames du Bois de
Boulogne*, 346; *Darling*, 550–51;
Daughters of Darkness, 268; *Desert
Hearts*, 212; *LaDolce Vita*, 566;
Fantasia, 435; *Gone with the Wind*,
146, 199, 430, 513; *The Good
Earth*, 363; *The Hunger*, 268; *The
Importance of Being Earnest*, 368,
535; *Indiscreet*, 533; *The Lady
from Shanghai*, 285; *Leave Her to
Heaven*, 368; *The Legend of Lylah
Clare*, 415–16; *Marnie*, 118; *Mo-
rocco*, 346; *National Velvet*, 350;
Orphée, 346; *Persona*, 294; *The
Philadelphia Story*, 80, 199;

Psycho, 399–400, 505, 669; *Queen Christina*, 416; *Repulsion*, 368; *The Servant*, 289; *Snow White*, 346; *Suddenly Last Summer*, 53, 263, 435; *Sylvia Scarlett*, 416; *The Ten Commandments*, 366; *The Three Musketeers*, 363; *Through a Glass Darkly*, 325; *The Towering Inferno*, 269; *Vertigo*, 368; *Who's Afraid of Virginia Woolf?* 291, 507; *Woman of the Year*, 144; *The Women*, 556; *Wuthering Heights*, 690; *Young Man with a Horn*, 346. See also individual actors, directors
Circe, 52, 108, 284, 339, 367, 385, 664. *See also* Homer
clams, 92–93
Clark, Kenneth, 56, 78, 79, 123, 150, 160, 163, 167, 532
Cleopatra, 130, 144, 397, 417–19, 421, 499, 565. *See also* Shakespeare
Clift, Montgomery, 689
Clytemnestra, 100–01, 102, 256, 466, 468, 563, 589. *See also* Aeschylus
Coburn, Kathleen, 341–42
Cocteau, Jean, 122, 498
Cody, John, 671
Colapietro, Vincenza, 660–61, 700
Coleridge, Samuel Taylor, 6, 41, 85, 105, 122, 169, 170, 197, 198, 232–33, 235, 265, 281, 300, 307–14 passim, 317–46, 347, 354, 358, 365, 381, 389, 421, 439, 449, 451, 454, 460, 461, 479, 554, 565, 569, 572, 578, 623, 624; *Christabel*, 50–51, 130, 187, 191, 266, 268, 317–24 passim, 326, 330, 331–46, 348, 353, 371, 374, 384, 386, 387, 398, 427, 444, 452, 456, 457, 477, 478, 485, 521, 523, 527, 573, 574, 582, 606–15 passim, 633, 643, 646, 662, 671; "The Eolian Harp," 318–19, 344; "Kubla Khan," 218, 328–31, 335, 343, 344, 345, 351, 367, 373, 382, 391, 413, 579, 586, 590, 604, 661; *The Rime of the An-cient Mariner*, 320, 321–28, 331–46 passim, 356, 450, 469, 515, 543, 573–91 passim; "To Words-worth," 319–21, 336, 345, 373, 379, 483
Colette, 489
Colonna, Vittoria, 47, 162
Courbet, Gustave, 428
court hermaphrodite, 142–44, 429, 506, 608
Coward, Noel, 545, 546
Crawford, Joan, 504
Crete. *See* Minoan-Mycenaean
Cybele, 56, 103, 132, 138, 235, 354, 359, 416, 458, 463, 493, 507

daemonic: defined, 3–4, 466
Daiches, David, 457
Damon, J. Foster, 291
dandy, 394–95, 410, 428–30, 537, 566
Dante Alighieri, 255–56, 365, 386, 551, 624, 673; *La Vita Nuova*, 121, 375–76; *Inferno*, 151, 219, 259, 292, 351, 372–73, 395, 399, 402, 426, 452, 579, 591; *Paradiso*, 301, 402, 586; Beatrice, 121–22, 321, 376, 492–93, 494, 513
Darwin, Charles, 172, 185, 235, 236, 574
Daumier, Honoré, 262
David, Jacques Louis, 146, 329, 410
Davis, Bette, 54, 87, 507, 551
Debussy, Claude, 483–84
decadence, 125, 130–39, 209, 231, 262, 389, 419
Decadent aesthete, 429, 531
Degas, Edgar, 434
Delacroix, Eugène, 78, 173, 350, 395, 396, 397, 418, 498, 501, 572, 635
Delcourt, Marie, 124–25
Delphi, 56, 117, 290, 383, 468, 646; oracle, 46–47, 102, 130, 162, 256, 259, 302, 366, 374, 386–87, 454, 518, 620, 661, 662
Demeter, 44, 50, 103, 156, 592
Deneuve, Catherine, 268, 368

Dennis, John, 269
Diana, 78–79, 80, 87, 127, 128, 178, 179, 190, 214, 223, 296, 443. *See also* Artemis
Dickens, Charles, 80, 313, 430, 442–43, 452, 469, 529, 567, 591, 636, 637.
Dickinson, Emily, 187, 279, 280, 365, 454, 540, 573, 605, 623–73
Dickinson, Susan Gilbert, 668, 669, 670–71, 673
Diderot, Denis, 182, 241, 400
Dido, 84, 128–30, 223, 314, 444. *See also* Vergil
Dietrich, Marlene, 54, 81, 346, 413, 415, 416
Diodorus Siculus, 125, 256, 350
Dionysus, 5–6, 30, 82, 88–98, 102–05, 107, 117, 124, 127, 130–31, 133, 231, 246, 382, 484, 602–03. *See also* Sade, Shakespeare, sparagmos
Disney, Walt, 346, 435
Dodds, E. R., 47, 97
Dodgson, Charles Lutwidge. *See* Carroll, Lewis
Donatello, 153, 156, 163, 168, 171, 172, 173, 311, 593; *David,* 118, 123, 146–50, 151–52, 158–59, 165, 515
Don Juan, 36, 253–54, 255. *See also* Byron
Donne, John, 144, 228, 284, 288, 308, 567, 574, 633
doppelgänger. *See* double
Dostoyevsky, Feodor, 346, 480, 515
double, 69, 156–57, 211, 287, 311, 348, 366, 377–78, 381, 395, 400, 403–04, 423–24, 446, 493, 518, 526, 558–59, 560, 562, 576, 577, 646. *See also* twins
Douglas, Lord Alfred, 516, 524–25, 543, 562–63, 568, 569
Dover, K. J., 110, 114, 124
drag queens, 45, 102, 104, 123, 194, 219, 266, 472, 535, 557. *See also* castrati; transvestism

Dumont, Margaret, 558
Dylan, Bob, 261–62, 651

Eglinton, J. Z., 115
Egypt, 31, 37, 38, 41, 50, 57–71, 72, 85, 99, 101, 105, 123–30 passim, 148, 153, 158, 172, 173, 174, 213–17, 225, 227, 267, 277, 286, 292, 345, 350, 355, 366–67, 377, 383, 407, 408, 417–20, 429, 485, 491, 496, 512, 529, 558, 575, 615, 616, 640
Eissler, K. R., 258
Elagabalus, 134–35
Eliade, Mircea, 45, 177, 262
Eliot, George, 439, 442, 454; *Middlemarch,* 92, 261, 273, 363, 440
Eliot, T. S., 46, 460, 471
Elizabeth I, 171, 175, 177, 178, 179, 184, 214, 362, 586
Ellis, Havelock, 399
Ellmann, Richard, 556, 570
Emerson, Ralph Waldo, 543, 598–602, 603, 604, 613, 616, 624, 640, 652, 658, 664
English epicene, the, 389, 549–52, 556, 557, 561, 562, 570–71
Ephesian Artemis. *See* Artemis
Epicoene (man of beauty), 165, 360–64
Erikson, Erik, 380
Erté, 409
Euripides, 6, 74, 90, 123, 228, 239; *Bacchae,* 89, 99–100, 102–04, 107, 108, 109, 158, 231, 238, 263, 297, 350, 380, 597, 606–07; *Medea,* 7, 107–09, 129, 217, 262, 297, 298, 397, 530, 576
Evans, Bertrand, 202
Evans, Dame Edith, 557
Eve, 11, 40, 160–62, 503, 504, 505
eye, 32, 33, 36, 50, 62–71 passim, 88, 93, 99, 101, 104, 130–31, 148, 166–93 passim, 212, 213, 247, 260, 310, 329, 338, 339, 412, 419–21, 434, 437, 485, 486, 488, 514, 563, 565, 574, 575, 582, 594, 599–

600, 602, 612–13, 618, 621, 643, 664. *See also* cinema; voyeurism

Faithfull, Theodore, 248
Farnell, Lewis, 44, 45, 123, 156, 387–88
Fauré, Gabriel, 116
Faust. *See* Goethe
Fellini, Federico, 251, 566
female impersonators. *See* drag queens
feminism, 1–2, 3, 12, 13, 16, 21, 24, 27, 32, 37, 42, 43, 142, 247, 592, 652
femme fatale, 13–15, 131–32, 212, 217, 247, 249, 262, 283, 296, 339, 367, 381, 417, 499, 562, 565. *See also* vampire
Fenichel, Otto, 378
Ferenczi, Sandor, 4, 15, 16, 92, 471
fetishism, 20, 30, 130, 247, 249, 258, 262, 436, 575, 664
Fiedler, Leslie, 572, 581, 593
film. *See* cinema
Firbank, Ronald, 546
Flaubert, Gustave, 129, 261, 314, 362, 408, 431, 443–44, 498, 581
Fletcher, Ian, 471
Fontenrose, Joseph, 51, 70
Forster, E. M., 355, 549–50, 588, 604, 616
Foster, Jodie, 122
Fraenkel, Eduard, 73
Francis, St., 642
Frazer, Sir James George, 45, 47, 53, 91, 96, 156, 237, 281, 315, 330, 355, 458, 463, 527–28, 621
Freud, Sigmund, 2, 4, 14, 16, 17, 21, 26, 27, 34, 53, 83, 89, 102, 115, 132, 156, 157, 172, 185, 203, 228– 36, 247, 257–69 passim, 282, 315, 317, 338, 378, 405, 436, 471, 521, 567, 579, 626, 644, 675
Fromm, Erich, 272
Fruman, Norman, 342
Furies, 47, 51, 101, 102, 103, 106, 239, 381, 466

Frye, Northrop, 206, 223, 270, 286, 352, 439, 448, 540, 565

Ganymede, 120, 138, 148, 200, 206, 207, 252, 511
Garbo, Greta, 81, 179, 368, 416
Gardner, Ava, 143
Garland, Judy, 54, 393, 416
Gaudí, Antoni, 489, 497
Gautier, Théophile: 408–21, 422, 429, 430, 435, 460, 461, 471, 485, 486, 498, 512, 514, 516, 530, 563, 570–78 passim; "Contralto," 413– 14, 478, 539, 593; *King Candaules,* 420, 487–88, 542, 666; *Mademoiselle de Maupin,* 252, 350, 390, 406, 408–17, 418, 420, 426, 437, 464, 473, 481, 506, 515, 529, 536, 609; *The Mummy's Foot,* 419–20, 513, 537, 574, 600, 625; *A Night with Cleopatra,* 417–19, 420–21, 426, 487, 490, 519, 537, 565, 576
Gay, Peter, 230
Genet, Jean, 41, 235, 243, 247, 506, 532, 607, 658
George, Lloyd, 143
Géricault, Théodore, 608
Giacometti, Alberto, 310
Giambologna, 88, 210, 356, 357, 358, 532, 534
Gide, André, 425
Gingold, Hermione, 538
Giorgione, 285, 378
Girodet, Anne-Louis, 363
glamour: defined, 177, 376, 393, 521. *See also* charisma
Goethe, Johann Wolfgang von: 43, 248–60, 262, 281, 294, 312, 390, 394, 549, 559, 568, 607; *Faust,* 36, 251, 253–57, 259, 265, 267, 283, 284, 305, 346, 347, 348, 358, 366, 409, 410, 455, 465, 505, 517, 581, 600; *The Sorrows of Young Werther,* 115, 248–49, 250, 255, 258, 259, 302, 313, 334, 357, 403, 409, 469; *Venetian Epigrams,* 252–53, 259;

Goethe, Johann Wolfgang von (*cont.*)
  264, 540, 595; *Wilhelm Meister's*
  Apprenticeship, 88, 143, 199, 249–
  52, 255, 258, 259, 313, 371, 403,
  405, 414, 443, 456, 470
Gogol, Nikolai, 419, 600, 625
Gorgon, 47–51, 64, 68, 70, 78, 83,
  85, 154, 160, 212, 230, 339, 485,
  486, 504, 535, 556, 557, 620. *See*
  also Medusa
Gothic novel, 247, 265–69, 270, 287,
  288, 325, 572, 578, 583, 612, 613,
  659
Goujon, Jean, 79
Goya, Francisco, 468
Graham, Martha, 94, 357
Graiai, 70, 591, 631
Grant, Cary, 533
Graves, Robert, 385, 672
Great Mother, 8, 41–54, 80, 88, 110,
  118, 135, 137–38, 160, 176, 182,
  225–37 passim, 246, 256, 258,
  270–71, 280, 281, 282, 290–301
  passim, 308, 315–16, 324, 375,
  388, 427, 435, 444, 462, 465, 472,
  507, 602, 605, 606
Greenacre, Phyllis, 548
Greenwood, Joan, 368, 535, 561
Guthrie, W. K. C., 73

Hadrian, 118, 126, 134, 375. *See*
  also Antinous
Hamilton, A. C., 172, 194
Hamilton, George, 255, 533
Harpies, 51, 52, 209, 256, 423, 612
Harrison, Jane, 5, 42, 49, 74, 84, 86–
  87, 89, 96, 97, 106, 123, 125, 226,
  246, 339
Harrison, Martin, 494
Harrison, Rex, 533
Hartman, Geoffrey, 25, 302–03,
  314–15, 386, 543–44, 612
Harvey, Laurence, 551
Hauser, Arnold, 60, 123, 152, 540
Hawthorne, Nathaniel, 265, 300,
  439, 448, 572, 585, 595, 623, 664;
  The Birthmark, 580, 587, 589,
  593; *The Blithedale Romance*, 338,

582, 594, 609, 610, 611, 614–15;
  The Minister's Black Veil, 580, 582;
  The Scarlet Letter, 542, 580–84,
  596, 626, 668
Hayworth, Rita, 151, 285, 329, 357
Hazlitt, William, 343
Helen of Troy, 38, 254, 255, 257,
  485, 499–500
Hellenistic art, 36, 74, 76, 79, 86, 88,
  99, 108, 112, 121–30 passim, 136,
  146, 169, 185, 260, 262, 329, 379,
  400, 413, 461, 478, 479, 497, 501,
  569, 571, 575
Hemingway, Ernest, 167, 264
Hendrix, Jimi, 263
Hepburn, Katharine, 80, 144, 199,
  416, 435
Hera, 41, 43, 46, 73, 82, 84, 89, 106
Heracleitus, 5, 218, 481–88 passim
Herbert, George, 228, 273, 279, 599
Hercules, 90, 114, 135, 437, 467
Herington, C. J., 83–84
Heriot, Angus, 393
Hermaphrodite, 124–25, 176, 277,
  287, 289–93, 337, 365, 366–71,
  374–76, 390, 401, 412–14, 560,
  607. *See also* alchemy; androgyny;
  court hermaphrodite
Hermes, 88, 136, 148, 199, 207, 220.
  See also Mercury
Herodotus, 45, 62, 420
Hervey, John, Baron, 136–37, 144,
  394, 532, 678
Hesiod, 46, 51, 81, 87
Higginson, Thomas Wentworth,
  636–45 passim, 657–70 passim
Himmelfarb, Gertrude, 372
Hinks, Roger, 73
Hitchcock, Alfred, 51, 118, 399
Hitler, Adolf, 74, 146, 303, 339–40,
  567, 583. *See also* Nazis
Hobbes, Thomas, 172
Hofmannsthal, Hugo von, 595
Homer: 72, 73, 101, 102, 123, 128,
  129, 172, 239, 466, 672; *Iliad*, 31,
  37, 45, 61, 64, 81, 83, 84, 100,
  106–07, 521, 542, 605, 606, 625,
  653; *Odyssey*, 45, 50, 51, 52, 81–

89 passim, 103, 121, 173, 187, 188, 290, 305, 334, 373, 423, 465, 501, 521, 573, 606, 626, 632, 641, 652. *See also* Achilles; Helen; Paris
homosexuality (male): defined, 14–15, 234, 378, 380; taste, style, behavior, 21, 22, 26, 32, 54, 81, 109–25, 142–43, 209, 221, 264, 389, 400, 430, 434, 484, 496, 515, 519, 543, 556, 557, 558, 672; in antiquity, 79, 100, 109–25, 193, 131, 133–35; in Renaissance, 157–58, 163, 165–66, 168–69, 202, 204–07, 217, 228, 289; in Sade, 237–46 passim; in German Romantics, 250, 259, 264; in English Romantics, 266, 267, 274, 289, 291, 303, 312, 319, 342, 349–50, 358, 379, 457; in French Romantics, 391, 393, 395, 411, 412, 425, 428, 443; in American Romantics, 343, 581, 587, 588, 594, 605–06, 673; late 19th century, 482, 486, 506, 515, 516–19, 549, 555–57, 571, 612, 613; in Mann, 596–97. *See also* lesbianism; camp; English epicene
Horace, 133, 172, 427, 473
Horney, Karen, 22, 106, 294
Hough, Graham, 321
House, Humphrey, 341
Houston, John Porter, 409
Howard, Leslie, 533
Hunt, Holman, 498
Huysmans, Joris-Karl, 24, 47, 48, 93, 245, 284, 320, 395, 429, 430–38, 444, 467, 475, 479, 486, 497–506 passim, 514, 521, 529, 533, 563–86 passim, 595, 619, 654, 656

Ibsen, Henrik, 286
I Love Lucy, 550. *See also* Ball, Lucille
incest, 41, 53, 82, 93–94, 131, 199, 210, 219, 233, 240, 251, 258, 264, 266–67, 309, 314, 338, 346, 347–49, 351, 363, 369–75, 377–79, 400, 404, 446–48, 456, 457, 468,

471, 496, 498, 504, 526, 574, 576, 579, 621, 659
Ingres, Jean-Auguste-Dominique, 61, 173, 277, 362, 363, 501, 620, 628, 689
Isherwood, Christopher, 209
Isis, 41, 43, 87, 95, 182, 184, 195, 217, 225, 256, 370, 463, 603
Italians, 217–18, 221, 234, 298, 308, 323, 390, 406, 660–61, 663, 667, 700. *See also* Catholicism, Roman

Jack the Ripper, 22, 245, 247
Jackson, Helen Hunt, 670
James, Henry, 49, 53, 300, 558, 607–22, 624, 637; *The Ambassadors*, 607, 616, 618, 619; *The Bostonians*, 339, 582, 610, 611, 615; *Daisy Miller*, 618–19, 621; *The Golden Bowl*, 615, 617, 618–19, 621, 664; *The Portrait of a Lady*, 608, 609–10, 620, 621; *The Turn of the Screw*, 268, 272, 611–15, 616–21 passim, 666; *The Wings of the Dove*, 608, 610, 617, 619, 620
Janson, H. W., 146
Jehovah, 38, 40–41, 159, 274, 298, 318, 327, 359, 463, 471, 487, 580, 584. *See also* Judaism
Jesus Christ, 18, 53, 89, 95, 96, 121, 156, 236, 245, 259, 279, 281, 294, 296, 324–25, 337, 426, 473, 569, 586, 594, 617, 626–33 passim, 642, 647, 651–52, 671
Joan of Arc, 78
Johnson, Lionel, 535
Johnson, Samuel, 544, 550
Johnson, Thomas H., 665
Jones, Ernest, 93
Jonson, Ben, 144, 165
Joyce, James, 17, 42, 43, 49, 256, 267, 282
Judaism, 8, 11, 30, 33, 41, 44, 61, 72, 117, 134, 138, 139, 172, 229, 298–99, 543. *See also* Jehovah
Judeo-Christianity. *See* Catholicism; Christianity; Jehovah; Jesus; Judaism; Mary; Protestantism

Judith and Holofernes, 146, 499, 504
Julius Caesar, 134, 259
Jung, Carl Gustav, 85, 88, 198, 210,
    222, 245, 258, 307, 489, 646
Juno, 128. See also Hera

Kafka, Franz, 279, 280, 301, 324,
    346, 419, 656
Kali, 8, 285
Kant, Immanuel, 653
Keats, John: 46, 131, 169, 192, 259,
    265, 319, 347, 365–66, 378–79,
    381–88, 413, 459, 465, 488, 490,
    497, 498, 505, 578, 603, 605, 635,
    639, 649, 651, 663; "La Belle
    Dame Sans Merci," 283–85, 385–
    86; The Eve of St. Agnes, 266,
    382–83; Hyperion poems, 386–88,
    407, 574; "Lamia," 285, 383–85;
    "To Autumn," 382
Keene, Donald, 174
Kernan, Alvin, 355
Kessler, Milton, 272–73, 274, 604
Kettle, Arnold, 440
Khepera, 41, 82, 243, 288, 506, 607,
    613, 614, 675. See also autoeroti-
    cism
Khnopff, Fernand, 504
Kinkead-Weekes, Mark, 452
Kleist, Heinrich von, 260–65, 281,
    282, 305, 348, 349, 363, 380, 465,
    504, 575, 652, 653, 668
Klimt, Gustav, 504
Knight, G. Wilson, 17, 25, 92, 98,
    190, 195, 206, 268, 309, 315, 336,
    350, 352, 353, 366, 376, 378, 455,
    554, 560, 644, 681
Knight, W. F. Jackson, 46, 49, 87,
    130, 334, 357
kouros, 72, 110–12, 125, 126, 158,
    168. See also beautiful boy
Krafft-Ebing, Richard von, 132, 189,
    700
Kritios Boy, 110–11, 118, 146, 163,
    374, 593
Kulp, Nancy, 538

Laclos, Choderlos de, 235, 518

Lamarr, Hedy, 329
Lamb, Lady Caroline, 199, 251, 350,
    361, 385
Lamb, Henry, 533
Lamia, 51. See also Keats
Lampridius, 135
Lange, Victor, 250
Laocoön, 99, 108, 159, 228, 240,
    326, 497
Latouche, Henri de, 252, 390, 402–
    13 passim, 478, 479
Lawrence, St., 629
Lawrence, D. H., 286, 297, 368, 586,
    588, 604; The Rainbow, 376–77;
    Women in Love, 195, 285, 291,
    368, 376, 405–06, 689
Leavis, F. R., 440
Leavis, Q. D., 445
Leda, 120, 154, 160, 485, 487. See
    also Yeats
LeFanu, J. Sheridan, 337
Leigh, Janet, 399
Leigh, Vivien, 199
Lennon, John, 551
Leonardo da Vinci, 153–58, 168,
    169, 172, 192, 276, 279, 293, 456,
    491, 500, 504, 511, 659; The Last
    Supper, 154, 157, 158; Medusa (at-
    tributed), 373; Mona Lisa, 15, 28,
    43, 49, 149, 154–55, 157, 158,
    160, 176, 212, 266, 485–88, 505;
    The Virgin and Child with St.
    Anne, 155–57, 211, 447, 493. See
    also Pater, Walter
lesbianism: taste, behavior, 26–27,
    54, 117, 516, 557; in pornography,
    125; in Rome, 133; in Renais-
    sance, 181–82, 192, 201–03, 210,
    247; in Sade, 238, 240, 241, 245;
    in English Romantics, 291, 331–
    46, 353, 371, 573, 609; in Austen,
    441, 546; in E. Brontë, 456–57; in
    French Romantics, 395–402, 414–
    16, 425–28, 437, 444, 610; in
    American Romantics, 338, 582,
    609, 670–72, 673; in late 19th
    century, 339, 464, 472–78, 488,
    582, 609–10, 611, 614; in art, 80,

277, 496, 509, 511; in modernism, 321, 376–77, 455–56, 688. *See also* homosexuality (male)
Lester, Richard, 363
Lewes, George Henry, 454
Lewis, C. S., 175, 190
Lewis, Matthew G., 265–67, 291, 307, 351, 353, 390, 400
liberalism, 2–3, 26, 31, 38, 227, 346, 429, 472. *See also* Rousseau
Liebert, Robert, 167
Lilith, 52, 492
Lindsay, Jack, 198
Lippincott, Kristen, 679
Locke, John, 2
Longaud, Félix, 404
Losey, Joseph, 289
Luce, Clare Boothe, 556
Lucian, 125, 133
Lucretius, 43, 363
Lucy, St., 33, 630
Lukács, Georg, 250
Luther, Martin, 139, 253. *See also* Protestantism
lyric, 104, 206, 365, 571
Lysippus, 123

McCarthy, Mary, 552, 556
McIntosh, Angus, 202
Mack, Maynard, 224
Madonna (Holy Virgin). *See* Mary
Madonna (pop star), 498
Maenads, 26, 94, 103, 105, 108, 130–31, 132, 251, 380, 427, 566
Malanga, Gerard, 516
male heroine, 264, 312, 321–23, 342, 344, 346, 423, 469, 470, 486, 543, 569, 573, 577, 581, 618, 651, 657
Mallarmé, Stéphane, 408, 538
Mame, Auntie, 88, 199, 220–21
Manet, Edouard, 489
Mankiewicz, Joseph L., 435, 551
Mann, Thomas: 258; *Death in Venice*, 118, 122, 168, 179, 251, 252, 258, 429, 595–97, 607
Mannerism, 150, 160, 163, 168, 169, 178, 196, 231, 260, 266, 288, 389,

399, 465, 482, 490, 496, 497, 532–39 passim, 572
Mantegna, Andrea, 150, 495, 625
manufactured object, 280, 283, 391, 464–65, 633, 643, 647, 664. *See also* android
Marie Antoinette, 144
Marinetti, Filippo, 86
Marlowe, Christopher, 196, 206, 207, 254
Martial, 133
Marvell, Andrew, 567
Marx Brothers, 558
Marxism, 16, 27, 36–37, 231
Mary, Virgin, 28, 43, 48, 53, 75, 138, 156–69 passim, 237, 259, 276, 277, 325, 332, 412, 462, 485, 487, 505, 508–09, 511, 572, 580, 581, 604, 627, 642, 668
Masaccio, 150
Masoch. *See* Sacher-Masoch
mastectomy, 262, 263, 305, 575, 654
masturbation. *See* autoeroticism
Mathis, Johnny, 98
matriarchy, 42–43
Mead, Margaret, 42, 45
Mecca, 56
Medea. *See* Euripides
Medusa, 14–15, 16, 35, 47–48, 51, 52, 94, 267, 277, 325, 373, 378, 434, 465, 497, 501, 503, 538, 563, 574, 585, 592, 607, 645, 664. *See also* Gorgon
Melville, Herman, 448, 584–95, 605; *Bartleby*, 301, 609; *Billy Budd*, 115, 179, 251, 343, 513, 586, 592–95, 596; *Moby-Dick*, 285, 424, 577, 584–90, 591, 592, 595, 600, 604, 606, 625; *Paradise of Bachelors, Tartarus of Maids*, 276, 286, 585, 590–93, 595, 597
menstruation, 10–12, 17, 26, 91, 92, 95, 591, 636
Mercurius, 88, 199, 208–12, 213, 220, 222, 226–27, 250–51, 354, 385, 440. *See also* alchemy
Mercury, 88, 151–52, 207–08, 210. *See also* Hermes

Metaphysical poetry, 228, 624, 629, 637, 663, 668. *See also* individual poets

Michael, St., 148

Michelangelo: 47, 57, 153, 156–68, 169, 172, 173, 205–09 passim, 246, 292, 294, 297, 314, 433, 478, 480, 496, 587, 588, 640; *Bacchus*, 167; *Creation of Man*, 99, 160–62; *Cumaean Sibyl*, 160–62; *David*, 99, 146, 158–59; *Dying Slave*, 165, 166, 167, 191; *Giuliano de' Medici*, 163–65, 261, 262, 360, 362, 501; *Last Judgment*, 99, 163, 168, 501; *Moses*, 159, 163, 169, 420; *Night*, 99, 160, 167–68, 176, 196, 217, 422, 507; *Pietà* (Rome), 55, 161, 167, 379; *Victory*, 148, 149, 165–66

Mill, John Stuart, 372, 573, 583, 661

Milton, John: 297, 309, 312–13, 315, 320, 355, 365, 374, 653; *Comus*, 83, 94, 278, 284, 573; *Lycidas*, 466; *Paradise Lost*, 52, 143, 185, 190, 228–29, 265, 270, 292, 303, 357, 366, 585, 639

Minerva, 83, 237. *See also* Athena

Minoan-Mycenaean age, 8, 83, 84, 88, 578

Mirbeau, Octave, 496

Mishima, Yukio, 245–46

Mitford, Nancy, 550

Monet, Claude, 528

Montagu, Lady Mary Wortley, 393, 532

Montaigne, Michel Eyquem de, 233–34

Montégut, Emile, 446

Montesquiou, Robert de, 429, 533

Moore, George, 484, 485, 622

Moore, Virginia, 454

Moreau, Gustave, 320, 401, 444, 490, 498–501, 504, 506, 508, 570, 613, 619, 655

Morris, William, 498

Mozart, Wolfgang Amadeus, 247, 352, 394

Mudrick, Marvin, 441

Munch, Edvard, 310, 489, 505

Murray, Gilbert, 81, 94, 105

Murray, Margaret, 336

Muse, 50, 160, 162, 171, 220, 249, 258, 297, 309, 318, 333, 338, 344, 345, 357, 386–87, 457, 466, 478, 573, 640, 657, 672, 673

Mycenaean. *See* Minoan-Mycenaean

Napoleon, 61, 146, 232, 329, 353, 362, 394, 440

narcissism, 189, 248–49, 284, 351, 376, 594, 596

Nazis, 25, 29, 389, 645. *See also* Hitler

necrophilia, 425, 438, 464, 469, 498, 664, 665, 700

Nefertiti, 66–71, 79, 80, 116, 149, 154, 160, 368, 494

Nero, 25, 134–36, 210, 238, 463, 529, 567, 650

Neumann, Erich, 42, 43, 47, 52, 88, 93, 380

Nichols, Fred, 133

Nietzsche, Friedrich, 2, 14, 29, 73, 105, 172, 185, 215, 235, 236, 267, 380, 515, 559, 598

Nilsson, Martin, 83

Niven, David, 533

Nixon, Richard, 308–09

Novak, Kim, 368, 415

Numa Pompilius. *See* cats

Nureyev, Rudolf, 357

Oberon, Merle, 690

Odysseus. *See* Homer

Oedipus, 3, 17, 46, 50, 93, 102, 290, 504, 581, 627, 632. *See also* Sophocles

Oliver, Edna May, 538

Olivier, Laurence, 690

Onassis, Jacqueline Kennedy, 506

Ono, Yoko, 551

Ortega y Gasset, José, 563

Osiris, 41, 52, 89, 95, 96, 603

Otto, Walter, 74, 81, 88, 185

Ovid, 52, 78, 80, 125, 132–33, 200, 228, 242, 289, 292, 374, 377, 403, 467

Packer, Barbara, 599, 600
paganism, 18, 23, 25–26, 30–31, 138–39
Paglia, Alfonsina, 127
Paglia, Pasquale J., 218, 700
Paracelsus, 124–25
Paris (of Troy), 129, 255, 513
Parthenon, 77, 83–84, 100, 104, 124, 125, 126, 179
Pascal, Blaise, 234, 653, 655
Pater, Walter, 320, 408, 412, 419, 435, 460, 479–88, 508, 520, 522, 530, 539, 549; "Conclusion," The Renaissance, 481–83, 485, 516–18; Mona Lisa, 15, 154–55, 485–88, 498, 501, 505, 524, 538, 541; Marius, 481, 484, 486, 527
Patterson, Rebecca, 671
Penthesilea, 128, 178, 183, 260–65. See also Amazons
Percival, Milton O., 291
Perkins, Anthony, 399
Perseus, 47, 48, 339, 401, 495–96, 497–98, 631
personae. See Amazon; androgyne of manners; android; beautiful boy; court hermaphrodite; dandy; Decadent aesthete; drag queen; Epicoene (man of beauty); Gorgon; Great Mother; Khepera; lesbian; male heroine; manufactured object; Mercurius; Pythoness; Teiresias; transsexual; twin; vampire, Venus Barbata; virago
Perugino, 169
Petrarch, 121, 142, 189, 201, 232, 283, 419, 513, 594, 643
Pheidias, 61, 72, 84, 123
Philip Neri, St., 630
Picasso, Pablo, 435
Piero della Francesca, 153, 177–78, 511
Pindar, 367, 603
Plath, Sylvia, 17, 645
Plato, 120–21, 122, 123, 136, 142, 206, 256, 373, 374, 404, 410, 414, 458, 519, 523, 524, 554, 555, 590–600 passim
Plotina, 136, 178, 252

Plutarch, 91, 95–97, 196, 207, 213, 216, 224, 225, 239, 259, 370, 382
Poe, Edgar Allan, 41, 53, 66, 122, 170, 232, 247, 263, 265, 284, 300, 320, 322, 323, 346, 356, 421, 429, 430, 448, 470, 477, 572–80, 608, 610, 611, 623, 655, 666; Berenice, 338–39, 438, 573–77 passim, 600, 629, 664; Cask of Amontillado, 577, 619; Descent into Maelström, 47, 52, 433, 466, 575–76, 577, 584, 589; Fall of the House of Usher, 348, 377, 431, 454, 576, 577, 614, 625; Ligeia, 266, 268, 338–39, 464, 491, 573–78 passim, 614–15; Masque of Red Death, 335, 421, 423, 432, 463, 514, 576–77, 631, 652, 654; Morella, 423, 452, 573, 574, 576; Murders in Rue Morgue, 578–79; Narrative of A. Gordon Pym, 325, 579–80, 584, 590–91; Oval Portrait, 525, 529; Pit and Pendulum, 47, 577, 606, 624, 628; Tell-Tale Heart, 70, 348, 480, 577, 625; William Wilson, 287, 526, 560
Pollaiuolo, Antonio del, 150
Polycleitus, 123
Polygnotus, 90
Pompeii, 264
Pontormo, Jacobo da, 150
Pope, Alexander, 356, 532, 545; Dunciad, 17, 144, 551; Epistle to Arbuthnot, 136–37, 303, 678; Essay on Man, 230; The Rape of the Lock, 39, 78, 178, 532, 561
Pope-Hennessy, John, 163
pornography, 20, 24–25, 26, 34–35, 47, 54, 124, 167, 190, 191, 264, 266, 300, 331, 498, 505, 546, 635
Porter, Cole, 546
Praxiteles, 79, 123, 306. See also Aphrodite, of Knidos
Praz, Mario, 247, 385, 464, 475
Pre-Raphaelitism, 173, 409, 480, 487, 490–98, 504, 506, 528. See also individual artists
Presley, Elvis, 115, 165, 361–64, 453, 521

Price, Vincent, 636
Pritchett, V. S., 455
Proclus, 179
prostitution, 23, 26, 137, 250, 280, 291, 416, 444
Protestantism, 33, 34, 173, 192, 228, 265, 268, 302, 320, 572–73, 578–84, 598, 599, 601, 603, 624, 629, 642. *See also* Catholicism; Christianity; Luther
Proust, Marcel, 132, 312, 425, 428, 429–30, 442, 455, 484, 533, 542, 555, 617
psychoiconicism, 130, 345, 523–24
psychological heliotropism, 375, 392
Puccini, Giacomo, 667
Pythoness. *See* Delphic oracle

Quarles, Francis, 92

Rabelais, François, 17
Rachilde, 437–38, 483, 514, 563, 664
Racine, Jean, 7, 255
Radcliffe, Ann, 265
Radio City Music Hall, 241, 496
rape, 22–24, 185–97 passim, 236–45 passim, 254–71 passim, 317, 321, 332, 334, 345, 346, 379–80, 397, 400, 401, 420, 452, 574, 575, 606, 628, 629, 636–58 passim, 671, 672
Raphael (Sanzio), 140, 151, 169, 178, 356, 383, 384, 490, 493, 659
Raphael, Frederick, 550
Ravel, Maurice, 483–84
Read, John, 62
Reed, Walter L., 453
Reisman, David, 135
Rembrandt, 78
Reni, Guido, 245–46
Richards, Renée, 369
Richmond, Hugh, 203
Richter, Gisela, 127
Riefenstahl, Leni, 146
Rigg, Diana, 416
Robertson, Alec, 116
rock music, 94, 102, 276, 281, 358–59. *See also* individual groups

rococo art, 506, 640
Roethke, Theodore, 273
Rogers, Ginger, 357
Rolling Stones, The, 231, 281, 358. *See also* rock music
Rome, ancient, 72, 125–39, 214–15
Rose, H. J., 44, 447
Rosenfield, Claire, 446
Rossetti, Christina, 456
Rossetti, Dante Gabriel, 122, 150, 157, 320, 447, 490–95, 496, 498, 503, 506, 512, 513, 559
Rougemont, Denis de, 121
Rousseau, Jean Jacques, 2, 14, 36, 38, 115, 192, 217, 230–35, 236, 240, 248, 249, 260–83 passim, 300–17 passim, 357, 379, 391, 393, 401, 402, 410–23 passim, 429–43 passim, 459, 472, 490, 501, 505, 532, 565, 567, 613, 652, 658. *See also* liberalism
Rowse, A. L., 221
Roxon, Lillian, 358
Rubens, Peter Paul, 293, 363
Rule, Jane, 212
Ruskin, John, 481, 483, 487, 490, 491, 504
Russell, Rosalind, 220, 556
Rutherford, Margaret, 538

Sacher-Masoch, Leopold von, 258, 436–37, 576
Sackville-West, Victoria, 337, 455, 548
Sade, Donatien Alphonse Francois, comte de, 2, 6, 14, 24, 37, 85, 132, 172, 185, 190, 231, 235–47, 248, 261–84 passim, 300, 315, 340, 345, 349, 379, 389–402 passim, 412–26 passim, 431, 460–75 passim, 490, 501, 515, 542, 565, 567, 576, 578, 585, 588, 605, 610, 624–53 passim, 665–73 passim, 689. *See also* sadomasochism
sadomasochism, 3, 44, 98, 186, 189, 191–92, 231, 234–35, 242–43, 245–46, 263, 436, 472, 480. *See also* Sade

Saint-Gaudens, Augustus, 79
Saki (H. H. Munro), 614
Salomé, 368, 397, 504, 506, 507,
    508, 562–65, 613. *See also* Mo-
    reau, Gustave
Samothrace, Winged Victory of, 69
Sand, George, 402, 406, 408, 437
Sanger, C. P., 447
Sappho, 38, 117, 121, 131, 228, 374,
    472, 594, 624, 672. *See also* Swin-
    burne, *Anactoria*
Sartre, Jean-Paul, 93, 94, 257, 383,
    429, 532, 607, 658
Schapiro, Meyer, 156
Schiller, Friedrich von, 259, 269
Schmidt, Heidi Jon, 635
Scott, Sir Walter, 331, 356, 448
Scylla, 52, 94, 241, 268, 577, 634
Sebastian, St., 33, 112, 114, 148,
    165, 244, 246, 625
Sedgwick, Edie, 251, 385
Serling, Rod, 344
Seurat, Georges, 490
Seyrig, Delphine, 268
sex. *See* androgyny; autoeroticism;
    castration; fetishism; homosex-
    uality; incest; lesbianism; men-
    struation; narcissism; necrophilia;
    pornography; prostitution; rape;
    sadomasochism; transsexualism;
    transvestism; urination; vagina
    dentata; vampire; voyeurism
sexual metathesis, 350, 396, 425,
    428, 455, 457, 477, 478, 573, 611,
    647, 671
sexual personae. *See* personae
Shakespeare, William, 99, 146, 158,
    162, 170, 176, 194–228, 248, 279,
    285, 312, 354, 355, 356, 365, 381,
    435, 439, 440, 474, 546, 554, 593,
    653; *Sonnets*, 205–07, 208, 371;
    Rape of Lucrece, 194, 205, 334,
    629; *Venus and Adonis*, 194, 197,
    366; *Antony and Cleopatra*, 7, 196,
    197, 199, 212–27, 230, 237–38,
    239, 261, 350–59 passim, 377,
    400, 418, 448, 450, 465, 473, 477,
    536, 589, 603, 640, 646, 660, 670–
    71; *As You Like It*, 88, 157, 181,

182, 184, 197, 199–212, 216–17,
    219, 222, 227, 238, 240, 249, 251,
    252, 266, 345, 371, 392, 403–17
    passim, 467, 536, 560, 609, 640;
    Hamlet, 25, 93–94, 99, 109, 143–
    44, 155, 196, 197, 203, 217, 253,
    254, 563, 637, 663; *I Henry IV*, 91–
    92; *Julius Caesar*, 44; *King Lear*,
    52, 94, 196, 208, 213, 217, 305,
    341, 445, 577, 631; *Macbeth*, 7,
    47, 77, 217, 256, 420; *Merchant of
    Venice*, 200; *Midsummer Night's
    Dream*, 208, 226; *Othello*, 196,
    203, 206, 289, 594, 671; *Richard
    II*, 143, 323; *Romeo and Juliet*,
    208, 413; *The Tempest*, 88, 209,
    250; *Titus Andronicus*, 194–95,
    197; *Troilus and Cressida*, 140,
    206, 475, 507, 554; *Twelfth Night*,
    197, 200–05, 206, 208, 252, 350,
    400, 402, 435; *Winter's Tale*, 197,
    206, 262
shamanism, 45, 54, 77, 382
Shelley, Mary, 256, 331–32, 359–60,
    369, 370, 372, 374, 508, 633, 661
Shelley, Percy Bysshe: 173, 259, 311,
    312, 315, 331–32, 339, 346, 347,
    355–56, 362, 365–81, 382, 409,
    459, 460–61, 508, 523, 583, 661;
    Adonais, 365–66, 373, 378; *The
    Cenci*, 377–78; *Epipsychidion*, 309,
    369–77, 378, 379, 387, 400–10
    passim, 446, 447, 449, 458, 461,
    462, 505, 513, 524, 571, 579, 669;
    "Mont Blanc," 269, 380; "Ode to
    the West Wind," 318, 379–80,
    429, 478, 599; "Ozymandias,"
    366–67; *Prometheus Unbound*,
    366, 379, 473; *The Witch of Atlas*,
    256, 367–69, 374, 376, 401, 404,
    465, 479, 494, 524, 560
Siddal, Elizabeth. *See* Rossetti,
    Dante Gabriel
Signorelli, Luca, 292
Silz, Walter, 264
Sirens, 51, 256
skopophilia. *See* voyeurism
Snow White, 345–46, 525, 164
soap opera, 470

social novel, 439–45, 448, 459, 607–
    22 passim, 672
Solomon, Eric, 447
Solomon, Simeon, 494, 498
Sophocles, 7, 45, 102, 109, 155. *See
    also* Oedipus
sparagmos, 95, 97, 101, 104, 268,
    449, 636
Spengler, Oswald, 60, 80, 105–06,
    109, 267, 354, 484, 505
Spenser, Edmund, *The Faerie
    Queene:* 35, 61, 73, 78, 94, 130,
    132, 166, 170–99, 214, 215, 219,
    227–29, 235–44 passim, 255, 261,
    265, 270, 271, 279–87 passim,
    292–93, 294, 299, 317, 333, 340,
    350, 353, 365, 367, 370–71, 381,
    401–13 passim, 436, 465, 470,
    474, 489, 491, 512, 513, 533, 535,
    567–73 passim, 607, 610, 621–29
    passim, 639, 648–58 passim, 667,
    673; Acrasia, 187, 190, 514;
    Amoret, 182, 186, 191, 628, 630;
    Artegall, 174, 183–84, 191, 216,
    377, 410, 467, 498; Belphoebe, 80,
    175–86 passim, 193, 197, 200,
    212, 249, 251, 267, 278, 296–97,
    333, 345, 373, 403, 407, 441, 442,
    467, 470, 520, 539, 596, 643;
    Bower of Bliss, 152, 187–88, 190,
    192, 196, 213, 216, 217, 223, 225,
    228, 229, 273, 275, 276, 284, 302,
    314, 333–34, 354, 380, 383, 386,
    396, 397, 438, 465, 493, 496, 506,
    514, 585, 628; Britomart, 175–86
    passim, 192, 193, 200, 201, 203,
    211–12, 297, 307, 377, 407, 540;
    Duessa, 176, 187, 336, 337; Flo-
    rimell, 182, 184, 186, 187, 254,
    266, 276, 278, 289, 367, 368, 404;
    Talus, 191, 283, 369, 643; Venus,
    176, 371–72, 387, 392, 579
Sphinx, 50, 210, 344, 422, 457, 499,
    504, 505, 601
Stendhal, 233, 443
Stern, Karl, 92, 480
Sternberg, Josef von, 415
Sterne, Laurence, 654

Stevens, Wallace, 656
Stokes, Adrian, 162, 167
Stoller, Robert J., 416
Storr, Anthony, 11, 436
Strachey, Lytton, 533
Strauss, Richard, 565
Stravinsky, Igor, 94
Streisand, Barbra, 54, 558
Strindberg, August, 505
Stuck, Franz von, 501, 503–04
Suetonius, 134–35, 224–25
Summers, Montague, 662
Swedenborg, Emanuel, 292, 318,
    402, 404
Swift, Jonathan, 94, 239, 244
Swinburne, Algernon, 43, 247, 263,
    320, 379, 408, 431, 436, 460–80,
    481, 491, 493, 494, 554, 573, 608,
    637, 661, 667; *Anactoria*, 342, 428,
    472–78, 479, 518, 519, 610, 641,
    650; *Atalanta in Calydon*, 262,
    321, 466–70, 486, 506, 528, 606;
    Dolores, 461–63, 464, 475, 486,
    487, 488, 508, 669; *Faustine*, 463–
    65, 472, 488, 669; *Triumph of
    Time*, 470–71, 569, 605
Symonds, John Addington, 159, 414,
    678
Symons, Arthur, 436, 493

Tasso, Torquato, 78, 179, 181, 249
Tave, Stuart M., 441
Taylor, Elizabeth, 87, 144, 350, 507
Teiresias, 45–46, 102, 255, 261, 262,
    306, 354, 382–83, 410, 465. *See
    also* transsexualism
temenos: defined, 23
Temple, Shirley, 659
Teresa of Avila, St. *See* Bernini
Thackeray, William Makepeace,
    441–42, 508
Thomas Aquinas, St., 177, 646–47
Thoreau, Henry David, 38
Thorslev, Peter, 361–62
Thucydides, 83
Tiepolo, 245
Tierney, Gene, 368
Titian, 78

Tolstoy, Leo, 88, 129, 199, 251, 312, 314, 440, 443–44, 581
Toulouse-Lautrec, Henri de, 489
tragedy, 6–7, 101, 103, 104, 620
Traherne, Thomas, 482–83
Trajan, 134, 136
transsexualism, 44–45, 86–87, 180, 182, 242, 301–02, 324, 333, 368, 582, 589, 602, 610–11, 640–41, 642–43, 671. *See also* Teiresias
transvestism, 44, 87, 89–91, 124, 134–35, 165, 180–87 passim, 200–16 passim, 233, 238, 242, 249–52, 258–59, 265–66, 345–54 passim, 366–78 passim, 390, 393, 396, 401, 408–22 passim, 443, 444, 467, 470, 478, 508, 580, 597, 620, 640, 648. *See also* drag queens
Trilling, Lionel, 269, 272, 315, 383, 384
Tristman, Richard, 47, 243
Turnell, Martin, 425
Turner, J. M. W., 635
Turner, Tina, 227
Twilight Zone, The, 344
twins, 74, 80, 201, 204, 258, 259, 262, 307–08, 370–75, 377, 390, 393, 401–02, 526, 559, 562, 671. *See also* double
Tyler, Parker, 368, 416

urination, 20–21, 62, 148
uroboros, 41, 82, 88, 187, 198, 209, 241, 253, 264, 282, 349, 540, 587, 600, 658

vagina dentata, 13, 47, 433–34, 574, 577
vampire, 11, 13, 49, 50, 69, 131, 193, 261, 271, 274, 280, 282, 289, 296, 325, 327, 331–46, 380, 383, 404, 422, 425, 433, 444, 457, 461, 465, 476–93 passim, 505, 508, 518, 519, 526, 560, 574–83 passim, 604–12 passim, 643, 646, 662, 665. *See also* femme fatale

Van den Berg, J. H., 115, 207, 233, 493
Van Dyck, Anthony, 118, 530
Van Ghent, Dorothy, 445
Vasari, Giorgio, 163, 173, 456
Veblen, Thorstein, 552, 553, 559
Venetian art, 110, 168, 292, 596, 597, 655
Venus: 92, 94, 128, 135, 148, 178, 190, 214, 223–24, 237, 347, 423, 465–66, 493; Armata, 87, 217; Barbata, 87, 291, 507. *See also* Aphrodite; Botticelli; Spenser
Venus de Milo, 43, 56, 155
Venus of Willendorf, 54–57, 60, 66, 69, 70, 79, 105, 116, 246, 359, 421, 507
Vergil, 44, 77, 84, 87, 128–30, 132, 141, 171, 178, 184, 195, 207, 228, 284, 290, 326, 368, 391, 441, 556, 583. *See also* Camilla; Dido
Verlaine, 342, 428
Verne, Jules, 655
Verrocchio, Andrea del, 149, 156
Vidal, Gore, 435
virago, 160, 162, 217, 220, 250, 352, 397, 422, 505, 507, 508
Virgin Mary, The. *See* Mary
Viviani, Emilia, 369–77, 404, 513, 523, 524
Voltaire, 260
voyeurism, 173, 189–91, 242, 253, 254, 265, 271, 274–75, 349–50, 411–12, 415, 419–20, 475, 540, 583, 604–05, 606, 613, 642, 647, 664–66, 673. *See also* eye

Wagner, Richard, 268, 394, 507
Waite, Arthur Edward, 199
Walter, Jessica, 556
Warhol, Andy, 251, 385, 516
Waters, Bill, 494
Watteau, Antoine, 423, 530
Wayne, John, 21
Weber, Max, 521
Webster, Noah, 638, 641
Weigert-Vowinkel, Edith, 44
Welles, Orson, 285

Wells, H. G., 489, 655
Welsford, Enid, 142–43
West, John Anthony, 223
West, Mae, 557
West, Rebecca, 615, 619
Whalley, George, 321
Whistler, James A. M., 43, 489, 497, 504–05, 507, 530
White, Newman Ivey, 375
Whitman, Walt, 41, 239, 274–75, 296, 321, 469, 470, 506, 588, 602–07, 613, 642–43, 656, 663, 664, 673
Wilde, Oscar, 61, 171, 173, 199, 244, 300, 313–20 passim, 379, 389, 408, 410, 412, 428, 435, 460, 474, 481, 506, 512–71, 616, 619, 621, 652, 660, 671; *De Profundis*, 524–25, 569–71; *Importance of Being Earnest*, 194, 219–20, 520–21, 523, 531–71, 611, 613, 667, 668, 698; *Picture of Dorian Gray*, 122, 249, 348, 377–78, 406, 424, 429, 441, 483, 487, 512–30, 531, 535–40 passim, 544, 557–69 passim, 579, 583, 593–600 passim, 646; *Salomé*, 368, 507–08, 562–65, 611. *See also* camp; English epicene, the
Wilding, Michael, 533
Williams, Tennessee, 53, 258, 263, 434–35, 689
Willson, David Harris, 363
Wilson, Colin, 426
Wilson, Edmund, 441, 610–11, 620
Winckelmann, Johann J., 109, 260
Windsor, Duchess of, 70
Wölfflin, Heinrich, 173
Woolf, Virginia, 49–50, 118, 313, 442, 445, 454, 480, 484, 548–49, 617, 645, 659; *Mrs. Dalloway*, 209,

249, 321; *Orlando*, 249, 345, 405, 455–56; *A Room of One's Own*, 295–96, 312, 653; *To the Lighthouse*, 50, 256, 308, 458, 529; *The Waves*, 404, 563
Wordsworth, William, 6, 11, 43, 46, 85, 93, 192, 231, 235, 259, 274, 281, 297, 300–16, 317–49 passim, 354, 359, 365, 370, 378–88 passim, 402, 418, 430, 439, 442, 449–60 passim, 469, 543–44, 565–74 passim, 584, 585, 598, 601, 607, 613, 623, 624, 636–60 passim, 667, 668, 670, 690; "I Wandered Lonely," 315, 335, 346, 650; "Nutting," 275; "Old Cumberland Beggar," 310, 313, 322; *The Prelude*, 233, 301–15 passim, 367, 382, 421; "Resolution and Independence," 310, 313, 322; "She was a Phantom of Delight," 307; "A Slumber Did My Spirit Seal," 307; *Tintern Abbey*, 301–02, 303, 307–08, 314, 348, 366, 367
Wright, Andrew H., 441
Wyman, Jane, 672

Xenophon, 521

Yeats, William Butler, 268, 281, 345, 380, 386, 402, 412, 487, 629

Zagorin, Perez, 363–64
Zeus, 41, 46, 71–106 passim, 120, 125, 132, 148, 154, 159, 200, 320, 380, 386, 436, 487, 504, 635
Ziegler, Philip, 141
Zilboorg, Gregory, 82–83
Zimmer, Heinrich, 116
Zola, Emile, 280, 444